Third Edition

TERRORISM AND COUNTERTERRORISM

UNDERSTANDING THE
NEW SECURITY ENVIRONMENT

READINGS & INTERPRETATIONS

About the Authors

Brigadier General (Retired) Russell D. Howard is the director of the Jebsen Center for Counter-Terrorism Studies at the Fletcher School at Tufts University. Previously, he was the head of the Department of Social Sciences and the founding director of the Combating Terrorism Center at West Point. As a Special Forces officer, Brigadier General (Retired) Howard served at every level of command including: A Detachment Commander in the 7th Special Forces Group, B Detachment Commander in the 1st Special Forces Group, Battalion Commander at the Special Warfare Center and School, and Commander of the 1st Special Forces Group (Airborne). In preparation for his academic position, he earned degrees from San Jose State University, the University of Maryland, the Monterey Institute of International Studies, and Harvard University. During the course of his career, Brigadier General (Retired) Howard has had anti-terror and counter-terror responsibilities and has taught and published on the subject. He is also the co-editor of *Defeating Terrorism, Homeland Security and Terrorism, and Weapons of Mass Destruction and Terrorism* all McGraw-Hill publications.

Major Reid Sawyer, a career military intelligence officer, is the former Executive Director and founding member of the Combating Terrorism Center at the United States Military Academy. He is currently a fellow with the Center and an adjunct assistant professor at the School of International and Public Affairs at Columbia University, where he teaches a graduate seminar on terrorism studies. As an intelligence officer, Major Sawyer previously served in a variety of special operations assignments. Major Sawyer earned his undergraduate degree from the United States Military Academy and holds a masters of public administration from Columbia University where he is completing his doctorate degree. Major Sawyer has lectured widely on the topic of terrorism and counterterrorism. He is also the co-editor of *Defeating Terrorism.*

Natasha E. Bajema is a Ph.D. candidate at the Fletcher School of Law and Diplomacy, Tufts University. Before coming to Fletcher, she was a Research Associate at the Center on International Cooperation at New York University, where she conducted research on the threat of WMD and policy responses. She has worked on WMD terrorism issues as a Junior Political Officer in the Weapons of Mass Destruction Branch of the Department for Disarmament Affairs at the United Nations. She holds an MA in international policy and a certificate in nonproliferation studies from the Monterey Institute of International Studies. She also served as a junior co-editor of *Weapons of Mass Destruction and Terrorism.*

Third Edition

TERRORISM AND COUNTERTERRORISM

UNDERSTANDING THE NEW SECURITY ENVIRONMENT

READINGS & INTERPRETATIONS

RUSSELL D. HOWARD
BRIGADIER GENERAL USA (RET.)

REID L. SAWYER
MAJOR USA

NATASHA E. BAJEMA
PH.D CANDIDATE AT THE FLETCHER
SCHOOL OF LAW AND DIPLOMACY,
TUFTS UNIVERSITY

FOREWORD BY
BARRY R. MCCAFFREY
GENERAL USA (RET.)

Boston   Burr Ridge, IL   Dubuque, IA   New York   San Francisco   St. Louis
Bangkok   Bogotá   Caracas   Kuala Lumpur   Lisbon   London   Madrid   Mexico City
Milan   Montreal   New Delhi   Santiago   Seoul   Singapore   Sydney   Taipei   Toronto

The McGraw-Hill Companies

Higher Education

TERRORISM AND COUNTERTERRORISM: UNDERSTANDING THE NEW SECURITY
ENVIRONMENT, READINGS AND INTERPRETATIONS, THIRD EDITION

This text is published by the **Contemporary Learning Series** group within the McGraw-Hill
Higher Education division.

1 2 3 4 5 6 7 8 9 0 DOC/DOC 0 9 8

MHID 0-07-337979-4
ISBN 978-0-07-337979-1

Managing Editor: *Larry Loeppke*
Production Manager: *Faye Schilling*
Senior Developmental Editor: *Jill Peter*
Editorial Assistant: *Nancy Meissner*
Production Service Assistant: *Rita Hingtgen*
Permissions Coordinator: *Leondard J. Behnke*
Senior Marketing Manager: *Julie Keck*
Marketing Communications Specialist: *Mary Klein*
Marketing Coordinator: *Alice Link*
Project Manager: *Jane Mohr*
Design Specialist: *Tara McDermott*
Senior Administrative Assistant: *DeAnna Dausener*
Cover Graphics: *Kristine Jubeck*

Compositor: Laserwords Private Limited
Cover Image: Department of Defense/PH2 Jim Watson, USN (DN-SD-04-12750)

Library of Congress Control Number 2002106286

www.mhhe.com

Contents in Brief

Contents

Foreword

On September 11, 2001, the United States was confronted with the stark reality of modern terrorism. The brutal murder of thousands of innocent lives stripped away our ability to ignore the threat posed by the emergence of transnational terrorist organizations. The terrorism we witnessed on September 11, 2001 was a giant escalation of an evolving threat. Prior to these tragic attacks, Americans had witnessed a steadily growing series of violent attacks culminating in more than 5,000 casualties in the terrorist bombings of our East African embassies in 1998. The attacks in Madrid and in London unequivocally demonstrate that the terrorist targets are shifting from the Global South to Western Europe and that new members are joining what has become a global movement. The question is not *if* further terrorist attacks will occur in the United States, but *when* and at *what* magnitude. One thing is certain, terrorists will continue to try to adapt to the changing counterterror security environment.

Terrorism, at its very roots, centers on fear and targets our liberal democratic values. The fear generated by terrorism speaks to our vulnerabilities and the government's apparent lack of ability to stop further attacks. The current proliferation of lethal technologies, combined with radical ideologies, potentially presents truly horrific scenarios. We will continue to witness new forms of terrorism, be it viruses that selectively attack target populations or suicide bombers attempting to slaughter our children in our nation's schools. It is imperative for all of us to study and learn about these new threats. We will be driven to understand why terrorism occurs and how best to counter terrorism's driving forces. No single solution or sole instrument of national power can hope to resolve these questions alone. Instead, we must search out new and different solutions that challenge our traditional assumptions. The goal of this superb collection of articles is to heighten the reader's awareness of the critical issues related to the threat of terrorism. Although it is impossible for any single work to address the entire breadth of the terrorism field, this volume captures the most salient pieces on the subject.

There are many terrorism experts in academia. However, there are only a handful of individuals who combine impressive academic credentials with extensive special operations combat and training experience. Two of the editors of this compilation, Brigadier General (Retired) Russ Howard and Major Reid Sawyer, are distinguished scholars who also have spent careers on the cutting edge of U.S. military special operations. Their combined experience of more than 40 years in the front lines of the struggle to prevent terrorism provides them with a distinct and uniquely informed perspective on the current war on terrorism.

The most recent member of the *Terrorism and Counterterrorism* editing team is Natasha E. Bajema, who is an expert on Weapons of Mass Destruction (WMD) and nonproliferation issues. Presently, Ms. Bajema is completing her Ph.D. at the Fletcher

School at Tufts University. Previously, she was a Research Associate at the Center on International Cooperation at New York University. Ms. Bajema also worked on WMD terrorism issues as a Junior Political Officer in the Weapons of Mass Destruction Branch of the Department for Disarmament Affairs at the United Nations.

Together, these scholars have gathered and edited the best works of more than fifteen of the leading commentators on terrorism at a critical time in our nation's history. This superbly researched book also reflects their experience in security-related courses in the Department of Social Sciences at West Point, at Columbia University, at Tufts University, and at the Fletcher School. Brigadier General Howard, Major Sawyer, and Natasha Bajema have refined their thinking on the topic through their experimentation with the curricula in these national security courses. Students of national security polity will find this book to be a unique combination of well-known and astute thinkers who have articulated the current and future policy implications of terrorism. The relevant experiences of Howard, Sawyer, and Bajema as editors place them in the best position to bring together this wide-ranging material.

There is much uncertainty about the future. However, we are sure that only through diligent and creative study can America effectively address this very real asymmetrical threat to our national security. We are challenged to develop a conceptual framework to reevaluate the security environment. Clearly, we must craft flexible and effective counter-terrorism strategies. The policy solutions to this complex threat of terrorism do not lie solely with our military, or even our government. Instead, we must create cooperative efforts to find a national solution to manage the terrorist threat; a solution that involves a partnership with the international community combined with an integrated and coherent strategy that unites community, state, and federal authorities supported by business, the health professions, and academia. We also cannot allow ourselves to become trapped in overly simplistic views of the threat. Our challenge is to dramatically embrace our domestic security while carefully preserving our precious freedoms guaranteed in the Bill of Rights as well as the safety and dignity of foreigners living among us.

Through the thoughtful study of the definitions, issues, and recommendations provided by these accomplished authors and the editors, hopefully we can move toward a better understanding of terrorism and its causes.

Barry R. McCaffrey

Preface

The haunting image of New York's falling twin towers defined for the world the reality of the "new terrorism." Americans had faced terrorism before September 11. However, terrorism's previous incarnations, were not nearly as organized, deadly, or personal as the attacks inflicted on New York City and Washington, D.C., or on that remote Pennsylvania field.

In 1984 when I first became involved in the antiterrorism and counterterrorism efforts, most international and national terrorism was ideological. It was part of the East versus West, left versus right confrontation—a small but dangerous side-show to the greater, bipolar, Cold War drama. In the past, terrorism was almost always the province of groups of militants who had the backing of political forces and states hostile to American interests. Under the old rules, "terrorists wanted a lot of people watching, not a lot of people dead."[1] They did not want large body counts because they wanted converts. They wanted a seat at the table. Today's terrorists are not particularly concerned about converts and don't want a seat at the table, "They want to destroy the table and everyone sitting at it."[2]

What is new to me and my generation, but not to Reid Sawyer and Natasha Bajema and theirs, is the emergence of terrorism that is not ideological in a political sense. Instead it is inspired by religious extremism and ethnic-separatist elements, who might be individuals such as the Unabomber, or like-minded people working in cells, small groups, or larger coalitions.[3] They do not answer completely to any government, operate across national borders, and have access to funding and advanced technology.[4] Such groups are not bound by the same constraints or motivated by the same goals as nation-states. And, unlike state-sponsored groups, religious extremists, ethnic separatists, and lone "Unabombers" are not susceptible to traditional diplomacy or military deterrence. There is no state with which to negotiate or to retaliate against. And, today's terrorists are not concerned about limiting casualties. Religious terrorists, such as al Qaeda in particular, want casualties—lots of them.[5]

The new terrorism is not an ideologicalism like communism or capitalism whose value can be debated in the classroom or decided at polls. It is an ancient tactic and instrument of conflict. Terrorism today has a global reach that it did not have before globalization and the information technology revolution. It can ride the back of the Web, use advanced communications to move immense financial sums from Sudan to the Philippines, to Australia, to banks in Florida.[6] And, for $28.50, any Internet surfer can purchase *Bacteriological Warfare: A Major Threat to North America,* which shows how to grow deadly bacteria that could be used in a weapon of mass destruction.

Clearly, the United States and its citizens are favored targets of the new terrorists. Many wonder why. "Why do They Hate Us?" was the banner headline in *Newsweek* and the *Christian Science Monitor* soon after 9/11. Why should Islamic extremists hate us? After all, was it not the United States that saved those who follow the Islamic faith in Kuwait, liberated them in Iraq, and continues to protect them in Bosnia and Kosovo? Is it a Jihad, a war of faiths between Christians and Moslems as some suggest? Or is the United States a target because of the resentment it has spread through societies demoralized by their recent history. As one knowledgeable journalist put it, "A sense of failure and injustice is rising in the throats of millions" because Arab nations have lost three wars against Israel, their arch-foe and America's ally.

Many also believe that globalization is not only a technological tool for terrorists, but that it is a root cause of terrorism either separately or in conjunction with religious extremism. Extreme Muslim extremists and others who have missed the rewards of globalization worry that unbridled globalization exploits workers and replaces ancient cultures with McDonald's and Mickey Mouse. According to some, globalization is based on the American economic system, and because the United States is the dominant world power, it has succeeded in expanding the reach of its version of globalization to more and more areas of the world. As the gap between the rich and poor has grown wider during the last twenty years of U.S.–led globalization, the poor have watched American wealth and hegemony expand, while they, themselves, have received little or no benefit.

There are other theories about rising terrorism and future targets, many of which will be covered in this book. One thing is certain however, America is a target. It has been attacked and will be again unless the attacks can be prevented or preempted. Rudi Giuliani made this very clear to West Point's 2002 graduating class when he was the guest speaker at their final dinner banquet. He theorized that America was attacked for a number of reasons: it prizes political and economic freedom, elects its political leaders, and has lifted people out of poverty; it also has religious freedom, respects human rights as well as the rights of women. America's adversaries do not, and they are threatened by the freedoms we have. "We are right and they are wrong," Giuliani said to thunderous applause. "There is no excuse and no justification for these attacks," he said. The [former] mayor told the cadets that America has already won the war on terrorism. "We still have a lot of battles to win, but we have actually won the war on terrorism because the terrorists tried, but could not break our spirit."

This book, first edited at West Point, will address those "battles to win"—how to fight and win them, and why America and the free world are in the dubious position of having to fight the battles in the first place. Why edit the first edition of this book (the book at West Point)? More importantly, why did two career soldiers originally edit the book? Brigadier General Dan Kaufman, West Point's former dean, answered these questions in a *Los Angeles Times* interview. "Suddenly, now the world is a much more dangerous place," he said. "The nation is at risk again. The notion that the American homeland is vulnerable is new to all of us. Given where West Point sits—fifty miles from ground zero—there is a sense of immediacy here."

Organization

Terrorism and Counterterrorism: Understanding the New Security Environment, 3rd ed., is in two parts. Unit I analyzes the philosophical, political, and religious roots of terrorist activities around the world and discusses the national, regional, and global effects of historical and recent terrorist acts. In addition to material on the threats from suicide bombers, as well as from chemical, biological, radiological, and nuclear weapons, there are also important contributions analyzing new and growing threats: criminal cartels terrorist recruitment on the Internet, and genomic terrorism. Unit II deals with the past, present, and future national and international responses to terrorism and defenses against it.

Unit I, "Defining the Threat"

Unit I contains five chapters. Chapter 1, "Terrorism Defined," consists of articles by Bruce Hoffman, Eqbal Ahmad, and Martha Crenshaw who define terrorism and address several specific questions, in some cases from very different perspectives: What is terrorism? What is counterterrorism? Who is a terrorist? And, why do these questions matter? Hoffman's "Defining Terrorism" emphasizes the changing nature of terrorism. He succinctly defines its past and present, explains its evolution, and delineates terrorism from other concepts such as insurgency, criminals, etc. His offering is an important primer that will prepare the reader for the rest of the book. Ahmad's "Terrorism: Theirs & Ours," like Hoffman's article also emphasizes change. "To begin with," writes Ahmad, "terrorists change. The terrorist of yesterday is the hero of today, and the hero of yesterday becomes the terrorist of today." His example is Osama bin Laden, who was once an American ally in the fight against the Soviet Union and is now public enemy number one. In "The Logic of Terrorism: Terrorist Behavior as a Product of Strategic Choice," Martha Crenshaw shows that terrorism is a perfectly rational and logical choice for some individuals and groups: "The central problem is to determine when extremist organizations find terrorism useful. . . . Terrorism is not the only method of working toward radical goals, and thus it must be compared to the alternative strategies available to dissidents."

Audrey Kurth Cronin's "Behind the Curve: Globalization and International Terrorism," argues that terrorism is not only a reaction to globalization but is also facilitated by it, while the U.S. response to the terrorist threat has been reactive and anachronistic. She introduces a theme echoed elsewhere in this volume that while military power is an important tool in this conflict, it can only be a supporting instrument in the campaign against terrorism.

Chapter 2, "Understanding the Facilitators of Modern Terrorism," explains how globalization, rapid changes in communications technology, and adapting modern business practices facilitate terrorist's global operations. Audrey Kurth Cronin's "Behind the Curve: Globalization and International Terrorism," argues that terrorism is not only a reaction to globalization but is also facilitated by it, while the U.S. response to the terrorist threat has been reactive and anachronistic. She introduces a theme echoed elsewhere in this volume that while military power is an important tool in this conflict, it can only be a supporting instrument in the campaign against terrorism. In "Weak States and Global Threats: Fact or Fiction?" Stewart Patrick explains there is little evidence supporting the notion that there is a strong correlation between weak states, denied areas and terrorism. Ray Takeyh and Nikolas Gvosdev have a slightly different view. In their article "Do Terrorist Networks Need a Home?" they argue that terrorist's networked cellular structure and ready access to modern communications precludes them from requiring a "territorial home." However, explain the authors, failed states can still provide areas for training, recruitment, logistics, and communications operations.

Chapter 3, "The New Terrorism," explores the rise and impact of new terrorism in greater depth and then looks at some of the technological and control mechanisms that make today's terrorists more difficult to detect and defeat than the left-wing terrorists of earlier eras.

I begin this dialogue in "The New Terrorism," by outlining eight ways today's terrorism differs from that of the Cold War. Specifically the new terrorism is more violent and better financed than in the Cold War era. The new terrorists operate globally, are better trained, more difficult to penetrate, and have access to and say they will use weapons of mass destruction. Perhaps most important for all to remember is that victory will be elusive. More than likely there will be no formal surrender by a defeated foe, no armistice ending combat on acceptable terms, and no arrest and incarceration of all the members of a terrorist organization. My article discusses the advantages present-day terrorists, particularly al Qaeda, have over their counterparts in the 1960s, '70s, and '80s.

A trio of RAND specialists—John Arquilla, David Ronfeldt, and Michele Zanini—suggest in "Networks, Netwar, and Information-Age Terrorism" that a new type of enemy and warfare will be the product of the information revolution, including the rise of new, more complex forms of terrorism. New systems and organizations and modes of conflict used by modern-day terrorists will inevitably affect the nature and styles of warfare. Using "netwar" and "cyberwar" as weapons, these terrorists will attack modern societies' vulnerabilities. The authors recommend that new organizations, strategies, technologies, and doctrines will be required to defeat this new form of enemy.

The third article, "Defeating Al Qaeda" by Rohan Gunaratna, examines the shift in al Qaeda from a group to that of an ideology. Counter-terror organizations will have to focus on al Qaeda the group and on their ideology to be effective, says Gunaratna. Finally, in "Rethinking Threat Assessments for Terrorist Targets: Applying the Lessons of Complex Terrorism," Natasha Bajema draws on theory to demonstrate how the increasing vulnerability of economic and technological systems combined with the growing capabilities of terrorists raises the appeal of potential targets, such as nuclear power plants. In contrast, Bajema concludes that increasing demands for electricity production, growing concerns about global warming, and the fragile state of the U.S. plan for nuclear waste disposal are interacting to increase the appeal of nuclear power plants as terrorist targets.

An old saying I learned as a child is that "More people have been killed in the name of God than for any other reason." Things have not changed. Indeed the articles in Chapter 4, "Religion and the Intersection with Terrorism," argue that religious terrorism is on the rise and is unprecedented in its militancy and activism. In his article, "Terrorism in the Name of Religion," Magnus Ranstorp explores the reasons for the dramatic increase of religiously motivated terrorism.

Quintan Wiktorowicz's "A Genealogy of Radical Islam" contends that al Qaeda and like-minded terrorist groups are not "outliers" at all. Instead they are part of a broader community of more extremist Islamists known as "Salafis" or "Wahhabis." In the end, speculates Wiktorowicz, the level of extremist activity may be the undoing of popular support for al Qaeda. The "Clash within Islam," by Emmanuel Sivan, explains why moderate Muslims have such a difficult time countering Muslim extremists. Some of the reasons are historical, political, and organizational. Other reasons have to do with basic communications skills and fear. Many moderates are afraid to stand up to the extremists for fear of losing their lives.

Chapter 5, "Modern Methods and Modes of Attack," explores many weapons available to and/or sought by terrorists. Weapons of mass destruction (WMD) are an important topic in this chapter, but Gavin Cameron and Natasha Bajema explain that WMD in the hands of terrorist groups are more often weapons of mass disruption rather than weapons of mass destruction. "Terrorism in the Genomic Age," by John Ellis, paints a frightening picture of the possible misuse of the human genome by terrorists. In "The Leaderless Nexus: When Crime and Terror Converge," Chris Dishman argues that the shift from hierarchical to more diverse organizational structures is not only happening within terrorist organizations but also in criminal organizations. This new phenomenon complicates counterterrorism efforts and creates a more flexible operating environment for terrorists to obtain logistics support.

Bruce Hoffman's piece, "The Logic of Suicide Terrorism," in Chapter 5, describes how the tactics of terrorists, particularly suicide bombing, are also very logical. According to Hoffman, suicide bombings are inexpensive and effective—the ultimate smart bomb. Finally in Chapter 5, Assaf Moghadam's "The Evolution of Suicide Terrorism and its Implications for Research" notes that suicide operations have a long history. He further suggests that dramatic changes in suicide terrorism, including the use of suicide attacks in the absence of foreign occupation, changing patterns of recruitment, and the use of small radicalized cells are not adequately understood by counterterrorism specialists.

Unit II, "Countering the Terrorist Threat"

Unit II is organized in five chapters. The essays and articles in Unit II analyze and debate the practical, political, ethical, and moral questions raised by military and nonmilitary responses, including preemptive actions outside the context of declared war. New to this volume from previous volumes of *Terrorism and Counterterrorism* are chapters on "Terrorism and the Media" and "Winning the War on Terrorism."

Chapter 6, "Terrorism and the Media," examines the role the media play on terrorists and counter-terrorists. In the chapter's first article, "Dilemmas Concerning Media Coverage of Terrorist Attacks," Boaz Ganor identifies the media's dilemma in covering terrorism—the need to report on the events, otherwise referred to as the "public's right to know," and the benefits terrorists derive from the media coverage. Ganor uses Israel as a case study to explore the "dilemma." In "Watchdogs on a Leash: Closing Doors on the Media," John Stacks notes the importance of the media in holding democratic governments accountable by keeping the public aware of the government's response to terrorism. In "High-Tech Terror: Al Qaeda's Use of New Technology," Jarret Brachman describes how adept al Qaeda and like-minded terrorist groups are at exploiting new communications and media technologies. Ending Chapter 6, Gabriel Weimann's "www.terror.net: How Modern Terrorism Uses the Internet" argues that policymakers don't pay enough attention to the "routine uses of the Internet" that terrorists exploit to their advantage.

Chapter 7, "The Challenges of Terrorism to a Free Society," examines the challenge to states when combating terrorism. Richard Betts in "The Soft Underbelly of American Primacy: Tactical Advantages of Terror," asserts that a strategy of terrorism "flows from the coincidence of two conditions: intense political grievance and gross imbalance of power." Says Betts, terrorism "may become instrumentally appealing by default—when one party in conflict lacks other military options." "This is why terrorism is the premier form of 'asymmetric warfare,' the Pentagon buzzword for the type of threats likely to confront the United States in the post–Cold War world."

In his final article in this book, "A Nasty Business," Bruce Hoffman notes the difficulty intelligence organizations in democracies have in collecting intelligence against terrorists: "Gathering 'good intelligence' against terrorists is an inherently brutish enterprise, involving methods a civics class might not condone." Written in 2002, Hoffman was prescient in the questions he asked about the limits of interrogation and the efficacy of torture. Hoffman also advances the question asked by many after September 11: How much of their civil rights, liberties, and freedoms are Americans willing to give up in order to prosecute the war on terrorism? This article is a must-read for any student of this subject.

In "The Limits of Military Power," Rob de Wijk states that "the West's armed forces are fundamentally flawed. Conceptually, the focus is still on conventional warfare, but the new wars will be unconventional. . . . The West needs special forces to confront unconventional irregular fighters such as terrorists, and those forces are not available in large quantities." Nevertheless, de Wijk contends that the military, including special forces, cannot win the war on terrorism alone. There must also be a "campaign to win the hearts and minds of the Islamic people."

Richard Shultz Jr., concludes this chapter with an interesting look at why the United States never deployed its special operations forces against al Qaeda prior to 9/11. This article is a must-read for any student seeking to understand the bureaucratic nature of policy making in this area. Shultz has spent his career studying terrorism, special operations, and military strategy. In his article "Showstoppers: Nine Reasons Why We Never Sent Our Special Operations after Al Qaeda before 9/11," he brings this vast amount of knowledge to bear in analyzing the interviews he conducted with senior policy makers who were involved in the decisions not to deploy our special operations forces against al Qaeda.

The selections in Chapter 8, "Strategies and Approaches for Combating Terrorism," discuss grand strategies (or the lack thereof) executed by the United States and its opponents in terrorism and counterterrorism warfare. Martha Crenshaw leads off the chapter with the aptly titled "Terrorism, Strategies, and Grand Strategies," in which she argues the strategic dimensions of terrorism were neglected by scholars and practitioners prior to 9/11. She challenges policymakers to rethink their approach to responding to terrorism and argues that "counterterrorist strategy must be linked to grand strategy and grand strategy to policy goals." Similarly, in "US Counter-terrorism Options: A Taxonomy," Daniel Byman criticizes the Bush administration for lack of a grand strategy (or much of any strategy) to counter the terrorist threat. Likening the Bush administration's counterterrorism effort to a "garbage-pail approach," Byman suggests consideration of seven different options for going after al Qaeda and like-minded terrorist groups.

In "Preemptive Military Doctrine: No Other Choice," I argue that deterrence and containment, the previous foundations of U.S. strategy, are no longer valid when confronting transnational, non-state terrorists. I agree with President Bush that the United States must identify and destroy the terrorist threat before it reaches our borders, and, if necessary, act alone and use preemptive force. In my view, the traditional economic, political, diplomatic, and military applications of American power used to leverage and influence states in the past are not effective against non-state actors. Whom do you sanction or embargo? With whom do you negotiate? How do you defend against or deter Osama bin Laden? You don't. The only effective way to influence the bin Ladens of the world is to preempt them before they can act.

Paul Pillar, a senior CIA official and a noted terrorism scholar, paints a picture of the new al Qaeda—one characterized by decentralization. His exploration of the changing nature of the threat and the implications of that change for governments is one of the first to explore the problems of fighting a decentralized enemy. In other words, we are no longer facing the al Qaeda of 2001—we are instead facing a disparate and dispersed enemy that may come from any corner of the radicalized factions of Sunni Islam. In his article, "Beyond Al Qaeda: Countering a Decentralized Terrorist Threat," Pillar begins with the challenges that this new form poses for intelligence agencies before moving on to a discussion of the international cooperation needed to address the threat. He concludes his article with a call to maintain the commitment to this struggle.

Steven Simon and Jeff Martini address one of the most critical questions in this fight against al Qaeda—how to deny the organization its popular support. In their article, "Terrorism: Denying Al Qaeda Its Popular Support," the authors explain that "Denying terrorists the support of these constituents is a crucial component in the war on terrorism and requires approaches that go beyond the standard strategies employed in the current campaign." Without such an approach, the terrorists' message will continue to hold sway and gain support from this broader population that provides the recruits, the money, and the legitimacy sought by the terrorists.

In the final article of this chapter, "Untangling the Terror Web: Identifying and counteracting the Phenomenon of Crossover between Terrorist Groups," Matt Levitt argues that counterterrorism efforts should focus on terrorist's logistics and support efforts. According to Levitt, the logistical and support networks of terrorist groups present unique opportunities to interdict and disrupt terrorist operations.

Chapter 9, "Leveraging the Role of the Private Sector," is new to previous volumes of this book and recognizes that the global private sector has become a critical player in counterterrorism efforts. Leading off the chapter is Mark Basile's article titled, "Going to the Source: Why Al Qaeda's Financial Network is Likely to Withstand the Current War on Terrorist Financing." In the article Basile examines a different challenge that governments face in combating terrorism—that of terrorist financing. He concludes that al Qaeda's method of moving money will be difficult to stop but that efforts must be made to do so in order to defeat them. Kelly Hicks and Roseann McSorley, practitioners from Deutsche Bank, argue in "Global Terrorism and the Private Sector: The Impact of 9/11 on Security Awareness and Operations in Financial Institutions" that financial institutions' support to local law enforcement is crucial to the campaign against terrorism. In much the same vein, Stacy Reiter Neal concludes Chapter 9 with "Cross-Sector Intelligence Partnerships: Is Public-Private Information Sharing a Neglected Counter-terrorism Tool." In her article Neal concludes that "the possibilities presented by successful public-private partnerships are immeasurable," but they are limited by clear information-sharing policies and procedures.

Chapter 10 concludes this edition with four articles suggesting ways to win the "so called" war on terrorism. In "Al-Qaeda Strikes Back," Bruce Riedel reminds us that the fight against al Qaeda is far from over. In fact, Riedel argues that al Qaeda is more powerful today as a result of the U.S. military going into Iraq. However, Riedel is optimistic that al Qaeda can eventually be defeated. In "How al-Qaeda ends: The Decline and Demise of Terrorist Groups," Audrey Kurth Cronin contends that al Qaeda will be defeated just like countless terrorist groups have been defeated in the past. Studying previous successes against terrorist groups, says Cronin, will benefit policy makers in defeating al Qaeda now.

"The Uncontested Battles: The Role of Actions, Networks and Ideas in the Fight Against al Qaeda," by Reid Sawyer and Jodi Vittori, first articulates that policy and strategy errors have made al Qaeda stronger despite losing its sanctuary in Afghanistan. To defeat al Qaeda, the authors contend that al Qaeda must be understood as a multi-faceted organization and a global social movement. To defeat al Qaeda, they must be fought on three levels: a war of action, a war of networks, and a war of ideas. I agree with all of the authors on most points. However in my article "Winning the Campaign against Terrorists: Five Considerations," I challenge the notion that there is a war against terrorism and suggest we stop calling it a "war." Like many in this book, I further suggest that kinetic energy alone will not defeat al Qaeda and offer other mechanisms for addressing and defeating the threat.

Notes

1. Brian Michael Jenkins, "Will Terrorists Go Nuclear?" RAND Paper P-5541 (1975), p. 4.
2. James Woolsey, 1994.
3. Stephen A. Cambone, *A New Structure for National Security Policy Planning,* Washington D.C.: Government Printing Office, 1996, p. 43.
4. Gideon Rose, "It Could Happen Here—Facing the New Terrorism," *Foreign Affairs,* March-April, 1999, p. 1.
5. Bruce Hoffman, *Inside Terrorism,* New York: Columbia University Press, 1998, p. 205.
6. Paul Mann, "Modern Military Threats: Not All They Might Seem?" *Aviation Week & Space Technology,* April 22, 2002, p. 1. (Gordon Adams quote)

Unit I

Defining the Threat

Chapter 1

Defining Terrorism: Means, Ends, and Motives

Chapter 1 introduces the problems inherent in defining a topic as complex as terrorism. In the news everywhere and used to describe events from the Philippines to Central America, from the Middle East to the United States, we "think we know what it is when we see it." But is that enough? Bruce Hoffman does not think so. In his reading "Defining Terrorism," he struggles to come up with a definition of the term that avoids the "promiscuous" and imprecise labeling of a range of acts. He provides dictionary definitions but finds them to be "unsatisfying" because ultimately a society's definition is a reflection of the political and social tenor of the times. Hoffman traces the historical use of the term "terrorism" from the reign of terror that followed the French Revolution; to the communist and fascist movements in Russia, Italy, and Germany; to the narco-terrorism of the 1990s. He concludes with a definition that seeks to distinguish terrorists from guerrillas, ordinary criminals, and assassins.

Eqbal Ahmad finds the official definition used by the U.S. government and their approach to terrorism to be an extremely limiting one, which stirs up emotion without "exercising our intelligence." Ahmad maintains that we do need to know what terrorism is before we can determine how to stop it. Most important, we must first study the motives of the terrorists. Throughout his reading, Ahmad uses Osama bin Laden and his transformation from U.S. ally to terrorist as a case study. His reading concludes with three recommendations to the United States for dealing with terrorism, which, although written in 1998, are remarkably prophetic in light of the events of September 11, 2001.

The psychology behind the motivation and behavior of terrorists has been examined extensively, but the public, as well as many specialists, have often been content to write-off terrorists as irrational fanatics. Rather than see terrorism as an unintended outcome or the last resort of pathological individuals, Martha Crenshaw examines the use of terrorism as a deliberate strategy. She describes a framework of rational decision making, examining the calculations of cost versus benefit that go into the choice of terrorism as a weapon. Crenshaw concludes that neither the psychological nor the strategic explanation alone is adequate for examining terrorist behavior, but offers the strategic choice framework as an "antidote" to the persistent psychological stereotypes that she believes are nonproductive and fairly persuasive.

Bruce Hoffman, 2006

Defining Terrorism

What is terrorism? Few words have so insidiously worked their way into our everyday vocabulary. Like "Internet"—another grossly overused term that has similarly become an indispensable part of the argot of the early twenty-first century—most people have a vague idea or impression of what terrorism is but lack a more precise, concrete, and truly explanatory definition of the word. This imprecision has been abetted partly by the modern media, whose efforts to communicate an often complex and convoluted message in the briefest amount of airtime or print space possible have led to the promiscuous labeling of a range of violent acts as "terrorism." Pick up a newspaper or turn on the television and—even within the same broadcast or on the same page—one can find such disparate acts as the bombing of a building, the assassination of a head of state, the massacre of civilians by a military unit, the poisoning of produce on supermarket shelves, or the deliberate contamination of over-the-counter medication in a drugstore, all described as incidents of terrorism. Indeed, virtually any especially abhorrent act of violence perceived as directed against society—whether it involves the activities of antigovernment dissidents or governments themselves, organized-crime syndicates, common criminals, rioting mobs, people engaged in militant protest, individual psychotics, or lone extortionists—is often labeled "terrorism."

Dictionary definitions are of little help. The preeminent authority on the English language, the much-venerated *Oxford English Dictionary,* is disappointingly unobliging when it comes to providing edification on this subject, its interpretation at once too literal and too historical to be of much contemporary use:

> Terrorism: A system of terror. 1. Government by intimidation as directed and carried out by the party in power in France during the revolution of 1789–94; the system of "Terror." 2. *gen.* A policy intended to strike with terror those against whom it is adopted; the employment of methods of intimidation; the fact of terrorizing or condition of being terrorized.

These definitions are wholly unsatisfying. Rather than learning what terrorism is, one instead finds, in the first instance, a somewhat pedestrian historical—and, in respect of the modern accepted usage of the term, a uselessly anachronistic—description. The second definition offered is only slightly more helpful. While accurately communicating the fear-inducing quality of terrorism, the definition is still so broad as to apply to almost any action that scares ("terrorizes") us. Though an integral part of "terrorism," this definition is still insufficient for the purpose of accurately defining the phenomenon that is today called "terrorism."

A slightly more satisfying elucidation may be found in the *OED*'s definition of the perpetrator of the act than in its efforts to come to grips with the act itself. In this respect, a "terrorist" is defined thus:

> 1. As a political term: a. Applied to the Jacobins and their agents and partisans in the French Revolution, esp. to those connected with the Revolutionary tribunals during the "Reign of Terror." b. Any one who attempts to further his views by a system of coercive intimidation; *spec,* applied to members of one of the extreme revolutionary societies in Russia.

This is appreciably more helpful. First, it immediately introduces the reader to the notion of terrorism as a *political* concept. As will be seen, this key characteristic of terrorism is absolutely paramount to understanding its aims, motivations, and purposes and is critical in distinguishing it from other types of violence.

Terrorism, in the most widely accepted contemporary usage of the term, is fundamentally and inherently political. It is also ineluctably about power: the pursuit of power, the acquisition of power, and the use of power to achieve political change. Terrorism is thus violence—or, equally important, the threat of violence—used and directed in pursuit of, or in service of, a political aim. With this vital point clearly illuminated, one can appreciate the significance of the additional definition of "terrorist" provided by the *OED:* "Any one who attempts to further his views by a system of coercive intimidation." This definition underscores clearly the other fundamental characteristic of terrorism: that it is a planned, calculated, and indeed systematic act.

Given this relatively straightforward elucidation, why, then, is terrorism so difficult to define? The most compelling reason perhaps is because the meaning of the term has changed so frequently over the past two hundred years.

The Changing Meaning of Terrorism

The word "terrorism" was first popularized during the French Revolution. In contrast to its contemporary usage, at that time terrorism had a decidedly *positive* connotation. The system or *régime de la terreur* of 1793–94—from which the English word came—was adopted as a means to establish order during the transient anarchical period of turmoil and upheaval that followed the uprisings of 1789, and indeed many other revolutions. Hence, unlike terrorism as it is commonly understood today, to mean a *revolutionary* or antigovernment activity undertaken by nonstate or subnational entities, the *régime de la terreur* was an instrument of governance wielded by the recently established revolutionary *state*. It was designed to consolidate the new government's power by intimidating counterrevolutionaries, subversives, and all other dissidents whom the new regime regarded as "enemies of the people." The Committee of General Security and the Revolutionary Tribunal ("People's Court" in the modern vernacular) were thus accorded wide powers of arrest and judgment, publicly putting to death by guillotine those convicted of treasonous (i.e., reactionary) crimes. In this manner, a powerful lesson was conveyed to any and all who might oppose the revolution or grow nostalgic for the ancien régime.

Ironically, perhaps, terrorism in its original context was also closely associated with the ideals of virtue and democracy. The revolutionary leader Maximilien Robespierre firmly believed that virtue was the mainspring of a popular government at peace, but that during the time of revolution virtue must be allied with terror in order for democracy to triumph. He appealed famously to "virtue, without which terror is evil; terror, without which virtue is helpless" and proclaimed: "Terror is nothing but justice, prompt, severe and inflexible; it is therefore an emanation of virtue."

Despite this divergence from its subsequent meaning, the French Revolution's "terrorism" still shared at least two key characteristics with its modern-day variant. First, the *régime de la terreur* was neither random nor indiscriminate, as terrorism is often portrayed today, but was organized, deliberate, and systematic. Second, its goal and its very justification—like that of contemporary terrorism—was the creation of a "new and better society" in place of a fundamentally corrupt and undemocratic political system. Indeed, Robespierre's vague and Utopian exegeses of the revolution's central goals are remarkably similar in tone and content to the equally turgid, millenarian manifestos issued by many contemporary revolutionary—primarily left-wing, Marxist-oriented—terrorist organizations. For example, in 1794 Robespierre declared, in language eerily presaging the communiqués issued by groups such as Germany's Red Army Faction and Italy's Red Brigades nearly two centuries later:

> We want an order of things . . . in which the arts are an adornment to the liberty that ennobles them, and commerce the source of wealth for the public and not of monstrous opulence for a few families. . . . In our country we desire morality instead of selfishness, honesty and not mere "honor," principle and not mere custom, duty and not mere propriety, the sway of reason rather than the tyranny of fashion, a scorn for vice and not a contempt for the unfortunate.

Like many other revolutions, the French Revolution eventually began to consume itself. On 8 Thermidor, year two of the new calendar adopted by the revolutionaries (July 26, 1794), Robespierre announced to the National Convention that he had in his possession a new list of traitors. Fearing that their own names might be on that list, extremists joined forces with moderates to repudiate both Robespierre and his *régime de la terreur.* Robespierre and his closest followers themselves met the same fate that had befallen some forty thousand others: execution by guillotine. The Terror was at an end; thereafter "terrorism" became a term associated with the abuse of office and power—with overt "criminal" implications. Within a year of Robespierre's demise, the word had been popularized in English by Edmund Burke, who, in his famous polemic against the French Revolution, described the "Thousands of those Hell hounds called Terrorists . . . let loose on the people."

One of the French Revolution's more enduring repercussions was the impetus it gave to antimonarchical sentiment elsewhere in Europe. Popular subservience to rulers who derived their authority from God through "divine right of rule," rather than from their subjects, was increasingly questioned by a politically awakened Continent. The advent of nationalism, and with it notions of statehood and citizenship based on the common identity of a people rather than the lineage of a royal family, were resulting in the unification and creation of new nation-states such as Germany and Italy. Meanwhile, the massive socioeconomic changes engendered by the Industrial Revolution were creating new "universalist" ideologies (such as communism/Marxism), born of the alienation and exploitative conditions of nineteenth-century capitalism. From this milieu a new era of terrorism emerged, in which the concept had gained many of the familiar revolutionary, antistate connotations of today. Its chief progenitor was arguably the Italian republican extremist Carlo Pisacane, who had forsaken his birthright as duke of San Giovanni only to perish in 1857 during an ill-fated revolt against Bourbon rule. A passionate advocate of federalism and mutualism, Pisacane is remembered less on this account than for the theory of "propaganda by deed," which he is credited with defining—an idea that has exerted a compelling influence on rebels and terrorists alike ever since. "The propaganda of the idea is a chimera," Pisacane wrote. "Ideas result from deeds, not the latter from the former, and the people will not be free when they are educated, but educated when they are free." Violence, he argued, was necessary not only to draw attention to, or generate publicity for, a cause, but also to inform, educate, and ultimately rally the masses behind the revolution. The didactic purpose of violence, Pisacane argued, could never be effectively replaced by pamphlets, wall posters, or assemblies.

Perhaps the first organization to put into practice Pisacane's dictum was the Narodnaya Volya, or People's Will (sometimes translated as "People's Freedom"), a small group of Russian constitutionalists that had been founded in 1878 to challenge czarist rule. For the Narodnaya Volya, the apathy and alienation of the Russian masses afforded few alternatives besides resorting to daring and dramatic acts of violence designed to attract attention to the group and its cause. However, unlike the many late-twentieth-century terrorist organizations that have cited the principle of "propaganda by deed" to justify the wanton targeting of civilians in order to assure them publicity through the shock and horror produced by wholesale bloodshed, the Narodnaya Volya displayed an almost quixotic attitude toward the violence it wrought. To this group, "propaganda by deed" meant the selective targeting of specific individuals whom the group considered the embodiment of the autocratic, oppressive state. Hence the victims—the czar, leading members of the royal family, senior government officials—were deliberately chosen for their "symbolic" value as the dynastic heads and subservient agents of a corrupt and tyrannical regime. An intrinsic element in the group's collective beliefs was that "not one drop of superfluous blood" should be shed in pursuit of aims, however noble or utilitarian they might be. Even having selected their targets with great care and the utmost deliberation, group members still harbored profound regrets about taking the life of a fellow human being. Their unswerving adherence to this principle is perhaps best illustrated by the failed attempt on the life of Grand Duke Serge Alexandrovich made by a successor organization to the Narodnaya Volya in 1905. As the royal carriage came into view, the terrorist tasked with the assassination saw that the duke was unexpectedly accompanied by his children and therefore aborted his mission rather than risk harming the intended victim's family (the duke was killed in a subsequent attack). By comparison, the midair explosion caused by a terrorist bomb on Pan Am Flight 103 over Lockerbie, Scotland, in December 1988 indiscriminately claimed the lives of all 259 people on board—innocent men, women, and children alike—plus eleven inhabitants of the village where the plane crashed.

Ironically, the Narodnaya Volya's most dramatic accomplishment also led directly to its demise. On March 1, 1881, the group assassinated Czar Alexander II. The failure of eight previous plots had led the conspirators to take extraordinary measures to ensure the success of this attempt. Four volunteers were given four bombs each and deployed along the alternative routes followed by the czar's cortege. As two of the bomber-assassins stood in wait on the same street, the sleighs carrying the czar and his Cossack escort approached the first terrorist, who hurled his bomb at the passing sleigh, missing it by inches. The whole entourage came to a halt as soldiers seized the hapless culprit and the czar descended from his sleigh to check on a bystander wounded by the explosion. "Thank God, I am safe," the czar reportedly declared—just as the second bomber emerged from the crowd and detonated his weapon, killing both himself and his target. The full weight of the czarist state now fell on the heads of the Narodnaya Volya. Acting on information provided by the arrested member, the secret police swept down on the group's safe houses and hideouts, rounding up most of the plotters, who were quickly tried, convicted, and hanged. Further information from this group led to subsequent arrests, so that within a year of the assassination only one member of the original executive committee was still at large. She too was finally apprehended in 1883, at which point the first generation of Narodnaya Volya terrorists ceased to exist, although various successor organizations subsequently emerged to carry on the struggle.

At the time, the repercussions of the czar's assassination could not have been known or appreciated by either the condemned or their comrades languishing in prison or exiled to Siberia. But in addition to precipitating the beginning of the end of czarist rule, the group also deeply influenced individual revolutionaries and subversive organizations elsewhere. To the nascent anarchist movement, the "propaganda by deed" strategy championed by the Narodnaya Volya provided a model to be emulated. Within four months of the czar's murder, a group of radicals in London convened an "anarchist conference," which publicly applauded the assassination and extolled tyrannicide as a means to achieve revolutionary change. In hopes of encouraging and coordinating worldwide anarchist activities, the conferees decided to establish the "Anarchist International" (or "Black International"). Although this idea, like most of their ambitious plans, came to naught, the publicity generated by even a putative "Anarchist International" was sufficient to create a myth of global revolutionary pretensions and thereby stimulate fears and suspicions disproportionate to its actual impact or political achievements. Disparate and uncoordinated though the anarchists' violence was, the movement's emphasis on individual action or operations carried out by small cells of like-minded radicals made detection and prevention by the police particularly difficult, thus further heightening public fears. For example, following the assassination of U.S. president William McKinley in 1901 (by a young Hungarian refugee, Leon Czolgosz, who, while not a regular member of any anarchist organization, was nonetheless influenced by the philosophy), Congress swiftly enacted legislation barring known anarchists or anyone "who disbelieves in or is opposed to all organized government" from entering the United States. However, while anarchists were responsible for an impressive string of assassinations of heads of state and a number of particularly notorious bombings from about 1878 until the second decade of the twentieth century, in the final analysis, other than stimulating often exaggerated fears, anarchism made little tangible impact on either the domestic or the international politics of the countries affected. It does, however, offer an interesting historical footnote: much as the "information revolution" of the late-twentieth and early-twenty-first centuries is alleged to have made the means and methods of bomb-making and other types of terrorist activity more readily available via the Internet, on CD-ROM, and through ordinary libraries and bookstores, one of anarchism's flourishing "cottage industries" more than a century earlier was the widespread distribution of similar "how-to"- or "do-it-yourself"-type manuals and publications of violence and mayhem.

Meanwhile, another series of developments was unfolding on the other side of Europe that would exert a similarly profound influence on future terrorist strategy and tactics. In this instance, the motivation was neither antimonarchical nor anarchist, but nationalist and separatist. Although Britain's rule of Ireland already had a centuries-long history of restiveness and rebellion, in the mid-nineteenth century the locus of revolutionary activities had expanded from Ireland to include the United States as well. Among the mass of Irish emigrants who had fled the failure of successive potato crops and the resultant famine was a group of radical nationalists who in 1858 founded a secret society called the Fenian Brotherhood. The Fenians—and their Ireland-based offshoot, the Irish Revolutionary Brotherhood (IRB)—were at once as daring and determined as they were impatient and incompetent. Their motto of "revolution sooner or never" accurately describes a string of half-baked plots that purported to kidnap the Prince of Wales, invade Canada, and orchestrate a popular uprising in Ireland. So successful were British efforts to penetrate the organization, and so abject were the Fenians' failed grand schemes, that the movement fell into desuetude within a decade of its founding. But the Fenians' unswerving commitment to both Irish republicanism and the use of violence to attain it created a legacy that subsequently inspired a new generation of U.S.-based Irish revolutionaries.

Thus by 1873 a new organization, calling itself the Clan na Gael (United Irishmen), had taken up the Fenians' mantle. Its driving force was a firebrand named Jeremiah O'Donovan Rossa. Sentenced to life imprisonment for sedition in 1865, O'Donovan Rossa was released only six years later after a commission of inquiry substantiated his claims of mistreatment. The abuse inflicted on imprisoned terrorists like O'Donovan Rossa in the nineteenth century actually bears a disquieting resemblance to the treatment reportedly meted out to some detainees in the war on terrorism today. Not only was O'Donovan Rossa held for more than a month with his hands handcuffed behind his back, but he was also "kept naked day and night" in a darkened cell and fed a meager ration of bread and water. Exiled to the United States, O'Donovan Rossa quickly resumed his subversive activities. He was assisted in these endeavors by Patrick Ford, the editor of the *Irish World,* a newspaper that became the main platform for Clan na Gael propaganda and incitement. Together, they developed a new strategy for the republican movement. "We are not now advising a general insurrection," Ford explained in a December 4, 1875, column.

> On the contrary, we should oppose a general insurrection in Ireland as untimely and ill advised. But we believe in action nonetheless. The Irish cause requires Skirmishers. It requires a little band of heroes who will initiate and keep up without intermission a guerrilla warfare.

In words that accurately presaged the advent of a form of transnational terrorism that has become a permanent fixture of our time, Ford also described how these "Skirmishers" would "fly over land and sea like invisible beings—now striking the enemy in Ireland, now in India, now in England itself as occasion may present."

O'Donovan Rossa and Ford displayed an uncommon understanding of the terrorist dynamic that went beyond even this early recognition of the media's power to communicate and amplify a violent message. Remarkably, both men grasped that just as money lubricates commerce, a solid financial base is required to sustain an effective terrorism campaign. It was thus not long before advertisements began to appear in the *Irish World* soliciting contributions on behalf of a "skirmisher fund." By March 1877 $23,350 had been collected—a sum equivalent to nearly half a million dollars in 2005. O'Donovan Rossa appears to have also fully appreciated terrorism's asymmetric virtues with regard to the disproportionate economic losses and damage that could be inflicted on the enemy state and the flood of contributions that a series of successful attacks might engender. "England," he explained in the *Irish World,* "will not know how or where she is to be struck. A successful strike that will do her half a million dollars' worth of damage will bring us enough funds to carry on the work."

Four years later, the Skirmishers commenced operations. On January 14, 1881, they bombed the Salford Infantry Barracks in Manchester. Their choice of target reflected yet another now-familiar pattern of contemporary terrorism: attacks on buildings or other inanimate objects designed to commemorate, and thereby draw attention to, some event of historic significance to the perpetrators. In this instance, the Salford Barracks was where three Fenians—the so-called Manchester Martyrs—had been hanged in 1867. Up until this point, the Irish terrorists seem to have differed only slightly from their Russian counterparts. Both attacked targets symbolizing their enemy (inanimate objects in the case of the Skirmishers and representatives of the czar by the Narodnaya Volya). Both also believed fervently in terrorism's didactic potential—whether directed toward the landless Irish or the Russian peasant. But two years later, the Irish campaign diverged significantly from the highly discriminate terrorism practiced by the Narodnaya Volya to something both more sinister and consequential. The principal weapons in the Russians' campaign, as we have seen, were the handgun and the nineteenth-century equivalent of the hand grenade; employed in acts of individual assassination deliberately calculated to avoid death or injury to all but their intended target. By comparison, the Skirmishers had already spilled innocent blood: a seven-year-old boy had been killed and three other people injured in the Salford Barracks blast. Still more innocent blood, however, was soon to be shed.

In 1883 the Clan na Gael and a rebranded IRB, now known as the Irish Republican Brotherhood, formed a tactical alliance and together embarked on a bombing campaign directed against the London Underground and mainline railway stations in both the United Kingdom's capital and other cities. Although the bombers' intention was not to wantonly or deliberately kill or harm innocent persons, but instead to throttle Britain's economy and dramatically call attention to themselves and their cause, their choice of both weapon (homemade bombs consisting of gunpowder detonated by primitive time-delay fuses) and target (locations in congested urban areas and public transportation) ensured that the effects of their operations could be neither constrained nor controlled. And, while it is true that these bombings claimed the lives of fewer than a dozen passersby or rail passengers, given that some of the explosive devices contained more than twenty pounds of commercial dynamite, this was more likely the result of luck and happenstance than any effort on the part of the bombers to limit by timing or placement the effect of their attacks.

The "dynamite campaign," as this spasm of Victorian-era urban terrorism came to be known, lasted until 1887. It spread beyond London to Liverpool and Glasgow before collapsing under the weight of intensified police surveillance, heightened border and port control, the effective use of informants, and unprecedented national and even international cooperation and liaison among hitherto entirely parochial law enforcement agencies. Indeed, the advances in police investigative, intelligence, and preemptive operations necessitated by the bombings led that same year to the formal establishment of Scotland Yard's famed Special Branch—the first such police unit dedicated specifically to political crime and counterterrorism. More significant for our purposes, however, is the impact that nineteenth-century Irish political violence had on terrorism's evolution and development. In retrospect, we can see that it was at this time that patterns and modi operandi first appeared that would become standard terrorist operating procedures decades later. The Irish groups, for example, were among the first to recognize the importance of establishing a foreign base beyond the reach of their enemy in order to better sustain and promote a protracted terrorist campaign. They were also ahead of their time in understanding the value of such a sanctuary not only for planning and logistical purposes but also for the effective dissemination of propaganda and the critical solicitation of operational funds. Their use of time-delayed explosive devices so that the perpetrator could easily effect escape, and thereby ensure the terrorist campaign's sustainment, was another important innovation that became a standard feature of twentieth-century terrorism. Finally, terrorist targeting of mass transport—and especially subway systems—along with an almost callous, if not even casual, disregard of innocent life have now become commonplace. The July 2005 suicide attacks on London's transit system, which killed 52 people and wounded 700 others, and the ten near-simultaneous bombings of commuter trains arriving at Madrid's Atocha rail station in March 2004, which killed 191 people and wounded hundreds more, are especially apposite, and tragic, examples. "At the grand strategic level," Lindsay Clutterbuck cogently notes, the Clan na Gael and IRB's

> ideas enabled terrorism to move away from being a phenomenon consisting of a single event, or at best a loosely connected series of events, and to evolve into sustained campaigns underpinned by their own well developed sense of timing and tempo. There was a quantum leap beyond the limited aim of assassinating an individual to achieve their objectives and into operational scenarios where terrorism could persist for years and encompass the deaths of thousands of people.

On the eve of the First World War, terrorism still retained its revolutionary connotations. By this time, growing unrest and irredentist ferment had already welled up within the decaying Ottoman and Hapsburg empires. In the 1880s and 1890s, for example, militant Armenian nationalist movements in eastern Turkey pursued a terrorist strategy against continued Ottoman rule of a kind that would later be adopted by most of the post-Second World War ethno-nationalist/separatist movements. The Armenians' objective was simultaneously to strike a blow against the despotic "alien" regime through repeated attacks on its colonial administration and security forces, in order to rally indigenous support, and to attract international attention, sympathy, and support. Around the same time, the Inner Macedonian Revolutionary Organization (IMRO) was active in the region overlapping present-day Greece, Bulgaria, and Serbia. Although the Macedonians did not go on to suffer the catastrophic fate that befell the Armenians during the First World War (when an estimated one million people perished in what is considered to be the first officially implemented genocide of the twentieth century), IMRO never came close to achieving its aim of an independent Macedonia and thereafter degenerated into a mostly criminal organization of hired thugs and political assassins.

The events immediately preceding the First World War in Bosnia are of course more familiar because of their subsequent cataclysmic impact on world affairs. There, similar groups of disaffected nationalists—Bosnian Serb intellectuals, university students, and even schoolchildren, collectively known as Mlada Bosna, or Young Bosnians—arose against continued Hapsburg suzerainty. While it is perhaps easy to dismiss the movement, as some historians have, as comprising "frustrated, poor, dreary and maladjusted" adolescents—much as many contemporary observers similarly denigrate modern-day terrorists as mindless, obsessive, and maladjusted—it was a member of Young Bosnia, Gavrilo Princip, who is widely credited with having set in motion the chain of events that began on June 28, 1914, when he assassinated the Hapsburg archduke Franz Ferdinand in Sarajevo, and culminated in the First World War. Whatever its superficially juvenile characteristics, the group was nonetheless passionately dedicated to the attainment of a federal South Slav political entity—uniting Slovenes, Croats, and Serbs—and resolutely committed to assassination as the vehicle with which to achieve that aim. In this respect, the Young Bosnians perhaps had more in common with the radical republicanism of Giuseppe Mazzini, one of the most ardent exponents of Italian unification in the nineteenth century, than with groups such as the Narodnaya Volya—despite a shared conviction in the efficacy of tyrannicide. An even more significant difference, however, was the degree of involvement in, and external support provided to, Young Bosnian activities by various shadowy Serbian nationalist groups. Principal among these was the pan-Serbian secret society, the Narodna Obrana (the People's Defense, or National Defense).

The Narodna Obrana had been established in 1908, originally to promote Serbian cultural and national activities. It subsequently assumed a more subversive orientation as the movement became increasingly involved with anti-Austrian activities—including terrorism—mostly in neighboring Bosnia and Herzegovina. Although the Narodna Obrana's exclusionist pan-Serbian aims clashed with the Young Bosnians' less parochial South Slav ideals, its leadership was quite happy to manipulate and exploit the Bosnians' emotive nationalism and youthful zeal for its own purposes. To this end, the Narodna Obrana actively recruited, trained, and armed young Bosnians and Herzegovinians from movements, such as the Young Bosnians, who were then deployed in various seditious activities against the Hapsburgs. As early as four years before the archduke's assassination, a Herzegovinian youth, trained by a Serbian army officer with close ties to the Narodna Obrana, had attempted to kill the governor of Bosnia. But while the Narodna Obrana included among its members senior Serbian government officials, it was not an explicitly government-controlled or directly state-supported entity. Whatever hazy government links it maintained were further and deliberately obscured when a radical faction left the Narodna Obrana in 1911 and established the Ujedinjenje ili Smrt (the Union of Death, or Death or Unification)—more popularly known as the Crna Ruka, the Black Hand. This more militant and appreciably more clandestine splinter group has been described by one historian as combining

> the more unattractive features of the anarchist cells of earlier years—which had been responsible for quite a number of assassinations in Europe and whose methods had a good deal of influence via the writings of Russian anarchists upon Serbian youth—and of the [American] Ku Klux Klan. There were gory rituals and oaths of loyalty, there were murders of backsliding members, there was identification of members by number, there were distributions of guns and bombs. And there was a steady traffic between Bosnia and Serbia.

This group, which continued to maintain close links with its parent body, was largely composed of Serbian military officers. It was led by Lieutenant Colonel Dragutin Dmitrievich (known by his pseudonym, Apis), himself the chief of the Intelligence Department of the Serbian general staff. With this key additional advantage of direct access to military armaments, intelligence, and training facilities, the Black Hand effectively took charge of all Serb-backed clandestine operations in Bosnia.

Although there were obviously close links between the Serbian military, the Black Hand, and the Young Bosnians, it would be a mistake to regard the relationship as one of direct control, much less outright manipulation. Clearly, the Serbian government was well aware of the Black Hand's objectives and the violent means the group employed in pursuit of them; indeed, the Serbian crown prince Alexander was one of the group's benefactors. But this does not mean that the Serbian government was necessarily as committed to war with Austria as the Black Hand's leaders were, or that it was prepared to countenance the group's more extreme plans for fomenting cross-border, anti-Hapsburg terrorism. There is some evidence to suggest that the Black Hand may have been trying to force Austria's hand against Serbia and thereby plunge both countries into war by actively abetting the Young Bosnians' plot to assassinate the archduke. Indeed, according to one revisionist account of the events leading up to the murder, even though the pistol used by Princip had been supplied by the Black Hand from a Serbian military armory in Kragujevac, and even though Princip had been trained by the Black Hand in Serbia before being smuggled back across the border for the assassination, at the eleventh hour Dmitrievich had apparently bowed to intense government pressure and tried to stop the assassination. According to this version, Princip and his fellow conspirators would hear nothing of it and stubbornly went ahead with their plans. Contrary to popular assumption, therefore, the archduke's assassination may not have been specifically ordered or even directly sanctioned by the Serbian government. However, the obscure links between high government officials and their senior military commanders and ostensibly independent, transnational terrorist movements, and the tangled web of intrigue, plots, clandestine arms provision and training, intelligence agents, and cross-border sanctuary that these relationships inevitably involved provide a pertinent historical parallel to the contemporary phenomenon known as "state-sponsored" terrorism (that is, the active and often clandestine support, encouragement, and assistance provided by a foreign government to a terrorist group).

By the 1930s, the meaning of "terrorism" had changed again. It was now used less to refer to revolutionary movements and violence directed against governments and their leaders and more to describe the practices of mass repression employed by totalitarian states and their dictatorial leaders against their own citizens. Thus the term regained its former connotations of abuse of power by government, and it was applied specifically to the authoritarian regimes that had come to power in Fascist Italy, Nazi Germany, and Stalinist Russia. In Germany and Italy, respectively, the accession to office of Hitler and Mussolini had depended in large measure on the "street"—the mobilization and deployment of gangs of brown- or black-shirted thugs to harass and intimidate political opponents and root out other scapegoats for public vilification and further victimization. "Terror? Never," Mussolini insisted, demurely dismissing such intimidation as "simply . . . social hygiene, taking those individuals out of circulation like a doctor would take out a bacillus." The most sinister dimension of this form of "terror" was that it became an intrinsic component of Fascist and Nazi governance, executed at the behest of, and in complete subservience to, the ruling political party of the land—which had arrogated to itself complete, total control of the country and its people. A system of government-sanctioned fear and coercion was thus created whereby political brawls, street fights, and widespread persecution of Jews, communists, and other declared "enemies of the state" became the means through which complete and submissive compliance was ensured. The totality of party control over, and perversion of, government was perhaps most clearly evinced by a speech given by Hermann Göring, the newly appointed Prussian minister of the interior, in 1933. "Fellow Germans," he declared,

> my measures will not be crippled by any judicial thinking. My measures will not be crippled by any bureaucracy. Here I don't have to worry about Justice; my mission is only to destroy and exterminate, nothing more. This struggle will be a struggle against chaos, and such a struggle I shall not conduct with the power of the police. A bourgeois State might have done that. Certainly, I shall use the power of the State and the police to the utmost, my dear Communists, so don't draw any false conclusions; but the struggle to the death, in which my fist will grasp your necks, I shall lead with those there—the Brown Shirts.

The "Great Terror" that Stalin was shortly to unleash in Russia both resembled and differed from that of the Nazis. On the one hand, drawing inspiration from Hitler's ruthless elimination of his own political opponents, the Russian dictator similarly transformed the political party he led into a servile instrument responsive directly to his personal will, and the state's police and security apparatus into slavish organs of coercion, enforcement, and repression. But conditions in the Soviet Union of the 1930s bore little resemblance to the turbulent political, social, and economic upheaval afflicting Germany and Italy during that decade and the previous one. On the other hand, therefore, unlike either the Nazis or the Fascists, who had emerged from the political free-for-alls in their own countries to seize power and then had to struggle to consolidate their rule and retain their unchallenged authority, the Russian Communist Party had by the mid-1930s been firmly entrenched in power for more than a decade. Stalin's purges, in contrast to those of the French Revolution, and even to Russia's own recent experience, were not "launched in time of crisis, or revolution and war . . . [but] in the coldest of cold blood, when Russia had at last reached a comparatively calm and even moderately prosperous condition." Thus the political purges ordered by Stalin became, in the words of one of his biographers, a "conspiracy to seize total power by terrorist action," resulting in the death, exile, imprisonment, or forcible impressment of millions.

Certainly, similar forms of state-imposed or state-directed violence and terror against a government's own citizens continue today. The use of so-called death squads (often off-duty or plainclothes security or police officers) in conjunction with blatant intimidation of political opponents, human rights and aid workers, student groups, labor organizers, journalists, and others has been a prominent feature of the right-wing military dictatorships that took power in Argentina, Chile, and Greece during the 1970s and even of elected governments in El Salvador, Guatemala, Colombia, and Peru during the upheavals that afflicted those countries, particularly in the 1980s. But these state-sanctioned or explicitly ordered acts of *internal* political violence directed mostly against domestic populations—that is, rule by violence and intimidation by those *already* in power against their own citizenry—are generally termed "terror" in order to distinguish that phenomenon from "terrorism," which is understood to be violence committed by nonstate entities.

Following the Second World War, in another swing of the pendulum of meaning, "terrorism" regained the revolutionary connotations with which it is most commonly associated today. At that time the term was used primarily in reference to the violent revolts then being prosecuted by the various indigenous nationalist/anticolonialist groups that emerged in Asia, Africa, and the Middle East during the late 1940s and 1950s to oppose continued European rule. Countries as diverse as Israel, Kenya, Cyprus, and Algeria, for example, owe their independence at least in part to nationalist political movements that employed terrorism against colonial powers. It was also during this period that the "politically correct" appellation of "freedom fighters" came into fashion as a result of the political legitimacy that the international community (whose sympathy and support were actively courted by many of these movements) accorded to struggles for national liberation and self-determination. Sympathy and support for the rebels extended to segments of the colonial state's own population as well, creating a need for less judgmental and more politically neutral language than "terrorist" and "terrorism" to describe these revolutionaries and the violence they committed in what were considered justified "wars of liberation." Many newly independent Third World countries and communist-bloc states in particular also adopted this vernacular, arguing that anyone or any movement that fought against "colonial" oppression and/or Western domination should not be described as "terrorists" but were properly deemed to be "freedom fighters." This position was perhaps most famously explained by Palestine Liberation Organization (PLO) chairman Yasir Arafat, when he addressed the United Nations General Assembly in November 1974. "The difference between the revolutionary and the terrorist," Arafat stated, "lies in the reason for which each fights. For whoever stands by a just cause and fights for the freedom and liberation of his land from the invaders, the settlers and the colonialists, cannot possibly be called terrorist."

During the late 1960s and 1970s, terrorism continued to be viewed within a revolutionary context. However, this usage now expanded to include nationalist and ethnic separatist groups outside a colonial or neocolonial framework as well as radical, entirely ideologically motivated organizations. Disenfranchised or exiled nationalist minorities—such as the PLO, the Quebecois separatist group FLQ (Front de Liberation du Quebec), the Basque ETA (Euskadita Askatasuna, or Freedom for the Basque Homeland), and even a hitherto unknown South Moluccan irredentist group seeking independence from Indonesia—adopted terrorism as a means to draw attention to themselves and their respective causes, in many instances with the specific aim, like their anticolonial predecessors, of attracting international sympathy and support. Around the same time, various left-wing political extremists—drawn mostly from the radical student organizations and Marxist/Leninist/Maoist movements in Western Europe, Latin America, and the United States—began to form terrorist groups opposing American intervention in Vietnam and what they claimed were the irredeemable social and economic inequities of the modern capitalist liberal-democratic state.

Although the revolutionary cum ethno-nationalist/separatist and ideological exemplars continue to shape our most basic understanding of the term, it was not long before "terrorism" was being used to denote broader, less distinct phenomena. In the early 1980s, for example, terrorism came to be regarded as a calculated means to destabilize the West as part of a vast global conspiracy. Books like *The Terror Network* by Claire Sterling propagated the notion to a receptive American presidential administration and similarly susceptible governments elsewhere that the seemingly isolated terrorist incidents perpetrated by disparate groups scattered across the globe were in fact linked elements of a massive clandestine plot, orchestrated by the Kremlin and implemented by its Warsaw Pact client states, to destroy the Free World. By the middle of the decade, however, a series of suicide bombings directed mostly against American diplomatic and military targets in the Middle East was focusing attention on the rising threat of state-sponsored terrorism. Consequently, this phenomenon—whereby various renegade foreign governments such as the regimes in Iran, Iraq, Libya, and Syria became actively involved in sponsoring or commissioning terrorist acts—replaced communist conspiracy theories as the main context within which terrorism was viewed. Terrorism thus became associated with a type of covert or surrogate warfare whereby weaker states could confront larger, more powerful rivals without the risk of retribution.

In the early 1990s the meaning and usage of the term "terrorism" were further blurred by the emergence of two new buzzwords: "narco-terrorism" and the so-called gray area phenomenon. The former term revived the Moscow-orchestrated terrorism conspiracy theories of previous years while introducing the critical new dimension of narcotics trafficking. Thus "narco-terrorism" was defined by one of the concept's foremost propagators as the "use of drug trafficking to advance the objectives of certain governments and terrorist organizations"—identified as the "Marxist-Leninist regimes" of the Soviet Union, Cuba, Bulgaria, and Nicaragua, among others. The emphasis on "narco-terrorism" as the latest manifestation of the communist plot to undermine Western society, however, had the unfortunate effect of diverting official attention away from a bona fide emerging trend. To a greater extent than ever in the past, entirely criminal (that is, violent, *economically* motivated) organizations were now forging strategic alliances with terrorist and guerrilla organizations or were themselves employing violence for specifically political ends. The growing power of the Colombian cocaine cartels, their close ties with left-wing terrorist groups in Colombia and Peru, and their repeated attempts to subvert Colombia's electoral process and undermine successive governments constitute perhaps the best-known example of this continuing trend.

Those who drew attention to this "gray area phenomenon" were concerned less with grand conspiracies than with highlighting the increasingly fluid and variable nature of subnational conflict in the post-cold war era. Accordingly, in the 1990s "terrorism" began to be subsumed by some analysts within the "gray area phenomenon." Thus the latter term came to be used to denote "threats to the stability of nation states by non-state actors and non-governmental processes and organizations"; to describe violence affecting "immense regions or urban areas where control has shifted from legitimate governments to new half-political, half-criminal powers"; or simply to group together in one category the range of conflicts across the world that no longer conformed to traditionally accepted notions of war as fighting between the armed forces of two or more established states, but instead involved irregular forces as one or more of the combatants. Terrorism had shifted its meaning again from an individual phenomenon of subnational violence to one of several elements, or part of a wider pattern, of nonstate conflict.

The terrorist attacks on September 11, 2001, inevitably, redefined "terrorism" yet again. On that day, nineteen terrorists belonging to a group calling itself al Qaeda (or al-Qa'ida) hijacked four passenger aircraft soon after they took off from airports in Boston,

Newark, New Jersey, and Washington, D.C. Two of the planes were then deliberately flown into the twin towers of New York City's World Trade Center. Both structures collapsed shortly afterward. A third aircraft similarly smashed into the Pentagon, where the U.S. Department of Defense is located, severely damaging the southwest portion of that building. Meanwhile, passengers on board the fourth aircraft learned of the other attacks and struggled to subdue the hijackers. In the ensuing melee, the plane spun out of control and crashed into a field in rural Pennsylvania. A total of nearly three thousand people were killed in the attacks. To put that death toll in perspective, in the entirety of the twentieth century no more than fourteen terrorist incidents had killed more than one hundred people. And until 9/11 no terrorist operation had ever killed more than five hundred people. Among the dead were citizens of some eighty different countries, although the largest number of fatalities by far were U.S. citizens. Indeed, more than twice as many Americans perished on 9/11 than had been killed by terrorists since 1968—the year acknowledged as marking the advent of modern, international terrorism.

So massive and consequential a terrorist onslaught required nothing less than an equally comprehensive and far-reaching response. "This is a new kind of evil . . . [and we] will rid the world of the evildoers," President George W. Bush promised just days later. "Our nation was horrified," he continued, "but it's not going to be terrorized." Yet when the president addressed a special joint session of the U.S. Congress on September 20, 2001, he repeatedly invoked the word "terror"—that is, the "state of being terrified or greatly frightened," according to the *OED*'s definition—rather than the specifically political phenomenon "terror*ism*." "Our war on terror," the president famously declared, "begins with al-Qaida, but it does not end there." The consequences of his semantic choice, whether deliberate or not, nonetheless proved as portentous as they were significant: heralding a virtually open-ended struggle against anyone and anything that arguably scared or threatened Americans. The range of potential adversaries thus expanded beyond Osama bin Laden, al Qaeda's leader, and his minions, who, the president explained, "hate us . . . [and] our freedoms," now to include "rogue" states arrayed in an "axis of evil" (e.g., Iraq, Iran, and North Korea) and especially heinous Middle East dictators thought to possess weapons of mass destruction (WMD). As Professor Sir Michael Howard, the world's leading authority on strategy and military history, later reflected,

> President Bush's declaration of a "war on terror" was generally seen abroad as a rhetorical device to alert the American people to the dangers facing them, rather than as a statement to be taken seriously or literally in terms of international law. But further statements and actions by the Bush Administration have made it clear that the President's words were intended to be taken literally.

The implications of this policy were clearly demonstrated by the relationship that the president and his advisers believed existed between al Qaeda and Saddam Hussein. Although White House suspicions that Iraq was somehow behind 9/11 never completely faded, they were eventually eclipsed by growing concerns about terrorists acquiring WMD from Iraqi stockpiles. Indeed, it was precisely this fear that President Bush cited to justify the March 2003 invasion. The Bush administration's conflation of terrorism and WMD was specifically cited by Richard Dearlove, then head of MI-6, Britain's Secret Intelligence Service, in his report to Prime Minister Tony Blair of high-level U.S.-U.K.

consultations held in Washington, D.C., seven months before the invasion. "Military action was now seen as inevitable," notes of Dearlove's meeting with the prime minister stated. "Bush wanted to remove Saddam, through military action, justified by the conjunction of terrorism and WMD." The chain of events that began on 9/11 and the declaration of a "war on terror" that thereafter set America on the path to war with Iraq thus prompted Michael Howard again to note how it was evidently "not enough" for Americans

> to be at war with an abstract entity described by their president as "Terror." They need a specific adversary who embodies the spirit of evil against whom national sentiment can be mobilised, as it was mobilised against Hitler in 1941. Osama bin Laden proved too evasive and evanescent a figure to provide the necessary catharsis, but prominent among the usual suspects was Saddam Hussein. There was little evidence to link him with this particular crime, but he was a bad guy, with whom many members of the Bush administration had unfinished business. . . . He was, in short, the most powerful and dangerous figure among the declared enemies of the US, which in itself gave them the right indeed the duty—to destroy him.

The "war on terror" thus became, in President Bush's infelicitous choice of words, as much a "crusade" against evil as it was an unwavering reaction to the multiplicity of new security threats confronting the nation—and therefore accounts for the way terrorism was redefined in the early twenty-first century, according to Stanford University linguist Geoffrey Nunberg, in order to "encompass both the dark forces that threaten 'civilization' and the fears they arouse."

Why Is Terrorism So Difficult to Define?

Not surprisingly, as the meaning and usage of the word have changed over time to accommodate the political vernacular and discourse of each successive era, terrorism has proved increasingly elusive in the face of attempts to construct one consistent definition. At one time, the terrorists themselves were far more cooperative in this endeavor than they are today. The early practitioners didn't mince their words or hide behind the semantic camouflage of more anodyne labels such as "freedom fighter" or "urban guerrilla." The nineteenth-century anarchists, for example, unabashedly proclaimed themselves to be terrorists and frankly proclaimed their tactics to be terrorism. The members of Narodnaya Volya similarly displayed no qualms in using these same words to describe themselves and their deeds. Such frankness did not last, however. Although the Jewish terrorist group of the 1940s known as Lehi (the Hebrew acronym for Lohamei Herut Yisrael, the Freedom Fighters for Israel), but more popularly called the Stern Gang after its founder and first leader, Abraham Stern, would admit to its effective use of terrorist tactics, its members never considered themselves to be terrorists. It is significant, however, that even Lehi, while it may have been far more candid than its latter-day counterparts, chose as the name of the organization not Terrorist Fighters for Israel but the far less pejorative Freedom Fighters for Israel. Similarly, although more than twenty years later the Brazilian revolutionary Carlos Marighela displayed little compunction about openly advocating the use of "terrorist" tactics, he still insisted on depicting himself and his disciples as "urban guerrillas" rather than "urban terrorists." Indeed, it is clear from Marighela's writings that he was well aware of the word's undesirable connotations and strove to displace them with positive resonances. "The words 'aggressor' and 'terrorist,' " Marighela wrote in his famous *Handbook of Urban Guerrilla War* (also known as the "Mini-Manual"), "no longer mean what they did. Instead of arousing fear or censure, they are a call to action. To be called an aggressor or a terrorist in Brazil is now an honour to any citizen, for it means that he is fighting, with a gun in his hand, against the monstrosity of the present dictatorship and the suffering it causes."

This trend toward ever more convoluted semantic obfuscations to sidestep terrorism's pejorative overtones has, if anything, become more entrenched in recent decades. Terrorist organizations almost without exception now regularly select names for themselves that consciously eschew the word "terrorism" in any of its forms. Instead these groups actively seek to evoke images of

- freedom and liberation (e.g., the National Liberation Front, the Popular Front for the Liberation of Palestine, Freedom for the Basque Homeland);
- armies or other military organizational structures (e.g., the National Military Organization, the Popular Liberation Army, the Fifth Battalion of the Liberation Army);
- actual self-defense movements (e.g., the Afrikaner Resistance Movement, the Shankhill Defence Association, the Organization for the Defence of the Free People, the Jewish Defense Organization);
- righteous vengeance (the Organization for the Oppressed on Earth, the Justice Commandos of the Armenian Genocide, the Palestinian Revenge Organization)

—or else deliberately choose names that are decidedly neutral and therefore bereft of all but the most innocuous suggestions or associations (e.g., the Shining Path, Front Line, al-Dawa (the Call), Alfaro Lives—Damn It!, Kach (Thus), al-Gamat al-Islamiya (the Islamic Organization), the Lantaro Youth Movement, and *especially* al Qaeda (the Arabic word for the "base of operation" or "foundation"—meaning the base or foundation from which worldwide Islamic revolution can be waged—or, as other translations have it, the "precept" or "method").

What all these examples suggest is that terrorists clearly do not see or regard themselves as others do. "Above all I am a family man," the archterrorist Carlos, the Jackal, described himself to a French newspaper following his capture in 1994. Similarly, when the infamous KSM—Khalid Sheikh Mohammed, mastermind of the 9/11 attacks whom bin Laden called simply "al Mukhtar" (Arabic for "the brain")—was apprehended in March 2003, a photograph of him with his arms around his two young sons was found next to the bed in which he had been sleeping. Cast perpetually on the defensive and forced to take up arms to protect themselves and their real or imagined constituents only, terrorists perceive themselves as reluctant warriors, driven by desperation—and lacking any viable alternative—to violence against a repressive state, a predatory rival ethnic or nationalist group, or an unresponsive international order. This perceived characteristic of self-denial also distinguishes the terrorist from other types of political extremists as well as from people similarly involved in illegal, violent avocations. A communist or a revolutionary, for example, would likely readily accept and admit that he is in fact a communist or a revolutionary. Indeed, many would doubtless take particular pride in claiming either of those appellations for themselves. Similarly, even a person engaged in illegal, wholly disreputable, or entirely selfish violent activities, such as robbing banks or carrying out contract killings, would probably admit to being a bank robber or a murderer for hire. The terrorist, by contrast, will *never* acknowledge that he is a terrorist and moreover will go to great lengths to evade and obscure any such inference or connection. Terry Anderson, the American journalist who was held hostage for almost seven years by the Lebanese terrorist organization Hezbollah, relates a telling conversation he had with one of his guards. The guard had objected to a newspaper article that referred to Hezbollah as terrorists. "We are not terrorists," he indignantly stated, "we are fighters." Anderson replied, "Hajj, you are a terrorist, look it up in the dictionary. You are a terrorist, you may not like the word and if you do not like the word, do not do it." The terrorist will always argue that it is society or the government or the socioeconomic "system" and its laws that are the *real* "terrorists," and moreover that if it were not for this oppression, he would not have felt the need to defend either himself or the population he claims to represent. Another revealing example of this process of obfuscation-projection may be found in the book *Invisible Armies,* written by Sheikh Muhammad Hussein Fadlallah, the spiritual leader of the Lebanese terrorist group responsible for Anderson's kidnapping. "We don't see ourselves as terrorists," Fadlallah explains, "because we don't believe in terrorism. We don't see resisting the occupier as a terrorist action. We see ourselves as *mujihadeen* [holy warriors] who fight a Holy War for the people." Indeed, Hezbollah's efforts to distance itself entirely from any terrorist associations and appellations have only intensified in the years since it first entered mainstream Lebanese politics. Perhaps because it now has thirteen elected members of the Lebanese Parliament, Hezbollah spokespersons persistently argue that it is a bona fide political party, cum "resistance movement."

On one point, at least, everyone agrees: "Terrorism" is a pejorative term. It is a word with intrinsically negative connotations that is generally applied to one's enemies and opponents, or to those with whom one disagrees and would otherwise prefer to ignore. "What is called terrorism," Brian Jenkins has written, "thus seems to depend on one's point of view. Use of the term implies a moral judgement; and if one party can successfully attach the label *terrorist* to its opponent, then it has indirectly persuaded others to adopt its moral viewpoint." Hence the decision to call someone or label some organization "terrorist" becomes almost unavoidably subjective, depending largely on whether one sympathizes with or opposes the person/group/cause concerned. If one identifies with the victim of the violence, for example, then the act is terrorism. If, however, one identifies with the perpetrator, the violent act is regarded in a more sympathetic, if not positive (or, at the worst, ambivalent) light, and it is not terrorism.

The implications of this associational logic were perhaps most clearly demonstrated in the exchanges between Western and non-Western member states of the United Nations following the 1972 Munich Olympics massacre, in which eleven Israeli athletes were killed. The debate began with the proposal by the UN secretary general, Kurt Waldheim, that the UN should not remain a "mute spectator" to the acts of terrorist violence then occurring throughout the world but should take practical steps that might prevent further bloodshed. While a majority of the UN member states supported the secretary general, a disputatious minority—including many Arab states and various African and Asian countries—derailed the discussion, arguing (much as Arafat would do two years later in his own address to the General Assembly) that "people who struggle to liberate themselves from foreign oppression and exploitation have the right to use all methods at their disposal, including force."

The Third World delegates justified their position with two arguments. First, they claimed that all bona fide liberation movements are invariably decried as "terrorists" by the regimes against which their struggles for freedom are directed. The Nazis, for example, labeled as terrorists the resistance groups opposing Germany's occupation of their lands. Moulaye el-Hassen, the Mauritanian ambassador, pointed out, just as "all liberation movements are described as terrorists by those who have reduced them to slavery." Therefore, by condemning "terrorism" the UN was endorsing the power of the strong over the weak and of the established entity over its nonestablished challenger—in effect, acting as the defender of the status quo. According to Chen Chu, the deputy representative of the People's Republic of China, the UN thus was proposing to deprive "oppressed nations and peoples" of the only effective weapon they had with which to oppose "imperialism, colonialism, neo-colonialism, racism and Israeli Zionism." Second, the Third World delegates argued forcefully that it is not the violence itself that is germane but its "underlying causes"—that is, the "misery, frustration, grievance and despair"—that produce the violent acts. As the Mauritanian representative again explained, the term "terrorist" could "hardly be held to apply to persons who were denied the most elementary human rights, dignity, freedom and independence, and whose countries objected to foreign occupation." When the issue was again raised the following year, Syria objected on the grounds that "the international community is under legal and moral obligation to promote the struggle for liberation and to resist any attempt to depict this struggle as synonymous with terrorism and illegitimate violence." The resultant definitional paralysis subsequently throttled UN efforts to make any substantive progress on international cooperation against terrorism beyond very specific agreements on individual aspects of the problem (concerning, for example, diplomats and civil aviation).

The opposite approach, in which identification with the victim determines the classification of a violent act as terrorism, is evident in the conclusions of a parliamentary working group of NATO (an organization comprising long-established, status quo Western states). The final report of the 1989 North Atlantic Assembly's Subcommittee on Terrorism states: "Murder, kidnapping, arson and other felonious acts constitute criminal behavior, but many non-Western nations have proved reluctant to condemn as terrorist acts what they consider to be struggles of national liberation." In this reasoning, the defining characteristic of terrorism is the act of violence itself, not the motivations or justification for or reasons behind it. After decades of debate and resistance, the UN itself finally embraced this rationale by adopting the International Convention for the Suppression of Terrorist Bombings. The convention outlawed the unlawful delivery, placement, discharge, or detonation of an

> explosive or other lethal device in, into or against a place of public use, a State or government facility, a public transportation system or an infrastructure facility with the intent to cause death or serious bodily injury; or with the intent to cause extensive destruction of such a place, facility or system, where such destruction results in or is likely to result in major economic loss.

It came into force just four months before the 9/11 attacks.

Indeed, this approach has long been espoused by analysts such as Jenkins who argue that terrorism should be defined "by the nature of the act, not by the identity of the perpetrators or the nature of their cause." But this is not an entirely satisfactory solution either, since it fails to differentiate clearly between violence perpetrated by states and by nonstate entities, such as terrorists. Accordingly, it plays into the hands of terrorists and their apologists who would argue that there is no difference between the "low-tech" terrorist pipe bomb placed in the rubbish bin at a crowded market that wantonly and indiscriminately kills or maims everyone within a radius measured in tens of feet and the "high-tech" precision-guided ordnance dropped by air force fighter-bombers from a height of twenty thousand feet or more that achieves the same wanton and indiscriminate effects on the crowded marketplace far below. This rationale thus equates the random violence inflicted on enemy population centers by military forces—such as the Luftwaffe's raids on Warsaw and Coventry, the Allied firebombings of Dresden and Tokyo, and the atomic bombs dropped by the United States on Hiroshima and Nagasaki during the Second World War, and indeed the countervalue strategy of the postwar superpowers' strategic nuclear policy, which deliberately targeted the enemy's civilian population—with the violence committed by substate entities labeled "terrorists," since both involve the infliction of death and injury on noncombatants. Indeed, this was precisely the point made during the above-mentioned UN debates following the 1972 Munich Olympics massacre by the Cuban representative, who argued that "the methods of combat used by national liberation movements could not be declared illegal while the policy of terrorism unleashed against certain peoples [by the armed forces of established states] was declared legitimate."

It is a familiar argument. Terrorists, as we have seen, deliberately cloak themselves in the terminology of military jargon. They consciously portray themselves as bona fide (freedom) fighters, if not soldiers, who—though they wear no identifying uniform or insignia—are entitled to treatment as prisoners of war (POWs) if captured and therefore should not be prosecuted as common criminals in ordinary courts of law. Terrorists further argue that, because of their numerical inferiority, far more limited firepower, and paucity of resources compared with an established nation-state's massive defense and national security apparatus, they have no choice but to operate clandestinely, emerging from the shadows to carry out dramatic (in other words, bloody and destructive) acts of hit-and-run violence in order to attract attention to, and ensure publicity for, themselves and their cause. The bomb in the rubbish bin, in their view, is merely a circumstantially imposed "poor man's air force": the only means with which the terrorist can challenge—and get the attention of—the more powerful state. "How else can we bring pressure to bear on the world?" one of Arafat's political aides once inquired. "The deaths are regrettable, but they are a fact of war in which innocents have become involved. They are no more innocent than the Palestinian women and children killed by the Israelis and we are ready to carry the war all over the world."

But rationalizations such as these ignore the fact that, even while national armed forces have been responsible for far more death and destruction than terrorists might ever aspire to bring about, there nonetheless is a fundamental qualitative difference between the two types of violence. Even in war there are rules and accepted norms of behavior that prohibit the use of certain types of weapons (for example, hollow-point or "dum-dum" bullets, CS "tear" gas, chemical and biological warfare agents) and proscribe various tactics and outlaw attacks on specific categories of targets. Accordingly, in theory, if not always in practice, the rules of war—as observed from the early seventeenth century when they were first proposed by the Dutch jurist Hugo Grotius and subsequently codified in the famous Geneva and Hague Conventions on Warfare of the 1860s, 1899, 1907, and 1949—not only grant civilian noncombatants immunity from attack but also

- prohibit taking civilians as hostages;
- impose regulations governing the treatment of captured or surrendered soldiers (POWs);
- outlaw reprisals against either civilians or POWs;
- recognize neutral territory and the rights of citizens of neutral states; and
- uphold the inviolability of diplomats and other accredited representatives.

Even the most cursory review of terrorist tactics and targets over the past quarter century reveals that terrorists have violated all these rules. They not infrequently have

- taken civilians as hostages, and in some instances then brutally executed them (e.g., the former Italian prime minister Aldo Moro and the German industrialist Hans Martin Schleyer, who, respectively, were taken captive and later murdered by the Red Brigades and the Red Army Faction in the 1970s and, more recently, Daniel Pearl, a *Wall Street Journal* reporter, and Nicholas Berg, an American businessmen, who were kidnapped by radical Islamic terrorists in Pakistan and Iraq, respectively, and grotesquely beheaded);
- similarly abused and murdered kidnapped military officers—even when they were serving on UN-sponsored peacekeeping or truce supervisory missions (e.g., the American Marine Lieutenant Colonel William Higgins, the commander of a UN truce-monitoring detachment, who was abducted by Lebanese Shi'a terrorists in 1989 and subsequently hanged);
- undertaken reprisals against wholly innocent civilians, often in countries far removed from the terrorists' ostensible "theater of operation," thus disdaining any concept of neutral states or the rights of citizens of neutral countries (e.g., the brutal 1986 machine-gun and hand-grenade attack on Turkish Jewish worshipers at an Istanbul synagogue carried out by the Palestinian Abu Nidal Organization (ANO) in retaliation for a recent Israeli raid on a guerrilla base in southern Lebanon); and
- repeatedly attacked embassies and other diplomatic installations (e.g., the bombings of the U.S. embassies in Nairobi and Dar es Salaam in 1998 and in Beirut and Kuwait City in 1983 and 1984, and the mass hostage-taking at the Japanese ambassador's residence in Lima, Peru, in 1996–97), as well as deliberately targeting diplomats and other accredited representatives (e.g., the British ambassador to Uruguay, Sir Geoffrey Jackson, who was kidnapped by leftist terrorists in that country in 1971, and the fifty-two American diplomats taken hostage at the Tehran legation in 1979).

Admittedly, the armed forces of established states have also been guilty of violating some of the same rules of war. However, when these transgressions do occur—when civilians are deliberately and wantonly attacked in war or taken hostage and killed by military forces—the term "war crime" is used to describe such acts and, as imperfect and flawed as both international and national judicial remedies may be, steps nonetheless are often taken to hold the perpetrators accountable for the crimes. By comparison, one of the fundamental raisons d'être of international terrorism is a refusal to be bound by such rules of warfare and codes of conduct. International terrorism disdains any concept of delimited areas of combat or demarcated battlefields, much less respect for neutral territory. Accordingly, terrorists have repeatedly taken their often parochial struggles to other, sometimes geographically distant, third-party countries and there deliberately enmeshed people completely unconnected with the terrorists' cause or grievances in violent incidents designed to generate attention and publicity.

The reporting of terrorism by the news media, which have been drawn into the semantic debates that divided the UN in the 1970s and continue to influence all discourse on terrorism, has further contributed to the obfuscation of the terrorist/"freedom fighter" debate, enshrining imprecision and implication as the lingua franca of political violence in the name of objectivity and neutrality. In striving to avoid appearing either partisan or judgmental, the American media, for example, resorted to describing terrorists—often in the same report—as variously "guerrillas," "gunmen," "raiders," "commandos," and even "soldiers." A random sample of American newspaper reports of Palestinian terrorist activities between June and December 1973, found in the terrorism archives and database maintained by the RAND Corporation, provides striking illustrations of this practice. Out of eight headlines of articles reporting the same incident, six used the word "guerrillas" and only two used "terrorists" to describe the perpetrators. An interesting pattern was also observed: those accounts that immediately followed a particularly horrific or tragic incident—that is, involving the death and injury of innocent people (in this instance, a 1973 attack on a Pan Am airliner at the Rome airport, in which thirty-two passengers were killed)—tended to describe the perpetrators as "terrorists" and their act as "terrorism" (albeit in the headline in one case only, before reverting to the more neutral terminology of "commando," "militants," and "guerrilla attack" in the text) more frequently than did reports of less serious or nonlethal incidents. One *New York Times* editorial, however, was far less restrained than the stories describing the actual incident, describing it as "bloody" and "mindless" and using the words "terrorists" and "terrorism" interchangeably with "guerrillas" and "extremists." Only six months previously, however, the same newspaper had run a story about another terrorist attack that completely eschewed the terms "terrorism" and "terrorist," preferring "guerrillas" and "resistance" (as in "resistance movement") instead. The *Christian Science Monitor*'s reports of the Rome Pan Am attack similarly avoided "terrorist" and "terrorism" in favor of "guerrillas" and "extremists"; an Associated Press story in the next day's *Los Angeles Times* also stuck with "guerrillas," while the two *Washington Post* articles on the same incident opted for the terms "commandos" and "guerrillas."

This slavish devotion to terminological neutrality, which David Rapoport first observed nearly thirty years ago,[112] is still in evidence today. A telling illustration of the semantics of terrorism reportage can be found in some of the press coverage of the terrorist violence that afflicted Algeria during the 1990s and claimed the lives of an estimated hundred thousand people. An article appearing in the *International Herald Tribune* (a Paris-based newspaper then published in conjunction with the *New York Times* and the *Washington Post*) reported a 1997 incident in Algeria in which thirty people had been killed by perpetrators who were variously described as "terrorists" in the article's headline, less judgmentally as "extremists" in the lead paragraph, and as the still more ambiguous "Islamic fundamentalists" in the article's third paragraph. In a country where terrorist-inflicted bloodshed was endemic, one might think that the distinctions between "terrorists," mere "extremists," and ordinary "fundamentalists" would be clearer. Equally interesting was the article that appeared on the opposite side of the same page of the newspaper that described the "decades of sporadic *guerrilla* [my emphasis] warfare by the IRA" in Northern Ireland. Yet sixty years ago this newspaper apparently had fewer qualms about using the word "terrorists" to describe the two young Jewish men in pre-independence Israel who, while awaiting execution after having been convicted of attacking British military targets, committed suicide. Other press accounts of the same period in *The Times* of London and the *Palestine Post* similarly had no difficulties, for example, in describing the 1946 bombing by Jewish terrorists of the British military headquarters and government secretariat located in Jerusalem's King David Hotel as a "terrorist" act perpetrated by "terrorists." And, in perhaps the most specific application of the term, the communist terrorists against whom the British fought in Malaya throughout the late 1940s and 1950s were routinely referred to as "CTs"—for "Communist terrorists." As Rapoport warned in the 1970s, "In attempting to correct the abuse of language for political purposes, our journalists may succeed in making language altogether worthless."

More recently, the coverage given by the *Washington Post* and the *New York Times* to the barricade-and-hostage situation that unfolded at a Beslan, North Ossetia, school in early September 2004 underscored these continuing semantic ambiguities. Even in the post-9/11 era, few terrorist attacks have evoked quite the horror and revulsion that the fifty-two-hour ordeal and its deliberate targeting of children produced. According to official Russian figures, at least 331 hostages—including more than 172 children—were killed, although many believe the actual numbers to be much higher. Yet the perpetrators, an indisputably cruel and ruthless group of Chechen terrorists, were repeatedly described in far more neutral and anodyne terms by both of America's national newspapers of record. The *Washington Post's* initial report of the seizure and its account of the rescue operations, for example, did not use the words "terrorism" and "terrorists" at all, except in the context of direct quotations or statements made by an aide to Russian president Vladimir Putin, various other Russian official spokespersons, or President Bush himself. Instead, a variety of other adjectives were employed in the two articles sampled, including "guerrillas" (seventeen references), "hostage takers" (eleven), "rebels" (six), "fighters" (three), and "separatists" (two). The *New York Times's* reporting and rhetorical choices were little different. Admittedly, its first article detailing the incident used the word "terrorist" twice, in both instances independently of quotes or statements made by Russian officials. But more inoffensive terms such as "guerrillas" (seventeen references), "fighters" (nine), "insurgents" (six), "rebels" (six), and "hostage takers" (two) predominated in both this story and the report of the siege's grisly denouement. The word "terrorist" again appeared twice in the second piece, but only when quoting Russian president Vladimir Putin and his spokesman. Indeed, the "unrelenting use of such euphemistic language" in the *Washington Post's* reporting of the Beslan incident prompted one reader to ask in a letter to the editor,

"Why can't your editors just identify these people for what they are . . . terrorists?" The *New York Times*'s first public editor, Daniel Okrent, devoted a column to the subject after readers similarly complained about the paper's reluctance to use the words "terrorist," "terrorism," and "terror." His explanation was that the *Times* in fact has no policy governing the use of such words—except to eschew them as much possible.

The cumulative effect of this proclivity toward equivocation is that today there is no one widely accepted or agreed-upon definition for terrorism. Different departments or agencies of even the same government will themselves often have very different definitions for it. The U.S. State Department, for example, uses the definition of terrorism contained in Title 22 of the United States Code, Section 2656f(d):

> premeditated, politically motivated violence perpetrated against noncombatant targets by subnational groups or clandestine agents, usually intended to influence an audience.

In an accompanying footnote is the explanation that:

> For purposes of this definition, the term "noncombatant" is interpreted to include, in addition to civilians, military personnel who at the time of the incident are unarmed and/ or not on duty. . . . We also consider as acts of terrorism attacks on military installations or on armed military personnel when a state of military hostilities does not exist at the site, such as bombings against US bases in Europe, the Philippines, or elsewhere.[123]

The U.S. Federal Bureau of Investigation (FBI) defines terrorism as

> the unlawful use of force or violence against persons or property to intimidate or coerce a Government, the civilian population, or any segment thereof, in furtherance of political or social objectives,

while the Department of Homeland Security (DHS) states that terrorism is

> any activity that involves an act that:
>
> Is dangerous to human life or potentially destructive of critical infrastructure or key resources; and . . . must also appear to be intended
>
> (i) to intimidate or coerce a civilian population; (ii) to influence the policy of a government by intimidation or coercion; or (iii) to affect the conduct of a government by mass destruction, assassination, or kidnapping.

And the U.S. Department of Defense defines it as

> the calculated use of unlawful violence or threat of unlawful violence to inculcate fear; intended to coerce or to intimidate governments or societies in the pursuit of goals that are generally political, religious, or ideological objectives.

Not surprisingly, each of the above definitions reflects the priorities and particular interests of the specific agency involved. The State Department's emphasis is on the premeditated and planned or calculated nature of terrorism in contrast to more spontaneous acts of political violence. Its definition is also the only one of the four to emphasize both the ineluctably political nature of terrorism and the perpetrators' fundamental "subnational" characteristic. The State Department's approach is also noteworthy in that it expands the definition of a terrorist act beyond the usual, exclusive focus on civilians to include "noncombatant targets." This broad category encompasses not only assassinations of military attachés and military forces deployed on peacekeeping missions, but also attacks on cafes, discotheques, and other facilities frequented by off-duty service personnel, as well as on military installations and armed personnel—provided that a "state of military hostilities does not exist at the site." Under this rubric, incidents such as the 1983 suicide truck bombing of the U.S. Marine barracks at Beirut International Airport; the similar attack thirteen years later against a U.S. Air Force housing complex in Khobar, Saudi Arabia; and the October 2000 seaborne suicide assault on a U.S. Navy destroyer, the USS *Cole* while it was at anchor in Aden, Yemen, are defined as terrorist acts. The State Department definition is deficient, however, in failing to consider the psychological dimension of terrorism. Terrorism is as much about the threat of violence as the violent act itself and, accordingly, is deliberately conceived to have far-reaching psychological repercussions beyond the actual target of the act among a wider, watching, "target" audience. "Terrorism," as Jenkins succinctly observed two decades ago, "is theatre."

Given the FBI's mission of investigating and solving crimes—both political (e.g., terrorism) and other—it is not surprising that its definition focuses on different elements. Unlike the State Department's, this definition does address the psychological dimensions of the terrorist act described above, laying stress on terrorism's intimidatory and coercive aspects. The FBI definition also identifies a much broader category of terrorist targets than only "noncombatants," specifying not only governments and their citizens but also inanimate objects, such as private and public property. Accordingly, politically motivated acts of vandalism and sabotage are included, such as attacks on:

- abortion clinics by militant opponents of legalized abortion in the United States;
- retail businesses and stores by anti-globalists and/or anarchists;
- medical research facilities by groups opposing experimentation on animals, such as the Animal Liberation Front (ALF); and
- ski resorts, condominium vacation developments, commercial logging operations, or automobile dealerships by radical environmentalists associated with the Earth Liberation Front (ELF).

Although the FBI definition recognizes social alongside political objectives as fundamental terrorist aims, it offers no clear elucidation of the differences between them to explain this distinction. The Department of Homeland Security (DHS) definition clearly reflects its mission: concentrating on attacks to critical infrastructure and key national resources that could have grave societal consequences. In this respect, the DHS cites specifically in its definition the threat of "mass destruction," the better to differentiate and distinguish its responsibilities from those of other agencies.

The Department of Defense definition of terrorism is arguably the most complete of the four. It highlights the terrorist threat as much as the actual act of violence and focuses on terrorism's targeting of whole societies as well as governments. Curiously, unlike the State Department definition, it does not include the deliberate targeting of individuals for assassination and makes no attempt to distinguish between attacks on combatant and noncombatant military personnel. The Defense Department definition, significantly, also cites the religious and ideological aims of terrorism alongside its fundamental political objectives—but omits the social dimension found in the FBI's definition.

It is not only individual agencies within the same governmental apparatus that cannot agree on a single definition of terrorism. Experts and other long-established scholars in the field are equally incapable of reaching a consensus. In the first edition of his magisterial survey, *Political Terrorism: A Research Guide,* Alex Schmid devoted more than a hundred pages to examining more than a hundred different definitions of terrorism in an effort to discover a broadly acceptable, reasonably comprehensive explication of the word. Four years and a second edition later, Schmid was no closer to the goal of his quest, conceding in the first sentence of the revised volume that the "search for an adequate definition is still on." Walter Laqueur despaired of defining terrorism in both editions of his monumental work on the subject, maintaining that it is neither possible to do so nor worthwhile to make the attempt. "Ten years of debates on typologies and definitions," he responded to a survey on definitions conducted by Schmid, "have not enhanced our knowledge of the subject to a significant degree." Laqueur's contention is supported by the twenty-two different word categories occurring in the 109 different definitions that Schmid identified in his survey (see table 1). At the end of this exhaustive exercise, Schmid asks "whether the above list contains all the elements necessary for a good definition. The answer," he suggests, "is probably 'no.'"

If it is impossible to define terrorism, as Laqueur argues, and fruitless to attempt to cobble together a truly comprehensive definition, as Schmid admits, are we to conclude that terrorism is impervious to precise, much less accurate definition? Not entirely. If we cannot define terrorism, then we can at least usefully distinguish it from other types of violence and identify the characteristics that make terrorism the distinct phenomenon of political violence that it is.

Distinctions as a Path to Definition

Guerrilla warfare and insurgency are good places to start. Terrorism is often confused or equated with, or treated as synonymous with, guerrilla warfare and insurgency. This is not entirely surprising, since guerrillas and insurgents often employ the same tactics (assassination, kidnapping, hit-and-run attack, bombings of public gathering places, hostage-taking, etc.) for the same purposes (to intimidate or coerce, thereby affecting behavior through the arousal of fear) as terrorists. In addition, terrorists as well as guerrillas and insurgents wear neither uniform nor identifying insignia and thus are often indistinguishable from noncombatants. However, despite the inclination to lump terrorists, guerrillas, and insurgents into the same catchall category of "irregulars," there are nonetheless fundamental differences among the three. "Guerrilla," for example, in its most widely accepted usage, is taken to refer to a numerically larger group of armed individuals, who operate as a military unit, attack enemy military forces, and seize and hold territory (even if only ephemerally during daylight hours), while also exercising some form of sovereignty or control over a defined geographical area and its population. "Insurgents" share these same characteristics; however, their strategy and operations transcend hit-and-run attacks to embrace what in the past has variously been called "revolutionary guerrilla warfare," "modern revolutionary warfare," or "people's war" but is today commonly termed "insurgency." Thus, in addition

Table 1

Frequencies of definitional elements in 109 definitions of "terrorism"

Element	Frequency (%)
1 Violence, force	83.5
2 Political	65
3 Fear, terror emphasized	51
4 Threat	47
5 (Psychological) effects and (anticipated) reactions	41.5
6 Victim-target differentiation	37.5
7 Purposive, planned, systematic, organized action	32
8 Method of combat, strategy, tactic	30.5
9 Extranormality, in breach of accepted rules, without humanitarian constraints	30
10 Coercion, extortion, induction of compliance	28
11 Publicity aspect	21.5
12 Arbitrariness; impersonal, random character; indiscrimination	21
13 Civilians, noncombatants, neutrals, outsiders as victims	17.5
14 Intimidation	17
15 Innocence of victims emphasized	15.5
16 Group, movement, organization as perpetrator	14
17 Symbolic aspect, demonstration to others	13.5
18 Incalculability, unpredictability, unexpectedness of occurrence of violence	9
19 Clandestine, covert nature	9
20 Repetitiveness; serial or campaign character of violence	7
21 Criminal	6
22 Demands made on third parties	4

Source: Alex P. Schmid, Albert J. Jongman, et al., *Political Terrorism: A New Guide to Actors, Authors, Concepts, Data Bases, Theories, and Literature* (New Brunswick, N.J.: Transaction Books, 1988), pp. 5–6.

to the irregular military tactics that characterize guerrilla operations, insurgencies typically involve coordinated informational (e.g., propaganda) and psychological warfare efforts designed to mobilize popular support in a struggle against an established national government, imperialist power, or foreign occupying force. Terrorists, however, do not function in the open as armed units, generally do not attempt to seize or hold territory, deliberately avoid engaging enemy military forces in combat, are constrained both numerically and logistically from undertaking concerted mass political mobilization efforts, and exercise no direct control or governance over a populace at either the local or the national level.

It should be emphasized that none of these are pure categories and considerable overlap exists. Established terrorist groups like Hezbollah, FARC (Revolutionary Armed Forces of Colombia), and the LTTE (Liberation Tigers of Tamil Eelam, or Tamil Tigers), for example, are also often described as guerrilla movements because of their size, tactics, and control over territory and populace. Indeed, nearly a third of the thirty-seven groups on the U.S. State Department's "Designated Foreign Terrorist Organizations" list could just as easily be categorized as guerrillas. The ongoing insurgency in Iraq has further contributed to this semantic confusion. The 2003 edition of the State Department's *Global Patterns of Terrorism* specifically cited the challenge of making meaningful distinctions between these categories, lamenting how the "line between insurgency and terrorism has become increasingly blurred as attacks on civilian targets have become more common." Generally, the State Department considers attacks against U.S. and coalition military forces as insurgent operations and incidents such as the August 2003 suicide vehicle-borne bombings of the UN headquarters in Baghdad and the Jordanian embassy in that city, the assassinations of Japanese diplomats, and kidnapping and murder of aid workers and civilian contractors as terrorist attacks. The definitional rule of thumb therefore is that secular Ba'athist Party loyalists and other former regime elements who stage guerrilla-like hit-and-run assaults or carry out attacks using roadside IEDs (improvised explosive devices) are deemed "insurgents," while foreign jihadists and domestic Islamic extremists who belong to groups like al Qaeda in Mesopotamia, led by Abu Musab Zarqawi, and who are responsible for most of the suicide attacks and the videotaped beheading of hostages, are labeled terrorists.

It is also useful to distinguish terrorists from ordinary criminals. Like terrorists, criminals use violence as a means to attain a specific end. However, while the violent act itself may be similar—kidnapping, shooting, and arson, for example—the purpose or motivation clearly is different. Whether the criminal employs violence as a means to obtain money, to acquire material goods, or to kill or injure a specific victim for pay, he is acting primarily for selfish, personal motivations (usually material gain). Moreover, unlike terrorism, the ordinary criminal's violent act is not designed or intended to have consequences or create psychological repercussions beyond the act itself. The criminal may of course use some short-term act of violence to "terrorize" his victim, such as waving a gun in the face of a bank clerk during a robbery in order to ensure the clerk's expeditious compliance. In these instances, however, the bank robber is conveying no "message" (political or otherwise) through his act of violence beyond facilitating the rapid handing over of his "loot." The criminal's act therefore is not meant to have any effect reaching beyond either the incident itself or the immediate victim. Further, the violence is neither conceived nor intended to convey any message to anyone other than the bank clerk himself, whose rapid cooperation is the robber's only objective. Perhaps most fundamentally, the criminal is not concerned with influencing or affecting public opinion; he simply wants to abscond with his money or accomplish his mercenary task in the quickest and easiest way possible so that he may reap his reward and enjoy the fruits of his labors. By contrast, the fundamental aim of the terrorist's violence is ultimately to change "the system"—about which the ordinary criminal, of course, couldn't care less.

The terrorist is also very different from the lunatic assassin, who may use identical tactics (e.g., shooting, bombing) and perhaps even seeks the same objective (e.g., the death of a political figure). However, while the tactics and targets of terrorists and lone assassins are often identical, their purpose is different. Whereas the terrorist's goal is again ineluctably *political* (to change or fundamentally alter a political system through his violent act), the lunatic assassin's goal is more often intrinsically idiosyncratic, completely egocentric and deeply personal. John Hinckley, who tried to kill President Reagan in 1981 to impress the actress Jodie Foster, is a case in point. He acted not from political motivation or ideological conviction but to fulfill some profound personal quest (killing the president to impress his screen idol). Such entirely *apolitical* motivations can in no way be compared to the rationalizations used by the Narodnaya Volya to justify its campaign of tyrannicide against the czar and his minions, nor even to the Irish Republican Army's efforts to assassinate Prime Minister Margaret Thatcher or her successor, John Major, in hopes of dramatically changing British policy toward Northern Ireland. Further, just as one person cannot credibly claim to be a political party, so a lone individual cannot be considered to constitute a terrorist group. In this respect, even though Sirhan Sirhan's assassination of presidential candidate and U.S. senator Robert Kennedy in 1968 had a political motive (to protest against U.S. support for Israel), it is debatable whether the murder should be defined as a terrorist act since Sirhan belonged to no organized political group and there is no evidence that he was directly influenced or inspired by an identifiable political or terrorist movement. Rather, Sirhan acted entirely on his own, out of deep personal frustration and a profound animus.

Finally, the point should be emphasized that, unlike the ordinary criminal or the lunatic assassin, the terrorist is not pursuing purely egocentric goals; he is not driven by the wish to line his own pocket or satisfy some personal need or grievance. The terrorist is fundamentally an *altruist:* he believes that he is serving a "good" cause designed to achieve a greater good for a wider constituency—whether real or imagined—that the terrorist and his organization purport to represent. The criminal, by comparison, serves no cause at all, just his own personal aggrandizement and material satiation. Indeed, a "terrorist without a cause (at least in his own mind)," Konrad Kellen has argued, "is not a terrorist." Yet the possession or identification of a cause is not a sufficient criterion for labeling someone a terrorist. In this key respect, the difference between terrorists and political extremists is clear. Many people, of course, harbor all sorts of radical and extreme beliefs and opinions, and many of them belong to radical or even illegal or proscribed political organizations. However, if they do not use violence in the pursuit of their beliefs, they cannot be considered terrorists. The terrorist is fundamentally a *violent intellectual,* prepared to use and, indeed, committed to using force in the attainment of his goals.

In the past, terrorism was arguably easier to define than it is today. To qualify as terrorism, violence had to be perpetrated by an individual acting at the behest of or on the behalf of some existent organizational entity or movement with at least some conspiratorial structure and identifiable chain of command. This criterion, however, is no longer sufficient. In recent years, a variety of terrorist movements have increasingly adopted a strategy of "leaderless networks" in order to thwart law enforcement and intelligence agency efforts to penetrate them. Craig Rosebraugh, the publicist for a radical environmentalist group calling itself the Earth Liberation Front (ELF), described the movement in a 2001 interview as a deliberately conceived "series of cells across the country with no chain of command and no membership roll . . . only a shared philosophy." It is designed this way, he continued, so that "there's no central leadership where [the authorities] can go and knock off the top guy and [the movement then] will be defunct." Indeed, an ELF recruitment video narrated by Rosebraugh advises "individuals interested in becoming active in the Earth Liberation Front to . . . form your own close-knit autonomous cells made of trust-worthy and sincere people. Remember, the ELF and each cell within it are anonymous not only to one another but to the general public." As a senior FBI official conceded, the ELF is "not a group you can put your fingers on" and thus is extremely difficult to infiltrate.

This type of networked adversary is a new and different breed of terrorist entity to which traditional organizational constructs and definitions do not neatly apply. It is popu-lated by individuals who are ideologically motivated, inspired, and animated by a move-ment or a leader, but who neither formally belong to a specific, identifiable terrorist group nor directly follow orders issued by its leadership and are therefore outside any established chain of command. It is a structure and approach that al Qaeda has also sought to imple-ment. Ayman al-Zawahiri, bin Laden's deputy and al Qaeda's chief theoretician, extolled this strategy in his seminal clarion call to jihad (Arabic for "striving," but also "holy war"), *Knights Under the Prophet's Banner: Meditations on the Jihadist Movement.* The chapter titled "Small Groups Could Frighten the Americans" explains:

> Tracking down Americans and the Jews is not impossible. Killing them with a single bullet, a stab, or a device made up of a popular mix of explosives or hitting them with an iron rod is not impossible. Burning down their property with Molotov cocktails is not difficult. With the available means, small groups could prove to be a frightening horror for the Americans and the Jews.

Whether termed "leaderless resistance," "phantom cell networks," "autonomous leadership units," "autonomous cells," a "network of networks," or "lone wolves," this new conflict paradigm conforms to what John Arquilla and David Ronfeldt call "netwar":

> an emerging mode of conflict (and crime) at societal levels, short of traditional mili-tary warfare, in which the protagonists use network forms of organization and related doctrines, strategies, and technologies attuned to the information age. These protago-nists are likely to consist of dispersed organizations, small groups, and individuals who communicate, coordinate, and conduct their campaigns in an internetted manner, often without precise central command.

Unlike the hierarchical, pyramidal structure that typified terrorist groups of the past, this new type of organization is looser, flatter, more linear. Although there is a leadership of sorts, its role may be more titular than actual, with less a direct command and control rela-tionship than a mostly inspirational and motivational one. "The organizational structure," Arquilla and Ronfeldt explain,

> is quite flat. There is no single central leader or commander; the network as a whole (but not necessarily each node) has little to no hierarchy. There may be multiple leaders. Decisionmaking and operations are decentralized and depend on consultative consen-sus-building that allows for local initiative and autonomy. The design is both acepha-lous (headless) and polycephalous (Hydra-headed)—it has not precise heart or head, although not all nodes may be "created equal."

As part of this "leaderless" strategy, autonomous local terrorist cells plan and execute attacks independently of one another or of any central command authority, but through their individual terrorist efforts seek the eventual attainment of a terrorist organization or movement's wider goals. Although these ad hoc terrorist cells and lone individuals may be less sophisticated and therefore less capable than their more professional, trained counterparts who are members of actual established terrorist groups, these "amateur" terrorists can be just as bloody-minded. A recent FBI strategic planning document, for instance, describes lone wolves as the "most significant domestic terrorism threat" that the United States faces. "They typically draw ideological inspiration from formal terrorist organizations," the 2004–09 plan states, "but operate on the fringes of those movements. Despite their ad hoc nature and generally limited resources, they can mount high-profile, extremely destructive attacks, and their operational planning is often difficult to detect."

Conclusion

By distinguishing terrorists from other types of criminals and irregular fighters and terrorism from other forms of crime and irregular warfare, we come to appreciate that terrorism is

- ineluctably political in aims and motives;
- violent—or, equally important, threatens violence;
- designed to have far-reaching psychological repercussions beyond the immediate victim or target;
- conducted *either* by an organization with an identifiable chain of command or conspiratorial cell structure (whose members wear no uniform or identifying insignia) or by individuals or a small collection of individuals directly influenced, motivated, or inspired by the ideological aims or example of some existent terrorist movement and/or its leaders; and
- perpetrated by a subnational group or nonstate entity.

We may therefore now attempt to define terrorism as the deliberate creation and exploitation of fear through violence or the threat of violence in the pursuit of political change. All terrorist acts involve violence or the threat of violence. Terrorism is specifically designed to have far-reaching psychological effects beyond the immediate victim(s) or object of the terrorist attack. It is meant to instill fear within, and thereby intimidate, a wider "target audience" that might include a rival ethnic or religious group, an entire country, a national government or political party, or public opinion in general. Terrorism is designed to create power where there is none or to consolidate power where there is very little. Through the publicity generated by their violence, terrorists seek to obtain the leverage, influence, and power they otherwise lack to effect political change on either a local or an international scale.

Bruce Hoffman is a professor of security studies at the Edmund A. Walsh School of Foreign Service at Georgetown University. Dr. Hoffman is the former Corporate Chair in Counter-Terrorism and Counter-Insurgency at the RAND Corporation, where he was also director of the Washington, DC office. He is editor of the journal *Conflict and Terrorism* and holds fellowships at the Combating Terrorism Center at West Point and the National Security Studies Center at Haifa University, Israel.

Eqbal Ahmad, 1998

Terrorism: Theirs & Ours

Eqbal Ahmad was one of the major activist scholars of this era. He was born in India probably in 1934. He was never quite sure. He left with his brothers for the newly created state of Pakistan in 1947. In 1996, the BBC did a powerful and moving TV documentary chronicling Ahmad's trek in a refugee caravan from his village in Bihar to Pakistan. The film, not shown on PBS in the U.S., is remarkable not just as an historical document but also for providing insight into the dangers of sectarian nationalism. Ahmad's secular thinking was surely shaped by the wrenching communal and political violence he experienced as a youngster. Even before the subcontinent was engulfed in the homicidal convulsions of 1947, Ahmad witnessed his own father murdered before him.

Ahmad came to the United States in the 1950s to study at Princeton. Later he went to Algeria. It was there that his ideas about national liberation and anti-imperialism crystallized. He worked with Frantz Fanon, author of The Wretched of the Earth, *during the revolt against the French. Returning to the U.S., he became active in the civil rights and anti-Vietnam War movements. It was during his involvement in the latter that I first heard his name. He was accused of plotting to kidnap Henry Kissinger. The trumped-up charges were dismissed.*

I did my first interview with him in the early 1980s in his apartment on New York's Upper West Side. It was memorable. I had just gotten a new tape recorder. I returned home thinking, Wow, I've got a great interview. I hit play and discovered the tape was blank. I had failed to turn the machine on. With considerable embarrassment I explained to him what happened. He said, "No problem." He invited me over the next day and we did another interview. This time, I pressed the right buttons. Whenever I tell that story, his friends would nod and say, "That's Eqbal."

Ahmad's radical politics and outspoken positions made him a pariah in academic circles. After years of being an intellectual migrant worker, Hampshire College in Amherst, Massachusetts, hired him in the early 1980s as a professor. He taught there until his retirement in 1997. He spent most of his final years in Islamabad where he wrote a weekly column for Dawn, *Pakistan's oldest English-language newspaper. His political work consisted chiefly of trying to bridge differences with India on the issues of Kashmir and nuclear weapons. He was also speaking out against the rise of Islamic fundamentalism and was concerned about the possible Talibanization of Pakistan.*

Eqbal Ahmad died in Islamabad, Pakistan, on May 11, 1999. His close friend Edward Said wrote, "He was perhaps the shrewdest and most original anti-imperialist analyst of the postwar world, particularly of the dynamics between the West and postcolonial Asia and

Africa; a man of enormous charisma, dazzling eloquence, incorruptible ideals, unfailing generosity and sympathy. . . . Whether on the conflict between Israelis and Palestinians or India and Pakistan, he was a force for a just struggle but also for a just reconciliation. . . . Humanity and genuine secularism . . . had no finer champion."

"Terrorism: Theirs & Ours" was one of Eqbal Ahmad's last public talks in the United States. He spoke at the University of Colorado at Boulder in October 1998. It was broadcast nationally and internationally on my weekly Alternative Radio program. Eqbal Ahmad's near prophetic sense is stunning. After the September 11 terrorist attacks, I aired the speech again. Listeners called in great numbers requesting copies. They almost all believed that the talk had just been recorded.

—David Barsamian

Until the 1930s and early 1940s, the Jewish underground in Palestine was described as "terrorist." Then something happened: around 1942, as news of the Holocaust was spreading, a certain liberal sympathy with the Jewish people began to emerge in the Western world. By 1944, the terrorists of Palestine, who were Zionists, suddenly began being described as "freedom fighters." If you look in history books you can find at least two Israeli prime ministers, including Menachem Begin,[1] appearing in "Wanted" posters saying, TERRORISTS, REWARD [THIS MUCH]. The highest reward I have seen offered was 100,000 British pounds for the head of Menachem Begin, the terrorist.

From 1969 to 1990, the Palestine Liberation Organization (PLO) occupied center state as a terrorist organization. Yasir Arafat has been repeatedly described as the "chief of terrorism" by the great sage of American journalism, William Safire of *The New York Times.* On September 29, 1998, I was rather amused to notice a picture of Yasir Arafat and Israeli prime minister Benjamin Netanyahu standing on either side of President Bill Clinton. Clinton was looking toward Arafat, who looked meek as a mouse. Just a few years earlier, Arafat would appear in photos with a very menacing look, a gun holstered to his belt. That's Yasir Arafat. You remember those pictures, and you'll remember the next one.

In 1985, President Ronald Reagan received a group of ferocious-looking, turban-wearing men who looked like they came from another century. I had been writing about the very same men for *The New Yorker.* After receiving them in the White House, Reagan spoke to the press, referring to his foreign guests as "freedom fighters." These were the Afghan mujahideen. They were at the time, guns in hand, battling the "Evil Empire." For Reagan, they were the moral equivalent of our Founding Fathers.

In August 1998, another American president ordered missile strikes to kill Osama bin Laden and his men in Afghanistan-based camps. Mr. bin Laden, at whom fifteen American missiles were fired to hit in Afghanistan, was only a few years earlier the moral equivalent of George Washington and Thomas Jefferson. I'll return to the subject of bin Laden later.

I am recalling these stories to point out that the official approach to terrorism is rather complicated, but not without characteristics. To begin with, terrorists change. The terrorist of yesterday is the hero of today, and the hero of yesterday becomes the terrorist of today.

In a constantly changing world of images, we have to keep our heads straight to know what terrorism is and what it is not. Even more importantly, we need to know what causes terrorism and how to stop it.

Secondly, the official approach to terrorism is a posture of inconsistency, one which evades definition. I have examined at least twenty official documents on terrorism. Not one offers a definition. All of them explain it polemically in order to arouse our emotions, rather than exercise our intelligence. I'll give you an example which is representative. On October 25, 1984, Secretary of State George Shultz gave a long speech on terrorism at the Park Avenue Synagogue in New York City. In the State Department Bulletin of seven single-spaced pages, there is not a single clear definition of terrorism. What we get instead are the following statements. Number one: "Terrorism is a modern barbarism that we call terrorism." Number two is even more brilliant; "Terrorism is a form of political violence." Number three: "Terrorism is a menace to Western moral values." Do these accomplish anything other than arouse emotions? This is typical.

Officials don't define terrorism because definitions involve a commitment to analysis, comprehension, and adherence to some norms of consistency. That's the second characteristic of the official approach to terrorism. The third characteristic is that the absence of definition does not prevent officials from being globalistic. They may not define terrorism, but they can call it a menace to good order, a menace to the moral values of Western civilization, a menace to humankind. Therefore, they can call for it to be stamped out worldwide. Anti-terrorist policies therefore, must be global. In the same speech he gave in New York City, George Shultz also said: "There is no question about our ability to use force where and when it is needed to counter terrorism." There is no geographical limit. On the same day, U.S. missiles struck Afghanistan and Sudan. Those two countries are 2,300 miles apart, and they were hit by missiles belonging to a country roughly 8,000 miles away. Reach is global.

A fourth characteristic is that the official approach to terrorism claims not only global reach, but also a certain omniscient knowledge. They claim to know where terrorists are, and therefore, where to hit. To quote George Shultz again, "We know the difference between terrorists and freedom fighters and as we look around, we have no trouble telling one from the other." Only Osama bin Laden doesn't know that he was an ally one day and an enemy another. That's very confusing for Osama bin Laden. I'll come back to him toward the end; it's a real story.

Fifth, the official approach eschews causation. They don't look at why people resort to terrorism. Cause? What cause? Another example: on December 18, 1985, *The New York Times* reported that the foreign minister of Yugoslavia—you remember the days when there was a Yugoslavia—requested the secretary of state of the U.S. to consider the causes of Palestinian terrorism. The secretary of state, George Shultz, and I'm quoting from *The New York Times,* "went a bit red in the face. He pounded the table and told the visiting foreign minister, "There is no connection with any cause. Period." Why look for causes?

A sixth characteristic of the official approach to terrorism is the need for the moral revulsion we feel against terror to be selective. We are to denounce the terror of those groups which are officially disapproved. But we are to applaud the terror of those groups of whom officials do approve. Hence, President Reagan's statement, "I am a contra." We know that the contras of Nicaragua were by any definition terrorists, but the media heed the dominant view.

More importantly to me, the dominant approach also excludes from consideration the terrorism of friendly governments. Thus, the United States excused, among others, the terrorism of Pinochet, who killed one of my closest friends, Orlando Letelier, one of Chilean President Salvador Allende's top diplomats, killed in a car bombing in Washington, DC in 1976. And it excused the terror of Zia ul-Haq, the military dictator of Pakistan, who killed many of my friends there. All I want to tell you is that according to my ignorant calculations, the ratio of people killed by the state terror of Zia ul-Haq, Pinochet, Argentinian, Brazilian, Indonesian type, versus the killing of the PLO and other organizations is literally, conservatively 1,000 to 1. That's the ratio.

History unfortunately recognizes and accords visibility to power, not to weakness. Therefore, visibility has been accorded historically to dominant groups. Our time—the time that begins with Columbus—has been one of extraordinary unrecorded holocausts. Great civilizations have been wiped out. The Mayas, the Incas, the Aztecs, the American Indians, the Canadian Indians were all wiped out. Their voices have not been heard, even to this day. They are heard, yes, but only when the dominant power suffers, only when resistance has a semblance of costing, of exacting a price, when a Custer is killed or when a Gordon is besieged. That's when you know that there were Indians or Arabs fighting and dying.

My last point on this subject is that during the Cold War period, the United States sponsored terrorist regimes like Somoza in Nicaragua and Batista in Cuba, one after another. All kinds of tyrants have been America's friends. In Nicaragua it was the contra, in Afghanistan, the mujahideen.

Now, what about the other side? What is terrorism? Our first job should be to define the damn thing, name it, give it a description other than "moral equivalent of founding fathers" or "a moral outrage to Western civilization." This is what *Webster's Collegiate Dictionary* says: "Terror is an intense, overpowering fear." Terrorism is "the use of terrorizing methods of governing or resisting a government." This simple definition has one great virtue: it's fair. It focuses on the use of violence that is used illegally, extra-constitutionally, to coerce. And this definition is correct because it treats terror for what it is, whether a government or private group commits it.

Have you noticed something? Motivation is omitted. We're not talking about whether the cause is just or unjust. We're talking about consensus, consent, absence of consent, legality, absence of legality, constitutionality, absence of constitutionality. Why do we keep motives out? Because motives make no difference. In the course of my work I have identified five types of terrorism: state terrorism, religious terrorism (Catholics killing Protestants, Sunnis killing Shiites, Shiites killing Sunnis), criminal terrorism, political terrorism, and oppositional terrorism. Sometimes these five can converge and overlap. Oppositional protest terrorism can become pathological criminal terrorism. State terror can take the form of private terror. For example, we're all familiar with the death squads in Latin America or in Pakistan where the government has employed private people to kill its opponents. It's not quite official. It's privatized. In Afghanistan, Central America, and Southeast Asia, the CIA employed in its covert operations drug pushers. Drugs and guns often go together. The categories often overlap.

Of the five types of terror, the official approach is to focus on only one form— political terrorism—which claims the least in terms of loss of human lives and property. The form that exacts the highest loss is state terrorism. The second highest loss is created by religious terrorism, although religious terror has, relatively speaking, declined. If you are looking historically, however, religious terrorism has caused massive loss. The next highest loss is caused by criminal terrorism. A Rand Corporation study by Brian Jenkins examining a ten-year period (1978 to 1988) showed fifty percent of terrorism was committed without any political cause. No politics. Simply crime and pathology. So the focus is on only one, the political terrorist, the PLO, the bin Laden, whoever you want to take.

Why do they do it? What makes terrorists tick?

I would like to knock out some quick answers. First, the need to be heard. Remember, we are dealing with a minority group, the political, private terrorist. Normally, and there are exceptions, there is an effort to be heard, to get their grievances recognized and addressed by people. The Palestinians, for example, the superterrorists of our time, were dispossessed in 1948. From 1948 to 1968 they went to every court in the world. They knocked on every door. They had been completely deprived of their land, their country, and nobody was listening. In desperation, they invented a new form of terror: the airplane hijacking. Between 1968 and 1975 they pulled the world up by its ears. That kind of terror is a violent way of expressing long-felt grievances. It makes the world hear. It's normally undertaken by small, helpless groupings that feel powerless. We still haven't done the Palestinians justice, but at least we all know they exist. Now, even the Israelis acknowledge. Remember what Golda Meir, prime minister of Israel, said in 1970: There are no Palestinians. They do not exist.

They damn well exist now.

Secondly, terrorism is an expression of anger, of feeling helpless, angry, alone. You feel like you have to hit back. Wrong has been done to you, so you do it. During the hijacking of the TWA jet in Beirut, Judy Brown of Belmar, New Jersey, said that she kept hearing them yell, "New Jersey, New Jersey." What did they have in mind? She thought that they were going after her. Later on it turned out that the terrorists were referring to the U.S. battleship *New Jersey,* which had heavily shelled the Lebanese civilian population in 1983.

Another factor is a sense of betrayal, which is connected to that tribal ethic of revenge. It comes into the picture in the case of people like bin Laden. Here is a man who was an ally of the United States, who saw America as a friend; then he sees his country being occupied by the United States and feels betrayal. Whether there is a sense of right and wrong is not what I'm saying. I'm describing what's behind this kind of extreme violence.

Sometimes it's the fact that you have experienced violence at other people's hands. Victims of violent abuse often become violent people. The only time when Jews produced terrorists in organized fashion was during and after the Holocaust. It is rather remarkable that Jewish terrorists hit largely innocent people or U.N. peacemakers like Count Bernadotte of Sweden, whose country had a better record on the Holocaust. The men of Irgun, the Stern Gang, and the Hagannah terrorist groups came in the wake of the Holocaust. The experience of victimhood itself produces a violent reaction.

In modern times, with modern technology and means of communications, the targets have been globalized. Therefore, globalization of violence is an aspect of what we call globalization of the economy and culture in the world as a whole. We can't expect everything else to be globalized and violence not to be. We do have visible targets. Airplane hijacking is something new because international travel is relatively new, too. Everybody now is in your gunsight. Therefore the globe is within the gunsight. That has globalized terror.

Finally, the absence of revolutionary ideology has been central to the spread of terror in our time. One of the points in the big debate between Marxism and anarchism in the nineteenth century was the use of terror. The Marxists argued that the true revolutionary does not assassinate. You do not solve social problems by individual acts of violence. Social problems require social and political mobilization, and thus wars of liberation are to be distinguished from terrorist organizations. The revolutionaries didn't reject violence, but they rejected terror as a viable tactic of revolution. That revolutionary ideology has gone out at the moment. In the 1980s and 1990s, revolutionary ideology receded, giving in to the globalized individual. In general terms, these are among the many forces that are behind modern terrorism.

To this challenge rulers from one country after another have been responding with traditional methods. The traditional method of shooting it out, whether it's with missiles or some other means. The Israelis are very proud of it. The Americans are very proud of it. The French became very proud of it. Now the Pakistanis are very proud of it. The Pakistanis say, Our commandoes are the best. Frankly, it won't work. A central problem of our time: political minds rooted in the past at odds with modern times, producing new realities.

Let's turn back for a moment to Osama bin Laden. *Jihad,* which has been translated a thousand times as "holy war," is not quite that. *Jihad* in Arabic means "to struggle." It could be struggle by violence or struggle by non-violent means. There are two forms, the small *jihad* and the big *jihad.* The small *jihad* involves external violence. The big *jihad* involves a struggle within oneself. Those are the concepts. The reason I mention it is that in Islamic history, *jihad* as an international violent phenomenon had for all practical purposes disappeared in the last four hundred years. It was revived suddenly with American help in the 1980s. When the Soviet Union intervened in Afghanistan, which borders Pakistan, Zia ul-Haq saw an opportunity and launched a *jihad* there against godless communism. The U.S. saw a God-sent opportunity to mobilize one billion Muslims against what Reagan called the Evil Empire. Money started pouring in. CIA agents starting going all over the Muslim world recruiting people to fight in the great *jihad.* Bin Laden was one of the early prize recruits. He was not only an Arab, he was a Saudi multimillionaire willing to put his own money into the matter. Bin Laden went around recruiting people for the *jihad* against communism.

I first met Osama bin Laden in 1986. He was recommended to me by an American official who may have been an agent. I was talking to the American and asked him who were the Arabs there that would be very interesting to talk with. By *there* I meant in Afghanistan and Pakistan. The American official told me, "You must meet Osama." I went to see Osama. There he was, rich, bringing in recruits from Algeria, from Sudan, from Egypt, just like Sheikh Abdul Rahman, an Egyptian cleric who was among those convicted for the 1993 World Trade Center bombing. At that moment, Osama bin Laden was a U.S. ally. He remained an ally. He turned at a particular moment. In 1990 the U.S. went into Saudi Arabia with military forces. Saudi Arabia is the holy place of Muslims, home of Mecca and Medina. There had never been foreign troops there. In 1990, during the build-up to the Gulf War, they went in in the name of helping Saudi Arabia defend itself. Osama bin Laden remained quiet. Saddam was defeated, but the American foreign troops stayed on in the land of the kaba (the sacred site of Islam in Mecca). Bin Laden wrote letter after letter saying, Why are you here? Get out! You came to help but you have stayed on. Finally he started a *jihad* against the other occupiers. His mission is to get American troops out of Saudi Arabia. His earlier mission was to get Russian troops out of Afghanistan.

A second point to be made about him is that he comes from a tribal people. Being a millionaire doesn't matter. His code of ethics is tribal. The tribal code of ethics consists of two words: loyalty and revenge. You are my friend. You keep your word. I am loyal to you. You break your word, I go on my path of revenge. For him, America has broken its word. The loyal friend has betrayed him. Now they're going to go for you. They're going to do a lot more. These are the chickens of the Afghanistan war coming home to roost.

What is my recommendation to America?

First, avoid extremes of double standards. If you're going to practice double standards, you will be paid with double standards. Don't use it. Don't condone Israeli terror, Pakistani terror, Nicaraguan terror, El Salvadoran terror, on the one hand, and then complain about Afghan terror or Palestinian terror. It doesn't work. Try to be even-handed. A superpower cannot promote terror in one place and reasonably expect to discourage terrorism in another place. It won't work in this shrunken world.

Do not condone the terror of your allies. Condemn them. Fight them. Punish them. Avoid covert operations and low-intensity warfare. These are breeding grounds for terrorism and drugs. In the Australian documentary about covert operations, *Dealing with the Demon,* I say that wherever covert operations have been, there is a drug problem. Because the structure of covert operations, Afghanistan, Vietnam, Nicaragua, Central America, etcetera, have been very hospitable to the drug trade. Avoid covert operations. It doesn't help.

Also, focus on causes and help ameliorate them. Try to look at causes and solve problems. Avoid military solutions. Terrorism is a political problem. Seek political solutions. Diplomacy works. Take the example of President Clinton's attack on bin Laden. Did they know what they were attacking? They say they know, but they don't know. At another point, they were trying to kill Qadaffi. Instead, they killed his young daughter. The poor child hadn't done anything. Qadaffi is still alive. They tried to kill Saddam Hussein. Instead they killed Laila bin Attar, a prominent artist, an innocent woman. They tried to kill bin Laden and his men. Twenty-five other people died. They tried to destroy a chemical factory in Sudan. Now they are admitting that they destroyed a pharmaceutical plant that produced half the medicine for Sudan.

Four of the missiles intended for Afghanistan fell in Pakistan. One was slightly damaged, two were totally damaged, one was totally intact. For ten years the American government has kept an embargo on Pakistan because Pakistan was trying, stupidly, to build nuclear weapons and missiles. So the U.S. has a technology embargo on my country. One of the missiles was intact. What do you think the Pakistani official told the *Washington Post?* He said it was a gift from Allah. Pakistan wanted U.S. technology. Now they have the technology, and Pakistan's scientists are examining this missile very carefully. It fell into the wrong hands. Look for political solutions. Military solutions cause more problems than they solve.

Finally, please help reinforce and strengthen the framework of international law. There was a criminal court in Rome. Why didn't the U.S. go there first to get a warrant against bin Laden, if they have some evidence? Enforce the United Nations. Enforce the International Court of Justice. Get a warrant, then go after him internationally.

Eqbal Ahmad was born in India but moved to the newly created state of Pakistan in 1947. His theories about national liberation and anti-imperialism developed over years of involvement in radical causes worldwide. Ahmad spent the last years of his life addressing the conflict between India and Pakistan regarding Kashmir and speaking out against the rise of Islamic fundamentalism and the influence of the Taliban in Pakistan. This reading is a transcript of a public talk he gave at the University of Colorado in October 1998. Ahmad died in 1999.

Note

1. Yitzhak Shamir is the other.

Martha Crenshaw, 1998

The Logic of Terrorism: Terrorist Behavior as a Product of Strategic Choice

This [selection] examines the ways in which terrorism can be understood as an expression of political strategy. It attempts to show that terrorism may follow logical processes that can be discovered and explained. For the purpose of presenting this source of terrorist behavior, rather than the psychological one, it interprets the resort to violence as a willful choice made by an organization for political and strategic reasons, rather than as the unintended outcome of psychological or social factors.[1]

In the terms of this analytical approach, terrorism is assumed to display a collective rationality. A radical political organization is seen as the central actor in the terrorist drama. The group possesses collective preferences or values and selects terrorism as a course of action from a range of perceived alternatives. Efficacy is the primary standard by which terrorism is compared with other methods of achieving political goals. Reasonably regularized decision-making procedures are employed to make an intentional choice, in conscious anticipation of the consequences of various courses of action or inaction. Organizations arrive at collective judgments about the relative effectiveness of different strategies of opposition on the basis of abstract strategic conceptions derived from ideological assumptions. This approach thus allows for the incorporation of theories of social learning.

Conventional rational-choice theories of individual participation in rebellion, extended to include terrorist activities, have usually been considered inappropriate because of the "free rider" problem. That is, the benefits of a successful terrorist campaign would presumably be shared by all individual supporters of the group's goals, regardless of the extent of their active participation. In this case, why should a rational person become a terrorist, given the high costs associated with violent resistance and the expectation that everyone who supports the cause will benefit, whether he or she participates or not? One answer is that the benefits of participation are psychological. . . .

A different answer, however, supports a strategic analysis. On the basis of surveys conducted in New York and West Germany, political scientists suggest that individuals can be *collectively* rational.[2] People realize that their participation is important because group size and cohesion matter. They are sensitive to the implications of free-riding and perceive their personal influence on the provision of public goods to be high. The authors argue that "average citizens may adopt a collectivist conception of rationality because they recognize that what is individually rational is collectively irrational."[3] Selective incentives are deemed largely irrelevant.

One of the advantages of approaching terrorism as a collectively rational strategic choice is that it permits the construction of a standard from which deviations can be measured. For example, the central question about the rationality of some terrorist organizations, such as the West German groups of the 1970s or the Weather Underground in the United States, is whether or not they had a sufficient grasp of reality—some approximation, to whatever degree imperfect—to calculate the likely consequences of the courses of action they chose. Perfect knowledge of available alternatives and the consequences of each is not possible, and miscalculations are inevitable. The Popular Front for the Liberation of Palestine (PFLP), for example, planned the hijacking of a TWA flight from Rome in August 1969 to coincide with a scheduled address by President Nixon to a meeting of the Zionist Organization of America, but he sent a letter instead.[4]

Yet not all errors of decision are miscalculations. There are varied degrees of limited rationality. Are some organizations so low on the scale of rationality as to be in a different category from more strategically minded groups? To what degree is strategic reasoning modified by psychological and other constraints? The strategic choice framework provides criteria on which to base these distinctions. It also leads one to ask what conditions promote or discourage rationality in violent underground organizations.

The use of this theoretical approach is also advantageous in that it suggests important questions about the preferences or goals of terrorist organizations. For example, is the decision to seize hostages in order to bargain with governments dictated by strategic considerations or by other, less instrumental motives?

The strategic choice approach is also a useful interpretation of reality. Since the French Revolution, a strategy of terrorism has gradually evolved as a means of bringing about political change opposed by established governments. Analysis of the historical development of terrorism reveals similarities in calculation of ends and means. The strategy has changed over time to adapt to new circumstances that offer different possibilities for dissident action—for example, hostage taking. Yet terrorist activity considered in its entirety shows a fundamental unity of purpose and conception. Although this analysis remains largely on an abstract level, the historical evolution of the strategy of terrorism can be sketched in its terms.[5]

A last argument in support of this approach takes the form of a warning. The wide range of terrorist activity cannot be dismissed as "irrational" and thus pathological, unreasonable, or inexplicable. The resort to terrorism need not be an aberration. It may be a reasonable and calculated response to circumstances. To say that the reasoning that leads to the choice of terrorism may be logical is not an argument about moral justifiability. It does suggest, however, that the belief that terrorism is expedient is one means by which moral inhibitions are overcome. . . .

The Conditions for Terrorism

The central problem is to determine when extremist organizations find terrorism useful. Extremists seek either a radical change in the status quo, which would confer a new advantage, or the defense of privileges they perceive to be threatened. Their dissatisfaction with the policies of the government is extreme, and their demands usually involve the displacement of existing political elites.[6] Terrorism is not the only method of working toward radical goals, and thus it must be compared to the alternative strategies available to dissidents. Why is terrorism attractive to some opponents of the state, but unattractive to others?

The practitioners of terrorism often claim that they had no choice but terrorism, and it is indeed true that terrorism often follows the failure of other methods. In nineteenth-century Russia, for example, the failure of nonviolent movements contributed to the rise of terrorism. In Ireland, terrorism followed the failure of Parnell's constitutionalism. In the Palestinian-Israeli struggle, terrorism followed the failure of Arab efforts at conventional warfare against Israel. In general, the "nonstate" or "substate" users of terrorism—that is, groups in opposition to the government, as opposed to government itself—are constrained in their options by the lack of active mass support and by the superior power arrayed against them (an imbalance that has grown with the development of the modern centralized and bureaucratic nation-state). But these constraints have not prevented oppositions from considering and rejecting methods other than terrorism. Perhaps because groups are slow to recognize the extent of the limits to action, terrorism is often the last in a sequence of choices. It represents the outcome of a learning process. Experience in opposition provides radicals with information about the potential consequences of their choices. Terrorism is likely to be a reasonably informed choice among available alternatives, some tried unsuccessfully. Terrorists also learn from the experiences of others, usually communicated to them via the news media. Hence the existence of patterns of contagion in terrorist incidents.[7]

Thus the existence of extremism or rebellious potential is necessary to the resort to terrorism but does not in itself explain it, because many revolutionary and nationalist organizations have explicitly disavowed terrorism. The Russian Marxists argued for years against the use of terrorism.[8] Generally, small organizations resort to violence to compensate for what they lack in numbers.[9] The imbalance between the resources terrorists are able to mobilize and the power of the incumbent regime is a decisive consideration in their decision making.

More important than the observation that terrorism is the weapon of the weak, who lack numbers or conventional military power, is the explanation for weakness. Particularly, why does an organization lack the potential to attract enough followers to change government policy or overthrow it?

One possibility is that the majority of the population does not share the ideological views of the resisters, who occupy a political position so extreme that their appeal is inherently limited. This incompatibility of preferences may be purely political, concerning, for example, whether or not one prefers socialism to capitalism. The majority of West Germans found the Red Army Faction's promises for the future not only excessively vague but distasteful. Nor did most Italians support aims of the neofascist groups that initiated the "strategy of tension" in 1969. Other extremist groups, such as the *Euzkadi ta Akatasuna* (ETA) in Spain or the Provisional Irish Republican Army (PIRA) in Northern Ireland, may appeal exclusively to ethnic, religious, or other minorities. In such cases, a potential constituency of like-minded and dedicated individuals exists, but its boundaries are fixed and limited. Despite the intensity of the preferences of a minority, its numbers will never be sufficient for success.

A second explanation for the weakness of the type of organization likely to turn to terrorism lies in a failure to mobilize support. Its members may be unwilling or unable to expend the time and effort required for mass organizational work. Activists may not possess the requisite skills or patience, or may not expect returns commensurate with their endeavors. No matter how acute or widespread popular dissatisfaction may be, the masses do not rise spontaneously; mobilization is required.[10] The organization's leaders, recognizing the advantages of numbers, may combine mass organization with conspiratorial activities. But resources are limited and organizational work is difficult and slow even under favorable circumstances. Moreover, rewards are not immediate. These difficulties are compounded in an authoritarian state, where the organization of independent opposition is sure to incur high costs. Combining violent provocation with nonviolent organizing efforts may only work to the detriment of the latter.

For example, the debate over whether to use an exclusively violent underground strategy that is isolated from the masses (as terrorism inevitably is) or to work with the people in propaganda and organizational efforts divided the Italian left-wing groups, with the Red Brigades choosing the clandestine path and Prima Linea preferring to maintain contact with the wider protest movement. In prerevolutionary Russia the Socialist-Revolutionary party combined the activities of a legal political party with the terrorist campaign of the secret Combat Organization. The IRA has a legal counterpart in Sinn Fein.

A third reason for the weakness of dissident organizations is specific to repressive states. It is important to remember that terrorism is by no means restricted to liberal democracies, although some authors refuse to define resistance to authoritarianism as terrorism.[11] People may not support a resistance organization because they are afraid of negative sanctions from the regime or because censorship of the press prevents them from learning of the possibility of rebellion. In this situation a radical organization may believe that supporters exist but cannot reveal themselves. The depth of this latent support cannot be measured or activists mobilized until the state is overthrown.

Such conditions are frustrating, because the likelihood of popular dissatisfaction grows as the likelihood of its active expression is diminished. Frustration may also encourage unrealistic expectations among the regime's challengers, who are not able to test their popularity. Rational expectations may be undermined by fantastic assumptions about the role of the masses. Yet such fantasies can also prevail among radical undergrounds in Western democracies. The misperception of conditions can lead to unrealistic expectations.

In addition to small numbers, time constraints contribute to the decision to use terrorism. Terrorists are impatient for action. This impatience may, of course, be due to external factors, such as psychological or organizational pressures. The personalities of leaders, demands from followers, or competition from rivals often constitute impediments to strategic thinking. But it is not necessary to explain the felt urgency of some radical organizations by citing reasons external to an instrumental framework. Impatience and eagerness for action can be rooted in calculations of ends and means. For example, the organization may perceive an immediate opportunity to compensate for its inferiority vis-à-vis the government. A change in the structure of the situation may temporarily alter the balance of resources available to the two sides, thus changing the ratio of strength between government and challenger.

Such a change in the radical organization's outlook—the combination of optimism and urgency—may occur when the regime suddenly appears vulnerable to challenge. This vulnerability may be of two sorts. First, the regime's ability to respond effectively, its capacity for efficient repression of dissent, or its ability to protect its citizens and property may weaken. Its armed forces may be committed elsewhere, for example, as British forces were during World War I when the IRA first rose to challenge British rule, or its coercive resources may be otherwise overextended. Inadequate security at embassies, airports, or military installations may become obvious. The poorly protected U.S. Marine barracks in Beirut were, for example, a tempting target. Government strategy may be ill-adapted to responding to terrorism.

Second, the regime may make itself morally or politically vulnerable by increasing the likelihood that the terrorists will attract popular support. Government repressiveness is thought to have contradictory effects; it both deters dissent and provokes a moral backlash.[12] Perceptions of the regime as unjust motivate opposition. If government actions make average citizens willing to suffer punishment for supporting antigovernment causes, or lend credence to the claims of radical opponents, the extremist organization may be tempted to exploit this temporary upsurge of popular indignation. A groundswell of popular disapproval may make liberal governments less willing (as opposed to less able) to use coercion against violent dissent.

Political discomfort may also be internationally generated. If the climate of international opinion changes so as to reduce the legitimacy of a targeted regime, rebels may feel encouraged to risk a repression that they hope will be limited by outside disapproval. In such circumstances the regime's brutality may be expected to win supporters to the cause of its challengers. The current situation in South Africa furnishes an example. Thus a heightened sensitivity to injustice may be produced either by government actions or by changing public attitudes.

The other fundamental way in which the situation changes to the advantage of challengers is through acquiring new resources. New means of financial support are an obvious asset, which may accrue through a foreign alliance with a sympathetic government or another, richer revolutionary group, or through criminal means such as bank robberies or kidnapping for ransom. Although terrorism is an extremely economical method of violence, funds are essential for the support of full-time activists, weapons purchases, transportation, and logistics.

Technological advances in weapons, explosives, transportation, and communications also may enhance the disruptive potential of terrorism. The invention of dynamite was thought by nineteenth-century revolutionaries and anarchists to equalize the relationship between government and challenger, for example. In 1885, Johann Most published a pamphlet titled *Revolutionary War Science,* which explicitly advocated terrorism. According to Paul Avrich, the anarchists saw dynamite "as a great equalizing force, enabling ordinary workmen to stand up against armies, militias, and police, to say nothing of the hired gunmen of the employers."[13] In providing such a powerful but easily concealed weapon, science was thought to have given a decisive advantage to revolutionary forces.

Strategic innovation is another important way in which a challenging organization acquires new resources. The organization may borrow or adapt a technique in order to exploit a vulnerability ignored by the government. In August 1972, for example, the Provisional IRA introduced the effective tactic of the one-shot sniper. IRA Chief of Staff Sean MacStiofain claims to have originated the idea: "It seemed to me that prolonged sniping from a static position had no more in common with guerrilla theory than mass confrontations."[14] The best marksmen were trained to fire a single shot and escape before their position could be located. The creation of surprise is naturally one of the key advantages of an offensive strategy. So, too, is the willingness to violate social norms pertaining to restraints on violence. The history of terrorism reveals a series of innovations, as terrorists deliberately selected targets considered taboo and locales where violence was unexpected. These innovations were then rapidly diffused, especially in the modern era of instantaneous and global communications.

It is especially interesting that, in 1968, two of the most important terrorist tactics of the modern era appeared—diplomatic kidnappings in Latin America and hijackings in the Middle East. Both were significant innovations because they involved the use of extortion or blackmail. Although the nineteenth-century Fenians had talked about kidnapping the prince of Wales, the People's Will (Narodnaya Volya) in nineteenth-century Russia had offered to halt its terrorist campaign if a constitution were granted, and [although] American Marines were kidnapped by Castro forces in 1959, hostage taking as a systematic and lethal form of coercive bargaining was essentially new. . . .

Terrorism has so far been presented as the response by an opposition movement to an opportunity. This approach is compatible with the findings of Harvey Waterman, who sees collective political action as determined by the calculations of resources and opportunities.[15] Yet other theorists—James Q. Wilson, for example—argue that political organizations originate in response to a threat to a group's values.[16] Terrorism can certainly be defensive as well as opportunistic. It may be a response to a sudden downturn in a dissident organization's fortunes. The fear of appearing weak may provoke an underground organization into acting in order to show its strength. The PIRA used terrorism to offset an impression of weakness, even at the cost of alienating public opinion: in the 1970s periods of negotiations with the British were punctuated by outbursts of terrorism because the PIRA did want people to think that they were negotiating from strength.[17] Right-wing organizations frequently resort to violence in response to what they see as a threat to the status quo from the left. Beginning in 1969, for example, the right in Italy promoted a "strategy of tension," which involved urban bombings with high numbers of civilian casualties, in order to keep the Italian government and electorate from moving to the left.

Calculation of Cost and Benefit

An organization or a faction of an organization may choose terrorism because other methods are not expected to work or are considered too time-consuming, given the urgency of the situation and the government's superior resources. Why would an extremist organization expect that terrorism will be effective? What are the costs and benefits of such a choice, compared with other alternatives? What is the nature of the debate over terrorism? Whether or not to use terrorism is one of the most divisive issues resistance groups confront, and numerous revolutionary movements have split on the question of means even after agreeing on common political ends.[18]

The costs of terrorism. The costs of terrorism are high. As a domestic strategy, it invariably invites a punitive government reaction, although the organization may believe that the government reaction will not be efficient enough to pose a serious threat. This cost can be offset by the advance preparation of building a secure underground. *Sendero Luminoso* (Shining Path) in Peru, for example, spent ten years creating a clandestine organizational structure before launching a campaign of violence in 1980. Furthermore, radicals may look to the future and calculate that present sacrifice will not be in vain if it inspires future resistance. Conceptions of interest are thus long term.

Another potential cost of terrorism is loss of popular support. Unless terrorism is carefully controlled and discriminate, it claims innocent victims. In a liberal state, indiscriminate violence may appear excessive and unjustified and alienate a citizenry predisposed to loyalty to the government. If it provokes generalized government repression, fear may diminish enthusiasm for resistance. This potential cost of popular alienation is probably least in ethnically divided societies, where victims can be clearly identified as the enemy and where the government of the majority appears illegal to the minority. Terrorists try to compensate by justifying their actions as the result of the absence of choice or the need to respond to government violence. In addition, they may make their strategy highly discriminate, attacking only unpopular targets.

Terrorism may be unattractive because it is elitist. Although relying only on terrorism may spare the general population from costly involvement in the struggle for freedom, such isolation may violate the ideological beliefs of revolutionaries who insist that the people must participate in their liberation. The few who choose terrorism are willing to forgo or postpone the participation of the many, but revolutionaries who oppose terrorism insist that it prevents the people from taking responsibility for their own destiny. The possibility of vicarious popular identification with symbolic acts of terrorism may satisfy some revolutionaries, but others will find terrorism a harmful substitute for mass participation.

The advantages of terrorism. Terrorism has an extremely useful agenda-setting function. If the reasons behind violence are skillfully articulated, terrorism can put the issue of political change on the public agenda. By attracting attention it makes the claims of the resistance a salient issue in the public mind. The government can reject but not ignore an opposition's demands. In 1974 the Palestinian Black September organization, for example, was willing to sacrifice a base in Khartoum, alienate the Sudanese government, and create ambivalence in the Arab world by seizing the Saudi Arabian embassy and killing American and Belgian diplomats. These costs were apparently weighed against the message to the world "to take us seriously." Mainstream Fatah leader Salah Khalef (Abu Iyad) explained: "We are planting the seed. Others will harvest it. . . . It is enough for us now to learn, for example, in reading the *Jerusalem Post,* that Mrs. Meir had to make her will before visiting Paris, or that Mr. Abba Eban had to travel with a false passport."[19] George Habash of the PFLP noted in 1970 that "we force people to ask what is going on."[20] In these statements, contemporary extremists echo the nineteenth-century anarchists, who coined the idea of propaganda of the deed, a term used as early as 1877 to refer to an act of insurrection as "a powerful means of arousing popular conscience" and the materialization of an idea through actions.[21]

Terrorism may be intended to create revolutionary conditions. It can prepare the ground for active mass revolt by undermining the government's authority and demoralizing its administrative cadres—its courts, police, and military. By spreading insecurity—at the extreme, making the country ungovernable—the organization hopes to pressure the regime into concessions or relaxation of coercive controls. With the rule of law disrupted, the people will be free to join the opposition. Spectacular humiliation of the government demonstrates strength and will and maintains the morale and enthusiasm of adherents and sympathizers. The first wave of Russian revolutionaries claimed that the aims of terrorism were to exhaust the enemy, render the government's position untenable, and wound the government's prestige by delivering a moral, not a physical, blow. Terrorists hoped to paralyze the government by their presence merely by showing signs of life from time to time. The hesitation, irresolution, and tension they would produce would undermine the processes of government and make the Czar a prisoner in his own palace.[22] As Brazilian revolutionary Carlos Marighela explained: "Revolutionary terrorism's great weapon is initiative, which guarantees its survival and continued activity. The more committed terrorists and revolutionaries devoted to anti-dictatorship terrorism and sabotage there are, the more military power will be worn down, the more time it will lose following false trails, and the more fear and tension it will suffer through not knowing where the next attack will be launched and what the next target will be."[23]

These statements illustrate a corollary advantage to terrorism in what might be called its excitational function: it inspires resistance by example. As propaganda of the deed, terrorism demonstrates that the regime can be challenged and that illegal opposition is possible. It acts as a catalyst, not substitute, for mass revolt. All the tedious and time-consuming organizational work of mobilizing the people can be avoided. Terrorism is a shortcut to revolution. As the Russian revolutionary Vera Figner described its purpose, terrorism was "a means of agitation to draw people from their torpor," not a sign of loss of belief in the people.[24]

A more problematic benefit lies in provoking government repression. Terrorists often think that by provoking indiscriminate repression against the population, terrorism will heighten popular disaffection, demonstrate the justice of terrorist claims, and enhance the attractiveness of the political alternative the terrorists represent. Thus, the West German Red Army Faction sought (in vain) to make fascism "visible" in West Germany.[25] In Brazil, Marighela unsuccessfully aimed to "transform the country's political situation into a military one. Then discontent will spread to all social groups and the military will be held exclusively responsible for failures."[26]

But profiting from government repression depends on the lengths to which the government is willing to go in order to contain disorder, and on the population's tolerance for both insecurity and repression. A liberal state may be limited in its capacity for quelling violence, but at the same time it may be difficult to provoke to excess. However, the government's reaction to terrorism may reinforce the symbolic value of violence even if it avoids repression. Extensive security precautions, for example, may only make the terrorists appear powerful.

Summary. To summarize, the choice of terrorism involves considerations of timing and of the popular contribution to revolt, as well as of the relationship between government and opponents. Radicals choose terrorism when they want immediate action, think that only violence can build organizations and mobilize supporters, and accept the risks of challenging the government in particularly provocative way. Challengers who think that organizational infrastructure must precede action, that rebellion without the masses is misguided, and that premature conflict with the regime can only lead to disaster favor gradualist strategies. They prefer methods such as rural guerrilla warfare, because terrorism can jeopardize painfully achieved gains or preclude eventual compromise with the government.

The resistance organization has before it a set of alternatives defined by the situation and by the objectives and resources of the group. The reasoning behind terrorism takes into account the balance of power between challengers and authorities, a balance that depends on the amount of popular support the resistance can mobilize. The proponents of terrorism understand this constraint and possess reasonable expectations about the likely results of action or inaction. They may be wrong about the alternatives that are open to them, or miscalculate the consequences of their actions, but their decisions are based on logical processes. Furthermore, organizations learn from their mistakes and from those of others, resulting in strategic continuity and progress toward the development of more efficient and sophisticated tactics. Future choices are modified by the consequences of present actions.

Hostage Taking as Bargaining

Hostage taking can be analyzed as a form of coercive bargaining. More than twenty years ago, Thomas Schelling wrote that "hostages represent the power to hurt in its purest form."[27] From this perspective, terrorists choose to take hostages because in bargaining situations the government's greater strength and resources are not an advantage. The extensive resort to this form of terrorism after 1968, a year that marks the major advent of diplomatic kidnappings and airline hijackings, was a predictable response to the growth of state power. Kidnappings, hijackings, and barricade-type seizures of embassies or public buildings are attempts to manipulate a government's political decisions.

Strategic analysis of bargaining terrorism is based on the assumption that hostage takers genuinely seek the concessions they demand. It assumes that they prefer government compliance to resistance. This analysis does not allow for deception or for the possibility that seizing hostages may be an end in itself because it yields the benefit of publicity. Because these limiting assumptions may reduce the utility of the theory, it is important to recognize them.

Terrorist bargaining is essentially a form of blackmail or extortion.[28] Terrorists seize hostages in order to affect a government's choices, which are controlled both by expectations of outcome (what the terrorists are likely to do, given the government reaction) and preferences (such as humanitarian values). The outcome threatened by the terrorist—the death of the hostages—must be worse for the government than compliance with terrorist demands. The terrorist has two options, neither of which necessarily excludes the other: to make the threat both more horrible and more credible or to reward compliance, a factor that strategic theorists often ignore.[29] That is, the cost to the government of complying with the terrorists' demands may be lowered or the cost of resisting raised.

The threat to kill the hostages must be believable and painful to the government. Here hostage takers are faced with a paradox. How can the credibility of this threat be assured when hostage takers recognize that governments know that the terrorists' control over the situation depends on live hostages? One way of establishing credibility is to divide the threat, making it sequential by killing one hostage at a time. Such tactics also aid terrorists in the process of incurring and demonstrating a commitment to carrying out their threat. Once the terrorists have murdered, though, their incentive to surrender voluntarily is substantially reduced. The terrorists have increased their own costs of yielding in order to persuade the government that their intention to kill all the hostages is real.

Another important way of binding oneself in a terrorist strategy is to undertake a barricade rather than a kidnapping operation. Terrorists who are trapped with the hostages find it more difficult to back down (because the government controls the escape routes) and, by virtue of this commitment, influence the government's choices. When terrorists join the hostages in a barricade situation, they create the visible and irrevocable commitment that Schelling sees as a necessary bond in bargaining. The government must expect desperate behavior, because the terrorists have increased their potential loss in order to demonstrate the firmness of their intentions. Furthermore, barricades are technically easier than kidnappings.

The terrorists also attempt to force the "last clear chance" of avoiding disaster onto the government, which must accept the responsibility for noncompliance that leads to the deaths of hostages. The seizure of hostages is the first move in the game, leaving the next move—which determines the fate of the hostages—completely up to the government. Uncertain communications may facilitate this strategy.[30] The terrorists can pretend not to receive government messages that might affect their demonstrated commitment. Hostage takers can also bind themselves by insisting that they are merely agents, empowered to ask only for the most extreme demands. Terrorists may deliberately appear irrational, either through inconsistent and erratic behavior or unrealistic expectations and preferences, in order to convince the government that they will carry out a threat that entails self-destruction.

Hostage seizures are a type of iterated game, which explains some aspects of terrorist behavior that otherwise seem to violate strategic principles. In terms of a single episode, terrorists can be expected to find killing hostages painful, because they will not achieve their demands and the government's desire to punish will be intensified. However, from a long-range perspective, killing hostages reinforces the credibility of the threat in the next terrorist incident, even if the killers then cannot escape. Each terrorist episode is actually a round in a series of games between government and terrorists.

Hostage takers may influence the government's decision by promising rewards for compliance. Recalling that terrorism represents an iterative game, the release of hostages unharmed when ransom is paid underwrites a promise in the future. Sequential release of selected hostages makes promises credible. Maintaining secrecy about a government's concessions is an additional reward for compliance. France, for example, can if necessary deny making concessions to Lebanese kidnappers because the details of arrangements have not been publicized.

Terrorists may try to make their demands appear legitimate so that governments may seem to satisfy popular grievances rather than the whims of terrorists. Thus, terrorists may ask that food be distributed to the poor. Such demands were a favored tactic of the *Ejercito Revolucionario del Pueblo (ERP)* in Argentina in the 1970s.

A problem for hostage takers is that rewarding compliance is not easy to reconcile with making threats credible. For example, if terrorists use publicity to emphasize their threat to kill hostages (which they frequently do), they may also increase the costs of compliance for the government because of the attention drawn to the incident.

In any calculation of the payoffs for each side, the costs associated with the bargaining process must be taken into account.[31] Prolonging the hostage crisis increases the costs to both sides. The question is who loses most and thus is more likely to concede. Each party presumably wishes to make the delay more costly to the other. Seizing multiple hostages appears to be advantageous to terrorists, who are thus in a position to make threats credible by killing hostages individually. Conversely, the greater the number of hostages, the greater the cost of holding them. In hijacking or barricade situations, stress and fatigue for the captors increase waiting costs for them as well. Kidnapping poses fewer such costs. Yet the terrorists can reasonably expect that the costs to governments in terms of public or international pressures may be higher when developments are visible. Furthermore, kidnappers can maintain suspense and interest by publishing communications from their victims.

Identifying the obstacles to effective bargaining in hostage seizures is critical. Most important, bargaining depends on the existence of a common interest between two parties. It is unclear whether the lives of hostages are a sufficient common interest to ensure a compromise outcome that is preferable to no agreement for both sides. Furthermore, most theories of bargaining assume that the preferences of each side remain stable during negotiations. In reality, the nature and intensity of preferences may change during a hostage-taking episode. For example, embarrassment over the Iran-*contra* scandal may have reduced the American interest in securing the release of hostages in Lebanon.

Bargaining theory is also predicated on the assumption that the game is two-party. When terrorists seize the nationals of one government in order to influence the choices of a third, the situation is seriously complicated. The hostages themselves may sometimes become intermediaries and participants. In Lebanon, Terry Waite, formerly an intermediary and negotiator, became a hostage. Such developments are not anticipated by bargaining theories based on normal political relationships. Furthermore, bargaining is not possible if a government is willing to accept the maximum cost the terrorists can bring to bear rather than concede. And the government's options are not restricted to resistance or compliance; armed rescue attempts represent an attempt to break the bargaining stalemate. In attempting to make their threats credible—for example, by sequential killing of hostages—terrorists may provoke military intervention. There may be limits, then, to the pain terrorists can inflict and still remain in the game.

Conclusions

This essay has attempted to demonstrate that even the most extreme and unusual forms of political behavior can follow an internal, strategic logic. If there are consistent patterns in terrorist behavior, rather than random idiosyncrasies, a strategic analysis may reveal them. Prediction of future terrorism can only be based on theories that explain past patterns.

Terrorism can be considered a reasonable way of pursuing extreme interests in the political arena. It is one among the many alternatives that radical organizations can choose. Strategic conceptions, based on ideas of how best to take advantage of the possibilities of a given situation, are an important determinant of oppositional terrorism, as they are of the government response. However, no single explanation for terrorist behavior is satisfactory. Strategic calculation is only one factor in the decision-making process leading to terrorism. But it is critical to include strategic reasoning as a possible motivation, at a minimum as an antidote to stereotypes of "terrorists" as irrational fanatics. Such stereotypes are a dangerous underestimation of the capabilities of extremist groups. Nor does stereotyping serve to educate the public—or, indeed, specialists—about the complexities of terrorist motivations and behaviors.

Martha Crenshaw is a senior fellow at Center for International Security and Cooperation and the Freeman Spogli Institute for International Studies at Stanford University, focusing her research on innovation in terrorist campaigns, the distinction between "old" and "new" terrorism, how terrorism ends, and why the United States is the target of terrorism. From 1974 to 2007, Dr. Crenshaw was a professor of government at Wesleyan University in Middletown, Connecticut.

Notes

1. For a similar perspective (based on a different methodology) see James DeNardo, *Power in Numbers: The Political Strategy of Protest and Rebellion* (Princeton, N.J.: Princeton University Press, 1985). See also Harvey Waterman, "Insecure 'Ins' and Opportune 'Outs': Sources of Collective Political Activity," *Journal of Political and Military Sociology* 8 (1980): 107–12, and "Reasons and Reason: Collective Political Activity in Comparative and Historical Perspective," *World Politics* 33 (1981): 554–89. A useful review of rational choice theories is found in James G. March, "Theories of Choice and Making Decisions," *Society* 20 (1982): 29–39.
2. Edward N. Muller and Karl-Dieter Opp, "Rational Choice and Rebellious Collective Action," *American Political Science Review* 80 (1986): 471–87.
3. Ibid., 484. The authors also present another puzzling question that may be answered in terms of either psychology or collective rationality. People who expected their rebellious behavior to be punished were more likely to be potential rebels. This propensity could be explained either by a martyr syndrome (or an expectation of hostility from authority figures) or intensity of preference—the calculation that the regime was highly repressive and thus deserved all the more to be destroyed. See pp. 482 and 484.
4. Leila Khaled, *My People Shall Live: The Autobiography of a Revolutionary* (London: Hodder and Stoughton, 1973), 128–31.
5. See Martha Crenshaw, "The Strategic Development of Terrorism," paper presented to the 1985 Annual Meeting of the American Political Science Association, New Orleans.
6. William A. Gamson, *The Strategy of Social Protest* (Homewood, Illinois: Dorsey Press, 1975).
7. Manus I. Midlarksy, Martha Crenshaw, and Fumihiko Yoshida, "Why Violence Spreads: The Contagion of International Terrorism," *International Studies Quarterly* 24 (1980): 262–98.
8. See the study by David A. Newell, *The Russian Marxist Response to Terrorism: 1878–1917* (Ph.D. dissertation, Stanford University, University Microfilms, 1981).
9. The tension between violence and numbers is a fundamental proposition in DeNardo's analysis; see *Power in Numbers,* chapters 9–11.
10. The work of Charles Tilly emphasizes the political basis of collective violence. See Charles Tilly, Louise Tilly, and Richard Tilly, *The Rebellious Century 1830–1930* (Cambridge: Harvard University Press, 1975), and Charles Tilly, *From Mobilization to Revolution* (Reading, Mass.: Addison-Wesley, 1978).
11. See Conor Cruise O'Brien, "Terrorism under Democratic conditions: The Case of the IRA," in *Terrorism, Legitimacy, and Power: The Consequences of Political Violence,* edited by Martha Crenshaw (Middletown, Conn.: Wesleyan University Press, 1983).
12. For example, DeNardo, in *Power in Numbers,* argues that "the movement derives moral sympathy from the government's excesses" (p. 207).
13. Paul Avrich, *The Haymarket Tragedy* (Princeton: Princeton University Press, 1984), 166.
14. Sean MacStiofain, *Memoirs of a Revolutionary* (N.p.: Gordon Cremonisi, 1975), 301.
15. Waterman, "Insecure 'Ins' and Opportune 'Outs' and "Reasons and Reason."
16. *Political Organizations* (New York: Basic Books, 1973).
17. Maria McGuire, *To Take Arms: My Year with the IRA Provisionals* (New York: Viking, 1973), 110–11, 118, 129–31, 115, and 161–62.
18. DeNardo concurs; see *Power in Numbers,* chapter 11.
19. See Jim Hoagland, "A Community of Terror," *Washington Post,* 15 March 1973, pp. 1 and 13; also *New York Times,* 4 March 1973, p. 28. Black September is widely regarded as a subsidiary of Fatah, the major Palestinian organization headed by Yasir Arafat.

20. John Amos, *Palestinian Resistance: Organization of a Nationalist Movement* (New York: Pergamon, 1980), 193; quoting George Habash, interviewed in *Life Magazine,* 12 June 1970, 33.

21. Jean Maitron, *Histoire du mouvement anarchiste en France (1880–1914),* 2d ed. (Paris: Société universitaire d'éditions et de librairie, 1955), 74–5.

22. "Stepniak" (pseud. for Sergei Kravshinsky), *Underground Russia: Revolutionary Profiles and Sketches from Life* (London: Smith, Elder, 1883), 278–80.

23. Carlos Marighela, *For the Liberation of Brazil* (Harmondsworth: Penguin, 1971), 113.

24. Vera Figner, *Mémoires d'une révolutionnaire* (Paris: Gallimard, 1930), 206.

25. *Textes des prisonniers de la "fraction armée rouge" et dernières lettres d'Ulrike Meinhof* (Paris: Maspéro, 1977), 64.

26. Marighela, *For the Liberation of Brazil,* 46.

27. Schelling, *Arms and Influence* (New Haven, Conn.: Yale University Press, 1966), 6.

28. Daniel Ellsberg, *The Theory and Practice of Blackmail* (Santa Monica: Rand Corporation, 1968).

29. David A. Baldwin, "Bargaining with Airline Hijackers," in *The 50% Solution,* edited by William I. Zartman, 404–29 (Garden City, N.Y.: Doubleday, 1976), argues that promises have not been sufficiently stressed. Analysts tend to emphasize threats instead, surely because of the latent violence implicit in hostage taking regardless of outcome.

30. See Roberta Wohlstetter's case study of Castro's seizure of American Marines in Cuba: "Kidnapping to Win Friends and Influence People," *Survey* 20 (1974): 1–40.

31. Scott E. Atkinson, Todd Sandler, and John Tschirhart, "Terrorism in a Bargaining Framework," *Journal of Law and Economics* 30 (1987): 1–21.

Chapter 2

Understanding the Facilitators of Modern Terrorism

In the 21st century, the forces of globalization—in particular the advent of advanced communications technology—have dramatically changed the nature of terrorism, in part by acting as facilitators. Easy access to critical information via the Internet and increasing diffusion of advanced technologies allows terrorists to plan their attacks with greater precision and to cause greater destruction than ever before. Weak states or ungoverned spaces provide terrorist groups the necessary safe havens from which to plan and execute their attacks. Chapter 2 examines various enablers of terrorism including globalization, information technologies, the global financial network and weak states and their implications for policy responses.

Audrey Kurth Cronin argues that the current wave of international terrorism is characterized by unpredictable and unprecedented threats from nonstate actors. According to Dr. Cronin, terrorism is not only a reaction to globalization but is facilitated by it, while the U.S. response to the terrorist threat has been reactive and anachronistic. Furthermore, she explains, the combined focus of the United States on state-centric threats and its attempt to cast twenty-first century terrorism into familiar strategic terms avoids and often undermines effective response to the current nonstate terrorist phenomena. Military power, writes Cronin, is an important but supporting instrument in the campaign against terrorism. More effective, however, will be nonmilitary instruments such as intelligence, public diplomacy, and cooperation with allies.

Given the flat, diffuse, transnational, networked structure of modern terrorist groups, Ray Takeyh and Nikolas Gvosdev question the assumption that terrorists need a failed state or other territorial home—in the same way that multinational corporations have a corporate headquarters—where it can based its operations. According to Takeyh and Gvosdev, failed states hold a number of attractions for terrorist organizations. In addition to providing terrorists an opportunity to acquire territory necessary for training complexes, arms depots, and communication centers, failed states create pools of recruits and supporters for terrorist groups. Retaining the outward signs of state sovereignty, failed states can also issue legitimate passports and other documents to enable terrorists to move around the world. Takeyh and Gvosdev conclude that the critical links between failed states and terrorism require the U.S. government to include efforts to reconstruct regimes in failed states in their counterterrorism strategies.

In the third article, Stewart Patrick notes how following the 9/11 attacks, the U.S. and other governments are increasingly organizing their counterterrorism policies around assumed links between weak states or "ungoverned spaces" and terrorism, WMD proliferation, crime, and regional instability. He argues that the most striking aspect of this trend is how little empirical evidence underpins the presumed connection between weak governance and transnational threats. According to Dr. Patrick, these governments "have rarely distinguished among categories of weak and failing states or asked whether (and how) certain types of developing countries are associated with particular threats." In his evaluation of which states are associated with which dangers, Dr. Patrick provides framework for a deeper understanding of the underlying mechanisms linking poor governance and state incapacity.

Audrey Kurth Cronin, 2002

Behind the Curve

Globalization and International Terrorism

The coincidence between the evolving changes of globalization, the inherent weaknesses of the Arab region, and the inadequate American response to both ensures that terrorism will continue to be the most serious threat to U.S. and Western interests in the twenty-first century. There has been little creative thinking, however, about how to confront the growing terrorist backlash that has been unleashed. Terrorism is a complicated, eclectic phenomenon, requiring a sophisticated strategy oriented toward influencing its means and ends over the long term. Few members of the U.S. policymaking and academic communities, however, have the political capital, intellectual background, or inclination to work together to forge an effective, sustained response. Instead, the tendency has been to fall back on established bureaucratic mind-sets and prevailing theoretical paradigms that have little relevance for the changes in international security that became obvious after the terrorist attacks in New York and Washington on September 11, 2001.

The current wave of international terrorism, characterized by unpredictable and unprecedented threats from nonstate actors, not only is a reaction to globalization but is facilitated by it; the U.S. response to this reality has been reactive and anachronistic. The combined focus of the United States on state-centric threats and its attempt to cast twenty-first-century terrorism into familiar strategic terms avoids and often undermines effective responses to this nonstate phenomenon. The increasing threat of globalized terrorism must be met with flexible, multifaceted responses that deliberately and effectively exploit avenues of globalization in return; this, however, is not happening.

As the primary terrorist target, the United Sates should take the lead in fashioning a forward-looking strategy. As the world's predominant military, economic, and political power, it has been able to pursue its interests throughout the globe with unprecedented freedom since the breakup of the Soviet Union more than a decade ago. Even in the wake of the September 11 terrorist attacks on the World Trade Center and the Pentagon, and especially after the U.S. military action in Afghanistan, the threat of terrorism, mostly consisting of underfunded and ad hoc cells motivated by radical fringe ideas, has seemed unimportant by comparison. U.S. strategic culture has a long tradition of downplaying such atypical concerns in favor of a focus on more conventional state-based military power.[1] On the whole, this has been an effective approach: As was dramatically demonstrated in Afghanistan, the U.S. military knows how to destroy state governments and their armed forces, and the American political leadership and public have a natural bias toward using power to achieve the quickest results. Sometimes it is important to show resolve and respond forcefully.

The United States has been far less impressive, however, in its use of more subtle tools of domestic and international statecraft, such as intelligence, law enforcement, economic sanctions, educational training, financial controls, public diplomacy, coalition building, international law, and foreign aid. In an ironic twist, it is these tools that have become central to the security of the United States and its allies since September 11. In an era of globalized terrorism, the familiar state-centric threats have not disappeared; instead they have been joined by new (or newly threatening) competing political, ideological, economic, and cultural concerns that are only superficially understood, particularly in the West. An examination of the recent evolution of terrorism and a projection of future developments suggest that, in the age of globalized terrorism, old attitudes are not just anachronistic; they are dangerous.

Terrorism as a phenomenon is not new, but for reasons explained below, the threat it now poses is greater than ever before. The current terrorist backlash is manifested in the extremely violent asymmetrical response directed at the United States and other leading powers by terrorist groups associated with or inspired by al-Qaeda. This backlash has the potential to fundamentally threaten the international system. Thus it is not just an American problem. Unless the United States and its allies formulate a more comprehensive response to terrorism, better balanced across the range of policy instruments, the results will be increasing international instability and long-term failure.

The article proceeds in five main sections. First, it provides a discussion of the definition, history, causes, and types of terrorism, placing the events of September 11, 2001, in their modern context. Second, it briefly describes key trends in modern terrorism, explaining how the phenomenon appears to be evolving. Third, it analyzes the implications of these trends for the stability and security of the international community generally, and the United States and its allies more specifically. Fourth, the article outlines the prospects of these trends. It concludes with a range of policy recommendations suggested by the analysis.

Definition, Origins, Motivations, and Types of Modern Terrorism

The terrorist phenomenon has a long and varied history, punctuated by lively debates over the meaning of the term. By ignoring this history, the United States runs the risk of repeating the plethora of mistakes made by other major powers that faced similar threats in the past. This section begins with an explanation of the definition of terrorism, then proceeds to an examination of terrorism's origins, major motivations, and predominant types.

Definition of Terrorism

Terrorism is notoriously difficult to define, in part because the term has evolved and in part because it is associated with an activity that is designed to be subjective. Generally speaking, the targets of a terrorist episode are not the victims who are killed or maimed in the attack, but rather the governments, publics, or constituents among whom the terrorists hope to engender a reaction—such as fear, repulsion, intimidation, overreaction, or radicalization. Specialists in the area of terrorism studies have devoted hundreds of pages toward trying to develop an unassailable definition of the term, only to realize the fruitlessness of their efforts: Terrorism is intended to be a matter of perception and is thus seen differently by different observers.[2]

Although individuals can disagree over whether particular actions constitute terrorism, there are certain aspects of the concept that are fundamental. First, terrorism always has a political nature. It involves the commission of outrageous acts designed to precipitate political change.[3] At its root, terrorism is about justice, or at least someone's perception of it, whether man-made or divine. Second, although many other uses of violence are inherently political, including conventional war among states, terrorism is distinguished by its nonstate character—even when terrorists receive military, political, economic, and other means of support from state sources. States obviously employ force for political ends: When state force is used internationally, it is considered an act of war; when it is used domestically, it is called various things, including law enforcement, state terror, oppression, or civil war. Although states can terrorize, they cannot by definition be terrorists. Third, terrorism deliberately targets the innocent, which also distinguishes it from state uses of force that inadvertently kill innocent bystanders. In any given example, the latter may or may not be seen as justified; but again, this use of force is different from terrorism. Hence the fact that precision-guided missiles sometimes go astray and kill innocent civilians is a tragic use of force, but it is not terrorism. Finally, state use of force is subject to international norms and conventions that may be invoked or at least consulted; terrorists do not abide by international laws or norms and, to maximize the psychological effect of an attack, their activities have a deliberately unpredictable quality.[4]

Thus, at a minimum, terrorism has the following characteristics: a fundamentally political nature, the surprise use of violence against seemingly random targets, and the targeting of the innocent by nonstate actors.[5] All of these attributes are illustrated by recent examples of terrorism—from the April 2000 kidnapping of tourists by the Abu Sayyaf group of the Philippines to the various incidents allegedly committed by al-Qaeda, including the 1998 bombings of the U.S. embassies in Kenya and Tanzania and the September 11 attacks. For the purposes of this discussion, the shorthand (and admittedly imperfect) definition of terrorism is the threat or use of seemingly random violence against innocents for political ends by a nonstate actor.

Origins of Terrorism

Terrorism is as old as human history. One of the first reliably documented instances of terrorism, however, occurred in the first century B.C.E. The Zealots-Sicarri, Jewish terrorists dedicated to inciting a revolt against Roman rule in Judea, murdered their victims with daggers in broad daylight in the heart of Jerusalem, eventually creating such anxiety among the population that they generated a mass insurrection.[6] Other early terrorists include the Hindu Thugs and the Muslim Assassins. Modern terrorism, however, is generally considered to have originated with the French Revolution.[7]

The term "terror" was first employed in 1795, when it was coined to refer to a policy systemically used to protect the fledgling French republic government against counter-revolutionaries. Robespierre's practice of using revolutionary tribunals as a means of publicizing a prisoner's fate for broader effect within the population (apart from questions of legal guilt or innocence) can be seen as a nascent example of the much more highly developed, blatant manipulation of media attention by terrorist groups in the mid- to late twentieth century.[8] Modern terrorism is a dynamic concept, from the outset dependent to some degree on the political and historical context within which it has been employed.

Decolonization and Antiglobalization: Drivers of Terrorism?

Although individual terrorist groups have unique characteristics and arise in specific local contexts, an examination of broad historical patterns reveals that the international system within which such groups are spawned does influence their nature and motivations. A distinguishing feature of modern terrorism has been the connection between sweeping political or ideological concepts and increasing levels of terrorist activity internationally. The broad political aim has been against (1) empires, (2) colonial powers, and (3) the U.S.-led international system marked by globalization. Thus it is important to understand the general history of modern terrorism and where the current threat fits within an international context.

David Rapoport has described modern terrorism such as that perpetuated by al-Qaeda as part of a religiously inspired "fourth wave." This wave follows three earlier historical phases in which terrorism was tied to the breakup of empires, decolonization, and leftist anti-Westernism.[9] Rapoport argues that terrorism occurs in consecutive if somewhat overlapping waves. The argument here, however, is that modern terrorism has been a power struggle along a continuum: central power versus local power, big power versus small power, modern power versus traditional power. The key variable is a widespread perception of opportunity, combined with a shift in a particular political or ideological paradigm. Thus, even though the newest international terrorist threat, emanating largely from Muslim countries, has more than a modicum of religious inspiration, it is more accurate to see it as part of a larger phenomenon of antiglobalization and tension between the have and have-not nations, as well as between the elite and underprivileged within those nations. In an era where reforms occur at a pace much slower than is desired, terrorists today, like those before them, aim to exploit the frustrations of the common people (especially in the Arab world).

In the nineteenth century, the unleashing of concepts such as universal suffrage and popular empowerment raised the hopes of people throughout the western world, indirectly resulting in the first phase of modern terrorism. Originating in Russia, as Rapoport argues, it was stimulated not by state repression but by the efforts of the czars to placate demands for economic and political reforms, and the inevitable disappointment of popular expectations that were raised as a result. The goal of terrorists was to engage in attacks on symbolic targets to get the attention of the common people and thus provoke a popular response that would ultimately overturn the prevailing political order. This type of modern terrorism was reflected in the activities of groups such as the Russian Narodnaya Volya (People's Will) and later in the development of a series of movements in the United States and Europe, especially in territories of the former Ottoman Empire.

The dissolution of empires and the search for a new distribution of political power provided an opportunity for terrorism in the nineteenth and twentieth centuries. It climaxed in the assassination of Archduke Franz Ferdinand on June 28, 1914, an event that catalyzed the major powers into taking violent action, not because of the significance of the man himself but because of the suspicion of rival state involvement in the sponsorship of the killing. World War I, the convulsive systemic cataclysm that resulted, ended the first era of modern terrorism, according to Rapoport.[10] But terrorism tied to popular movements seeking greater democratic representation and political power from coercive empires has not ceased. Consider, for example, the Balkans after the downfall of the former state of Yugoslavia. The struggle for power among various Balkan ethnic groups can be seen as the final devolution of power from the former Ottoman Empire. This postimperial scramble is also in evidence elsewhere—for example, in Aceh, Chechnya, and Xinjiang, to mention just a few of the trouble spots within vast (former) empires. The presentation of a target of opportunity, such as a liberalizing state or regime, frequently evokes outrageous terrorist acts.

According to Rapoport, a second, related phase of modern terrorism associated with the concept of national self-determination developed its greatest predominance after World War I. It also continues to the present day. These struggles for power are another facet of terrorism against larger political powers and are specifically designed to win political independence or autonomy. The mid–twentieth-century era of rapid decolonization spawned national movements in territories as diverse as Algeria, Israel, South Africa, and Vietnam.[11] An important by-product was ambivalence toward the phenomenon in the international community, with haggling over the definition of terrorism reaching a fever pitch in the United Nations by the 1970s.

The question of political motivation became important in determining international attitudes toward terrorist attacks, as the post–World War II backlash against the colonial powers and the attractiveness of national independence movements led to the creation of a plethora of new states often born from violence. Arguments over the justice of international causes and the designation of terrorist struggles as "wars of national liberation" predominated, with consequentialist philosophies excusing the killing of innocent people if the cause in the long run was "just." Rapoport sees the U.S. intervention in Vietnam, and especially the subsequent American defeat by the Vietcong, as having catalyzed a "third wave" of modern terrorism; however, the relationship between the Vietnam conflict and other decolonization movements might just as easily be considered part of the same phase. In any case, the victory of the Vietcong excited the imaginations of revolutionaries throughout the world and, according to Rapoport, helped lead to a resurgence in terrorist violence. The Soviet Union underwrote the nationalist and leftist terrorist agendas of some groups, depicting the United States as the new colonial power—an easy task following the Vietnam intervention—and furthering an ideological agenda oriented toward achieving a postcapitalist, international communist utopia. Other groups, especially in Western Europe, rejected both the Soviet and capitalist models and looked admiringly toward nationalist revolutionaries in the developing world.[12] Leftist groups no longer predominate, but the enduring search for national self-determination continues, not only in the areas mentioned above but also in other hot spots such as the Basque region, East Timor, Sri Lanka, and Sudan.

Terrorism achieved a firmly international character during the 1970s and 1980s,[13] evolving in part as a result of technological advances and partly in reaction to the dramatic explosion of international media influence. International links were not new, but their centrality was. Individual, scattered national causes began to develop into international organizations with links and activities increasingly across borders and among differing causes. This development was greatly facilitated by the covert sponsorship of states such as Iran, Libya, and North Korea, and of course the Soviet Union, which found the underwriting of terrorist organizations an attractive tool for accomplishing clandestine goals while avoiding potential retaliation for the terrorist attacks.

The 1970s and 1980s represented the height of state-sponsored terrorism. Sometimes the lowest common denominator among the groups was the concept against which they were reacting—for example, "Western imperialism"—rather than the specific goals they sought. The most important innovation, however, was the increasing commonality of international connections among the groups. After the 1972 Munich Olympics massacre of eleven Israeli athletes, for example, the Palestinian Liberation Organization (PLO) and its associated groups captured the imaginations of young radicals around the world. In Lebanon and elsewhere, the PLO also provided training in the preferred techniques of twentieth-century terrorism such as airline hijacking, hostage taking, and bombing.

Since the September 11 attacks, the world has witnessed the maturation of a new phase of terrorist activity, the jihad era, spawned by the Iranian Revolution of 1979 as well as the Soviet defeat in Afghanistan shortly thereafter. The powerful attraction of religious and spiritual movements has overshadowed the nationalist or leftist revolutionary ethos of earlier terrorist phases (though many of those struggles continue), and it has become the central characteristic of a growing international trend. It is perhaps ironic that, as Rapoport observes, the forces of history seem to be driving international terrorism back to a much earlier time, with echoes of the behavior of "sacred" terrorists such as the Zealots-Sicarii clearly apparent in the terrorist activities of organizations such as al-Qaeda and its associated groups. Religious terrorism is not new; rather it is a continuation of an ongoing modern power struggle between those with power and those without it. Internationally, the main targets of these terrorists are the United States and the U.S.-led global system.

Like other eras of modern terrorism, this latest phase has deep roots. And given the historical patterns, it is likely to last at least a generation, if not longer. The jihad era is animated by widespread alienation combined with elements of religious identity and doctrine—a dangerous mix of forces that resonate deep in the human psyche.

What is different about this phase is the urgent requirement for solutions that deal both with the religious fanatics who are the terrorists and the far more politically motivated states, entities, and people who would support them because they feel powerless and left behind in a globalizing world. Thus if there is a trend in terrorism, it is the existence of a two-level challenge: the hyperreligious motivation of small groups of terrorists and the much broader enabling environment of bad governance, nonexistent social services, and poverty that punctuates much of the developing world. Al-Qaeda, a band driven by religious extremism, is able to do so much harm because of the secondary support and sanctuary it receives in vast areas that have not experienced the political and economic benefits of globalization. Therefore, the prescription for dealing with Osama bin Laden and his followers is not just eradicating a relatively small number of terrorists, but also changing the conditions that allow them to acquire so much power. Leaving aside for the moment the enabling environment, it is useful to focus on the chief motivations of the terrorists themselves, especially the contrasting secular and spiritual motivations of terrorism.

Leftist, Rightist, Ethnonationalist/Separatist, and "Sacred" Terrorism

There are four types of terrorist organizations currently operating around the world, categorized mainly by their source of motivation: left-wing terrorists, right-wing terrorists, ethnonationalist/separatist terrorists, and religious or "sacred" terrorists. All four types have enjoyed periods of relative prominence in the modern era, with left-wing terrorism intertwined with the Communist movement,[14] right-wing terrorism drawing its inspiration from Fascism,[15] and the bulk of ethnonationalist/separatist terrorism accompanying the wave of decolonization especially in the immediate post–WorldWar II years. Currently, "sacred" terrorism is becoming more significant.[16] Although groups in all categories continue to exist today, left-wing and right-wing terrorist groups were more numerous in earlier decades. Of course, these categories are not perfect, as many groups have a mix of motivating ideologies—some ethnonationalist groups, for example, have religious characteristics or agendas[17]—but usually one ideology or motivation dominates.

Categories are useful not simply because classifying the groups gives scholars a more orderly field to study (admittedly an advantage), but also because different motivations have sometimes led to differing styles and modes of behavior. Understanding the type of terrorist group involved can provide insight into the likeliest manifestations of its violence and the most typical patterns of its development. At the risk of generalizing, left-wing terrorist organizations, driven by liberal or idealist political concepts, tend to prefer revolutionary, antiauthoritarian, antimaterialistic agendas. (Here it is useful to distinguish between the idealism of individual terrorists and the frequently contradictory motivations of their sponsors.) In line with these preferences, left-wing organizations often engage in brutal criminal-type behavior such as kidnapping, murder, bombing, and arson, often directed at elite targets that symbolize authority. They have difficulty, however, agreeing on their long-term objectives.[18] Most left-wing organizations in twentieth-century Western Europe, for example, were brutal but relatively ephemeral. Of course, right-wing terrorists can be ruthless, but in their most recent manifestations they have tended to be less cohesive and more impetuous in their violence than leftist terrorist groups. Their targets are often chosen according to race but also ethnicity, religion, or immigrant status, and in recent decades at least, have been more opportunistic than calculated.[19] This makes them potentially explosive but difficult to track.[20] Ethnonationalist/separatist terrorists are the most conventional, usually having a clear political or territorial aim that is rational and potentially negotiable, if not always justifiable in any given case. They can be astoundingly violent, over lengthy periods. At the same time, it can be difficult to distinguish between goals based on ethnic identity and those rooted in the control of a piece of land. With their focus on gains to be made in the traditional state-oriented international system, ethnonationalist/separatist terrorists often transition in and out of more traditional paramilitary structures, depending on how the cause is going. In addition, they typically have sources of support among the local populace of the same ethnicity with whom their separatist goals (or appeals to blood links) may resonate. That broader popular support is usually the key to the greater average longevity of ethnonationalist/separatist groups in the modern era.[21]

All four types of terrorist organizations are capable of egregious acts of barbarism. But religious terrorists may be especially dangerous to international security for at least five reasons.

First, religious terrorists often feel engaged in a Manichaean struggle of good against evil, implying an open-ended set of human targets: Anyone who is not a member of their religion or religious sect may be "evil" and thus fair game. Although indiscriminate attacks are not unique to religious terrorists, the exclusivity of their faith may lead them to dehumanize their victims even more than most terrorist groups do, because they consider nonmembers to be infidels or apostates—as perhaps, for instance, al-Qaeda operatives may have viewed Muslims killed in the World Trade Center.

Second, religious terrorists engage in violent behavior directly or indirectly to please the perceived commands of a deity. This has a number of worrisome implications: The whims of the deity may be less than obvious to those who are not members of the religion, so the actions of violent religious organizations can be especially unpredictable. Moreover, religious terrorists may not be as constrained in their behavior by concerns about the reactions of their human constituents. (Their audience lies elsewhere.)

Third, religious terrorists consider themselves to be unconstrained by secular values or laws. Indeed the very target of the attacks may be the law-based secular society that is embodied in most modern states. The driving motivation, therefore, is to overturn the current post-Westphalian state system—a much more fundamental threat than is, say, ethnonationalist terrorism purporting to carve out a new secular state or autonomous territory.

Fourth, and related, religious terrorists often display a complete sense of alienation from the existing social system. They are not trying to correct the system, making it more just, more perfect, and more egalitarian. Rather they are trying to replace it. In some groups, apocalyptic images of destruction are seen as a necessity—even a purifying regimen—and this makes them uniquely dangerous, as was painfully learned on September 11.[22]

Fifth, religious terrorism is especially worrisome because of its dispersed popular support in civil society. On the one hand, for example, groups such as al-Qaeda are able to find support from some Muslim nongovernmental foundations throughout the world,[23] making it truly a global network. On the other hand, in the process of trying to distinguish between the relatively few providers of serious support from the majority of genuinely philanthropic groups, there is the real risk of igniting the very holy war that the terrorists may be seeking in the first instance.

In sum, there are both enduring and new aspects to modern terrorism. The enduring features center on the common political struggles that have characterized major acts of international terrorism. The newest and perhaps most alarming aspect is the increasingly religious nature of modern terrorist groups. Against this historical background, the unique elements in the patterns of terrorist activity surrounding September 11 appear starkly.

Key Trends in Modern Terrorism

By the late 1990s, four trends in modern terrorism were becoming apparent: an increase in the incidence of religiously motivated attacks, a decrease in the overall number of attacks, an increase in the lethality per attack, and the growing targeting of Americans.

Statistics show that, even before the September 11 attacks, religiously motivated terrorist organizations were becoming more common. The acceleration of this trend has been dramatic: According to the RAND–St. Andrews University Chronology of International Terrorism,[24] in 1968 none of the identified international terrorist organizations could be classified as "religious"; in 1980, in the aftermath of the Iranian Revolution, there were 2 (out of 64), and that number had expanded to 25 (out of 58) by 1995.[25]

Careful analysis of terrorism data compiled by the U.S. Department of State reveals other important trends regarding the frequency and lethality of terrorist attacks. The good news was that there were fewer such attacks in the 1990s than in the 1980s: Internationally, the number of terrorist attacks in the 1990s averaged 382 per year, whereas in the 1980s the number per year averaged 543.[26] But even before September 11, the absolute number of casualties of international terrorism had increased, from a low of 344 in 1991 to a high of 6,693 in 1998.[27] The jump in deaths and injuries can be partly explained by a few high-profile incidents, including the bombing of the U.S. embassies in Nairobi and Dar-es-Salaam in 1998;[28] but it is significant that more people became victims of terrorism as the decade proceeded. More worrisome, the number of people killed per incident rose significantly, from 102 killed in 565 incidents in 1991 to 741 killed in 274 incidents in 1998.[29] Thus, even though the number of terrorist attacks declined in the 1990s, the number of people killed in each one increased.

Another important trend relates to terrorist attacks involving U.S. targets. The number of such attacks increased in the 1990s, from a low of 66 in 1994 to a high of 200 in the year 2000.[30] This is a long-established problem: U.S. nationals consistently have been the most targeted since 1968.[31] But the percentage of international attacks against U.S. targets or U.S. citizens rose dramatically over the 1990s, from about 20 percent in 1993–95 to almost 50 percent in 2000.[32] This is perhaps a consequence of the increased role and profile of the United States in the world, but the degree of increase is nonetheless troubling.

The increasing lethality of terrorist attacks was already being noticed in the late 1990s, with many terrorism experts arguing that the tendency toward more casualties per incident had important implications. First it meant that, as had been feared, religious or "sacred" terrorism was apparently more dangerous than the types of terrorism that had predominated earlier in the twentieth century. The world was facing the resurgence of a far more malignant type of terrorism, whose lethality was borne out in the larger death toll from incidents that increasingly involved a religious motivation.[33] Second, with an apparent premium now apparently placed on causing more casualties per incident, the incentives for terrorist organizations to use chemical, biological, nuclear, or radiological (CBNR) weapons would multiply. The breakup of the Soviet Union and the resulting increased availability of Soviet chemical, biological, and nuclear weapons caused experts to argue that terrorist groups, seeking more dramatic and deadly results, would be more drawn to these weapons.[34] The 1995 sarin gas attack by the Japanese cult Aum Shinrikyo in the Tokyo subway system seemed to confirm that worry. More recently, an examination of evidence taken from Afghanistan and Pakistan reveals al-Qaeda's interest in chemical, biological, and nuclear weapons.[35]

In addition to the evolving motivation and character of terrorist attacks, there has been a notable dispersal in the geography of terrorist acts—a trend that is likely to continue. Although the Middle East continues to be the locus of most terrorist activity, Central and South Asia, the Balkans, and the Transcaucasus have been growing in significance over the past decade. International connections themselves are not new: International terrorist organizations inspired by common revolutionary principles date to the early nineteenth century; clandestine state use of foreign terrorist organizations occurred as early as the 1920s (e.g., the Mussolini government in Italy aided the Croat Ustasha); and complex mazes of funding, arms, and other state support for international terrorist organizations were in place especially in the 1970s and 1980s.[36] During the Cold War, terrorism was seen as a form of surrogate warfare and seemed almost palatable to some, at least compared to the potential prospect of major war or nuclear cataclysm.[37] What has changed is the self-generating nature of international terrorism, with its diverse economic means of support allowing terrorists to carry out attacks sometimes far from the organization's base. As a result, there is an important and growing distinction between where a terrorist organization is spawned and where an attack is launched, making the attacks difficult to trace to their source.

Reflecting all of these trends, al-Qaeda and its associated groups[38] (and individuals) are harbingers of a new type of terrorist organization. Even if al-Qaeda ceases to exist (which is unlikely), the dramatic attacks of September 2001, and their political and economic effects, will continue to inspire similarly motivated groups—particularly if the United States and its allies fail to develop broad-based, effective counterterrorist policies over the long term. Moreover, there is significant evidence that the global links and activities that al-Qaeda and its associated groups perpetuated are not short term or anomalous. Indeed they are changing the nature of the terrorist threat as we move further into the twenty-first century. The resulting intersection between the United States, globalization, and international terrorism will define the major challenges to international security.

The United States, Globalization, and International Terrorism

Whether deliberately intending to or not, the United States is projecting uncoordinated economic, social, and political power even more sweepingly than it is in military terms. Globalization,[39] in forms including Westernization, secularization, democratization, consumerism, and the growth of market capitalism, represents an onslaught to less privileged people in conservative cultures repelled by the fundamental changes that these forces are bringing—or angered by the distortions and uneven distributions of benefits that result.[40] This is especially true of the Arab world. Yet the current U.S. approach to this growing repulsion is colored by a kind of cultural naïveté, an unwillingness to recognize—let alone appreciate or take responsibility for—the influence of U.S. power except in its military dimension. Even doing nothing in the economic, social, and political policy realms is still doing something, because the United States is blamed by disadvantaged and alienated populations for the powerful Western-led forces of globalization that are proceeding apace, despite the absence of a focused, coordinated U.S. policy. And those penetrating mechanisms of globalization, such as the internet, the media, and the increasing flows of goods and peoples, are exploited in return. Both the means and ends of terrorism are being reformulated in the current environment.

The Means

Important changes in terrorist methods are apparent in the use of new technologies, the movement of terrorist groups across international boundaries, and changes in sources of support. Like globalization itself, these phenomena are all intertwined and overlapping but, for ease of argument, they are dealt with consecutively here.

First, the use of information technologies such as the internet, mobile phones, and instant messaging has extended the global reach of many terrorist groups. Increased access to these technologies has so far not resulted in their widely feared use in a major cyberterrorist attack: In Dorothy Denning's words, terrorists "still prefer bombs to bytes."[41] Activists and terrorist groups have increasingly turned to "hacktivism"—attacks on internet sites, including web defacements, hijackings of websites, web sit-ins, denial-of-service attacks, and automated email "bombings"—attacks that may not kill anyone but do attract media attention, provide a means of operating anonymously, and are easy to coordinate internationally.[42] So far, however, these types of attacks are more an expense and a nuisance than an existential threat.

Instead the tools of the global information age have led to enhanced efficiency in many terrorist-related activities, including administrative tasks, coordination of operations, recruitment of potential members, communication among adherents, and attraction of sympathizers.[43] Before the September 11 attacks, for example, members of al-Qaeda communicated through Yahoo email; Mohammed Atta, the presumed leader of the attacks, made his reservations online; and cell members went online to do research on subjects such as the chemical-dispersing powers of crop dusters. Although not as dramatic as shutting down a power grid or taking over an air traffic control system, this practical use of technology has significantly contributed to the effectiveness of terrorist groups and the expansion of their range.[44] Consider, for example, the lethal impact of the synchronized attacks on the U.S. embassies in 1998 and on New York and Washington in 2001, neither of which would have been possible without the revolution in information technology. When he was arrested in 1995, Ramzi Yousef, mastermind of the 1993 World Trade Center attack, was planning the simultaneous destruction of eleven airliners.[45]

The internet has become an important tool for perpetuating terrorist groups, both openly and clandestinely. Many of them employ elaborate list serves, collect money from witting or unwitting donors, and distribute savvy political messages to a broad audience online.[46] Groups as diverse as Aum Shinrikyo, Israel's Kahane Chai, the Popular Front for the Liberation of Palestine, the Kurdistan Workers' Party, and Peru's Shining Path maintain user-friendly official or unofficial websites, and almost all are accessible in English.[47] Clandestine methods include passing encrypted messages, embedding invisible graphic codes using steganography,[48] employing the internet to send death threats, and hiring hackers to collect intelligence such as the names and addresses of law enforcement officers from online databases.[49] All of these measures help to expand and perpetuate trends in terrorism that have already been observed: For example, higher casualties are brought about by simultaneous attacks, a diffusion in terrorist locations is made possible by internet communications, and extremist religious ideologies are spread through websites and videotapes accessible throughout the world.

More ominous, globalization makes CBNR weapons increasingly available to terrorist groups.[50] Information needed to build these weapons has become ubiquitous, especially through the internet. Among the groups interested in acquiring CBNR (besides al-Qaeda) are the PLO, the Red Army Faction, Hezbollah, the Kurdistan Workers' Party, German neo-Nazis, and the Chechens.[51]

Second, globalization has enabled terrorist organizations to reach across international borders, in the same way (and often through the same channels) that commerce and business interests are linked. The dropping of barriers through the North American Free Trade Area and the European Union, for instance, has facilitated the smooth flow of many things, good and bad, among countries. This has allowed terrorist organizations as diverse as Hezbollah, al-Qaeda, and the Egyptian al-Gama'at al-Islamiyya to move about freely and establish cells around the world.[52] Movement across borders can obviously enable terrorists to carry out attacks and potentially evade capture, but it also complicates prosecution if they are apprehended, with a complex maze of extradition laws varying greatly from state to state. The increased permeability of the international system has also enhanced the ability of nonstate terrorist organizations to collect intelligence (not to mention evade it); states are not the only actors interested in collecting, disseminating, and/or acting on such information. In a sense, then, terrorism is in many ways becoming like any other international enterprise—an ominous development indeed.

Third, terrorist organizations are broadening their reach in gathering financial resources to fund their operations. This is not just an al-Qaeda phenomenon, although bin Laden's organization—especially its numerous business interests—figures prominently among the most innovative and wealthy pseudocorporations in the international terrorist network. The list of groups with global financing networks is long and includes most of the groups identified by the U.S. government as foreign terrorist organizations, notably Aum Shinrikyo, Hamas, Hezbollah, and the Tamil Tigers. Sources of financing include legal enterprises such as nonprofit organizations and charities (whose illicit activities may be a small or large proportion of overall finances, known or unknown to donors); legitimate companies that divert profits to illegal activities (such as bin Laden's large network of construction companies); and illegal enterprises such as drug smuggling and production (e.g., the Revolutionary Armed Forces of Colombia—FARC), bank robbery, fraud, extortion, and kidnapping (e.g., the Abu Sayyaf group, Colombia's National Liberation Army, and FARC).[53] Websites are also important vehicles for raising funds. Although no comprehensive data are publicly available on how lucrative this avenue is, the proliferation of terrorist websites with links or addresses for contributions is at least circumstantial evidence of their usefulness.

The fluid movement of terrorists' financial resources demonstrates the growing informal connections that are countering the local fragmentation caused elsewhere by globalization. The transit of bars of gold and bundles of dollars across the border between Afghanistan and Pakistan as U.S. and allied forces were closing in on the Taliban's major strongholds is a perfect example. Collected by shopkeepers and small businessmen, the money was moved by operatives across the border to Karachi, where it was transferred in the millions of dollars through the informal *hawala* or *hundi* banking system to the United Arab Emirates.[54] There it was converted into gold bullion and scattered around the world before any government could intervene. In this way, al-Qaeda preserved and dispersed a proportion of its financial resources.[55] In addition to gold, money was transferred into other commodities—such as diamonds in Sierra Leone and the Democratic Republic of Congo, and tanzanite from Tanzania —all while hiding the assets and often making a profit,[56] and all without interference from the sovereign governments that at the time were at war with al-Qaeda and the Taliban.[57]

As this example illustrates, globalization does not necessarily require the use of high technology: It often takes the form of traditional practices used in innovative ways across increasingly permeable physical and commercial borders. Terrorist groups, whose assets comparatively represent only a small fraction of the amount of money that is moved by organized crime groups and are thus much more difficult to track, use everything from direct currency transport (by couriers) to reliance on traditional banks, Islamic banks, money changers (using accounts at legitimate institutions), and informal exchange (the *hawala* or *hundi* system).

This is by no means a comprehensive presentation of global interpenetration of terrorist means, and some of the connections described above have existed for some time and in other contexts. The broad strategic picture, however, is of an increasing ability of terrorist organizations to exploit the same avenues of communication, coordination, and cooperation as other international actors, including states, multinational corporations, nongovernmental organizations, and even individuals. It would be naïve to assume that what is good for international commerce and international communication is not also good for international terrorists[58]—who are increasingly becoming opportunistic entrepreneurs whose "product" (often quite consciously "sold") is violence against innocent targets for a political end.

The Ends

The objectives of international terrorism have also changed as a result of globalization. Foreign intrusions and growing awareness of shrinking global space have created incentives to use the ideal asymmetrical weapon, terrorism, for more ambitious purposes.

The political incentives to attack major targets such as the United States with powerful weapons have greatly increased. The perceived corruption of indigenous customs, religions, languages, economies, and so on, are blamed on an international system often unconsciously molded by American behavior. The accompanying distortions in local communities as a result of exposure to the global marketplace of goods and ideas are increasingly blamed on U.S.-sponsored modernization and those who support it. The advancement of technology, however, is not the driving force behind the terrorist threat to the United States and its allies, despite what some have assumed.[59] Instead, at the heart of this threat are frustrated populations and international movements that are increasingly inclined to lash out against U.S.-led globalization.

As Christopher Coker observes, globalization is reducing tendencies toward instrumental violence (i.e., violence between states and even between communities), but it is enhancing incentives for expressive violence (or violence that is ritualistic, symbolic, and communicative).[60] The new international terrorism is increasingly engendered by a need to assert identity or meaning against forces of homogeneity, especially on the part of cultures that are threatened by, or left behind by, the secular future that Western-led globalization brings.

According to a report recently published by the United Nations Development Programme, the region of greatest deficit in measures of human development—the Arab world—is also the heart of the most threatening religiously inspired terrorism.[61] Much more work needs to be done on the significance of this correlation, but increasingly sources of political discontent are arising from disenfranchised areas in the Arab world that feel left behind by the promise of globalization and its assurances of broader freedom, prosperity, and access to knowledge. The results are dashed expectations, heightened resentment of the perceived U.S.-led hegemonic system, and a shift of focus away from more proximate targets within the region.

Of course, the motivations behind this threat should not be oversimplified: Anti-American terrorism is spurred in part by a desire to change U.S. policy in the Middle East and Persian Gulf regions as well as by growing antipathy in the developing world vis-à-vis the forces of globalization. It is also crucial to distinguish between the motivations of leaders such as Osama bin Laden and their followers. The former seem to be more driven by calculated strategic decisions to shift the locus of attack away from repressive indigenous governments to the more attractive and media-rich target of the United States. The latter appear to be more driven by religious concepts cleverly distorted to arouse anger and passion in societies full of pent-up frustration. To some degree, terrorism is directed against the United States because of its engagement and policies in various regions.[62] Anti-Americanism is closely related to antiglobalization, because (intentionally or not) the primary driver of the powerful forces resulting in globalization is the United States.

Analyzing terrorism as something separate from globalization is misleading and potentially dangerous. Indeed globalization and terrorism are intricately intertwined forces characterizing international security in the twenty-first century. The main question is whether terrorism will succeed in disrupting the promise of improved livelihoods for millions of people on Earth. Globalization is not an inevitable, linear development, and it can be disrupted by such unconventional means as international terrorism. Conversely, modern international terrorism is especially dangerous because of the power that it potentially derives from globalization—whether through access to CBNR weapons, global media outreach, or a diverse network of financial and information resources.

Prospects for the Future

Long after the focus on Osama bin Laden has receded and U.S. troops have quit their mission in Afghanistan, terrorism will be a serious threat to the world community and especially to the United States. The relative preponderance of U.S. military power virtually guarantees an impulse to respond asymmetrically. The lagging of the Arab region behind the rest of the world is impelling a violent redirection of antiglobalization and antimodernization forces toward available targets, particularly the United States, whose scope and policies are engendering rage. Al-Qaeda will eventually be replaced or redefined, but its successors' reach may continue to grow via the same globalized channels and to direct their attacks against U.S. and Western targets. The current trajectory is discouraging, because as things currently stand, the wellspring of terrorism's means and ends is likely to be renewed: Arab governments will probably not reform peacefully, and existing Western governments and their supporting academic and professional institutions are disinclined to understand or analyze in depth the sources, patterns, and history of terrorism.

Terrorism is a by-product of broader historical shifts in the international distribution of power in all of its forms—political, economic, military, ideological, and cultural. These are the same forms of power that characterize the forces of Western-led globalization. At times of dramatic international change, human beings (especially those not benefiting from the change—or not benefiting as much or as rapidly from the change) grasp for alternative means to control and understand their environments. If current trends continue, widening global disparities, coupled with burgeoning information and connectivity, are likely to accelerate—unless the terrorist backlash, which is increasingly taking its inspiration from misoneistic religious or pseudoreligious concepts, successfully counters these trends. Because of globalization, terrorists have access to more powerful technologies, more targets, more territory, more means of recruitment, and more exploitable sources of rage than ever before. The West's twentieth-century approach to terrorism is highly unlikely to mitigate any of these long-term trends.

From a Manichean perspective, the ad hoc and purportedly benign intentions of the preponderant, secular West do not seem benign at all to those ill served by globalization. To frustrated people in the Arab and Muslim world, adherence to radical religious philosophies and practices may seem a rational response to the perceived assault, especially when no feasible alternative for progress is offered by their own governments. This is not to suggest that terrorists should be excused because of environmental factors or conditions. Instead, Western governments must recognize that the tiny proportion of the population that ends up in terrorist cells cannot exist without the availability of broader sources of active or passive sympathy, resources, and support. Those avenues of sustenance are where the center of gravity for an effective response to the terrorist threat must reside. The response to transnational terrorism must deal with the question of whether the broader enabling environment will increase or decrease over time, and the answer will be strongly influenced by the policy choices that the United States and its allies make in the near future.

Conclusions and Policy Prescriptions

The characteristics and causes of the current threat can only be analyzed within the context of the deadly collision occurring between U.S. power, globalization, and the evolution of international terrorism. The U.S. government is still thinking in outdated terms, little changed since the end of the Cold War. It continues to look at terrorism as a peripheral threat, with the focus remaining on states that in many cases are not the greatest threat. The means and the ends of terrorism are changing in fundamental, important ways; but the means and the ends of the strategy being crafted in response are not.

Terrorism that threatens international stability, and particularly U.S. global leadership, is centered on power-based political causes that are enduring: the weak against the strong, the disenfranchised against the establishment, and the revolutionary against the status quo. Oversimplified generalizations about poverty and terrorism, or any other single variable, are caricatures of a serious argument.[63] The rise in political and material expectations as a result of the information revolution is not necessarily helpful to stability, in the same way that rising expectations led terrorists to take up arms against the czar in Russia a century ago. Indeed the fact that so many people in so many nations are being left behind has given new ammunition to terrorist groups; produced more sympathy for those willing to take on the United States; and spurred Islamic radical movements to recruit, propagandize, and support terrorism throughout many parts of the Muslim world. The al-Qaeda network is an extremist religious terrorist organization, its Taliban puppet regime was filled with religious zealots, and its suicide recruits were convinced that they were waging a just holy war. But the driving forces of twenty-first-century terrorism are power and frustration, not the pursuit of religious principle. To dismiss the broad enabling environment would be to focus more on the symptoms than the causes of modern terrorism.

The prescriptions for countering and preventing terrorism should be twofold: First, the United States and other members of the international community concerned about this threat need to use a balanced assortment of instruments to address the immediate challenges of the terrorists themselves. Terrorism is a complex phenomenon; it must be met with short-term military action, informed by in-depth, long-term, sophisticated analysis. Thus far, the response has been virtually all the former and little of the latter. Second, the United States and its counterterrorist allies must employ a much broader array of longer-term policy tools to reshape the international environment, which enables terrorist networks to breed and become robust. The mechanisms of globalization need to be exploited to thwart the globalization of terrorism.

In the short term, the United States must continue to rely on capable military forces that can sustain punishing air strikes against terrorists and those who harbor them with an even greater capacity for special operations on the ground. This requires not only improved stealthy, long-range power projection capabilities but also agile, highly trained, and lethal ground forces, backed up with greater intelligence, including human intelligence supported by individuals with language skills and cultural training. The use of military force continues to be important as one means of responding to terrorist violence against the West, and there is no question that it effectively preempts and disrupts some international terrorist activity, especially in the short term.[64]

Over time, however, the more effective instruments of policy are likely to remain the nonmilitary ones. Indeed the United States needs to expand and deepen its nonmilitary instruments of power such as intelligence, public diplomacy, cooperation with allies, international legal instruments, and economic assistance and sanctions. George Kennan, in his 1947 description of containment, put forth the same fundamental argument, albeit against an extremely different enemy.[65] The strongest response that the United States can muster to a serious threat has to include political, economic, and military capabilities—in that order; yet, the U.S. government consistently structures its policies and devotes its resources in the reverse sequence.

The economic and political roots of terrorism are complex, increasingly worrisome, and demanding of as much breadth and subtlety in response as they display in their genesis. The United States must therefore be strategic in its response: An effective grand strategy against terrorism involves planning a global campaign with the most effective means available, not just the most measurable, obvious, or gratifying. It must also include plans for shaping the global environment after the so-called war on terrorism has ended—or after the current political momentum has subsided.

The United States, working with other major donor nations, needs to create an effective incentive structure that rewards "good performers"—those countries with good governance, inclusive education programs, and adequate social programs—and works around "bad performers" and intervenes to assist so-called failed states. Also for the longer term, the United States and its allies need to project a vision of sustainable development—of economic growth, equal access to basic social needs such as education and health, and good governance—for the developing world. This is particularly true in mostly Muslim countries whose populations are angry with the United States over a perceived double standard regarding its long-standing support for Israel at the expense of Palestinians, policies against the regime of Saddam Hussein at the expense of some Iraqi people, and a general abundance of American power, including the U.S. military presence throughout the Middle East. Whether these policies are right or wrong is irrelevant here; the point is that just as the definition of terrorism can be subjective and value laden, so too can the response to terrorism take into account perceptions of reality. In an attempt to craft an immediate military response, the U.S. government is failing to put into place an effective long-term grand strategy.

This is not just a problem for the U.S. government. The inability to develop a strategy with a deep-rooted, intellectually grounded understanding of the history, patterns, motivations, and types of terrorism is reflective of the paucity of understanding of the terrorist phenomenon in the academic community. Terrorism is considered too policy-oriented an area of research in political science,[66] and it operates in an uncomfortable intersection between disciplines unaccustomed to working together, including psychology, sociology, theology, economics, anthropology, history, law, political science, and international relations. In political science, terrorism does not fit neatly into either the realist or liberal paradigms, so it has been largely ignored.[67] There are a few outstanding, well-established senior scholars in the terrorism studies community—people such as Martha Crenshaw, David Rapoport, and Paul Wilkinson—but in the United States, most of the publicly available work is being done in policy-oriented research institutes or think tanks that are sometimes limited by the narrow interests and short time frames of the government contracts on which they depend. Some of that research is quite good,[68] but it is not widely known within the academy. The situation for graduate students who wish to study terrorism is worse: A principal interest in terrorism virtually guarantees exclusion from consideration for most academic positions. This would not necessarily be a problem if the bureaucracy were more flexible and creative than the academy is, but as we know from the analysis of the behavior of U.S. agencies shortly before September 11, it is not. In the United States, academe is no more strategic in its understanding of terrorism than is the U.S. government.

The globalization of terrorism is perhaps the leading threat to long-term stability in the twenty-first century. But the benefit of globalization is that the international response to terrorist networks has also begun to be increasingly global, with international cooperation on law enforcement, intelligence, and especially financial controls being areas of notable recent innovation.[69] If globalization is to continue—and there is nothing foreordained that it will—then the tools of globalization, including especially international norms, the rule of law, and international economic power, must be fully employed against the terrorist backlash. There must be a deliberate effort to move beyond the current episodic interest in this phenomenon: Superficial arguments and short attention spans will continue to result in event-driven policies and ultimately more attacks. Terrorism is an unprecedented, powerful nonstate threat to the international system that no single state, regardless of how powerful it may be in traditional terms, can defeat alone, especially in the absence of long-term, serious scholarship engaged in by its most creative minds.

Audrey Kurth Cronin is Director of Studies of the Changing Character of War Program at Oxford University. Previously, Dr. Cronin was a professor of strategy and taught courses on international terrorism, strategy, and policy-making at U.S. National War College, National Defense University. She also worked at the Congressional Research Service, Library of Congress, where she advised Members of Congress and their staffs on terrorism matters.

Notes

1. The issue of U.S. strategic culture and its importance in the response to international terrorism is explored in more depth in Audrey Kurth Cronin, "Rethinking Sovereignty: American Strategy in the Age of Terror," *Survival,* Vol. 44, No. 2 (Summer 2002), pp. 119–139.
2. On the difficulty of defining terrorism, see, for example, Omar Malik, *Enough of the Definition of Terrorism!* Royal Institute of International Affairs (London: RIIA, 2001); and Alex

P. Schmid, *Political Terrorism: A Research Guide* (New Brunswick, N.J.: Transaction Books, 1984). Schmid spends more than 100 pages grappling with the question of a definition, only to conclude that none is universally accepted.

3. Saying that terrorism is a political act is not the same as arguing that the political ends toward which it is directed are necessarily negotiable. If violent acts do not have a political aim, then they are by definition criminal acts.

4. The diabolical nature of terrorism has given resonance to Robert Kaplan's view that the world is a "grim landscape" littered with "evildoers" and requiring Western leaders to adopt a "pagan ethos." But such conclusions deserve more scrutiny than space allows here. See Steven Mufson, "The Way Bush Sees the World," *Washington Post,* Outlook section, February 17, 2002, p. B1.

5. R.G. Frey and Christopher W. Morris, "Violence, Terrorism, and Justice," in Frey and Morris, eds., *Violence, Terrorism, and Justice* (Cambridge: Cambridge University Press, 1991), p. 3.

6. Walter Laqueur, *Terrorism* (London: Weidenfeld and Nicolson, 1977, reprinted in 1978), pp. 7–8; and David C. Rapoport, "Fear and Trembling: Terrorism in Three Religious Traditions," *American Political Science Review,* Vol. 78, No. 3 (September 1984), pp. 658–677.

7. David C. Rapoport, "The Fourth Wave: September 11 in the History of Terrorism," *Current History,* December 2001, pp. 419–424; and David C. Rapoport, "Terrorism," *Encyclopedia of Violence, Peace, and Conflict* (New York: Academic Press, 1999).

8. Ironically, Robespierre's tactics during the Reign of Terror would not be included in this article's definition of terrorism, because it was state terror.

9. Rapoport, "The Fourth Wave."

10. Ibid., pp. 419–420.

11. Ibid., p. 420.

12. Adrian Gulke, *The Age of Terrorism and the International Political System* (London: I.B. Tauris, 1995), pp. 56–63.

13. This is not to imply that terrorism lacked international links before the 1970s. There were important international ties between anarchist groups of the late nineteenth century, for example. See David C. Rapoport, "The Four Waves of Modern Terrorism," in Audrey Kurth Cronin and James Ludes, eds., *The Campaign against International Terrorism* (Washington, D.C.: Georgetown University Press, forthcoming).

14. Groups such as the Second of June Movement, the Baader-Meinhof Gang, the Red Brigades, the Weathermen, and the Symbionese Liberation Army belong in this category.

15. Among right-wing groups would be other neo-Nazi organizations (in the United States and Europe) and some members of American militia movements such as the Christian Patriots and the Ku Klux Klan.

16. The list here would be extremely long, including groups as different as the Tamil Tigers of Sri Lanka, the Basque separatist party, the PLO, and the Irish Republican Army (IRA) and its various splinter groups.

17. Bruce Hoffman notes that secular terrorist groups that have a strong religious element include the Provisional IRA, Armenian factions, and perhaps the PLO; however, the political/separatist aspect is the predominant characteristic of these groups. Hoffman, "Terrorist Targeting: Tactics, Trends, and Potentialities," *Technology and Terrorism* (London: Frank Cass, 1993), p. 25.

18. An interesting example is France's Action Directe, which revised its raison d'être several times, often altering it to reflect domestic issues in France—anarchism and Maoism, dissatisfaction with NATO and the Americanization of Europe, and general anticapitalism. See Michael Dartnell, "France's Action Directe: Terrorists in Search of a Revolution," *Terrorism and Political Violence,* Vol. 2, No. 4 (Winter 1990), pp. 457–488.

19. For example, in the 1990s Germany and several other European countries experienced a rash of random arson attacks against guest houses and offices that provided services to immigrants, many of whom were Middle Eastern in origin. Other examples include the violence associated with groups such as Europe's "football hooligans." A possible American example of the opportunistic nature of right-wing terrorism may be the anthrax letter campaign conducted in October 2001. See Susan Schmidt, "Anthrax Letter Suspect Profiled: FBI Says Author Likely

Is Male Loner; Ties to Bin Laden Are Doubted," *Washington Post,* November 11, 2001, p. A1; and Steve Fainaru, "Officials Continue to Doubt Hijackers' Link to Anthrax: Fla. Doctor Says He Treated One for Skin Form of Disease," *Washington Post,* March 24, 2002, p. A23.

20. It is interesting to note that, according to Christopher C. Harmon, in Germany, 1991 was the first year that the number of indigenous rightist radicals exceeded that of leftists. Harmon, *Terrorism Today* (London: Frank Cass, 2000), p. 3.

21. For example, in discussing the longevity of terrorist groups, Martha Crenshaw notes only three significant terrorist groups with ethnonationalist ideologies that ceased to exist within ten years of their formation (one of these, EOKA, disbanded because its goal—the liberation of Cyprus—was attained). By contrast, a majority of the terrorist groups she lists as having existed for ten years or longer have recognizable ethnonationalist ideologies, including the IRA (in its many forms), Sikh separatist groups, Euskadi Ta Askatasuna, the various Palestinian nationalist groups, and the Corsican National Liberation Front. See Crenshaw, "How Terrorism Declines," *Terrorism and Political Violence,* Vol. 3, No. 1 (Spring 1991), pp. 69–87.

22. On the characteristics of modern religious terrorist groups, see Bruce Hoffman, *Inside Terrorism* (New York: Columbia University Press, 1998), especially pp. 94–95; and Bruce Hoffman, "Terrorism Trends and Prospects," in Ian O. Lesser, Bruce Hoffman, John Arguilla, Michelle Zanini, and David Ronfeldt, eds., *Countering the New Terrorism* (Santa Monica, Calif.: RAND, 1999), especially pp. 19–20. On the peculiar twists of one apocalyptic vision, see Robert Jay Lifton, *Destroying the World to Save It: Aum Shinrikyo, Apocalyptic Violence, and the New Global Terrorism* (New York: Henry Holt, 1999).

23. There is a long list of people and organizations sanctioned under Executive Order 13224, signed on September 23, 2001. Designated charitable organizations include the Benevolence International Foundation and the Global Relief Foundation. The list is available at http:// www. treas.gov/offices/enforcement/ofac/sanctions/t11ter.pdf (accessed November 26, 2002).

24. The RAND–St. Andrews University Chronology of International Terrorism is a databank of terrorist incidents that begins in 1968 and has been maintained since 1972 at St. Andrews University, Scotland, and the RAND Corporation, Santa Monica, California.

25. Hoffman, *Inside Terrorism,* pp. 90–91; and Nadine Gurr and Benjamin Cole, *The New Face of Terrorism: Threats from Weapons of Mass Destruction* (London: I.B. Tauris, 2000), pp. 28–29.

26. Statistics compiled from data in U.S. Department of State, *Patterns of Global Terrorism,* published annually by the Office of the Coordinator for Counterterrorism, U.S. Department of State.

27. Ibid. For a graphical depiction of this information, created on the basis of annual data from *Patterns of Global Terrorism,* see Cronin, "Rethinking Sovereignty," p. 126.

28. In the 1998 embassy bombings alone, for example, 224 people were killed (with 12 Americans among them), and 4,574 were injured (including 15 Americans). U.S. Department of State, *Patterns of Global Terrorism, 1998.*

29. Ibid. For a graphical depiction of deaths per incident, created on the basis of annual data from *Patterns of Global Terrorism,* see Cronin, "Rethinking Sovereignty," p. 128.

30. Ibid.

31. Hoffman, "Terrorist Targeting," p. 24.

32. U.S. Department of State, *Patterns of Global Terrorism,* various years.

33. Examples include Bruce Hoffman, *"Holy Terror": The Implications of Terrorism Motivated by a Religious Imperative,* RAND Paper P-7834 (Santa Monica, Calif.: RAND, 1993); and Mark Juergensmeyer, "Terror Mandated by God," *Terrorism and Political Violence,* Vol. 9, No. 2 (Summer 1997), pp. 16–23.

34. See, for example, Steven Simon and Daniel Benjamin, "America and the New Terrorism," *Survival,* Vol. 42, No. 1 (Spring 2000), pp. 59–75, as well as the responses in the subsequent issue, "America and the New Terrorism: An Exchange," *Survival,* Vol. 42, No. 2 (Summer 2000), pp. 156–172; and Hoffman, "Terrorism Trends and Prospects," pp. 7–38.

35. See Peter Finn and Sarah Delaney, "Al-Qaeda's Tracks Deepen in Europe," *Washington Post,* October 22, 2001, p. A1; Kamran Khan and Molly Moore, "2 Nuclear Experts Briefed Bin Laden,

Pakistanis Say," *Washington Post,* December, 12, 2001, p. A1; James Risen and Judith Miller, "A Nation Challenged: Chemical Weapons—Al Qaeda Sites Point to Tests of Chemicals," *New York Times,* November 11, 2001, p. B1; Douglas Frantz and David Rohde, "A Nation Challenged: Biological Terror—2 Pakistanis Linked to Papers on Anthrax Weapons," *New York Times,* November 28, 2001; and David Rohde, "A Nation Challenged: The Evidence—Germ Weapons Plans Found at a Scientist's House in Kabul," *New York Times,* December 1, 2001.

36. Laqueur, *Terrorism,* pp. 112–116.

37. Ibid., pp. 115–116.

38. Groups with known or alleged connections to al-Qaeda include Jemaah Islamiyah (Indonesia, Malaysia, and Singapore), the Abu Sayyaf group (Philippines), al-Gama'a al-Islamiyya (Egypt), Harakat ul-Mujahidin (Pakistan), the Islamic Movement of Uzbekistan (Central Asia), Jaish-e-Mohammed (India and Pakistan), and al-Jihad (Egypt).

39. For the purposes of this article, globalization is a gradually expanding process of interpenetration in the economic, political, social, and security realms, uncontrolled by (or apart from) traditional notions of state sovereignty. Victor D. Cha, "Globalization and the Study of International Security," *Journal of Peace Research,* Vol. 37, No. 3 (March 2000), pp. 391–393.

40. With respect to the Islamic world, there are numerous books and articles that point to the phenomenon of antipathy with the Western world, either because of broad cultural incompatibility or a specific conflict between Western consumerism and religious fundamentalism. Among the earliest and most notable are Samuel P. Huntington, "The Clash of Civilizations?" *Foreign Affairs,* Vol. 72, No. 3 (Summer 1993); Benjamin R. Barber, *Jihad vs. McWorld: Terrorism's Challenge to Democracy* (New York: Random House, 1995); and Samuel P. Huntington, *The Clash of Civilizations and the Remaking of World Order* (New York: Simon and Schuster, 1996).

41. For more on cyberterrorism, see Dorothy Denning, "Activism, Hacktivism, and Cyberterrorism: The Internet as a Tool for Influencing Foreign Policy," paper presented at Internet and International Systems: Information Technology and American Foreign Policy Decision-making Workshop at Georgetown University, http://www.nautilus.org/info-policy/workshop/papers/denning.html (accessed January 5, 2003); Dorothy Denning, "Cyberterrorism," testimony before the U.S. House Committee on Armed Services, Special Oversight Panel on Terrorism, 107th Cong., 1st sess., May 23, 2001, available on the Terrorism Research Center website, http://www.cs.georgetown.edu/?denning/infosec/cyberterror.html (accessed January 5, 2003); Jerold Post, Kevin Ruby, and Eric Shaw, "From Car Bombs to Logic Bombs: The Growing Threat of Information Terrorism," *Terrorism and Political Violence,* Vol. 12, No. 2 (Summer 2000), pp. 97–122; and Tom Regan, "When Terrorists Turn to the Internet," *Christian Science Monitor,* July 1, 1999, http://www.csmonitor.com (accessed January 5, 2003).

42. Ibid. Dorothy Denning cites numerous examples, among them: In 1989, hackers released a computer worm into the NASA Space Physics Analysis Network in an attempt to stop a shuttle launch; during Palestinian riots in October 2000, pro-Israeli hackers defaced the Hezbollah website; and in 1999, following the mistaken U.S. bombing of the Chinese embassy in Belgrade during the war in Kosovo, Chinese hackers attacked the websites of the U.S. Department of the Interior, showing images of the three journalists killed during the bombing.

43. Paul R. Pillar, *Terrorism and U.S. Foreign Policy* (Washington, D.C.: Brookings, 2001), p. 47.

44. Ibid.

45. Simon Reeve, *The New Jackals: Ramzi Yousef, Osama bin Laden, and the Future of Terrorism* (Boston: Northeastern University Press, 1999), p. 260.

46. Dorothy Denning, "Cyberwarriors: Activists and Terrorists Turn to Cyberspace," *Harvard International Review,* Vol. 23, No. 2 (Summer 2001), pp. 70–75. See also Brian J. Miller, "Terror.org: An Assessment of Terrorist Internet Sites," Georgetown University, December 6, 2000.

47. Miller, "Terror.org," pp. 9, 12.

48. Steganography is the embedding of messages usually in pictures, where the messages are disguised so that they cannot be seen with the naked eye. See Denning, "Cyberwarriors."

49. I am indebted to Dorothy Denning for all of this information. The Provisional IRA hired contract hackers to find the addresses of British intelligence and law enforcement officers. See Denning, "Cyberterrorism"; and Denning, "Cyberwarriors."

50. There are many recent sources on CBNR. Among the best are Jonathan B. Tucker, ed., *Toxic Terror: Assessing Terrorist Use of Chemical and Biological Weapons* (Cambridge, Mass.: MIT Press, 2000); Joshua Lederberg, *Biological Weapons: Limiting the Threat* (Cambridge, Mass.: MIT Press, 1999); Richard A. Falkenrath, Robert D. Newman, and Bradley A. Thayer, *America's Achilles' Heel: Nuclear, Biological, and Chemical Terrorism and Covert Attack* (Cambridge, Mass.: MIT Press, 1998); Gurr and Cole, *The New Face of Terrorism;* Jessica Stern, *The Ultimate Terrorists* (Cambridge, Mass.: Harvard University Press, 1999); and Brad Roberts, ed., *Terrorism with Chemical and Biological Weapons: Calibrating Risks and Responses* (Alexandria, Va.: Chemical and Biological Arms Control Institute, 1997).

51. See Falkenrath, Newman, and Thayer, *America's Achilles' Heel,* pp. 31–46.

52. A clear example of this phenomenon was the uncovering in December 2001 of a multinational plot in Singapore by the international terrorist group Jemaah Islamiyah to blow up several Western targets, including the U.S. embassy. A videotape of the intended targets (including a description of the plans in Arabic) was discovered in Afghanistan after al-Qaeda members fled. Thus there are clear connections between these organizations, as well as evidence of cooperation and coordination of attacks. See, for example, Dan Murphy, "'Activated' Asian Terror Web Busted," *Christian Science Monitor,* January 23, 2002, http://www.csmonitor.com (accessed January 23, 2002); and Rajiv Chandrasekaran, "Al Qaeda's Southeast Asian Reach," *Washington Post,* February 3, 2002, p. A1.

53. Rensselaer Lee and Raphael Perl, "Terrorism, the Future, and U.S. Foreign Policy," issue brief for Congress, received through the Congressional Research Service website, order code IB95112, Congressional Research Service, Library of Congress, July 10, 2002, p. CRS-6.

54. Roger G. Weiner, "The Financing of International Terrorism," Terrorism and Violence Crime Section, Criminal Division, U.S. Department of Justice, October 2001, p. 3. According to Weiner, the *hawala* (or *hundi*) system "relies entirely on trust that currency left with a particular service provider or merchant will be paid from bank accounts he controls overseas to the recipient specified by the party originating the transfer." Ibid. See also Douglas Frantz, "Ancient Secret System Moves Money Globally," *New York Times,* October 3, 2001, http://www.nytimes.com (accessed October 3, 2001).

55. International efforts to freeze bank accounts and block transactions between suspected terrorists have hindered, at least to some degree, al-Qaeda's ability to finance attacks; however, a proportion remains unaccounted for. "Cash Moves a Sign Al-Qaeda Is Regrouping," *Straits Times,* March 18, 2002, http://www.straitstimes.asia1.com.sg (accessed March 18, 2002).

56. U.S. Department of State, *Patterns of Global Terrorism, 2001.* According to the U.S. Department of State, Hezbollah also may have transferred resources by selling millions of dollars' worth of Congolese diamonds to finance operations in the Middle East.

57. Douglas Farah, "Al Qaeda's Road Paved with Gold," *Washington Post,* February 17, 2002, pp. A1, A32.

58. Pillar, *Terrorism and U.S. Foreign Policy,* p. 48.

59. Many in the United States focus on the technologies of terrorism, with a much less developed interest in the motivations of terrorists. Brian M. Jenkins, "Understanding the Link between Motives and Methods," in Roberts, *Terrorism with Chemical and Biological Weapons,* pp. 43–51. An example of a study that focuses on weapons and not motives is Sidney D. Drell, Abraham D. Sofaer, and George W. Wilson, eds., *The New Terror: Facing the Threat of Biological and Chemical Weapons* (Stanford, Calif.: Hoover Institution, 1999).

60. Christopher Coker, *Globalisation and Insecurity in the Twenty-first Century: NATO and the Management of Risk,* Adelphi Paper 345 (London: International Institute for Strategic Studies, June 2002), p. 40.

61. The indicators studied included respect for human rights and human freedoms, the empowerment of women, and broad access to and utilization of knowledge. See United Nations Development

Programme, Arab Fund for Economic and Social Development, *Arab Human Development Report, 2002: Creating Opportunities for Future Generations* (New York: United Nations Development Programme, 2002).

62. Martha Crenshaw, "Why America? The Globalization of Civil War," *Current History,* December 2001, pp. 425–432.

63. A number of recent arguments have been put forth about the relationship between poverty and terrorism. See, for example, Anatol Lieven, "The Roots of Terrorism, and a Strategy against It," Prospect (London), October 2001, http://www.ceip.org/files/Publications/lieventerrorism.asp? from=pubdate (accessed November 17, 2002); and Daniel Pipes, "God and Mammon: Does Poverty Cause Militant Islam?" *National Interest,* No. 66 (Winter 2001/02), pp. 14–21. This is an extremely complex question, however, and much work remains to be done. On the origins of the new religious terrorism, see Hoffman, *Inside Terrorism;* and Mark Juergensmeyer, *Terror in the Mind of God: The Global Rise of Religious Violence* (Berkeley: University of California Press, 2000). Important earlier studies on the sources of terrorism include Martha Crenshaw, "The Causes of Terrorism," *Comparative Politics,* July 1981, pp. 379–399; Martha Crenshaw, *Terrorism in Context* (University Park: Pennsylvania State University Press, 1995); and Walter Reich, ed., *Origins of Terrorism: Psychologies, Ideologies, Theologies, States of Mind,* 2d ed. (Washington, D.C.: Woodrow Wilson Center for International Scholars, 1998).

64. For more discussion on the traditional elements of U.S. grand strategy, especially military strategy, see Barry R. Posen, "The Struggle against Terrorism: Grand Strategy, Strategy, and Tactics," *International Security,* Vol. 26, No. 3 (Winter 2001/02), pp. 39–55.

65. George F. Kennan, "The Sources of Soviet Conduct," *Foreign Affairs,* Vol. 25, No. 4 (July 1947), pp. 575–576.

66. See the extremely insightful article by Bruce W. Jentleson, "The Need for Praxis: Bringing Policy Relevance Back In," *International Security,* Vol. 26, No. 4 (Spring 2002), pp. 169–183.

67. I am indebted to Fiona Adamson for this observation.

68. Important terrorism scholars in the think tank community include Walter Laqueur (Center for Strategic and International Studies), Brian Jenkins (RAND), Bruce Hoffman (RAND) and, from the intelligence community, Paul Pillar. This list is illustrative, not comprehensive.

69. On these issues, see Cronin and Ludes, T*he Campaign against International Terrorism.*

I am grateful for helpful comments and criticisms on previous drafts from Robert Art, Patrick Cronin, Timothy Hoyt, James Ludes, and an anonymous reviewer. I have been greatly influenced by conversations and other communications with Martha Crenshaw, to whom I owe a huge debt. None of these people necessarily agrees with everything here. Also beneficial was a research grant from the School of Foreign Service at Georgetown University. My thanks to research assistants Christopher Connell, William Josiger, and Sara Skahill and to the members of my graduate courses on political violence and terrorism. Portions of this article will be published as "Transnational Terrorism and Security: The Terrorist Threat to Globalization," in Michael E. Brown, ed., *Grave New World: Global Dangers in the Twenty-First Century* (Washington, D.C.: Georgetown University Press, forthcoming).

Ray Takeyh and Nikolas K. Gvosdev

Do Terrorist Networks Need a Home?

How are international business organizations and global terrorist networks similar? This question is not a riddle but an analogy made by policymakers ranging from Secretary of State Colin Powell to Russian presidential advisor Gleb Pavlovsky. The comparison seems apropos because the multinational corporation and the transnational terrorist network both utilize the existing global economic, transportation, and communications systems to organize and manage far-flung subsidiaries and to move funds, men, and material from one location to another.

The 2001 trial of Madji Hasan Idris, an Egyptian member of the radical Al Wa'd organization, revealed the extent to which terror has operationally adopted the global business model. Al Wa'd would send young Egyptian recruits to camps in Kosovo or Pakistan and then dispatch them to serve in the Philippines, Kashmir, or wherever else they were needed after their training and indoctrination were complete. Cell phones and e-mail kept the network in constant contact, while couriers provided cash advances, air-plane tickets, and passports to facilitate operations.

The objectives of terrorist organizations such as Al Qaeda and the symbiotic organized-crime networks that help sustain these groups are also not confined territorially or ideologically to a particular region. They are instead explicitly global in orientation. In contrast, "traditional" terrorist organizations such as the Irish Republican Army (IRA) or the Kurdish Workers' Party (PKK) have pursued largely limited, irredentist aims. Each terrorist group drew its membership largely from a specific population, even if they sought the sponsorship of a foreign patron for arms and logistical support. Al Qaeda, in contrast, recruits adherents from around the globe and seeks out failed states everywhere to house its own, self-sufficient infrastructure.

Extending the analogy, then, these failed states are the global terrorist network's equivalent of an international business's corporate headquarters, providing concrete locations, or stable "nodes," in which to situate their factories, training facilities, and storehouses. Where the analogy differs is the type of state that each seeks. While the multinational corporation seeks out states that offer political stability and a liberal business climate with low taxes and few regulations, failing or failed states draw terrorists, where the breakdown of authority gives them the ability to conduct their operations without risk of significant interference. Today's terrorist does not need a strong state to provide funding and supplies. Rather, it seeks a weak state that cannot impede a group's freedom of action but has the veneer of state sovereignty that prevents other, stronger states from taking effective countermeasures.

The successful U.S. military campaign in Afghanistan has, in the short run, deprived Al Qaeda of one of its principal centers for bases and training camps. Does it matter? Naturally, Al Qaeda operatives are reportedly seeking to move personnel and equipment to new "hosts"—Somalia, Indonesia, Chechnya, the mountains of Central Asia, Bosnia, Lebanon, or Kosovo. In these places, the writ of state authority is lax or nonexistent, and vibrant civil societies do not exist to deny militants the ability to move and operate in the public mainstream. At the same time, these groups also seek to utilize "brown zones" in Western societies, whether specific neighborhoods or particular types of organizations, where state governments are reluctant to intervene.[1] Do terrorist networks need a failed state or other territorial home where it can base its operations, or can these organizations completely blend into global society?

Why Terrorist Networks Need Failed States

Failed states hold a number of attractions for terrorist organizations. First and foremost, they provide the opportunity to acquire territory on a scale much larger than a collection of scattered safe houses—enough to accommodate entire training complexes, arms depots, and communications facilities. Generally, terrorist groups have no desire to assume complete control of the failed state but simply to acquire de facto control over specified areas where they will then be left alone.

In Bosnia, for example, radical groups took control of a number of districts, such as the village of Bocinja Donja, where they could operate with little scrutiny from the central government and live apart from the rest of society. Control over territory not only permits the construction of institutions, but it also allows groups to develop business interests such as gum mastic plantations in Sudan or small factories in Albania, which help generate income for operations. The failed state also enables terrorist groups and organized crime networks to establish transshipment points. Italian intelligence, for example, is extremely concerned about how Albania has become the hub of the primary, illicit traffic routes that cross the Balkans and involve the dispersal of drugs, weapons, dirty money, and illegal migrants.

For the most part, terrorist groups have gained control over territory in a failed state through a Faustian bargain with authorities, usually by offering its services to the failed state during times of conflict. In Bosnia, Kosovo, Chechnya, Sudan, and Afghanistan, Islamist fighters would arrive to partake in local wars, bringing with them not only manpower but much-needed equipment and finances. Once on the ground, they could exploit the chaos caused by the fighting to set up their operations. The near-collapse of the Albanian government during the 1990s; the chaos unleashed in Colombia, Sierra Leone, and Bosnia because of civil wars; the protection of warlords in a Chechnya that is de facto independent of Russia; and the continuing absence of an effective judicial system in Kosovo have enabled terrorists of all stripes to continue their work without significant interference.

Second, failed states have weak or nonexistent law-enforcement capabilities, permitting terrorist groups to engage in smuggling and drug trafficking in order to raise funds for operations. Turkish intelligence sources report that Osama bin Laden extended logistical support and guerrilla training to the Islamic Movement of Uzbekistan (IMU), whose leaders have maintained close ties with Islamic radicals in Afghanistan. Using the southern Fergana Valley as a transit point, Afghans have transferred weapons and personnel into Central Asia. They also use the valley as a transshipment point for drugs produced in Afghanistan en route for sale in Europe, the proceeds of which Al Qaeda can then use to finance further operations. Russian law enforcement officers maintain that groups in Afghanistan used opium-derived income to arm, train, and support fundamentalist groups including the IMU and the Chechen resistance. Another key narcotics route has been via Turkey into the Balkans, where the drugs can then be marketed in Western Europe. Moreover, the continuing conditions in Bosnia, Albania, and Kosovo have created ripe conditions for human trafficking, arms smuggling, and narcotics distribution—all areas in which bin Laden reputedly has been a "silent investor," utilizing profits to help fund Al Qaeda operations.[2] Colombia has experienced a similar pattern, with both leftist and rightist terrorist groups protecting coca fields and cocaine processing facilities in return for a share of the proceeds. The "brown zones" represented by offshore banking centers further facilitate the interconnection of terrorist groups with the narcotics trade by allowing terrorist groups to deposit funds and ensure their availability to their operatives.

Third, failed states create pools of recruits and supporters for terrorist groups, who can use their resources and organizations to step into the vacuum left by the collapse of official state power and civil society. In Central Asia, radicals have taken advantage of the weak successor states to try to establish new outposts, particularly in the Fergana Valley, where mass unemployment and a shortage of land have afflicted the natives. By playing on the widespread dissatisfaction with the corruption, economic stagnation, and political repression of the Central Asian republics, the Islamists have tapped into new pools of recruits and used the rural and mountainous areas of the region to create safe havens for training terrorists.

Observers view Central Asia as a staging area for militant organizations in Tajikistan, Uzbekistan, Kazakhstan, Kyrgyzstan, China, and Russia. Poor economic conditions in failed states also mean that terrorist groups take advantage of their financial resources to hire recruits and bribe officials. In Colombia, for example, new members of the right-wing "United Self-Defense Forces" receive pay of $180 per month, described as a "healthy sum" in a country with more than 20 percent unemployment. Islamist groups, particularly in the Balkans, found that a useful tool for recruitment was to offer the possibility of high-paying work to unemployed young men in the Persian Gulf states, with the hope of then diverting them into joining mujahideen units.

Finally, failed states retain the outward signs of sovereignty. The presumption against interference in the internal affairs of another state, enshrined in the United Nations (UN) Charter, remains a major impediment to cross-border action designed to eliminate terrorist networks. Despite the high volume of traffic in drugs, weapons, and migrants undertaken by Italian, Albanian, and Russian mafia groups via the port of Durres, for example, no European state has shown much inclination to enter Albania by force and take control of the city. Failed states may be notoriously unable to control their own territory, but they remain loath to allow access to any other state to do the same.

The governments of failed states also can issue legitimate passports and other documents—or provide the templates needed to forge credible copies—that enable terrorists to move around the world and disguise their true identities.[3] Abu Zubaydah, Al Qaeda's chief of staff, had a number of passports and false aliases that have enabled him to move freely, coordinating the activities of sleeper cells; at the time of his capture, he had a number of blank (and possibly forged) Saudi passports.[4] Bin Laden reportedly holds passports issued by Sudan, Bosnia, and Albania.

Moreover, failed states have had—and in some cases continue to possess—official military units that under international law can legitimately purchase weaponry. In some cases, such equipment is transferred to terrorist groups; in other cases, the failed state is simply too weak to secure armories, as occurred in Albania. Interpol estimates that, during January–March 1997, terrorists and organized-crime gangs seized hundreds of thousands of assault rifles, machine guns, and rocket launchers from state depots.

Bin Laden's experiences in Sudan following his expulsion from Saudi Arabia in 1991 demonstrated the value of relocating operations to a failed state. Sudan, riven by political instability and civil war, was a classic example of a failed state. Bin Laden established training camps, set up front companies to move assets and generate new revenues, and used the cloak of state sovereignty to shield his operations. Sudan became known as a way station for bin Laden's operatives, a place where terrorists could gather, train, and plan in relative safety and comfort. This pattern repeated itself in Albania and Bosnia, where radical groups, utilizing large donations from Saudi Arabia and the Persian Gulf region, established charitable organizations that doled out humanitarian relief, created schools and orphanages, and even developed a network of banks and credit agencies for the populace. By creating an alternative to a failed state, these groups won supporters both in the ranks of the government and among the general population.[5]

At the same time, terrorist organizations utilized the "brown zones" found in Western societies as secondary bases of operations. Taking advantage of lax asylum laws and immigration procedures, and the low level of scrutiny given to religious and charitable organizations, Al Qaeda has dispatched operatives and sleepers into Western countries, creating a network of safe houses and acquiring vehicles as well as equipment. Moreover, it has intensified its efforts to recruit operatives who are fully integrated members of society—whether second-generation Muslim immigrants or converts—and can move without attracting undue attention. Even after the decisive military strikes launched against Al Qaeda installations in Afghanistan, therefore, the organization and others like it remain a threat.

The Afghanistan Question: Stopgap or Solution?

Washington's global antiterrorism coalition has legitimately focused the initial response to the September 11 attacks on the failed state of Afghanistan and the Al Qaeda network. An effective and judicious use of force by the United States and its allies has been largely successful so far in destroying Al Qaeda's infrastructure on Afghan territory. Islamists themselves have admitted that the loss of the "Islamic Emirate of Afghanistan" represents a major setback to the cause but are confident that Al Qaeda can revive under the proper conditions.[6]

Terrorists are relying on two developments: that long-term occupation and reconstruction in Afghanistan will not follow short-term military action and that the United States has no real stomach for pursuing terrorist enclaves in other, more inaccessible locations. Islamist sources have proclaimed their confidence in the survival of their networks in places such as Kashmir, Kosovo, Chechnya, and Palestine, where they believe that the

United States and its allies will choose not to risk significant losses in urban or guerrilla warfare and where no "fifth columns" can undermine the terrorist groups, as occurred in Afghanistan.[7]

The operations in Afghanistan result from a unique and serendipitous convergence of several factors: the existence of anti-Taliban resistance on the ground; the absence of international recognition of the Taliban regime in Afghanistan as a legal government; the general consensus among the world's major powers that decapitation of the Taliban served international order and stability; and, finally, the very real sense of shock in the aftermath of the destruction wrought in Washington, D.C., and New York City. Somalia, which lacks any central government, and the Philippines, where the government asked for U.S. assistance to combat Abu Sayyaf and where a peace plan for granting autonomy to the Muslim southern regions enjoys the support of the state as well as of Muslim moderates, are other areas where concerted military action can be predominantly successful. These areas are the exception, however, rather than the rule.

Solving the problem of global terrorism by conducting military operations in failed states will be difficult to repeat elsewhere. Russian defense minister Sergei Ivanov said, "Any actions, including the use of force, by states and international organizations must be based on the norms and principles of international law and be appropriate for the threats."[8] Few states are eager to extend any sort of carte blanche to the United States to engage in military action anywhere in the world. Moreover, states may have their own security concerns that conflict with the aims of the war on terrorism.

Forces have spotted Al Qaeda operatives in two areas in the south Caucasus: the Pankisi gorge (which links Chechnya and Georgia) and the Kodori gorge (which runs between Georgia and the breakaway republic of Abkhazia). In an ideal world, the simple solution is that Georgia should work closely with Russian security forces, utilizing U.S. equipment and training, to deny Chechen militants the ability to transit Pankisi and to prevent the transfer of weapons and funds into Chechnya from the Georgian side. At the same time, one would argue, the international community should recognize the reality of a separate Abkhazian state, which has effectively existed since 1993, thereby giving Abkhazia the wherewithal to police its borders adequately. Anyone remotely familiar with Caucasian politics, however, knows how unlikely this scenario is. Georgia, for instance, will not undertake any action that either weakens its sovereignty (e.g., grant extra-territorial privileges for Russian security forces to engage in hot pursuit across the border) or undermines its territorial integrity (e.g., recognize the existence of a separate Abkhazia). Last autumn, Georgian paramilitary forces allegedly even sought to engage the services of Chechen fighters, including Al Qaeda operatives, by bringing a group from Pankisi across Georgia into Kodori to utilize them in the struggle against the Abkhazians, with the government turning a blind eye to the whole operation. Indeed, the Georgian government might redirect U.S. aid intended for use against terrorist groups in Pankisi toward retaking Abkhazia by force instead, which could precipitate a larger regional crisis.

Moreover, no one in the region supports the principle of recognizing de facto statelets as de jure independent because the same precedent could then apply to the Armenians of Nagorno-Karabakh against Azerbaijan and even to the Chechens themselves vis-à-vis the Russian Federation. Similar problems in the Balkans regarding Kosovo, the constituent entities of the Bosnian republic, and the Albanian-majority regions of southern Serbia and

Macedonia indicate that, for the foreseeable future, areas effectively outside of any state's purview will continue to litter Southeastern Europe and the Caucasus.

The continuing weakness of other states also will prove to be a major liability in the war against terrorism. The arrest of Al Qaeda sympathizers in Yemen risks escalating tribal tensions, which could lead the government to back away from enforcing a true crackdown against proterrorist elements. The arrest of Yemeni and Egyptian fighters in Bosnia last autumn led to vociferous protests in Sarajevo, highlighting the continuing fragility of the coalition government and raising the possibility that, should the Party of Islamic Action return to power, future antiterrorist cooperation could end. In February 2002, riots broke out in Pristina when authorities from the UN Mission in Kosovo took three former Kosovo Liberation Army members into custody for suspected terrorist acts and war crimes. Around the world, therefore, governments will likely play a double game—appeasing Washington by cooperating to some extent, while striking bargains with terrorists to prevent further destabilization.

Pakistan, one of the key members of the antiterrorist alliance, is a weak link. Indeed, President Pervez Musharraf is discovering the difficulties in containing the forces that he himself helped to unleash when he was army chief of staff. The Pakistan of the 1990s was a state mired in ethnic tension, sectarian violence, and an absence of cohesive central rule. The theological centers (the *madrassahs*), political parties, intelligence services, and retired generals had utilized the services of Al Qaeda, with motivations ranging from religious fanaticism to strategic advantage. Pakistan found Al Qaeda useful as a source of guerrilla fighters that Pakistan could send into Kashmir while providing the government in Islamabad with "plausible deniability"; according to the best estimates, up to 40 percent of the Kashmiri guerrillas came from Afghanistan. Reversing course after September 11 is no easy task. Many of the leading extremists and their cadres have avoided the police dragnets unleashed by Musharraf and simply bide their time, often in refuges where Islamabad's writ runs sluggishly. The December 2001 assassination of the brother of Interior Minister Moinuddin Haider, who is overseeing the crackdown on militants; the attack against the Indian parliament that same month; and the kidnapping and murder of journalist Daniel Pearl in January 2002 are reminders that Pakistan has by no means been "rehabilitated."

Finally, military campaigns to deny terrorists access to failed states do not address the role of Middle Eastern states in financing Islamist terror or their interest in using failed states as dumping grounds for their own militants. By subsidizing disillusioned young men to "fight for Islam" in Afghanistan, Yugoslavia, and Chechnya, many leading Middle Eastern politicians and business figures burnished their own Islamic credentials and removed potentially disruptive figures from the domestic arena.

Military operations against or within failed states designed to destroy bases and infrastructure and neutralize terrorist operatives can only be one aspect of the war on terrorism. At times, military force is not appropriate. Carrier-launched fighter-bombers are useless for uncovering Al Qaeda sleeper cells in Hamburg or shutting down Web sites that provide instructions to terrorist recruits. Food airdrops cannot compensate for the bribes that terrorist groups pay underfunded police officers. The willingness to close the loopholes allowing terrorists to function in the "brown zones" of the West has already begun to recede. In most Western countries, especially Germany, "the right to nearly absolute civil and personal privacy amounts to a state theology."[9] Restrictions may tighten, but fundamental change in a whole host of policies ranging from privacy laws to asylum procedures is unlikely. Proponents must seek the long-term victory against international terrorism in the rehabilitation, not the conquest, of the failed state.

A New Type of Nation Building

The United States and its allies cannot conduct the fight against global terrorism in a vacuum. Effective combat is impossible as long as the failed states that terrorist movements use for refuge are left to flounder. If the United States is serious about rooting out terrorism, it cannot stop at the destruction of a few camps or the freezing of bank accounts. Once the military strikes end, state reconstruction must occur.

Nation building has received a bad reputation in U.S. policy circles, notably because of failures in the Balkans and Somalia, among others, and in part due to the quasi-utopian air surrounding nation building in the 1990s, with greater stress given to empowering downtrodden ethnic groups than on constructing viable state institutions. In fact, many of the idealistic democracy-promotion programs of this period may have had a counterproductive effect by encouraging the diffusion and decentralization of power and the weakening of executive branch institutions.

The situation requires realistic nation building, focusing on existing conditions and working to rebuild and reconstruct viable institutions. The Bush administration has recognized that war against terrorism implies a war against political chaos in favor of strengthening legitimate states. Despite all the claims about globalization creating a new world order, states remain the key actors in the international arena.

In Afghanistan, for example, nation building cannot stop with signing papers in Bonn. A token central government is insufficient. Afghanistan requires effective regional administrations based in Kandahar, Herat, Mazar-e Sharif, and Jalalabad, working with, not around, the regional leaders and warlords. The nation- and state-building efforts of Mexican president Plutarco Elias Calles during the 1920s may set a precedent: regional strongmen were incorporated into the army, given positions within the political administration, or bribed with lucrative business opportunities. Until local institutions are strong enough to assume responsibility for law and order, the international community must ensure that the necessary forces are in place.

The first task in rehabilitating failed states is not holding elections but assisting in the swift reconstruction of the basic infrastructure of society—the health care system, the police force, and so forth—followed by longer-term investment. Linked to that process should be generous aid to reconstruct the bases of community life and to ensure that the wellsprings of civil society—religious organizations, schools, and the media—do not fall victim to extremist forces. In explaining the spread of Islamist extremism across Eurasia, Ravil Gainutdin, the chair of the Muslim Religious Board for European Russia, maintains that financial difficulties have rendered moderate groups unable to afford the costs of print and broadcast media. Reconstructing states will be a wasted effort if extremist groups dominate the airwaves and provide the textbooks used in schools.

The second task is effective military and security assistance. The IMU has been so difficult to crush because, among other reasons, the weak militaries of states such as Kyrgyzstan are no match for a well-armed, well-trained, and well-financed insurgency. Police and security forces need training and equipment that will enable them to intercept and destroy terrorist formations and to crack down on the narcotics trade that supplies much of the income radical groups use to purchase arms and supplies and to bribe impoverished government officials.

The scale of smuggling across the Eurasian arc (from Asia to the Balkans) demonstrates how the culture of lawlessness, abetted by failed states, has taken root. Last year, the Russian Federal Security Service alone confiscated some two tons of narcotics en route from Afghanistan to Europe. Effective financial and logistical support to regional efforts, such as the one envisioned by the draft agreement reached in December 2001 between Indonesia, Malaysia, and the Philippines that created a joint rapid-response force to fight terrorism and border crime, can help strangle the international networks that have benefited from porous borders and undefined jurisdiction to smuggle personnel, funds, and equipment from place to place.

Terrorism will be problematic as long as people are disaffected. Strengthening states around the world, however, prevents scattered, localized cells from transforming into a potent network with a global reach. Recent history demonstrates that relatively weak and isolated insurgencies from Kosovo to the South Philippines became much more deadly and effective once they drew upon an international network for a continuous supply of recruits, funds, and equipment coordinated and dispatched from bases located in failed states. The best means for emasculating international terrorist networks are effective regimes policing their borders and exercising supervision over their territory.

The United States faces the new challenge of transnational terrorists who establish sanctuaries in failed states and attract support worldwide. The traditional approach of combating terrorism, namely, using a combination of economic sanctions, military reprisals, and political pressure, may have succeeded in dissuading individual state sponsors of discrete terrorist groups—states with vested economic and political interests, such as Libya—but will likely fail at coping with this new brand of terror. Special military operations are only the first step in rooting out terror. Substantial economic and political investment designed to reconstruct regimes in failed states will be necessary if the United States and its allies hope not simply to disable terror's infrastructure temporarily, but to prevent such forces from seeking out new adherents and bases of operations in other failed states.

Ray Takeyh is a senior fellow for Middle Eastern studies at the Council on Foreign Relations, focusing his research on Iran, the Persian Gulf, and U.S. foreign policy. Dr. Takeyh was previously professor of national security studies at the National War College; professor and director of studies at the Near East and South Asia Center, National Defense University; fellow in international security studies at Yale University; fellow at the Washington Institute for Near East Policy; and fellow at the Center for Middle Eastern Studies, University of California, Berkeley.

Nikolas K. Gvosdev is Editor of *The National Interest* and a Senior Fellow of Strategic Studies at The Nixon Center. Dr. Gvosdev is a frequent commentator on U.S. foreign policy and international relations, Russian and Eurasian affairs, and developments in the Middle East.

Notes

1. See Guillermo O'Donnell, *On the State, Democratization, and Some Conceptual Problems* (*A Latin American View with Glances at Some Post-Communist Countries*), working paper #192 (Notre Dame, Ind.: Helen Kellogg Institute for International Studies, 1993).
2. See, for example, the report issued by the Macedonian Information Agency (MIA), September 20, 2001.
3. Of great concern, for example, is the fate of some 100,000 Albanian passports that "disappeared" during the 1997 unrest, some of which Interpol fears have been used to "legalize" terrorists in Europe. *Ta Nea,* September 14, 2001, p. 11. Thailand, for instance, is trying to take steps to combat the "illicit network . . . that produced forged passports and documents [that] has made the country attractive to foreign terrorists." *Nation* (Bangkok), March 11, 2002 (editorial).
4. See *Al-Sharg Al-Awsat,* March 8, 2002, p. 3 (interview of Muhammad Al-Shafi'i with a former "Afghan Arab").
5. For a discussion of this process in Albania, see *Hurriyet,* October 25, 2001; *Albania,* October 31, 2001.
6. See *Al-Quds Al-Arabi,* February 27, 2002 (communiqué reportedly issued by Mullah Omar). Concerning the fragility of the Karzai government, the Iranian newspaper *Jomhuri-ye Eslami* editorialized:

   > Even if, due to coercion and foreign military pressure, no reaction is seen for a while, the freedom-loving and independent-spirited people of Afghanistan will not remain passive and idle for long. The turmoil is there, and at the right moment and appropriate opportunity they will rise like a burning fire from under the ashes and devour all the foreigners and their domestic lackeys.

   Jomhuri-ye Eslami, February 24, 2002.
7. Mamduh Isma'il, *Al-Quds Al-Arabi,* January 22, 2002 (providing an Islamist perspective regarding the post-September 11 future of the international Islamist movement, including its ability to survive the losses of its Afghan bases).
8. ITAR-TASS, February 3, 2002.
9. Jane Kramer, "Letter from Europe: Private Lives," *New Yorker,* February 11, 2002, p. 36.

Stewart Patrick

Weak States and Global Threats

Fact or Fiction?

It has become a common claim that the gravest dangers to U.S. and world security are no longer military threats from rival great powers, but rather transnational threats emanating from the world's most poorly governed countries. Poorly performing developing countries are linked to humanitarian catastrophes; mass migration; environmental degradation; regional instability; energy insecurity; global pandemics; international crime; the proliferation of weapons of mass destruction (WMD); and, of course, transnational terrorism. Leading thinkers such as Francis Fukuyama have said that, "[s]ince the end of the Cold War, weak and failing states have arguably become the single-most important problem for international order."[1] Official Washington agrees. Secretary of State Condoleezza Rice declares that nations incapable of exercising "responsible sovereignty" have a "spillover effect" in the form of terrorism, weapons proliferation, and other dangers.[2] This new focus on weak and failing states represents an important shift in U.S. threat perceptions. Before the September 11 attacks, U.S. policymakers viewed states with sovereignty deficits exclusively through a humanitarian lens; they piqued the moral conscience but possessed little strategic significance. Al Qaeda's ability to act with impunity from Afghanistan changed this calculus, convincing President George W. Bush and his administration that "America is now threatened less by conquering states than we are by failing ones."[3]

This new strategic orientation has already had policy and institutional consequences, informing recent U.S. defense, intelligence, diplomatic, development, and even trade initiatives. The U.S. government's latest *National Defense Strategy* calls on the U.S. military to strengthen the sovereign capacities of weak states to combat internal threats of terrorism, insurgency, and organized crime. Beyond expanding its training of foreign security forces, the Pentagon is seeking interagency buy-in for a U.S. strategy to address the world's "ungoverned spaces."[4] The Central Intelligence Agency (CIA), which has identified 50 such zones globally, is devoting new collection assets to long-neglected parts of the world.[5] The National Intelligence Council is assisting the Department of State's new Office of the Coordinator for Reconstruction and Stabilization in identifying states at risk of collapse so that the office can launch conflict prevention and mitigation efforts. Not to be outdone, the U.S. Agency for International Development (USAID) has formulated its own "Fragile States Strategy" to bolster countries that could breed terror, crime, instability, and disease. The Bush administration has even justified the Central American Free Trade Area as a means to prevent state failure and its associated spillovers.[6]

This new preoccupation with weak states is not limited to the United States. In the United Kingdom, the Prime Minister's Strategy Unit has advocated a government-wide approach to stabilizing fragile countries,[7] and Canada and Australia are following suit. The United Nations has been similarly engaged; the unifying theme of last year's proposals for UN reform was the need for effective sovereign states to deal with today's global security agenda. Kofi Annan remarked before the Council on Foreign Relations in New York in 2004 that, "[w]hether the threat is terror or AIDS, a threat to one is a threat to all. . . . Our defenses are only as strong as their weakest link."[8] In September 2005, the UN endorsed the creation of a new Peacebuilding Commission to help war-torn states recover. The Development Assistance Committee (DAC) of the Organization for Economic Cooperation and Development (OECD) in January 2005 also launched a "Fragile States" initiative in partnership with the World Bank's Low-Income Countries Under Stress (LICUS) program.[9]

It is striking, however, how little empirical evidence underpins these sweeping assertions and policy developments. Policymakers and experts have presumed a blanket connection between weak governance and transnational threats and have begun to implement policy responses accordingly. Yet, they have rarely distinguished among categories of weak and failing states or asked whether (and how) certain types of developing countries are associated with particular threats. Too often, it appears that the entire range of Western policies is animated by anecdotal evidence or isolated examples, such as Al Qaeda's operations in Afghanistan or cocaine trafficking in Colombia. The risk in this approach is that the United States will squander energy and resources in a diffuse, unfocused effort to attack state weakness wherever it arises, without appropriate attention to setting priorities and tailoring responses to poor governance and its specific, attendant spillovers.

Before embracing a new strategic vision and investing in new initiatives, conventional wisdom should be replaced by sober, detailed analysis. The ultimate goal of this fine-grained approach should be to determine which states are associated with which dangers. Weak states do often incubate global threats, but this correlation is far from universal. Crafting a more effective U.S. strategy will depend on a deeper understanding of the underlying mechanisms linking poor governance and state incapacity in the developing world with cross-border spillovers.

Defining Weak and Failing States

There is no consensus on the precise number of weak and failing states. The Commission on Weak States and U.S. National Security estimates that there are between 50 and 60; the United Kingdom's Department for International Development classifies 46 nations with 870 million inhabitants as "fragile"; and the World Bank treats 30 countries as LICUS.[10] These divergent estimates reflect differences in the criteria used to define state weakness, the indicators used to gauge it, and the relative weighting of various aspects of governance.

State strength is relative and can be measured by the state's ability and willingness to provide the fundamental political goods associated with statehood: physical security, legitimate political institutions, economic management, and social welfare. Many countries have critical gaps in one or more of these four areas of governance. In effect, they possess legal but not actual sovereignty. In the security realm, they struggle to maintain a monopoly on the use of force, control borders and territory, ensure public order, and provide safety from crime. In the political sphere, they lack legitimate governing institutions that provide effective administration, ensure checks on power, protect basic rights and freedoms, hold leaders accountable, deliver impartial justice, and permit broad citizen participation. In the economic arena, they strain to carry out basic macroeconomic and fiscal policies or establish a legal and regulatory climate conducive to entrepreneurship, private enterprise, open trade, natural resource management, foreign investment, and economic growth. Finally, in the social domain, they fail to meet the basic needs of their populations by making even minimal investments in health, education, and other social services.

Yet, not all weak states look alike. They range in a spectrum from collapsed states, such as Somalia, that have gaps in all four capacities to fragile "good performers," such as Senegal, that are making some progress in most or all areas. In between, most weak states struggle on many fronts or muddle through. Not by coincidence, weak and failing states tend to be ineligible for the Millennium Challenge Account (MCA), an innovative aid window announced by Bush in March 2002 to reward countries that have a demonstrated commitment to "ruling justly," "investing in their people," and "promoting economic freedom."[11]

State weakness is not just a question of capacity but also of will. History provides repeated examples of corrupt, incompetent, or venal regimes—Zimbabwe today under President Robert Mugabe, for example—that have driven promising countries into the ground.[12] By distinguishing between capacity and will, four categories of weak states can be differentiated: relatively good performers, states that are weak but willing, states that have the means but not the will, and those with neither the will nor the way to fulfill the basic functions of statehood (see table 1). Such analytical distinctions have policy utility, informing the mix of incentives external actors might deploy in engaging poor performers. The goal is to move weak states toward the upper left quadrant of table 1 by filling capacity gaps, persuading unreconstructed states to mend their ways, or both.

Table 1

Capacity and Will as Dimensions of State Weakness

	Strong Will	**Low Will**
High Capacity	**Relatively Good Performers** (e.g., Senegal, Honduras)	**Unresponsive/Corrupt/ Repressive** (e.g., Burma, Zimbabwe)
Low Capacity	**Weak but Willing** (e.g., Mozambique, East Timor)	**Weak and Not Willing** (e.g., Haiti, Sudan)

Compared to other developing countries, weak and failing states are more likely to suffer from low or no growth and to be furthest away from reaching the Millennium Development Goals, a set of commitments made by UN member states in 2000 to make concrete progress by 2015 in critical development objectives, such as eradicating extreme poverty and hunger, achieving universal primary education, and reducing child mortality. The inhabitants of these weak and failing states are likely to be poor and malnourished, live with chronic illness and die young, go without education and basic health care, suffer gender discrimination, and lack access to modern technology. Compared to OECD, or developed, countries, fragile states are 15 times more prone to civil war, with such violence both more extreme and longer lasting than even in other developing countries. Such states are the over-whelming source of the world's refugees and internally displaced peoples. Many are also among the world's worst abusers of human rights.[13]

The most comprehensive and well-respected system for evaluating state performance is the World Bank's "Governance Matters" data set. The most recent installment, in 2005, ranks 209 countries and territories along six dimensions: voice and accountability, political instability and violence, government effectiveness, regulatory burden, rule of law, and control of corruption.[14] Table 2 lists the 44 countries that rest in the bottom quintile, ranked from weakest (Somalia) to strongest (Algeria).

Table 2

Bottom Quintile of Aggregate Governance Rankings

Somalia (weakest)	Cote d'Ivoire	Venezuela
Iraq	Nigeria	Guinea
Myanmar	Laos	Togo
Democratic Republic of Congo	Angola	Azerbaijan
	Equatorial Guinea	Bangladesh
Afghanistan	Tajikistan	Cuba
Liberia	Republic of Congo	Iran
Haiti	Belarus	Nepal
Zimbabwe	Chad	Libya
Turkmenistan	Yemen	Syria
Sudan	Solomon Islands	Sierra Leone
North Korea	West Bank/Gaza	Guinea-Bissau
Uzbekistan	Pakistan	Cameroon
Burundi	Ethiopia	Comoros
Central African Republic	Eritrea	Algeria (strongest)

Source: Kaufmann, Kray, and Mastruzzi, *Governance Matters IV,* 2005.

Three observations can be drawn from this data. First, the weakest states are not necessarily the poorest. Accordingly, the fifth quintile includes several lower-middle-income countries, such as Venezuela, and excludes a few very poor countries, such as Gambia and Niger. This definition of state weakness differs from that adopted by the World Bank and OECD/DAC donors, which restrict the category "fragile state" to very poor countries that are eligible for the bank's concessional (International Development Association) window and that score lowest on the bank's Country Policy and Institutional Assessment indicators.

That approach, although consistent with the poverty reduction mandate of aid agencies, is overly restrictive for policy analysts and officials interested in the security implications of weak governance across the entire range of developing countries.

Second, the list of weak and failing states in table 2 captures a diverse collection of countries that pose a similarly diverse array of potential challenges to U.S. foreign and national security policy. Most of these countries are either in conflict or recovering from it, have experienced recurrent bouts of political instability, or rank very low in terms of "human security," as measured by risk of violent death and abuses to core human rights.[15] Several are "outposts of tyranny," in the Bush administration's parlance (e.g., North Korea, Belarus, Cuba, Zimbabwe), authoritarian states that may appear superficially strong but rest on a brittle foundation. Others are sites of ongoing U.S. combat and reconstruction efforts (Iraq, Afghanistan); active or potential WMD proliferators (North Korea, Iran, Pakistan); past or present safe havens for terrorism (Afghanistan, Yemen); anchors of regional stability or instability (Nigeria, Pakistan); bases for narcotics trafficking and crime (Burma); potential sources of uncontrolled migration (Haiti); critical energy suppliers (Venezuela, Nigeria); locations of epidemic disease (Angola, Democratic Republic of Congo [DRC]); or settings for recent atrocities and humanitarian crises (Sudan, Liberia, Burundi, Sierra Leone). Needless to say, a single state frequently falls into more than one of these categories of concern.

Third, the relationship between state weakness and spillovers is not linear. It varies by threat. Some salient transnational dangers to U.S. and global security come not from states at the bottom quintile of the Governance Matters rankings but from the next tier up, countries such as Colombia, the world's leading producer of cocaine; Saudi Arabia, home to a majority of the September 11 hijackers; Russia, a host of numerous transnational criminal enterprises; and China, the main source both of SARS and avian flu. These states tend to be better run and more capable of delivering political goods; nearly half are eligible or on the threshold of eligibility for the MCA in 2006. Nevertheless, even these middling performers may suffer from critical gaps in capacity or political will that enable spillovers.

How do these sets of states correlate with significant transnational threats to the United States and the international community? The answer depends in part on which threat you are talking about.

Transnational Threats and U.S. National Security

The growing concern with weak and failing states is really based on two separate propositions: first, that traditional concepts of security such as interstate violence should expand to encompass cross-border threats driven by nonstate actors (such as terrorism), activities (crime), or forces (pandemics); and second, that such threats have their origins in large measure in weak governance in the developing world.

Since the Reagan administration, successive versions of the *National Security Strategy* have incorporated nonmilitary concerns such as terrorism, organized crime, infectious disease, energy security, and environmental degradation. The common thread linking these challenges is that they originate primarily in sovereign jurisdictions abroad but have the potential to harm U.S. citizens. Some national security traditionalists resist this definitional expansion on the grounds that such concerns pose at best an indirect rather than existential threat to U.S. national interests or even human life. Proponents of a wider view respond that unconventional threats may contribute to violence by destabilizing states and regions. More fundamentally, they argue that the traditional "violence paradigm" for national security must adapt to accommodate other threats to the safety, well-being, and way of life of U.S. citizens. Such threats include not only malevolent, purposive ones such as transnational terrorism, something many traditionalists now accept, but also "threats without a threatener"—malignant forces that emerge from nature, such as global pandemics, or as by-products of human activity, such as climate change.[16]

Traditionalists may similarly be dubious that weak and failing states in general endanger U.S. national security.[17] More relevant, they contend, are a handful of pivotal weak states, such as nuclear-armed Pakistan or North Korea, whose fortunes may affect regional balances of power or prospects for large-scale destruction.[18] Yet, it is not always easy to predict where threats may emerge. In the 1990s, few anticipated that remote, poor, and war-ravaged Afghanistan would be the launching pad for the most devastating attack on the United States in the nation's history.

The challenge for policy analysts is to discern more carefully which states are likely to present which baskets of transnational problems. Such distinctions will allow them to direct limited resources to address the priority challenges in critical countries and tailor responses to the key incentive structures in those countries accordingly. A start here is to look more closely at the potential links of weak and failing states to terrorism, WMD proliferation, crime, disease, energy insecurity, and regional instability.

Hotbeds of Terrorism?

Both the Bush administration and outside commentators frequently contend that countries with weak or nonexistent governance are greater risks to generate and serve as hosts of transnational terrorist organizations. As the *New York Times* argued in July 2005, "Failed states that cannot provide jobs and food for their people, that have lost chunks of territory to warlords, and that can no longer track or control their borders, send an invitation to terrorists."[19]

Such claims have some justification. Data on global terrorist attacks from the University of Maryland show that, from 1991 to 2001, most individual terrorists came from low-income authoritarian countries in conflict, such as Sudan, Algeria, and Afghanistan.[20] Similarly, data compiled annually by the State Department reveals that for 2003–2005 most U.S. designated Foreign Terrorist Organizations use weak and failing states as their primary bases of operations.[21] Weak and failing states appeal to transnational terrorist organizations for the multiple benefits they offer: safe havens, conflict experience, settings for training and indoctrination, access to weapons and equipment, financial resources, staging grounds and transit zones, targets for operations, and pools of recruits. Al Qaeda, for example, enjoyed the hospitality of Sudan and Afghanistan, where it built training camps and enlisted new members; exploited Kenya and Yemen to launch attacks on U.S. embassies in Nairobi and Dar es Salaam as well as on the USS *Cole;* and financed its operations through illicit trade in gemstones, including diamonds and tanzanite, from African conflict zones.[22]

Accordingly, the United States is seeking to deny terrorists access to weak states. Africa has emerged as a primary arena of concern. An analysis of the 9/11 Commission report by the Congressional Research Service warns that that "the international terror threat against the [United States] and local interests is likely to continue to grow in several parts of Africa because of porous borders, lax security, political instability, and a lack of state resources and capacities."[23] The Department of Defense is responding by training

African security forces in a dozen countries in the Sahel to control their borders and territories more effectively.[24] More comprehensively, the *National Strategy for Combating Terrorism* commits the United States to "diminishing the underlying conditions that terrorists seek to exploit"[25] by bolstering state capacities, alleviating poverty, and promoting good governance. Bush echoed this theme in his September 2005 speech at the UN High-Level Plenary Meeting, declaring, "We must help raise up the failing states and stagnant societies that provide fertile ground for terrorists."[26]

A closer look suggests that the connection between state weakness and transnational terrorism is more complicated and tenuous than often assumed. First, obviously not all weak and failed states are afflicted by terrorism. As historian Walter Laqueur points out, "In the 49 countries currently designated by the United Nations as the least developed hardly any terrorist activity occurs."[27] Weak capacity per se cannot explain why terrorist activity is concentrated in particular regions, particularly the Middle East and broader Muslim world, rather than others such as Central Africa. Other variables and dynamics, including political, religious, cultural, and geographical factors, clearly shape its global distribution.

Similarly, not all terrorism that occurs in weak and failing states is transnational. Much is self-contained action by insurgents motivated by local political grievances, such as the Revolutionary Armed Forces of Colombia (FARC), or national liberation struggles, such as the Liberation Tigers of Tamil Eelam (LTTE) in Sri Lanka. It is thus only tangentially related to the "global war on terrorism," which, as defined by the Bush administration, focuses on terrorists with global reach, particularly those motivated by an extreme Salafist strand of Wahhabi Islam.

Third, not all weak and failing states are equal. Conventional wisdom holds that terrorists are particularly attracted to collapsed, lawless polities such as Somalia or Liberia, or what the Pentagon terms "ungoverned spaces." In fact, as Davidson College professor Ken Menkhaus and others note, terrorists are more likely to find weak but functioning states, such as Pakistan or Kenya, congenial bases of operations. Such badly governed states are not only fragile and susceptible to corruption, but they also provide easy access to the financial and logistical infrastructure of the global economy, including communications technology, transportation, and banking services.[28]

Fourth, transnational terrorists are only partially and perhaps decreasingly reliant on weak and failing states. For one, the Al Qaeda threat has evolved from a centrally directed network, dependent on a "base," into a much more diffuse global movement consisting of autonomous cells in dozens of countries, poor and wealthy alike. Moreover, the source of radical Islamic terrorism may reside less in state weakness in the Middle East than in the alienation of de-territorialized Muslims in Europe. The "safe havens" of global terrorists are as likely to be the *banlieues* of Paris as the wastes of the Sahara or the slums of Karachi.[29]

In other words, weak and failing states can provide useful assets to transnational terrorists, but they may be less central to their operations than widely believed. If there is one failed state today that is important to transnational terrorism, it is probably Iraq. As CIA director Porter Goss testified in early 2005, the U.S.-led invasion and occupation transformed a brutal but secular authoritarian state into a symbol and magnet for the global jihadi movement.[30]

Although all four governance gaps associated with weak and failing states may contribute to transnational terrorism, political and security gaps are the most important. In the absence of peaceful outlets for political expression, frustrated groups are more likely to adopt violence against repressive regimes and their perceived foreign sponsors. Similarly, states that do not control borders or territory facilitate terrorist infiltration and operations. Two other gaps may play supporting roles. When states do not meet basic social needs, they provide openings for charitable organizations or educational systems linked to radical networks. Similarly, states lacking effective economic institutions are more likely to suffer from stagnant growth, breed political extremism, and be unable to regulate terrorist financing.

In seeking to bolster weak states against transnational terrorism, policymakers must distinguish between capacity and will. The U.S. Anti-Terrorist Assistance program is predicated on the belief that well-intentioned but poor governments, in the Sahel or East Africa, for example, simply lack the tools to do the job. Yet, the cases of Pakistan and Saudi Arabia suggest a more serious impediment: a lack of determination by governing regimes, worried about alienating an already radicalized population, to take forceful steps such as cracking down on jihadi groups or imposing central authority over restive regions.[31]

Weapons Proliferation Risks?

Fears that weak and failing states may incubate transnational terrorism merge with a related concern: that poorly governed countries may be unable or disinclined to control stocks of nuclear, biological, or chemical weapons or prevent the onward spread or leakage of WMD-related technology. This is not an idle worry. According to the British government, of the 17 states that have current or suspended WMD programs beyond the five permanent members of the UN Security Council, 13 are "countries at risk of instability."[32] The most frightening prospect is that a nuclear-armed state such as Pakistan or North Korea might lose control of its nuclear weapons through collapse or theft, placing the weapons into the hands of a successor regime or nonstate actors with little compunction about their use. A more likely scenario might involve the transfer of biological weapons, which are easier to make and transport but difficult to track.

Direct transfer of functioning WMD should not be the only concern. Revelations about the extensive international nuclear arms bazaar of Abdul Qadeer Khan suggest that poor governance may be the Achilles' heel of global nonproliferation efforts. For more than two decades, Khan, Pakistan's leading nuclear scientist, orchestrated a clandestine operation to sell sensitive expertise and technology, including the means to produce fissile material and to design and fabricate nuclear weapons, to Iran, Libya, and North Korea. As David Albright and Corey Hinderson stated, "The Khan network could not have evolved into such a dangerous supplier without the utter corruption and dishonesty of successive Pakistani governments, which, for almost two decades, were quick to deny any involvement of its scientists in illicit procurement."[33] Furthermore, it could not have gone global without institutional weaknesses in more advanced middle-income countries, including Malaysia, South Africa, and Turkey, that possessed manufacturing capabilities but lacked the knowledge, capacity, or will to implement relevant export control and nonproliferation laws.

Although U.S. officials are understandably preoccupied with the dangers of WMD proliferation, for most of the world the spread of more mundane but still deadly conventional weapons poses the greatest threat to human security and civil peace. There is clear evidence that weak, failing, and postconflict states play a critical role in the global proliferation of small arms and light weapons. According to the Geneva-based *Small Arms*

Survey, more than 640 million such weapons circulate globally, many among private hands and for illicit purposes.[34] Weak states are often the source, transit, and destination countries for the illegal arms trade. On the borderlands of the former Soviet Union, for example, vast stockpiles of weapons remain in ill-secured depots, providing tempting targets for rebel groups, terrorists, and international criminal organizations. Such matériel frequently surfaces on the global black or grey markets, as corrupt officials manipulate legitimate export licenses to obscure the military purpose or ultimate recipient of the shipment. In one notable instance in 1999, Ukraine's export agency transferred 68 tons of munitions to Burkina Faso. The weapons were then shipped to Liberia and ultimately to Sierra Leone, landing in the hands of Foday Sankoh's Revolutionary United Front.[35]

The availability of conventional weapons further weakens state capacity by fueling civil wars and insurgencies, fostering a culture of criminality and impunity. As the experiences of Afghanistan, Haiti, and the DRC, among others, show, easy access to instruments of violence complicates efforts by governments and international partners to establish public order and the rule of law, provide relief, and pursue more ambitious development goals.

As with terrorism, the risk of proliferation from weak states is often more a matter of will than of objective capacity. This is particularly true for WMD proliferation. The technological sophistication and secure facilities needed to construct such weapons would seem to require access to and some acquiescence from the highest levels of the state apparatus. This may be less true for small arms proliferation. Some weak states simply lack the capacity to police the grey or black market and to control flows of such weapons across their borders.

Of the four governance gaps, WMD proliferation is most likely to be correlated with security and political shortcomings, particularly poor civilian oversight of the defense establishment and the presence of an authoritarian and corrupt regime. In the case of small arms, weak economic institutions may also create incentives and opportunities for proliferation.

Dens of Thieves?

Beyond posing terrorist or proliferation risks, weak and failing states are said to provide ideal bases for transnational criminal enterprises involved in the production, transit, or trafficking of drugs, weapons, people, and other illicit commodities and in the laundering of the profits from such activities. The surging scope and scale of global organized crime underpins these concerns. The worldwide narcotics trade alone is now estimated to be a $300–500 billion business, on a par with at least the global automobile industry or at most the global oil industry. Former International Monetary Fund managing director Michel Camdessus estimates that money laundering accounts for 2–5 percent of world gross domestic product, or between $800 billion and $2 trillion.[36]

The rise in organized crime is being driven by the dynamics of globalization. Recent advances in communications and transportation, the removal of commercial barriers, and the deregulation of financial services have created unprecedented opportunities for illicit activity, from money laundering to trafficking in drugs, arms, and people. National authorities, particularly in weak states, strain to encourage legitimate commerce while curbing illicit trade.[37]

The relationship between transnational organized crime and weak states is parasitic. All things being equal, criminal networks are drawn to environments where the rule of law is absent or imperfectly applied, law enforcement and border controls are lax, regulatory systems are weak, contracts go unenforced, public services are unreliable, corruption is rife, and the state itself may be subject to capture. As University of Pittsburgh professor Phil Williams said, such capacity gaps provide "functional holes" that criminal enterprises can exploit. Poor governance has made Africa, in the words of the UN Office on Drugs and Crime, "an ideal conduit through which to extract and/or transship a range of illicit commodities, such as drugs, firearms, minerals and oil, timber, wildlife, and human beings."[38] Transnational organized crime further reduces weak-state capacity, as criminals manipulate corruption to gain protection for themselves and their activities and to open new avenues for profit. Criminal groups have become adept at exploiting weak-state capacity in conflict zones, such as Colombia or the DRC, where political authority is contested or formal institutions have collapsed, and in fluid postconflict settings, such as Bosnia or Kosovo, where they have not yet been firmly reestablished.

Yet, if state weakness is often a necessary condition for the influx of organized crime, it is not a sufficient one. Even more than a low-risk operating environment, criminals seek profits. In a global economy, realizing high returns depends on tapping into a worldwide market to sell illicit commodities and launder the proceeds, which in turn depends on access to financial services, modern telecommunications, and transportation infrastructure. Such considerations help explain why South Africa and Nigeria have become magnets for transnational and domestic organized crime and why Togo has not.[39] Criminals will accept the higher risks of operating in states with stronger capacity in return for greater rewards.

In addition, the link between global crime and state weakness varies by sector. The category "transnational crime" encompasses a vast array of activities, not limited to narcotics trafficking, alien smuggling, piracy, environmental crime, sanctions violations, contraband smuggling, counterfeiting, financial fraud, high-technology crime, and money laundering. Some of these activities, such as narcotics trafficking, are closely linked to state weakness. Poorly governed states dominate the annual list of countries Washington designates as "major" drug-producing and -transiting nations. Nearly 90 percent of global heroin, for example, comes from Afghanistan and is trafficked to Europe via poorly governed states in Central Asia or along the "Balkan route." Burma is the second-largest producer of opium and a key source of methamphetamine. Weak states similarly dominate the list of countries designated as the worst offenders in human trafficking, a $7–8 billion business that sends an estimated 800,000 women and children across borders annually for purposes of forced labor or sexual slavery.[40]

Other criminal sectors such as money laundering, financial fraud, cyber crime, intellectual property theft, and environmental crime are less obviously correlated with state weakness. With few exceptions, for example, money laundering occurs primarily in small offshore financial centers, wealthy nations, or middle-income countries. The reason is straightforward: most weak and failing states lack the requisite banking systems. On the other hand, many of the profits being laundered come from activities that emanate from or transit through weak states.

Among the four governance gaps, the rise of transnational organized crime in weak states appears to be most closely correlated with poor economic and political institutions. Poor regulatory environments and unaccountable political systems constrain the growth of the licit economy and create opportunities for corruption, both grand and petty. Inadequate public security and social welfare may play a secondary role by fostering a culture of lawlessness and permitting criminals to win support by meeting basic needs of a beleaguered population. Finally, the relative role of capacity versus will in facilitating transnational organized crime in weak states tends to vary. As crime becomes more entrenched, a compromised political elite is less likely to deploy the capacities at its disposal to fight it.

Plague and Pestilence?

The threat of the rapid spread of avian influenza, which could conceivably kill tens of millions of people, has placed infectious disease into the first tier of national security issues. There is growing concern that weak and failing states may serve as important breeding grounds for new pandemics and, lacking adequate capacity to respond to these diseases, endanger global health. As development economists Clive Bell and Maureen Lewis said, "Failed or faltering states cannot or will not perform basic public health functions . . . placing the rest of the world at risk."[41]

Since 1973, more than 30 previously unknown disease agents, including HIV/AIDS, Ebola, and the West Nile virus, have emerged for which no cures are available. Most have originated in developing countries. During the same time span, more than 20 well-known pathogens, including tuberculosis, malaria, and cholera, have reemerged or spread, often in more virulent and drug-resistant forms.[42] In an age of mass travel and global commerce, when more than 2 million people cross international borders a day and air freight exceeds 100 billion ton-kilometers a year, inadequate capacity or insufficient will to respond with vigorous public health measures can quickly threaten lives across the globe. National security and public health experts worry that weak and failed states, which invest little in epidemiological surveillance, health information and reporting systems, primary health care delivery, preventive measures, or response capacity, will lack the means to detect and contain outbreaks of deadly disease.

These worries are well founded. Although there is little solid data on the link between state capacity and epidemic patterns, it is known that the global infectious disease burden falls overwhelmingly (90 percent) on low- and middle-income countries that account for only 11 percent of global health spending. The Armed Forces Medical Intelligence Center has devised a typology of countries by health care status, ranking nations into five categories on the basis of resources and priority devoted to public health, quality of health care, access to drugs, and capacity for surveillance and response. States in the bottom two quintiles are the main victims of the world's seven deadliest infectious diseases: respiratory infections, HIV/AIDS, diarrheal diseases, tuberculosis, malaria, hepatitis B, and measles. Sub-Saharan Africa is the hardest hit, with just 10 percent of the world's population but 90 percent of its malaria and 75 percent of its HIV/AIDS cases.[43]

The spread of infectious disease is being driven partly by breakdowns in public health, especially during periods of political turmoil and war. HIV/AIDS is a case in point. Nearly all instances of the disease in South and Southeast Asia can be traced to strains that evolved in northern Burma, an ungoverned warren of drug gangs, irregular militias, and human traffickers. Similarly, the collapse of the DRC made it a petri dish for the evolution of numerous strains of HIV. Nor does peace always improve matters, at least initially. In Ethiopia and several other African countries, rising HIV/AIDS prevalence has paralleled the return and demobilization of ex-combatants and their reintegration into society, exposing the wider citizenry to disease contracted during military deployments.[44]

Beyond countries in conflict, many developing and transitional states possess decrepit and decaying public health systems that can easily be overwhelmed. Following the end of the Cold War, the states of the former Soviet Union all experienced spikes in the incidence of measles, tuberculosis, and HIV. In the spring of 2005, weak health infrastructure in Angola amplified an outbreak of the hemorrhagic fever Marburg. The same year, the government of Nigeria failed to enforce a national immunization program, allowing polio, a disease on the brink of eradication, to spread across a broad swath of Africa and beyond to Yemen, Saudi Arabia, and Indonesia.

Diseases incubated in weak and failing states pose both direct and indirect threats to the United States. Significant numbers of U.S. citizens may become infected and die. Even if they do not, such epidemics may impose high economic costs and undermine key countries or regions. The World Bank estimates that SARS cost the East Asian regional economy some $20–25 billion, despite killing only 912 people.[45] The political costs of disease are more nuanced but no less real. In the most heavily affected African countries, HIV/AIDS has decimated human capital and fiscal systems, undermining the already limited capacity of states to deliver basic services, control territory, and manage the economy. It has strained health and education systems, eroded social cohesion, undermined agriculture and economic growth, and weakened armies. The pandemic is spreading rapidly into Eurasia and could surge to 110 million cases by 2010, with dramatic increases in countries of strategic significance such as India, China, and Russia.[46]

In the growing transnational threat posed by epidemics, the weak-state problem tends to be one of capacity more than will. Although there have been prominent cases of official denial and foot-dragging (e.g., over HIV/AIDS in Russia or SARS in China), the greater problem is a genuine inability to prevent and respond adequately to disease outbreaks. The most salient governance gap in the case of epidemics is in providing social welfare, notably underdeveloped public health infrastructure.

Energy Insecurity?

The doubling of world oil prices in 2005 exposed strains and volatility in the global energy market at a time of surging global demand, intensifying competition over dwindling reserves, and instability in key producer countries from Iraq to Nigeria to Venezuela. To some, these trends suggest that reliance on oil and gas from weak and failing states may endanger U.S. and global energy security by increasing the volatility, costs, and risk of interruption of supplies. Beyond requiring the United States to pay an "insecurity premium," such dependence may complicate the pursuit of broader U.S. national security and foreign policy objectives.

Anxiety about U.S. energy security is nothing new. Much hand-wringing accompanied the oil crisis of the mid-1970s, when domestic U.S. production peaked and the country confronted an Arab oil embargo. Despite temporary shortages and an oil price shock, the Nixon-era United States managed to find alternate sources of supply. Most economists are confident that today's markets are similarly capable of absorbing temporary interruptions, albeit at a price.

Nevertheless, some new dynamics deserve consideration. First, the U.S. quest for energy security is occurring at a time of increased global competition for limited supplies. Since 2000, the world's consumption of fossil fuels has risen much faster than most analysts had predicted, driven not only by sustained U.S. demand but also by China's seemingly unquenchable thirst for energy. During 2004 alone, Chinese oil imports surged by 40 percent, making China the world's second-largest oil importing country.[47] The removal of excess production and refining capacity has resulted in a dramatic tightening of the global energy market and has left prices vulnerable to sudden spikes in the event of disturbances in producer countries.

Second, price shocks are increasingly likely, given the world's growing reliance on energy supplies from weak states, as proven reserves in stable countries peak or become depleted. As Hampshire College professor of security studies Michael Klare said, the geographic concentration of exploitable fossil fuels means that the availability of energy is "closely tied to political and socioeconomic conditions within a relatively small group of countries."[48] Significantly, many of the world's main oil exporters, including Iraq, Nigeria, Russia, Saudi Arabia, and Venezuela, are less stable today than in 2000. The United Kingdom calculates that some 60 percent of global oil reserves are located in countries "facing stability challenges," such as Azerbaijan, where untapped reserves could generate $124 billion in revenue by 2024. Complicating matters, a large percentage of the world's oil and gas transits unstable regions, such as Transcaucasia, and vulnerable choke points, such as the Straits of Hormuz and Malacca, via pipeline or tanker.[49]

The U.S. exposure to volatility and interruption of energy supplies has grown markedly since 1973, when it imported only 34 percent of its crude oil. By 2005 this figure was 58 percent, with fully one-third coming from Venezuela, Nigeria, Iraq, and Angola. Increasingly, U.S. energy security is hostage to foreign political developments.[50] During the past several years, oil markets have tightened in response to strikes in Venezuela, violence in Nigeria, and insurgency in Iraq. This dependence on weak states will only increase. By 2015 the United States is forecast to be importing 68 percent of its oil, a quarter of it from the Gulf of Guinea, up from today's 15 percent. All of the countries in that region—Angola, Cameroon, Congo-Brazzaville, Gabon, Equatorial Guinea, and Nigeria—face tremendous governance challenges.[51] Nigeria, a fragile democracy that Washington hopes will become an anchor of stability in the region, is beset by rampant corruption and crime, simmering ethnic tensions, and grinding poverty. During the past three years, rebels in the Niger Delta have repeatedly disrupted Nigeria's oil flow.

Rising dependence on energy from weak and failing states promises to have unpleasant ramifications for wider U.S. foreign policy objectives. It will surely complicate U.S. democracy promotion by encouraging Washington to cozy up to authoritarian dictators or to intervene to shore up unstable regimes in regions such as the Caucasus or Central

Asia. Even where the United States sticks to its principles, it may find good governance elusive in countries awash in petrodollars. For such "trust fund states," as Fareed Zakaria terms them, it is all too easy to rely on easy natural resource revenue rather than to do the hard work of building the economic and political institutions necessary to create enduring wealth and foster human liberty.[52]

By definition, the transnational threat of energy insecurity is peculiar to a subset of weak states that either possess large energy resources or sit astride transit routes. The nature of this threat varies according to whether state weakness is a function of insufficient will, inadequate capacity, or both. For Venezuela or Iran, for example, the main risk of interrupted supplies comes from the unpredictability of autocratic regimes. For Nigeria or post-Saddam Hussein Iraq, in contrast, the risk is that weak elected governments will be unable to ensure oil flows in the face of domestic instability. In either case, the governance gaps most closely correlated with energy insecurity tend to be political and economic, reflecting the tendency of natural resource riches to produce endemic corruption, abusive state power, and long-term stagnation.

Bad Neighbors?

Experience since the end of the Cold War has shown that conflict in developing countries can have critical transnational dimensions.[53] A common contention is that violent conflict and complex emergencies often spill over the porous borders of weak and failing states, destabilizing regions. Such claims have merit. As state structures collapse and borders become more porous, these countries often export violence as well as refugees, political instability, and economic dislocation to states in their vicinity. This risk is compounded when weak, vulnerable, or collapsed states are adjacent to countries with similar characteristics that possess few defenses against spillovers. Weaknesses in one state can thus encourage the rise of an entire bad neighborhood. Such a pattern emerged in West Africa during the 1990s, as the conflict in Liberia under Charles Taylor poured across national borders in the form of people, guns, and conflict diamonds, undermining neighboring Sierra Leone, Guinea, and Cote d'Ivoire.[54]

In reciprocal fashion, bad neighborhoods can undermine governance and encourage violence in already weak states. Many recent internal conflicts, from that of Burundi in the Great Lakes Region of Africa to that of Tajikistan in Central Asia, have been embedded in such regional conflict formations. In some cases, contiguous countries have fomented civil war by supporting armed groups across borders that share their political goals. In other cases, transnational networks, whether based on ethnic identity, political affinity, or economic interest, have undermined the central government and fueled violent conflict by facilitating illicit traffic in small arms, drugs, people, or lootable commodities. Where regional conflict formations are present, sustainable peace may depend on successful peacebuilding in the larger region.[55]

Given their propensity to descend into violence and embroil neighboring countries, weak and failing states are disproportionately at risk of external military intervention. State failure preceded virtually every case of the 30-odd instances of U.S. military intervention between 1960 and 2005.[56] Failed and failing states have also been the overwhelming focus of the 55 UN peacekeeping operations over the same period.[57]

Even in the absence of violence, failing states impose significant economic hardship on their regions, undoing years of development efforts. Recent analysis by the World Bank suggests that the average total cost of a failed state to itself and its neighbors amounts to a staggering $82.4 billion, or more than the total global foreign aid budget of $79 billion. In other words, the collapse of a single state can effectively erase an entire year's worth of worldwide official development assistance.[58]

The link here between state failure or weakness and regional instability is not universal but obvious: when weak or failed states are contiguous, the risk of regional instability is higher. The spillover of violent conflict itself may reflect a lack of capacity or will. Some governments are unable to control cross-border activities of rebel groups operating from their territory. The most salient governance gap here is inability to provide public security. Other governments adopt a conscious policy of destabilizing their neighbors. In this case, internal weakness and external aggression tend to reflect authoritarian political institutions.

A Road Map for Policy

Although more research is clearly warranted, it is not too soon to offer some recommendations for a more effective U.S. strategy toward weak and failing states. In developing this new strategy, policymakers must be better equipped with the tools to calculate what countries are at risk from which particular threats when determining when and how the United States should become involved. The strategy should have at least three components lacking in current U.S. policy: deeper intelligence collection and analysis on the links between state weakness and transnational threats; improved policy coherence to integrate all instruments of U.S. national influence in crisis countries; and robust international engagement to leverage efforts of partners and allies who share Washington's interest in stemming the negative spillovers of state weakness in the developing world.

To determine where U.S. involvement is warranted and to tailor state-building efforts in a manner that mitigates the most salient dangers, policymakers must first be able to anticipate which threats are likely to arise from particular countries. For one, they should recall the distinction between state capacity and will as determinants of good governance and state functionality. One testable hypothesis is that a weak state's propensity to generate spillovers, as well as the nature of these threats, will vary according to whether that weakness is a function of capacity, will, or both. The initial analysis above suggests that weak capacity is especially conducive to health epidemics and small arms proliferation, that inadequate will is often central to terrorism and WMD proliferation, and that both play roles in transnational organized crime, energy insecurity, and regional instability (see table 3). All things being equal, it is reasonable to predict that countries lacking both capacity and will for good governance should generate the most transnational threats. Accordingly, it should be expected that the six categories of spillovers—terrorism, proliferation, crime, health, energy, and regional instability—will cluster around such states. A related hypothesis is that states that are irresponsible as well as or instead of being powerless should be more likely to generate transnational threats that are not merely malignant, such as epidemics, but also malevolent, such as terrorism and weapons proliferation.

Table 3

Tentative Links between Capacity/Will and Transnational Threats

	Capacity	Will
Terrorism		X
WMD Proliferation		X
Small Arms Proliferation	X	
Crime	X	X
Disease	X	
Energy Insecurity	X	X
Regional Instability	X	X

A second set of hypotheses links particular transnational threats to specific shortcomings in state performance. Weak states suffer from one or more of four functional gaps, in their ability to provide physical security, legitimate political institutions, effective economic management, or basic social welfare. Although any such hypotheses would need to be refined, it seems reasonable to predict that those states most associated either with transnational terrorism, proliferation risks, or regional instability would have shortcomings in security and political capacities; that infectious disease would rank low on social welfare, particularly health investments; and that transnational-crime as well as energy-insecurity candidates would lack stable political and economic institutions (see table 4). Assessing these hypotheses will require breaking state strength down into its component parts and testing whether gaps in these areas correlate with the relevant threats.

Table 4

Tentative Links between Governance Gaps and Transnational Threats

	Political	Security	Economic	Social
Terrorism	X	X		
Weapons Proliferation	X	X		
Crime	X		X	
Disease				X
Energy Insecurity	X		X	
Regional Instability	X	X		

A third testable hypothesis would be that some categories of threats are more closely correlated with the weakest quintile of states, whereas others are more typical of the next higher tier. The concept of spillover, after all, implies a transnational connection.

In some cases, such as violent conflicts or epidemics, spillovers can travel fairly easily from the weakest states. In other cases, including WMD proliferation and some forms of crime, the transnational diffusion of threats is more likely to come from states that are superficially strong but possess critical "sovereignty holes" and that provide easy access to the transportation, communications, and financial infrastructure of the global economy. If this hypothesis is borne out in empirical analysis, the implication is profound. A state need not possess capacity or commitment gaps across the board to pose a major risk of spillovers. A few critical gaps can make all the difference and should be targeted by external actors.

Working from these hypotheses, policymakers can begin to assemble a more effective strategy to address the specific threats presented by different characteristics of weak and failing states. Since late 2004, the National Intelligence Council has prepared a semiannual "Instability Watch List" that identifies countries at risk of state failure within two years. Although this development is welcome, busy policymakers find only marginal utility in periodic warning products that resemble the "conventional wisdom watch," with the requisite up and down arrows, that appears in *U.S. News and World Report* or *Newsweek*. To be useful, such a list should also be accompanied by a consequences matrix that outlines not only the potential negative developments within each country but also the implications of such turmoil for transnational threats such as disruption of oil supplies, regional instability, or WMD proliferation likely to affect U.S. national security interests. A sophisticated early-warning system could help policymakers determine where to devote U.S. efforts and help them build the political will for effective preventive action.

In addition, the U.S. government must replace its current fragmented approach to weak and failing states with a truly integrated strategy that allows it to bring all relevant tools of national power to bear in the service of coherent country plans. The State Department and Pentagon have made recent, modest progress in creating standing capacities to stabilize and rebuild war-torn societies, and they are beginning to coordinate the civilian and military sides of these undertakings. There has been no similar effort to define a unified interagency strategy to prevent states from sliding into failure and violence in the first place. Too often, Washington's engagement with weak states is in practice little more than a collection of independent bilateral diplomatic, military, aid, trade, and financial relationships, influenced by the institutional mandates and bureaucratic hobbyhorses of respective agencies. What is missing is a coordinated approach uniting the three Ds of U.S. foreign policy—defense, development, and diplomacy—as well as intelligence, financial, and trade policies. Integration must occur not only in Washington but also at U.S. embassies, within country teams under the direction of the ambassador. The precise country strategy will vary according to the perceived root causes of weakness. Where capacity is lacking, the United States should enable states to fill the gaps. Where will is lacking, the United States should deploy incentives to persuade or compel a stronger commitment. Where both are absent, the United States must try to change the attitudes of the country's leadership while working with civil society to build basic capacities and empower agents of reform.

Finally, the United States must spearhead a more coherent multilateral response to the linked challenges of state weakness and global threats. National governments and intergovernmental organizations are groping for new mechanisms and instruments to prevent and respond to state failure, but similar to internal U.S. efforts, progress has been hampered by fragmented institutional mandates. The United States should advance common approaches to state-building and transnational threats within the G-8, the UN, NATO, the Organization of American States, the OECD, and the World Bank and within regional bodies to which it does not belong, such as the European Union, the African Union, and the Association of Southeast Asian Nations. Such leadership would provide a tangible expression of the administration's espoused commitment to effective multilateral cooperation and of its willingness to help faltering states offer better futures to their citizens. This mission can unite developed and developing countries. Although transnational dangers are reshaping the rich world's security agenda, the poor countries nevertheless remain the main victims of global dangers such as crime, disease, and terrorism.

Weak and failing states can and do generate transnational spillovers such as terrorism, weapons proliferation, crime, disease, energy insecurity, and regional instability that endanger U.S. national interests and international security. At the same time, the blanket equation of weak states and global threats provides only modest analytic insights and even less practical guidance for policymakers. Each poorly performing country suffers from a distinctive set of pathologies and generates a unique mixture of challenges, of varying gravity.[59] There can be no one-size-fits-all response to addressing either the sources or consequences of these weaknesses. At a practical level, neither the United States nor its allies have the unlimited resources or attention spans required to launch ambitious state-building exercises in all corners of the world. U.S. officials will thus need to investigate the sources and consequences of transnational threats better and subsequently be able to set priorities and make tough choices about where, when, and how to engage weak and failing states to improve U.S. and international security.

Stewart Patrick is a research fellow at the Center for Global Development in Washington D.C, where he directs the project on Weak States and U.S. National Security. From 2002 to 2005, Dr. Patrick served on the U.S. Secretary of State's Policy Planning Staff. He is also a former International Affairs Fellow of the Council on Foreign Relations and research associate at the Center on International Cooperation at New York University.

Notes

1. Francis Fukuyama, *State-Building: Governance and World Order in the 21st Century* (Ithaca, N.Y.: Cornell University Press, 2004), p. 92. See John J. Hamre and Gordon R. Sullivan, "Toward Postconflict Reconstruction," *The Washington Quarterly* 25, no. 4 (Autumn 2002): 85–96; Susan E. Rice, "The New National Security Strategy: Focus on Failed States," *Brookings Policy Brief,* no. 116 (February 2003); Chester A. Crocker, "Engaging Failing States," *Foreign Affairs* 82, no. 5 (September/October 2003): 32–44; "Grappling With State Failure," *Washington Post,* June 9, 2004, p. A20; Mark Turner and Martin Wolf, "The Dilemma of Fragile States," *Financial Times,* February 18, 2005; Lee Hamilton, "The Dangerous Connection—Failed and Failing States, WMD, and Terrorism" (webcast, Woodrow Wilson International Center for Scholars, Washington, D.C., April 25, 2005), http://www.wilsoncenter. org/index.cfm?fuseaction=events.event&event_id=116497.
2. Adam Garfinkle, "A Conversation With Condoleezza Rice," *American Interest* 1, no. 1 (Autumn 2005): 47–50. See Richard Haass, "Sovereignty: Existing Rights, Evolving Responsibilities"

(speech, Georgetown University, Washington, D.C., January 14, 2003), http://www.state.gov/s/p/rem/2003/16648.htm; U.S. Agency for International Development (USAID), *Foreign Aid in the National Interest: Promoting Freedom, Security and Opportunity* (Washington, D.C.: USAID, 2003), p. 1; Caroline Daniel, "U.S. in Final Stage of National Security Revamp," *Financial Times,* January 5, 2006.

3. *National Security Strategy of the United States of America* (September 2002), p. 1, http://www.whitehouse.gov/nsc/nss.html.

4. *National Defense Strategy of the United States of America* (March 2005), http://www.defenselink.mil/news/Mar2005/d20050318nds1.pdf. See Bradley Graham, "Pentagon Strategy Aims to Block Internal Threats to Foreign Forces," *Washington Post,* March 19, 2005, p. A2; Jim Garamone, "Rumsfeld Describes Changing Face of War," Armed Forces Press Service, May 25, 2005.

5. George Tenet, "The World Wide Threat in 2003: Evolving Dangers in a Complex World," testimony before the Senate Select Committee on Intelligence, February 12, 2003; "Possible Remote Havens for Terrorists and Other Illicit Activity," May 2003 (unclassified Central Intelligence Agency [CIA] map).

6. Stephen D. Krasner and Carlos Pascual, "Addressing State Failure," *Foreign Affairs* 84, no. 4 (July/August 2005): 153–163; USAID, *Fragile States Strategy* (Washington, D.C.: USAID, February 2005); Robert Zoellick, "CAFTA is a Win-Win," *Washington Post,* May 24, 2005, p. A17.

7. Prime Minister's Strategy Unit (PMSU), *Investing in Prevention: An International Strategy to Manage Risks of Instability and Improve Crisis Response* (London: PMSU, February 2005).

8. Kofi Annan (speech, Council on Foreign Relations, New York, December 16, 2004). See High-Level Panel on Threats, Challenges and Change, "A More Secure World: Our Shared Responsibility," 2004, p. 9.

9. "Development Effectiveness in Fragile States," http://www.oecd.org/department/0,2688,en_2649_33693550_1_1_1_1_1,00.html.

10. Commission on Weak States and U.S. National Security, *On the Brink: Weak States and U.S. National Security* (Washington, D.C.: Center for Global Development, 2004); British Department for International Development (DFID), *Why We Need to Work More Effectively in Fragile States* (London: DFID, January 2005), pp. 27–28; "World Bank Group Work in Low-Income Countries Under Stress: A Task Force Report," September 2002. See "The Failed States Index," *Foreign Policy,* no. 149 (July/August 2005): 56–65 (developed by the Fund for Peace and *Foreign Policy,* focusing on susceptibility to instability and conflict as opposed to broader state capacities); Robert Rotberg, "Strengthening Governance: Ranking States Would Help," *The Washington Quarterly* 28, no. 1 (Winter 2004–05): 71–81; Ashraf Ghani, Clare Lockhart, and Michael Carnahan, "Closing the Sovereignty Gap: An Approach to State-Building," *Overseas Development Institute Working Paper,* no. 253, September 2005.

11. Office of the Press Secretary, The White House, "President Proposes $5 Billion Plan to Help Developing Nations," March 14, 2002, http://www.whitehouse.gov/news/releases/2002/03/20020314-7.html.

12. Michael Clemens and Todd Moss, "Costs and Causes of Zimbabwe's Crisis," *CGD Notes,* July 2005, http://www.cgdev.org/content/publications/detail/2918/.

13. DFID, *Why We Need to Work More Effectively in Fragile States,* p. 9; United Nations High Commission for Refugees, "2004 Global Refugee Trends," June 17, 2005, http://www.unhcr.org/cgi-bin/texis/vtx/events/opendoc.pdf?tbl=STATISTICS&id=42b283744; Paul Collier and Anke Hoeffler, "The Challenge of Reducing the Global Incidence of War," *Copenhagen Consensus Challenge Paper,* March 26, 2004, http://www.copenhagenconsensus.com/Files/Filer/CC/Papers/Conflicts_230404.pdf; Freedom House, *The Worst of the Worst: The World's Most Repressive Societies* (Washington, D.C.: Freedom House, 2004).

14. Daniel Kauffmann, Aart Kray, and Massimo Mastruzzi, *Governance Matters IV: Governance Indicators for 1996–2004* (Washington, D.C.: World Bank, 2005).

15. Center for Human Security, *Human Security Report 2005,* p. 92.
16. Gregory F. Treverton, "Enhancing Security Through Development: Probing the Connections" (Annual Bank Conference on Development Economics, Amsterdam, May 23–24, 2005), http://siteresources.worldbank.org/INTAMSTERDAM/Resources/GregTreverton.pdf; Peter Bergen and Laurie Garrett, "Report of the Working Group on State Security and Transnational Threats," Princeton Project on U.S. National Security, September 2005.
17. Justin Logan and Christopher Preble, "Failed States and Flawed Logic: The Case Against a Standing Nation-Building Office," *Policy Analysis,* no. 560 (January 11, 2006), http://www.cato.org/pubs/pas/pa560.pdf.
18. John Mearshimer, *The Tragedy of Great Power Politics* (New York: W.W. Norton, 2001); Gary T. Dempsey, "Old Folly in a New Disguise: Nation Building to Combat Terrorism," *Policy Analysis,* no. 429 (March 21, 2002), http://www.cato.org/pubs/pas/pa429.pdf.
19. "Fighting Terrorism at Gleneagles," *New York Times,* July 5, 2005, p. A22.
20. Monty G. Marshall, "Global Terrorism: An Overview and Analysis," September 12, 2002, p. 25, http://www.cidcm.umd.edu/inscr/papers/GlobalTerrorismmgm.pdf (report from the Center for International Development and Conflict Management, University of Maryland).
21. *Patterns of Global Terrorism* (Washington, D.C.: U.S. Department of State, 2003); *Country Reports on Terrorism* (Washington, D.C.: U.S. Department of State, 2005).
22. Ray Takeyh and Nicholas Gvosdev, "Do Terrorist Networks Need a Home?" *The Washington Quarterly* 25, no. 3 (Summer 2002): 97–108; Sebastian Mallaby, "The Reluctant Imperialist: Terrorism, Failed States and the Case for American Empire," *Foreign Affairs* 81, no. 2 (March/April 2002): 2–7.
23. Francis T. Miko, "Removing Terrorist Sanctuaries: The 9/11 Commission Recommendations and U.S. Policy," *CRS Report for Congress,* RL32518, August 10, 2004, http://www.maxwell.af.mil/au/awc/awcgate/crs/rl32518.pdf. See Princeton N. Lyman and J. Stephen Morrison, "The Terrorist Threat in Africa," *Foreign Affairs* 83, no. 1 (January/February 2004): 75–86.
24. Eric Schmitt, "As Africans Join Iraqi Insurgency, U.S. Counters With Military Training in Their Lands," *New York Times,* June 10, 2005, p. A11.
25. *National Strategy for Combating Terrorism* (February 2003), p. 22, http://www.whitehouse.gov/news/releases/2003/02/counter_terrorism/counter_terrorism_strategy.pdf.
26. Office of the Press Secretary, The White House, "President Addresses United Nations High-Level Plenary Meeting," September 14, 2005, http://www.whitehouse.gov/news/releases/2005/09/20050914.html.
27. Walter Laqueur, *No End to War: Terrorism in the Twenty-First Century* (New York: Continuum, 2003), p. 11.
28. Ken Menkhaus, "Somalia: State Collapse and the Threat of Terrorism," *Adelphi Paper* no. 364 (2004). See Greg Mills, "Africa's New Strategic Significance," *The Washington Quarterly* 27, no. 4 (Autumn 2004): 157–169.
29. Olivier Roy, *Globalized Islam: The Search for a New Ummah* (London: Hurst, 2004); Timothy M. Savage, "Europe and Islam: Crescent Waxing, Cultures Clashing," *The Washington Quarterly* 27, no. 3 (Summer 2004): 25–50.
30. Dana Priest, "Iraq New Terror Breeding Ground; War Created Haven, CIA Advisers Report," *Washington Post,* January 14, 2005, p. A1.
31. Daniel Byman, "Passive Sponsors of Terrorism," *Survival* 47, no. 4 (Winter 2005–06): 117–144.
32. PMSU, *Investing in Prevention,* p. 12. See *Deadly Arsenals* (Washington, D.C.: Carnegie Endowment for International Peace, 2005).
33. David Albright and Corey Hinderson, "Unraveling the A.Q. Khan and Future Proliferation Networks," *The Washington Quarterly* 28, no. 2 (Spring 2005): 111–128.
34. Graduate Institute of International Studies, *Small Arms Survey 2003: Development Denied* (Oxford: Oxford University Press, 2003), p. 57.
35. C. J. Chivers, "Ill-Secured Soviet Arms Depots Tempting Rebels and Terrorists," *New York Times,* July 16, 2005, p. A1.

36. *International Crime Threat Assessment* (Washington, D.C.: December 2000), p. 18, http://www.fas.org/irp/threat/pub45270index.html; Moises Naim, *Illicit: How Smugglers, Copycats and Traffickers Are Hijacking the Global Economy* (New York: Doubleday, 2005).

37. Peter Andreas, "Transnational Crime and Economic Globalization," in *Transnational Organized Crime and International Security: Business as Usual?*, eds. Mats Berdal and Monica Serrano (Boulder, Colo.: Lynne Rienner, 2002).

38. Phil Williams, "Transnational Criminal Enterprises, Conflict, and Instability," in *Turbulent Peace: The Challenges of Managing International Conflict,* eds. Chester Crocker, Fen Osler Hampson, and Pamela Aall (Washington, D.C.: United States Institute of Peace, 2001), pp. 97–112; UN Office on Drugs and Crime (UNODC), *Why Fighting Crime Can Assist Development in Africa: Rule of Law and Protection of the Most Vulnerable* (Vienna: UNODC, May 2005).

39. Williams, "Transnational Criminal Enterprises, Conflict, and Instability," p. 100.

40. U.S. Department of State, "Presidential Determination on Major Drug Transit or Major Illicit Drug Producing Countries for Fiscal Year 2006," *International Country Narcotics Strategy Reports,* September 15, 2005; UNODC, *2005 World Drug Report;* U.S. Department of State, "Trafficking in Persons Report," March 2005.

41. Clive Bell and Maureen Lewis, "The Economic Implications of Epidemics Old and New," *Center for Global Development Working Paper* no. 54, p. 31. See Allen Sipress, "Indonesia Stretched to the Limit in Battle Against Two Diseases," *Washington Post,* November 6, 2005, p. A19.

42. National Intelligence Council (NIC), *The Global Infectious Disease Threat and Its Implications for the United States* (Washington, D.C.: NIC, 2000).

43. Dennis Pirages, "Containing Infectious Disease," in *State of the World 2005: Redefining Global Security* (New York: W.W. Norton, 2005), p. 46; NIC, *Global Infectious Disease Threat,* fig. 9, http://www.cia.gov/cia/reports/nie/report/752049.gif.

44. Laurie Garrett, "HIV and National Security: Where Are the Links?" *Council on Foreign Relations Report,* 2005; Paul Collier et. al., *Breaking the Conflict Trap: Civil War and Development Policy* (Washington, D.C.: The World Bank and Oxford University Press, 2003); NIC, *Global Infectious Disease Threat,* p. 37.

45. World Bank, "The World Bank Responds to SARS," June 4, 2003, http://web.worldbank.org/WBSITE/EXTERNAL/NEWS/contentMDK:20114259~menuPK:34457~pagePK:34370~piPK:34424~theSitePK:4607,00.html.

46. NIC, *The Next Wave of HIV/AIDS: Nigeria, Ethiopia, Russia, India and China* (Washington, D.C.: NIC, 2002).

47. "China Reports Soaring Oil Imports," *BBC News,* September 14, 2004, http://news.bbc.co.uk/1/hi/business/3654060.stm.

48. Michael Klare, *Resource Wars: The New Landscape of Global Conflict* (New York: Henry Holt, 2001), p. 44.

49. PMSU, *Investing in Prevention,* p. 11; U.S. Department of Energy, "World Oil Transit Chokepoints," August 1999.

50. John Mintz, "Outcome Grim at Oil War Game," *Washington Post,* June 24, 2005, p. A19.

51. David L. Goldwyn and J. Stephen Morrison, "A Strategic Approach to U.S. Governance and Security in the Gulf of Guinea," July 2005 (report of the CSIS task force on Gulf of Guinea Security).

52. Fareed Zakaria, *The Future of Freedom: Illiberal Democracy at Home and Abroad* (New York: W.W. Norton, 2003), p. 75.

53. Michael E. Brown, ed., *The International Dimensions of Internal Conflict* (Cambridge, Mass: MIT Press, 1996).

54. Myron Weiner, "Bad Neighbors, Bad Neighborhoods: An Inquiry Into the Causes of Refugee Flows," *International Security* 21, no. 1 (Summer 1996): 5–42.

55. Barnett Rubin, *Blood on the Doorstep: The Politics of Preventive Action* (New York: Century Foundation/Council on Foreign Relations, 2002), pp. 134–137.

56. Jeffrey D. Sachs, "The Strategic Significance of Global Inequality," *The Washington Quarterly* 24, no. 3 (Summer 2001): 187–198.

57. UN Department of Peacekeeping Operations, "Operations Timeline," http://www.un.org/Depts/dpko/dpko/timeline/pages/timeline.html.

58. Paul Collier and L. Chauvet, "Presentation to the DAC Learning and Advisory Process on Difficult Partnerships," November 5, 2004.

59. Simon Chesterman, Michael Ignatieff, and Ramesh Thakur, eds., *Making States Work: State Failure and the Crisis of Governance* (Tokyo: United Nations University, 2005), p. 359.

Chapter 3

The New Terrorism

Brigadier General (Retired) Russell Howard [this books co-editor] presents a framework for understanding the new terrorism. This framework distinguishes between the old politically motivated terrorist and the new transnational religiously motivated terrorist. He argues that terrorism is more violent, groups operate globally; they are better financed, better trained, and more difficult to penetrate; and the potential future use of weapons of mass destruction completely changes the calculus of today's terrorists. The nexus of these elements creates an enemy that is difficult to find, difficult to defeat, and very dangerous. In thinking about this more dangerous world, it is important to understand how terrorism has changed so that we can move to a better understanding of how to address the problem in a comprehensive manner. Howard's framework is the starting point for any such analysis.

John Arquilla, David Ronfeldt, and Michele Zanini examine changes in terrorism in the information age. The classic motivation and rationales will not change, but conduct and operational characteristics of terrorism will change. The authors explore—often in what they outline as a deliberately speculative manner—organizational changes that allow for less hierarchical structures and flatter networks of power with dense communications; they look at changes in strategy and technology and the manner in which terrorism is evolving toward what they label as *netwar.*

The third article, "The Post-Madrid Face of al-Qaeda" by Rohan Gunaratna, examines the shift in al-Qaeda from a group to that of an ideology. He argues that al-Qaeda's role as a terrorist group is complete—that the group has inspired other groups, individuals, and a rising generation of militants to join the fight. The Madrid attacks symbolizes the changing nature of the battlefield from the Global South—places such as Bali, Casablanca, and Saudi Arabia—to the Global North. He argues that a singular focus on al-Qaeda as a group will preclude intelligence and law enforcement agencies from comprehending the changing nature of the threat. To be truly effective in this conflict, counterterror governments must focus their attention not only on the established groups but also on their support cells and ideologues.

Finally, Natasha Bajema argues that increasing terrorist technological and financial capabilities to plan and execute lethal attacks are not the only significant aspect of new terrorism. Drawing on Homer-Dixon's concept of complex terrorism, she demonstrates how the increasing vulnerability of economic and technological systems combined with the growing capabilities of terrorists raises the appeal of potential targets, such as nuclear power plants. In contrast to traditional threat assessments that typically account for terrorist capabilities to attack a nuclear facility and security measures taken at nuclear facilities, Bajema assesses the threat of nuclear sabotage by considering broader elements of the strategic context for a nuclear power plant including nuclear waste disposal, global climate change, and energy security. Bajema concludes that increasing demands for electricity production, growing concerns about global warming, and the fragile state of the U.S. plan for nuclear waste disposal are interacting to increase the appeal of nuclear power plants as terrorist targets.

Brigadier General (Retired) Russell D. Howard

The New Terrorism

Professor Bruce Hoffman, a professor at Georgetown University and a contributor to this book and arguably one of the world's leading terrorism experts, put it this way: "I don't mean to sound perverse, but there is maybe certain nostalgia for the old style of terrorism, where there wasn't the threat of loss of life on a massive scale. It's a real commentary on how much the world has changed."[1] In much the same way that many Cold Warriors miss the predictability and transparency of the U.S.-Soviet confrontation, many intelligence professionals, military operators, pundits, and academics miss the familiar type of terrorism that, although quite dangerous, in the end was merely a nasty sideshow to the greater East-West conflict.[2] Much of this "Cold War" terrorism was inspired by Marxist-Leninist ideology; its perpetrators sought to draw attention to their cause and to gain political concessions. They were motivated by secular rather than apocalyptic ends and were quick to claim responsibility for their attacks.[3] The commando-style terrorism, waged by the likes of Andreas Baader and Ulrike Meinhof of the German extreme left Rote Armee Fraction or by Abu Nidal of the Fatah National Council (who was killed in Baghdad in 2002), was ruthless. But it was not nearly as deadly as the threat the world faces today.[4] Now the old, predominantly state-sponsored terrorism has been supplanted by a religiously and ethnically motivated terrorism that "neither relies on the support of sovereign states nor is constrained by the limits on violence that state sponsors observed themselves or placed on their proxies."[5]

American security experts and intelligence analysts have not yet come to terms with the nature of al-Qaeda and like-minded groups or with how they differ from the terrorist groups, with which I was familiar with during the Cold War. One difference is the alleged objective. While Cold War terrorist groups had goals that were theoretically attainable and mostly political in nature, "al-Qaeda goes beyond the political into what Ralph Peters, military strategist and author, calls the transcendental—a vision formed by religion."[6]

Many new terrorist motives have also emerged. Terrorist groups such as al-Qaeda have international objectives, and globalization has enabled and facilitated terrorists' worldwide goals. "Rather than using terrorism to create change within a single society or focus on a specific government, terrorism has gone international to support global causes, and the U.S. and the West have become primary targets."[7] Terrorist attacks have become increasingly sophisticated and designed to achieve mass casualties, and this is likely to continue. However, the distinction between old and new terrorism goes beyond an increasing magnitude of deliberate mass-casualty attacks against civilians and non-combatants. These attacks are targeted against societies ever more vulnerable since they depend on openness and globalization for their existence. [8]

This new terrorism has a much greater potential to cause harm to America, the West, and all secular countries, including those in the Muslim world. Led by al-Qaeda and Osama bin Laden, it "is built around loosely linked cells that do not rely on a single leader or state sponsor." The new terrorism is transnational, borderless, and prosecuted by non-state actors, and it is very, very dangerous.[9]

The old and new styles of terrorism are distinguishable in at least eight different ways:

1. The terrorist attacks on September 11, 2001 effectively shattered the illusion of an invulnerable U.S. homeland, protected by two oceans and bordered by friendly or weak neighbors. In the past, the nation was not vulnerable to terrorists, except for the homegrown, mostly right-wing variety such as the Oklahoma City bomber. Now, the American homeland is very much at risk. "When, not if" is how many terrorism experts regard the likelihood of another 9/11 type attack.

2. The new terrorism is more violent. Under the old paradigm, terrorists wanted attention, not mass casualties. Now they want both.

3. Unlike their Cold War counterparts, who were usually sub-state actors trying to effect change in local politics, today's terrorists are transnational, non-state actors who operate globally and want to destroy the West and all Islamic secular states.

4. The new terrorists are much better financed than their predecessors, who relied mainly on crime or the largess of state sponsors. Today's terrorists have income streams from legal and illegal sources, and are not accountable to state sponsors—or anybody else.

5. Today's terrorists are better trained. We know this from the materials captured in al-Qaeda's training camps in Afghanistan and from the similar training materials of other Muslim extremist groups found in Europe and Central Asia.

6. This generation's terrorists are more difficult to penetrate than terrorists of previous generations. The networked, cellular structure used by al-Qaeda and its allies is especially difficult to penetrate for a hierarchical security apparatus like that of the United States. Bribes and sex traps could catch terrorists for prosecution and information in the old days; it is difficult to "turn" religious extremists with these methods. The $50 million reward on Osama bin Laden has yet to be collected, and it is unclear how successful other methods have been in getting bin Laden's followers to talk.

7. Most insidious, however, is the widespread availability of weapons-usable materials and increasing concern that terrorists might use weapons of mass destruction (WMD). In the 1980s, when I first became engaged in counterterrorism, we were concerned about small arms, explosives (particularly plastique), rocket propelled grenades, and the occasional shoulder-fired anti-aircraft missile. Today, the concern is about nuclear, radiological, chemical, and biological weapons—all potentially catastrophic, with massive killing potential.

8. Victory will be elusive. More than likely there will be no formal surrender by a defeated foe, no armistice ending combat on acceptable terms, no arrest and incarceration of all the members of a terrorist organization. There will be no victory

parade. At best, the U.S. and the West can probably return to a life of inconvenience with infrequent incidents. However, free societies will have to remain vigilant and permanently on alert. Not doing so will invite those who want to harm us to attack again, possibly with a nuclear, radiological, chemical, or biological weapon.

This article discusses these eight distinguishing characteristics of the new terrorism and argues that they must be understood and addressed if the United States and the West hope to prevail. Osama bin Laden's al-Qaeda is the principal case study for this work because his ideology, organization, surrogates, and followers epitomize the new terrorism and are the number-one threat to America's security. Other terrorist groups, particularly Hezbollah, are also discussed. Aside from al-Qaeda, no terrorist group has killed more Americans and none pose a more formidable threat.[10]

America at Risk

The 9/11 terrorist attacks shattered the illusion that Americans are safe from troubles originating beyond our shores, traditionally protected by geography and by weak or friendly neighbors. The attacks forced American citizens and policymakers to learn how to fight a new kind of war. Some have compared September 11, 2001, to December 7, 1941, the only other occasion since the War of 1812 that American territory has been attacked.[11] There are many similarities. Both were surprise attacks, were predictable and possibly avoidable, were extraordinarily costly in life and national treasure, and were defining points in American history. However, as David Halberstam notes in *War in a Time of Peace,* there are also many differences. According to Halberstam, the historical demarcation point that the U.S. crossed on 9/11 is even greater than the one it crossed with the bombing of Pearl Harbor.[12] The post–Pearl Harbor war was easily understood. The enemy was a state, and interstate warfare was more traditional, definable, and susceptible to American's industrial and technological advantages. Today's enemy is not a state but a transnational, non-state actor. The method of warfare is not traditional: it is more elusive, operates in the shadows often at a great distance, but also sometimes right among us with secret cells and aliases, and it exploits America's industrial and technological advantages.[13]

Also different, seems to be the resolve of the American people to wage war. Throughout our history, Americans have traditionally displayed an extraordinary degree of resourcefulness and self-sacrifice in times of war.[14] The best example of that tradition is World War II, when the war effort became an immediate extension of America's national will and purpose.[15] Today, says Stephen Flynn, "we are breaking with that tradition. Our nation faces grave peril, but we seem unwilling to mobilize at home to confront the threat before us."[16] For example, at the height of World War II, the United States committed roughly 36 percent of its gross domestic product (GDP) to the war effort, and when the Japanese surrendered on the battleship Missouri in 1945, America had more than 12 million men and women in uniform. Presently, less than 4 percent of U.S. GDP is committed to the campaign against terrorism, and of the 2.6 million men and women presently in uniform 1.4 million are in the National Guard and Reserve.[17] Unlike during World War II, when America's productive capacity was focused on the war effort, today there are no shortages, no rationing, and the production of goods and services for the consumer market runs unabated.

Why are the American people unwilling to mobilize at home? Three reasons come to mind. First, they understand conventional war but not the war on terror. Second, they fail to realize the security implications of globalization and information technology. Third, they are not generally affected by the war unless their children—less than one half of 1 percent of the U.S. population—are fighting it. Some, including this author have said that it might take another catastrophic terrorist event in the U.S. before the nation wakes up to the security realities of the 21st century.

The war on terror is not like engaging an enemy amassed on a foreign battlefield. Destroying or confiscating the enemy's battlefield capabilities and dispersing its troops will not ensure victory.[18] Today, as Halberstam explained, "the more visible the enemy is, the further he is from the magnetic field of our intelligence operations and any potential military strike."[19]

> It is not that America, as it enters a very different kind of battle, lacks weaponry; it is that the particular kind of weaponry we specialize in lacks targets. This will be a difficult military-intelligence-security challenge: What we do best, they are not vulnerable to. What we do least well, they are vulnerable to. What they do best, we are—to a considerable degree—vulnerable to.[20]

Combating terrorism, particularly the Islamic extremist variety, is as much about fighting an international idea as it is about an organized military force maneuvering within defined geographical boundaries. The danger posed by al-Qaeda, its followers, and its surrogates and other Islamic extremists cannot be managed by relying primarily on military campaigns overseas. "There are no fronts in the war on terrorism."[21]

> The 9/11 attacks highlighted the fact that our borders offer no effective barrier to terrorists intent on bringing their war to our soil. Nor do their weapons have to be imported, since they have proven how easy it is to exploit the modern systems we rely upon in our daily lives and use them against us.[22]

These modern systems are the sophisticated networks that move people, goods, energy, money, and information at higher volumes and greater velocities[23]—the very systems that ensure America's competitive edge in the age of globalization. For years, our growing dependence on these networks has not been matched by a parallel focus on securing them.[24]

> The architects of these networks have made efficiency and diminishing costs their highest priority. Security considerations have been widely perceived as annoying speed bumps in achieving their goals. As a result, the systems that underpin our prosperity are soft targets for those bent on challenging U.S. power.[25]

The attacks on the World Trade Center and the Pentagon ended a unique historical span for the U.S. as a great power. For nearly a century, America has been a major player in the world; but until 9/11, the homeland had escaped the ravages of modern warfare and weaponry because of its unique geographical position and unparalleled industrial technological base. When confronted with threats, the U.S. dealt with them on our adversaries "or allies" turf. Except for the occasional disaster or heinous crime, life in America had been terror-free. It has taken a group of rebels without a country—a ghost nation as it were—to pose a threat to America and our way of life.[26]

More Violent

In the past, "terrorists wanted a lot of people watching, not a lot of people dead."[27] Unlike the terrorists of the 1960s to the 1990s, who generally avoided high-casualty attacks for fear of the negative publicity they would generate, al-Qaeda is not in the least worried about that.[28] Terrorists in past decades did not want large body counts because they wanted converts; they also wanted a seat at the table. Today's terrorists are not particularly concerned about converts, and rather than wanting a seat at the table, "they want to destroy the table and everyone sitting at it."[29] Religious terrorists, al-Qaeda, in particular, want casualties—lots of them.[30]

The dominant terrorist activities in the past were abductions of individuals or groups, such as air passengers, to extort political concessions and/or financial concessions.[31] Unfortunate civilians usually became victims of terrorist operations because they were captives of hostage-taking events, and because they happened to be in the wrong place at the wrong time. Terrorists took hostages for three reasons: to gain attention for their cause, the release of imprisoned comrades, or ransom. The odds were—96 percent of the time in the 1980s—that hostages would survive the event. Victims were generally casualties because they happened to be in the proximity of an explosion, ambush, or bank robbery. However, the motive of these terrorists was to get attention or money, not cause the deaths of civilians.

The destruction of the World Trade Center marks the preliminary peak of a trend which started some years ago: making terror absolute.[32] As Osama bin Laden points out in the following quote: the aim is the maximization of damage, preferably by causing the maximum number of casualties.

> By causing mass casualties on a regular basis [bin Laden] could hope to persuade the Americans to keep clear of overseas conflicts. There was also a retributive element to the strategy . . . the militants of al-Qaeda and like-minded groups clearly wanted to punish the Americans for a whole range of policies, particularly for those it pursued in the Middle East, as well as for what they saw as its irreligious decadence.[33]

For example, nine months after the attack on New York, Osama bin Laden forwarded a chilling announcement on a now defunct al-Qaeda-affiliated Web site, www.alneda.com, stating: "We have the right to kill four million Americans—two million of them children—and to exile twice as many and wound and cripple hundreds of thousands."[34]

Despite successes against al-Qaeda by coalition military forces in Afghanistan, in Iraq and by police agencies around the world, the frequency and reach of al-Qaeda's attacks have continued to increase. Fortunately, despite continuing al-Qaeda efforts to perpetuate mass casualty attacks—the foiled plot to hijack several U.S. airliners in the UK and continued efforts to acquire WMD for example—the lethality of the 9/11 attack has not been eclipsed.[35]

Truly Global: Conducted by Transnational, Non-State Actors

In the 1970s and 1980s, terrorism was mostly local. It was mainly ideologically motivated and nationalistic in nature; terrorists pursued clearly identifiable political, economic and social goals.[36] The terrorists were usually state-sponsored, sub-state actors intent on overturning a state's political and/or economic system. Today, there has been a shift from localized terrorist groups, supported by states such as the Soviet Union, to loosely organized global networks. Today, the new terrorists have global motives and capabilities. They are backed by like-minded organizations throughout the world and in many respects, have achieved *de facto* sovereign status by acquiring the means to conduct war—and have in fact declared war—posing significant military and security policy challenges for which the U.S. and the West had no preplanned response.[37] The "new terrorism" of the 1990s and beyond has been dominated—not only since 9/11—by Islamic extremists whose motives are more abstract and absolute. This parallels a change from primarily politically motivated terrorism to a more religiously motivated variety and a change also in structure.[38] The most active international terrorist groups are no longer centralized, hierarchically structured organizations, but networks of relatively autonomous cells, inspired and directed but not controlled by charismatic leaders.[39]

Al-Qaeda's global network consists of independently operating permanent or semi-permanent cells of trained militants in more than 76 countries.[40] In fact, since 9/11 more than 4,300 al-Qaeda operatives, hailing from 49 countries, have been arrested in 97 countries.[41] Moreover, the concept of global terrorism applies not just to al-Qaeda but collectively to many terrorist organizations throughout the world. These organizations operate through an interconnected network that often provides mutual aid and support making it difficult to isolate a particular group or faction.[42] There is also growing evidence that al-Qaeda is now subcontracting work to like-minded terrorists. According to Jessica Stern:

> Bin Laden's organization has also nurtured ties with a variety of other groups around the world, including: Ansar al Islam, based mainly in Iraq and Europe, Jemaah Islamiah in Southeast Asia, Abus Sayyaf and the Moro Islamic Liberation Front in the Philippines, and many Pakistani jihadi groups.[43]

These affiliated or like-minded groups have the capacity to carry out attacks and inflict pain on the U.S. under al-Qaeda's banner, says Bruce Hoffman. In fact, new revelations about the emerging al-Qaeda network—the depth of its ranks and its ties to "franchise" terrorists in up to 70 countries—show that the intent to attack America, the West, and secular states around the world has not diminished.[44] According to some, successes against al-Qaeda in Afghanistan, Iraq, and elsewhere may have made defeating the organization even more difficult. Since al-Qaeda lost its sanctuary in Afghanistan, Jason Burke believes "there is no longer a central hub for Islamic militancy."[45] Instead, the al-Qaeda worldview, or "al-Qaedaism," is what sustains acts of terrorism against the West and the United States.[46]

This radical internationalist ideology—sustained by anti-Western, anti-Zionist, and anti-Semitic rhetoric—has adherents among many individuals and groups, few of whom are currently linked in any substantial way to bin Laden or those around him. They merely follow his precepts, models, and methods. They act in the style of al-Qaeda, but they are only part of al-Qaeda in the very loosest sense.[47] Perhaps most troubling is recent evidence that al-Qaeda—a Sunni organization—has cooperated and continues to cooperate with Hezbollah, a Shiite group considered by many to be the most sophisticated terrorist organization in the world.[48] Israel learned this the hard way in its recent military operations against Hezbollah in Lebanon. "Shock and Awe" operations against Hezbollah and Lebanon were no more effective than "Shock and Awe" operations in Iraq at the opening of the second Gulf War. "Hezbollah, which enjoys backing from Syria and Iran, is based in southern Lebanon and in the lawless 'tri-border' region of South America, where Paraguay, Brazil, and Argentina meet."[49] Hezbollah also has a worldwide network and has sleeper cells in Asia, Africa Europe, North America, and South America.[50]

Al-Qaeda's targeting is global, which is also different from the local, tactical focus of earlier terrorist groups. Now, not only are targets selected to cause casualties without limit, they are selected to undermine the global economy. "They might be called strategic acts of destruction, rather than the tactical terrorist acts of the past."[51] According to Air Marshall Sir Timothy Garden, "it may have been possible for the international community to live with occasional acts of local terrorism around the world; it is much more difficult to live with non-state actors who have a mission to destroy a large part of the global system."[52]

In summary, we have seen a threat posed by non-state actors spanning the globe that exploit open societies, porous borders and differences in state legal structures and international law to perpetrate their acts. The terrorists who masterminded the 9/11 attacks were part of a diffuse network bound by a common terrorist ideology rather than a particular citizenship or ethnicity. "They reduced their risks by plotting their crime in Germany, which has the greatest controls preventing undercover policing and surveillance in Europe, and committing their crimes in the United States, exploiting its open borders and uncontrolled movements of visitors and citizens."[53] We have also seen the emergence of terrorism that is not ideological in a political sense but is inspired by religious extremists working in cells, small groups, and larger coalitions.[54] They do not answer to any government, they operate across national borders, and they have access to funding and advanced technology.[55] Such groups are not bound by the same constraints or motivated by the same goals as nation-states. And unlike state-sponsored groups, religious extremists such as al-Qaeda are not susceptible to traditional diplomacy or military deterrence. There is no state with which to negotiate or against which to retaliate.

Well-Financed

Al-Qaeda learned from the failings of previous terrorist groups, such as the Baeder Meinhof, Red Brigades, and the Abu Nidal group, all of which were perennially undercapitalized. According to Bruce Hoffman, al-Qaeda under Osama bin Laden saw the need to be much more flexible and to maintain a steady supply of money, which is crucial to lubricate the wheels of terrorism.[56]

Estimates of Osama bin Laden's personal wealth range from $18 million to as high as $200 million, but "it is most commonly agreed that bin Laden inherited approximately $57 million at age sixteen"[57] and received a million dollars a year between 1970 and 1994.[58] Bin Laden has been able to leverage his millions into a global financial empire by investing in legitimate businesses, taking advantage of the globalized financial system, abusing the Islamic banking (*hawala*) system, and coercing an entire network of Islamic philanthropic and charitable institutions. The total net worth of the al-Qaeda financial empire is unclear—I would put it in the hundreds of millions. Between September 11, 2001, and October 2002, more than 165 countries enacted blocking actions against terrorist assets, and approximately $112 million of these assets have been frozen worldwide

($34 million in the U.S. and $78 million overseas).[59] According to at least one report, international efforts to curtail terrorists' fund-raising, money-laundering, and financing activities have resulted in a 90 percent reduction in al-Qaeda's income, compared with before 9/11.[60] However, most experts disagree and believe that al-Qaeda and like-minded terrorist groups have moved out of normal channels into other sources of revenue that sustain operations at near pre-9/11 levels. For example, in a dissertation published by RAND, Steven Kiser concluded that al-Qaeda's financial infrastructure has shown an impressive ability to adapt to adverse conditions, quickly taking advantage of available opportunities, pursuing creative, nontraditional, and unorthodox methods of money management, and geographically moving operations to areas where laws are lax or nonexistent.[61] Interestingly, between January and September 2001, anticipating that U.S. would engage in robust initiatives to counter the financing of terrorism following the 9/11 attacks, bin Laden began moving al-Qaeda's easily traceable assets into not-traceable diamonds from Charles Taylor's Liberia to the Antwerp diamond market.[62]

In fact, Osama bin Laden's entrepreneurial skills are legendary. During his five-year stint in Sudan, he cornered the market on gum arabic, the basic ingredient in fruit juices produced in the United States.[63] "He also started an Islamic Bank, built a tannery, created an export company, launched construction projects and developed agricultural schemes."[64] Other business ventures included a trading company in Kenya and a ceramic plant, publishing outlet, and appliance firm in Yemen.[65]

Al-Qaeda's misuse of the ancient *hawala* underground banking system, which allows money transfers without actual money movement, is particularly instructive. Seemingly custom-made for al-Qaeda, the *hawala* is an ancient system that originated in South Asia and is still used worldwide to conduct legitimate business as well as for money laundering. The components of *hawala,* which distinguish it from other parallel remittance systems, are trust and the extensive use of connections, such as family relationships or regional affiliations. Unlike traditional banking, *hawala* makes minimal use of any sort of negotiable instruments or documentation. Transfers of money take place based on communications between members of a network of *hawaladars,* or *hawala* dealers.[66] A recent Council on Foreign Relations study illustrates how the *hawala* system works:

> Customers in one city hand their local *hawaladar* some money. That individual then contacts his counterpart across the world, who in turn distributes money out of his own resources to the intended recipient. The volume of transactions flowing through the system in both directions is such that the two *hawaladars* rarely have to worry about settlement.[67]

Hawaladars charge their customers a nominal cash transaction fee for the service. They are willing to carry each other's debts for long periods of time because they are often related through familial, clan, or ethnic associations.[68]

Al-Qaeda also uses other methods to move funds. Cash smuggling is one; moving assets in the form of precious metals and gemstones is another. The gold trade and the *hawala* are especially symbiotic: they flourish in the same locales and offer complementary services to those moving assets across borders. Al-Qaeda also uses traditional smuggling routes and methods favored by international drug traffickers, arms dealers, and other organized criminal groups.[69]

Charities and philanthropic organizations have also been used to move funds and are sources of al-Qaeda funding. "The al-Qaeda organization uses charities to move money. Funds going to charities are, indeed, directed toward social welfare activities in the community, but a traditional 10 percent tithe, or sometimes a much greater share, is used to support terrorist activity."[70] "Since December 2001, the assets of more than a dozen Islamic charities worldwide have been frozen, three of them based in the United States."[71] For example, U.S. authorities have designated the U.S.-based Benevolence International Foundation (BIF) as a terrorist financier with links to the al-Qaeda network, and its assets have been frozen in the U.S., Canada, and Bosnia. But the bin Laden network is not the only terrorist group skimming funds from U.S.-based charities.[72] In fact, the U.S. Treasury Department found overwhelming evidence that the Holy Land Foundation for Relief and Development, the self-proclaimed largest Muslim charity in the United States, was an arm of Hamas, a radical Islamic organization that operates in the West Bank and Gaza strip.[73]

Al-Qaeda-trained cells choose from a variety of methods to obtain local funding. "Credit card fraud, car theft and document forgery are popular among Algerian cells in Europe.[74] In North America, terrorist financiers practice cigarette smuggling and coupon scams, both of which provide large profits but result in minor penalties if apprehended."[75]

More recently, there is evidence that financial operations are taking place between Islamist organizations—notably al-Qaeda and affiliates—and criminal organizations. According to Steven Kiser:

> Al-Qaeda appears to have a cooperative but limited relationship with some organized criminal networks, using these organizations to acquire materials they require for terrorist attacks, as well as aiding in the laundering money. The biggest links are with rebel groups that also served as diamond smuggling networks in western Africa. Al-Qaeda's affiliates also are beginning to cooperate with organized crime. For example, Abu Sayyaf now raises funds through kidnapping ransoms, piracy and gunrunning.[76]

Additionally, the terrorists responsible for the bombings on March 11, 2004 in Madrid are believed to have funded their operation at least partially through the sale of narcotics.[77]

Well-Trained

Formalized terrorist training during the Cold War was generally conducted by the states sponsoring terrorist groups. It is known, for instance, that the former Soviet Union ran terrorism training camps at Simferpol in the Crimea, Ostrova in Czechoslovakia, and Pankow in East Germany. Captured PLO terrorist Adnan Jaber has given a comprehensive account of his Soviet training:

> He did a six-month course there, during which Russian military and civilian instructors covered propaganda methods, political affairs, tactics and weapons. Other such courses dealt with advanced explosives work, bomb-making, and training in biological and chemical warfare.[78]

However, it would be incorrect to assume that most terrorists during the Cold War years went through such formal training. More than likely, many went into action without such instruction and simply learned by doing.[79]

This is not at all the case today. In fact, graduating from a training camp is the common denominator and rite of passage for al-Qaeda operatives and their allies. The camps have trained both formal al-Qaeda members and members of allied Islamist organizations.[80]

Al-Qaeda manuals and records captured in Afghanistan training camps portray a comprehensive program that emphasizes paramilitary training, Islamic studies, and current politics. Common to all members of al-Qaeda and its associated groups are the following personality traits and qualifications, which are required before one can become an Islamist military operative:

> Knowledge of Islam, ideological commitment, maturity, self-sacrifice, discipline, secrecy and concealment of information, good health, patience, unflappability, intelligence and insight, caution and prudence, truthfulness and wisdom, and the ability to observe and analyze, and the ability to act.[81]

Aspiring operatives are also taught forgery, assassination techniques, and the conducting of maritime or vehicle suicide attacks.[82] As a means of avoiding sophisticated National Security Administration signal intelligence capabilities, al-Qaeda teaches its operatives how to use couriers and sophisticated telecommunications, the Internet, and encryption technologies to try to outfox U.S. surveillance.[83]

An al-Qaeda manual, *Military Studies in the Jihad Against the Tyrants,* which was seized in Manchester, England, at the home of a bin Laden follower, is a condensed version of thousands of pages of al-Qaeda training materials seized in Afghanistan. An English translation of the 180-page Arabic document was placed in evidence during the recent Kenya and Tanzania bombing trials in New York City. The manual is extraordinarily comprehensive and instructs terrorist operatives in an array of techniques, including Jihad (Holy War), military organization, financial precautions and forged documents, security measures in public transportation, special operations and weapons, guidelines for beating and killing hostages, how to assassinate with poisons, spoiled food, and feces, and methods of physical and psychological torture.[84]

Al-Qaeda's training is very eclectic and comprehensive; its tacticians and trainers have taken much from the special operations forces of several nations, including the U.S., U.K., and Russia. Indeed, al-Qaeda fighters are as well or better trained than those of many national armies (as was the case in Afghanistan) and in many cases the case in Iraq against new, American-trained Iraqi armed forces and police. What is even more startling is its intelligence and "black operations" acumen. "Unlike the rag-tag terrorist groups of the Cold War period" says Rohan Gunaratna, "sophisticated terrorist groups of the post-Cold War period, such as al-Qaeda, have developed intelligence wings comparable to government intelligence agencies."[85]

Losing the Afghanistan sanctuary and their training camps did not stop al-Qaeda from training new recruits because they shifted their training venue from stationary camps to the Internet.[86] Nearly four years after their defeat in Afghanistan, al-Qaeda became the first terrorist movement in history to migrate from physical space to cyberspace. With laptops and DVDs, in secret hideouts and at neighborhood Internet cafes, young code-writing jihadists replicate the training, communication, planning and preaching facilities they lost in Afghanistan with countless new locations on the Internet.[87]

Al-Qaeda suicide bombers and ambush units in Iraq routinely use the Web for training, relying on the Internet's anonymity and flexibility to operate with near impunity in cyberspace. Also, in Qatar, Egypt and Europe, cells affiliated with al-Qaeda that have recently carried out or seriously planned bombings have relied heavily on the Internet.[88]

According to longtime terrorism expert Dennis Pluchinsky, Western intelligence agencies and outside terrorism experts now conclude that the "global jihad movement"—led by al-Qaeda, "surrogate groups and ad hoc cells"—has become a "Web-directed" phenomenon.[89] "Hampered by the nature of the Internet itself, the government has proven ineffective at blocking or even hindering significantly this vast online presence."[90]

Among other things, al-Qaeda and like-minded jihadis are building a massive and dynamic online library of training materials—some supported by experts who answer questions on message boards or in chat rooms—covering such varied subjects as how to mix ricin poison, how to make a bomb from commercial chemicals, how to pose as a fisherman and sneak through Syria into Iraq, how to shoot at a U.S. soldier, and how to navigate by the stars while running through a night-shrouded desert. These materials are cascading across the Web in Arabic, Urdu, Pashto and other first languages of jihadist volunteers.[91]

Difficult to Penetrate

Another difference between old and new terrorism is that the latter has adopted a networked and less hierarchical form. "Both the anti-capitalist and national liberation terrorist groups of the 1970s and 1980s mostly had hierarchical forms and chains of command."[92] But in response to improvements in counterterrorism capabilities and increased cooperation among governments, groups like al-Qaeda have adopted networked structural models instead of hierarchical structures. They resemble modern "flat" business structures such as "Craigslist" rather than the multilayer organizations found in older corporations such as Ford Motor Company.[93] Rapid advances in digital communication have also increased the viability of these networks, though they are not totally dependent on the latest information technology. "While information technology has made networks more effective, low-tech means such as couriers and landline telephones can enable networks in certain circumstances."[94]

Strict adherence to a flat, diffused, cellular, networked structure has allowed al-Qaeda to maintain a high degree of secrecy and security. "These cells are independent of other local groups al-Qaeda may be aligned with and range in size from two to fifteen members."[95] Using code, targets are announced in the general media, and individuals or independent cells are expected to use initiative, stealth, and flexibility to destroy them.

The network will obviously be more likely to achieve long-term effectiveness if its members share a unifying ideology, common goals, and mutual interests, as is the case with al-Qaeda.[96] Networks are most effective when they distribute the responsibility for operations and provide redundancies for key functions. "Operating cells need not contact or coordinate with other cells except for those essential to a particular operation or function."[97] Avoiding unnecessary coordination or approval provides deniability to terrorist leaders and enhances the security of terrorist operations.

Washington's predilection for technical means of intelligence collection at the expense of covert and clandestine operations with human sources, compounded by an acute lack of culturally attuned operatives, analysts, and linguists, has contributed greatly to the inability of U.S. operators to penetrate tightly knit cells of al-Qaeda and other militant Islamic groups.[98]

Al-Qaeda's loss of sanctuary in Afghanistan has forced it to disperse and go underground, thus making it more difficult to penetrate. Also, like-minded terrorist organizations operating on their own in loosely affiliated groups have increased. "In particular, Islamic terrorist groups tend to be loosely organized, recruit their members from many different countries, and obtain support from an informal international network of like-minded extremists."[99] The new terrorism resembles a virus that morphs as its environment changes. Individual cells and nodes evolve their own strategy, and if hit, will adapt, regroup, generate new leadership, shift locations, adjust tactics, and evolve into a new set of cells and networks capable of reconstitution, dispersal, and innovation.[100] The resulting transnational and decentralized structure helps terrorists to avoid detection and penetration.[101]

Though weakened by the disruption of its finances and communications, its base destroyed, and its leaders in flight, al-Qaeda is still dangerous and very difficult to penetrate.[102] While sharing a common militant Islamic ideology, al-Qaeda has become a loose and "ever-shifting alliance of like-minded groups."[103] Instead of large, well-orchestrated attacks like those of 9/11, al-Qaeda operations are now smaller and less ambitious. They remain extremely dangerous, however, and their "killer cells" seem to be growing and spawning imitations around the world.[104]

Access to Weapons of Mass Destruction

The seventh way the new terrorists differ from old is the most worrisome: they are determined to obtain and use nuclear, radiological, chemical, and biological weapons of mass destruction (WMD). According to Graham Allison's recent book *Nuclear Terrorism,* polls taken in 2003 found that four out of every ten Americans worry about the chances of nuclear attack.[105] In the judgment of many experts, these fears are not exaggerated. For example, a study conducted in 2000 by Howard Baker and Lloyd Cutler determined that the most urgent unmet national security threat to the United States today is the danger that weapons of mass destruction or weapons-usable material in Russian could be stolen, sold to terrorists, and used against Americans abroad or at home.[106]

With a single act, terrorists using a weapon of mass destruction can cause the deaths of thousands, even millions.[107] Acquiring WMD has been made easier thanks to Information Age technologies and the availability of suppliers.[108] Discoveries in Afghanistan have confirmed that al-Qaeda and other terrorist groups are actively pursuing biological agents for use against the United States and its allies.[109] According to David Kay, this should not be a surprise:

> Only a blind, deaf and dumb terrorist group could have survived the last five years and not been exposed at least to the possibility of the use of WMD, while the more discerning terrorists would have found some tactically brilliant possibilities already laid out on the public record.[110]

"We must be prepared for new types of attacks; anything could happen," says Koichi Oizumi, an international relations professor at Nihon University in Tokyo, the city where the Aum Shinrikio used sarin nerve gas to kill twelve and injure hundreds in the first major use of a chemical agent in a terrorist attack.[111]

Steven Miller, director of the International Security Program at Harvard's Kennedy School, says that policymakers should be particularly concerned about terrorist access to nuclear weapons. "Opportunities for well-organized and well-financed terrorists to infiltrate a Russian nuclear storage facility are greater than ever."[112] Miller believes that there have been more than two dozen thefts of weapons-usable materials in the former Soviet Union in recent years. Although "several suspects have been arrested in undercover sting operations," he wonders about those who may have gotten away.[113] These thefts go back to at least 1994, "when 350 grams of plutonium were smuggled on board a Lufthansa flight from Moscow to Munich. Fortunately, SWAT teams confiscated the material as soon as it arrived."[114]

In the past, any state that allowed a terrorist group it sponsored to use WMD against the United States knew it would be committing suicide, and the fear of nuclear retaliation was ample motivation for sponsors to keep the lid on. Today, any terrorist group with a known base of operations, even if it does not have a state sponsor, would similarly risk annihilation for waging a WMD terrorist attack. But al-Qaeda has no state sponsor and is a loosely organized global network, which makes retaliation much more problematic.

Finally, there is still considerable debate concerning jihadist groups such as al-Qaeda and their ability to acquire WMD and carry out an attack. Unfortunately, the organization's record and its statements are very straightforward and confirm the notion that al-Qaeda would indeed use WMD to escalate their terrorist attacks on the United States and the West. Al-Qaeda's view on WMD and its operational and symbolic importance is expressed by operational leader and ideologue Abu Musab al Suri in his open letter to the U.S. State Department:

> If I were consulted in the case of that operation, I would advise the use of planes in flights from outside the U.S. that would carry WMD. Hitting the U.S. with WMD was and is still very complicated. Yet, it is possible after all, with Allah's help, and more important than being possible—it is vital.[115]

According to Al Suri, WMD are the only means that would allow al-Qaeda to alter the current balance of power in the organization's favor, and this explains why, in the aftermath of 9/11, al-Qaeda's interest for WMD has increased exponentially.[116] The reciprocity argument is a second justification for using WMD. Accordingly, al-Qaeda has a right to use WMD and indiscriminately kill civilians in retaliation for the West's alleged crimes against Muslims all over the world.[117]

Al-Qaeda also obtained religious justification to use WMD from Islamic scholars such as Saudi Islamist Shaykh Naser bin Hamad al-Fahd, who penned the first fatwa on the use of WMD on May 21, 2003.[118] When asked by an anonymous person about the permissibility of the use of WMD, and al-Fahd replied: "If the Muslims could defeat the infidels only by using these kinds of weapons, it is allowed to use them even if they kill them all, and destroy their crops and cattle."[119] He then wrote an additional memorandum explaining the Islamic sources he has used to substantiate his conclusions, and he added that since the U.S. had killed about 10 million of Muslims, the Muslim world was indeed allowed to retaliate and kill as many American citizens. This line of thinking was drawn from a 2002 statement of al-Qaeda leader Suleiman Abu Gheith, who had claimed that al-Qaeda was allowed to kill at least 4 million of Americans, including 2 million of children.[120]

In past years, attempts to acquire, fabricate, and deploy WMD have been carried out by al-Qaeda-affiliated organizations in Europe, the Caucasus, as well as in Central and Southeast Asia. In the Caucasus, Pankisi Gorge in Georgia has been identified as the past center of al-Qaeda's biological and chemical weapons activity.[121] French anti-terrorism judge, Jean-Louis Bruguiére, collected evidence showing that chemical-biological terrorists in Europe have "been trained in special camps in the zone (Caucasus) in order to build biological and chemical systems and bombs."[122] Allegedly, al-Qaeda's scientist Abu Khatab operated in this area and was involved in Chechen cyanide plot against the Russian government before he was killed in 2006.[123] The chemical and biological training in camps in the Pankisi Gorge are particularly relevant because many of the mujahiddin who complete their training there return to Europe, where they might try to use their knowledge and carry out local attacks.

In the past, Pakistan has been strategic location for al-Qaeda's WMD programs, and Pakistani scientists have been involved in attempts to support al-Qaeda's efforts to acquire nuclear weapons. For example, nuclear scientist and atomic weapons expert Sultan Bashiruddin Mahmood has been accused of providing assistance to bin Laden to further his efforts to develop nuclear weapons. After retiring, Mahmood founded a charitable organization, Ummah Tameer E-Nau (UTN), whose real objective was: "to assist the Taliban, bin Laden, and his al-Qaeda terrorist network in developing high-tech weapons."[124]

In Southeast Asia, the al-Qaeda-affiliated Jeemah Islamiya (JI) has been involved with several foiled plots to carry out local WMD attacks and to provide international assistance to develop WMD. The *9/11 Report* indicates that: "Atef [Abu Hafs, senior al-Qaeda leader] turned to Hambali [Jeemah Islamiya leader] when al-Qaeda needed a scientist to take over its biological weapons program. Hambali obliged by introducing a U.S.-educated JI member, Yazid Sufaat, to Ayman al Zawahiri in Kandahar. In 2001 Sufaat spent several months attempting to cultivate anthrax for al-Qaeda in a laboratory he helped set up near the Kandahar airport."[125]

Moreover, JI has already attempted to carry out chemical or biological attacks. According to terrorism expert Rohan Gunaratna, there is a JI manual that explains how to carry out chemical attacks with chemical hydrogen cyanide. The manual said that "30ml of the agent can kill 60 million people, God willing," confirming the group's intention to cause the highest number of casualties possible.[126]

In sum, there is ample evidence indicating al-Qaeda has been concerned with developing, acquiring, and deploying WMD weapons, and that if the group were to succeed in their efforts, they would not hesitate to use them against U.S. and Western targets. As President Bush correctly pointed out in the 2002 National Security Strategy: "The gravest danger our Nation faces lies at the crossroads of radicalism and technology. Our enemies have openly declared that they are seeking weapons of mass destruction, and evidence indicates that they are doing so with determination."[127]

Defining Victory and Defeat

Much has been written about winning the war on terrorism, defeating al-Qaeda, and ending terrorism. In the last presidential campaign, both candidates implied that the war on terror may not be winnable, and were criticized for saying so. In my opinion, however, they were correct. Victory and defeat are elusive terms in a war on terrorism. Unlike World Wars I and II and the first Gulf War, when victory was sealed with an agreement, and the Vietnam War, when defeat was understood as Saigon fell, the war on terror will have no such defining moments. I believe, the war against terrorism will never be over, at least not in my lifetime. "There will always be a threat that someone will blow up an airplane or a building or a container ship."[128] The fact is, "one cannot defeat terrorism. Terrorism in one form or another has been around for centuries and will be around for many more."[129] Counterterrorism is not about defeating terrorism; it is about defeating terrorists, such as al-Qaeda. The measures of success in the war against terror are also different than those of a conventional war. Instead of body counts and casualty rates, success in the war on terror may be measured in numbers voting, schools opened, and women in the work force.[130] Success against al-Qaeda and like-minded terrorist groups will come when their operational, logistical, and financial activities are difficult to conduct and their freedom of movement to conduct operations is severely restricted.[131] The best we may be able to achieve is to understand that we live in danger, without living in fear.

Conclusion

To recap, eight key factors differentiate the al-Qaeda terrorist network from the terrorist organizations of past generations. First, al-Qaeda attacked the United States homeland, seriously undermining American's sense of security and well-being. The attack raised serious questions about the ability of the U.S. to respond to radically different threats and to meet "the paramount responsibility of any government—assuring the security of all persons, citizens or not, who legally reside within its sovereign territory."[132] Second, terrorism today is more violent. It has been responsible for the most lethal terrorist attack in history and has achieved the highest ever rate of lethality per attack.[133]

Third, while earlier terrorist organizations had local aspirations, al-Qaeda has global reach and strategic objectives. Its operators are transnational, non-state actors whose allegiance is to a cause, not a state. This is problematic because the traditional forms of state interaction—diplomatic, economic, and military—to solve differences prior to conflict are difficult to apply with a non-state actor. When things get dicey, with whom do you negotiate, on whom do you impose sanctions, and whom do you threaten with force? And if a transnational, non-state actor like bin Laden uses a weapon of mass destruction against you, whom do you nuke?

Fourth, al-Qaeda is a wealthy multinational organization with several income streams. It has investments and concealed accounts worldwide, many in the Western societies that bin Laden despises most.[134] He and his followers will continue to use their wealth to coerce governments into providing access and safe haven, just as they have done in the Sudan and Afghanistan. They will also pay to subcontract and franchise the services of like-minded terrorist organizations, all for the purpose of killing Americans.

Fifth, as Rohan Gunaratna says, al-Qaeda is not a ragtag outfit. Al-Qaeda operatives are well trained in military, special operations, and intelligence functions. Notwithstanding the coalition's victory in Afghanistan, the allies learned what made the al-Qaeda global terrorist network a daunting foe: "a relatively sophisticated, well-trained, and well-financed organization that drew on ongoing grassroots support and a fanatical willingness to fight to the death."[135]

Sixth, a strict adherence to its networked, cellular structure makes penetrating al-Qaeda extremely difficult. Composed of many cells whose members do not know one another, never assemble in one place together, and use strict discipline in their communications, the al-Qaeda model is more than a match for Western intelligence agencies that rely mainly on technical means of intelligence collection.[136] "America's new enemies can't be bought, bribed, or even blackmailed."[137] They want to kill Americans and will do so at any cost.

Seventh and most worrisome is al-Qaeda's determination to acquire nuclear, radiological, chemical, and biological weapons of mass destruction. The potential for acquiring these weapons is greater because of globalization, information technology, and the availability of shady suppliers. Globalization and the related spread of free-market economies, liberal values and institutions, and a developing global cultural network have provided unprecedented advancements in the developed world. Globally linked economies continue to grow at exponential rates, advances in international science are racing forward, and people—at least those benefiting from globalization—are more connected than ever before. Information and money flow quicker and at lower cost. It is much easier for people to travel, communicate and do business internationally.[138]

Yet, this growing interdependence, inexorably linked to technology, poses risks because security, business, and communication's infrastructures are increasingly more fragile. Global interdependence makes us stronger, but also in some aspects, more vulnerable. There is also a backlash from those who view globalization as a threat to traditional culture and their vested interests. Some discontented, illiberal non-state actors perceive themselves under attack and, therefore, resort to offensive action. This is the case with al-Qaeda and affiliated organizations.[139]

Indeed, the new terrorism has an unparalleled global reach. It can ride the back of the Web, using advanced communications to move immense financial flows from Sudan to the Philippines or from Australia to banks in Florida.[140] And for $28.50, any Internet surfer can purchase *Bacteriological Warfare: A Major Threat to North America,* which teaches how to grow deadly bacteria. Shady suppliers come from many countries, particularly Russia, which cannot offer employment to many ex-Soviet scientists and weaponeers. In fact, there are reports of plutonium for sale across Eastern Europe and of Russian scientists who once worked in Soviet labs linked to germ warfare now selling their services in the Middle East for hefty fees.[141]

Eighth and most frustrating is that we will not know when or whether we have achieved victory or if the enemy is defeated. More than likely, victory in the traditional warfare sense will never be achieved in our lifetime. In fact, defeating terrorism is most likely an unachievable objective. Terrorism is a tactic that has been used for centuries and will continue to be used in the future, particularly when weaker adversaries attack stronger foes. As Philip Heymann, the former Deputy Attorney General of the United States, argues, "There will be terrorism. We can deal with it; we can discourage it; but we cannot end it completely."[142] At a minimum, reducing the risks from terrorism so that an atmosphere of pre–9/11 security exists will define victory. In the long-run, al-Qaeda and like-minded terrorist groups will go the way of the Baedar Meinhof, the Red Brigades, and the Japanese Red Army. However, terrorism in some form will continue to exist.

As envisioned by al-Qaeda, the "perfect new warfare" would entail multiple attacks against America designed to produce the greatest number of casualties. For maximum effect, these attacks would take place nearly simultaneously and at several locations, much like the attacks of September 11, 2001 in New York City, Washington D.C., and Pennsylvania.[143]

One might say that America's war against the new terrorism is far colder than the Cold War—"cold" as in the cold-blooded murder of the 9/11 attacks. At least with the Soviets, we always knew who was in charge and that we couldn't be attacked without his orders. In fact, the U.S. president had a direct line to Soviet leaders and could work through difficult moments with them personally. By contrast, on September 11, 2001, we lost thousands of people. Although we know that Osama bin Laden ordered the killing, we have no direct line to him or anyone else in his leadership. We also know that he and his followers will continue to hit the United States, its allies, and secular Islamic states again and again until he and his network are stopped.

It has been said that generals always make the mistake of preparing for the last war instead of the next one. This article has emphasized changes in the terrorist threat since the Cold War decades so that today's generals and their civilian masters can better understand how to fight and win the current war, and so that having won it, we will never have to fight a war like this again.

Brigadier General Russell D. Howard (Retired) was a career Special Forces officer and is now the Director of the Jebsen Center for Counter-terrorism Studies at the Fletcher School at Tufts University. His recent publications include *Defeating Terrorism,* (McGraw-Hill, 2004), *Homeland Security and Terrorism* (McGraw-Hill, 2005), and *Weapons of Mass Destruction and Terrorism* (McGraw-Hill, 2006).

Notes

1. "Terror Cells of Today Hard to Combat." *The New York Times,* August 20, 2002. Available at www.nytimes.com/aponline/international/AP-Evolution-of-Terror.html
2. John Mearsheimer, "Why We Will Soon Miss the Cold War," *Atlantic Monthly,* August 1990. See also Glenn Sacks, "Why I Miss the Cold War," October 2, 2001. Available at www.glennsacks.com.
3. Brian H. Hook, Margaret J. A. Peterlin, and Peter L. Welsh, "Intelligence and the New Threat: The USA PATRIOT Act and Information Sharing Between the Intelligence and Law Enforcement Communities," *Federalist Society for Law and Public Policy Studies* (December 2001): 3.
4. Brian Murphy, "The Shape of Terrorism Changes," *Fayetteville Observer,* August 21, 2002, 9A.
5. Steven Simon and Daniel Benjamin, "America and the New Terrorism," *Survival, 42,* no. 1 (Spring 2000): 69.
6. Sebestyen L. v. Gorka, "al-Qaeda's Rhetoric and its Implications," *Jane's Terrorism and Security Monitor,* January 13, 2005, 1.

7. "Combating Terrorism and its Implications for Intelligence," DCAF Internal Paper, June 2004, 8. Available at http://se2.isn.ch/serviceengine/FileContent?serviceID=DCAF&fileid=2DC89 8E2-BB8D-D231-DA79-72C1AB46E3D6&lng=en.
8. "Combating Terrorism and its Implications for Intelligence," 8.
9. Ibid.
10. "Hezbollah in America," *Washington Times,* May 20, 2005. Available at www.washtimes.com/op-ed/20050519-092915-7312r.htm
11. Some in the Southwest may include Pancho Villa's excursion into New Mexico as an attack.
12. David Halberstam, *War in Time of Peace* (New York: Simon and Schuster, 2001), 498.
13. Ibid. 496–497.
14. Stephen Flynn, *America the Vulnerable* (New York: Harper Collins, 2004), x.
15. Halberstam, 496
16. Flynn, x.
17. "Air Force Association Statement of Policy," September 12, 2004. Available at www.afa.org/AboutUs/PolicyIssues05.asp See also *Wikipedia, The Free Encyclopedia* at <en.wikipedia.org/wiki/United_States_military>
18. Brian H. Hook, Margaret J. A. Peterlin, and Peter L. Welsh, "Intelligence and the New Threat: The USA PATRIOT Act and Information Sharing Between the Intelligence and Law Enforcement Communities," *Federalist Society for Law and Public Policy Studies* (December 2001): 3.
19. Halberstam, 497.
20. Ibid.
21. Flynn, x.
22. Ibid.
23. Ibid, 5.
24. Ibid.
25. Ibid.
26. Halberstam, 498.
27. Quote attributed to Brian Jenkins in 1974.
28. Rohan Gunaratna, *Inside al-Qaeda—Global Network of Terror* (New York: Columbia Press, 2002), 91.
29. Quote attributed to James Woolsey, 1994.
30. Bruce Hoffman, *Inside Terrorism* (New York: Columbia University Press, 1998), 205.
31. Stefan Mair, "The New World of Privatized Violence," *International Politics and Society, 2* (2003): 17.
32. Ibid.
33. Lawrence Freeman, "Out of Nowhere—Bin Laden's Grievances," *BBC Online.* Available at www.bbc.co.uk/history/war/sept_11/build_up_05.shtml
34. Graham Allison, *Nuclear Terrorism* (New York: Times Books, 2004), 13.
35. David Albright, "Al-Qaeda's Quixotic Quest to go Nuclear," *Asia Times,* November 22, 2002. Available at www.atimes.com/atimes/Middle_East/DK22Ak01. See also, Tina Tarvainen, "al-Qaeda and WMD, a Primer," *Terrorism Monitor, 3,* 11 (June 2, 2005). Available at www.jamestown.org/terrorism/news/article.php?articleid=2369714
36. Stefan Mair, "The New World of Privatized Violence,"*International Politics and Society, 2* (2003): 12.
37. "Combating Terrorism and its Implications for Intelligence," 8.
38. Michael Whine, "The New Terrorism," Available at www.ict.org.il/articles/articledet.cfm?articleid=427
39. Stefen Mair, 17.
40. Jerrold M. Post, "Killing in the Name of God: Osama Bin Laden and al-Qaeda," in *Know Thy Enemy: Profiles of Adversary Leaders and Their Strategic Cultures,* edited by Barry R. Schneider and Jerrold M. Post, (Maxwell Air Force Base: USAF Counterproliferation Center), 33.

41. Conversation with Dr. Rohan Gunaratna, November 15, 2002 in Garmisch, Germany.
42. "Combating Terrorism and its Implications for Intelligence," 9.
43. Jessica Stern, "The Protean Enemy," *Foreign Affairs* (July/August 2003): 33.
44. See Ann Tyson, "al-Qaeda Broken, but Dangerous," *Christian Science Monitor,* June 24, 2002. Available at www.csmonitor.com/2002/0624/p01s02-usgn.htm.
45. Jason Burke, "al-Qaeda," *Foreign Policy,* May/June 2004, 18.
46. Ibid.
47. Ibid.
48. Jessica Stern, "The Protean Enemy (al-Qaeda)," *Foreign Affairs,* July–August, 2003, 31. See also Dan Eggan, "9/11 Panel Links Al-Qaeda and Iran," *Washington Post,* June 26, 2004, A12.
49. Ibid.
50. Matthew Levitt, "Islamic Extremism in Europe: Beyond alQaeda, Hamas, and Hezbollah in Europe," Testimony before the Joint Hearing of the House Committee on International Relations, Subcommittee on Europe and Emerging Threats, April 27, 2005. Available at www.washingoninstitute.org/teplateC07.php?CID-234
51. Ibid.
52. Timothy Garden, "Security and the War Against Terrorism," www.tgarden.demon.co.uk/writings/articles/2002/020320riia.html
53. Louise I. Shelley and John T. Picarelli, "Methods not Motives: Implications of the Convergence of International Organized Crime and Terrorism," *Police Practice and Research, 3,* no. 4, 306.
54. Stephen A. Cambone, *A New Structure for National Security Policy Planning* (Washington DC: Government Printing Office, 1996), 43.
55. Gideon Rose, "It Could Happen Here—Facing the New Terrorism," *Foreign Affairs* (March/April 1999): 1.
56. Discussions with Bruce Hoffman over multiple dates, the most recent October 23, 2007.
57. Multiple Conversations with John Dorschner, 2001–2002. Also, see John Dorschner, "A Shadowy Empire of Hate was Born of a War in Afghanistan," *Knight Ridder Newspapers,* September 24, 2001.
58. "Bin Laden no Longer Seen as al-Qaeda's Main Financier," *Associated Press,* September 2, 2004. Available at <http://www.msnbc.msn.com/id/5896423>
59. "CDI Primer: Terrorist Finances," October 25, 2002. Available at www.cdi.org/terrorism/finance_primer-pr.cfm
60. Martin Rudner, "Using Financial Intelligence Against the Funding of Terrorism," *International Journal of Intelligence and CounterIntelligence, 19,* no. 1, 222. See also, "al-Qaeda Income Cut, Says Foreign Office," *Daily Telegraph,* London, April 7, 2003.
61. Steve Kiser, "al-Qaeda's Financial Empire," *Pardee RAND Graduate School Series,* March 2005, 111.
62. Douglas Farah, "al-Qaeda and the Gemstone Trade," in *Countering the Financing of Terrorism,* edited by Thomas J. Biersteker and Sue E. Eckert (London: Routledge, 2007), 199.
63. Robin Wright, *Sacred Rage* (New York: Simon and Schuster, 2001), 252.
64. Ibid.
65. Ibid.
66. Patrick M Yost and Harjit Singh Sandhu, "The *hawala* Alternative Remittance System and its Role in Money Laundering," Interpol General Secretariat, January 2002. Available at www.interpol.int/Public/FinancialCrime/MoneyLaundering/hawala/default.asp
67. Maurice Greenberg, "Terrorist Financing," Council on Foreign Relations Report, 2002, 11.
68. Ibid.
69. Ibid.
70. Louise I. Shelley and John T. Picarelli, "Methods Not Motives: Implications of the Convergence of International Organized Crime and Terrorism," *Police Practice and Research, 3,* no. 4 (2002): 307.
71. Neil A. Lewis, "The Money Trail—Court Upholds Freeze on Assets of Muslim Group Based in U.S." *New York Time,* June 21, 2003, A11.
72. "US Accuses Charity of Financing Terror," *BBC Online,* November 20, 2002.

73. Lewis, A11.
74. Kiser, 79.
75. Ibid, 79.
76. Ibid, 81.
77. Ibid.
78. Christopher Dobson and Ronald Payne, *The Terrorists, Their Weapons, Leaders and Tactics* (New York: Facts on File, 1982), 80.
79. Ibid.
80. Post, 35.
81. Gunaratna, 73.
82. Ibid.
83. Martin Rudner, 203. See also, Robert Fisk, "With Runners and Whispers, al-Qaeda Outfoxes U.S. Forces," *The Independent,* London, December 6, 2002.
84. Abdullah Ali Al-Salama, *Military Espionage in Islam,* http://www.skfriends.com/bin-laden-terrorist-manual.htm
85. Gunaratna, 76.
86. Gabriel Weimann, "www.terror.net—How Modern Terrorism Uses the Internet," U.S. Institute of Peace Special Report, March 2004, 3.
87. Steve Coll and Susan Glasser, "Terrorists Turn to the Web as a Base of Operations," *Washington Post,* August 7, 2005, A01.
88. Ibid.
89. Ibid.
90. Ibid.
91. Ibid.
92. See Whine, "The New Terrorism."
93. Shelly and Picarelli, 307.
94. *A Military Guide to Terrorism in the Twenty-First Century,* U.S. Army Tradoc Manual, Ft. Leavonworth Kansas. Version 1.0, May 13, 2003, 40.
95. Ibid, 33.
96. John Arqilla and David Ronfeldt, *Networks and Netwars* (Santa Monica: RAND, 2001), 9.
97. *A Military Guide to Terrorism in the the Twenty-First Century,* Version 1.0, May 13, 2003, 40.
98. Martin Rudner, p. 216.
99. "Combating Terrorism and its Implications for Intelligence," 9.
100. Ibid.
101. Ibid.
102. "Al-Qaeda, An Ever-Shifting Web," *The Economist,* October 19–25, 2002, 26
103. Ibid.
104. Ibid.
105. Graham Allison, *Nuclear Terrorism* (New York: Henry Holt and Company, 2004), 8.
106. Ibid, 9.
107. Richard B. Myers, "Fighting Terrorism in an Information Age," International Information Programs, U.S. Department of State, August 19, 2002, 2. Available at <usinfo.state.gov/regional/nea/sasia/text/0819info.htm>
108. Ibid.
109. Judith Miller, "Lab Suggests Qaeda Planned to Build Arms, Officials Say," *New York Times,* September 14, 2002, 1.
110. David Kay, "WMD Terrorism: Hype or Reality," in James M. Smith and William C. Thomas, eds., *The Terrorism Threat and US Government Response: Operational and Organizational Factors* (US Air Force Academy: INSS Book Series, 2001), 12.
111. "Terror Cells of Today Hard to Combat," *The New York Times,* August 20, 2002. Available at www.nytimes.com/aponline/international/AP-Evolution-of-Terror.html
112. Doug Gavel, "Can Nuclear Weapons be Put Beyond the Reach of Terrorists," *Kennedy School of Government Bulletin,* Autumn 2002, 43.
113. Ibid, 45.

114. Ibid, 48.
115. James J. F. Forest, "Confronting the Threat of an al-Qaeda WMD Attack," *Accuracy in Media,* December 12, 2006. Available at http://www.aim.org/guest_column/A5077_0_6_0_C/ See also, Reuven Paz, "Global Jihad and WMD: Between Martyrdom and Mass Destruction," *Current Trends in Islamist Ideology, 2,* Hudson Institute, September 2005. http://www.sofir.org/sarchives/005026.php
116. Ibid. James J. F. Forest.
117. Hamid Mir, "Osama Claims he has Nukes: If US uses N-arms it will get same response," *Dawn Internet,* November 10, 2001. http://www.dawn.com/2001/11/10/top1.htm
118. Robert Wesley, "Al-Qaeda's WMD Strategy After the U.S. Intervention in Afghanistan," *Terrorism Monitor, 3,* no. 20, October 21, 2005. http://jamestown.org/terrorism/news/article.php?issue_id=3502
119. Reuven Paz, "Global Jihad and WMD: Between Martyrdom and Mass Destruction," *Current Trends in Islamist Ideology, 2,* September 2005. Available at http://www.sofir.org/sarchives/005026.php
120. Robert Wesley, "Al-Qaeda's WMD Strategy After the U.S. Intervention in Afghanistan," *Terrorism Monitor, 3,* no. 20, October 21, 2005. http://jamestown.org/terrorism/news/article.php?issue_id=3502
121. Akaki Dvali, "Instability in Georgia: A New Proliferation Threat?" Issue Brief, Center for Nonproliferation Studies, Monterey Institute of International Studies, August 2003. Available at www.nti.org/e_research/e3_31a.html
122. "Interview with Jean-Louis Bruguiére," *PBS Frontline,* October 12, 2004. Available at www.pbs.org/wgbh/pages/frontline/shows/front/map/bruguiere.html
123. Dan Darling, "al-Qaeda's Mad Scientist. The significance of Abu Khabab's Death," (September 30, 2006), *The Weekly Standard,* January 19, 2006. Available at www.weeklystandard.com/Content/Public/Articles/000/000/006/602zqghe.asp.
124. U.S. Department of Treasury, "Protecting Charitable organizations," *Terrorism and Financial Intelligence.* Available at www.treasury.gov/offices/enforcement/key-issues/protecting/charities_execorder_13224-p.shtml
125. Reuven Paz.
126. Natalie O'Brien, "JI Planned Holocaust Gas Attack in Buildings," *Weekend Australian,* May 27, 2006. Available at www.theaustralian.news.com.au/story/0,20867,19270458-5001561,00.html
127. *The National Security Strategy of the United States of America,* September 2002. Available at www.whitehouse.gov/nsc/nss.pdf.
128. James Fallows, "Success Without Victory," *The Atlantic Monthly,* January/February, 2005.
129. Matthew Levitt, "Untangling the Terror Web: Identifying and counteracting the Phenomenon of Crossover Between Terrorist Groups," *SAIS Review, 24,* no. 1 (Winter/Spring 2004): 35.
130. Rowan Scarborough, "Metrics Help Guide the Pentagon," *Washington Times,* April 5, 2005, 3.
131. Ibid,
132. Richard H. Ullman, "9/11 a New Day for Counterterrorism,?" *Great Decisions,* 2002 Edition, 5.
133. Bruce Newsome, "Executive Summary," *Mass-Casualty Terrorism: Second Quarterly Forecast by the University of Reading Terrorism Forecasting Group,* June 13, 2003, 3. Available at www.rdg.ac.uk/GSEIS/University_of_Reading_Terrorism_Forecast_2003Q2.pdf
134. Robin Wright, 253.
135. Ann Tyson, "al-Qaeda, Resilient and Organized," *Christian Science Monitor,* March 7, 2002, 1.
136. Gunaratna, 76.
137. Sacks, 1.
138. Henry A. Crumpton, *Remarks at the Royal United Services Institute Conference on Transnational Terrorism,* London, United Kingdom, January 16, 2006. Available at www.state.gov/s/ct/rls/rm/2006/59987.htm

139. Ibid.
140. Paul Mann, "Modern Military Threats: Not All They Might Seem?" *Aviation Week & Space Technology,* April 22, 2002, 1. (Gordon Adams quote)
141. For example, see the 1997 National Academies Press report, "Proliferation Concerns: Assessing U.S. Efforts to Help Contain Nuclear and Other Dangerous Materials and Technologies in the Former Soviet Union." Available at http://www.nap.edu/catalog.php?record_id=5590.
142. Philip B. Heymann, *Terrorism and America a Common Sense Strategy for a Democratic Society* (Cambridge, MA: MIT Press, 1998), 5.
143. "A Military Assessment of the al-Qaeda Training Tapes," *Strategy Page,* June 28, 2003. Available at www.strategypage.com/articles/tapes/5.asp

John Arquilla, David Ronfeldt, and Michele Zanini, 1999

Networks, Netwar, and Information-Age Terrorism

The rise of network forms of organization is a key consequence of the ongoing information revolution. Business organizations are being newly energized by networking, and many professional militaries are experimenting with flatter forms of organization. In this [selection], we explore the impact of networks on terrorist capabilities, and consider how this development may be associated with a move away from emphasis on traditional, episodic efforts at coercion to a new view of terror as a form of protracted warfare. Seen in this light, the recent bombings of U.S. embassies in East Africa, along with the retaliatory American missile strikes, may prove to be the opening shots of a war between a leading state and a terror network. We consider both the likely context and the conduct of such a war, and offer some insights that might inform policies aimed at defending against and countering terrorism.

A New Terrorism (With Old Roots)

The age-old phenomenon of terrorism continues to appeal to its perpetrators for three principal reasons. First, it appeals as a weapon of the weak—a shadowy way to wage war by attacking asymmetrically to harm and try to defeat an ostensibly superior force. This has had particular appeal to ethnonationalists, racist militias, religious fundamentalists, and other minorities who cannot match the military formations and firepower of their "oppressors"—the case, for example, with some radical Middle Eastern Islamist groups vis-à-vis Israel, and, until recently, the Provisional Irish Republican Army (PIRA) vis-à-vis Great Britain.

Second, terrorism has appealed as a way to assert identity and command attention—rather like proclaiming, "I bomb, therefore I am." Terrorism enables a perpetrator to publicize his identity, project it explosively, and touch the nerves of powerful distant leaders. This kind of attraction to violence transcends its instrumental utility. Mainstream revolutionary writings may view violence as a means of struggle, but terrorists often regard violence as an end in itself that generates identity or damages the enemy's identity.

Third, terrorism has sometimes appealed as a way to achieve a new future order by willfully wrecking the present. This is manifest in the religious fervor of some radical Islamists, but examples also lie among millenarian and apocalyptic groups, like Aum Shinrikyo in Japan, who aim to wreak havoc and rend a system asunder so that something new may emerge from the cracks. The substance of the future vision may be only vaguely defined, but its moral worth is clear and appealing to the terrorist.

In the first and second of these motivations or rationales, terrorism may involve retaliation and retribution for past wrongs, whereas the third is also about revelation and rebirth, the coming of a new age. The first is largely strategic; it has a practical tone, and the objectives may be limited and specific. In contrast, the third may engage a transcendental, unconstrained view of how to change the world through terrorism.

Such contrasts do not mean the three are necessarily at odds; blends often occur. Presumptions of weakness (the first rationale) and of willfulness (in the second and third) can lead to peculiar synergies. For example, Aum's members may have known it was weak in a conventional sense, but they believed that they had special knowledge, a unique leader, invincible willpower, and secret ways to strike out.

These classic motivations or rationales will endure in the information age. However, terrorism is not a fixed phenomenon; its perpetrators adapt it to suit their times and situations. What changes is the conduct of terrorism—the operational characteristics built around the motivations and rationales.

This [selection] addresses, often in a deliberately speculative manner, changes in organization, doctrine, strategy, and technology that, taken together, speak to the emergence of a "new terrorism" attuned to the information age. Our principal hypotheses are as follows:

- **Organization.** Terrorists will continue moving from hierarchical toward information-age network designs. Within groups, "great man" leaderships will give way to flatter decentralized designs. More effort will go into building arrays of transnationally internetted groups than into building stand-alone groups.

- **Doctrine and strategy.** Terrorists will likely gain new capabilities for lethal acts. Some terrorist groups are likely to move to a "war paradigm" that focuses on attacking U.S. military forces and assets. But where terrorists suppose that "information operations" may be as useful as traditional commando-style operations for achieving their goals, systemic *disruption* may become as much an objective as target *destruction*. Difficulties in coping with the new terrorism will mount if terrorists move beyond isolated acts toward a new approach to doctrine and strategy that emphasizes campaigns based on swarming.

- **Technology.** Terrorists are likely to increasingly use advanced information technologies for offensive and defensive purposes, as well as to support their organizational structures. Despite widespread speculation about terrorists using cyberspace warfare techniques to take "the Net" down, they may often have stronger reasons for wanting to keep it up (e.g., to spread their message and communicate with one another).

In short, terrorism is evolving in a direction we call *netwar*. Thus, after briefly reviewing terrorist trends, we outline the concept of netwar and its relevance for understanding information-age terrorism. In particular, we elaborate on the above points about organization, doctrine, and strategy, and briefly discuss how recent developments in the nature and behavior of Middle Eastern terrorist groups can be interpreted as early signs of a move toward netwar-type terrorism.

Given the prospect of a netwar-oriented shift in which some terrorists pursue a war paradigm, we then focus on the implications such a development may have for the U.S. military. We use these insights to consider defensive antiterrorist measures, as well as proactive counterterrorist strategies. We propose that a key to coping with information-age terrorism will be the creation of interorganizational networks within the U.S. military and government, partly on the grounds that it takes networks to fight networks.

Recent Views About Terrorism

Terrorism remains a distinct phenomenon while reflecting broader trends in irregular warfare. The latter has been on the rise around the world since before the end of the Cold War. Ethnic and religious conflicts, recently in evidence in areas of Africa, the Balkans, and the Caucasus, for awhile in Central America, and seemingly forever in the Middle East, attest to the brutality that increasingly attends this kind of warfare. These are not conflicts between regular, professional armed forces dedicated to warrior creeds and Geneva Conventions. Instead, even where regular forces play roles, these conflicts often revolve around the strategies and tactics of thuggish paramilitary gangs and local warlords. Some leaders may have some professional training; but the foot soldiers are often people who, for one reason or another, get caught in a fray and learn on the job. Adolescents and children with high-powered weaponry are taking part in growing numbers. In many of these conflicts, savage acts are increasingly committed without anyone taking credit—it may not even be clear which side is responsible. The press releases of the protagonists sound high-minded and self-legitimizing, but the reality at the local level is often about clan rivalries and criminal ventures (e.g., looting, smuggling, or protection rackets).[1]

Thus, irregular warfare has become endemic and vicious around the world. A decade or so ago, terrorism was a rather distinct entry on the spectrum of conflict, with its own unique attributes. Today, it seems increasingly connected with these broader trends in irregular warfare, especially as waged by nonstate actors. As Martin Van Creveld warns:

> In today's world, the main threat to many states, including specifically the U.S., no longer comes from other states. Instead, it comes from small groups and other organizations which are not states. Either we make the necessary changes and face them today, or what is commonly known as the modern world will lose all sense of security and will dwell in perpetual fear.[2]

Meanwhile, for the past several years, terrorism experts have broadly concurred that this phenomenon will persist, if not get worse. General agreement that terrorism may worsen parses into different scenarios. For example, Walter Laqueur warns that religious motivations could lead to "superviolence," with millenarian visions of a coming apocalypse driving "postmodern" terrorism. Fred Iklé worries that increased violence may be used by terrorists to usher in a new totalitarian age based on Leninist ideals. Bruce Hoffman raises the prospect that religiously-motivated terrorists may escalate their violence in order to wreak sufficient havoc to undermine the world political system and replace it with a chaos that is particularly detrimental to the United States—a basically nihilist strategy.[3]

The preponderance of U.S. conventional power may continue to motivate some state and nonstate adversaries to opt for terror as an asymmetric response. Technological advances and underground trafficking may make weapons of mass destruction (WMD— nuclear, chemical, biological weapons) ever easier for terrorists to acquire.[4] Terrorists' shifts toward looser, less hierarchical organizational structures, and their growing use of advanced communications technologies for command, control, and coordination, may further empower small terrorist groups and individuals who want to mount operations from a distance.

There is also agreement about an emergence of two tiers of terror: one characterized by hard-core professionals, the other by amateur cut-outs.[5] The deniability gained by terrorists operating through willing amateurs, coupled with the increasing accessibility of ever more destructive weaponry, has also led many experts to concur that terrorists will be attracted to engaging in more lethal destruction, with increased targeting of information and communications infrastructures.[6]

Some specialists also suggest that "information" will become a key target—both the conduits of information infrastructures and the content of information, particularly the media.[7] While these target-sets may involve little lethal activity, they offer additional theaters of operations for terrorists. Laqueur in particular foresees that, "If the new terrorism directs its energies toward information warfare, its destructive power will be exponentially greater than any it wielded in the past—greater even than it would be with biological and chemical weapons."[8] New planning and scenario-building is needed to help think through how to defend against this form of terrorism.[9]

Such dire predictions have galvanized a variety of responses, which range from urging the creation of international control regimes over the tools of terror (such as WMD materials and advanced encryption capabilities), to the use of coercive diplomacy against state sponsors of terror. Increasingly, the liberal use of military force against terrorists has also been recommended. Caleb Carr in particular espoused this theme, sparking a heated debate.[10] Today, many leading works on combating terrorism blend notions of control mechanisms, international regimes, and the use of force.[11]

Against this background, experts have begun to recognize the growing role of networks—of networked organizational designs and related doctrines, strategies, and technologies—among the practitioners of terrorism. The growth of these networks is related to the spread of advanced information technologies that allow dispersed groups, and individuals, to conspire and coordinate across considerable distances. Recent U.S. efforts to investigate and attack the bin Laden network (named for the central influence of Osama bin Laden) attest to this. The rise of networks is likely to reshape terrorism in the information age, and lead to the adoption of netwar—a kind of information-age conflict that will be waged principally by nonstate actors. Our contribution . . . is to present the concept of netwar and show how terrorism is being affected by it.

The Advent of Netwar—Analytical Background[12]

The information revolution is altering the nature of conflict across the spectrum. Of the many reasons for this, we call attention to two in particular. First, the information revolution is favoring and strengthening network forms of organization, often giving them an advantage over hierarchical forms. The rise of networks means that power is migrating to nonstate actors, who are able to organize into sprawling multi-organizational networks (especially all-channel networks, in which every node is connected to every other node) more readily than can traditional, hierarchical, state actors. Nonstate-actor networks are thought to be more flexible and responsive than hierarchies in reacting to outside developments, and to be better than hierarchies at using information to improve decisionmaking.[13]

Second, as the information revolution deepens, conflicts will increasingly depend on information and communications matters. More than ever before, conflicts will revolve around "knowledge" and the use of "soft power."[14] Adversaries will emphasize "information operations" and "perception management"—that is, media-oriented measures that aim to attract rather than coerce, and that affect how secure a society, a military, or other actor feels about its knowledge of itself and of its adversaries. Psychological disruption may become as important a goal as physical destruction.

Thus, major transformations are coming in the nature of adversaries, in the type of threats they may pose, and in how conflicts can be waged. Information-age threats are likely to be more diffuse, dispersed, multidimensional, and ambiguous than more traditional threats. Metaphorically, future conflicts may resemble the Oriental game of *Go* more than the Western game of chess. The conflict spectrum will be molded from end to end by these dynamics:

- *Cyberwar*—a concept that refers to information-oriented military warfare—is becoming an important entry at the military end of the spectrum, where the language has normally been about high-intensity conflicts (HICs).
- *Netwar* figures increasingly at the societal end of the spectrum, where the language has normally been about low-intensity conflict (LIC), operations other than war (OOTW), and nonmilitary modes of conflict and crime.[15]

Whereas cyberwar usually pits formal military forces against each other, netwar is more likely to involve nonstate, paramilitary, and irregular forces—as in the case of terrorism. Both concepts are consistent with the views of analysts such as Van Creveld, who believe that a "transformation of war" is under way.[16] Neither concept is just about technology; both refer to comprehensive approaches to conflict—comprehensive in that they mix organizational, doctrinal, strategic, tactical, and technological innovations, for offense and defense.

Definition of Netwar

To be more precise, netwar refers to an emerging mode of conflict and crime at societal levels, involving measures short of traditional war, in which the protagonists use network forms of organization and related doctrines, strategies, and technologies attuned to the information age. These protagonists are likely to consist of dispersed small groups who communicate, coordinate, and conduct their campaigns in an internetted manner, without a precise central command. Thus, information-age netwar differs from modes of conflict and crime in which the protagonists prefer formal, stand-alone, hierarchical organizations, doctrines, and strategies, as in past efforts, for example, to build centralized movements along Marxist lines.

The term is meant to call attention to the prospect that network-based conflict and crime will become major phenomena in the decades ahead. Various actors across the spectrum of conflict and crime are already evolving in this direction. To give a string of examples, netwar is about the Middle East's Hamas more than the Palestine Liberation Organization (PLO), Mexico's Zapatistas more than Cuba's Fidelistas, and the American Christian Patriot movement more than the Ku Klux Klan. It is also about the Asian Triads more than the Sicilian Mafia, and Chicago's Gangsta Disciples more than the Al Capone Gang.

This spectrum includes familiar adversaries who are modifying their structures and strategies to take advantage of networked designs, such as transnational terrorist groups, black-market proliferators of WMD, transnational crime syndicates, fundamentalist and ethno-nationalist movements, intellectual property and high-sea pirates, and smugglers of black-market goods or migrants. Some urban gangs, back-country militias, and militant single-issue groups in the United States are also developing netwar-like attributes. In addition, there is a new generation of radicals and activists who are just beginning to create information-age ideologies, in which identities and loyalties may shift from the nation-state to the transnational level of global civil society. New kinds of actors, such as anarchistic and nihilistic leagues of computer-hacking "cyboteurs," may also partake of netwar.

Many—if not most—netwar actors will be nonstate. Some may be agents of a state, but others may try to turn states into *their* agents. Moreover, a netwar actor may be both subnational and transnational in scope. Odd hybrids and symbioses are likely. Furthermore, some actors (e.g., violent terrorist and criminal organizations) may threaten U.S. and other nations' interests, but other netwar actors (e.g., peaceful social activists) may not. Some may aim at destruction, others at disruption. Again, many variations are possible.

The full spectrum of netwar proponents may thus seem broad and odd at first glance. But there is an underlying pattern that cuts across all variations: the use of network forms of organization, doctrine, strategy, and technology attuned to the information age.

More About Organizational Design

The notion of an organizational structure qualitatively different from traditional hierarchical designs is not recent; for example, in the early 1960s Burns and Stalker referred to the organic form as "a network structure of control, authority, and communication," with "lateral rather than vertical direction of communication." In organic structure,[17]

> omniscience [is] no longer imputed to the head of the concern; knowledge about the technical or commercial nature of the here and now task may be located anywhere in the network; [with] this location becoming the ad hoc centre of control authority and communication.

In the business world, virtual or networked organizations are being heralded as effective alternatives to bureaucracies—as in the case of Eastman Chemical Company and the Shell-Sarnia Plant—because of their inherent flexibility, adaptiveness, and ability to capitalize on the talents of all members of the organization.[18]

What has long been emerging in the business world is now becoming apparent in the organizational structures of netwar actors. In an archetypal netwar, the protagonists are likely to amount to a set of diverse, dispersed "nodes" who share a set of ideas and interests

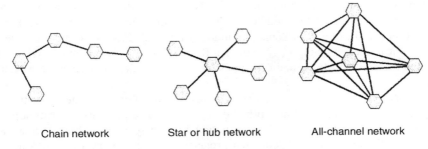

Chain network   Star or hub network   All-channel network

Figure 1

and who are arrayed to act in a fully internetted "all-channel" manner. Networks come in basically three types (or topologies) (see Figure 1):[19]

- The *chain* network, as in a smuggling chain where people, goods, or information move along a line of separated contacts, and where end-to-end communication must travel through the intermediate nodes.
- The *star,* hub, or wheel network, as in a franchise or a cartel structure where a set of actors is tied to a central node or actor, and must go through that node to communicate and coordinate.
- The *all-channel network,* as in a collaborative network of militant small groups where every group is connected to every other.

Each node in the diagrams of Figure 1 may be to an individual, a group, an institution, part of a group or institution, or even a state. The nodes may be large or small, tightly or loosely coupled, and inclusive or exclusive in membership. They may be segmentary or specialized—that is, they may look alike and engage in similar activities, or they may undertake a division of labor based on specialization. The boundaries of the network may be well defined, or blurred and porous in relation to the outside environment. All such variations are possible.

Each type may be suited to different conditions and purposes, and all three may be found among netwar-related adversaries—e.g., the chain in smuggling operations, the star at the core of terrorist and criminal syndicates, and the all-channel type among militant groups that are highly internetted and decentralized. There may also be hybrids. For example, a netwar actor may have an all-channel council at its core, but use stars and chains for tactical operations. There may also be hybrids of network and hierarchical forms of organization, and hierarchies may exist inside particular nodes in a network. Some actors may have a hierarchical organization overall, but use networks for tactical operations; other actors may have an all-channel network design, but use hierarchical teams for tactical operations. Again, many configurations are possible, and it may be difficult for an analyst to discern exactly what type of networking characterizes a particular actor.

Of the three network types, the all-channel has been the most difficult to organize and sustain historically, partly because it may require dense communications. However, it gives the network form the most potential for collaborative undertakings, and it is the type that is gaining strength from the information revolution. Pictorially, an all-channel netwar actor resembles a geodesic "Bucky ball" (named for Buckminster Fuller); it does not resemble a pyramid. The design is flat. Ideally, there is no single, central leadership, command, or headquarters—no precise heart or head that can be targeted. The network as a whole (but not necessarily each node) has little to no hierarchy, and there may be multiple leaders. Decision-making and operations are decentralized, allowing for local initiative and autonomy. Thus the design may sometimes appear acephalous (headless), and at other times polycephalous (Hydra-headed).[20]

The capacity of this design for effective performance over time may depend on the presence of shared principles, interests, and goals—at best, an overarching doctrine or ideology—that spans all nodes and to which the members wholeheartedly subscribe. Such a set of principles, shaped through mutual consultation and consensus-building, can enable them to be "all of one mind," even though they are dispersed and devoted to different tasks. It can provide a central ideational, strategic, and operational coherence that allows for tactical decentralization. It can set boundaries and provide guidelines for decisions and actions so that the members do not have to resort to a hierarchy—"they know what they have to do."[21]

The network design may depend on having an infrastructure for the dense communication of functional information. All nodes are not necessarily in constant communication, which may not make sense for a secretive, conspiratorial actor. But when communication is needed, the network's members must be able to disseminate information promptly and as broadly as desired within the network and to outside audiences.

In many respects, then, the archetypal netwar design corresponds to what earlier analysts called a "segmented, polycentric, ideologically integrated network" (SPIN):[22]

> By segmentary I mean that it is cellular, composed of many different groups. . . . By polycentric I mean that it has many different leaders or centers of direction. . . . By networked I mean that the segments and the leaders are integrated into reticulated systems or networks through various structural, personal, and ideological ties. Networks are usually unbounded and expanding. . . . This acronym [SPIN] helps us picture this organization as a fluid, dynamic, expanding one, spinning out into mainstream society.

Caveats About the Role of Technology

To realize its potential, a fully interconnected network requires a capacity for constant, dense information and communications flows, more so than do other forms of organization (e.g., hierarchies). This capacity is afforded by the latest information and communications technologies—cellular telephones, fax machines, electronic mail (e-mail), World Wide Web (WWW) sites, and computer conferencing. Moreover, netwar agents are poised to benefit from future increases in the speed of communication, dramatic reductions in the costs of communication, increases in bandwidth, vastly expanded connectivity, and integration of communication with computing technologies.[23] Such technologies are highly advantageous for a netwar actor whose constituents are geographically dispersed.

However, caveats are in order. First, the new technologies, however enabling for organizational networking, may not be the only crucial technologies for a netwar actor.

Old means of communications such as human couriers, and mixes of old and new systems, may suffice. Second, netwar is not simply a function of the Internet; it does not take place only in cyberspace or the infosphere. Some key battles may occur there, but a war's overall conduct and outcome will normally depend mostly on what happens in the real world. Even in information-age conflicts, what happens in the real world is generally more important than what happens in the virtual worlds of cyberspace or the infosphere.[24] Netwar is not Internet war.

Swarming, and the Blurring of Offense and Defense

This distinctive, often ad-hoc design has unusual strengths, for both offense and defense. On the offense, networks are known for being adaptable, flexible, and versatile vis-à-vis opportunities and challenges. This may be particularly the case where a set of actors can engage in *swarming*. Little analytic attention has been given to swarming, yet it may be a key mode of conflict in the information age. The cutting edge for this possibility is found among netwar protagonists.[25]

Swarming occurs when the dispersed nodes of a network of small (and perhaps some large) forces converge on a target from multiple directions. The overall aim is the *sustainable pulsing* of force or fire. Once in motion, swarm networks must be able to coalesce rapidly and stealthily on a target, then dissever and redisperse, immediately ready to recombine for a new pulse. In other words, information-age attacks may come in "swarms" rather than the more traditional "waves."

In terms of defensive potential, well-constructed networks tend to be redundant and diverse, making them robust and resilient in the face of adversity. Where they have a capacity for interoperability and shun centralized command and control, network designs can be difficult to crack and defeat as a whole. In particular, they may defy counterleadership targeting—attackers can find and confront only portions of the network. Moreover, the deniability built into a network may allow it to simply absorb a number of attacks on distributed nodes, leading the attacker to believe the network has been harmed when, in fact, it remains viable, and is seeking new opportunities for tactical surprise.

The difficulties of dealing with netwar actors deepen when the lines between offense and defense are blurred, or blended. When *blurring* is the case, it may be difficult to distinguish between attacking and defending actions, particularly when an actor goes on the offense in the name of self-defense. The *blending* of offense and defense will often mix the strategic and tactical levels of operations. For example, guerrillas on the defensive strategically may go on the offense tactically; the war of the *mujahideen* in Afghanistan provides a modern example.

The blurring of offense and defense reflects another feature of netwar: it tends to defy and cut across standard boundaries, jurisdictions, and distinctions between state and society, public and private, war and peace, war and crime, civilian and military, police and military, and legal and illegal. A government has difficulty assigning responsibility to a single agency—military, police, or intelligence—to respond.

Thus, the spread of netwar adds to the challenges facing the nation-state in the information age. Nation-state ideals of sovereignty and authority are traditionally linked to a bureaucratic rationality in which issues and problems can be neatly divided, and specific offices can be charged with taking care of specific problems. In netwar, things are rarely so clear. A protagonist is likely to operate in the cracks and gray areas of society, striking where lines of authority crisscross and the operational paradigms of politicians, officials, soldiers, police officers, and related actors get fuzzy and clash.

Networks Versus Hierarchies: Challenges for Counternetwar

Against this background, we are led to a set of three policy-oriented propositions about the information revolution and its implications for netwar and counternetwar.[26]

Hierarchies have a difficult time fighting networks. There are examples across the conflict spectrum. Some of the best are found in the failings of governments to defeat transnational criminal cartels engaged in drug smuggling, as in Colombia. The persistence of religious revivalist movements, as in Algeria, in the face of unremitting state opposition, shows the robustness of the network form. The Zapatista movement in Mexico, with its legions of supporters and sympathizers among local and transnational nongovernmental organizations (NGOs), shows that social netwar can put a democratizing autocracy on the defensive and pressure it to continue adopting reforms.

It takes networks to fight networks. Governments that would defend against netwar may have to adopt organizational designs and strategies like those of their adversaries. This does not mean mirroring the adversary, but rather learning to draw on the same design principles of network forms in the information age. These principles depend to some extent upon technological innovation, but mainly on a willingness to innovate organizationally and doctrinally, and by building new mechanisms for interagency and multijurisdictional cooperation.

Whoever masters the network form first and best will gain major advantages. In these early decades of the information age, adversaries who have adopted networking (be they criminals, terrorists, or peaceful social activists) are enjoying an increase in their power relative to state agencies.

Counternetwar may thus require effective interagency approaches, which by their nature involve networked structures. The challenge will be to blend hierarchies and networks skillfully, while retaining enough core authority to encourage and enforce adherence to networked processes. By creating effective hybrids, governments may better confront the new threats and challenges emerging in the information age, whether generated by terrorists, militias, criminals, or other actors.[27] The U.S. Counterterrorist Center, based at the Central Intelligence Agency (CIA), is a good example of a promising effort to establish a functional interagency network,[28] although its success may depend increasingly on the strength of links with the military services and other institutions that fall outside the realm of the intelligence community.

Middle Eastern Terrorism and Netwar

Terrorism seems to be evolving in the direction of violent netwar. Islamic fundamentalist organizations like Hamas and the bin Laden network consist of groups organized in loosely interconnected, semi-independent cells that have no single commanding hierarchy.[29]

Hamas exemplifies the shift away from a hierarchically oriented movement based on a "great leader" (like the PLO and Yasser Arafat).[30]

The netwar concept is consistent with patterns and trends in the Middle East, where the newer and more active terrorist groups appear to be adopting decentralized, flexible network structures. The rise of networked arrangements in terrorist organizations is part of a wider move away from formally organized, state-sponsored groups to privately financed, loose networks of individuals and subgroups that may have strategic guidance but enjoy tactical independence. Related to these shifts is the fact that terrorist groups are taking advantage of information technology to coordinate the activities of dispersed members. Such technology may be employed by terrorists not only to wage information warfare [IW], but also to support their own networked organizations.[31]

While a comprehensive empirical analysis of the relationship between (a) the structure of terrorist organizations and (b) group activity or strength is beyond the scope of this paper,[32] a cursory examination of such a relationship among Middle Eastern groups offers some evidence to support the claim that terrorists are preparing to wage netwar. The Middle East was selected for analysis mainly because terrorist groups based in this region have been active in targeting U.S. government facilities and interests, as in the bombings of the Khobar Towers, and . . ., the American embassies in Kenya and Tanzania.

Middle Eastern Terrorist Groups: Structure and Actions

Terrorist groups in the Middle East have diverse origins, ideologies, and organizational structures, but can be roughly categorized into traditional and new-generation groups. Traditional groups date back to the late 1960s and early 1970s, and the majority of these were (and some still are) formally or informally linked to the PLO. Typically, they are also relatively bureaucratic and maintain a nationalist or Marxist agenda. In contrast, most new-generation groups arose in the 1980s and 1990s, have more fluid organizational forms, and rely on Islam as a basis for their radical ideology.

The traditional, more-bureaucratic groups have survived to this day partly through support from states such as Syria, Libya, and Iran. The groups retain an ability to train and prepare for terrorist missions; however, their involvement in actual operations has been limited in recent years, partly because of successful counterterrorism campaigns by Israeli and Western agencies. In contrast, the newer and less hierarchical groups, such as Hamas, the Palestinian Islamic Jihad (PIJ), Hizbullah, Algeria's Armed Islamic Group (GIA), the Egyptian Islamic Group (IG), and Osama bin Laden's Arab Afghans, have become the most active organizations in and around the Middle East.

The traditional groups. Traditional terrorist groups in the Middle East include the Abu Nidal Organization (ANO), the Popular Front for the Liberation of Palestine (PFLP), and three PFLP-related splinters—the PFLP-General Command (PFLP-GC), the Palestine Liberation Front (PLF), and the Democratic Front for the Liberation of Palestine (DFLP).

The ANO was an integral part of the PLO until it became independent in 1974. It has a bureaucratic structure composed of various functional committees.[33] The activism it displayed in the 1970s and 1980s has lessened considerably, owing to a lessening of support from state sponsors and to effective counterterrorist campaigns by Israeli and Western intelligence services.[34] The very existence of the organization has recently been put into question, given uncertainty as to the whereabouts and fate of Abu Nidal, the leader of the group.[35]

The PFLP was founded in 1967 by George Habash as a PLO-affiliated organization. It has traditionally embraced a Marxist ideology, and remains an important PLO faction. However, in recent years it has suffered considerable losses from Israeli counterterrorist strikes.[36] The PFLP-General Command split from the PFLP in 1968, and in turn experienced a schism in the mid-1970s. This splinter group, which called itself the PLF, is composed of three subgroups, and has not been involved in high-profile acts since the 1985 hijacking of the Italian cruise ship *Achille Lauro*.[37] The PFLP was subjected to another split in 1969, which resulted in the Democratic Front for the Liberation of Palestine. The DFLP resembles a small army more than a terrorist group—its operatives are organized in battalions, backed by intelligence and special forces.[38] DFLP strikes have become less frequent since the 1970s, and since the late 1980s it has limited its attacks to Israeli targets near borders.[39]

What seems evident here is that this old generation of traditional, hierarchical, bureaucratic groups is on the wane. The reasons are varied, but the point remains—their way of waging terrorism is not likely to make a comeback, and is being superseded by a new way that is more attuned to the organizational, doctrinal, and technological imperatives of the information age.

The most active groups and their organization. The new generation of Middle Eastern groups has been active both in and outside the region in recent years. In Israel and the occupied territories, Hamas, and to a lesser extent the Palestinian Islamic Jihad, have shown their strength over the last four years with a series of suicide bombings that have killed more than one hundred people and injured several more.[40] Exploiting a strong presence in Lebanon, the Shi'ite Hizbullah organization has also staged a number of attacks against Israeli Defense Forces troops and Israeli cities in Galilee.[41]

The al-Gama'a al-Islamiya, or Islamic Group (IG), is the most active Islamic extremist group in Egypt. In November 1997 IG carried out an attack on Hatshepsut's Temple in Luxor, killing 58 tourists and 4 Egyptians. The Group has also claimed responsibility for the bombing of the Egyptian embassy in Islamabad, Pakistan, which left 16 dead and 60 injured.[42] In Algeria, the Armed Islamic Group (GIA) has been behind the most violent, lethal attacks in Algeria's protracted civil war. Approximately 70,000 Algerians have lost their lives since the domestic terrorist campaign began in 1992.[43]

Recently, the loosely organized group of Arab Afghans—radical Islamic fighters from several North African and Middle Eastern countries who forged ties while resisting the Soviet occupation of Afghanistan[44]—has come to the fore as an active terrorist outfit. One of the leaders and founders of the Arab Afghan movement, Osama bin Laden, a Saudi entrepreneur who bases his activities in Afghanistan,[45] is suspected of sending operatives to Yemen to bomb a hotel used by U.S. soldiers on their way to Somalia in 1992, plotting to assassinate President Clinton in the Philippines in 1994 and Egyptian President Hosni Mubarak in 1995, and of having a role in the Riyadh and Khobar blasts in Saudi Arabia that resulted in the deaths of 24 Americans in 1995 and 1996.[46] U.S. officials have pointed to bin Laden as the mastermind behind the U.S. embassy bombings in Kenya and Tanzania, which claimed the lives of more than 260 people, including 12 Americans.[47]

To varying degrees, these groups share the principles of the net-worked organization—relatively flat hierarchies, decentralization and delegation of decisionmaking authority, and loose lateral ties among dispersed groups and individuals.[48] For instance, Hamas is loosely structured, with some elements working openly through mosques and social service institutions to recruit members, raise funds, organize activities, and distribute propaganda. Palestinian security sources indicate that there are ten or more Hamas splinter groups and factions with no centralized operational leadership.[49] The Palestine Islamic Jihad is a series of loosely affiliated factions, rather than a cohesive group.[50] The pro-Iranian Hizbullah acts as an umbrella organization of radical Shiite groups, and in many respects is a hybrid of hierarchical and network arrangements; although the formal structure is highly bureaucratic, interactions among members are volatile and do not follow rigid lines of control.[51] According to the U.S. Department of State, Egypt's Islamic Group is a decentralized organization that operates without a single operational leader,[52] while the GIA is notorious for the lack of centralized authority.[53]

Unlike traditional terrorist organizations, Arab Afghans are part of a complex network of relatively autonomous groups that are financed from private sources forming "a kind of international terrorists' Internet."[54] The most notorious element of the network is Osama bin Laden, who uses his wealth and organizational skills to support and direct a multinational alliance of Islamic extremists. At the heart of this alliance is his own inner core group, known as Al-Qaeda ("The Base"), which sometimes conducts missions on its own, but more often in conjunction with other groups or elements in the alliance. The goal of the alliance is opposition on a global scale to perceived threats to Islam, as indicated by bin Laden's 1996 declaration of a holy war against the United States and the West. In the document, bin Laden specifies that such a holy war will be fought by irregular, light, highly mobile forces using guerrilla tactics.[55]

Even though bin Laden finances Arab Afghan activities and directs some operations, he apparently does not play a direct command and control role over all operatives. Rather, he is a key figure in the coordination and support of several dispersed activities.[56] For instance, bin Laden founded the "World Islamic Front for Jihad Against Jews and Crusaders."[57] And yet most of the groups that participate in this front (including Egypt's Islamic Group) remain independent, although the organizational barriers between them are fluid.[58]

From a netwar perspective, an interesting feature of bin Laden's Arab Afghan movement is its ability to relocate operations swiftly from one geographic area to another in response to changing circumstances and needs. Arab Afghans have participated in operations conducted by Algeria's GIA and Egypt's IG. Reports in 1997 also indicated that Arab Afghans transferred training operations to Somalia, where they joined the Islamic Liberation Party (ILP).[59] The same reports suggest that the Arab Afghan movement has considered sending fighters to Sinkiang Uighur province in western China, to wage a holy war against the Chinese regime.[60] This group's ability to move and act quickly (and, to some extent, to swarm) once opportunities emerge hampers counterterrorist efforts to predict its actions and monitor its activities. The fact that Arab Afghan operatives were able to strike the U.S. embassies in Kenya and Tanzania substantiates the claim that members of this network have the mobility and speed to operate over considerable distances.

Although the organizational arrangements in these groups do not match all the basic features of the network ideal,[61] they stand in contrast to more traditional groups. Another feature that distinguishes the newer generation of terrorist groups is their adoption of information technology.

Middle Eastern Terrorist Groups and the Use of Information Technology

Information technology (IT) is an enabling factor for networked groups; terrorists aiming to wage netwar may adopt it not only as a weapon, but also to help coordinate and support their activities. Before exploring how Middle Eastern terrorist groups have embraced the new technology, we posit three hypotheses that relate the rise of IT to organization for netwar:

- The greater the degree of organizational networking in a terrorist group, the higher the likelihood that IT is used to support the network's decisionmaking.

- Recent advances in IT facilitate networked terrorist organizations because information flows are becoming quicker, cheaper, more secure, and more versatile.

- As terrorist groups learn to use IT for decisionmaking and other organizational purposes, they will be likely to use the same technology as an offensive weapon to destroy or disrupt.

Middle Eastern terrorist groups provide examples of information technology being used for a wide variety of purposes. As discussed below, there is some evidence to support the claim that the most active groups—and therefore the most decentralized groups—have embraced information technology to coordinate activities and disseminate propaganda and ideology.[62] At the same time, the technical assets and know-how gained by terrorist groups as they seek to form into multi-organizational networks can be used for offensive purposes—an Internet connection can be used for both coordination and disruption. The anecdotes provided here are consistent with the rise in the Middle East of what has been termed *techno-terrorism,* or the use by terrorists of satellite communications, e-mail, and the World Wide Web.[63]

Arab Afghans appear to have widely adopted information technology. According to reporters who visited bin Laden's headquarters in a remote mountainous area of Afghanistan, the terrorist financier has computers, communications equipment, and a large number of disks for data storage.[64] Egyptian "Afghan" computer experts are said to have helped devise a communication network that relies on the World Wide Web, e-mail, and electronic bulletin boards so that the extremists can exchange information without running a major risk of being intercepted by counterterrorism officials.[65]

Hamas is another major group that uses the Internet to share operational information. Hamas activists in the United States use chat rooms to plan operations and activities.[66] Operatives use e-mail to coordinate activities across Gaza, the West Bank, and Lebanon. Hamas has realized that information can be passed securely over the Internet because it is next to impossible for counterterrorism intelligence to monitor accurately the flow and content of Internet traffic. Israeli security officials have difficulty in tracing Hamas messages and decoding their content.[67]

During a recent counterterrorist operation, several GIA bases in Italy were uncovered, and each was found to include computers and diskettes with instructions for the construction of bombs.[68] It has been reported that the GIA uses floppy disks and computers to store and process instructions and other information for its members, who are dispersed in Algeria and Europe.[69] Furthermore, the Internet is used as a propaganda tool by Hizbullah, which manages three World Wide Web sites—one for the central press office (at www. hizbollah.org), another to describe its attacks on Israeli targets (at www.moqawama.org), and the last for news and information (at www.almanar.com.lb).[70]

The presence of Middle Eastern terrorist organizations on the Internet is suspected in the case of the Islamic Gateway, a World Wide Web site that contains information on a number of Islamic activist organizations based in the United Kingdom. British Islamic activists use the World Wide Web to broadcast their news and attract funding; they are also turning to the Internet as an organizational and communication tool.[71] While the vast majority of Islamic activist groups represented in the Islamic Gateway are legitimate, one group—the Global Jihad Fund—makes no secret of its militant goals.[72] The appeal of the Islamic Gateway for militant groups may be enhanced by a representative's claim, in an Internet Newsnet article in August 1996, that the Gateway's Internet Service Provider (ISP) can give "CIA-proof" protection against electronic surveillance.[73]

Summary Comment

This review of patterns and trends in the Middle East substantiates our speculations that the new terrorism is evolving in the direction of netwar, along the following lines:[74]

- An increasing number of terrorist groups are adopting networked forms of organization and relying on information technology to support such structures.
- Newer groups (those established in the 1980s and 1990s) are more networked than traditional groups.
- A positive correlation is emerging between the degree of activity of a group and the degree to which it adopts a networked structure.[75]
- Information technology is as likely to be used for organizational support as for offensive warfare.
- The likelihood that young recruits will be familiar with information technology implies that terrorist groups will be increasingly networked and more computer-friendly in the future than they are today.

Terrorist Doctrines—The Rise of a "War Paradigm"

The evolution of terrorism in the direction of netwar will create new difficulties for counterterrorism. The types of challenges, and their severity, will depend on the kinds of doctrines that terrorists develop and employ. Some doctrinal effects will occur at the operational level, as in the relative emphasis placed on disruptive information operations as distinct from destructive combat operations. However, at a deeper level, the direction in which terrorist netwar evolves will depend upon the choices terrorists make as to the overall doctrinal paradigms that shape their goals and strategies.

At least three terrorist paradigms are worth considering: terror as coercive diplomacy, terror as war, and terror as the harbinger of a "new world." These three engage, in varying ways, distinct rationales for terrorism—as a weapon of the weak, as a way to assert identity, and as a way to break through to a new world—discussed earlier in this [selection]. While there has been much debate about the overall success or failure of terrorism,[76] the paradigm under which a terrorist operates may have a great deal to do with the likelihood of success. Coercion, for example, implies distinctive threats or uses of force, whereas norms of "war" often imply maximizing destruction.

The Coercive-Diplomacy Paradigm

The first paradigm is that of coercive diplomacy. From its earliest days, terrorism has often sought to persuade others, by means of symbolic violence, either to do something, stop doing something, or undo what has been done. These are the basic forms of coercive diplomacy,[77] and they appear in terrorism as far back as the Jewish Sicarii Zealots who sought independence from Rome in the first century AD, up through the Palestinians' often violent acts in pursuit of their independence today.

The fact that terrorist coercion includes violent acts does not make it a form of war—the violence is exemplary, designed to encourage what Alexander George calls "forceful persuasion," or "coercive diplomacy as an alternative to war."[78] In this light, terrorism may be viewed as designed to achieve specific goals, and the level of violence is limited, or proportional, to the ends being pursued. Under this paradigm, terrorism was once thought to lack a "demand" for WMD, as such tools would provide means vastly disproportionate to the ends of terror. This view was first elucidated over twenty years ago by Brian Jenkins—though there was some dissent expressed by scholars such as Thomas Schelling—and continued to hold sway until a few years ago.[79]

The War Paradigm

Caleb Carr, surveying the history of the failures of coercive terrorism and the recent trends toward increasing destructiveness and deniability, has elucidated what we call a "war paradigm."[80] This paradigm, which builds on ideas first considered by Jenkins,[81] holds that terrorist acts arise when weaker parties cannot challenge an adversary directly and thus turn to asymmetric methods. A war paradigm implies taking a strategic, campaign-oriented view of violence that makes no specific call for concessions from, or other demands upon, the opponent. Instead, the strategic aim is to inflict damage, in the context of what the terrorists view as an ongoing war. In theory, this paradigm, unlike the coercive diplomacy one, does not seek a proportional relationship between the level of force employed and the aims sought. When the goal is to inflict damage generally, and the terrorist group has no desire or need to claim credit, there is an attenuation of the need for proportionality—the worse the damage, the better. Thus, the use of WMD can be far more easily contemplated than in a frame of reference governed by notions of coercive diplomacy.

A terrorist war paradigm may be undertaken by terrorists acting on their own behalf or in service to a nation-state. In the future, as the information age brings the further empowerment of nonstate and transnational actors, "stateless" versions of the terrorist war paradigm may spread. At the same time, however, states will remain important players in the war paradigm; they may cultivate their own terrorist-style commandos, or seek cut-outs and proxies from among nonstate terrorist groups.

Ambiguity regarding a sponsor's identity may prove a key element of the war paradigm. While the use of proxies provides an insulating layer between a state sponsor and its target, these proxies, if captured, may prove more susceptible to interrogation and investigative techniques designed to winkle out the identity of the sponsor. On the other hand, while home-grown commando-style terrorists may be less forthcoming with information if caught, their own identities, which may be hard to conceal, may provide undeniable evidence of state sponsorship. These risks for states who think about engaging in or supporting terrorism may provide yet more reason for the war paradigm to increasingly become the province of nonstate terrorists—or those with only the most tenuous linkages to particular states.

Exemplars of the war paradigm today are the wealthy Saudi jihadist, Osama bin Laden, and the Arab Afghans that he associates with. As previously mentioned, bin Laden has explicitly called for war-like terrorism against the United States, and especially against U.S. military forces stationed in Saudi Arabia. President Clinton's statement that American retaliation for the U.S. embassy bombings in East Africa represented the first shots in a protracted war on terrorism suggests that the notion of adopting a war paradigm to counter terror has gained currency.

The New-World Paradigm

A third terrorist paradigm aims at achieving the birth of what might be called a "new world." It may be driven by religious mania, a desire for totalitarian control, or an impulse toward ultimate chaos.[82] Aum Shinrikyo would be a recent example. The paradigm harks back to the dynamics of millennialist movements that arose in past epochs of social upheaval, when *prophetae* attracted adherents from the margins of other social movements and led small groups to pursue salvation by seeking a final, violent cataclysm.[83]

This paradigm is likely to seek the vast disruption of political, social, and economic order. Accomplishing this goal may involve lethal destruction, even a heightened willingness to use WMD. Religious terrorists may desire destruction for its own sake, or for some form of "cleansing." But the ultimate aim is not so much the destruction of society as a rebirth after a period of chaotic disruption.

The Paradigms and Netwar

All three paradigms offer room for netwar. Moreover, all three paradigms allow the rise of "cybotage"—acts of disruption and destruction against information infrastructures by terrorists who learn the skills of cyberterror, as well as by disaffected individuals with technical skills who are drawn into the terrorist milieu. However, we note that terrorist netwar may also be a battle of ideas—and to wage this form of conflict some terrorists may want the Net *up,* not down.

Many experts argue that terrorism is moving toward ever more lethal, destructive acts. Our netwar perspective accepts this, but also holds that some terrorist netwars will stress disruption over destruction. Networked terrorists will no doubt continue to destroy things and kill people, but their principal strategy may move toward the nonlethal end of the spectrum, where command and control nodes and vulnerable information infrastructures provide rich sets of targets.

Indeed, terrorism has long been about "information"—from the fact that trainees for suicide bombings are kept from listening to international media, through the ways that terrorists seek to create disasters that will consume the front pages, to the related debates about countermeasures that would limit freedom of the press, increase public surveillance and intelligence gathering, and heighten security over information and communications systems. Terrorist tactics focus attention on the importance of information and communications for the functioning of democratic institutions; debates about how terrorist threats undermine democratic practices may revolve around freedom of information issues.

While netwar may be waged by terrorist groups operating with any of the three paradigms, the rise of networked groups whose objective is to wage war may be the one most relevant to and dangerous from the standpoint of the military. Indeed, if terrorists perceive themselves as warriors, they may be inclined to target enemy military assets or interests. . . .

[Conclusion] Targeting Terrorists in the Information Age

The transition from hierarchical to networked terrorist groups is likely to be uneven and gradual. The netwar perspective suggests that, for the foreseeable future, various networked forms will emerge, coexisting with and influencing traditional organizations. Such organizational diversity implies the need for a counterterrorism strategy that recognizes the differences among organizational designs and seeks to target the weaknesses associated with each.

Counterleadership strategies or retaliation directed at state sponsors may be effective for groups led by a charismatic leader who enjoys the backing of sympathetic governments, but are likely to fail if used against an organization with multiple, dispersed leaders and private sources of funding. Networked organizations rely on information flows to function, and disruption of the flows cripples their ability to coordinate actions. It is no coincidence, for instance, that while the separation between Hamas political and military branches is well documented, this terrorist group jealously guards information on the connections and degree of coordination between the two.[84]

At the same time, the two-way nature of connectivity for information networks such as the Internet implies that the dangers posed by information warfare are often symmetric—the degree to which a terrorist organization uses information infrastructure for offensive purposes may determine its exposure to similar attacks by countering forces. While it is true that terrorist organizations will often enjoy the benefit of surprise, the IW tactics available to them can also be adopted by counterterrorists.

The key task for counterterrorism, then, is the identification of organizational and technological terrorist networks. Once such structures are identified, it may be possible to insert and disseminate false information, overload systems, misdirect message traffic, preclude access, and engage in other destructive and disruptive activities to hamper and prevent terrorist operations.

John Arquilla is a senior consultant to the International Security Group at RAND Corporation and an associate professor of defense analysis at the Naval Postgraduate School in Monterey, California.

David Ronfeldt is a senior social scientist at RAND whose research focuses on issues such information revolution, netwar, and the rise of transnational networks of nongovernmental organizations.

Michele Zanini is a research at RAND. These experts are all contributors to the book *Countering the New Terrorism* (1999).

Notes

1. For an illuminating take on irregular warfare that emphasizes the challenges to the Red Cross, see Michael Ignatieff, "Unarmed Warriors," *The New Yorker,* March 24, 1997, pp. 56–71.
2. Martin Van Creveld, "In Wake of Terrorism, Modern Armies Prove to Be Dinosaurs of Defense," *New Perspectives Quarterly,* Vol. 13, No. 4, Fall 1996, p. 58.
3. See Walter Laqueur, "Postmodern Terrorism," *Foreign Affairs,* Vol. 75, No. 5, September/October 1996, pp. 24–36; Fred Iklé, "The Problem of the Next Lenin," *The National Interest,* Vol. 47, Spring 1997, pp. 9–19; Bruce Hoffman, *Responding to Terrorism Across the Technological Spectrum,* RAND, P-7874, 1994; Bruce Hoffman, *Inside Terrorism,* Columbia University Press, New York, 1998; Robert Kaplan, "The Coming Anarchy," *Atlantic Monthly,* February 1994, pp. 44–76.
4. See J. Kenneth Campbell, "Weapon of Mass Destruction Terrorism," Master's thesis, Naval Postgraduate School, Monterey, California, 1996.
5. Bruce Hoffman and Caleb Carr, "Terrorism: Who Is Fighting Whom?" *World Policy Journal,* Vol. 14, No. 1, Spring 1997, pp. 97–104.
6. For instance, Martin Shubik, "Terrorism, Technology, and the Socioeconomics of Death," *Comparative Strategy,* Vol. 16, No. 4, October–December 1997, pp. 399–414; as well as Hoffman, 1998.
7. See Matthew Littleton, "Information Age Terrorism," MA thesis, U.S. Naval Postgraduate School, 1995, and Brigitte Nacos, *Terrorism and the Media,* Columbia University Press, New York, 1994.
8. Laqueur, 1996, p. 35.
9. For more on this issue, see Roger Molander, Andrew Riddile, and Peter Wilson, *Strategic Information Warfare: A New Face of War,* RAND, MR-661-OSD, 1996; Roger Molander, Peter Wilson, David Mussington, and Richard Mesic, *Strategic Information Warfare Rising,* RAND, 1998.
10. Caleb Carr, "Terrorism as Warfare," *World Policy Journal,* Vol. 13, No. 4, Winter 1996–1997, pp. 1–12. This theme was advocated early by Gayle Rivers, *The War Against the Terrorists: How to Fight and Win,* Stein and Day, New York, 1986. For more on the debate, see Hoffman and Carr, 1997.
11. See, for instance, Benjamin Netanyahu, *Winning the War Against Terrorism,* Simon and Schuster, New York, 1996, and John Kerry (Senator), *The New War,* Simon & Schuster, New York, 1997.
12. This analytical background is drawn from John Arquilla and David Ronfeldt, *The Advent of Netwar,* RAND, MR-678-OSD, 1996, and David Ronfeldt, John Arquilla, Graham Fuller, and Melissa Fuller, *The Zapatista "Social Netwar" in Mexico,* RAND, MR-994-A, forthcoming. Also see John Arquilla and David Ronfeldt (eds.), *In Athena's Camp: Preparing for Conflict in the Information Age,* RAND, MR-880-OSD/RC, 1997.

13. For background on this issue, see Charles Heckscher, "Defining the Post-Bureaucratic Type," in Charles Heckscher and Anne Donnelon (eds.), *The Post-Bureaucratic Organization,* Sage, Thousand Oaks, California, 1995, pp. 50–52.

14. The concept of soft power was introduced by Joseph S. Nye in *Bound to Lead: The Changing Nature of American Power,* Basic Books, New York, 1990, and further elaborated in Joseph S. Nye and William A. Owens, "America's Information Edge," *Foreign Affairs,* Vol. 75, No. 2, March/April 1996.

15. For more on information-age conflict, netwar, and cyberwar, see John Arquilla and David Ronfeldt, "Cyberwar is Coming!" *Comparative Strategy,* Vol. 12, No. 2, Summer 1993, pp. 141–165, and Arquilla and Ronfeldt, 1996 and 1997.

16. Martin Van Creveld, *The Transformation of War,* Free Press, New York, 1991.

17. T. Burns and G. M. Stalker, *The Management of Innovation,* Tavistock, London, 1961, p. 121.

18. See, for instance, Jessica Lipnack and Jeffrey Stamps, *The Age of the Network,* Wiley & Sons, New York, 1994, pp. 51–78, and Heckscher, "Defining the Post-Bureaucratic Type," p. 45.

19. Adapted from William M. Evan, "An Organization-Set Model of Interorganizational Relations," in Matthew Tuite, Roger Chisholm, and Michael Radnor (eds.), *Interorganizational Decisionmaking,* Aldine Publishing Company, Chicago, 1972.

20. The structure may also be cellular, although the presence of cells does not necessarily mean a network exists. A hierarchy can also be cellular, as is the case with some subversive organizations. A key difference between cells and nodes is that the former are designed to minimize information flows for security reasons (usually only the head of the cell reports to the leadership), while nodes in principle can easily establish connections with other parts of the network (so that communications and coordination can occur horizontally).

21. The quotation is from a doctrinal statement by Louis Beam about "leaderless resistance," which has strongly influenced right-wing white-power groups in the United States. See *The Seditionist,* Issue 12, February 1992.

22. See Luther P. Gerlach, "Protest Movements and the Construction of Risk," in B. B. Johnson and V. T. Covello (eds.), *The Social and Cultural Construction of Risk,* D. Reidel Publishing Co., Boston, Massachusetts, 1987, p. 115, based on Luther P. Gerlach and Virginia Hine, *People, Power, Change: Movements of Social Transformation,* The Bobbs-Merrill Co., New York, 1970. This SPIN concept, a precursor of the netwar concept, was proposed by Luther Gerlach and Virginia Hine in the 1960s to depict U.S. social movements. It anticipates many points about network forms of organization that are now coming into focus in the analysis not only of social movements but also some terrorist, criminal, ethno-nationalist, and fundamentalist organizations.

23. See Wolf V. Heydenbrand, "New Organizational Forms," *Work and Occupations,* No. 3, Vol. 16, August 1989, pp. 323–357.

24. See Paul Kneisel, "Netwar: The Battle Over Rec.Music.White-Power," *ANTIFA INFO BULLETIN,* Research Supplement, June 12, 1996, unpaginated ASCII text available on the Internet. Kneisel analyzes the largest vote ever taken about the creation of a new Usenet newsgroup—a vote to prevent the creation of a group that was ostensibly about white-power music. He concludes that "The *war* against contemporary fascism will be won in the 'real world' off the net; but *battles* against fascist netwar are fought and won on the Internet." His title is testimony to the spreading usage of the term netwar.

25. Swarm networks are discussed by Kevin Kelly, *Out of Control: The Rise of Neo-Biological Civilization,* A William Patrick Book, Addison-Wesley Publishing Company, New York, 1994. Also see Arquilla and Ronfeldt, 1997.

26. Also see Alexander Berger, "Organizational Innovation and Redesign in the Information Age: The Drug War, Netwar, and Other Low-End Conflict," Master's Thesis, Naval Postgraduate School, Monterey, California, 1998, for additional thinking and analysis about such propositions.

27. For elaboration, see Arquilla and Ronfeldt, 1997, Chapter 19.

28. Vernon Loeb, "Where the CIA Wages Its New World War," *Washington Post,* September 9, 1998. For a broader discussion of interagency cooperation in countering terrorism, see Ashton

Carter, John Deutch, and Philip Zelikow, "Catastrophic Terrorism," *Foreign Affairs,* Vol. 77, No. 6, November/December 1998, pp. 80–94.

29. Analogously, right-wing militias and extremist groups in the United States also rely on a doctrine of "leaderless resistance" propounded by Aryan nationalist Louis Beam. See Beam, 1992; and Kenneth Stern, *A Force Upon the Plain: The American Militia Movement and the Politics of Hate,* Simon and Schuster, New York, 1996. Meanwhile, as part of a broader trend toward netwar, transnational criminal organizations (TCOs) have been shifting away from centralized "Dons" to more networked structures. See Phil Williams, "Transnational Criminal Organizations and International Security," *Survival,* Vol. 36, No. 1, Spring 1994, pp. 96–113; and Phil Williams, "The Nature of Drug-Trafficking Networks," *Current History,* April 1998, pp. 154–159. As noted earlier, social activist movements long ago began to evolve "segmented, polycephalous, integrated networks." For a discussion of a social netwar in which human-rights and other peaceful activist groups supported an insurgent group in Mexico, see David Ronfeldt and Armando Martinez, "A Comment on the Zapatista 'Netwar'," in John Arquilla and David Ronfeldt, 1997, pp. 369–391.

30. It is important to differentiate our notions of information-age networking from earlier ideas about terror as consisting of a network in which all nodes revolved around a Soviet core (Claire Sterling, *The Terror Network,* Holt, Rinehart & Winston, New York, 1981). This view has generally been regarded as unsupported by available evidence (see Cindy C. Combs, *Terrorism in the Twenty-First Century,* Prentice-Hall, New York, 1997, pp. 99–119). However, there were a few early studies that did give credit to the possibility of the rise of terror networks that were bound more by loose ties to general strategic goals than by Soviet control (see especially Thomas L. Friedman, "Loose-Linked Network of Terror: Separate Acts, Ideological Bonds," *Terrorism,* Vol. 8, No. 1, Winter 1985, pp. 36–49).

31. For good general background, see Michael Whine, "Islamist Organisations on the Internet," draft circulated on the Internet, April 1998 (*www.ict.org.il/articles*).

32. We assume that group activity is a proxy for group strength. Group activity can be measured more easily than group strength, and is expected to be significantly correlated with strength. The relationship may not be perfect, but it is deemed to be sufficiently strong for our purposes.

33. Office of the Coordinator for Counterterrorism, *Patterns of Global Terrorism,* 1996, U.S. Department of State, Publication 10433, April 1997.

34. Loeb, 1998; and John Murray and Richard H. Ward (eds.), *Extremist Groups,* Office of International Criminal Justice, University of Illinois, Chicago, 1996.

35. Youssef M. Ibrahim, "Egyptians Hold Terrorist Chief, Official Asserts," *New York Times,* August 26, 1998.

36. Murray and Ward, 1996.

37. *Patterns of Global Terrorism,* 1996, and Murray and Ward, 1996.

38. Murray and Ward, 1996.

39. *Patterns of Global Terrorism,* 1995, 1996, 1997.

40. For instance, in 1997 Hamas operatives set off three suicide bombs in crowded public places in Tel Aviv and Jerusalem. On March 21, a Hamas satchel bomb exploded at a Tel Aviv café, killing three persons and injuring 48; on July 30, two Hamas suicide bombers blew themselves up in a Jerusalem market, killing 16 persons and wounding 178; on September 4, three suicide bombers attacked a Jerusalem pedestrian mall, killing at least five persons (in addition to the suicide bombers), and injuring at least 181. The Palestinian Islamic Jihad has claimed responsibility (along with Hamas) for a bomb that killed 20 and injured 75 others in March 1996, and in 1995 it carried out five bombings that killed 29 persons and wounded 107. See *Patterns of Global Terrorism,* 1995, 1996, 1997.

41. See "Hizbullah," Israeli Foreign Ministry, April 11, 1996. Available on the Internet at *http://www.israel-mfa.gov.il.*

42. See *Patterns of Global Terrorism,* 1995, 1996, 1997.

43. *Patterns of Global Terrorism,* 1997.

44. "Arab Afghans Said to Launch Worldwide Terrorist War," *Paris al-Watan al-'Arabi,* FBIS-TOT-96-010-L, December 1, 1995, pp. 22–24.

45. William Gertz, "Saudi Financier Tied to Attacks," *Washington Times,* October 23, 1996.

46. Tim Weiner, "U.S. Sees bin Laden as Ringleader of Terrorist Network," *New York Times,* August 21, 1998; M. J. Zuckerman, "Bin Laden Indicted for Bid to Kill Clinton," *USA Today,* August 26, 1998.

47. Pamela Constable, "Bin Laden 'Is Our Guest, So We Must Protect Him'," *Washington Post,* August 21, 1998.

48. We distinguish between deliberate and factional decentralization. Factional decentralization— prevalent in older groups—occurs when subgroups separate themselves from the central leadership because of differences in tactics or approach. Deliberate or operational decentralization is what distinguishes netwar agents from others, since delegation of authority in this case occurs because of the distinct advantages this organizational arrangement brings, and not because of lack of consensus. We expect both influences on decentralization to continue, but newer groups will tend to decentralize authority even in the absence of political disagreements.

49. "Gaza Strip, West Bank: Dahlan on Relations with Israel, Terrorism," *Tel Aviv Yedi'ot Aharonot,* FBIS-TOT-97-022-L, February 28, 1997, p. 18.

50. The leader of the PIJ's most powerful faction, Fathi Shaqaqi, was assassinated in October 1995 in Malta, allegedly by the Israeli Mossad. Shaqaqi's killing followed the assassination of Hani Abed, another PIJ leader killed in 1994 in Gaza. Reports that the group has been considerably weakened as a result of Israeli counterleadership operations are balanced by the strength demonstrated by the PIJ in its recent terrorist activity. See "Islamic Group Vows Revenge for Slaying of Its Leader," *New York Times,* October 30, 1995, p. 9.

51. Magnus Ranstorp, "Hizbullah's Command Leadership: Its Structure, Decision-Making and Relationship with Iranian Clergy and Institutions," *Terrorism and Political Violence,* Vol. 6, No. 3, Autumn 1994, p. 304.

52. *Patterns of Global Terrorism,* 1996.

53. "Algeria: Infighting Among Proliferating 'Wings' of Armed Groups," *London al-Sharq al-Aswat,* FBIS-TOT-97-021-L, February 24, 1997, p. 4.

54. David B. Ottaway, "US Considers Slugging It Out With International Terrorism," *Washington Post,* October 17, 1996, p. 25.

55. "Saudi Arabia: Bin-Laden Calls for 'Guerrilla Warfare' Against US Forces," *Beirut Al-Diyar,* FBIS-NES-96-180, September 12, 1996.

56. It is important to avoid equating the bin Laden network solely with bin Laden. He represents a key node in the Arab Afghan terror network, but there should be no illusions about the likely effect on the network of actions taken to neutralize him. The network conducts many operations without his involvement, leadership, or financing—and will continue to be able to do so should he be killed or captured.

57. "Militants Say There Will Be More Attacks Against U.S.," *European Stars and Stripes,* August 20, 1998.

58. For instance, there have been reports of a recent inflow of Arab Afghans into Egypt's Islamic Group to reinforce the latter's operations. See Murray and Ward, 1996, and "The CIA on Bin Laden," *Foreign Report,* No. 2510, August 27, 1998, pp. 2–3.

59. This move was also influenced by the Taliban's decision to curb Arab Afghan activities in the territory under its control as a result of U.S. pressure. See "Arab Afghans Reportedly Transfer Operations to Somalia," *Cairo al-Arabi,* FBIS-TOT-97-073, March 10, 1997, p. 1.

60. "Afghanistan, China: Report on Bin-Laden Possibly Moving to China," *Paris al-Watan al-'Arabi,* FBIS-NES-97-102, May 23, 1997, pp. 19–20.

61. While it is possible to discern a general trend toward an organizational structure that displays several features of a network, we expect to observe substantial differences (and many hierarchy/ network hybrids) in how organizations make their specific design choices. Different network designs depend on contingent factors, such as personalities, organizational history, operational requirements, and other influences such as state sponsorship and ideology.

62. Assessing the strength of the relationship between organizational structure and use of information technology is difficult to establish. Alternative explanations may exist as to why newer groups would embrace information technology, such as age of the group (one could

speculate that newer terrorist groups have on average younger members, who are more familiar with computers), or the amount of funding (a richer group could afford more electronic gadgetry). While it is empirically impossible to refute these points, much in organization theory supports our hypothesis that there is a direct relationship between a higher need for information technology and the use of network structures.

63. "Saudi Arabia: French Analysis of Islamic Threat," *Paris al-Watan al-'Arabi,* FBIS-NES-97-082, April 11, 1997, pp. 4–8.

64. "Afghanistan, Saudi Arabia: Editor's Journey to Meet Bin-Laden Described," *London al-Quds al-'Arabi,* FBIS-TOT-97-003-L, November 27, 1996, p. 4.

65. "Arab Afghans Said to Launch Worldwide Terrorist War," 1995.

66. "Israel: U.S. Hamas Activists Use Internet to Send Attack Threats," *Tel Aviv IDF Radio,* FBIS-TOT-97-001-L, 0500 GMT October 13, 1996.

67. "Israel: Hamas Using Internet to Relay Operational Messages," *Tel Aviv Ha'aretz,* FBIS-TOT-98-034, February 3, 1998, p. 1.

68. "Italy: Security Alters Following Algerian Extremists' Arrests," *Milan Il Giornale,* FBIS-TOT-97-002-L, November 12, 1996, p. 10.

69. "Italy, Vatican City: Daily Claims GIA 'Strategist' Based in Milan," *Milan Corriere della Sera,* FBIS-TOT-97-004-L, December 5, 1996, p. 9.

70. "Hizbullah TV Summary 18 February 1998," *Al-Manar Television World Wide Webcast,* FBIS-NES-98-050, February 19, 1998. Also see "Developments in Mideast Media: January–May 1998," Foreign Broadcast Information Service (FBIS), May 11, 1998.

71. "Islamists on Internet," FBIS Foreign Media Note-065EP96, September 9, 1996.

72. "Islamic Activism Online," FBIS Foreign Media Note-02JAN97, January 3, 1997.

73. The Muslim Parliament has recently added an Internet Relay Chat (IRC) link and a "Muslims only" List-Serve (automatic e-mail delivery service). See "Islamic Activism Online," FBIS Foreign Media Note-02JAN97, January 3, 1997.

74. Similar propositions may apply to varieties of netwar other than the new terrorism.

75. We make a qualification here. There appears to be a significant positive association between the degree to which a group is active and the degree to which a group is decentralized and networked. But we cannot be confident about the causality of this relationship or its direction (i.e., whether activity and strength affect networking, or vice-versa). A host of confounding factors may affect both the way groups decide to organize and their relative success at operations. For instance, the age of a group may be an important predictor of a group's success—newer groups are likely to be more popular; popular groups are more likely to enlist new operatives; and groups that have a large number of operatives are likely to be more active, regardless of organizational structure. Another important caveat is related to the fact that it is difficult to rank groups precisely in terms of the degree to which they are networked, because no terrorist organization is thought to represent either a hierarchical or network ideal-type. While the conceptual division between newer-generation and traditional groups is appropriate for our scope here, an analytical "degree of networking" scale would have to be devised for more empirical research.

76. See, for instance, William Gutteridge (ed.), *Contemporary Terrorism,* Facts on File, Oxford, England, 1986; Hoffman and Carr, 1997; and Combs, 1997.

77. See Alexander George and William Simons, *The Limits of Coercive Diplomacy,* Westview Press, Boulder, 1994.

78. Alexander George, *Forceful Persuasion: Coercive Diplomacy as an Alternative to War,* United States Institute of Peace Press, Washington, DC, 1991.

79. Brian Jenkins, *The Potential for Nuclear Terrorism,* RAND, P-5876, 1977; Thomas Schelling, "Thinking about Nuclear Terrorism," *International Security,* Vol. 6, No. 4, Spring 1982, pp. 68–75; and Patrick Garrity and Steven Maaranen, *Nuclear Weapons in a Changing World,* Plenum Press, New York, 1992.

80. Carr, 1996.

81. Brian Jenkins, *International Terrorism: A New Kind of Warfare,* RAND, P-5261, 1974.

82. For a discussion of these motives, see Laqueur, 1996; Iklé, 1997; and Hoffman, 1998, respectively.

83. See, for instance, Michael Barkun, *Disaster and the Millennium,* Yale University Press, New Haven, 1974; and Norman Cohn, *The Pursuit of the Millennium: Revolutionary Messianism in Medieval and Reformation Europe and Its Bearing on Modern Totalitarian Movements,* Harper Torch Books, New York, 1961.

84. Bluma Zuckerbrot-Finkelstein, "A Guide to Hamas," *Internet Jewish Post,* available at *http://www.jewishpost.com/jewishpost/jp0203/jpn0303.htm.*

Rohan Gunaratna

Defeating Al-Qaeda—The Pioneering Vanguard of the Islamic Movements[1]

Despite being the most hunted terrorist group in history, the leadership, organization and ideology of Jama'at al-Qaeda al-Jihad has been able to survive.[2] After al-Qaeda was dislodged from its traditional base of Afghanistan in early 2002, the group has been able to reconstitute itself and fight back largely because it has found a safe haven in Pakistan's Federally Administered Tribal Areas (FATA).

Three profound developments characterize the global threat landscape after the September 11, 2001 attacks (9-11) in the United States. First, after the US-led intervention in Afghanistan, the center of gravity for terrorism has moved from Afghanistan to Pakistan's FATA. While Afghanistan remains a battlefield, core al-Qaeda members, with the help of the Taliban, have created FATA as the global headquarters of like-minded groups. Second, following the targeted assassination of al-Qaeda's leader Abu Musab al Zarkawi (Abu Musab) in Iraq, the group's leadership in FATA, nominee Abu Ayub al Masri has assumed the leadership role of al-Qaeda in Iraq. As the US and its Western allies are inching towards troop withdrawal, Iraq has become core al-Qaeda's central battlefield. Third, after the US invasion and occupation of Iraq, al-Qaeda in FATA has gained a foothold in the Middle East, establishing a forward operational base 2,290 kilometres (1,420 miles) closer to the West. While the war in Iraq is providing inspiration and instigation to jihadists worldwide, FATA has emerged as a key centre for planning and preparing operations to strike the US as well as its allies and friends.

At the heart of these developments is the leadership of al-Qaeda led by Usama Bin Laden and his Egyptian deputy Dr Ayman al-Zawahiri (al-Zawahiri), who is also the principal architect of the global jihad movement. Al-Zawahiri has assumed control of Majlis al-Shurra (consultative council), al-Qaeda's highest decision-making body. Although its strength has depleted from 3,000 to 4,000 members during 9-11 to a few hundred members today, al-Qaeda remains resilient. Its strong desire to prosecute spectacular attacks against Western targets is feared. Furthermore, al-Qaeda attracts the most media attention in the West compared to other threat groups. It has an unmatched ability to reach out to the Muslim masses as well as work with Islamist groups globally. It accepts like-minded groups who seek to name themselves after al-Qaeda, and to adopt its ideology of global jihad and operational tactics of suicide.

Background

Since the emergence of the contemporary wave of terrorism in the Middle East in 1968, the world has witnessed three categories of terrorist organisations—ideological (left and right wing), ethnonationalist (irredentist, separatist, autonomy) and politico-religious groups. Two landmark events—the Islamic revolution in Iran—and Soviet intervention in Afghanistan—both in 1979 marked the emergence of the contemporary wave of Islamist guerrilla and terrorist groups.[3] While Iran's clerical regime held 66 Americans as hostages for 444 days in Tehran, the anti-Soviet multinational Afghan campaign checkmated the world's largest army—the Soviet army—in a protracted guerrilla campaign that lasted a decade. While an Islamic regime defied one superpower in the Middle East, an Islamic movement defeated another superpower in Afghanistan. In response to the Soviet occupation of Afghanistan (December 1979–February 1989), US presence in the Arabian Peninsula (December 1990), Gulf War I (January 1991) and the US-led coalition occupation of Iraq (March 2003–), Islamism grew in strength, size and influence. As a result, virulent and extremist ideologies found greater acceptance, existing Islamist political parties and terrorist groups became more influential, and new Islamist organisations proliferated.

A militant Sunni group, al-Qaeda was based in Pakistan (1988–1991), Sudan (1991–1996), Afghanistan (1996–2002) and again Pakistan (2002-to-date). Since its foundation in March 1988, one year before Soviet troop withdrawal from Afghanistan, al-Qaeda built a "network of networks."[4] By co-opting leaders of like-minded Islamic movements, al-Qaeda built an umbrella of which Osama bin Laden gradually assumed the leadership. In its earlier life—Maktab – il – khidamat (Afghan Service Bureau)—established in 1984, it built a global network that channeled resources and recruits from around the world to Afghanistan. After defeating the Soviet Army, the largest land army in the world, and stripping the Soviet Empire of its super power status, the Islamists aimed its sights at the remaining superpower—the United States of America. As the vicious by-product of the anti-Soviet multinational Afghan campaign, al-Qaeda had inherited a state-of-the-art training infrastructure, wealthy sponsors, proven trainers, experienced combatants and a vast support base stretching from Australia throughout the Muslim world into Canada.

After its victory against the Soviet army in Afghanistan in the 1980s, al-Qaeda transformed from a guerrilla group to a terrorist group capable of operating in urban terrain and targeting civilians after its headquarters relocated from Peshawar, Pakistan, to Khartoum, Sudan in December 1991. After the 1993 meeting in Khartoum, between Osama bin Laden and Imad Mugneyev, the head of the Special Security Apparatus of Hezbollah, the most dangerous terrorist group at that time, al-Qaeda members and recruits received terrorist instruction in Sudan and Southern Lebanon.[5] The camps in Sudan were sponsored and conducted by the Iranian Ministry of Intelligence and Security Affairs (MOIS) and the Iranian Revolutionary Guards Corps (IRGC). As the Taliban regime perceived the clerical regime in Iran as inimical, Iranian sponsorship declined after Osama bin Laden relocated from Sudan to Afghanistan in May 1996.[6] After US occupation of Iraq in March 2003, Iran became the immediate neighbour of the United States of America. In conducting its operations from Afghanistan, a landlocked country, al-Qaeda had to rely either on Pakistan or Iran as a launching pad. With severe losses on its Pakistan front, since October 2001, al-Qaeda has opened a new staging area, the Iranian front.

Al-Qaeda maintained an extensive presence in Iran and even ties with the intelligence service of Iran. There is no evidence of Iranian support for Osama bin Laden. Although Iran and the Lebanese Hezbollah supported al-Qaeda before 1996, after al-Qaeda relocated to

Afghanistan in May 1996, al-Qaeda received no support from the Iranian government. After he fled from Afghanistan, an al-Qaeda ally Abu Musab al Zarqawi was operating out of Iran briefly but received no official Iranian support. Before Zarqawi became a well-known terrorist in Iraq, the Iranian authorities arrested Zarqawi very briefly but released him. Contrary to reporting by some security and intelligence services of Europe, Zarqawi was not provided official safe haven by the Iranians. Until to this date, Iran has never provided official support to Tawhid Wal Jihad (now al-Qaeda in Iraq). In fact, after Zarqawi bombed the most holy Shia shrines in Iraq, both MOIS and IRGC supported Shia groups to hunt Zarqawi and his associates. Although al-Qaeda is operating out of Iran, it is not receiving any official Iranian support as yet. These detainees are not tortured or otherwise kept in tough confinement, but they are not allowed to participate in al-Qaeda planning. The al-Qaeda organization today does not include any of their previously detained members in Iranian jails. While some of the Kurdish Jihadists the Iranians have captured have been released, and sent back into Iraq, the Iranians have constantly increased the amount of al-Qaeda detainees in their possession. The Iranians seem to be maintaining over 100 top al-Qaeda detainees as a bargaining chip. The way the Western nations are approaching Iran over the nuclear issue, this may change.

Background

Al-Qaeda has suffered formidable losses since September 11, 2001. Over 3000 leaders, members and key supporters of al-Qaeda have been killed or captured in 102 countries since the United States of America's declared "War on Terrorism."[7] Nonetheless, the robust Islamist milieu, in which al-Qaeda operates, has enabled the group to replenish its human losses (members captured and killed) and material wastage (assets seized and funds frozen). Furthermore, having imparted guerilla and terrorist training to several tens of thousands of Islamists from around the world in its camps in Afghanistan, al-Qaeda built sufficient strategic depth worldwide for the generation of support and recruits. As a well-endowed and well-resourced group from its inception, al-Qaeda invested in creating a cadre of highly dedicated and committed fighters willing to kill and die in the name of religion. Whether they live in the West or the East, al-Qaeda supporters and sympathizers believe in the often repeated al-Qaeda dictum: "It is the duty of every Muslim to wage jihad."

Despite the US-led intensive and sustained global hunt, al-Qaeda continues to present an unprecedented threat. Its unique historical origins, religious character, and organizational structure guarantee its sustenance and survival. When compared with all the other terrorist groups we have been studying since the emergence of the contemporary wave of terrorism in 1968, al-Qaeda is different in composition, diversity, and reach. With the exception of Aum Shinrikyo of Japan, al-Qaeda is the first multinational terrorist group of the 21st century.[8] It has recruited from the Muslim territories of Asia, Africa, Middle East, Caucuses and the Balkans as well as the Muslim migrant and diaspora communities of Europe, North America and Australia. In contrast to other groups that recruited from one single nationality[9] or groupings of nationalities from one particular region,[10] al-Qaeda is truly multinational. Despite global efforts to detect, disrupt, degrade and destroy al-Qaeda, the group has survived because it has a global presence. Periodically it has attacked symbolic, strategic and high-profile targets across geographic regions to make its presence known to its support base and to its enemies. Its capacity to survive is largely due to its loosely networked structure, diverse composition and universal ideology. To counter and evade the growing threat to al-Qaeda, the group itself has transformed structurally, strategically and geographically. Al-Qaeda is global in reach, from Asia to Canada; multi-national in composition, from Uigurs in Xingjiang to American Hispanics; and therefore, enjoys diverse capabilities, access to resources, and multiple modus operandi. There is no standard textbook for fighting al-Qaeda. To effectively destroy a group like al-Qaeda, a global approach and a global strategy is a pre-requisite.

Post-9/11 Al-Qaeda

Today, al-Qaeda is in a period of consolidation. It has lost its base—Afghanistan—but with the help of its erstwhile host, the Islamic Movement of the Taliban, the then-ruling party of the Islamic Emirate of Afghanistan, al-Qaeda has re-established itself. Together with a number of their associated groups, both al-Qaeda and the Taliban are operating from the Pakistani-Afghan border. On the Pakistani side, this region comprises of the North West Frontier Province (NWFP), FATA and Baluchistan. FATA consists of seven agencies—Bajaur, Mohamed, Orakzai, Kurram, North and South Waziristan, and Khyber. The core of al-Qaeda leadership has moved to the 'ungoverned territories' of NWFP and FATA-areas, which in spite of being part of the Pakistani state, follow a distinctive colonial era administrative and legal system. These tribal areas do not recognize provincial or federal laws. Other threat groups operating in FATA today include: Islamic Movement of the Taliban, the erstwhile ruling regime of Afghanistan seeking to return to power; Islamic Movement of Uzbekistan and its splinter Islamic Jihad Movement, groups seeking to create an Islamic state in Uzbekistan; Eastern Turkistan Islamic Movement, a group from China seeking to create an Islamic State in Western China; and Libyan Islamic Fighters Group, a group seeking to establish an Islamic state in Libya; as well as several other groups.

Despite the dismantling of its training and operational infrastructure in Afghanistan, al-Qaeda remains a serious, immediate and a direct threat to its enemies. Although al-Qaeda's physical and personnel infrastructure worldwide has suffered, its multilayered global network still retains sufficient depth to plan, prepare and execute operations directly and through associate groups. By ideologically and physically penetrating a number of regional conflicts where Muslims participate, al-Qaeda's decentralized network works with like-minded groups. With sustained action by the US, its allies and its friends in Afghanistan and Pakistan, the core of al-Qaeda, its organisers of attacks, trainers, financiers, operatives and other experts are moving to lawless zones of Asia, Middle East, Horn of Africa and the Caucuses. Despite the death and capture of at least half its operational leaders, members and key supporters, the group remains operationally effective.

Like a strike on a hive of bees, al-Qaeda members are gravitating, seeking new bases in the Afghanistan-Pakistan border, Iraq, Yemen, Somalia, etc. Like sharks rapidly moving in search of new opportunities, post-9/11 al-Qaeda cells survive and strike on opportunity. After identifying the weaknesses and the loopholes of the new security architecture, a constantly probing al-Qaeda is likely to infiltrate. While retaining a presence in Afghanistan, post 9/11 al-Qaeda members are active and its fresh recruits train in the conflict zones. For al-Qaeda, regional conflicts are healthy greenhouses to rebuild, regroup, and strike.

Although al-Qaeda as an organization per se has suffered, it is still retaining its pioneering vanguard status of the Islamic movements. In keeping with its founding charter authored by its founder leader Dr Abdullah Azzam, al-Qaeda remains the spearhead of the Islamic movements. Despite repeated high quality losses, al-Qaeda is still able to set the ideological and operational agenda for three-dozen foreign Islamist groups it trained and financed during the last decade. Al-Qaeda is able to preserve its global status by relying on its associated groups to sustain its fight against the US, its allies and its friends. To compensate for the loss of its state-of-the-art training infrastructure in Afghanistan, al-Qaeda is exploiting the Islamic movements within its ideological, military and financial spheres of influence. Until US intervention in October 2001, the international neglect of Afghanistan turned the country into a "terrorist Disneyland" with about 40 Islamist groups receiving both guerrilla and terrorist training throughout the 1990s. These Asian, Middle Eastern, African and Caucasian groups, hitherto fighting local campaigns, influenced by al-Qaeda's vision of a global jihad, today pose a threat comparable to al-Qaeda.

The post-9/11 trajectory of al-Qaeda operations demonstrates its staying power. With sustained US and allied action in Afghanistan and Pakistan, al-Qaeda has an infinite capacity to change its shape. In the coming months, al-Qaeda will fragment, decentralise, regroup in lawless zones of the world, work with like-minded groups, select a wider range of targets, focus on economic targets and population centres, and conduct most attacks in the global south. Although the group will be constrained from conducting coordinated simultaneous attacks against high-profile, symbolic or strategic targets in the West, al-Qaeda together with its regional counterparts will attack in Asia, Africa, Middle East, and even in Latin America, a region where it only has a limited presence. Despite the likely capture or death of its core and penultimate leaders, al-Qaeda's anti-Western universal jihad ideology inculcated among the politicised and radicalised Muslims will sustain support for al-Qaeda.

While its organisers of attacks will remain in Pakistan and Iraq, its operatives and messengers will travel back and forth coordinating with al-Qaeda nodes in safe zones such as Europe, North Africa, Yemen, Somalia, Bangladesh and Chechnya. To make its presence felt, al-Qaeda will increasingly rely on its global terrorist network of groups in Southeast Asia, South Asia, Horn of Africa, Middle East, and the Caucuses to strike at its enemies. Already attacks in Kenya, Indonesia, India, Pakistan, Kuwait and Yemen seek to compensate for the loss and lack of space and opportunity to operate in the West. Its operatives are currently working together with Jemmah Islamiyah (JI: Southeast Asia), Supreme Islamic Courts (Horn of Africa), Al Ansar Mujahidin (Caucuses), Tawhid Wal Jihad renamed al-Qaeda in Iraq (Middle East), Jayash-e-Mohommad (South Asia), Salafi Group for Call and Combat (GSPC, North Africa, Europe and North America) and other Islamist groups it had trained and financed in the past decade. As al-Qaeda has a very small number of cells in the West, the group will operate through the GSPC and Takfir Wal Hijra—two groups it had infiltrated in Europe and North America.[11] With the transfer of terrorist technology and expertise from the centre to the periphery, the attacks by the associated groups of al-Qaeda are posing a threat comparable to al-Qaeda.

The fragmentation of al-Qaeda support and operational infrastructure under sustained military and law enforcement action is making it rely on its strategic linkages, diversity, and global reach. The decentralisation of al-Qaeda has contributed to its flexibility of targeting. Despite being the most hunted terrorist group in history, its cellular structure, rigid compartmentalization, and the robust Islamist milieu, ensure its resilience to destruction. With sustained military action in Afghanistan, the threat of terrorism has diffused increasing the threshold for political violence worldwide. The new threshhold terrorism is a multidimensional, complex, and a global challenge. Despite sustained attrition of Islamist networks since October 2001, their high capacity for replenishing losses by regenerating fresh support and recruits has ensured the continuity of the intellectual and operational capabilities of al-Qaeda. As such, many governments and publics will have to live with a medium to high threat index for several years in different parts of the world.

Current Situation

In response to the high threat to al-Qaeda, the group is becoming more creative and lethal. The group is adapting dual technologies—airplanes, commercially available chemicals, agricultural fertilizers, liquid petroleum gas, and liquid nitrogen gas—as its new weapons. The group is also searching for new weapons such as chemical and biological agents (especially contact poisons), which are easy to conceal and breach security. The statements of Osama in February 2003, "think intelligently and kill the Americans secretly," and Sheikh Nasr bin Hamid al Fahd's May 2003 fatwa legitimizing the use of chemical, biological, radiological, and nuclear weapons are examples of al-Qaeda's intent. Reflecting the existing and emerging threat, Eliza Manningham-Buller, the head of the British Security Services (MI5), said in London on July 17, 2003, that a terrorist attack on a Western city using chemical, biological, radiological and nuclear (CBRN) technology is "only a matter of time."[13] She added: "We know that renegade scientists have cooperated with al-Qaeda and provided them with some of the knowledge they need to develop these weapons."[14] The al-Qaeda associate group—the Salafi Group for Call and Combat (GSPC)—successfully developed ricin, one of the contact poisons found in the al-Qaeda manuals and its rudimentary manufacturing apparatus in London in January 2003. The ricin network in Europe, especially in London, Manchester, East Anglia and Edinburgh in the UK, worked together with al-Qaeda experts in the Pankishi Gorge in Georgia, the border of Chechnya.

In the current environment, terrorist groups will continue to recruit and mission its members and supporters living in the West to support and conduct attacks. With the exception of the bombing of the Federal Building in Oklahoma in 1995, almost all the major terrorist attacks in the West have been conducted by members of diaspora and migrant communities. The 9/11 coordinator Ramzi bin al Shibh and the suicide pilots were migrants living in the West. As foreign terrorist groups based in North America, Western Europe, and Australia did not pose a direct and an immediate threat to Western security until 9/11, these host governments tolerated their activity and presence. Even after 9/11, due to the reluctance of Europe, Canada, and Australia to disrupt terrorist support networks, terrorist organizations continue to target émigré communities for recruits and support. Other than al-Qaeda front, cover and sympathetic groups, other Islamist groups are aggressively politicizing, radicalizing and mobilizing their migrants and diaspora. Assif Mohammed Hanif, 21, and Omar Khan Sharif, 27, two British suicide bombers of Asian origin from

Derbyshire, UK, infiltrated Israel and attacked Mike's Place, a nightclub, on April 30, 2003. While Hanif detonated a suicide device killing two musicians and one waiter and injuring 60, Sharif's explosive device failed to detonate. Since the 31-month uprising in Israel, Hanif's bombing was the first suicide attack by a foreigner. Similarly, in Asia, the first suicide bomber who targeted the State Assembly in Srinagar, was Kashmir, a British Muslim, also of Asian origin. The émigré communities remain vulnerable to ideological penetration, recruitment, and provision of financial support. Despite stepped up government surveillance, disenfranchised segments of the émigré' communities in Western countries still identify themselves with the struggles in their homelands. Until and unless, host governments develop a better understanding of the threat and target terrorist propaganda (both its tools and its ideologues) the threat to the West from within will persist.

As illustrated by the statements of both Osama bin Laden and his successor and deputy Dr Ayman Al Zawahiri, although al-Qaeda's capability to attack the West has diminished, its intention to attack has not. On October 6, 2002, Osama bin Laden, the Emir-General of al-Qaeda said: "I am telling you, and God is my witness, whether America escalates or de-escalates this conflict, we will reply to it in kind, God willing. God is my witness, the youth of Islam are willing and preparing things that will fill your hearts with tears. They will target the key sectors of your economy until you stop your injustice and aggression or until the more short-lived of the US die."[15] Ayman Al Zawahiri said on Al Jazeera on October 8, 2002: "Our message to our enemies is this: America and its Allies should know that their crimes will not go unpunished, god willing. We advice them to hasten to leave Palestine, the Arabian Peninsula, Afghanistan, and all Muslim countries, before they loose everything. We addressed some messages to America's Allies to stop their involvement in its crusader campaign. The Mujahid youths have addressed a message to Germany and another to France. If these measures have not been sufficient, we are ready with the help of God, to increase them."[16] In many ways their periodic pronouncements and statements are the best guide to future al-Qaeda actions.

Targeting Trends

Having recruited from a cross-section of society—the rich, the poor, the educated and the less educated—al-Qaeda has developed a reasonably good understanding of Western security measures and countermeasures. After the bombing of the US embassies in East Africa in August 1998, the US government enhanced the perimeter security of its land targets. Then al-Qaeda attacked the USS Cole, a maritime target in October 2000. When the US government enhanced the perimeter of its land and maritime targets, al-Qaeda attacked America's icons from the sky. The tactical trajectory of al-Qaeda suggests a cunning foe always keen to harass, hurt, and humiliate the enemy by deception.

Al-Qaeda's tactical repertoire was deeply influenced by the Iranian-sponsored Lebanese Hezbollah. Hezbollah's modus operandi of coordinated simultaneous suicide attacks influenced al-Qaeda's modus operandi in a big way. As al-Qaeda's aim was also to force the withdrawal of US troops from the Arabian Peninsula, the group emulated the success of Hezbollah in Beirut in 1983 where the group forced the US-led multinational peace-keeping force to withdrew from Lebanon in 1983 following coordinated simultaneous suicide attacks on US and French targets. In the attack on its marine barracks, the US lost

243 personnel, the single biggest loss since Vietnam. As a result, for several years, the US disengaged itself from the politics of the Middle East. With the exception of the attack on the USS Cole, all the mega attacks by al-Qaeda have been coordinated simultaneous suicide attacks. For instance, al-Qaeda attacked the US embassies in Kenya and Tanzania in August 1998; attempted to destroy the Los Angeles international airport, Radisson Hotel in Amman, Jewish and Christian holy sites in Jordan, and the USS The Sullivans in Aden, Yemen on the eve of the Millennium; and attacked America's most outstanding economic and military target and attempted to attack its political landmark on 9/11. Similarly al-Qaeda influenced its associated groups to conduct coordinated simultaneous attacks. For instance, Jemmah Islamiyah successfully attacked 16 churches in Indonesia on Christmas Day in 2000 and five targets in Manila, Philippines on December 30, 2000.

In the early 1990s, al-Qaeda's aim was to create Islamic states in the Middle East by targeting the false Muslim rulers and the corrupt Muslim regimes. After suffering significant losses—both its operatives and material—in the Middle East, al-Qaeda decided to abandon its policy of targeting near targets in favour of targeting the distant enemy—the West—especially the "head of the poisonous snake"—the USA. Gradually, al-Qaeda attacks escalated in intensity and sophistication—East Africa in August 1998, USS Cole in October 2000, and America's mainland on 9-11. The two-wave attacks in October 2001 and May 2003 are major turning points. Today, al-Qaeda is returning to its near-targets in the Middle East, Asia, Africa and the Caucuses. Having suffered significant losses to its support and operational infrastructure in North America, Western Europe and Australasia (the primary target countries) in the last two years, al-Qaeda has been aggressively seeking Western and Jewish targets in the Muslim World.

Although attacking inside North America, Europe, Australasia and Israel remains a priority, Western security measures and countermeasures have made it expensive and difficult for al-Qaeda to mount an operation on Western soil. Nonetheless, al-Qaeda and its associate groups will attack Western targets outside the West where security is largely in the hands of foreign governments. Al-Qaeda finds it less costly to operate in parts of Asia, Africa, and the Middle East, where there is lack of security controls. Therefore, most attacks will be against Western targets located in the global south such as the attack in Saudi Arabia. While focusing on Western targets, al-Qaeda will continue to conduct operations against Muslim rulers and regimes supporting the US-led "war or terror." The physical security of the Saudi royalty, Pakistani and Afghan leaders (Musharaaf and Karzai, respectively) will remain particularly vulnerable and their regimes will come under sustained political challenges in the coming years.

With the hardening of US targets, the threat is shifting to both government and population targets of allies and friends of the US. Similarly, al-Qaeda is increasingly looking for opportunity targets. For instance, when al-Qaeda failed to target a US warship off Yemen, it targeted a French oil super tanker in October 2002. The hardening of government land and commercial aerial targets has shifted al-Qaeda targeting to both soft land and maritime targets. Although the primary intention of al-Qaeda is to target inside the US, it lacks the quality operatives of the Mohommad Atta caliber to operate inside the US. Therefore, al-Qaeda is targeting US land, sea and aviation overseas. Increased hardening of US military and diplomatic targets after 9/11 is steadfastly shifting the threat to other classes of targets. For instance, al-Qaeda cells in Morocco attempted to target both British and US shipping in the Straits of Gibraltar in mid-2002. Due to perimeter and structural hardening of Israeli and US embassies in Europe and Asia, al-Qaeda decided to target friends and allies of Israel and the US. More than ever before, the allies and the friends of the US are vulnerable to al-Qaeda attack today.

Hardening of government targets will also displace the threat to softer targets making civilians prone to terrorist attack. For instance, al-Qaeda planned to attack US diplomatic targets in Bangkok, Singapore, Kuala Lumpur, Phnom Penh, Hanoi and Manila, American Institute in Taiwan, and the US consulate in Surabaya in September 2002,[17] but visible security presence made the group consider soft targets. Although not in all cases, hardening of targets works but as the world witnessed with horror, countermeasures make terrorists creative and innovative. As the traditional explosives-laden vehicle was a non-option to breach the hardened perimeter security of America's most outstanding landmarks, al-Qaeda was forced to develop an aerial airborne capability. Similarly, hardening of military and diplomatic targets in Southeast Asia prompted Jemmah Islamiyiah to seek entertainment targets such as Bali. The reality is that government countermeasures have increased the vulnerability of population centres and economic targets. As Islamist groups weaken they are likely to hit soft targets, killing civilians, if possible in large number. As it is impossible to prevent bombing of public places, civilian and civilian infrastructure targets will remain the most vulnerable to terrorist attack in the immediate, mid-, and long term.

Hardening of land and aviation targets will shift the threat to sea targets, particularly to commercial maritime targets. As any aviation incident attracts significant attention, al-Qaeda assigns a high priority to aviation-impact terrorism. Due to the difficulty of hijacking aircraft to ram them against targets, al-Qaeda will increasingly invest conducting stand-off attacks and using handheld Surface to Air Missiles (SAMs). For instance, al-Qaeda Sudanese member fired a SA-7 missile at a US military transport plane at the Prince Sultan base in Saudi Arabia in mid 2001. His arrest in Khartoum in December 2001 led the Saudi authorities to recover another complete missile system buried in the Riyadh desert. If appropriate and immediate countermeasures are not taken to target the al-Qaeda shipping network, SAMs under al-Qaeda control held in the Pakistan-Kashmir-Afghanistan theatre, the Arabian Peninsula, and the Horn of Africa will find its way to the Far Asia and to Europe, and possibly even to North America. Protective measures, especially target hardening of vulnerable government personnel and infrastructure, by law enforcement and protective services are a temporary solution. To reduce the threat, governments have no option but to hunt terrorists and prevent public support and sympathy for terrorism.

The post-9/11 robust security architecture has forced al-Qaeda to transform its targeting strategy. Al-Qaeda's capacity to conduct spectacular or theatrical attacks has diminished due to three factors. First, heightened human vigilance. The high state of alertness of the public and law enforcement authorities has led to the disruption of several operations. For instance, the alert passengers and crew prevented the bombing of the transatlantic flight by Richard Reid, the al-Qaeda shoe bomber on board American Airlines 63 on December 22, 2001. Second, unprecedented law enforcement, security and intelligence cooperation and coordination. As a direct result of inter- and intra-agency cooperation, a large number of suspects have been detained and arrested, and over 100 attacks by al-Qaeda and its associated groups have been interdicted, prevented or abandoned since 9/11. Cooperation beyond the Anglo-Saxon countries, Europe and Israel, especially with the Middle East and Asia, has led to significant arrests. For instance, Jose Padilla, who intended to mount surveillance and reconnaissance to detonate a radiological dispersal device in Washington DC, en-route from Pakistan via Zurich, was arrested at the Chicago O'Hare international airport in the US on May 8, 2002. Third, hunting al-Qaeda and its associate groups has limited their time, space and resources to conceptualise, plan and prepare elaborate terrorist strikes. As long as the international community can maintain the public vigilance, anti- and counterterrorism cooperation and coordination worldwide, and sustained pressure on the group, al-Qaeda will not be able to mount large-scale coordinated simultaneous attacks on symbolic, strategic and high-profile targets. Large attacks require long term planning and preparation by several operatives and across several countries. In the current security environment, where there are periodic desertions, arrests, and penetration, a terrorist group can only plan, prepare and execute medium to small-scale operations. Preventing complacency from setting in—especially after a long period of al-Qaeda inactivity—is difficult but it is a must if we are to prevent the next attack.

The nature of the al-Qaeda threat has clearly changed since 9/11. In comparison, the post-9/11 threat to the US, its allies and its friends is fragmented and diffused. Although it has no resources to carry out theatrical or spectacular attacks, it has a clandestine network to move experts, messages and money to associate groups. All indications are that al-Qaeda is not deserting from the 1520-mile-long Pakistan-Afghanistan border, but its leadership is actively and aggressively tasking its membership and ideologising associate groups.[18] From the centre of Afghanistan and Pakistan, al-Qaeda's technical experts and financiers, organizers of attacks, and operatives are gravitating to lawless zones in Asia, Horn of Africa, Caucuses, Balkans and the Middle East, widening the perimeter of the conflict. The regional groups—such as Jemmah Islamiyah—and local groups—such as al-Qaeda in Iraq—are providing a platform for al-Qaeda to plan, prepare, and execute operations against targets of the West and Muslim countries friendly to the West. For instance, the attack on the French tanker Limburg was staged by al-Qaeda working with the Islamic Army of the Abyan in Aden. Similarly, the Bali bombing was staged by Jemmah Islamiya, working together with al-Qaeda experts. Likewise, in Pakistan, a dozen attacks have been conducted by al-Qaeda through individual members of Jaish-e-Mohammed, Lashkar-e-Jhangvi, Harakat-ul-Jihad-I-Islami, Lashkar-e-Tayyaba, and Harakat-ul Mujahidin.[19] A decentralised al-Qaeda working with Islamist and other groups worldwide is a force multiplier. In the years ahead, al-Qaeda which has a long history of providing experts, trainers and funds to other groups—is likely to operate effectively and efficiently through their associates. To compensate for the losses suffered by the group, post-9/11 al-Qaeda operatives are heavily reliant on the social and familial contacts in associate groups. Therefore, mapping the family and social trees of leaders, members, supporters and sympathizers is key to understanding the deepening operational nexus between al-Qaeda and its associate groups. The nexus has manifested in tactical and opportunity targeting as well as the globalisation of the terrorist strategy—developments that call for closer political, diplomatic, law enforcement, military, security and intelligence cooperation and coordination.

Wave Attacks

Today, al-Qaeda conducts two types of attacks—stand-alone attacks and wave attacks. For maximum impact and effect, al-Qaeda prefers to conduct attacks in waves. The first wave of attacks by al-Qaeda after 9/11 was in October and November 2003, when al-Qaeda working together with Islamic Army of the Abayan in Yemen, Jemmah Islamiyah in Indonesia (Islamic Group), Al Ansar Mujahidin in Chechnya (The Supporters of the Warriors of God), Shurafaa al-Urdun (The Honourables of Jordan), and Al Ittihad Al Islami (Islamic Union) staged five attacks. A suicide boat meant for a US warship attacked the French oil super tanker Limburg off Mukalla, Yemen on October 6; gunmen killed two US marines on exercises in Failaka, Kuwait on October 8; multiple suicide bombings in Bali, Indonesia on October 12, 2003; hostage taking in a theatre in Moscow on October 24; assassination of USAID official Lawrence Foley in Amman, Jordan on October 28; suicide bombing of an Israeli-owned Kikambala Paradise hotel; and Surface to Air Missile attack on Israeli Arkia Flight 582 on November 28.

After maintaining a year of silence, al-Qaeda presented Koranic justifications in October 2002 immediately before launching the coordinated multiple attacks in the Middle East and Asia. The attacks in Yemen, Kuwait and Jordan indicated the ability of al-Qaeda and its associated groups to function amidst security countermeasures. Islamist groups in Chechnya and Thailand also conducted terrorist operations in Russia and in Southern Thailand respectively. On October 6, an explosives-laden suicide boat rammed the 157,833-ton French oil super tanker Limburg before mooring at al Shihr off the coast of Yemen. The explosion killed one Bulgarian and injured one crew member, and spilling 90,000 barrels of crude oil.[20] Although the time and the place of the attack could not be determined, governments in Asia and in the Middle East anticipated maritime suicide attacks on military and commercial shipping in the Straits of Malacca and in the Persian Gulf by al-Qaeda.[21] Based on debriefing of al-Qaeda operatives detained in the Middle East and in Asia, the US intelligence community warned of impending attacks. For instance, before US and Indonesian joint military and naval exercises were held from May 30-June 3, 2002, al-Qaeda's former Southeast Asian representative Omar Al Faruq was trying to source terrorists to conduct suicide attacks against US warships in Surabaya in Indonesia's second largest city in May 2002.[22] Two days after the Limburg attack, two terrorists in a pickup truck attacked a marine unit of the US military on training maneuvers on Failaka, an island 10 miles east of Kuwait City.[23] The October 8 attack killed Lance Corporal Antonio J. Sledd, 20 years old, from Hillsborough County Florida. The terrorists drove to a second location to attack again but were killed by US marines.

Al-Qaeda, operating through Jemmah Islamiyah (JI), its Southeast Asian network, staged the worst terrorist attack in Indonesia's tourist resort of Bali, killing 202 and injuring over 300 people (mostly Australian tourists) on October 12, 2002, also the anniversary of the USS Cole attack.[24] Before and after the mass casualty bombing at the Sari Club, Bali at 23.15 Hrs, small bombs exploded near other targets reflecting both al-Qaeda and JI modus operandi and widespread capability to conduct coordinated simultaneous or near-simultaneous attacks. The targets were the Philippine Consulate, Manado City, North Sulawesi, at 18.45, 23.00 Hrs at the Paddy Restaurant, Kuta Beach Strip in Bali, and 23.25 Hrs near the US Consulate in Denpasar, Bali.[25] Bali, a predominately Hindu city where 22,000 Australians were holidaying, was the ideal target for JI-al-Qaeda. The neighbouring Philippines witnessed five bombings killing 22 including a US serviceman and injuring over 200 in October 2002. Although the perpetrators have not been identified, the Philippine intelligence community suspects that the bombings were carried out by the al-Qaeda-affiliated Abu Sayyaf Group, a group that has suffered significantly as a result of post 9-11 US assistance to the Armed Forces of the Philippines. On October 28, a terrorist opened fire on Laurence Foley, a 60-year old US diplomat in Jordan working as an administrator for the US Agency for International Development (USAID).[26] Foley was shot point blank seven times in his chest when he was heading for his car parked in his garage in his house in Amman. The Shurafaa al-Urdun (The Honourables of Jordan), a suspected front for al-Qaeda, claimed that Foley was killed in protest of US support for Israel and the "bloodshed in Iraq and Afghanistan."[27] The attack came amidst a warning in August 2002, when the US government stated that al-Qaeda was planning to kidnap US citizens in Jordan.

Following the tradition of Prophet Muhammad of calling its enemies to convert to Islam before subduing them, al-Qaeda launched multiple attacks in Kuwait, Yemen, and Bali, all in the second week of October 2002. Bin Laden said: "In the name of God, the merciful, the compassionate; a message to the American people: peace be upon those who follow the right path. I am an honest advisor to you. I urge you to seek the joy of life and the afterlife, and to rid yourself of your dry, miserable, and spiritless materialistic life. I urge you to become Muslims, for Islam calls for the principle of 'There is no God but Allah,' and for justice and forbids injustice and criminality. I also call on you to understand the lesson of the New York and Washington raids, which came in response to some of your previous crimes. The aggressor deserves punishment. However, those who follow the movement of the criminal gang at the White House, the agents of the Jews, who are preparing to attack and partition the Islamic World, without you disapproving of this, realize that you have not understood anything from the message of the two raids. . . . We beseech Almighty God to provide us with his support. He is the protector and has the power to do so. Say: O People of the Book! Come to common terms as between us and you: That we worship none but Allah; that we associate no partners with him; that we associate no partners with him; that we erect not from among ourselves lords and patrons other than Allah. If then they turn back, say ye: bear witness that we at least are Muslims bowing to Allah's will."[28]

To assess the statements of bin Laden and Zawahiri, the CIA approached the senior most al-Qaeda leaders in US detention, Abu Zubaidah, former head of al-Qaeda's external operations, and Ramzi bin Al Shibh, the chief logistics officer of 9/11 operation. They interpreted with dead accuracy that bin Laden would not make such a statement unless the organisation was "ready and able to carry out such attacks" and according to Abu Zubaidah, "bin Laden's modus operandi considered of reviewing operational plans, weighing the consequences of each, selecting targets, and finally releasing his message regarding an impending attack. The plan has been approved and the timing is now determined by the operatives and the local security situation."[29] They said that the same way the prophet urged his opponents to embrace Islam before being subdued by his army, Osama was calling his opponents to convert to Islam before attacking them. Although the tape was meant for an external constituency, Osama was trying to justify Koranically his course of action to his internal constituency.

Diffusion of Threat

Both the spreading out of al-Qaeda cells and the conduct of spectacular attacks have certainly made anti- and counter-terrorism initiatives difficult and complex. As terrorists are copycats, the direct and indirect influence of al-Qaeda is reflected in the changing behaviour of several groups. As terrorist groups closely guard their foreign linkages, often it has become difficult even by government intelligence agencies to identify the exact nature of their external relationships. While the Russian secret service is convinced of the al-Qaeda-Chechen terrorist nexus, there has been a grave reluctance in the Western press to call Chechen groups that practice terrorism as "terrorists."[30] On October 23, 2002, 53 male and female suicide terrorists from Chechnya, 600 miles away from Moscow, stormed the 1163 seat auditorium of Act II screening Nord-Ost (North East), a popular musical.[31] After mining the theatre with 850 hostages, they wanted Russian forces to withdraw from Chechnya. The next day, they sent a video tape to Al Jazeera where a hostage taker said: I swear by God we are more keen on dying than you are keen on living . . . each one of us is willing to sacrifice himself for the sake of God and the independence of Chechnya."[32] On October 26, after the terrorists began to execute their hostages, Spetsnaz commandos in the elite Alfa and Vympel anti terror squads of the Federal Security Service rescued the hostages after injected sleeping gas though the ventilation system and holes bored underneath the auditorium. Of the 119 dead hostages, only two died of gun shot injuries—others perished from the gas, due to lack of timely medical care. The Moscow operation was conducted by 25-year-old Movsar Baraye, the nephew of Arbi Barayev, the Chechen Islamic Special Units leader who oversaw the beheading of three British and one New Zealand telecommunication workers in Chechnya in 1998.[33] The deputies of the Chechen rebel President Aslan Maskhadov were Shamil Basayev, leader, and Ibn ul-Khattab, military leader, Majlis ul-Shura of Mujahidin of Ichkeria and Dagestan respectively.[34] Khattab, the then commander of the Al Ansar Mujahidin (Islamic International Brigade) and a protégé of bin Laden, was assassinated by the Russian secret service on March 19, 2002. Movsar was close to Khattab, who remained a part of the al-Qaeda network until his death.[35] Khattab was succeeded by Mohomad al Ghamdi, alias Abu Walid, the cousin of two 9/11 hijackers, the Ghamdi brothers. With Chechens developing capabilities, they too have been replaced by Chechen leaders. The Moscow operation bore the first three hallmarks of al-Qaeda: (1) grandiose operations, (2) suicide, (3) targeting the heart, and (4) coordinated simultaneous attacks. It demonstrated once again al-Qaeda's role as an inspirator and an instigater.

Second Wave

The post 9/11 second wave targeted Riyadh, Casablanca, Chechnya and Karachi in May 2003. Demonstrating that the group remains a resilient threat, al-Qaeda coordinated its attack in Riyadh with its associated groups the timings of the bombings in North Africa, Caucuses and in Asia. To compensate for the loss of significant personnel and physical infrastructure, al-Qaeda is relying on its associate groups to conduct operations.

Despite being hunted by the Saudi intelligence and its law enforcement agencies, al-Qaeda was able to plan, prepare and execute an operation in the heart of the Kingdom on May 12, 2003. Amidst domestic and foreign intelligence, both technical and human, that al-Qaeda was in the final phases of an operation, Saudi authorities failed to detect and disrupt the operation that destroyed three poorly protected foreign residential complexes in Riyadh at 11:25 p.m. on May 12, 2003. The triple suicide attacks in Al Hamra, Coroval, and Jedawal killed 34 including nine bombers and injured 194 people. A fourth explosion hit the offices of Siyanco, a Saudi Maintenance Company, a venture between Frank E. Basil, Inc of Washington and local Saudi Partners, but there were no casualties.

In Morocco, suicide bombers attacked Casa de Espana, a Spanish social club; Hotel Farah; a Jewish community center and cemetery and a restaurant next to the Belgium consulate in Casablanca, all within 20 minutes, on May 16. In addition to 12 bombers who perished in the raid, the attacks killed 27 and injured 100. Of the 14 man attack team, one failed suicide bomber was captured, and later one bomber was arrested. The attacks in Saudi Arabia and Morocco bear the hallmarks of al-Qaeda. Al-Qaeda in Saudi Arabia and its associated group Assirat al-Moustaquim (The Straight Path) in Morocco conducted the coordinated simultaneous suicide attacks against western and Jewish targets with the aim of inflicting maximum fatalities.

In Chechnya, Al Ansar Mujahidin, an associate group of al-Qaeda, mounted suicide operations on Znamenskoye killing 59 and injuring 200 also on May 12 and Iliskhan-Yurt killing 18 and injuring 100 on May 14. The bombings in Chechnya were aimed at producing mass fatalities and fear—offices and homes in Znamenskoye, northern district of Nadterechny, and an assassination of Akhmad Kadyrov, the Chechen administration leader near a shrine in Iliskhan-Yurt where 15,000 Muslims gathered to mark the birth of Prophet Muhammed. An Ansar Mujahidin is led by Abu Walid alias Mohommad al Ghamdi, the successor of Ibn Omar al Khattab, Afghan veterans and protégés of Osama bin Laden. Abu Walid is the cousin of the 9-11 hijackers—Ahmed and Hamza al Ghamdi—all from the Southern Saudi Province of Asir.

In Pakistan, the Muslim United Army (MUA) simultaneously bombed 19 Shell and two Caltex gasoline stations in Nazimabad, Joharabad, SITE, Sharea Faisal, Gulshan-I-Iqbal, all in Southern Karachi between 4–5 a.m. on May 15. MUA is believed to be Lashkar-e-Jhangvi, an al-Qaeda associated group in Pakistan. The improved explosives devices, weighing 200 grams, with 15-minute timers, were placed inside garbage cans beside fuel pumps by motorcyclists. The bombings damaged the Pakistani infrastructure owned by Anglo Dutch and American companies and injured one customer, three station attendants, and one security guard. To prevent such attacks, Pakistan had increased security of food chains—Pizza Hut, MacDonalds, KFC—but the group had selected its tactic and targets creatively. The bombing was in revenge of Pakistan hunting al-Qaeda and its associate members in Pakistan.

Middle East—Striking the Heartland

Although the epicenter of international terrorism has shifted from Afghanistan to Iraq, al-Qaeda remains active in other territories. Al-Qaeda's attack in Riyadh on May 12, 2003 demonstrated that al-Qaeda remains an enduring threat to areas outside conlict zones. Despite recurrent indications and warnings, including from the CIA that "they are coming for you," the Saudis were defiant, stating that "everything was under control."[36] Two weeks before the attack, it was very clear to both the American and the Saudi authorities that al-Qaeda was in the final phases of launching am operation.

There were multiple indications and at least one warning the week preceding the attack. This included a US government warning of the likelihood of an attack in Saudi Arabia. Although the warning was not target specific, it was country specific. Under the no double standards policy, the US was mandated to place all general and specific warnings to its citizens both at home and overseas in the public domain. On April 29, US Embassy in Riyadh requested Saudi authorities to increase the security of the residential complexes. On May 1, the US State Department issued a travel warning requesting private US citizens in Saudi Arabia to consider departing and Americans to defer non essential travel. On May 6, nineteen members of al-Qaeda escaped after a firefight with the Saudi security forces. During the confrontation, demonstrating their willingness to kill and to die, one member exploded a device killing himself. The 19 had fought with Osama bin Laden in the Tora Bora battles in Afghanistan. They were the same members who conducted the operation. One al-Qaeda member surrendered and provided information about the al-Qaeda organization in Saudi Arabia but not about the attack. The Saudis released the identities of the 19 wanted men requesting the public for assistance. On May 7, a spokesman for al-Qaeda, Thabet bin Qais, stated that Osama bin Laden's forces were gearing up for a series of attacks. On May 7, the US Embassy in Riyadh requested Saudi authorities to increase the security of the residential complexes. On May 8, Saudi authorities seized 800 lbs of explosives, automatic weapons, grenades, ammunition, computers, communication equipment and money from both a house and a vehicle about a quarter mile from Jedawal, one of the complexes later attacked. On May 10, the US Embassy in Riyadh requested Saudi authorities to increase the security of the residential complexes. The US Embassy specifically requested the Saudi authorities for additional protection for the Jedawal complex. On May 11, an al-Qaeda member Abu Mohammed Ablaj wrote to the London-based Al-Majalla magazine that the armed martyrdom squads were about to attack. "Beside targeting the heart of America, among the strategic priorities now is to target and execute operations in the Gulf countries and allies of the United States," Ablaj wrote in an email the day before the attack.

Even prior to these indications, the intelligence reports suggested that Saudi Arabia was coming under increasing threat. Both the CIA and the FBI informed their Saudi counterparts nearly a year before the attack that Abdel Rahman Jabarah, a Canadian al-Qaeda member of Kuwait origin, had entered the Kingdom. Together with Mohammed al-Johani, who led the operation, Abdel Rahman, one of the organizers of the bombing, was the elder brother of Mohomad Mansour Jabarah, a 21-year old al-Qaeda operative in US custody. After the al-Qaeda operation to destroy the US and Israeli diplomatic targets in Manila and the US, British, Australian and Israeli diplomatic targets in Singapore were thwarted in December 2001, its operations coordinator Mohomad Mansour fled to the Middle East and he was arrested in Oman in March 2002. Both the operations commander Mohommed al-Johani and the Canadian brothers worked under Khalid Sheikh Mohommad, the head of the Military Committee of al-Qaeda, and his successor and Deputy Tawfiq Attash, both of whom were arrested in Rawalpindi and Karachi in Pakistan in March, 2003. Al-Johani, who left Saudi Arabia when he was 18, returned to Saudi Arabia on a forged passport in March 2003 to conduct the operation. Operating under the al-Qaeda front "The Mujahideen in the Peninsula," al Johani built the organization to conduct attacks in the region starting with the Saudi Arabia. Thirty-six hours after the attack, 'Al-Muwahhidun' (Those who profess the oneness of God), a front for al-Qaeda, claimed responsibility for the attack.

As the attack was intended against the Westerners, and the first attack against a Western target after US intervened and occupied Iraq, the attack will be viewed with mix feelings within the Kingdom and the Middle East. The elite who want to retain their power and status will want to control the group. However, the suppression and repression of the Islamists of the al-Qaeda brand are likely to generate a fresh wave of recruits and support for al-Qaeda and its associated groups in the Gulf. While the Saudi over-reaction is likely to decrease the threat in the short term, it will increase Saudi public support for al-Qaeda in the long term. Unless, Saudi Arabia reforms the education system of the country, Osama bin Laden, the popular hero of all the Saudis who oppose the House of al Saud, will remain their symbol of resistance.

Outside the Middle East, al-Qaeda members are concentrated in the Horn of Africa, the Caucuses (Chechnya and Pankishi Gorge in Georgia) and in Asia. In the international intelligence community the Achilles Heel has always been Africa, especially the Horn. Intelligence on the Horn has improved since August 1998 but not appreciably. While based in Sudan (December 1991–May 1996), having made significant inroads to the countries in East Africa, al-Qaeda continues to operate in the Horn. While the Russian military has sustained heavy losses in Chechnya, the US Special Operations Forces working with the Georgian forces are conducing operations to clear the gorge. In Djibouti, there are several hundred US personnel engaged in activities in the Horn of Africa and Yemen. In addition to Afghanistan and Pakistan, al-Qaeda elements have a presence throughout Asia. For instance, al-Qaeda members regularly infiltrate Kashmir and Bangladesh in South Asia. In addition to the Middle East, when it comes to regions, the Horn of Africa and Southeast Asia present the biggest challenges. Even before the gravity of terrorism moved from the Middle East to Asia in the early 1990s, the Middle Eastern groups were active in Southeast Asia.

Southeast Asia: A New Theatre

Of the two-dozen Islamist terrorist groups active in Southeast Asia, JI presents the biggest threat. There are about 400 al-Qaeda trained JI members in Southeast Asia. With the exception of Afghanistan and Pakistan, Southeast Asia is the home of the single largest concentration of al-Qaeda trained active members in any given region. The presence of 240 million Muslims, emerging democracies, corrupt governments, weak rulers, and lack security are making Southeast Asia emerge as a new centre for al-Qaeda activity. Historically, Southeast Asia has featured prominently in all al-Qaeda operations including 9/11, when Khalid Sheikh Mohommad, the head of the al-Qaeda military committee, convened a meeting of 12 al-Qaeda operatives in Kula Lumpur from January 5–12, 2000, to coordinate both the USS Cole and the 9/11 operation. Immediately before 9/11, bin Laden dispatched its key financier Mohammed Mansour Jabarah (a Kuwaiti of Canadian citizenship; alias Sammy) to Malaysia to plan and prepare the attacks against US and Israeli diplomatic targets in Manila, Philippines. After visiting the embassies with an al-Qaeda suicide bomber Ahmed Sahagi, Jabarah concluded that "the attack on the US Embassy in Manila would have been much more difficult" and that "a plane would be needed to attack this building because the security was very tough."[37] Therefore, al-Qaeda decided to shift the operation to Singapore where the "embassy is very close to the streets and did not have many barriers to prevent the attack."[38] Due to the difficulty of shipping the explosives to Singapore to the Philippines, Nurjaman Riduan Isamuddin (alias Hambali) a 36-year-old Indonesian serving both on the al-Qaeda and JI Shura (Consultative) Councils, decided to cancel the Singapore operation of destroying US, British, Australian and Israeli diplomatic targets—and pick "better" targets in the Philippines. The detection and disruption of the Singapore operation by Singapore's Internal Security Department led to the discovery of al-Qaeda's JI regional network in December 2001. Although the Malaysian and the Philippine governments arrested JI members, Indonesia's President Megawatti Sukarnoputri was reluctant to follow suit, and as a result about 180 JI members moved to Indonesia and Thailand. In Southern Thailand, Hambali together with Jabarah discussed bombings in "bars, cafes, or nightclubs frequented by westerners in Thailand, Malaysia, Singapore, Philippines and Indonesia."[39] Although Hambali's original plan was to conduct a number of small bombings in line with the in-house capability and modus operandi of JI, the arrival of bomb making experts and finance from al-Qaeda into the region improved JI technical expertise to conduct large-scale bombings.

The Moro Islamic Liberation Front (MILF), an associate group of al-Qaeda, provided training to JI recruits in Mindanao, Philippines. After Camp Abu Bakar was overrun in April 2000, MILF and JI established training camps in Indonesia: Poso, Sulawesi and in Balikpapan and Sampit in Kalimanthan.[40] Before the MILF-Manila government resumed peace talks, MILF camps—Vietnam, Hudeibiya and Palestine—provided facilities to hundreds of foreign nationals including Arab members of al-Qaeda. The arrest in Indonesia in January of Muhammad Saad Iqbal Madni, a Pakistani, and in June 2002, Omar Al Farook alias Mahmoud bin Ahmed Assegaf, a Kuwait, the former leader of Camp Vietnam, provided insight into MILF Special Operations Group-JI linkages and future al-Qaeda plans.[41] Omar Al Farook also divulged attack plans and information of financial transfers, including US$ 73,000 from Sheikh Abu Abdallah Al Emarati of Saudi Arabia to Abu Bakar Bashir in Indonesia to purchase explosives. An Indonesian intelligence report states: "In the absence of an Internal Security Act, it is almost impossible for the Indonesian government to take legal action against anybody involved in al-Qaeda unless he has committed a crime. Therefore, Farook was deported on immigration grounds and the illegal acquisition of documents. He was arrested on June 5 [2002]. On June 8 [2002], he was deported to the US Air Force base in Baghram, Afghanistan."[42] After escaping from Baghram, on July 11, 2005, he worked for al-Qaeda in FATA. After he relocated to Basra, Iraq, he was killed by the British troops on September 25, 2006.

The JI spiritual, ideological and political leader is Abu Bakar Bashir, who also had an operational role, is still free. Hambai, the operational commander of JI and al-Qaeda in Southeast Asia is in US custody. Like Indonesia, Thailand denied the existence of a terrorist network, but is today confronted with an escalating terrorist threat in its south. With US, support and cooperation of its neighbours, Philippines is fighting ASG, JI and the Raja Solaiman Revolutionary Movement. Manila is negotiating with MILF, the largest of the threat groups.

The lack of a zero tolerance terrorism policy in the region and beyond facilitated the spawning and sustenance of a robust terrorist support and operational network. When the JI network was discovered in December 2001, Indonesia permitted the continued operation of a fully fledged JI infrastructure. This was despite the Al Farook and Jabarah debriefings implicating the continued use of Indonesia and Thailand by JI and al-Qaeda. These governments as well as the neighbouring governments failed to engage in sustained targeting of terrorist operatives and assets. Despite the US intelligence community providing strategic intelligence including the threat to "bars, cafes, or nightclubs" there was a failure on the part of the regional governments to develop the ground, contact or tactical intelligence by technical and human source penetration. The Australian government should have invested sufficient resources in its immediate neighbourhood to dampen Islamism and use the JI infrastructure in Perth, Sydney, Melbourne and Adelaide to penetrate the network. Despite a dozen Australian citizens and residents participating in JI and al-Qaeda training camps from Mindanao, Philippines to Afghanistan,[43] the government assessment and operational agencies did not believe that the threat was "significant" until Bali.[44]

Liberal Democracies: North America, Europe, Australasia

Examination of terrorist support and operational infrastructure worldwide reveals that liberal democracies offer the ideal conditions for foreign terrorist groups to establish their support networks in the West. For terrorism to flourish, pre-requisites are terrorists, who conduct attacks, and non-terrorists, who provide support. To defeat terrorism, both these categories must be targeted. During the past two decades, Asian, Middle Eastern and Latin American terrorist groups established open offices or secret cells for disseminating propaganda, raising funds, specialized training, procuring and transporting supplies in the West. For instance, Australia became the home of several foreign terrorist groups: Palestinian Hamas, Lebanese Hezbollah, Chechen mujahidin, Kurdish Workers Party (Turkey), Euzkadi Ta Askatasuna (Spain), Liberation Tigers of Tamil Eelam (Sri Lanka), Babbar Khalsa International (India) and International Sikh Youth Federation (India), dissident factions of the Irish Republican Army. The foreign terrorist groups disseminate terrorist propaganda, recruit, raise funds, procure and transport technologies from the West to perpetrate terrorism elsewhere. As these groups did not pose a direct and an immediate threat to host countries, Western security and intelligence agencies monitored these groups without disrupting their propaganda, fund raising, procurement and transportation infrastructure. As a result, several terrorists, their supporters and sympathisers infiltrated Western society and government. These foreign terrorist groups diverted the resources raised in the West to attack targets countries in the global south.

In addition to establishing al-Qaeda cells, the group also co-opted the leaderships of two European networks. As a result, both Takfir Wal Hijra and GSPC in Europe and to a lesser extent in North America present a significant threat to Western security. These two networks are fed by migrants from North Africa and ideologically fuelled by the developments in the lands of jihad, especially of their home countries. Like Europe witnessed a spill over of terrorism from the Middle East, the developments in Southeast Asia has increased the threat to Australia, New Zealand and their interests overseas. Australia has been an al-Qaeda target since 1999 but certain events increased the threat to the country since 2000. For example Australia's high-profile participation in the US-led anti-terrorist campaign in

Afghanistan in October 2001 and the angry reaction of Australian Muslims were used as examples supporting bin Laden's claim in early November 2001 that Australia conspired and led a crusade against the Islamic nation to dismember East Timor in November 2001. A grenade was lobbed from a motorbike into the garden of the Australian International School in Jakarta in November 2001; large firecrackers were hurled into the Australian Embassy in Jakarta in November 2001; and an Arab al-Qaeda suicide bomber in an explosives-laden truck planned to destroy the Australian High Commission in Singapore in early 2002.[45] Al-Qaeda and Taliban detainee and prisoner interrogation in Afghanistan, Pakistan, Camp Delta and in US revealed that Australian Muslims trained in Camp Al Farooq in Afghanistan and elsewhere were tasked to conduct terrorist operations against Australian targets.

Before al-Qaeda targeted Australians overseas, al-Qaeda established a support network in Australia using its Southeast Asian arm—JI. At the invitation of the JI Australia, JI founder leader the late Abdullah Sungkar, his successor Abu Bakar Bashir and operations commander Hambali visited Australia a dozen times. Furthermore, JI penetration of local Muslim groups led to a significant generation of propaganda within Australia aimed at politicising and radicalising Australian Muslims. Sungkar spoke of the "obligation of jihad within the framework of aiming to re-erect dawlah islamiyyah" by applying the strategies of faith and its expression in word and action and jihad.[46] He added: "In this, quwwaatul musallaha or military strength is essential."[47] The JI leaders said Indonesian Muslims had two choices: "life in a nation based upon the Koran and the sunnah or death while striving to implement, in their entirety, laws based on the Koran and the sunnah."[48] Bin Laden gave an exclusive interview to his supporters in Australia that was published on a website in Australia. JI also raised funds in Australia and funds were transferred from Australia, first to JI Malaysia and then with the disruption of the JI network in Malaysia, to JI Indonesia.[49] Furthermore, Australia features prominently in the JI regional structure. JI network in the Asia-Pacific is divided into four geographic regions, which includes Australia. JI's Area 4 or Mantiqi 4 (M4) covers Irian Jaya and Australia. As such, Australia has no option but to work jointly with the Southeast Asian countries to detect, disrupt, degrade and destroy the JI organisation. Its failure to do so will result in further attacks both in Australia and in its neighbourhood.

Another reason the terrorist threat is rising in Australia is that several terrorist groups in its immediate neighbourhood—notably in the Philippines, Indonesia and Malaysia—have stepped up their activities at home and abroad. In addition, half a dozen groups with links to al-Qaeda perceive Australia as an enemy. In order to strengthen security in the Asia-Pacific, Australia and the Southeast Asian region do need to improve cooperation. Until Bali, there is definitely a very poor understanding of the threat in Australia. The Australian malaise is one of not being sufficiently educated on the Asia-Pacific region with a poor understudying of the culture, politics and economics of its neighbours.[50] When you factor in a serious transnational terrorist threat it seems the 'she'll be right' or 'it can't happen to us' attitude prevails.[51] In the task ahead, Australia lacks the expertise and capacity but it may require a shift of thinking on how its finite resources will be deployed. As a technologically advanced country with significant economic, political, diplomatic, and a military capability, Australia could also assist countries in Southeast Asia, especially Indonesia, to improve its capability to fight terrorism. Australia can make a significant contribution to the ensuing criminal investigation to assist Indonesia. Australia should take a leadership role in this region as a whole, especially with its Southeast Asian friends, in moving Indonesia into action. This tragic event could see a rapid maturation of cooperation in the region spurred on by Australia.

To meet the current threat, the Australian Security Intelligence Organisation (ASIO), its counter-intelligence and anti-terrorist agency and the Australian Security and Intelligence Service (ASIS), its overseas intelligence service, needs to double its strength without loss of quality and resources as well as greater powers to operate effectively and efficiently. To improve the security of Australia and New Zealand, Australian agencies must work closely with their New Zealand counterparts.

Afghanistan-Pakistan-Iran

With US intervention in Afghanistan in October 2001, Osama bin Laden requested the bulk of the al-Qaeda members to travel to their home countries and await instructions. Those who had come to the adverse attention of their home security and intelligence agencies were asked to remain in Pakistan. Al-Qaeda's operational leaders Abu Zubaidah and Khalid Sheikh Mohommad relocated to Pakistan and coordinated the global terrorist campaign until their arrests in March 2002 and May 2003 respectively. After the arrest of Khalid Sheikh Mohommad's successor Tawfiq bin Attash, Osama bin Laden appointed his Chief of Security Seif Al-'Adel as the new operations chief in April 2003. Operating out of Iranian soil, Seif Al-'Adel executed the Riyad bombings in May 2003. A former officer of the Egyptian military, and thereafter a member of the Egyptian Islamic Jihad, he fought against the Soviet army before joining al-Qaeda and thereafter trained with the Hezbollah in Southern Lebanon. Seif Al-'Adel was joined in the Riyadh operation by another senior member Abu Khaled, and Osama bin Laden's son Sa'ad bin Laden, a bodyguard of the al-Qaeda leader. The operational leadership that coordinated the Riyadh bombing and dispatched experts to Casablanca, Morocco, to advise Assirat al-Moustaquim remains in Iran. Due to the loss of a large number of al-Qaeda leaders and operatives in Pakistan, al-Qaeda is increasingly looking towards Iran. However, after the operations in 2003, the Iranian government detained them. An Iraqi Islamist group Ansar al-Islami (renamed Jamiat Ansar al Sunnah), and al-Qaeda in Iraq, another al-Qaeda associate group, are also operating on the Iran-Iraq border.

The international community has gravely failed to rebuild Afghanistan by transforming the war-ravaged state into a modern state of the 21st century. Al-Qaeda has re-invented itself in Afghanistan by working with Mullah Omar's Taliban and Gulbaddin Hekmatiyar's Hezbi-e-islami. Similarly, al-Qaeda continues to work with Sipai Sahaba, Lashkar-e-jenghvi, Lashkar-e-Toiba, Jayash-e-Mohommad, Harakart-ul-Mujahidin and a number of other Pakistani groups. With US security forces and the intelligence community targeting al-Qaeda's nerve centre in Afghanistan-Pakistan, al-Qaeda will decentralise even further. While its organisers of attacks will remain in Pakistan and its immediate neighbourhood, its operatives will travel back and forth coordinating with al-Qaeda nodes in the south. To make its presence felt, al-Qaeda will increasingly rely on its global terrorist network of like-minded groups in Southeast Asia, South Asia, Horn of Africa, Middle East, and the Caucuses to strike its enemies. Already attacks in Kenya, Indonesia, India, Pakistan, Kuwait and Yemen seek to compensate for the loss and lack of space and opportunity to operate in Afghanistan. With the transfer of terrorist technology and expertise from the centre to the periphery, the attacks by the associated groups of al-Qaeda will pose a threat as great as al-Qaeda.

Impact on Separatist Conflicts

Although al-Qaeda is waging a universal jihad, the influence of al-Qaeda on Muslim separatist groups active in their territories is growing. It is a worrying trend as Islamists tend to "hijack" the resources of the ethnonationalists. There is very little governments can do to arrest the trend. Whether it is in the Moroland in the Philippines, Aceh in Indonesia, Pattini in Thailand, Kashmir in India-Pakistan, or Chechnya in Russia, Muslim secessionist conflicts have been penetrated by Islamist groups to different degrees. Either by emulation or direct contact, factions, splinters and main groups of the separatist category are learning from al-Qaeda tactics, techniques and styles. Al-Qaeda did not engage in kidnapping, hostage taking or assassination frequently, but its camps in Afghanistan and elsewhere taught these tactics to several tens of thousands of youth.[52] Even before 9-11, it has been observed that al-Qaeda has been attempting to develop alliances with non-Islamist Muslim groups. Rabitat-ul Mujahidin is an alliance of Islamist and Muslim separatist groups from the Philippines, Indonesia, Malaysia, Myanmar and Thailand.[53] Thailand, especially Bangkok and Narathiwat Province, a safe haven for Jemmah Islamiyah, is the home of a number of other groups. The Pattani United Liberation Organisation (PULO) formed in 1967, New PULO formed in 1995, Barisan Revolusi Nasional Malayu Pattani (BRN) formed in 1960, Gerakan Mujahideen Islam Pattani (GMIP) formed in 1986, and Bersatu (Unity) formed in 1997.[54] GMIP has members, such as Wae Ka Raeh, who trained in Afghanistan and fought for al-Qaeda.[55] In spite of the successes of the Thai government of bringing the secessionist violence to an end in the 1980s, there has been a revival in 2001. On October 29, 2002, a series of arson incidents and bombs exploded in Southern Thailand. Five schools were set on fire in Songkhla Province and bombs damaged both My Garden Hotel and a Buddhist temple in the neighbouring Pattani Province in 2001. Since April 2001, about two-dozen law enforcement officers have been killed in southern Thailand but the authorities in Bangkok have dismissed the violence as criminal and not terrorist. After Bali I and II, the threat to popular tourist destination, including to Pukhet and Pataya in Thailand, has increased. Although there is acknowledgement now, the terrorist threat has grown significantly in Southern Thailand. Although the al-Qaeda network in Thailand, where two of the 9-11 hijackers were launched after a meeting in Malaysia in January 2000, was disrupted, Thailand is a very important venue for terrorists to hide and meet. After living in denial for one and a half years, Thailand was forced to arrest Thai JI members in June 2003, after a Singaporean JI member was arrested in Bangkok. As a result, an attack being planned by JI Thailand on diplomatic targets in Bangkok and two tourist resorts was disrupted.

Ideological Threat

More than an organization, the ideology of al-Qaeda remains a resilient threat. Although al-Qaeda can still mount operations, with the increase in pressure, al-Qaeda will become relegated to an ideology. As al-Qaeda increasingly depends on like-minded groups to conduct attacks, other Islamist groups will become like al-Qaeda. For instance, Mas Salamat Kasthari, the Chief of Jemmah Islamiyah (JI) of Singapore, was planning to hijack an Aerofloat plane from Bangkok and crash it into the Changi International Airport in Singapore in 2002. The tactic of using an air vehicle as a weapon was clearly an al-Qaeda invention. When asked by his interrogators why he chose to hijack an Aerofloat plane, he responded that JI had decided to teach Russia a lesson for killing civilians in Chechnya. Furthermore, the killing of 202 civilians in Bali by the same group was not Southeast Asian in character. Southeast Asia had never witnessed a mass fatality terrorist attack before. Likewise, the JI attack in Bali witnessed the first suicide attack by a Southeast Asian terrorist.[56] During the past decade, JI and other associated Islamist groups had come under al-Qaeda influence in a substantial way.

Traditionally, al-Qaeda with better trained, more experienced and highly committed operatives wanted to attack more difficult targets—especially strategic targets—and leave the easier and tactical targets to its associated groups. With al-Qaeda decentralizing, its operatives are working closely together at a tactical level with other groups. As a result, the lethality of the attacks conducted by the associate groups of al-Qaeda is increasing. As Bali in 2002 and Casablanca in 2003 demonstrated, the attacks conducted by the associate groups of al-Qaeda can be as lethal as the attacks conducted by the parent group itself. With attacks conducted by al-Qaeda's associated groups posing a threat as great as al-Qaeda, the theatre of war will widen. Government security and intelligence agencies will be forced to monitor the technologies, tactics and techniques of a wide range of groups.

Although US is under severe pressure to withdraw from Saudi Arabia, the US will prefer to remain in the Kingdom because withdrawal after the recent attack will mean defeat in the eyes of its opponents. Nonetheless, US visibility in the Middle East, US assistance to Israel, and continued US presence in Iraq will generating wide-ranging reactions from the Islamists, both terrorist groups and political parties. Especially after US, Allied, and Coalition intervened in Afghanistan on October 7, 2001, Iraq is an attractive base for al-Qaeda. The Islamists desperately need a new theater to produce psychologically and physically war-trained Islamists.

Successes and Failures

Although branded a "War against Terrorism" by the US, the fight is against a radical ideology producing Muslim youth willing to kill and die and wealthy Muslims willing to support and suffer incarceration. For the al-Qaeda umbrella—the World Islamic Front for Jihad Against the Jews and the Crusaders—the fight is against a civilisation. The reality is that it is a fight between the vast majority of progressive Muslims and the miniscule percentage of radical Muslims. It is not a clash of civilisations but a clash among civilisations—a fight that must essentially be fought within the Muslim world. While the immediate (1–2 years) consequences are apparent, the mid (5 years) and long term (10 years) consequence of fighting primarily an ideological campaign militarily is yet to be seen. All indications are that Islamism—whether it is in Turkey, Pakistan, Malaysia, or in Indonesia—is moving from the periphery to the centre. US intervention in Iraq has spiked the ideological fuel prolonging the strength, size and life of Islamist political parties and terrorist groups.

The greatest failure of the US-led coalition is its lack of capability to neutralise the core leadership of both al-Qaeda and the Islamic Movement of the Taliban. While preparations for protracted guerrilla operations against the coalition forces inside Afghanistan is coordinated by the Taliban leader Mullah Mohommad Omar, terrorist operations worldwide including in Afghanistan is coordinated by Osama bin Laden and his deputy, principal strategist and designated successor Dr Ayman Zawahiri. Multiple sources, including the CIA, reveal that both bin Laden and al-Zawahiri are alive.[57] Furthermore, Zawahiri refers to suicide attacks on the oldest Jewish synagogue in North Africa in Djerba, Tunisia, killing 21 including 14 German tourists on April 11, 2002 and the killing of 14 including 11 French naval technicians working on the submarine project outside Sheraton Hotel in Karachi, Pakistan, on May 9, 2002. He states "Thank God, America could not reach the leaders of al-Qaeda and Taliban, including Mullah Muhammad Omar and Shayak Osama bin Laden, who enjoy good heath and, alongside the rest of the patient mujahidin, are managing the battle against the US crusader raid on Afghanistan."[58] Members of the former Army of the Islamic Emirate Afghanistan loyal to Mullah Omar and al-Qaeda's 055 Brigade that survived death or capture are supporting or engaged in guerrilla and terrorist operations against the US-led coalition both inside and outside Afghanistan respectively. Mullah Omar is building a clandestine network slowly and steadily in Afghanistan utilizing its vast and porous borders to wage a protracted campaign of sustained urban warfare. Bin Laden and Zawahiri are developing targets overseas, especially soft targets with a twin focus on population centres and economic targets.

Change of Mindset

To make it difficult for its enemies, al-Qaeda has constantly innovated its military tactics, financial methods, and propaganda techniques in the past year. Al-Qaeda—focusing on strategic targets prior to 9/11—is operating across the entire spectrum targeting both strategic to tactical targets. Although the West seized US$ 150 million of terrorist money in the first four months after 9/11, with the transformation of al-Qaeda financial practices only about $10 million has been seized. With the targeting of the above ground open banking system, the underground unregulated banking network (hawala) has grown bigger. With mosques, madrasas, charities and community centres that disseminate Islamist propaganda coming under threat, al-Qaeda is increasingly relying on the Internet. As al-Qaeda is a learning organization, the law enforcement, intelligence, and security agencies fighting al-Qaeda must be goal-oriented and not rule-oriented.

With the terrorists adapting to the threat posed by government law enforcement authorities, government security and intelligence agencies are increasing their human and technical source penetration. Capabilities for terrorist tracking, re-emption and disruption of terrorist operations are increasing. For instance, an al-Qaeda team travelling in their vehicle in Yemen's northern Province of Marib was attacked by a hellfire missile from the CIA-controlled unmanned Predator drone on November 4, 2002. The attack killed Ali Senyan al-Harthi alias Qaed Senyan al-Harthi alias Abu Ali, the mastermind of the USS Cole operation and a key al-Qaeda leader in the region. To meet the current threat, the Pentagon has increased its intelligence capability and the CIA has increased its paramilitary capability. In the foreseeable future, human intelligence and covert strike forces will remain at the heart of fighting secret and highly motivated organisations like al-Qaeda. It is critical for the US to increase its sharing of intelligence especially with their Middle Eastern and Asian counterparts. Traditionally, the US has been averse to sharing high-grade intelligence especially source-based intelligence with the Muslim World. This has changed since 9/11 but not adequately.

If al-Qaeda is to be defeated, a change in the thinking of the US-led "War of Terrorism" is paramount. Despite the US-led coalition campaign worldwide, the al-Qaeda alliance—the World Islamic Front for Jihad Against the Jews and Crusaders—has managed to repair the damage to their support and operational infrastructure. As no serious international effort has been made to counter the Islamist ideology (the belief that "every Muslim's duty is to wage jihad") the robust Islamist milieu is providing recruits and financial support for Islamist groups worldwide to replenish their human losses and material wastage. Today, 2–4 al-Qaeda and Taliban members are captured or killed in Afghanistan but at the end of the week the Islamists are successful in attracting a dozen recruits as members, collaborators, supporters and sympathisers.[59] To put it crudely, the rate of production of Islamists is greater than the rate of their kill or capture. Into the counter-terrorism toolbox, the powerful message that al-Qaeda is not Koranic but heretical has not been integrated. As such there is popular support for the al-Qaeda model of Islam among the politicised and radicalised Muslims. As there is no effort to counter or dilute the ideology of extremism, the military campaign against al-Qaeda even if pursued single-mindedly and unrelentingly is likely to take decades. The "deep reservoir of hatred and a desire for revenge"[60] will remain unless the US can start to think beyond the counter-terrorist military and financial dimensions.

The international community must seek to build a zero tolerance level for terrorist support activity. The tragedy of 9/11, Bali I and II, Moscow, Riyadh, Casablanca and several other attacks demonstrate that contemporary terrorists are indiscriminate. As terrorists do not recognise and respect ethnicity, religion or national borders, terrorism irrespective of location should be fought. There is no appeasement with those who seek to advance their political aims and objectives using violence. Like Indonesia, countries that condone, tolerate or fail to take tough action against terrorism will be touched by it. It is not only the countries in the South but even countries in the North that have been complacent in the fight against terrorism. Within four months of 9/11, Western governments froze US\$ 150 million of terrorist money in Europe and North America indicative of the magnitude of terrorist wealth in liberal democracies. Although the al-Qaeda support network has suffered in the US, its propaganda, recruitment, and fundraising activities are still continuing in Europe. Despite efforts to the contrary, segments of Muslims in the migrant communities of North America, Western Europe and Australasia and territorial communities of the Middle East and Asia continue to provide support to al-Qaeda and other Islamist groups. As Europe has not suffered a large-scale attack, Europeans do not perceive al-Qaeda as a high threat. As a result, Islamist support activities are continuing in Western Europe. With the increase in threat, both governments and their publics that do not take the threat information seriously are bound to suffer.

Managing the Threat

Al-Qaeda has had a head start of ten years. Until one month after US diplomatic targets in East Africa were destroyed by al-Qaeda in August 1998, the CIA did not even know the correct name of Osama bin Laden's group.[61] However, during the past two years the understanding of the US intelligence community of its principal enemy—al-Qaeda—has grown dramatically. The tragedy of 9/11 has empowered the Counter Terrorism Center at the CIA to develop the much-needed organization and more importantly the mindset to hunt al-Qaeda. Largely due to detainee debriefings, the West today understands the threat it faces much better than ever before. The US government, especially its security and intelligence community, has learned at a remarkable pace. There is a remarkable improvement in collection and analysis both by the CIA and the FBI. For instance, immediately before the Yemeni, Kuwaiti and Bali attack, the CIA and FBI alerted friendly counterpart agencies and the US State Department issued worldwide alerts. The West together with its Middle Eastern and Asian counterparts seriously started to fight al-Qaeda only after 9/11 and al-Qaeda has suffered gravely. The global strategy of the West to meet the global threat posed by al-Qaeda is taking shape slowly but steadily. Like it contained the Soviet threat in the second half of the 20th century, it will develop the organisation and a doctrine to contain the Islamist threat. With sustained efforts to target the core and penultimate leadership, it is very likely that the al-Qaeda echelon Osama bin Laden, Dr Ayman Al Zawahiri and even the Taliban leader Mullah Omar will be captured or more likely killed. Nonetheless, Islamist terrorism will outlive al-Qaeda, and Islamism as an ideology will persist in the foreseeable future.

The global fight against terrorism will be carried out by the West and Japan—the rich and influential nations with the greatest staying power. With the diffusion of the terrorist threat, the US political, military, economic and diplomatic presence will grow and its influence will expand globally in the months and years ahead.[62] It is a long fight and will have to be fought on all fronts by multiple actors across many countries. To ensure the success of the campaign, the international community must remain focused on targeting al-Qaeda and be committed to rebuilding Afghanistan and Pakistan, and now Iraq. Western nations must move beyond rhetoric into concrete action, pour in resources, and build modern model nation-states for the Muslim World in these countries. Protecting Karzai of Afghanistan and Musharaff of Pakistan—the most threatened world leaders—is paramount. Several attempts by al-Qaeda and its associated groups to assassinate these leaders have been frustrated. International assistance to their regimes to politically and economically develop their countries and invest in their publics is key to reducing the space for and challenge the Islamists continuously appealing to the politically and economically marginalised.

On the eve of the US intervention in Afghanistan, Osama bin Laden correctly stated that the fight has moved beyond al-Qaeda. Al-Qaeda's propaganda war since 9/11 especially after US intervention in Iraq has escalated several folds. With al-Qaeda and pro-al-Qaeda web sites proliferating—many of them operationally unconnected but ideologically connected to al-Qaeda—support for al-Qaeda's ideology is slowly growing. Support for Islamism will grow even further if the US intervenes in Iraq. The world has recently witnessed several isolated terrorist incidents by those influenced by terrorist propaganda. For instance, Hesham Mohamed Hadayet, an Egyptian, walked to the El Al counter at the Los Angeles International Airport and shot two people dead on America's independence day on July 4, 2002.[63] There were arrests worldwide including in the heart of Europe of several politicised and radicalised Muslims providing funds or were planning and preparing terrorist attacks. Osman Petmezci, a 24-year-old Turkish national, and his American fiancée

Astrid Eyzaguirre, 23, were preparing to attack the US Army Europe Headquarters in Heidelberg but were arrested by the German authorities on September 5, 2002.[64] Inside the couple's third-floor apartment, police recovered 130 kilograms of bomb making chemicals, five pipe bombs, a bomb making manual, detonators and a picture of bin Laden. German authorities believe that the "couple was acting alone, despite citing evidence that they admired Osama bin Laden and shared some of convictions, including a hatred for the Jews."[65] There are several similar unreported or under reported terrorist attacks. For instance, a US helicopter carrying US oil company employees was attacked after taking off from the San'a airport injuring two persons on November 3, 2002. With the steadfast erosion of al-Qaeda personnel and physical infrastructure, al-Qaeda can become a state-of-mind spawning both individual terrorists and successor terrorist organisations. To avoid this real danger, the ideological response to al-Qaeda and Islamism as a doctrine must not be made a secondary task.

To win the campaign, the fight against radical Islam should not be confused with the Muslim world, one fifth of humanity or 1.44 billion people.[66] It is not a clash of civilisation but a clash among civilisation. It is a fight waged between the progressive Muslims and the radical Muslims. Only a miniscule number of the Muslim public actively supports terrorism.[67] The vast majority of Muslims have suffered as a result of political violence unleashed by a small group of power hungry leaders wearing the garb of religion. If the fight is to be won, efforts must be made to protect the moderate Muslims from virulent ideologies propagated by Mullah's of the al-Qaeda brand of Islam. With the threat of Islamism increasing, the hands of the progressive Muslim leaders both in government and outside government especially in the non-governmental organisations must be strengthened. It must involve the best of relations between the Western governmental and non-governmental leaders with their Middle Eastern and Asian counterparts and moreover public diplomacy where governments directly communicate with the public, even of publics across borders.[68] Despite the oil boom, the failure of the Arab leaders to invest in their citizens has increased both the ideological appeal and the welfare programs of terrorist groups. The Arab regimes must take the blame for their failure to build modern education systems, create new jobs, and develop the quality of life of their people. Arab regime's reliance on blaming the West for many of their problems and their reluctance to counter anti-Western rhetoric make Western public diplomacy in the Arab World even more necessary. In parallel to Al Jazeera, a CNN, BBC or CBS Arab satellite television station is central to correcting and fashioning the traditional Middle Eastern view of the West. Instead of shying away, the West must engage the Middle East to develop transparency and accountability.[69] Furthermore, joint prophylactic measures—greater investment in the political, socio-economic reform especially education and welfare—by the West, and working together with the Muslim World is likely to reduce support for terrorism in the long term.[70] Failure to develop a multi-pronged, multi-dimensional, multi-agency and a multinational response to al-Qaeda and its associate groups will lead to a continuity of the threat, and even an escalation.

Rohan Gunaratna is Head of Terrorism Research at the Institute of Defence and Strategic Studies in Singapore. Dr. Gunaratna is also Jebsen Center Senior Fellow for Counter-Terrorism Studies; Senior Fellow (emeritus), Combating Terrorism Center at West Point; and Honorary Fellow, International Policy Institute for Counter Terrorism, Israel.

Notes

1. I am grateful to Brigadier General Russell D. Howard of the Jebsen Centre for Counter Terrorism Studies at the Fletcher School of Law and Diplomacy and Major Reid L. Sawyer of the United States Military Academy at West Point for their invitation to write this chapter.
2. In May 2001, Al-Qaeda and Egyptian Islamic Jihad merged. The official name of Al-Qaeda led by Usama bin Laden and his deputy Dr. Ayman al-Zawahiri is Jama'at al-Qaeda al-Jihad (al-Qaeda al-Jihad Group) or Tanzim Qaedat al-Jihad (al-Qaeda and Jihad Organization).
3. While guerrilla groups target combatants, terrorist groups target non-combatants.
4. The term was coined by the Counter Terrorism Centre at the Central Intelligence Agency, Langley, Virginia, USA sometime in the late 1990s. Michael Sheehan, former US Ambassador for Counter Terrorism and currently Deputy Commissioner for Counter Terrorism at the New York Police Department, Senior's Conference, US Military Academy, West Point, June 2003.
5. The meeting was arranged by the former Egyptian Army Captain Ali Mohommad who subsequently became a naturalised American, joined the US military and served as a Supplies Sergeant at Fort Bragg, North Carolina, before joining al-Qaeda and becoming the Chief bodyguard of Osama bin Laden and the Principal Instructor of al-Qaeda, both in Afghanistan and Sudan. He is currently in US custody in the mainland USA.
6. However, 10% of phone calls from Osama bin Laden's satellite phone went to Iran from 1996–1998.
7. Compared to its numerical strength of 4000 members, estimated at October 2001, the loss of over 3000 members and key supporters is significant. The figure 4000 members come from al-Qaeda detainee debriefs, including the FBI interrogation of Mohommad Mansour Jabarah, the 21 year old Canadian operative of Kuwaiti-Iraqi origin detained in mainland USA since 2002.
8. However, Aum Shinrikyo does not have the same global composition or the global reach of al-Qaeda.
9. For instance, Egyptian Islamic Jihad and the Islamic Group of Egypt has only Egyptians; Armed Islamic Group of Algeria and Salafi Group for Call and Combat has only Algerians, Moro Islamic Liberation Front and the Abu Sayaaf Group has only Moros.
10. For instance, Takfir Wal Hijra, a group active in Europe and North America recruited from North Africa—Egyptians, Algerians, Libyans, Algerians, Moroccans, and Tunisians—and Jemmah Islamiyah recruited from Southeast Asia and Australia—Indonesian, Malaysian, Thais, Singaporeans, Filipinos, and Australians (both cradle and convert Muslims).
11. Hasan Hattab, the head of the European network of the Armed Islamic Group of Algeria (GIA), broke away from the GIA in 1998 and formed GSPC. Although GSPC is strongest in Europe, a cell in the US planning to target the MGM hotel and casino in Las Vegas was broken by the FBI in 2002.
12. Interview, Dr Reuven Paz, International Policy Institute for Counter Terrorism, Israel, May 2003.
13. Eliza Manningham-Buller, Terrorism Conference, Royal United Services Institute, London, July 17, 2003
14. Ibid.
15. Osama bin Laden's two-minute audiotape broadcast to mark the first anniversary of the US intervention in Afghanistan, Al Jazeera, Arab Satellite Television Station, Qatar, October 6, 2002.
16. Ayman Al Zawahiri's question and answer with an unidentified reporter, Al Jazeera, October 8, 2002.
17. Debriefing of Umar Al Faruq, held at Baghram Airbase, Afghanistan, on September 9, 2002, enabled the US government to issue an alert immediately before September 11, 2002, the first anniversary of 9–11. Tactical Interrogation Report Umar Al Faruq, CIA, Langley, September 2002.
18. Kashmir, only six hours by road from Afghanistan and the theatre of conflict nearest to Afghanistan, was visited by the author in August 2002. Both reviewing detainee tactical

interrogation reports and debriefing of foreign detainees by the author revealed that al-Qaeda is neither abandoning nor deserting Afghanistan or Pakistan but the routine flow of foreigners to fight in Indian Kashmir is continuing.

19. For instance, the 9/11 mastermind Khalid Sheikh Mohomad, al-Qaeda's head of the military committee, tasked Jayashi-e-Mohommad member Ahmed Saeed Omar Sheikh to kill Daniel Pearl, the first US casualty in a terrorist attack since 9/11. Operating through Lashkar-e-Omar, an umbrella group mooted by al-Qaeda, six terrorists opened fire and killed 17 Christians including five children and a policeman and injuring 17 in a church in Bahawalpur, Punjab on October 28, 2001. Similarly, a grenade attack on a church in the heavily guarded diplomatic enclave in Islamabad killed 5 including a US official's wife and daughter and injured 41 on March 17, 2002. Al-Qaeda also financed a car bombing to kill President Musharaff, and when it failed used the same car bomb to attack the US consulate. While Pakistanis mounted reconnaissance and organised the explosives and the vehicle, an Arab al-Qaeda member finally arrived and conducted the suicide bombing, killing 12 Pakistanis and injuring 51, including one US marine guard in Karachi on June 14 2002.

20. Al-Qaeda website al.neda.com claimed that it attacked the "French oil tanker off the coast of Yemen."

21. Terrorist connections of Abubakar Basyir; and further details on terrorist connection and activities of Umar Faruq, Orange Alert Document, September 2002, p. 2.

22. Umar Faruq's Terrorist Activities in Indonesia, Badan Inteligen Nasional (BIN: National Intelligence Agency), Jakarta, June 2002, p.1.

23. al.neda.com claimed that it attacked the "Fialka base in Kuwait."

24. al.neda.com claimed that it attacked the "nightclubs and whorehouses in Indonesia."

25. Analysis of the Latest Bombing Incident in Indonesia and Its Possible Connections with Al-Qaeda and Jemmah Islamiyah, National Intelligence Coordinating Agency, Philippines, October 2002.

26. USAID is the lead disaster relief agency engaged in agriculture, water and humanitarian programs.

27. The same group had claimed responsibility for killing Israeli diamond merchant Yitzhak Snir, a man in his 50s, who was slain near Foley's home on August 6, 2001. The group said the attack was in response to Israeli behaviour against Palestinians. Israeli security officials suspected that two previous attacks conducted against Israeli citizens in Jordan were also by the same group. On December 5, 2000, an unidentified gunman shot and slightly wounded Israeli diplomat Shlomo Razabi in the left foot as he was leaving an Amman store. On November 19, 2000, Israeli diplomat Yoram Havivian was slightly wounded in the arm and the leg when a gunman fired on his vehicle.

28. Osama bin Laden's two-minute audiotape broadcast to mark the first anniversary of the US intervention in Afghanistan, Al Jazeera, Arab Satellite Television Station, Qatar, October 6, 2002.

29. Al-Qa'ida Declarations of Continued Attacks, CIA, Langley, October 2002, p. 1.

30. Valeria Korchagina, "Hostage-takers 'keen on dying.' USA Today, October 25, 2002, p. 14 A. Article uses the term "rebels."

31. After the first Chechen war (December 1994–November 1996), Russian troops withdrew from Chechnya but returned in 1999 in response to a series of apartment bombings in Moscow that killed 300 Russians.

32. Chechen Tape, Al Jezeera, October 24, 2002.

33. Movsar's aunt Khava Barayev, 19, conducted a suicide attack killing two Russian soldiers at the Russian base in Alkhan-Yurt in June 2000.

34. Poisoned Letter Killed Chechen Commander Khattab, Kavkaz-Tsentr News Agency Web Site in Russian April 28, 2002.

35. Al-Qaeda's former Southeast Asian representative Umar Al Faruq's cell phone number 081-2802-7614 was in the phone memory of Ibn-ul-Khattab as well as the phone book of another al-Qaeda leader Abu Talha alias Muhammad Abdallah Nasir Ubayd al Dusari arrested by the Kuwaitis. Tactical Interrogation Report Umar Al Faruq, CIA, Langley, September 2002.

36. George Tenant, CIA Director, visited Riyadh a few weeks before the attack and appraised the House of al Saud of the impending threat. Interview, CIA officer, May 2003.

37. Information Derived from Mohammed Mansour Jabarah, Federal Bureau of Investigations, US Department of Justice, August 21, 2002, p. 2.

38. Ibid

39. Ibid.

40. Umar Faruq's Terrorist Activities in Indonesia, BIN, Jakarta, June 2002, p. 2.

41. Ibid, p. 2.

42. Although BIN headed by A.M. Hendropriyono targeted al-Qaeda cells, the Indonesian government was reluctant to target JI and its associated Majlis Mujahidin Indonesia (MMI: Mujahidin Council of Indonesia) headed by Abu Bakar Bashir and Lashkar Jundullah headed by Agus Dwikarna.

43. Debriefing of John Walker Lindh, Virginia, US, July 25–25, 2002.

44. Margo O'Neill, Lateline, Australian Broadcasting Corporation, October 9, 2002. Australian government saw no significant threat to Australia or to its interests.

45. Despite a JI surveillance video of the Australian target that was recovered in the residence of the late al-Qaeda military commander Mohomad Atef alias Abu Haf's in Afghanistan, the Australian government did not take the threat seriously—some officials believed that al-Qaeda/JI had included the Australian High Commission in the target list because it was next to the US Embassy. Even in March 2002, some Australian intelligence officials who participated at a counter-terrorism meeting organised by the Institute for Defence and Strategic Studies in Singapore disbelieved that JI was under al-Qaeda control.

46. Nida'ul Islam (Call to Islam), Islamic Youth Movement magazine, Sydney, February–March 1997

47. Ibid.

48. "The latest Indonesian crisis: causes and solutions", JI political manifesto, May 1998,

49. Debriefing of JI members, September–October 2002.

50. Interview, Jeff Pentrose, Former Director, Australian Federal Police Intelligence, October 2002

51. Ibid.

52. The author reviewed over 200 tapes, including training tapes, recovered by CNN's Nic Robertson from al-Qaeda's registry in Afghanistan, CNN Centre, Atlanta, August–September 2002.

53. The second meeting of the Rabitat-ul Mujahidin held in Kuala Lumpur, Malaysia, presided by the JI leader Abu Bakar Basyir in mid-2000 included both Islamists and separatist leaders—Agus Dwikarna from Sulawesi, Tenku Idris from Aceh, Ibrahim Maidin from Singapore, Abdul Fatah from Thailand, Nik Adli Abdul Aziz from Malaysia, representatives from Myanmar and Egyptian Islamic Jihad. Interview, Intelligence official, Department of the Prime Minister, Malaysia, November 2002.

54. Tony Davis, "The Complexities of Unrest in Southern Thailand" Jane's Intelligence Review, Volume 14 Number 9, September 2002. p. 17.

55. Ibid. p. 17.

56. Iqbal, the JI member, detonated a backpack of explosives that he carried into the Paddy's Bar in Bali.

57. Al-Qa'ida Declarations of Continued Attacks, CIA, Langley, October 2002, p. 1.

58. Ayman Al Zawahiri's question and answer with an unidentified reporter, Al Jazeera, October 8, 2002.

59. Interviews, US military and intelligence officials, Washington DC, October 29–November 1, 2002.

60. Brian Michael Jenkins. Countering al-Qaeda: An Appreciation of the Situation and Suggestions for Strategy, RAND, 2002.

61. None of the CIA documents until August 1998 refers to Osama Bin Laden's organisation as al-Qaeda. It refers to the group as UBL or OBL network and as Islamic Army. Furthermore, the US designated foreign terrorist groups in 1997 do not list "al-Qaeda."

62. In addition to the rise of Islamism, another factor that is driving an increased US presence worldwide is the re-emergence of the Peoples Republic of China and US efforts to contain the next superpower.

63. Shooting at Los Angeles International Airport Kills Two, Injures Others on July 4, FBI Press Release, Los Angeles Field Office, July 5, 2002.

64. Tony Czuczka, Germans had hints about suspected bomb plot against US, Associated Press, September 8, 2002.

65. Ibid.

66. For statistics, US Centre for World Mission 2002 Report.

67. Husain Haqqani, "The Gospel of Jihad," Foreign Policy, September–October, 2002, p. 74.

68. Perception that the Indonesian military was behind the Bali bombing found resonance in Indonesia because US government only engaged the Indonesian government and not the public. While strengthening government to government cooperation, it is necessary also to engage the public in a dialogue and keep them informed of the active presence of an al-Qaeda-JI network in Indonesia.

69. For instance, charities should not be permitted to raise funds or transfer funds unless and until the end user has been verified and validated.

70. Marina Ottaway, "Nation Building," Foreign Policy, September–October 2002, pp. 16–24.

Natasha E. Bajema

Rethinking Threat Assessments for Terrorist Targets: Applying the Lessons of Complex Terrorism

The objectives of threat assessments for terrorist targets such as nuclear power plants are typically two-fold: They analyze prevailing terrorist capabilities and motivations for attacking particular targets and assess the adequacy of security measures taken to defend these targets. Traditional threat assessments for terrorist targets generally do not consider broader issues, such as, in the case of nuclear power plants (NPPs), the problem of nuclear waste disposal. What does the problem of nuclear waste disposal have to do with the threat of nuclear sabotage? When we think about NPPs as terrorist targets, the issue of nuclear waste certainly represents an important part of the equation. After all, terrorists view NPPs as desirable targets primarily because of the large inventories of radioactive materials that they contain and the potential economic, environmental, and psychological consequences if these materials were to be released into the environment.[1] The problem of nuclear waste disposal, on the other hand, is not an issue that immediately comes to mind when assessing terrorist threats against NPPs.

Drawing on the lessons of *complex terrorism,* this paper departs from the path of traditional threat assessments to evaluate the broader implications of a terrorist attack on an NPP for environmental security, energy security, and U.S. policy on nuclear waste disposal.[2] By showing how the problem of nuclear waste disposal—generally considered an environmental issue—may become a concern of counterterrorism efforts in the future, this paper aims to demonstrate the need to use systemic approaches for assessing terrorist threats in the 21st century.

Understanding the Implications of Complex Terrorism for Threat Assessments

If the terrorists of the 21st century are *strategic actors* as claimed by the *National Strategy for Homeland Security,* then it is likely that these actors evaluate their preferred targets from both operational and systemic perspectives and select targets for their chances for operational success and greatest strategic impact.[3] It would follow, then, that assessments on the threat of terrorism should assume systemic as well as operational approaches. Yet, traditional threat assessments are missing crucial systemic elements of the terrorist threat that are illuminated by Thomas Homer-Dixon's concept of *complex terrorism.* According to Homer-Dixon, complex terrorism arises from two key trends: the growing technological capabilities of terrorists and the increasing vulnerability of economic and technological systems. Homer-Dixon warns that analysts have focused a great deal on the first trend, less on the second and have "virtually ignored their combined effect."[4]

Nuclear power plants have long been considered attractive targets for terrorists due to the potentially significant economic, environmental, and psychological consequences of a *successful* attack. Given the relative robustness of nuclear facilities and the complexity of achieving a massive release of radiation, however, analysts have typically assumed that terrorists would not actively target NPPs.[5] Understated assumptions about terrorist capabilities and level of interest have been seriously challenged by the nature of the 9/11 terrorist attacks and subsequent intelligence from al-Qaeda operatives about the planning process. The 9/11 attacks "demonstrated that terrorists are capable of successfully attacking fixed infrastructure with large civilian jetliner."[6] In addition, the 9/11 attacks "raised the possibility of a new kind of threat to commercial power plants and spent fuel storage: premeditated, carefully planned, high-impact attacks by terrorists to damage these facilities for the purpose of releasing radiation to the environment and spreading fear and panic among civilian populations."[7] In his 2002 State of the Union speech, President George W. Bush warned about the implications of finding diagrams of U.S. NPPs in al-Qaeda camps in Afghanistan. Indeed, according to Khalid Sheik Mohammed, one of the chief organizers of the 9/11 attacks, NPPs were among the selected targets in an initial plan that included 10 hijacked aircrafts before it was scaled down.[8] Other recent evidence of interest in NPPs as targets includes the arrest of 19 Pakistani-born men living in Canada in August 2003 for involvement in suspicious activities such as surveillance and flying lessons that would transport them over a nuclear power plant.[9]

Despite insights gleaned from the 9/11 attacks and subsequent intelligence, however, the Nuclear Regulatory Commission (NRC) and the nuclear industry continue to vigorously downplay the threat against NPPs. Understated claims about the threat against NPPs are supported by much of the existing threat analysis on nuclear sabotage. Some experts emphasize the relative robustness of NPPs compared to other key infrastructure.[10] The National Research Council notes that there are "many other types of large industrial facilities that are potentially vulnerable to attack, for example, petroleum refineries, chemical plants, oil and liquefied natural gas supertankers. These facilities do not have the robust construction and security features characteristic of NPPs, and many are located near highly populated urban areas."[11] Furthermore, analysts argue that terrorists will forgo targeting of NPPs due to a low probability of a successful attack.[12] Since attacks on NPPs do not offer a high probability of success, "sophisticated terrorists will not see them as attractive targets."[13] Finally, many threat assessments focus on the complexity of carrying out a "successful attack" and suggest that even if terrorists did attack an NPP, they would not achieve their objectives.[14] For example, a study conducted by the Electric Power Research Institute (EPRI) in 2002 found that "nuclear plant structures that house reactor fuel can withstand aircraft impacts, even though they were not specifically designed for such impacts."[15] Using this reasoning, the NRC determined in January 2007 that NPPs "do not need to protect themselves from potential attacks by terrorists using airplanes."[16]

Based on traditional threat assessments, it is tempting to conclude that rising terrorist capabilities and motivations to exploit technology and open societies in order to cause death and destruction present only a minimal, if any, increase in the threat against NPPs. However, many of these threat assessments are incomplete and supported by flawed assumptions. Traditional threat assessments typically evaluate the likelihood of a massive release of radiation resulting from various modes of attack. Since "an attack that damages a power plant or its spent fuel facilities would not necessarily result in the release of any radioactivity to the environment," it is widely assumed that unless terrorists were assured a perfect outcome—i.e., a massive release of radiation—they would not target NPPs.[17] If this logic were applied to 9/11, it would follow that terrorists would not attempt to crash aircraft into the World Trade Center if they did not have a guarantee that the weather conditions would be ideal or that one or both towers would collapse. Clearly, the brutal success of the 9/11 attacks was highly dependent on several factors that were beyond the control of al-Qaeda operatives. In other words, al-Qaeda has demonstrated a willingness to assume a high level of risk in implementing sophisticated attacks. In addition, although the 9/11 attacks led to thousands of deaths and the collapse of the World Trade Center towers, the nature of other targets that were selected (including the Pentagon and the White House) suggests that al-Qaeda terrorists may possibly be more interested in the symbolic value and strategic impact of their attacks than in causing mass destruction.

Planning an attack on an NPP requires a significant level of technical expertise and involves a high risk of failure. Therefore, it appears reasonable to assume a terrorist group attacking an NPP would want to maximize the impact of an attack and would probably aim to cause a massive release of radioactivity into the environment. However, it is quite possible that terrorist groups have a wider range of strategic or symbolic objectives in targeting NPPs and would therefore be willing to accept a lower level of operational success than is typically assumed.

In addition to relying on faulty assumptions, traditional threat assessments on nuclear sabotage remain overly focused on evaluating terrorist capabilities for carrying out a successful attack against an NPP, which in this context means causing a massive release of radiation. Lacking the insights provided by Homer-Dixon's concept of complex terrorism, these threat assessments fail to consider important systemic elements of the threat. In particular, threat assessments overlook the increasing vulnerability of economic and technological systems. Increases in vulnerability to terrorist attacks are caused by "the growing complexity and interconnectedness of our modern societies" and "increasing geographic concentration of wealth, human capital, knowledge, and communication links."[18] In order to apply the lessons of complex terrorism to threat assessments of nuclear sabotage in the United States, we need consider the broader strategic context of NPPs and their role in assuring U.S. energy security. To that end, this chapter examines the physical, psychological, and policy linkages and interdependencies that shape the strategic context for NPPs and contribute to their appeal as terrorist targets.

The Problem of Nuclear Waste Disposal: Solved by Default

Framing the strategic context for NPPs begins with a brief look at U.S. plans for the disposal of nuclear waste and the impact of those plans on the future of the nuclear energy industry. Since the 1970s, the long-term viability of the nuclear energy industry has been irreversibly linked to finding a solution for the disposal of nuclear waste that is acceptable to the general public.[19] Finding a solution to the problem of nuclear waste has traditionally been a concern of both nuclear power proponents and opponents, albeit for different reasons.[20] "Nuclear advocates see such a policy as essential to maintaining a role for nuclear power in the United States, while critics contend that the United States has neglected for too long what they view as unacceptable risks posed by accumulated spent nuclear fuel."[21] In the U.S., the strategy for handling nuclear waste has gone through three phases, each focusing on a different solution: reprocessing, storage in a geologic repository, and interim storage on the site of NPPs.

Until 1976, the U.S. government planned to reprocess nuclear waste for re-use in nuclear reactors.[22] When President Gerald Ford imposed a moratorium on spent fuel reprocessing in 1976 due to the associated risk of nuclear proliferation, the U.S. nuclear energy industry, having no alternative plan for handling spent fuel, was rather suddenly confronted with a serious nuclear waste disposal crisis. The spent fuel pools at commercial nuclear power reactors, designed with limited storage capacity based on the assumption that spent fuel would be sent away for reprocessing, were rapidly reaching full capacity. NPP operators faced having to shut down operations if no solution was found. The nuclear energy industry also "appeared in jeopardy because of a widespread perception that the government did not know how—or at least was not doing much—to solve the waste disposal problem."[23] By the time the Three Mile Island accident had occurred in 1979, the federal government and the nuclear power industry were viewed by the public as having mishandled the nuclear waste issue and were facing a crisis of credibility on nuclear safety issues. Serious doubts about the long-term viability of nuclear energy contributed to the stagnation of the nuclear energy industry.[24]

The ban on spent fuel reprocessing essentially nullified the only existing plan for addressing the problem of nuclear waste in the United States.[25] Consequently, in the 1980s, the U.S. government began to reconfigure its plan for handling nuclear waste and shifted its focus to finding a geologic site for its permanent disposal.[26] This process culminated in 1987 in the hasty selection of Yucca Mountain as the site for the repository for the permanent disposal nuclear waste and the mandated deadline of January 31, 1998 for the Department of Energy (DOE) to begin accepting nuclear waste.[27] In recent years, the DOE has argued that Yucca Mountain represents the most suitable site for a geologic repository for the permanent disposal of nuclear waste and "recommended to President Bush that the Yucca Mountain project go forward."[28] In February 2002, President Bush recommended to Congress that it approve Yucca Mountain as the final repository for nuclear waste.[29] As provided for in the Nuclear Waste Policy Act of 1982, the Governor of Nevada submitted his notice of disapproval and "vetoed" the selection of Yucca Mountain as the site for the geologic repository.[30] The U.S. Congress overrode Nevada's veto and approved the site at Yucca Mountain for the development of a repository for nuclear waste in July 2002.

Despite these developments, the problem of nuclear waste disposal remains largely unsolved. As of 2007, the U.S. government has spent twenty years studying and evaluating the site at Yucca Mountain as a potential repository and billions of dollars "without yet placing even a single spent fuel assembly in its final disposal site."[31] The U.S. government, having abandoned a selection process based on scientific criteria for political expediency in 1987, has no alternative plan to storing nuclear waste at Yucca Mountain. Significant questions remain about Yucca Mountain's relative suitability as a geologic repository. Officials from the state of Nevada assert that "the site is unsafe, pointing to potential volcanic activity, earthquakes, water infiltration, [and] underground flooding. . . ."[32] Although the DOE "contends that the scientific evidence indicates that Yucca Mountain is suitable for isolating nuclear waste for at least 10,000 years," there have been quality assurance concerns about the scientific assessments used to validate the site.[33] Furthermore, not only has the DOE failed to meet its mandated deadline of January 31, 1998 to begin accepting spent fuel from commercial reactors for final disposal, it has yet to submit a license application to the NRC to build a repository at Yucca Mountain. Once the repository has finally opened for operations (in the best-case scenario, in 2017), the DOE must successfully receive 175 shipments of nuclear waste per year over a twenty-four-year period.[34] This transport plan is almost certain to meet with political resistance from state and local officials of the many regions through which the nuclear waste must be transported. Any incident involving the transport of spent fuel, whether accidental or intentional, could bring the process to a standstill and undermine the basic tenets of U.S. policy on nuclear waste disposal.

Given the delays in implementing the plan for permanent disposal, the problem of nuclear waste has so far been solved by default: interim storage of nuclear waste at the site of NPPs. NPP operators began to run out of storage space for spent fuel in the late 1970s and feared that some reactors "might have to be shut down by the mid 1990s unless more storage space was made available."[35] Since NPP operators could not ship away their spent fuel for reprocessing as had been originally planned, they had little choice but to shut down operations or "expand the onsite storage capacities to allow continued operation of their plants."[36] To increase storage capacities, NPP operators were forced to begin re-racking spent fuel pools.[37] However, this increased storage capacity only in the short term. With spent fuel pools at maximum capacity again in the mid-1980s, NPP operators began to shift some spent fuel to dry cask storage in 1986.[38] Almost 53,000 metric tons of spent fuel in the United States is currently located in spent fuel pools or in dry storage casks at NPP sites, awaiting disposal in a geologic repository.[39]

The lack of a viable solution to the problem of nuclear waste disposal negatively affects public support for nuclear power and may continue to hinder the expansion of the nuclear energy industry as it has in the past. Thus, any future for the nuclear energy industry in the United States hinges irrevocably on a viable plan for nuclear waste disposal.

Interim Storage of Spent Fuel: Enhancing the Appeal of NPPs as Terrorist Targets

Terrorists are often posited to engage in a rational cost-benefit analysis in the planning of their attacks. Analysts generally assume that contemporary terrorists aim to minimize the risk of failure and maximize the impact of their attacks. Thus, it follows that any factor related to a potential target that minimizes risk of failure or maximizes the impact of an attack may shift the cost-benefit calculation of a terrorist group and increase the appeal of that target. The interim storage of spent fuel, by increasing the environmental and human-health consequences of an attack and by hindering the expansion of the nuclear energy industry, helps to maximize the impact of an attack on an NPP. At the same time, the interim storage of nuclear waste in vulnerable spent fuel pools serves to minimize the risk of failure. Thus, the interim storage of nuclear waste enhances the appeal of NPPs as terrorist targets across three dimensions.

Environmental and Human-Health Risks

Spent fuel from nuclear power generation imposes a unique burden on the environment and human health since it remains highly radioactive for several hundred years and requires safe isolation from the environment for many thousands of years.[40] Under normal operations, however, nuclear power makes only a small contribution to the annual radiation doses received by surrounding populations.[41] For this reason, accidental or intentional releases of radiation are the main source of concern for the nuclear energy industry. The growing inventories of spent fuel at NPPs increases environmental and human-health risks in the event of an accident or sabotage for several reasons.

First, the decentralized storage of nuclear waste increases the number of regions and populations that face a risk of accidental or intentional releases of radiation into the environment. Many NPPs are located about 15 to 20 miles from large urban areas, and "more than 161 million Americans reside within 75 miles of where spent nuclear fuel and high-level radioactive waste are stored."[42] Furthermore, NPPs need substantial supplies of water for cooling and are usually located "near rivers, lakes, and seacoasts. In case of an accident or attack, this material could seep into groundwater and travel in storm and snowmelt run-off into nearby bodies of water."[43] In a worst-case scenario, the release of radioactivity may severely contaminate a large area and render it uninhabitable for hundreds of years. The 1986 Chernobyl disaster resulted in the contamination of thousands of acres of arable land, the closure of dozens of farms, and the dislocation of tens of thousands of people.[44]

Second, the widespread practice of high-density storage in spent fuel pools (due to re-racking) introduces heightened safety concerns. The use of high-density storage racks eliminates extra space between fuel assemblies that was intended to promote water circulation necessary for cooling. If a spent fuel pool loses its cooling capacity or its water contents, and the spent fuel becomes exposed to air, the fuel will heat up and may catch fire. The risk of fire depends on the amount of fuel in the pool, its age, and spacing for circulation. The dense packing of spent fuel increases "the risk that temperatures could climb to high levels in the event that the spent fuel becomes uncovered."[45]

Third, high-density spent fuel racks "allow approximately five times as many assemblies to be stored as would have been possible with the original racks."[46] Thus, spent fuel pools contain much larger inventories of highly radioactive materials than the nuclear reactors themselves. A typical nuclear reactor "contains about 80 metric tons of uranium in its fuel, while a typical U.S. spent fuel pool today contains about 400 tons of spent fuel."[47] Although spent fuel pools have lower levels of radioactivity than a nuclear reactor, they do contain "an average of 10 times more long-lived radioactivity" than a reactor.[48] The significantly larger volumes of material stored in spent fuel pools increases the amount of Cesium-137 that may be released into the environment in the case of an accident or sabotage.[49] On average, 400 tons of spent fuel in a pool would contain about 35 MCi.[50] The estimated average consequences of a spent fuel fire would be $100 billion in damages and 2,000 cancer deaths for a release of 3.5 MCi, and $400 billion in damages and 6,000 cancer deaths for a release of 35 MCi.[51] In other words, terrorist attacks on targets with larger inventories of radioactive materials are likely to yield greater environmental and human-health consequences.

Energy Security and the Threat of Global Climate Change

The threat of global climate change increases the relative value of nuclear power vis-à-vis other sources of energy for assuring U.S. energy security and thus, enhances the appeal of NPPs as terrorist targets. Nuclear power has the potential to make a significant contribution toward efforts to address the threat of global climate change. Since NPPs do not emit greenhouse gases, electricity generation from nuclear power has substantial environmental benefits if it is used to offset carbon emissions from fossil fuels.[52] Generating 7 billion metric tons of carbon dioxide equivalent in 2004, the United States relies heavily on fossil fuels to generate electricity, producing about 52 percent of its total supply from coal and 17 percent from natural gas.[53] In fact, about 40 percent of U.S. energy-related greenhouse gases are attributable to the electric power industry.[54] Nuclear power is the "only non-fossil fuel that generates more than 10 percent of total electricity."[55] From 1960 to 2000, nuclear power generation has offset a total of 3,142 million metric tons of carbon.[56] Without an expansion of the nuclear industry, the United States will be unable to harness future environmental benefits of nuclear power for mitigating the threat of global climate change.

The role of nuclear power as a solution to the greenhouse gas problem is a subject of contentious debate, and much of the focus rests on the environmental costs of managing nuclear waste. Any expansion of nuclear power would inevitably lead to the production of larger volumes of nuclear waste. Public reluctance to accept the environmental costs of expanding the nuclear industry may prevent nuclear power from playing a role in mitigating climate change. In the past, public concerns about the nuclear waste problem have served as a major impediment to an expansion of the nuclear industry. Although U.S. electric utility companies placed orders for as many as 162 NPPs between 1965 and 1973, the growth of the nuclear energy industry slowed significantly during the 1970s for several reasons, including surplus base load capacity, relatively high capital costs, regulatory uncertainty, and public concerns about safety and disposal of nuclear waste.[57] In fact, no new orders for NPPs were placed after 1973.[58] According to the DOE, "even with the projected increase in nuclear capacity and generation, the nuclear share of total electricity generation" will decline if there are no new orders.[59] The *Annual Energy Outlook 2007* predicts that the nuclear share of total electricity generation will fall from 19 percent in 2005 to 15 percent in 2030.[60] Although there are currently no orders for new NPPs, as many as 15 U.S. utility companies are considering building new NPPs for the first time in two decades.[61] However, any setbacks related to nuclear safety or the problem of nuclear waste are likely to undermine these plans.

Given unsustainable policy on nuclear waste disposal in the United States, any attack on an NPP or nuclear waste transport could threaten the fragile future of the nuclear energy industry and U.S. efforts to address global climate change. By enhancing the strategic impact of an attack, the threat of global climate change increases the appeal of NPPs as terrorist targets.

Terrorism and the Threat of Nuclear Sabotage

The interim storage of nuclear waste in vulnerable spent fuel pools increases the likelihood of a successful terrorist attack. Thus, finding a viable solution to the disposal of nuclear waste may also become a direct concern of counterterrorism efforts in the near future. Many experts assert that increasing inventories of spent fuel stored at NPPs and the relative vulnerability of spent fuel pools raises the risk of nuclear sabotage.[62] Since 9/11, there have been increasing concerns that terrorists could target these weaker structures and cause a massive release of radiation while avoiding the complexity of attacking the nuclear reactor itself. The interim storage of spent fuel enhances the appeal of NPPs as terrorist targets in several ways.

At a purely superficial level, the interim storage of spent fuel at NPPs adds greater numbers of potentially lucrative targets beyond the nuclear reactor(s) to the site of NPPs: spent fuel pools and dry cask storage. Every NPP contains one or more pools to store spent fuel after it is discharged from the reactor core. Though some storage of spent fuel in pools is necessary for the operation of NPPs, the attractiveness of spent fuel pools as targets could be diminished by reducing the volume of radioactive materials they contain. The transfer of spent fuel from these pools to dry cask storage in the 1980s added a new set of targets to the sites of NPPs. The steel-reinforced concrete dry casks are located outside on concrete pads within the protected area of the NPP. Each cask contains about 10 to 15 metric tons of spent fuel.[63] Similar to casks used for transporting nuclear waste, these casks are extremely robust and "designed to withstand transport accidents, earthquakes, tornadoes and other extreme incidents with minimal release of radiation." If penetrated, the area of contamination would likely remain within the boundary of the facility.[64] Although the dry casks are generally considered unattractive targets for a terrorist attack, they are easy to identify and located near the outside perimeter of the plant. Any incident causing damage to these casks could have a cascading psychological impact on plans to transport nuclear waste in the future and may thus contribute to the increasing appeal of NPPs as terrorist targets.

Until recently, much of the debate regarding the vulnerabilities of NPPs to terrorist attacks focused on the risk of sabotage to the nuclear reactor, the most visible and critical part of an NPP and therefore intuitively, the most sensational target.[65] After all, the nuclear reactor produces energy and represents the target of highest economic value at an NPP. Given the increasing volumes of spent fuel stored at the site of NPPs, however, this calculation may be changing for terrorists. Absent a geologic repository for the final disposal of nuclear waste, spent fuel pools have been reconfigured to contain many more fuel assemblies than the reactor core and thus hold far greater volumes of radioactive material than originally planned. Greater volumes of highly radioactive materials increase the environmental and human-health risks of an accident or sabotage that involves a release of radiation into the environment. Ferguson et al. suggest that "by some estimates, the consequences of a successful terrorist attack on a spent fuel storage area that caused the fuel to ignite could create a radioactive disaster comparable to, if not worse than, one caused by the meltdown of an operating reactor's core and the breaching of its containment, allowing the widespread dispersion of radiation."[66] Terrorist groups that target NPPs hope to exploit all the environmental, economic, and psychological consequences that could result from a massive release of radiation into the environment. Since causing a release of radiation from a spent fuel pool could have greater environmental consequences, terrorists may view them as a more effective means to capitalize on the sensational economic and psychological impact of attacking an NPP while avoiding a more complex attack against a robustly protected nuclear reactor.

Compared to the nuclear reactor, a spent fuel pool presents a more vulnerable target to terrorist attack. While nuclear reactors are protected by several layers of containment, including a steel reactor vessel and a dome-shaped containment structure with walls of reinforced concrete about four to six feet thick, most spent fuel pools in the United States are located outside the containment structure in a typical industrial building. In some designs, the pool walls serve as the external walls of the building, exposing the pool to attack from the air or by projectiles. Although spent fuel pools are more vulnerable than nuclear reactors, the pools themselves are robustly constructed and fairly resistant to terrorist attack. The pool walls are between four and eight feet thick, made of reinforced concrete, and are "designed for seismic stability and to resist horizontal strikes" of projectiles from tornados.[67] In addition, the pools are typically lined with a one-quarter to one-half-inch stainless steel liner, "which is attached to the walls with studs embedded in the concrete."[68] Unlike easy-to-recognize reactor buildings, the buildings that house the spent fuel pool(s) are more difficult to distinguish from other auxiliary buildings on the site of an NPP. Furthermore, "some plants have structures surrounding the spent fuel pool building that would provide some shielding of pools from low-angle line-of-site attacks."[69]

Spent fuel pools may also offer less complex targets than nuclear reactors for achieving a massive release of radiation into the environment. For a successful attack on a nuclear reactor, terrorists would have to trigger a meltdown of a reactor core, cause a breach in multiple layers of the containment, and cause a fire—all of which are faced with significant technical obstacles. Upon learning of a terrorist attack, plant operators are likely to react immediately by turning off the nuclear reactor. Even after a reactor is shut down, nuclear reactor fuel continues to produce an enormous amount of heat generated by highly radioactive fission products and requires continuous cooling. Nuclear reactors are well-protected against core meltdown and are typically outfitted with layers of redundant safety systems: emergency core cooling systems, redundant pumps, emergency generators, and batteries. Whereas a terrorist group would have disable all emergency cooling systems to cause a core meltdown, NPP operators and guards would be required to protect only one cooling system in order to prevent overheating of the reactor core. If a terrorist group were successful in causing a core meltdown, the heat generated by fission products would melt the uranium fuel through the vessel walls into the containment building and cause the release of radioactivity inside the reactor building. However, without a major explosion and subsequent damage to the containment building, the radiation would be contained within the facility and would likely resemble the Three Mile Island accident in 1979.

In a worst-case scenario, the pressure in the reactor building could increase to dangerous levels, cause a steam explosion and break through the walls of containment building allowing for the release of radioactive gases into the environment. Although this scenario is possible, "only a small number of meltdowns, barely 2 percent, would actually breach the containment building with a steam explosion and lead to a catastrophic release of radioactivity."[70] Finally, a sustained fire would be necessary to cause Chernobyl-like release of radiation into the environment. Since all nuclear reactors in the United States use water for cooling and moderating the fission reaction, reactors themselves do not contain any combustible materials. Experts suggest that a "sustained fire would be impossible" without foreign objects such as an attacking plane that "penetrated the containment completely, including its fuel-bearing wings."[71]

Although attacking a spent fuel pool would be less technically complex, a terrorist group would still face significant challenges. In particular, terrorists would need a significant amount of time (more than several hours) to successfully carry out a chain of events and cause a massive release of radiation. First, a terrorist group would have to cause a loss-of-coolant accident by disabling all cooling systems for the spent fuel pool and/or causing the pool to drain. Both scenarios could lead to an eventual uncovering of the spent fuel, which would cause the fuel to heat up, possibly catch fire, and release its radioactive inventory. However, even if a terrorist group successfully disabled all cooling systems, "it would take several days of continuous boiling to uncover the fuel" since spent fuel produces far less heat than a nuclear reactor.[72] As long as the spent fuel remained under water, NPP operators would be able to access the building and simply add water to the pool using emergency fire hoses. For this reason, the most serious risk for a spent fuel pool would be the loss of water or complete draining of the pool. Even in this case, terrorists would face substantial obstacles. Spent fuel is stored in thousands of gallons of water and sits at the bottom of the pool under about 26 feet of water. Also, since most spent fuel pools are located at ground level or partially underground (either at or below the water table), they are difficult, if not impossible, to drain to a level that exposes the top of the spent fuel rods.[73]

Second, terrorists would have to cause significant damage to the building housing the spent fuel pool to release radiation. Third, to release radiation into the environment, terrorists would have to either cause the fuel to heat up to produce a spent fuel fire as just described or mechanically disperse the spent fuel with an explosion. Although an explosion would be easier to accomplish, "an explosion or high-energy impact directly on the spent fuel could mechanically pulverize and loft fuel out of the pool," limiting the radioactive contamination to the plant and surrounding area. A sustained fire would be necessary to cause Chernobyl-like release of radiation into the environment.[74] Bringing about a zirconium spent fuel fire would be extremely challenging and require a great deal of time. From the time that spent fuel was uncovered, it would likely take several hours for the temperature of the spent fuel assemblies to reach about 900 degrees Celsius in order to a spent fuel fire to be self-sustaining.[75] Given these time requirements, more likely than not, "the consequences of a terrorist attack on a spent fuel pool would likely unfold slowly enough that there would be time to take mitigative actions to prevent a large release of radioactivity."[76]

Several countries with advanced nuclear power industries have taken the vulnerabilities of spent fuel pools seriously. For example, after 9/11, France installed anti-aircraft missiles to protect its spent fuel pools at its reprocessing facility.[77] In Germany, all spent fuel pools are located inside the reactor containment structures and thus are more resistant to attack.[78] Furthermore, 9 out of 18 NPPs in Germany "were designed to withstand the crash of a Phantom jet at the typical cruising speed,"[79] and all NPP operators in Germany are required to defend against this type of attack. In contrast, NPP operators in the United States are not required by the NRC to defend against air attacks.[80]

The U.S. government insists that onsite storage in spent fuel pools or dry storage is safe and sufficiently resistant to accidental releases of radiation and terrorist attacks.[81] The NRC requires that NPP operators implement security measures against a design-basis threat based on prevailing threat assessments. The design-basis threat is currently defined as "a commando attack by a number of attackers with hand-carried equipment and automatic weapons, the use of a four-wheel drive vehicle, a vehicle bomb and with the assistance of an insider."[82] The NRC insists that security measures at NPPs have been improved since 9/11, and that improvements include "more guards, more weapons, greater standoff distance from the facilities, [and] improved communications. . . ."[83] However, according to a recent study by the National Research Council, "there are no requirements in place to defend against the kinds of larger-scale, premeditated, skillful attacks that were carried out on September 11, 2001."[84]

Nuclear Power Plants: Non-Redundant Nodes in the U.S. Energy Network?

By identifying critical links between the problem of nuclear waste disposal, environmental security, energy security, and nuclear sabotage, this chapter has demonstrated how the appeal of NPPs as terrorist targets can increase through linkages that raise the strategic value of NPPs. The lack of a viable solution to the problem of nuclear waste disposal has resulted in an unsustainable default solution: interim storage of nuclear waste. The interim storage of growing inventories of nuclear waste in vulnerable spent fuel pools at NPPs amplifies the potential environmental consequences of a successful attack and increases the risk of sabotage. The threat of climate change increases the relative value of nuclear power as an energy source, while the fragile state of U.S. nuclear waste disposal policy threatens the future of the nuclear energy industry. These linkages suggest that even a minor attack on an NPP could lead to a resurgence of public opposition to nuclear energy, jeopardize the long-term viability of nuclear energy industry, and severely undermine the current plan for the final disposal of nuclear waste in the United States. Beyond these linkages, however, NPPs represent key components of a larger, more complex system: the U.S. energy network. A threat assessment taking a systemic approach also requires consideration of the physical (electrical grid) and economic interdependencies underlying the U.S. energy network and the role of NPPs within that network.

Homer-Dixon's concept of complex terrorism highlights the increasing interdependencies and linkages among technological and economic systems in advanced societies that enhance terrorist capabilities to cause destruction that are overlooked by traditional threat assessments for nuclear sabotage. Advanced societies have a tendency toward increasing concentrations of assets and people in small geographic areas "in order to achieve economies of scale."[85] Multiple centers containing high concentrations of assets and people become densely linked together to form complex systems or networks that entail "sets of nodes and links among those nodes."[86] Further, "[a]s societies modernize and become richer, their networks become more complex and interconnected. The number of nodes increases, as does the density of links among the nodes and the speed at which materials, energy, and information are pushed along these links."[87]

Homer-Dixon argues that tightly coupled networks have complex feedback loops that can lead to disproportionate and cascading effects if a network experiences even a small shock.[88] For example, in 2003, a minor equipment failure on the electrical grid "plunged New York, as well as much of Ontario and New England, into darkness"—in some cases for more than 24 hours. More than 30 million people were affected by the 2003 blackout. Economic losses caused by the blackout are "estimated in the range of $2 billion to $10 billion."[89] As networks become more tightly coupled, this increases the non-redundancy of some nodes in the system and creates potential for greater feedback and nonlinear response. The potential for feedback and nonlinear response is reflected in increasing costs of power outages over time "from $30 billion in 1995 to $119 billion in 2001."[90] According to Homer-Dixon, "terrorists and other malicious individuals can magnify their own disruptive power by exploiting these features of complex and interconnected networks . . . Terrorists must be clever to exploit these weaknesses. They must attack the right nodes in the right networks"—in other words, they must attack the non-redundant nodes in the right network.[91]

Energy networks are considered to be among the most vulnerable systems since "they so clearly underpin the vitality of modern economies."[92] Since energy networks comprise "everything from the national network of gas pipelines to the electricity grid," they are "replete with high-value nodes like oil refineries, tank farms, and electrical substations."[93] Increasingly dense connections among an ever-greater number of nodes in the U.S. energy network leads to system interdependencies: the reliance of one network (such as electric power) upon another (such as telecommunications), or even mutual reliance of networks upon one another.[94] For example, the 1996 power outage in western U.S. states "nearly led to the collapse of the telecommunications system."[95] A study conducted by the National Research Council in 2002 assessed the comparative vulnerability of U.S. energy systems and found the electrical system of greatest concern—even more so than oil and gasoline supply—because the use of gasoline is not as universal as electricity in the United States.[96] Technological innovation combined with "social (political and financial) forces throughout the 21st century has led to ever larger centralized electricity generation plants connected by ever larger synchronized grids."[97]

Beyond power outages and associated economic losses, a terrorist attack causing damage to an NPP could have severe ramifications for U.S. energy security, whether or not the attack led to a massive release of radiation into the environment. Nuclear power plants, each with a production capacity of 1,000 MWe or greater, concentrate significant portions of U.S. electricity supply in a few power plants. Producing 20 percent of U.S. electricity and more than 40 percent of electricity in five states, NPPs represent vital and indispensible components of the U.S. energy infrastructure, especially in light of a looming energy supply crisis. According to the *National Energy Policy,* electricity supply in the United States has "failed to keep pace with growing demand."[98] In the next two decades, between 1,300 and 1,900 new electric plants must be built to meet the projected electricity demand.[99] Most of these new power plants will be fueled by natural gas and will lead to a greater reliance on natural gas imports, since only 85 percent of total U.S. natural gas consumption is produced domestically.[100] The Energy Information Administration predicts that U.S. natural gas demand will increase by 50 percent between 2000 and 2020.[101] Nuclear power has a proven record of reducing U.S. dependence on oil and natural gas. In 1977, oil-fired power plants supplied about 17 percent of U.S. electricity.[102] By 1980, oil-fired power plants had been overtaken by NPPs supplying only 11 percent of electricity compared to 12 percent generated by nuclear power. Nuclear power surpassed natural gas in generating electricity in 1983 and hydropower in 1984 "to make it the largest supplier of electricity in the United States behind coal."[103]

If the nuclear power industry were to be crippled following a successful terrorist attack, NPPs would not be easily replaced by other plants due to the structure of electricity markets and operational efficiency of NPPs. Due to higher capacity factor of NPPs, "1,000 MWe of nuclear capacity usually displaces or is displaced by more than 1,000 MW of coal or gas capacity."[104] Furthermore, nuclear power offers the most suitable energy source for base load supply. The electricity market consists of two sub-markets: base load and peak load markets. Base load markets cover the base demand for electricity, and peak load markets supply demand spikes on daily, weekly, and seasonal basis. Peak capacity remains unused when demand is off-peak. For this reason, power plants with higher operating costs are better peak load sources, and vice versa for base load. Despite having higher capital costs, NPPs have lower operating costs than natural gas plants. The operating cost advantage of NPPs comes from the low cost of uranium fuel. Since "fuel is the principal component of short-term marginal costs for power generation . . . there is usually an incentive to use [nuclear] capacity in preference to other, more expensive fuels. Fuel costs are particularly high for natural gas-based plants but are also higher for coal. Nuclear power is thus advantaged for base power load generation because there is less incentive to shut down the plant off peak."[105] Finally, "nuclear power output levels are usually difficult to rapidly increase or decrease without venting surplus steam."[106] For these reasons, natural gas and other energy sources are "more suitable for changeable peak requirements."[107]

In addition to operational efficiency, nuclear power is less resource-intensive than other energy sources. "Generating one TWh of electricity requires only 32 tons of uranium concentrate, but would require 122,000 tons of natural gas or 330,000 tons of coal."[108] Given the stable supply of uranium fuel, nuclear energy represents an energy source with a higher "domestic profile" since it is not subject to the political instability of oil and natural gas supplies.[109] Although natural gas produces lower carbon emissions than coal or oil plants, increased reliance on natural gas due to a loss of existing and future potential nuclear power generation capacity will not only have ramifications for efforts to mitigate global climate change, it will compromise the long-term energy security of the United States.

Nuclear power plants are becoming increasingly non-redundant nodes in the U.S. energy network. While the "outage of a single nuclear station would have an impact similar to the outage of any other large generation site . . . the uniqueness of nuclear power, both from a public and regulatory perspective, could result in a much wider impact."[110] The accidents at Three Mile Island and Chernobyl "contributed to the stagnation of the nuclear industry . . . A devastating terrorist attack (or another serious accident) could, once again, hobble the nuclear industry."[111]

Conclusion

In a post–9/11 world, the United States may be nearing supercriticality on the issue of nuclear waste disposal.[112] In this context, supercriticality implies a point of no return, a point past which the U.S. government may have unwittingly limited its options for addressing global climate change and providing for U.S. energy security in the event of a terrorist attack on an NPP. Any attack on an NPP will likely set off an uncontrolled chain reaction fueled by the unique psychological impact of all things nuclear on public opinion. Although the nuclear energy industry and the U.S. government have somewhat restored their credibility on nuclear issues since Three Mile Island, this status remains fragile and is tightly linked with the need to solve the nuclear waste problem. Thus, the chain reaction begins and ends with the problem of nuclear waste disposal. Interim storage of nuclear waste at NPPs increases the strategic impact of any attack on an NPP, the appeal of NPPs as terrorist targets, and, consequently the risk of nuclear sabotage. An attack on an NPP, whether or not it leads to a release of radiation into the environment or destruction of the nuclear reactor, could threaten the future of the nuclear energy industry, efforts to address climate change, and U.S. energy security.

Traditional threat assessments, typically limited to assessing terrorist capabilities and security measures taken at NPPs, fail to consider these broader policy linkages that increase the appeal of NPPs as terrorist targets. As a result, these assessments do not address important elements of the threat and are deficient. Whereas traditional threat assessments yield recommendations related to security measures taken at NPPs, intelligence and emergency preparedness, a threat assessment taking a systemic approach suggests remedies that decrease the strategic value of NPPs as terrorist targets. In addition to improving the reliability of the electrical grid and increasing the U.S. energy production capacity, a viable solution to the problem of nuclear waste disposal remains critical for reducing the effects of an attack on an NPP. Absent a geologic repository for the disposal of nuclear waste, there are several options for reducing the risk of nuclear sabotage associated with interim storage of spent fuel.

First, most nuclear waste stored in spent fuel pools should be transferred to dry cask storage. Although dry casks remain on the site of NPPs, they are more robust structures and contain smaller amounts of nuclear waste than spent fuel pools. Second, nuclear waste could be stored at several centralized dry cask storage facilities. Several interim storage sites are nearing completion and could receive up to 40,000 metric tons of nuclear waste.[113] Third, the U.S. government should accelerate progress related to new proliferation-resistant reprocessing technologies under the Global Nuclear Energy Partnership.[114]

Natasha E. Bajema is a co-editor of this volume and a Ph.D. Candidate at the Fletcher School of Law and Diplomacy, Tufts University. Before coming to Fletcher, she was a Research Associate at the Center on International Cooperation at New York University. She has also served as a Junior Political Officer in the Weapons of Mass Destruction Branch of the Department for Disarmament Affairs at the United Nations. She holds an M.A. in international policy from the Monterey Institute of International Studies.

Notes

1. National Research Council, *Safety and Security of Commercial Spent Nuclear Fuel Storage*, Public Report (Washington DC: The National Academies Press, 2006), 36.
2. Thomas Homer-Dixon, "The Rise of Complex Terrorism," *Foreign Policy* (January/February 2002).

3. *National Strategy for Homeland Security* (Washington DC: Office of Homeland Security, 2002), 7.
4. See Homer-Dixon.
5. National Research Council (2006), 35.
6. Ibid, 30.
7. Ibid, 47.
8. *The 9/11 Commission Report* (Washington DC: U.S. Government Printing Office, 2004), 154.
9. Charles D. Ferguson, William C. Potter, and Amy Sands, *The Four Faces of Nuclear Terrorism* (New York: Routledge, 2005), 195.
10. See Remarks by Richard Meserve, Chairman, United States Nuclear Regulatory Commission, "Panel Discussion: Nuclear Terror Threats," Carnegie International Non-Proliferation Conference, Washington D.C., November 15, 2002.; See also Paul Gaukler, D. Sean Barnett, and Douglas J. Rosinski, "Nuclear Energy and Terrorism," *Natural Resources & Environment,* Winter 2002. Available at <www.abanet.org/environ/pubs/nre/specissue/gauklerbarnettrosinski. pdf>. See also National Research Council, *Making the Nation Safer: The Role of Science and Technology in Countering Terrorism* (Washington D.C.: The National Academies Press, 2002).
11. National Research Council (2002), 43.
12. See Gaukler et al; See also Gerald E. Marsh and George S. Stanford, *Terrorism and Nuclear Power: What Are the Risks?* National Policy Analysis No. 374 (Washington D.C.: National Center for Public Policy Research, November 2001). Available at <www.nationalcenter.org/ NPA374.html>
13. See Marsh and Stanford.
14. National Research Council (2006), 35.
15. Electric Power Research Institute, *Deterring Terrorism: Aircraft Crash Impact Analyses Demonstrate Nuclear Power Plant's Structural Strength,* December 2002. Available at <www. nei.org/documents/eprinuclearplantstructuralstudy200212.pdf>
16. Steven Mufson, "Nuclear Agency: Air Defenses Impractical," *The Washington Post,* January 30, 2007.
17. National Research Council (2006), 35.
18. See Homer-Dixon.
19. In 1976, California state legislators approved a law imposing constraints on the development of nuclear power until the federal government had approved a solution for nuclear waste disposal. As many as ten states followed suit and adopted similar legislation, effectively blocking the expansion of the nuclear energy industry. The CA law was upheld by the U.S. Supreme Court in April 1983. By 1983, 10 additional states had passed similar legislation. See the Office of Technology Assessment, 216.
20. Nuclear waste and spent fuel are used interchangeably throughout this paper.
21. Matthew Bunn, John P. Holdren, Allison Macfarlane, Susan E. Pickett, Atsuyuki Suzuki, Tatsujiro Suzuki, and Jennifer Weeks, *Interim Storage of Spent Nuclear Fuel,* A Joint Report from the Harvard University Project on Managing the Atom and the University of Tokyo Project on Sociotechnics of Nuclear Energy (Cambridge, MA: Harvard University and University of Tokyo, 2001), 46.
22. Using reprocessing technology, about 96 percent of the leftover uranium can be recovered, re-enriched, and reused in the reactor. Plutonium, an element that is synthetically created during the fission process in the nuclear reactor, represents about 1 percent of the spent fuel and can also be reused as nuclear reactor fuel after it is mixed with depleted uranium and made into fresh nuclear fuel in a mixed oxide (MOX) fuel fabrication plant. Unlike the uranium used in commercial nuclear reactors, however, the plutonium separated out during spent fuel reprocessing is weapons-grade and can be used to develop nuclear weapons. For more technical information on the nuclear fuel cycle, see the Appendix to Chapter 1 of *The Future of Nuclear Power,* An Interdisciplinary MIT Study (Cambridge, MA: MIT, 2003), available at <http://web. mit.edu/nuclearpower>
23. Ted Greenwood, "Nuclear Waste Management in the United States," in *The Politics of Nuclear Waste,* E. William Colglazier, Jr., ed., (New York: Pergamon Press, 1982), 9.

24. John P. Holdren, "Radioactive-Waste Management in the United States: Evolving Policy Prospects and Dilemmas," *Annual Review of Energy and the Environment,* 17 (November 1992): 238.

25. President Reagan withdrew the ban on commercial reprocessing in 1981. However, the nuclear industry no longer viewed reprocessing as an economically or politically viable endeavor. Since operations ceased at the first reprocessing facility in 1972 for technical reasons, "no reprocessing of commercial spent fuel has occurred in the United States." See the Office of Technology Assessment, *Managing the Nation's Commercial High-Level Radioactive Waste* (Washington, DC: U.S. Congress Office of Technology Assessment, OTA-O-171, March 1985), 84–85; See also Holdren, 241.

26. In 1982, U.S. Congress passed the Nuclear Waste Policy Act (NWPA). Under NWPA, "Congress sought to create a comprehensive legal framework for managing spent fuel and high-level radioactive waste." Most significantly, NWPA set timetables for siting and licensing a geologic repository, required the Department of Energy (DOE) to begin studying potential repository sites, and mandated the DOE to begin accepting nuclear waste by January 31, 1998. See Office of Technology Assessment, 88.

27. The DOE selected nine candidate sites for the first geologic repository in 1983 and recommended three sites to President Reagan in 1986 for further study: Yucca Mountain in Nevada, Deaf Smith County in Texas, and Hanford, Washington. See the website of the DOE's Office of Civilian Radioactive Waste Management at <www.ocrwm.doe.gov>. Becoming concerned about delays and rising costs of the program to study multiple repository sites, the U.S. Congress amended NWPA in 1987 to limit the DOE's site characterization activities to Yucca Mountain, Nevada. The Nuclear Waste Policy Act Amendments (NWPAA) determined that "if found suitable, Yucca Mountain would become the country's one permanent repository." See Holdren, 248.

28. Mark Holt, *Civilian Nuclear Waste Disposal,* CRS Report for Congress, RL33461, August 8, 2006, 10.

29. Office of the Press Secretary, White House, "Yucca Mountain Statement," Press Release, February 15, 2002. Available at <www.whitehouse.gov/news/releases/2002/02/20020215-11.html>

30. NWPA 1982 provides for "consultation and concurrence" in which "a state would be consulted by the government and given opportunity to concur with each step in developing a repository. By not concurring, a state could effectively exercise a veto." A state's concurrence could be overridden "by the Federal Government only through a Presidential determination backed by both Houses of Congress." See Office of Technology Assessment, 87.

31. David A. Lochbaum, *Nuclear Waste Disposal Crisis* (Tulsa, OK: PennWell Books, 1996), 12.

32. Agency for Nuclear Projects, State of Nevada, *What's Wrong with Putting Nuclear Waste in Yucca Mountain?* 2003. Available at <www.state.nv.us/nucwaste/news2003/pdf/nv_wwrong.pdf> See also Holt, 2.

33. See Holt, 2 and 10; See also U.S. Government Accountability Office, *Yucca Mountain: Quality Assurance at DOE's Planned Nuclear Waste Repository Needs Increased Management Attention,* GAO-06-313, March 2006. Available at <www.gao.gov/new.items/d06313.pdf>

34. Ferguson,et. al., 207.

35. Office of Technology Assessment, 89.

36. Lochbaum, 58.

37. Spent fuel racks were originally designed to provide generous space between spent fuel assemblies for water circulation and cooling. High-density storage racks eliminate much of this space to pack fuel assemblies closer together. The new dense configuration increased storage capacities in some pools by up to about a factor of five. See National Research Council (2006).

38. Ibid.

39. This figure is as of February 2006 and based on data found at www.ocrwm.doe.gov

40. Spent fuel is nuclear fuel that has been irradiated or "burned" in the core of a nuclear reactor. "When the fissile material has been consumed to a level where it is no longer economically viable (typically 4.5 to 6 years of operation for current fuel designs), the fuel is considered

spent and is removed from the reactor core." Spent fuel requires shielding, cooling and remote handling. See National Research Council (2006), 16–17.

41. International Energy Agency, *Nuclear Power in the OECD* (Paris: OECD/IEA, 2001), 171.
42. U.S. Department of Energy, *Why Yucca Mountain?,* Office of Public Affairs Brochure, 1. Available at <www.ocrwm.doe.gov/ym_repository/sr/brochure.pdf>
43. Ibid, 1.
44. See Robert Alvarez, Jan Beyea, Klaus Janberg, Jungmin Kang, Ed Lyman, Allison Macfarlane, Gordon Thompson, and Frank N. von Hippel, "Reducing the Hazards from Stored Spent Power-Reactor Fuel in the United States," *Science and Global Security, 11* (2003).
45. Ferguson et. al., 205.
46. National Research Council (2006), 43.
47. This is the amount for a PWR. See Alvarez et. al., 7.
48. Robert Alvarez, "What about the Spent Fuel?" *Bulletin of Atomic Scientists, 58,* no. 1 (January/February 2002): 45–47.
49. Cesium-137 has a 30-year half-life, is relatively volatile, and is a potent land contaminant. See Alvarez et. al., 7.
50. Ibid.
51. Jan Beyea, Ed Lyman, and Frank von Hippel, "Damages from a Major Release of ^{137}Cs into the Atmosphere of the United States," *Science and Global Security, 12* (2004): 125.
52. Ronald Hagen, *Nuclear Power and the Environment* (Washington DC: Energy Information Administration, 2007), 4. Available at <www.eia.doe.gov/cneaf/nuclear/page/nuclearenvissues.html>
53. *Annual Energy Review 2005* (Washington, DC: Energy Information Administration, 2005). See tables 8.2b and 12.1. Available at <tonto.eia.doe.gov/FTPROOT/multifuel/038405.pdf>
54. Ronald E. Hagen, John R. Moens, and Zdenek D. Nikodem, *Impact of U.S. Nuclear Generation on Greenhouse Gas Emissions* (Washington DC: Energy Information Administration, 2001), 3. Available at <tonto.eia.doe.gov/FTPROOT/nuclear/ghg.pdf>
55. Energy Information Administration, "Greenhouse Gases, Climate Change and Energy," brochure, available at <www.eia.doe.gov/oiaf/1605/ggccebro/chapter1.html>
56. See Hagen et al., 5; 10.
57. Energy Information Administration, "Nuclear Power: 12 percent of America's Generating Capacity, 20 percent of the Electricity, " available at <www.eia.doe.gov/cneaf/nuclear/page/analysis/nuclearpower.html> See also Lochbaum, 9.
58. Lochbaum, 10–11.
59. *Annual Energy Outlook 2007* (Washington, DC: Energy Information Administration, 2007), 3. Available at <www.eia.doe.gov/oiaf/aeo/pdf/0383(2007).pdf>
60. Ibid.
61. Some have applied for an early site permit. As many as seven license applications for construction/operation of NPPs may be submitted in 2007. For more information on new nuclear plant status, see Nuclear Energy Institute website at <www.nei.org/index.asp?catnum=2&catid=344>
62. See Hui Zhang, "Radiological Terrorism: Sabotage of Spent Fuel Pools," *INESAP: International Network of Engineers and Scientists Against Proliferation,* no. 22 (December 2003): 75–78. Available at <www.inesap.org/pdf/INESAP_Bulletin22.pdf>
63. National Research Council (2006), 63.
64. National Research Council, "Making the Nation Safer: The Role of Science and Technology in Countering Terrorism," 48.
65. Alvarez et al., 45–47.
66. Ferguson et. al., 204.
67. National Research Council (2006), 40–41.
68. Ibid, 41.
69. National Research Council (2006), 43.
70. Michio Kaku and Jennifer Trainer, eds., *Nuclear Power: Both Sides* (New York: W.W. Norton & Company, 1982), 82.
71. Carl Behrens, "Nuclear Power Plants: Vulnerability to Terrorist Attack," *Congressional Research Service Report,* RS21131, January 31, 2002, 3.

72. National Research Council (2006), 48.
73. Ferguson et al., 204.
74. National Research Council (2006), 49–50.
75. Mycle Schneider, "The Threat of Nuclear Terrorism: From Analysis to Precautionary Measures." Paper presented at the French National Assembly Meeting sponsored by Mr. Pierre Lellouche, Member of Parliament. Paris, France, December 10, 2001, 5.
76. National Research Council (2006), 34.
77. See Zhang.
78. National Research Council (2006), 40.
79. Ibid, 93.
80. Ibid, 31.
81. In 2003, the U.S. Government Accountability Office (GAO) concluded that "NRC and DOE studies indicate a low likelihood of widespread harm to human health from terrorist attacks or severe accidents involving spent fuel—either in transit or dry or wet storage. Spent fuel is heavy, ceramic material that is neither explosive nor volatile and resists easy dispersal . . . While the release of a large quantity of radioactive material from a wet storage pool is theoretically possible, such a release would require an extremely unlikely chain of events." See U.S. Government Accountability Office, *Spent Nuclear Fuel: Options Exist to Further Enhance Security,* GAO-03-426, July 2003, 2. Available at <www.gao.gov/new.items/d03426.pdf>
82. See Meserve.
83. See Meserve.
84. National Research Council (2006), 47.
85. See Homer-Dixon.
86. Ibid.
87. Ibid.
88. Ibid.
89. Alexander E. Farrell, Hisham Zerriffi, and Hadi Dowlatabadi, "Energy Infrastructure and Security," *Annual Review of Environment and Resources, 29:* 450.
90. National Research Council (2002), 180.
91. Homer-Dixon quotes Langdon Winner, a theorist of politics and technology, who provides the first rule of modern terrorism: "Find the critical but nonredundant parts of the system and sabotage . . . them according to your purposes." See Homer-Dixon.
92. Ibid.
93. Ibid.
94. Farrell et al., 434.
95. Ibid.
96. National Research Council (2002), 178.
97. Farrell et al., 436.
98. *National Energy Policy,* 1–5.
99. Ibid, xi.
100. The import share of consumption rose from 5 percent in 1987 to 15 percent in 2000. See *National Energy Policy,* 1–7.
101. *National Energy Policy,* 1–8.
102. *Annual Energy Review 2005,* 229.
103. Lochbaum, 11.
104. Hagen et al., 6.
105. Ibid, 22.
106. Ibid, 14.
107. Ibid, 14.
108. Jonathan Pershing, "Nuclear Power and Environmental Policy," *Business as Usual and Nuclear Power,* OECD Proceedings of a Joint IEA/NEA Meeting, October 14–15, 1999 (Paris: OECD/NEA, 2000), 37. Available at <www.iea.org/textbase/nppdf/free/2000/busassual2000.pdf>
109. Hagen et al., 24.
110. National Research Council (2002), 182.
111. Ferguson et al., 235.

112. In nuclear physics, supercriticality implies an increasing rate of fission within a nuclear reactor that can lead to meltdown of the reactor core if the rate of fission is not controlled or slowed by neutron-absorbing control rods.

113. See Bunn et al.; see also National Research Council (2002).

114. In 2006, President Bush announced the Global Nuclear Energy Partnership (GNEP), which is a comprehensive strategy for developing the long-term potential of nuclear energy for replacing carbon-intensive fossil fuels while minimizing the proliferation risk and reducing the volumes of nuclear waste. Under GNEP, the DOE hopes to develop proliferation-resistant technologies to reuse and recycle nuclear fuel and reduce the amount of nuclear waste requiring permanent geologic disposal. For more information, see U.S. Department of Energy, "The Global Nuclear Energy Partnership," fact sheet, available at <www.gnep.energy.gov/pdfs/06-GA50506-01.pdf>

Chapter 4

Religion and the Intersection with Terrorism

The 1993 bombings of Manhattan's World Trade Center, Aum Shinrikyo's release of sarin nerve gas in the Tokyo underground, and the bombing of the U.S. federal building in Oklahoma City were acts of terrorism carried out by players with vastly different origins, doctrines, and practices, writes Magnus Ranstorp. Yet Ranstorp recognizes one common thread among these terrorist acts: The perpetrators believed "their actions were divinely sanctioned, even mandated by God." Ranstorp charts the rise in terrorism for religious motives and reports that between the mid-1960s and mid-1990s the number of fundamentalist movements of all religious affiliations tripled. Nearly a quarter of all terrorist groups active in the world today are primarily motivated by religious concerns, yet these groups are also driven by practical political considerations—and it is difficult for observers to distinguish the political from the religious in the terrorist acts these groups commit. Ranstorp explores the motives, the "serious sense of crisis in their environment," which nearly all these groups experience and that fuels an escalation in their activities; the threats of secularization from foreign sources these group identify and rail against; the hierarchy of power that emanates from a dynamic so-called leader; the role religious symbolism plays in selecting their targets; and the sense of home and change for vengeance these groups offer to followers who suffer under a history of grievances. Contrary to popular opinion, Ranstorp concludes, "[r]eligious terrorism is anything but disorganized or random, but rather driven by an inner logic common among diverse groups and faiths who use political violence to further their sacred causes."

Quintan Wiktorowicz's article is a very significant and important contribution to the field. "A Genealogy of Radical Islam" traces the development of radical jihadi thought. Central to his argument is the concept that al Qaeda is not a "theological outlier" but instead part of a larger global community of Salafists. In the article, Wiktorowicz identifies what he terms as the "key points of divergence" among the Salfi community. He concludes by noting that the "development of jihadi thought is characterized by the erosion of critical constraints used to limit warfare and violence in classical Islam." The expansion of al Qaeda's targets from military or political to civilian targets is indicative of the future path toward targeting wider groups of people.

Whereas Wiktorowicz examines the emergence of al Qaeda from a broader global community of Salafists, Emmanuel Sivan considers the state of radical Islam within Muslim lands. Rather than the alleged clash of civilizations, Sivan suggests that it is the clash within Islam—the struggle between radical Islam and the powers-that-be—that counts. Sivan describes the emergence of the Salafiyya movement, which "born of a deep concern that Muslim societies were losing their Islamic essence" in the face of modernity, calls for a revitalization of Islam to end its cultural stagnation and decline. Sivan compares the success of radical and liberal offshoots of the Salafiyya movement. "Despite its elitist character and lack of a broad social base," liberal Islamists have "wielded a certain influence over intellectual life and over cultural mediators such as high school teachers and journalists." However, liberal Islamists have been less successful in appealing to the broader Muslim publics due to lacking communication and organizational skills. In contrast, radical Islamists have skillfully engaged in the *da'wa*—which includes propaganda, education, and medical and welfare actions—to the extent that they have changed the nature of Muslim societies, molding hearts and minds, and created a network of grateful clients.

Magnus Ranstorp, 1996

Terrorism in the Name of Religion

Introduction

On 25 February 1994, the day of the second Muslim sabbath during Islam's holy month of Ramadan, a Zionist settler from the orthodox settlement of Qiryat Arba entered the crowded Ibrahim (Abraham's) Mosque, located in the biblical town of Hebron on the West Bank. He emptied three 30-shot magazines with his automatic Glilon assault-rifle into the congregation of 800 Palestinian Muslim worshippers, killing 29 and wounding 150, before being beaten to death. A longstanding follower of the radical Jewish fundamentalist group, the Kach movement,[1] Baruch Goldstein was motivated by a complex mixture of seemingly inseparable political and religious desiderata, fuelled by zealotry and a grave sense of betrayal as his prime minister was "leading the Jewish state out of its God-given patrimony and into mortal danger."[2] Both the location and the timing of the Hebron massacre were heavily infused with religious symbolism. Hebron was the site of the massacre of 69 Jews in 1929. Also, the fact that it occured during the Jewish festival of Purim symbolically cast Goldstein in the role of Mordechai in the Purim story, meting out awesome revenge against the enemies of the Jews.[3] Israeli Prime Minister Yithzak Rabin, speaking for the great mass of Israelis, expressed revulsion and profound sadness over the act committed by a "deranged fanatic." However, a large segment of militant and orthodox Jewish settlers in West Bank and Gaza settlements portrayed Goldstein as a righteous man and hailed him as a martyr.[4] During his funeral, these orthodox settlers also voiced religious fervor in uncompromising and militant terms directed not only against the Arabs, but also against the Israeli government, which they believed had betrayed the Jewish People and the Jewish state.

Israeli leaders and the Jewish community tried to deny or ignore the danger of Jewish extremism by dismissing Goldstein as belonging, at most, to "the fringe of a fringe"[5] within Israeli society. Sadly, any doubts of the mortal dangers of religious zealotry from within were abruptly silenced with the assassination of prime minister Yitzhak Rabin by a young Jewish student, Yigal Amir, who claimed he had acted on orders of God. He had been influenced by militant rabbis and their *halalic* rulings, which he interpreted to mean that the "pursuer's decree" was to be applied against Israel's leader.[6] Most Israelis may be astonished by the notion of a Jew killing another Jew, but Rabin was ultimately the victim of a broader force which has become one of the most vibrant, dangerous and pervasive trends in the post–Cold War world: religiously motivated terrorism.

Far afield from the traditionally violent Middle East, where religion and terrorism share a long history,[7] a surge of religious fanaticism has manifested itself in spectacular acts of terrorism across the globe. This wave of violence is unprecedented, not only in its scope and the selection of targets, but also in its lethality and indiscriminate character.

Examples of these incidents abound: in an effort to hasten in the new millenium, the Japanese religious cult Aum Shinrikyo released sarin nerve gas on the Tokyo underground in June last year;[8] the followers of Sheikh 'Abd al-Rahman's al-Jama'a al-Islamiyya[9] caused mayhem and destruction with the bombing of Manhattan's World Trade Center and had further plans to blow up major landmarks in the New York City area; and two American white supremacists carried out the bombing of a U.S. Federal building in Oklahoma City.[10] All are united in the belief by the perpetrators that their actions were divinely sanctioned, even mandated, by God. Despite having vastly different origins, doctrines, institutions, and practices, these religious extremists are unified in their justification for employing sacred violence, whether in efforts to defend, extend or revenge their own communities, or for millenarian or messianic reasons.[11] This article seeks to explore these reasons for the contemporary rise in terrorism for religious motives and to identify the triggering mechanisms that bring about violence out of religious belief in both established and newly formed terrorist groups.

The Wider Trend of Religious Terrorism

Between the mid-1960s and the mid-1990s, the number of fundamentalist movements of all religious affiliations tripled worldwide. Simultaneously, as observed by Bruce Hoffman, there has been a virtual explosion of identifiable religious terrorist groups from none in 1968 to today's level, where nearly a quarter of all terrorist groups active throughout the world are predominantly motivated by religious concerns.[12] Unlike their secular counterparts, religious terrorists are, by their very nature, largely motivated by religion, but they are also driven by day-to-day practical political considerations within their context-specific environment. This makes it difficult for the general observer to separate and distinguish between the political and the religious sphere of these terrorist groups.

Nowhere is this more clear than in Muslim terrorist groups, as religion and politics cannot be separated in Islam. For example, Hizb'allah or Hamas operate within the framework of religious ideology, which they combine with practical and precise political action in Lebanon and Palestine. As such, these groups embrace simultaneously short-term objectives, such as the release of imprisoned members, and long-term objectives, such as continuing to resist Israeli occupation of their homelands and liberating all "believers." This is further complicated with the issue of state-sponsorship of terrorism: Religious terrorist groups become cheap and effective tools for specific states in the advancement of their foreign policy political agendas. They may also contain a nationalist-separatist agenda, in which the religious component is often entangled with a complex mixture of cultural, political, and linguistic factors. The proliferation of religious extremist movements has also been accompanied by a sharp increase in the total number of acts of terrorism since 1988, accounting for over half of the 64,319 recorded incidents between 1970 and July 1995.[13] This escalation by the religious terrorists is hardly surprising given the fact that most of today's active groups worldwide came into existence very recently. They appeared with a distinct and full-fledged organizational apparatus. They range from the Sikh Dal Khalsa and the Dashmesh organizations, formed in 1978 and 1982 respectively[14] and the foundation of the Shi'ite Hizb'allah movement in Lebanon in 1982; to the initial emergence of the militant Sunni organizations, known as Hamas and Islamic Jihad, in conjunction with the

1987 outbreak of the Palestinian Intifada as well as the establishment of the Aum Shinrikyo in the same year.

The growth of religious terrorism is also indicative of the transformation of contemporary terrorism into a method of warfare and the evolution of the tactics and techniques used by various groups, as a reaction to vast changes within the local, regional and global environment over the last three decades. These changes can be seen in numerous incidents, from the spate of hijackings by secular Palestinian terrorists and the mayhem of destruction caused by left- and right-wing domestic terrorists throughout Europe, to today's unprecedented global scope and level of religious extremism.

The evolution of today's religious terrorism neither has occurred in a vacuum nor represents a particularly new phenomenon. It has, however, been propelled to the forefront in the post–Cold war world, as it has been exacerbated by the explosion of ethnic-religious conflicts and the rapidly approaching new millenium.[15] The accelerated dissolution of traditional links of social and cultural cohesion within and between societies with the current globalization process, combined with the historical legacy and current conditions of political repression, economic inequality and social upheaval common among disparate religious extremist movements, have all lead to an increased sense of fragility, instability and unpredictability for the present and the future.[16] The current scale and scope of religious terrorism, unprecedented in militancy and activism, is indicative of this perception that their respective faiths and communities stand at a critical historical juncture: Not only do the terrorists feel the need to preserve their religious identity, they also see this time as an opportunity to fundamentally shape the future.[17] There are a number of overlapping factors that have contributed to the revival of religious terrorism in its modern and lethal form at the end of the millennium. At the same time, it is also possible to discern a number of features which are found in all religious terrorist groups across different regions and faiths. These features serve not only to define the cause and the enemy, but also fundamentally shape the means, methods and the timing of the use of the violence itself.

The Causes and the Enemies of Religious Terrorists

A survey of the major religious terrorist groups in existence worldwide in the 1990s would reveal that almost all experience a serious sense of crisis in their environment, which has led to an increase in the number of groups recently formed and caused an escalation in their activities. This crisis mentality in the religious terrorist's milieu is multifaceted, at once in the social, political, economic, cultural, psychological and spiritual sphere. At the same time, it has been greatly exacerbated by the political, economic and social tumult, resulting in a sense of spiritual fragmentation and radicalization of society experienced worldwide in the wake of the end of the Cold War and the extremist's "fear of the forced march toward 'one worldism.'"[18] Yet, this sense of crisis, as a perceived threat to their identity and survival, has been present to varying degrees throughout history. It has led to recurring phases of resurgence in most faiths. In these revivals, the believers use the religion in a variety of ways: they take refuge in the religion, which provides centuries-old ideals by which to determine goals; they find physical or psychological sanctuary against repression; or they may use it as a major instrument for activism or political action. Thus, religious terrorists perceive their actions as defensive and reactive in character and justify them in this way.[19] Islam's *jihad,* for example, is essentially a defensive doctrine, religiously sanctioned by leading Muslim theologians, and fought against perceived aggressors, tyrants, and "wayward Muslims." In its most violent form, it is justified as a means of last resort to prevent the extinction of the distinctive identity of the Islamic community against the forces of secularism and modernism. As outlined by Sheikh Fadlallah, the chief ideologue of Hizb'allah: "When Islam fights a war, it fights like any other power in the world, defending itself in order to preserve its existence and its liberty, forced to undertake preventive operations when it is in danger."[20] This is echoed by Sikh extremists, who advocate that, while violence is not condoned, when all peaceful means are exhausted, "you should put your hand on the sword."[21] The defensive character of protecting one's faith through religious violence is also evident in the Sikh's fear of losing their distinct identity in the sea of Hindus and Muslims.[22] In the United States, the paranoid outlook of white supremacist movements is driven by a mixture of racism and anti-Semitism, as well as mistrust of government and all central authority.[23] This sense of persecution is also visible among the Shi'ites as an historically dominant theme for 13 centuries, manifest in the annual Ashura processions by the Lebanese Hizb'allah, commemorating the martyrdom of Imam Husayn. This event and mourning period have been used as justification and as a driving force behind its own practice of martyrdom through suicide attacks.[24]

Other than a few strictly millenarian or messianic groups (such as Aum Shinrikyo or some Christian white supremacist movements), almost all the contemporary terrorist groups with a distinct religious imperative are either offshoots or on the fringe of broader movements. As such, the militant extremists' decisions to organize, break away or remain on the fringe are, to a large extent, conditioned by the political context within which they operate. Their decisions are shaped by doctrinal differences, tactical and local issues, and the degree of threat that they perceive secularization poses to their cause. This threat of secularization may come either from within the movements themselves and the environment within which they come into contact, or from outside influences. If the threat is external, it may amplify their sense of marginality within, and acute alienation from, society. It may also fuel the need to compensate for personal sufferings through the radical transformation of the ruling order.[25] The internal threat of secularization is often manifest in a vociferous and virulent rejection of the corrupt political parties, the legitimacy of the regime, and also the lackluster and inhibited character of the existing religious establishment. Thus, religious terrorism serves as the only effective vehicle for violent political opposition.[26] As explained by Kach's leader, Baruch Marzel, "(w)e feel God gave us in the six-day war, with a miracle, this country. We are taking this present from God and tossing it away. They are breaking every holy thing in this country, the Government, in a very brutal way."[27] Similarly, as voiced by the late Palestinian Islamic Jihad's leader, Fathi al-Shaqaqi, with reference to the Gaza-Jericho agreement between the PLO [Palestine Liberation Organization] and Israel: "Arafat has sold his soul for the sake of his body and is trying to sell the Palestinian people's soul in return for their remaining alive politically."[28] The religious terrorist groups' perception of a threat of secularization from within the same society is also manifest in the symbolism used in the selection of their names, indicating that they have an absolute monopoly of the revealed truth by God. It is, therefore, not surprising that some of the most violent terrorist groups over the last decade have also adopted names accordingly: Hizb'allah (Party of God), Aum Shinrikyo (The Supreme Truth) and Jund al-Haqq

(Soldiers of Truth). These names also endow them with religious legitimacy, historical authenticity, and justification for their actions in the eyes of their followers and potential new recruits. They also provide valuable insight into their unity of purpose, direction and degree of militancy, with names like Jundallah (Soldiers of God), Hamas (Zeal), Eyal (Jewish Fighting Organization) and Le Groupe Islamique du Armé (Armed Islamic Group, GIA) which promises unabated struggle and sacrifice.

The threat of secularization from foreign sources is also the catalyst for springing religious terrorists into action. Intrusion of secular values into the extremist's own environment and the visible presence of secular foreign interference provoke self-defensive aggressiveness and hostility against the sources of these evils. This is especially true against colonalism and neo-colonialism by western civilizations or against other militant religious faiths. These defensive sentiments are often combined with the visible emergence and presence of militant clerical leaders. Such leaders have more activist and militant ideologies than the mainstream movement from which they have emerged as either clandestine instruments or breakaway groups. It is often the case that these clerical ideologues and personalities act as a centrifugal force in attracting support, strengthening the organizational mechanisms and in redefining the methods and means through terrorism. At the same time, they provide theological justification, which enables their followers to pursue the sacred causes more effectively and rapidly. The so-called spiritual guides, who ultimately overlook most political and military activities while blessing acts of terrorism, can be found in almost all religious terrorist groups: Examples include Hizb'allah's Sheikh Fadlallah and Hamas' Sheikh Yassin, the militant Sikh leader Sant Bhindranwale and Aum Shinrikyo's leader, Shoko Ashara.

Most active terrorist groups with a religious imperative were actually propelled into existence in reaction to key events. These events either served as a catalyst or inspirational model for the organization or gravely escalated the perception of the threat of foreign secularization, or for messianic or millenarian groups, a heightened sense that time was running out. The latter is evident in the growth and increased activism of doomsday cults, awaiting the imminent apocalypse, whose self-prophetic visions about the future have triggered them to hasten the new millennium.[29] This messianic anticipation, for example, was clearly evident in the attack on the Grand Mosque of Mecca in 1979 (the Islamic year 1400) by armed Muslim militants from al-Ikhwan, who expected the return of their Madhi.[30] The formation of Lebanese Hizb'allah can be attributed to the context of the civil war environment and the inspiring example of Ayatollah Khomeini's Islamic revolution in Iran. However, it was Israel's invasion of Lebanon in 1982 and the subsequent foreign intrusion in the form of the western-led Multinational Forces (MNF) that served as a catalyst for Hizb'allah's actual organizational formation and which to this day has continued to fuel its militancy and religious ideology. Similarly, the 1984 desecration by the Indian army of the Golden Temple in Amritsar, Sikhism's holiest shrine, led not only to the assassination of Prime Minister Indira Gandhi in revenge, but also to a cycle of endless violence between the warring faiths, which hitherto has claimed over 20,000 lives.[31]

In many ways, religious terrorists embrace a total ideological vision of an all-out struggle to resist secularization from within as well as from without. They pursue this vision in totally uncompromising holy terms in literal battles between good and evil. Ironically, there is a great degree of similarity between the stands of the Jewish Kach and

Islamic Hamas organizations: Both share a vision of a religious state between the Jordan River and the Mediterranean Sea; a xenophobia against everything alien or secular which must be removed from the entire land, and a vehement rejection of western culture. This distinction between the faithful and those standing outside the group is reinforced in the daily discourse of the clerics of these terrorist groups. The clerics' language and phrase-ology shapes the followers' reality, reinforcing the loyalty and social obligation of the members to the group and reminding them of the sacrifices already made, as well as the direction of the struggle.[32] In this task, many religious terrorist groups draw heavily upon religious symbolism and rituals to reinforce the sense of collectiveness. Examples of this emphasis on collectivity include the local reputation of the fighters of the underground military wing of Hamas, famous for never surrendering to arrest,[33] the growth of Hamas martyrology, which lionizes martyrs with songs, poems and shrines,[34] and the frequent symbolic burning and desecration of Israeli and American flags by several Islamic groups across the Middle East. This collectiveness is also reinforced by the fact that any deviation or compromise amounts to treachery and a surrender of the principles of the religious faith is often punishable by death.

The sense of totality of the struggle for these religious warriors is one purely defined in dialectic and cosmic terms as believers against unbelievers, order against chaos, and jus-tice against injustice, which is mirrored in the totality and uncompromising nature of their cause, whether that cause entails the establishment of Eretz Israel, an Islamic state based on *sharia* law or an independent Khalistan ("Land of the Pure"). As such, the religious terrorists perceive their struggle as all-out war against their enemies. This perception, in turn, is often used to justify the level and intensity of the violence. For example, this theme of war is con-tinuously detectable in the writings and statements by the terrorists, as exemplified by Yigal Amir's justification for assassinating Rabin;[35] or by Article 8 of Hamas' manifesto justifying that *jihad* is its path and that "[d]eath for the sake of Allah is its most sublime belief."

This totality of the struggle naturally appeals to its acutely disenfranchised, oppre-ssed, and alienated communities with the promises of change and the provision of con-structive alternatives. Unlike their recent historical predecessors, like the fringe al-Jihad organization which assassinated the Egyptian President Anwar Sadat in 1981,[36] many of the existing religious terrorist cells are different in that they can often complement their violence with realistic alternatives to secular submission. This is especially true at the grassroots level, due to the penchant for organization inherent in religion and the backing of a vast network of resources and facilities.[37] This has meant that some religious terror-ist groups are not solely relying on violence, but also have gradually built an impressive constituency through a strategy of "re-Islamization or re-Judaization from below."[38] The political dimension is complemented with terrorism in confrontation with the enemy or in defense of the sacred cause. This is a process which began in the early 1970s and culmi-nated in the 1990s with a visible shift in strategy among groups, from relying on terrorism while re-Islamizing their environment to complementing terrorism with the use of the elec-toral process to advance their sacred causes.

Religious terrorism also offers its increasingly suffering and impatient constituents more hope and a greater chance of vengeance against the sources of their historical griev-ances than they would otherwise have. This is most effectively illustrated by the 1985 Sikh inflight bombing of an Air India airliner, causing 328 deaths, as well as by Hizb'allah's twin suicide-bombings of the U.S. Marine barracks and the French MNF headquarters in Beirut in 1983, killing 241 and 56 soldiers respectively. Violent acts give these groups a sense of power that is disproportionate to their size. The basis for this feeling of power is enhanced by a strategy of anonymity by the religious terrorist which confuses the enemy. In other words, the covernames are used according to where the religious terrorists have come from and where they are heading. Terrorists of the Muslim faith, particularly Shi'ite groups, employ a wide variety of cover names (in the Shi'ite case rooted in history with the notion of *taqiyyah,* or dissimulation) in efforts to protect their communities against repression or retaliation by the enemy after terrorist acts.[39] Yet, these covernames reveal significantly the currents or directions within movements in alignment with their struggles.[40] As such, the religious terrorists tend to "execute their terrorist acts for no audience but themselves."[41] Although the act of violence in and of itself is executed primarily for the terrorists own community as a sign of strength, it naturally embodies wider elements of fear in their actual or potential enemy targets. The perpetrators adeptly exploit this fear by invoking religious symbolism, such as the release of videotaped images of an endless pool of suicide bombers, ready to be dispatched against new targets.

While the religious extremists uniformly strike at the symbols of tyranny, they are relatively unconstrained in the lethality and the indiscriminate nature of violence used, as it is conducted and justified in defence of the faith and the community. Reflecting the dialectic nature of the struggle itself, various religious terrorist groups also refer to their alien or secular enemies in de-humanizing terms which may loosen the moral constraints for them in their employment of particularly destructive acts of terrorism.[42] As explained by an extremist rabbi in conjunction with the funeral of Baruch Goldstein: "There is a great difference in the punishment becoming a person who hurts a Jew and a person who hurts a gentile. . . . [t]he life of a Jew is worth much more than the lives of many gentiles." This moral self-purification points to the belief that the perpetrators view themselves as divinely "chosen people," who not only possess religious legitimacy and justification for their propensity for violence, but also often act out of the belief that the violence occurs in a divinely sanctioned juncture in history. For example, the Japanese cult leader Shoko Ashara and his followers believed the world would end in 1997 and launched a sarin nerve gas attack on Tokyo's subway system to hasten the new millennium.[43]

In fact, the lack of any moral constraints in the use of violence cannot only be attributed to the totality of the struggle itself but also to the preponderance of recruits of young, educated and newly-urbanized men (often with very radical, dogmatic, and intolerant worldviews), in contemporary religious terrorist organizations.[44] This increased militancy of a younger generation of religious terrorists can be explained by both the fragmentation of groups into rival splinter factions and also the killing or imprisonment of key founding leaders and ideologues.[45] Apart from removing the older generation of terrorist leadership, the experience of persecution and imprisonment has led to the radicalization of younger recruits into the organizations.[46] Also there seems to be an inverse relationship between size and militancy.[47] The Shi'ite terrorist groups are more prone to martyrdom than their Sunni counterparts, due to their different historical legacies and to the more powerful role of Shi'ite clergymen in directly interceding between man and God. However, some Sunni groups have recently broken the mold, as evident in the unprecedented series of 13 Hamas suicide-attacks inside Israel (which killed 136 people between 6 April 1994 and 4 March

1996) after the Hebron massacre and, to a lesser extent, the foiled plan by the GIA to explode its hijacked Air France plane over metropolitan Paris in December 1994. However, as explained by Sheikh Fadlallah: "There is no difference between dying with a gun in your hand or exploding yourself. In a situation of struggle or holy war you have to find the best means to achieve your goals."[48]

While the resort to martyrdom by certain groups can be explained by the heightened sense of threat to the groups and their causes within their own environment, it can also be explained by an increasing level of internationalization between groups both in terms of contact, similarity of causes and as examples of strategies. This is particularly evident among Muslim terrorist groups. For example, many Algerian, Egyptian and Palestinian Muslim extremists have participated alongside the Mujahadin fighters in the Afghanistan conflict. They trained with these Afghan fighters and supported them both physically and ideologically in a war "as much about the forging of a new and revolutionary social order as about national liberation."[49] As a significant example of a revolutionary cause within a Sunni context, as opposed to the more narrow Shi'ite example of the Iranian revolution, the Afghan conflict served as a training ground for their own struggles during the 1980s: Following the collapse of communism, these fighters returned to their respective countries to radicalize the Islamic struggle at home, resorting to increasing violence in the process, either within existing movements or as splinter groups.

Yet, the mechanisms of unleashing acts of religious terrorism, in terms of intensity, methods and timing, are tightly controlled by the apex of the clerical hierarchy and most often dependent on their blessing. This was clearly demonstrated in the 1984 Gush Emunim plot to blow up the Temple Mount (or Dome of the Rock), Islam's third holiest site, in part for messianic reasons (to cause a cataclysmic war between Jews and Muslims to hasten the coming of the Messiah) and in part to foil the return of Jewish sacred land to Arabs in return for peace under the Camp David accord. This act of terrorism never materialized due to the lack of rabbinical backing.[50] Similarly, the role of the spiritual leaders within Islamic terrorist organizations is equally pivotal, as displayed by the central role of Sheikh Omar 'Abd al-Rahman of the Egyptian al-Jama'a al-Islamiyya in issuing the directive, or *fatwa*, for both the 1981 assassination of Anwar Sadat and the 1993 bombing of New York's World Trade Center.[51] As such, in most cases the strictly hierarchical nature of religious terrorist groups with a highly disciplined structure and obedient cadres means not only that the main clerical leaders command full control over the political as well as military activities of the organization but also that the strategies of terrorism are unleashed in accordance with general political directives and agendas.[52]

Yet, the use and sanctioning of religious violence requires clearly defined enemies. The newly-formed religious terrorist groups today do not appear in a vacuum nor are their members naturally born into extremism. The identity of the enemy and the decision to use religious violence against them are dependent on, and shaped by, the heightened degree of the sense of crisis threatening their faiths and communities. This, in turn, is influenced by the historical legacy of political repression, economic inequality or social upheaval, and may be exacerbated by ethnic and military disputes. This sense of grievance is uniquely experienced between the faiths and the individual groups, as well as in alignment with the political strategies and tactics adopted to confront them according to local, regional and international contexts. Internally, this militancy may be directed against the corruption or injustices of the political system, or against other religious communities; externally, it may be focused against foreign influences, which represent a cultural, economic, or political threat to the respective religious communities. The West, particularly the United States as well as Israel, tends to be the favourite target of this militancy, especially by terrorists of the Muslim faith.[53]

Anti-western sentiments and intense hostility towards Israel for the Muslim terrorist is the result of the historical legacy of political oppression and socio-economic marginalization within the Arab world. These hostilities are combined with the discrediting of secular ideologies and the illegitimacy of current political and economic elites, especially after the 1967 defeat of the Arabs by Israel.[54] This sense of crisis has been exacerbated by the Arab-Israeli conflict which served to reinforce a Muslim inferiority complex due to the inability of either Arab regimes or secular Palestinians to defeat Israel. Simultaneously, the West is perceived to be practising neocolonialism through its Israeli surrogate and its unqualified support for existing "un-Islamic" and "illegitimate" regimes across the Arab world. As such, the Islamist movements and their respective armed "terrorist" wings have gradually propelled themselves to the forefront of politics as the true defender of the oppressed and dispossessed and as the only effective spearhead against Israel's continued existence in the heart of Muslim territory and against the West's presence and interference in the region. Apart from the obvious religious dimensions of the loss of Palestine to Zionism, Muslim militants draw heavily on the symbolism of the historical legacy of the Crusades, pitting Christendom against Islam, to explain their current condition of oppression and disinheritance, and to provide workable solutions and defences against the threat of western encirclement and secularization.[55] The Muslim terrorists rework these historic religious symbols to fit present-day conditions as a vehicle to inspire political action and revolutionary violence against its enemies.

While the identity of the enemy is deeply rooted in both distant and recent history, the turn towards, and the direction of, terrorism by militant Muslim movements against foreign enemies have been following distinct phases according to changes in the political and ideological context in the region. These phases are directly influenced by the Iranian revolution in 1979, the Muslim resistance struggle led by the Mujahadin against the Soviets in Afghanistan, the electoral victory of the Front Islamique du Salut (FIS) in Algeria (1990 to 1991), and the signing of the Israeli-Palestinian Declaration of Principles in September 1993. The Iranian revolution provided a revolutionary model of Islam and inspired Islamic movements to seriously challenge existing regimes at home. Additionally, the internationalization of Muslim terrorist violence against the West and Israel during the 1980s supported Iran's efforts to export the revolution abroad and was a cost-effective instrument to change the foreign policies of western states hostile towards the Islamic Republic.[56] The Lebanese Hizb'allah movement in particular, was very useful to the Iranian regime in achieving these ends. It also provided Iran with the opportunity to participate, both indirectly and militarily, in the Arab-Israeli conflict.[57] Additionally, Muslim fighters in Afghanistan during the 1980s forged important networks between various groups and individuals which accelerated the activism among Muslim groups on the homefront when these fighters returned home. The FIS electoral victory in Algeria demonstrated to Muslim terrorist groups that they could use the ballotbox rather than relying solely on bullets in efforts to come to power in various Arab states. The election's subsequent nullification by the Algerian military junta led to radicalization of the Islamists and their turn towards terrorism against the state itself and the French government for extending support.

Simultaneously, the gradual resolution of the Israeli-Palestinian conflict threatens the pan-Islamic goal of militant Islamic movements of liberating Jerusalem. This threat has led to accelerated co-ordination between Islamic terrorist groups in efforts to sabotage the peace process and an increased militancy and confrontation against the West, Israel, and supportive Arab regimes. At the same time, the political wings of these terrorist groups seek to continue and extend the process of re-Islamization of society from below. The confluence of these factors over the last two decades has accelerated the militancy of the Muslim terrorist while it clearly demonstrates that they are closely attuned to changes in the local, regional, and international environment, as well as very adept to reformulating their strategies for political and military action accordingly in efforts to protect, extend or avenge their religious communities.

The Means, Methods, and Timing of the Religious Terrorist

In comparison to their secular counterparts, the religious terrorists have not been particularly inventive when it comes to using new types of weaponry in their arsenals, instead relying on the traditional bombs and bullets.[58] Yet the religious terrorists have demonstrated a great deal of ingenuity in terms of the tactics used in the selection of means, methods and timing of violence to cause maximum effect. They have utilized the notion of martyrdom and self-sacrifice through suicide bombings as a means of last resort against their conventionally more powerful enemies. The first time this tactic was employed by the Hizb'allah was against the American, French and later Israeli military contingents present in Lebanon in 1983. It was emulating the actions of the shock troops of the Iranian Revolutionary Guards in their war with Iraq. While the Hizb'allah clerics gradually encountered theological dilemmas in continuing the sanctioning of this method, as suicide is generally forbidden in Islam except for under exceptional circumstances, the Hamas movement felt compelled to adopt suicide bombings in 1994 as a means of last resort in order to sabotage the Israeli-Palestinian peace process.[59] They believed that its actual implemention on the ground would severely threaten Hamas' revolutionary existence. The tactic of suicide bombing was also used to take revenge against its "Zionist enemy" for the Hebron attack. While few terrorist groups adopt large-scale campaigns of suicide missions, the religious terrorist utilizes the traditional methods of assassination, kidnappings, hijackings, and bombings in a skillful combination in alignment with the current political context on the local, regional, and international level. Despite the growth and array of religious terrorist groups with diverse demands and grievances, they are all united not only in the level and intensity of violence used, but also in the role played by religious symbolism in selecting the targets and the timing of the violence itself.

Many of these terrorist groups are compelled to undertake operations with a distinct political agenda for organizational reasons to release imprisoned members or eliminating opponents. Nonetheless, the targets are almost always symbolic and carefully selected to cause maximum psychological trauma to the enemy and to boost the religious credentials of the terrorist group among their own followers. This is clearly evident from the selection by Muslim terrorists of western embassies, airlines, diplomats and tourists abroad as symbolically striking at the heart of their oppressors. This was evident in the selection of major New York City landmarks by Sheikh Rahman's followers or the multiple attacks by the Hizb'allah against U.S. diplomatic and military facilities.[60] In many instances, these groups have adopted a multi-pronged approach of using terrorism. For example, in Algeria the FIS has targeted foreign tourists, businessmen and diplomats, as well as Algerian officials and other Algerians who engage in un-Islamic behaviour (e.g unveiled women or any form of western culture). At the same time, it engages in the re-Islamization of society from below and simultaneously wages a war of attrition on French soil against symbolic civilian and official targets. In other cases, religious terrorists have used powerful symbolism to provoke deliberate reactions by the enemy, such as Dal Khalsa's severing of cows' heads outside two Hindu temples in Amritsar, which provoked massive disturbances between the Sikhs and the Hindus in April 1982.[61] This type of symbolism is also seen in the 1969 arson attack on the al-Aqsa mosque in East Jerusalem by a Jewish extremist and the 1982 plan by Jewish fanatics to blow up Temple Mount in order to spark a cataclysmic war between Muslims and Jews.[62]

Finally, the timing of the violence by religious terrorists is carefully selected to coincide with their own theological requirements or to desecrate their enemies' religious holidays and sacred moments. For example, the 1995 bombing of the Alfred P. Murrah Federal Building in Oklahoma by white supremacists was reportedly scripted after *The Turner Diaries,* but also timed to "commemorate the second anniversary of FBI's assault on the Branch Davidian's Waco, Texas compound; [and] to mark the date 220 years before when the American revolution began at Lexington and Concord."[63] Similarly, the symbolism of the timing of religious violence was also evident in the Algerian GIA's decision to hijacking an Air France plane during Christmas after the killing of two Catholic priests, or the cycle of violence by Hamas' suicide bombings against Israel, occurring in February 1996, on the second commemoration of the Hebron massacre.

Conclusions

This article has sought to demonstrate that, contrary to popular belief, the nature and scope of religious terrorism is anything but disorganised or random but rather driven by an inner logic common among diverse groups and faiths who use political violence to further their sacred causes. The resort to terrorism by religious imperative is also not a new phenomenon, but rather deeply embedded in the history and evolution of the faiths. Religions have gradually served to define the causes and the enemies as well as the means, methods and timing of the violence itself. As such, the virtual explosion of religious terrorism in recent times is part and parcel of a gradual process of what can be likened to neo-colonial liberation struggles. This process has trapped religious faiths within meaningless geographical and political boundaries and constraints, and has been accelerated by grand shifts in the global political, economic, military and socio-cultural setting, compounded by difficult local indigenous conditions for the believers. The uncertainty and unpredictability in the present environment as the world searches for a new world order, amidst an increasingly complex global environment with ethnic and nationalist conflicts, provide many religious terrorist groups with the opportunity and the ammunition to shape history according to their divine duty, cause, and mandate while it indicates for others that the end of time itself is near. As such, it is imperative to move away from treating this new religious force in global politics as a monolithic entity but rather seek to understand the inner logic of these individual groups and the mechanisms that produce terrorism in order to undermine their breeding ground and strength, as they are here to stay. At present it is doubtful that the United States or any western government is adequately prepared to meet this challenge.

Magnus Ranstorp is the Research Director of the Centre for Asymmetric Threat Studies at the Swedish National Defence College. Previously Dr. Ranstorp was the Director of Centre for the Study of Terrorism and Political Violence at the University of St Andrews, Scotland. His most recent edited book is *Mapping Terrorism Research: State of the Art, Gaps and Future Direction* (Routledge, 2006).

Notes

1. The Kach movement was founded in 1971 by the ultra-orthodox American Rabbi Meir Kahane when he emigrated to Israel. The group calls for the establishment of a theocratic state in Eretz (Greater) Israel and the forced expulsion of Arabs. For a useful overview see Raphael Cohen-Almagor, "Vigilant Jewish Fundamentalism: From the JDL to Kach (or 'Shalom Jews, Shalom Dogs'), *Terrorism and Political Violence*, 4, No.1 (Spring 1992): pp.44–66; and Ehud Sprintzak, *The Ascendance of Israel's Radical Right* (New York: Oxford University Press, 1991).
2. "The Impossible Decision," *The Economist*, 11–17 November 1995, p.25.
3. For a discussion of Goldstein's decision to carry out the attack during Purim, see Sue Fiskhoff, "Gentle, Kind and Full of Religious Fervor," *Jerusalem Post*, 27 February 1994; and Chris Hedges and Joel Greenberg, "West Bank Massacre: Before Killing, a Final Prayer and a Final Taunt," *New York Times*, 28 February 1994, p. A1.
4. One of Goldstein's rabbinical mentors, Rabbi Dov Li'or, described him in compassionate terms as a man "who could no longer take the humiliation and the disgrace. Everything he did was in honor of Israel and for the glory of God," in *Yediot Aharanot*, 18 March 1994. Also see: Richard Z. Chesnoff, "It Is a Struggle for Survival," *U.S. News & World Report*, 14 March 1994.
5. Charles Krauthammer, "Deathly Double Standard," *Jerusalem Post*, 6 March 1994.
6. Prior to Rabin's assassination, Yigal Amir had tried two previous times. For a very useful biography of the assassin, see John Kifner, "A Son of Israel: Rabin's Assassin," *New York Times*, 19 November 1995; *idem.*, "Israelis Investigate Far Right; May Crack Down on Speech," *New York Times*, 8 November 1995. One of these traditional exemptions for killing is Din Rodef, or Law of the Pursuer. The rule was first set forth in the 12th century by the great Moses Maimonides, a Spanish Jewish scholar. Going beyond the principle of self-defense, it states that even a witness to the act of someone's trying to kill another is allowed to kill the potential assassin. For Yigal Amir's use of the principle as a defense for killing Rabin, see Raine Marcus, "Amir: I Wanted to Murder Rabin," *Jerusalem Post*, 16 March 1996.
7. As aptly observed by David C. Rapoport in his seminal work, the words "zealot," "assassin" and "thug" all derive from historic fanatic movements within, respectively, Judaism, Islam and Hinduism, respectively. See Bruce Hoffman, *"Holy Terror": The Implications of Terrorism Motivated by a Religious Imperative* (Santa Monica: RAND, 1993) pp. 1–2; and David C. Rapoport, "Fear and Trembling: Terrorism in Three Religious Traditions," *American Political Science Review*, 78, no. 3 (September 1984) pp. 668–72. For a useful historical overview, see David C. Rapoport, "Why Does Religious Messianism Produce Terror?" in *Contemporary Research on Terrorism*, ed. Paul Wilkinson and A.M. Stewart, (Aberdeen: Aberdeen University Press, 1987) pp. 72–88.

8. The attack on the Tokyo subway was the first recorded instance of a terrorist group committing mass murder with a weapon of mass destruction. The Aum Shinrikyou religious cult was established in 1987 by Shoko Ashara, a nearly blind acupuncturist and yoga master, and is composed of a synthesized mixture of Buddhist and Hindu theology. For a useful brief biographical sketch of Ashara, see James Walsh, "Shoko Asahara: The Making of a Messiah," *Time,* 3 April 1995. The sarin nerve gas attack on Tokyo's subway killed 8 and injured over 5,500. Also see Martin Wollacott, "The Whiff of Terror," *The Guardian,* 21 March 1995.

9. For a useful overview of al-Jama'a al-Islamiyya and its activities in Egypt, see Barry Rubin, *Islamic Fundamentalism in Egyptian Politics* (London: Macmillan 1990).

10. See Stephen Robinson, "The American Fundamentalist," *Daily Telegraph,* 24 April 1995.

11. For a very comprehensive discussion, see Mark Juergensmeyer, ed. "Violence and the Sacred in the Modern World," *Terrorism and Political Violence,* 3, no. 3 (Autumn 1991).

12. Bruce Hoffman (1993), p. 2. The year 1968 is widely recognized as the point of origin for modern international terrorism. It was the beginning of an explosion of hijackings from Cuba to the United States, as well as attacks against Israeli and Western airlines by various Palestinian groups. Also see Barry James, "Religious Fanaticism Fuels Terrorism," *International Herald Tribune,* 31 October 1995, p. 3.

13. See Professor Yonah Alexander, "Algerian Terrorism: Some National, Regional and Global Perspectives," Prepared statement before the House Committee on International Relations, Subcommittee on Africa, *Federal News Service,* 11 October 1995. This figure should be compared with 8,339 acts of international terrorism during the period 1970 to 1994 with 3,105 incidents occurring after 1988, see RAND-St. Andrews, *Chronology of International Terrorism* (St. Andrews: Centre for the Study of Terrorism and Political Violence, University of St. Andrews, March 1996).

14. The Dashmesh (meaning "10th") organization was named after the Sikhs' last guru, Gobind Singh, who, in the eighteenth century, transformed the Sikh community into a warrior class by justifying force when necessary. Both the Dashmesh and the Sikh Dal Khalsa advocate the establishment of an independent Khalistan.

15. The emergence of ethnic-religious conflict over conventional inter-state warfare was illuminated by a 1994 report by the United Nations Development Programme in which only 3 out of a total of 82 conflicts worldwide were between states. See Roger Williamson, "The Contemporary Face of Conflict—Class, Colour, Culture and Confession," in *Jane's Intelligence Review Yearbook— The World in Conflict 94/95* (London: Jane's Information Group, 1995) pp. 8–10. Also see Julia Preston, "Boutros Ghali: 'Ethnic Conflict' Imperils Security," *Washington Post,* 9 November 1993, p. 13. Also see Hans Binnendijk & Patrick Clawson, eds., *Strategic Assessment 1995: U.S. Security Challenges in Transition* (Washington: National Defense University Press, 1995); and Martin Kramer, "Islam & the West (including Manhattan)," *Commentary* (October 1993) pp. 33–37.

16. For the wider debate of the religious resurgence, see Scott Thomas, "The Global Resurgence of Religion and the Study of World Politics," *Millenium,* 24, no. 2 (Summer 1995) and Peter Beyer, *Religion and Globalization* (London: Sage, 1994).

17. As observed: At a time when no one knows precisely what form the future may take, the strength of fundamentalism lies in its ability to promise radical change without having to specify its outlines—since God is claimed as its guarantor," in Mahmoud Hussein, "Behind the Veil of Fundamentalism," *UNESCO Courier,* December 1994, p. 25. Also as stated by an ideologue of Jewish extremist group, Kahane Chai: "We are accountable only to our Creator, to He who chose us for our mission in history," in Amir Taheri, "Comentary: The Ideology of Jewish Extremism," *Arab News,* 12 March 1994.

18. Robin Wright, "Global Upheaval Seen as Engine for Radical Groups," *Los Angeles Times,* 6 November 1995.

19. "Fundamentalism Unlimited," *The Economist,* 27 March 1993, p. 67; and Hussein, p. 25.

20. Muhammad Hussein Fadlallah, "To Avoid a World War of Terror," *Washington Post,* 4 June 1986. As reiterated by Sheikh Fadallah: "We are not preachers of violence. Jihad in Islam is a

defensive movement against those who impose violence." Laura Marlowe, "A Fiery Cleric's Defense of Jihad," *Time,* 15 January 1996. For further elaboration on this by Sheikh Fadlallah, see *al-Majallah,* 1–7 October 1986.

21. This is often seen in the Sikh slogan: "The Panth [religion] is in danger." See Paul Wallace, "The Sikhs as a 'Minority' in a Sikh Majority State in India," *Asian Survey,* 26, no. 3 (March 1986) p. 363.

22. Laurent Belsie, "At a Sikh Temple, Opinions Reflect Conflicting Religious Traditions," *Christian Science Monitor,* 11 November 1984. For a detailed discussion of the use of violence, see Sohan Singh Sahota, *The Destiny of the Sikhs* (Chandigarh: Modern Publishers, 1970).

23. Bruce Hoffman, "American Right-Wing Terrorism," *Jane's Intelligence Review,* 7, no. 7 (July 1995) pp. 329–30.

24. See John Kifner, "Shiite Radicals: Rising Wrath Jars the Mideast," *New York Times,* 22 March 1987.

25. This theme is developed by David Rapoport, "Comparing Militant Fundamentalist Movements," in *Fundamentalism and the State,* ed. Martin E. Marty and R. Scott Appleby (Chicago: The University of Chicago Press, 1993).

26. See Maha Azzam, "Islamism, the Peace Process and Regional Security," *RUSI Journal* (October 1995) pp. 13–16.

27. Kifner, 19 November 1995.

28. *Al-Hayah,* 4 May 1994. Similarly, according to Hamas' manifesto: "Palestine is a Holy Muslim asset to the end of time, so that no man has the right to negotiate about her or to relinquish [any part of] her," in Amos Oz, "Israel's Far Right Collaborates With Hamas in Thwarting Peace," *The Times,* 11 April 1995.

29. For a useful insight into the dynamics of cults, see Richardo Delgado, "Limits to Proselytizing," *Society* (March/April 1980) pp. 25–33; Margaret Thaler Singer, "Coming of the Cults," *Psychology Today* (January 1979) pp. 73–82.

30. See Robin Wright, "U.S. Struggles to Deal With Global Islamic Resurgence," *Los Angeles Times,* 26 January 1992.

31. For a useful overview, see Pranay Gupte, "The Punjab: Torn by Terror," *New York Times,* 9 August 1985; Vijah Singh, "Les Sikhs, une Secte Traditionnelle Saisié par la Terrorisme," *Liberation,* 1 November 1984.

32. For example, this uncompromising position is clearly evident by Hamas' own charter in Article 11: "The land of Palestine is an Islamic trust (*waqf*) to be maintained by succeeding generations of Muslims until the Day of Judgement. In this responsibility, or any part of it, no negligence will be tolerated, and no surrender." *Mithaq Harakat al-Muqawamah al-Islamiyah* (Hamas, 1988).

33. See Michael Kelly, "In Gaza, Peace Meets Pathology," *New York Times,* 29 November 1994, p. 56.

34. See Michael Parks, "Ready to Kill, Ready to Die, Hamas Zealots Thwart Peace," *Los Angeles Times,* 25 October 1994, p. A10. For interesting insight into mentality of suicide bombers, see Joel Greenberg, "Palestinian 'Martyrs,' All Too Willing," *New York Times,* 25 January 1995; and *Ma'ariv,* 30 December 1994, p. 8. For an example of this martyrology with an extensive list of Izzeldin al-Qassem martyrs since 1990, see *Filastin al'Muslimah,* November 1994, p. 14.

35. In a statement in Israeli court, Amir provided the justification: "When you kill in war, it is an act that is allowed," in Russell Watson, "Blame Time," *Newsweek,* 20 November 1995. As explained by Amir, "I did not commit the act to stop the peace process because there is no concept as the peace process, it is a process of war," *Mideast Mirror,* 6 November 1995.

36. For a useful overview of the incident, see Jihad B. Khazen, *The Sadat Assassination: Background and Implications* (Washington: Georgetown University's Center for Contemporary Arab Studies, 1981); and Dilip Hiro, "Faces of Fundamentalism," *The Middle East,* May 1988, pp. 11–12.

37. See Robert Fisk, "'Party of God' Develops Its Own Political Style," *Irish Times,* 9 February 1995.

38. For a very interesting discussion of this phenomenon, see Gilles Keppel, *The Revenge of God: The Resurgence of Islam, Christianity and Judaism in the Modern World* (London: Polity Press, 1995).

39. For a useful exposition of concealment in Shi'ism, refer to lecture by Prof. Etan Kohlberg, Hebrew University, delivered at the Tel Aviv University (Tel Aviv, Israel: 23 May 1993).

40. See Maskit Burgin, A. Merari, and A Kurz, eds., *Foreign Hostages in Lebanon,* JCSS Memorandum, no. 25, August 1988 (Tel Aviv: Tel Aviv University, 1988).

41. Bruce Hoffman (1993), p. 3.

42. See Bruce Hoffman, "'Holy Terror': The Implications of Terrorism Motivated by a Religious Imperative," in *The First International Workshop on Low Intensity Conflict,* ed. A. Woodcock et al. (Stockholm: Royal Society of Naval Sciences, 1995) p. 43.

43. See Andrew Pollack, "Cult's Prophesy of Disaster Draws Precautions in Tokyo," *New York Times,* 15 April 1995; and Andrew Brown, "Waiting for the End of the World," *The Independent,* 24 March 1995.

44. For example, a survey of imprisoned members of the Egyptian group al-Takfir wal-Hijra (Repentance and Holy Flight) revealed that the average member was in his 20s or early 30s, a university student or recent graduate; had better than average marks in school work; felt intensely about causes but was intolerant of conflicting opinions; and a willingness to employ violence if necessary. See Ray Vicker, "Islam on the March," *Wall Street Journal,* 12 February 1980. For a similar profile of Sikh terrorists, see Carl H. Haeger, "Sikh Terrorism in the Struggle for Khalistan," *Terrorism,* 14 (1991) p. 227. Also see Hala Mustafa, "The Islamic Movements Under Mubarak," in *The Islamist Dilemma: The Political Role of Islamic Movements in the Contemporary Arab World,* ed. Laura Guazzone (Reading: Ithaca Press, 1995) p. 173.

45. For example, see Paul Wilkinson, "Hamas: An Assessment," *Jane's Intelligence Review* (July 1993) pp. 313–14; and Ziad Abu-Amr, *Islamic Fundamentalism in the West Bank and Gaza* (Indianapolis: Indiana University Press, 1994).

46. As demonstrated in the case of Egypt, "Jihad and other movements were born in [former Presidents] Nasser's and Sadat's prisons," see Robin Wright, "Holy Wars': The Ominous Side of Religion in Politics," *Christian Science Monitor,* 12 November 1987, p. 21. Also see Mustafa, p. 174.

47. Richard Hrair Dekmeijan, *Islam in Revolution: Fundamentalism in the Arab World* (Syracuse: Syracuse University Press, 1985) p. 61–62.

48. George Nader, *Middle East Insight* (June–July 1985).

49. See Anthony Davis, "Foreign Combatants in Afghanistan," *Jane's Intelligence Review* (July 1994) p. 327. Also see Raymond Whitaker, "Afghani Veterans Fan Out to Spread the Word—and Terror," *The Independent,* 16 April 1995.

50. For a detailed discussion of this plan, see Ehud Sprinzak, "Three Models of Religious Violence: The Case of Jewish Fundamentalism in Israel," in Marty and Appleby (1993), pp. 475–76. As stated by Sprinzak: "There has been no act by the Jewish underground which did not have a rabbinical backing." *Yediot Aharanot,* 18 March 1994.

51. See Youssef M. Ibrahim, "Muslim Edicts Take on New Force," *New York Times,* 12 February 1995; and Philip Jacobson, "Muhammad's Ally," *The Times Magazine,* 4 December 1993.

52. For example, see *Ma'ariv,* 28 February 1996; Ze'ev Chafets, "Israel's Quiet Anger," *New York Times,* 7 November 1995.

53. As revealed by Hizb'allah manifesto in 1985, "Imam Khomeini, the leader, has repeatedly stressed that America is the reason for all our catastrophes and the source of all malice. By fighting it, we are only exercising our legitimate right to defend our Islam and the dignity of our nation." See Hizb'allah's manifesto reprinted in Augustus Richard Norton, *Amal and the Shi'a: Struggle for the Soul of Lebanon* (Austin: University of Texas Press, 1987) pp. 167–87. See also Martin Kramer, "The Jihad Against the Jews," *Commentary* (October 1994) pp. 38– 42.

54. For example, see David Wurmser, "The Rise and Fall of the Arab World," *Strategic Review* (Summer 1993) pp. 33–46.

55. See Fred Halliday, *Islam and the Myth of Confrontation* (London: I.B. Tauris, 1995).

56. For example see Alvin H. Bernstein, "Iran's Low-Intensity War Against the United States," *Orbis,* 30 (Spring 1986) pp. 149–67; and Sean K. Anderson, "Iran: Terrorism and Islamic Fundamentalism," in *Low-Intensity Conflict: Old Threats in a New World,* ed. Edwin G. Corr and Stephen Sloan (Oxford: Westview Press, 1992) pp. 173–95.

57. See Magnus Ranstorp, *Hizballah in Lebanon: The Politics of the Western Hostage-Crisis* (London: Macmillan, 1996).

58. See Bruce Hoffman (1993).

59. See Martin Kramer, "The Moral Logic of Hizbollah," in *Origins of Terrorism: Psychologies, Ideologies, Theologies, States of Mind,* ed. Walter Reich (Cambridge: Cambridge University Press, 1990) pp. 131–57.

60. See Robert M. Jenkins, "The Islamic Connection," *Security Management* (July 1993) pp. 25– 30.

61. See Guy Arnold et al, eds., *Revolutionary & Dissident Movements: An International Guide* (Harlow: Longman Group, 1991) p. 141.

62. See Mir Zohair Husain, *Global Islamic Politics* (New York: Harper Collins, 1995) pp. 186–200.

63. Bruce Hoffman, "Intelligence and Terrorism: Emerging Threats and New Security Challenges in the Post–Cold War Era," *Intelligence and National Security,* 11, no. 3 (April 1996) p. 214. For a broader discussion of millenarian terrorism, see Michael Barkun, ed. *Millennialism and Violence* (London: Frank Cass, 1996).

Quintan Wiktorowicz, 2005

A Genealogy of Radical Islam

A genealogy of the radical ideas that underline al-Qaeda's justification for violence shows that the development of jihadi thought over the past several decades is character-ized by the erosion of critical constraints used to limit warfare and violence in classical Islam. This erosion is illustrated by the evolution of jihadi arguments related to apos-tasy and waging jihad at home, global jihad, civilian targeting, and suicide bombings.

Introduction

Al Qaeda and the radical fundamentalists that constitute the new "global jihadi movement" are not theological outliers. They are part of a broader community of Islamists known as "Salafis" (commonly called "Wahhabis").[1] The term "salafi" is used to denote those who follow the example of the companions (*salaf*) of the Prophet Mohammed. Salafis believe that because the companions learned about Islam directly from the Prophet, they com-manded a pure understanding of the faith. Subsequent practices, in contrast, were sullied by religious innovations that infected the Muslim community over time. As a result, Mus-lims must purify the religion by strictly following the Qur'an, the Sunna (path or traditions of the Prophet Mohammed), and the consensus of the companions. Every behavior must be sanctioned by these religious sources.

Although there is consensus among Salafis about this understanding of Islam, there are disagreements over the use of violence. The jihadi faction believes that violence can be used to establish Islamic states and confront the United States and its allies. Nonviolent Salafis, on the other hand, emphatically reject the use of violence and instead emphasize propagation and advice (usually private) to incumbent rulers in the Muslim world.[2] These two groups demarcate the most important fissures within the Salafi community, although there are individuals and movements that do not fall neatly into either, including influ-ential figures like Mohammed Sorour (now in London), Safar al-Hawali, and Salman al-Auda.

Understanding the genealogy of the radical jihadis necessitates identifying the key points of divergence within the Salafi community. Given a common understanding about following the strict model of the Prophet and his companions, what are the major points of disagreement? This article identifies four major points of contention among Salafis: (1) whether Muslims can call leaders apostates and wage jihad against them; (2) the nature of a "defensive" and global jihad; (3) the permissibility of targeting civilians; and (4) the legitimacy of suicide bombings (what radicals call "martyrdom operations"). How and why did the radicals diverge from the majority of Salafis on these issues? Who supported the divergent ideological trends, and how have these trends evolved over time?

The answers to these questions lie, to a large extent, in the inherently subjective process of religious interpretation whereby immutable religious texts and principles are applied to new circumstances and issues. The Qur'an and the Sunna of the Prophet Mohammed outline numerous rules about politics, economics, society, and individual behavior, but they do not directly respond to many questions relevant to the modern period. As a result, Salafis (and other Muslims) ask themselves what the Prophet would do if he were alive today. Given the way he lived his life and the principles he followed, how would he respond to the issues facing contemporary society? It is a process of extrapolation based on independent judgment (*ijtihad*) and reasoning by analogy (*qiyas*). So, for example, what would the Prophet say about the use of weapons of mass destruction? Clearly neither the Qur'an nor the Sunna speaks directly to this issue. Some radicals, however, argue that there is evidence that the Prophet would have supported the use of weapons of mass destruction if he were alive today. Specifically, they cite the siege of Ta'if in which the Prophet authorized the use of a catapult against a walled city where enemy fighters mixed with civilians, what jihadis call the "weapon of mass destruction of his day."[3] This process of reasoning invariably leads to differences of opinion about how the Prophet would respond to current issues.

The subjective nature of this process is nicely captured by a member of the Shura Council and Military Wing of the Gamiyya Islamiyya in Egypt during a group interview in June 2002 in which leaders explained why they abandoned the violent struggle initiated by the movement during the earlier 1990s:

> Shari'ah [the straight path of Islam, Islamic law] cannot be separated from reality. You must read both the reality and the relevant text before applying the right verses to the appropriate reality. Mistakes stem from the fact that the right text is sometimes applied on irrelevant reality.[4]

The leaders cited the decision by certain members of the movement to seize property belonging to Coptic Christians as an example. One responded that, "The person who did this used to apply certain texts to the wrong reality. The Islamic ruling on seizing loot belonging to the infidels applies to wars against the infidels, such as the war against the Jews in 1973 because it was a clear war. As for applying this principle to fellow citizens who are a part of this country's fabric, it is wrong."[5]

In tracing the evolution of jihadi thought over the past few decades, it appears that many of the shifts and changes are the result of new understandings about context rather than new readings of the religious texts and concomitant principles. Jihadis continue to use the same texts, quotes, and religious evidence as other Salafis, but they have developed new understandings about context and concepts such as "belief," "defense against aggression," and "civilians." The evolution of jihadi thought is less about changing principles embedded in the religious texts than the ways in which these principles are operative in the contemporary period.

This is not to argue that theology is completely irrelevant. Certainly, individual thinkers like Taqi al-Din Ibn Taymiyya (1263–1328), Muhammad bin Abdul Wahhab (1703–1792), Mawlana Abul A'la Mawdudi (1903–1979), and Sayyid Qutb (1906–1966) offered new understandings of the religious texts that challenged dominant interpretations, but subsequent thinkers, for the most part, merely adapted these understandings to new issues, often stretching them to their logical conclusion in a way that increased the scope of permissible violence.

Charges of Apostasy (*Takfir*) and Waging Jihad at Home

The vast majority of Muslims are conservative in their approach to declaring someone an apostate, a process known as takfir. The seriousness of the endeavor is underscored by a number of Qur'anic cautionary notes and stories about the Prophet. A few examples include:

> If a Muslim calls another *kafir* [unbeliever], then if he is a *kafir* let it be so; otherwise, he [the caller] is himself a *kafir.* (saying of the Prophet from Abu Dawud, *Book of Sunna,* edition published by Quran Mahal, Karachi, vol. iii, p. 484)

> No man accuses another man of being a sinner, or of being a *kafir,* but it reflects back on him if the other is not as he called him. (saying of the Prophet from Bukhari, *Book of Ethics;* Book 78, ch. 44)

> Withhold [your tongues] from those who say "There is no god but Allah"— do not call them *kafir.* Whoever calls a reciter of "There is no god but Allah" as a *kafir,* is nearer to being a *kafir* himself. (reported from Ibn Umar)[6]

Most Muslims believe that, as the Prophet said, "whoever accuses a believer of disbelief, it is as if he killed him."[7] Therefore, so long as a leader has a "mustard seed of faith" and implements the prayer, he is still considered a Muslim. (Throughout this article, the pronoun "he" is used because this is the jihadi standard. It must be recognized, however, that it encompasses both males and females.) From this perspective, a leader only becomes an apostate if he willingly implements non-Islamic law, understands that it does not represent Islam, and announces that it is superior to Islam. Otherwise, the leader could be ignorant, coerced, or driven by self-interest, failings that signify sinfulness, not apostasy. This is the line of argument represented by the Salafi mainstream.[8]

This reading of apostasy requires absolute proof of intentions, something that is nearly impossible unless the ruler publicly announces his disbelief. Nonviolent Salafis have, in fact, created a complex decision-making tree for excommunication that makes it extremely difficult to declare someone an apostate. They may charge a person with committing an act of apostasy, but unless that individual willingly proclaims that the act is Islamic, after clear evidence to the contrary, or announces that it is superior to Islam, he remains a Muslim. The culprit may go to Hell if he does not repent before dying, but that is for God to decide.

The nonviolent Salafis also believe it is forbidden to fight against rulers. Most cite the well-accepted prohibition against killing other Muslims, as outlined in Qur'an 4:92: "It is not for a believer to kill a believer unless (it be) by mistake."

The current jihadi argument about apostasy developed out of Egyptian and Saudi intellectual streams. The Egyptian lineage has its roots in British-controlled India. Conservative Indian Muslims were concerned that many Hindu converts to Islam were retaining earlier cultural practices and that Shi'ism and the British were undermining the purity of Sunni Islam. Hardliners reacted by drawing a sharp distinction between "true believers" and the infidels, which included Muslims who deviated from a rigid interpretation of Islam (apostates). Radical Sunni groups supporting this Manichean perspective emerged in Northern India during the 1820s and 1830s, including a movement led by Sayyid Ahmad Rai-Barelvi.[9] The conservative bent to these groups prompted the British to denote them as "Wahhabis" after the puritanical sect found on the Arabian Peninsula.

These conservatives were the intellectual predecessors to Mawlana Abul A'la Mawdudi, who in the 1930s seemed to give a "modernist cast to Sayyid Ahmad Rai-Barelvi's approach."[10] Whereas Rai-Barlevi and others rejected anything Western as antithetical to Islam, Mawdudi sought to appropriate Western technology, science, and other aspects of modernity while returning to the fundamentals of Islam. For modernists, the positive aspects of the West could be used to strengthen the Muslim community against Western imperialism. At the same time, despite this difference with earlier conservatives, Mawdudi adopted the strict distinction between belief and disbelief developed by Rai-Barelvi and his ilk.

Mawdudi's work drew extensively from Taqi al-Din Ibn Taymiyya, the best known medieval Salafi scholar, particularly his writings on the sovereignty of God.[11] One of Ibn Taymiyya's most important contributions to Salafi thought is his elaboration of the concept of *tawhid*—the unity of God. He divided the unity of God into two categories: the unity of lordship and the unity of worship. The former refers to belief in God as the sole sovereign and creator of the universe. All Muslims readily accept this. The second is affirmation of God as the only object of worship and obedience. Ibn Taymiyya reasoned that this latter component of divine unity necessitates following God's laws. The use of human-made laws is tantamount to obeying or worshipping other than God and thus apostasy. Mawdudi adopted this position and drew a sharp bifurcation between the "party of God" and the "party of Satan," which included Muslims who adhered to human-made law.

In making this argument, Mawdudi introduced his concept of "the modern jahiliyya" (circa 1939). The term "jahiliyya" refers to the "period of ignorance" (or period of paganism) preceding the advent of Islam. He argued that the deviations of self-proclaimed Muslims, the influence of imperialist powers, and the use of non-Islamic laws were akin to this earlier period of ignorance. For Mawdudi, true Muslims must struggle against this ignorance, just as the Prophet and his companions struggled against the paganism of the dominant Quraysh tribe in Mecca. In 1941, he formed the Jamaat-i-Islami as the spearhead of this struggle, a vanguard viewed as necessary to promote God's sovereignty on Earth.[12]

Mawdudi's importance for the Egyptian stream is his impact on Sayyid Qutb, often seen as the godfather of revolutionary Sunni Islam (he was executed by Nasser in 1966).[13] Qutb read Mawdudi's most influential works, including *Jihad in Islam, Islam and Jahiliyya,* and *Principles of Islamic Government,* which were translated into Arabic beginning in the 1950s. A more direct connection existed through one of Mawdudi's most important protégés, Abdul Hasan Ali Nadvi, who was a central figure in transmitting his mentor's theories to the Arab world. In 1950, Nadvi wrote *What Did the World Lose Due to the Decline of Islam?,* a book published in Arabic that expounded on Mawdudi's theory of modern jahiliyya. When he first traveled to the Middle East in 1951, Nadvi met with Qutb, who had already read his book. Both Mawdudi and Nadvi are quoted at length in Qutb's *In the Shade of the Qu'ran,* published in 1953.[14]

In *In the Shade of the Qu'ran,* Qutb outlines his view of the modern jahiliyya, which provides the cornerstone for declaring rulers apostates and waging jihad.

> Jahiliyya (barbarity) signifies the domination (hakamiyya) of man over man, or rather the subservience to man rather than to Allah. It denotes rejection of the divinity of God and the adulation of mortals. In this sense, jahiliyya is not just a specific historical period (referring to the era preceding the advent of Islam), but a state of affairs. Such a state of human affairs existed in the past, exists today, and may exist in the future,

taking the form of jahiliyya, that mirror-image and sword enemy of Islam. In any time and place human beings face that clear-cut choice: either to observe the Law of Allah in its entirety, or to apply laws laid down by man of one sort or another. In the latter case, they are in a state of jahiliyya. Man is at the crossroads and that is the choice: Islam or jahiliyya. Modern-style jahiliyya in the industrialized societies of Europe and America is essentially similar to the old-time jahiliyya in pagan and nomadic Arabia. For in both systems, man is under the dominion of man rather than Allah.[15]

Qutb brought together Mawdudi's "modern jahiliyya" and Ibn Taymiyya's argument that the unity of God requires that Muslims follow divine law, creating a synthesis that reinforced the stark distinction between the Party of God and the Party of Satan: all those who do not put faith into action through an Islamic legal system and strictly obey the commands of God are part of the modern jahiliyya and no longer Muslims. In the Middle Eastern context, this meant apostasy because most members of the "jahiliyya community" were born Muslims.

Qutb's solution to the modern jahiliyya, however, was a stark departure from Mawdudi, who sought to work within the system. Whereas Mawdudi formed a political party and social movement to promote reform, Qutb advocated jihad to establish an Islamic state. In doing so, he argued against well-established Islamic legal opinions that jihad was primarily a struggle against the soul (*jihad al-nafs*) or a defensive war to protect the Muslim community. In a kind of Islamic liberation theology, he argued that force was necessary to remove the chains of oppression so that Islamic truth could predominate. Even more importantly, because the rulers in the Muslim world used non-Islamic legal codes, they were part of the modern jahiliyya and therefore not real Muslims. As infidels, they could be fought and removed from power, because the primary objective of Muslims is to establish God's rule on earth (divine *hukm*).

Qutb's argument found its most infamous manifestation in Mohammed al-Faraj's *The Neglected Duty*.[16] Faraj was a member of Islamic Jihad and used the book as a kind of internal discussion paper to explain and defend the group's ideology.[17] The book uses several lines of argument that have become staples of jihadi discourse. First, Faraj draws on Ibn Taymiyya to argue for the centrality of jihad in faith. He uses an assortment of quotes and hadiths (stories about the Prophet) in an effort to demonstrate that "jihad is second only to belief" in Islam. This is used to elevate the importance of jihad as a "pillar of Islam," a mandatory requirement to be a Muslim. Faraj argues that jihad has become "the neglected duty" (a phrase adopted by today's jihadis), something that must be resurrected as a central pillar of the faith.

Second, he reiterates Qutb's argument that rulers who do not implement Islamic law are unbelievers and must be removed from power. This is based on a Qur'anic verse consistently cited by Al Qaeda: "Whoever does not rule by what God hath sent down—they are unbelievers" (Qur'an 5:48). In making this argument, Faraj turns to Ibn Taymiyya's fatwa against the Mongols (or Tatars). As they conquered Muslim territory, the Mongols converted to Islam, thus raising questions about whether combat against them was a legitimate jihad. Ibn Taymiyya responded by arguing that someone who professes to be a Muslim is no longer a believer if he fails to uphold Islamic law or breaks any number of major injunctions concerning society and behavior. As Johannes Jansen notes, "The list of injunctions he draws is quite long; and it is not altogether clear how many nonapplied injunctions bring the ruler (or the individual believer) to the point of no return. When does he become an apostate to be combated?"[18] For the jihadis, the rationale was clear: the Mongols continued to implement the Yasa code of Genghis Khan and were therefore no longer Muslim because they did not adhere to the unity of worship. Jihadis viewed (and continue to view) this as analogous to contemporary states where rulers have adopted Western legal codes rather than Islamic law alone.

Qutb's influence on Faraj and other Egyptian jihadis is unquestionable. He inspired an assortment of radical groups, including The Islamic Liberation Organization, Takfir wal Hijra (Excommunication and Flight), Salvation from Hell, the Gamiyya Islamiyya (Islamic Group), and Islamic Jihad. He also had an important impact on two Egyptian thinkers who have been critical for the international jihadi movement. The first is Omar Abdul Rahman, the former mufti of Islamic Jihad and the Gamiyya Islamiyya who is currently serving a life sentence for conspiracy to commit terrorism in the United States. As a graduate from al-Azhar University, Rahman had substantial cachet among the radicals inspired by Qutb. Because most of his pronouncements were oral (he is blind), there is little textual data about his views. He did, however, fervidly support Qutb's emphasis on the necessity of God's governance on earth and the use of jihad to remove apostate rulers. Rahman also argued that, "the enemy who is at the forefront of the work against Islam is America and the allies."[19] For many jihadis, Rahman replaced Abdullah Azzam, one of Al Qaeda's founders, as the theological leader of the global jihad after the latter was assassinated in 1989. His incarceration, of course, has diminished this role.

Qutb also dramatically impacted Ayman Zawhiri, Al Qaeda's second in command. In his *Knights under the Prophet's Banner*, Zawahiri calls Qutb "the most prominent theoretician of the fundamentalist movements."[20] For Zawahiri, Qutb's greatest contribution seems to have been that,

> He affirmed that the issue of unification [tawhid] in Islam is important and that the battle between Islam and its enemies is primarily an ideological one over the issue of unification. It is also a battle over to whom authority and power should belong—to God's course and the shari'ah, to man-made laws and material principles, or to those who claim to be intermediaries between the Creator and mankind. . . . This affirmation greatly helped the Islamic movement to know and define its enemies.
>
> Sayyid Qutub's [sic] call for loyalty to God's oneness and to acknowledge God's sole authority and sovereignty was the spark that ignited the Islamic revolution against the enemies of Islam at home and abroad. The bloody chapters of this revolution continue to unfold day after day.[21]

Zawahiri adopted both Qutb's Manichean view of the world and his unwavering desire to establish an Islamic state at any cost, using violence if necessary. This dichotomous struggle for God's sovereignty on earth eliminates the middle ground and sets the stage for a millennial, eschatological battle between good and evil.

Qutb's arguments inform jihadis in other countries as well. Many of his disciples fled Egypt during the massive crackdown by Nasser in the 1960s and moved to Saudi Arabia, where at least a few prominent thinkers took positions as university professors. Sayyid Qutb's brother, Mohammed, is perhaps the best example. In 1964, he published *The Jahiliyya of the Twentieth Century,* which rearticulated Sayyid's arguments (radicals often cite his *Islam: The Misunderstood Religion* as influential as well).[22] Not only did Mohammed Qutb teach Osama bin Laden at university, but he taught some future Islamist dissidents as well, including Safar al-Hawali. The Saudi government tolerated (perhaps even supported) the spread of Qutb's ideology because it coincided with their antipathy toward Nasser and foreign policy objectives vis-à-vis Egypt. Although it is tempting to place all the blame on Sayyid Qutb for the radicalization of Islamism, the Saudis developed their own jihadi intellectual stream through Ibn Wahhab, who remains extremely influential. The Saudi jihadis recognize Qutb as a good Muslim who did good work, but they do not rely on him to the same extent as the Egyptian groups, instead using Ibn Wahhab as their direct pipeline to Ibn Taymiyya,[23] although there is some evidence that Taymiyya was less of an influence on Ibn Wahhab than is conventionally thought.[24]

Ibn Wahhab's most relevant work for the radicals is a small book titled *The Ten Voiders [or Nullifiers] of Islam* (see Table 1), which outlines ten things that automatically expel someone from the religion[25] Three are of particular importance for the jihadis. First, a Muslim becomes a disbeliever if he associates someone or something in worshipping God. During his life, Ibn Wahhab was combating some Islamic practices he viewed as deviant polytheism, such as Sufism. Given the jihadis' emphasis on Ibn Taymiyya's argument about the unity of worship, this "voider" is also used to condemn any ruler who uses non-Islamic law.

Table 1

The ten voiders according to Ibn Wahhab (i.e., automatic apostasy)

1) Polytheism (associating others with God in worship)

2) Using mediators for God (for example, praying to saints)

3) Doubting that non-Muslims are disbelievers

4) Judging by non-Islamic laws and believing these are superior to divine law

5) Hating anything the Prophet Mohammed practiced

6) Mocking Islam or the Prophet Mohammed

7) Using or supporting magic

8) Supporting or helping non-believers against Muslims

9) Believing that someone has the right to stop practicing Islam

10) Turning away from Islam by not studying or practicing it

Second, any Muslim who judges by "other than what God revealed" and believes this is superior to divine law is an apostate. For nonviolent Salafis, the two parts of this "voider" are critical: to be an apostate a ruler must not only implement non-Islamic law but also believe he is using legal means that are better than Islam. Unless the leader flagrantly admits that he has rejected Islam or believes in the supremacy of human-made law (extremely unlikely), he remains a Muslim.[26]

Jihadis, on the other hand, argue that actions are grounds for apostasy. For radicals, there are certain things about Islam that are "known by necessity," such as the ten voiders (some radicals use a much longer list). As a result, if a leader violates one of these, it is evidence of apostasy because he willingly flouts God's will. Like Qutb and the Egyptian radicals, the Saudi jihadis root this argument in Ibn Taymiyya's perspective on the unity of God: it requires both belief in the Creator as well as action (obeying and worshipping God).

Third, supporting or helping nonbelievers against Muslims is apostasy. This one, above all others, seems to have become the central "evidence" used by Al Qaeda to charge regimes in the Muslim world with apostasy. The movement and its supporters continually refer to the same Qur'anic verse: "O you who believe! Take not the Jews and Christians for your friends and protectors [*awliya'*]; they are but friends and protectors to each other" (Qur'an 5:51). It is important to note that there is an important grammatical ambiguity in this verse: it uses the term "wali" (pl. *awliya'*), which is an old Arabic technical term for patron, although in contemporary usage it has developed a broader connotation.[27] The jihadis use an expansive definition of *wali* to include virtually any relationship with non-Muslims.

The jihadis cite, in particular, the Saudi regime's decision to allow American troops in the kingdom to fight Iraq in 1990–1991. This was seen as taking nonbelievers as friends and helping them in a war against other Muslims (though Al Qaeda would never view Saddam Hussein as a Muslim). Bin Laden makes direct reference to this in his 1996 "Declaration of War": "The regime betrayed the Ummah [Muslim community] and joined the Kufr [unbelievers], assisting and helping them against the Muslims. It is well known that this is one of the ten 'voiders' of Islam, deeds of de-Islamisation" (his use of the term "voider" comes from Ibn Wahhab).[28]

The terms "helping" and "supporting" are inherently subjective, and Al Qaeda uses this to create an expansive understanding that includes any kind of support for the United States in its "war on terrorism." Even a word of support is considered apostasy. Take the following statement from a bin Laden tape that emerged in February 2003 as the United States was positioning to invade Iraq:

> We also point out that whosoever supported the United States, including the hypocrites of Iraq or the rulers of Arab countries, those who approved their actions and followed them in this crusade war by fighting with them or providing bases and administrative support, or any form of support, even by words, to kill the Muslims in Iraq, should know that they are apostates and outside the community of Muslims. It is permissible to spill their blood and take their property. God says, "O ye who believe! Take not the Jews and the Christians for your friends and protectors: they are but friends and protectors to each other."[29]

Although it is difficult to verify, it seems that the radicalization of the Saudi Salafis comes from three sources, in addition to Ibn Wahhab himself. First, there were always some radical elements among the Saudi Salafis, what Guido Steinberg refers to as the "radical wing" of the Wahhabiyya. These elements have existed since at least the 1920s and joined the Ikhwan revolts in 1928–1929. Second, Qutb's influence was felt through his books as well as Egyptians working and teaching in Saudi Arabia after the Nasser crackdown against Islamists.[30] Third, there was a radicalization process as a result of the war against the Soviets in Afghanistan. The conflict brought together Egyptians, Saudis, and other nationalities in a conflict zone where they learned about Islam in a context of violence. This period also witnessed the influence of more radical elements coming out of the Deobandi madrasa system in Pakistan. This provided greater opportunity for exposure to the jihadi elements from Egypt and elsewhere, which likely shifted the ideology of some of the Saudi fighters. Prior to that experience, Saudi Salafis were, for the most part, pro-regime, often ferociously so because the regime supported Salafism and helped export it as part of the kingdom's foreign policy. It took Afghanistan to significantly shake that support (exacerbated in the immediate aftermath by the stationing of American troops in Saudi Arabia).

Global Jihad

In Islam, there are two types of external jihad: offensive and defensive. In Islamic juris-prudence, the offensive jihad functions to promote the spread of Islam, enlightenment, and civility to the *dar al-harb* (domain of war). In most contemporary interpretations, the offensive jihad can only be waged under the leadership of the caliph (successor to the Prophet), and it is tempered by truces and various reciprocal agreements between the Islamic state and non-Muslim governments, such as guaranteed freedom of worship for Muslim minorities. Today, very few Islamists focus on this form of jihad.

The defensive jihad (*jihad al-dafa'a*), however, is a widely accepted concept that is analogous to international norms of self-defense and Judeo-Christian just war theory.[31] According to most Islamic scholars, when an outside force invades Muslim territory it is incumbent on all Muslims to wage jihad to protect the faith and the faithful. Mutual protection is seen as a religious obligation intended to ensure the survival of the global Muslim community. At the root of defensive jihad is a theological emphasis on justness, as embodied in chapter 6, verse 151 of the Qur'an: "Do not slay the soul sanctified by God except for just cause." Defending the faith-based community against external aggression is considered a just cause *par excellence.*

Although Muslim scholars almost uniformly agree that a defensive jihad is an obli-gation for Muslims, the issue remained relatively dormant until the Soviet invasion of Afghanistan in 1979. At the time, the majority of scholars had accepted the argument that jihad should focus on the struggle of the soul and inner purification, what has been dubbed "the greater jihad."[32] For the jihadis, the most important objective was to challenge this perspective and inspire participation in the war against the Soviets on behalf of Muslim brothers and sisters in Afghanistan. As a result, much of the writing at this time included extensive exhortations to jihad that outlined both the duty and glory of participation.

In making this argument, jihadis relied extensively on Ibn Taymiyya, whose contri-bution to the ideology of jihad has more to do with the religious and moral elements of jihad rather than legalistic issues related to just war or rules of engagement in combat.[33] In his writings, he argued that, "The command to participate in jihad and the mention of its merits occur innumerable times in the Koran and Sunna. Therefore it is the best voluntary [religious] act that man can perform. All scholars agree that it is better than the hajj (greater pilgrimage) and the *'umra* (lesser pilgrimage) [performed at a time other than the Hajj], than voluntary salat [prayer] and voluntary fasting, as the Koran and Sunna indicate. The Prophet, Peace be upon him, has said: "*The head of the affair is Islam, its central pillar is the salat and its summit is the jihad.' And he has said: 'In Paradise there are a hundred grades with intervals as wide as the distance between the sky and earth. All these God prepared for those who take part in jihad*'."[34] [original italics]

Jihadis also drew extensively from the work of Ibn Nuhaas al-Demyati (d. 1412). In *Advice to Those Who Abstain from Fighting in the Way of Allah,* Ibn Nuhaas methodically addresses the various concerns of those who resist participating in jihad.[35] He touches on fears of death; concern for children, spouses, relatives, friends, social status, and lineage; love for material things; and desire to improve oneself before participating in battle. For each of these, Ibn Nuhaas quotes the Qur'an and Sunna of the Prophet to argue that this life means nothing when compared with the hereafter.

Abdullah Azzam is the most important figure to resurrect active participation in defensive jihad in the contemporary period. Following in the tradition of Ibn Taymiyya and Ibn Nuhaas, parts of his writings are intended to inspire participation. In his *Join the Caravan,* he opens by arguing that, "Anybody who looks into the state of the Muslims today will find that their greatest misfortune is their abandonment of Jihad (due to love of this world and abhorrence of death)."[36] To muster support, Azzam turns to Qur'anic verses consistently cited by Al Qaeda today, such as, "Proscribed for you is fighting, though it be hateful to you. Yet it may happen that you will hate a thing which is better for you; and it may happen that you will love a thing which is worse for you. God knows and you know not" (Qur'an 2:216).

He also makes a more legalistic argument to demonstrate that jihad is an undeniable duty. Azzam uses Ibn Taymiyya's distinction between collective and individual duties (*fard kifayah* and *fard 'ayn*) in Islam. Collective duties are obligations that can be fulfilled by a group of Muslims on behalf of the entire Muslim community. Individual duties are those that each and every Muslim must fulfill to avoid falling into sin. In the context of jihad, Ibn Taymiyya argued that, "jihad is obligatory if it is carried out on our initiative and also if it is waged as defense. If we take the initiative, it is a collective duty [which means that] if it is fulfilled by a sufficient number [of Muslims], the obligation lapses for all others and the merit goes to those who have fulfilled it. . . . But if the enemy wants to attack the Muslims, than repelling him becomes a[n] [individual] duty for all those under attack and for the others in order to help him."[37]

Azzam adopted Ibn Taymiyya's reasoning and argued that if a group of Muslims trying to fulfill a duty to repel aggressors fails to do so alone, it becomes an individual obligation for those nearest the conflict zone:

> Ibn 'Abidin, the Hanafi scholar says, "(Jihad is) fard 'ayn [an individual obligation] when the enemy has attacked any of the Islamic heartland, at which point it becomes fard 'ayn on those close to the enemy. . . . As for those beyond them, at some distance from the enemy, it is fard kifayah [a collective duty] for them unless they are needed. The need arises when those close to the enemy fail to counter the enemy, or if they do not fail but are negligent and fail to perform jihad. In that case it becomes obligatory on those around them—fard 'ayn, just like prayer and fasting, and they may not abandon it. (The circle of people on whom jihad is fard 'ayn expands) until in this way, it becomes compulsory on the entire people of Islam, of the West and the East.[38] (original sentence structure from translation)

According to Azzam, the Afghans could not fulfill the obligation without help from other Muslims: "the jihad is in need of men and the inhabitants of Afghanistan have not met the requirement which is to expel the Disbelievers from Afghanistan. In this case, the communal obligation (fard kifayah) is overturned. It becomes individually obligatory (fard 'ayn) in Afghanistan, and remains so until enough Mujahideen [holy warriors] have gathered to expel the communists in which case it again becomes fard kifayah."[39]

Azzam also argues that this obligation is eternal. In making this claim, he is clearly influenced by Sayyid Qutb and quotes the following passage from Qutb's writing:

> If Jihad had been a transitory phenomenon in the life of the Muslim Ummah, all these sections of the Qur'anic text would not be flooded with this type of verse! Likewise, so much of the sunnah [sic] of the Messenger of Allah (may Allah bless him and grant him peace), would not be occupied with such matters. . . . If Jihad were a passing phenomenon of Islam, the Messenger of Allah (may Allah bless him and grant him peace) would not have said the following words to every Muslim until the Day of Judgment, "Whoever dies neither having fought (in Jihad), nor having made up his mind to do so, dies on a branch of hypocrisy."[40]

So, Azzam concludes, the jihad in Afghanistan is an eternal individual obligation. Under these circumstances, it is elevated to the status of the five pillars of Islam, necessary to be a Muslim. Azzam, like Al Qaeda later, uses a quote from Ibn Taymiyya to emphasize the importance of the defensive jihad as a religious obligation: "As for the occupying enemy who is spoiling the religion and the world, there is nothing more compulsory after faith (iman) than repelling him."[41] Building on this, Azzam argues that, "everyone not performing jihad today is forsaking a duty, just like the one who eats during the days of Ramadan without excuse, or the rich person who withholds the Zakat [religiously obligated charity] from his wealth." This means that, "The obligation of jihad today remains fard 'ayn until the liberation of the last piece of land which was in the hands of Muslims but has been occupied by the Disbelievers" (such as Spain, for example). This argument sets the stage for what Olivier Roy has termed "the nomadic jihad," an eternal struggle to "defend" Muslims from the disbelievers.[42]

The influence on Al Qaeda's current thinking is unmistakable. This is not surprising given that Azzam helped found Al Qaeda and provided the underlying rationale for the movement in an April 1988 article titled "The Solid Base" (al-Qa'ida al-Bulba), published in *al-Jihad*. Various Al Qaeda statements extend Azzam's argument about the obligations of the nomadic jihad to justify attacks against the United States. To apply this argument, however, the jihadis have to demonstrate that the Americans are occupying Muslim land. For bin Laden, this rationale became clear in 1990 after King Fahd ignored his offer to use Afghan war veterans to repel Saddam and instead authorized the presence of American troops in Saudi Arabia. In a 1998 fatwa, bin Laden and several other jihadis argued that, "for over seven years the United States has been occupying the lands of Islam in the holiest of places, the Arabian Peninsula, plundering its riches, dictating to its rulers, humiliating its people, terrorizing its neighbors, and turning its bases in the Peninsula into a spearhead through which to fight the neighboring Muslim peoples. If some people have formerly debated the fact of the occupation, all the people of the Peninsula have now acknowledged it."[43]

In this argument, the jihadis received support from less radical Islamists like Safar al-Hawali and Salman al-Auda, who opposed the American presence. In his 1996 "Declaration of War," for example, bin Laden explicitly references Hawali: "The imprisoned Sheikh Safar al-Hawali, may Allah hasten his release, wrote a book of seventy pages; in it he presented evidence and proof that the presence of the Americans in the Arab Peninsula is a pre-planned military occupation."[44]

Bin Laden and Al Qaeda also found comfort with the oppositional Islamists who signed the Memorandum of Advice in July 1992, which represented an unprecedented public critique of the Saudi regime's domestic and foreign policies.[45] Although many of these oppositional clerics do not support Al Qaeda's tactics and use of violence, their critique of the regime and overall opposition to the U.S. presence in the kingdom provided the fodder bin Laden needed to frame America as an occupying force supported by an un-Islamic regime, thereby justifying a defensive jihad.

The critical need for a defensive posture to legitimize jihad is apparent in Al Qaeda's penchant for framing all its actions as defensive. In a 1998 interview, bin Laden argued that, "We are carrying out the mission of the Prophet Muhammad (peace be upon him). The mission is to spread the word of God, not to indulge in massacring people. We ourselves are the target of killings, destruction, and atrocities. We are only defending ourselves. This is a defensive jihad. We want to defend our people and our land. That is why we say, if we don't get security, the Americans, too, would not get security. This is the simple formula that even an American child can understand. Live and let live."[46]

For most jihadis, this "defensive argument" was absolutely necessary to legitimate 11 September in particular. For example, immediately after the 11 September attacks, Abu Hamza al-Misri, a radical Al Qaeda supporter in London, argued that it "was done in self defense. If they did it for that reason then they are justified." He added that, "If you ask how could it be self defense in doing this in America, it is as much as it was in self defense in Hiroshima."[47]

Killing Civilians[48]

The Qur'an and Sunna of the Prophet Mohammed are replete with enjoinments against killing civilians. Nonviolent Salafis and other Muslims repeatedly emphasize the following pieces of religious evidence to argue for a prohibition against targeting noncombatants:

> We decreed for the Children of Israel that whosoever kills a human being for other than manslaughter or corruption in the earth, it shall be as if he had killed all mankind, and whoso saves the life of one, it shall be as if he had saved the life of all mankind. (Quran 5:32).

> And fight in God's cause against those who wage war against you, but do not transgress, for God loves not the transgressors. (Qur'an 2:190).

> Set out for jihad in the name of Allah and for the sake of Allah. Do not lay hands on the old verging on death, on women, children and babes. Do not steal anything from the booty and collect together all that falls to your lot in the battlefield and do good, for Allah loves the virtuous and the pious. (Sunna of the Prophet Mohammed)

> Stop, O people, that I may give you ten rules for your guidance in the battlefield. Do not commit treachery or deviate from the right path. You must not mutilate dead bodies. Neither kill a child, nor a woman, nor an aged man. Bring no harm to the trees, nor burn them with fire, especially those which are fruitful. Slay not any of the enemy's flock, save for your food. You are likely to pass by people who have devoted their lives to monastic services; leave them alone. (Instructions given by Abu Bakr, the first caliph or successor to the Prophet Muhammad, to a Muslim army setting out to battle against the Byzantine Empire in Syria.)

Although nonviolent Salafis view this kind of religious evidence as a prohibition against *purposely* targeting civilians, they do recognize the possibility of civilian casualties in the course of warfare, considered an acceptable consequence in a legitimate jihad. Islamic fighters must do everything they can to limit noncombatant casualties, but "collateral damage" (to use Western terminology) is often inevitable. This is particularly the case where the enemy uses human shields. Under these circumstances, the Islamic fighters are permitted to attack, and the responsibility for noncombatant deaths lies with the enemy.

From this perspective, only combatants can be targeted. This includes not only soldiers, political leaders responsible for waging war, and intelligence officers, but support staff outside the military and political structure as well, such as advisors who help plan the war. Although they may not be directly involved in actual fighting and combat, support personnel are considered part of the war effort, thereby making them legitimate targets.

The move toward civilian targeting seems to be a recent development with little precedent. Neither Sayyid Qutb nor Ibn Wahhab argued that civilians could be targeted during combat and war, and there was little discussion about the subject until the 1990s. As a result, Al Qaeda has reached directly back to the example of the Prophet and classical and medieval scholars such as Ibn Taymiyya, Ibn Kathir, Ibn al-Qayyim, Shawkani, Ibn al-Qasim, and Ibn Qudamah. Given the vast religious evidence from the Qur'an and Sunna emphasizing the sanctity of life and limiting attacks against noncombatants, Al Qaeda could hardly argue against noncombatant immunity. But it has broken new ground over the past decade or so to develop an expanded understanding about permissible targets in war.

The jihadi debate about civilian targeting began in the mid-1990s in response to the Algerian civil war, which erupted after the regime cancelled Parliamentary elections in January 1992 as it became clear that the Islamic Salvation Front would dominate the new government.[49] Following the coup, Islamist rebels limited attacks to government officials, military personnel, and the police. The scope and tenor of the conflict, however, escalated dramatically in 1993 with the emergence of the Armed Islamic Group (Groupes Islamiques Armé or GIA). Initially, the GIA launched broader attacks against the security services and assassinated junior ministers and members of the National Consultative Council (formed by President Mohammed Boudiaf to provide a democratic façade following the coup).

During this period, there is some evidence that bin Laden and Al Qaeda provided limited support to the GIA through Qamareddin Kharban, the leader of the "Algerian Afghans" (Algerians who had fought in Afghanistan against the Soviets). This included financial support; Al Qaeda fighters sent to Algeria; and theological cover through Al Qaeda-linked scholars like Abu Qatada, who also helped publish and distribute the GIA's *al-Ansar* bulletin (in conjunction with Abu Musab) in London.[50]

This growing relationship changed dramatically in 1996 when Antar Zouabri became the emir of the GIA. He initiated his new leadership position by issuing a fatwa charging the entire society with apostasy and authorizing attacks against any Algerian who refused to join or aid the GIA (including other armed Islamist groups). In this manner, Zouabri took Qutb's Manichean view of the world to an extreme: you are either with the GIA and thus Islamic truth or against it and thus God. The position was summed up in a GIA communiqué posted in an Algiers suburb in 1997: "There is no neutrality in this war we are waging. With the exception of those who are with us, all others are apostates and deserve to die."[51]

The fatwa shifted GIA operations away from the state and toward softer targets in society, eventually leading to widespread civilian massacres. Whereas civilians comprised only 10% of the casualties in 1992, by 1997 this figure rose to 84%.[52] Thousands were massacred. Ordinary citizens were maimed, decapitated, and burned alive. According to GIA chief Abou el-Moudhir, all of these people "have become the enemies of our fighters, from the youngest of their children to the oldest of their elderly."[53] Although there is some evidence of possible regime complicity in a few attacks, the GIA claimed responsibility for most of them.

The underlying justification for the massacres portended the later Al Qaeda justification for 11 September and purposeful civilian targeting: individuals who support the government act as surrogates and representatives of the enemy; they are thus legitimate targets. Take the GIA's rationale for attacking journalists and editors:

> The rotten apostate regime did not stop using the mercenary media to cover its crimes and rationalize its aggression. This has turned all written, seen, and heard media outlets into a tool of aggression spreading lies and rumors. It would have been an obligation for these writers to stand with their nation in these hard times and embrace the blessed jihad, but instead they have turned their pens into swords defending the low lives of apostasy and treason. Based on that, mujahidin consider every reporter and journalist working for radio and television as no different than regime apostates. GIA calls on every reporter working there to immediately stop work, otherwise the group will continue hitting hard those who do not comply. Whoever fights us with the pen will be fought with the sword.[54]

In other words, "civilian" journalists and editors were no longer noncombatants because they served the interest of the government.

The same kind of reasoning was used to attack teachers and school children: by attending government-controlled schools, they signaled support for the regime. In a statement published in the Arabic daily *al-Hayat,* the GIA warned that those who "continue their studies are helping the tyrant to ensure stability and thereby are not accomplishing the jihad." They are considered heretics and deserve death.[55]

More broadly, the GIA argued that any Algerian who did not support the GIA was tacitly supporting the regime, thereby removing their noncombatant immunity. The menu of legitimate targets was thus expanded to include almost the entire society.

The massacres sparked a debate within international jihadi circles. Supporters were frustrated by the GIA's apparent unwillingness to elaborate on the religious justification for their attacks. Some supporters initially denied GIA involvement, dismissing such claims as government propaganda (Abu Hamza al-Misri is a case in point, although he eventually withdrew his support for the movement in 1997). But when it became clear that Algerian jihadis were involved, there was widespread condemnation and opposition from the international jihadi network. Abu Qatada, considered the GIA's mufti, withdrew his support as a direct response to the massacres.[56] Allegedly dismayed by the un-Islamic nature of the massacres, bin Laden provided support for the rival GSPC (Groupe Salafiste pour la Predication et le Combat, Salafi Group for Combat and Propagation) led by former GIA emir Hassan Hattab. Zouabri became increasingly isolated and the GIA disintegrated into rival factions. He was eventually killed in February 2002.[57]

The primary concern for bin Laden and the international jihadis seems to have been that the targets were Muslims rather than infidels. According to Islamic law, Muslims cannot kill other Muslims, except under very stringent conditions (such as banditry, but even then there are restrictions). The idea of using *takfir* against such a broad portion of the population was rejected by the international jihadis. For Al Qaeda, killing apostate government officials is one thing; attacking ordinary Muslim citizens is entirely different because they have been led astray by the regime and its battalion of state clerics, who purposely obfuscate and hide Islamic truth from the people. The massacres also threatened Al Qaeda's strategy to win the hearts and minds of Muslims in its battle against the United States and its "puppets."[58]

Emerging from the debate about civilian targeting in Algeria, Al Qaeda began sharpening its position in the late 1990s with support from a consortium of contemporary scholars. The movement uniformly rejected targeting Muslim civilians, unless they assisted the infidel (in which case they were no longer Muslims in any event). It also displayed great sensitivity to concerns that Muslims could be caught in the crossfire, arguing that Muslims should not mix with non-Muslims and should stay away from potential targets. Those who are killed inadvertently are considered martyrs for the cause, and blood money should be paid to the families. This argument about blood payment appears to have come from Ayman Zawhiri, who offered this solution after members of Islamic Jihad inadvertently killed a young child during an attack against Prime Minister Atif Sidqi's motorcade in Egypt in 1993.[59] This was also the solution offered for Muslims killed in the 11 September attacks.[60]

The jihadis predominantly use two lines of argument to justify targeting non-Muslim civilians (see also Table 2). First, they use a "doctrine of proportional response." Although accepting the general prohibition against killing noncombatants, the jihadis consistently draw on Ibn al-Qayyim, al-Shawkani, al-Qurtubi, Ibn Taymiyya, and others to argue that when the infidel kills Muslim civilians it becomes permissible to attack their civilians in kind. This is supported by Qur'an 2:194: "And one who attacks you, attack him in like manner as he attacked you." In his *Shadow of the Lances,* Al Qaeda spokesman Suleiman Abu Gheith argues that, "Anyone who peruses these sources reaches a single conclusion: The sages have agreed that reciprocal punishment to which the verses refer is not limited to a specific instance. It is a valid rule for punishments for infidels, for the licentious Muslims, and for oppressors."[61] In other words, if the enemy uses tactics that are prohibited according to Islam, these tactics become legal for Muslims.

Table 2

Conditions for killing civilians according to Al Qaeda (only one condition is necessary)

1) The enemy has purposefully killed Muslim civilians*

2) Civilians have assisted the enemy in "deed, word, or mind"*

3) Islamic fighters cannot distinguish between combatants and non-combatants

4) There is a need to burn enemy strongholds or fields where there are civilians

5) Heavy weaponry needs to be used

6) The enemy uses civilians as human shields

7) The enemy violates a treaty with the Muslims and civilians must be killed as a lesson

* These are the most often cited conditions.

To make the doctrine of proportional response operable against Americans, the jihadis have to demonstrate that the United States is purposely targeting Muslim civilians. It does so by citing a number of conflicts involving the United States in which civilians have been killed, including Afghanistan and Iraq, among others. Without actually demonstrating intent, which is critical for the use of the proportionality doctrine, the radicals conclude that the United States has strategically killed Muslims to terrorize the Islamic nation (umma). It makes this argument with particular emphasis on the Palestinian territories (and unwavering American support for Israel), in effect tapping into the widespread sense of despair felt by millions of Muslims exposed to the images of children and other civilians killed during confrontations with Israeli soldiers. In the justification for 11 September, Al Qaeda argues that,

> There currently exists an extermination effort against the Islamic peoples that has America's blessing, not just by virtue of its effective cooperation, but by America's activity. The best witness to this is what is happening with the full knowledge of the world in the Palestinian cities of Jenin, Nablus, Ramallah, and elsewhere. Every day, all can follow the atrocious slaughter going on there with American support that is aimed at children, women, and the elderly. Are Muslims not permitted to respond in the same way and kill those among the Americans who are like the Muslims they are killing? Certainly! By Allah, it is truly a right for Muslims.[62]

For Al Qaeda, the evidence points to a clear conclusion:

> It is allowed for Muslims to kill protected ones among unbelievers as an act of reciprocity. If the unbelievers have targeted Muslim women, children, and elderly, it is permissible for Muslims to respond in kind and kill those similar to those whom the unbelievers killed.[63]

For Suleiman Abu Gheith, the sheer volume of Muslims killed by the United States means that Muslims have the right to kill four million Americans in order to reach parity.[64]

Al Qaeda's use of the doctrine of proportional response hinges on its interpretation of U.S. intentions: are American troops purposely targeting civilians? If the answer is yes, even nonviolent Salafis would agree that it is permissible to target American civilians. If the answer is no, then Muslims are limited by religious edicts against killing women, children, the elderly and other noncombatants. Bombarded by images of young, stone-throwing boys shot by Israeli soldiers, most Muslims accept the argument that Israel purposely targets civilians. Increasingly, many have also come to believe that the United States is doing the same. Some argue, for example, that U.S. technology is so effective that the only way civilians can be killed is if American troops target them. Al Qaeda thus plays into widespread frustration and apprehension about American military power and the "collateral damage" of war.

The second major line of argument builds on Ibn Taymiyya, who argued that, "Since lawful warfare is essentially jihad and since its aim is that the religion is God's entirely and God's word is uppermost, therefore, according to all Muslims, those who stand in the way of this aim must be fought. As for those who cannot offer resistance or cannot fight, such as women, children, monks, old people, the blind, the handicapped and their likes, they shall not be killed, unless they actually fight with words [e.g., propaganda] and acts [e.g., spying or otherwise assisting in the warfare]."[65] This defines enemy populations in terms of their capacity to fight, in effect introducing subjectivity into the definition of "civilian."

The jihadis argue that anyone who assists the enemy in any way loses the protection of noncombatant status: "It is allowed for Muslims to kill protected ones among unbelievers on the condition that the protected ones have assisted in combat, whether in deed, word, mind, or any other form of assistance, according to the prophetic command." Perhaps the most oft-cited piece of evidence for this line of argument is a story about Duraid Ibn al-Simma, a well-known Arab poet who strongly opposed Mohammed and the message of Islam. According to tradition, he was brought to the battlefield to advise the Hawazin troops about battle procedures in a conflict against the Muslims. As a very old man, he posed no physical threat to the Muslim forces, but the intelligence he provided to the enemy made him a target and led to his death in battle.[66]

Although even nonviolent Salafis agree that individuals who directly assist combat through advice in war planning or other supportive functions are legitimate targets, Al Qaeda uses the subjectivity inherent in the "capacity to fight" threshold to dramatically broaden the menu of legitimate targets. Anyone the movement itself deems as supporting the "war against Islam" is fair game, including NGOs, journalists, academics, government consultants, and businesses.

The most important new line of thinking, without precedent in Islamic law, is the jihadi argument about personal and individual culpability in a democracy. This argument is best represented in a fatwa about 11 September issued by Hammoud al-Uqla al-Shuaybi, considered the godfather of the Saudi jihadis. In the fatwa, al-Uqla argues that:

> [W]e should know that whatever decision the non-Muslim state, America, takes—especially critical decisions which involve war—it is taken based on opinion poll and/or voting within the House of Representatives and Senate, which represent directly, the exact opinion of the people they represent—the people of America—through their representatives in the Parliament [Congress]. Based on this, any American who voted for war is like a fighter, or at least a supporter.[67]

In addition to citing Ibn Taymiyya's stance vis-à-vis the capacity of the enemy population to fight, al-Uqla also cites another ruling in which Ibn Taymiyya argued that Christians could be fought because "they assisted the enemies of the Muslims against them, and helped them with their wealth and weapons, despite the fact that they did not fight us." Al-Uqla's perspective has influenced some of his more radical jihadi students, including Ali bin Khudayr al-Khudayr, Nasir Hamad al-Fahd, and Suleiman Alwan. Alwan and al-Khudayr issued fatwas after 11 September saying that anyone who assisted the United States was an apostate. Al-Fahd issued a fatwa supporting the use of weapons of mass destruction.

This kind of argument is replicated in several Al Qaeda publications. In its justification for 11 September, the movement reasons that because a democratically elected government reflects the will of the people, a war against Islam of this magnitude must have popular support. Using the term "public opinion" (*al-ra'y al-'amm*) to represent the will of the people in a democracy, Al Qaeda argues that,

> It is stupidity for a Muslim to think that the Crusader-Zionist public opinion which backs its government was waiting for some action from Muslims in order to support the Crusader war against Islam and thereby enkindle a spirit of hostility against Islam and Muslims. The Crusader-Zionist public opinion has expended all it has in order to stand behind the nations of the cross, executing their war against Islam and Muslims

from the beginning of the colonization of Islamic countries until the present day. If the successive Crusader-Zionist governments had not received support from their people, their war against Islam and Muslims would not have taken such an obvious and conspicuous form. It is something that would not attain legitimacy except by the voices of the people.[68]

Abd al Aziz bin Saleh al-Jarbu, author of *Basing the Religious Legitimacy of Destroying America,* recounts a story in which the Prophet ordered his followers to kill a woman because she sang songs to inspire the enemy warriors. "If this was the decree against anyone who sang songs of vituperation against the Messenger," he reasoned, "then it is all the more a decree against those who to this added participating in a vote approving massacres of Muslims and against those who spread shame and prostitution to Islam and the Muslims."[69]

Obviously Ibn Taymiyya did not discuss the culpability of individuals in a democracy because this was not a medieval or classical issue. The jihadis have transmogrified his line of argument and a well-established principle in Islamic jurisprudence that those who assist in combat, even if they are not soldiers, are legitimate targets. By declaring all Americans personally responsible simply because they live in a democracy, Al Qaeda has manipulated the subjective nature of defining "the capacity to fight" to justify widescale attacks on non-combatants.

Although GIA emir Zouabri was never considered a theological luminary and had little direct influence on theological debates about civilian targeting, his rationale for the massacres in Algeria runs throughout Al Qaeda's justification for 11 September. In both cases, the definition of "civilian" was stretched to include broad swathes of the population. So whereas Al Qaeda may have objected to killing Muslim civilians in Algeria, its logic for killing non-Muslim civilians mirrors Zouabri's reasoning.

Suicide Bombings

Like civilian targeting, the issue of suicide bombings or "martyrdom operations" is relatively recent. The use of suicide bombings by Muslims began in Lebanon and was popularized by Hizballah. Tactically speaking, this influenced Palestinian groups. Theologically speaking, however, it is unlikely that Hizballah directly influenced Al Qaeda and the Sunni jihadis because its arguments derived from Shi'ite traditions of martyrdom (and it focused on military and political targets). The real debate about the religious permissibility of these kinds of operations among Salafis, in fact, did not emerge until the mid-1990s and was a response to its widespread usage by Hamas and other Palestinian factions.

What is interesting about the current jihadi arguments about suicide bombings is how little attention seems to be given to constructing a theological argument justifying such attacks. Instead, the vast majority of materials focus on extolling the virtues of martyrdom. Abdullah Azzam's *Virtues of Martyrdom in the Path of Allah* is a classic example.[70] In it, he elaborates twenty-seven points of evidence about the benefits of martyrdom. Most writings argue that the martyr has a seat in Paradise, avoids the torture of the grave, marries seventy black eyed virgins, and can advocate on behalf of seventy relatives so that they too might reach Paradise. Scholars from all ideological persuasions agree about the virtues of martyrdom.

Since the 1990s, Al Qaeda and the jihadis have been forced to address two central questions. First, are martyrdom operations suicide? This is critical because Islam explicitly prohibits suicide. Some of the more senior Salafi clerics in Saudi Arabia have argued that these attacks are prohibited. Muhammad Bin Salih Bin Uthaymin (d. 2000), for example, argues that, "as for what some people do regarding activities of suicide, tying explosives to themselves and then approaching disbelievers and detonating amongst them, then this is a case of suicide. . . . So whoever commits suicide then he will be considered eternally to Hell-Fire, remaining there forever."[71] In making this condemnation, the focus is on the *act* itself: consciously killing oneself.

The jihadis, however, focus on the *intent* of the perpetrator. Although he is not as radical as Al Qaeda, Yusuf al-Qaradawi outlines the basic reasoning:

> He who commits suicide kills himself for his own benefit, while he who commits martyrdom sacrifices himself for the sake of his religion and his nation. While someone who commits suicide has lost hope with himself and with the spirit of Allah, the *Mujahid* [holy warrior] is full of hope with regard to Allah's spirit and mercy. He fights his enemy and the enemy of Allah with this new weapon, which destiny has put in the hands of the weak, so that they would fight against the evil of the strong and arrogant. The *Mujahid* becomes a "human bomb" that blows up at a specific place and time, in the midst of the enemies of Allah and the homeland, leaving them helpless in the face of the brave *Shahid* [martyr] who . . . sold his soul to Allah, and sought the *Shahada* [Martyrdom] for the sake of Allah.[72]

Here Al Qaeda shares its view of suicide bombings as legitimate martyrdom operations with less radical, conservative Sunnis. This includes not only figures like al-Qaradawi, but also Mohammed Sayyed Tantawi, the Sheikh of al-Azhar in Egypt.[73] The jihadis thus find ample support among Muslims for the *tactic* itself.

The second question is related to targeting. Can Islamic fighters kill civilians in "martyrdom operations"? Much of the jihadi argument in answering this question is based on its justification for killing civilians in general, outlined in the previous section of this article: it challenges mainstream definitions of "innocent civilians" to include anyone who assists the enemy in "word, deed, or mind," an extremely expansive category. Its reliance on this line of reasoning stems from widespread opposition to killing civilians, even in suicide bombings. Although someone like Tantawi may support suicide bombings in principle, he and others object to killing civilians in the process. Even Muhammed al-Maqdisi, an extreme jihadi Salafi in Jordan, has cautioned against civilian targeting, although noting that in some contexts the Islamic fighters may not be able to distinguish between combatants and noncombatants.[74] From this perspective, collateral damage is permissible but should be avoided where possible.

It is because of the general consensus that Muslims cannot purposely target civilians that Al Qaeda and others must emphasize that alleged "civilians" are not really noncombatants. In the context of Israel, for example, al-Qaradawi and the jihadis frame Israel as a militarized country. Because there is mandatory military service for men and women (and reserve service after that), all men and women become legitimate targets in martyrdom operations. Some more radical elements argue that because children will one day grow up and serve in the Israeli army, they too are legitimate targets. Regardless of the nuances, Al Qaeda is careful to frame the targets of the attacks as combatants through deeds, words, and thoughts.

Conclusion and Future Prospects

The development of jihadi thought is characterized by the erosion of critical constraints used to limit warfare and violence in classical Islam. Whereas most Islamic scholars throughout history have defined apostates as those who clearly leave the faith by declaring themselves non-Muslims or rejecting key tenets of Islam (prayer, the prophethood of Mohammed, monotheism, etc.), jihadis claim that any leader who does not implement and follow Islamic law (as they understand it) is an apostate. Whereas most scholars reject violent uprisings to remove rulers so long as they allow the prayer and have "a mustard seed of faith," jihadis believe it is a divine duty to wage jihad against rulers who refuse to implement the radicals' interpretation of Islamic law. Whereas there is a general acceptance throughout Islamic history that civilians should not be targeted in war, Al Qaeda has defined the term "civilian" in such a way as to make everyone living in a Western democracy subject to attack (reinforced by a doctrine of proportional response that requires Muslims to kill millions of Americans). And although there is broad support for the use of suicide bombings, Al Qaeda has expanded its use to encompass attacks on ordinary civilians in Western countries rather than just military or political targets.

This trajectory indicates that the jihadis will attack increasingly wider categories of people. This is already being witnessed with regard to the Shi'ite community in Pakistan and Saudi Arabia (and to some extent Iraq because of Zarqawi's intention to seed discord between Sunnis and Shi'ites). A number of radicals declared their intention to kill Shi'ites in the early 1990s, and this has become an increasingly common position.[75] More attacks might also be expected against others in the Sunni community, in addition to state officials and government personnel.

However it plays out, the historical development of jihadi thought has been one of increasingly expansive violence, not one of limitations. In the end, this may erode popular support for Al Qaeda, as increased violence did to the GIA in Algeria, but in the meantime more groups of people will likely find themselves on the jihadi list of legitimate targets. Given the jihadi argument about proportional response and intentions to acquire weapons of mass destruction, attacks may become increasingly deadly as well.

Quintan Wiktorowicz is the author of *Radical Islam Rising: Muslim Extremism in the West; The Management of Islamic Activism: Salafis, the Muslim Brotherhood, and State Power in Jordan; Global Jihad: Understanding September 11;* and numerous articles and book chapters on radical Islamic groups in Jordan, Egypt, Algeria, and Europe.

Notes

1. Those typically called "Wahhabis" reject the term because it suggests that they follow Ibn Wahhab, a person, rather than God. This, for conservative Muslims, would be tantamount to apostasy. They instead use the term "Salafi." For more on Salafis, see Quintan Wiktorowicz, *The Management of Islamic Activism: Salafis, the Muslim Brotherhood, and State Power in Jordan* (Albany: State University of New York Press, 2001), chapter four; Marc Sageman, *Understanding Terror Networks* (Philadelphia: University of Pennsylvania Press, 2004).
2. See Quintan Wiktorowicz, "The New Global Threat: Transnational Salafis and Jihad," *Middle East Policy* 8(4) (December 2001), pp. 18–38; Michael Doran, "Somebody Else's Civil War," *Foreign Affairs* 81(1) (January/February 2002), pp. 22–42.

3. For the first fatwa on weapons of mass destruction, see the analysis of Sheikh Naser bin Hamad al-Fahd's fatwa, issued on 21 May 2003, by Reuven Paz, "YES to WMD: The First Islamist Fatwah on the Use of Weapons of Mass Destruction," *Prism Special Dispatches* 1(1) (May 2003), available at ⟨http://www.e-prism.org/images/PRISM%20Special%20dispatch%20no%201.doc⟩.

4. *Al-Musawwar,* 21 June 2002, pp. 4–22, in FBIS-NES-2002-0625.

5. Ibid.

6. From quotes provided at ⟨http://tariq.bitshop.com/misconceptions/fatwas/prohibition.htm⟩. These are the standard kinds of evidence used by nonviolent Salafis.

7. *Sahih Bukhari* 8, p. 73; 8, p. 126.

8. For the mainstream Salafi perspective on these issues and others (translated into English), see various publications at ⟨www.salafipublications.com⟩. The website is well known among Salafis as supporting the Saudi religious establishment, which is tied to the Saudi regime.

9. Email from Juan Cole, 25 March 2003.

10. Ibid.

11. For Mawdudi's perspective, see Charles J. Adams, "Mawdudi and the Islamic State," in *Voices of Resurgent Islam,* edited by John L. Esposito (Oxford: Oxford University Press, 1983), pp. 99–133; and Seyyed Vali Reza Nasr, *Mawdudi & the Making of Islamic Revivalism* (Oxford: Oxford University Press, 1995). Mawdudi's most important works are readily available online. For example, see ⟨http://www.masmn.org/Books/⟩.

12. For more on the Jamaat-i-Islami, see Seyyed Vali Nasr, *The Vanguard of the Islamic Revolution: The Jama'at-I Islami of Pakistan* (Berkeley: University of California Press, 1994).

13. For Sayyid Qutb's ideology, see Yvonne Y. Haddad, "Sayyid Qutb: Ideologue of Islamic Revival," in *Voices of Resurgent Islam,* edited by John L. Esposito (Oxford: Oxford University Press, 1983), pp. 67–98; Ahmad S. Moussalli, *Radical Islamic Fundamentalism: The Ideological and Political Discourse of Sayyid Qutb* (Syracuse: Syracuse University Press, 1994); Ibrahim M. Abu-Rabi, *Intellectual Origins of Islamic Resurgence in the Modern Arab World* (Albany: State University Of New York Press, 1995); and William E. Shepard, *Sayyid Qutb and Islamic Activism: A Translation and Critical Analysis of Social Justice in Islam* (London: Brill, 1996). For his influence on radical jihadis in particular, see Emmanuel Sivan, *Radical Islam: Medieval Theology and Modern Politics* (New Haven: Yale University Press, 1985), Gilles Kepel, *Muslim Extremism in Egypt: The Prophet and Pharaoh,* trans. Jon Rothschild (Berkeley: University of California Press, 1993); Sageman, *Understanding Terror Networks,* chapter one.

14. Sivan, *Radical Islam,* p. 28.

15. As quoted in Sivan, *Radical Islam,* pp. 23–24.

16. Faraj's tract is translated in Johannes J.G. Jansen, *The Neglected Duty: The Creed of Sadat's Assassins and Islamic Resurgence in the Middle East* (New York: MacMillian Publishing Company, 1986). Also, see Kepel, *Muslim Extremism,* chapter seven.

17. Jansen, *The Neglected Duty,* p. 6.

18. Ibid., p. 97.

19. As quoted in Malika Zeghal, "Religion and Politics in Egypt: The Ulema of al-Azhar, Radical Islam, and the State (1952–1994)," *International Journal of Middle East Studies* 31(3) (August 1999), p. 395.

20. From *al-Sharq al-Awsat* published extracts of Ayman Zawahiri's *Knights under the Prophet's Banner,* FBIS-NES-2002-108, available at ⟨www.fas.org/irp/world/para/ayman_bk.html⟩. Qutb's influence on Zawahiri is corroborated in Montasser al-Zayyat, *The Road to Al Qaeda: The Story of Bin Laden's Right-Hand Man,* trans. Ahmed Fekry, edited by Sara Nimis (London: Pluto Press, 2004). Al-Zayyat has acted as the lawyer for a number of radical jihadis in Egypt and is well placed in the jihadi community, although many now view him as a security agent because of his central role in developing a nonviolent ideology among jihadis.

21. From *al-Sharq al-Awsat* published extracts of Ayman Zawahiri's *Knights under the Prophet's Banner,* FBIS-NES-2002-108, available at ⟨www.fas.org/irp/world/para/ayman_bk.html⟩.

22. *Islam: The Misunderstood Religion* is published by New Era publications and is available at ⟨www.barnesandnoble.com⟩.

23. Michael Doran made this observation in an e-mail. For more on Ibn Wahhab's ideology and influence, see Natana J. DeLong-Bas, *Wahhabi Islam: From Revival and Reform to Global Jihad* (Oxford: Oxford University Press, 2004).
24. DeLong-Bas, *Wahhabi Islam*.
25. See (http://www.islambasics.com/view.php?bkID=64).
26. See various publications on the topic at www.salafipublications.com
27. E-mail from Juan Cole, 12 February 2003.
28. The "Declaration" is available at (http://www.pbs.org/newshour/terrorism/international/fatwa_1996.html).
29. Originally played on *al-Jazeera*. Translated transcript available at (http://news.bbc.co.uk/2/hi/middle_east/2751019.stm).
30. E-mail from Guido Steinberg, 25 March 2003. Also, for those who read German, see Guido Steinberg, *Religion und Staat in Saudi-Arabien. Die Wahhabitischen Gelehrten 1902–1953* (Würzburg: Ergon, 2002).
31. See, for example, John Kelsay and James Turner Johnson, eds., *Just War and Jihad: Historical and Theoretical Perspectives on War and Peace in Western and Islamic Traditions* (New York: Greenwood Press, 1991); and James Turner Johnson, *The Holy War Idea in Western and Islamic Traditions* (University Park, PA: The Pennsylvania State University Press, 1997).
32. Jihadis believe that the story about the Prophet's reference to the "greater jihad" was fabricated.
33. Rudolph Peters, *Jihad in Classical and Modern Islam* (Princeton: Markus Wiener Publishers, 1996), chapter five.
34. Peters, *Jihad*, p. 47.
35. Available at (http://www.islamworld.net/advice_jihad.html).
36. Online version available at (http://www.religioscope.com/info/doc/jihad/azzam_caravan 1_foreword.htm).
37. Peters, *Jihad*, pp. 52–53.
38. Online version available at (http://www.religioscope.com/info/doc/jihad/azzam_caravan_ 4 part2.htm).
39. Online version available at (http://www.religioscope.com/info/doc/jihad/azzam_caravan_ 5 part3.htm).
40. Online version available at (http://www.religioscope.com/info/doc/jihad/azzam_caravan_ 3 part1.htm).
41. Ibid.
42. Olivier Roy, "The Radicalization of Sunni Conservative Fundamentalism," *ISIM Newsletter* No. 2, March 1999. Available online at (http://www.isim.nl/files/newsl_2.pdf).
43. The fatwa is available at (http://www.fas.org/irp/world/para/docs/980223-fatwa.htm).
44. Online version at (http://www.pbs.org/newshour/terrorism/international/fatwa_1996.html).
45. See Mamoun Fandy, *Saudi Arabia and the Politics of Dissent* (New York: Palgrave, 1999); and Gwenn Okruhlik, "Making Conversation Permissible: Islamism and Reform in Saudi Arabia," in *Islamic Activism: A Social Movement Theory Approach,* edited by Quintan Wiktorowicz (Bloomington: Indiana University Press, 2004).
46. As quoted in John Esposito, *Unholy War: Terror in the Name of Islam* (Oxford: Oxford University Press, 2002), p. 24.
47. *London Press Association,* 14 September 2001, FBIS-WEU_2001-0914.
48. For a more elaborate discussion of this, see Quintan Wiktorowicz and John Kaltner, "Killing in the Name of Islam: Al Qaeda's Justification for September 11," *Middle East Policy* 10(2) (Summer 2003), pp. 76–92. The article is available at (http://www.mepc.org/public_asp/journal_vol10/0306_wiktorowiczkaltner.asp).
49. For the ideological struggle in the conflict, see Mohammed Hafez, "Armed Islamist Movements and Political Violence in Algeria," *Middle East Journal* 54(4) (Autumn 2000), pp. 572–592; idem., *Why Muslims Rebel: Repression and Resistance in the Islamic World* (Boulder: Lynne Rienner, 2003), chapter five.

50. Quintan Wiktorowicz, "The GIA and GSPC in Algeria," In *In the Service of Al Qaeda: Radical Islamic Movements,* edited by Magnus Ranstorp (New York: Hurst Publishers and New York University Press, forthcoming).
51. AFP, 21 January 1997, in FBIS-NES-97-013.
52. Calculated by the author using the *Middle East Journal* "Chronology of Events."
53. AFP, 7 August 1997.
54. Armed Islamic Group communiqué issued 16 January 1995.
55. AFP, 6 August 1994, in *Joint Publications Research Service*-TOT-94-034-L.
56. Interview by author with one of Abu Qatada's associates in Jordan, 1997.
57. Wiktorowicz, "The GIA and GSPC."
58. This strategy was discussed by Zawahiri in *Knights under the Prophet's Banner,* FBISNES-2002-108, available at www.fas.org/irp/world/para/ayman_bk.html).
59. Ibid.
60. Translation and original Arabic available at (http://www.mepc.org/public_asp/journal_vol10/0306_wiktorowiczkaltner.asp).
61. MEMRI, "'Why We Fight America': Al-Qa'ida Spokesman Explains September 11 and Declares Intentions to Kill 4 Million Americans with Weapons of Mass Destruction," *Special Dispatch Series—No. 388,* 12 June 2002. Available at (http://www.memri.org/bin/articles.cgi?Page=subjects&Area=jihad&ID=SP38802).
62. Available at (http://www.mepc.org/public_asp/journal_vol10/0306_wiktorowiczkaltner.asp).
63. Available at (http://www.mepc.org/public_asp/journal_vol10/0306_wiktorowiczkaltner.asp).
64. MEMRI, "Why We Fight America."
65. Peters, *Jihad,* p. 49.
66. Wiktorowicz and Kaltner, "Killing in the Name of Islam," p. 88.
67. An English translation of the fatwa was posted at (www.azzam.com) after 11 September. The fatwa was dismissed by reformist Salafis in Saudi Arabia. The Council of Ulema argued that the statement was "not worth adhering to." The council also contested al-Uqla's authority to issue fatwas. See (www.fatwa-online.com/news/0011017_1.htm).
68. Translation and original Arabic available at (http://www.mepc.org/public_asp/journal_vol10/0306_wiktorowiczkaltner.asp).
69. Yigal Carmon, "Contemporary Islamist Ideology Permitting Genocidal Murder," paper presented at the Stockholm International Forum on Preventing Genocide," MEMRI *Special Report—*No. 25, 27 January 2004, available at (http://www.memri.org/bin/articles.cgi?Page=subjects&Area=jihad&ID=SR2504).
70. Available at (http://www.islamicawakening.org/viewarticle.php?articleID=1012&).
71. Available at (www.fatwa-online.com/fataawa/worship/jihaad/jih004/0010915_1.htm). See (www.fatwa-online.com) for additional fatwas along these lines.
72. As quoted in MEMRI, "Debating the Religious, Political and Moral Legitimacy of Suicide Bombings Part 1: The Debate over Religious Legitimacy," *Inquiry and Analysis Series—No. 53,* 2 May 2001. Available at (http://www.memri.org/bin/articles.cgi?Page=subjects&Area=jihad& ID=IA5301).
73. Ibid.
74. Interview with Nida'ul Islam magazine, issue 22, February–March 1998, available at (http://www.islam.org.au/articles/22/maqdisy.htm).
75. See Michael Doran, "The Saudi Paradox," *Foreign Affairs* 83(1) (January/February 2004). Available online at (http://www.foreignaffairs.org/20040101faessay83105/michael-scott-doran/thesaudi-paradox.html).

Emmanuel Sivan

The Clash within Islam

Despite the international terrorist threat from al-Qaeda, some analysts claim that radical Islam is on the wane.[1] We are already, so they say, in the era of post-Islamism. They have a point—provided one considers only the violent, *jihadi* aspect of that broad socio-cultural and political movement that is radical Islam. However, the movement as a whole—which is made up of a plethora of groups, more or less structured, loosely coordinated (at least within the boundaries of individual states), often overlapping—is still vigorous and exercises a measure of influence in various Muslim societies, including on politics. This influence continues, despite the fact that in most places, the movement is unlikely to take power, either by ballots or bullets.

Even the original *jihad* launched by the movement some 50 years ago, against the 'apostate', or secularised regimes in the lands of Islam, is far from over. It did suffer heavy defeats in the late 1990s—the end of the fifth, decade-long wave of Islamic violence, following previous waves in the early 1950s, the mid-1960s, the late 1970s and the early 1980s. Yet, in Algeria the civil war goes on, though on a smaller scale. The Armed Islamic Group (GIA) has been largely exterminated, and the Islamic Salvation Army (AIS) has laid down its arms, but these two groups have been superseded by a new, no less murderous organisation, the Salafi Group for Combat and Propaganda (GSPC), which operates outside the big urban centres. In Egypt, security services remain on alert, despite the fact that the Jama'a Islamiyya has laid down its arms and renounced recourse to violence against fellow Muslims. The other major terror organisation in Egypt, the Jihad, is split between militants abroad, headed by Ayman al-Zawahiri (who joined al-Qaeda), and those on Egyptian soil, many of whom are underground, awaiting the propitious hour to re-launch the *jihad* against the regime. Other Jihad members—mostly those militants in prison—have formally abjured *jihad* against fellow Muslims. Jihad suspects are arrested from time to time, as well as presumed militants of other terror groups such as Takfir wa-Hijra and the Islamic Liberation Party. A state of alert is evident in Morocco and Tunisia, two countries that fear infiltration and overspill of groups from the North African diaspora in France, with or without an al-Qaeda connection. Jordan and the Gulf states are also on high alert. The semi-legal and legal civil-society associations affiliated with radical Islam, where many former terror activists and sympathisers have found refuge, are subject to constant police surveillance and harassment, as well as the occasional arrest and military trial. Though the security services might be over-suspicious, the possibility of a new conflagration of violence cannot be excluded, especially if economic conditions worsen. Causes for economic downturn could include another slump in oil prices, like those in the late 1970s and mid-1980s, which boosted support for the radicals, and the decline in tourism to the Middle East following the 11 September attacks.

Then there are Hamas and Islamic Jihad, which seized control of events in the second Palestinian *intifada*. Although badly bruised, these two groups are continuing the fight against the infidel, Israeli occupation, a fight quite distinct from that of most radicals who fight fellow Muslims in Islamic states. (The other exceptions are the anti-Russian *jihad* in Afghanistan in the 1980s, the Pakistani militants fighting the Indians in Kashmir and some of the Chechen groups fighting the Russian army). Hamas, the more powerful of these two Palestinian groups, is based upon a powerful socio-political movement active within non-governmental organisations (NGOs) and municipal and cultural life. As in other Muslim lands, this movement contributed to the renaissance of civil society, which throughout the Middle East had been greatly enfeebled by populist military regimes (including, in the case of Gaza, the same Nasserist regime that smashed civil society in Egypt in the 1950s).

Social and Cultural Vigour

This essay is concerned with the state of radical Islam within Muslim lands themselves, and therefore does not consider al-Qaeda, a phenomenon of the Muslim diaspora. Almost all the radical Islamic movements, except for the Algerian Salafist Group for Preaching and Combat (GSPC) and perhaps also the Indonesian Jama'a Islamiyya, hold grave reservations about al-Qaeda strategy.[2] Of course, the al-Qaeda dream is that success against the 'far enemies'—the United States and Israel—will rebound into the successful toppling of the 'near enemy', apostate Arab regimes. But this is the dream of an apocalyptic future, a dream most radical Muslims do not share.

This essay also deliberately avoids the term 'political Islam', which has the effect of flattening out the diversity and density of a multi-layered movement. This movement was born of a deep concern that Muslim societies were losing their Islamic essence under the impact of imported modernity. If the radicals, among others, turned to politics—and ultimately, to violent action to seize power—it was because many came to perceive the state as the major modernising agency, controlling education and media. Not all of them made this choice. While many radical Muslims concluded that they had to wrest power from the 'apostate' rulers, whether by force or through the electoral process, others have preferred to create a political or social lobby, or to fall back upon that age-old solution practised by dissident *ulama* (men of religion) as far back as ninth-century Baghdad—creating their own socio-cultural presence within civil society.

Over the last four decades, Islamic radicals vacillated between these options according to the changing local circumstances, often combining two or more at the same time. In periods of ferocious repression, as at present, semi-legal political activity, educational and welfare action have the added merit of serving as a refuge for persecuted militants. The key merits of NGO activity in the eyes of the radicals are, firstly, that it may change the nature of society, moulding hearts and minds, especially of the young, effectively countering government efforts at modernisation. Secondly, it creates networks of grateful clients, a 'counter-society' immune to the secularist credo, and a potential social and political power base oriented towards re-Islamisation. The experience of past periods of repression has proven that it is out of this social base that a future violent outburst might arise. This explains the vigilance of various governments with regard to the *da'wa*—an Islamist term which denotes a combination of propaganda, education, medical and welfare action—and its practitioners. Yet the *da'wa* has an importance beyond that of being a possible cradle for violence. It is bringing about change in many Muslim societies, and sometimes plays a role—albeit indirect—in politics.

The greatest feat of radical Islam is its sheer survival over half a century of ferocious state repression. It has, at the same time, made tremendous inroads into the hearts and minds of Muslims, especially in Arabic-speaking countries. By the early 1970s militant Islamic discourse dominated the public sphere, replacing pan-Arabism and Marxism, and it has maintained this hegemony to the present day. It has influenced gender roles, relations with local Christians (growing erosion of these relations is evident in Egypt, Jordan and Palestine), consumption habits and public mores. Governments in various Islamic countries have succumbed to militant pressure, censoring books, plays and films critical of Islam. The Islamist media—notably audio- and video-cassettes—is growing, and religious activism is becoming a major avenue for venting protest. Young militants engage in grassroots vigilantism against alcohol, pornography and TV satellite dishes, impose Islamic dress codes and monitor the behaviour of non-Islamic tourists. Activists mount court cases and press campaigns against 'permissive' writers and artists, and mobilise mass demonstrations against the rising cost of living or in favour of introducing a constitution.

This success resides, above all, in the strength of voluntary Islamic associations, the backbone of the radical Islamic movement. They carry on the *da'wa* work, create support networks and show that Islamic values can be fully implemented in the modern era. Despite the high turnover rate, due to attrition and police harassment, there is always a large pool of new recruits, mostly young urban males aged 15 to 25. This is to be accounted for, in part, by the organisational genius of the Islamists, who devised an intricate yet elastic structure for its *jama'at* (association), which is decentralised with minimal hierarchy, endowing members with the empowerment they lack and crave in contemporary society. This is a sort of 'enclave', a term devised by anthropologist Mary Douglas, which ensures equality of status among members without hampering decision-making.[3]

Moreover, the Islamists have a knack for tailoring the message to changing circumstances. In the last 15 years or so, the message has been that the failure of the all-providing state in the lands of Islam is due to its moral dissoluteness and secularism. This message appeals to a deeply ingrained cultural tradition connecting private anxieties to public woes. The message falls on ready ears, because the failure of states in Muslim countries is clear. This state failure to provide has been exacerbated by the decline in oil and gas prices, which has impoverished some oil-rich states and also caused the drying up both of Gulf state aid to poor Islamic countries and employment for expatriate 'guest workers' from those countries. For some states, these woes were worsened by the demise of the USSR and the resultant loss of assured East European markets.

The revenue crisis helped the Islamists almost everywhere. Governments responded to the crisis by breaking the unwritten covenant of the 1950s and 1960s, in which subjects relinquished their claims to basic human and civil rights in return for the state providing them with education, health care, employment and subsidies for such necessities as staple foodstuffs, cooking gas and transportation. The poor and the young are suffering the most from these retrenchments. The 'retreating state' creates disgruntled citizens by the legion: university students no longer assured of government jobs; workers barely able to eke out a living, let alone save for a dowry and start a family; masses of rural immigrants who lack such basics as shelter. Radical Islam provides a plausible moral explanation for their predicament. It also furnishes, through the *jama'at,* some of the services curtailed by the state, such as pre-school education and free-of-charge medical clinics.

The inroads made by radical Islamists are not restricted to the lower urban classes. *Jama'at* have sprung up among professional classes, whose higher income and sophistication enable them to act independently. After trying to shape decision-making within their respective professions, such professionals then stake out positions on wider public affairs. Lawyers' associations tend to take a stand in favour of application of the *sharia*—a major plank of the Islamist platform. They also back court cases presented by militants against so-called heretics such as Egyptian scholar Nasr Hamid Abu Zayd, who was condemned for apostasy and ordered to divorce his wife (he has since gone into exile in the Netherlands).

There is a measure of collaboration across borders, thanks not just to the munificence of Saudi princes, but also to religious luminaries, who act as higher legal and moral authorities in other countries. For example, Egyptian Sheikh Yusuf al-Qardawi, who lives in Qatar, serves as supreme mufti for the Palestinian Hamas. Sheikh Ibn Qatada, a Palestinian-Jordanian living in London, is mufti to the Algerian GIA.

Perhaps more important is the osmosis of radical Islamic ideas into the conservative Islamic establishment. Despite the efforts of a few moderate clerics (such as the current rector of al-Azhar University in Cairo, Sheikh Tantawi), the tilt to the right is unmistakable. In the case of al-Azhar, this is due to the action of the Ulama Front group, headed by the firebrand Isma'il al-Habalush, a popular preacher. Habalush and his Front have opposed any liberal amendment of the divorce law, and demanded that a female al-Azhar researcher, Dr Amina al-Nasir, be fired for casting doubt upon the authenticity of a famous *hadith* (oral tradition) proclaiming the innate inferiority of women. They clamoured for the banning of *A Thousand and One Nights,* defined as a lewd book, and for the removal from theatres of the film on the Prophet Muhammad made by the famous filmmaker, Yusuf Shahin. In these and other cases, al-Azhar, which has been empowered by the Egyptian government to wield censorship on matters religious and moral, followed suite, with the Chief Mufti (the rector's second in command) giving full support to radicals. Conservative members of the judiciary take their cues from al-Azhar and tend to interpret moot points of the law by referring to the *sharia,* in a distinctly anti-modernist interpretation.

The same drift towards radical Islamic positions is evident in Algeria, thanks to presence there in the 1980s and early 1990s, as state-appointed head of the establishment, of a major Egyptian radical thinker, Sheikh Muhammad al-Ghazali. The Kuwaiti and Jordanian religious establishments have moved in the same direction. As the institutional *ulama* control religious education in the state system, these men of religion are able to promote openly a sort of indoctrination hostile to pluralism in religious affairs: one-size-fits-all solutions, infused with dogmatic hostility towards modern culture as well as against the West, which is seen to include Japan and Russia.[4]

Political parties that used to be conservative on religious matters, such as the ruling National Democratic Party (NDP) in Egypt, changed course. During the public debate on the Nasir Hamid Abu Zayd affair in 1994–96, the party's religious weekly, *Liwa Al-Islam,* did not publish a single article, editorial or op-ed in support of the scholar. The same holds true for *Aqidati,* the religious organ of the so-called al-Ahrar (Liberal) Party. The radicals' hope is that this gradual infiltration into the elites will ultimately have further political implications. Perhaps, one day, even the army top brass might be won over to the radical cause.

Politics: Against Long Odds

The Turks might need some convincing that political Islam is on the wane, after the landslide victory of the Islamist Justice and Development Party (AKP) in the November 2002 elections. It remains to be seen, of course, how free a rein the AKP government will be allowed by the army, the self-appointed guardian of secularity, and for how long. It also remains to be seen whether the moderate tone—introduced over the last three or four years in the AKP plank by its present leader, Recep Tayyip Erdoghan, a former anti-democratic firebrand—is more than cosmetic. Most seasoned Turkish observers are sceptical.

In Egypt, the Muslim Brotherhood are banned as a political organisation. Were it otherwise, by the estimate of the Al-Ahram Institute for Strategic Studies, the Muslim Brotherhood could win one quarter of the vote. (Currently the Muslim Brotherhood has just 17 deputies, all of whom ran as 'independents', out of 454 in the People's Assembly). The Wasat (centre) Party, founded by younger members of the Muslim Brotherhood and former Jama'a Islamiyya militants who had abjured violence, was likewise refused registration as political party. After a long court battle, it was registered as a 'cultural association', which meant that the regime would tolerate it, much like the Muslim Brotherhood, in a sort of a semi-legal limbo.

None of these three groups offers a persuasive democratic credo. All three have more than dabbled in violence: the AKP in the late 1960s to early 1970s; the Muslim Brotherhood in the 1950s and 1960s; and some Wasat members in the 1980s and 1990s. All of them have come around to a de facto acceptance of the rules of the democratic (or rather semi-democratic) game after crashing against the iron wall of the regime and its mainstay, the army and security services. They have, presumably, cut off all relations with the extremist, violent fringes of radical Islam, but their differences are in method, not in platform. Chastised by repression, long imprisonment and the execution of comrades and torture, they seem to bank on the ballot as the way to power. Still, the ruling regimes are adamant that this is merely a *pro forma* conversion. They point out the denunciation of democracy by Islamist leaders and preachers as a 'poisonous Western import'. They cite Muslim Brotherhood hostility towards the Copts, whom it wants reduced to their age-old status as second-class citizens, or the Muslim Brotherhood position (shared by the AKP, Wasat and the Tunisian Nahda movement) that no right of free speech should be extended to atheists or agnostics. The Nahda has in fact been driven underground under the stringent rule of president Zayn al-Abidin Ali. And the same is true, with a vengeance, for similar movements in Syria and Iraq.

Translating socio-cultural vigour into political presence, let alone influence, is not easy. This represents a real conundrum for radical Islam, given the importance of the state as a major agent of secularisation. The radicals have learnt, from their own bitter experience, the futility of the armed struggle, yet the electoral road into the political process remains blocked. Infiltrating the top bureaucracy and the courts may provide a side entrance, but regimes are vigilant, especially with regard to the army, where periodical purges of 'religious minded' officers are a matter of routine.

Not all regimes practise exclusionary policy towards the radicals. Pakistan, Jordan, Morocco, Yemen, Kuwait, Bahrain and even Algeria follow a line of partial inclusion: granting some, though not all, Islamist groupings legal status and the right to run in elections. However, the regime sees to it that their parliamentary presence is minimised through single-member constituencies with preference given to rural and more docile candidates, as well by gerrymandering, ballot rigging and other such methods. Nevertheless, in September 2002, Pakistan's United Action Front Islamist parties had significant electoral success, garnering a parliamentary contingent trailing just behind the two major parties. Similar success was attained in October 2002 by the Moroccan Justice and Development Party and by the Islamists in Bahrain, both having been allowed to run on a platform calling for application of *sharia* law. This right was not extended, however, to the veteran Moroccan party Al-Adl wa-1-Ihsan (Justice and Charity), whose charismatic leader, Sheikh Abd al-Rahman Yasin, was in jail for years and is currently under house arrest. The Islamic Front in Jordan, the Jama'a Islamiyya (Sunni) and Hizbollah (Shi'ite) in Lebanon, and the Islah (reform) Party in Yemen have been running in elections for years. So has Algeria's Movement for Social Peace. (However, the Islamic Salvation Front [FIS], which won a plurality in the first round of elections in December 1991, prior to the army takeover, remains outlawed.)

Election tampering and limited parliamentary presence are not the only political obstacles faced by Islamist groups. The regimes' policies of semi-inclusion also mean that when these groups enter government, they are usually assigned minor ministries, or their minister is not allowed any budgetary discretion (as was the case in Jordan when the Islamist party was given the Ministry of Education). There is little wonder that Islamists tend to leave office after a while, or stay merely for the sake of the (rather limited) patronage it allows. They have no real results to show for their effort, at least not in what matters most: blocking slippage down the slope of de facto laicisation. Promises to make legislation conform to the *shari'a* are buried in committee. Participation in government tends to discredit Islamist parties in the eyes of their electorate either as a sell-out or as ineffectual, and they lose votes in the following elections—as happened in Jordan in 1993 and Yemen in 1997. The radicals may find solace in government concessions to their cause in education and media, concessions which may slow down the erosion of Islamic values and mores. Yet whether this is attributable to parliamentary activism is doubtful. Islamist parties may also find comfort in the fact that left-wingers are likewise repressed or at least similarly harassed. It is, however, cold comfort indeed to have political life stifled all around. The only (less than meagre) consolation the radicals do enjoy is that they have maintained a hegemonic position among the submerged opposition forces, even where the Left is well organised and active, as in Algeria, Morocco and Lebanon. This is not exactly the 'failure of political Islam' as pronounced by analysts. Hegemonic they might be, but their supposed conversion from *jihad* to *da'wa* is doubted not just by security services, but by the bulk of the secularists and the pragmatic new middle class.

This state of affairs was illustrated during a conference held in Cairo on 8 September 2002, entitled 'The Future of the Islamist Movement in the Aftermath of September 11'. The star of the gathering was the organiser, Muntasir al-Zayat, barrister for many Islamists brought to trial, and close to the fledgling Wasat Party. Zayat argued forcefully that the conversion of the Jama'a Islamiyya from violence to peaceful means (partly through its role in the Wasat) is wholeheartedly sincere and that the organisation wishes to become a pragmatic socio-political movement. Respect for the law of the country they live in is incumbent upon Muslims everywhere, he said, whether in Egypt or in the West. Violence or hatred against Copts must be eschewed. While members of the pro- Muslim Brotherhood Labour party supported from the podium his claim that that warfare against the Mubarak was over, sceptical voices were heard from the floor, mostly from liberal intellectuals. The most powerful challenge came from Nasserist human-rights lawyer Negad al-Bora'i, who cast doubt upon the speakers' renunciation of violence and respect for freedom of expression. 'Where do you stand on democracy and specifically on peaceful transmission of power?' he asked. 'Where do you stand on freedom of belief, particularly the right to change one's religion?'[5] 'These are crucial questions that must be answered with honesty and integrity,' al-Bora'i said.[6] All he received from the Islamist speakers were evasive answers.

The Dilemma of the Middle Class

If the radicals are thus caught between a rock and a hard place, so is the modern middle class which favours broader human and civil rights and the evolution of a participatory polity. Fearful of radical Islam—all the more so given the experience of Islam in power in Iran, Afghanistan and Sudan—the middle classes have had to acquiesce to the dashing of all hopes for democratisation. Even new, younger rulers such as the kings of Jordan and Morocco have made only paltry progress towards democratisation, lest they play into the hands of the radicals, who would benefit from freer debate in the public sphere, greater accountability of the rulers and fair electoral process. The harsher regimentation of political life, which was the response of most regimes to the Islamic threat in the 1990s, has not been alleviated after the defeat of domestic terrorism. The middle class dares not protest too much, viewing this regimentation as a precautionary measure and the lesser evil. 'Hubzism' (from *hubz*, bread) is the term coined in Tunisia for the tacit bargain struck between the middle class and the new president, who seized power in late 1987, a time of mounting Islamist turmoil. The bourgeoisie agreed to harsh repression, which entails heavy-handed restrictions on human and civil rights, not only of Islamists, but also of human-rights activists and other liberals, in return for physical security and political stability. The *hubz* in question goes beyond sheer necessities and includes owning a flat and car. Eighty percent of the new bourgeois possess both. Much like the spectre of Marxism in Latin America in the 1970s and 1980s, radical Islam has the effect of making the soft conservative-liberal centre embrace authoritarian regimes for fear of the alternative.

Even in countries where partial inclusion is the rule, there is no Latin American-style Democracia Pactada with a road map and time table for the transition to democracy. No final target, no stages; all depends upon the goodwill of the powers-that-be. And indeed, in some places, such as Jordan, there has recently been some retreat from the relaxation of political participation. In Morocco, where recent elections were singularly clean, one could nevertheless note a slowing in the pace of reform.

It is an open question whether this blocking of the political channels might not sooner or later push a young cohort of militants to opt once again for violence. The shake-up of a regime under an international crisis (such as a war in Iraq), an economic crisis (due perhaps to another oil slump), or a succession crisis and bloody squabbles among the rulers—all are likely to goad the young towards the same violent option that attracted them in 1964–65, after years of ferocious repression under Nasser; in 1974–77 (in Egypt); in 1981–82 (in Egypt and Syria); in 1987–92 (in Tunisia, Iraq, Algeria and Egypt); and in 1995–97 (in Egypt and Algeria). Another wave of armed revolt cannot be excluded. The security services certainly do not exclude it: watching closely even semi-legal groups of the Muslim Brotherhood type, harassing and making so-called pre-emptive arrests in their ranks.

Is There a Liberal Islamic Alternative?

The clash within Islam—and this is the clash that counts, not the alleged clash of civilisations—is between radical Islam and the powers-that-be. Conservative Islam—for example, Friday and Ramadan preachers on state-sponsored TV stations—supports the governing regime on political matters and radical Islamists on social and cultural matters. Yet what of the liberal Islamic alternative, an 'Enlightened Islam' (*al-Islam al-mustanir*)?

Both the radical and the liberal trends are offshoots of the Salafiyya movement. Born in the last quarter of the nineteenth century, it called for a substantial reform of Islam to end its cultural stagnation and decline, which was seen as the root cause for Islam's lagging behind European civilisation. Reform was to centre around the return to the Salaf al-Salih (the virtuous ancestors). In the glorious early age of Islam, the religion is said to have been flexible, capable of progress and development by relying on rational adaptation to changing circumstances while preserving its essence. It lost this ability somewhere late in the third century of its existence. The aim of the Salafis was to help win back this ability.

As Islam is an orthopraxis (that is, behaviour is given precedence over belief) rather than an orthodoxy, the way to regain Islam's original flexibility, according to the Salafis, was to revitalise law and education rather than theology. The major tool was to be the *ijtihad,* the authority jurists had to amend, even change, the *sharia* by applying personal legal reasoning in evaluating the urgent needs of the Islamic community. Innovation in such matters should not be considered nefarious, as most traditionalist *ulama* held, but beneficial. Ideas to be absorbed into innovation could be indigenous or European, for Islam had taken on great ideas in the Middle Ages (such as Greek philosophy). As far as possible, said the Salafis of the early twentieth century, such borrowing should be made in accordance with the norms of the Salaf al-Salih, as expressed in the rich, pluralistic legal and *hadith* literature. This would assure a measure of control and preserve Islamic identity while at the same time encouraging progress.

This intellectual movement had quite an influence upon the young educated generation, especially in Egypt, Syria and Lebanon, and kept its unity till the eve of the First World War. It is typical that in 1913 the new leader of the Salafiyya, the Syrian Rashid Rida, then living in Egypt, wrote a rave review of a translation made by Ahmad Fathi Zaghloul, brother of the Egyptian nationalist leader Sa'ad Zaghloul, of a book entitled *The Roots of Anglo-Saxon Superiority.* One should learn from the pace-setting civilisation of our era, wrote Rida, and borrow as many of its ideas as possible that are congruent with our identity. The fight against British occupation of Egypt, which he lauded, should not extend to culture. According to Rida, Egyptians had much to learn from the British while flatly rejecting their political rule and claims about the 'White Man's Burden'.

The war years and their immediate aftermath made Rida and many other Salafi militants revise such ideas. The Ottoman Empire, a bulwark of Islamic identity, suffered a crashing defeat, lost most of its territory and was soon to be abrogated by the secular moderniser Kemal Ataturk. Larger chunks of Dar al-Islam (the Islamic world), notably the Fertile Crescent (from whence came Rashid Rida) fell under European domination. Egypt was no more the exception in the Middle East but the rule. Europe showed what Rida and his ilk came to see as its real face—arrogant, domineering and expansionist. For the radical Salafis, it was no longer possible to preserve the distinction between Europe's cultural and political facets, all the more so as the Great War seemed to unveil underlying irrational and destructive streaks in European culture. Could it be that Europe itself was in decline and didn't have much to offer? This doubt was sustained by recently translated writings such as Oswald Spengler's *The Decline of the West*. Spenglerian prophets of doom and gloom, such as Alexis Carrel, Stuart Chamberlain and later, Arnold Toynbee, became best-selling authors in the Arab Middle East during the interwar years.

Yet the major doubt preoccupying the *Al-Manar* trend, named after the weekly newspaper edited by Rida, was internal: are we still Muslims, the radical Salafis came to ask. Could it be that, enfeebled by centuries of decline, Muslims had already surrendered to the temptations of a European civilisation? In line with the liberal Salafis who preserved their hope that Islam and modernity were reconcilable, Rida answered in the affirmative, that most Muslims were no more than 'geographical [nominal] Muslims', following solely external rules of behaviour learnt by rote, devoid of belief and understanding of the rules' significance. They cut corners in ritual and, above all, did not apply the *sharia,* certainly not under foreign rule. In such a state of affairs, the *ijtihad* was still needed, yet it should be more uniform for all Islamic lands, far more controlled. The weak identity of present day Islam was incapable of assimilating too many innovations, and definitely not pluralistic ones. These are the core ideas of radical Islam, striving to build up mental and behavioural siege-walls to defend a beleaguered faith.

The Salafiyya was thus split between radicals and liberals. While the radicals grew in strength, thanks to the Muslim Brotherhood (founded in 1928), the liberals, who claimed allegiance to the Salafi founders, moved further to the left, embracing world culture and progress. Some of them, like Egyptian thinker Taha Hussein, now put early Islam under scrutiny, according to norms learnt from the Western Orientalist scholars, whom Rida saw as enemies of the Faith, burrowing into and sabotaging Islam in the service of missionaries and imperialists. Others, like Ali Abd al-Raziq, an Al-Azhar scholar, raised the question of whether it would be better for Islam to be separate from the state. The Prophet Muhammad, after all, was a spiritual rather than temporal leader, and many of the corrupt despotic caliphs were the ones to blame for the Islamic decline. Others still, like the great jurist al-Sanhuri, less polemical and more constructive, worked assiduously to amend major Egyptian laws in a liberal fashion by creative use of modes of reasoning and devices unearthed in the vast literature produced over the ages by Muslim jurisprudence. New policies, such as equality of women before the law and equal status for minorities, were bandied about. Despite its elitist character and lack of a broad social base (which the Muslim Brotherhood had succeeded in building for the radicals), the liberals wielded a certain influence over intellectual life and over cultural mediators such as high school teachers and journalists.

Like other vital forces of Middle Eastern civil societies, liberal Islam was badly bludgeoned by the militaristic, populist regimes that came to power in the 1950s. These regimes espoused belligerent nationalism, were ferocious in preserving indigenous heritage and were deeply suspicious of any ideas originating in those Western empires it had dislodged. They stood for unity, uniformity and one-man, one-party rule, and sought to manipulate religion to win the populace to their cause. When civil society returned to life in the 1970s, in the context of the 'retreating state' and initiatives by the radical Muslim *jama'at* coming out of the underground, the liberals were slow to emerge. This is to be partly explained by the importance in Arab intellectual and political life of Marxism, which attracted those of the budding intelligentsia who were open to the outside world.

It was in the 1980s, when the decline of Marxism and the populist ideologies of the Nasserist and Ba'athist type became evident—and with some states embracing, at least in theory, the market economy, democracy and pluralism—that a generational mix of liberal Muslim thinkers and polemicists started to come to the fore. This process accelerated in the following decade. Liberal Eygptians worthy of particular mention are: the jurist Muhammad Sa'id; the High Court judge Ashmawi; Husayn Ahmad Amin, a senior diplomat and Islamic scholar (the son of Ahmad Amin, a prominent liberal thinker of the interwar era); Hasan Hanafi, a French-trained philosopher; and Faraj Foda, an agricultural engineer and self-taught Islamic scholar. Another engineer and autodidact, the Syrian Muhamad Shahrur, produced a best-selling study of the Koran and its relevance today. Two brilliant al-Azhar graduates, the Egyptians Muhammad Sayyid al-Qimni and Khalil Abd al-Karim, combined scholarly credentials and polemical ability to great effect in both their journalistic and scholarly articles. The Lebanese Ridwan al-Sayyid, a graduate of al-Azhar and Tubingen University, straddled both worlds of discourse, as did the Abd al-Hamid al-Ansari of Qatar. North Africans soon joined the fray, combining Islamic and French educational backgrounds, among them the Moroccan Abdou Filai-Ansari; and the Tunisians Muhammad Talbi; Muhammad Charfi; and Abdal-Majid Charfi. One could add to the list the now-exiled scholar, Nasr Hamid Abu Zayd.

These fourteen intellectuals do not offer a uniform message. Nevertheless, they all share the overriding aim of Jamal al-Din al-Afghani and Muhammad Abduh, the Salafi founding fathers: an in-depth reform of Islam, to shake this culture out of its torpor and bring it into the modern world. But such a reform, say these intellectuals, would also counteract the deleterious effects of radical Islam. To achieve this dual aim, three preconditions must be met.

First, Islamic heritage should be contextualised, that is, explained and interpreted in terms of the times and places in which it was produced. Following in the footsteps of Taha Hussein and Ahmad Amin, these intellectuals undertook broad and systematic studies of the evolution of law, political and social history, *hadith* and philosophy. These studies produced rich evidence that Islam has been constantly evolving in response to changing circumstances, and that it has encompassed a myriad of variations according to time and place, while maintaining allegiance to a core prophetic message (itself not devoid of stages of internal development and even contradictions). Liberals are convinced that findings to date amply justify a recourse to free, flexible *ijtihad,* seeking pluralistic solutions—not uniform ones, as desired by the radicals—for the variety of situations obtaining in the Islamic world today. Such a broad minded, open-ended *ijtihad* should rely, as far as possible, upon Islam's rich heritage of solutions and devices. Making use of this heritage will serve to ensure that cultural identity is not lost during the process of reform and revitalisation—as both radicals and traditionalists fear. Every generation has the right and duty to make Islam evolve, as was the case in the early days of the Salaf, from the seventh to the ninth century.

Second, Islam should join world civilisation, interact with it and borrow whatever it needs, subject to the cultural filters mentioned above. There is no unbridgeable chasm separating Islam from the more modernised countries, which include not only the West and Russia, but also Japan, South Korea and Malaysia—the latter three being particularly edifying examples of non-European countries achieving modernisation without loss of cultural identity. The radical bogeyman of a worldwide or Western conspiracy to culturally invade Islamic space simply does not exist. By all means, foreign political and economic domination should be opposed—but not foreign cultures. In a world of osmotic media borders, a degree of cultural globalisation is a given. The challenge is how to make globalisation work in favour of an Islamic variation of modernity. What is needed is not slavish imitation of the West, but rather, a selective appropriation of its cultural fare: integration not assimilation; joining the world, to which Muslims have a lot to offer, without being swallowed by it.

Third, Islam has very little to offer in the realm of politics, despite the political obsession of radicals. The state of Muhammad was prophetic, hence unique; not a model for future emulation. After Muhammad's death, political history was shaped by circumstances created by, among other factors, the conquests, the interplay of personal ambitions, the ethnic composition of the armies and economic development (notably, the transition from nomad to urban polity). Islamic thinkers had very little to offer by way of political doctrine. Islamic law had little to say on constitutional matters. Political practice was mostly authoritarian if not despotic. An Islamic state is a mirage, a figment of the radicals' imagination. So is their slogan 'application of the *sharia'*; for not only is the *sharia* not uniform, it also has little to say on economics, certainly not in their present sophisticated version. Its real strength is in matters of ritual and personal status, which do require renovation (for example, on the status of women, which evolved even under the Prophet). The real focus of political reform should be democracy, human and civil rights, tolerance, transparency and accountability in government. This is not to say that there is a specific Islamic precedent. The liberals doubt whether the *shura* (election of the caliph by the notables) can really be deemed a historical justification, let alone a model, for democracy, as radicals and traditionalists claim. This is an area where transcending Islamic heritage is called for. Free debate and popular sovereignty are the *sine qua non* for the revitalisation of society and culture. If Islamic heritage has anything to offer in this respect, it is the form of a history lesson: Islamic decline has always been closely associated with the rise of despotism. Moreover, democracy is congruent with the Islamic value of human dignity.

Liberal Islam has come a long way towards developing a coherent and relevant doctrine. So why are its thinkers so downcast? 'We're nothing but a bunch of dissidents writing on water,' said Husayn Ahmad Amin.[7] And Abd al-Majid Charfi concurred, in another such interview: 'We are always beleaguered; able sometimes to conduct a debate in the public sphere in Paris, but not in Tunis.' Sympathisers of the liberal cause are similarly disenchanted, as one can judge from articles in the Cairo book review monthly *Wujuhat Nazar.*[8]

Beleaguered they are, above all, by their arch-rivals, the radicals. Faraj Foda was assassinated in 1992 by the Jama'a Islamiyya. Soon after, the Nobel Prize-winning novelist

Najib Mahfuz, a strong supporter of the liberals, was stabbed and seriously wounded by a Jama'a militant. Ashmawi was subject to death threats from the Jihad group and had to be barricaded in his flat for months under a government security detail. When, in 1989, Qimni published his trail-blazing book *Al-Hizb Al-Hashemi,* where he ventured into a hitherto taboo area, the life of the Prophet (he interpreted the Prophet's struggle with Mecca in terms of power politics), a leading Islamist spokesman dubbed him 'the Arab Salman Rushdie'.[9] His later books, and those of his associate Khalil Abd al-Karim, who died recently, incurred radical ire for employing their vast erudition in a liberal reading of Islamic heritage.[10] The Azharite Ulama Front strived to have them banned (and failed on a technicality), as it likewise later called for firing female scholar Amina al-Nasir, their acolyte, from her university job. The radical sheikh Yusuf al-Badri lodged the complaint against Abu Zayd and thus launched the proceedings which led ultimately to his going into exile.

Nor do the liberals enjoy official support, unless they are under a clear and present terrorist threat—and even then, not always efficiently. After all, it was two court judgements that condemned Abu Zayd for apostasy. Semi-official censorship has driven Tunisian liberals to publish their books in Casablanca and Paris. Human-rights activists such as Charfi in particular suffered from state oppression. And when the Abu Zayd and later, the Sa'd al-Din Ibrahim affairs broke out, it was the religious weekly of the Egyptian ruling party which wholly supported their conviction. The pressure had a notable muzzling effect, with the exception of Ashmawi, on whom this pressure had the opposite effect, pushing him from a prudent style, as befits a judge, towards assertive polemics.[11] Most liberals tended to buckle under duress. Hanafi explained to the present writer that Abu Zayd brought the calamity upon himself out of sheer obstinacy. He, Hanafi, had advised him not to include his controversial publications on the Koran and Islamic myths in the list presented for his university promotion. Abu Zayd refused. The radical sheikh Yusuf Badri got wind of the affair, lodged his complaint, and the rest is history. Hanafi in fact developed in his writings a cautious, circumlocutory style, designed to not challenge the radicals, but this comes at a price: obfuscating the liberal message. The same is true of Ridwan al Sayyid, master of an abstract, somewhat pedantic style, who never debates directly with the radicals (in his case, the Sunni Jama'a Islamiyya and the Shi'ite Hizbollah), let alone offends them.

Many liberal writers outside Islamic lands, who are not subject to such pressures, similarly dilute their message. A case in point is Islamic scholar and liberal thinker Mohammad Arkoun, an Algerian living in France who has perfected an abstruse and rather pompous prose, sidestepping any polemic against the radicals. He claims he had to operate in such a manner out of fear for the safety of his relatives in Algiers. And indeed very few of the liberals anywhere rallied to support Abu Zayd during his ordeal. In a telling episode in 1996, Qimni appeared on a TV discussion programme (on an Arabic international commercial satellite channel—government TV does not air such contentious material) with fellow liberal Kamal Abu Majd. To Qimni's surprise, Abu Majd justified the condemnation of Abu Zayd on the narrow technical grounds that he was guilty in terms of the *hisba* (control of public morality), under which the affair was tried. However, he dissociated himself from the views of the radical sheikhs that Abu Zayd was guilty of apostasy.[12] No wonder few liberals were active in the defence of Sa'd al-Din Ibrahim, the human-rights activist condemned to seven years in jail for working for fairer elections and for publishing unflattering reports about discrimination against Copts.[13]

Another, perhaps more important self-inflicted wound suffered by liberal Islam is its elitism and lack of organisational skills—the latter being an area in which the radicals excel. Very few liberal spokesmen have the communication abilities to propagate their message effectively. This weakness is especially evident in audio-visual narrowcasting. Of the four hundred or so known 'tape-cassette preachers', none are liberal. The majority are radical, a minority traditionalist. While Amin and Qimni have stellar journalistic and literary qualities, being in demand as columnists for publications such as *Ruz Al-Yusuf, Sutur* and *Al-Qahira,* others are mediocre writers or scholars who publish mostly in learned journals. Rarely does one find a liberal scholar on TV. Few TV historical series are inspired by liberal ideas; a major exception was one on the life of Qasim Amin, an early proponent of women's rights, which was shown in Egypt during Ramadan 2002. Moreover, none of the liberals, at the higher or middle ranks, has organisational abilities and thus their grassroots presence is very thin. No wonder the liberals' mood is bleak. Their chances of becoming a significant opposition force are not promising. The radicals win not just by dint of skill and effort, but *faute de combattants.*

The Exception and the Rule

The situation is different in one Islamic country: Indonesia. In the June 1999 elections, the first democratic contest held since the fall of Suharto, Islamist parties calling for application of the *sharia* won 16%. They were overtaken, however, by the so-called 'pluralist Muslim' parties, which won 22%. These pluralist parties proclaim allegiance to the state's ideology, or civil religion, of Pancasila. Although they use Islamic symbols, they accept a de facto separation of state and religion. (President Megawati Sukarnoputri's Indonesian Democratic Party of Struggle [PDI-P], a secular-nationalist grouping, won a plurality of 34%).

In Indonesia, Islamic radicals do not hold sway. In August 2002, the upper house of parliament rejected by a large majority the Islamist radicals' proposal to amend the constitution and implement the *sharia* for the 88% of Indonesians who are Muslims. The parliamentary majority was made up of PDI-P and pluralist Muslims and enjoyed the strong support of the two largest Muslim education-cum-welfare organisations, Nahdlatul Ulama (NU) and the Muhammadiyah.

During the early years of independence, there was debate between Islamists and the *kebangsaan* (national-secularist) movements about the adoption of the *sharia*. The *Kebangsaan* won and the state adopted an ideology dedicated to 'unity in diversity' and religious pluralism. This was seen as the sole means of holding together a multi-ethnic, multi-religious society. Pancasila respects all five religions of Indonesia, giving none preferential treatment. Suharto worked hard to inculcate this ideology, to fight the Marxist left as well as extremist Muslims. In the mid-1980s, all mass civil society groupings were required to recognise Pancasila as the 'sole foundation' of the Indonesian state. Islamist movements did survive, but mostly as a semi-underground.

While the left was physically eliminated, antagonism between the regime and the Islamists endured. It was in this context that a cultural-political trend arose during the 1970s that offered an Islam-oriented alternative. It was moulded by a new generation of intellectuals calling themselves Neo-Modernist, in reference to the thinking of Fazlur Rahman, a Pakistani liberal who tried and failed to shape the legislative policy of the ruler, Ayyub Khan, and was forced into exile in the US. (The foremost thinker of this group, Nurcholish Madjid, wrote his dissertation at the University of Chicago under Rahman).

The prime concerns of the neo-modernists were the demands of modernity and the particularities of Indonesia. To that end, they argued for what they dubbed 'contextualised *ijtihad*', meaning legal reasoning sensitive to the time and place in which the religious texts they treat were created. Moreover, they claim that the very nature of Islam opposes the intermingling of divine values with the profane domain of politics. Islam does not need to regulate every aspect of life; its role is to provide moral guidelines. No particular type of regime is required by Islam; hence, Islamisation should be a cultural process within civil society. Consequently, the student groups gravitating around these young intellectuals accepted without reservation the Pancasila ideology and its political implications, especially with regard to the non-sectarian and harmonious relations between the various faiths, in the interests of national unity. What began as an elite phenomenon soon gained wide following among the educated young and greatly influenced the moderate Islamic parties which gained ground after the fall of Suharto, culminating in their electoral success in 1999.

This achievement is due, in part, to the personality of its intellectuals: N. Madjid, Abdurrahman Wahid, Harun Nasution, Munwir Syazali and Ahmad Wahib. The movement's ideas also fitted the nation-state ideals unique to Indonesia among Muslim countries: its traditions of pluralism, tolerance and social harmony. The movement's commitment to democracy and human rights during the Suharto years served it well after his fall in 1998. Yet no less significant, since the late 1980s, was the role neomodernism played in revitalising civil society through its development of education and welfare NGOs, often taking up tasks the regime was unable to undertake successfully. Abdurrahman Wahid, leader of the religious mass organisation Nahdlatul Ulama and later, the first democratically elected president, was part of the neo-modernist trend and played a role in creating the new NGOs. These NGOs, together with the Muhammadiyah, the other major mainstream religious movement, played a crucial role in the agitation that led to Suharto's fall.

Last but not least, one must note the particular pluralism of Indonesian Islam. Two-thirds of Muslims are *abangan,* or syncretic, while only a third are *santri,* devout (Sunni) orthodox. The latter tend not to question the Islamic credentials of the former, so as to keep social peace. Application of the *sharia* endangers this delicate balance. Most of the syncretic Muslims usually vote for Megawati. In recent years, though, the Islamic cultural resurgence embodied by Nahdlatul Ulama and other groups has converted many syncretics into *santri.* The new converts tend to be attracted by the neo-modernist version of the orthodoxy.

Indonesian circumstances are unique; the success of liberal Islam in this country is, quite simply, exceptional. Elsewhere in the Muslim world, the particular conditions of Indonesia do not exist. The regimes have a unitary–populist, if not plainly tyrannical outlook; the religious tradition is not pluralistic; and liberals lack communicating and organising skills. The liberal message in the Middle East and North Africa is as learned and sophisticated as that in Indonesia, yet it is a voice calling in the desert. The clash within Islam thus pits the radicals against the powers-that-be. And this, sadly, is the only struggle that counts.

Emmanuel Sivan is a professor of Islamic History at the Hebrew University of Jerusalem and has authored many books on contemporary Islam. Dr. Sivan's publications include *Radical Islam* (1990), *The 1948 Generation* (1991), and *Mythes Politiques Arabes* (1995).

Notes

1. O. Roy, *L'islam mondialisé* (Paris: Seuil, 2002); G. Kepel, *Jihad: The Trail of Political Islam* (Cambridge, MA: Harvard University Press, 2001).
2. See the article by a major radical Muslim thinker, Munir Shafiq in *Al-Hayat* (London), 20 October 2002, and the secret correspondence between Ayman al-Zawahiri and Jihad acivists in Egypt, published in *Al-Wasat* (London), 10 June, 2002. See also Zawahiri's memoirs published in *Al-Sharq Al-Awsat* (London), 2–9 December 2001.
3. See author's chapter 'The Culture of the Enclave', in M. M. Marty and R.S. Appleby, *Fundamentalisms Comprehended* (Chicago, IL: Chicago University Press, 1995).
4. See, for instance, on Algeria the study by D. Djerbal, 'Systeme educatif et société civile . . . dans l'Algérie des années 1980–1990', paper presented to the workshop of Turk Siyasi Ilimler Dernegi, Istanbul, May 1997.
5. Conversion from Islam to another religion is punishable by death according to the *sharia.*
6. *Cairo Times,* 12–18 September 2002.
7. Interview with author.
8. Article by Muhammad Hilmi Mahumud in *Wujuhat Nazar,* April 2002.
   One should note that Foda wasn't the only liberal Islamic martyr. Muhammad Taha, who called for a return to the non-political Islam of Muhammad in Mecca (prior to the *Hijra*) was executed by Numeiri in Sudan in 1985.
9. F. Huwaydi in *Al-Ahram,* 23 March 1989.
10. Qimni, *Hurub Dawlat Al-Rasu* (Cairo: Dar Sina, 1993); *Abd Al-Karim, Dawlat Yathrib* (Cairo: Dar Sina, 1999); *Al-Judhur Al-Ta' rikhiyya Lil-Shari'a Al-Islamiyya* (Cairo: Dar Sina, 1990).
11. See his articles in *Ruz Al-Yusuf,* 5 January, 1 June, 8 June 2002, and his book *Hijab al-Mar'ah* (Cairo: Ruz al-Yusuf, 2002).
12. Full transcript of the debate in his book *Al-Su'al Al-Akhir* (Cairo: Ruz al-Yusuf, 1998), p. 109.
13. See the list of signatories in favour of Ibrahim in *Al-Usbu* (Cairo), 7 October 2002.

Chapter 5

Modern Methods and Modes of Attack

This chapter explores various methods and modes of attack of the new terrorism: ways in which terrorist groups could expand their power and their capability for destruction. Whereas weapons of mass destruction (WMD) are often touted as the weapons of choice for today's terrorists, suicide bombers have been termed "the ultimate smart bomb." Notably, the September 11 attacks were essentially sophisticated and coordinate versions of suicide bomb attacks—resulting in the mass casualties and mass destruction that could be expected from terrorists' use of WMD. In addition to these deadly modes of attack, the changing structures of both transnational criminal organizations and terrorist organizations is creating new opportunities for collaboration between criminals and terrorists. These dangerous dimensions of the modern terrorist threat are likely to complicate the counterterrorism efforts of the U.S. government and other nations well into the future.

The threat of WMD is a complex issue—not just in the discussion of how to detect, deter, and defend against their use, but also in the complicated difference between the devices, technology, and processes needed to obtain and use these weapons. In their assessment of the post–9/11 threat of WMD terrorism, Gavin Cameron and Natasha Bajema contend that WMD in the hands of terrorist groups are more often likely to be weapons of mass disruption rather than weapons of mass destruction. Although al Qaeda has pursued an all-options strategy in their pursuit of chemical, biological, radiological and nuclear weapons (CBRN), "several plots involving CBRN were considered for the 9/11 attacks and later discarded by al Qaeda leadership in favor of conventional options." Given the evidence that "al Qaeda has been simply trying to develop any type of weapon that might help its cause," Cameron and Bajema assert that terrorist groups are likely to continue to choose between CBRN and conventional options for instrumental reasons. "Terrorists have many viable conventional options at their disposal, which are effective means for causing mass casualties and destruction, are easier to implement, are less expensive, and produce more predictable results." Nonetheless,

Cameron and Bajema argue that terrorist cells loosely affiliated with al Qaeda demonstrate a growing interest in CBRN for small-scale tactical attacks with significant potential to cause injury, disruption, and fear.

In perhaps the most frightening essay in this volume, John Ellis presents the future of biological warfare—genomic terrorism. Ellis describes genetically altered weapons that are engineered to strike, selectively killing one race and not another. While to many this may sound like science fiction, the future is already upon us. Today, much of the food we eat is genetically modified, and before its demise, the Soviet Union developed a vaccine-resistant form of smallpox. This type of genetic engineering, when combined with the complete sequencing of the human genome, creates a power that, as Ellis terms it, is unprecedented.

Opportunistic connections between transnational criminal organizations and terrorist organizations are increasingly prominent in the Information Age, in which "speed, flexibility, integration, and innovation are ingredients for success" for any organization. Chris Dishman examines the shift from a vertical to a horizontal organizational structure of criminal organizations and concludes that this changing structure creates new and important opportunities for terrorist organizations. Whereas criminal organizations once had very strict command-and-control hierarchies, the newer more loosely organized groups afford more opportunity for individual members to collaborate with terrorist organizations. The implications of this trend are many and will increasingly complicate counterterrorism efforts.

The foremost authority on suicide terrorism, Bruce Hoffman, provides a rare insight into this very dangerous and potentially imminent threat to the United States. In the past few years, the world has seen this tactic used in Israel, Saudi Arabia, Indonesia, London and most recently in Afghanistan and Iraq, to name but a few. The threat of suicide bombers is front and center for individuals at all levels of government—from city policy and fire departments to the Department of Homeland Security. Ultimately, "suicide terrorism is embraced as a psychological weapon designed to induce paralysis in one's opponent," explains Hoffman. One question often asked is when will such a threat come to the United States or other Western democracies? Hoffman's answer is that the United States has already experienced such events and not just the attacks of September 11. Through examination of Palestinian suicide bombers, Hoffman offers the reader insight as to what other countries might be able to expect and the challenges faced in defending such attacks.

Though suicide bombers are typically thought of as a recent trend in terrorism, Assaf Moghadam explains that precursors of today's suicide bombings stretch as far back as biblical times. According to Moghadam, the historical antecedents of suicide attacks "can be divided into three distinct periods: 1) from biblical times to the beginning of suicide attacks in Lebanon in 1981; 2) from the early 1980s to the advent of Al Qaeda's use of suicide attacks in 1998; and 3) from the late 1990s to the present day." In his subsequent review of contending theoretical explanations for suicide terrorism, Moghadam argues that recent changes in the patterns of suicide attacks are not adequately addressed by these existing explanations. Moghadam suggests that future explanations must account for dramatic changes in suicide terrorism including the use of suicide attacks in the absence of foreign occupation, the changing nature of terrorist goals for using this tactic, growing trend of radicalization in small cells, and changing patterns in the recruitment of suicide bombers.

Gavin Cameron and Natasha E. Bajema

Assessing the Post–9/11 Threat of CBRN Terrorism

A Threat of Mass Destruction or Mass Disruption?

Although weapons of mass destruction and terrorism has been a source of concern within the scholarly and policy communities since the 1970s and a heightened focus of threat analysis since the mid-1990s following Aum Shinrikyo's sarin gas attacks, it was the terrorist attacks on September 11, 2001 that permanently altered "global perceptions of threat and vulnerability."[1] Given the "profound threshold in terrorist constraint and lethality" crossed by al Qaeda on 9/11, terrorism has thus become nearly synonymous with the threat of weapons of mass destruction (WMD).[2] Most recently, the *National Strategy for Homeland Security,* released in October 2007, suggests that the intent by terrorists to inflict catastrophic damage on the United States "has fueled their desire to acquire WMD" and warns that "WMD in the hands of terrorists is one of the gravest threats we face, and we cannot permit the world's most dangerous terrorists to threaten us with the world's most destructive weapons."[3] Such statements generate the impression that all contemporary terrorists seek to cause indiscriminate casualties and thus, would naturally pursue WMD as their weapons of choice. However, the inevitability of links between terrorism, WMD, mass casualties, and mass destruction suggested by these statements does not reflect actual patterns of terrorist pursuit and use of these weapons. Whereas terrorists regularly inflict significant casualties and destruction using standard conventional means, there have been no incidents of a terrorist group successfully wielding WMD for the purpose of causing mass casualties and destruction.

WMD are generally defined as weapons that have the capability to cause mass casualties and destruction and include nuclear, chemical, and biological weapons. Since the concept of WMD was originally used to define advanced weapons developed by states for military purposes, the use of this term to refer to crude versions of these weapons developed by terrorists has been a source of criticism among experts. In assessing threat of potential terrorist use of such weapons, the term *WMD* tends to confuse more than it clarifies for several reasons.[4] First and most obviously, chemical, biological and radiological weapons are generally not physically destructive in the same way as nuclear weapons or even conventional explosives. Nonetheless, the potential effects of such devices go beyond the immediate physical impact to include disruption and fear-generation. Second, the availability of equipment and materials and technical obstacles associated with each distinct weapon type vary in ways that are significantly distorted by the term *WMD*. Third, terrorists have yet to cause mass casualties or mass destruction in attacks that use chemical, biological, radiological and nuclear weapons, nor are they likely to do so in the near future. In contrast, terrorists have demonstrated themselves increasingly capable of harnessing conventional weapons and technologies to cause mass casualties and destruction. Finally, the threat spectrum for terrorist use of WMD ranges from high-end use (mass destruction), potentially threatening the welfare of many people, to the use of such weapons for the purpose of causing fear and terror at the lower-end of the spectrum (mass disruption).[5] The empirical record of incidents involving terrorist use of WMD does not support threat analyses that primarily emphasize the high-end use of such devices. For these reasons, this chapter argues that such weapons in the hands of terrorists are more accurately denoted as weapons of mass disruption, or for the purposes of this chapter, separately as chemical, biological, radiological and nuclear weapons (CBRN).

To assess the threat of CBRN terrorism, it is first necessary to identify whether there is a nexus between the intent and capabilities of terrorist groups. As long as only a few terrorists exhibit interest in CBRN, and those interested parties lack the requisite technical capabilities to implement attacks, the threat of CBRN terrorism will remain relatively insignificant. This chapter begins by assessing terrorist motivations for using CBRN and reviewing the historical record of groups seeking such weapons. After establishing that a growing intent to pursue and use CBRN exists, this chapter discusses the technical barriers to the acquisition of each type of CBRN weapon. Finally, this chapter assesses the current threat of al Qaeda using CBRN, the ultimate nexus between intent and capabilities.

CBRN and the "New Terrorism"

Until recently, experts were convinced that terrorist groups would refrain from using unconventional weapons since the use of CBRN would "violate one of the basic principles of classic terrorism—namely, 'propaganda by deed.'"[6] Traditional terrorists did not seek to maximize the number of casualties in their attacks, using their violence instead as a means of coercing concessions from governments or serving as a catalyst for political change. As Brian Jenkins famously stated in 1975: "terrorists want a lot of people watching, not a lot of people dead."[7] This argument formed a critical basis for the terrorism literature for the next 20 years.

In the late 1990s, however, experts identified three trends in international terrorism that suggested a growing potential for the future terrorist use of CBRN. These trends comprise part of what is referred to as the "new terrorism."[8] The first trend suggests that the number of terrorist groups with a religious orientation has increased dramatically. Traditional terrorist groups, motivated by limited political goals, on the other hand, have been on the decline. For the purpose of comparison, Bruce Hoffman notes that none of the active international terrorist groups in 1968 "could be classified as religious—that is, having aims and motivations of a predominantly religious nature."[9] In 2004, almost half of the active terrorist organizations (46 percent) had religious motivations.[10] Second, the lethality of terrorist attacks is increasing. Over time, there have been fewer terrorist incidents and more casualties. According to Amy Smithson, "the RAND-St. Andrews database, which tracks incidents of international terrorism, recorded 250 incidents of terrorism in 1996—the lowest number of terrorist incidents since 1973."[11] The total number of nonfatal casualties between 1970 to 1983 amounted to 18,925. This total tripled to 69,833 nonfatal casualties between 1990 and 1996.[12] Third, there appears to be a direct linkage between religious terrorism and increasing lethality. Nadine Gurr and Benjamin Cole found that all attacks with more than 100 casualties in the 1990s were attributable to groups with a religious ideology.[13] Al Qaeda was responsible for 19 percent of fatalities from terrorist attacks between 1998 and 2004, yet it committed only 0.1 percent of terrorist attacks in that period.[14] Even excluding the fatalities caused on 9/11 does not alter the basic point that al Qaeda's violence during these years was disproportionately lethal.

Lacking the self-imposed constraints of traditional terrorist groups, religious terrorist groups are more likely to commit attacks involving mass casualties and to seek CBRN for the perpetration of attacks for two main reasons. First, these groups lack a constituency of supporters who are more moderate in their beliefs, but agree with the overall objectives. In other words, a religious group carries out its agenda on behalf of itself. Second, these groups believe that they are fulfilling the will of a higher power. This belief provides a justification for committing acts of indiscriminate violence. Using religion as a justification, individuals are absolved from their vicious acts and feel that they are fulfilling a divine duty.

The assumption that the religious nature of the "new terrorism" will inevitably lead to the use of CBRN for the purposes of causing indiscriminate mass murder, however, is misleading. For one, terrorists have many viable conventional options at their disposal, which are effective means for causing mass casualties and destruction, are easier to implement, are less expensive, and produce more predictable results. In contrast, terrorists attempting to use CBRN have failed to cause mass casualties due to significant technical and operational obstacles. In most cases, terrorists have pursued CBRN as one of many means of coercion and intimidation rather than a tool of mass destruction and sought these weapons for instrumental reasons—in particular their capacity for causing psychological terror. Historically, terrorist groups have seldom pursued unconventional weapons in their attacks. Until the sarin gas attacks in Tokyo in 1995, there were few significant incidents of CBRN terrorism.[15]

Significant historical incidents involving chemical or biological agents include the Rajneeshees, a religious cult that used salmonella to contaminate salad bars in Oregon, in 1984, sickening 751 people with the intention of influencing a local election.[16] In 1986, the Covenant, the Sword, and the Arm of the Lord acquired a barrel of potassium cyanide with the intention of poisoning U.S. urban water supplies to further the group's ideological and religious objectives.[17] In 1991, the Minnesota Patriots Council, another Christian Identity group, plotted to harm government officials with ricin. The group leaders were arrested before the attack could be implemented.[18] Both the Kurdistan Worker's Party (PKK) in Turkey and Liberation Tigers of Tamil Eelam in Sri Lanka, groups motivated by nationalism rather than religion, have used chemical weapons on at least one occasion. However, in each case, the use of chemical weapons was for a small-scale tactical attack and was not an attempt to cause mass casualties and destruction. Both organizations returned to the use of conventional weapons for subsequent attacks.[19]

The most important radiological threat occurred on November 23, 1995 when Chechen separatists announced that four cases of radioactive cesium had been hidden around Moscow. Russian officials largely dismissed the nuclear threat, claiming that the material was cesium-137.[20] The Chechen's primary intention was to display their capabilities and unless Russia withdrew from Chechnya, to ensure that its threats to launch further attacks against Moscow would be taken seriously.[21] Radiological sources have also been used in small-scale, often personal, attacks in a range of states including Japan, Russia, the United States, and several in Europe.[22]

Many experts considered the Aum Shinrikyo sarin gas attacks on the subway in Tokyo in 1995 to be a watershed event since it contradicted previous assumptions about terrorist use of CBRN.[23] Aum Shinrikyo, a religious cult, actively engaged in efforts to obtain, test and use chemical and biological weapons for the purpose of causing mass casualties. Aum Shinrikyo pursued a wide range of CBRN options and eventually settled on sarin gas, a chemical agent. After the sarin attacks, authorities discovered that the cult also had carried out biological attacks on multiple occasions using anthrax and botulism toxin. Despite vast financial resources estimated to be anywhere from $20 million to $1 billion, however, Aum Shinrikyo was unable to successfully carry out a biological attack.[24]

Since Aum Shinrikyo in 1995, there has been only a single significant incident involving the use of CBRN. In the fall of 2001, a series of letters containing anthrax were sent through the U.S. Postal Service. The sender of the anthrax letters was anonymous and remains unidentified.[25] Probable motivations for the attack include a desire to cause widespread panic and/or to emphasize vulnerability of the United States to a biological attack. The anthrax letters attack is especially troubling for two reasons. First, the strain of anthrax found in the letters had been milled to a fine powder and processed with chemical additives to enable the substance to be more readily inhaled into the lungs of potential victims, suggesting that the perpetrator had access to specialized knowledge and technology—possibly with insider access to the U.S. biodefense program.[26] Second, the perpetrator was not affiliated with a definable terrorist organization. Although there were initial fears that al Qaeda was responsible for the attacks, little evidence supported such a claim, and even Osama bin Laden denied involvement.[27] A lack of obvious terrorist involvement is more worrisome than if there had been such a link because analysts of CBRN terrorism have typically assumed that any incident with high-end agents would require resources and connections precluding all but the most sophisticated groups from exploiting this option.[28] The anthrax attacks appear to undermine the validity of such assumptions, even though the chief barrier to effective use of a biological agent, such as anthrax—the problem of widespread dissemination (as described later in this chapter)—was not solved. Although only five people died of anthrax inhalation, and another 18 were infected, "the mailings caused serious disruptions, including the closing of government building and the quarantine of tens of thousands of pieces of mail."[29] The total costs associated with the 2001 anthrax attack are estimated to exceed $6 billion.[30]

Despite a number of significant CBRN incidents, Jenkins's age-old argument against mass-casualty terrorism and its implication for CBRN terrorism has been largely supported by historical record of terrorist CBRN activities. None of the CBRN incidents noted above come even close to the high-consequence scenarios described by popular fiction and the media. Furthermore, terrorists have employed conventional weapons for all *major* terrorist attacks since 1995: Oklahoma City in 1995, the 1998 attacks on US embassies in Tanzania and Kenya, the 2002 Bali bombing, and the 2004 Madrid bombings. The technical difficulties associated with CBRN acquisition and uncertainties over the effectiveness of such weapons, as well as the technological conservatism of many terrorist organizations may explain this situation.[31]

Technical Obstacles and Operational Challenges

The technical obstacles to obtaining CBRN capability and operational challenges to implementing a successful attack are formidable even for terrorist groups with extensive resources. As Bruce Hoffman suggests, "a strong interest in, and clear willingness to use" CBRN is not "always matched by the capabilities required either to fabricate or effectively disseminate them."[32]

The clearest example of this point comes from the Japanese cult, Aum Shinrikyo.[33] Although well financed, organized and connected, the cult essentially failed in its objectives. Aum Shinrikyo pursued a broad range of chemical and biological agents: anthrax, botulinum toxin, Q-fever, Ebola virus, VX, hydrogen cyanide as well as the nerve agent, sarin. Aum also briefly sought a nuclear-yield device, for which the group had planned to obtain natural uranium and enrich it to weapons-grade. Despite extensive resources and technical expertise, the cult members struggled both in developing virulent batches of the chemical and biological agents and in achieving an effective delivery mechanism. Although organizational pressures and idiosyncratic decision making by Aum Shinrikyo's leadership, especially Shoko Asahara, played an important role in these failures, the nature of the technical obstacles created a situation in which such organizational factors mattered, by compelling the cult toward premature attacks. The group's sarin gas attacks in June 1994 in Matsumoto and March 1995 in Tokyo were conducted with insufficiently pure sarin and extremely crude delivery methods.

The technical and operational challenges associated with acquiring and using a significant CBRN capability vary considerably between the different types of weapons. Each type of weapon offers a distinct set of technical and operational challenges associated with acquiring, weaponizing and delivering such a capability. However, the technical bar is much lower for terrorists that pursue CBRN simply to cause injury, disruption, and fear.

Chemical Weapons

Chemical agents "are poisonous, man-made gases, liquids, or powders that, when absorbed through the lungs or skin, have incapacitating or lethal effects on humans and animals."[34] In order to develop chemical weapons, a terrorist group must successfully accomplish a series of steps: (1) acquisition of equipment, materials, and agents; (2) production; and (3) delivery/dissemination. The ease of acquiring or producing chemical agents and implementing a successful terrorist attack depends on the selected agent. Chemical agents range from commonly used chemicals such as ammonia and pesticides, which are available "off-the-shelf," to advanced agents developed for military applications such as nerve gases. In order to cause massive casualties with chemical weapons, a terrorist group would need to manufacture enormous quantities of the most lethal chemicals such as sarin or VX (nerve gases). While most of the modern chemical weapons used by militaries are highly complex chemical compounds, first-generation weapons were often much more straightforward. Chlorine, used as a weapon in World War I and recently by insurgents in Iraq, is required for a broad range of legitimate industrial processes, and thus represents one of the world's most widely used chemicals.[35] If a terrorist group does not seek to maximize casualties, then the scope for easily accessible options increases still further. Given the technical hurdles of manufacturing large quantities of military-grade agents, most terrorists are more likely to select from a variety of toxic household or industrial chemicals that can be purchased from commercial markets including cyanides, tear gas, insecticides or pesticides, sulfuric acid, arsenic, rat poison, and weed killer.[36] Imposing meaningful controls on access to chlorine and other commonly used chemicals is extremely difficult. A well-organized group, using a front company or complicit supplier, would have a strong prospect of successfully purchasing such chemicals for developing a chemical weapon.

For the most part, the key barrier to a terrorist organization seeking to acquire a chemical agent is the manufacturing process, rather than the acquisition of the basic chemicals. The recipes for producing chemical weapons, available in the open literature or on the Internet, are often unreliable. Moreover, working with toxic chemicals poses serious health hazards to a terrorist group attempting to develop a workable weapon.[37] In spite of significant technical hurdles, Aum Shinrikyo demonstrated itself capable of manufacturing and delivering small quantities of sarin nerve gas, enough to cause death and injury. Due to operational difficulties with weaponization and delivery, however, Aum was unable to bring about one of its desired goal of mass casualties. Originally, Shoko Asahara had "planned to acquire a stockpile of 70 tons of sarin and then employ a Russian military helicopter to spray the deadly agent over downtown Tokyo."[38] Fearing a raid on its headquarters, Asahara hastily ordered an attack against the Tokyo subway in 1995. Aum members released liquid sarin (600 grams) from sealed plastic bags by puncturing holes in them with umbrellas on five subway cars during morning rush hour.[39] Although there were a large numbers of injuries, the subway attack only resulted in twelve deaths. In another attack on the Tokyo subway a few weeks later, Aum failed again to cause significant death or injury. This time, Aum attempted to release hydrogen cyanide using a device rigged to combine sodium cyanide crystals with sulfuric acid. The device malfunctioned when it caught on fire, and the subway station was promptly evacuated.[40]

The means of delivery for chemical weapons are numerous and range from advanced military explosive devices and lacing of conventional explosives to the localized release of aerosols, poisoning of food, or emplacement in ventilation systems. However, in order to cause mass casualties, a chemical weapon must be delivered in a way that avoids the agent being rendered into ineffective quantities either due to environmental factors or to the delivery mechanism itself. A device that relies on an explosive means of dispersing an agent, for example, is likely to result in a high "burn-off" rate, so that the quantity of the agent left to harm victims would be significant.

Biological Weapons

Biological weapons employ living microorganisms (pathogens) or toxins produced by living organisms to attack human beings, animals, and/or plants. Similar to chemical weapons, in order to achieve a basic bioweapon capability, terrorists must accomplish several steps: acquire a virulent agent, produce significant quantities of the agent, and devise a mechanism for delivery and dissemination. Although the acquisition of dual-use materials and equipment for producing biological weapons is relatively easy, the development of an *effective* weapon and the implementation of a *successful* biological attack are faced with significant obstacles. Even terrorists planning small-scale attacks with rudimentary devices will encounter obstacles, some that are out of their control. The obstacles encountered at each stage (acquisition, production, delivery) depends on the biological agent selected by the terrorist group.

Biological agents can be acquired from a wide variety of sources including nature, culture collections, laboratories, hospitals, and military or biodefense programs. The ease of acquiring biological agents also varies significantly depending on the agent involved. For example, while the smallpox virus, post-eradication, is kept at just two sites in the world, anthrax and the plague both occur naturally in areas where the disease is endemic, and other agents, such as ricin (toxin), are derived from relatively available sources.[41] However, simple access to raw materials does not equate to an ability to create a high-grade or weaponized agent. Not all strains of an agent are equally effective for weaponization, and the process itself is not as easy as is sometimes suggested. For example, the production of ricin from castor beans is discussed in a plethora of literature such as the *Poisoner's Handbook*. Much of this literature is derivative and of limited practical value for high casualty violence. The Minnesota Patriots' Council, following such instructions, developed only an impure version of the ricin toxin.[42] In spite of all its resources, Aum Shinrikyo failed to isolate virulent strains of *Bacillis anthracis* and *Clostridium botulinum*.

After acquiring the biological agent, terrorists must produce and stabilize the pathogen or toxin. Since the equipment required for the production and stabilization of biological agents is used by the pharmaceutical, food, cosmetics and pesticide industries for legitimate applications, terrorists can acquire equipment and materials needed for developing a biological weapon on commercial markets. Fermenters, which can be used to grow pathogens, are widely available for a range of legitimate industries from brewing to biotechnology. Stabilization of the pathogen or toxin is essential for retaining the lethal capacity of the agent over longer periods of time. If the biological agent is not properly stabilized, it will quickly deteriorate and eventually die (pathogen) or lose its potency (toxin). Biological agents are stabilized by being converted into a liquid form or through freeze-drying. Freeze-drying and milling machines, extremely helpful in the conversion of agents into a dry, finely ground powder, are widely used in the pharmaceutical industry. The dual-use problem makes it difficult to impose meaningful restrictions on access to weapons-usable equipment, particularly if the terrorist organization operates from behind a front company to make its purchases. In the future, new technologies such as genetic engineering or microfermenters may make novel agents more accessible to terrorists.

For a biological agent to be used offensively, it must be delivered to the desired target area and effectively disseminated. At this stage, terrorists face many technical and operational obstacles. Assuming that terrorists using biological weapons seek to cause mass casualties, aerosol dissemination represents the most effective method of dissemination. An aerosol attack involves the dispersal of a biological agent as a cloud of particles over a target area.[43] Since the agent would need to be inhaled in order to infect potential victims, the group would need to create an aerosolized cloud of particles of between one and five microns in diameter, small enough to be inhaled and then retained in the lungs. This task alone represents a significant, though not insurmountable problem for the would-be biological weapons scientist. Other technical obstacles to effective dissemination and delivery of biological agents by terrorists include avoiding the clogging of the nozzle during aerosol dissemination, testing to ensure that the device is effective and avoiding detection, and avoiding infection and/or injury to group members. Furthermore, weather conditions such as rain, sunlight, temperature, wind, pollutants, and instability of atmosphere can all hinder the success of a biological attack depending on the agent. For example, while anthrax is relatively hardy, other agents may become significantly less effective when subjected to bright light, strong heat, or dryness.

Radiological and Nuclear Weapons

As Charles Ferguson and William Potter suggest in *The Four Faces of Nuclear Terrorism,* the threat of terrorists using radiological or nuclear weapons is a multidimensional one.[44] Each of the four dimensions of this threat involves differences in the requisite levels of terrorist capabilities, likelihood of success, and potential consequences if an attack is successful.

Devising a radiological dispersal device (RDD) is the most plausible scenario since such devices are likely to be the easiest type of CBRN weapon for terrorists to acquire. At its simplest, an RRD consists of no more than conventional explosives and a radioactive source, such as cesium-137 from a hospital X-ray machine. Although an RDD is not likely to cause physical destruction beyond the blast radius of the conventional explosives, the disruptive potential of a radioactive weapon or "dirty bomb" is considerable. Radioactive sources are widely available and poorly protected, certainly compared to other types of nuclear materials. The International Atomic Energy Agency (IAEA) reported that the "materials needed to build a 'dirty bomb' can be found in almost any country in the world, and more than 100 countries may have inadequate control and monitoring programs necessary to prevent or even detect the theft of these materials."[45]

Attacking a nuclear facility is another option for terrorists, one that could lead to a significant release of radiological material, contaminate a wide area, disable power production at a nuclear power plant, and potentially cause a widespread loss of confidence in the safety of nuclear energy production. However, the nature of security and safeguard measures taken at these facilities are such that while the sabotage of nuclear power plant is relatively technically and theoretically straightforward, such attacks remain sufficiently, practically, and logistically challenging as to make other CBRN options seem more attractive.

Acquiring a nuclear yield device would be substantially more challenging for a terrorist group and thus represents a highly unlikely scenario. Nonetheless, there are currently around 30,000 nuclear weapons in the world. According to Graham Allison, several hundred of those, primarily in the former republics of the Soviet Union, are vulnerable to theft by terrorists or by criminals who might sell them on to terrorist organizations.[46] Evidence suggests that some terrorist groups are interested in acquiring a nuclear-yield device; both Aum Shinrikyo and al Qaeda have both actively sought to purchase a weapon.

Nuclear-weapon states are not likely to deliberately provide a nuclear-yield weapon to a terrorist group for several reasons. State sponsors would fear retribution by the attacked state and/or the international community, have concerns about losing control over the nuclear-armed terrorist group, and exhibit a general reluctance to surrender nuclear weapons to another party due to the intrinsic difficulty of acquiring them. In a more likely scenario, military or scientific elites in some states might be willing, for ideological or financial reasons, to provide nuclear weapons, material, and/or expertise to terrorist organizations. Given the links between Pakistan's security service and al Qaeda, the uncertain chain of command over its nuclear arsenal, and Dr. A. Q. Khan's former role within the global nuclear black market, Pakistan is a particular state of concern in this respect. However, the largest nuclear arsenals in the world are in Russia and the United States. While many nuclear weapons in Russia are adequately protected from theft, others are not. Many Soviet-era tactical nuclear devices are especially vulnerable, and given the size of such weapons, would be particularly suitable for use by terrorists.[47]

The acquisition of fissile material represents the second and more probable route to the possession by terrorists of a nuclear-yield device. Acquiring weapons-grade material continues to serve as the chief barrier to developing such a weapon for states and terrorists alike. Nonetheless, nuclear-yield devices with military-level efficiency are beyond the capability of most terrorist organizations. Given the U.S.-led war on terrorism, fewer states than before are likely to grant terrorist organizations the time, space, resources, and expertise necessary to develop such a sophisticated device. Therefore, terrorists are more likely to devise an improvised nuclear device (IND). This device would be less efficient and sophisticated than a military-level weapon, but could be highly effective in causing mass casualties. An IND would not require knowledge beyond that available in the open literature and involves relatively straightforward engineering (a gun-type weapon, using U-235, rather than a more complex implosion weapon that requires Pu-239). A gun-type device does, however, require large quantities (approximately 50 kg) of highly enriched uranium. Thus, without state assistance of some kind, it is unlikely that even the most sophisticated terrorist organizations will be capable of enriching enough uranium to develop a crude device. Thus, the primary risk comes from the terrorist acquisition, whether through sale or theft, of state-produced weapons-grade nuclear material.[48]

The risks of terrorists gaining assess to nuclear material remains considerable. Global quantities of such material are enormous and scattered around the world, in both military and civilian sectors. Graham Allison has cited a figure of enough plutonium and highly enriched uranium for 240,000 nuclear weapons.[49] In many states, nuclear material is adequately protected, controlled, and accounted for, but in other states, where terrorists are most likely to be active, such measures are much looser. There have been regular reports of the theft and/or smuggling of nuclear materials from inadequately secured facilities. In this respect, the former republics of the Soviet Union represent a particular concern, largely due to the quantities of poorly protected material present there, but similar reports have emanated from states around the world. So far, the majority of incidents have involved small quantities of weapons-grade material, or larger quantities of non-weapons-grade nuclear material.

The technical challenges of acquiring, developing, and using CBRN weapons are likely to continue to play a key role in the relative paucity of high-end incidents in the near future. Thus, the most significant threats of CBRN terrorism exist wherever there is a nexus between a terrorist group's intent to cause mass casualties and extensive technical and financial resources—the most critical example of such a threat is al Qaeda.

Al Qaeda and CBRN Terrorism: Pre–9/11 to Present

Since the nature of Aum Shinrikyo's resources, motivations, and objectives could be viewed as an aberration rather than a sign of things to come, many analysts might still argue that Jenkins's concept of instrumental proportionality would continue to serve as the dominant rationale for the majority of terrorist activities—at least until September 11, 2001. The 9/11 attacks and subsequent nature of al Qaeda activities have permanently altered perceptions of the dominant trends within terrorism, one of the most prominent being the presumption that terrorists prefer using minimum force to achieve their political objectives. Since 9/11, most experts would concur that there are now at least some terrorists, if not quite a few, who want to inflict as many casualties as possible and might therefore cross the threshold of using CBRN. Thus, in the post–9/11 context, CBRN terrorism must now be seen not just as a means of intimidation and coercion, one that has rarely been used by terrorist groups, but also as a method with significant potential for killing large numbers of people and a growing sensational appeal among terrorist groups—especially terrorists associated with al Qaeda, the ultimate nexus of intent and capabilities.

As a terrorist organization, al Qaeda has evolved dramatically since 9/11, most obviously as a result of U.S. efforts in the war on terrorism. Whereas an identifiable organization and leadership structure linked to semi-autonomous cells operated before 9/11, al Qaeda has since become "an amorphous movement tenuously held together by a loosely networked transnational constituency rather than a monolithic, international terrorist organization with either a defined or identifiable command and control apparatus."[50] Bruce Hoffman argues that there are, in fact, "many al Qaedas rather the single al Qaeda of the past."[51] In order to better understand the multifaceted threat posed by al Qaeda, Hoffman suggests that the post–9/11 movement should be conceptualized as four distinct interwoven threads: al Qaeda Central, al Qaeda Affiliates and Associates, al Qaeda Locals, and the al Qaeda Network.[52] In the following, this typology will be used to evaluate the CBRN activities of terrorists associated with al Qaeda.

Al Qaeda Central and CBRN

In Hoffman's typology, al Qaeda Central refers to the central organizational structure and its core leadership that existed before 9/11 as well as any remnants and new players following U.S. efforts to dismantle the organization in Afghanistan. According to Hoffman, the operations of al Qaeda Central, typically follow the template of the 1998 East Africa bombings and 9/11 attacks, involving "high value, 'spectacular' attacks [that] are entrusted only to al Qaeda's professional cadre."[53] Hoffman argues that "these 'professional terrorists' are deployed in predetermined and carefully selected teams . . . with very specific targeting instructions."[54] Based on this model, the CBRN operations of al Qaeda Central are likely to be well planned, extensive, directly connected to key leaders such as Bin Laden or Zawahiri, and to be aimed at causing mass casualties and destruction.

Several plots involving CBRN were considered for the 9/11 attacks and later discarded by al Qaeda leadership in favor of conventional options. According *The 9/11 Commission Report,* Yazid Sufaat, a member of Jemaah Islamiya, was recruited in early 2001 by Hambali, a subordinate commander of al Qaeda, to take over its biological weapons program. Using a bachelor's degree in biological sciences and a minor in chemistry from California State University in Sacramento, Sufaat spent several months attempting to cultivate anthrax in a laboratory near Kandahar.[55] Plans for a biological attack were likely discarded due to concerns about feasibility. According to Khalid Sheik Mohammed, one of the chief organizers of the 9/11 attacks, nuclear power plants were among the selected targets in an initial plan that included 10 hijacked aircrafts before it was scaled down.[56] The plan to attack a nuclear facility was also discarded by senior leadership in favor of the eventual targets attacked on 9/11.[57] However, as late as July 2001, Mohamed Atta, one of the pilots of the 9/11 attacks, pitched a nuclear facility near New York as a potential target for the pending attacks. According to Ramzi Bin al-Shaiba, a chief coordinator of the 9/11 plot, Atta's suggestion was rejected by the other pilots who felt that targeting a nuclear facility would be too difficult given the restricted airspace around the facility, which would both preclude reconnaissance flights and increase "the likelihood that any plane would be shot down before impact."[58] Furthermore, not only had the targeting of a nuclear facility not received approval from senior al Qaeda leadership, nuclear power plants lacked the desired symbolic value of other targets.[59] The plan to attack the World Trade Center towers and other symbolic targets using planes was selected not only because it offered a means to strike at the U.S. economy, but also because it was considered more feasible.[60]

Following 9/11, al Qaeda leadership continued to reject lofty plans to use CBRN in favor of more feasible conventional attacks. From 1998 to 2002, Padilla traveled throughout Egypt, Saudi Arabia, Yemen, Pakistan, and Afghanistan for various terrorist training and was arrested on his return to the United States in May 2002. He was accused of attempting to acquire a radiological dispersal device that would be used within the United States and of plotting to blow up a series of apartment blocks using natural gas. For the latter purpose, he had received money, documents, contact details for other operatives in the United States, and training in explosives from al Qaeda leadership. Padilla wanted instead "to detonate a nuclear improvised bomb that they had learned to make from research on the Internet" or build a "dirty bomb." However, when he presented the plan to al Qaeda leaders, Khalid Sheikh Mohammed and Abu Zabaida, both were skeptical about the feasibility of the schemes and urged Padilla undertake the original apartment building operation instead.[61] In his recent book, Ron Suskind provides another example of al Qaeda making practical calculations about whether to use conventional versus unconventional means for their attacks. Suskind describes a plot in which Youseuf al-Ayiri, leader of al Qaeda in Saudi Arabia, devised a plan to attack the New York subway using a crude hydrogen cyanide dispersal device in 2003. According to Suskind, the scheme was called off 45 days before the attack by Zawahiri, al Qaeda's second-in-command.[62] However, significant questions remain about the alleged plot. For example, "it is not clear if this alleged al Qaeda cell actually acquired the precursor materials to construct" the device.[63]

Despite its use of conventional technologies for perpetrating the 9/11 attacks and repeated rejection of plans to use CBRN in favor of conventional options, al Qaeda Central has actively pursued an all-options strategy in its efforts to acquire CBRN, simultaneously seeking chemical, biological, radiological, and nuclear weapons.[64] Before 9/11, the U.S. intelligence community was largely skeptical of al Qaeda's "ability to use unconventional weapons to inflict mass casualties" and had thus underestimated the extent and nature of al Qaeda's CBRN activities.[65] In recent years, a more detailed picture of al Qaeda's CBRN capabilities and intentions has been made possible by several investigative commissions, interrogations, interviews, and trial testimonies. The unclassified report of the *Commission on the Intelligence Capabilities of the United States Regarding Weapons of Mass Destruction* issued in March 2005 is particularly useful for assessing al Qaeda's early efforts to acquire CBRN.

According to the *Commission on the Intelligence Capabilities,* al Qaeda attempted both to acquire chemical and biological weapons and to manufacture their own. In fact, the 11th edition of the group's *Encyclopedia of Jihad* was devoted to chemical and biological weapons.[66] By the late 1990s, the U.S. intelligence community was aware that some al Qaeda members had received rudimentary training in producing biological agents such as botulinum toxin and other toxins obtained from venomous animals.[67] Following the U.S.-led invasion of Afghanistan in 2001, analysts learned that al Qaeda's biological program was further along than previous intelligence had suggested. According to the *Commission on the Intelligence Capabilities,* the biological weapons program involved several well-equipped sites in Afghanistan and was found to be "extensive, well-organized, and operated for two years before September 11."[68] Based on notes and scientific literature found at one of al Qaeda's training camps, the operatives appeared to be particularly focused on the development of a single biological agent (not identified for security reasons). Although al Qaeda appeared to have prioritized research on this unidentified agent, a group of well-trained individuals had pursued work on a range of different agents. The findings of the *Commission on the Intelligence Capabilities* suggest that al Qaeda had isolated a strain of the unidentified agent and managed to produce a limited quantity of it by 2001. In addition, al Qaeda had acquired several other biological agents possibly by 1999.[69]

Evidence of al Qaeda's chemical weapons activities was disclosed at the trial of Ahmed Ressam in 2001. Ressam claimed to have witnessed a chemical weapons test during which a dog was killed using a cyanide-based gas.[70] CNN later released videotapes, made by al Qaeda before November 2001, which showed dogs being killed with an unspecified chemical agent.[71] The following month, the U.S. Department of Defense admitted that equipment and a lab found near Kandahar, Afghanistan, indicated that the group might have acquired sufficient capabilities for "a very limited production of biological and chemical agents."[72] In assessing al Qaeda's chemical weapons capability, the *Commission on the Intelligence Capabilities* found that the pre-2001 assessment by the U.S. intelligence community had been reasonably accurate. Al Qaeda had in its possession "small quantities of toxic chemicals, and had produced small amounts of World War I–era agents such as hydrogen cyanide, chlorine and phosgene."[73] In addition, al Qaeda appeared to have investigated more advanced chemical agents, possessed literature detailing the steps for producing a range of agents, and had the necessary equipment for production at training camps, all of which indicate that the group had engaged in at least some production of basic agents.[74]

Before 2001, the U.S. intelligence community believed al Qaeda to be capable of acquiring or developing radiological weapons for a number of reasons: the widespread availability of the radioactive sources, the straightforward means of dispersal using conventional explosives, and multiple references to radiological weapons within al Qaeda training manuals.[75] According to *The Times,* al Qaeda appears to have spent over $1.5 million on efforts to acquire enough materials for building a radiological weapon.[76] However, conclusive evidence that al Qaeda has a radiological capability remains elusive.[77] In January 2003, the British government alleged that al Qaeda, having prioritized a radiological device by 1999, had acquired not only the expertise but also the materials to do so prior to 9/11.[78] Although the evidence for this is not clear-cut, the discovery of the so-called "Superbomb" manual, which discusses radiological and nuclear devices and was found in Kabul in November 2001, adds credibility to these assertions.[79]

As its ultimate goal, al Qaeda leaders have long sought to acquire a nuclear weapon.[80] In February 2001, Jamal Ahmed Fadl, in his testimony at the trial of the 1998 East African embassy bombers, claimed that al Qaeda had tried to acquire nuclear material from the early 1990s onwards.[81] Prior to 9/11, the U.S. intelligence community thought it unlikely that the group had acquired a complete nuclear-yield weapon, let alone enough fissile material to build a nuclear weapon themselves.[82] Given substantial information gaps in U.S. intelligence on al Qaeda's nuclear capability, however, Osama bin Laden's claim in November 2001 that he possessed both nuclear and chemical weapons led the CIA's Weapons Intelligence, Nonproliferation, and Arms Control Center and the DCI's Counterterrorism Center to conclude that it was likely that al Qaeda had access to the relevant expertise and facilities necessary for developing a crude nuclear-yield capability.[83] Following the U.S.-led war in Afghanistan, both Coalition forces and Western media found multiple al Qaeda documents in Afghanistan, which suggested that the group had sought to develop a meaningful nuclear weapons program. Furthermore, the documents indicated that senior al Qaeda members met with Pakistani scientists to discuss both designs and gaining access to weapons-grade nuclear materials. However, by May 2002, U.S. intelligence had determined that there was no evidence that the group had acquired such material, let alone an intact nuclear weapon.[84]

Al Qaeda Network and CBRN

The discussion about al Qaeda's CBRN aspirations thus far has dealt with efforts directly connected to its central leadership or al Qaeda Central. Hoffman's three other versions of al Qaeda, however, have become increasingly significant since September 2001, particularly in terms of numbers of incidents. However, unlike al Qaeda Central, terrorists more loosely associated with al Qaeda have not pursued the entire range of CBRN or attempted to develop a long-standing and sophisticated capability. Rather, these groups have employed unsophisticated devices using easily accessible CBRN in their tactical attacks in order to capitalize on the psychological and disruptive effects of these weapons. Although some of these groups have threatened to cause mass casualties in their rhetoric, none of these groups have made a serious effort to plan attacks designed to cause mass casualties with CBRN. In most cases, these terrorists have plotted to use lower-end chemical and radiological agents that are likely to be disruptive rather than inflict mass casualties.

According to Hoffman, al Qaeda Affiliates and Associates are best described as "formally established insurgent or terrorist groups" such as Jemaah Islamiya in Indonesia and

Abu Musab Zarqawi's al Qaeda in Iraq.[85] These groups have typically received direct support from bin Laden in one form or another including spiritual guidance, training, arms, money, and other assistance. Al Qaeda insurgents in Iraq have on a number of occasions attempted or plotted to use chemical weapons in their attacks. In May 2004, U.S. forces claimed that Iraqi insurgents had attempted to use a 155 mm binary artillery shell containing two chemicals that would produce sarin gas, as part of an improvised explosive device. The shell, one of only a small number left from the Ba'athist regime, had little effect.[86] Starting in late 2006, Iraqi insurgents began to use chlorine bombs in Al-Anbar province. Before 2006, chlorine was readily available in Iraq for water treatment, lowering the associated costs of the tactic to the insurgents despite only modest gains in casualties.[87] Although an attack in April 2007 killed 27 in Ramadi, and another attack in May 2007 killed over 30 in Abu Sayda, the majority of casualties were caused by the explosive blast rather than the chlorine component of the devices. Nonetheless, the psychological impact of the burns, breathing difficulties, and other effects of the chemical demonstrated that chlorine bomb attacks are an effective means for terrorizing the Iraqi population. More significantly, in terms of potential impact, al Qaeda terrorists in the region plotted to attack multiple government targets in Jordan in April 2004, using a powerful combination of chemical and conventional weapons (twenty tons of chemicals). Jordanian authorities estimate that up to 80,000 people could have been killed or injured. The resulting disruption and fear generated by the attack would have had a dramatic impact on the political situation in Jordan, a forceful opponent of al Qaeda in the region.[88]

Both before and after 9/11, semiautonomous or wholly autonomous cells (al Qaeda Locals and al Qaeda Network) have increasingly pursued CBRN weapons for their attacks. According to Hoffman, al Qaeda Locals are local groups supporting the al Qaeda movement, most of whom have some terrorism experience and "a previous connection of some kind with al Qaeda."[89] In Hoffman's typology, the al Qaeda Network refers to autonomous cells of "home-grown Islamic radicals . . . as well as local converts to Islam . . . who have no direct connection with al Qaeda (or any other identifiable terrorist group), but nonetheless are prepared to carry out attacks in solidarity with or support of al Qaeda's radical jihadi agenda."[90] However, the distinction between al Qaeda Locals and al Qaeda Network as it pertains to CBRN activities is tenuous. In both cases, suspects were arrested before they had a chance to implement any CBRN attacks. At the time of their arrests, many of their attacks were still in the rudimentary planning stages. As such, the feasibility of many of these plots if implemented remains doubtful. Furthermore, these cells have generally plotted to use widely available chemical (cyanides, ricin) or radiological materials and were not found to have any sophisticated agents in their possession (sarin) or any large-scale production capability.

Minor incidents of al Qaeda Locals attempting or plotting to use CBRN abound in Europe. In December 2000, German police broke up an alleged plot by the Salafist Group for Call and Combat (GSPC), an Algerian-based group operating in Europe and associated with al Qaeda, to attack the European Parliament in Strasbourg with sarin.[91] In 2001, an Italian-based cell planned to launch an attack in France using "a suffocating gas," before being interdicted by the Italian security services. In addition to a lack of precise plans and specified targets, Italian authorities determined that the cell had made little progress toward acquiring a chemical weapon.[92] In February 2002, Italian police arrested nine Moroccan nationals for allegedly plotting a chemical terrorist attack on the U.S. embassy in Rome. The suspects were apprehended with approximately nine pounds of a cyanide compound (potassium ferrocyanide), as well as maps detailing the location of the water pipes for the U.S. embassy. The selection of potassium ferrocyanide, a highly ineffective means of poisoning water supplies, raises questions about the group's intentions and/or competence.[93] It also remains unclear whether the cell had any links to al Qaeda.

The most significant incident of al Qaeda Locals plotting to use CBRN occurred in Great Britain. In January 2003, British authorities, tipped off by French intelligence, arrested seven North African men suspected of producing ricin in their north London flat.[94] Further arrests tied to the ricin plot were conducted across Europe in Britain, Italy, and Spain.[95] At first, this incident appeared to be part of a major plot to use chemical weapons in the United Kingdom with assistance from an extensive network reaching directly to al Qaeda Central. In 2002, several members of a French Islamist cell, part of the same network as those arrested in London, had been arrested by French authorities for allegedly plotting to use chemical weapons. Although it was later established that the French cell had planned attacks using conventional weapons, protective biochemical suits had been found in their possession indicating a possible CBRN plot. Given links between the French cell and al Qaeda operatives in the Pankisi Gorge area and reports of al Qaeda leaders based in the Caucasus plotting a chemical weapons campaign, French authorities issued a warning to other European intelligence agencies to watch out for the smuggling of ricin and potassium cyanide into Europe.[96] Having found castor beans, processing equipment, as well as trace elements of ricin in their search of the London flat in 2003, British authorities assumed this to be part of a larger terrorist conspiracy to use chemical weapons.[97] Moreover, U.S. officials had claimed that four of the Islamists arrested in their north London flat were "associates" of the fugitive al Qaeda leader and chemical warfare specialist, Abu Mus'ab al-Zarqawi.[98] Such a link would have directly tied the London ricin plot to al Qaeda Central, to Ansar al-Islam in Iraq, and to the Pankisi Gorge in Georgia. In their search of the Finsbury Park Mosque in London, British police also discovered a range of conventional weapons and NBC (nuclear, biological, and chemical) suits.[99] Many of the arrested suspects were charged, including the original detainees, with conspiring to develop or produce chemical weapons.[100] However, of those brought to trial in Britain, all but one, Kamel Bourgass, were acquitted of involvement in any plot relating to chemical weapons. Bourgass was convicted of murdering a British policeman in Manchester and of conspiring to "commit a public nuisance by the use of poisons and/or explosives to cause disruption, fear or injury." The trial revealed the true nature of the London ricin plot. While Bourgass possessed castor beans, processing equipment, equipment, and "recipes" to develop ricin, he had not attempted to do so. Rather than implement a major chemical attack, he had intended simply to apply ricin to door handles in order to cause panic, rather than kill people. Moreover, although he had been a member of the GSPC in Algeria, Bourgass had little or no direct links to any definable al Qaeda entity.[101] Nonetheless, Bourgass had succeeded in sparking a vast security response and generating widespread public concern and media interest. In this respect, the case shows the efficacy of employing CBRN as a means of psychological terrorism.

The al Qaeda Network, autonomous cells of "home-grown Islamic radicals," has also plotted to use CBRN in their attacks on numerous occasions. Notably, none of these plots has made it to the implementation stage. In March 2004, al Qaeda sympathizers allegedly plotted to target civilians in London, using a combination of explosives and the chemical osmium tetroxide. Although osmium tetroxide is not a chemical that has been used for warfare, it does have the potential to cause significant damage to eyes, skin, and lungs, especially if used in a confined space. The plot, aiming to attack Gatwick airport, the London subway, or another high traffic area, was foiled before the group had acquired any of the chemical.[102] The plan to use osmium tetroxide as a chemical weapon suggests a limited knowledge of chemicals since it is highly volatile and unlikely to be effective if disseminated via an explosion. However, the unusual agent selection indicates sufficient understanding of chemistry to appreciate the weapons potential of nonstandard chemicals and an ability to think outside the box. Although osmium tetroxide is not easy to acquire, the chemical is not controlled to the same extent as other potential chemical agents.[103]

In August 2004, eight British men were charged in London with plotting to commit a public nuisance by using radioactive materials, toxic gases, chemicals, and/or explosives to cause disruption, fear, or injury. Two of the eight, Dhiren Barot (also known as Abu Musa al-Hindi or Abu Eissa al-Hindi) and Nadeem Tarmohammed possessed reconnaissance plans of the Prudential building in New Jersey, the New York Stock Exchange, and the International Monetary Fund and Citigroup in New York. Barot also possessed two notebooks containing information on explosives, poisons, chemicals, and related matters.[104] The full extent of the plot emerged at the trial, at which Barot and the others were ultimately convicted in 2006. In addition to the New York scheme, they had planned to launch widespread and simultaneous conventional weapon attacks, along with gas cylinder and explosive devices, in London. They also hoped to develop a radiological dispersal device and had conducted considerable research into such weapons. Barot had not only undergone training in Pakistan in the 1990s with al Qaeda, but also had supposedly presented his plan to members of the group, possibly as late as 2004.[105] However, the group had not apparently received funding for the project, nor acquired the vehicles or the bomb-making equipment for the attacks. In spite of this, the case was significant because the plan was so extensive, and would have led to widespread casualties, if successfully implemented. Although an attack was prevented, the case is clearly indicative of a more lethal plot by a cell with better connections back to a discernable central entity.

Conclusion

Terrorism with CBRN weapons is not a new phenomenon. Even before 9/11, there were several high-profile plots or attacks involving a range of groups with different ideologies. Both secular and religious motivations were represented in this mix of groups. Furthermore, the goals for using CBRN weapons extended from small-scale tactical attempts to extort limited gains to larger-scale efforts to achieve mass casualties. The post–9/11 situation can be seen therefore as an extension of these earlier trends. As Bruce Hoffman argues, "we face a two-fold challenge from both al Qaeda, given its long-standing and documented ambitions to develop capabilities spanning all four weapons categories . . . as well as from associated and affiliated jihadis, who are attracted to these weapons no necessarily because of their putative killing potential, but because of the profoundly corrosive and unsettling psychological effects that even a limited, discrete attack using a [CBRN] could have on a targeted society and nation."[106]

Given the scale of the 9/11 attacks, mass-casualty terrorism is now part of our reality. It thus seems likely that, given the option, al Qaeda use CBRN weapons to cause mass casualties. However, the evidence also suggests that al Qaeda has been simply trying to develop any type of weapon that might help its cause. In other words, al Qaeda appears to be pursing CBRN weapons simply as part of a broad range of options and for instrumental purposes (conventional and unconventional), rather than as an end in itself. Despite its vast resources and access to technical expertise, however, al Qaeda Central appears to have acquired only a small CBW capability in the past. The 9/11 attacks also show that CBRN weapons are not necessary to cause mass casualties. Al Qaeda has many viable conventional alternatives at its disposal, which are capable of achieving mass casualties and destruction, are easier to implement, are less expensive, and produce more predictable results. Given the difficulty and expense of acquiring and effectively using such weapons, along with the uncertain outcome of such a use, al Qaeda is likely continue to seek CBRN weapons, but will probably not rely on doing so successfully.

Despite the scale of the 9/11 attacks, it is a mistake to think of CBRN terrorism only in terms of potential mass-casualty events, a widespread tendency due to an excessive use of the flawed concept of WMD. Even before 9/11, one prominent scholar noted that:

> There is, in fact, a growing interest in chemical and biological weapons among terrorist and insurgent organizations worldwide for small-scale tactical attacks . . . [T]he flourishing mystique of chemical and biological weapons suggests that angry and alienated groups are likely to manipulate them for conventional political purposes.[107]

This prediction has largely played out in the past few years. The majority of recent attempts to acquire CBRN materials for terrorist purposes have been not from al Qaeda Central but rather from al Qaeda Local or al Qaeda Network—cells with only a loose link or no links to al Qaeda Central. This trend seems likely to continue for the foreseeable future. Small-scale attacks with unconventional materials offer the prospect of disruption, fear generation, and a psychological impact that would exceed a conventional attack with a similar level of resources. Such small-scale attacks are, generally, not likely to be resource or skill-intensive, and thus also fit the more ad hoc or amateur nature of at least some contemporary terrorism. Terrorist groups with minimal resources and expertise may be especially able to develop a basic capability for using chemical or radiological weapons. Arguably, the trend of CBRN being sought predominantly for tactical purposes, rather than as a means of causing mass casualties extends beyond the al Qaeda network.

In conclusion, given the operational challenges of successfully using CBRN weapons, conventional weapons remain more straightforward instruments for terrorists intent on causing mass casualties. In contrast, a low-grade CBRN capability offers considerable scope for causing disruption and coercion. Thus, when considering the threat of CBRN in the hands of terrorists, these weapons should be thought of mostly as weapons of mass disruption rather than mass destruction.

Gavin Cameron is an associate professor of Political Science and fellow of the Centre for Military & Strategic Studies (CMSS) at the University of Calgary in Canada. He is the author of *Nuclear Terrorism: A Threat Assessment for the 21ˢᵗ Century* (1999) and co-editor of *Agro-terrorism: What Is the Threat?* (2003). He is the 2006-8 President of the Canadian Association for Security and Intelligence Studies (CASIS).

Natasha E. Bajema is a co-editor of this volume and a Ph.D. Candidate at the Fletcher School of Law and Diplomacy, Tufts University. Before coming to Fletcher, she was a Research Associate at the Center on International Cooperation at New York University. She has also served as a Junior Political Officer in the Weapons of Mass Destruction Branch of the Department for Disarmament Affairs at the United Nations. She holds an M.A. in international policy from the Monterey Institute of International Studies.

Notes

1. Bruce Hoffman, "CBRN Terrorism Post–9/11," in Russell D. Howard and James J.F. Forest, eds., *Weapons of Mass Destruction and Terrorism* (Dubuque, IA: McGraw Hill, 2007), 264.
2. Hoffman, "CBRN Terrorism Post–9/11," 264.
3. *National Strategy for Homeland Security* (Washington DC: Homeland Security Council, 2007), 15.
4. For a broader discussion of the problems associated with WMD terrorism, as a concept, see Gavin Cameron, "WMD Terrorism in the United States: The Threat and Possible Countermeasures," *The Nonproliferation Review, 7,* no. 1 (Spring 2000): 162–163.
5. Hoffman, "CBRN Terrorism Post–9/11," 275.
6. Walter Laqueur, *The New Terrorism: Fanaticism and the Arms of Mass Destruction* (Oxford: Oxford University Press, 1999), 81.
7. Brian Jenkins, *Will Terrorists Go Nuclear?* no. P–5541 (Santa Monica, CA: RAND, 1975).
8. For further discussion on the changing nature of terrorism, see Bruce Hoffman, *Inside Terrorism,* 2nd ed. (New York: Columbia University Press, 2006). See also Walter Laqueur.
9. Bruce Hoffman, "Old Madness, New Methods: Revival of Religious Terrorism Begs for Broader U.S. Policy," *RAND Review,* Winter 1998–1999, 14.
10. Hoffman, *Inside Terrorism,* 86.
11. Amy Smithson, *Ataxia: The Chemical and Biological Terrorism Threat and the US Response,* Report No. 35 (Washington DC: The Henry L. Stimson Center, 2000), 16.
12. Amy E. Smithson and Leslie-Anne Levy, *Ataxia: The Chemical and Biological Terrorism Threat and the US Response,* Report No. 35 (Washington DC: The Henry L. Stimson Center, 2000), 16.
13. Nadine Gurr and Benjamin Cole, *The New Face of Terrorism:Threats from Weapons of Mass Destruction* (London: I.B. Tauris Publishers, 2002), 31.
14. Hoffman, *Inside Terrorism,* 88
15. The Center for Nonproliferation Studies of the Monterey Institute of International Studies maintains the largest unclassified database of incidents involving weapons of mass destruction and publishes a yearly WMD chronology.
16. W. Seth Carus, "The Rajneeshees," in Jonathan B. Tucker, ed., *Toxic Terror: Assessing Terrorist Use of Chemical and Biological Weapons* (Cambridge, MA: MIT Press, 2001), 115–138.
17. Jessica Eve Stern, "The Covenant, the Sword, and the Arm of the Lord," in Tucker, *Toxic Terror,* 139–158.

18. Jonathan B. Tucker and Jason Pate, "The Minnesota Patriots Council," in Tucker, *Toxic Terror,* 159–183.

19. "Turks Report Attempt to Poison Air Force Unit," *Reuters,* March 28, 1992; Alexander Chelyshev, "Terrorists Poison Water in Turkish Army Cantonment," *TASS,* March 29, 1992. See also Bruce Hoffman, "The Debate Over Future Terrorist Use of Chemical, Biological, Nuclear and Radiological Weapons" in Brad Roberts, ed., *Hype or Reality: The "New Terrorism" and Mass Casualty Attacks* (Alexandria, VA: The Chemical and Biological Arms Control Institute, 2000); Hoffman, *Inside Terrorism,* 268.

20. *Agence France Presse,* November 23, 1995. Mark Hibbs, "Chechen Separatists Take Credit For Moscow Cesium-137 Threat," *Nuclear Fuel, 20,* no. 25 (December 5, 1995): 5.

21. Stephane Orjollet, "Nuke Package Raises Fear of Chechen Attacks—But How Real Are They?" *Agence France Presse,* November 24, 1995.

22. See the Center for Nonproliferation Studies' "ChemBio Weapons & WMD Terrorism News Archive." Available at www.nti.org/db/cbw/index.htm.

23. The Center for Nonproliferation Studies has published a *Chronology of Aum Shinrikyo's CBW Activities,* March 2001. Available at http://cns.miis.edu/pubs/reports/aum_chrn.htm. See Smithson and Levy for a detailed analysis of Aum Shinrikyo.

24. David E. Kaplan, "Aum Shinrikyo," in Tucker, *Toxic Terror,* 210.

25. Richard Hollingham, "FBI draws blank in anthrax probe*," BBC News,* August 5, 2003.

26. Jason Pate, "Anthrax and Mass-Casualty Terrorism: What is the Bioterrorism Threat after September 11?" *US Foreign Policy Agenda,* November 2001. Available at http://usinfo.state.gov/journals/itps/1101/ijpe/pj63pate-2.htm.

27. Zahid Hussein, "Bin Laden met nuclear scientists from Pakistan," *The Times,* November 25, 2001.

28. David Charters argues that the case actually validates such assumptions since the quality of the anthrax and the fact that the perpetrator has yet to be caught suggests someone who was well-trained with special access to the material. Charters believes that the incident reinforces the belief that terrorist groups would need to acquire the expertise and access to resources that such an individual possesses in order to use biological weapons effectively. I am indebted to David Charters for his helpful comments on this point.

29. Leonard Cole, "WMD and Lessons from Anthrax Attacks," in Howard and Forest, *Weapons of Mass Destruction and Terrorism,* 88. See also Javed Ali, "No Clear Pattern Emerging in Anthrax Investigation," *CNN,* December 25, 2001.

30. Cole, 96.

31. For further discussion, see Hoffman, "CBRN Terrorism Post–9/11," 265–269.

32. Ibid, 271.

33. See, for example, Ian Reader, *Religious Violence in Contemporary Japan: The Case of Aum Shinrikyo* (Richmond, UK: Curzon Press, 2000); Robert Jay Lifton, *Destroying the World to Save It: Aum Shinrikyo, Apocalyptic Violence, and the New Global Terrorism* (New York: Henry Holt & Co, 1999); David E. Kaplan, "Aum Shinrikyo (1995)" in Tucker, *Toxic Terror.*

34. Jonathan Tucker, "Chemical Terrorism: Assessing Threats and Responses," in Howard and Forest, *Weapons of Mass Destruction and Terrorism,* 213.

35. See, for example, "Chlorine Bomb Hits Iraq village, *BBC News,* May 16, 2007. Available at http://news.bbc.co.uk/2/hi/middle_east/6660585.stm.

36. Tucker, "Chemical Terrorism," 213, 217.

37. This point was well made by Jonathan Tucker, shortly after 11 September 2001. See "The Proliferation of Chemical and Biological Weapons Materials and Technologies to State and Sub-State Actors," Testimony before the Subcommittee on International Security, Proliferation and Federal Services of the U.S. Senate Committee on Governmental Affairs, November 7, 2001.

38. Tucker, "Chemical Terrorism," 215.

39. Ibid.

40. Ibid.

41. The two known sites include the Centers for Disease Control in Atlanta and the State Research Center for Virology and Biotechnology (VECTOR) in Russia.

42. Jonathan B. Tucker and Jason Pate, "The Minnesota Patriots' Council" in Tucker, *Toxic Terror.*

43. Office of Technology Assessment, *Technologies Underlying Weapons of Mass Destruction,* 97–98.

44. Charles D. Ferguson, William C. Potter, with Amy Sands, Leonard S. Spector and Fred L. Wehling, *The Four Faces of Nuclear Terrorism* (Monterey, CA: Center for Nonproliferation Studies, 2004).

45. International Atomic Energy Agency, "Inadequate Control of World's Radioactive Sources," Press Release, 2002.

46. Graham Allison, "How to Stop Nuclear Terror," *Foreign Affairs,* 83, no. 1 (January-February 2004).

47. See Ferguson and Potter, 46.

48. Gavin Cameron, *Nuclear Terrorism: A Threat Assessment for the 21st Century* (Basingstoke: Macmillan Press, 1999), 131–132.

49. Allison, "How to Stop Nuclear Terror."

50. Bruce Hoffman, "The Changing Face of al Qaeda," *Studies in Conflict & Terrorism,* 27, no. 6 (Nov/Dec 2004): 552

51. Bruce Hoffman, "Combating Al Qaeda and the Militant Islamic Threat," Testimony before the Subcommittee on Terrorism, Unconventional Threats and Capabilities of the House Armed Services Committee, February 16, 2006, 3.

52. Ibid, 3–7.

53. Ibid, 4.

54. Ibid.

55. *The 9/11 Commission Report: Final Report of the National Commission on Terrorist Attacks Upon The United States* (New York: W. W. Norton, 2004), 151, see footnote on page 490.

56. Ibid, 154.

57. Mark Henderson, "Nuclear Reactors Vulnerable to Attack," *The Times* (London), September 27, 2001, 4; "Masterminds of 11 September Reveal Terror Secrets," *Sunday Times* (London), September 8, 2002, A1.

58. *The 9/11 Commission Report,* 245.

59. Ibid.

60. Ibid, 153–155.

61. "Transcript of News Conference on Jose Padilla," *CNN,* June 1, 2004. Available at http://www.cnn.com/2004/LAW/06/01/comey.padilla.transcript/index.html.

62. See Ron Suskind, *The One Percent Doctrine* (New York: Simon & Schuster, 2005), 218. It should also be noted that there are some grounds for skepticism over the details of the 2003 plot against the New York subway. There is little evidence that the plotters had made an attempt to acquire the necessary materials for the attack and the delivery device, the mubtakkar, that was discovered as a plan on a seized hard-drive may not have worked as effectively as Suskind described. See 193–196. See also Sammy Salama, "Special Report: Manual for Producing Chemical Weapons to be used in New York Subway Plot Available on Al-Qaeda Website Since Late 2005," *WMD Insights,* Center for Nonproliferation Studies. Available at http://cns.miis.edu/pubs/other/salama_060720.htm; "Cyanide Gas Plot Not Much of a Threat, Experts Say," *Global Security Newswire,* June 26, 2006.

63. See Salama.

64. Hoffman, "CBRN Terrorism Post–9/11," 269.

65. *The Commission on the Intelligence Capabilities of the United States Regarding Weapons of Mass Destruction,* Report to the President of the United States, March 31, 2005, 268.

66. Ibid.

67. Ibid, 269.

68. Ibid.

69. Ibid, 269–270.

70. Pamela Hess, "Al Qaida May Have Chemical Weapons," *United Press International,* August 19, 2002.

71. "Insight," *CNN,* August 19, 2002.

72. Judith Miller, "Lab Suggests Qaeda Planned to Build Arms, Officials Say," *New York Times,* September 14, 2002.
73. *The Commission on the Intelligence Capabilities,* 270.
74. Ibid, 270–271.
75. Ibid, 272.
76. Anthony Lloyd, "Bin Laden's Nuclear Secrets Found," *The Times,* November 15, 2001.
77. Bob Woodward, Robert G. Kaiser, and David Ottaway, "US Fears Bin Laden Made Nuclear Strides: Concern Over 'Dirty Bomb' Affects Security," *Washington Post,* December 4, 2001, A1.
78. Frank Gardner, "AL-Qaeda 'Was Making Dirty Bomb,'" *BBC News,* January 31, 2003. Available at http://news.bbc.co.uk/1/hi/uk/2711645.stm.
79. "Osama Bin Laden's Bid to Acquire Weapons of Mass Destruction Represents the Greatest Threat that Western Civilization has faced," *Mail on Sunday* (London), June 23, 2002.
80. Hoffman, "The Changing Face of al Qaeda," 552.
81. Daniel McGrory, "Al-Qaeda's $1 Million Hunt for Atomic Weapons," *The Times,* November 15, 2001.
82. *The Commission on the Intelligence Capabilities,* 271.
83. Ibid.
84. Ibid, 271–272.
85. Hoffman, "Combating Al Qaeda and the Militant Islamic Threat," 4.
86. Jonathan Marcus, "'Sarin bomb' reopens Iraq WMD Debate," *BBC News,* May 17, 2004. Available at http://news.bbc.co.uk/1/hi/world/middle_east/3722855.stm.
87. See, for example, Damien Cave and Ahmad Fadam, "Iraq Militants Use Chlorine in 3 bombings" *New York Times,* February 21, 2007; Steven R. Hurst, "Suicide Chlorine Bombing Kills 27: Suicide Bomber Attacks Ramadi Police Checkpoint with Truck Loaded with TNT, Chlorine, 27, Dead," *ABC News,* April 7, 2007. Available at http://abcnews.go.com/International/wireStory?id=3016594; See also "Chlorine Bomb Hits Iraq Village."
88. Hoffman, *Inside Terrorism,* 279.
89. Bruce Hoffman, "Combating Al Qaeda and the Militant Islamic Threat," 5.
90. Ibid.
91. Charles Bremner and Daniel McGrory, "Bin Laden Cell Plotted French Poison Attack," *The Times,* November 30, 2001.
92. Ibid.
93. Melinda Henneberger, "4 Arrested in Plot Against U.S. Embassy in Rome," *New York Times,* February 21, 2002, A15; Richard Boudreaux, "Italians Release Details on Suspects," *Los Angeles Times,* February 26, 2002, A3.
94. "Terror Police Find Deadly Poison," *BBC News Online,* January 7, 2003. Available at http://news.bbc.co.uk/2/hi/uk_news/2636099.stm; Stewart Tendler, Dominic Kennedy & Daniel McGrory, "Terror Raid on Poison Factory," *The Times* (London), January 8, 2003; Nick Hopkins and Tania Branigan, "Poison Sparks Terror Alert," *The Guardian,* January 8, 2003; "Experts Attempt to Track Deadly Poison," *BBC News,* January 8, 2003; "UK Terror Alert after Ricin Found," *CNN,* January 8, 2003; Nick Hopkins and Audrey Gillan, "New Arrest as Toxin Hunt Intensifies," *The Guardian,* January 9, 2003; "Police search for Accomplices in Ricin Probe," *Washington Post,* January 9, 2003; "Seventh Arrest in Ricin Case," *BBC News Online,* January 8, 2003. Available at http://news.bbc.co.uk/2/hi/uk_news/2637515.stm.
95. Helen Carter, David Ward, and Nick Hopkins, "Murder Suspect 'Is Senior Player' In Ricin Plot Network," *The Guardian* (London), January 16, 2003.
96. Leppard, Rufford and Cracknell, "How Poison Trail Spread to Britain," *The Sunday Times* (London), January 19,2003, A16–A17.
97. "Terror Police Find Deadly Poison," *BBC News Online.*
98. "Ricin Suspects Linked to al Qaeda," *CNN,* January 17, 2003; See also Leppard, Rufford and Cracknell.
99. Hala Jabar and David Leppard, "Bio-war suits found in London mosque," *The Sunday Times* (London), January 26, 2003, A1.

100. "Chemical Weapons Suspect in Court," *BBC News,* January 29, 2003.
101. Chris Summers, "Questions over Ricin Conspiracy," *BBC News,* April 13, 2005. Available at http://news.bbc.co.uk/2/hi/uk_news/4433499.stm; "The Ricin Case Timeline," *BBC News,* April 13, 2005. Available at http://news.bbc.co.uk/2/hi/uk_news/4433459.stm.
102. Brian Ross and Christopher Isham, "'Very Nasty,' Potential Bomb Plot Involved Deadly Chemical," *ABCNews.com,* April 5, 2004; See also, "Chemical 'Bomb Plot' in UK Foiled," *BBC News,* April 6, 2004. Available at http://news.bbc.co.uk/1/hi/uk/3603961.stm.
103. Michelle Baker and Margaret Kosal, "Osmium Tetroxide—a New Chemical Terrorism Weapon?" Center for Nonproliferation Studies, Monterey Institute of International Studies, April 13, 2004. Available at http://cns.miis.edu/pubs/week/040413.htm.
104. "Terror Suspects Charges in Full," *BBC News,* August 17, 2004. Available at http://news.bbc.co.uk/1/hi/uk/3573704.stm; "8 Remanded over US Terror Plot," *CNN,* August 25, 2004; "Terror Accused in Year Trial Wait," *BBC,* September 3, 2004. Available at http://news.bbc.co.uk/1/hi/uk/3625986.stm.
105. "Key Questions from the Barot case," *BBC News,* November 7, 2006. Available at http://news.bbc.co.uk/2/hi/uk_news/6126040.stm; "Prosecution Case Against al Qaeda Briton," *BBC News,* November 6, 2006. Available at http://news.bbc.co.uk/2/hi/uk_news/6122270.stm.
106. Hoffman, "CBRN Terrorism Post–9/11," 264.
107. Ehud Sprinzak, "The Great Superterrorism Scare," *Foreign Policy,* 112 (Fall 1998): 118.

John Ellis, 2003

Terrorism in the Genomic Age

Two stories were published with little fanfare in the spring of 2003. One, a Reuters dispatch, began as follows: "Scientists have completed the finished sequence of the human genome, or genetic blueprint of life, which holds the keys to transforming medicine and understanding disease. Less than three years after finishing the working draft of the three billion letters that make up human DNA and two years earlier than expected, an international consortium of scientists said on Monday (4/13/2003) the set of instructions on how humans develop and function is done."[1]

The other story, which appeared in the British weekly *The Economist,* reported that after intensive debate, The Institute for Genomic Research (TIGR) had decided to publish the anthrax genome on its website. The Bush Administration had contracted TIGR to produce a finished sequence of the anthrax genome as part of its overall effort to better understand the dimensions of the bio-terror threat. The Administration argued that publishing the anthrax genome might be detrimental to the national security interests of the United States. TIGR argued that publishing scientific research made for better scientific research.[2]

Neither story attracted much media attention, but both stories were emblematic of a profound shift in human affairs. One might call it the dawning of the Genomic Age. As Juan Enriquez, director of the Life Sciences Project at the Harvard Business School wrote in 1998, genomic science promises to "tell us about the past, who evolved from whom, and how." More important, when combined with nanotechnologies, genomic science gives mankind unprecedented power. "By understanding and being able to recreate and modify the instructions that make life, humans will soon be able to directly and deliberately influence their own evolution and that of other species."[3]

Enriquez and others have written at length on how genomics is altering and will eventually transform the global economy. Whole categories of business—including agriculture, pharmaceuticals, petrochemicals and energy—are already reconfiguring themselves to adapt to genomic science and what it implies. The immediate consequence has been a rush of corporate consolidation; a pooling of resources to help fund genomic research. It is likely that by the end of 2010, as few as seven companies will control virtually all of the value-added of agriculture; which is to say that they will own the patents to genetically modified seed that will grow into food that will be more pest-resistant, more nutritious and may well have pharmaceutical benefits as well. It is equally likely that by the end of 2010, as few as seven companies will control much of the value-added of the pharmaceutical business. And with each passing decade of this century, the difference between economic success and economic stagnation will be determined by who possesses genomic knowledge and who does not.[4]

The speed with which genomic knowledge is advancing is breathtaking. It cost a consortium of private interests, the United States and the United Kingdom roughly $5 billion over 13 years to undertake The Human Genome Project, which in the year 2000 produced the first draft of the human genome. It might have taken that consortium forty years, had not the Celera Corporation, under the direction of Dr. Craig Venter, greatly accelerated the process. But once accelerated, it is now moving at breakneck speed. A company in Cambridge, Massachusetts, called U.S. Genomics believes that it will be able to produce a complete genomic sequence of a new-born baby, stamped onto a compact disk, within two days of that child's birth, at a cost of $1000.00 per fully sequenced genome. Mom goes in, has a baby, and two days later walks out with a $1000 CD that will inform that child's medical care for the rest of his or her life. U.S. Genomics expects to be able to do this before the end of this decade.[5]

Vast (and cheap) computing power enables and turbo-charges this extraordinary advance of genomic knowledge. Countries around the world are beginning to grasp the revolutionary implications and are acting accordingly. Singapore has what might be called a genomic industrial policy. Australia has the same thing. And China, fearing it might fall behind not only the United States but its much smaller neighbors, has decided to build an entire city devoted to genomic research and development. The city is known as Genome City, and its construction is perhaps the highest priority of the Chinese government and its military. Work on the project goes 24 hours a day, 7 days a week. When it is all done, Genome City will employ and house over 50,000 people. Construction should be completed by the end of 2004.[6]

Changing the instruction sets that control the evolution of all living things will eventually be the most important business in the world. Changing the instruction sets that control the evolution of pathogens was the most secret business of two countries in the last two decades of the 20th Century. In the former Soviet Union, in direct violation of the 1972 Biological Weapons Convention, a huge team of Soviet scientists working at a facility known as the Biopreparat developed genetically altered anthrax, smallpox and plague. Working under the guidance of the Soviet military, the Biopreparat employed over 30,000 people and produced a vast arsenal of weaponized chemical and biological agents. The head of the Biopreparat, Dr. Ken Alibek, detailed the breadth and scope of the undertaking in a book[7] after he defected to the United States.

It is a terrifying book, not least because Alibek maintains that at least some of the work that was done at the Biopreparat facility carries on to this day. But it is especially terrifying for what it implies. All research into chemical and biological warfare, into virus and pathogen, is essentially "dual use." One must develop the weapon to develop the vaccine or antidote. As research and development of weaponized biological and chemical agents advances, the likelihood of a stable biological or chemical weapon increases. And as the research advances, the possibility of targeting these weapons becomes very real indeed.

The ability to target biological and chemical weapons was the focus of South Africa's top secret chemical and biological program known as Project Coast. Project Coast was created by the then white-minority government in the late 1980s. The idea was to develop a biological or chemical weapon that would kill blacks but not whites, in the event that revolutionary fervor amongst the vast black majority endangered the white population. Project Coast worked on other "ideas," such as anti-fertility drugs that would slow black population growth. But the "big idea," if one can call it that, was to find the genetic key that would enable one ethnic group to exterminate another ethnic group without putting itself at risk.[8]

Just as pharmaceuticals might be targeted at individuals, based on genetic makeup, bioweaponeers in both the Soviet Union and South Africa were exploring the possibility of targeting specific ethnic groups with biological agents. This possibility was given new momentum, in a back-handed way, in 1995, when the Aum Shinrikyo cult attacked the Tokyo subway system with Sarin gas. The attack killed 12 people and injured more than 5000 others.[9]

In his Harvard Business School case study, Juan Enriquez described what didn't happen and why: "One of the mysteries was why more people were not hurt (in the Tokyo subway attack). The crowded subway should have acted as a giant aerosol can and infected many more people. Part of the answer is that the technology used by the cult was second rate. Another part of the puzzle may be that 25% of Asians and 10% of Caucasians have an enzyme called paraoxonase in their blood that allows them to break down Sarin and other pollutants ten times faster than most people."[10]

The key finding, clearly, was that some people would die and some would not in a Sarin gas attack, depending in part on whether they did or did not have the paraoxonase enzyme. Thankfully, some of those who were inside the Tokyo subway system on that fateful day in March of 1995, did have the enzyme and so were injured but not killed in the attack. But for bioweaponeers, the larger point was that biological and chemical agents could indeed be targeted, albeit crudely, by ethnic type.

Ken Alibek and others believe that after the break-up of the Soviet Union, a not insignificant number of the scientists affiliated with the Biopreparat program were, in baseball terminology, picked up on waivers by rogue states, including Iran, Iraq and North Korea. Western intelligence agencies believe that prior to the U.S. invasion of Iraq, the regime of Saddam Hussein was especially active in the development of weaponized chemical and biological agents. It was largely for this reason that President Clinton authorized the U.S. missile attacks on Iraq in 1998 and that President Bush followed up with a full-scale invasion in 2003.[11]

Militarily, it makes sense for economically backward or stagnant states to invest heavily in bioweapons. As Enriquez points out in his HBS case study, "a UN study (conducted in 1969) estimated that the cost of using biological weapons against civilians was 1/2000 that of conventional weapons and 1/800 the cost of using nuclear weapons." As a simple of matter of return on investment, developing bioweapons offer the cheapest path to deadly peril.[12]

This is especially true now that secondary and tertiary states can access genomic information that is routinely published as a matter of scientific protocol. If they need to see a complete sequence of the anthrax genome, as noted at the start of this essay, they need only have scientists acting as cut-outs visit the website of The Institute for Genomic Research. A few such scientists thus piggy-back on the combined enterprise of the wealthiest nations on earth to extract exactly the information necessary to produce more deadly (which is to say, vaccine resistant) anthrax spores. Weaponize those spores, whether in an aerosoal can or in a warhead of some kind, and suddenly a secondary or tertiary state possesses a strategic weapon of frightening lethality.

Perhaps more frightening is the distinct possibility that a secondary or tertiary state would not want to be held accountable for the development and deployment of such a weapon and so, instead of using it, sells it to a terrorist organization that shares a common enemy (more than likely, that enemy would be the United States, the United Kingdom, Russia or China). If an anthrax aerosol bomb is released in the New York City subway system, it would be difficult if not impossible to determine who put it there. Two years after the anthrax mailings nearly paralyzed Washington, DC, the FBI and the CIA still do not know (definitively) who was responsible. Militarily, the United States (or Russia or China) would not know what to do in response to a biological attack on one of its cities, at a time when political pressure to do *something* would be at its zenith.

It is exactly this possibility that drove the Bush Administration to adopt its policy of pre-emptive action. In his speech to the graduating class of 2002 at West Point, President Bush shifted the national security policy of the United States from containment to preemption to put secondary and tertiary states on notice that if they were caught trafficking in the business of weaponizing chemical and biological agents (and/or nuclear/radiological devices), they would be subject to the full force of U.S. military power.[13] The policy of preemption has sparked considerable controversy in the United States, but it addresses the new reality of warfare. Weaponized chemical and biological agents are inherently de-stabilizing and wreak havoc on conventional military strategy and tactics. Unconventional policies are necessary to confront a thoroughly unconventional threat.

In the near term, there are two key groups whose financial wherewithal and global reach make it possible if not likely that they will use genomic knowledge for destructive and destabilizing purposes. First among these are the drug cartels. The Columbian cartels alone oversee a cash flow business of roughly $25 billion, according to DEA and independent estimates. The margins on cocaine and heroin production and distribution are well into the 70% range. This gives the cartels extraordinary financial leverage. (Obviously, the $25 billion figure is an guesstimate. The U.S. Drug Enforcement Agency and other law enforcement/intelligence services don't have a complete audit of the Cartel cash machine.[14]

That leverage, when applied to genomic drug research, enables them to not only research and develop ever more potent (and addictive) narcotics, but to research and develop next generations of drugs like Ecstasy, Viagra and methamphetamine. It is important to remember that Ecstasy was a legal drug for a number of years before Congress finally passed legislation banning its sale and use. As genomic knowledge advances, the ability to build Ecstasy-like chemical compounds (that produce a much stronger high, but more benign "hangover") will advance with it.

The rewards for building such a drug will be even more enormous than the present returns on the sale of heroin and cocaine. Scientists could stand to make tens of millions of dollars for developing a drug that produces Ecstasy-like euphoria, Viagra-like sexual enhancement and methamphetamine-like alertness. It's even possible that passing a law to outlaw such a drug would not pass, if enough people could be convinced that the after-effects were negligible. Whatever happens, it is certain that the drug environment into which the present generation of children (the so-called "echo boom" generation, which is the largest generational cohort in American history) will be loaded with chemical compounds and narcotic substances of unprecedented potency and/or addictiveness. And that the major financial beneficiaries will be the already cash-heavy cartels of Columbia and Mexico.

The second group with the financial wherewithal and global reach who can be expected to seize upon genomic knowledge for destructive and destabilizing purpose are, of course, terrorist organizations, the leading edge of which (at least for the moment) is Osama bin Laden's Al Qaeda.[15] General Wayne Downing (USA-Rtd), who served as the director of President George W. Bush's Global War on Terror (and who was largely responsible for authoring the U.S. Strategy for Fighting Global Terrorism, told the *Washington Post* at the end of 2002 that the thing that leaped off the pages and discs of the recovered (from Afghanistan) Al Qaeda documents and C-drives was Al Qaeda's zeal for either building or acquiring weapons of mass destruction.[16]

It is very difficult for an organization like Al Qaeda to build a nuclear weapon. It requires the indulgence of a host state and considerable scientific sophistication. It is considerably less difficult for an organization like Al Qaeda to build a radiological weapon, but it is much more difficult without a stable and secure "host." Least difficult is the acquisition or purchase of genetically-altered biological weapons. The price tag is very high, but the black market for such products exists. And again, as genomic knowledge advances, the cost of relatively crude genetically-altered biological and chemical weaponry will decline accordingly.[17]

What distinguishes Al Qaeda and other elements of radical Islam (from, say, nation-states like North Korea or Iran) is their willingness to use such weapons. What makes that willingness even more terrifying is that they have already shown that they can deliver such weapons through the use of what might be called "human missiles." The media call them suicide bombers. They're not. They're delivery mechanisms for strategic weapons.

The willingness of Islamic and Palestinian "terrorists" to use themselves as detonation devices makes problematic even the most basic tactics of "homeland defense." A terrorist willing to die of genetically-altered and vaccine-resistant smallpox can kill literally hundreds of thousands of people. If he or she kills hundreds of thousands of people in lower Manhattan, then the global financial markets have a seizure. If the global financial markets have a seizure, the global economy goes into a tailspin. The attacks on the twin towers of the World Trade Center cost New York City roughly $83 billion, according to a study conducted by the city's leading management consulting firms.[18] A genetically-altered smallpox attack would probably cause the City's finances to collapse altogether. And that would be the least of such an attack's consequences.

Aside from the specific threat posed by drug cartels and terrorist organizations armed with destabilizing and destructive genomic knowledge, there is another, perhaps larger, issue raised by the Age of Genomics. That issue is the separation between those who have genomic knowledge and those who don't. Countries like the United States and China that will be at the forefront of molecular biology, nanotechnologies, next generation information technology and pervasive computing will be on the winning side of what one might call the genomic/digital divide. On the other side will be a host of Islamic and African countries that will be literally unable to compete in or contribute to (except as laborers) the global economy. They will be genomic losers. One side will be able to cure cancer. The other side will beg for the medicial expertise. One side will be able to feed its population a hundred times over. The other side will experience horrific famine. One side will enjoy extraordinary wealth. The other will experience abject poverty. The seeds of resentment sown, when added to an already enraged movement of radical Islamists, will likely prove to be a highly volatile mix.

The underlying reality of modern life in most Islamic nations today is relentlessly grim. Life expectancy is short, illiteracy is high, famine is common, economic stagnation and deprivation is the norm. Governments, many of which have enjoyed long-standing support of the U.S. and its western allies, are notoriously corrupt and frequently barbaric in their abuses of human rights. For large numbers of Muslims, especially Shia Muslims, the inability to attain a better life for themselves or their children has caused them to embrace a much more virulent theocratic ideology. And in so doing, they effectively disconnect from the economically developed world. They have no stake in its success and find only solace and sweet revenge in its destruction. Genomics accentuates this separation to the ultimate degree; on one side are people capable of manipulating the evolution of all living things, on the other are people who have no power at all. Except, of course, the power to create and replicate catastrophic events.[19]

So what does all this suggest, in terms of policy?

First, it is of paramount concern that the United States and its allies do everything possible to enforce strict protocols and conventions with regards to the use of biological and chemical weapons. Any country that indulges in this kind of research, development or deployment must be subject to the harshest possible sanctions, including the possibility of armed intervention.

Second, it is critical that the United States and its allies do everything it can to enhance its capability of responding to bioterrorism. A recent study by the Partnership for Public Service found, according to a *New York Times* report, that "the (U.S.) government is likely to be overwhelmed in the event of a bioterrorism attack because of serious shortages in skilled medical and scientific personnel." Even if one allows considerable leeway for hyperbole (when was the last time a public service advocacy group thought the government was doing a bang-up job?), the fact remains that the anthrax mail attacks in the fall of 2001 did indeed reveal an almost woeful lack of preparedness for biological attack. While U.S. government preparedness has substantially improved since them, the shortage of skilled personnel remains a source of real worry in the event of another attack.[20]

Third, it is critical that molecular biologists and genomic scientists engage in a Manhattan Project–effort to create new scientific protocols that will specifically address the national security issues raised by genomic research and development. Since Hiroshima and Nagasaki, physicists have engaged with the government to control and contain the spread of nuclear weapons. As Henry Kelly, president of the Federation of American Scientists, recently argued in the *New York Times,* the time has come for genomic scientists and molecular biologists to do the same thing.[21]

Fourth and perhaps finally, genomic research must advance. As Henry Kelly wrote in the *New York Times,* "the difference between a lab for producing lifesaving vaccines and one capable of making deadly toxins is largely one of intent." The more genomic knowledge we have, the more ways we will have to combat pathogens, either through vaccine or antidote, the less likely it is that a genetically-altered pathogen will yield a catastrophic result. Our intent must be to act in the best interests of mankind. We must grow the food, fight the disease, enrich and elongate life. The Genomic Age will largely be defined on how well we measure up.[22]

John Ellis is a Jebsen Center Senior Fellow for Counter-Terrorism Studies. He is a leading expert in genomic and biological warfare and a nationally-recognized journalist and media consultant on political, economic, and terrorism-related issues. From 2002 to 2004, Mr. Ellis was a Senior Fellow at the Combating Terrorism Center at West Point. Mr. Ellis is currently a partner in Sand Hills Partners, a small venture capital firm, and the Chairman of Sand Hills Celera Capital Corporation, a privately-held business development corporation.

Notes

1. http://www.msnbc.com/news/899806.asp?0cv=HA00.
2. http://www.economist.com/displaystory.cfm?story_id=1748489.
3. *Gene Research, the Mapping of Life and the Global Economy* is a Harvard Business School Case Study, N9-599-016, written by Juan Enriquez and is available at www.hbsp.harvard.edu.
4. For more on how genomics is transforming agriculture and pharmaceuticals, see http://harvardbusinessonline.hbsp.harvard.edu/b01/en/common/item_detail.jhtml?id=R00203.
5. The exact cost of the Human Genome Project is, at some level, unknowable, since knowledge begets knowledge and the cost of academic research is fungible. The U.S. government contributions are detailed at http://www.ornl.gov/TechResources/Human_Genome/project/budget.html. The ballpark number of $5 billion includes the contributions of the United Kingdom and private charitable trusts. For more on Eugene Chan and his work at U.S. Genomics, visit http://www.cio.com/archive/010103/37.html. The specifics about stamping out a CD of an infant's genome were taken from notes at the Genomic Sequencing and Analysis Conference in Boston, Massachusetts, in September of 2002. The author attended the conference.
6. This information was gleaned from interviews with Juan Enriquez of the Harvard Business School, who was given a tour of Genome City by Chinese Government Officials.
7. *Biohazard: The Chilling True Story of the Largest Covert Biological Weapons Program in the World—Told from the Inside by the Man Who Ran It.*
8. See the *Washington Post,* April 20 and 21, 2003.
9. http://www.cdc.gov/ncidod/EID/vol5no4/olson.htm.
10. Enriquez, HBS Case Study N9-599-016.
11. See *The Demon in the Freezer,* by Richard Preston as well as *Biohazard,* by Ken Alibek.
12. Enriquez, HBS Case Study N9-599-016.
13. http://www.jinsa.org/articles/print.html?documentid=1492.
14. For a good overview of the drug threat, see http://www.usdoj.gov/dea/pubs/intel/02046/02046.html.
15. See *Inside Al Qaeda,* by Rohan Gunaratna.
16. http://usembassy.state.gov/mumbai/wwwfns.pdf for National Strategy for Combating Terrorism. For Downing comments, see *Washington Post,* December 24, 2002.
17. *Washington Post,* April 20–21, 2003.
18. http://www.nycp.org/impactstudy/release.htm.
19. See the annual *Economist* survey of 2002 for updated statistics of relative wealth and poverty; http://www.theworldin.com/.
20. *New York Times,* July 5, 2003.
21. *New York Times* op-ed, July 2, 2003.
22. *New York Times* op-ed, July 2, 2003.

Chris Dishman, 2005

The Leaderless Nexus: When Crime and Terror Converge

This article argues that the breakdown of hierarchical structures in illicit organizations is creating new opportunities for criminals and terrorists to collaborate. The rise of networked organizations has given greater independence to criminals and terrorists who previously answered to a clear chain of command. These members are now willing to engage in operations that before had been off-limits because the leadership believed the activity would hurt the organization's broader mandate. The result is that a "leaderless nexus" is beginning to emerge between criminals and terrorists. The phenomenon has far-reaching and dangerous implications for U.S. security, and should be thoughtfully considered as lawmakers debate homeland security reform.

International law enforcement pressure is forcing criminal and terrorist organizations to decentralize their organizational structures. Mexican law enforcement efforts are causing drug cartels in Mexico to break into smaller units. Many of the leaders who constituted Al Qaeda's command and control leadership are under arrest or dead, forcing bin Laden to play a more inspirational role, no longer micromanaging attacks as he did for the 11 September spectacular. Even groups that still maintain some hierarchical structure, like the terrorist group Hezbollah, have little control over their extensive networks.

The "flattening" of these groups is creating new and dangerous opportunities for collaboration between criminals and terrorists. The actions of criminal underlings or terrorist operatives are not as constrained because criminal or terrorist "headquarters" are no longer able to micromanage employees. Lower to mid-level criminals and terrorists are taking advantage of their independence to form synergistic ties between the two groups. Some political militant groups have also introduced financial incentive systems to recruit and retain militants. Because members join to make money, they will quickly set ideological goals to the side if it affects profits.

Criminals and terrorists have collaborated on some level for centuries. As many observers point out, the two groups work toward nefarious ends in the same underground community. This cooperation, however, was usually restricted to lower level criminals and terrorists and even then only for short durations. A Don, Colombian cartel boss, or Snakehead would not put his organization in bed with a terrorist group—not because of higher moral values—but because it was bad for business; cooperation with political radicals would turn unwanted attention onto his group. In the last two decades, however, these bosses have been forced to decentralize their organizations, and the managerial role of the leader has been replaced by a networked organization. In short, Don Corleone can no longer order his *mafiosi* to stay away from drug trafficking.

Nowhere is this dynamic more apparent than in the financing of terrorist and criminal cells that are forced to generate funds independently without assistance from leadership. International money laundering crackdowns are making it more difficult for terrorist financiers to quickly and continually send money to their operatives. Low- to mid-level terrorist and criminal actors are forced to find their funding sources, fraudulent documents, transportation, and safe houses. Mid to lower-level criminals—who have quickly risen to greater levels of prominence in decentralized structures—have few qualms working with terrorists, in spite of the fact their ultimate boss would certainly disapprove of such an arrangement. The result is that a *leaderless nexus* has emerged between criminals and terrorists; a phenomenon with far-reaching implications that should be a major concern for law enforcement and intelligence.

The Rise of Networks in Corporations, Transnational Criminal Organizations (TCOs), and Terrorist Groups

Early in the twentieth century, industrialists like Henry Ford brought hierarchies to new heights. Hierarchies enabled businesses to mass produce and mass distribute goods and services. Companies were large, maintained tight control over their operations, provided clear roles for each worker, and asked workers to perform specialized tasks.[1]

The dawn of the Information Age, which brought a different set of factors for corporate success, quickly strained the rigid hierarchical organization. Speed, flexibility, integration, and innovation became ingredients for success in the modern era. In a hierarchy, boundaries exist between managers and the rank and file (ceilings and floors) and "walls" divide each function or specialization within the company.[2] Information is compartmented within the upper levels of the organization while the workers perform specialized tasks or functions.

Profits plummeted when hierarchical corporations could not adjust to the demands of the Information Age. Some companies realized that the hierarchy was impeding their success and radically changed their organizational structure to adapt to the new environment.[3] General Electric (GE), for example, implemented a "Workout" program that created permeable boundaries and shifted resources to support its processes versus functions. Workers learned new capabilities and assumed new responsibilities. Information was no longer compartmented and senior managers shared the company's goals and objectives with the rank and file.

The Information Age has not just had severe implications in the business sector, but also for terrorism and organized crime. In the last 20 years, criminal and terrorist organizations have undergone their own versions of GE's "Workout" program. Terrorist and criminal organizations began to transform their own hierarchical structures into networks. Some, like Al Qaeda, expanded the size and importance of networks already imbedded in their traditional hierarchical organizations, whereas others evolved from a networked group into a more complex horizontal design. Unlike the business community, low profits did not drive these organizations to seek change; law enforcement and intelligence, which began to successfully root out subversive organizations, forced illegal armed groups to find new ways to evade authority and become more resilient. Criminals and terrorists needed to ensure that their organization would not collapse if the main leader or leaders were arrested or killed.

John Arquilla and David Ronfeldt, pioneers in the discussion of network design, describe networks as the organizational cornerstone of a new mode of conflict.[4] Networks contain dispersed nodes—either cells or individuals—internetted together by similar beliefs, ideology, doctrine, and goals. There is no central command, headquarters, or single leader. Cells communicate horizontally and rely extensively on technology to facilitate the heavy communication necessary for networks to carry out operations or tasks. Participants in a network can range from the ultra-committed, to individuals who participate for only short periods.

Modern religious terrorist organizations, more so than criminal ones, have aggressively adopted networked structures in the face of intense counterterror actions. Domestic terrorist groups aiming to overthrow closed-political regimes learned quickly that a network provides resilience. Islamist groups in Egypt, for example, have been forced to radically change their organizational structure to be resilient in the face of suffocating counterterror operations.[5] Since 11 September, pressure against international terror organizations like Al Qaeda has also forced those groups to rely more on networks to organize, prepare for, and carry out attacks.

Terrorists have not always used networks extensively. Marxist terrorist groups, for example, were organized along hierarchical lines.[6] Many of these groups were state sponsored, which necessitated a tight line of control from the state liaison to the group's leader. The state needed a single person or group of persons to interface and give assurances about operations and goals. Any rogue actions by the terrorists could undermine the state's larger political objectives.

A networked organization can still contain hierarchical components. A command cadre, for example, can be imbedded within one node of the organization. There could also be an overarching hierarchy that only uses a network for tactical operations. Terrorist organizations that emerged in the 1980s and 1990s adopted this mix of network and hierarchy. Hezbollah, which emerged in earnest in 1982, is a purposeful blend of hierarchy and network.[7] While the hierarchy enables Hezbollah to control parts of Lebanon and participate in state politics, the network gives Hezbollah financial, religious, social, and military support inside and outside of the country. The network is comprised of Hezbollah followers guided by religious clerics on important political, social, or military subjects. As Hezbollah has no "membership," its leaders rely on the clerics and their own following to influence others to work toward the organization's interests. Hezbollah's hierarchy, in contrast, has formal and direct links between its organs. Its structure includes the highest authority, the decision-making *shoura* (council), which is made up of seven special committees: ideological, financial, military, political, judicial, informational, and social affairs. The committee's members are elected every two years and it is headed by the Secretary General. Hezbollah also contains other hierarchical elements including a Politburo and an Executive *shoura* that is responsible for implementing the high council's decisions. The Deputy Secretary General of Hezbollah outlined the decision to pursue a mixed structure: "We concluded at the end (of organizational discussions) that we needed a structural organization which was in some respects rigid enough to be able to prevent infiltration by the enemy and at the same time flexible enough to embrace the maximum sector of people without having to go through a long bureaucratic process of red tape."[8]

Another organization that maintained a mix of network and hierarchy was the Shining Path, a Maoist guerrilla group in Peru that aimed to overthrow the government with a People's Revolution. Before its dismantlement, the Shining Path's hierarchy consisted of a National Directorate, a Central Committee, and several regional commands.[9] Unlike Hezbollah, however, the hierarchy was not a collective body where everyone was given an equal vote. In fact, the hierarchy was designed to implement the decisions of one person, Abimael Guzman, who alone decided the group's strategy, objectives, and aims. The "rank and file" members comprised the network of the organization. They were organized into cells that had little contact with the hierarchy. The network allowed the Shining Path to operate over a vast geographic area because the widespread rank and file could make decisions without guidance from the command cadre.

Like modern terrorists, law enforcement crackdowns on transnational criminal organizations (TCOs) have forced criminals to expand their use of networks. Networks facilitate illegal commerce and help TCOs avoid and respond to law enforcement. Drug trafficking organizations in Mexico, in particular, have been forced to decentralize as law enforcement continues to decapitate the leadership of their organizations.[10] Mexican authorities have arrested key members of 3 different cartels within a 14-month period.[11] Mexico's senior counter drug official noted that a result of the spate of drug arrests is that drug leaders are realizing that their organization will become disorganized and chaotic if its hierarchy is decapitated.[12] Cells begin to act independently without regard for the organization in order to make money. Leaders understand that this disarrayed organization is even more susceptible to continuing law enforcement pressure.[13] According to the official, one cartel has organized into a "horizontally-structured business council" to sustain its operations in face of intense law enforcement pressure.[14]

Members of drug trafficking organizations (DTOs), including Mexican drug trafficking organizations, are being pushed further from their traditional center of gravity, with the leadership forced to maintain distance from the members in order to evade law enforcement. Criminal expert Phil Williams notes that many criminal organizations still use some form of hierarchical design, only incorporating or expanding networks where needed. Williams outlines a framework for a networked criminal organization: a core, composed of tight-knit leadership and a periphery consisting of expendable, networked criminals.[15] This organizational mutation is probably only temporary—a transition point from a traditional hierarchical criminal group to a fully networked organization. The vulnerability of a core, even within a networked organization, will probably compel criminal leaders to further flatten their organizational structures.

The Role of a Terrorist Leader in Different Organizational Structures

Marsha Crenshaw, an authority on terrorist organizations, believes that one of the most important jobs of a terrorist leader is preventing the defection of persons to the aboveground world or to another radical organization by creating an attractive incentive structure.

> Leaders ensure organizational maintenance by offering varied incentives to followers, not all of which involve the pursuit of the group's stated political purposes. Leaders seek to prevent both defection and dissent by developing intense loyalties among group members. . . . Leaders maintain their position by supplying various tangible and intangible incentives to members, rewards that may enhance or diminish the pursuit of the organization's public ends.[16]

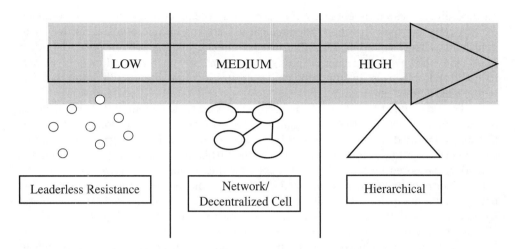

Figure 1. The degree of a leader's control in different forms of terrorist and criminal organizations. In a hierarchy, the leader controls almost all aspects of the organization, including recruitment, promotion, delegation of authority, and the planning of major events (i.e., Terrorist attack or criminal undertaking). In a decentralized cell structure, there is no single leader or command element that controls all the various nodes in the network. Cell leaders guide the activities of individual cells. In a leaderless resistance movement, the leader's role is restricted to providing inspiration to its members (or potential members) to undertake tasks on behalf of the group.

The creation of an incentive structure, as highlighted by Crenshaw, was an important characteristic of a leader managing an illicit hierarchy. Now, many terrorists groups have transformed into networked organizations, radically changing the role of the leader. At a minimum, a network has no single leader or command cadre that manages and oversees the organization. Sometimes there are no leaders at all, or leaders might be imbedded in various network nodes, or cells, but without authority over the broader organization (see Figure 1). One of the advantages of a network is that there is no leader who assumes so much responsibility that his or her arrest or death derails the organization's mission and capability. The use of networks is almost a natural evolution in response to a law enforcement strategy designed to decapitate the leadership of criminal or terrorist organizations—a hierarchy attacking a hierarchy. In addition to networks, there is another type of organization with no leader—leaderless resistance. This form of organization has no network, no leaders, and cannot be described as "flat" because it only consists of single individuals or very small groups who are not tied to any other organizations—vertically or horizontally.

The role of leaders in these types of organizations merits some discussion.

Hierarchical

In a hierarchical organization, the leader plays a direct role managing the activities of the organization. The leader acts as a Chief Executive Officer, delegating authority to subordinates and maintaining clear chains of command. The hierarchical organization is structured to facilitate top-to-bottom guidance. Ideas are rarely presented from the bottom-up, but even if they are, the group's leaders retain veto power over the idea. The leaders rely on subordinates with different areas of responsibility (i.e., security, financial, recruitment, etc.) to carry out their direction. Hierarchical leaders can be micro-managers; they will punish a low-level subordinate for a mistake, or direct a small activity or operation. Most importantly, however, the leader ensures the organization's operations ultimately support its goals and objectives. In sum, a hierarchy creates a cohesive monolithic unit that acts within well-defined parameters.

The Provisional Irish Republican Army (PIRA), a typical hierarchical organization, offers some insights. The PIRA is organized like a business, with positions, responsibilities, and authority dispersed in a pyramid-shaped organization. The Army Council controls and directs the military strategy and tactics of the PIRA, including ordering or vetoing the operations proposed by subordinate elements.[17] Military guidance is passed to either the PIRA's Northern or Southern Command—military elements with areas of responsibility, not dissimilar in organization to the U.S. Unified Command Plan. There is also a General Headquarters staff that oversees all PIRA activities through its ten departments. Overall, the organization proved very effective (although not resilient), because as one expert notes,[18] disputes were always ruled on by higher authorities ensuring a cohesive unit to carry out the leadership's guidance.

Decentralized Cell Structure

A decentralized cell structure is one characteristic of a networked organization, although not a defining trait. Understanding the leader's role in this form of organization—which is usually prominent in some form of a network—provides insights into the evolving role of leaders within a network.

Arquilla and Ronfeldt describe the structure and role of leaders in one form of network:

> The network as a whole (but not necessarily each node) has little to no hierarchy; there may be multiple leaders. Decision making and operations are decentralized, allowing for local initiative and autonomy. Thus the design may look acephalous (headless) at times, and polycephalous (Hydraheaded) at other times, though not all nodes may be "created equal." In other words, it is a heterarchy, or what may be better termed a panarchy.[19]

As Arquilla and Ronfeldt note, the major difference in leadership in a decentralized cell structure versus a hierarchy is that a cell structure can have multiple leaders—a panarchy—whose functions and responsibilities change depending on circumstances. The leader is usually the person with the most experience in the cell, and its members naturally defer to this veteran. Within the cell, the leader ensures tasks are carried out appropriately without attracting law enforcement attention. The cell leader is also responsible for external relations, although contact is usually kept to a minimum and the cell retains extensive independence. Along these lines, Marc Sageman, whose examination of Al Qaeda focuses on social networks, believes that hub leaders are dynamic, outgoing personalities with extensive social reach. These persons are able to attract recruits and can help guide them to the training necessary to participate in jihad.[20]

The absence of the top-down guidance existing in a hierarchical organization makes it imperative for the nodes in the network to communicate on a regular basis to ensure that each is operating within the context of a larger plan. He or she is also the ideological or doctrinal espouser and watchdog—ensuring that everyone maintains the ideological fervor necessary for the success of the cell and its broader networked organization. This is perhaps the most important responsibility, because the broader networked organization, of which the cell is a part, will only be successful if cell members retain similar goals, aims, and beliefs.[21]

Leaderless Resistance

A third type of organization has been coined by experts as "leaderless resistance." Jeffrey Kaplan defines leaderless resistance as:

> . . . A lone wolf operation in which an individual, or a very small, highly cohesive group, engage in acts of anti-state violence independent of any movement, leader, or network of support.[22]

In a leaderless organization, there are no leaders—only perpetrators—involved in an attack. Ideologues goal or motivate the radical masses into conducting attacks. As terrorism expert Jessica Stern notes, "inspirational leaders" encourage their followers to attack targets but the leaders do not provide funding, direct orders, or any other form of tangible support. Anti-abortionists, for example, will raise money for jailed militants, but never participate in any pre-attack measures.[23]

The White Aryan Nation (WAR) urged followers to conduct violent attacks after Proposition 187, which would bar illegal immigrants from receiving government services in California, was stopped by a Federal court. The leader stated that "Today, California ceased to exist as an Aryan-dominated state. W.A.R. releases all associates from any constraints, real or imagined, in confronting the problem in any way you see fit."[24]

Leaderless resistance was popularized by the right-wing preacher and radical Louis Beam. Right wing groups such as the Phineas Priesthood and the White Aryan Resistance embraced Beam's vision by ensuring that no formal organization existed in their movements. There is no hierarchy or chain of command between the group's activists and its leadership. Activists do not rely on support from other cells so there is very little—if any—communication between operatives or their cells. Each operative is self-sufficient; they will choose the site of an attack and plan the attack on their own. Interestingly, left wing groups also adopted Beam's vision of a leaderless organization. The radical environmental group, the Earth Liberations Front (ELF) encourages its followers to create their own cell rather than joining an existing cell because efforts to locate an existing cell could compromise the organization.[25] ELF's cells are independent and autonomous, and members do not know the identities of members in a different cell; the cells are "linked" together by a shared ideology.[26]

Al Qaeda Is Forced to Decentralize

Al Qaeda is the most salient example of a terrorist organization that has been forced to decentralize. Since 11 September Al Qaeda has lost roughly 70 percent of its leadership, which comprised the heart of Al Qaeda's command cadre. Experts have given different names to this centralized element, including the Al Qaeda hard core, Al Qaeda hierarchy,

Al Qaeda's professional cadre, or Al Qaeda's central staff. This centralized element, created in 1998, coordinates and oversees the functions and tasks of Al Qaeda, including preparing for and executing terrorist attacks.[27]

Terrorist expert Peter Bergin believes Al Qaeda's centralized structure functions like a corporation, where bin Laden, acting as director, formulates policies in consultation with his top advisors.[28] These policies are implemented by a series of subordinate "committees," the most senior of which is the *shura majlis,* or "Advisory Council," which is attended by Al Qaeda's most veteran leaders and reports directly to bin Laden.[29] Under this council are at least four committees, including a military; finance and business; fatwa and Islamic study; and media and publicity committee.[30] Committee members can serve on more than one committee and sometimes individuals work directly for bin Laden on special assignments.[31] Committee membership is based on family, nationality, and friendship. In this regard, Al Qaeda's command element resembles the mafia: merit and performance play little role in success in the hierarchy.[32]

Bin Laden utilizes this structure to carry out spectacular mass attacks. The military committee, for example, plans and executes attacks for Al Qaeda, conducts surveillance, gathers intelligence, and trains members in military tactics.[33] The head of Al Qaeda's military committee prior to 11 September, Khalid Sheikh Muhammad, conceived and helped plan the plot to crash airliners into symbolic U.S. targets.[34] Bin Laden operates both within and outside this structure. For the most important terrorist attacks, bin Laden dealt directly with those executing the plot. The National Commission on Terrorist Attacks revealed, for example, that bin Laden played a very "hands-on" role in planning the 11 September attacks: he handpicked the operatives that participated in the operation; he cancelled a planned operation to crash airliners in Southeast Asia; he personally interceded to keep an operative in the plot who Muhammad wanted removed; and rejected several shura members' recommendations to abort the attacks.[35] Although the degree of bin Laden's involvement, as revealed by the Commission, could be overstated, it's clear that at a minimum he was heavily involved in operational decision making.

The loss of Al Qaeda's Afghanistan haven, and the death or arrest of many of its senior leaders, has forced Al Qaeda to decentralize. Because communication links between Al Qaeda's centralized command and its operatives have been disrupted, bin Laden and his central staff now play a less direct role in planning attacks.[36] Al Qaeda's operational commanders and cell leaders exert more authority and make decisions that used to be under bin Laden's purview.[37] Although it's unclear to what extent the committees are still functioning, bin Laden's essential need for secrecy since 11 September suggests that at a minimum, the committees are not operating as efficiently as before. According to J. Cofer Black, the State Department's Counterterrorism Coordinator, some terrorist cells have delayed attacks because of communication mix-ups between the group and Al Qaeda's leadership. Black cites the attack on the Muhaya housing compound in Riyadh as an example of the lack of clear direction Al Qaeda is providing to its network. The attack resulted in the deaths of many Muslims during Ramadan and as Cofer dryly noted, "was a public relations disaster"—the attack awoke the dormant Saudi counterterrorism apparatus that began to flush out Al Qaeda cells.[38] Additionally, the international financial crackdown on Al Qaeda's finances has probably hurt the finance committee's ability to fund operations worldwide.

The Negative Results of Decentralization:
Criminal, Terrorist Boundaries Less Clear

Al Qaeda provides a sharp illustration of a terrorist group forced to decentralize. Many other criminal and terrorist organizations also use networks to plan terrorist attacks or run illicit rackets. In the case of Al Qaeda, decentralization has probably hurt the organization's ability to carry out spectacular terrorist attacks. Nevertheless, the proliferation of international criminal and terrorist networks like Al Qaeda pose new threats to stability. Because networks marginalize or eliminate the command cadre, cells and nodes now have expanded roles and responsibilities. These lower to mid-level members define the organization, its actions, its direction and its goals. The activities of these operatives, who are the critical pillars of terrorist and criminal organizations, are no longer constrained by a leader or elder. This freedom allows individuals or small cells to pursue multiple nefarious ends, even at the expense of broader organizational goals. Although political[39] and financial aims are two distinct, usually incompatible ends, lower and midlevel operators do not wrestle with such academic distinctions. A criminal seeks to keep the status quo, stay out of the limelight, not commit collateral violence, and make money. A terrorist in contrast seeks attention, wants to commit collateral violence, and wants to alter the status quo. Lower to mid-level cell leaders are not concerned with incompatible goals, however, and without oversight will pursue personal and organizational agendas.

Historically, the distinction between a criminal and a terrorist has not always been clear. Many terrorists use crime to generate revenue to support their ultimate political goal, whereas some criminals use illicit funds to support radical political causes. Even prior to 11 September, Al Qaeda directed its cells to be financially self-sufficient.[40] Some criminals use terrorism (as a violent tactic) against authorities if a large-scale crackdown on their organization occurs. Nevertheless, within hierarchical organizations there is still some degree of leadership control that could bring the organization back on course should the organization's goals begin to stray from the original cause.[41] An organization that is completely decentralized, or contains a large decentralized component, is usually unwilling or unable to control the activities of its members. This dynamic is most applicable to criminal syndicates, where the transition from hierarchy to a decentralized network has sometimes created an "every cell for itself" atmosphere. Cash-strapped cells are now willing to conduct any crime in order to stay afloat.[42] These crimes could include operations previously "out of bounds" for most transnational organized criminal groups, including smuggling weapons of mass destruction, creating fraudulent documents for terrorists, or smuggling terrorist personnel. These cells are also no longer constrained by a leadership that prohibited interaction with terrorists because of the unwanted law enforcement attention such activities would bring.[43]

In addition to being unable to control its members, a decentralized network is unable to provide continuous financial assistance to its nodes. The need for secrecy and resiliency between nodes in the network means that money is not often passed between nodes or amassed in a single node in the network. There is no "terrorist bank" that a member can go to request funds in a decentralized network. Because of these financial difficulties, many terrorist nodes have taken an unprecedented foray into organized crime to raise money for their financially depleted cell or hub. Al Qaeda cells and hubs, for example, are deeply involved with drug trafficking in Afghanistan and have purchased illegitimate diamonds from rebels in Africa.[44] In December 2003 coalition forces seized three vessels smuggling heroin and hashish in the Persian Gulf that were probably tied to Al Qaeda operatives.[45] Far-flung Hezbollah networks have also generated a significant amount of money. According to one official, Hezbollah received anywhere from $50–$100 million from the tri-border region in South America. Two Hezbollah operatives in Cuidad del Este, Paraguay are estimated to have moved $50 million to Hezbollah from 1995 until their arrest in 2001. The cell raised money through counterfeiting, money laundering, and extortion.[46] A Hezbollah cell in North Carolina took advantage of the tax difference on cigarettes sold in North Carolina and Michigan to net over $7.9 million. Law enforcement authorities believe that terrorist groups in the United States continue to smuggle cigarettes, netting an average of $2 million on each truckload of the product.[47]

Dangerous Dynamics Emerge

Two phenomenon result from the increasing authority of low- to mid-level criminal and terrorist leaders and their need to survive in a decentralized environment. First, these leaders will increasingly seek to collaborate with criminal or terrorist counterparts outside of the organization for extended periods of time. These new cadre of leaders will be more likely to create strategic alliances with other terrorist or criminal subversives. Second, the decentralized organization will internally transform so that both criminals and terrorists are critical ingredients in the organization's structure.

External Convergence

Past criminal/terrorist alliances were usually short-term relationships that existed on a case by case basis only. These were "one spot" arrangements, where terrorists or criminals would collaborate for only short periods of time.[48] Terrorists might provide bomb-making skills to a criminal group for a set fee, but the relationship would end after the training was over. In 1993, for example, some reports alleged that Pablo Escobar hired National Liberation Army (ELN) guerrillas to plant car bombs because Escobar's organization could not carry out such attacks.[49] One-spot arrangements can also include single transactions between criminal and terrorist groups. In one example, four members of the United Self-Defense Groups of Colombia were arrested in Houston, Texas when they tried to exchange $25 million of cocaine and cash for shoulder-fired anti-aircraft missiles and other weapons.[50]

From now on, criminal and terrorist cell or hub leaders will build long-term alliances with their criminal or terrorist counterpart, allowing each group to benefit from the other's knowledge and experience. In January 2002, members of a Hezbollah drug ring were arrested in "Operation Mountain Express" by U.S. and Canadian authorities. The Hezbollah ring was smuggling pseudoephedrine, a precursor chemical for methamphetamines, from Canada to Mexican criminal gangs in the Midwest. The Hezbollah operatives had established a long-standing criminal alliance with the Mexican drug dealers from which they netted at least millions of dollars that were laundered to terrorists in the Middle East.[51] Although this Hezbollah group laundered the proceeds to a Middle Eastern terrorist group, the cell could have also kept the money to sustain the cell and possibly prepare for an attack. In this respect, long-term alliances radically improve the effectiveness of each cell or small group. Terrorists will be able to raise more money from criminal actions. Ramzi Yousef, mastermind of the 1993 bombing of the World Trade Center, wanted to build a bigger bomb to topple one tower into the other, but he could not because he lacked the necessary funding.[52]

"External" alliances could become internal as the outside party becomes integrated into the network. A decentralized network facilitates these relationships by allowing cells or individuals to participate in the network in any capacity. As Williams states, "networks can be highly structured and enduring in nature or they can be loose, fluid, or amorphous in character, with members coming and going according to particular needs, opportunities and demands. Some individuals or even small organizations will drift in and out of networks when it is convenient for them to do so."[53] Businessmen and criminals who benefit from a guerrilla war economy would probably be folded into a network because their financial security is directly tied to the ongoing war and the guerrilla rebellion.

Hybrid Organizations

A second and equally important dynamic is the "hybridization" of criminal or terrorist networks. A model example of a functioning network would consist of cells and members with similar ideologies, motives, and views of success or failure. When cells or nodes begin to pursue their own agendas, the like-minded identity that binds the network together dissolves and a hybrid organization emerges. The new hybrid organization is dominated by persons in cells, fronts, or other organizational components that retain multiple motives and desired end-states. Some Islamic militants, for example, are heavily involved in drug trafficking and reap major profits from the illegal activity. These militants justify drug trafficking because they believe their enemies suffer from drug consumption. In their view, they receive a dual benefit from the crime: they generate profits and hurt their enemies. These profits can be used to support the cell's activities, be invested in personal bank accounts, or given to friends and families. Hezbollah, for example, which has been involved in drug trafficking in Lebanon, views drug trafficking as another weapon to use against its enemies. One Hezbollah *fatwa* (religious edict) stated that "We are making these drugs for Satan America and the Jews. If we cannot kill them with guns, so we will kill them with drugs."[54] In more recent illustration, law enforcement officials investigating the Madrid bombings noted that one of the suspect bombers "justified drug trafficking if it was for Islam . . . he saw it as part of jihad."[55]

Identifying a hybrid is difficult. Cells within hybrid organizations are chameleons—criminal by day, terrorist by night. A sleeper cell may not look like a sleeper cell at all; its activities focused on organized crime: extortion, counterfeiting, drug trafficking, and so on. Authorities investigating the Madrid train bombings stated that one of the suspect's drug trafficking activities masked his involvement in terrorism; authorities never considered him part of a terrorist plot.[56] Identifying a hybrid is also challenging because it has no hierarchy from which an analyst can determine aims, goals, and degree of control.

Hybrid organizations form synergistic ties internally to build criminal or terrorist expertise (see Figure 2). Cell leaders collaborate with other cells or nodes to maximize criminal gains or prepare for violent attacks. One result is that terrorist cells increase their

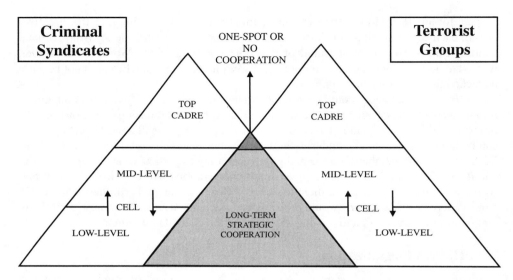

Figure 2. Graphic depiction of a new dynamic where low- to mid-level criminals and terrorists create strategic alliances with each other. These lower to mid-level members are the pillars of decentralized criminal and terrorist organizations, and cooperation between the two will lead to new challenges for law enforcement authorities.

financial intake by participating in sophisticated organized criminal rings. The examples shown earlier (Al Qaeda and Hezbollah) illustrate the millions of dollars that can be generated from organized crime. As noted earlier, emerging information about the Madrid bombings shows that many of the plotters were heavily involved in drug trafficking. Jamal Ahmidan, one of the cell's ringleaders, allegedly traded hashish for 220 pounds of dynamite used in the attack. He also brought in six drug traffickers who participated in the plot.[57] The result of this criminal, terrorist synergy was a devastating blast that killed 191 people.

Enforcement Implications

The breakdown of hierarchical organizations poses a unique challenge for law enforcement and intelligence. Law enforcement's successful strategy of arresting high value targets has forced criminal and terrorist leaders to be less involved in the day to day direction of the organization. The result is a growing independence, sophistication, and number of small cells or criminal gangs that multiplies the number of targets law enforcement must pursue. Decentralized organizations leave few evidentiary trails between the leadership and its cells, and between the cells themselves. Many cell leaders cannot identify other cell members or their support personnel. In Colombia, for example, a senior law enforcement official noted that Colombian traffickers now operate in small, autonomous cells that make it more difficult for law enforcement to discover them.[58] Gathering information about a hierarchical organization was easier because law enforcement agents only needed to recruit one well-placed informant to break up the entire organization.[59]

The combustible mix of lower and mid-level profit-minded criminals and terrorists makes it difficult to delineate between the two. As a result, law enforcement agents working criminal cases could provide critical information on a terrorist cell or plot. Terrorists have traditionally used a criminal support structure in their operations, but now longer term relationships are being established between terrorist cells and criminal organizations. Terrorist cells could in fact become fully involved in profit-driven activities.

Since 11 September, many experts, think tanks, and commissions have debated the need to create a domestic counterterrorism intelligence service separate from the FBI. The 9-11 Commission, which is sure to make heavy recommendations for U.S. intelligence, has already hinted at the possibility of recommending the creation of a domestic intelligence service. Many proposals have emerged, some of which are tweaks of Britain's internal security service, MI5. Two proposals have received the most attention:

- *John Deutch's Proposal.* He proposed the creation of a domestic intelligence service under the Director of Central Intelligence, making the DCI responsible for both the foreign and domestic collection of terrorist threats. This is organizationally different than Britain's MI5 as Deutch's proposal places the service under the Director of Central Intelligence, versus Britain's Home Secretary—which is the closest equivalent of the Department of Homeland Security.

- *Gilmore Commission.* The Gilmore commission recommended the creation of a stand-alone agency to analyze domestic and foreign collected information on foreign terrorist groups. The agency would have the more muscular collection powers established under the post-11 September Foreign Intelligence Surveillance Act (FISA) regulations. It would be the primary coordinating point for sharing information with state and local officials, but would not collect or analyze information on national domestic terrorist groups.

Each proposal contains different components. Some place the new organization under the Director for Central Intelligence; others make it a stand-alone agency, and others not mentioned here recommend that the agency stay within the Department of Justice or the FBI. The common thread between all recommendations is that they separate the investigation of profit-driven crimes from terrorism investigations. At first glance, such a separation seems warranted. For years terrorism has been considered a law enforcement phenomenon, an issue that did not deserve the attention of other higher priority national security interests.

The problem, however, is that separating criminal from terrorist investigations could hinder, rather than help, identify and arrest terrorists. As this article has noted, it is increasingly difficult to label a terrorist a terrorist and a criminal a criminal. Many terrorists and guerrilla movements are engaged in organized crime, and many profit-minded criminals no longer have inhibitions about working with terrorists. Thus a criminal lead could very well trace back to a terrorist. The creation of a terrorism-only agency would create an institutional barrier between the criminal and terrorism analysts.

Conclusion

The transformation of terrorists and criminal organizations from hierarchy to network has dangerous and largely unnoticed implications. With the emergence of decentralized organizations, a centuries-old dynamic between hierarchical terrorist and criminal organizations has begun to change. Criminals and terrorists now have few reservations about cooperating with each other. Many will create long-term strategic alliances to harness each other's expertise—making their groups more dangerous and elusive than ever.

Notes

1. Ron Ashkenas, Dave Ulrich, Todd Jick, and Steve Kerr, *The Boundaryless Organization: Breaking the Chains of Organizational Structure* (Jossey-Bass, San Francisco, 2002).
2. Ibid.
3. Horizontal organization experts, however, still stress that some amount of hierarchy is necessary to guide and orchestrate the horizontal organizations. Ibid.
4. There are many works that provided the basis for this analysis. See John Arquilla and Theodore Karasik, "Chechnya: A Glimpse of Future Conflict," *Studies in Conflict & Terrorism,* 22, pp. 207–229 (1999). "Networks and Netwars," edited by John Arquilla and David Ronfeldt, RAND Report (2001). "In Athena's Camp: Preparing for Conflict in the Information Age," edited by John Arquilla and David Ronfeldt, RAND report (1997). "Networks, Netwar, and Information-Age Terrorism," John Arquilla, David Ronfeldt, and Michele Zanini, *Countering the New Terrorism* (Washington, DC: RAND, 1999).
5. Other paths were also chosen. Some organizations like Islamic Jihad chose to leave Egypt, while others, like the Muslim Brotherhood, gave up violence to pursue a political path.
6. Michele Zanini and Sean J. A. Edwards, "The Networking of Terror in the Information Age," in *Networks and Netwars,* edited by John Arquilla and David Ronfeldt, RAND Report (2001).
7. Magnus Ranstorp, "Hizbollah's Command Leadership: It's Structure, Decision-Making and Relationship with Iranian Clergy and Institutions," *Terrorism and Political Violence* (Autumn 1994) and from Hala Jaber, "Hezbollah: Born with a Vengeance" (New York: Columbia Press, 1997), pp. 63–66.
8. Hala Jaber, *Hezbollah: Born with a Vengeance* (New York: Columbia Press, 1997), p. 64.
9. Gordon McCormick, "The Shining Path and Peruvian Terrorism," *Inside Terrorist Organizations,* edited by David Rapaport. Also see Gordon McCormick, "The Shining Path and the Future of Peru," RAND report (March 1990).
10. The same dynamic exists in Colombia. See Joseph Contreras and Steven Ambrus, "The DEA's Nightmare: Colombian Targets Get Smart, Techno-Hip and Phenomenally Successful," *Newsweek,* 21 February 2000. Also see Jeremy McDermott and Oscar Becerra, "Mexican Drug Trade Faces Fragmentation," *Jane's Intelligence Review* (May 2003).
11. Ibid.
12. *Tijuana La Frontera,* UEDO Director Says Mexican Drug Cartels Operate Like Companies, 1 July 2003.
13. Ibid.
14. Ibid.
15. Phil Williams, "Transnational Criminal Networks," *Networks and Netwars,* edited by John Arquilla and David Ronfeldt, RAND Report (2001).
16. Marsha Crenshaw, "Theories of Terrorism: Instrumental and Organizational Approaches," *Inside Terrorist Organizations,* edited by David Rapaport, p. 14.
17. John Horgan and Max Taylor, "The Provisional Irish Republican Army: Command and Functional Structure," *Terrorism and Political Violence,* 9(3) (Autumn 1997), pp. 1–32.
18. Ibid., p. 3.
19. The network form described in this section is an "all-channel network." See John Arquilla and David Ronfeldt "The Advent of Netwar: Analytic Background," *Studies in Conflict and Terrorism,* 2(1999), p. 193.
20. See Marc Sageman, *Understanding Terror Networks* (Philadelphia: University of Pennsylvania Press, 2004), pp. 70–71.

21. Jeremy Pressman, "Leaderless Resistance: The Next Threat?" *Current History* (December 2003).
22. Jeffrey Kaplan, "Leaderless Resistance," *Terrorism and Political Violence* (Autumn 1997), p. 43.
23. Jessica Stern, *Terror in the Name of God: Why Religious Militants Kill* (New York: Harper Collins, 2003), pp. 148, 165.
24. Jo Thomas, "New Face of Terror Crimes: 'Lone Wolf' Weaned on Hate," *New York Times* (16 August 1999).
25. Stefan Leader and Peter Probst, "The Earth Liberation Front and Environmental Terrorism," *Terrorism and Political Violence* (Winter 2003).
26. Ibid.
27. "Overview of the Enemy," The National Commission on Terrorist Attacks Upon the United States, Staff Statement No. 15. Rohan Gunaratna, *Inside Al Qaeda* (New York: Berkeley Books, 2002), p. 76.
28. Peter Bergin, *Holy War, Inc.* (New York: Simon and Schuster, 2002), p. 31.
29. Rohan Gunaratna, *Inside Al Qaeda* (New York: Berkeley Books, 2002), p. 77.
30. A recent report by the National Commission on Terrorist Attacks cites two other committees: A foreign purchase committee and security committee. Rohan Gunaratna, *Inside Al Qaeda* (New York: Berkeley Books, 2002), p. 77. U.S.A. v. Usama bin Laden, 98 Cr. 1023 (SDNY) Indictment. Bergin, *Holy War, Inc.* (New York: Simon and Schuster, 2002), p. 31.
31. Rohan Gunaratna, *Inside Al Qaeda,* p. 77.
32. Rohan Gunaratna, *Inside Al Qaeda,* p. 76. U.S.A. v. Usama bin Laden, 98 Cr. 1023 (SDNY) Indictment.
33. Rohan Gunaratna, *Inside Al Qaeda* (New York, Berkeley Books, 2002), p. 77. U.S.A. v. Usama bin Laden, 98 Cr. 1023 (SDNY) Indictment.
34. "Outline of the 9/11 plot," The National Commission on Terrorist Attacks Upon the United States, Staff Statement No. 16.
35. "Overview of the Enemy," The National Commission on Terrorist Attacks Upon the United States, Staff Statement No. 16.
36. Testimony to the House Committee on International Relations, J. Cofer Black, "Al-Qaida: The Threat to the United States and Its Allies," 1 April 2004.
37. It is important to note that it's unclear to what extent Al Qaeda's centralized element still exists and functions. Rohan Gunaratana believes the four committees still existed after the U.S. invasion of Afghanistan. See Rohan Gunaratna, *Inside Al Qaeda,* p. 78. Also see "Overview of the Enemy."
38. Testimony to the House Committee on International Relations, J. Cofer Black.
39. The word "political" will be used loosely in this article. The purpose of "political" is to differentiate it from the financial goals of an organized crime group. As defined here, the word will encompass a wide range of motivations including irredentism, desire to overthrow a government, sectarian violence, and the host of religious motivations including establishment of an Islamic caliphate, pushing the United States out of the Middle East, overthrowing Western-minded Middle Eastern government, etc.
40. Mark Basile, "Going to the Source: Why Al Qaeda's Financial Network Is Likely to Withstand the Current War on Terrorist Financing," *Studies in Conflict & Terrorism,* 2004.
41. Some leaders might not be interested in steering the organization back to its original cause in which case the organization's ends and objectives have transformed. See Chris Dishman, "Terrorism, Crime, and Transformation," *Studies in Conflict & Terrorism,* 24, pp. 43-58 (January 2001).
42. *Tijuana La Frontera,* UEDO Director Says Mexican Drug Cartels Operate Like Companies.
43. Chris Dishman, "Terrorism, Crime and Transformation," *Studies in Conflict & Terrorism* (January 2001).
44. Rachel Ehrenfield, *Funding Evil—How Terrorism Is Financed and How to Stop It* (Chicago: Bonus Books, 2003), pp. 33-71. Al Qaeda reportedly taxes Afghanistan poppy growers and heroin refiners; launders money for the Taliban; purchases poppy crops directly; and distributes

refined heroin throughout the Balkans to Europe. Al Qaeda cells also laundered over $20 million by purchasing illegitimate diamonds from Liberia and Revolutionary United Front rebels.

45. Series of CNN wire reports describe the boat seizures: 29 December 2003. "U.S. holds al Qaeda drug suspects: Navy intercepts hauls of hashish, heroin and methamphetamines," 20 December 2003, "U.S. seizes drugs on boats in Persian Gulf," 2 January 2004, "More drugs seized in Gulf-U.S."

46. Rachel Ehrenfield, *Funding Evil—How Terrorism Is Financed and How to Stop It* (Chicago: Bonus Books, 2003), pp. 147–149.

47. Sari Horwit, "Cigarette smuggling linked to terrorism." *Washington Post,* 8 June 2004 (New York: St. Martins Press), p. 53.

48. Prepared testimony of Dr. Phil Williams before the House International Relations Committee, 31 January 1996.

49. Patrick Clawson and Rensselear Lee, The Andean Cocaine Industry, p. 53.

50. "Narco-Terrorism: International Drug Trafficking And Terrorism—A Dangerous Mix," United States Senate, Committee on the Judiciary, Opening Statement of Senator Orrin G. Hatch, Tuesday, 20 May 2003. Available at (http://frwebgate.access.gpo.gov/cgibin/useftp.cgi?IPaddress=62.140.64.88&filename=90052.wais&directory=diskb/wais/data/108_senate_hearings).

51. See Ehrenfeld, *Funding Evil,* pp. 11–12. "Drug Money For Hezbollah?," CBSNEWS.COM, Washington, D.C., 1 September 2002. Also see DEA transcript release, "More Than 100 Arrested In Nationwide Methamphetamine Investigation," available at (http://www.usdoj.gov/dea/major/me3.html).

52. Members of the cash-strapped cell were discovered when they attempted to get back their deposit on the rental van. Cited in Testimony of Matthew A. Levitt Senior Fellow in Terrorism Studies, The Washington Institute for Near East Policy Before the United States Subcommittee on International Trade and Finance, Committee on Banking, Housing, and Urban Affairs "Charitable And Humanitarian Organizations in the Network of International Terrorist Financing," 1 August 2002.

53. Williams, "Transnational Criminal Networks," p. 70.

54. Fatwa quoted in Rachel Ehrenfield, *Funding Evil,* pp. 143–145.

55. Sebastian Rotella, "The World; Jihad's Unlikely Alliance; Muslim extremists who attacked Madrid funded the plot by selling drugs, investigators say," *Los Angeles Times,* 23 May 2004.

56. Ibid.

57. One of the Madrid suspect bombers was also an informant for authorities investigating a drug gang. See Rotella, "The World; Jihad's Unlikely Alliance."

58. See Douglas Farah, "Colombian Drug Cartels Exploit Tech Advantage," *Washington Post,* 15 November 1999.

59. See Joseph Contreras and Steven Ambrus, "The DEA's Nightmare: Colombian Targets Get Smart, Techno-Hip and Phenomenally Successful," *Newsweek,* 21 February 21, 2000.

Bruce Hoffman, 2003

The Logic of Suicide Terrorism

First you feel nervous about riding the bus. Then you wonder about going to a mall. Then you think twice about sitting for long at your favorite café. Then nowhere seems safe. Terrorist groups have a strategy—to shrink to nothing the areas in which people move freely—and suicide bombers, inexpensive and reliably lethal, are their latest weapons. Israel has learned to recognize and disrupt the steps on the path to suicide attacks. We must learn too.

Nearly everywhere in the world it is taken for granted that one can simply push open the door to a restaurant, café, or bar, sit down, and order a meal or a drink. In Israel the process of entering such a place is more complicated. One often encounters an armed guard who, in addition to asking prospective patrons whether they themselves are armed, may quickly pat them down, feeling for the telltale bulge of a belt or a vest containing explosives. Establishments that cannot afford a guard or are unwilling to pass on the cost of one to customers simply keep their doors locked, responding to knocks with a quick glance through the glass and an instant judgment as to whether this or that person can safely be admitted. What would have been unimaginable a year ago is now not only routine but reassuring. It has become the price of a redefined normality.

In the United States in the twenty months since 9/11 we, too, have had to become accustomed to an array of new, often previously inconceivable security measures—in airports and other transportation hubs, hotels and office buildings, sports stadiums and concert halls. Although some are more noticeable and perhaps more inconvenient than others, the fact remains that they have redefined our own sense of normality. They are accepted because we feel more vulnerable than before. With every new threat to international security we become more willing to live with stringent precautions and reflexive, almost unconscious wariness. With every new threat, that is, our everyday life becomes more like Israel's.

The situation in Israel, where last year's intensified suicide-bombing campaign changed the national mood and people's personal politics, is not analogous to that in the United States today. But the organization and the operations of the suicide bombers are neither limited to Israel and its conflict with the Palestinians nor unique to its geostrategic position. The fundamental characteristics of suicide bombing, and its strong attraction for the terrorist organizations behind it, are universal: Suicide bombings are inexpensive and effective. They are less complicated and compromising than other kinds of terrorist operations. They guarantee media coverage. The suicide terrorist is the ultimate smart bomb. Perhaps most important, coldly efficient bombings tear at the fabric of trust that holds societies together. All these reasons doubtless account for the spread of suicide terrorism from the Middle East to Sri Lanka and Turkey, Argentina and Chechnya, Russia and Algeria—and to the United States.

To understand the power that suicide terrorism can have over a populace—and what a populace can do to counter it—one naturally goes to the society that has been most deeply affected. As a researcher who has studied the strategies of terrorism for more than twenty-five years, I recently visited Israel to review the steps the military, the police, and the intelligence and security services have taken against a threat more pervasive and personal than ever before.

I was looking at x-rays with Dr. Shmuel Shapira in his office at Jerusalem's Hadassah Hospital. "This is not a place to have a wristwatch," he said as he described the injuries of a young girl who'd been on her way to school one morning last November when a suicide terrorist detonated a bomb on her bus. Eleven of her fellow passengers were killed, and more than fifty others wounded. The blast was so powerful that the hands and case of the bomber's wristwatch had turned into lethal projectiles, lodging in the girl's neck and ripping a major artery. The presence of such foreign objects in the bodies of his patients no longer surprises Shapira. "We have cases with a nail in the neck, or nuts and bolts in the thigh . . . , a ball bearing in the skull," he said.

Such are the weapons of war in Israel today: nuts and bolts, screws and ball bearings, any metal shards or odd bits of broken machinery that can be packed together with homemade explosive and then strapped to the body of a terrorist dispatched to any place where people gather—bus, train, restaurant, café, supermarket, shopping mall, street corner, promenade. These attacks probably cost no more than $150 to mount, and they need no escape plan—often the most difficult aspect of a terrorist operation. And they are reliably deadly. According to data from the Rand Corporation's chronology of international terrorism incidents, suicide attacks on average kill four times as many people as other terrorist acts. Perhaps it is not surprising, then, that this means of terror has become increasingly popular. The tactic first emerged in Lebanon, in 1983; a decade later it came to Israel, and it has been a regular security problem ever since. Fully two thirds of all such incidents in Israel have occurred in the past two and a half years—that is, since the start of the second intifada, in September of 2000. Indeed, suicide bombers are responsible for almost half of the approximately 750 deaths in terrorist attacks since then.

Last December, I walked through Jerusalem with two police officers, one of them a senior operational commander, who were showing me the sites of suicide bombings in recent years. They described the first major suicide-terrorist attack in the city, which occurred in February of 1996, early on a Sunday morning—the beginning of the Israeli work week. The driver of the No. 18 Egged bus was hurrying across a busy intersection at Sarei Yisrael Street as a yellow light turned red. The bus was about halfway through when an explosion transformed it into an inferno of twisted metal, pulverized glass, and burning flesh. A traffic camera designed to catch drivers running stop lights captured the scene on film. Twenty-five people were killed, including two U.S. citizens, and eighty were wounded.

The early years of suicide terrorism were a simpler time, the officers explained. Suicide bombers were—at least in theory—easier to spot then. They tended to carry their bombs in nylon backpacks or duffel bags rather than in belts or vests concealed beneath their clothing, as they do now. They were also typically male, aged seventeen to twenty-three, and unmarried. Armed with these data, the authorities could simply deny work permits to Palestinians most likely to be suicide bombers, thus restricting their ability to cross the Green Line (Israel's pre-1967 border) into Israel proper from the West Bank or the Gaza Strip.

Today, though, suicide bombers are middle-aged and young, married and unmarried, and some of them have children. Some of them, too, are women, and word has it that even children are being trained for martyrdom. "There is no clear profile anymore—not for terrorists and especially not for suicide bombers," an exasperated senior officer in the Israel Defense Forces told me last year. Sometimes the bombers disguise themselves: male *shaheed* (Arabic for "martyrs") have worn green IDF fatigues; have dressed as *haredim* (ultra-Orthodox Jews), complete with yarmulkes and tzitzit, the fringes that devout Jews display as part of their everyday clothing; or have donned long-haired wigs in an effort to look like hip Israelis rather than threatening Arabs. A few women have tried to camouflage bombs by strapping them to their stomachs to fake pregnancy. And contrary to popular belief, the bombers are not drawn exclusively from the ranks of the poor but have included two sons of millionaires. (Most of the September 11 terrorists came from comfortable middle- to upper-middle-class families and were well educated.) The Israeli journalist Ronni Shaked, an expert on the Palestinian terrorist group Hamas, who writes for *Yedioth Ahronoth,* an Israeli daily, has debunked the myth that it is only people with no means of improving their lot in life who turn to suicide terrorism. "All leaders of Hamas," he told me, "are university graduates, some with master's degrees. This is a movement not of poor, miserable people but of highly educated people who are using [the image of] poverty to make the movement more powerful."

Buses remain among the bombers' preferred targets. Winter and summer are the better seasons for bombing buses in Jerusalem, because the closed windows (for heat or air-conditioning) intensify the force of the blast, maximizing the bombs' killing potential. As a hail of shrapnel pierces flesh and breaks bones, the shock wave tears lungs and crushes other internal organs. When the bus's fuel tank explodes, a fireball causes burns, and smoke inhalation causes respiratory damage. All this is a significant return on a relatively modest investment. Two or three kilograms of explosive on a bus can kill as many people as twenty to thirty kilograms left on a street or in a mall or a restaurant. But as security on buses has improved, and passengers have become more alert, the bombers have been forced to seek other targets.

The terrorists are lethally flexible and inventive. A person wearing a bomb is far more dangerous and far more difficult to defend against than a timed device left to explode in a marketplace. This human weapons system can effect last-minute changes based on the ease of approach, the paucity or density of people, and the security measures in evidence. On a Thursday afternoon in March of last year a reportedly smiling, self-satisfied bomber strolled down King George Street, in the heart of Jerusalem, looking for just the right target. He found it in a crowd of shoppers gathered in front of the trendy Aroma Café, near the corner of Agrippas Street. In a fusillade of nails and other bits of metal two victims were killed and fifty-six wounded. Similarly, in April of last year a female suicide bomber tried to enter the Mahane Yehuda open-air market—the fourth woman to make such an attempt in four months—but was deterred by a strong police presence. So she simply walked up to a bus stop packed with shoppers hurrying home before the Sabbath and detonated her explosives, killing six and wounding seventy-three.

Suicide bombing initially seemed the desperate act of lone individuals, but it is not undertaken alone. Invariably, a terrorist organization such as Hamas (the Islamic Resistance Movement), the Palestine Islamic Jihad (PIJ), or the al Aqsa Martyrs Brigade has recruited the bomber, conducted reconnaissance, prepared the explosive device, and identified a target—explaining that if it turns out to be guarded or protected, any crowded place nearby will do. "We hardly ever find that the suicide bomber came by himself," a police officer explained to me. "There is always a handler." In fact, in some cases a handler has used a cell phone or other device to trigger the blast from a distance. A policeman told me, "There was one event where a suicide bomber had been told all he had to do was to carry the bomb and plant explosives in a certain place. But the bomb was remote-control detonated."

The organizations behind the Palestinians' suicide terrorism have numerous components. Quartermasters obtain the explosives and the other materials (nuts, bolts, nails, and the like) that are combined to make a bomb. Now that bomb-making methods have been so widely disseminated throughout the West Bank and Gaza, a merely competent technician, rather than the skilled engineer once required, can build a bomb. Explosive material is packed into pockets sewn into a canvas or denim belt or vest and hooked up to a detonator—usually involving a simple hand-operated plunger.

Before the operation is to be launched, "minders" sequester the bomber in a safe house, isolating him or her from family and friends—from all contact with the outside world—during the final preparations for martyrdom. A film crew makes a martyrdom video, as much to help ensure that the bomber can't back out as for propaganda and recruitment purposes. Reconnaissance teams have already either scouted the target or received detailed information about it, which they pass on to the bomber's handlers. The job of the handlers, who are highly skilled at avoiding Israeli army checkpoints or police patrols, is to deliver the bomber as close to the target as possible.

I talked to a senior police-operations commander in his office at the Russian Compound, the nerve center of law enforcement for Jerusalem since the time when first the Turks and then the British ruled this part of the world. It was easy to imagine, amid the graceful arches and the traditional Jerusalem stone, an era when Jerusalem's law-enforcement officers wore tarbooshes and pressed blue tunics with Sam Browne belts rather than the bland polyester uniforms and blue baseball-style caps of today. Although policing this multi-faith, historically beleaguered city has doubtless always involved difficult challenges, none can compare with the current situation. "This year there were very many events," my host explained, using the bland generic noun that signifies terrorist attacks or attempted attacks. "In previous years we considered ten events as normal; now we are already at forty-three." He sighed. There were still three weeks to go before the end of the year. Nineteen of these events had been suicide bombings. In the calculus of terrorism, it doesn't get much better. "How easy it has become for a person to wake up in the morning and go off and commit suicide," he observed. Once there were only "bags on buses, not vests or belts" to contend with, the policeman said. "Everything is open now. The purpose is to prove that the police can do whatever they want but it won't help."

This, of course, is the age-old strategy of terrorists everywhere—to undermine public confidence in the ability of the authorities to protect and defend citizens, thereby creating a climate of fear and intimidation amenable to terrorist exploitation. In Jerusalem, and in Israel as a whole, this strategy has not succeeded. But it has fundamentally changed daily behavior patterns—the first step toward crushing morale and breaking the will to resist.

The terrorists appear to be deliberately homing in on the few remaining places where Israelis thought they could socialize in peace. An unprecedented string of attacks in the first four months of last year illustrated this careful strategy, beginning at bus stops and malls and moving into more private realms, such as corner supermarkets and local coffee bars. In March, for example, no one paid much attention to a young man dressed like an ultra-Orthodox Jew who was standing near some parked cars as guests left a bar mitzvah celebration at a social hall in the ultra-Orthodox Jerusalem neighborhood of Beit Yisrael. Then he blew himself up, killing nine people, eight of them children, and wounding fifty-nine. The tight-knit religious community had felt that it was protected by God, pointing to the miraculous lack of injury a year before when a booby-trapped car blew up in front of the same hall. Using a strategy al Qaeda has made familiar, the terrorists revisited the site.

Less than a month after the Beit Yisrael attack the suicide bombers and their leaders drove home the point that Israelis cannot feel safe anywhere by going to the one large Israeli city that had felt immune from the suspicion and antipathy prevalent elsewhere—Haifa, with its successful mixture of Jews, Christian and Muslim Arabs, and followers of the Bahai faith. The University of Haifa has long had the highest proportion of Arab students of any Israeli university. The nearby Matza restaurant, owned by Jews but run by an Israeli Arab family from Galilee, seemed to embody the unusually cordial relations that exist among the city's diverse communities. Matza was popular with Jews and Arabs alike, and the presence of its Arab staff and patrons provided a feeling of safety from attack. That feeling was shattered at two-thirty on a quiet Sunday afternoon, when a suicide bomber killed fifteen people and wounded nearly fifty.

As we had tea late one afternoon in the regal though almost preternaturally quiet surroundings of Jerusalem's King David Hotel, Benny Morris, a professor of history at Ben Gurion University, explained, "The Palestinians say they have found a strategic weapon, and suicide bombing is it. This hotel is empty. The streets are empty. They have effectively terrorized Israeli society. My wife won't use a bus anymore, only a taxi." It is undeniable that daily life in Jerusalem, and throughout Israel, has changed as a result of last year's wave of suicide bombings. Even the police have been affected. "I'm worried," one officer told me in an aside—whether in confidence or in embarrassment, I couldn't tell—as we walked past Zion Square, near where some bombs had exploded. "I tell you this as a police officer. I don't come to Jerusalem with my children anymore. I'd give back the settlements. I'd give over my bank account to live in peace."

By any measure 2002 was an astonishing year for Israel in terms of suicide bombings. An average of five attacks a month were made, nearly double the number during the first fifteen months of the second intifada—and that number was itself more than ten times the monthly average since 1993. Indeed, according to a database maintained by the

National Security Studies Center, at Haifa University, there were nearly as many suicide attacks in Israel last year (fifty-nine) as there had been in the previous eight years combined (sixty-two). In Jerusalem alone there were nine suicide attacks during the first four months of 2002, killing thirty-three and injuring 464. "It was horrendous," a young professional woman living in the city told me. "No one went out for coffee. No one went out to restaurants. We went as a group of people to one another's houses only."

Again, terrorism is meant to produce psychological effects that reach far beyond the immediate victims of the attack. "The Scuds of Saddam [in 1991] never caused as much psychological damage as the suicide bombers have," says Ami Pedahzur, a professor of political science at Haifa University and an expert on political extremism and violence who manages the National Security Studies Center's terrorism database. As the French philosopher Gaston Bouthoul argued three decades ago in a theoretical treatise on the subject, the "anonymous, unidentifiable threat creates huge anxiety, and the terrorist tries to spread fear by contagion, to immobilise and subjugate those living under this threat." This is precisely what the Palestinian terrorist groups are trying to achieve. "The Israelis . . . will fall to their knees," Sheikh Ahmad Yassin, the spiritual leader of Hamas, said in 2001. "You can sense the fear in Israel already; they are worried about where and when the next attacks will come. Ultimately, Hamas will win." The strategy of suicide terrorists is to make people paranoid and xenophobic, fearful of venturing beyond their homes even to a convenience store. Terrorists hope to compel the enemy society's acquiescence, if not outright surrender, to their demands. This is what al Qaeda hoped to achieve on 9/11 in one stunning blow—and what the Palestinians seek as well, on a more sustained, if piecemeal, basis.

After decades of struggle the Palestinians are convinced that they have finally discovered Israel's Achilles' heel. Ismail Haniya, another Hamas leader, was quoted in March of last year in *The Washington Post* as saying that Jews "love life more than any other people, and they prefer not to die." In contrast, suicide terrorists are often said to have gone to their deaths smiling. An Israeli policeman told me, "A suicide bomber goes on a bus and finds himseslf face-to-face with victims and he smiles and he activates the bomb—but we learned that only by asking people afterwards who survived." This is what is known in the Shia Islamic tradition as the *bassamat al-farah,* or "smile of joy"—prompted by one's impending martyrdom. It is just as prevalent among Sunni terrorists. (Indeed, the last will and testament of Mohammed Atta, the ringleader of the September 11 hijackers, and his "primer" for martyrs, *The Sky Smiles, My Young Son,* clearly evidence a belief in the joy of death.)

This perceived weakness of an ostensibly powerful society has given rise to what is known in the Middle East as the "spider-web theory," which originated within Hizbollah, the Lebanese Shia organization, following a struggle that ultimately compelled the Israel Defense Forces to withdraw from southern Lebanon in May of 2000. The term is said to have been coined by Hizbollah's secretary general, Sheikh Hassan Nasrallah, who described Israel as a still formidable military power whose civil society had become materialistic and lazy, its citizens self-satisfied, comfortable, and pampered to the point where they had gone soft. IDF Chief of Staff Moshe "Boogie" Ya'alon paraphrased Nasrallah for the Israeli public in an interview published in the newspaper *Ha'aretz* last August.

> The Israeli army is strong, Israel has technological superiority and is said to have strategic capabilities, but its citizens are unwilling any longer to sacrifice lives in order

to defend their national interests and national goals. Therefore, Israel is a spider-web society: it looks strong from the outside, but touch it and it will fall apart.

Al Qaeda, of course, has made a similar assessment of America's vulnerability.

A society facing such a determined foe can respond. Israel, with its necessarily advanced military and intelligence capacities, was able in the first four months of last year to meet the most concerted effort to date by Palestinian terrorists to test the resolve of its government and the mettle of its citizens. Twelve Israelis were killed in terrorist attacks in January, twenty-six in February, 108 in March, and forty-one in April. The population of the United States is roughly forty-seven times that of Israel, meaning that the American equivalent of the March figure would have exceeded 5,000—another 9/11, but with more than 2,000 additional deaths. After April of 2002, however, a period of relative quiet settled over Israel. The number of suicide attacks, according to the National Security Studies Center, declined from sixteen in March to six in April, six in May, five in June, and six in July before falling still further to two in August and similarly small numbers for the remainder of the year. "We wouldn't want it to be perceived [by the Israeli population] that we have no military answers," a senior IDF planner told me. The military answer was Operation Defensive Shield, which began in March and involved both the IDF's huge deployment of personnel to the West Bank and its continuing presence in all the major Palestinian population centers that Israel regards as wellsprings of the suicide campaign. This presence has involved aggressive military operations to pre-empt suicide bombing, along with curfews and other restrictions on the movement of residents.

The success of the IDF's strategy is utterly dependent on regularly acquiring intelligence and rapidly disseminating it to operational units that can take appropriate action. Thus the IDF must continue to occupy the West Bank's major population centers, so that Israeli intelligence agents can stay in close—and relatively safe—proximity to their information sources, and troops can act immediately either to round up suspects or to rescue the agent should an operation go awry. "Military pressure facilitates arrests, because you're there," one knowledgeable observer explained to me. "Not only do you know the area, but you have [covert] spotters deployed, and the whole area is under curfew anyway, so it is difficult for terrorists to move about and hide without being noticed, and more difficult for them to get out. The IDF presence facilitates intelligence gathering, and the troops can also conduct massive sweeps, house to house and block to block, pick up people, and interrogate them."

The IDF units in West Bank cities and towns can amass detailed knowledge of a community, identifying terrorists and their sympathizers, tracking their movements and daily routines, and observing the people with whom they associate. Agents from Shabak, Israel's General Security Service (also known as the Shin Bet), work alongside these units, participating in operations and often assigning missions. "The moment someone from Shabak comes with us, everything changes," a young soldier in an elite reconnaissance unit told me over coffee and cake in his mother's apartment. "The Shabak guy talks in Arabic to [the suspect] without an accent, or appears as an Arab guy himself. Shabak already knows everything about them, and that is such a shock to them. So they are afraid, and they will tell Shabak everything." The success of Defensive Shield and the subsequent Operation Determined Way depends on this synchronization of intelligence and operations. A junior officer well acquainted with this environment says, "Whoever has better intelligence is the winner."

The strategy—at least in the short run—is working. The dramatic decline in the number of suicide operations since last spring is proof enough. "Tactically, we are doing everything we can," a senior officer involved in the framing of this policy told me, "and we have managed to prevent eighty percent of all attempts." Another officer said, "We are now bringing the war to them. We do it so that we fight the war in *their* homes rather than in *our* homes. We try to make certain that we fight on their ground, where we can have the maximum advantage." The goal of the IDF, though, is not simply to fight in a manner that plays to its strength; the goal is to actively shrink the time and space in which the suicide bombers and their operational commanders, logisticians, and handlers function—to stop them before they can cross the Green Line, by threatening their personal safety and putting them on the defensive.

Citizens in Israel, as in America, have a fundamental expectation that their government and its military and security forces will protect and defend them. Soldiers are expected to die, if necessary, in order to discharge this responsibility. As one senior IDF commander put it, "It is better for the IDF to bear the brunt of these attacks than Israeli civilians. The IDF is better prepared, protected, educated." Thus security in Israel means to the IDF an almost indefinite deployment in the West Bank—a state of ongoing low-level war. For Palestinian civilians it means no respite from roadblocks and identity checks, cordon-and-search operations, lightning snatch-and-grabs, bombing raids, helicopter strikes, ground attacks, and other countermeasures that have turned densely populated civilian areas into war zones.

Many Israelis do not relish involvement in this protracted war of attrition, but even more of them accept that there is no alternative. "Israel's ability to stand fast indefinitely is a tremendous advantage," says Dan Schueftan, an Israeli strategist and military thinker who teaches at Haifa University, "since the suicide bombers believe that time is on their side. It imposes a strain on the army, yes, but this is what the army is for." Indeed, no Israeli with whom I spoke on this visit doubted that the IDF's continued heavy presence in the West Bank was directly responsible for the drop in the number of suicide bombings. And I encountered very few who favored withdrawing the IDF from the West Bank. This view cut across ideological and demographic lines. As we dined one evening at Matza, which has been rebuilt, a centrist graduate student at Haifa University named Uzi Nisim told me that Palestinian terrorists "will have the power to hit us, to hurt us, once [the IDF] withdraws from Jenin and elsewhere on the West Bank." Ami Pedahzur, of Haifa University, who is a leftist, agreed. He said, "There is widespread recognition in Israel that this is the only way to stop terrorism." I later heard the same thing from a South African couple, relatively new immigrants to Israel who are active in a variety of human-rights endeavors. "Just the other day," the husband told me, "even my wife said, 'Thank God we have Sharon. Otherwise I wouldn't feel safe going out.'"

Nevertheless, few Israelis believe that the current situation will lead to any improvement in Israeli-Palestinian relations over the long run. Dennis Zinn, the defense correspondent for Israel's Channel 1, told me, "Yes, there is a drop-off [in suicide bombings]. When you have bombs coming down on your heads, you can't carry out planning and suicide attacks. But that doesn't take away their motivation. It only increases it."

Given the relative ease and the strategic and tactical attraction of suicide bombing, it is perhaps no wonder that after a five-day visit to Israel last fall, Louis Anemone, the security chief of the New York Metropolitan Transit Authority, concluded that New Yorkers—and, by implication, other Americans—face the same threat. "This stuff is going to be imported over here," he declared—a prediction that Vice President Dick Cheney and FBI Director Robert Mueller had already made. In March, Secretary of Homeland Security Tom Ridge also referred to the threat, saying in an interview with Fox News that we have to "prepare for the inevitability" of suicide bombings in the United States. Anemone even argued that "today's terrorists appear to be using Israel as a testing ground to prepare for a sustained attack against the U.S." In fact, Palestinians had tried a suicide attack in New York four years before 9/11; their plans to bomb a Brooklyn subway station were foiled only because an informant told the police. When they were arrested, the terrorists were probably less than a day away from attacking: according to law-enforcement authorities, five bombs had been primed. "I wouldn't call them sophisticated," Howard Safir, the commissioner of police at the time, commented, "but they certainly were very dangerous." That suicide bombers don't need to be sophisticated is precisely what makes them so dangerous. All that's required is a willingness to kill and a willingness to die.

According to the Rand Corporation's chronology of worldwide terrorism, which begins in 1968 (the year acknowledged as marking the advent of modern international terrorism, whereby terrorists attack other countries or foreign targets in their own country), nearly two thirds of the 144 suicide bombings recorded have occurred in the past two years. No society, least of all the United States, can regard itself as immune from this threat. Israeli Foreign Minister Benjamin Netanyahu emphasized this point when he addressed the U.S. Congress nine days after 9/11. So did Dan Schueftan, the Israeli strategist, when I asked him if he thought suicide terrorism would come to America in a form similar to that seen in Israel this past year. He said, "It is an interesting comment that the terrorists make: we will finish defeating the Jews because they love life so much. Their goal is to bring misery and grief to people who have an arrogance of power. Who has this? The United States and Israel. Europe will suffer too. I don't think that it will happen in the U.S. on the magnitude we have seen it here, but I have no doubt that it will occur. We had the same discussion back in 1968, when El Al aircraft were hijacked and people said this is your problem, not ours."

The United States, of course, is not Israel. However much we may want to harden our hearts and our targets, the challenge goes far beyond fortifying a single national airline or corralling the enemy into a territory ringed by walls and barbed-wire fences that can be intensively monitored by our armed forces. But we can take precautions based on Israel's experience, and be confident that we are substantially reducing the threat of suicide terrorism here.

The police, the military, and intelligence agencies can take steps that work from the outside in, beginning far in time and distance from a potential attack and ending at the moment and the site of an actual attack. Although the importance of these steps is widely recognized, they have been implemented only unevenly across the United States.

- Understand the terrorists' operational environment. Know their *modus operandi* and targeting patterns. Suicide bombers are rarely lone outlaws; they are preceded by long logistical trails. Focus not just on suspected bombers but on the infrastructure required to launch and sustain suicide-bombing campaigns. This is the essential spadework. It will be for naught, however, if concerted efforts are not made to circulate this information quickly and systematically among federal, state, and local authorities.

- Develop strong, confidence-building ties with the communities from which terrorists are most likely to come, and mount communications campaigns to eradicate support from these communities. The most effective and useful intelligence comes from places where terrorists conceal themselves and seek to establish and hide their infrastructure. Law-enforcement officers should actively encourage and cultivate cooperation in a nonthreatening way.

- Encourage businesses from which terrorists can obtain bomb-making components to alert authorities if they notice large purchases of, for example, ammonium nitrate fertilizer; pipes, batteries, and wires; or chemicals commonly used to fabricate explosives. Information about customers who simply inquire about any of these materials can also be extremely useful to the police.

- Force terrorists to pay more attention to their own organizational security than to planning and carrying out attacks. The greatest benefit is in disrupting pre-attack operations. Given the highly fluid, international threat the United States faces, counterterrorism units, dedicated to identifying and targeting the intelligence-gathering and reconnaissance activities of terrorist organizations, should be established here within existing law-enforcement agencies. These units should be especially aware of places where organizations frequently recruit new members and the bombers themselves, such as community centers, social clubs, schools, and religious institutions.

- Make sure ordinary materials don't become shrapnel. Some steps to build up physical defenses were taken after 9/11—reinforcing park benches, erecting Jersey barriers around vulnerable buildings, and the like. More are needed, such as ensuring that windows on buses and subway cars are shatterproof, and that seats and other accoutrements are not easily dislodged or splintered. Israel has had to learn to examine every element of its public infrastructure. Israeli buses and bus shelters are austere for a reason.

- Teach law-enforcement personnel what to do at the moment of an attack or an attempt. Prevention comes first from the cop on the beat, who will be forced to make instant life-and-death decisions affecting those nearby. Rigorous training is needed for identifying a potential suicide bomber, confronting a suspect, and responding and securing the area around the attack site in the event of an explosion. Is the officer authorized to take action on sighting a suspected bomber, or must a supervisor or special unit be called first? Policies and procedures must be established. In the aftermath of a blast the police must determine whether emergency medical crews and firefighters may enter the site; concerns about a follow-up attack can dictate that first responders be held back until the area is secured. The ability to make such lightning determinations requires training—and, tragically, experience. We can learn from foreign countries with long experience of suicide bombings, such as Israel and Sri Lanka, and also from our own responses in the past to other types of terrorist attacks.

America's enemies are marshaling their resources to continue the struggle that crystallized on 9/11. Exactly what shape that struggle will take remains to be seen. But a recruitment video reportedly circulated by al Qaeda as recently as spring of last year may provide some important clues. The seven-minute tape, seized from an al Qaeda member by U.S. authorities, extols the virtues of martyrdom and solicits recruits to Osama bin Laden's cause. It depicts scenes of *jihadists* in combat, followed by the successive images of twenty-seven martyrs with their names, where they were from, and where they died. Twelve of the martyrs are featured in a concluding segment with voice-over that says, "They rejoice in the bounty provided by Allah. And with regard to those left behind who have not yet joined them in their bliss, the martyrs glory in the fact that on them is no fear, nor have they cause to grieve." The video closes with a message of greeting from the Black Banner Center for Islamic Information.

The greatest military onslaught in history against a terrorist group crushed the infrastructure of al Qaeda in Afghanistan, depriving it of training camps, operational bases, and command-and-control headquarters; killing and wounding many of its leaders and fighters; and dispersing the survivors. Yet this group still actively seeks to rally its forces and attract recruits. Ayman Zawahiri, bin Laden's chief lieutenant, laid out a list of terrorist principles in his book, *Knights Under the Prophet's Banner* (2001), prominent among them the need for al Qaeda to "move the battle to the enemy's ground to burn the hands of those who ignite fire in our countries." He also mentioned "the need to concentrate on the method of martyrdom operations as the most successful way of inflicting damage against the opponent and the least costly to the mujahideen in terms of casualties." That martyrdom is highlighted in the recruitment video strongly suggests that suicide attacks will continue to be a primary instrument in al Qaeda's war against—and perhaps in—the United States. Suleiman Abu Gheith, al Qaeda's chief spokesman, has said as much. In rhetoric disturbingly reminiscent of the way that Palestinian terrorists describe their inevitable triumph over Israel, Abu Gheith declared, "Those youths that destroyed Americans with their planes, they did a good deed. There are thousands more young followers who look forward to death like Americans look forward to living."

Bruce Hoffman is a professor of security studies at the Edmund A. Walsh School of Foreign Service at Georgetown University. Dr. Hoffman is the former Corporate Chair in Counter-Terrorism and Counter-Insurgency at the RAND Corporation, where he was also director of the Washington, DC office. He is editor of the journal *Conflict and Terrorism* and holds fellowships at the Combating Terrorism Center at West Point and the National Security Studies Center at Haifa University, Israel.

Assaf Moghadam

The Evolution of Suicide Terrorism and Its Implications for Research

Suicide terrorism is oftentimes described as a modern phenomenon, but its antecedents have existed for several millennia. Throughout this period, there have been a multitude of states and organizations that have employed different forms of suicide attacks for both religious and secular reasons. The questions of why some individuals are willing to die in order to kill and why they enjoy the support of organizations in the process—have preoccupied an increasing number of scholars in recent years.

The purpose of this chapter is threefold. First, this chapter offers a review of the historical antecedents of suicide attacks, which can be divided into three distinct periods: (1) from biblical times to the beginning of suicide attacks in Lebanon in 1981; (2) from the early 1980s to the advent of al Qaeda's use of suicide attacks in 1998; and (3) from the late 1990s to the present day. The second part of this chapter reviews contending theoretical explanations of suicide terrorism. Part three of this chapter highlights recent changes in the patterns of suicide attacks that are not addressed by these existing explanations and argues that given these dramatic changes, existing approaches to explaining suicide attacks can offer only partial insights. The chapter concludes with a number of suggestions for future research.

In this chapter, suicide attacks are defined as a violent modus operandi designed to inflict harm on individuals and/or physical infrastructure, whereby the death of the perpetrator or perpetrators is necessary for the success of the act.[1] Attacks during which the perpetrators had a high likelihood to die in the process of the act, but where death was not technically required in order to inflict harm on others, are treated here as related phenomena. To the extent that they occurred before the onset of modern suicide terrorism in the early 1980s, they are described as precursors or antecedents of suicide attacks, rather than suicide attacks per se.[2]

Historical Evolution of Suicide Attacks

This section reviews the historical evolution of suicide attacks and is divided into three sections. The first of these covers the period from the biblical Samson to the beginning of suicide attacks in Lebanon in 1981. The second covers the period from the early 1980s to the advent of al Qaeda's use of suicide attacks in 1998. The third section covers the period since the late 1990s to the present.

Suicide Attacks and Their Precursors until 1981

The modern phenomenon of suicide terrorism is often dated at the early 1980s, when a series of suicide attacks in Lebanon struck the Iraqi and American embassies as well as other U.S., French, and Israeli military targets. Antecedents of suicide attacks, however, can be found as early as biblical times. This section briefly reviews some precursors of suicide attacks from the biblical Samson until 1981. In that period, suicide attacks were rarely used as part of a terrorist campaign in the modern sense of the word. Instead, prototypes of the modern tactic of suicide terrorism were carried out by various actors, including individuals, groups, sects, and armies associated with nation states such as Japan, Vietnam, or Iran.

Perhaps the first documented story of a suicide attacker, however, is that of an individual. The Book of Judges of the Old Testament tells the story of Samson, the biblical strongman who was betrayed by Delilah, a woman to whom he had revealed the secret of his strength. Delilah delivered that secret to the Philistines, who promptly imprisoned and tortured Samson. When the Philistines brought a sacrifice unto their god Dagon, they forced Samson to entertain them, placing him near the central pillars of their Gazan temple. Samson used his humiliation as an opportunity to exact revenge on his captors. According to the Bible, Samson asked God to give him strength to avenge the Philistines. "Let me die with the Philistines," he cried out, before collapsing the temple, burying himself along with the assembled crowd that surrounded him. Samson's attack fits the classic definition of a suicide attack because his death was a precondition for the success of his vengeful act. Had Samson not died himself, he could not have killed the assembled Philistines. His utterance of the sentence "Let me die with the Philistines" embodies the very essence of the tactic of suicide operations, namely the confluence of the willingness to kill and to die.

Since biblical times, suicide attacks have been employed as a tactic by nearly all religions at one point or another. Between the 11th and 13th centuries C.E., the so-called Assassins, a radical Shia sect, employed suicide attacks, among other methods, to spread their own version of Islam. Their weapon of choice was the dagger, which they used in order to kill their enemies in broad daylight. The Assassins rarely attempted to escape from the scene after killing their victims, and seemed fearless in the face of their own death. According to Bernard Lewis, "the killing by the Assassin of his victim was not only an act of piety; it also had a ritual, almost sacramental quality. It is significant that in all their murders . . . the Assassins always used a dagger; never poison, never missiles, though there must have been occasions when these would have been easier and safer. The Assassin," Lewis continues, "is almost always caught, and usually indeed makes no attempt to escape; there is even a suggestion that to survive a mission was shameful."[3] This seemingly fanatical courage of the Assassins gave birth to the now debunked myth that members of this sect had been drugged with hashish—a belief that gave the Assassins (*Hashashiyoun* or *Hashishiyyin* in Arabic) their name.[4]

Over the course of several centuries, antecedents of suicide attacks were also employed in three Muslim communities in the Malabar coast of southwestern India, Aceh in northern Sumatra, and Mindanao and Sulu in the southern Philippines.[5] Dale ascribed the use of what he terms 'suicidal attacks' in large part to the systematic exploitation of

Western nation states of the local Muslim population and economy, coupled with the early religious zeal with which the Spanish and Portuguese attempted to convert Muslim populations to Christianity following the arrival of Vasco da Gama in the Indian Ocean in 1498. The attacks in Muslim India and Indonesia described by Dale, however, are not entirely consistent with the types of suicide attacks common today. The attack mode consisted of Muslim warriors "rush[ing] at the enemy, trying to kill as many of them as possible, until they themselves were killed."[6] Because their death was not necessary for the success of the attack, the attacks by these mujahideen are perhaps better described as precursors to modern-day suicide attacks.

Additional forerunners of the contemporary suicide attack phenomenon appeared in Russia during the late 19th and early 20th centuries. Several attacks by the Anarchist group *Narodnaya Volya* ("The People's Will")—including, most prominently, the assassination of Tsar Alexander II in 1881—involved the death of its perpetrator as an integral part of its mission. The assassination followed eight previous, unsuccessful attempts at the Tsar's life. The ninth attempt at tyrannicide succeeded because one of the four Russian revolutionaries who equipped themselves with bombs on that day decided to detonate the bomb in such close proximity to the Tsar that it would ensure not only his target's death but also his own.[7]

Prior to the 1980s, the most prominent use of this modus operandi was by the Japanese *kamikaze* suicide pilots, who staged over 3,000 suicide sorties between October 1944 and August 1945. Japan, however, was not the only nation producing suicide attackers during World War II. During the Battle of the Coral Sea in May 1942 and the Battle at Midway the following month, two U.S. airmen crashed their planes onto Japanese ships.[8] Meanwhile, Soviet and German fighter pilots were ordered to crash their planes into enemy aircraft during desperate times, though that order seems to have been rarely carried out.[9] The use of suicide attacks by Japan and, to lesser extent, by other countries during World War II helps dispel some popular misconceptions about this modus operandi. These cases demonstrate that this tactic has not been used exclusively by terrorist organizations, but also by states. Second, and perhaps more importantly, along with the example of the Russian anarchists, the kamikaze missions provided early evidence that the use of suicide missions was not sanctioned exclusively by religion. Although almost all Japanese are nominally both Buddhist and Shinto, and many cherish Confucian values such as filial piety, submission for authority, and diligence, Japanese suicide attackers seemed to be motivated more by a desire to protect their country and their families than merely by a keen devotion to their Emperor.[10]

Precursors to modern-day suicide attacks have also emerged in the post–World War II period in Vietnam. According to Weinberg, during the Tet Offensive in 1968, special Viet Cong sapper units were sent on suicide missions against high-prestige or high-visibility targets.[11] It is likely that in the majority of cases, the suicide teams dispatched by the North Vietnamese and their allies were what German soldiers describe as *Himmelfahrtskommandos*—units dispatched on missions that are so risky that they will result in almost certain death. That said, based on Weinberg's findings, at least a number of these attacks seem to have been "conventional" suicide attacks, i.e., operations in which the death of the perpetrators were a precondition for the success of the attack.[12]

Lebanon and the Modern Phenomenon of Suicide Terrorism after 1981

In 1981, the history of suicide attacks underwent a dramatic shift. From Lebanon, where the tactic was adopted by the radical Shia Hizballah, the tactic spread rapidly to violent groups in many other countries and increasingly adopted the form of suicide *terrorism*—a trend that continues to this very day. The roots of the contemporary phenomenon of suicide terrorism that emerged in the early 1980s in Lebanon can be found in the Islamic Revolution of Iran. More than any other regime that preceded it, Iran under Khomeini provided the religious and ideological justification for the use of violence in the name of Islam. Waging *jihad* fulfilled a core role within this framework, while self-sacrifice and martyrdom were extolled as the highest service that a Muslim could perform for God. The idea of martyrdom as the most meritorious service to God reached its pinnacle during the early years of the Iran-Iraq war. Between 1981 and 1984, the Islamic Republic of Iran called upon masses of youth to volunteer for the so-called "human wave attacks." These attacks consisted of up to 20,000 children as young as 12 or 13 who were sent into the line of fire and across minefields, with no backup. Exploding the mines with their own bodies, these children were used to clear the way for the soldiers that followed them. In return for their almost certain death, the children were provided with a key, which they wore around their neck. After their martyrdom, they were told, that key would open the gate to paradise.

The cynical call for martyrdom made its next appearance in Lebanon, where the first suicide attack took place in Beirut in December 1981. Twenty-seven people died and more than 100 were wounded when a member of the Iranian-backed Shia group, Al Dawa (The Call), drove a bomb-laden car into the Iraqi embassy in Beirut. Not before long, suicide attacks would also be aimed at Western targets in Lebanon. In April 1983, a suicide bomber drove an explosives-laden van into the U.S. embassy in Beirut, killing 63 people and wounding another 120. On October 23 of that year, suicide bombers killed nearly 300 American and French servicemen with two coordinated car and truck bombings targeted at the compounds housing these forces. These suicide attacks were the beginning of a new trend, namely the systematic use of suicide attacks as part of terrorist and/or insurgent campaign. Until 1999, dozens of additional suicide attacks were conducted in Lebanon, most of which were carried out by Hizballah, which targeted mostly Israeli forces and its Lebanese allies.

Lebanon was the staging ground for many innovations in the history of suicide attacks, including the use of female suicide bombers and the systematic proliferation of a cult of sacrifice. On March 10, 1985, the Syrian Socialist Nationalist Party dispatched 18-year-old Sumayah Sa'ad, who drove a car loaded with dynamite into an Israeli military position in Southern Lebanon, killing 12 Israeli soldiers and wounding 14 others. No other female suicide bombers are known to have been used prior to that date. Two weeks later, 17-year-old San'ah Muheidli drove a TNT-laden car into an IDF convoy, killing two soldiers and wounding two more. Upon their deaths, the two women were awarded the title of "Brides of Blood" (*Arous ad-Damm*).[13]

No other organization that preceded it was more proficient at deploying suicide bombers than Hizballah. The group not only developed a mechanism to systematically recruit and train suicide bombers, but it also ensured ideological support on the part of

Shia imams close to the group. To justify the need to sacrifice its own fighters and to overcome the religious sanctioning against suicide in Islam, the group developed a cult of martyrdom, which it had copied from revolutionary Iran. Generating a martyrdom cult had two added effects: increasing the number of potential recruits for Hizballah and acting as a mechanism by which the group could morally disengage from the act and its victims. One of the ways in which this culture was propagated was through the use of euphemisms. Thus, the group used the phrase *al-amalyiat al-istishhadiyya* (martyr operation) as a euphemism instead of the word *intihar,* which describes ordinary suicide on the basis of personal distress. Similarly, the martyr (*shahid,* lit. witness) was described as a "happy martyr" (*shahid as-said*) or *istishhaadi,* i.e., he who gives himself over to martyrdom. Suicide attacks, along with the names of their perpetrators, were announced and celebrated on radio stations and since 1990, on television stations. In addition, as many Palestinian, Iraqi, and other suicide bombers would do in subsequent years, Lebanese "shahids" recorded a farewell video. These videos were frequently broadcast alongside the footage of the attack itself. The group also established martyrs' funds, while its spiritual and strategic supporters praised the martyrs' deeds in mosques and other public institutions.[14]

Suicide attacks were relatively successful in Lebanon in that they raised the costs of military presence for foreign states. They helped lead to the withdrawal of French and American troops from Lebanon, and likely contributed to Israel's withdrawal from Lebanon to a smaller, self-proclaimed "security zone," which it held until it fully withdrew from Lebanon in 2000. The success of the tactic in Lebanon soon prompted other groups to adopt suicide missions. The first group who emulated this tactic was the Liberation Tigers of Tamil Eelam (LTTE), whose leader, Vellupillai Prabhakaran, was greatly impressed by Hizballah's successful use of suicide attacks as a tool to fight an asymmetric battle.[15] Beginning in July 1987, the LTTE's charismatic leader decided to adopt suicide tactics in order to offset the militarily more powerful Sri Lankan state, which is dominated by ethnic Sinhalese. Between 1987 and 2001, the LTTE planned and executed an estimated 200 suicide attacks[16]—a number that, until 2003, accounted for more suicide operations than those by all other organizations employing this tactic combined. In 2003, the LTTE was bypassed by Palestinian organizations as the lead perpetrators of this tactic.[17]

The first Palestinian organization to adopt this tactic was Hamas, which carried out its first such mission at the Mehola Junction on April 16, 1993. Between 1993 and 1998, Hamas and the Palestinian Islamic Jihad (PIJ) carried out nearly 30 suicide attacks. The tactic became even more widely used in the next wave of attacks that occurred during the Second Intifada. Henceforth, suicide attacks were also used by secular organizations such as Fatah's Al Aqsa Martyrs Brigades and the Popular Front for the Liberation of Palestine (PFLP).

Suicide missions have also been used in the context of the Turkish-Kurdish conflict between 1996 and 1999, when the Kurdistan Workers Party (PKK) executed 15 suicide attacks and planned another seven attacks that failed.[18] The PKK was led by a highly charismatic leader, Abdullah Ocalan, and its cadres included many women. The PKK's attacks peaked in 1999, following Ocalan's capture in Kenya. They came to a halt when in August 1999, the PKK's imprisoned leader announced a "peace initiative" and denounced violence.

Al Qaeda and Suicide Attacks in Iraq

In the course of the 1980s and 1990s, suicide bombings had become a common tactic in some parts of the world, but it was not until the 1998 bombings that this modus operandi turned into a truly global phenomenon—as measured in the exponential rise in the number of suicide attacks and the number of organizations perpetrating suicide missions, as well as the rapidly rising number of countries targeted since 1998.[19]

On August 7, 1998, a set of explosions, only minutes apart, rocked the U.S. embassies in Nairobi, Kenya, and Dar-es-Salaam, Tanzania. The embassy bombings were a milestone in the confrontation between al Qaeda and the United States, as they marked the beginning of al Qaeda's involvement in the planning, direction, and execution of suicide attacks. More importantly, however, the embassy bombings also revealed another trend, namely the growing influence of Salafi-Jihadist ideology among individuals and groups involved in suicide attacks. Since 1998, Salafi-Jihadist groups have not only become the most dominant perpetrators of suicide attacks, but also the most lethal ones.[20] In Iraq, for example, where more suicide bombings occurred between 1981 and 2006 than in all other states combined, Salafi-Jihadist groups were the main organizers of this tactic.[21]

Besides their importance in indicating a new trend in the ideological affiliation of groups perpetrating suicide attacks, the embassy bombings were also significant because they affirmed a fundamental shift in al Qaeda's strategy. Until the mid-1990s, the terrorist network had focused its ire on the "near enemy"—Arab and Muslim regimes whose real or perceived alliance with the United States rendered them apostates in the understanding of the group's Salafi-Jihadist ideology. On August 7, 1998, it became painfully clear that al Qaeda had completed a change in strategy that now involved punishing the "far enemy"—the infidel regimes in the West, led by the United States. The attacks foreshadowed future spectacular suicide attacks by al Qaeda that would target the United States and its allies over the next decade. They included the attack on the U.S.S. *Cole* in October 2000; the attacks of September 11, 2001; an attack on a synagogue in Djerbia, Tunisia, in April 2002; and a series of suicide and other terrorist operations in Kenya in November 2002. Since then, al Qaeda and/or associated groups were also involved in a number of other suicide bombings, including in Casablanca and Istanbul in May and November 2003, and in London in July 2005. Numerous other attempts were foiled, including an attempt by shoe bomber Richard Reid to detonate an explosive device over the Atlantic, a desire to hit U.S. landmarks in New York and New Jersey, and a plot to blow up as many as a dozen airliners bound from London to the United States over American cities in 2006.

The growing influence of Salafi-Jihadist ideology on groups employing suicide attacks was soon noticeable in Chechnya, where Salafi-Jihadist veterans of the Afghan–Soviet war flocked to wage a holy war against Russia. On June 7, 2000, a Chechen man and a Chechen woman detonated a bomb-laden truck at a checkpoint at Alkhan-Yurt in Chechnya. Attacks by Chechens were different from other suicide attacks since the 1980s because like al Qaeda's anti-Western campaign, the Chechen conflict bore elements of a global struggle. Rather than attempting to keep the focus on its Russian enemy, the Chechen rebels noted on their official Web site after their first suicide attack that the operation was meant as a message to all Muslims. The operation, according to the rebels, "was a cry that said no to the crimes against the Muslim Ummah, but will the people of the Ummah heed to this call and rush to support their brothers and sisters who are in need? Will the hearts of the believers come alive with this example of pure faith and courageous sacrifice?"[22]

Suicide attacks by Salafi-Jihadist groups were heavily influenced by al Qaeda's strong emphasis on "martyrdom operations." Like other groups, al Qaeda has adopted this tactic because of its high lethality, its ability to instill fear in the target audience, and sow confusion among its enemy. More so than other groups, however, al Qaeda has also been successful at instilling the spirit of self-sacrifice and the cult of martyrdom in the collective psyche of virtually all of its fighters. Abdullah Azzam, co-founder of al Qaeda, was the first theoretician who succeeded in turning martyrdom and self-sacrifice into a "formative ethos" of al Qaeda. After Azzam's death, Osama bin Laden and other al Qaeda members continued to inculcate this importance of martyrdom into the minds of the network's rank and file. In 2004, for instance, bin Laden urged his followers to "become diligent in carrying out martyrdom operations; these operations, praise be to God, have become a great source of terror for the enemy. . . . These are the most important operations."[23] Bin Laden's deputy, Ayman al-Zawahiri, similarly elevated martyrdom as the most honorable act for Muslims on many occasions.[24]

The preeminence of suicide attacks among al Qaeda's tactics has been most dramatically on display in Iraq after the U.S.-led invasion in March 2003. On March 22, 2003, less than a week after the beginning of the Iraq campaign, four civilians, including Paul Moran, a 39-year-old Australian cameraman on assignment for the Australian Broadcasting Corporation, were killed in a suicide car bombing on the outskirts of the village of Khurmal in northern Iraq. Over the next years, the number of suicide attacks in Iraq would easily surpass that of all known suicide attacks in other countries combined. High-profile suicide attacks in Iraq initially targeted mostly U.S. and allied forces, as well as international organizations. In subsequent years, these attacks began to target Iraqi "collaborators" and members of Iraq's Shia community, oftentimes during Shia high holidays.

As in a growing number of other regions—notably Afghanistan, Pakistan, Chechnya, but also Western Europe—suicide attacks in Iraq are increasingly associated with Salafi-Jihadist ideology. Most suicide attacks in Iraq are perpetrated by groups that adhere to a strict Salafi-Jihadist doctrine of Islam. These include Ansar al-Islam, Ansar al-Sunnah Army, the Victorious Sect, Jaish-e-Muhammad, Ahl al-Sunna wal-Jamaah Army, and the Conquest Army, among others.[25] The quintessential Salafi-Jihadist group active in Iraq is al Qaeda in Iraq, whose goals are paradigmatic for those of other Salafi-Jihadist organizations. They were summarized in an online magazine in March 2005 by a commander of the group, Abu Maysara. al Qaeda in Iraq's goals include the renewal of pure monotheism; waging jihad for the sake of Allah; coming to the aid of the Muslims wherever they are; reclaiming Muslim dignity; and finally, "to re-establish the Rightly-Guided Caliphate in accordance with the Prophet's example, because 'whoever dies without having sworn allegiance to a Muslim ruler dies as an unbeliever.'"[26]

The adoption of suicide attacks by al Qaeda and Salafi-Jihadist groups marks the true beginning of globalized suicide attacks. In light of the internationalization of this phenomenon and the unprecedented proliferation of this tactic, it is worthwhile to revisit some of the arguments brought forward to date to explain the genesis of suicide terrorism. To that end, the next part of this chapter will briefly review the existing literature on the causes of suicide terrorism.

Explaining Suicide Attacks—A Review

Studies dedicated to explaining the causes of suicide attacks were almost impossible to find a decade ago, but have skyrocketed in numbers following the attacks of 9/11. Some of these studies examine the level of the individual bomber, considering such personal motivations as humiliation, despair, personal crisis, commitment, or psychopathology.[27] The second category consists of studies that have stressed the need to focus on the group or organization as the key variable in explaining suicide bombings.[28] A third category of studies emphasizes the socio-structural level. In contrast to studies that focus on a single level of analysis, in recent years, a growing number of scholars argues that a proper understanding of suicide terrorism requires an integration of multiple levels of analysis.[29]

Explanations at the Individual Level

Conducting analysis at the individual level, analysts from a variety of disciplines have been able to reject a number of previously held beliefs about suicide terrorism. First, they have concluded that suicide bombers cannot be compared to ordinary suicides. While ordinary suicides are usually drawn to their deaths due to a personal crisis, suicide bombers tend to act for what they believe to be altruistic reasons—a distinction dating back to the French sociologist Emile Durkheim.[30] Second, neither do suicide bombers act irrationally. On the contrary, most analysts believe that suicide attackers act rationally in the sense that they believe the benefits of perpetrating suicide attacks to outweigh the costs of doing so.[31] Third, terrorism scholars have also been able to dispel the often held belief that "all suicide bombers are alike." Thus, while a number of earlier studies of suicide attackers have argued that there is a common profile to suicide bombers,[32] more recent studies based on additional data have concluded that suicide attackers do not share many similar characteristics in common.

A variety of motivations for suicide terrorism have been proposed by analysts studying suicide terrorism at the individual level including mental illness, personal crises, revenge, subsequent benefits, and financial gain. Many researchers have been occupied with the role that psychological factors play in the genesis of suicide bombers, but have failed to produce evidence that conclusively links psychopathology with the resort to terrorism. While clearly highly alienated from society, most experts agree, terrorists are sane and relatively "normal" in the sense that they do not exhibit signs of suffering from a salient psychopathology.[33] For that reason, mental illness as a factor in suicide terrorism has been dismissed.[34] Studies of individual bombers have highlighted that some suicide bombers have suffered from personal crisis, which is likely to have played a role in the decision to become a suicide bomber. Personal crisis appears to be a particularly common motivation among women suicide bombers such as the Chechen Black Widows.[35] Other studies indicate the seeking of revenge as a prevailing motive for the resort to suicide attacks—at times, this motive is reinforced by perceived humiliation.[36] Kimhi and Even, for instance, identified the individual seeking retribution for suffering as one of four prototypes of Palestinian suicide bombers.[37]

According to some researchers, suicide attackers tend to act out of a deep sense of commitment to a larger cause, to their social network, or to a terrorist organization and its ideology.[38] According to Pedahzur, this sense of commitment applies particularly to those suicide bombers who have been members of organizations, as opposed to those that have been recruited for the particular task of a suicide mission.[39] Strong commitment can be the result of psychological pressure exerted by the group's leadership, which can help present self-sacrificial attacks as a way for an ordinary individual to defend his country and his people. Suicide bombings can be highly empowering in that regard. Hafez, for example, argues that militant groups call upon suicide bombers to "perform their duty to their own values, family, friends, community, or religion. Failure to act, consequently, creates dissonance because it is perceived as a betrayal of one's ideals, loved ones, country, God, or sense of manhood."[40] Suicide attacks may thus be conceived as a way for individuals to overcome and reverse their perceived sense of humiliation, shame, and injustice to achieve honor, respect, and redemption.[41]

Several authors have stressed the expectation of posthumous benefits as a motive for suicide attackers particularly when the perpetrators of the attacks are Muslims. Such benefits can include the suicide attacker's elevated social status after death, rewards for the family, as well as the attainment of heavenly pleasures in the afterlife. The expectation of personal benefits in the afterlife that seems to motivate many Muslim suicide bombers,[42] such as a guaranteed place in heaven, the eventual reunification with one's family, or sexual pleasures, does not necessarily apply to nonreligious cases of suicide attacks. In the case of the nationalist Black Tigers, for example, there is no expectation of a posthumous compensation.[43] Finally, some students of suicide attacks have argued that suicide bombers may act partly out of financial incentives,[44] which have already been shown to have affected some non-suicidal terrorists in their decision to join or remain in terrorist organizations.[45] Monetary rewards for the families of suicide bombers have been common among Palestinian suicide bombers as well as those of Hizballah.[46]

In sum, studies examining individual motivations of suicide terrorism have established that suicide bombers can be motivated by a range of factors that often includes a strong commitment and the seeking of revenge, and sometimes a sense of personal crisis. These studies, however, have not been able to identify either necessary or sufficient conditions for an individual's resort to suicide terrorism. Thus, no studies have established why some highly committed individuals become suicide bombers while others do not, or why revenge leads to suicide terrorism in some cases and not in others. Although studies focusing on the individual level of analysis have made important contributions to the understanding of why individuals may be motivated to sacrifice their lives for a larger cause, they also left behind a fair number of question marks.

The Organizational-Strategic Level

Partly in response to these limitations, a second category of studies has focused on the organizational-strategic level of analysis. Studies falling within this approach are particularly important because suicide attacks are mostly acts of terrorism, which in turn are rarely carried out by individuals acting on their own, but rather by individuals who are members of organizations, groups, or cells attached to a larger network.[47] Studies at the organizational-strategic level typically build on the pioneering theoretical work of Crenshaw, who argued that terrorism can be understood as the result of a deliberate choice by terrorist organizations who believe that violence is the best means to advance their political goals.[48] Based on this rational framework, terrorist organizations select suicide attacks as a means to fulfill various rational interests ranging from the basic need to survive to sophisticated strategic and tactical interests.

Suicide attacks perpetrated by terrorist organizations may be the result of the organization's perceived need to survive.[49] A minimum degree of violent presence is necessary for all terrorist groups to remain effective. Failure to maintain such a degree of violence will eventually lead—or will be perceived to lead—to the group's irrelevance and eventual disappearance as a political force. The timing of the suicide attack may be a function of opportunity. The organization may possess a rare opportunity to stage a successful suicide attack or it may have a unique opportunity to strike a target of particularly high value, deciding to use a suicide operation to increase the chances of success, as the Narodnaya Volya did in the previously mentioned assassination of Tsar Alexander II on March 1, 1881.

Researchers examining suicide terrorism from an organizational perspective also emphasize the strategic and tactical benefits of this mode of operations. Several authors have argued that their relatively high degree of lethality has rendered suicide attacks a rational or "logical" choice for organizations and states under certain circumstances.[50] Pape, for example, asserts that "the main reason that suicide terrorism is growing is that terrorists have learned that it works."[51] Other scholars, however, have challenged that contention by arguing that the degree of success of suicide terrorism is overstated.[52] In any event, suicide attacks are hardly employed for military purposes alone. More likely, organizations utilize this tactic for a combination of military effectiveness and political purpose. The frequent videotaping of suicide bombers prior to their mission underscores the fact that terrorist organizations attempt to elicit maximum propaganda benefits. Similarly, suicide bombings are often timed to derail political events contrary to the cause of the terrorist group—be it the Israeli-Palestinian peace process or elections in Iraq.[53]

Beyond strategic benefits, some terrorist groups prefer suicide attacks for their tactical benefits, which are numerous. First, even more than ordinary terrorist attacks, suicide operations are likely to draw attention to a group's cause, aided in large part by the extraordinarily high attention such operations enjoy in the media. In this regard, suicide attacks can be thought of as a form of "strategic signaling," whereby terrorist attacks are used to communicate a group's character and goals to the target audience.[54] As pointed out by Hoffman and McCormick, for instance, the LTTE used suicide attacks to signal an image of elitism, professionalism, invincibility, and fanatical single-mindedness to the Sri Lankan government.[55] Second, suicide missions, even more than ordinary terrorist attacks, serve the organization's attempt to create extreme fear in the larger population—a key feature, in fact, of all terrorist attacks. This occurs in part due to the group's demonstration of the inefficacy of the targeted government, and in part due to the demoralization of the public and of law enforcement agencies. A suicide attack creates not only a disproportionately intense amount of fear among the targeted population, but its effect may be particularly traumatizing and long-lasting,[56] thus serving, as Holmes put it, as an "intensifier of enemy despair."[57] Adding to the frustration of the targeted population, Holmes adds, is the inability of the targeted community to exact revenge on the perpetrators, arguably rendering the recovery from these attacks more difficult than from ordinary terrorism.[58] Third, suicide attacks may serve as an internal morale booster for the terrorist group. The use of this tactic indicates the complete dedication of the suicide attackers to their cause. It can lead to a sense of moral superiority of the groups' members over their adversaries, which may result in a group's perception that it will eventually prevail over its enemies.[59] Finally, terrorist organizations adopt suicide operations because of a number of unique operational benefits. They are a cost-efficient tool, with suicide vests costing as little as $50–$150.[60] They are also high-precision weapons of sorts, and have therefore often been called the "ultimate smart bomb."[61] The explosive devices, which are usually strapped on to the perpetrator's body, can be detonated at the time and place of the attacker's choosing, thus maximizing the lethality of the improvised explosive device (IED). Other tactical benefits of suicide attacks are that their use obviates the need for the complicated task of planning an escape route. Furthermore, the suicide bomber's ensured death nullifies the risk of his or her capture. The risk that the bomber will be intercepted, interrogated, and compelled to disclose incriminating information about the organization is minuscule.[62]

In sum, organizational approaches to suicide bombing have highlighted the strategic and tactical benefits of suicide attacks. The reasons why groups adopt suicide attacks have little to do with the motivations that lead individuals to become suicide bombers. Similar to the individual level studies, however, organizational approaches have limitations. They fail to explain why, if the benefits of suicide terrorism are so numerous, many organizations avoid their use. Neither do they provide a satisfying answer to the question of when a terrorist group decides to adopt a suicide attack.

The Socio-Cultural Level

Socio-cultural approaches, the third major category of studies of suicide attacks, have attempted to provide an answer to the limits of approaches at the individual and organizational-strategic levels of analysis by arguing that individuals and organizations will embark on suicide terrorism if they enjoy social support for this tactic. Indeed, this explanation appears to account for the widespread use of suicide attacks in places like Lebanon or Israel, where a cult of martyrdom has been apparent—manifesting itself in venerations of suicide bombers, the prominent use of euphemistic labels for suicide attacks and their perpetrators, and the penetration of the suicide bomber into popular culture, such as movies, comics, or plays. Some researchers claim that sustained levels of suicide terrorism are entirely dependent upon strong support among the attacker's domestic population.[63] It is apparent, however, that an increasing number of suicide attacks in recent years have been performed in countries where there does not seem to be strong popular support for these activities—such as Afghanistan, Pakistan, and even Iraq.[64] A culture of martyrdom may well surround the world of the suicide bombers in these cases, but increasingly that culture seems to be found on cyberspace, as opposed to the street level.

In recent years, more and more analysts have offered explanations that attempt to integrate several levels of analysis. Proponents of multi-causal approaches correctly note that mono-causal approaches to the study of suicide attacks are insufficient. These scholars argue that a comprehensive understanding of suicide terrorism requires an understanding of individual-level motives, organizational-level strategic and tactical factors, as well as the role played by the external environment. Scholars adopting such approaches, however, have not been able to solve the problem of specificity, i.e., explaining why some situations produce suicide terrorism while others do not.[65]

Towards New Explanations of Suicide Attacks

In recent years, the tactic of suicide terrorism appears to have undergone additional changes that necessitate a thorough review of existing explanations of suicide terrorism. At first glance, the argument that suicide terrorism is a response to foreign occupation appears to have some merit, given the widespread use of suicide terrorism among communities vying for a national homeland, such as Palestinians and Tamils.[66] Upon closer inspection, however, suicide attacks increasingly occur in places where there is no discernible occupation. Bangladesh, Indonesia, Jordan, Morocco, Saudi Arabia, Turkey, the United Kingdom, and Uzbekistan are some of the countries that suffered such attacks in recent years that are not occupied by foreign armies. Second, in those countries where there is an occupation, attacks are not always directed at occupiers but at other ethnic communities, as is the case in Iraq, where Shias are among the prime targets. In addition, those attacks that are aimed at military targets linked to occupation are not always carried out by the occupied. In Iraq, most attacks that do target occupation forces are carried out not by Iraqis, but instead by Saudi, Syrian, Kuwaiti, North African, and other foreign jihadists.[67]

Another prominent group of theories whose explanatory ability has diminished to some extent are organizational explanations suggesting that groups adopt suicide terrorism in order to better compete with other groups for the support of a local population.[68] The theory assumes that local populations support suicide bombings, yet in a growing number of places such strong domestic support appears to be lacking. Such explanations may have accounted for the adoption of suicide terrorism in the case of some Lebanese and Palestinian groups, but in the case of suicide attacks in Iraq or in Western countries, for instance, strong popular support for suicide attacks is not observable. An openly propagated cult of martyrdom, so visible in Lebanon, the West Bank, and Gaza, is virtually absent in places like Iraq and Afghanistan—regions that currently dominate the landscape of suicide terrorism in terms of numbers of attacks.

Explanations of suicide terrorism offered in the future should account for several fundamental changes noticeable in the pattern of suicide attacks. They must account for the fact that while suicide attacks in the past were perpetrated mostly by subnational organizations with limited goals, they are now increasingly perpetrated by Salafi-Jihadist organizations with transnational goals.[69] New theories of suicide attacks should also explain why suicide attacks during the 1980s and much of the 1990s were mostly localized affairs, involving attacks that were locally planned and locally executed with the help of local handlers, recruiters, and suicide bombers. Today's suicide attacks tend to have goals that are more global, and indeed unlimited in scope. Salafi-Jihadists have become the predominant ideological perpetrators of suicide terrorism, and their world view is based on an exceedingly loose definition of the enemy.[70] Whereas traditional suicide bombers such as Lebanese members of Hizballah or members of Palestinian groups had a clear and limited notion of who they should target—namely the American, French, or Israeli occupiers—many suicide bombers today have adopted the rhetoric of al Qaeda and its guiding Salafi-Jihadist ideology, which present the enemy in broad terms, as an infidel or a member of the "Zionist-Crusader alliance."

Future explanations of suicide attacks must also explain why today's recruitment occurs increasingly from the bottom up, rather than from the top down. Whereas groups such as Hamas or the LTTE once sent out recruiters to identify suicide bombers, many suicide bombers today volunteer for "martyrdom operations" proactively, instead of waiting to be contacted by recruitment officers. Theoretical explanations must also address the worrisome fact that a growing number of suicide bombers do not share the same kinds of experiences that have arguably contributed to the willingness to become suicide bombers in earlier cases. Increasingly, grievances of present-day bombers are vicariously, rather than directly, experienced. Mohammed Sidique Khan, Hasib Mir Hussein, Shahzeed Tanweer, and Germaine Lindsay—the four London suicide bombers—have not experienced the hardships of military occupation that their suicidal counterparts in the West Bank and Gaza have endured. Neither is it likely that the large numbers of Saudis and other foreign jihadists who flock to Iraq to become martyrs have themselves experienced the humiliation of roadblocks or other manifestations of foreign occupation. On the contrary, many of today's martyrs, in fact, have enjoyed a relatively comfortable upbringing.[71]

Finally, forthcoming explanations of suicide attacks will be more valuable if they can help address the growing trend of radicalization in small cells. What role do preexisting social ties such as friendship or kinship play in the radicalization of individuals towards suicide terrorism, and are networks a necessary and/or sufficient factor? These and other vexing questions revolving around suicide attacks are not likely to be answered conclusively any time soon, but additional insights into these phenomena may help contain the scourge of suicide terrorism in the future.

Assaf Moghadam is a research fellow at the Combating Terrorism Center at West Point, a postdoctoral fellow at Harvard University's Initiative on Religion in International Affairs, and a research associate of the Jebsen Center for Counterterrorism Studies at The Fletcher School at Tufts University. Dr. Moghadam is the author of *The Roots of Terrorism* (New York: Chelsea House, 2006) and the forthcoming *The Globalization of Martyrdom: Al Qaeda, Salafi Jihad, and the Diffusion of Suicide Attacks* (Baltimore: Johns Hopkins University Press, 2008).

Notes

1. This definition follows from Yoram Schweitzer, "Suicide Terrorism: Development and Main Characteristics," in International Policy Institute for Counter-Terrorism (ICT), ed. *Countering Suicide Terrorism: An International Conference* (Herzliyya, Israel: ICT, 2001), 78; and Boaz Ganor, "Suicide Attacks in Israel," in ICT, ed. *Countering Suicide Terrorism,* 140.
2. For a discussion of definitional issues surrounding suicide terrorism, see Assaf Moghadam, "Defining Suicide Terrorism," in Ami Pedahzur, ed. *Root Causes of Suicide Terrorism: Globalization of Martyrdom* (London: Routledge, 2006).
3. Bernard Lewis, *The Assassins: A Radical Sect in Islam* (New York: Oxford University Press, 1987), 127.
4. The Assassins did not call themselves Assassins, but *feda'i,* which can roughly be translated as "devotee."
5. Stephen Frederic Dale, "Religious Suicide in Islamic Asia: Anticolonial Terrorism in India, Indonesia, and the Philippines," *Journal of Conflict Resolution, 32,* no. 1 (March 1988).
6. Ibid, 51.
7. On the assassination of Tsar Alexander II, see, for example, Bruce Hoffman, *Inside Terrorism* (New York: Columbia University Press, 1998), 17–19.

8. Peter Hill, "Kamikaze, 1943–5," in *Making Sense of Suicide Missions,* ed. Diego Gambetta (Oxford ; New York: Oxford University Press, 2005), 1.

9. Barry Smith, "Kamikaze—Und Der Westen," in *Terror Und Der Krieg Gegen Ihn: Öffentliche Reflexionen,* ed. G. Meggle (Paderborn, Germany: Mentis, 2003), 4-5; Hill, "Kamikaze, 1943–5," 42.

10. Hill, "Kamikaze, 1943–5," 5–8.

11. Leonard Weinberg, "Suicide Terrorism for Secular Causes," in Pedahzur, ed. *Root Causes of Suicide Terrorism,* 117.

12. Ibid, 119.

13. Taheri, *Holy Terror,* 126–129.

14. Christoph Reuter, *My Life Is a Weapon: A Modern History of Suicide Bombing* (Princeton, NJ: Princeton University Press, 2004), 65–66.

15. Bruce Hoffman and Gordon H. McCormick, "Terrorism, Signaling, and Suicide Attack," *Studies in Conflict and Terrorism,* 27, no. 4 (July–August 2004): 259.

16. Ibid, 256. There are no precise data on the number of attacks perpetrated by the LTTE. For a discussion, see Hoffman and McCormick, "Terrorism, Signaling, and Suicide Attack," 275, fn. 52. See also Stephen Hopgood, "Tamil Tigers, 1987–2002," in Gambetta, ed. *Making Sense of Suicide Missions,* 53–55.

17. Based on information gathered from the suicide terrorism database by the National Security Studies Center, University of Haifa. The author thanks Ami Pedahzur and Arie Perliger for access to the database.

18. Ami Pedahzur, *Suicide Terrorism* (Cambridge; Malden, MA: Polity, 2005), 89.

19. Assaf Moghadam, *The Globalization of Martyrdom: al Qaeda, Salafi Jihad, and the Diffusion of Suicide Attacks* (Baltimore: Johns Hopkins University Press, 2008) [forthcoming].

20. Ibid.

21. See, for example, Mohammed M. Hafez, *Suicide Bombers in Iraq: The Strategy and Ideology of Martyrdom* (Washington, DC: United States Institute of Peace Press, 2007); and International Crisis Group, "In Their Own Words: Reading the Iraqi Insurgency," *ICG Middle East Report No. 50* (Amman/Brussels: International Crisis Group, 15 February 2006).

22. Quoted in Reuven Paz, "Suicide Terrorist Operations in Chechnya," *International Policy Institute for Counterterrorism,* 20 June 2000. Available at http://www.ict.org.il.

23. Quoted in Christopher M. Blanchard, "al Qaeda: Statements and Evolving Ideology," in CRS Report for Congress RL32759 (Washington, DC: Congressional Research Service, Library of Congress, 2005), 10.

24. See, for example, his statements regarding the four London bombers. "Al-Qaeda Film on the First Anniversary of the London Bombings Features Messages by Bomber Shehzad Tanweer, American Al-Qaeda Member Adam Gadahn and Al-Qaeda Leader Ayman Al-Zawahiri," MEMRI TV Monitor Project Clip No. 1186 (6 July 2006).

25. Hafez, *Suicide Bombers in Iraq.*

26. The article was translated by the Middle East Media Research Institute (MEMRI). See "The Iraqi Al-Qa'ida Organization: A Self-Portrait," *MEMRI Special Dispatch Series* No. 884 (24 March 2005).

27. See, for example, Joan Lachkar, "The Psychological Make-up of a Suicide Bomber," *Journal of Psychohistory, 29,* no. 4 (Spring 2002); David Lester, Bijou Yang, and Mark Lindsay, "Suicide Bombers: Are Psychological Profiles Possible?," *Studies in Conflict and Terrorism, 27,* no. 4 (July-August 2004); Eyad Sarraj, "Suicide Bombers: Dignity, Despair, and the Need of Hope," *Journal of Palestine Studies,* 31, no. 4 (Summer 2004); and Anat Berko, *The Path to Paradise: The Inner World of Suicide Bombers and their Dispatchers* (Westport, CT: Praeger Security International, 2007).

28. Ehud Sprinzak, "Rational Fanatics," *Foreign Policy,* (September/October 2000); Mia Bloom, *Dying to Kill: The Allure of Suicide Terror* (New York: Columbia University Press, 2005); Robert A. Pape, *Dying to Win: The Strategic Logic of Suicide Terrorism* (New York: Random House, 2005); Pedahzur, *Suicide Terrorism.*

29. Assaf Moghadam, "Palestinian Suicide Terrorism in the Second Intifada: Motivations and Organizational Aspects," *Studies in Conflict and Terrorism, 26,* no. 2 (2003); Assaf

Moghadam, "The Roots of Suicide Terrorism: A Multi-Causal Approach," in Pedahzur, ed. *Root Causes of Suicide Terrorism;* Mohammed M. Hafez, "Rationality, Culture, and Structure in the Making of Suicide Bombers: A Preliminary Theoretical Synthesis and Illustrative Case Study," *Studies in Conflict and Terrorism, 29,* no. 3 (April-May 2006); and Hafez, *Suicide Bombers in Iraq.*

30. See, for example, Ami Pedahzur, Arie Perliger, and Leonard Weinberg, "Altruism and Fatalism: The Characteristics of Palestinian Suicide Terrorists," *Deviant Behavior, 24,* no. 4 (July–August 2003); and Ariel Merari, "Suicide Terrorism," in *Assessment, Treatment, and Prevention of Suicidal Behavior,* ed. Robert I. and David Lester Yufit (New York: Wiley, 2004).

31. Sprinzak, "Rational Fanatics;" Moghadam, "Palestinian Suicide Terrorism in the Second Intifada"; Bloom, *Dying to Kill;* Pedahzur, *Suicide Terrorism;* Hoffman and McCormick, "Terrorism, Signaling, and Suicide Attack."

32. Harvey Kushner, "Suicide Bombers: Business as Usual," *Studies in Conflict and Terrorism, 19,* no. 4 (1996); and Raphael Israeli, "Islamikaze and Their Significance," *Terrorism and Political Violence, 9,* no. 3 (Autumn 1997).

33. Clark R. McCauley, and M.E. Segal, "Social Psychology of Terrorist Groups," in *Group Processes and Intergroup Relations: Review of Personality and Social Psychology,* ed. C. Hendrick (Newbury Park: Sage, 1987).

34. Jeff Victoroff, "The Mind of the Terrorist: A Review and Critique of Psychological Approaches," *Journal of Conflict Resolution, 49,* no. 1 (February 2005).

35. See especially Barbara Victor, *Army of Roses: Inside the World of Palestinian Women Suicide Bombers* (Emmaus, PA: Rodale, 2003); Anat Berko and Edna Erez, "'Ordinary People' and 'Death Work': Palestinian Suicide Bombers as Victimizers and Victims," *Violence and Victims, 20,* no. 6 (December 2005).

36. For an application of humiliation-revenge theory, see especially Mark Juergensmeyer, *Terror in the Mind of God: The Global Rise of Religious Violence* (Berkeley: University of California Press, 2001); Jessica Stern, *Terror in the Name of God: Why Religious Militants Kill* (New York: Ecco/Harper Collins, 2003); and Farhad Khosrokhavar, *Suicide Bombers: Allah's New Martyrs* (London: Pluto, 2005).

37. Shaul Kimhi and Shmuel Even, "Who Are the Palestinian Suicide Bombers?," *Terrorism and Political Violence, 16,* no. 4 (Winter 2004).

38. See, for example, Kimhi and Even, "Who are the Palestinian Suicide Bombers?"; Pedahzur, *Suicide Terrorism,* 126–134.

39. Pedahzur, *Suicide Terrorism,* 125.

40. Mohammed M. Hafez, "Manufacturing Human Bombs: Strategy, Culture, and Conflict in the Making of Palestinian Suicide Bombers" (Revised paper submitted to the United States Institute of Peace for publication in the Peaceworks series, Version 2, 4 April 2005): 18–19. Available at http://www.utexas.edu/cola/depts/government/content/events/workshop_papers/hafez.pdf.

41. Juergensmeyer, *Terror in the Mind of God;* Nasra Hassan, "An Arsenal of Believers: Talking to the 'Human Bombs" *New Yorker,* 77, no. 36 (2001); Moghadam, "Palestinian Suicide Terrorism in the Second Intifada"; Stern, *Terror in the Name of God.*

42. For a discussion of these benefits in the case of Palestinian suicide bombers, see Boaz Ganor, "Suicide Attacks in Israel," 144–45.

43. Hopgood, "Tamil Tigers, 1987–2002," 43–76.

44. Bruce Bueno de Mesquita, for example, argues that suicide bombers are "young men with no economic prospects and little education. There is a rational expectation on the part of suicide bombers that they are providing for their families." Quoted in Bloom, *Dying to Kill,* 35.

45. See especially Stern, *Terror in the Name of God,* 189, 216.

46. On Palestinian groups, see Assaf Moghadam, "Suicide Bombings in the Israeli-Palestinian Conflict: A Conceptual Framework" (Herzliyya, Israel: Project for the Research of Islamist Movements (PRISM), May 2002), 25-26. On Hizballah, see Reuter, *My Life is a Weapon,* 70.

47. Very few exceptions of individuals acting entirely on their own exist, including the "Unabomber," Theodore Kaczynski, as well as 15-year-old Charles Bishop, who crashed a light plane into the 28th floor of the Bank of America Plaza in Tampa, Florida, on 5 January 2002.

48. Martha Crenshaw, "An Organizational Approach to the Analysis of Political Terrorism," *Orbis* (Fall 1985); Martha Crenshaw, "Theories of Terrorism: Instrumental and Organizational Approaches," in *Inside Terrorist Organizations,* ed. David C. Rapoport (New York: Frank Cass, 1988); and Martha Crenshaw, "The Logic of Terrorism: Terrorist Behavior as a Product of Strategic Choice," in *Origins of Terrorism: Psychologies, Ideologies, Theologies, States of Mind,* ed. Walter Reich (Washington, DC: Woodrow Wilson Center Press, 1998).

49. On the organizational strive for survival and maintenance, see Chester I. Barnard, *The Functions of the Executive* (Cambridge, MA: Harvard University Press, 1938), 216; and James Q. Wilson, *Political Organizations* (New York: Basic Books, 1973), 30–36. On the need for terrorist organizations to survive, see Crenshaw, "An Organizational Approach to the Analysis of Political Terrorism," 465–89.

50. Pape, *Dying to Win;* Scott Atran, "Genesis of Suicide Terrorism," *Science,* 299, no. 5612 (2003).

51. Pape, *Dying to Win,* 61.

52. Assaf Moghadam, "Suicide Terrorism, Occupation, and the Globalization of Martyrdom: A Critique of 'Dying to Win'," *Studies in Conflict and Terrorism, 29,* no. 8 (2006).

53. Andrew Kydd and Barbara F. Walter, "Sabotaging the Peace: The Politics of Extremist Violence," *International Organization* 56, no. 2 (2002); Hafez, *Suicide Bombers in Iraq.*

54. Hoffman and McCormick, "Terrorism, Signaling, and Suicide Attack," 262.

55. Ibid.

56. See, for example, Keith B. Richburg, "Suicide Bomb Survivors Face Worlds Blown Apart," *Washington Post,* January, 31 2004, A15; Amos Harel, "Suicide Attacks Frighten Israelis More Than Scuds," *Haaretz,* February 13, 2003; "Young Israelis 'Traumatised' by Conflict," *BBC News,* June 2, 2004.

57. Stephen Holmes, "Al-Qaeda, September 11, 2001," in Gambetta, ed. *Making Sense of Suicide Missions,* 162.

58. Ibid, 163.

59. Adam Dolnik, "Die and Let Die: Exploring Links between Suicide Terrorism and Terrorist Use of Chemical, Biological, Radiological, and Nuclear Weapons," *Studies in Conflict and Terrorism, 26,* no. 1 (2003).

60. Hassan, "An Arsenal of Believers," 36–41.

61. See, for example, Bruce Hoffman, "The Logic of Suicide Terrorism," *Atlantic Monthly,* June 2003, 40–47.

62. See, for example, Sprinzak, "Rational Fanatics," 66-67; Ganor, "Suicide Attacks in Israel," 143–144; and Audrey Kurth Cronin, "Terrorism and Suicide Attacks," *CRS Report for Congress* RL32058 (Washington, D.C.: Congressional Research Service, Library of Congress 2003), 8–12.

63. Bloom, *Dying to Kill.*

64. See Moghadam, "Suicide Terrorism, Occupation, and the Globalization of Martyrdom," 707–729.

65. Moghadam, "The Roots of Suicide Terrorism;" Hafez, "Rationality, Culture, and Structure in the Making of Suicide Bombers."

66. Pape, *Dying to Win.*

67. American commanders in Iraq say that foreigners make up over 90 percent of the suicide bombers. See Dexter Filkins, "Foreign Fighters Captured in Iraq Come from 27, Mostly Arab, Lands," *New York Times,* October 21, 2005.

68. Bloom, *Dying to Kill.*

69. Assaf Moghadam, "The New Martyrs Go Global," *Boston Globe,* November 18, 2005, A19; Moghadam, "Suicide Terrorism, Occupation, and the Globalization of Martyrdom."

70. Moghadam, *The Globalization of Martyrdom.*

71. See, for example, Reuven Paz, "Arab Volunteers in Iraq: An Analysis," *PRISM Occasional Papers, 3,* No. 1 (March 2005); and Marc Sageman, *Understanding Terror Networks.*

Unit II

Countering the Terrorist Threat

Chapter 6

Terrorism and the Media

Brian Jenkins has famously argued that "terrorists want a lot of people watching, not a lot of people dead." For this purpose, terrorist groups have sought and often depended on traditional media coverage to amplify the impact of their message. With the primary task of reporting events as they take place—including terrorist attacks—the media has thus inadvertently served as a conduit for terrorist groups. On the other hand, by providing extensive coverage of the most sensational events, the media has typically increased its viewership and consequently, its revenues.

The relationship between terrorists and the traditional media has always been one of much controversy. Two schools of thought have emerged on this issue. The first theory addresses the idea that terrorist organizations seek to achieve widespread media coverage that, in turn, will further intimidate the public and influence policymakers. The second theory challenges the centrality of the media to terrorists' strategy. Boaz Ganor explores the tension between these two theories through an examination of the terrorist events in Israel. This article presents difficult questions to policymakers with regard to the role of the media and media coverage of terrorist incidents.

In addition to reporting on events, the traditional media plays a critical role in holding democratic governments accountable by keeping the public aware of the policies and actions taken in the war on terrorism. According to John Stacks, following the 9/11 attacks, the U.S. government "has been cloaking more and more of its actions in official secrecy: secret immigration hearings, secret court proceedings, secret detentions, secret wars." Furthermore, the Bush administration has dramatically increased the amount of government material that is classified and been increasingly reluctant to talk to the press. Stacks argues that "while there is no doubt some tactical necessity for protecting more of the government's information in a time of terrorist threat, there is also an undeniable need for the public to fully trust and understand its government in such a sensitive time."

The advent of advanced communications technology and the Internet has altered the symbiotic relationship between terrorism and the media in significant ways. With access to their own information cybernetworks, terrorist groups no longer depend entirely on traditional media to disseminate their message. Jarret Brachman contends that "Internet-based activism has changed the nature of social and political movements: no longer does one need to physically relocate to support a cause—now anyone can bolster a movement at any time, virtually anywhere, using a computer." Brachman describes how al Qaeda has exploited new technological tools—email, chat rooms, online magazines, cell phone videos, CD-ROMs, and video games—to recruit new members, receive donations, coordinate and plan attacks, collect information on their targets, as well as "to radicalize and empower armies of new recruits by shaping their general worldview."

Gabriel Weimann argues that policymakers, by overemphasizing the threat of cyberterrorism, have "paid insufficient attention to the more routine uses of the Internet." Wiemann discusses how the particular characteristics of the Internet—easy access, little or no regulation, access to huge audiences, anonymity of communication, fast flow of information, cheap—make it an ideal arena for activity by terrorist organizations. "Today, almost all active terrorist organizations. . .maintain websites" and thus are directly linked to their audiences. Wiemann also details "eight different, albeit sometimes overlapping, ways in which contemporary terrorists use the Internet." According to Wiemann, the Internet is "an almost perfect embodiment of the democratic ideals of free speech and open communication." Wiemann warns that although policymakers need to become better informed about how terrorists use the Internet, any circumscription of our own freedom to use the Internet would "hand the terrorists a victory and deal democracy a blow."

Boaz Ganor, 2005

Dilemmas Concerning Media Coverage of Terrorist Attacks

Terrorist and guerrilla organizations throughout the world differ from one another in their methods, their aims, the weaponry at their disposal, the extent of outside help they receive, and so on. Therefore, scholars are at odds regarding the very existence of a collective strategy among terrorist organizations.

One school of thought asserts that terrorist organizations operate according to a multi-phase rational strategy, which begins with perpetrating a terrorist attack aimed at achieving widespread media coverage. The media coverage is supposed to intimidate the public, and in this way influence the political perspectives and attitudes of the citizens. The anxiety felt by the nation's citizens will be translated into public pressure on decision makers to accede to terrorists' demands and make decisions that coincide with the interests of the terrorist organizations. This theory perceives the media and public opinion as central elements in the terrorist organizations' attack policy. Another school of thought is doubtful as to the central importance of the media in the terrorists' operational strategy and the extent to which public opinion can influence the attitudes of decision makers, especially on matters of security and foreign affairs.

According to the first school of thought, the written and electronic media play a major role in modern democratic society, among other things, as an agent that mediates between the public and its leadership, and has an impact on shaping public opinion and government decisions. Given the media's importance in modern society, it is a major element in the strategy used by terrorist and guerrilla organizations. This was expressed by Carlos Marighella, who noted that the rescue of prisoners, executions, kidnappings, sabotage, terrorism, and the war of nerves—all these are acts of armed propaganda, carried out solely for propaganda effect.

Terrorist attacks, then, are aimed at achieving maximum coverage in the written and electronic press. Terrorist organizations, aware of the media's importance as a tool for broadcasting their message, do their utmost to attract media attention. As part of this, they act to increase the number of victims in terrorist attacks and escalate the nature of these acts, using means that are increasingly ruthless or terrifying.

Weimann outlines the advantages that terrorists gain from media coverage of terrorist attacks: generating public interest in the terrorists' activities and enhancing their influence; attributing a positive spin to the restrictive acts of the terrorist organizations and shaping their image; portraying terrorists as the weak side in the conflict and promoting support for their motives; providing important information regarding counter-terrorism activities, etc. Crenshaw notes that the history of terrorism reveals a series of developments whereby terrorists deliberately choose targets that had previously been considered taboo or locations where violence is unexpected, and the innovation is then disseminated via the international media. Post mentions the fact that terrorists have succeeded in gaining a virtual monopoly over the weapon of the television camera, and in manipulating their target audience through the media. According to Post, terrorist organizations have demonstrated the power and importance of the media and have used this means to highlight the legitimacy of their goals.

This theory postulates that the relationship between terrorist organizations and the media is one of mutual profit. On the one hand, terrorists gain a great deal from the media coverage they receive. The media serve as a stage from which the terrorists broadcast their messages to various target audiences, earning support for the terrorist organization and its actions among its supporters and enhancing its scope and capability far beyond its actual power. Media coverage also helps in gathering vital intelligence information for planning attacks and assessing the offensive intentions of the other side; for imitating successful attacks perpetrated by other organizations; and securing international legitimacy for the terrorist organization while damaging the international image and status of the nation coping with terrorism. On the other hand, terrorists give the media newsworthy and interesting information—drama that involves human lives; a basis for political commentary; human-interest stories on the victims and their families, as well as the terrorists involved in the attack, background coverage, and more. In general, terrorism offers the media gripping stories with an interesting plot, and as a result, they also get higher ratings. Terrorist organizations do not have to do very much in order to attract media attention. It is given to them all too easily, among other things, because of the competition between the different media channels and the desire for financial profit.

Violent incidents (especially terrorist attacks) "sell newspapers" and interest the public. Schmid and De Graff argue that one cannot ignore the fact that the media operate on considerations of profits, which are based on advertising revenue. This revenue depends on the number of television viewers and radio listeners, and newspaper sales. Terrorist acts attract the public's interest, and thus increase sales figures.

As a result of the importance of the media aspect of any terrorism strategy, news coverage may have an impact on the different components of an attack: the target (depending on the symbolism of the target, its security sensitivity, the degree to which it is well-populated, its location, etc.), the duration, the timing, the method chosen. Hoffman stresses, therefore, that modern media play a key role in terrorist activity. Moreover, when the media prepare for coverage and the attack does not take place, it is sometimes forced to justify the money spent by bringing background coverage with a "human interest angle." Thus, there is a distorted focus on the human aspect instead of the overall picture, and the large networks, in fact, become agents that influence the shaping of policy rather than agents that merely report.

Most of the public in the United States identified during the 1980s with the arguments heard against the media regarding their coverage of terrorist attacks. In a public opinion poll conducted by ABC and *The Washington Post* in January 1986, most of the American public (76 percent of those surveyed) felt that the terrorists' success was dependent upon the publicity they received in the media, and that the media sometimes exaggerated terrorist attacks and played into the terrorists' hands by giving them the coverage they were seeking. It was proposed that such television coverage be made illegal, empowering the police to prevent television coverage when necessary. Nonetheless, most respondents felt that media coverage of terrorism serves the public interest, and most believed that television should continue covering terrorist acts even if this led to additional attacks. The vast majority felt that terrorism existed both with television and without it.

This double standard in the public's feelings about the media coverage of terrorist attacks is reflected in academic studies as well. In contrast with the accepted approach regarding the reciprocal relationship between the media and terrorist organizations, another approach was put forth claiming that terrorist organizations do not consider media coverage of their acts to such a large extent, and they certainly do not plan their strategies according to the media. Supporters of this approach rely, *inter alia,* on statements made by terrorist leaders who minimize the media's importance, and at times even attack the media. Moreover, those who side with this theory emphasize that the ability of the terrorist organizations to influence decision makers on political matters by exerting pressure and intimidating the public is not high, and is actually doubtful.

Crenshaw notes in this context that studies conducted with regard to the IRA and the ETA have shown that these organizations find no benefit in media coverage. In reality, they perceive the media as being hostile, prejudiced, and subjective. From their point of view, news reports broadcast through the media are part of the policies of the nations to which they are opposed. Representatives of these organizations claimed the line characterizing the media was one that supported the status quo while exaggerating their reports of the violence so as to damage the organizations' image in the eyes of the public, while at the same time ignoring their non-violent activity. Furthermore, coverage of terrorist attacks usually paints terrorists in a very negative light, which casts doubt on the claim that limiting media coverage reduces the number of attacks.

Hoffman highlights the fact that media coverage sometimes plays a positive role in coping with terrorism. This was the case, for example, when the Unabomber was exposed in the United States following his demand that his ideological manifesto be published in the daily press. The same holds true for the American media's near-obsession with the hostages of the TWA flight hijacked in 1985 which, according to the families of the hostages, kept the issue at the top of the agenda of American decision makers and ultimately led to the release of the hostages. In addition, we must consider the fact that avoiding media coverage of terrorist attacks, or reducing its scope, is liable to cause an escalation in the number of attacks and their nature by the terrorist organizations, in an effort to force the media to cover these acts regardless. And if this were not enough, there is the fear that avoiding media coverage would lead to rumors and that the lack of reliable and up-to-date information would cause widespread, and unnecessary, panic.

Those supporting this theory claim that not only do the media not serve the true goals of the terrorist organization, but even if terrorism also influences the political attitudes of the public through media coverage, it is not at all clear whether public opinion ultimately has any effect on decision makers and their political attitudes. This is because alongside the influence of public opinion, decision makers are exposed to additional—and, at times, contradictory— influences from other sources. Furthermore, even if media coverage of terrorist attacks has an effect on the public and that is indeed translated as pressure on decision makers, it isn't at all clear that this is the influence that terrorist organizations actually hoped for. Quite the reverse, media coverage is likely to arouse public protests that would increase the resources allocated to fight terrorism. Wilensky believes that terrorism does not achieve its goals by employing fear and threats. He claims, on the contrary, that terrorism hardens the population's attitude and leads to counter-terrorism measures. Laquer states that society is willing to suffer terrorism as long as it remains a nuisance. But when a feeling of insecurity begins to spread and when terrorism becomes a genuine danger, people no longer denounce the government for ignoring human rights in order to fight it. Quite the contrary, in such a situation there is increased demand to use more aggressive counter-terrorism measures, without consideration of human rights.

Gur notes that waves of terrorist attacks in Western Europe were accompanied by a rise in public support for taking serious steps against terrorist organizations. According to Gur, waves of terrorism in democratic societies often sow the seeds of its own demise because such violence jeopardized support for the terrorists, and security forces can then gather intelligence information about them more easily. Hoffman, who bases himself on a study conducted at the RAND Institute in 1989, stresses that in spite of the comprehensive coverage of terrorist attacks by the American media during the five years preceding the study, no support or sympathy was generated among the American public for the attitudes and motives of the terrorists. Gur and Hoffman naturally refer to internal terrorism (which takes place within the nation itself), and their study doesn't necessarily relate to international terrorism (which involves at least two nations), or terrorism that has been "imported" into a country.

Perhaps Abu Iyad, Yasser Arafat's former deputy, can actually bridge the gap between the two opposing theories regarding the question of whether media coverage of terrorist attacks and their influence on public opinion serves the interests of the terrorist organizations or not. In this context, Abu Iyad stated (referring to the attack at the Munich Olympics in September 1972) that one of the goals of the attack was: "To exploit the unusual concentration of media coverage in Munich to give our struggle an international resonance—*positive or negative, it didn't matter!* . . . In essence, Abu Iyad stresses that in terms of the organization perpetrating the attack, the type of criticism the act evokes is un-important so long as it succeeds in drawing the public's attention to the problem of the Palestinian people. In other words, it isn't important what the world says about you, the main thing is that they talk about you and are aware of your problems and demands. Hoffman continues this line of thought when he states that the success in achieving the impact you desire is usually measured by terrorists in terms of the amount of publicity and attention garnered, and not in terms of the type of publicity, and whether it is positive or negative.

The Media as Part of the Strategy of Terrorism

The media plays a key role in the strategy of terrorism. Damage from a terrorist attack is usually limited to the scene of the attack itself, but the act also aims to influence a target audience that goes way beyond the victims themselves. The way to reach target audiences and to broadcast the messages the terrorist organization wants to transmit is through the media. Thus, the media serve as a vital means for transmitting messages simultaneously to three different target audiences (see Figure 1). For the native population from which

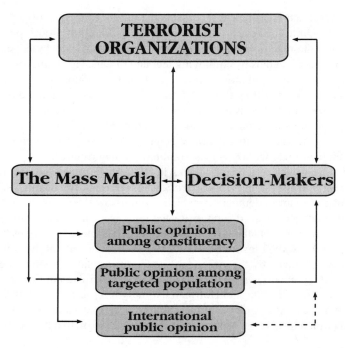

Figure 1. The strategy of modern terrorism.

the organization originates and activists within the organization itself, the media transmit messages of power; the ability to achieve their strategic goals in spite of their technology inferiority, fewer numbers, and lack of resources; a call to support the organization and join its ranks; and above all—to raise the morale of this target audience. A completely opposite message is broadcast concomitantly to another of the organization's target audiences—the population targeted with terrorism. A terrorist attack is supposed to transmit to this target audience the feeling that they are vulnerable as individuals anywhere and anytime, and therefore their military-economic strength cannot guarantee their lives, their well-being, their health or their property. The message being sent to this audience is usually accompanied by a series of concrete demands, whether political or operational, acquiescence to which would allegedly ensure the end of the attacks and the restoration of peace. With regard to this target audience, the goal of the terrorist organization is to demoralize them and compromise their ability to cope with terrorism. The third message transmitted by the media is geared towards international public opinion, that same audience that is not involved in the conflict and observes events from the sidelines. The terrorist organization uses the attack to focus this audience's attention on the conflict in which it is embroiled, the arguments presented by the terrorists and their representatives around the world, and the suffering of the terrorist organization's native population.

Thus, the media serve as a magnifying glass that can intensify the impact of the attack and turn terrorism into an effective tool. Without the media aspect, terrorism remains one more cause of death, one of many, and not necessarily the most important or most dangerous one. Weimann compares the domain of terrorism to a stage. Indeed, almost all of the components found in a theatrical show can be found in a terrorist show, including: a producer—the initiator of the attack; a director—the organizer of the attack; a casting director—who locates and recruits the terrorists for the mission; an audience—the different types of target audiences who observe the attack; the setting—the backdrop chosen to perpetrate the attack; a plot—the story behind the attack, the background and events; a message—the various messages broadcast to the different types of audiences; actors—the terrorists, the victims, and other involved. But beyond all of this, there is the stage. The stage in a theater is usually raised in order to enable a larger and wider audience to observe what is taking place and absorb the message. The stage of terrorism is the media, which serve the terrorist organization in precisely the same way.

The Journalist's Dilemma

In an attempt to justify and explain the way in which the media cover terrorist acts, the media usually cite two main arguments. One is that the media play a major role in the democratic way of government—guaranteeing the "public's right to know." This value necessitates, they believe, media coverage of terrorist attacks without censorship, restrictions, or moral or other types of obstacles. Even if the media act as an essential stage for terrorist organizations and indirectly assists them, their central role in a democracy requires journalists to behave as they do. The other argument, which is held by many in the media, is that in this modern age the main factor that determines the scope of media coverage and its nature is ratings. So long as the public is interested in watching the atrocities of terrorism, there will always be someone to supply this need and therefore, it is impossible to restrict or change the nature of the media's coverage.

These two statements call for thorough study and examination. On the face of it, the equation that "blood equals ratings" appears correct, but only up to a certain limit. When the public is exposed to images that are particularly harsh—close-ups of body parts, for example, or repeated broadcasts of the death and destruction at the scene of an attack, at least some prefer to turn off the television, switch to another channel, or do something else. This can be concluded, for example, from the severe criticism aimed at the media by the public in Israel during the 1990s, concerning the unlimited and unrestrained media coverage from the scenes of terrorist acts, particularly suicide bombings. Such disapproval was expressed in television interviews, calls from radio listeners, review articles in the press, and at times, even from direct contact by citizens to the different media outlets. This criticism ultimately led to positive changes in the nature of Israeli television coverage from the end of 2000 (with the beginning of a wave of terrorist activity and intensive violence by the Palestinians, which became known as "the Al Aksa intifada").

The public's demand that reporters cover terrorist attacks in a sober and responsible manner challenges journalists with a very serious dilemma—the journalist's dilemma. This dilemma has two aspects: On one level, the reporter must find the proper balance of his professional obligation as a journalist to cover the events as they happen with the need to respond to the legitimate demands of those in his country who receive this information. On another level, he must find a balance between contingencies derived from competition among the many channels and media outlets, and his civic duty not to become a pawn in the hands of the terrorist organizations and assist them, even indirectly, in achieving their short-term and long-term objectives. The call for the media to perform their civic duty is reflected in statements made by Weimann, who declared that along with the public's right to receive precise, genuine, and up-to-date information as far as possible, that is, the public's "right to know," the public also has a "right not to know," that is, the victim's right to privacy; the right of the public not to be exposed to the personal and intimate details of the terror victims through media coverage that infringes upon their dignity; the right of the public to uphold the state's security secrets that preserve their safety, etc. The journalist's need to cope with these two types of obligations was illustrated most vividly following the terrorist attacks in the United States on September 11, 2001. Television camera crews who covered the horrors of the attack decided at that time to stick small American flags on their cameras, or to cover the live broadcasting vans of the various television networks with American flags or photographs of the missing. Such acts illustrate more than anything else the awareness and responsiveness by American journalists of their two parallel obligations—their professional obligation and their civic duty.

In 1997, the International Policy Institute for Counter-Terrorism at the Herzliya Inter-disciplinary Center held a professional conference, called "The Shefayim Conference," which was attended by Israeli media personnel (journalists and editors), and counter-terrorism experts to discuss the media coverage of terrorist attacks in Israel. The goal was to try and find a proper balance between these two obligations. . . . Among recommendations made by conference participants were two main proposals: to avoid close-up images of terrorist victims, and to limit as much as possible the repeated broadcasting of images of death and destruction from the scene of the attack. These two recommendations actually enable journalists to maintain the delicate balance between the journalist's professional obligation and his civic duty. On the one hand, acceptance of these recommendations will help protect the public's right to receive information, since media coverage of the attacks in real time will not be halted. But, on the other hand, without close-up photos of the horrors of the attack, the media will not encourage anxiety and fear and, thus, will not be used as a pawn by the terrorists. Avoiding frequent broadcasts from the scene of the attack will limit the damage to the people's morale from terrorist attacks, and on the other hand, will reduce television viewers' tendency to stop watching or switch to another channel.

The Live Broadcast Dilemma

Among all the different types of media, it would appear that television has the greatest influence on public morale. The terrible images broadcast from the scene of an attack into every home in the targeted nation, and the entire world, serves the propaganda and fear-provoking goals of the terrorist organization more than any other outlet.

Israel's experience during the mid-1990s with regard to television coverage of terrorist attacks is instructive regarding the problem of live coverage at the scene of an attack. The paradox is that through the use of live close-up footage the viewer is exposed, at times, to more horrible scenes than those to which the people at the scene itself are witness. People at the scene are busy carrying out their specific tasks—security, reporting, rescue, recovery—and they are neither interested nor able to actually focus on the particularly horrible images from the scene such as body parts strewn around the ground or other grisly sights. In contrast with these, when a television cameraman arrives on the scene of the attack who is unaware of the conflict between his professional obligation and his civic duty, he naturally wanders around the scene in search of the most shocking images.

From this perspective, Israel has seen an improvement in its media coverage since the early 2000s. From time to time, if television cameras begin to focus on particularly harsh images during the course of a live broadcast from the scene of an attack, the live broadcast is sometimes suspended and the newscaster or a studio commentator appears on the screen until the camera is no longer focused on the difficult scene. These were correct editing decisions as a result of public criticism.

In this context one must, of course, be careful not to throw the baby out with the bath water. The warranted criticism of the nature of the media coverage must not detract from the importance of media coverage in general, and live broadcasts in particular, when it comes to terrorists attacks. If there is anything more dangerous than irresponsible coverage of terrorist attacks, it is a lack of any coverage. Lack of coverage in real time could lead to the spreading of rumors that are unfounded, and their effect on public morale is liable to be even more damaging and destructive.

To summarize this dilemma, the advantages of live broadcasts of terrorist attacks out-weigh the disadvantages, even when the correspondent is unaware of his civic responsibility. When covering terrorist attacks it is possible, and certainly necessary, to employ editorial considerations in real time, to avoid camera close-ups of dead bodies and the wounded, to avoid broadcasting expressions of panic and extreme fear, and to photograph from somewhere slightly removed from the center of the attack. . . .

Boaz Ganor is the deputy dean of the Lauder School of Government and Diplomacy at the Interdisciplinary Center Herzliya. He is also the founder and the Executive Director of the International Policy Institute for Counter-Terrorism. Dr. Ganor is a member of Israel's National Committee for Homeland Security Technologies, of the International Advisory Board of Institute of Defense and Strategic Studies, (IDSS), Singapore, and of the International Advisory team of the Manhattan Institute (CTCT) to the New-York Police Department (NYPD). Dr. Ganor is author of numerous articles on counter-terrorism and *The Counter-Terrorism Puzzle: A Guide for Decision Makers* (2005).

John F. Stacks

Watchdogs on a Leash

Closing Doors on the Media

This administration is more closed-mouthed, more closed-doored than any in memory.

—Michael Duffy,
Washington bureau chief, *Time* magazine

In the aftermath of the terrorist attacks on the United States, the national government has been cloaking more and more of its actions in official secrecy: secret immigration hearings, secret court proceedings, secret detentions, secret wars. Government officials have been prosecuted for sharing "sensitive" but not classified information with the press. Guidelines for abiding by the Freedom of Information Act (FOIA) have been tightened so as to virtually gut the intent of the law. Even presidential papers from prior administrations, which of course belong to the nation, are now sealed unless the sitting and former president agree to their use by historians. The list goes on. The spectacular acts of terrorism on September 11, 2001, have succeeded in keeping the American public from knowing very much about what its government is doing or planning to do, or why.

While there is no doubt some tactical necessity for protecting more of the government's information in a time of terrorist threat, there is also an undeniable need for the public to fully trust and understand its government in such a sensitive time.

The growing uses of official secrecy are well documented and discussed in other chapters of this book. But there is another pernicious and damaging kind of secrecy being practiced by the administration of George W. Bush. Officials in Washington have largely stopped talking to the press except in set-piece briefings. Interviews are refused. Phone inquiries are left unanswered. The public is thus being denied access to the workings of the government it elected. While there are televised briefings, and plenty of photo opportunities, real discussion and real access are denied. The Bush administration has perfected the technique of flooding the cable news operations with enough sound bites and pictures to fill the air with its own message. But it is refusing access to the more thoughtful, long-form journalists who might penetrate beneath the polished message the administration wants delivered. "The sources who really talk with anything resembling honesty are few and far between," says one Washington bureau chief.

A standard tool in drying up the flow of information to the public has always been the practice of stamping government paperwork "secret." After years of attempting to reduce the amount of government material that is classified, and to declassify the mountains of historical documents in the hands of the government, both trends have reversed, according to a paper by former *Los Angeles Times* Washington bureau chief Jack Nelson. In a paper prepared for the Joan Shorenstein Center on the Press, Politics, and Public Policy at the Kennedy School of Government at Harvard, Nelson reports that in the fiscal year 2001 the total number of classification actions in the government amounted to more than 33,000, an increase of 44 percent over the previous year.

Meanwhile, cabinet officers like Defense Secretary Donald Rumsfeld are calling for jail terms for leakers, and the Federal Bureau of Investigation is investigating members of Congress for allegedly leaking. And as usual, the government is using leaks for its own purposes. As the campaign to gather support for the war in Iraq progressed, the Pentagon repeatedly leaked rough outlines of its war plans as a way of demonstrating its determination to oust Saddam Hussein. The double standard was also in evidence over the handling of periodic taped messages from Osama bin Laden. Shortly after the attacks of September 11, 2001, National Security Advisor Condoleezza Rice convinced the heads of the network news divisions and the cable news channels to sharply censor a videotape of the Al-Qaeda leader. But in another context, as the effort to sell the world on an invasion of Iraq intensified in 2003, the administration made no effort to restrict the broadcast of an audiotape thought to be from bin Laden, urging his followers to avenge an attack on Iraq. The idea was to show the link between bin Laden and Saddam. Fox News, helpfully, broadcast the tape in its entirety.

At the same time, the Bush administration, leveraging national fears about terrorism, reversed existing policy on surrendering documents under the Freedom of Information Act. In a memorandum from White House chief of staff Andrew Card, agencies and departments were instructed to include "sensitive information" in the same category as information affecting national security in rejecting FOIA requests.

Averted Eyes

There was a time, not so long ago, when Washington officials believed it was their duty to talk to the press and thereby to talk to the country. A hardworking reporter in the capital could get an interview, if not this minute, then soon enough to make deadline, if not today, then maybe tomorrow. Officials were selective, of course, calling back first the reporters for the wire services and the big dailies or the three networks, later the newsmagazines with longer deadlines, and then, if time allowed, answering the questions of reporters for smaller news organizations. Reporters for the large news organizations would routinely have background discussions, often in the offices of the top policymakers and from time to time over informal lunches and dinners.

This discourse with the press was regarded not only as part of the job of governing; it was also seen to be in the self-interest of the official and of the government itself. Stories and scripts were being written, and the officials wanted to have their own input, to guide the story toward their point of view, or to steer it against an opponent's position. And if advancing an argument was not sufficient reason to talk with the press, personal ambition was. Press secretaries to the powerful figures in the government saw their primary job as getting their principals' names and faces into the news.

Today the doors of the government in Washington are being slammed in the reporters' faces. The job of the press secretary is now to shut out the press and to keep the bosses' names out of the news. The Bush administration is not interested in communicating with the press except through official spokespersons well versed in the message of the day. Survival in the Bush administration requires, in the words of one veteran Washington correspondent, "keeping your head down and your mouth shut." Press-accessible and unprogrammable officials are quickly sacked. As one Washington bureau chief put it: "This administration's belief in news management is absolutely evangelical." Seymour Hersh, who produced for *The New Yorker* the one piece of unconventional reporting about the special operations missions inside Afghanistan, is one of the most persistent reporters now working in Washington. He has been there for decades and has a vast number of sources. During a panel discussion sponsored by the Libel Defense Resource Center, Hersh said that he felt cut off from the real workings of the administration. "This is scary," he said, "I have never had less of a pulse [of what's going on in government]."

Of course, every administration in history has tried to manage the news by preventing leaks and by trying to orchestrate its message. Some have succeeded more than others. But it is obvious from reading and watching the press, and from the accounts of Washington reporters, that the current administration has become the grand champion of closed government. And what is perhaps even more troubling, the public—full of distrust of the press and the fear of terrorism—is not complaining. More ominously still, journalists themselves have said almost nothing about their inability to cover the Bush administration. So why is this government so closed to the press? Because this government has found it can get away with it.

Every bureau chief has his or her own stories about access denied. In one case, one large news organization was preparing a major piece on Defense Secretary Rumsfeld. A request to interview the secretary was made to the public affairs office at the Pentagon. The answer was "No." What if we ran the text of the interview, rather than just selected quotes in the story, the bureau chief countered? "Well," said the Pentagon, "only if you run the entire interview verbatim, no cuts, no editing, no trimming for space." How about we run the unedited text on our website and an edited version in print? "No" again. "Thanks anyway," said the bureau chief. Even routine Pentagon coverage has become more difficult. Only regularly accredited Pentagon reporters are permitted to move about the building without an escort; other correspondents who do not cover the Defense Department regularly can enter only with an escort.

Not that it makes much difference to be able to roam freely. One top defense correspondent reports that officers he has known and talked to for years will avert their eyes when they are encountered in the hall, to avoid even the suspicion of being close to someone from the press. One bureau chief recounted the story of a reporter having to interview a department source in the men's room, hoping there would be sufficient privacy so that the source's cooperation would go unnoticed.

Rumsfeld and the top military spokesmen totally controlled the information about the conduct of U.S. forces in Afghanistan and in so doing left out major pieces of information, none of which was in any way damaging to the image of our fighting forces. Thomas E. Ricks, the defense correspondent for the *Washington Post,* noted to Ted Gup, writing for the *Columbia Journalism Review* in the fall of 2002, that Rumsfeld and the other briefers failed to mention the first stationing of U.S. troops in a part of the former Soviet Union, the first firing of a missile from an unmanned aircraft, and the first significant fielding of Central Intelligence Agency paramilitary forces since Vietnam.

In the Department of Justice, all press interviews are conducted with a minder from the press office in attendance, a practice that was once regarded as completely out of bounds and unacceptable by the press. In the twenty years I covered Washington, including the White House, I don't recall more than one or two instances in which press-office people sat in on an interview, including those with the president himself. There is no practice that is more chilling to a free flow of information. The last time I conducted an interview with a minder present was in 1998—in Baghdad.

In another case, *Time* magazine was preparing its annual *Person of the Year* cover. Typically, the magazine prepares two or three pieces and continues to debate the virtues of each choice and to weigh the reporting coming in. Although villains like Joseph Stalin and Ayatollah Khomeini were chosen in the days before the magazine became hypersensitive to its advertisers, *Person of the Year* has in later years become a happy choice, an honorific. In 2002, Vice President Dick Cheney was one possible choice. "Would the vice president sit for a *Person of the Year* interview," the magazine asked? Cheney is so press-shy and determined to not upstage his boss that he passed up the honor.

The Old Rules of Engagement

Recalling the good old days is often not much use in analyzing current events. Memories are gauzy, and nostalgia is a powerful impulse. But it was not so long ago that the closed-door policy of this administration was simply unthinkable.

It is ironic that the greatest days of press access to government occurred in the years between the end of World War II and the war in Vietnam. If danger to the nation is the rationale for secrecy now, surely the Cold War posed an even graver threat to the existence of the republic. Yet in those years the government was a relatively open enterprise.

Reporters, especially the best reporters from the best news organizations, had regular access to the top leaders of government. Presidents had informal discussions with reporters alone and in groups. Cabinet secretaries were easily available to top reporters and columnists. Presidential candidates, rather than moving around the country in a cocoon of handlers and spokespersons, rode the trains and planes of the campaign trail in close proximity to the working press. It was commonplace for even young reporters to get direct and prolonged access to the candidates.

By today's standards, access by the press to public officials was truly astounding. Although he was far from alone in his ability to talk with the powerful, James B. Reston, columnist and Washington bureau chief for the *New York Times,* best exemplified the way the press and the government worked in those days. When he was covering the Department of State during Dwight Eisenhower's administration, Reston would have frequent private meetings with Secretary John Foster Dulles. The two would share a drink, and Dulles, stirring his whiskey with his finger, would share his opinions about world problems, about other members of the Eisenhower administration, and even about the president himself, once complaining to Reston that he thought Ike was a bit too detached from the regular business of government. On another occasion, Dulles outlined to Reston a debate that was raging inside the administration over whether it might be a good idea to launch a nuclear attack on the Soviet Union as a way of ending the Cold War quickly. It was perhaps a precursor to the new Bush doctrine of preemptive war. Reston wrote about the debate and eventually, at a White House press conference, asked Eisenhower his views. Ike denounced the idea and ended the argument in his administration.

Reston, along with others in Washington in his time, had frequent access to the president himself. After a harsh, three-day summit meeting with Soviet leader Nikita Khrushchev, the first person John Kennedy spoke with was none other than Reston, who proceeded to write brilliantly nuanced news reports reflecting Kennedy's pessimistic views of the summit meeting. Reston never mentioned that his source was the president himself.

These days ended in the bitter struggles between the press and the government over Vietnam and Watergate. And the Reston paradigm itself was destroyed when Henry Kissinger, when he was national security adviser under Richard Nixon, seduced Reston into reporting inaccurately Kissinger's role in the infamous Christmas bombing of North Vietnam at the end of 1972. Part of the reason Reston fell prey to Kissinger's manipulations was that the Nixon administration had pretty well bottled up other potential sources for Reston and other reporters inside the administration, not by prohibiting them from talking to reporters—although they tried that tactic—but by excluding even Secretary of State William Rogers from key deliberations about foreign policy.

Gerald Ford restored much of the old amity between press and government, and that cessation of hostilities was at least in part responsible for the healing effect of his administration after the Nixon era. Jimmy Carter, although greeted with suspicion and even condescension by much of the establishment press corps in Washington, was likewise open to reporters.

Ronald Reagan, however, probably ran the most open administration in recent history. Reagan himself avoided much direct contact with the press because his command of detailed information was limited. Still, he would permit the occasional private interview, using his considerable charm and avuncular sweetness to disarm reporters. The White House staff, however, was incredibly accessible to the press corps. The major news-magazines, for example, had regularly scheduled weekly background sessions with White House Chief of Staff James A. Baker—"feedings," they were called playfully. These sessions were tremendously useful in understanding how the administration worked, what it intended to do, and even provided candid insights into how the president operated in the Oval Office. Others on the Reagan White House staff differed, one from another, in their press-friendliness, but most were as available as Baker. This willingness to talk with reporters played no small part in the success of the Reagan presidency and its generally positive press coverage, despite the fact that most reporters who covered Reagan on a daily basis disagreed deeply with many of his policies and found him to be intellectually limited.

The first President Bush was a good deal more press shy as president than he had been as a candidate for the presidency in 1980. As Reagan's vice president he, too, would see the press fairly regularly but was always cautious about what he said. He feared that he would drift away from the Reagan program which he was working hard to support, despite what must have been deep personal misgivings. It was First Lady Barbara Bush who loathed the press deeply, especially as criticism of her husband mounted. "This George Bush is more like his mother, than like his father, in his feeling for the press," said one Washington bureau chief, "and this feeling extends way down into the administration culture."

Certainly the press has in part earned the contempt now shown it by many politicians and government officials. The unmerciful battering the press administered to Bill Clinton over Whitewater, what was an essentially inconsequential land deal, delivered the message to politicians that once the press frenzy has started it is almost impossible to stop. It does seem in retrospect, and actually appeared to be true at the time, that had the president and first lady made a clean breast of the matter they could have stopped the fuss. But the longer they stonewalled, the more the press growled and chewed. The right-wing scandal machines fed the press's eagerness for dirt, and thus the cycle worsened.

Moreover, some media outlets, with a few notable exceptions, have been gradually taking themselves out of the news-gathering business. Cable television news, for example, seems most happy to substitute noisy provocateurs like Chris Matthews and Bill O'Reilly for serious news shows. CNN, which according to polls by the Pew Research Center is still seen as the most credible source of television news, is bleeding audience to Fox News. Roger Ailes, who runs Fox News, achieved his greatest public relations triumph since he sold America on "the new Nixon" in 1968 with his successful campaign to market his programming as "fair and balanced." Third place MSNBC, taking its cue from Fox, added Joe Scarborough, a conservative former member of Congress, to its evening lineup. His cheerleading support for the war seemed more appropriate for "Sports Center" than for a serious news network.

With the exceptions of the *New York Times* and the Associated Press and, to a lesser extent, the *Washington Post* and the *Los Angeles Times,* the major press organizations have been pruning away their international coverage and severely limiting the amount of space and airtime devoted to foreign news. This turn inward is not because editors are no longer interested in foreign news but because the cost of maintaining foreign bureaus and using up limited space with those stories is not justified by the amount of reader interest they attract. To many business executives in the offices of major news organizations, foreign stories amount to, as one executive at Time Inc. put it a few years ago, "homework." Splashier graphics, shorter stories, and more "service" journalism have replaced the news from abroad. European and Asian editions of the newsmagazine are much more cosmopolitan. In early 2003, a *Time* magazine cover story in Europe featured a well-reported examination of the tensions between Europe and the United States over Iraq. That edition is not available in the United States, where *Time*'s domestic cover was about the power of the mind in healing the body. It is easier for politicians to ignore news organizations that are preoccupied with trying to entertain rather than inform their readers. The television networks have nearly abandoned the actual act of covering news abroad, stationing a few correspondents in key capitals who read the news provided them by wire services. As correspondent Bob Simon said of his CBS network during the Libel Defense Resource Center discussion: "We are no longer a news-gathering organization."

This retreat from seriousness extends as well to domestic news. Once fine newspapers like the *Miami Herald* and the *Philadelphia Inquirer,* both part of the constantly-cost-cutting Knight-Ridder chains, have had their news holes and their news staffs trimmed dramatically over the past decade. The goal has been to increase the rate of profitability of the holding company, and the consequence has been a clear deterioration in the quality of the newspapers the company publishes. Knight-Ridder is far from alone in this cost-cutting, and the result has been a clear loss of quality journalism at second-level newspapers across the country.

Pressure for higher rates of return from already profitable news publications is, of course, directly connected to the conglomeration of these businesses into the media giants that increasingly dominate the news industry. Again with the notable exception of the *New York Times* and the *Washington Post,* where the Sulzberger and Graham families have maintained voting control of their stock, the newspapers, networks, and newsmagazines are under severe cost and profit pressures from their business management. This problem has been exacerbated in recent years by a dramatic decline in advertising revenue that resulted from the post-bubble slump in the economy.

Timid or Intimidated?

One of the great frauds that has been committed against the mainstream media has been the persistent and widely believed allegation that the press tilts toward the political left. Books making these charges, like former CBS correspondent Bernard Goldberg's *Bias* and Ann Coulter's *Slander,* appear with stunning regularity and rise to best-seller status quickly. Leaving aside the question of what might these days constitute a truly liberal political complexion, what gives some credibility to the persistent cries of left-wing bias is that the mass media are not conservative in the sense that they agree, either editorially or in their news judgment, with the movement and religious conservatives who now constitute the core of the national Republican constituency. Except for opinion journals, which target specific ideological audiences, most organs of the American press hug the political center, to the extent they understand where that center is. And the reason is simple: That's where most of their readers and viewers are politically. In the more fractured markets for cable news, Fox has been able to tilt to the right while being more entertaining with its opinionated talk-show hosts. But for most major news outlets, the center is where the money is.

This constant quest for a large audience breeds a real timidity on the part of much of the press, even in the face of a virtual information lockout by the Bush administration. Bush is popular, or has been since September 11, and the press is following the polls. It voiced only mild criticism of the president's policies, even as he prepared a military adventure unlike any in the nation's history. Even the *New York Times* avoided opposing the idea of a preemptive strike on Iraq, contenting itself with pleas for permitting the United Nations inspection process to go on longer. In the wake of the quick military success of the invasion into Iraq, it is reasonable to expect even greater deference to the president—at least for a while longer.

As it tries not to stray too far from the opinion set of its mass market, the press has another problem with its audience. In the period immediately following September 11, the Pew Research Center found widespread support for the idea that the press was professional, patriotic, and compassionate, in the words of the survey. But even before the first anniversary of the terrorist attacks, the measures for all those qualities had declined to under 50 percent of the respondents. The cautionary effects these numbers have on the decisions of the mass media are obvious.

Still, the prevailing attitude, as has always been the case when the nation is at war—however "war" is defined—has been to join what Kathleen Hall Jamieson and Michael Waldman describe as the rally-'round-the-flag effect. They note that this is so not only in the opinion sections of the publications but also in the news sections. They marshal some startling quotes in support of this observation. Dan Rather: "George Bush is president, he makes the decisions, and you know, as just one American, if he wants me to line up, just tell me where." Cokie Roberts: "Look, I am, I'll just confess to you, a total sucker for the guys who stand up with all the ribbons on and stuff, and they say it's true and I'm ready to believe it."

This tendency to be supportive of the government in times of war has been exacerbated, at least in Washington, by a sense of personal danger resulting from the attack on the Pentagon, the planned attack on either the Capitol or the White House, and the sure knowledge that Washington will always be a prime target for another terrorist attack. Speaking to Ted Gup for his piece in the *Columbia Journalism Review,* Evan Thomas of *Newsweek* noted that the press has been muted about the secret detentions of terrorism suspects and immigration law violators. "I think this relates to people being afraid," Thomas said. "They [the journalists] want to keep these potential terrorists—even if they're not—behind bars. Journalists are occasionally people. They share the same fears of terrorism, and they are more willing to look the other way because of that. I am sure that we will decide in retrospect that we went soft on the administration and let them get away with too much. It's inevitable."

The desire to operate on the same emotional wavelength as the audience is part of the economic imperative inherent in the avoidance of offending readers and viewers. This instinct is compounded by another impulse that leads to tiptoe journalism. Most of the conglomerates that own the major media outlets have major business before the government—whether on taxes, or mergers, or communications law. While editors and publishers are being careful not to alienate audiences, their corporate supervisors are cautioning them not to offend the government.

This problem did not arrive the day President Bush moved into the White House; it existed before and will exist under whatever successor follows the current administration. During the Clinton years, for example, *Time* magazine, which had been quite mild, and occasionally even dismissive, of the Whitewater scandal, ran a tough and well-reported cover story on how the White House political staff had been attempting to interfere with the Treasury Department's examination of the failed savings and loan company that had a major part in the Whitewater land deal. Clinton's spokesman never denied the story but instead launched an assault on the cover photo that had been chosen by *Time.* It was a black-and-white, White House stock photo of Clinton and George Stephanopoulos meeting in the Oval Office used to illustrate the fact that Stephanopoulos had been involved in the intercession with Treasury. The White House claimed, preposterously, that *Time* ran this photo intending to show that the president and his aide were actually conspiring on the Whitewater matter.

Soon after the story ran, Clinton himself appeared at the White House Correspondent's Association annual dinner, projected a blowup of the *Time* cover, and then showed a series of obviously fake *Time* covers with Clinton and an assortment of celebrities. The gambit was amusing to many, but not to Time Warner chairman Gerald Levin. Worried about the effect of an angry White House on his company's various pieces of government business, he sent stern word down through the ranks of the magazine's editors, instructing that a more "normal" relationship be established between the magazine and the Clinton White House.

Coverage of Washington is now timid and tentative, careful and controlled. When the U.S. government sent a drone airplane into Yemen, tracked a suspected terrorist, and then destroyed him and the other passengers in his car, most stories raised the obvious questions about the authority for such an assassination inside a country with which the United States is not at war. One person also killed was an American citizen, charged with no crime. Officials made no attempt to justify his killing, other than pointing out that he was in a car with a terrorist. How did we know it was the known terrorist in the car? Was there no way to intercept and apprehend the known terrorist? Who authorized the firing of the missile? In the war on terrorism, questions like that are uncomfortable and unwelcome by the mass audience. Within two days, after Bush administration officials stonewalled the questions, the story died. In his State of the Union address, President Bush even boasted of the assassination and implied there have been others. Only Hendrik Hertzberg of *The New Yorker* took notice of this unprecedented admission by an American president. As White House spokesman Ari Fleischer explained at the time of the bombing, "The president has said very plainly to the American people that this is a war in which . . . sometimes there are going to be things that are done that the American people may never know about."

In one of the rare instances where reporters were able to get administration officials to speak candidly and even against their own interests, the *Washington Post* ran a story in early 2003 describing how the U.S. government was outsourcing some of the more intense interrogations of Al-Qaeda suspects to foreign countries with long records of torture. The piece provoked an editorial in *The Economist,* but there was very little mention of the interrogation policy by other U.S. news organizations. The revelation that John Poindexter, the Reagan aide responsible for much of the Iran-Contra scandal, was employed by the Pentagon to fashion an Orwellian database to gather the most routine information about the activities of ordinary citizens would have caused a media feeding frenzy five years ago. In the current climate, the story got relatively little attention in the general media until the Congress quietly postponed the program.

The press in Washington is not complaining, at least publicly. One bureau chief contacted for this piece was candid in saying that speaking on the record about lack of access to administration officials would only make managing that difficult relationship that much harder. Instead of complaining, Washington reporters are trying to get along with the Bush administration. Some reporters are busy doing puff pieces about various members of the administration—"beat builders," one correspondent calls them—in hopes that they will be let into the tent. In times past, hostility between the press and government often led to tough coverage. Now, the reverse is true. The old danger of getting too close to sources and writing puff pieces about those sources seems to have been reversed. The more the press is kept at bay, the more pliant the coverage has become. Says a veteran Washington bureau chief: "A starving press corps only becomes desperately hungry for small bits. Little anecdotes have become prized commodities because they are so rare. Starvation has been very successful [for the administration]."

The president himself is totally shut away from the mainstream press, having only the most occasional news conferences and, as the selling of the war on Iraq proceeded, a luncheon with conservative columnists. On a long trip to Europe and Russia in his first year in office, Bush never met with the traveling press corps. More astoundingly, neither did his press secretary, Ari Fleischer. "The press secretary was one of the royal attendants," said one bureau chief who made the trip. Bush's televised and carefully scripted press conference just before the attack on Iraq was his first in eighteen months. He has had no on-the-record interview with the big dailies or the news-magazines since he was sworn in. Only Watergate ace Bob Woodward appears to have achieved great access to administration officials and even got to review presumably classified National Security Council minutes for his recent book *Bush at War,* but his reporting was done retrospectively and not for the daily newspaper. He has traded timeliness for access, and what he is producing is not quite journalism, not quite history.

"I am telling you," Seymour Hersh told the audience during the Libel Defense Resource Center's panel discussion, "this [Bush] crowd has the utmost contempt for us. . . . They really do not care about us. They really do have us figured out." The sad fact of the matter is that the policy of limiting access and limiting discussion is succeeding brilliantly from the administration's point of view. With a political opposition in Congress cowed by many of the same forces that intimidate the press, the usual technique of at least reporting what opponents say is not available to the media. Without lawyers to represent those incarcerated as suspects in the war on terrorism, there are no advocates for the media willing to question, on the record, the misuse of the nation's system of justice. The silence is powerful indeed.

John F. Stacks reported for *Time* magazine for three decades. He supervised the magazine's coverage of Watergate as Washington news editor, and later served as chief of correspondents and deputy managing editor.

Jarret M. Brachman

High-Tech Terror

Al-Qaeda's Use of New Technology

"We must get our message across to the masses of the nation and break the media siege imposed on the jihad movement. This is an independent battle that we must launch side by side with the military battle."

—Ayman Al-Zawahiri[1]

"Our enemies have skillfully adapted to fighting wars in today's media age, but . . . our country has not. . . ."

—Donald Rumsfeld[2]

Despite the considerable resources that the United States has dedicated to combating *jihadi* terrorism since the attacks of September 11, 2001, its primary terrorist enemy, al-Qaeda, has mutated and grown more dangerous. Al-Qaeda today is no longer best conceived of as an organization, a network, or even a network-of-networks. Rather, by leveraging new information and communication technologies, al-Qaeda has transformed itself into an organic social movement, making its virulent ideology accessible to anyone with a computer.

Since its popularization in the mid-1990s, Internet-based activism has changed the nature of social and political movements: no longer does one need to physically relocate to support a cause—now anyone can bolster a movement at any time, virtually anywhere, using a computer. One can even pledge allegiance to Osama bin Laden by filling out an online form.[3] While Western governments should be concerned with who is viewing this hateful content, they need to recognize the more dangerous trend—namely, that *jihadis* are empowering one another to be producers, not simply consumers, of this material.

In the wake of recent attacks by *jihadi* terrorists against targets in London, Madrid, and Jakarta, the United States government has invested significant resources in the preemption and prevention of attacks at home. It should not be surprising, then, that the American counterterrorism establishment approaches the *jihadi* movement's use of technology with a primarily operational mindset. Agencies tasked with monitoring the *jihadi* movement's use of email, chat rooms, online magazines, cell phone videos, CD-ROMs, and even video games look for immediate intelligence indicators and warnings. However, there has been little directive (or bureaucratic incentive) for these agencies to situate the technological activity they monitor in a broader strategic context. Unfortunately, it is the strategic—not operational—objectives of the *jihadi* movement's use of technology that engenders the most enduring and lethal threat to the United States over the long term.

If Western governments made reading the online statements posted by al-Qaeda ideologues a priority, they would better realize how the *jihadi* movement is not simply using technological tools to recruit new members, receive donations, and plan attacks. In actuality, al-Qaeda's use of the Internet and other new technologies has also enabled it to radicalize and empower armies of new recruits by shaping their general worldview.[4]

From a counterterrorism perspective, there is no easy way to cauterize the surge of *jihadi* web presence or the movement's broader exploitation of modern technologies. Dismantling radical Internet homepages, for instance, is ineffective because these sites almost always reappear at other web addresses. Additionally, the eradication of such sites is incredibly counterproductive for the analysts trying to track the content on them. On the other hand, leaving hostile websites in place allows for those interested in learning about, thinking about, and discussing violent *jihad* to do so unabated. Either choice is problematic.

For the United States to defeat al-Qaeda and the broader *jihadi* movement, it must first gain a better appreciation of the ways in which the movement is successfully fueling itself by harnessing new technologies. This article is intended as a first step toward that objective.

Technology and Social Movements

Throughout history, individuals, groups, and networks from across the ideological spectrum have harnessed emerging technologies in order to advance their own political and social agendas. The printing press, cassette tape, and the fax machine have, at different points in time, served to spark revolutions in thought and action. The Internet today penetrates all levels of society while being subject to relatively few constraints. By bypassing other more conventional mediums, the Internet creates not just the tools, but an entirely new forum for fostering global awareness of issues unconstrained by government censorship or traditional cultural norms. Over the past decade, various groups and movements have used the Internet to:

- Coordinate movement activities, events, and actions;
- Discuss topics of interest and news with movement participants;
- Disseminate propaganda, educational, and training materials;
- Identify, recruit, and socialize new membership; and
- Find and exploit information about their opposition.

In fact, the use of the Internet for social and political activism has actually generated an entire subfield of study within the academic disciplines of sociology and political science.[5]

However, widespread misconceptions about the movement's use of technology have served to focus too much public (and thus policy) attention on the more sensational features of *jihadi* Internet activity, such as the online deluge of Iraqi attack videos, and not enough on its more mundane aspects, such as *jihadi* web forums. Any meaningful discussion of al-Qaeda's use of the Internet must first seek to rectify such errors.

The *jihadi* web world is structured much like that of any other movement's virtual presence, although it is significantly more unstable. Web forum sites like the *Al-Hesbah Discussion Forum* (<www.alhesbah.org>) or the now-defunct *Syrian Islamic Forum* serve as initial entry points from which interested viewers from around the world can read about the breaking news from Iraq, follow links to attack videos from active *jihad* campaigns, view motivational imagery of martyr operatives in heaven, and even download scripted talking points about the religious justifications for waging violent *jihad*. Some of these forums even post *jihadi* job openings.[6] However, these sites vacillate between active and inactive states, often because of disagreements with their service providers or as a result of hostile action against them. They change web addresses frequently, making them incredibly difficult to follow for one not immersed in the *jihadi* web world.

For those seeking a more accessible way to communicate with others who have a similar affinity for *jihad* and al-Qaeda, Google's Orkut software—a popular, worldwide Internet service—provides a useful tool.[7] This online community has helped rally support for Osama bin Laden and facilitated the sharing of *jihadi* videos as well as communication among non-Arab *jihad* sympathizers.

To get the latest news and current events from a *jihadi* perspective, interested viewers have a number of options. They can follow the links on web discussion forums to a series of al-Qaeda-friendly news broadcasts (called the "Voice of the Caliphate") highlighting recent attacks, criticizing Arab governments for collaborating with Jews and Christians, and discussing future goals of the *jihadi* movement.[8] Those searching for *jihadi*-oriented news updates can easily sign up for daily email feeds from one of the many *jihadi* email listserve groups, many of which use the Yahoo! web service. They can also sign up for the free "lightning" mobile Internet service at <www.islammemo.cc/mobile>, which allows users to access selected news content via their cell phones.

Individuals interested in setting up their own terrorist cells—like those responsible for the Madrid train bombing—can find more than news updates online. *Jihadi* web forums provide links to several al-Qaeda magazines, which outline step-by-step instructions for communicating with cell members, defining tactics and procedures, and constructing explosives, among other topics. In fact, with little trouble, they can identify the *jihadi* Yahoo! Group that hosts the *Encyclopedia of Preparation,* a voluminous training manual for everything from kidnapping officials to building nuclear devices.[9]

Increasingly, those who monitor *jihadi* websites find detailed instructional documents and videos that explain how to use specific software packages or access certain types of files online. These tutorials are accompanied with a "*jihadi*-approved" version of the software to download, which often includes computer programs for video editing or webpage design. To this end, *jihadi* computer programmers have launched new stand-alone web browsing software, similar to Internet Explorer, which searches only particular sites. By restricting the freedom to navigate to other online destinations, such programs facilitate the intellectual separation of *jihadi* visitors from the chaos of cyberspace. These efforts to define and bound *jihadi* ideological space, critical for *jihadi* success in light of the multiplicity of alternative viewpoints that can be accessed online, should be expected to accelerate as ideologues seek dominance over this technology.

More thoughtful visitors can read about *jihadi* ideology from the al-Qaeda library site (<http://tawhed.ws>), which hosts over 3,000 books and monographs from respected *jihadi* thinkers. One recent posting in a radical Islamic discussion forum, *Tajdid al-Islami,* demonstrated for participants how *jihadi*-themed books can now be downloaded onto cell phones.[10] In addition to books, anyone can download propaganda and recruitment videos directly onto their mobile devices.[11]

Similar to other web-oriented movements, the *jihadi* online world would not exist were it not for the dedicated efforts of its technical experts and webmasters who maintain these sites. As an information technology specialist, British citizen Babar Ahmad used his computer skills to maintain one of the earliest English-language pro-*jihad* websites from his south London home. His Internet homepage provided news and radical imagery about *jihad* with the goal of cultivating a deeper awareness among would-be participants about the movement's goals.[12] These technical experts play an important role in making the latest advances in information and computer technology available to movement participants. Al-Qaeda's use of the Internet, as evidenced by individuals like Ahmad or the virtual army of other computer-savvy *jihadi* youth, is consistent with the broader pattern of grassroots activism occurring around the world; the *jihadi* use of technology, however, had deadly consequences.

Weaponizing the Internet

Despite the fact that *jihadi* websites have only recently received widespread public attention, pro-*jihad* webmasters have been hosting websites since before the attacks of September 11, 2001. It was not until the United States and its allies unseated the Taliban in Afghanistan, however, that senior al-Qaeda leaders found themselves in a scramble to keep their movement motivated and coherent. As such, they used the Internet to replace their dismantled training camps, reconnect their weakened organization, and reconstitute their leadership. Although these virtual combat classrooms do not render physical training camps obsolete, information technologies do change the nature of education, indoctrination, and participation.

Al-Qaeda has increasingly looked to the Internet as a way of shaping military operations on the battlefield. As Iraqi insurgents perfect their combat techniques, they communicate them to a larger audience through a variety of channels, including the Internet. Increasingly, military commanders have reported a growing trend of Iraqi insurgent tactics being replicated in Afghanistan.[13] The Taliban's use of remote triggered improvised explosive devices (IEDs), for example, demonstrates a notable evolution from the hard-wired detonators they had previously used.[14] In recent months, government officials in Thailand have reported a similar upsurge in the technical sophistication of tactics used by radical Islamic insurgents in the south of the country.[15] Thai security forces attribute these seemingly overnight advancements, particularly in terms of how guerrillas are wiring and deploying IEDs, to a combination of the availability of *jihadi* training manuals, which they have found in safe houses in CD-ROM and hardcopy form, and direct instruction from Thai *jihadis* with al-Qaeda training camp experience.

In recent years, a burgeoning web network of "resistance sites" has emerged to facilitate the insurgency in Iraq by providing detailed directions, advice, and maps to those looking to participate.[16] Suggesting routes through Syria, facilitators guide interested participants from Saudi Arabia or Europe into the heart of the battle via a winding underground railroad of safe houses and sympathetic mosques.

Jihadi media brigades also foster awareness about their cause through a continuous stream of emails, propaganda videos, and pictures.[17] Focused on turning their enemy's strengths against them, *jihadis* actively use the latest Western software—including Windows Movie Maker, Adobe Acrobat, and others—to create anti-Western products intended to inspire their followers and humiliate their enemies. These al-Qaeda affiliated or inspired media outlets have found a wealth of imagery from Western media sources, which they manipulate to craft their own propaganda products. Over the past year, this imagery has increasingly focused on profiling wounded and dead American soldiers in disturbingly graphic ways. Perhaps even more shocking to Western audiences is the black humor that often accompanies this imagery.[18]

One recent al-Qaeda propaganda campaign highlighting sniper operations in Iraq has fostered broad popular awareness in the West and the Muslim world of the *jihadi* movement's ideological successes. A series of videos, photos, and discussions about alleged attacks conducted by *jihadi* heroes, the "Baghdad Sniper" and the "Sniper of Fallujah," have been proliferating on hostile websites.[19] The videos show attacks by a sniper against American forces in Iraq, each ending with a successful hit against a soldier. The stark contrast between the imposing *jihadi* sniper and the suffering American soldier fits precisely with the goals of the movement: providing a sense of meaning and proof of victory to those sympathetic to the *jihadi* cause.

These types of propaganda products are typically burned to CD-ROM and distributed by hand not only to *jihadi* activists but also to anyone who may be curious about the movement. Available in markets and under the counters of some shops, these videos can be purchased throughout the Middle East and Southeast Asia. The sniper has become a folk hero for some Iraqis, who may not necessarily subscribe to the *jihadi* ideology, but do feel a connection with the active resistance waged by the sniper against what they perceive to be imperialistic U.S. forces.

In addition to using technology for education and indoctrination purposes, *jihadi* groups have also exploited these technologies to revolutionize the way in which their supporters participate in the struggle. For example, in November 2005, the information bureau of "The Army of the Victorious Group," a Sunni insurgent group operating in Iraq, used several radical Islamic websites to announce a contest for designing the organization's website. The winner would not only have his design implemented, but he would receive a prize in the form of the opportunity to fire missiles via computer at a U.S. army base in Iraq.[20] The announcement emphasized that:

> The winner will fire three long-range missiles from any location in the world at an American army base in Iraq, by pressing a button [on his computer] with his own blessed hand, using technology developed by the *jihad* fighters, Allah willing.[21]

By stressing the "opportunity for our brothers outside Iraq to join their brothers on the front line[s] in Iraq, the land of the frontier and of *jihad,* and to [participate in] destroying the strongholds of polytheism and heresy," the contest sponsors demonstrated their view that the very *use* of technology is an integral part of the education and indoctrination process. Such applications of technology allow those interested in supporting the insurgency in Iraq to do so from outside the actual field of battle.

Importantly, *jihadi* web users have become increasingly aware of attempts by governments to monitor their behavior. In order to enhance operational security in the use of technology, *jihadis* have recently posted protocol about safe ways to use technology. For example, a guide for using the Internet safely and anonymously recently emerged on a *jihadi* forum site.[22] The guide explains how governments identify users; penetrate their usage of software chat programs, including Microsoft Messenger and PalTalk; and advises readers not to use Saudi Arabian based email addresses (those that end with a ".sa" extension) because they are not secure. Rather, the author of this guide suggests that *jihadis* should register for anonymous accounts from commercial providers like Hotmail or Yahoo!.

Video Games and *Jihad*

Although counterterrorism analysts correctly focus on the ways in which *jihadis* employ new technologies to advance their operational agendas, they must also pay better attention to the strategic application of technology in cultivating widespread ideological support among Muslim youth. To date, the burgeoning *jihadi* video game industry has made relatively little impact on policymakers, but this application of technology does reflect a growing effort by radical Islamic propagandists to reach a younger demographic with their message.

Before continuing, it is important to note that many video games available to youth in the West are equally or even more violent than the *jihadi* versions. Additionally, there is no clear consensus among experts on whether playing violent games leads an individual to perpetrate violence in real life. Despite these limitations, what makes *jihadi* games uniquely problematic is the nature of the assumptions it asks players to make. Take, for instance, this paraphrased setting from a real *jihadi* video game available for download on the Internet:

> The year is 2214. United under the banner of Islam, soldiers of Allah have successfully conquered the world, reestablishing the global Caliphate. No longer do infidel forces threaten the *ummah,* the global community of Islamic believers. No longer are "good" Muslims tempted by the manipulative forces of commercialism or sexuality. By clicking on "New Game," this puritanical Islamic utopia is whisked into a state of chaos as it faces an impending attack by infidel space invaders. Only "you" can save it. . . .[23]

Children who play this game are supposed to accept that, at some point in history, Muslims conquered the world and killed or converted all those who opposed them. While players may understand that such games are based on fiction, the act of playing them arguably increases their propensity to accept ideologies that consist of extreme goals, such as the establishment of a global Islamic caliphate.

These types of radical Islamic video games would make most game savvy Western youth chuckle. Their graphics are rudimentary, and their game play is stilted. When compared to any commercial action game in the West, or even video games employed by the U.S. Army to predispose youths toward military service, *jihadi* games pale in comparison. But when one peers beyond the graphic interface, a coherent and ideological world in thought comes into relief. In the *jihadi* games, Muslims are faced with a variety of aggressors—the American military, alien invaders, Israeli settlers, or even robots programmed to kill—that they must fend off for the sake of Islam. Beyond the primary plot of the game—whether assassinating Israeli political leaders, clearing Israeli settlements, or knowing trivia about early Christian invaders—would-be gamers are assumed to be steeped in the appropriate knowledge base before even approaching the game. That way, upon interacting with the game itself, the game's premise is intuitive to the player.

In a game called "Under Ash" and its sequel "Under Siege," players assume the identity of "Ahmed," a young Palestinian man tasked with delivering "a collection of important ideas in the history of the Palestinian Cause." As Ahmed, players follow his escalation of violence from stone-throwing to face-to-face combat. The game's website reminds prospective players that:

> A nation in Palestine is being uprooted: their houses are being devastated, their establishments are being destroyed, their lands are being occupied, their trees are being pulled out, their property is being confiscated, their cities are being besieged, their schools are being closed, their sanctuaries are being violated, their sacred structures are being made permitted, [*sic*] their children are being beaten, their hands are being broken, their bones are being crushed and they are imprisoned, tortured, and slain.[24]

Not all games in the radical Islamic bent are so overtly violent. For instance, a package of mini-games sold under the title "The Islamic Fun!" and produced by Innovative Minds is targeted at providing children with an alternative to secular video games.[25] Robert Spencer describes this CD-ROM:

> Its games have names such as "Fishing Bear," "Tree Hop," and "Two Bunny Race." In "Tree Hop," a tiger bounds atop a series of trees in pursuit of a beach ball. "Fishing Bear" features a bear sporting green pajamas (complete with nightcap) and a wide grin.[26]

Tucked inside this package of seemingly innocuous games, however, is one entitled "The Resistance." Players between the ages of five and seven become farmers in South Lebanon who join the Islamic resistance against invading Israelis. Their objective is to destroy all invading "Zionist forces."

Video games, like other popular media, become part of a culture's discourse. Different from other tools such as pamphlets, books, or websites, video games allow for two-way engagement—both intellectual and physical—in a simulated world. Players strike keys or click buttons to shoot, syncing physical action with intellectual and visual cues. Repeated play reinforces the connection between thought and action, between intent and implementation. Video games serve as a record of popular sentiment and therefore serve to influence the understanding of historical memories for those who play them.

Drawing selective historical lessons, highlighting particular characters, or simulating certain battles allow game developers to control the "reality" in which players engage. The more realistic these games become, the less dissonance players see between the game and the world around them. The opportunity for players to be lulled into a sense that the game harmonizes with reality is an extremely dangerous prospect, whether the game is designed for simply passing time or for radicalizing youth.

The use of websites, chat rooms, and video games cannot be seen as simply an *ad hoc* outcome of globalization or the adoption of technology by the *jihadi* movement. As shown in the next sections, al-Qaeda's harnessing of technology has been a calculated strategic move—the goal being to catalyze awareness of the need for Muslims to "resist" and open new ways for them to participate in that resistance.

Strategic Exploitation of Technology

"The revolution in communications and the global satellite channels and the Internet have opened the minds of people. . . ."

—Abu Musab Al-suri[27]

In recent decades, *jihadi* ideologues have devoted significant energy to promulgating an aggressive, historically informed, and universally applicable strategy for expanding their influence, both territorially and ideologically. Senior thinkers within this group of Islamic zealots publish voluminous texts outlining their agendas.[28] Given their obscure historical meandering and opaque style, however, these grand-strategy texts do not receive the attention they should from Western policymakers. *jihadi* propagandists, however, eagerly consume these texts and bring their message to a mass audience by producing and applying technology in new ways as described in the sections above.[29]

Abu Musab al-Suri, a senior al-Qaeda thinker, can be seen as the chief architect of al-Qaeda's contemporary Internet movement. Therefore, if one is to understand the logic informing the *jihadi* use of technology, one must become intimately familiar with the man choreographing this technological movement.

Abu Musab al-Suri is the *nom de guerre* of the Syrian *jihadi* Mustafa 'Abd al-Qadir Mustafa Husayn, also known as Umar 'Abd al-Hakim and Mustafa Setmariam Nassar. He is a career *jihadi* who spent much of his life fighting, training, and writing about violent *jihad*.[30] Suri's unique personal background shapes his approach to fomenting social change, particularly regarding the role of strategic communication and propaganda. He is reportedly proficient in multiple languages, including Spanish, French, English, and his native Arabic. He is known to hold a black belt in judo (a martial arts approach that relies on turning an enemy's strength against them) and possesses advanced expertise in guerrilla warfare.

Having lived in both Arab and Western cultures, his perspective on spreading the *jihadi* movement is global in scope. Suri argues that *jihad* should be understood as a comprehensive war, where its soldiers employ military, political, media, civil, and ideological tools. For Suri, the Internet and other media resources should be used to help establish what he calls "resistance blockades" in order to keep the enemy (Western culture) from further corrupting Islamic institutions, organizations, and ideas through this technology. Suri advocates that *jihadis* reclaim technological tools of communication and use them to radicalize the Muslim masses—a guerilla war of ideas as well as of violence.

Suri is both student and master in the propaganda business. In the early 1990s, he moved to England to help establish the media wing of the Armed Islamic Group (GIA). He wrote articles in the publications of a variety of *jihadi* groups, including the Algerian *Al-Ansar* newsletter, the Libyan *Al-Fajr* newsletter, and the Egyptian *Mujahidun* newsletter, which were all published in Europe during that period. He was reportedly detained by

Algerian security forces, but denied his involvement with the GIA, condemning the group for killing Muslims in their attacks. Fearing future arrest, Suri then decided to dedicate his time to literary work and independent journalism, earning the nickname "pen *jihadist*" from U.S. counterterrorism officials.[31]

In 1996, Suri reportedly established the Bureau for the Study of Islamic Conflicts in London.[32] The office is perhaps most well known for facilitating two press interviews with Osama bin Laden for the BBC and CNN. At that time, Suri reportedly planned to pursue university studies in journalism and political science in Britain, but due to pressure from British security agencies he fled to Afghanistan in 1997, where he stayed until the country's collapse in December 2001. From 1997 to 2001, with the help of the Taliban's Ministry of Defense, Suri established the Al-Ghurabaa terrorist training camp in the infamous Qarghah Military Base in Kabul. It was here that he pledged allegiance to the Taliban leader, Mullah Muhammad Omar, in 2000. Suri worked in the Taliban's Ministry of Information and wrote for the Taliban's official newspaper, *Shari'ah.* He also participated in preparing the Arabic-language programming of Kabul's radio station. During that period, Suri established a new "Al-Ghurabaa" (known as the "Center for Islamic Studies and Information"), issued the *Concerns of the Defenders of Truth* magazine, and wrote a number of books, including a 1,600-page tome dedicated to launching a "Global Islamic Resistance."[33]

Suri's lifelong goal has been to bring *jihad* to the people. The establishment of al-Qaeda and its attacks around the world—particularly those on September 11, 2001—were critical, but not necessarily sufficient, steps toward catalyzing the global Islamic revolution he envisions. Drawing upon the operational, tactical, and strategic lessons of past *jihadi* movements, including his experience working with the Algerian *jihad* and several attempts to overthrow the Syrian government in the 1980s, Suri has gained a very clear sense of what the movement needs to do in order to be successful.[34] The obvious next step for Suri is to cultivate an intellectual, cultural, and military guerrilla movement around the world.

Suri's Method: Establish a Culture of Preparation

Although Suri used the Internet and new technologies in a limited way himself, he was acutely aware of their potential to empower the masses to conduct their own research, communicate with one another, and identify with an idea larger than themselves.

In his most recent work, *A Call to Global Islamic Resistance,* Suri frequently characterizes the Internet and satellite television, as well as computers in general, as critical vehicles for inciting a global resistance.[35] Such incitement, he argues, can only happen once the masses understand the problems they face and why their help is needed to overcome them. But Suri takes a curiously process-based approach to defining incitement, arguing that people cannot fully understand the political repression and economic exploitation they face unless they participate in resistance activities, which could include anything from accessing and distributing *jihadi* propaganda to actively fighting against the West.

Suri argues throughout his works that a truly effective grassroots campaign relies on technology, exploited in small-scale, directed operations by a large number of people. The circulation of propaganda, for instance, should be sent to personal email contact lists.

Jihadi movement participants, he argues, should also use computers, CD-ROMs, and DVDs to circulate large quantities of *jihadi* information—in the form of books, essays, brochures, photographs, and videos—in a highly compressed fashion. For Suri, those who recognize the need to participate in the Global Islamic Resistance should work within small propaganda cells in order to:

- Deploy written statements that call on Muslims worldwide to join the Global Islamic Resistance in every possible publication;
- Publish works on military and training curricula to inform the popular resistance;
- Translate those works into Turkish, Urdu, Indonesian, and other languages spoken in Muslim-majority countries; and
- Disseminate any scholarly writing that supports the spirit of resistance, including senior scholarly opinions regarding the enemies of *jihad* and writings identifying unbelievers and boycotting cooperation with them.

For Suri, Muslim youth ought to develop computer proficiency so that they can access and disseminate information using the latest technology from an early age. The Internet, Suri notes, is one of the most useful ways to craft a historical record of the *jihadi* movement across the military, social, media, and ideological fronts. By making *jihadi* videos readily accessible, Suri suggests, the Internet helps aspiring *jihadis* to learn how to deliver speeches in the "appropriate" manner.

Conclusion

This article has sought to introduce readers to the various ways the *jihadi* movement leverages communication and information technologies. Its aim was to demonstrate the strategic significance of these technologies for advancing an organic, global *jihadi* movement that can adapt to environmental changes, including enhanced counterterrorism policies.

The examples provided here are only a few of the ways this growing army of *jihadi* propagandists—proficient in the use of computers and acutely aware of the power of the Internet—uses technology to communicate their ideology around the world. Sites like al-Qaeda's library offer a tremendous resource to scholars and researchers who want to gain a better understanding of the strategic goals of various thinkers in the movement. The discussion forums provide a valuable resource for monitoring how conceptual thinking is translated into popular action.

It seems clear that senior *jihadi* strategists like Abu Musab al-Suri, who have urged propagandists not only to spread the ideology, but to actually educate others about how to become propagandists themselves, are having an influence on the way the movement leverages technology. *jihadi* use of new technologies must therefore be monitored by bureaucracies tasked with combating *jihadi* terrorism, not just to obtain the operational information that is available, but also to obstruct this larger process of indoctrinating a generation of young *jihadi* soldiers worldwide.

Unless the United States crafts a strategy that stymies long-term ideological radicalization among large numbers of Muslim youth, America's "Long War" against terrorism is likely to be just that.

Jarret M. Brachman is the Director of Research in the Combating Terrorism Center at West Point. Dr. Brachman specializes in Jihadist ideology, strategy and propaganda. He has spoken on those topics before the British House of Lords, the U.S. Congress and he regularly consults with federal, state and local law enforcement on issues related to terrorism and al-Qaeda. His research has been profiled on a variety of international television and print media, including *60 Minutes, al-Jazeera* and the *New York Times.*

Notes

1. Ayman al-Zawahiri, "Knights Under the Banner of the Prophet," *Al-Sharq al-Awsat,* December 2, 2001.
2. BBC News, "U.S. Losing Media War to al-Qaeda," February 17, 2006, <http://news.bbc.co.uk/2/hi/americas/4725992.stm> (accessed February 24, 2006).
3. *Now Online: Swear Loyalty to Al-Qaeda Leaders,* The Middle East Media Research Institute Special Dispatch 1027, November 18, 2005, <http://memri.org/bin/articles.cgi?Page=subjects &Area=jihad&ID=SP102705> (accessed March 27, 2006).
4. Senior *jihadi* strategist Abu Musab al-Suri dedicated his most recent book, *Da'wah lil-Muqawamah al-Islamiyyah al-'Alamiyyah (A Call to Global Islamic Resistance),* to catalyzing a global Islamic revolution via new media technologies, particularly through the Internet and satellite television. He published the book online in 2004 at the culmination of his career directing and thinking about *jihad.* The book can be accessed online at <www.fsboa.com/vw/index.php?subject=7&rec=27&tit=tit&pa=0> (accessed March 29, 2006).
5. See Steven Hick and John G. McNutt, eds., *Advocacy, Activism, and the Internet: Community Organization and Social Policy* (Chicago: Lycecum, 2002); Martha McCaughey and Michael D. Ayers, eds., *Cyberactivism: Online Activism in Theory and Practice* (New York: Routledge, 2003); and Quintan Wiktorowicz, *Islamic Activism: A Social Movement Theory Approach* (Bloomington: Indiana University Press, 2003).
6. Anton LaGuardia, "Al-Qaeda Places Recruiting Ads," *The London Telegraph,* August 10, 2005.
7. Kasie Hunt, "Osama bin Laden Fan Clubs Build Online Communities," *USA Today,* March 8, 2006, <www.usatoday.com/tech/news/2006-03-08-orkut-al-qaeda_x.htm> (accessed March 29, 2006).
8. *New Al-Qaeda Weekly Internet News Broadcast Celebrates U.S. Hurricanes and Gaza Pullout, Reports on Al-Zarqawi's Anti-Shiite Campaign and Chemical Mortar Shells in Iraq,* The Middle East Media Research Institute Special Dispatch Series 993, September 23, 2005, <http://memri.org/bin/articles.cgi?Page=subjects&Area=jihad&ID=SP99305> (accessed March 27, 2006).
9. See Stephen Ulph, "A Guide to *Jihad* on the Web," *Jamestown Foundation Terrorism Monitor* 2 (7), March 31, 2005.
10. *Tajdid Al-Islami,* "Here Are Books That Can be Read on a Cell Phone," February 16, 2006, <www.tajdeed.org.uk/forums/showthread.php?s=8bf3d9789390e5e7dad7d22476adeb3b&thr eadid=38954> (accessed March 27, 2006).
11. The *jihadi* website, Mohajroon, has featured links to video clips that can be viewed on cell phones. See the website's "Visuals Section," <www.mohajroon.com/modules.php?name=Islamic_Gaw al&operation=subsection&subsection=1> (accessed March 8, 2006).
12. In October 2004, a U.S. federal grand jury indicted Ahmad for providing material support to terrorists through his homepage, azzam.com, among other charges. See <www.usdoj.gov/usao/ct/Press2004/20041006.html> (accessed April 10, 2006) for the indictment. He has yet to be extradited to the United States.
13. Sami Yousafzai and Ron Moreau, "Unholy Allies," *Newsweek,* September 26, 2005, <www.msnbc.msn.com/id/9379240/site/newsweek/> (accessed March 26, 2006); and David S. Cloud, "Insurgents Are Continually Getting More Sophisticated with Their Devices," *The New York Times,* August 3, 2005.

14. Vicky O'Hara, "Troop Protections from Homemade Bombs Sought," broadcast on National Public Radio, March 4, 2005, <www.npr.org/templates/story/story.php?storyId=4522369> (accessed March 26, 2006).

15. Shaun Waterman, "Thai Militants Learn from Iraq Insurgency," *United Press International,* February 15, 2006, <www.upi.com/SecurityTerrorism/view.php?StoryID=20060215-020216-8561r> (accessed March 26, 2006).

16. For example, on June 16, 2005, "Al-Muhjhir al-Islami," a participant in the online radical discussion forum "Firdaws," described in great detail how "the central border area between Syria's Dir al-Zur province and Iraq's al-Anbar province is the entry point most used by the mujahadeen," in a posting entitled, "The way toward the country of the two rivers." See <http://sireinstitute.org/bin/articles.cgi?ID=publications56205&Category=publications&Subcategory=0> (accessed March 27, 2006).

17. The most popular of these media groups is known as Global Islamic Media Front (GIMF). Its propaganda is among the most sophisticated and pervasive in online *jihadi* media.

18. Goafalaldyn.com, "The Sarcastic Bloody Comedy Video Tape Hidden Camera of the Mujahideen in Iraq," September 6, 2005, <www.goafalaladyn.com/vb/showthread.php?t=5324> (currently inaccessible).

19. Goafalaladyn.com, "Jaysh Al-Islami in Iraq, Gift of Eid to the Monotheist People," November 2, 2005, <www.goafalaladyn.com/vb/showthread.php?t=6848> (currently inaccessible).

20. The *Al-Hesbah Forum* is currently inaccessible but had been found at <www.alhesbah.org>. The Flash document had been posted at: <http://heretic.maid.to/cgi-bin/stored/serio0835.swf>.

21. *Islamist Website Design Contest: Winner Fires Missiles U.S. Army Base in Iraq,* The Middle East Media Research Institute Special Dispatch 1038, December 1, 2005, <http://memri.org/bin/articles.cgi?Page=archives&Area=sd&ID=SP103805> (accessed March 26, 2006).

22. "A Guide for Internet Safety and Anonymity Posted to Jihadist Forum," SITE Institute, 24 March 2006, <http://siteinstitute.org/bin/articles.cgi?ID=publications160206&Category=publications&Subcategory=0> (accessed March 27, 2006).

23. This is a paraphrased summary of the opening scenes in a video game called: "Ummah Defense." One can receive the game "Ummah Defense" and "Ummah Defense 2" as a bonus when they purchase the game "Maze of Destiny" from the website <www.simplyislam.com/iteminfo.asp?item=54854> (accessed March 26, 2006).

24. This explanation can be found on the game's website at <www.underash.net/emessage.htm> (accessed March 25, 2006).

25. This package of games can be purchased from the website <www.inminds.co.uk/islamic-fun.html> (accessed March 26, 2006).

26. Robert Spencer, "*Jihadi* For Kids," June 7, 2002 <www.freecongress.org/commentaries/2002/020607RS.asp> (accessed March 26, 2006).

27. Al-Suri, *A Call to Global Islamic Resistance.*

28. See the *jihadi* strategic library at <tawhed.ws>.

29. The now dead terrorist propagandist, Yusuf al-Ayiri, is one of the most well-known jihadis with the ability to engage in high-level ideological discussions and translate his ideas into propaganda directed toward the Muslim masses. This influential Saudi served as an ideologue, recruiter, and webmaster for al-Qaeda's first website, al-Neda.com, until his death in June 2003. He is generally considered a model within the *jihadi* movement for bridging the gap between the deep thinkers and fighters on the ground.

30. The biography that informs much of this discussion was posted originally on Suri's own homepage, <www.fsboa.com/vw> in March 2005. That site is currently unavailable and is now located on al-Qaeda's library site, <tawhed.ws>, (accessed March 30, 2006), which was down at the time of writing.

31. Robert Windrem, "U.S. Hunt for Pen Jihadist Ends," *NBC News,* November 3, 2005.

32. "Fuel to Fire," *Al-Abram Weekly,* Issue 763, October 6–12, 2005, <http://weekly.ahram.org.eg/2005/763/in3.htm> (accessed March 26, 2006).

33. Ibid.

34. Al-Suri, A Call to Global Islamic Resistance.

35. Ibid.

Gabriel Weimann

www.terror.net

How Modern Terrorism Uses the Internet

Summary

- The great virtues of the Internet—ease of access, lack of regulation, vast potential audiences, and fast flow of information, among others—have been turned to the advantage of groups committed to terrorizing societies to achieve their goals.
- Today, all active terrorist groups have established their presence on the Internet. Our scan of the Internet in 2003–4 revealed hundreds of websites serving terrorists and their supporters.
- Terrorism on the Internet is a very dynamic phenomenon: websites suddenly emerge, frequently modify their formats, and then swiftly disappear—or, in many cases, seem to disappear by changing their online address but retaining much the same content.
- Terrorist websites target three different audiences: current and potential supporters; international public opinion; and enemy publics.
- The mass media, policymakers, and even security agencies have tended to focus on the exaggerated threat of cyberterrorism and paid insufficient attention to the more routine uses made of the Internet. Those uses are numerous and, from the terrorists' perspective, invaluable.
- There are eight different ways in which contemporary terrorists use the Internet, ranging from psychological warfare and propaganda to highly instrumental uses such as fundraising, recruitment, data mining, and coordination of actions.
- While we must better defend our societies against cyberterrorism and Internet-savvy terrorists, we should also consider the costs of applying counterterrorism measures to the Internet. Such measures can hand authoritarian governments and agencies with little public accountability tools with which to violate privacy, curtail the free flow of information, and restrict freedom of expression, thus adding a heavy price in terms of diminished civil liberties to the high toll exacted by terrorism itself.

Introduction

The story of the presence of terrorist groups in cyberspace has barely begun to be told. In 1998, around half of the thirty organizations designated as "Foreign Terrorist Organizations" under the U.S. Antiterrorism and Effective Death Penalty Act of 1996 maintained websites; by 2000, virtually all terrorist groups had established their presence on the Internet. Our scan of the Internet in 2003–4 revealed hundreds of websites serving terrorists and their supporters. And yet, despite this growing terrorist presence, when policymakers, journalists, and academics have discussed the combination of terrorism and the Internet, they have focused on the overrated threat posed by cyberterrorism or cybewarfare (i.e., attacks on computer networks, including those on the Internet) and largely ignored the numerous uses that terrorists make of the Internet every day.

In this report we turn the spotlight on these latter activities, identifying, analyzing, and illustrating ways in which terrorist organizations are exploiting the unique attributes of the Internet. The material presented here is drawn from an ongoing study (now in its sixth year) of the phenomenon, during which we have witnessed a growing and increasingly sophisticated terrorist presence on the World Wide Web. Terrorism on the Internet, as we have discovered, is a very dynamic phenomenon: websites suddenly emerge, frequently modify their formats, and then swiftly disappear—or, in many cases, seem to disappear by changing their online address but retaining much the same content. To locate the terrorists' sites, we have conducted numerous systematic scans of the Internet, feeding an enormous variety of names and terms into search engines, entering chat rooms and forums of supporters and sympathizers, and surveying the links on other organizations' websites to create and update our own lists of sites. This is often a herculean effort, especially because in some cases (e.g., al Qaeda's websites) locations and contents change almost daily.

The report begins by sketching the origins of the Internet, the characteristics of the new medium that make it so attractive to political extremists, the range of terrorist organizations active in cyberspace, and their target audiences. The heart of the report is an analysis of eight different uses that terrorists make of the Internet. These range from conducting psychological warfare to gathering information, from training to fundraising, from propagandizing to recruiting, and from networking to planning and coordinating terrorist acts. In each instance, we offer concrete examples drawn from our own research, from cases reported in the media, and from contacts with Western intelligence organizations. Although the bulk of the report amounts to a strong argument for the political, intelligence, and academic communities to pay much more attention to the dangers posed by terrorists' use of the Internet, the report concludes with a plea to those same communities not to overreact. The Internet may be attractive to political extremists, but it also symbolizes and supports the freedom of thought and expression that helps distinguish democracies from their enemies. Effective counterterrorist campaigns do not require, and may be undermined by, draconian measures to restrict Internet access.

Modern Terrorism and the Internet

Paradoxically, the very decentralized network of communication that the U.S. security services created out of fear of the Soviet Union now serves the interests of the greatest foe of the West's security services since the end of the Cold War: international terror. The roots of the modern Internet are to be found in the early 1970s, during the days of the Cold War, when the U.S. Department of Defense was concerned about reducing the vulner-ability of its communication networks to nuclear attack. The Defense Department decided to decentralize the whole system by creating an interconnected web of computer networks. After twenty years of development and use by academic researchers, the Internet quickly expanded and changed its character when it was opened up to commercial users in the late 1980s. By the mid-1990s, the Internet connected more than 18,000 private, public, and national networks, with the number increasing daily. Hooked into those networks were about 3.2 million host computers and perhaps as many as 60 million users spread across all seven continents. The estimated number of users in the early years of the twenty-first century is over a billion.

As it burgeoned, the Internet was hailed as an integrator of cultures and a medium for businesses, consumers, and governments to communicate with one another. It appeared to offer unparalleled opportunities for the creation of a forum in which the "global village" could meet and exchange ideas, stimulating and sustaining democracy throughout the world. However, with the enormous growth in the size and use of the network, utopian visions of the promise of the Internet were challenged by the proliferation of pornographic and violent content on the web and by the use of the Internet by extremist organizations of various kinds. Groups with very different political goals but united in their readiness to employ terrorist tactics started using the network to distribute their propaganda, to communicate with their supporters, to foster public awareness of and sympathy for their causes, and even to execute operations.

By its very nature, the Internet is in many ways an ideal arena for activity by terrorist organizations. Most notably, it offers

- easy access;
- little or no regulation, censorship, or other forms of government control;
- potentially huge audiences spread throughout the world;
- anonymity of communication;
- fast flow of information;
- inexpensive development and maintenance of a web presence;
- a multimedia environment (the ability to combine text, graphics, audio, and video and to allow users to download films, songs, books, posters, and so forth); and
- the ability to shape coverage in the traditional mass media, which increasingly use the Internet as a source for stories.

An Overview of Terrorist Websites

These advantages have not gone unnoticed by terrorist organizations, no matter what their political orientation. Islamists and Marxists, nationalists and separatists, racists and anarchists: all find the Internet alluring. Today, almost all active terrorist organizations (which number more than forty) maintain websites, and many maintain more than one website and use several different languages.

As the following illustrative list shows, these organizations and groups come from all comers of the globe. (This geographical categorization, it should be noted, reveals the geographical diversity but obscures the fact that many groups are truly transnational, and even transregional, in character.)

- *From the Middle East,* Hamas (the Islamic Resistance Movement), the Lebanese Hezbollah (Party of God), the al Aqsa Martyrs Brigades, Fatah Tanzim, the Popular Front for the Liberation of Palestine (PFLP), the Palestinian Islamic Jihad, the Kahane

Lives movement, the People's Mujahedin of Iran (PMOI—Mujahedin-e Khalq), the Kurdish Workers' Party (PKK), and the Turkish-based Popular Democratic Liberation Front Party (DHKP/C) and Great East Islamic Raiders Front (IBDA-C).

- *From Europe,* the Basque ETA movement, Armata Corsa (the Corsican Army), and the Irish Republican Army (IRA).

- *From Latin America,* Peru's Tupak-Amaru (MRTA) and Shining Path (Sendero Luminoso), the Colombian National Liberation Army (ELN-Colombia), and the Armed Revolutionary Forces of Colombia (FARC).

- *From Asia,* al Qaeda, the Japanese Supreme Truth (Aum Shinrikyo), Ansar al Islam (Supporters of Islam) in Iraq, the Japanese Red Army (JRA), Hizb-ul Mujehideen in Kashmir, the Liberation Tigers of Tamil Eelam (LTTE), the Islamic Movement of Uzbekistan (IMU), the Moro Islamic Liberation Front (MILF) in the Philippines, the Pakistan-based Lashkare-Taiba, and the rebel movement in Chechnya.

Content

What is the content of terrorist sites? Typically, a site will provide a history of the organization and its activities, a detailed review of its social and political background, accounts of its notable exploits, biographies of its leaders, founders, and heroes, information on its political and ideological aims, fierce criticism of its enemies, and up-to-date news. Nationalist and separatist organizations generally display maps of the areas in dispute: the Hamas site shows a map of Palestine, the FARC site shows a map of Colombia, the LTTE site presents a map of Sri Lanka, and so forth. Despite the ever-present vocabulary of "the armed struggle" and "resistance," what most sides do *not* feature is a detailed description of their violent activities. Even if they expound at length on the moral and legal basis of the legitimacy of the use of violence, most sites refrain from referring to the terrorists' violent actions or their fatal consequences—this reticence is presumably inspired by propagandist and image-building considerations. Two exceptions to this rule are Hezbollah and Hamas, whose sites feature updated statistical reports of their actions ("daily operations") and tallies of both "dead martyrs" and "Israeli enemies" and "collaborators" killed.

Audiences

Whom do the Internet terrorists target at their sites? An analysis of the content of the websites suggests three different audiences.

- *Current and potential supporters.* Terrorist websites make heavy use of slogans and offer items for sale, including T-shirts, badges, flags, and videotapes and audiocassettes, all evidently aimed at sympathizers. Often, an organization will target its local supporters with a site in the local language and will provide detailed information about the activities and internal politics of the organization, its allies, and its competitors.

- *International public opinion.* The international public, who are not directly involved in the conflict but who may have some interest in the issues involved, are courted with sites in languages other than the local tongue. Most sites offer versions in several languages. ETA's site, for instance, offers information in Castilian, German, French, and Italian; the MRTA site offers Japanese and Italian in addition to its English and Spanish versions; and the IMU site uses Arabic, English, and Russian. For the benefit of their international audiences, the sites present basic information about the organization and extensive historical background material (material with which the organization's supporters are presumably already familiar).

Judging from the content of many of the sites, it appears that foreign journalists are also targeted. Press releases are often placed on the websites in an effort to get the organization's point of view into the traditional media. The detailed background information is also very useful for international reporters. One of Hezbollah's sites specifically addresses journalists, inviting them to interact with the organization's press office via-email.

- *Enemy publics.* Efforts to reach enemy publics (i.e., citizens of the states against which the terrorists are fighting) are not as clearly apparent from the content of many sites. However, some sites do seem to make an effort to demoralize the enemy by threatening attacks and by fostering feelings of guilt about the enemy's conduct and motives. In the process, they also seek to stimulate public debate in their enemies' states, to change public opinion, and to weaken public support for the governing regime.

How Terrorists Use the Internet

We have identified eight different, albeit sometimes overlapping, ways in which contemporary terrorists use the Internet. Some of these parallel the uses to which everyone puts the Internet—information gathering, for instance. Some resemble the uses made of the medium by traditional political organizations—for example, raising funds and disseminating propaganda. Others, however, are much more unusual and distinctive—for instance, hiding instructions, manuals, and directions in coded messages or encrypted files.

Psychological Warfare

Terrorism has often been conceptualized as a form of psychological warfare, and certainly terrorists have sought to wage such a campaign through the Internet. There are several ways for terrorists to do so. For instance, they can use the Internet to spread disinformation, to deliver threats intended to distill fear and helplessness, and to disseminate horrific images of recent actions, such as the brutal murder of the American journalist Daniel Pearl by his captors, a videotape of which was replayed on several terrorist websites. Terrorists can also launch psychological attacks through cyberterrorism, or, more accurately, through creating the fear of cyberterrorism. "Cyberfear" is generated when concern about what a computer attack *could* do (for example, bringing down airliners by disabling air traffic control systems, or disrupting national economies by wrecking the computerized systems that regulate stock markets) is amplified until the public believes that an attack *will* happen. The Internet—an uncensored medium that carries stories, pictures, threats, or messages regardless of their validity or potential impact—is peculiarly well suited to allowing even a small group to amplify its message and exaggerate its importance and the threat it poses.

Al Qaeda combines multimedia propaganda and advanced communication technologies to create a very sophisticated form of psychological warfare. Osama bin Laden and his followers concentrate their propaganda efforts on the Internet, where visitors to al Qaeda's numerous websites and to the sites of sympathetic, aboveground organizations can access prerecorded videotapes and audiotapes, CD-ROMs, DVDs, photographs, and announcements. Despite the massive onslaught it has sustained in recent years—the arrests and deaths of many of its members, the dismantling of its operational bases and training camps in Afghanistan, and the smashing of its bases in the Far East—al Qaeda has been able to conduct an impressive scare campaign. Since September 11, 2001, the organization has festooned its websites with a string of announcements of an impending "Large attack" on U.S. targets. These warnings have received considerable media coverage, which has helped to generate a widespread sense of dread and insecurity among audiences throughout the world and especially within the United States.

Interestingly, al Qaeda has consistently claimed on its websites that the destruction of the World Trade Center has inflicted psychological damage, as well as concrete damage, on the U.S. economy. The attacks on the Twin Towers are depicted as an assault on the trademark of the U.S. economy, and evidence of their effectiveness is seen in the weakening of the dollar, the decline of the U.S. stock market after 9/11, and a supposed loss of confidence in the U.S. economy both within the United States and elsewhere. Parallels are drawn with the decline and ultimate demise of the Soviet Union. One of bin Laden's recent publications, posted on the web, declared that "America is in retreat by the Grace of Almighty and economic attrition is continuing up to today. But it needs further blows. The young men need to seek out the nodes of the American economy and strike the enemy's nodes."

Publicity and Propaganda

The Internet has significantly expanded the opportunities for terrorists to secure publicity. Until the advent of the Internet, terrorists' hopes of winning publicity for their causes and activities depended on attracting the attention of television, radio, or the print media. These traditional media have "selection thresholds" (multistage processes of editorial selection) that terrorists often cannot reach. No such thresholds, of course, exist on the terrorists' own websites. The fact that many terrorists now have direct control over the content of their message offers further opportunities to shape how they are perceived by different target audiences and to manipulate their own image and the image of their enemies.

As noted earlier, most terrorist sites do not celebrate their violent activities. Instead, regardless of the terrorists' agendas, motives, and location, most sites emphasize two issues: the restrictions placed on freedom of expression and the plight of comrades who are now political prisoners. These issues resonate powerfully with their own supporters and are also calculated to elicit sympathy from Western audiences that cherish freedom of expression and frown on measures to silence political opposition. Enemy publics, too, may be targets for these complaints insofar as the terrorists, by emphasizing the antidemocratic nature of the steps taken against them, try to create feelings of unease and shame among their foes. The terrorists' protest at being muzzled, it may be noted, is particularly well suited to the Internet, which for many users is *the* symbol of free, unfettered, and uncensored communication.

Terrorist sites commonly employ three rhetorical structures, all used to justify their reliance on violence. The first one is the claim that the terrorists have no choice other than to turn to violence. Violence is presented as a necessity foisted upon the weak as the only means with which to respond to an oppressive enemy. While the sites avoid mentioning how the terrorists victimize others, the forceful actions of the governments and regimes that combat the terrorists are heavily emphasized and characterized with terms such as "slaughter," "murder," and "genocide." The terrorist organization is depicted as constantly persecuted, its leaders subject to assassination attempts and its supporters massacred, its freedom of expression curtailed, and its adherents arrested. This tactic, which portrays the organization as small, weak, and hunted down by a strong power or a strong state, turns the terrorists into the underdog.

A second rhetorical structure related to the legitimacy of the use of violence is the demonizing and delegitimization of the enemy. The members of the movement or organization are presented as freedom fighters, forced against their will to use violence because a ruthless enemy is crushing the rights and dignity of their people or group. The enemy of the movement or the organization is the real terrorist, many sites insist: "Our violence is tiny in comparison to his aggression" is a common argument. Terrorist rhetoric tries to shift the responsibility for violence from the terrorist to the adversary, which is accused of displaying its brutality, inhumanity, and immorality.

A third rhetorical device is to make extensive use of the language of nonviolence in an attempt to counter the terrorists' violent image. Although these are violent organizations, many of their sites claim that they seek peaceful solutions, that their ultimate aim is a diplomatic settlement achieved through negotiation and international pressure on a repressive government.

Data Mining

The Internet may be viewed as a vast digital library. The World Wide Web alone offers about a billion pages of information, much of it free—and much of it of interest to terrorist organizations. Terrorists, for instance, can learn from the Internet a wide variety of details about targets such as transportation facilities, nuclear power plants, public buildings, airports, and ports, and even about counterterrorism measures. Dan Verton, in his book *Black Ice: The Invisible Threat of Cyberterrorism* (2003), explains that "al-Qaeda cells now operate with the assistance of large databases containing details of potential targets in the U.S. They use the Internet to collect intelligence on those targets, especially critical economic nodes, and modern software enables them to study structural weaknesses in facilities as well as predict the cascading failure effect of attacking certain systems." According to Secretary of Defense Donald Rumsfeld, speaking on January 15, 2003, an al Qaeda training manual recovered in Afghanistan tells its readers, "Using public sources openly and without resorting to illegal means, it is possible to gather at least 80 percent of all information required about the enemy."

The website operated by the Muslim Hackers Club (a group that U.S. security agencies believe aims to develop software tools with which to launch cyberattacks) has featured links to U.S. sites that purport to disclose sensitive information such as code names and radio frequencies used by the U.S. Secret Service. The same website offers tutorials in creating and spreading viruses, devising hacking stratagems, sabotaging networks, and developing codes; it also provides links to other militant Islamic and terrorist web addresses. Specific targets that al Qaeda-related websites have discussed include the Centers for Disease Control and Prevention in Atlanta; FedWire, the money-movement clearing system maintained by the Federal Reserve Board; and facilities controlling the flow of information over the Internet. Like many other Internet users, terrorists have access not only to maps and diagrams of potential targets but also to imaging data on those same facilities and networks that may reveal counterterrorist activities at a target site. One captured al Qaeda computer contained engineering and structural features of a dam, which had been downloaded from the Internet and which would enable al Qaeda engineers and planners to simulate catastrophic failures. In other captured computers, U.S. investigators found evidence that al Qaeda operators spent time on sites that offer software and programming instructions for the digital switches that run power, water, transportation, and communications grids.

Numerous tools are available to facilitate such data collection, including search engines, e-mail distribution lists, and chat rooms and discussion groups. Many websites offer their own search tools for extracting information from databases on their sites. Word searches of online newspapers and journals can likewise generate information of use to terrorists; some of this information may also be available in the traditional media, but online searching capabilities allow terrorists to capture it anonymously and with very little effort or expense.

Fundraising

Like many other political organizations, terrorist groups use the Internet to raise funds. Al Qaeda, for instance, has always depended heavily on donations, and its global fundraising network is built upon a foundation of charities, nongovernmental organizations, and other financial institutions that use websites and Internet-based chat rooms and forums. The Sunni extremist group Hizb al-Tahrir uses an integrated web of Internet sites, stretching from Europe to Africa, which asks supporters to assist the effort by giving money and encouraging others to donate to the cause of jihad. Banking information, including the numbers of accounts into which donations can be deposited, is provided on a site based in Germany. The fighters in the Russian breakaway republic of Chechnya have likewise used the Internet to publicize the numbers of bank accounts to which sympathizers can contribute. (One of these Chechen bank accounts is located in Sacramento, California.) The IRA's website contains a page on which visitors can make credit card donations.

Internet user demographics (culled, for instance, from personal information entered in online questionnaires and order forms) allow terrorists to identify users with sympathy for a particular cause or issue. These individuals are then asked to make donations, typically through e-mails sent by a front group (i.e., an organization broadly supportive of the terrorists' aims but operating publicly and legally and usually having no direct ties to the terrorist organization). For instance, money benefiting Hamas has been collected via the website of a Texas-based charity, the Holy Land Foundation for Relief and Development (HLF). The U.S. government seized the assets of HLF in December 2001 because of its ties to Hamas. The U.S. government has also frozen the assets of three seemingly legitimate charities that use the Internet to raise money—the Benevolence International Foundation, the Global Relief Foundation, and the Al-Haramain Foundation—because of evidence that those charities have funneled money to al Qaeda.

In another example, in January 2004, a federal grand jury in Idaho charged a Saudi graduate student with conspiring to help terrorist organizations wage jihad by using the Internet to raise funds, field recruits, and locate prospective U.S. targets—military and civilian—in the Middle East. Sami Omar Hussayen, a doctoral candidate in computer science in a University of Idaho program sponsored—ironically—by the National Security Agency, was accused of creating websites and an e-mail group that disseminated messages from him and two radical clerics in Saudi Arabia that supported jihad.

Recruitment and Mobilization

The Internet can be used not only to solicit donations from sympathizers but also to recruit and mobilize supporters to play a more active role in support of terrorist activities or causes. In addition to seeking converts by using the full panoply of website technologies (audio, digital video, etc.) to enhance the presentation of their message, terrorist organizations capture information about the users who browse their websites. Users who seem most interested in the organization's cause or well suited to carrying out its work are then contacted. Recruiters may also use more interactive Internet technology to roam online chat rooms and cybercafes, looking for receptive members of the public, particularly young people. Electronic bulletin boards and user nets (issue-specific chat rooms and bulletins) can also serve as vehicles for reaching out to potential recruits.

Some would-be recruits, it may be noted, use the Internet to advertise themselves to terrorist organizations. In 1995, as reported by Verton in *Black Ice,* Ziyad Khalil enrolled as a computer science major at Columbia College in Missouri. He also became a Muslim activist on the campus, developing links to several radical groups and operating a website that supported Hamas. Thanks in large part to his Internet activities, he came to the attention of bin Laden and his lieutenants. Khalil became al Qaeda's procurement officer in the United States, arranging purchases of satellite telephones, computers, and other electronic surveillance technologies and helping bin Laden communicate with his followers and officers.

More typically, however, terrorist organizations go looking for recruits rather than waiting for them to present themselves. The SITE Institute, a Washington, D.C.-based terrorism research group that monitors al Qaeda's Internet communications, has provided chilling details of a high-tech recruitment drive launched in 2003 to recruit fighters to travel to Iraq and attack U.S. and coalition forces there. Potential recruits are bombarded with religious decrees and anti-American propaganda, provided with training manuals on how to be a terrorist, and—as they are led through a maze of secret chat rooms—given specific instructions on how to make the journey to Iraq. In one particularly graphic exchange in a secret al Qaeda chat room in early September 2003 an unknown Islamic fanatic, with the user name "Redemption Is Close," writes, "Brothers, how do I go to Iraq for Jihad? Are there any army camps and is there someone who commands there?" Four days later he gets a reply from "Merciless Terrorist." "Dear Brother, the road is wide open for you—there are many groups, go look for someone you trust, join him, he will be the protector of the Iraqi regions and with the help of Allah you will become one of the Mujahidin." "Redemption

Is Close" then presses for more specific information on how he can wage jihad in Iraq. "Merciless Terrorist" sends him a propaganda video and instructs him to download software called Pal Talk, which enables users to speak to each other on the Internet without fear of being monitored.

Many terrorist websites stop short of enlisting recruits for violent action but they do encourage supporters to show their commitment to the cause in other tangible ways. "How can I help the struggle: A few suggestions," runs a heading on the Kahane Lives website; "Action alert: What you can do" is a feature on the Shining Path's website. The power of the Internet to mobilize activists is illustrated by the response to the arrest of Abdullah Ocalan, leader of the Kurdish terrorist group the PKK. When Turkish forces arrested Ocalan, tens of thousands of Kurds around the world responded with demonstrations within a matter of hours—thanks to sympathetic websites urging supporters to protest.

Networking

Many terrorist groups, among them Hamas and al Qaeda, have undergone a transformation from strictly hierarchical organizations with designated leaders to affiliations of semi-independent cells that have no single commanding hierarchy. Through the use of the Internet, these loosely interconnected groups are able to maintain contact with one another—and with members of other terrorist groups. In the future, terrorists are increasingly likely to be organized in a more decentralized manner, with arrays of transnational groups linked by the Internet and communicating and coordinating horizontally rather than vertically.

Several reasons explain why modern communication technologies, especially computer-mediated communications, are so useful for terrorists in establishing and maintaining networks. First, new technologies have greatly reduced transmission time, enabling dispersed organizational actors to communicate swiftly and to coordinate effectively. Second, new technologies have significantly reduced the cost of communication. Third, by integrating computing with communications, they have substantially increased the variety and complexity of the information that can be shared.

The Internet connects not only members of the same terrorist organizations but also members of different groups. For instance, dozens of sites exist that express support for terrorism conducted in the name of jihad. These sites and related forums permit terrorists in places such as Chechnya, Palestine, Indonesia, Afghanistan, Turkey, Iraq, Malaysia, the Philippines, and Lebanon to exchange not only ideas and suggestions but also practical information about how to build bombs, establish terror cells, and carry out attacks.

Sharing Information

The World Wide Web is home to dozens of sites that provide information on how to build chemical and explosive weapons. Many of these sites post *The Terrorist's Handbook* and *The Anarchist Cookbook,* two well-known manuals that offer detailed instructions on how to construct a wide range of bombs. Another manual, *The Mujahadeen Poisons Handbook,* written by Abdel-Aziz in 1996 and "published" on the official Hamas website, details in twenty-three pages how to prepare various homemade poisons, poisonous gases, and other deadly materials for use in terrorist attacks. A much larger manual, nicknamed "The Encyclopedia of Jihad" and prepared by al Qaeda, runs to thousands of pages; distributed through the Internet, it offers detailed instructions on how to establish an underground organization and execute attacks. One al Qaeda laptop found in Afghanistan had been used to make multiple visits to a French site run by the Société Anonyme (a self-described "fluctuating group of artists and theoreticians who work specifically on the relations between critical thinking and artistic practices"), which offers a two-volume *Sabotage Handbook* with sections on topics such as planning an assassination and antisurveillance methods.

This kind of information is sought out not just by sophisticated terrorist organizations but also by disaffected individuals prepared to use terrorist tactics to advance their idio-syncratic agendas. In 1999, for instance, a young man by the name of David Copeland planted nail bombs in three different areas of London: multiracial Brixton, the largely Bangladeshi community of Brick Lane, and the gay quarter in Soho. Over the course of three weeks, he killed 3 people and injured 139. At his trial, he revealed that he had learned his deadly techniques from the Internet, downloading *The Terrorist's Handbook* and *How to Make Bombs: Book Two*. Both titles are still easily accessible. A search for the keywords "terrorist" and "handbook" on the Google search engine found nearly four thousand matches that included references to guidebooks and manuals. One site gives instructions on how to acquire ammonium nitrate, Copeland's "first choice" of explosive material.

In Finland in 2002, a brilliant chemistry student who called himself "RC" discussed bomb-making techniques with other enthusiasts on a Finish Internet website devoted to bombs and explosives. Sometimes he posted queries on topics such as manufacturing nerve gas at home. Often he traded information with the site's moderator, whose messages carried a picture of his own face superimposed on Osama bin Laden's body, complete with turban and beard. Then RC set off a bomb that killed seven people, including himself, in a crowded shopping mall. The website frequented by RC, known as the Home Chemistry Forum, was shut down by its sponsor, a computer magazine. But a backup copy was immediately posted again on a read-only basis.

Planning and Coordination

Terrorists use the Internet not only to learn how to build bombs but also to plan and coordinate specific attacks. Al Qaeda operatives relied heavily on the Internet in planning and coordinating the September 11 attacks. Thousands of encrypted messages that had been posted in a password-protected area of a website were found by federal officials on the computer of arrested al Qaeda terrorist Abu Zubaydah, who reportedly masterminded the September 11 attacks. The first messages found on Zubaydah's computer were dated May 2001 and the last were sent on September 9, 2001. The frequency of the messages was highest in August 2001. To preserve their anonymity, the al Qaeda terrorists used the Internet in public places and sent messages via public e-mail. Some of the September 11 hijackers communicated using free web-based e-mail accounts.

Hamas activists in the Middle East, for example, use chat rooms to plan operations and operatives exchange e-mail to coordinate actions across Gaza, the West Bank, Lebanon, and Israel. Instructions in the form of maps, photographs, directions, and technical details of how to use explosives are often disguised by means of steganography, which involves hiding messages inside graphic files. Sometimes, however, instructions are delivered concealed in only the simplest of codes. Mohammed Atta's final message to the other eighteen terrorists who carried out the attacks of 9/11 is reported to have read: "The semester begins in three more weeks. We've obtained 19 confirmations for studies in the faculty of law, the faculty of urban planning, the faculty of fine arts, and the faculty of engineering." (The reference to the various faculties was apparently the code for the buildings targeted in the attacks.)

Since 9/11, U.S. security agencies have monitored a number of websites that they believe are linked to al Qaeda and appear to contain elements of cyberplanning (e.g., directions for operatives, information for supporters and activists, calls for action, threats, and links to other websites):

- alneda.com, which, until it was closed down in 2002, is said by U.S. officials to have contained encrypted information to direct al Qaeda members to more secure sites, featured international news about al Qaeda, and published a variety of articles, books, and fatwas (the latter typically declaring war on the United States, Christianity, or Judaism);

- assam.com, which served as a mouthpiece for jihad in Afghanistan, Chechnya, and Palestine;

- almuhrajiroun.com, which in the late 1990s and early 2000s urged sympathizers to assassinate Pakistani president Pervez Musharraf;

- qassam.net, a site that U.S. officials claim is linked not only to al Qaeda but also to Hamas;

- jihadunspun.net, which offered a thirty-six-minute video of Osama bin Laden lecturing, preaching, and making threats;

- 7hj.7hj.com, which aimed to teach visitors how to hack into Internet networks and how to infect government and corporate websites with "worms" and viruses;

- aloswa.org, which featured quotations from bin Laden and religious legal rulings justifying the attacks of 9/11 and other assaults on the West;

- drasat.com, run (some experts suspect) by a fictional institution called the Islamic Studies and Research Center and reported to be the most credible of dozens of Islamist sites posting al Qaeda news; and

- jehad.net, alsaha.com, and islammemo.com, which are alleged to have posted al Qaeda statements as well as calls for action and directions for operatives.

Conclusion

In a briefing given in late September 2001, Ronald Dick, assistant director of the FBI and head of the United States National Infrastructure Protection Center (NIPC), told reporters that the hijackers of 9/11 had used the Internet, and "used it well." Since 9/11, terrorists have only sharpened their Internet skills and increased their web presence. Today, terrorists of very different ideological persuasions—Islamist, Marxist, nationalist, separatist, racist—have learned many of the same lessons about how to make the most of the

Internet. The great virtues of the Internet—ease of access, lack of regulation, vast potential audiences, fast flow of information, and so forth—have been turned to the advantage of groups committed to terrorizing societies to achieve their goals.

How should those societies respond? This is not the place to attempt anything like a definitive answer, but two things seem clear. First, we must become better informed about the uses to which terrorists put the Internet and better able to monitor their activities. As noted at the outset of this report, journalists, scholars, policymakers, and even security agencies have tended to focus on the exaggerated threat of cyberterrorism and paid insufficient attention to the more routine uses made of the Internet. Those uses are numerous and, from the terrorists' perspective, invaluable. Hence, it is imperative that security agencies continue to improve their ability to study and monitor terrorist activities on the Internet and explore measures to limit the usability of this medium by modern terrorists.

Second, while we must thus better defend our societies against terrorism, we must not in the process erode the very qualities and values that make our societies worth defending. The Internet is in many ways an almost perfect embodiment of the democratic ideals of free speech and open communication; it is a marketplace of ideas unlike any that has existed before. Unfortunately, as this report has shown, the freedom offered by the Internet is vulnerable to abuse from groups that, paradoxically, are themselves often hostile to uncensored thought and expression. But if, fearful of further terrorist attacks, we circumscribe our own freedom to use the Internet, then we hand the terrorists a victory and deal democracy a blow. We must not forget that the fear that terrorism inflicts has in the past been manipulated by politicians to pass legislation that undermines individual rights and liberties. The use of advanced techniques to monitor, search, track, and analyze communications carries inherent dangers. Although such technologies might prove very helpful in the fight against cyberterrorism and Internet-savvy terrorists, they would also hand participating governments, especially authoritarian governments and agencies with little public accountability, tools with which to violate civil liberties domestically and abroad. It does take much imagination to recognize that the long-term implications could be profound and damaging for democracies and their values, adding a heavy price in terms of diminished civil liberties to the high toll exacted by terrorism itself.

Of Related Interest

A number of other publications from the United States Institute of Peace address issues related to terrorism and to the Internet and other forms of information technology. Note: Most of our reports can be downloaded from our website at www.usip.org/reports.

Recent Special Reports on Terrorism

- *Terrorism in the Horn of Africa* (Special Report 113, January 2004)
- *Global Terrorism after the Iraq War* (Special Report 111, October 2003)
- *The Diplomacy of Counterterrorism: Lessons Learned, Ignored, and Disputed* (Special Report 80, January 2002)
- For terrorism and counterterrorism links, visit www.usip.org/library/topics/terrorism.html.

Recent Reports from the Virtual Diplomacy Initiative

- *Creating a Common Communications Culture: Interoperability in Crisis Management* (January 2004)
- *Net Diplomacy I (Beyond Foreign Ministries), II (Beyond Old Borders), and III (2015 and Beyond)* (August 2002)
- *Information Technology and Peace Support Operations* (July 2002)
- For more resources, visit www.usip.org/virtualdiplomacy/index.html.

Gabriel Weimann is professor of communication at Haifa University, where he has taught since 1984. Dr. Weimann is a prolific analyst of terrorism and the mass media, and his publications include five books and more than 100 book chapters and articles. From 2003 to 2004, Dr. Weimann was a senior fellow at the United States Institute of Peace.

Chapter 7

The Challenges of Terrorism
to a Free Society

In Chapter 7, the authors explore the tragedies of September 11 as a cornerstone—on how the events of a single day can focus new light on America's stature in the world, and how the tragedies that occurred in the space of a few hours have caused a deep ripple effect in the nation's government and its policy-making efforts. In particular, the United States is grappling with the challenges of terrorism to a free society.

Richard K. Betts maps out the landscape, explaining why terror can be an effective means against a nation as powerful as the United States, why such tactics have an impact despite a significant power imbalance. "American global privacy is one of the causes of this war," he writes. It is not just the way the United States and its moves are perceived by certain parties around the world: "Remaking the world in the Western image is what Americans assume to be just, natural, and desirable, indeed in only a matter of time. But that presumption is precisely what energizes many terrorists' hatred," writes Betts, but it is also the perception here at home. Betts discusses the tactics and countermeasures of this situation, when "intense political grievance and gross imbalance of power" become an explosive equation for terror.

At a time when nations are under the threat of terrorist actions, timely intelligence collection is central to any successful counterterrorism strategy. Bruce Hoffman examines the more difficult questions that Western democracies are grappling with in regard to limits of interrogations. "The struggles against Osama bin Laden and his minions will rely on good intelligence," writes Hoffman, but the experiences of other countries, fighting similar conflicts against similar enemies, suggest that "Americans still do not appreciate the enormously difficult—and morally complex—problem that the imperative to gather 'good intelligence' entails." Hoffman cites scenarios, both fictional and real, about those who have been responsible for information gathering in times of crises, and the unsavory but perhaps necessary measures they have taken. They act in times when extraordinary circumstances create extraordinary pressure to deliver results.

Military expert Rob de Wijk asserts that "the struggle against insurgents made clear the urgent need to refocus and restructure the way the United States and its allies think about and plan to wage military counterinsurgency operations." In his article, de Wijk explores the limits of military power and why the West does not appear to be capable of dealing with insurgencies. According to de Wijk, the United States requires a new approach and new assets: developing irregular forces that are well-practiced in guerilla tactics and asymmetrical retaliation; strengthening both special operations forces and human intelligence capabilities; abandoning some beliefs about traditional warfare; and sharpening the skills of coercive diplomacy, when dealing with states. Finally, de Wijk delves into the cultural aspect of the new war, of which a central component is "the campaign to win the support of the populace of the opponent . . . In other words, the United States and its allies must wage a battle for the hearts and minds of the people . . . in the Islamic world."

Finally, Richard H. Shultz Jr. describes the processes and decisions that went into not deploying our special operations forces against terrorists prior to 9/11. This article is not only a poignant reminder of how bureaucratic inertia in a democracy can affect the execution of a military strategy as well as a historical examination of past events, but it is also an important statement about how we must think about the future—about how the will to win a war must be present across all instruments of national power.

Richard K. Betts, 2002

The Soft Underbelly of American Primacy: Tactical Advantages of Terror

In given conditions, action and reaction can be ridiculously out of proportion. . . .
One can obtain results monstrously in excess of the effort. . . . Let's consider this auto
smash-up. . . . The driver lost control at high speed while swiping at a wasp which had
flown in through a window and was buzzing around his face. . . . The weight of a wasp
is under half an ounce. Compared with a human being, the wasp's size is minute, its
strength negligible. Its sole armament is a tiny syringe holding a drop of irritant, formic
acid. . . . Nevertheless, that wasp killed four big men and converted a large, powerful
car into a heap of scrap.

—Eric Frank Russell[1]

To grasp some implications of the new first priority in U.S. foreign policy, it is necessary to understand the connections among three things: the imbalance of power between terrorist groups and counterterrorist governments; the reasons that groups choose terror tactics; and the operational advantage of attack over defense in the interactions of terrorists and their opponents. On September 11, 2001, Americans were reminded that the overweening power that they had taken for granted over the past dozen years is not the same as omnipotence. What is less obvious but equally important is that the power is itself part of the cause of terrorist enmity and even a source of U.S. vulnerability.

There is no consensus on a definition of "terrorism," mainly because the term is so intensely pejorative.[2] When defined in terms of tactics, consistency falters, because most people can think of some "good" political cause that has used the tactics and whose purposes excuse them or at least warrant the group's designation as freedom fighters rather than terrorists. Israelis who call the Khobar Towers bombers of 1996 terrorists might reject that characterization for the Irgun, which did the same thing to the King David Hotel in 1946, or some Irish Americans would bridle at equating IRA bombings in Britain with Tamil Tiger bombings in Sri Lanka. Anticommunists labeled the Vietcong terrorists (because they engaged in combat out of uniform and assassinated local officials), but opponents of the Saigon government did not. Nevertheless, a functional definition is more sensible than one conditioned on the identity of the perpetrators. For this article, terrorism refers to the illegitimate, deliberate killing of civilians for purposes of punishment or coercion. This holds in abeyance the questions of whether deliberate killing of civilians can ever be legitimate or killing soldiers can be terrorism.

In any case, for all but the rare nihilistic psychopath, terror is a means, not an end in itself. Terror tactics are usually meant to serve a strategy of coercion.[3] They are a use of force designed to further some substantive aim. This is not always evident in the heat of rage felt by the victims of terror. Normal people find it hard to see instrumental reasoning behind an atrocity, especially when recognizing the political motives behind terrorism might seem to make its illegitimacy less extreme. Stripped of rhetoric, however, a war against terrorism must mean a war against political groups who choose terror as a tactic.

American global primacy is one of the causes of this war. It animates both the terrorists' purposes and their choice of tactics. To groups like al Qaeda, the United States is the enemy because American military power dominates their world, supports corrupt governments in their countries, and backs Israelis against Muslims; American cultural power insults their religion and pollutes their societies; and American economic power makes all these intrusions and desecrations possible. Japan, in contrast, is not high on al Qaeda's list of targets, because Japan's economic power does not make it a political, military, and cultural behemoth that penetrates their societies.

Political and cultural power makes the United States a target for those who blame it for their problems. At the same time, American economic and military power prevents them from resisting or retaliating against the United States on its own terms. To smite the only superpower requires unconventional modes of force and tactics that make the combat cost exchange ratio favorable to the attacker. This offers hope to the weak that they can work their will despite their overall deficit in power.

Primacy on the Cheap

The United States has enjoyed military and political primacy (or hegemony, unipolarity, or whatever term best connotes international dominance) for barely a dozen years. Those who focus on the economic dimension of international relations spoke of American hegemony much earlier, but observers of the strategic landscape never did. For those who focus on national security, the world before 1945 was multipolar, and the world of the cold war was bipolar. After 1945 the United States had exerted hegemony within the First World and for a while over the international economy. The strategic competition against the Second World, however, was seen as a titanic struggle between equal politicomilitary coalitions and a close-run thing until very near the end. Only the collapse of the Soviet pole, which coincided fortuitously with renewed relative strength of the American economy, marked the real arrival of U.S. global dominance.

The novelty of complete primacy may account for the thoughtless, indeed innocently arrogant way in which many Americans took its benefits for granted. Most who gave any thought to foreign policy came implicitly to regard the entire world after 1989 as they had regarded Western Europe and Japan during the past half-century: partners in principle but vassals in practice. The United States would lead the civilized community of nations in the expansion and consolidation of a liberal world order. Overwhelming military dominance was assumed to be secure and important across most of the domestic political spectrum.

Liberal multilateralists conflated U.S. primacy with political globalization, indeed, conflated ideological American nationalism with internationalist altruism.[4] They assumed that U.S. military power should be used to stabilize benighted countries and police international violence, albeit preferably camouflaged under the banner of institutions such as the United Nations, or at least NATO. They rejected the idea that illiberal impulses or movements represented more than a retreating challenge to the West's mission and its capacity to extend its values worldwide.

Conservative unilateralists assumed that unrivaled power relieved the United States of the need to cater to the demands of others. When America acted strategically abroad, others would have to join on its terms or be left out of the action. The United States should choose battles, avoid entanglements in incompetent polities, and let unfortunates stew in their own juice. For both multilateralists and nationalists, the issue was whether the United States would decide to make an effort for world welfare, not whether a strategic challenge could threaten its truly vital interests. (Colloquial depreciation of the adjective notwithstanding, literally vital U.S. interests are those necessary to life.)

For many, primacy was confused with invulnerability. American experts warned regularly of the danger of catastrophic terrorism—and Osama bin Ladin explicitly declared war on the United States in his *fatwa* of February 1998. But the warnings did not register seriously in the consciousness of most people. Even some national security experts felt stunned when the attacks occurred on September 11. Before then, the American military wanted nothing to do with the mission of "homeland defense," cited the Posse Comitatus act to suggest that military operations within U.S. borders would be improper, and argued that homeland defense should be the responsibility of civilian agencies or the National Guard. The services preferred to define the active forces' mission as fighting and winning the nation's wars—as if wars were naturally something that happened abroad—and homeland defense involved no more than law enforcement, managing relief operations in natural disasters, or intercepting ballistic missiles outside U.S. airspace. Only in America could the nation's armed forces think of direct defense of national territory as a distraction.

Being Number One seemed cheap. The United States could cut the military burden on the economy by half after the cold war (from 6 percent to 3 percent of GNP) yet still spend almost five times more than the combined military budgets of all potential enemy states. And this did not count the contributions of rich U.S. allies.[5] Of course the margin in dollar terms does not translate into a comparable quantitative margin in manpower or equipment, but that does not mean that a purchasing power parity estimate would reduce the implied gap in combat capability. The overwhelming qualitative superiority of U.S. conventional forces cuts in the other direction. Washington was also able to plan, organize, and fight a major war in 1991 at negligible cost in blood or treasure. Financially, nearly 90 percent of the bills for the war against Iraq were paid by allies. With fewer than 200 American battle deaths, the cost in blood was far lower than almost anyone had imagined it could be. Less than a decade later, Washington waged another war, over Kosovo, that cost no U.S. combat casualties at all.

In the one case where costs in casualties exceeded the apparent interests at stake—Somalia in 1993—Washington quickly stood down from the fight. This became the reference point for vulnerability: the failure of an operation that was small, far from home, and elective. Where material interests required strategic engagement, as in the oil-rich Persian Gulf, U.S. strategy could avoid costs by exploiting its huge advantage in conventional capability. Where conventional dominance proved less exploitable, as in Somalia, material interests did not require strategic engagement. Where the United States could not operate militarily with impunity, it could choose not to operate.

Finally, power made it possible to let moral interests override material interests where some Americans felt an intense moral concern, even if in doing so they claimed, dubiously, that the moral and material stakes coincided. To some extent this happened in Kosovo, although the decision to launch that war apparently flowed from overoptimism about how quickly a little bombing would lead Belgrade to capitulate. Most notably, it happened in the Arab-Israeli conflict. For more than three decades after the 1967 Six Day War, the United States supported Israel diplomatically, economically, and militarily against the Arabs, despite the fact that doing so put it on the side of a tiny country of a few million people with no oil, against more than ten times as many Arabs who controlled over a third of the world's oil reserves.

This policy was not just an effect of primacy, since the U.S.–Israel alignment began in the cold war. The salience of the moral motive was indicated by the fact that U.S. policy proceeded despite the fact that it helped give Moscow a purchase in major Arab capitals such as Cairo, Damascus, and Baghdad. Luckily for the United States, however, the largest amounts of oil remained under the control of the conservative Arab states of the Gulf. In this sense the hegemony of the United States within the anticommunist world helped account for the policy. That margin of power also relieved Washington of the need to make hard choices about disciplining its client. For decades the United States opposed Israeli settlement of the West Bank, terming the settlements illegal; yet in all that time the United States never demanded that Israel refrain from colonizing the West Bank as a condition for receiving U.S. economic and military aid.[6] Washington continued to bankroll Israel at a higher per capita rate than any other country in the world, a level that has been indispensable to Israel, providing aid over the years that now totals well over $100 billion in today's dollars.[7] Although this policy enraged some Arabs and irritated the rest, U.S. power was great enough that such international political costs did not outweigh the domestic political costs of insisting on Israeli compliance with U.S. policy.

Of course, far more than subsidizing Israeli occupation of Palestinian land was involved in the enmity of Islamist terrorists toward the United States. Many of the other explanations, however, presuppose U.S. global primacy. When American power becomes the arbiter of conflicts around the world, it makes itself the target for groups who come out on the short end of those conflicts.

Primacy and Asymmetric Warfare

The irrational evil of terrorism seems most obvious to the powerful. They are accustomed to getting their way with conventional applications of force and are not as accustomed as the powerless to thinking of terror as the only form of force that might make their enemies do their will. This is why terrorism is the premier form of "asymmetric warfare," the Pentagon buzzword for the type of threats likely to confront the United States in the post–cold war world.[8] Murderous tactics may become instrumentally appealing by default—when one party in a conflict lacks other military options.

Resort to terror is not necessarily limited to those facing far more powerful enemies. It can happen in a conventional war between great powers that becomes a total war, when the process of escalation pits whole societies against each other and shears away civilized restraints. That is something seldom seen, and last seen over a half-century ago. One does not need to accept the tendentious position that allied strategic bombing in World War II constituted terrorism to recognize that the British and Americans did systematically assault the urban population centers of Germany and Japan. They did so in large part because precision bombing of industrial facilities proved ineffective.[9] During the early phase of the cold war, in turn, U.S. nuclear strategy relied on plans to counter Soviet conventional attack on Western Europe with a comprehensive nuclear attack on communist countries that would have killed hundreds of millions. In the 1950s, Strategic Air Command targeteers even went out of their way to plan "bonus" damage by moving aim points for military targets so that blasts would destroy adjacent towns as well.[10] In both World War II and planning for World War III, the rationale was less to kill civilians per se than to wreck the enemy economies—although that was also one of Osama bin Laden's rationales for the attacks on the World Trade Center.[11] In short, the instrumental appeal of strategic attacks on noncombatants may be easier to understand when one considers that states with legitimate purposes have sometimes resorted to such a strategy. Such a double standard, relaxing prohibitions against targeting noncombatants for the side with legitimate purposes (one's own side), occurs most readily when the enemy is at least a peer competitor threatening vital interests. When one's own primacy is taken for granted, it is easier to revert to a single standard that puts all deliberate attacks against civilians beyond the pale.

In contrast to World War II, most wars are limited—or at least limited for the stronger side when power is grossly imbalanced. In such cases, using terror to coerce is likely to seem the only potentially effective use of force for the weaker side, which faces a choice between surrender or savagery. Radical Muslim zealots cannot expel American power with conventional military means, so they substitute clandestine means of delivery against military targets (such as the Khobar Towers barracks in Saudi Arabia) or high-profile political targets (embassies in Kenya and Tanzania). More than once the line has been attributed to terrorists, "If you will let us lease one of your B-52s, we will use that instead of a truck bomb." The hijacking and conversion of U.S. airliners into kamikazes was the most dramatic means of asymmetric attack.

Kamikaze hijacking also reflects an impressive capacity for strategic judo, the turning of the West's strength against itself.[12] The flip-side of a primacy that diffuses its power throughout the world is that advanced elements of that power become more accessible to its enemies. Nineteen men from technologically backward societies did not have to rely on home-grown instruments to devastate the Pentagon and World Trade Center. They used computers and modern financial procedures with facility, and they forcibly appropriated the aviation technology of the West and used it as a weapon. They not only rebelled against the "soft power" of the United States, they trumped it by hijacking the country's hard power.[13] They also exploited the characteristics of U.S. society associated with soft power—the liberalism, openness, and respect for privacy that allowed them to go freely about the business of preparing the attacks without observation by the state security apparatus. When soft power met the clash of civilizations, it proved too soft.

Strategic judo is also apparent in the way in which U.S. retaliation may compromise its own purpose. The counteroffensive after September 11 was necessary, if only to demonstrate to marginally motivated terrorists that they could not hope to strike the United States for free. The war in Afghanistan, however, does contribute to polarization in the Muslim world and to mobilization of potential terrorist recruits. U.S. leaders can say that they are not waging a war against Islam until they are blue in the face, but this will not convince Muslims who already distrust the United States. Success in deposing the Taliban may help U.S. policy by encouraging a bandwagon effect that rallies governments and moderates among the Muslim populace, but there will probably be as many who see the U.S. retaliation as confirming al Qaeda's diagnosis of American evil. Victory in Afghanistan and follow-up operations to prevent al Qaeda from relocating bases of operation to other countries will hurt that organization's capacity to act. The number of young zealots willing to emulate the "martyrdom operation" of the nineteen on September 11, however, is not likely to decline.

Advantage of Attack

The academic field of security studies has some reason to be embarrassed after September 11. Having focused primarily on great powers and interstate conflict, literature on terrorism was comparatively sparse; most of the good books were by policy analysts rather than theorists.[14] Indeed, science fiction has etched out the operational logic of terrorism as well as political science. Eric Frank Russell's 1957 novel, from which the epigraph to this article comes, vividly illustrates both the strategic aspirations of terrorists and the offense-dominant character of their tactics. It describes the dispatch of a single agent to one of many planets in the Sirian enemy's empire to stir up fear, confusion, and panic through a series of small covert activities with tremendous ripple effects. Matched with deceptions to make the disruptions appear to be part of a campaign by a big phantom rebel organization, the agent's modest actions divert large numbers of enemy policy and military personnel, cause economic dislocations and social unrest, and soften the planet up for invasion. Wasp agents are infiltrated into numerous planets, multiplying the effects. As the agent's handlers tell him, "The pot is coming slowly but surely to the boil. Their fleets are being widely dispersed, there are vast troop movements from their overcrowded home-system to the outer planets of their empire. They're gradually being chivvied into a fix. They can't hold what they've got without spreading all over it. The wider they spread the thinner they get. The thinner they get, the easier it is to bite lumps out of them."[15]

Fortunately al Qaeda and its ilk are not as wildly effective as Russell's wasp. By degree, however, the phenomenon is quite similar. Comparatively limited initiatives prompt tremendous and costly defensive reactions. On September 11 a small number of men killed 3,000 people and destroyed a huge portion of prime commercial real estate, part of the military's national nerve center, and four expensive aircraft. The ripple effects, however, multiplied those costs. A major part of the U.S. economy—air travel—shut down completely for days after September 11. Increased security measures dramatically increased the overall costs of the air travel system thereafter. Normal law enforcement activities of the Federal Bureau of Investigation were radically curtailed as legions of agents were transferred to counterterror tasks. Anxiety about the vulnerability of nuclear power plants, major bridges and tunnels, embassies abroad, and other high-value targets prompted plans for big investments in fortification of a wide array of facilities. A retaliatory war in Afghanistan ran at a cost of a couple billion dollars a month beyond the regular defense budget for months. In one study, the attacks on the World Trade Center and the Pentagon were estimated to cost the U.S. economy 1.8 million jobs.[16]

Or consider the results of a handful of 34-cent letters containing anthrax, probably sent by a single person. Besides killing several people, they contaminated a large portion of the postal system, paralyzed some mail delivery for long periods, provoked plans for huge expenditures on prophylactic irradiation equipment, shut down much of Capitol Hill for weeks, put thousands of people on a sixty-day regimen of strong antibiotics (potentially eroding the medical effectiveness of such antibiotics in future emergencies), and overloaded police and public health inspectors with false alarms. The September 11 attacks and the October anthrax attacks together probably cost the perpetrators less than a million dollars. If the cost of rebuilding and of defensive investments in reaction came to no more than $100 billion, the cost-exchange ratio would still be astronomically in favor of the attack over the defense.

Analysts in strategic studies did not fall down on the job completely before September 11. At least two old bodies of work help to illuminate the problem. One is the literature on guerrilla warfare and counterinsurgency, particularly prominent in the 1960s, and the other is the offense-defense theory that burgeoned in the 1980s. Both apply well to understanding patterns of engagement between terrorists and counterterrorists. Some of the axioms derived from the empirical cases in the counterinsurgency literature apply directly, and offense-defense theory applies indirectly.

Apart from the victims of guerrillas, few still identify irregular paramilitary warfare with terrorism (because the latter is illegitimate), but the two activities do overlap a great deal in their operational characteristics. Revolutionary or resistance movements in the preconventional phase of operations usually mix small-unit raids on isolated outposts of the government or occupying force with detonations and assassinations in urban areas to instill fear and discredit government power. The tactical logic of guerrilla operations resembles that in terrorist attacks: the weaker rebels use stealth and the cover of civilian society to concentrate their striking power against one among many of the stronger enemy's dispersed assets; they strike quickly and eliminate the target before the defender can move forces from other areas to respond; they melt back into civilian society to avoid detection and reconcentrate against another target. The government or occupier has far superior strength in terms of conventional military power, but cannot counterconcentrate in time because it has to defend all points, while the insurgent attacker can pick its targets at will.[17] The contest between insurgents and counterinsurgents is "tripartite," polarizing political alignments and gaining the support of *attentistes* or those in the middle. In today's principle counterterror campaign, one might say that the yet-unmobilized Muslim elites and masses of the Third World—those who were not already actively committed either to supporting Islamist radicalism or to combating it—are the target group in the middle. As Samuel Huntington noted, "a revolutionary war is a war of attrition."[18] As I believe Stanley Hoffman once said, in rebellions the insurgents win as long as they do not lose, and the government loses as long as it does not win. If al Qaeda-like groups can stay in the field indefinitely, they win.

Offense-defense theory applied nuclear deterrence concepts to assessing the stability of conventional military confrontations and focused on what conditions tended to give the attack or the defense the advantage in war.[19] There were many problems in the specification and application of the theory having to do with unsettled conceptualization of the offense-defense balance, problematic standards for measuring it, and inconsistent applications to different levels of warfare and diplomacy.[20] Offense-defense theory, which flourished when driven by the urge to find ways to stabilize the NATO-Warsaw Pact balance in Europe, has had little to say directly about unconventional war or terrorism. It actually applies more clearly, however, to this lower level of strategic competition (as well as to the higher level of nuclear war) than to the middle level of conventional military power. This is because the exchange ratio between opposing conventional forces of roughly similar size is very difficult to estimate, given the complex composition of modern military forces and uncertainty about their qualitative comparisons; but the exchange ratio in both nuclear and guerrilla combat is quite lopsided in favor of the attacker. Counterinsurgency folklore held that the government defenders need something on the order of a ten-to-one advantage over the guerrillas if they were to drive them from the field.

There has been much confusion about exactly how to define the offense-defense balance, but the essential idea is that some combinations of military technology, organization, and doctrine are proportionally more advantageous to the attack or to the defense when the two clash. "Proportionally" means that available instruments and circumstances of engagement give either the attack or the defense more bang for the buck, more efficient power out of the same level of resources. The notion of an offense-defense balance as something conceptually distinct from the balance of power means, however, that it cannot be identified with which side wins a battle or a war. Indeed, the offense-defense balance can favor the defense, while the attacker still wins, because its overall margin of superiority in power was too great, despite the defense's more efficient use of power. (I am told that the Finns had a saying in the Winter War of 1939–40: "One Finn is worth ten Russians, but what happens when the eleventh Russian comes?") Thus, to say that the offense-defense balance favors the offensive terrorists today against the defensive counterterrorists does not mean that the terrorists will prevail. It does mean that terrorists can fight far above their weight, that in most instances each competent terrorist will have much greater individual impact than each good counterterrorist, that each dollar invested in a terrorist plot will have a bigger payoff than each dollar expended on counterterrorism, and that only small numbers of competent terrorists need survive and operate to keep the threat to American society uncomfortably high.

In the competition between terrorists on the attack and Americans on the defense, the disadvantage of the defense is evident in the number of high-value potential targets that need protection. The United States has "almost 600,000 bridges, 170,000 water systems, more than 2,800 power plants (104 of them nuclear), 190,000 miles of interstate pipelines for natural gas, 463 skyscrapers . . . nearly 20,000 miles of border, airports, stadiums, train tracks."[21] All these usually represented American strength; after September 11 they also represent vulnerability:

> Suddenly guards were being posted at water reservoirs, outside power plants, and at bridges and tunnels. Maps of oil and gas lines were removed from the Internet. In Boston, a ship carrying liquefied natural gas, an important source of fuel for heating New England homes, was forbidden from entering the harbor because local fire officials feared that if it were targeted by a terrorist the resulting explosion could lay low much of the city's densely populated waterfront. An attack by a knife-wielding lunatic on the driver of a Florida-bound Greyhound bus led to the immediate cessation of that national bus service. . . . Agricultural crop-dusting planes were grounded out of a concern that they could be used to spread chemical or biological agents.[22]

Truly energetic defense measures do not only cost money in personnel and equipment for fortification, inspection, and enforcement; they may require repealing some of the very underpinnings of civilian economic efficiency associated with globalization. "The competitiveness of the U.S. economy and the quality of life of the American people rest on critical infrastructure that has become increasingly more concentrated, more interconnected, and more sophisticated. Almost entirely privately owned and operated, there is very little redundancy in this system."[23] This concentration increases the potential price of vulnerability to single attacks. Tighter inspection of cargoes coming across the Canadian border, for example, wrecks the "just-in-time" parts supply system of Michigan auto manufacturers. Companies that have invested in technology and infrastructure premised on unimpeded movement "may see their expected savings and efficiencies go up in smoke. Outsourcing contracts will have to be revisited and inventories will have to be rebuilt."[24] How many safety measures will suffice in improving airline security without making flying so inconvenient that the air travel industry never recovers as a profit-making enterprise? A few more shoe-bomb incidents, and Thomas Friedman's proposal to start an airline called "Naked Air—where the only thing you wear is a seat belt" becomes almost as plausible as it is ridiculous.[25]

The offense-dominant character of terrorism is implicit in mass detentions of Arab young men after September 11, and proposals for military tribunals that would compromise normal due process and weaken standard criminal justice presumptions in favor of the accused. The traditional liberal axiom that it is better to let a hundred guilty people go free than to convict one innocent reflects confidence in the strength of society's defenses—confidence that whatever additional crimes may be committed by the guilty who go free will not grossly outweigh the injustice done to innocents convicted, that one criminal who slips through the net will not go on to kill hundreds or thousands of innocents. Fear of terrorists plotting mass murder reversed that presumption and makes unjust incarceration of some innocents appear like unintended but expected collateral damage in wartime combat.

Offense-defense theory helps to visualize the problem. It does not help to provide attractive solutions, as its proponents believed it did during the cold war. Then offense-defense theory was popular because it seemed to offer a way to stabilize the East-West military confrontation. Mutual deterrence from the superpowers' confidence in their counteroffensive capability could substitute for defense at the nuclear level, and both sides' confidence in their conventional defenses could dampen either one's incentives to attack at that level. Little of this applies to counterterrorism. Both deterrence and defense are weaker strategies against terrorists than they were against communists.

Deterrence is still relevant for dealing with state terrorism; Saddam Hussein or Kim Jong-Il may hold back from striking the United States for fear of retaliation. Deterrence offers less confidence for preventing state sponsorship of terrorism; it did not stop the Taliban from hosting Osama bin Laden. It offers even less for holding at bay transnational groups like al Qaeda, which may lack a return address against which retaliation can be visited, or whose millennialist aims and religious convictions make them unafraid of retaliation. Defense, in turn, is better than a losing game only because the inadequacy of deterrence leaves no alternative.[26] Large investments in defense will produce appreciable reductions in vulnerability, but will not minimize vulnerability.

Deterrence and defense overlap in practice. The U.S. counteroffensive in Afghanistan constitutes retaliation, punishing the Taliban for shielding al Qaeda and sending a warning to other potential state sponsors. It is also active defense, whittling down the ranks of potential perpetrators by killing and capturing members of the Islamist international brigades committed to jihad against the United States. At this writing, the retaliatory function has been performed more effectively than the defensive, as the Taliban regime has been destroyed, but significant numbers of Arab Afghans and al Qaeda members appear to have escaped, perhaps to plot another day.

Given the limited efficacy of deterrence for modern counterterrorism, it remains an open question how much of a strategic success we should judge the impressive victory in Afghanistan to be. Major investments in passive defenses (airline security, border inspections, surveillance and searches for better intelligence, fortification of embassies, and so forth) are necessary, but will reduce vulnerability at a cost substantially greater than the costs that competent terrorist organizations will have to bear to probe and occasionally circumvent them. The cost-exchange ratio for direct defense is probably worse than the legendary 10:1 ratio for successful counterinsurgency, and certainly worse than the more than 3:1 ratio that Robert McNamara's analysts calculated for the advantage of offensive missile investments over antiballistic missile systems—an advantage that many then and since have thought warranted accepting a situation of mutual vulnerability to assured destruction.[27]

The less prepared we are to undertake appropriate programs and the more false starts and confusions that are likely, the worse the cost-exchange ratio will be in the short term. The public health system, law enforcement organizations, and state and local bureaucrats are still feeling their way on what, how, and in which sequence to boost efforts. The U.S. military will also have to overcome the natural and powerful effects of inertia and attachments to old self-conceptions and preferred programs and modes of operation. Impulses to repackage old priorities in the rhetoric of new needs will further dilute effectiveness of countermeasures.

Nevertheless, given low confidence that deterrence can prevent terrorist attacks, major improvements in defenses make sense.[28] This is especially true because the resource base from which the United States can draw is vastly larger than that available to transnational terrorists. Al Qaeda may be rich, but it does not have the treasury of a great power. Primacy has a soft underbelly, but it is far better to have primacy than to face it. Even at an unfavorable cost-exchange ratio, a number of defensive measures are a sensible investment, but only because our overwhelming advantage in resources means that we are not constrained to focus solely on the most efficient countermeasures.

At the same time, as long as terrorist groups remain potent and active, a serious war plan must exploit efficient strategies as well. Given the offense-dominant nature of terrorist operations, this means emphasis on counteroffensive operations. When terrorists or their support structures can be found and fixed, preemptive and preventive attacks will accomplish more against them, dollar for dollar, than the investment in passive defenses. Which is the more efficient use of resources: to kill or capture a cell of terrorists who might otherwise choose at any time to strike whichever set of targets on our side is unguarded, or to try to guard all potential targets? Here the dangers are that counteroffensive operations could prove counterproductive. This could easily happen if they degenerate into brutalities and breaches of laws of war that make counterterrorism begin to appear morally equivalent to its target, sapping political support and driving the uncommitted to the other side in the process of polarization that war makes inevitable. Whether counteroffensive operations gain more in eliminating perpetrators than they lose in alienating and mobilizing "swing voters" in the world of Muslim opinion depends on how successful the operations are in neutralizing significant numbers of the organizers of terrorist groups, as opposed to foot soldiers, and in doing so with minimal collateral damage.

Primacy and Policy

September 11 reminded those Americans with a rosy view that not all the world sees U.S. primacy as benign, that primacy does not guarantee security, and that security may now entail some retreats from the economic globalization that some had identified with American leadership. Primacy has two edges—dominance and provocation. Americans can enjoy the dominance but must recognize the risks it evokes. For terrorists who want to bring the United States down, U.S. strategic primacy is a formidable challenge, but one that can be overcome. On balance, Americans have overestimated the benefits of primacy, and terrorists have underestimated them.

For those who see a connection between American interventionism, cultural expansiveness, and support of Israel on one hand, and the rage of groups that turn to terrorism on the other, primacy may seem more trouble than it's worth, and the need to revise policies may seem more pressing. But most Americans have so far preferred the complacent and gluttonous form of primacy to the ascetic, blithely accepting steadily growing dependence on Persian Gulf oil that could be limited by compromises in lifestyle and unconventional energy policies. There have been no groundswells to get rid of SUVs, support the Palestinians, or refrain from promoting Western standards of democracy and human rights in societies where some elements see them as aggression.

There is little evidence that any appreciable number of Americans, elite or mass, see our primacy as provoking terrorism. Rather, most see it as a condition we can choose at will to exploit or not. So U.S. foreign policy has exercised primacy in a muscular way in byways of the post-cold war world when intervention seemed cheap, but not when doing good deeds threatened to be costly. Power has allowed Washington to play simultaneously the roles of mediator and partisan supporter in the Arab-Israeli conflict. For a dozen years nothing, with the near exception of the Kosovo War, suggested that primacy could not get us out of whatever problems it generated.

How far the United States goes to adapt to the second edge of primacy probably depends on whether stunning damage is inflicted by terrorists again, or September 11 gradually fades into history. If al Qaeda and its ilk are crippled, and some years pass without more catastrophic attacks on U.S. home territory, scar tissue will harden on the soft underbelly, and the positive view of primacy will be reinforced. If the war against terrorism falters, however, and the exercise of power fails to prevent more big incidents, the consensus will crack. Then more extreme policy options will get more attention. Retrenchment and retreat will look more appealing to some, who may believe the words of Sheik Salman al-Awdah, a dissident Saudi religious scholar, who said, "If America just let well enough alone, and got out of their obligations overseas . . . no one would bother them."[29]

More likely, however, would be a more violent reaction. There is no reason to assume that terrorist enemies would let America off the hook if it retreated and would not remain as implacable as ever. Facing inability to suppress the threat through normal combat, covert action, and diplomatic pressure, many Americans would consider escalation to more ferocious strategies. In recent decades, the march of liberal legalism has delegitimized tactics and brutalities that once were accepted, but this delegitimation has occurred only in the context of fundamental security and dominance of the Western powers, not in a situation where they felt under supreme threat. In a situation of that sort, it is foolhardy to assume that American strategy would never turn to tactics like those used against Japanese and German civilians, or by the civilized French in the *sale guerre* in Algeria, or by the Russians in Chechnya in hopes of effectively eradicating terrorists despite astronomical damage to the civilian societies within which they lurk.

This possibility would highlight how terrorists have underestimated American primacy. There is much evidence that even in the age of unipolarity, opponents have mistakenly seen the United States as a paper tiger. For some reason—perhaps wishfully selective perception—they tend to see retreats from Vietnam, Beirut, and Somalia as typical weakness of American will, instead of considering decisive exercises of power in Panama, Kuwait, Kosovo, and now, Afghanistan.[30] As Osama bin Laden said in 1997, the United States left Somalia "after claiming that they were the largest power on earth. They left after some resistance from powerless, poor, unarmed people whose only weapon is the belief in Allah. . . . The Americans ran away."[31]

This apparently common view among those with an interest in pinning America's ears back ignores the difference between elective uses of force and desperate ones. The United States retreated where it ran into trouble helping others, not where it was saving itself. Unlike interventions of the 1990s in Africa, the Balkans, or Haiti, counterterrorism is not charity. With vital material interests involved, primacy unleashed may prove fearsomely potent.

Most likely America will see neither absolute victory nor abject failure in the war against terror. Then how long will a campaign of attrition last and stay popular? If the United States wants a strategy to cut the roots of terrorism, rather than just the branches, will American power be used effectively against the roots? Perhaps, but probably not. This depends of course on which of many possible root causes are at issue. Ironically, one problem is that American primacy itself is one of those roots.

A common assertion is that Third World poverty generates terrorism. While this must certainly be a contributing cause in many cases, there is little evidence that it is either a necessary or sufficient condition. Fundamentalist madrassas might not be full to overflowing if young Muslims had ample opportunities to make money, but the fifteen Saudis who hijacked the flights on September 11 were from one of the most affluent of Muslim countries. No U.S. policy could ever hope to make most incubators of terrorism less poor than Saudi Arabia. Iran, the biggest state sponsor of anti-American terrorism, is also better off than most Muslim countries. Poverty is endemic in the Third World, but terrorism is not.

Even if endemic poverty were the cause, the solution would not be obvious. Globalization generates stratification, creating winners and losers, as efficient societies with capitalist cultures move ahead and others fall behind, or as elite enclaves in some societies prosper while the masses stagnate. Moreover, even vastly increased U.S. development assistance would be spread thin if all poor countries are assumed to be incubators of terrorism. And what are the odds that U.S. intervention with economic aid would significantly reduce poverty? Successes in prompting dramatic economic development by outside assistance in the Third World have occurred, but they are the exception more than the rule.

The most virulent anti-American terrorist threats, however, do not emerge randomly in poor societies. They grow out of a few regions and are concentrated overwhelmingly in a few religiously motivated groups. These reflect political causes—ideological, nationalist, or transnational cultural impulses to militant mobilization—more than economic causes. Economic development in an area where the political and religious impulses remain unresolved could serve to improve the resource base for terrorism rather than undercut it.

A strategy of terrorism is most likely to flow from the coincidence of two conditions: intense political grievance and gross imbalance of power. Either one without the other is likely to produce either peace or conventional war. Peace is probable if power is imbalanced but grievance is modest; the weaker party is likely to live with the grievance. In that situation, conventional use of force appears to offer no hope of victory, while the righteous indignation is not great enough to overcome normal inhibitions against murderous tactics. Conventional war is probable if grievance is intense but power is more evenly balanced, since successful use of respectable forms of force appears possible.[32] Under American primacy, candidates for terrorism suffer from grossly inferior power by definition. This should focus attention on the political causes of their grievance.

How are political root causes addressed? At other times in history we have succeeded in fostering congenial revolutions—especially in the end of the cold war, as the collapse of the Second World heralded an End of History of sorts.[33] The problem now, however, is the rebellion of anti-Western zealots against the secularist end of history. Remaking the world in the Western image is what Americans assume to be just, natural, and desirable, indeed only a matter of time. But that presumption is precisely what energizes many terrorists' hatred. Secular Western liberalism is not their salvation, but their scourge. Primacy could, paradoxically, remain both the solution and the problem for a long time.*

Richard K. Betts is the director of the Institute of War and Peace Studies and the director of the International Security Policy Program in the School of International and Public Affairs at Columbia University. Dr. Betts was a senior fellow and research associate at the Brookings Institution in Washington D.C. He has served on the National Commission on Terrorism and the U.S. Senate Select Committee on Intelligence. A specialist on national security policy and military strategy, Dr. Betts is author, editor and co-author of several books on the subject, including *The Irony of Vietnam: The System Worked* (1979), which won the Woodrow Wilson Prize, and the recently published *Enemies of Intelligence: Knowledge and Power in American National Security.*

*The author thanks Robert Jervis for comments on the first draft.

Notes

1. William Wolf in Eric Frank Russell, *Wasp* (London: Victor Gollancz, 2000, originally published 1957), 7.
2. "The word has become a political label rather than an analytical concept." Martha Crenshaw, *Terrorism and International Cooperation* (New York: Institute for East-West Security Studies, 1989), 5.
3. For a survey of types, see Christopher C. Harmon, "Five Strategies of Terrorism," *Small Wars and Insurgencies* 12 (Autumn 2001).
4. Rationalization of national power as altruism resembles the thinking about benign Pax Britannica in the Crowe Memorandum: ". . . the national policy of the insular and naval State is so directed as to harmonize with the general desires and ideals common to all mankind, and more particularly . . . is closely identified with the primary and vital interests of a majority, or as many as possible, of the other nations. . . . England, more than any other non-insular Power, has a direct and positive interest in the maintenance of the independence of nations, and therefore must be the natural enemy of any country threatening the independence of others, and the natural protector of the weaker communities." Eyre Crowe, "Memorandum on the Present State of British Relations with France and Germany," 1 January 1907, in G. P. Gooch and Harold Temperley, eds., *British Documents on the Origins of the War, 1898–1914*, vol. 3: *The Testing of the Entente, 1904–6* (London: His Majesty's Stationery Office, 1928), 402–403.
5. At the end of the twentieth century, the combined military budgets of China, Russia, Iraq, Yugoslavia (Serbia), North Korea, Iran, Libya, Cuba, Afghanistan, and Sudan added up to no more than $60 billion. *The Military Balance, 1999–2000* (London: International Institute for Strategic Studies, 1999), 102, 112, 132, 133, 159, 186, 275.
6. Washington certainly did exert pressure on Israel at some times. The administration of Bush the Elder, for example, threatened to withhold loans for housing construction, but this was a marginal portion of total U.S. aid. There was never a threat to cut off the basic annual maintenance payment of several billion dollars to which Israel became accustomed decades ago.
7. The United States has also given aid to friendly Arab governments—huge amounts to Egypt and some to Jordan. This does not counterbalance the aid to Israel, however, in terms of effects on opinions of strongly anti-Israeli Arabs. Islamists see the regimes in Cairo and Amman as American toadies, complicit in betrayal of the Palestinians.
8. Theoretically, this was anticipated by Samuel P. Huntington in his 1962 analysis of the differences between symmetrical intergovernmental war and asymmetrical antigovernmental war. "Patterns of Violence in World Politics" in Huntington, ed., *Changing Patterns of Military Politics* (New York: Free Press of Glencoe, 1962), 19–21). Some of Huntington's analysis of insurrectionary warfare within states applies as well to transnational terrorism.
9. The Royal Air Force gave up on precision bombing early and focused deliberately on night bombing of German cities, while the Americans continued to try precision daylight bombing. Firestorms in Hamburg, Darmstadt, and Dresden, and less incendiary attacks on other cities, killed several hundred thousand German civilians. Over Japan, the United States quickly gave up attempts at precision bombing when weather made it impractical and deliberately resorted to an incendiary campaign that burned most Japanese cities to the ground and killed at least 300,000 civilians (and perhaps more than half a million) well before the nuclear attacks on Hiroshima and Nagasaki, which killed another 200,000. Michael S. Sherry, *The Rise of American Air Power: The Creation of Armageddon* (New Haven: Yale University Press, 1987), 260, 413–43.
10. The threat of deliberate nuclear escalation remained the bedrock of NATO doctrine throughout the cold war, but after the Kennedy administration, the flexible response doctrine made it conditional and included options for nuclear first-use that did not involve deliberate targeting of population centers. In the Eisenhower administration, however, all-out attack on the Soviet bloc's cities was integral to plans for defense of Western Europe against Soviet armored divisions.

11. In a videotape months after the attacks, bin Laden said, "These blessed strikes showed clearly that this arrogant power, America, rests on a powerful but precarious economy, which rapidly crumbled . . . the global economy based on usury, which America uses along with its military might to impose infidelity and humiliation on oppressed people, can easily crumble. . . . Hit the economy, which is the basis of military might. If their economy is finished, they will become too busy to enslave oppressed people. . . . America is in decline; the economic drain is continuing but more strikes are required and the youths must strike the key sectors of the American economy." Videotape excerpts quoted in "Bin Laden's Words: 'America Is in Decline,' the Leader of Al Qaeda Says," *New York Times,* 28 December 2001.

12. This is similar to the concept of political judo discussed in Samuel L. Popkin, "Pacification: Politics and the Village," *Asian Survey* 10 (August 1970); and Popkin, "Internal Conflicts— South Vietnam" in Kenneth N. Waltz and Steven Spiegel, eds., *Conflict in World Politics* (Cambridge, MA: Winthrop, 1971).

13. Soft power is "indirect or cooptive" and "can rest on the attraction of one's ideas or on the ability to set the political agenda in a way that shapes the preferences that others express." It "tends to be associated with intangible power resources such as culture, ideology, and institutions." Joseph S. Nye, Jr., "The Changing Nature of World Power," *Political Science Quarterly,* 105 (Summer 1990): 181. See also Nye, *Bound to Lead: The Changing Nature of American Power* (New York: Basic Books, 1990).

14. For example, Bruce Hoffmann, *Inside Terrorism* (New York: Columbia University Press, 1998); Paul R. Pillar, *Terrorism and American Foreign Policy* (Washington, DC: Brookings Institution Press, 2001); Richard A. Falkenrath, Robert D. Newman, and Bradley S. Thayer, *America's Achilles' Heel: Nuclear, Biological, and Chemical Terrorism and Covert Attack* (Cambridge: MIT Press, 1998).

15. Russell, *Wasp,* 64. The ripple effects include aspects of strategic judo. Creating a phony rebel organization leads the enemy security apparatus to turn on its own people. "If some Sirians could be given the full-time job of hunting down and garroting other Sirians, and if other Sirians could be given the full-time job of dodging or shooting down the garroters, then a distant and different life form would be saved a few unpleasant chores. . . . Doubtless the military would provide a personal bodyguard for every big wheel on Jaimec; that alone would pin down a regiment." Ibid., 26, 103.

16. Study by the Milken Institute discussed in "The Economics: Attacks May Cost 1.8 Million Jobs," *New York Times,* 13 January 2002.

17. Mao Tse-Tung's classic tracts are canonical background. For example, "Problems of Strategy in China's Revolutionary War" (especially chap. 5) in *Selected Works of Mao Tse-Tung* (Beijing: Foreign Languages Press, 1967), vol. i, and "Problems of Strategy in Guerrilla War Against Japan," in *Selected Works,* vol. ii (1967). Much of the Western analytical literature grew out of British experience in the Malayan Emergency and France's role in Indochina and Algeria. For example, Franklin Mark Osanka, ed., *Modern Guerrilla Warfare* (New York: Free Press, 1962); Gerard Chaliand, ed., *Guerrilla Strategies: An Historical Anthology from the Long March to Afghanistan* (Berkeley: University of California Press, 1982); Roger Trinquier, *Modern Warfare: A French View of Counterinsurgency,* Daniel Lee, trans. (New York: Praeger, 1964); David Galula, *Counterinsurgency Warfare: Theory and Practice* (New York: Praeger, 1964); Sir Robert Thompson, *Defeating Communist Insurgency* (New York: Praeger, 1966); Richard L. Clutterbuck, *The Long Long War: Counterinsurgency in Malaya and Vietnam* (New York: Praeger, 1966); George Armstrong Kelly, *Lost Soldiers: The French Army and Empire in Crisis, 1947–1962* (Cambridge: MIT Press, 1965), chaps. 5–7, 9–10; W. P. Davison, *Some Observations on Viet Cong Operations in the Villages* (Santa Monica, CA: RAND Corporation, 1968). See also Douglas S. Blaufarb, *The Counter-Insurgency Era: U.S. Doctrine and Performance, 1950 to the Present* (New York: Free Press, 1977); D. Michael Shafer, *Deadly Paradigms: The Failure of U.S. Counterinsurgency Policy* (Princeton: Princeton University Press, 1988); Timothy J. Lomperis, *From People's War to People's Rule: Insurgency, Intervention, and the Lessons of Vietnam* (Chapel Hill: University of North Carolina Press, 1996).

18. Huntington, "Patterns of Violence in World Politics," 20–27.

19. George Quester, *Offense and Defense in the International System,* 2nd ed. (New Brunswick, NJ: Transaction Books, 1988); Robert Jervis, "Cooperation Under the Security Dilemma," *World Politics* 30 (January 1978); Jack L. Snyder, *The Ideology of the Offensive: Military Decision Making and the Disasters of 1914* (Ithaca, NY: Cornell University Press, 1984); Stephen Van Evera, *Causes of War: Power and the Roots of Conflict* (Ithaca, NY: Cornell University Press, 1999), chaps. 6–8; Charles L. Glaser and Chaim Kaufmann, "What Is the Offense-Defense Balance and Can We Measure It?" *International Security* 22 (Spring 1998).

20. For critiques, see Jack S. Levy, "The Offensive/Defensive Balance of Military Technology," *International Studies Quarterly* 28 (June 1984); Scott D. Sagan, "1914 Revisited," *International Security* 11 (Fall 1986); Jonathan Shimshoni, "Technology, Military Advantage, and World War I: A Case for Military Entrepreneurship," *International Security* 15 (Winter 1990/91); Richard K. Betts, "Must War Find a Way?" *International Security* 24 (Fall 1999); Betts, "Conventional Deterrence: Predictive Uncertainty and Policy Confidence," *World Politics* 37 (January 1985).

21. Jerry Schwartz, Associated Press dispatch, 6 October 2001, quoted in Brian Reich, "Strength in the Face of Terror: A Comparison of United States and International Efforts to Provide Homeland Security" (unpublished paper, Columbia University, December 2001), 5.

22. Stephen E. Flynn, "The Unguarded Homeland" in James F. Hoge, Jr. and Gideon Rose, eds., *How Did This Happen? Terrorism and the New War* (New York: PublicAffairs, 2001), 185.

23. Ibid., 185–186.

24. Ibid., 193–194.

25. Thomas L. Friedman, "Naked Air," *New York Times,* 26 December 2001.

26. See Steven Simon and Daniel Benjamin, "America and the New Terrorism," *Survival* 42 (Spring 2000); 59, 66–69, 74.

27. Estimates in the 1960s indicated that even combining ABM systems with counterforce strikes and fallout shelters, the United States would have to counter each Soviet dollar spent on ICBMs with three U.S. dollars to protect 70 percent of the industry, assuming highly ABMs (.8 kill probability). To protect up to 80 percent of the population, far higher ratios would be necessary. Fred Kaplan, *The Wizards of Armageddon* (New York: Simon and Schuster, 1983), 321–324.

28. For an appropriate list of recommendations see *Countering the Changing Threat of International Terrorism,* Report of the National Commission on Terrorism, Pursuant to Public Law 277, 105th Congress (Washington, DC, June 2000). This report holds up very well in light of September 11.

29. Quoted in Douglas Jehl, "After Prison, a Saudi Sheik Tempers His Words," *New York Times,* 27 December 2001.

30. See data in the study by Barry M. Blechman and Tamara Cofman Wittes, "Defining Moment: The Threat and Use of Force in American Foreign Policy," *Political Science Quarterly* 114 (Spring 1999).

31. Quoted in Simon and Benjamin, "America and the New Terrorism," 69.

32. On why power imbalance is conducive to peace and parity to war, see Geoffrey Blainey, *The Causes of War,* 3rd. ed. (New York: Free Press, 1988), chap. 8.

33. Francis Fukuyama's thesis was widely misunderstood and caricatured. He noted that the Third World remained mired in history and that some developments could lead to restarting history. For the First World, the defeated Second World, and even some parts of the Third World, however, the triumph of Western liberalism could reasonably be seen by those who believe in its worth (as should Americans) as the final stage of evolution through fundamentally different forms of political and economic organization of societies. See Fukuyama, "The End of History?" *National Interest* no. 16 (Summer 1989); and Fukuyama, *The End of History and the Last Man* (New York: Free Press, 1992).

Bruce Hoffman, 2002

A Nasty Business

Intelligence is capital," Colonel Yves Godard liked to say. And Godard undeniably knew
what he was talking about. He had fought both as a guerrilla in the French Resistance during World War II and against guerrillas in Indochina, as the commander of a covert special
operations unit. As the chief of staff of the elite 10th Para Division, Godard was one of the
architects of the French counterterrorist strategy that won the Battle of Algiers, in 1957. To
him, information was the sine qua non for victory. It had to be zealously collected, meticulously analyzed, rapidly disseminated, and efficaciously acted on. Without it no antiterrorist
operation could succeed. As the United States prosecutes its global war against terrorism,
Godard's dictum has acquired new relevance. Indeed, as is now constantly said, success in
the struggle against Osama bin Laden and his minions will depend on good intelligence.
But the experiences of other countries, fighting similar conflicts against similar enemies,
suggest that Americans still do not appreciate the enormously difficult—and morally
complex—problem that the imperative to gather "good intelligence" entails.

The challenge that security forces and militaries the world over have faced in
countering terrorism is how to obtain information about an enigmatic enemy who fights
unconventionally and operates in a highly amenable environment where he typically is
indistinguishable from the civilian populace. The differences between police officers and
soldiers in training and approach, coupled with the fact that most military forces are generally uncomfortable with, and inadequately prepared for, counterterrorist operations,
strengthens this challenge. Military forces in such unfamiliar settings must learn to acquire
intelligence by methods markedly different from those to which they are accustomed. The
most "actionable," and therefore effective, information in this environment is discerned not
from orders of battle, visual satellite transmissions of opposing force positions, or intercepted signals but from human intelligence gathered mostly from the indigenous population. The police, specifically trained to interact with the public, typically have better access
than the military to what are called human intelligence sources. Indeed, good police work
depends on informers, undercover agents, and the apprehension and interrogation of terrorists and suspected terrorists, who provide the additional information critical to destroying
terrorist organizations. Many today who argue reflexively and sanctimoniously that the
United States should not "over-react" by over-militarizing the "war" against terrorism assert that such a conflict should be largely a police, not a military, endeavor. Although true,
this line of argument usually overlooks the uncomfortable fact that, historically, "good" police work against terrorists has of necessity involved nasty and brutish means. Rarely have
the importance of intelligence and the unpleasant ways in which it must often be obtained
been better or more clearly elucidated than in the 1966 movie *The Battle of Algiers*. In an
early scene in the film the main protagonist, the French paratroop commander, Lieutenant

Colonel Mathieu (who is actually a composite of Yves Godard and two other senior French army officers who fought in the Battle of Algiers), explains to his men that the "military aspect is secondary." He says, "More immediate is the police work involved. I know you don't like hearing that, but it indicates exactly the kind of job we have to do."

I have long told soldiers, spies, and students to watch *The Battle of Algiers* if they want to understand how to fight terrorism. Indeed, the movie was required viewing for the graduate course I taught for five years on terrorism and the liberal state, which considered the difficulties democracies face in countering terrorism. The seminar at which the movie was shown regularly provoked the most intense and passionate discussions of the semester. To anyone who has seen *The Battle of Algiers,* this is not surprising. The late Pauline Kael, doyenne of American film critics, seemed still enraptured seven years after its original release when she described *The Battle of Algiers* in a 900-word review as "an epic in the form of a 'created documentary'"; "the one great revolutionary 'sell' of modern times"; and the "most impassioned, most astute call to revolution ever." The best reviews, however, have come from terrorists—members of the IRA; the Tamil Tigers, in Sri Lanka; and 1960s African-American revolutionaries—who have assiduously studied it. At a time when the U.S. Army has enlisted Hollywood screenwriters to help plot scenarios of future terrorist attacks, learning about the difficulties of fighting terrorism from a movie that terrorists themselves have studied doesn't seem far-fetched.

In fact, the film represents the apotheosis of cinema verite. That it has a verisimilitude unique among onscreen portrayals of terrorism is a tribute to its director, Gillo Pontecorvo, and its cast—many of whose members reprised the real-life roles they had played actually fighting for the liberation of their country, a decade before. Pontecorvo, too, had personal experience with the kinds of situations he filmed: during World War II he had commanded a partisan brigade in Milan. Indeed, the Italian filmmaker was so concerned about not giving audiences a false impression of authenticity that he inserted a clarification in the movie's opening frames: "This dramatic re-enactment of The Battle of Algiers contains NOT ONE FOOT of Newsreel or Documentary Film." The movie accordingly possesses an uncommon gravitas that immediately draws viewers into the story. Like many of the best films, it is about a search—in this case for the intelligence on which French paratroops deployed in Algiers depended to defeat and destroy the terrorists of the National Liberation Front (FLN). "To know them means we can eliminate them," Mathieu explains to his men in the scene referred to above. "For this we need information. The method: interrogation." In Mathieu's universe there is no question of ends not justifying means: the Paras need intelligence, and they will obtain it however they can. "To succumb to humane considerations," he concludes, "only leads to hopeless chaos."

The events depicted on celluloid closely parallel those of history. In 1957 the city of Algiers was the center of a life-and-death struggle between the FLN and the French authorities. On one side were the terrorists, embodied both on screen and in real life in Ali La Pointe, a petty thief turned terrorist cell leader; on the other stood the army, specifically the elite 10th Para Division, under General Jacques Massu, another commander on whom the Mathieu composite was based. Veterans of the war to preserve France's control of Indochina, Massu and his senior officers—Godard included—prided themselves on having acquired a thorough understanding of terrorism and revolutionary warfare, and how to counter both. Victory, they were convinced, would depend on the acquisition of intelligence. Their method was to build a meticulously detailed picture of the FLN's apparatus in Algiers which would help the French home in on the terrorist campaign's masterminds Ali La Pointe and his bin Laden, Saadi Yacef (who played himself in the film). This approach, which is explicated in one of the film's most riveting scenes, resulted in what the Francophile British historian Alistair Horne, in his masterpiece on the conflict, *A Savage War of Peace,* called a "complex organigramme [that] began to take shape on a large blackboard, a kind of skeleton pyramid in which, as each fresh piece of information came from the interrogation centres, another [terrorist] name (and not always necessarily the right name) would be entered." That this system proved tactically effective there is no doubt. The problem was that it thoroughly depended on, and therefore actively encouraged, widespread human-rights abuses, including torture.

Massu and his men—like their celluloid counterparts—were not particularly concerned about this. They justified their means of obtaining intelligence with utilitarian, cost-benefit arguments. Extraordinary measures were legitimized by extraordinary circumstances. The exculpatory philosophy embraced by the French Paras is best summed up by Massu's uncompromising belief that "the innocent [that is, the next victims of terrorist attacks] deserve more protection than the guilty." The approach, however, at least strategically, was counterproductive. Its sheer brutality alienated the native Algerian Muslim community. Hitherto mostly passive or apathetic, that community was now driven into the arms of the FLN, swelling the organization's ranks and increasing its popular support. Public opinion in France was similarly outraged, weakening support for the continuing struggle and creating profound fissures in French civil-military relations. The army's achievement in the city was therefore bought at the cost of eventual political defeat. Five years after victory in Algiers the French withdrew from Algeria and granted the country its independence. But Massu remained forever unrepentant: he insisted that the ends justified the means used to destroy the FLN's urban insurrection. The battle was won, lives were saved, and the indiscriminate bombing campaign that had terrorized the city was ended. To Massu, that was all that mattered. To his mind, respect for the rule of law and the niceties of legal procedure were irrelevant given the crisis situation enveloping Algeria in 1957. As anachronistic as France's attempt to hold on to this last vestige of its colonial past may now appear, its jettisoning of such long-standing and cherished notions as habeas corpus and due process, enshrined in the ethos of the liberal state, underscores how the intelligence requirements of counterterrorism can suddenly take precedence over democratic ideals.

Although it is tempting to dismiss the French army's resort to torture in Algeria as the desperate excess of a moribund colonial power, the fundamental message that only information can effectively counter terrorism is timeless. Equally disturbing and instructive, however, are the lengths to which security and military forces need often resort to get that information. I learned this some years ago, on a research trip to Sri Lanka. The setting—a swank oceanfront hotel in Colombo, a refreshingly cool breeze coming off the ocean, a magnificent sunset on the horizon—could not have been further removed from the carnage and destruction that have afflicted that island country for the past eighteen years and have claimed the lives of more than 60,000 people. Arrayed against the democratically elected Sri Lankan government and its armed forces is perhaps the most ruthlessly efficient terrorist organization-cum-insurgent force in the world today: the Liberation Tigers of Tamil Eelam, known also by the acronym LTTE or simply as the Tamil Tigers. The Tigers are unique in the annals of terrorism and arguably eclipse even bin Laden's al Qaeda in professionalism, capability, and determination. They are believed to be the first nonstate group in history to stage a chemical-weapons attack when they deployed poison gas in a 1990 assault on a Sri Lankan military base—some five years before the nerve-gas attack on the Tokyo subway by the apocalyptic Japanese religious cult Aum Shinrikyo. Of greater relevance, perhaps, is the fact that at least a decade before the seaborne attack on the U.S.S. *Cole,* in Aden harbor, the LTTE's special suicide maritime unit, the Sea Tigers, had perfected the same tactics against the Sri Lankan navy. Moreover, the Tamil Tigers are believed to have developed their own embryonic air capability—designed to carry out attacks similar to those of September 11 (though with much smaller, noncommercial aircraft). The most feared Tiger unit, however, is the Black Tigers—the suicide cadre composed of the group's best-trained, most battle-hardened, and most zealous fighters. A partial list of their operations includes the assassination of the former Indian Prime Minister Rajiv Gandhi at a campaign stop in the Indian state of Tamil Nadu, in 1991; the assassination of Sri Lankan President Ranasinghe Premadasa, in 1993; the assassination of the presidential candidate Gamini Dissanayake, which also claimed the lives of fifty-four bystanders and injured about one hundred more, in 1994; the suicide truck bombing of the Central Bank of Sri Lanka, in 1996, which killed eighty-six people and wounded 1,400 others; and the attempt on the life of the current President of Sri Lanka, Chandrika Kumaratunga, in December of 1999. The powerful and much venerated leader of the LTTE is Velupillai Prabhakaran, who, like bin Laden, exercises a charismatic influence over his fighters. *The Battle of Algiers* is said to be one of Prabhakaran's favorite films.

I sat in that swank hotel drinking tea with a much decorated, battle-hardened Sri Lankan army officer charged with fighting the LTTE and protecting the lives of Colombo's citizens. I cannot use his real name, so I will call him Thomas. However, I had been told before our meeting, by the mutual friend—a former Sri Lankan intelligence officer who had also long fought the LTTE—who introduced us (and was present at our meeting), that Thomas had another name, one better known to his friends and enemies alike: Terminator. My friend explained how Thomas had acquired his sobriquet; it actually owed less to Arnold Schwarzenegger than to the merciless way in which he discharged his duties as an intelligence officer. This became clear to me during our conversation. "By going through the process of laws," Thomas patiently explained, as a parent or a teacher might speak to a bright yet uncomprehending child, "you cannot fight terrorism." Terrorism, he believed, could be fought only by thoroughly "terrorizing" the terrorists—that is, inflicting on them the same pain that they inflict on the innocent. Thomas had little confidence that I understood what he was saying. I was an academic, he said, with no actual experience of the life-and-death choices and the immense responsibility borne by those charged with protecting society from attack. Accordingly, he would give me an example of the split-second decisions he was called on to make. At the time, Colombo was on "code red" emergency status, because of intelligence that the LTTE was planning to embark on a campaign of bombing public gathering places and other civilian targets. Thomas's unit had apprehended three terrorists who, it suspected, had recently planted somewhere in the city a bomb that was then ticking away, the minutes counting down to catastrophe. The three men were brought before Thomas. He asked them where the bomb was. The terrorists—highly dedicated and steeled to resist interrogation—remained silent. Thomas asked the question again, advising them that if they did not tell him what he wanted to know, he would kill them. They were unmoved. So Thomas took his pistol from his gun belt, pointed it at the forehead of one of them, and shot him dead. The other two, he said, talked immediately; the bomb, which had been placed in a crowded railway station and set to explode during the evening rush hour, was found and defused, and countless lives were saved. On other occasions, Thomas said, similarly recalcitrant terrorists were brought before him. It was not surprising, he said, that they initially refused to talk; they were schooled to withstand harsh questioning and coercive pressure. No matter: a few drops of gasoline flicked into a plastic bag that is then placed over a terrorist's head and cinched tight around his neck with a web belt very quickly prompts a full explanation of the details of any planned attack.

I was looking pale and feeling a bit shaken as waiters in starched white jackets smartly cleared the china teapot and cups from the table, and Thomas rose to bid us good-bye and return to his work. He hadn't exulted in his explanations or revealed any joy or even a hint of pleasure in what he had to do. He had spoken throughout in a measured, somber, even reverential tone. He did not appear to be a sadist, or even manifestly homicidal. (And not a year has passed since our meeting when Thomas has failed to send me an unusually kind Christmas card.) In his view, as in Massu's, the innocent had more rights than the guilty. He, too, believed that extraordinary circumstances required extraordinary measures. Thomas didn't think I understood—or, more to the point, thought I never could understand. I am not fighting on the front lines of this battle; I don't have the responsibility for protecting society that he does. He was right: I couldn't possibly understand. But since September 11, and especially every morning after I read the "Portraits of Grief" page in *The New York Times,* I am constantly reminded of Thomas—of the difficulties of fighting terrorism and of the challenges of protecting not only the innocent but an entire society and way of life. I am never bidden to condone, much less advocate, torture. But as I look at the snapshots and the lives of the victims recounted each day, and think how it will take almost a year to profile the approximately 5,000 people who perished on September 11, I recall the ruthless enemy that America faces, and I wonder about the lengths to which we may yet have to go to vanquish him.

The moral question of lengths and the broader issue of ends versus means are, of course, neither new nor unique to rearguard colonial conflicts of the 1950s or to the unrelenting carnage that has more recently been inflicted on a beautiful tropical island in the Indian Ocean. They are arguably no different from the stark choices that eventually confront any society threatened by an enveloping violence unlike anything it has seen before. For a brief period in the early and middle 1970s Britain, for example, had something of this experience—which may be why, among other reasons, Prime Minister Tony Blair and his country today stand as America's staunchest ally. The sectarian terrorist violence in Northern Ireland was at its height and had for the first time spilled into England in a particularly vicious and indiscriminate way. The views of a British army intelligence officer at the time, quoted by the journalist Desmond Hamill in his book *Pig in the Middle* (1985), reflect those of Thomas and Massu.

Naturally one worries—after all, one is inflicting pain and discomfort and indignity on other human beings . . . [but] society has got to find a way of protecting itself . . . and it can only do so if it has good information. If you have a close-knit society which doesn't give information then you've got to find ways of getting it. Now the softies of the world complain—but there is an awful lot of double talk about it. If there is to be discomfort and horror inflicted on a few, is this not preferred to the danger and horror being inflicted on perhaps a million people?

It is a question that even now, after September 11, many Americans would answer in the negative. But under extreme conditions and in desperate circumstances that, too, could dramatically change—much as everything else has so profoundly changed for us all since that morning. I recently discussed precisely this issue over the telephone with the same Sri Lankan friend who introduced me to Thomas years ago. I have never quite shaken my disquiet over my encounter with Thomas and over the issues he raised—issues that have now acquired an unsettling relevance. My friend sought to lend some perspective from his country's long experience in fighting terrorism. "There are not good people and bad people," he told me, "only good circumstances and bad circumstances. Sometimes in bad circumstances good people have to do bad things. I have done bad things, but these were in bad circumstances. I have no doubt that this was the right thing to do." In the quest for timely, "actionable" intelligence will the United States, too, have to do bad things—by resorting to measures that we would never have contemplated in a less exigent situation?

Bruce Hoffman is a professor of security studies at the Edmund A. Walsh School of Foreign Service at Georgetown University. Dr. Hoffman is the former Corporate Chair in Counter-Terrorism and Counter-Insurgency at the RAND Corporation, where he was also director of the Washington, DC office. He is editor of the journal *Conflict and Terrorism* and holds fellowships at the Combating Terrorism Center at West Point and the National Security Studies Center at Haifa University, Israel.

Rob de Wijk

The Limits of Military Power

Why the West Cannot Deal with Insurgencies

Defense planning had only fleetingly dealt with the threat of apocalyptic terrorism before September 11. Over the past six years, the United States and its Allies shifted its focus from conventional warfare to irregular challenges associated with international jihadism. Late 2001, a U.S.-led coalition removed the Taliban from power. In the spring of 2003 a U.S.-led intervention ousted Saddam Hussein. After the regime changes in Afghanistan and Iraq, Western forces became involved in a protracted counterinsurgency campaign. The result of this has been an attempt, both in the United States and in Europe, to relearn the lessons of counterinsurgency (COIN) operations. By 2007, despite efforts to develop strategy and doctrine to address these new challenges, coalition forces were unable to end the insurgencies and restore stability in Afghanistan and Iraq. After six years a comprehensive approach for dealing with the insurgency is still lacking, and it remains a priority today. In his September 2007 report on Afghanistan, U.N. Secretary General Ban Ki-Moon wrote that "the most urgent priority must be an effective, integrated civilian-military strategy and security plan for Afghanistan."[1] The struggle against insurgents made clear the urgent need to refocus and restructure the way the United States and its allies think about and plan to wage military COIN operations.

- First, something remains fundamentally wrong with the West's armed forces. Conceptually, many NATO member states focus on conventional warfare and territorial defense, but the new wars will be unconventional wars, requiring expeditionary armed forces.

- Second, contemporary concepts, such as limited collateral damage and proportionality, have little value when preparing for the new wars.

- Third, how concepts such as coercive diplomacy and coercion can be used effectively is unclear.

In sum, the United States and its allies face significant practical as well as conceptual challenges. The September 11 attacks made clear that terrorism no longer can be considered a tactical or local challenge, requiring cooperation between the national intelligence services and the police. The new terrorism is a strategic or international challenge, requiring international cooperation between intelligence services and armed forces. The insurgencies following the regime changes in Afghanistan and Iraq also raise questions about the West's ability to deal with the new threats. Afghanistan and Iraq define the West's ability to protect its interests in the future. If the West cannot deal with insurgencies, the best option is withdrawal after regime change. The new regime would be offered help for transforming the country, but if the next government is hostile to the West's interests as well, a new intervention will be carried out. Such a cynical strategy of coercion by punishment may be the result of failures in Afghanistan and Iraq, yet will be considered as a sign of Western failure. For the time being, muddling through is the only viable option. But meeting the challenges requires a new approach as well as new assets.

"Savage Warfare"

Western armed forces demonstrated their superiority clearly during the Gulf War in 1991, when, after the extensive use of airpower, U.S. ground forces gained a decisive victory over Iraq within 100 hours. In contrast to conventional warfare, which relies on technological capabilities—manned arms and standoff weaponry—to engage the enemy, terrorists fight unconventionally. Technology plays a supporting role at best, for personal protection, communications, and targeting. In the final analysis, however, successes depend on old-fashioned fighting skills and the use of knives or small-caliber arms in search-and-destroy operations.

In the case of conventional warfare, armies take and hold ground, air forces conduct strategic bombing operations and engage the enemy, and navies support land forces by conducting offshore attacks and cutting off lines of communications. This is the Western way of waging war. The new wars on terrorism, however, will have to deal with irregular forces that practice guerrilla tactics, instill panic, and retaliate asymmetrically—when, where, and how they choose.

Actually, referring to the military campaign now under way as the "new" war demonstrates little understanding of the history of warfare. In 1898, in *Lockhart's Advance Through Tirah,* Captain L. J. Shadwell wrote about "savage warfare" (that is, non-European warfare) "that differs from that of civilized people." Some areas in the world have not changed much since Shadwell's time. More than 100 years ago, he wrote:

> A frontier tribesman can live for days on the grain he carries with him, and other savages on a few dates; consequently no necessity exists for them to cover a line of communications. So nimble of foot, too, are they in their grass shoes, and so conversant with every goat-track in their mountains that they can retreat in any direction. This extraordinary mobility enables them to attack from any direction quite unexpectedly, and to disperse and disappear as rapidly as they came. For this reason the rear of a European force is as much exposed to attack as its front or flanks.[2]

In Afghanistan today, the biggest change is that army boots or Nikes have replaced "grass shoes." Furthermore, local fighters possess limited numbers of modern weapons systems, such as Stinger antiaircraft missiles, which were acquired during the 1980s when the United States considered Afghani freedom fighters who needed support in their struggle against Soviet occupation. The basic Afghani and Iraqi weapons "platform" is the pickup truck, which carries fighters armed with guns; in mountainous regions, the mule is still the most important mode of transportation.

In most Western countries, irregular warfare has always been considered "savage warfare," for which there is no preparation. Historically, the British and the Dutch, in particular, combatted insurgents quite successfully in their colonies. With the loss of Indonesia in the 1950s, the Dutch lost not only all their experience in waging this kind of war but also their mental preparedness for such action.

In drafting a new field manual on counterinsurgency and counterterrorism, the Netherlands army's staff utilized the old manuals that General Johannes van Heutsz used during the 1920s and 1930s, when he was combating insurgents and terrorists in what is now the Republic of Indonesia. Van Heutsz also reorganized his conventional ground forces to deal with the insurgents, creating small units of a dozen armed men to carry out search-and-destroy missions. This military action led to an episode that the Dutch do not want to repeat.

Today, the army's counterinsurgency operations could be perceived as war crimes. Because no distinction could be made between combatants and noncombatants, the Dutch burnt down entire villages in order to eliminate fighters' bases. For this reason, Secretary Rumsfeld argued that direct attacks on terrorists are useless; forces are required to "drain the swamp they live in."[3]

In October 2007 history repeated itself when The Netherlands was held responsible for the large number of civilian casualties inflicted during heavy fighting in the southern provinces of Afghanistan. Although investigations by the United Nations Assistance Mission in Afghanistan (UNAMA) did not accuse the Dutch of seriously violating international humanitarian law, they did conclude that the indiscriminate use of heavy artillery and fighter aircraft had resulted in unacceptably high number of civilian deaths. The issue at stake is how to fight insurgents that cannot be distinguished from civilians or use civilians as a shield. Proxy wars, the use of standoff weaponry, and aerial bombing will reduce the number of friendly casualties, but unavoidably increase the number of civilian victims.

In addition to consulting Van Heutsz's tactics, the Dutch used the British counterinsurgency manual, which is still considered the most detailed manual for this type of warfare. Of the former colonial powers, only the British have retained their historic knowledge of fighting COIN operations; at the same time, British forces have maintained the mental preparedness needed to carry out counterinsurgency operations.

In the United States a similar debate took place. The Americans left Vietnam with an improved understanding of and a distaste for counterinsurgency. The latter explains why COIN operations got little attention in subsequent Field Manuals. The Army's 1983 Field Manual (FM) 100-5 maintained that the AirLand Battle doctrine for conventional warfare applied equally to low-intensity conflict, including peace support operations, disaster relief, counterguerrilla warfare, and counterterrorist operations. The same assumptions were made by Field Manuals on Counterguerrilla Operations, Special Forces Operations and Low Intensity Operations. These assumption were wrong, because operations not only required a different doctrine, but different skills and different mind set as well. By 1990 Field Manuals no longer mentioned low-intensity warfare. The preferred terminology was now Operations Other Than War (OOTW). In 1994 FM 100-20 *Military Operations Other Than War,* replaced *Military Operations in Low Intensity Conflict.* But the attitude did not change. COIN operations were not considered "the real thing." This was reinforced by another assumption, namely that the actual COIN operation should be carried out by a host country. Doctrine assumed that U.S. combat forces would only be introduced into the insurgency if the host country failed. As a result armed forces were ill prepared for unconventional warfare in Afghanistan and Iraq. Moreover, its obsolete doctrine was designed around Mao's concept of rural "people's war," which differs conceptually from the challenge in Afghanistan and Iraq.

Lessons learned, however, were incorporated in a new Interim Army Field Manual on Counter Insurgency Operations (FMI 13-07.22). In the wording of the manual: "The stunning victory over Saddam Hussein's army in 2003 validated U.S. conventional force TTP, but the ensuing aftermath of instability has caused review of lessons from the Army's historical experience and those of the other services and multinational partners."

Indeed, Operations Enduring Freedom and Iraqi Freedom provided a fertile test ground. In Iraq, different types of war were fought in one and the same theatre. The third U.S. Infantry Division carried out conventional operations against regular Republican Guard Divisions deployed around Baghdad; in the northern Kurdish territories counterterror operations took place against the Ansar-al-Islam movement and their training camps in the mountains; in the south, especially in and around Basra, British and American forces were engaged in urban warfare; throughout the country, the Fedayeen Saddam militias were hunted down.

Nevertheless, the quick and decisive regime change together with few friendly losses and modest levels of collateral damage, surprised many. Although Saddam Hussein turned out to be an extremely incompetent strategist, the keys to success were joint operations combining precision air power, infantry, mechanized forces, marines, special operations forces, the use of innovative concepts such as Network Centric Warfare (NCW) and Effects Based Operations (EBO), and the application of new command, control, communication, and reconnaissance technologies. Networking of forces contributed to the tempo, which is fundamental to the success of military operations. The combination of intensive air strikes with the continuous employment of highly mobile, high-tech ground forces made it possible for relatively small forces to defeat larger ones.

Operation Iraqi Freedom made clear that American military force was developing into a more usable instrument for coercion. Most Europeans were not aware of the revolution in military affairs that took place in the United States. The revolution had led to a situation where everything that moves can be seen and hit. This new kind of warfare was truly "post-modern," because the colossal maneuvers of the traditional battlefields during were relegated to history.

Operation Iraqi Freedom made many Europeans also aware of the ever increasing transatlantic gap, not only in military technology, but in doctrine as well. Interoperability between European and American forces was jeopardized; joint and combined operations would no longer be possible. But following the American example could also make Europeans less reluctant to use force if necessary. As has been argued before, the European allies have limited capabilities for advanced expeditionary warfare, i.e., capabilities to conduct high-tempo, large-scale conventional and unconventional combat operations in distant parts of the world with minimal risk for friendly forces and acceptable levels of collateral damage. But the application of innovative concepts together with new technologies could make the European Union less reluctant to use force to achieve its foreign policy objectives.

The key issue, however, is that successful regime change could be followed by defeat during the stabilization phase. If a stabilization force is seen as an occupation force, the war will not stop with the regime change. On the contrary, it is just beginning. Due to disastrous experiences and acknowledgment that most wars will not be fought in a conventional manner, unconventional warfare and asymmetry have become established concepts. In addition, there is growing recognition that COIN operations are part of the broader concept of stabilization. Stabilization forces are likely to be deployed in a potentially hostile environment, and most likely will have to deal with "spoilers" or insurgents using asymmetrical techniques. Providing security in such an environment requires COIN operations as part of the overall stabilization effort.

Thus, stabilization is a challenging mix of counterinsurgency operations, peacekeeping, humanitarian aid, reconstruction, and transformation or state building, including efforts such as Security Sector Reform (SSR) and Demobilization, De-mining and Reconstruction (DDR). A new stabilization and transformation/reconstruction doctrine for fighting spoilers and state building in parallel is needed to spell out the precise interaction between these efforts. Such a doctrine should emphasize a broad and comprehensive approach, which combines the relevant elements of the interagency and is multinational at all levels. In Afghanistan, NATO experimented with concepts like "concerted planning and action," but had little support from other organizations such as the European Union. Thus, the stabilization operation remained largely a military effort and failed to win the hearts-and-minds of large segments of the populace.

Today, the West needs special and specialized forces to deal with irregular fighters such as terrorists; these forces are not available in large quantities. A distinction should be made here between special operations forces (SOF), which are used for covert or clandestine action, and specialized forces, which carry out specialized overt missions. The most famous of all SOF, Great Britain's Special Air Service (SAS), dates from World War II. Conceived by Captain David Stirling, the SAS has been used since 1941. Most special operations forces—such as Australia's Special Air Service Regiment, Holland's Bijzondere Bijstands Eenheid (BBE), the units of France's new joint Commandement des Operation Speciale (COS), Germany's Grenzschutsgruppe GSG-9, Israel's Sayeret Matkal/Unit 269, and the U.S. Army's 1st Special Forces Operational Detachment, Delta Force, and Naval Special Warfare Development Group—were established in the 1970s as a direct response to terrorist incidents. When radical supporters of Iran's revolution captured 53 staff members and guards at the U.S. embassy in Tehran in November 1979, however, the United States still had no standing counterterrorist task force. As a result, a rescue team had to be assembled from scratch, and it took six months of preparation before the rescue operation could be launched. Charged with rescuing the hostages was the newly created Delta Force, with the support of U.S. Navy and Air Force airlifts. The tragic end of this attempt is well known. Technical problems and tactical failures caused the operation's abortion, and it ended in disaster in April 1980. Nevertheless, after this failed rescue operation, special operations forces received more funding, and better equipment and training. Consequently, special operations forces became an important foreign policy tool for U.S. policymakers.[4]

SOF specialize in clandestinely rescuing hostages. SOF's military tasks focus on infiltrations into enemy territory to carry out sabotage, search-and-destroy and rescue missions, and forward air control. Western militaries have extremely limited true SOF capabilities, probably no more than 3,000–5,000 troops for all NATO countries. In addition, Western governments have specialized forces that carry out overt actions. The United States has approximately 45,000 such troops; its NATO allies have 20,000–30,000.

For European NATO-allies, deployability is a key issue. Of a troop strength of 1.5 million, only 150,000 can be used for combat missions abroad. This is due to the fact that many European allies not only rely largely on conscripts, but still invest mainly in territorial defense. For example, due to conscription and logistical shortfalls, Germany, with a land force of more than 220,000, can only deploy 12,000 troops at the same time. At present some 50,000 European troops are deployed in Iraq, Afghanistan, and elsewhere. Sustainability requirements demand that the other 100,000 troops are kept in reserve for future force rotations. In other words, there is an urgent need that more European allies transform their armed forces from in place forces into deployable armed forces for expeditionary warfare.

The U.S. Army Rangers battalions, which specialize in seizing airfields, are among the better known of the specialized units; another is the 82nd Airborne Division, the world's largest parachute force. These forces seize key targets and prepare the ground for the general-purpose forces that follow.

Nevertheless, new concepts such as Effect Based Operations (EBO) and Network Centric Warfare (NCW) also need to be developed.[5] The success of the interventions in Afghanistan and Iraq gave credence to these concepts. As has been argued before, the combination of maneuverable high-tech forces, including SOF, precision-guided munitions and real-time targeting proved an extremely effective force multiplier. Deployed SOF and specialized forces must disperse and form a network that covers large areas. These forces must make use of advanced communications, including uplinks and downlinks with unmanned and manned aircraft and satellites to enable quick-response strikes against high-value targets. For the military, netwar requires a different mindset, because unlike traditional formations, there is less hierarchy and less emphasis on combined arms operations.

EBO and NCW will enhance the efficacy of stabilization operations as well. Stabilization operations require the minimum use of force and "social patrols." Increased situational awareness and the ability to call in reinforcements rapidly will greatly enhance the military effectiveness of small units with limited combat power in a potentially hostile environment.

So, only a very small portion of all forces assigned to NATO are SOF or specialized armed forces—too small a number to engage in sustained combat operations. Clearly, it is too late to increase this capability for the campaign in Afghanistan and other countries hosting terrorists. Even if a decision were made to create more of these units, only a small number of young people would be willing or able to join these forces; according to some estimates, less than 10 percent make it through the grueling selection process. The consequences of the lack of deployable special and specialized forces became visible in Afghanistan and Iraq. Of the NATO member states, only the United States, the United Kingdom, France, Canada, and the Netherlands have fully transformed armed forces for expeditionary warfare. These countries took on most of the burden in the volatile South of Afghanistan. Operational reasons or national political caveats prevented other NATO-partners from deployment in the South.

The situation is similar as far as the West's human intelligence (HUMINT) capabilities are concerned. For data collection, the intelligence communities of the United States and its NATO allies focus primarily on satellite imagery, signals intelligence (SIGINT), and electronic intelligence (ELINT). Satellite imagery guides both SOF and HUMINT to targets. Although satellite imagery obtains important strategic information, SOF and HUMINT are the best way to obtain tactical information on the ground, especially because terrorist groups make only limited use of cellular telephones and satellite communications. Since the U.S. cruise missile attacks on his training camps in August 1998, Osama bin Laden no longer uses his satellite telephone, which had made him easy to detect. Instead, he issues "mission orders," instructing his lieutenants orally, in writing, or on videotape that television stations broadcast widely. Consequently, the United States and its allies have no choice but to infiltrate his network.

Tapping into this network is an enormous task, however, because the al Qaeda organization has bases and cells in 50–60 countries, including the United States and most European nations, where so-called sleeper agents live. The individuals who carried out the attacks on the World Trade Center and the Pentagon had been ordinary residents in the United States and other Western countries. Therefore, agents from Islamic states' intelligence communities must infiltrate networks and cells both inside and outside the Islamic world, while Western governments must at the same time recruit agents in the Islamic communities in their own countries. Effective use of HUMINT requires intensive cooperation among intelligence services worldwide. Effective HUMINT requires foreign language skills. But only 1.6 percent of Americans speak critical languages.[6] The situation in Europe is not much better. Consequently, stabilization forces and the intelligence community rely on local informants and interpreters with questionable reliability.

Without sufficient HUMINT capabilities, and SOF and specialized forces to effectively address unexpected threats and unconventional warfare—the only option open to the West's opponents—the United States and its allies will find the campaign on terrorism almost impossible. In its most basic form, "asymmetrical" warfare utilizes one side's comparative advantage against its enemy's relative weakness. Successful asymmetrical warfare exploits vulnerabilities—which are easy to determine—by using weapons and tactics in ways that are unplanned or unexpected. The weakness of Western societies is perceived as their desire to reduce collateral damage by emphasizing technological solutions, the need to maintain coalitions, and the need to adhere to the international rule of law. Moreover, Western industrialized societies are economically and socially vulnerable. Thus, dealing with these new threats requires groups of well-trained, well-equipped, and highly motivated individuals who can infiltrate and destroy terrorist networks.

At the tactical level, the opponent conducting asymmetrical warfare tries to change the course of action in order to prevent the achievement of political objectives. These tactics—including guerrilla warfare, hit-and-run attacks, sabotage, terrorism, and the capture of soldiers, who are then shown on television—will confront allied ground forces in Afghanistan and other places that harbor terrorist training camps and headquarters.

At the strategic level, the opponent using asymmetrical tactics exploits the fears of the civilian population, thereby undermining the government, compromising its alliances, and affecting its economy. The September 11 attacks were only partly successful on this score. The fear of further attacks has led to uncertainty about the future among the population of most Western nations; and, as a result, their economies have fallen into recession. On the other hand, the attackers very likely miscalculated not only the resolve of the leadership and population of the United States but also most of the world's willingness to form and maintain coalitions to fight terrorism.

In sum, direct military action—that is, the new war—against insurgents and terrorists requires both special operations forces and human intelligence gathering. Both assets are scarce, however, and not available in the quantities necessary to fight and win sustained wars. Moreover, deploying SOF is extremely risky, and effective engagement requires skills and techniques that come very close to war crimes. Therefore, the United States and its allies need to develop a new defense-planning concept.

The Limited Value of Contemporary Western Concepts

For historical and cultural reasons, the armed forces of Western countries have been disinclined to prepare for military action that was considered uncivilized warfare. As a consequence, policymakers, the military, and the public are psychologically ill-prepared for the new war. They have become used to concepts such as limited collateral damage, proportionality of response, and the absence of body bags. However, the current situation calls for a willingness to abandon these ideas, at least partially, a sacrifice that may be difficult for some individuals and nations to make.

These concepts have little value when carrying out military operations against insurgents and terrorists, however, for a number of reasons.

- *Collateral Damage.* Because opposing fighters do not usually wear uniforms, combatants are indistinguishable from civilians. Fighters depend on the local civilian population for logistics and shelter in rural areas; and in urban areas the population is used as a shield. Moreover, because the population's loyalties are to tribes and clans, differentiating between combatants and noncombatants is almost impossible. Thus, the concept of limited collateral damage is almost useless in unconventional warfare, in which civilian casualties cannot be avoided.

- *Proportionality of Response.* Proportionality refers to the size and character of the attack and the interests at stake. On September 11, the terrorists turned aircraft into weapons of mass destruction. Indeed, for two conventional bombs to cause the death of thousands of civilians is probably impossible. Additionally, the United States must now defend its national security, leadership, and credibility. If one takes the concept of proportionality literally, retaliation with a few low-yield nuclear weapons would certainly be justifiable, because only nuclear weapons could cause the damage of the September 11 attacks. However, keeping the fragile coalition with Islamic countries together requires *less* than a proportional response, so that using nuclear weapons is a non-option.

- *Absence of Body Bags.* Because vital interests of the United States and its allies are at stake, the concept of an absence of body bags carries little value either. Both President George W. Bush and former Prime Minister Tony Blair have the popular support to politically withstand heavy human losses, which there will be. General Joseph Ralston, NATO's former supreme allied commander, warned, "We cannot be in the mindset of a zero-casualty operation."[7] Yet whether most European allies are also willing to pay this high price is doubtful. Initially, the Belgian and Dutch governments saw invoking Article 5 of the NATO treaty as a symbolic measure and a demonstration of transatlantic solidarity. Other governments agreed so that they would be consulted on U.S. decisions and have some influence on U.S. decision making. Except for the United Kingdom, few European NATO allies acknowledged that the decision to invoke Article 5 implies sending their own troops to Southwest Asia.

Thus, combating insurgents and terrorists requires a mental firmness, a quality that is evident in the United States and the United Kingdom today but uncertain in other allies. The traditional concepts of proportionality and limited collateral damage, however, do not have much value in the present circumstances.

Coercion and Coercive Diplomacy

Another obstacle to effectively using military means to combat the new threats that terrorism pose is the limited insight that academics, and therefore policymakers, offer into the theories of coercion and coercive diplomacy as well as governments' lack of experience using them to achieve the desired outcome. Coercion is defined as the deliberate and purposeful use of economic and military power to influence the choices of one's adversaries; coercive diplomacy focuses on the latent use of the instruments of power to influence those choices. The studies on which these theories are based do not have much relevance for policymakers today, however. The terrorist attacks on the United States demonstrate the need for policymakers and the military to reevaluate the concepts that underlie their approaches to balancing political ends and military means.

Most theories of coercion find their origin in the Cold War period; but preoccupation with deterrence has distorted the concept. Deterrence as a concept is useless for today's challenges because the world cannot deter individuals such as bin Laden and his lieutenants. The same holds true in the case of failed states, many of which provide sanctuaries for insurgents and terrorists. Because negotiating with failed states and terrorists is impossible, both coercive diplomacy and coercion are meaningless. The only solution in those cases is direct action with SOF support, backed up by airpower.

Coercive diplomacy and coercion can be used only against functioning states that actively support or shelter terrorists. For that reason Vice President Dick Cheney's warning that the "full wrath" of the United States would be brought down against nations sheltering attackers is an indication of the administration's emerging strategy for combating terrorism.

The problem, however, is the West's lack of experience with this approach. Many cases of coercion and coercive diplomacy have failed. For example, the Gulf War was an unprecedented success, but attempts to coerce Saddam Hussein to comply with United Nations (UN) resolutions during the 1990s failed. The humanitarian intervention in Somalia during the early 1990s resulted in failure. The success of Operation Allied Force in the war in Kosovo was limited because it took 78 days to convince Serbian president Slobodan Milosevic to accept a diplomatic solution based on the Rambouillet agreements signed in early 1999.

Existing theories are based primarily on studies that Thomas Schelling, Alexander George, and Robert Pape conducted,[8] yet even these "classics" do not apply to the circumstances that the West faces today. Schelling distinguishes between "brute force" and "compellance." Brute force is aimed at forcing a military solution; compellance is aimed at using the threat of force to influence an actor's choice.[9] According to Schelling, armed conflict can only be averted when the opponent refrains from taking action. This situation requires a deadline because, without a clear ultimatum, threats are hollow.[10] Accordingly, the United States gave Afghanistan's Taliban regime a deadline, which it rejected, to surrender bin Laden and his lieutenants.

For Schelling, coercive diplomacy concerns not only undoing a particular action but also threatening the opponent with the use of force, which can bring about complete surrender. The crux of Schelling's approach is "risk strategy": by threatening the civilian population and presenting the prospect of terror, the actor expects the opponent's behavior to change. This notion made sense during the Cold War setting, when Schelling's book—in which he sought alternatives to the concept of deterrence—was published in 1966. However, a risk strategy is meaningless in the war against terrorism, because the coercers, the United States and its allies, must make it clear that the war is not against the Afghan people, but against terrorists and the regime supporting them. Thus, there are no civilian populations (such as the Soviet people in the Cold War) to threaten to use coercion effectively. What is worse, excessive military force could split the fragile Islamic alliance, which is cooperating with the United States in the war against terrorism. In other words, coercion might not only be ineffective, it might also backfire. For that reason, humanitarian aid for the civilian population accompanied the initial attacks on Afghanistan in early October 2001.

George's study of coercive diplomacy first appeared in 1971, and a new edition was published in 1994, in which George tested his theory on more recent cases. George distinguishes between defensive "coercive diplomacy" and offensive "military strategy." Coercive diplomacy consists of using diplomatic means, reinforced with instruments of power. Coercion, in the form of threats or military interventions, must force an adversary to cease unacceptable activities.

The main argument of George's theory is that coercion and diplomacy go hand in hand with rewards for the opponent when complying with demands.[11] In the case of the Taliban, Bush and Blair have made it clear that there is no room for compromise and that no rewards will be given for handing over bin Laden. Consequently, the Taliban had no incentive not to fight for its survival, forcing the United States and its allies to confront the prospect of a prolonged struggle and also undermining the fragile coalition forged between Western and Islamic states.

Schelling's and George's theories focus primarily on the *latent* use of instruments of power, whereas Robert Pape's theory concerns their *actual* use. Pape posits that coercion is effective when it aims at the benefit side of the cost-benefit calculation that every actor makes. The opposing side must consider the cost of giving in to the demands of the intervening states to be lower than the cost of resistance. Pape argues that this outcome is possible when the actor withholds military success from the opponent, while at the same time offering a reward after the demands have been met. However, both the Taliban as well as the U.S. and British governments have vital interests at stake; therefore, the Taliban's will to defend and the West's will to coerce are at maximum levels. Consequently, both sides are willing to pay a high price, and neither will give up easily.

As far as military strategy is concerned, Pape focuses on strategic bombing, which can be decisive only in long wars of attrition. The overall superiority of materiel determines its success. This was Russia's strategy in Chechnya during the strategic bombing campaign in Grozny, which most Western governments severely condemned as inhuman.

Nevertheless, a military coalition may have no option but to use elements of an attrition strategy. Given the unavailability of other assets, the destruction of training camps and underground facilities may require the use of low-yield tactical nuclear weapons or fuel air explosives. Moreover, some U.S. strategists are beginning to consider using the threat of a limited nuclear strike as a way to deter potential adversaries that support terrorist organizations from using chemical and biological weapons or to destroy the storage site of these weapons.[12] Thus, the use of nuclear weapons might actually be militarily useful in the war against terrorism, but the potentially grave consequences—such as fracturing the coalition—prevent policymakers from using them.

Pape argues that deposing political regimes is not feasible "because leaders are hard to kill, governments are harder to overthrow, and even if the target government can be overthrown, the coercer can rarely guarantee that its replacement will be more forthcoming."[13] In other words, Blair's warning to the Taliban "to surrender terrorists or to surrender power"[14] does not have many successful historical precedents. The removal of Panama's president Manuel Noriega from power in 1989 is one of the few successful examples.

Pape concluded that airpower can be successful when it denies the opponent the use of military capabilities. This approach requires a strategy of denial—that is, the destruction of key military targets, including headquarters and command and control centers, logistics, and staging areas. In the case of unconventional warfare, however, the number of high-value targets is extremely limited; therefore, there is little to bomb. Consequently, the only strategy that can be successful is a military strategy of control, which requires search-and-destroy missions using land forces such as special operations forces, reinforced by specialized forces and airpower. As argued earlier in this discussion, however, the United States and its allies have very limited military capabilities in these areas.

Schelling, George, and Pape's studies are useful as a starting point for further academic research; but their work has limited utility for contemporary policymaking. Consequently, the September 11 incidents have prompted both policymakers and the military to rethink their basic concepts and to seek another approach to the old challenge of balancing political objectives and military means. For example, a mechanism of second-order change could be developed, aimed at mobilizing neighboring states against a target state. The Islamic Republic of Iran, which is strongly opposed to the Taliban regime, could play a crucial role by putting pressure on Afghanistan, for instance. Pressure from Iran would have the added advantage of involving an Islamic country and thus strengthening the coalition. Thus, reexamining old concepts and traditional approaches are essential to successfully employing military means in the campaign on terrorism.

The Battle for Hearts and Minds

Americans expected a warm welcome for U.S. forces in Iraq. The Iraqi people welcomed the intervention but opposed a long stay of foreign "occupation" forces. The Europeans in Afghanistan had a similar experience. Most European politicians believed that they would carry out a relatively risk-free peacekeeping and reconstruction missions with full support of the local population. But both Americans and Europeans have forgotten the lesson that at least part of the populace see foreign presence as an occupation and consequently as a humiliation.

A significant component of the new war—one that has been historically successful for both allies and adversaries of the United States—is the campaign to win the support of the populace of the opponent. Losing the support of the populace is easy. In Iraq, British forces, with their vast experience in Northern Ireland got the situation under control in Basra, but American troops faced enormous difficulties when dealing with insurgents in the so-called Sunni Triangle. For the Americans, the battle for Fallujah was a turning point. In April 2004 the Americans were forced to withdraw from Fallujah, the center of the pro-Saddam insurgency. Due to the large-scale application of force used the support of the populace was lost completely and discontent was funnelled toward organized resistance. It demonstrated the relative weakness of American forces and inapplicability of old COIN concepts.

In other words, the United States and its allies must also wage a battle for the hearts and minds of the people, in this case, those in the Islamic world. This effort—using several approaches, including humanitarian aid and propaganda—must be made along with diplomatic measures and military operations. The humanitarian aid that accompanies the bombs being dropped in Afghanistan in the current fight demonstrates that the United States recognizes the importance of this campaign.

Israel serves as an example of the difficulties that a nation confronts in a war against terrorists and of the way the battle to win the hearts and minds of the population can accompany military measures. Terror persists in Israel, despite the fact that the country built a security fence separating Israel from Palestinian territories and has military assets that are important for waging this type of war, including defense forces and intelligence services that are among the best in the world; policymakers and a public who are willing to take risks and to accept casualties; and widespread public support for the military even if mistakes are made. And yet the country cannot prevent or deter terrorist acts and attacks with rockets from southern Lebanon and the Gaza Strip, for example. Israel's experience shows that armed forces—trained, structured, and equipped for conventional war—are incapable of dealing with insurgents. Israel had no choice but to develop new tactics, employ different weapons systems, and use small task forces to carry out small-scale operations. However even this shift in modus operandi has not guaranteed success.

Bin Laden, who is accused of being the force behind the September 11 attacks, fights a similar battle to the Intifada on a global scale. His objective is clear: to unite the Islamic world under a political-religious figure, or caliph, by removing pro-Western regimes, the state of Israel, and the U.S. presence from the Islamic world.

Israel's experience also shows that, at best, the problem of terror can be made manageable. Its solution requires offensive military action, heavy security measures to prevent radical elements from carrying out their attacks, and the building of coalitions with moderate political figures.

Important to this discussion is Israel's experience with the issue under discussion: gaining the support of the civilian population. For example, when the security zone in southern Lebanon still existed, Israel carried out a counterinsurgency campaign within it, while at the same time providing aid to the Lebanese population therein, including projects to rebuild infrastructure and programs to provide health care. On the other side of the coin, radical movements such as Hamas use nongovernmental organizations extensively for these purposes.

Bin Laden is popular because of his "good works" in the Islamic world, especially in Pakistan and Afghanistan. Indeed, in most Islamic countries, radical groups of fundamentalists have developed a social and cultural infrastructure to build an Islamic civil society and fill a vacuum that their countries' governments have neglected. For example, during the 1990s in Egypt, Jordan, the West Bank and Gaza, Afghanistan, and Pakistan, radical movements provided health care, education, and welfare for those nations' poor. After the 1992 earthquake in Cairo, these organizations were on the streets within hours, whereas the Egyptian government's relief efforts lagged behind. In fact, Qur'an study centers have become the single most important source for recruiting new members for the radical movements.

These types of campaigns that radical Islamic movements have waged have extremely successfully undermined the legitimacy of governments and gained the support of the local civilian population. Consequently, the diplomatic and military actions of the United States and its allies should go hand in hand with a campaign for hearts and minds in order to win the support of the Islamic world's population. In addition to food rations, U.S. aircraft have dropped leaflets and small transistor radios to enable the Afghans to receive Washington's message. Nevertheless, even a dual strategy of humanitarian aid and military intervention does not guarantee success. Other factors must be taken into account.

Clashing Civilizations, the Ultimate Civilization

The major obstacle to success in the campaign against terrorism is not military, political, or diplomatic, but cultural. Because of strong anti-Western sentiments in the Islamic world, a coalition to counter terrorism is fragile by nature and such a coalition is critical to the success of military measures. The geostrategic changes that occurred in the 1990s have contributed to anti-Western feelings in large parts of the world. First, the West "won" the Cold War, with the United States remaining the sole superpower; and in international relations the "hegemon" is always met with distrust. Second, in 1998, the differences between the United States and non-Western nations countries became clearer as a result of a new version of interventionism.

The year 1998 seems to be a turning point in recent history. Events that took place in 1998 and 1999 seemed to indicate that the U.S. approach had once and for all shifted to a narrower and more selective foreign and national security policy of unilateralism and preservation of the nation's dominant position in the world. A number of events contributed to this image:

- In response to the bombings of the U.S. embassies in Kenya and Tanzania, the United States intervened unilaterally—and without a UN Security Council mandate—in Sudan and Afghanistan in August 1998. The U.S. goal was to strike a blow against bin Laden's alleged terrorist network.

- In December that same year, Operation Desert Fox took place, in which the United States and the United Kingdom carried out bombing raids on Iraq. The military action was meant as retribution for Saddam Hussein's obstruction of UNSCOM's (UN Special Commision's) inspections of Iraq's development of weapons of mass destruction. In 1999 and 2000, the bombings continued, albeit with limited intensity.

- In 1998, the U.S. government decided to increase its defense budget (which had undergone a period of decline) by 5.6 percent, a development that some nations viewed with apprehension.[15]

- In March 1999, Operation Allied Force—led by the United States and without a mandate by the UN Security Council—intervened in Kosovo to force Milosevic to end his terror against the Albanian Kosovars and to find a solution to the situation in Kosovo.

- In July 1999, the United States presented its national missile defense (NMD) initiative, designed to protect the country against limited attacks by rogue states using ballistic missiles. This development demanded a review of the 1972 Anti-Ballistic Missile (ABM) Treaty, which allows the deployment of a limited number of anti-missile interceptors in the United States and Russia. With the U.S. Senate's refusal to ratify the Comprehensive Test Ban Treaty (CTBT), a general prohibition on conducting nuclear tests was dropped.

As a result of these events and reinforced by U.S.–led interventions in Afghanistan and Iraq, many non-Western countries began to perceive the United States as a superpower that wants to change the status quo and create a "new world order" according to its own views. Because of the fundamental difference between Western and non-Western ideas, Russia, China, and Islamic countries distrust interventions that are based on normative principles, such as democracy and humanitarianism. According to Chinese commentators, for example, interventions by the United States indicate that the West can impose its liberal values on the rest of the world without fear of confrontation with Russia.[16]

The fact is that only Western governments appeal to normative principles as a reason for intervention. The notion that these principles are universal and that sovereignty is secondary to human interest won ground in the 1990s. The concepts of democracy, respect for human rights, free-market economy, pluralism, the rule of law, and social modernization are deeply rooted in Western culture and are the product of a civilization that developed over centuries. Universal pretensions and a feeling of superiority are not alien to Western culture. In 1860 Isaac Taylor wrote about the "ultimate civilization." He dealt with the moral supremacy of Western civilization and considered other civilizations to be barbarian because they held polygamy, prostitution, slavery, and torture to be legal. After the fall of the Berlin Wall in 1989, many came to the conclusion that Western values, particularly democracy, had triumphed. In fact, in *The End of History and the Last Man,* published in 1992, Francis Fukuyama even referred to the end of history, because liberal democracies had prevailed and the collapse of dictatorships was supposedly inevitable.[17] In September 2001 the Italian Prime Minister Silvio Belusconi, praised Western civilization as superior to that of the Islamic world and urged Europe to "reconstitute itself on the basis of its Christian roots." In a briefing to journalists he talked about the "superiority of our civilization, which consists of a value system that has given people widespread prosperity in those countries that embrace it and guarantees respect and religion."[18] Berlusconi's frankness was not appreciated both by Western politicians and the Islamic world, so that he had to qualify his statement.

Notwithstanding, after 1989, Western countries believed that they had the evidence for their claim to universal acceptance of their principles because a steadily growing group of countries, including Russia, claimed that they had embraced Western values.

Such declarations by non-Western governments means little ultimately. First, these governments can pay lip service for purely opportunistic reasons that may relate to other issues of importance to them—trade policy, for example. Second, declarations of acceptance of these principles do not necessarily indicate that governments actually embrace them. Their unwillingness to accept the consequences of noncompliance with these principles at times or, in certain situations, their willingness to set aside sovereignty—for example, in the event of a humanitarian disaster—belie these claims. This particularly is true for countries—such as Russia and China—that have rebellious minorities, leading to internal unrest, and aspirations to remain great powers.

The British–Canadian scholar and journalist Michael Ignatieff, therefore, appropriately posed the following question: Whose universal values are actually involved? He pointed out that views of Western countries, Islamic countries, and authoritarian regimes in East Asia have fundamental differences.[19] In Asia, for the most part, authoritarian state and family structures dominate, and democracy and individual rights are secondary. In general, Islamic countries reject the Western concept of the separation of church and state. Apart from Ignatieff's observation, however, the claim of universal acceptance of Western values constitutes a threat in the eyes of many non-Western countries, if acceptance is accompanied by dismissal of the cornerstones of international law, such as sovereignty and noninterference in domestic affairs. These countries perceive even humanitarian interventions as a new form of imperialism that should not be endorsed without question.

The war against terrorism is a golden opportunity for Western nations to enter a new era of cooperation with Russia and China, which are equally concerned about terrorism. Indeed, bin Laden and the Islamic insurgents in Chechnya are linked. Furthermore, the Islamic insurgency in Xinjiang in eastern China has a connection with the Taliban regime and, most probably, bin Laden as well.

This biggest challenge however, is the resurgence of Islam, which is a mainstream movement and not at all extremist. This resurgence is both a product of modernity and Muslims' attempt to deal with it by rejecting Western culture and influence, committing to Islam as the guide to life in the modern world. Fundamentalism, commonly misperceived as political Islam, is only one aspect of this resurgence, which began in the 1970s, when Islamic symbols, beliefs, practices, and institutions won more support throughout the Islamic world. As a product of modernity, the core constituency of Islamic resurgence consists of middle-class students and intellectuals. Indeed, the fundamentalists who carried out the September 11 attacks were well-educated, middle-class men. The Salafi movement, especially its jihadist faction, is the biggest challenge for the West. Salafis reject Islamic pluralism and follow the rules and guidance of the Qur'an and Sunna strictly. Quintan Wiktorowicz arged that Salafis believe "that following these rules they eliminate the biases of human subjectivity and self-interest, thereby allowing them to indentify the singular truths of God's command."[20]

Because the resurgence of Islam is fundamentally an anti-Western movement, building coalitions incorporating Islamic nations in the battle against terrorism is not easy. The coalition that was built in the aftermath of the September 11 attacks was primarily based on attitudes against bin Laden, the leader of the jihadist faction of the Salafists who seeks to establish an undivided *umma*—community of believers—under a political-religious leader, thereby presenting a challenge to most regimes in the Islamic world. Nevertheless, most regimes and large parts of their populations share some of bin Laden's anti-Western sentiments. Consequently, the coalition is fragile and, at best, willing to give only passive support. Thus, many Islamic people will consider a military campaign that is carried out by Western forces as—to use bin Laden's words—"a Zionist Crusade." Unfortunately, a controversial assertion—which Samuel P. Huntington made more than five years ago—that conflicts between cultures will dominate future international relations remains germane in the new millennium.[21]

The war on terrorism could improve the West's relations with China and Russia, but, if handled unwisely, it could also lead to a confrontation with the Islamic world. Today, the support of Russia and China for the U.S.-led coalitions in Afghanistan and Iraq is small, suggesting that the leadership of both countries prefer to see the Americans muddle along or, at worst, fail. A major consequence of the two interventions is that the West's international position is weakened considerably, thus enhancing the position of emerging powers. The United States' nightmare scenario is that friendly regimes in the Islamic world will fall and anti-Western regimes willing to play the oil card and support terrorists will emerge. Thus, the immediate consequence of the war on terrorism could be both ineffective and become a struggle for these energy resources, which are so vital to the Western world.

Limiting Expectations

As the war against terrorism gets into full gear, the United States and its allies must meet significant practical and conceptual challenges if the campaign is to be successful. A war against terrorists or insurgents can be manageable, at best, if certain approaches are adopted. In principle, the following options, which are not all mutually exclusive, are available to the United States and its allies, depending on the target of the campaign:

- Pursue a military strategy of *control* in failed states that terrorists use as sanctuaries. Control involves search-and-destroy missions by special operations forces, backed up by specialized forces and airpower. This option requires the United States and its allies to expand the number of SOF and specialized forces significantly.

- Adopt a strategy of *coercive diplomacy* or *coercion* against unfriendly regimes to pressure these regimes to give up their support of terrorist movements. If they do not comply with these demands, these regimes should be removed from power, which is easier said than done. This strategy requires new thinking about the optimum way to coerce regimes.

- Use *human intelligence* gathering methods extensively to infiltrate the terrorists' networks in friendly countries and then destroy the terrorist bases from within. This option also requires the United States and its allies to expand their HUMINT capabilities substantially and to embark on even closer cooperation with intelligence services in other countries.

- Wage a *campaign to win the hearts and minds* of the Islamic people. This option would enable the United States and its allies to gain the support of the populace and thereby drive a wedge between the population and the terrorists or insurgents.

- Prepare for a *protracted campaign*. Wining the hearts and minds at home is as important as winning the hearts and minds abroad.

Nevertheless, even if these options are adopted and prove successful, at least in the short term, an overriding issue must be addressed in order to achieve long-term success. The primary obstacle to success in the war against terrorism is a cultural one. To some degree, the battle is a clash of civilizations. Political Islam is fundamentally anti-Western, thus the prospect for success is limited. Using military means may exacerbate the potential that this campaign will be cast as a clash of civilizations, ultimately making the problem of terrorism even worse.

Rob de Wijk is an expert on military aspects of security issues at the Clingendael Institute for International Relations (The Netherlands). Dr. de Wijk is a professor of strategic studies at Leiden University and a professor of international relations at the Royal Military Academy (KMA) in Breda. A former head of the Defence Concepts Division of the Netherlands Ministry of Defence, he is the co-author of *NATO on the Brink of the New Millennium: The Battle for Consensus* (1998).

Notes

1. The situation in Afghanistan and its implications for international peace and security, Report of the Secretary-General, 21 September 2007.
2. L. J. Shadwell, *Lockhart's Advance Through Tirah* (London: W. Thacker & Co., 1898), 100–105.
3. As quoted in "Rumsfeld," *International Herald Tribune,* September 19, 2001, 6.
4. S. L. Marquis, *Unconventional Warfare: Rebuilding U.S. Special Operations Forces* (Washington, DC: Brookings Institution, 1997), 2.
5. See for a concise analysis for instance Norman Friedman, *Terrorism, Afghanistan, and America's New Way of War* (Annapolis, MD: Naval Institute Press, 2003), in particular chapter 10.
6. D. Byman, "US Counter-terrorism Options: A Taxonomy," *Survival, 49,* no. 3 (Autumn 2007): 124.
7. As quoted in "Rumsfeld," 6.
8. See Thomas A. Schelling, *Arms and Influence* (New Haven: Yale University Press, 1966); Alexander L. George and W.E. Simons, eds., *The Limits of Coercive Diplomacy* (Boulder, CO: Westview Press, 1994); Robert A. Pape, *Bombing to Win: Air Power and Coercion in War* (Ithaca, NY: Cornell University Press, 1996); Lawrence Freedman, *Strategic Coercion* (Oxford: Oxford University Press, 1998); Colin S. Gray, *Modern Strategy* (Oxford: Oxford University Press, 1999); Richard N. Haass, *Intervention: The Use of American Military Force in the Post-Cold War World* (Washington DC: Carnegie Endowment for International Peace, 1994); Michael O'Hanlon, *Saving Lives With Force: Military Criteria for Humanitarian Intervention* (Washington, DC: Brookings Institution, 1997); and B. R. Pirnie and W. E. Simons, *Soldiers for Peace* (Santa Monica, CA: Rand Corporation 1996).
9. Schelling, *Arms and Influence,* 2–3.
10. Ibid., 69–91; See also Thomas Schelling, *The Strategy of Conflict* (New York and London: Oxford University Press, 1965).
11. George and Simons, *Limits of Coercive Diplomacy,* 7.
12. "U.S. Strategists Begin to Favor Threat to Use Nuclear Weapons," *International Herald Tribune,* October 6–7, 2001, 4.
13. Pape, *Bombing to Win,* 316.
14. Prime Minister Tony Blair's speech to the Labor Party Conference, London, October 2, 2001.
15. International Institute for Strategic Studies, "U.S. Military Spending," *Strategic Comments, 6,* no. 4 (May 2000).

16. J. Teufel Dreyer, *The PLA and the Kosovo Conflict* (U.S. Army War College, Carlisle, May 2000), 3.
17. F. Fukuyama, *The End of History and the Last Man* (New York: The Free Press, 1992).
18. "Berlusconi vaunts West's Superiority," *International Herald Tribune,* September 27, 2001.
19. M. Ignatieff, *Whose Universal Values? The Crisis in Human Rights* (The Hague: Paemium Erasmianum, 1999).
20. Q. Wiktorowicz, "Anatomy of the Salafi Movement" *Studies in Conflict and Terrorism, 29* (2006): 207.
21. S. P. Huntington, *The Clash of Civilizations and the Remaking of World Order* (New York, Simon & Schuster, 1996).

Richard H. Shultz Jr., 2004

Showstoppers: Nine Reasons Why We Never Sent Our Special Operations Forces after al Qaeda before 9/11

Since 9/11, Secretary of Defense Donald Rumsfeld has repeatedly declared that the United States is in a new kind of war, one requiring new military forces to hunt down and capture or kill terrorists. In fact, for some years, the Department of Defense has gone to the trouble of selecting and training an array of Special Operations Forces, whose forte is precisely this. One president after another has invested resources to hone lethal "special mission units" for offensive—that is, preemptive—counterterrorism strikes, with the result that these units are the best of their kind in the world. While their activities are highly classified, two of them—the Army's Delta Force and the Navy's SEAL Team 6—have become the stuff of novels and movies.

Prior to 9/11, these units *were never used even once* to hunt down terrorists who had taken American lives. Putting the units to their intended use proved impossible—even after al Qaeda bombed the World Trade Center in 1993, bombed two American embassies in East Africa in 1998, and nearly sank the USS *Cole* in Yemen in 2000. As a result of these and other attacks, operations were planned to capture or kill the ultimate perpetrators, Osama bin Laden and his top lieutenants, but each time the missions were blocked. A plethora of self-imposed constraints—I call them showstoppers—kept the counterterrorism units on the shelf.

I first began to learn of this in the summer of 2001, after George W. Bush's election brought a changing of the guard to the Department of Defense. Joining the new team as principal deputy assistant secretary of defense for special operations and low-intensity conflict was Bob Andrews, an old hand at the black arts of unconventional warfare. During Vietnam, Andrews had served in a top-secret Special Forces outfit codenamed the Studies and Observations Group that had carried out America's largest and most complex covert paramilitary operation in the Cold War. Afterwards, Andrews had joined the CIA, then moved to Congress as a staffer, then to the defense industry.

I'd first met him while I was writing a book about the secret war against Hanoi, and we hit it off. He returned to the Pentagon with the new administration, and in June 2001 he called and asked me to be his consultant. I agreed, and subsequently proposed looking into counterterrorism policy. Specifically, I wondered why had we created these superbly trained Special Operations Forces to fight terrorists, but had never used them for their primary mission. What had kept them out of action?

Andrews was intrigued and asked me to prepare a proposal. I was putting the finishing touches on it on the morning of September 11, when al Qaeda struck. With that blow, the issue of America's offensive counterterrorist capabilities was thrust to center stage.

By early November, I had the go-ahead for the study. Our question had acquired urgency: Why, even as al Qaeda attacked and killed Americans at home and abroad, were our elite counterterrorism units not used to hit back and prevent further attacks? That was, after all, their very purpose, laid out in the official document *"Special Operations in Peace and War"* (1996). To find the answer, I interviewed civilian and military officials, serving and retired, at the center of U.S. counterterrorism policy and operational planning in the late 1980s and 1990s.

They included senior members of the National Security Council's Counterterrorism and Security Group, the interagency focal point for counterterrorism policy. In the Pentagon, I interviewed the top leaders of the offices with counterterrorism responsibility, as well as second-tier professionals, and their military counterparts in the Joint Staff. Finally, the U.S. Special Operations Command, headquartered in Tampa, Florida, is responsible for planning and carrying out counterterrorism strikes, and I interviewed senior commanders who served there during the 1990s.

Some were willing to speak on the record. Others requested anonymity, which I honored, in order to put before the top leadership of the Pentagon the detailed report from which this article is drawn. My findings were conveyed to the highest levels of the Department of Defense in January 2003.

Among those interviewed, few were in a better position to illuminate the conundrum than General Pete Schoomaker. An original member of the Delta Force, he had commanded the Delta Force in 1991–92, then led the Special Operations Command in the late 1990s. "Counterterrorism, by Defense Department definition, is offensive," Schoomaker told me during a discussion we had over two days in the summer of 2002. "But Special Operations was never given the mission. It was very, very frustrating. It was like having a brand-new Ferrari in the garage, and nobody wants to race it because you might dent the fender."

As terrorist attacks escalated in the 1990s, White House rhetoric intensified. President Clinton met each successive outrage with a vow to punish the perpetrators. After the *Cole* bombing in 2000, for example, he pledged to "find out who is responsible and hold them accountable." And to prove he was serious, he issued an increasingly tough series of Presidential Decision Directives. The United States would "deter and preempt . . . individuals who perpetrate or plan to perpetrate such acts," said Directive 39, in June 1995. Offensive measures would be used against foreign terrorists posing a threat to America, said Directive 62, in May 1998. Joint Staff contingency plans were revised to provide for offensive and preemptive options. And after al Qaeda's bombings of the U.S. embassies in Kenya and Tanzania, President Clinton signed a secret "finding" authorizing lethal covert operations against bin Laden.

These initiatives led to the planning of several operations. Their details rest in the classified records of the National Security Council's Counterterrorism and Security Group.

Its former coordinator, Dick Clarke, described them as providing the White House with "more aggressive options," to be carried out by Special Operations Forces (or SOF, a category that includes the Green Berets, the Rangers, psychological operations, civilian affairs, the SEALS, special helicopter units, and special mission units like the Delta Force and SEAL Team 6).

Several plans have been identified in newspaper accounts since 9/11. For example, "snatch operations" in Afghanistan were planned to seize bin Laden and his senior lieutenants. After the 1998 embassy bombings, options for killing bin Laden were entertained, including a gunship assault on his compound in Afghanistan.

SOF assaults on al Qaeda's Afghan training camps were also planned. An official very close to Clinton said that the president believed the image of American commandos jumping out of helicopters and killing terrorists would send a strong message. He "saw these camps as conveyor belts pushing radical Islamists through," the official said, "that either went into the war against the Northern Alliance [an Afghan force fighting the Taliban in northern Afghanistan] or became sleeper cells in Germany, Spain, Britain, Italy, and here. We wanted to close these camps down. We had to make it unattractive to go to these camps. And blowing them up, by God, would make them unattractive."

And preemptive strikes against al Qaeda cells outside Afghanistan were planned, in North Africa and the Arabian Gulf. Then in May 1999, the White House decided to press the Taliban to end its support of bin Laden. The Counterterrorism and Security Group recommended supporting the Northern Alliance.

These examples, among others, depict an increasingly aggressive, lethal, and preemptive counterterrorist policy. But *not one* of these operations—all authorized by President Clinton—was ever executed. General Schoomaker's explanation is devastating. "The presidential directives that were issued," he said, "and the subsequent findings and authorities, in my view, were done to check off boxes. The president signed things that everybody involved knew full well were never going to happen. You're checking off boxes, and have all this activity going on, but the fact is that there's very low probability of it ever coming to fruition. . . ." And he added: "The military, by the way, didn't want to touch it. There was great reluctance in the Pentagon."

From my interviews, I distilled nine mutually reinforcing, self-imposed constraints that kept the special mission units sidelined, even as al Qaeda struck at American targets around the globe and trumpeted its intention to do more of the same. These showstoppers formed an impenetrable phalanx ensuring that all high-level policy discussions, tough new presidential directives, revised contingency plans, and actual dress rehearsals for missions would come to nothing.

1. Terrorism as Crime

During the second half of the 1980s, terrorism came to be defined by the U.S. government as a crime, and terrorists as criminals to be prosecuted. The Reagan administration, which in its first term said that it would meet terrorism with "swift and effective retribution," ended its second term, in the political and legal aftermath of Iran-contra, by adopting a counterterrorism policy that was the antithesis of that.

Patterns of Global Terrorism, a report issued by the State Department every year since 1989, sets forth guidance about responding to terrorism. Year after year prior to 9/11, a key passage said it was U.S. policy to "treat terrorists as criminals, pursue them aggressively, and apply the rule of law." Even now, when President Bush has defined the situation as a war on terrorism, *"Patterns of Global Terrorism"* says U.S. policy is to "bring terrorists to justice for their crimes."

Criminalization had a profound impact on the Pentagon, said General Schoomaker. It came to see terrorism as "not up to the standard of our definition of war, and therefore not worthy of our attention." In other words, militaries fight other militaries. "And because it's not war," he added, "and we don't act like we're at war, many of the Defense Department's tools are off the table." The Pentagon's senior leadership made little if any effort to argue against designating terrorism as a crime, Schoomaker added derisively.

"If you declare terrorism a criminal activity, you take from Defense any statutory authority to be the leader in responding," a long-serving department official agreed. Whenever the White House proposed using SOF against terrorists, it found itself facing "a band of lawyers at Justice defending their turf." They would assert, said this old hand at special operations, that the Pentagon lacked authority to use force—and "lawyers in the Defense Department would concur. They argued that we have no statutory authority because this is essentially a criminal matter."

In effect, the central tool for combating terrorism would not be military force. Extradition was the instrument of choice. This reduced the Pentagon's role to providing transportation for the Justice Department.

To be sure, Justice had its successes. With the help of the Pakistani government, it brought back Mir Amal Kansi, the gunman who opened fire outside CIA headquarters in 1993; with the help of the governments of the Philippines and Kenya, it brought several of the terrorists responsible for the first World Trade Center bombing and the attacks on the U.S. embassies in East Africa back to stand trial. But those were lesser al Qaeda operatives. Against the group's organizational infrastructure and leadership, there were no such successes. Law enforcement had neither the access nor the capability to go after those targets.

2. Not a Clear and Present Danger or War

Since terrorism had been classified as crime, few Pentagon officials were willing to call it a clear and present danger to the United States—much less grounds for war. Any attempt to describe terrorism in those terms ran into a stone wall.

For instance, on June 25, 1996, a truck bomb killed 19 Americans and wounded another 250 at the U.S. military's Khobar Towers housing facility near Dhahran, Saudi Arabia. In the aftermath, a tough-minded subordinate of Allen Holmes, then the assistant secretary of defense for special operations and low-intensity conflict, asserted that the Defense Department needed a more aggressive counterterrorism policy to attack those responsible for these increasingly lethal terrorist attacks. Holmes told him, "Write it down, and we'll push it."

The aide laid out a strategy that pulled no punches. Khobar Towers, the World Trade Center bombing, and other attacks were acts of war, he wrote, and should be treated as such. He called for "retaliatory and preemptive military strikes against the terrorist leadership and infrastructure responsible, and even against states assisting them." In his strategy, he assigned a central role for this to SOF.

Holmes ran the proposal up the flagpole. A meeting to review it was held in the office of the undersecretary of defense for policy. As the hard-charging aide explained his recommendations, a senior policy official blurted out: "Are you out of your mind? You're telling me that our Middle East policy is not important and that it's more important to go clean out terrorists? Don't you understand what's going on in terms of our Middle East policy? You're talking about going after terrorists backed by Iran? You just don't understand." And that was that.

In the wake of Khobar Towers, Secretary of Defense William Perry asked retired General Wayne Downing to head a task force to assess what had happened. Formerly the head of the U.S. Special Operations Command, Downing had been in counterterrorism a long time. He was more than willing to pull the trigger and cajole policymakers into giving him the authority to do so. Interviewed in 2002 during a year-long stint as President Bush's deputy national security adviser for combating terrorism, he reflected on his report: "I emphasized that people are at war with us, and using terrorism as an asymmetrical weapon with which to attack us because they can't in a direct or conventional manner." It was war, he told the department's senior leadership; they needed to wake up to that fact. But his plea fell on deaf ears. He lamented, "No one wanted to address terrorism as war."

Even after bin Laden declared war on America in a 1998 *fatwa,* and bombed U.S. embassies to show his followers that he meant business in exhorting them to "abide by Allah's order by killing Americans . . . anywhere, anytime, and wherever possible," the Pentagon still resisted calling terrorism war. It wasn't alone. A CIA assessment of the *fatwa* acknowledged that if a *government* had issued such a decree, one would have had to consider it a declaration of war, but in al Qaeda's case it was only propaganda.

During the late 1990s, the State Department coordinator for counterterrorism was Mike Sheehan. A retired Special Forces officer who had learned unconventional warfare in El Salvador in the late 1980s, he was considered one of the most hawkish Clinton officials, pushing for the use of force against the Taliban and al Qaeda. His mantra was "drain the Afghan swamp of terrorists."

I visited Sheehan at his office at the U.N. building in New York, where he had become assistant secretary-general for peacekeeping. He recounted how aggressive counterterrorism proposals were received in the Defense Department: "The Pentagon wanted to fight and win the nation's wars, as Colin Powell used to say. But those were wars against the armies of other nations—not against diffuse transnational terrorist threats. So terrorism was seen as a distraction that was the CIA's job, even though DOD personnel were being hit by terrorists. The Pentagon way to treat terrorism against Pentagon assets abroad was to cast it as a force protection issue."

"Force protection" is Pentagon lingo for stronger barriers to shield troops from Khobar Towers-type attacks. Even the attack on the USS *Cole* did not change that outlook. As far as causing anyone to consider offensive measures against those responsible, "the *Cole* lasted only for a week, two weeks," Sheehan lamented. "It took a 757 crashing into the Pentagon for them to get it." Shaking his head, he added: "The near sinking of a billion-dollar warship was not enough. Folding up a barracks full of their troops in Saudi Arabia was not enough. Folding up two American embassies was not enough."

Of course, Washington continued to try to arrest those who had carried out these acts. But the places where terrorists trained and planned—Afghanistan, Lebanon, Sudan, Yemen—remained off-limits. Those were not areas where the Defense Department intended to fight. A very senior SOF officer who had served on the Joint Staff in the 1990s told me that more than once he heard terrorist strikes characterized as "a small price to pay for being a superpower."

3. The Somalia Syndrome

In the first year of his presidency, Bill Clinton suffered a foreign policy debacle. The "Fire Fight from Hell," *Newsweek* called it. The *Los Angeles Times* described it as culminating in "dozens of cheering, dancing Somalis dragging the body of a U.S. soldier through the city's streets." Those reports followed the 16-hour shootout portrayed in the movie "*Black Hawk Down*," pitting SOF units against Somali warriors in the urban jungle of Mogadishu on October 3–4, 1993. The American objective had been capturing Mohammed Aidid, a warlord who was interfering with the U.N.'s humanitarian mission. The new administration had expected a quick surgical operation.

The failure caused disquieting questions and bad memories. How could this happen? What had gone wrong? Some Clinton officials recalled that the last time the Democrats had held the White House, similar forces had failed in their attempt to rescue American hostages in Tehran ("Desert One"), a catastrophe instrumental in President Carter's 1980 reelection defeat.

Some senior generals had expressed doubts about the Mogadishu operation, yet as it had morphed from a peacekeeping mission into a manhunt for Aidid, the new national security team had failed to grasp the implications. The Mogadishu disaster spooked the Clinton administration as well as the brass, and confirmed the Joint Chiefs in the view that SOF should never be entrusted with independent operations.

After Mogadishu, one Pentagon officer explained, there was "reluctance to even discuss pro-active measures associated with countering the terrorist threat through SOF operations. The Joint Staff was very happy for the administration to take a law enforcement view. They didn't want to put special ops troops on the ground. They hadn't wanted to go into Somalia to begin with. The Joint Staff was the biggest foot-dragger on all of this counterterrorism business."

Another officer added that Somalia heightened a wariness, in some cases outright disdain, for SOF in the senior ranks. On the Joint Staff, the generals ranged from those who "did not have a great deal of respect" for SOF, to those who actually "hated what it represented, . . . hated the independent thought process, . . . hated the fact that the SOF guys on the Joint Staff would challenge things, would question things."

During Desert Storm, for example, General Norman Schwarzkopf was reluctant to include SOF in his war plan. He did so only grudgingly, and kept SOF on a short leash, wrote the commander of all Special Operations Forces at the time, General Carl Stiner, in his book *Shadow Warriors*. But SOF performed well in Desert Storm, and afterwards Schwarzkopf acknowledged their accomplishments. In 1993, Mogadishu turned back the clock.

4. No Legal Authority

August 1998 was a watershed for the White House. The embassy bombings led to the reexamination of preemptive military options. President Clinton proposed using elite SOF counterterrorism units to attack bin Laden, his lieutenants, and al Qaeda's infrastructure.

Also considered was unconventional warfare, a core SOF mission very different from counterterrorism. The Special Operations Command's *Special Operations in Peace and War* defines unconventional warfare as "military and paramilitary operations conducted by indigenous or surrogate forces who are organized, trained, equipped, and directed by an external source." For the White House, this meant assisting movements like the Northern Alliance in Afghanistan.

Both the Special Operations Command's counterterrorism units and Special Forces training for and executing unconventional warfare operate clandestinely. That is what their doctrine specifies. But because such operations are secret, the question arose in the 1990s whether the department had the legal authority to execute them.

This may seem baffling. If these missions are specified in the military doctrine of the Special Operations Command, and actual units train for them, isn't it obvious that the Department of Defense must have the authority to execute them? Perhaps, yet many in government emphatically deny it.

A gap exists, they believe, between DOD's *capability* for clandestine operations and its *authority* under the United States Code. In the 1990s, some Pentagon lawyers and some in the intelligence community argued that Title 10 of the U.S. Code, which covers the armed forces, did not give Defense the legal authority for such missions, Title 50, which spells out the legal strictures for covert operations, gave this power exclusively to the CIA.

Title 50 defines covert action as "an activity of the United States Government to influence political, economic, or military conditions abroad, where it is intended that the role of the United States Government will not be apparent or acknowledged publicly." Covert action and deniability go hand in hand. If a story about a covert action hits the newspapers, the president must be able to avow that the United States is not mixed up in it.

But is it the case that *only* the CIA has this authority? Title 50, Chapter 15, Section 413b of the U.S. Code stipulates: "The President may not authorize the conduct of a covert action by departments, agencies, or entities of the United States Government unless the President determines such an action is necessary to support identifiable foreign policy objectives of the United States and is important to the national security of the United States, which determination shall be set forth in a finding that shall meet each of the following conditions." The key condition is: "Each finding shall specify each department, agency, or entity of the United States Government authorized to fund or otherwise participate in any significant way in such action." Title 50 leaves the choice of agency to the president and does not exclude the Pentagon.

At the heart of this debate, said a former senior Defense official, was "institutional culture and affiliation." The department took the position that it lacked the authority because it did not *want* the authority—or the mission. He told me, "All of its instincts push it in that direction."

One senior member of the National Security Council's counterterrorism group recalled encountering this attitude during deliberations over counterterrorism operations and clandestine support for the Northern Alliance. To the Joint Staff, neither was "in their minds a military mission. It was a covert action. The uniformed military was adamant that they would not do covert action." And, he added, if you presented them with "a legal opinion that says 'You're wrong,' then they would say, 'Well, we're not going to do it anyway. It's a matter of policy that we don't.'"

The authority argument was a "cop-out," said a retired officer who served in the Pentagon from 1994 to 2000. Sure enough, the Defense Department could have bypassed Title 50 by employing SOF on a *clandestine* basis. While both clandestine and covert missions are secret, only the latter require that the U.S. role not be "acknowledged publicly," which is Title 50's key requirement. Using SOF to preempt terrorists or support resistance movements clandestinely in peacetime is within the scope of Title 10, as long as the U.S. government does not deny involvement when the mission is over.

But this interpretation of Title 10 was considered beyond the pale in the 1990s. The Pentagon did not want the authority to strike terrorists secretly or to employ Special Forces against states that aided and sheltered them.

5. Risk Aversion

The mainstream military often dismisses special operations as too risky. To employ SOF requires open-minded political and military leadership willing to balance risks against potential gains. Supple judgment was in short supply in the Pentagon in the 1990s.

Walter Slocombe served as Clinton's undersecretary of defense for policy, and took part in all counterterrorism policy discussions in the Department of Defense. "We certainly looked at lots of options which involved the possible use of SOF," he stressed. But in the end they were never selected because they seemed too hard to pull off, he acknowledged. Options that put people on the ground to go after bin Laden were "much too hard." It was much easier and much less risky to fire off cruise missiles.

During Clinton's first term, someone would always find something wrong with a proposed operation, lamented General Downing. The attitude was: "Don't let these SOF guys go through the door because they're dangerous. . . . They are going to do something to embarrass the country." Downing recalls that during his years in command, he "sat through the preparation of maybe 20 operations where we had targeted people who had killed Americans. Terrorists who had done bad things to this country, and needed either to be killed or apprehended and brought back here, and we couldn't pull the trigger." It was too risky for the Pentagon's taste.

The other side of the risk-aversion coin is policymakers' demand for fail-safe options. A general who served in the Special Operations Command in the 1990s encountered "tremendous pressure to do something," he said, but at the same time, the requirement was for "perfect operations, no casualties, no failure." There were some "great opportunities" to strike at al Qaeda, "but you couldn't take any risk in doing so. You couldn't have a POW, you couldn't lose a man. You couldn't have anybody hurt." It was Catch-22. There were frequent "spin-ups" for SOF missions, but "in the end, the senior political and military leadership wouldn't let you go do it."

In the mid-1990s, and again at the end of the decade, the Clinton administration flirted with supporting the Iraqi resistance and then the Northern Alliance. An officer who served on the Joint Staff recounted how the senior military leadership put the kibosh on these potentially bold moves.

The CIA ran the Iraqi operation. But its unconventional warfare capabilities were paltry, and it turned to the military for help, requesting that SOF personnel be seconded to bolster the effort. The Joint Staff and its chairman wanted nothing to do with it, he said. "The guidance I got from the chairman's director of operations was that we weren't going to support this, and do everything you can to stall or keep it in the planning mode, don't let it get to the point where we're briefing this at the National Security Council or on the Hill."

Later, the National Security Council's counterterrorism group proposed supporting the Northern Alliance. They pushed the proposal up to the "principals" level. But attached to it was a "non-concurrence" by the Joint Staff, opposing it as too complex and risky. That was the kiss of death.

None of this was new to the Joint Staff officer, who had been in special operations for a long time. "Risk aversion emerges as senior officers move into higher positions," he explained. "It's a very common thing for these guys to become non-risk takers. They get caught up in interagency politics and the bureaucratic process, and get risk-averse."

A member of the counterterrorism group in the late 1990s noted that General Hugh Shelton, a former commander of the Special Operations Command, considered the use of SOF for counterterrorism less than anyone when he was chairman of the Joint Chiefs. The official said Shelton directed the Joint Staff "not to plan certain operations, I'm sure you've heard this from others." In fact, I had. "It got to the point," he said, where "the uniforms had become the suits, they were more the bureaucrats than the civilians."

6. Pariah Cowboys

When events finally impelled the Clinton administration to take a hard look at offensive operations, the push to pursue them came from the civilians of the National Security Council's Counterterrorism and Security Group.

One of the hardest of the hard-liners was the group's chief, Dick Clarke. For nearly a decade, this career civil servant began and ended his work day with the burgeoning terrorist threat to America. He knew in detail the danger the bin Ladens of the world posed, and it worried him greatly. Defensive measures were just not enough. "Clarke's philosophy was to go get the terrorists," one former senior Pentagon special operations official told me, "Go get them anywhere you can."

Asked if that meant using SOF, he replied: "Oh yeah. In fact, many of the options were with special mission units." But "Dick Clarke was attempting to take on a Pentagon hierarchy that wasn't of the same philosophical mindset."

Clarke was not alone. Mike Sheehan also pushed for assisting the Northern Alliance and striking al Qaeda with SOF. Such measures worried the senior brass, who proceeded to weaken those officials by treating them as pariahs. That meant portraying them as cowboys, who proposed reckless military operations that would get American soldiers killed.

Sheehan explained: Suppose one civilian starts beating the drum for special operations. The establishment "systematically starts to undermine you. They would say, 'He's a rogue, he's uncooperative, he's out of control, he's stupid, he makes bad choices.' It's very damaging. . . . You get to the point where you don't even raise issues like that. If someone did, like me or Clarke, we were labeled cowboys, way outside our area of competence."

Several officials who served on the Joint Staff and in the Pentagon's special operations office remembered the senior brass characterizing Clarke in such terms. "Anything Dick Clarke suggested, the Joint Staff was going to be negative about," said one. Some generals had been vitriolic, calling Clarke "a madman, out of control, power hungry, wanted to be a hero, all that kind of stuff." In fact, one of these former officials emphasized, "when we would carry back from the counterterrorism group one of those SOF counterterrorism proposals, our job was to figure out not how to execute it, but how we were going to say no."

By turning Clarke into a pariah, the Pentagon brass discredited precisely the options that might have spared us the tragedy of September 11, 2001. And when Clarke fought back at being branded "wild" and "irresponsible," they added "abrasive" and "intolerant" to the counts against him.

7. Intimidation of Civilians

Another way the brass stymied hard-line proposals from civilian policymakers was by highlighting their own military credentials and others' lack of them. One former defense official recounted a briefing on counterterrorism options given the secretary of defense by senior civilians and military officers. "The civilian, a political appointee with no military experience, says, 'As your policy adviser, let me tell you what you need to do militarily in this situation.' The chairman sits there, calmly listening. Then it's his turn. He begins by framing his sophisticated PowerPoint briefing in terms of the 'experience factor,' his own judgment, and those of four-star associates. The 'experience factor' infuses the presentation. Implicitly, it raises a question intended to discredit the civilian: 'What makes you qualified? What makes you think that your opinion is more important than mine when you don't have the experience I have?' 'Mr. Secretary,' concludes the chairman, 'this is my best military advice.'" In such situations, the official said, civilians were often dissuaded from taking on the generals.

Wayne Downing, the former special operations commander, had plenty of experience providing such briefings. "Occasionally you would get a civilian champion," he said, who would speak up enthusiastically in favor of the mission being presented. "And then the chairman or the vice chairman would say, 'I don't think this is a good idea. Our best military judgment is that you not do this.' That champion is not going any further."

During the 1990s, the "best military advice," when it came to counterterrorism, was always wary of the use of force. Both risk-aversion and a deep-seated distrust of SOF traceable all the way back to World War II informed the military counsel offered to top decision makers. Almost all those I consulted confirmed this, and many, including General Stiner, have described it in print.

When President Clinton began asking about special operations, one former senior official recounted, "those options were discussed, but never got anywhere. The Joint Staff would say, 'That's cowboy Hollywood stuff.' The president was intimidated because these guys come in with all those medals, [and] the White House took the 'stay away from SOF options' advice of the generals."

Another former official during both Clinton terms described several instances where "best military advice" blocked SOF options under White House review. "The Pentagon resisted using Special Forces. Clinton raised it several times with [Joint Chiefs chairmen] Shalikashvili and Shelton. They recommended against it, and never really came up with a doable plan."

Occasionally, policymakers kept pushing. When support for the Northern Alliance was on the table after the embassy bombings in Africa, the senior military leadership "refused to consider it," a former counterterrorism group member told me. "They said it was an intelligence operation, not a military mission."

The counterterrorism group at the National Security Council pushed the proposal anyway, but the Joint Staff strongly demurred and would not support it. They argued that supporting the Northern Alliance would entangle the United States in a quagmire. That was the end of the line. Let's suppose, said the former counterterrorism group member, that the president had ordered a covert strike "despite the chairman going on record as opposing it. Now, if the president orders such an operation against the best military advice of his chief military adviser, and it gets screwed up, they will blame the president who has no military experience, who was allegedly a draft dodger." The Northern Alliance was left to wither on the vine.

8. Big Footprints

The original concept for SOF counterterrorism units was that they would be unconventional, small, flexible, adaptive, and stealthy, suited to discreet and discriminate use, say those "present at the creation" following the Desert One disaster. Force packages were to be streamlined for surgical operations. The "footprint" of any operation was to be small, even invisible.

By the 1990s, this had dropped by the wayside. One former official recalled that when strikes against al Qaeda cells were proposed, "the Joint Staff and the chairman would come back and say, 'We highly recommend against doing it. But if ordered to do it, this is how we would do it.' And usually it involved the 82nd and 101st Airborne Divisions. The footprint was ridiculous." In each instance the civilian policymakers backed off.

To some extent, SOF planners themselves have been guilty of this. "Mission-creep," one official called it. Since you can't "totally suppress an environment with 15 guys and three helicopters," force packages became "five or six hundred guys, AC-130 gunships, a 900-man quick-reaction force ready to assist if you get in trouble, and F-14s circling over the Persian Gulf." The policymakers were thinking small, surgical, and stealthy, so they'd take one "look at it and say that's too big."

One original Delta Force member traced this problem back to Desert One. "We took some bad lessons from that," he said. ". . . One was that we needed more. That maybe it would have been successful if we'd had more helicopters. That more is better. And now we add too many bells and whistles. We make our footprint too large. We price ourselves out of the market."

It's a way of dealing with the military's aversion to risk. "One way we tend to think we mitigate risk," he said, "is by adding more capabilities for this contingency and that contingency." Asked if this thinking had found its way into the Special Operations Command, he replied, "Yes. Absolutely."

9. No Actionable Intelligence

A top official in the Office of the Under Secretary of Defense for Policy in the 1990s described the intelligence deficit with respect to targeting Osama bin Laden: "If you get intelligence, it's by definition very perishable. He moves all the time and he undoubtedly puts out false stories about where he's moving," making it extremely difficult "to get somebody from anyplace outside of Afghanistan into Afghanistan in time. The biggest problem was always intelligence."

But if the target had been broadened to al Qaeda's infrastructure, the intelligence requirements would have been less demanding, noted Dick Clarke. "There was plenty of intelligence. We had incredibly good intelligence about where bin Laden's facilities were. While we might never have been able to say at any given moment where he was, we knew half a dozen places that he moved among. So there was ample opportunity to use Special Forces."

In effect, to turn the need for "actionable intelligence" into a showstopper, all you have to do is define the target narrowly. That makes the intelligence requirements nearly impossible to satisfy. Broaden the picture, and the challenge of actionable intelligence became more manageable.

Special Operators are actually the first to seek good intelligence. But according to an officer on the Joint Staff at the time, "no actions [were] taken to pre-position or deploy the kinds of people that could have addressed those intelligence shortfalls"—people who could have provided the operational-level intelligence needed for SOF to deploy rapidly against fleeting targets in the safe havens where terrorists nest.

What was essential for counterterrorism operations was to establish intelligence networks in places harboring targets. This "operational preparation of the battlespace" is accomplished by infiltrating special operators who pass for locals. Their job includes recruiting indigenous elements who can help SOF units enter an area of interest, and organize, train, and equip local resistance and surrogate forces to assist them.

But no such preparation took place in the 1990s in terrorist havens like Afghanistan, Yemen, Lebanon, and Sudan. Operating in those lands "would have taken official approval that prior to 9/11 would have never been given to us," one knowledgeable individual explained. "Prior to 9/11 there was no willingness to put Department of Defense personnel in such places. No such request would have been authorized."

Why? Because it's dicey, was the bottom line for a former senior Clinton appointee at the Pentagon. Asked if there were proposals at his level for it, he said: "Not that I remember," adding, "I can understand why. It raises a lot of questions. Without saying you shouldn't do it, it is one of those things that is going to cause concern . . . . You're talking not just about recruiting individuals to be sent, but recruiting whole organizations, and you think about it in the context of Somalia. I'm sure that would have raised a lot of questions. I can see why people would have been reluctant."

During Clinton's second term, then, the possibility of hunting down the terrorists did receive ample attention at the top echelons of government. But somewhere between inception and execution, the SOF options were always scuttled as too problematic.

War and tragedy have a way of breaking old attitudes. September 11, 2001, should have caused a sea change in SOF's role in fighting terrorism. To some extent, it has. Consider the stellar contribution of Special Operations Forces to the campaign in Afghanistan in 2001-02. In the early planning stages, SOF was only ancillary to the war plan; but by the end of October 2001, it had moved to center stage. It played a decisive role in toppling the Taliban and routing al Qaeda.

Since then, SOF have deployed to places like Yemen and the Philippines to train local militaries to fight al Qaeda and its affiliates. And last year, Secretary Rumsfeld ordered the Special Operations Command to track down and destroy al Qaeda around the globe. In effect, he ordered a global manhunt to prevent future 9/11s, including attacks with weapons of mass destruction.

In the war against terrorism, a global SOF campaign against al Qaeda is indispensable. Happily, our special counterterrorism units are tailor-made for this. And now that the United States is at war, it should be possible to overcome the showstoppers that blocked the "peacetime" use of those forces through the 1990s.

It should be—but will it? The answer is mixed. Some showstoppers have been neutralized. While law enforcement still has a role to play, we are clearly fighting a war, in which the Department of Defense and the armed forces take the lead. Thus, there should be far less latitude for turning advocates of tough counterterrorism missions into pariahs. September 11 and the president's response to it changed the terms of the policy discussion.

Yet the other showstoppers have not ceased to matter. Competing power centers continue to jockey for influence over counterterrorism policy. In a war in which the CIA may feel it has both a role to play and lost ground to regain, the Title 10/Title 50 debate and arguments over actionable intelligence are likely to persist. In our democratic society, fear of another Somalia remains. And the conventional military's mistrust of SOF has not evaporated.

Once again, a civilian is pushing for greater use of Special Operations Forces. Secretary of Defense Rumsfeld wants the Special Operations Command, for the first time in its history, to play the role of a "supported command," instead of supporting the geographic commands, as it has in the past. Neither those commands nor their friends on the Joint Staff are likely to welcome a reversal of the relationship in order to facilitate SOF missions. "Who's in command here?" could become a new wartime showstopper. Some in SOF believe it already has.

Once again, the problem involves institutions, organizational cultures, and entrenched ways of thinking. "Rumsfeld might think we're at war with terrorism," observed one former general, "but I'll bet he also thinks he is at war within the Pentagon. . . . The real war's happening right there in his building. It's a war of the culture. He can't go to war because he can't get his organization up for it."

Donald Rumsfeld may believe that Special Operations Forces should be in the forefront of the global war on terrorism. But for that to happen, he will have to breach what remains of the phalanx of resistance that blocked the offensive use of special mission units for over a decade—and he'll have to overcome the new showstoppers as well.

For now, it appears that the most powerful defense secretary ever has failed in his attempt to do this. In a disquieting October 16, 2003, memo to the Pentagon elite in the war on terror—General Dick Meyers, Joint Chiefs chairman; Deputy Defense Secretary

Paul Wolfowitz; General Pete Pace, vice chairman of the Joint Chiefs; and Doug Feith, undersecretary of defense for policy—Rumsfeld laments that progress has been slow and the Defense Department has not "yet made truly bold moves" in fighting al Qaeda. And he wonders whether his department "is changing fast enough to deal with the new 21st century security environment."

It's a good question. As al Qaeda regroups and deploys to new battlefields in Iraq and elsewhere, our special mission units—the Delta boys, the SEALs, and the rest—remain on the shelf. It's time to take them off.

Richard H. Shultz Jr. is director of international security studies at the Fletcher School, Tufts University, and was director of research at the Consortium for the Study of Intelligence in Washington, D.C.

Chapter 8

Strategies and Approaches for Combating Terrorism

Martha Crenshaw argues that the strategic dimensions of terrorism were neglected by both scholars of U.S foreign policy and terrorism specialists prior to September 11, 2001. In spite of significant divergence on preferred strategies, scholars concerned with the future of U.S. foreign policy—or grand strategy—shared "a lack of concern about terrorism." Terrorism specialists, on the other hand, typically considered "terrorist political violence as a stand-alone phenomenon, without reference to its geopolitical and strategic context." Crenshaw contends that prior to 9/11 "counterterrorism policy [was] rarely discussed in terms of its place in broader national security planning." As a result, a pattern of incrementalism, rather than a strategy, characterizes the American response to terrorism before the 9/11 attacks. Crenshaw insists that the 9/11 attacks call for a rethinking of terrorism and the response to it and argues that "counterterrorist strategy must be linked to grand strategy and grand strategy to policy goals."

Along similar lines, Daniel Byman suggests that a "garbage-pail approach" characterizes the efforts of the Bush administration to fight al Qaeda and its allies after 9/11. "These efforts are not part of an overarching strategic framework that lays out a path to victory. They are at best not integrated and at worst working against one another." According to Byman, "most elements of counterterrorism strategy address one of two different goals: disrupting the group itself and its operations; or changing the overall environment to defuse the group's anger or make it harder to raise money or attract recruits." In his article, Byman "lays out and compares seven strategic options for going after al Qaeda and its allies" and "finds that the best approach is to work with allies to fight terrorism in the hopes of containing the terrorists."

Brigadier General Russell D. Howard (ret.) argues that the Bush administration—or any administration—has no choice but to have a preemptive military doctrine when addressing terrorists who are transnational, non-state actors who possess weapons of mass destruction. According to Howard, Westphalian rules don't apply when dealing with transnational, non-state actors. The normal means of influence in dealing with states—diplomatic, economic, and military—are not applicable when dealing with al Qaeda or any other terrorist group that owes no allegiance to a state.

Paul Pillar delves into these issues even deeper with an article addressing counterterrorism in a post–al Qaeda environment. He, like others in this volume, describes the current al Qaeda threat as less of an organization and more of an ideological threat. Pillar argues that whereas "The fortunes of Osama bin Laden's Al Qaeda . . . have fluctuated,. . . . The trajectory of the larger movements over the past few years has been mostly up." The shift from organization to ideology presents distinctly different problems than the United States and other Western democracies have faced thus far in the conflict against terrorism. Governments like to fight against defined enemies, be they other states or non-state actors.

An article by Steven Simon and Jeff Martini explores the most critical issue raised in this volume—the need to deny al Qaeda its appeal. Without the development of a comprehensive strategy to accomplish this critical goal through the reordering of the U.S. national security norms, the al Qaeda derivative organizations will continue to regenerate and continue to attack U.S. interests.

This chapter concludes with an article by Matthew Levitt that presents an argument that counterterrorism efforts should be thought of in terms of shaping, defining, and ultimately constricting terrorists' support environments. In his article, Levitt demonstrates that the numerous groups share a "network of interlocking logistical support groups." The logistical and support intersections present unique opportunities to interdict and disrupt terrorist group plans and operations. Many times, policymakers and intelligence specialists look to "pigeonhole" terrorists as members of one group or another. Levitt argues that this myopic approach to terrorism analysis is problematic and misses the true nature of the terrorist environment today. Failing to identify and understand these connections undercuts the existing counterterrorism programs.

Martha Crenshaw

Terrorism, Strategies, and Grand Strategies

After September 11, 2001, terrorism took center stage in the debate among security studies, international relations, and foreign policy specialists over a grand strategy for the United States in the post-cold war era. Stephen Walt, for example, asserted that the September 11 attack had triggered the most rapid and dramatic change ever in the history of U.S. foreign policy.[1] The transition commonly was termed a "watershed."

The threat of terrorism was not prefigured, however, by the debate over grand strategy. Prevailing theories of international relations did not predict the outcome of developments that had begun much earlier, much as they failed to foresee the end of the cold war. Terrorism was not generally considered an important national security threat unless it combined two dangers: a threat to the U.S. homeland *and* the use of "weapons of mass destruction"—defined as nuclear, chemical, biological, or radiological weapons. Even then, the idea that terrorism was critically important to national security was not widely accepted by foreign policy specialists inside and outside of government.

Nor did analysts in the "terrorism studies" community—a group distinct from national security specialists—offer much substantive input to the debate over grand strategy. They tended to focus on explaining terrorism rather than prescribing solutions, and they rarely considered terrorism in the context of other foreign policy issues. In fact, these specialists often doubted that a consistent approach to terrorism was possible.

The September 11 attacks call for a rethinking of terrorism and the response to it. This task requires the combined efforts of foreign policy and terrorism specialists in government and in academia. Whether the response to terrorism is a set of individual counterterrorist operations, designed for specific circumstances, or a general strategy applied to a variety of cases, it must be shaped in terms of a larger conception of American security and interests. Such an integrated conception must be based on new ideas of both power and security. Strategic thinking in the post-cold war world must account for the unconventional power of nonstate actors: risk-takers who are willing to violate norms and who may be immune to military threats. A new conception of security also must consider the harmful consequences of the lack of power, as well as the damage that can be inflicted by power.

In this chapter I first establish the requirements for the development of a coherent response that would link means and ends. Next I analyze the period before the shock of September 11 in terms of the debate over grand strategy, the arguments of the "terrorism studies" specialists about responding to terrorism, and the government's actions. I then evaluate the impact of September 11 on grand strategy proposals and on the government's response to terrorism. Last, I ask whether the current American stance on terrorism meets the requirements for effective strategy, grand strategy, and policy.

Defining Strategy, Grand Strategy, and Policy

A necessary preliminary to analyzing the response to terrorism is a definition of the respective conceptual requirements for strategies, grand strategies, and policy in the abstract. It is worth noting, however, that in practice many accounts use the terms interchangeably.

A strategy—which typically refers to military operations—requires a precisely specified political objective. Strategy is a scheme for making the means produce the desired ends.[2] It is concerned with the relationship between means and ends—that is, with how the government's actions are designed to produce desired outcomes. The means must be sufficient to accomplish the ends, but a good design does not have goals that are so ambitious that resources cannot support them or so ambiguous that purposive actions cannot be crafted to reach them. The costs of any strategy must be acceptable in terms of the expected benefits, and the risks must be sensible. Yet however necessary strategy may be, it is not always possible. The constraints may be prohibitive.

"Grand strategy" represents a more inclusive conception that explains how a state's full range of resources can be adapted to achieve national security. It determines what the state's vital security interests are, identifies critical threats to them, and specifies the means of dealing with them. Thus, a "grand strategy" is complex, multifaceted, and directed toward a distant time horizon. It establishes a comprehensive framework that coordinates the objectives of individual strategies. It would explain how defending the nation against terrorism can and should relate to other foreign policy objectives—such as, for example, preventing the emergence of great power challengers, spreading democracy, and controlling the proliferation of weapons of mass destruction (WMD).

Policy defines the goals of strategy and "grand" or higher strategy. It is a statement of purpose. The central purpose of counterterrorist strategy is to prevent attacks on U.S. territory that cause large numbers of civilian casualties. Terrorism does not pose the threat of annihilation that the Soviet Union's nuclear capabilities did during the cold war. What was and is at stake is not national survival, material power, or the integrity of our armed forces and national defense system but the individual security of American civilians at home. This objective, however, must be coordinated with other policy purposes. Policy must determine priorities among competing values.

The Grand Strategy Debate before September 11

Scholars engaged in the debate over the future of American foreign policy in the 1990s agreed about the purpose of grand strategy—it should define and rank American interests, identify the major threats to them, and establish policy guidelines for protecting those interests—while they disagreed with regard to its content. They shared, however, a lack of concern about terrorism. The policy recommendations of scholars in the security studies and international relations fields typically did not cite terrorism as a major threat to American security.[3] Advocates of American primacy or preponderance focused on potential great power challengers, not terrorism. Advocates of "selective engagement" urged the United States to concentrate its efforts only on the most powerful states. Proponents of "offshore balancing," who thought that the United States should play the role of balancer in the international system and avoid foreign commitments, were more likely to cite the risk of terrorism as a reason for decreased international involvement, but only as a peripheral argument. For instance, Layne supported the case for disengagement with the general claim that "the risk of conflict, and the possible exposure of the American homeland to attack, derive directly from the overseas commitments mandated by preponderance's expansive definition of U.S. interests."[4] A similar argument for "restraint" mentioned terrorism in a footnote as an exception to "the great news is that America faces almost no discernible security threats."[5] One paragraph subsequently was devoted to explaining that the United States should continue to try to prevent and respond to terrorism but that restraint in world affairs would reduce the incentives to attack U.S. targets.[6]

One reason for this neglect may be that studies of grand strategy usually proceeded from realist assumptions,[7] despite some attempts to include domestic variables.[8] In such a framework, threats emanate from states, not non-states, and the most powerful states are the most important for American interests. Weak or failed states and shadowy underground conspiracies do not constitute challenges to the American position in the world. From this perspective, threats are simple to interpret. They stem from rival states that can challenge one's power now or in the future. The dominant mode of thought is worst-case analysis, by which one necessarily associates hostile intent with rising power.

Furthermore, the security studies and international relations fields were not especially hospitable to scholars interested in terrorism precisely because it was not considered an important problem for the discipline or for the development of grand strategy. As an intellectual approach, it did not lend itself to abstract theory or modeling.[9] The study of terrorism was too policy oriented to be of serious academic significance.

There were some exceptions to this general rule. Robert J. Art, defending a grand strategy of selective engagement, argued that a key American interest was preventing a WMD attack on the American homeland and that such an attack might come from "fanatical terrorists" using nuclear, biological, or chemical weapons.[10] In this framework, however, terrorism became a danger only when combined with WMD proliferation, and states continued to pose a greater threat than transnational actors. The most prescient analysts were Ashton B. Carter and William J. Perry, who defined "catastrophic" terrorism as a key threat and called for the response to terrorism to be incorporated into a general strategy of "preventive defense."[11] Their contribution had little impact on the overall "grand strategy" debate, however, perhaps because both authors were former high government officials rather than scholars.

"Terrorism Studies" before September 11

In their turn, terrorism specialists tended to neglect the strategic dimensions of the issue. The study of terrorism was divorced from the study of foreign policy and national security, as well as from theories of international relations. As Ian Lesser, an analyst for the Rand Corporation, concluded, "Most contemporary analyses of terrorism focus on terrorist political violence as a stand-alone phenomenon, without reference to its geopolitical and strategic context. Similarly, counterterrorism policy is rarely discussed in terms of its place in broader national security planning."[12] Lesser implied that this oversight was due to the perception that terrorism was not an existential threat unless it used WMD.

In contrast, Richard Falkenrath argued that scholars focusing on terrorism were skeptical of the WMD threat.[13] In his view, the specialists were critical of the Clinton administration's domestic preparedness program because they regarded the threat of WMD terrorism as highly unlikely and distracting—a judgment they based on observations of the past. Falkenrath suggested that the study of terrorism was useful for a variety of things, such as understanding motivation, but that it could not provide tactical warning, assess threats, or set priorities. Its predictions tended to be linear: a straight projection of the future from the past.

A possible explanation for the neglect of international relations was that specialists on terrorism usually represented interdisciplinary interests. Contributors came from backgrounds in sociology, psychology, anthropology, history, law, criminal justice, and communications, as well as political science. Within political science, scholars focusing on terrorism did not often work in the field of international relations. They were equally or more likely to be specialists in civil conflict. Multidisciplinarity made it hard to build a unifying set of theoretical assumptions that could coordinate different approaches to understanding the threat of terrorism or analyzing responses.

Nevertheless, before September 11 most specialists on terrorism, inside and outside of government, had concluded that an undifferentiated response to terrorism was either inappropriate or politically impossible. The reasons for this conclusion were based on the character of the threat and on the nature of domestic policies.

Character of the Threat

In 2000, Paul Pillar warned against inflexibility: "The terrorist threat is not really 'a threat' but rather a method used by an assortment of actors who threaten U.S. interests in varying ways and degrees."[14] Critical differences among contexts should "form the basis for tailoring what is, in effect, a different counterterrorist policy for each group or state."[15] Because the response should be shaped to individual circumstances, it is complicated and difficult and does not lend itself to generalization or rhetorical flourish. In Pillar's view, "Much attention has been paid to making counterterrorist measures stronger, broader, or more numerous. . . . More needs to be paid to gauging how effective or applicable such measures are to individual cases."[16]

Earlier analyses had made similar points. In 1986 Livingstone and Arnold observed that "the task of designing and implementing effective national policies to deal with terrorism is overwhelming in its scope and permutations and argues less for a general all-embracing strategy to address the problem than a multitude of less-ambitious component strategies, which in sum provide an overall framework for controlling and suppressing terrorism on a global scale."[17] Likewise, Marc Celmer—also analyzing the response of the Reagan administration—agreed that the issue did not lend itself to strategy.[18] Grant Wardlaw, an Australian defense specialist and terrorism analyst, also cautioned that "the idea of a general policy against terrorism is inherently faulty—terrorism has to be countered in a discriminating, case-by-case way."[19] Wardlaw warned that policy should remain at a general level to retain flexibility and imagination in dealing with what he regarded as a "literally infinite range of possible terrorist scenarios." Similar observations continued in the 1990s. Jeffrey D. Simon, for example, concluded that one of the key lessons learned from the experience of countering terrorism was "do not declare any official 'policy' on terrorism."[20]

In fact, critics considered public statements of general policy not only ineffectual but also counterproductive in that they undermined domestic political support. Wardlaw argued that strident policy rhetoric was likely to embarrass the government when principles had to be compromised, as they inevitably would. He also noted that when the government announced to the public that it had a strategy for managing terrorism, each subsequent terrorist incident made that policy look ineffective. Similarly, as Simon pointed out, the no-concessions principle—an ostensible cornerstone of U.S. policy since 1974—often was violated.[21] The Iran–Contra affair was only the most conspicuous of such public contradictions. Consistency in policy is necessary only if the government has promised it.

An additional aspect of the conceptual difficulty of dealing with terrorism was the tension between criminal justice and national security approaches to the issue, which was reflected in institutional rivalries within the government. Since the early 1980s specialists had debated whether terrorism should be defined as crime or as warfare. Each type of problem calls for a different set of policy responses. If it is a crime, a law enforcement strategy is appropriate. If it is warfare, a military response is warranted.

Domestic Politics

An alternative position within the "terrorism studies" school aspired to the development of a more systematic and overarching policy structure but considered it unlikely for reasons of domestic politics rather than the inherent intractability of the problem. Yehezkel Dror, an Israeli scholar specializing in policy analysis, argued that "terrorism is an unusual, though not extraordinary, phenomenon with some features of an extreme case"—which makes it difficult to understand and almost impossible to predict.[22] He concluded, however, that "grand policies" or "grand strategies" were unlikely because democratic governments were not disposed to construct them, not because the phenomenon was indeterminate. He observed that as long as "disjointed incrementalism" and normal decision making seemed to work, governments had no incentive for more ambitious strategies. Thus, "when a problem is handled in what is perceived to be a satisfying way, there will be little propensity to engage in policy innovation."[23] Because governments confront so many pressing problems, they are tempted to keep an issue in the "realm of the ordinary" as long as possible. At the same time, democracies lack the requirements for preparing grand policies. They learn poorly and handle complexity badly. Furthermore, Dror suspected that democracies, characterized by dispersed authority and ad hoc reactions, would not implement grand policies even if they were available. He predicted that a catastrophic shock might jolt a democratic government into action, if the shock revealed decisively that incremental policies had failed.

Over the years analysts emphasized the same domestic obstacles to effective strategy.[24] One barrier was the ever-expanding number of government agencies tasked with a counterterrorism mission. In many ways bureaucratic proliferation was the result of the complexity of the threat, but the expansion of responsibilities also was the result of inertia and incrementalism, as new functions were layered on old ones. The policymaking process also required coordinating the activities of agencies with both domestic and foreign policy jurisdictions. In this context, critics noted the absence of strong leadership from the top. The process was highly decentralized, permitting and encouraging rivalries among different executive branch agencies. The result of intermittent attention from the White House and the president was uncoordinated policy. With each terrorist crisis, terrorism rose to the top of the presidential agenda. In between crises, it sank to the bottom, as other critical issues competed for attention. Presidential advisers tended to regard terrorism as a no-win issue. Sequential attention also was encouraged by the news media, especially television. During the 1980s more interest groups became involved in the policy process, including victims' families (for example, the families of the victims of Pan Am 103). Largely as a result of public awareness, Congress also came to play a stronger role in pressing the executive to be more proactive and forward-looking. With such widely dispersed and autonomous centers of authority, all sensitive to public constituencies, any American government would find planning and implementing a consistent strategy a formidable task.

Government Response before September 11

The Clinton and elder Bush administrations tended to interpret terrorism in light of their preconceptions about American policy in a post–cold war world. As scholars did, policymakers defined the threat of terrorism and formulated counterterrorist strategies in a way that supported worldviews that were established in other contexts. Terrorism was fitted into a preexisting framework.

Although terrorism became an increasingly serious threat in the post–cold war world, the Clinton administration was not initially inclined to regard terrorism as a major national security issue. For example, David Tucker, a former Foreign Service officer writing a history of American policy toward terrorism, concluded that a "strategic vacuum" followed the Reagan administration strategy, which linked terrorism to the Soviet Union and the cold war.[25] Terrorism was not part of general foreign policy planning, as Paul Pillar confirmed.[26]

The Clinton administration entered office holding to the principle that terrorism best fit into a category of "modern" problems such as global organized crime, epidemics of disease, and environmental disasters. These dangers were not represented as threats directed specifically against American interests but common perils all states face. This framing of the issue was consistent with the administration's preferences for a multilateral approach. Thus, the Clinton administration took a modest position. Its policy was based on four simple principles: no concessions or rewards for terrorists, sanctions against state sponsors, international cooperation, and implementation of the rule of law.

Events quickly commanded the government's attention, however. The 1993 bombing of the World Trade Center and then the 1995 Aum Shinrikyo sarin gas attack on the Tokyo subway system and the Oklahoma City bombing brought terrorism onto the domestic policy agenda. Pressure from Congress and from local law enforcement agencies and "first responders" created a sense of urgency about the prospect of terrorist use of WMD—particularly chemical and biological weapons. "Homeland defense" against chemical and biological threats preoccupied policymakers, even though terrorism specialists remained dubious about the prospect of WMD terrorism.[27] Even the simultaneous bombings of American embassies in Kenya and Tanzania in 1998, the "millennium" plots of 1999, and the October 2000 attack on the USS *Cole* in Yemen did not make terrorism a national security priority or an essential element of foreign policy planning. A series of congressionally mandated reports and studies warned that terrorism should rank higher on the national agenda, but other international issues competed for attention: for example, crises in Somalia, Haiti, Bosnia, Kosovo, and South Asia and managing relations with Russia, North Korea, and China. The president also focused on mediating a settlement of the Israeli–Palestinian conflict.

The Clinton administration was not passive. The government responded to the East Africa bombings with cruise missile attacks on a pharmaceuticals plant in the Sudan suspected of links to al-Qaeda and on training camps in Afghanistan, some run by Pakistani intelligence services. Covert operations by the Central Intelligence Agency (CIA) to disrupt bin Laden's operations expanded steadily from 1996 to 2001. These operations focused on apprehending bin Laden and bringing him to trial—or possibly killing him, should these efforts fail. Arrests of suspected al-Qaeda militants led to more than thirty successful prosecutions in U.S. courts. These convictions included the persons responsible for the first World Trade Center bombing as well as some of the perpetrators of the 1998 East African bombings. Economic and diplomatic sanctions against the Taliban regime in Afghanistan were gradually tightened, with the support of the United Nations. The administration believed, however, that the public would not support an escalation of military counterterrorist efforts—especially not the use of ground troops. The government also declined to put strong pressure on Pakistan to cease its support for the Taliban.

In the period between the resolution of the drawn-out contest over the 2000 presidential election and September 2001, the second Bush administration also had other concerns, most domestic. There appears to have been no great sense of urgency about dealing with terrorism.[28] In the last months of the Clinton administration, the National Security Council (NSC) staff had developed a plan for a more active counterterrorist strategy, including arming the Northern Alliance against the Taliban. The new NSC decided to put the proposal through a policy review process that did not conclude until the following September.

Impact of September 11 on the Grand Strategy Debate

The attacks of September 11 propelled terrorism from obscurity to prominence in the wider field of international relations and foreign and security policy. It now took center stage in the grand strategy debate. Scholars who had previously ignored terrorism now acknowledged it as a major national security concern; in fact, some saw the threat of terrorism as occasion for a complete reorientation of post–cold war foreign policy. Barry Posen, for example, called for an end to treating terrorism as "administered policy" and the inauguration of a genuine strategy—the prior absence of which he blamed on domestic politics, bureaucratic inertia, and a weak intelligence effort.[29] Similarly, Stephen Walt cited faults associated with the domestic political process: the lack of serious public interest in foreign policy, the failure of leaders to see the risks inherent in foreign engagements, their partisanship, the influence of special interests, and congressional irresponsibility. He proposed that the United States take the role of being a great power more seriously.[30]

As Barry Posen observed, however, after September 11 the advocates of alternative grand strategies generally superimposed them on their interpretation of terrorism rather than using the case to reexamine their prior assumptions.[31] Each proponent of a foreign policy vision saw the "new" threat of terrorism as justification for the opinions or theories he proposed before September 11.[32] Several analysts thought that American policy was unlikely to change course. Walt, for example, did not think that the United States needed a new grand strategy, merely a reordering of priorities to include managing the antiterrorism coalition, controlling weapons of mass destruction, reconstructing Afghanistan, and improving relations with the Arab and Muslim worlds. Although not necessarily favoring the status quo, Steven Miller agreed that the September 11 attacks would not alter the basic policy of unilateralism that the Bush administration had originally pursued.[33] Although in the short run the issue captured the public and presidential agendas, grand strategy was not likely to change. Miller predicted that the impact of the attacks would be transitory.

On the other hand, Ashton Carter regarded the events of September 11 as confirmation of his prior view that the United States was pursuing the wrong grand strategy and urgently needed a new one, along the lines of the one he proposed before September 11.[34] In his view, catastrophic terrorism, not great-power rivalry, was likely to be the centerpiece of international security studies for the foreseeable future.

Proponents of a restrained American foreign policy predictably cited the U.S. pursuit of preponderance as a partial cause of the September 11 attacks, which they interpreted as a wake-up call for a new and radically different grand strategy of reduced international involvement.[35] In their view, American hegemony was the cause; reorientation of American foreign policy toward a less prominent world role would be the solution. Responsibility for maintaining order and stability should be devolved onto other states, so as to encourage multipolarity rather than primacy. The United States should become a fatalistic bystander in international affairs.

American Response after September 11

The history of American foreign policy exhibits a pattern of reaction to shock, and it may have been inevitable that only a devastating blow from terrorism, causing thousands of civilian casualties on American soil, could bring about fundamental policy change.[36] The United States was slow in responding to emerging threats in the past, and comparisons to the galvanizing effects of the 1941 attack on Pearl Harbor and the 1950 North Korean invasion of South Korea became commonplace after September 11.

After the shock of the multiple hijackings, the Bush administration declared a war on terrorism. The purpose of a war on terrorism is to destroy the enemy's capacity to act, not influence his decision making to deter or compel. Using the metaphor of war defined the problem as a threat to national security, prescribed the solution as military engagement, and predicted eventual victory over the adversary, although officials cautioned the public that the war would be long. In this framework, the alternative to an offensive strategy was defeat, which was unacceptable. The war metaphor also was compatible with American political culture and discourse, which also endorsed wars on drugs, poverty, crime, and other social problems.

The extraordinarily high number of casualties caused by the September 11 surprise attacks, as well as the nature of the targets (actual and intended), raised the stakes considerably. The United States was now willing to use means previously considered politically unacceptable: intervention with ground forces to overthrow a regime that actively supported a terrorist organization and destruction of that organization's territorial base. Both the Clinton and Bush administrations previously had considered and employed alternative options to end the Taliban's support for bin Laden. The military campaign in Afghanistan in October 2001 followed a series of unsuccessful demands that the Taliban surrender bin Laden, accompanied by the imposition of multilateral sanctions endorsed by the UN. In fact, Secretary of State Colin Powell suggested after bombing began that "moderate elements" of the Taliban might have a place in a future government.

Regional and international alliances were cemented to support the campaign. Pakistan—formerly an ally of the Taliban—was induced to support the American war effort, as were Uzbekistan and Tajikistan. The war effort went beyond direct military operations to defeat the Taliban regime in Afghanistan and destroy the infrastructure of the al-Qaeda organization; it also incorporated military assistance, including training, to regimes confronting local insurgencies with links to al-Qaeda—principally Yemen, the Philippines, and Georgia. The United States also organized an international coalition to legitimize the war on terrorism, provide operational assistance in Afghanistan, and disrupt al-Qaeda operations. National police and intelligence services from Europe to Asia were mobilized to apprehend al-Qaeda suspects and cut off their financial resources. The CIA's covert operations against terrorism were intensified. Hundreds of suspects were seized—some kept as "unlawful combatants" at Guantanamo Bay in Cuba, others left in the hands of governments willing to hold and interrogate them. The American government also emphasized public diplomacy to reduce the popular support bases of Islamic militancy in Muslim countries, especially in the Middle East.

The State Department's annual report for 2001 described American policy as (1) make no concessions to terrorists and no "deals" if hostages are seized; (2) bring terrorists to justice (i.e., to trial in the United States); (3) isolate and apply pressure to states that support terrorism to induce them to change their behavior; and (4) bolster the counterterrorist efforts of countries that help the United States.[37] The statement summarized efforts in the fields of diplomacy, intelligence, law enforcement, and finance. Military instruments, principally Operation Enduring Freedom, were mentioned last. The document emphasized international cooperation on all fronts.

After the Taliban regime was overthrown and al-Qaeda's territorial base in Afghanistan eliminated, the Bush administration began to expand its foreign policy conceptions. The formal statement of a new set of principles came in September 2002 with the release of *The National Security Strategy of the United States of America*.[38] Many elements of this plan predated the war on terrorism.[39] According to National Security Adviser Condoleeza Rice, however, September 11 was an "earthquake" or tectonic plate shift, analogous to the events that precipitated the cold war in 1945–47. This jolt clarified and sharpened the American conception of its role in the world.[40] Opposing terrorism and preventing irresponsible states from acquiring WMD, in her view, now defined the national interest.

The 2002 national security strategy recognized that nonstates are important enemies and that weak states are dangerous. It called for a response to threats before they are fully formed and justified preemption as anticipatory self-defense. To this end, the United States would seek international support but would act alone if American interests and "unique" responsibilities required. The strategy required a more global military presence. At the same time, it included public diplomacy or a "war of ideas" to delegitimize terrorism and alter the conditions and ideologies that permit it to flourish. The Bush administration explained this strong response as a moral necessity in dealing with "evil." The designated "rogue state" enemies—Iran, Iraq, and North Korea—were states that demonstrated generally hostile intent, oppressed their own citizens, threatened their neighbors, and possessed or were in the process of acquiring WMD as well as the means of delivery.[41]

A first requirement of the national security strategy was regime replacement in Iraq.[42] Replacing Saddam Hussein was considered to be a solution not only to the threat of a rogue state with the potential to use highly lethal weapons but also to a range of problems in the Middle East, including the Palestinian-Israeli conflict and lack of democracy. The expectation was that a new, democratic Iraq could serve as a model for other Arab states and a new source of regional stability. The administration also claimed that Iraq was linked to al-Qaeda and was likely to supply the organization with WMD. Thus, Saddam Hussein's removal also would serve the purposes of the war on terrorism.

In February 2003 the administration published a complementary *National Strategy for Combating Terrorism*. The strategy is based on the assumption that the September 11 attacks were acts of war, that terrorism, rather than a named adversary, is the enemy, and that defeating terrorism is the primary and immediate priority of the U.S. government. The strategy's purpose is to identify and defuse threats before they materialize into attacks on U.S. territory and interests. It stipulates that the United States will act unilaterally if need be and that it will act preemptively in self-defense. The United States will not wait for terrorists to act; instead it will employ an aggressive offensive strategy that is based on law enforcement and intelligence, military power, and international cooperation to block terrorist financing. All aspects of U.S. power will be employed in the struggle, and the United States will assist states that lack the resources to combat terrorism. Preventing terrorists from acquiring and using WMD is a central goal of the strategy; this threat is regarded as real and immediate. The "4D" strategy is summarized as "defeat, deny, diminish, and defend": The United States will destroy terrorist organizations; deny them the support of states; address the underlying conditions that permit and encourage terrorism (including finding a solution to the Israeli—Palestinian conflict); and defend the country, its citizens, and its interests abroad against attack. Victory is defined as the achievement of a world in which terrorism does not define the daily lives of Americans and their friends and allies. The goal, attainable only after long and sustained effort, is to eliminate terrorism as a threat to the American way of life.

Shortly after the announcement of the counterterrorist strategy, the Bush administration demonstrated the new reality of its preemptive and unilateralist strategy by launching the war against Iraq. The military campaign was justified as necessary to remove a regime that did and was likely to continue to support terrorism and had acquired and intended to keep acquiring WMD. The United States was successful in quickly ending Saddam Hussein's reign in Iraq and in doing so with a minimum of U.S. and allied casualties.

The cost, however, was the alienation of many of the United States' closest allies. Furthermore, the postwar occupation proved arduous and vexed, in part because of the emergence of violent opposition groups and individuals using guerrilla tactics. The prospect that Saddam Hussein survived the assault to lead a war of attrition against the occupying forces seemed increasingly likely. The failure to discover WMD also undermined U.S. credibility in the eyes of its critics—although not in the view of the American public, whose support for the war and the occupation remained strong in the war's immediate aftermath.

Critical Evaluation

How well did the American response fulfill the requirements of strategy? Can the response to terrorism—whether a comprehensive general approach or a set of case-by-case reactions tailored to circumstances—be fitted into a grand strategy for the United States? What is the relationship between defeating terrorism and intervening to overthrow the Iraqi regime or other "rogue states"?

Consider first counterterrorist strategy. The September 11 attacks broke what appeared to be a pattern of incrementalism in the American response to terrorism. The ambitiousness of the war on terrorism is not in doubt, although there was more continuity between the Clinton and Bush administrations' responses than the latter preferred to recognize. The definition of the objective and the logic of the relationship between ends and means in the war on terrorism, however, are not entirely clear. Are the ends so ambitious that no means could reach them? What is victory over terrorism? How can the removal of terrorism as a threat to the American way of life be measured?

The war in Afghanistan had two objectives. As a war against the Taliban regime, the strategy apparently succeeded in the short run because the Taliban regime was overthrown. Mullah Omar, however, remained unaccounted for. The outcome of the military campaign against al-Qaeda was problematic. Elements of the organization remained in areas of Afghanistan and Pakistan and continued to use terrorism against Western interests. Significant attacks occurred in Tunisia, Morocco, Saudi Arabia, Kenya, and Indonesia. Furthermore, such an adversary—a nonstate actor structured as a global network or conglomeration of franchise operations, with considerable local autonomy and flexibility—seemed to be able to reconstitute itself even after a physical defeat in a specific location. Al-Qaeda appeared to be independent of state support; conceivably, the organization could exist without a fixed territorial base, relying on multiple decentralized operational centers. Thus, preemptive strikes against states might have little effect.

The United States initiated the war not just against the Taliban and al-Qaeda but in principle against "terrorism of global reach." This war was waged not against al-Qaeda as a distinct nonstate entity but against the means the organization—or, for that matter, any other organization—chose to employ. This goal was so open-ended that accomplishing it might never be possible.

Moreover, an unintended and potentially costly consequence of counterterrorist strategy specifically as well as the new national security strategies could be the encouragement of future incarnations of the threat, as a reaction to extended U.S. military involvement around the world, outside Iraq. Encouraging states to crush terrorism could lead to the suppression of all opposition, provoking the establishment of new underground conspiracies with radical objectives and hatred for the United States. The strategy did not define limits to American assistance to regimes battling various violent challenges linked to terrorism "with global reach"—a phrase also left undefined. For example, how strong should the link be between a local conflict and al-Qaeda for the United States to intervene?

The strategy of preemption announced in 2002 applied to all threats, not just terrorism. It aimed to destroy the enemy's capacity to attack in advance, not influence its "will" or calculus of decision. The strategy's advocates perceived it as an attempt to alter a threatening status quo to defend American interests. Reliance on preemption also is a way of escaping the dilemma created by lack of tactical warning of terrorist attack or absence of a "smoking gun" of proven state complicity.[43] At the same time, fear of a preemptive attack can lead adversaries to strike first. North Korea, Syria, and Iran could be cases in point.

Thus, the war on terrorism was the centerpiece of a grand strategy of preponderance and unilateralism that the administration favored well before the September 11 attacks.[44] However, the use of military force to preempt state adversaries, particularly Iraq, could be costly in terms of defeating terrorism. If the new national security strategy can be defined as a grand strategy, it may not be compatible with an effective counterterrorist strategy. One consequence was that the war against Iraq alienated members of the antiterrorist coalition, which are essential to American law enforcement and intelligence efforts. NATO was painfully divided over the issue.

American strategic planners seemed not to have thought deeply about what happens after a preemptive war is fought and won. The United States appeared unprepared to cope with the level of insecurity and disorder that followed the collapse of the Iraqi regime. The consequences for the war on terrorism could be extremely negative. For example, the postwar occupation of Iraq could inspire terrorism from al-Qaeda or other extremist groups if it is perceived as evidence that the United States is hostile to Islam. Ironically, American actions might produce a surge of Iraqi nationalism that would unite and motivate violent opposition, including terrorism. Similarly, Afghanistan remained unstable and volatile after a military victory was declared. Neither Saddam Hussein nor Osama bin Laden was conclusively killed or taken into custody.

If in the long term the removal of Saddam Hussein's regime results not in the democratization of Iraq and neighboring regimes but in heightened instability and repressiveness, the prospect of continued terrorism is further heightened.[45] If one conceives of terrorism directed against U.S. interests as a form of internationalized civil conflict—a spillover of local grievances onto the international scene, facilitated by the processes of globalization[46]—then violence that initially is limited and localized could be transformed into "terrorism of global reach" in areas beyond Iraq. It is worth noting that past demonstrations of U.S. power did not dissuade terrorists. The raid on Libya in 1986 was followed by the bombing of Pan Am 103 in 1988. The 1998 strikes against the Sudan and Afghanistan did not halt al-Qaeda.

American efforts to "diminish" the conditions that are presumed to give rise to terrorism included resolving the Israeli-Palestinian conflict as well as establishing democratic stability in Iraq. After the war in Iraq, the Bush administration took on a much more active role than it had initially anticipated. The risks of failure remained high, however. The consequences could extend far beyond the scope of the conflict itself. If the United States—by virtue of its involvement, its power, and its alliance with Israel—is held responsible for continued Israeli violence against Palestinians, its attractiveness as a target of terrorism will grow.

Conclusions

This review of the American response to terrorism raises several critical questions. What sort of American foreign policy or grand strategy would be compatible with controlling terrorism? How might the material and the ideological or normative environment be shaped to discourage and prevent resort to such means? How can all the resources of the United States be coordinated? In particular, how should military means relate to economic and political instruments?

A first conclusion is that policymakers should avoid decontextualizing terrorism. For this reason, counterterrorist strategy must be linked to grand strategy and grand strategy to policy goals. These distinctions are not always clear in the American response to terrorism. It is tempting to attach the response to terrorism to an overarching conceptual structure that dictates top-down reasoning. However, the local political context within which terrorism emerges shapes its trajectory, and threat assessments should not overgeneralize or assume that terrorism is a monolithic force. Strategy must be flexible. Policymakers must learn to deal with complexity and ambiguity.

For example, al-Qaeda evolved under specific and perhaps unique historical circumstances. The Soviet invasion of Afghanistan, the American support for the moudjahidin, and the allied victory in the 1991 Gulf War were key precipitating events that will not be duplicated. Thus, the assumption that al-Qaeda will be a model for future terrorism may be incorrect. A successful strategy for defeating al-Qaeda might not be effective against other threats. In fact, responding uniformly can be dangerous if adversaries thereby are enabled to design around the threats they know.

Moreover, wars are waged against adversaries, not methods. Whether or not one can outlaw a practice by waging war against those who use it is an open question. Eradicating all "terrorism of global reach" establishes an open-ended policy goal. It may be too ambitious for any strategy. Measuring success may not be possible, especially if one considers the number and variety of actors that could practice terrorism.[47]

Although in the past states may have been the only adversaries who counted, the United States can no longer afford to act under this assumption. Yet efforts to justify a strategy of preemption toward Iraq in terms of a war on terrorism demonstrated just such a reliance on old thinking. The threat was no longer the autonomous nonstate actor al-Qaeda but a familiar adversary: Iraq. Reference to the possibility that Iraq might provide chemical, biological, nuclear, or radiological weapons to al-Qaeda was a way of shifting the focus of policy back to a state-centric world and its power balances. In this framework, nonstate actors acquire significance only if they are proxies of states; they are not regarded as independent actors.

Encouraging the liberalization of regimes that are intolerant of dissent, opening space for the expression of moderate opposition, and promoting democracy also form part of a grand strategy that shapes the international environment to make it less conducive to terrorism. The United States must work toward providing an attractive alternative future to persons dissatisfied with the status quo.[48] Otherwise many of the aggrieved are likely to be attracted to radical and anti-American causes. It is not clear that a grand strategy of preemption furthers this purpose.

It is equally critical that U.S. counterterrorist efforts be legitimate in the eyes of the international community. The support of other nations is indispensable to the disruption of terrorist operations and controlling the spread of weapons of mass destruction, but the war against Iraq ignored the dissent of allies. U.S. grand strategy should not ignore interdependence in the domain of international security.

Martha Crenshaw is a senior fellow at Center for International Security and Cooperation and the Freeman Spogli Institute for International Studies at Stanford University. Her current research focuses on innovation in terrorist campaigns, the distinction between "old" and "new" terrorism, how terrorism ends, and why the United States is the target of terrorism. From 1974 to 2007, Dr. Crenshaw was the Colin and Nancy Campbell Professor of Global Issues and Democratic Thought and professor of government at Wesleyan University in Middletown, Connecticut.

Notes

I want to thank Audrey Kurth Cronin and Douglas Foyle for their helpful comments on earlier drafts.

1. Stephen M. Walt, "Beyond bin Laden: Reshaping U.S. Foreign Policy," *International Security* 26, no. 3 (winter 2001-2002): 56.
2. See Richard K. Betts, "Is Strategy an Illusion?" *International Security* 25, no. 2 (fall 2000): 5–50.
3. See Michael Mastanduno, "Preserving the Unipolar Moment: Realist Theories and U.S. Grand Strategy after the Cold War," *International Security* 21, no. 4 (spring 1997): 49–88, and Barry R. Posen and Andrew L. Ross, "Competing Visions for U.S. Grand Strategy," *International Security* 21, no. 3 (winter 1996-97): 5–53.
4. Christopher Layne, "From Preponderance to Offshore Balancing: America's Future Grand Strategy," *International Security* 22, no. 1 (summer 1997): 116. This brief mention occurs in a lengthy article (pp. 86–124).
5. Eugene Gholz, Daryl G. Press, and Harvey M. Sapolsky, "Come Home, America: The Strategy of Restraint in the Face of Temptation," *International Security* 21, no. 4 (spring 1997): 8.
6. Ibid., 30. The article runs from pp. 5–48.
7. Mastanduno, "Preserving the Unipolar Moment."
8. According to Richard Rosecrance and Arthur Stein, grand strategy is not just an optimal response to international pressures, threats, and power configurations but the outcome of domestic orientations, resources, constraints, and conditions. See Richard Rosecrance and Arthur A. Stein (eds.), *The Domestic Bases of Grand Strategy* (Ithaca, N.Y.: Cornell University Press, 1993).
9. Bruce W. Jentleson, "The Need for Praxis: Bringing Policy Relevance Back In," *International Security* 26, no. 4 (spring 2002): 169–83. See also Peter Katzenstein, "September 11th in Comparative Perspective," paper presented to the American Political Science Association 98th Annual Meeting, Boston, August-September 2002; available at http://apsaproceedings.cup.org.
10. Robert J. Art, "Geopolitics Updated: The Strategy of Selective Engagement," *International Security* 23, no. 3 (winter 1998–99): 85.
11. Ashton B. Carter and William J. Perry, *Preventive Defense: A New Security Strategy for America* (Washington, D.C.: Brookings Institution Press, 1999). The concept of preventive defense

goes beyond terrorism to target the full range of threats to national security. Furthermore, the authors define "catastrophic terrorism" as acts that are an order of magnitude more severe than "ordinary" terrorism and are unprecedented outside of warfare (p. 150). Catastrophic terrorism need not involve the use of WMD.

12. Ian O. Lesser, "Countering the New Terrorism: Implications for Strategy," in Ian O. Lesser, Bruce Hoffman, John Arquilla, David Ronfeldt, and Michele Zanini, *Countering the New Terrorism* (Santa Monica, Calif.: Rand, 1999), 140. Lesser advocated a "core" strategy and "multidimensional" approach that would include not just direct responses to terrorism but shaping of the international environment (ibid., 140–42).

13. Richard Falkenrath, "Analytic Models and Policy Prescription: Understanding Recent Innovation in U.S. Counterterrorism," *Studies in Conflict and Terrorism* 24, no. 3 (May–June 2001): 159–82.

14. Paul R. Pillar, *Terrorism and U.S. Foreign Policy* (Washington, D.C.: Brookings Institution Press, 2001), 223.

15. Ibid.

16. Ibid., 229.

17. Neil C. Livingstone and Terrell E. Arnold, *Fighting Back: Winning the War against Terrorism* (Lexington, Mass.: D.C. Heath and Co., 1986), 229.

18. Marc A. Celmer, *Terrorism, U.S. Strategy, and Reagan Policies* (Westport, Conn.: Greenwood Press, 1987).

19. Grant Wardlaw, "State Response to International Terrorism: Some Cautionary Comments." in *Current Perspectives on International Terrorism,* ed. Robert A. Slater and Michael Stohl (London: Macmillan, 1988), 214.

20. Jeffrey D. Simon, *The Terrorist Trap: America's Experience with Terrorism* (Bloomington: Indiana University Press. 1994), 376.

21. The principle of no concessions to terrorist demands in cases of hostage seizures was developed under the Nixon administration, primarily by Henry Kissinger. It was first applied in 1977, when American diplomats were held hostage and subsequently murdered by members of the Black September Organization in Khartoum. Its application has been inconsistent.

22. Yehezkel Dror, "Terrorism as a Challenge to the Democratic Capacity to Govern," in *Terrorism, Legitimacy, and Power. The Consequences of Political Violence,* ed. Martha Crenshaw (Middletown, Conn.: Wesleyan University Press, 1983), 65. Dror also blamed social science: "This ignorance [of terrorism] principally stems from the state of the social sciences, which lack the frames of appreciation, cognitive maps, concept packages, and methodology to comprehend complex phenomena that cannot be understood through decomposition into easier-to-analyze subelements. Our generation, like earlier generations, is overwhelmed by events we cannot adequately comprehend with contemporary modes of thinking and tacit models" (ibid., 67).

23. Ibid., 81.

24. See, for example, William R. Farrell, *The U.S. Government Response to Terrorism: In Search of an Effective Strategy* (Boulder, Colo.: Westview Press, 1982); Martha Crenshaw, "Counterterrorism Policy and the Political Process," *Studies in Conflict and Terrorism* 24, no. 5 (2001): 329–38; Laura K. Donohue, "In the Name of National Security: U.S. Counterterrorist Measures, 1960–2000," *Terrorism and Political Violence* 13, no. 3 (autumn 2001): 47; Laura K. Donohue and Juliette N. Kayyem, "Federalism and the Battle over Counterterrorist Law: State Sovereignty, Criminal Law Enforcement, and National Security," *Studies in Conflict and Terrorism* 25, no. 1 (2002): 1–18; and Richard A. Falkenrath, "Problems of Preparedness: U.S. Readiness for a Domestic Terrorist Attack," *International Security* 25, no. 4 (spring 2001): 147–86.

25. David Tucker, *Skirmishes at the Edge of Empire: The United States and International Terrorism* (Westport, Conn.: Praeger, 1997), 134. Marc Celmer disagreed, however, and argued that even the Reagan administration lacked a strategy (Marc A. Celmer, *Terrorism, U.S. Strategy, and Reagan Policies* [Westport, Conn.: Greenwood Press, 1987]).

26. Pillar, *Terrorism and U.S. Foreign Policy,* 220–21.

27. See Falkenrath, "Analytic Models and Policy Prescription."

28. For example, Condoleezza Rice, then foreign policy adviser to the Bush campaign, wrote an article on "Promoting the National Interest" for the January–February 2000, issue of *Foreign Affairs*. Among the five key priorities the United States should focus on, she cited dealing with rogue regimes, whose threat increasingly was taking the form of potential for terrorism and the development of WMD. She devoted the most attention to China and Russia. The only specific reference to terrorism was in the context of rogue regimes, particularly Iraq, and their capacity to use chemical and biological weapons. Here she called for expanding intelligence capabilities rather than an active response.

29. Barry R. Posen, "The Struggle against Terrorism: Grand Strategy, Strategy, and Tactics," *International Security* 26, no. 3 (winter 2001–2002): 39–55. No mention is made of the fact that security specialists also had ignored the absence of strategy before September 11.

30. Walt, "Beyond bin Laden," especially 77–78.

31. Posen, "The Struggle against Terrorism," 53, 55.

32. In this respect, the debate over the failure to predict a major terrorist attack recalls the debate over the end of the cold war.

33. Steven E. Miller, "The End of Unilateralism or Unilateralism Redux?" *Washington Quarterly* 25, no. 1 (winter 2002): 15–29.

34. Ashton B. Carter, "The Architecture of Government in the Face of Terrorism," *International Security* 26, no. 3 (winter 2001–2002): 5–23. Carter, however, continued to dismiss the threat of "ordinary" terrorism, failing to see the causal links between terrorism that does not cause mass casualties and terrorism that does.

35. See Benjamin Schwarz and Christopher Layne, "A New Grand Strategy," *The Atlantic Monthly* 289, no. 1 (January 2002): 36–42. Available at www.theatlantic.com.

36. See Audrey Kurth Cronin, "Rethinking Sovereignty: American Strategy in the Age of Terrorism," *Survival* 44, no. 2 (summer 2002): 119–39. This outcome is what Dror also expected.

37. *Patterns of Global Terrorism 2001*. U.S. Department of State publication 10940, May 2002.

38. White House, 17 September 2002. The report is mandated by Congress.

39. See Nicholas Lemann, "Letter from Washington: The Next World Order," *The New Yorker,* April 1, 2002. Lemann suggested that the ideas behind the plan stemmed from officials in the first Bush administration. See also Rice, "Promoting the National Interest."

40. Lemann, "Letter from Washington."

41. The Clinton administration had abandoned the term "rogue states" in favor of "states of concern."

42. See the president's address to the United Nations General Assembly, New York, 12 September 2002; available at www.whitehouse.gov.

43. Whether this new idea should be called preemptive or preventive war is open to question. Preemption assumes that the defender has almost certain knowledge of an impending attack within a short time frame.

44. See Frances FitzGerald, "George Bush and the World," *New York Review of Books,* 26 September 2002.

45. See Marina Ottaway, Thomas Carothers, Amy Hawthorne, and Daniel Brumberg, *Democratic Mirage in the Middle East,* Carnegie Endowment for International Peace Policy Brief 20, October 2002.

46. Martha Crenshaw, "Why America? The Globalization of Civil War," *Current History* 100 (December 2001): 425–32.

47. One need only look at the Department of State's annual reports on international terrorism to see that hundreds of different groups have used terrorism fitting the definition of "international," which means involving the citizens or territory of more than one country. It is not clear how "terrorism of global reach" is distinguished from international terrorism.

48. This is not to argue that underlying grievances are a direct cause of terrorism, but they motivate audiences whose support is anticipated and sought by organized radical groups. Terrorism can be regarded as a way of soliciting and mobilizing support. Al-Qaeda is by no means a mass movement.

Daniel Byman

US Counter-terrorism
Options: A Taxonomy

The George W. Bush administration has tried to fight al-Qaeda and its allies with efforts ranging from aggressive intelligence and military campaigns to programmes to win over the youth of the Arab world through radio and television broadcasts. These efforts, however, are not part of an overarching strategic framework that lays out a path to victory.[1] They are at best not integrated and at worst working against one another.

The Bush administration's garbage-pail approach to counter-terrorism reflects a broader confusion on how to win the war on terrorism, and in particular how to defeat al-Qaeda and its allies. As frequently noted, this war will not end with a formal surrender; the enemy is too diffuse to simply attack and conquer. But the vast majority of work on the problem focuses on historical cases or explanations of the behaviour of different terrorist groups, even though by most accounts al-Qaeda is unique, or at least unusual.[2] Studies on counter-terrorism are fewer and tend to be narrow in focus.[3] A simple and succinct explanation and evaluation of various options in a way that can provide broad guidance to policymakers has not been available.

Most elements of counter-terrorism strategy address one of two different goals: disrupting the group itself, and its operations; or changing the overall environment to defuse the group's anger or make it harder to raise money or attract recruits. For example, the United States could back its most aggressive and capable allies that are committed to stopping al-Qaeda, providing them with financial support, intelligence assistance and other aid. In the long term, Washington could try to decrease political alienation in the Muslim world by spreading democracy, to reduce the level of popular grievance on which terrorists feed. Both approaches are good in theory, and in fact were endorsed in the White House's 2006 National Security Strategy.[4]

Yet a closer look suggests some inherent tensions between these two apparently straightforward approaches. Egypt, for example, is one of America's closest allies in the war on terrorism and has aggressively gone after al-Qaeda and its affiliates, both for its own sake and on Washington's behalf. At the same time, Egyptian President Hosni Mubarak is a turgid dictator whose cronyism, corruption, stagnation and repression alienate and anger many Egyptians and lead some to violence.[5] Should the United States push to replace Mubarak with a more democratic government, or should it back him to crush al-Qaeda cells by any means necessary? This is a difficult trade-off, but an effective strategy depends on identifying such trade-offs and consistently choosing the better option.

For the purposes of analysis, this essay lays out and compares seven strategic options for going after al-Qaeda and its allies: (1) crushing terrorist groups directly with massive force; (2) relying on allies to strike terrorist groups; (3) containing the terrorist group to limit its effectiveness and encourage internal divisions; (4) improving defences against terrorism; (5) diverting the group away from the United States to another target; (6) dele-gitimising the group's cause; and (7) transforming terrorist-breeding countries by promot-ing democracy. They are presented here in somewhat abstract and 'pure' form; in the real world, policy is more hybrid in nature. But describing the options in somewhat unnatural isolation helps us better understand the tensions among them. Most of these options can work in conjunction with others, but elements of some work in opposition to others.

Although the primary purposes of this essay is to lay out different options, the assess-ment below finds that the best approach is to work with allies to fight terrorism in the hope of containing the terrorists. In the long term, the terrorists' own weaknesses will come to the fore—something to encourage by working hard to delegitimise them. Defences can be improved, but there are limits to what is realistic, and many defensive measures are useless, wasted or can even make things worse. Diversion is possible in a few cases, particularly if the United States withdraws or draws down from Iraq and thus moves off the jihadists' centre stage. However, in general, diversion is hard to implement, risky in the long term as the jihadists may simply become stronger, and costly given that many of the countries that would suffer are close US allies—and immoral to boot. Crushing the adversary unilaterally is simply too massive a task given the global nature of the foe and is more likely to backfire and anger key allies. Despite their allure, massive efforts to democratise the world are also risky. Indeed, such efforts may have beneficial effects well beyond counter-terrorism, but they may often backfire when it comes to winning over potential radicals or gaining sup-port on counter-terrorism from area governments.

What, then, are the strategic options available to the United States? What are their strengths and weaknesses? How feasible are the different options? Which is the best course for Washington to pursue?

Strategy one: crushing al-Qaeda unilaterally

The most obvious way to defeat al-Qaeda, and the one with tremendous emotional appeal to many Americans, is to directly target the group and its supporters. The goal is to kill (or arrest) those who mean to do harm. In practice, such an approach means going well beyond current counter-terrorism policies and using military forces to kill al-Qaeda members and large numbers of supporters wherever they can be found. According to proponents, kill-ing on a mass scale will both reduce the number of terrorists and intimidate those who remain. In his book *Imperial Hubris,* Michael Scheuer, who led the CIA's hunt for Osama bin Laden for several years in the 1990s, notes that 'unchanged U.S. policies toward the Muslim world leave America only a military option for defending itself' and that military force cannot be applied 'daintily'. Scheuer calls for the United States to return to a Second World War-style use of force, with fast-paced killing and 'extremely large' body counts.[6] US allies, Scheuer contends, will not do this dirty work on America's behalf.

There are rare but encouraging examples where strong government campaigns have crushed terrorist groups. Turkey's campaign against the once-daunting Kurdish Workers Party (PKK) is instructive. For decades after the founding of the modern Turkish state in

1923, Turkey's Kurds had repeatedly chafed at the government's efforts to assimilate them. In 1984, the PKK launched a terrorism campaign and formed a large guerrilla army. Fighting in the name of Kurdish self-determination, the PKK sparked a mini-civil war, which by the time it diminished in 2000 had killed over 30,000 people. The Turkish government's response was a tough counter-insurgency campaign involving much of the Turkish army and intelligence service.[7]

Concurrently, Turkey also pressed the PKK's two main sponsors, Iraq and Syria, to cease providing safe havens and to surrender high-level PKK personnel hiding in their countries, particularly the group's leader, Abdullah Ocalan, who for years benefited from Damascus' hostility toward Turkey. Turkey engaged in a massive war against PKK cadres, repeatedly crossing the border into Iraq to target PKK bases in the Kurdish areas there. In 1998, Turkey threatened Syria with military action (a position the United States backed), and the regime sent Ocalan packing. He fled, going from Syria to Russia, Greece and Italy, eventually ending up in 1999 in Kenya, where he was arrested and returned to Turkey. This coincided with a period where the Turkish government became less repressive of Kurdish rights, allowing the use of Kurdish language and otherwise reducing pressures to assimilate.

The Turkish strategy illustrates how a group can be crushed by force applied by one government alone. After large numbers of terrorist cadre are killed or arrested, the organisation is simply less able to function. Over time, would-be members are dissuaded from joining the group out of fear that they too will be killed, arrested or otherwise punished. Particularly important was getting the PKK's leadership: as long as they were able to recruit, fundraise and train new cadre in havens outside Turkey, the group was able to survive despite the government's fierce counter-terrorism measures.[8]

A closer look, however, reveals that such a direct strategy is untenable when applied to al-Qaeda. There are truly massive pre-requisites for the United States to crush al-Qaeda largely by itself. First and foremost, the required intelligence capabilities are daunting. Because of al-Qaeda's global presence (to say nothing of the far-flung presence of its sympathisers), the United States would need a massive intelligence presence in every country with a significant jihadist presence, including Pakistan, Afghanistan, Saudi Arabia, Yemen and Indonesia. The US government regularly works with dozens of countries around the world to detail suspected terrorists.[9] If the United States went it alone, in all these countries US operatives would be spying on local mosques, tapping phone lines, trailing suspects, and otherwise doing the day-to-day work of counter-terrorism. US operatives would be breaking local laws and thus having to hide their activities from the police and intelligence services—many of whom might be trailing the same suspects.

Although the United States can improve its capacity in various countries, it cannot summon the necessary manpower. To monitor subversive and criminal activity in the United States, the FBI in 2005 had just under 30,000 employees.[10] Many more would be needed to gather intelligence in remote areas around the world where the police and people are not cooperative. Where would all those talented employees come from?

In 2001, less than a third of the CIA's new operations officers had any language expertise.[11] Efforts to remedy the shortfall in the intelligence community have not been very successful. Finding Americans with the necessary language skills can be difficult. According to census data, only 1.6% of Americans speak critical languages. And the number of those who have academic degrees, as Betsy Davis, the CIA's second-ranking recruiting officer recently noted, is 'frighteningly small'.[12]

To fight affiliates linked to al-Qaeda, the United States would be engaged in several Iraq-like operations and many smaller ones. Kashmir, Afghanistan, Chechnya and Algeria would all be theatres of action, as would Indonesia, Yemen, Nigeria and other places. Maintaining over 100,000 troops in Iraq has proven daunting for the US military, which has found it hard to maintain readiness for other missions and attract qualified recruits. Multiple Iraqs would be overwhelming.

Strategy two: crushing al-Qaeda multilaterally

Working with others would solve some of the problems the United States would have in crushing the adversary on its own, at least in the short term. Rather than monitor the mosque in Yemen with US agents or kill Algerian insurgents with American troops, Washington would rely on the forces of allies to act in its stead. The destruction of Egyptian Islamic Jihad's network in Europe and Egypt is one model that demonstrates the power of this approach. Like many Egyptian militant groups, Islamic Jihad grew out of Egypt's Muslim Brotherhood, a political organisation that has flirted with violence repeatedly and has suffered from repression again and again since its founding in 1928. Along with the like-minded, but at times bitter rival, Islamic Group, Egyptian Islamic Jihad led an uprising in the early 1990s that led to over 1,000 deaths. The militants attacked not only regime security forces, but also writers, secular judges, Copts and foreign tourists.

The government steadily gained the upper hand over the militants. Through massive detentions and brutal interrogation, the regime rounded up most of the suspects, as well as thousands of other Egyptians. To take the wind out of the militants' sails, the regime also made numerous concessions to individuals affiliated with the more moderate Muslim Brotherhood and to the religious establishment. The result was a more Islamicised Egypt, but a more peaceful one.[13]

By 1996, the groups no longer posed a threat to the survival of the Mubarak regime, but they remained lethal. The Islamic Group continued to attack Western tourists, most notoriously killing 58 (along with four Egyptians) in an attack on the Hatshepsut Temple in Luxor in 1997.

But as Egyptian Islamic Jihad wound down at home, its international role expanded. One strand of the group led by Ayman al-Zawahiri effectively merged with al-Qaeda. This strand embraced al-Qaeda's global agenda and saw the United States, not the Egyptian government, as the primary enemy. Others within the battered movement continued the struggle in Egypt, while still others called for a ceasefire.

The United States worked closely with the Egyptian government and other allies to contain this international movement. For example, the *Wall Street Journal* reports that in July 1998 the CIA worked with the government of Albania to deport several members of an Egyptian Islamic Jihad cell from the Balkans to Egypt. The CIA helped Albania's intelligence service with equipment to tap phones and trained them on surveillance. Interrogation of the prisoners in Egypt, much of which was brutal, led to mass trials of alleged terrorists there.[14]

As the Egyptian experience demonstrates, the United States can play multiple roles. With Egypt, the United States is a recipient of intelligence: information from interrogations goes to US intelligence officials, who in turn use it in their efforts in other countries or to prevent terrorists from infiltrating the United States. At times, the United States uses the intelligence it collects to direct allies like the Albanians to crack down on terrorist cells. As a result of this cooperation, more terrorists are off the streets. They no longer pose a threat to the United States or its citizens.

Allied police, soldiers and security services act in the stead of American agents to shut down fundraising, proselytising and websites. The military equivalent of the Egyptian Islamic Jihad operation would be working with local military forces against al-Qaeda-linked insurgents.[15] Instead of American special-operations forces closing in on the al-Qaeda camp in Pakistan's North West Frontier Province, the uniforms would be those of the Pakistani military.

Because much of the heavy lifting would be done by allies, the cost of this option would be far less than crushing al-Qaeda directly. The United States may pay to augment local capabilities, but this is a fragment of the cost of doing the work itself. Also, these allies are likely to be better in many respects than their US counterparts at certain functions, particularly when it comes to gathering intelligence—they have the home-field advantage. Allies can use their own laws to legally and easily acquire information, drawing on co-operation from local businesses and citizens. Their police know the communities well, and they have a massive presence simply to keep order and, in many cases, to protect the regime from unrest.

One of the biggest problems of this reliance is competence. In some respects, allies are as good as Americans and, in several important ways, better. But in many instances they suffer in comparison. Militarily, few allies hold a candle to American forces, particularly elite special-operations force units like the Navy Seals or the US Army's Delta Force. Most allies, particularly in the developing world where al-Qaeda camps are most likely to be found, lack sophisticated technologies like the *Predator* unmanned aerial vehicle and often are not able to coordinate their forces well. Some members of allied security services may even be sympathetic to the jihadists, providing them with advance warning or otherwise assisting their efforts to escape. A Jordanian journalist reports Saudi Arabia's past attempts to capture or kill bin Laden may have failed because jihadist sympathisers within Pakistani intelligence tipped him off.[16]

Some allies might also hesitate to work with the United States.[17] Open cooperation may draw the jihadists' wrath, turning allies from bystanders to targets. The good news is that most allies share America's views on al-Qaeda. For alliance purposes, bin Laden's organisation is in many ways an ideal adversary: it hates everyone. Muslim regimes are corrupt and impious, Western states support a variety of decadent leaders and are oppressing the Muslim world, and so on. Al-Qaeda's policy of supporting insurgencies means that many non-Western powers such as Russia, China, Indonesia, Nigeria and India all have a strong interest in seeing the jihadists destroyed.

Another problem is that anarchy reigns in parts of the world, making reliance on allies at best an incomplete approach. Afghanistan, Mauritania, Pakistan, Somalia, Tajikistan and Yemen are only a few of the countries around the world where the government's writ is limited to the capital and other major cities. In these areas, allies can, or will, do only so much. Thus, working through allies solves part of the problem, but huge gaps remain.

As with crushing al-Qaeda directly, working through allies requires making counter-terrorism a priority, albeit in a different way. The challenge here is not dealing with the fallout of offending allies, but rather paying the price of their cooperation. If the United States relies on allies to cooperate because it is the right thing to do, it will be sorely disappointed. Some will do it fitfully, others on their own schedule, and still others not at all. To gain support, the United States will often need to make concessions. Pakistan may provide additional cooperation against various jihadist movements—but not if the United States is simultaneously punishing Islamabad for its nuclear programme.

Strategy three: containment

An alternative to crushing al-Qaeda completely is to try to contain it, transforming it from a grave strategic threat to a dangerous nuisance, comparable to the dozens of other terrorist groups around the world.[18] Many of the particular methods would overlap with other strategy options; the main difference would be in priorities. The struggle against the jihadists would join the host of other US foreign-policy concerns, at times taking precedence but often being secondary. With Pakistan, for example, the United States would prioritise the regime's nuclear programme; with Saudi Arabia, oil-price stability.

Containment recognises the difficulty in finding every terrorist or even reducing group capabilities to the point that relatively low-tech attacks like the transportation bombings in Madrid and London are impossible. A containment strategy assumes the threat is manageable. As Philip Heymann, the former US deputy attorney general, argues, 'there will be terrorism. We can deal with it; we can discourage it; but we cannot end it completely.'[19] Indeed, by some measures, the threat is more than manageable—it is negligible. John Mueller acidly notes that before 11 September, the number of Americans who died from international terrorism was less than those killed by lightning strikes or, more prosaically, drowning in toilets.[20] Excluding Iraq and Afghanistan, the number of Americans killed by al-Qaeda-linked terrorism since 11 September is in the dozens. While tragic, losing relatively few people from terrorism in the six years since 11 September suggests that, from an actuarial point of view, more lives could be saved by putting resources elsewhere. Even in the month of September 2001 itself, more Americans died on the road and from cancer than from terrorism.[21]

Containment does not mean ignoring terrorists, but rather not putting terrorism front and centre. Containment, in essence, was the US counter-terrorism strategy for decades. The United States went after individual terrorists, be they members of the Abu Nidal Organisation, the Lebanese Hizbullah, Greece's November 17 Organisation, or other groups whose members had killed Americans. In all these cases the United States tried to arrest particular individuals, or have its allies do so, but there was no pretence of going after the group as a whole. Hizbullah, for example, has been nestled comfortably in Lebanon since its founding in the early 1980s. It killed Americans and took Western hostages in the 1980s, and since then continued to war constantly with Israel, but US efforts were confined to pressing the group's state sponsors, Iran and Syria, and trying to disrupt and arrest individual members when they left the Lebanese sanctuary.[22]

The exception to this limited focus was domestic terrorism. The FBI relentlessly tracked leftist groups like the Weathermen and the Symbionese Liberation Army, driving them deep underground and eventually rounding up all their important members. When the threat from right-wing militia movements became clear after the 19 April 1995 bombing of the Alfred P. Murrah Federal Building in Oklahoma City—the most devastating domestic terrorist attack in US history, killing 167 people, including 19 children—the FBI moved quickly to increase investigations of, and then disrupt and arrest, various right-wing movements throughout the country.[23]

In addition to managing the risk itself, containment has a potential strategy for long-term victory: any adversary has internal contradictions that, given time, will discredit and divide it. In al-Qaeda's case, the adversary is divided on what target should receive priority, who is a true Muslim, whether it is against Western values or just US policies, and other core issues. Islam expert Gilles Kepel notes that the presence of representatives from a wide range of Islamist groups in London has 'led to a tempest of reciprocal excommunications and anathemas'.[24] In addition, there are numerous leaders who are coming to the fore now that bin Laden cannot exert the same level of direct control because of the blows the organisation has sustained since losing the Taliban's backing and being subjected to greater international policing and intelligence disruption after 11 September—and these leaders may fight one another. Such differences have the potential to divide the movement; a generation from now, these contradictions will not have destroyed the jihadist cause, but they may have weakened it dramatically. The jihadist movement will cooperate less internally. Moreover, parts of the movement may literally war on other parts, and some elements may work with foreign intelligence agencies against their rivals.

Equally importantly, containment recognises the limits of many alternatives and that some of them may even backfire. One of containment's greatest strengths is that it avoids some of these risks. It is thus a relatively low-cost alternative: it demands less in the way of troops and intelligence. At home, little needs to be spent on costly homeland defence measures. Even more importantly, it requires few policy sacrifices. If Pakistan threatens to reduce its aid to the United States on terrorism because of US pressure on its nuclear programme, the United States can take that risk because counter-terrorism is not the dominant policy.

Containment, however, is far from perfect. In the past, containment of terrorist groups worked—but the reasons for this success provide little comfort today. The primary target of most terrorist groups in the world is not the United States, but rather their local government or, in many cases, Israel. Thus while Hizbullah has not been linked to anti-US attacks, with the possible exception of aiding Shia insurgent strikes in Iraq, for over a decade—and even its role in the 1996 attack on Khobar Towers, where a member was implicated, seems secondary—this is in large part because the organisation prefers to go after other targets first, particularly Israel.[25] Other groups, like November 17, are small and only capable of mounting a few attacks.

Al-Qaeda, however, both seeks to kill Americans itself and turn more local groups against the United States. While it also has other priorities, it can and will kill large numbers of Americans if not confronted or disabled. This problem is particularly acute today. Containment's vision is a long-term one and, over time, the movement may focus elsewhere or collapse under the weight of its own divisions. In the short term, however, and the short term may last a decade or more, the jihadist cause is alive and well, and attacks are likely to continue.

Getting some allies to cooperate with a containment policy would be difficult, because it has a large element of diversion to it. Other states will naturally have their own security interests and will resent efforts focused on protecting American citizens' lives at their expense. Containment would not be viewed favourably by governments looking for help in destroying the threat, not in keeping it local.

One of the biggest problems with containment is the home front. Containment is the antithesis of a 'crush' strategy, and thus appears as weakness to domestic audiences who are scared, angry and hungry for vengeance after a terrorist attack. This public response is not based on a rational calculation of the risks. Yet terrorism scares people. Even a limited number of deaths, particularly on home soil, thus has a disproportionate psychological effect. Work stops, and people refuse to travel. Public confidence in government plunges. This may be irrational from an actuarial point of view, but policymakers must adjust policy to cope with the behaviour of their citizens. Moreover, every government must ensure the security of its citizens to be credible, and the deliberate murder of civilians is a direct challenge to a government's legitimacy.

It is impossible for politicians not to respond to such provocations. The Bush administration has spent the years since 11 September telling the American people how dangerous the threat is, and most Democratic politicians have joined in the chorus. When politicians try to soften their rhetoric on terrorism, they face tremendous criticism. During the waning days of the 2004 elections, Democratic presidential candidate John Kerry told the *New York Times* that he wanted to turn terrorism into a 'nuisance' like crime; President Bush told reporters that the United States would never achieve a clear victory in the war. The public outcry forced both to 'clarify'—that is, to disown—their statements.

One cannot take the politics out of counter-terrorism. The painful reality might be that 'doing something'—whether spending money on homeland security or acting aggressively abroad—is necessary to reassure people after a massive attack on the homeland, since a perception that the government was passive could contribute to a massive overreaction. Reaction may be necessary to prevent overreaction.

Nor is it simply a matter of politics. Beyond simply preventing peace, terrorism can spark far more massive conflicts. Indeed, terrorist groups often hope to provoke larger popular struggles, seeing themselves as the vanguards of broader movements that they can create through violence. Through the murder and intimidation of civilians—and by provoking a harsh state response—they force people to choose sides, shattering what was a peaceful accommodation. There may be few fatalities from such terrorism, but the strategic consequences are massive. Two of the world's most deadly insurgencies—Kashmir and Chechnya—began with limited terrorism and quickly escalated to conflicts that claimed hundreds of thousands of victims. Israel, Colombia and other nations and regions have seen terrorists derail peace talks.

Indeed, small but violent groups can have an influence disproportionate to their size. Mueller points out that demagogic politicians can use very small bands of thugs to spawn refugee flights, which in turn leads to a cycle of revenge. In some towns in the Balkans little more than a dozen thugs forced thousands to flee.[26] In Iraq, limited violence in summer 2003 escalated just as the terrorists—now the insurgents—intended. Some parts of the opposition also seek to use terrorism to spark civil war. Jihadists have perpetrated repeated suicide bombings of Shia mosques in Iraq.

The lack of a response to terrorism can fuel this. Successful terrorism spawns imitation. An ineffectual response can thus spawn more of the problem. In addition, a lack of response can undermine the credibility of a government, beginning a cycle that terrorists exploit to build an organisation and become a full-fledged insurgent movement.

Al-Qaeda is well aware of the rewards of terrorism and seeks to exploit them. The bulk of al-Qaeda's activities are not related to anti-US or even international terrorism. Rather, the organisation proselytises and fosters insurgencies around the globe. Chechnya, Algeria, Kashmir, Bosnia, the Philippines, Indonesia and now Iraq are only some of the countries where the organisation has focused. These insurgencies, of course, kill tens or hundreds of thousands—and terrorism is how several of them began.

This is where containment advocates overstate how well things are going today. There have been no further attacks on the US homeland, in part due to the changes the United States has forced on al-Qaeda and to increased vigilance. However, al-Qaeda and affiliated groups have, if anything, become *more* active overseas since 11 September. Indonesia, Spain, Morocco, Saudi Arabia, Jordan, Yemen, Russia, Pakistan, Egypt and the United Kingdom are only a few of the countries that have suffered terrorism. More important in many ways are the ongoing insurgencies in Iraq, Afghanistan, Chechnya and Kashmir and the strife in Pakistan and Nigeria. In these countries the problem is immense and exceptionally costly.

Strategy four: defence

If terrorists can easily enter a country and operate with impunity, the number of attacks will almost certainly increase. 'Defence' is a broad term, however. It can include emergency preparedness, domestic intelligence, better border control, port-security initiatives and other measures designed to make it harder for the terrorists to successfully attack.

Much of what is now considered 'al-Qaeda' is really a collection of unaffiliated wannabes, inspired by bin Laden's dream but not in touch with the broader organisation.[27] They might be able to scrounge together the money to fly to the United States for an attack or, more commonly, seek to strike a US target in their home country. While in the United States, they could probably acquire a weapon or materials for a bomb.

With better defences, however, the chance of finding such amateurs is much higher. Shoddy passports would be inspected more carefully. Weapons dealers would be more vigilant with regard to individuals who might be terrorists, and illegal arms merchants would be under closer scrutiny. If terrorists seek help from individuals in the United States who might assist them—providing them with a place to sleep or helping them survey various targets—they are more likely to be caught, as these individuals are likely be under surveillance.

Effective offence cannot catch all these individuals. Many of them do not appear on the radar screen of intelligence agencies until after they undertake attacks.[28] However, it can help ensure that they are not linked to a broader operational, as opposed to ideological, network. In the absence of a local support infrastructure, terrorists must do everything on their own: acquire documents, raise money, find fellow-travellers to help them live day-to-day, and so on. Even more importantly, they are less likely to be trained and thus make more mistakes.

Perhaps the best example of how defence can work in a tactical sense is Israel's security barrier, which separates much of the West Bank from major Israeli population centres.[29] The barrier stopped many would-be attackers from penetrating Israel proper, forcing them to abandon their efforts or go through checkpoints, where they were often detected. Others tried to circumvent the barrier by travelling through areas where it was still incomplete. These detours added many miles and hours to their trips, however, and forced them to work with and inform more people about their activities—delays and opportunities that Israeli counter-terrorism forces were able to seize on in disrupting attacks.[30]

Defences are necessary because even superb intelligence is always incomplete. Investigations of attacks before 11 September emphasised that warning of a particular attack may be lacking even though there is broad recognition that one may occur. In 1985, the Report of the Secretary of State's Advisory Panel on Overseas Security (the Inman Report) examined the bombings of the US Embassy and Marine Barracks in Lebanon and concluded that 'if determined, well-trained and funded teams are seeking to do damage, they will eventually succeed'. The inquiries into the 1996 Khobar Towers attack and the 1998 Embassy bombings both found strategic warning was sound even though tactical warning was lacking.[31] In 1999, the Report of the Accountability Review Boards on the Embassy Bombings in Nairobi and Dar es Salaam (better known as the Crowe Commission) contended that 'we cannot count on having such intelligence to warn us of such attacks'.[32]

One advantage of defences over other strategies is they do not rely on the same level of cooperation with a broad set of allies, though neighbouring countries become very important. Regardless of the good opinion of Germany or the level of cooperation from Pakistan, the United States can still make itself safer by making its borders more secure. Canada and Mexico, however, must cooperate wholeheartedly for defences to function to their full extent.

Yet a strategy of defence raises some rather obvious questions. Firstly, what is to be defended? Some sites seem obvious. The White House and Congress, of course, should be well defended. So, too, should nuclear power plants and chemical manufacturing plants. But then it gets harder. Should state capitols be defended, or lesser federal government buildings (say, the Department of Transportation)? What about public transportation, which has long been a favourite target of terrorists around the world? Difficult choices must be made. For example, the cost of purchasing and installing explosive-detection systems for Boston's Logan International Airport is estimated to be $146 million, while the cost for Dallas/Fort Worth International Airport will be more than $193m, and the nationwide price tag is $3 billion.[33] Is this the best use of tax dollars, or are they better spent on more border guards or on social welfare programmes that decrease immigrant alienation?

The more comprehensive the list, the more costly the defences become. Increasing airline screening since 11 September has cost more than $10bn so far and the Transportation Security Agency expects to spend another $7bn billion in the next few years.[34] At the Rochester, New York airport the cost of security screening in 2003 exceeded the remaining cost of running the entire airport.[35] Even after spending billions of dollars, however, airport security has not dramatically improved. A 2004 confidential report prepared for the House Homeland Security Committee by a Government Accounting Office auditor found that screeners are failing to detect weapons at roughly the same rate as shortly after the attacks.[36] The Transportation Security Agency bought 1,344 hi-tech baggage-screening machines costing more than $1m each but experienced false alarms in 15–30% of all luggage. The culprit? Yorkshire puddings and bottles of shampoo which happen to have similar densities to certain explosives.[37]

The primary cost of many defences is not wasted dollars but lost time. Metal detectors for a subway system, for example, would lead to massive delays and make what is supposed to be convenient transportation quite inconvenient. These delays, in turn, would create perverse effects that would almost certainly lead to more deaths. Less convenient subway systems would make more people drive, and driving is far more dangerous than taking the train.

Terrorist innovation is also a challenge.[38] Israel found that the security barrier led Palestinian groups to shift their tactics. The barrier contributed to a dramatic plunge in the number of Israeli deaths from suicide attackers. But some still get through. Moreover, Palestinian groups have increased their use of mortars, firing over the barrier to strike into Israel.[39] The mortar attacks are less successful than the suicide bombings, but they do demonstrate how terrorists continue to innovate in response to defences.

Similar, but more successful, terrorist innovation led to the failure of US defences on 11 September. With metal detectors and improved security, the United States and other countries greatly reduced the number of airline hijackings from the level in the 1970s. Indeed, part of the reason for the success of the 11 September plot was that the hijackers were able to figure out a way to take over an aeroplane without guns, an innovation that would only work if they then crashed the aeroplane. If they had landed the plane and negotiated, as past hijackers had done, rescue teams could have easily stormed the plane without fear of the hostages being shot. US airline defences worked as planned—no one smuggled a gun or explosive material onto an aeroplane—but the plan itself did not capture the range of possibilities.

The United States faces particular problems because, unlike Israel, its citizens and interests are global. Defences, of course, do little to help critical allies in fighting terrorism. And while the United States defends its embassies and military bases around the world, terrorists can still go after less prestigious targets. Rather than attack a military base, they can attack individual soldiers, as Libya did in 1986 when it killed two soldiers and a Turkish woman at La Belle discotheque in Germany; rather than blow up embassies, jihadists can kill individual diplomats in their homes, as they did Lawrence Foley, a US Agency for International Development official in Jordan, in 2002.

Bureaucratically, improving defences can be costly. The Department of Homeland Security was intended to better coordinate the myriad agencies with pieces of the defence puzzle, but it has suffered from poor morale and confusion as to its mission. Moreover, the emphasis on terrorism has had dramatic costs. The Federal Emergency Management Agency was placed under the department because a terrorist strike could involve catastrophic damage requiring a sustained effort to care for victims and restore services. Under Homeland Security, however, the agency lost personnel and budgets for its traditional role of responding to natural disasters, reflected in its disastrous performance following Hurricane Katrina.[40]

One of the most effective forms of defence is domestic intelligence: identifying suspicious individuals and carefully monitoring their activities. The FBI currently is the lead US domestic intelligence agency as well as the leading criminal investigative agency.

Improving domestic intelligence involves a raft of changes, some of which involve diverting the FBI away from other priorities, such as white-collar crime.

But many of the biggest changes for domestic intelligence have costs in civil liberties and in the openness of society. In December 2005 the *New York Times* reported that the Bush administration had used the National Security Agency to spy on suspected terrorists on US soil without going through the Congressionally-mandated process that involved the Foreign Intelligence and Surveillance Act Court.[41] These revelations, and the lesser but long-standing flap over the US Patriot Act, highlighted a fundamental tension: gaining better information on suspected terrorists at times necessitates collecting more information in general, including on many individuals who, in the end, may not be involved in terrorism.

Domestic surveillance of US Muslim and Arab communities, the communities from which al-Qaeda would recruit new members and its sympathisers would emerge, may backfire in the end. American Muslim suspicions of the government are growing, and if this continues it could lead to increased radicalisation of some individuals. A 2005 survey of Muslim youth activists found that 70% felt that the American public had 'significant hostility' toward Muslims.[42] Because of measures taken to interview Arab Americans and to fingerprint and photograph immigrants, this community believes it is being unfairly harassed. Efforts to monitor non-governmental organisations that may have links to terrorist groups have drawn criticism for interfering with Muslims' religious obligation to contribute to charity. Increased surveillance or perceived official hostility may lead these communities, which for now are well integrated into society, to perceive a gap between being Muslims and being Americans.

Most proposed defensive measures come down particularly hard on immigrants and visitors. Reducing the number of visas to visitors from Pakistan, Saudi Arabia, Indonesia, Egypt or other countries with al-Qaeda-linked groups does reduce opportunities for radicals to slip in—but it also reduces opportunities for individuals who might be sympathetic to the United States to visit as well. Students from the Middle East, for example, have increasingly chosen to study in Europe, Canada and Australia rather than in the United States since 11 September. The number of students from the Middle East studying in the United States in the 2002/03 academic year fell by 10% from the previous year. Saudi Arabia and Kuwait saw a decrease of 25%, while the number of students from the United Arab Emirates dropped by 15%. Other Muslim countries were also affected.[43]

In the long term this could be disastrous, as many students who come to the United States are current or future elites in their home countries: they typically have more money, are better educated, and are otherwise able to shape opinion. Turning these people away or treating them poorly while they are here confirms their suspicions that the United States is hostile to Muslims. This can harm other policy goals as well, as these same elites might later help on trade, oil pricing, or other important US interests.

If part of a counter-terrorism strategy is to sell US values and explain the US system by exposing foreigners to Americans, closing off the United States is a problem. Indeed, those whom we seek most to influence—Islamists of various stripes who are often highly critical of al-Qaeda but also critical of the United States—face difficulty travelling because of their views and thus are more likely to sympathise with al-Qaeda.

Offence and defence work in tandem. If defences make it harder for terrorists to enter the United States—and successful US and allied strikes reduce the number of skilled terrorists—then the remaining amateurs are far more likely to fail. However, give terrorists enough time and freedom, and they are far more able to overcome even sophisticated defences.

Strategy five: diversion

A particularly nasty approach to counter-terrorism is to divert the jihadist onto someone else—the so-called 'campfire strategy'. If a bear attacks you and your friends around a campfire in the woods, you don't need to be faster than the bear, just faster than your friends. This is the strategy of diversion. Though the jihadists may loathe the United States, they will not target America because they have other priorities.

Diversion would involve playing up other conflicts that inflame the enemy. The United States would criticise Russia openly and frequently in Chechnya, play up the problems Muslims face in Europe, cluck sadly over India's abuses in Kashmir, and otherwise portray itself as sympathetic to Islamist views of the world's conflicts. At the same time, the United States would back away from policies—such as support for Israel, its presence in Iraq and backing authoritarian Muslim regimes—that most anger the jihadists. Over time, other countries would enter the jihadists' crosshairs.

Diversion is an exceptionally common counter-terrorism strategy, but one that few leaders articulate because its goal is to cause problems for others. France in the 1970s and much of the 1980s deliberately allowed terrorists sanctuary on its soil, believing, at times correctly, that as a reward for its cooperation terrorist groups would not attack French citizens or interests.[44] Arab governments in the 1980s tried to send potential young troublemakers to Afghanistan, lauding them as heroes for their efforts against the Soviets but all the while hoping that the youngsters would achieve their goal of martyrdom. The United States inadvertently follows this logic with many terrorist groups. The Liberation Tigers of Tamil Eelam in Sri Lanka (arguably the deadliest group in the world) or Chile's Manuel Rodriguez Patriotic Front-Dissidents are both hostile to US influence and US policies, but they focus first and foremost on their home countries. Even an explicitly anti-US group like the Marxist Devrimci Halk Kurtulus Partisi—Cephesi in Turkey is only of limited concern because it is focused first and foremost on the Turkish government. Such groups have other fish to fry, and the United States is quite content to let them do so.

A strategy of diversion has a logic suggested by the illogic of the jihadists' views. Goals such as removing invaders from Muslim lands, toppling what they see as illegitimate regimes, and establishing Islamic rule in their place do not, with the exception of the US presence in Iraq, inherently concern the United States. Mubarak in Egypt, King Abdullah of Saudi Arabia, or the prime minister of Israel are far more logical targets of anger than is America.[45]

Even in Iraq, some commentators argue that it is possible for terrorists to become engaged in a civil war there rather than going after the United States as international terrorists.[46] If the United States left Iraq, or perhaps if it lowered its profile considerably, Sunni jihadists might focus even more on killing Shíites, whom they see as apostates. In Iraq, the terrorists' propensity for internecine warfare may lead them away from US targets.

Iraq has also been justified as a way of diverting terrorists from attacking the US homeland. As President Bush argued in a 2005 speech about Iraq, 'there is only one course of action against [the terrorists]: to defeat them abroad before they attack us at home'.[47] By this logic, jihadists from around the world who would otherwise plot attacks against New York, Washington or other cities are instead sending their best people and devoting their time to defeating the US military in Iraq. No one wants to make US soldiers targets, but even soldiers prefer that the military be attacked rather than civilians.

Arab governments, in particular, are ripe for diversion. Many are already engaged in harsh repression against jihadist movements: Jordan, Morocco, Syria, Egypt, Tunisia and Libya are all good examples. Countries like Algeria, Iraq and, to a lesser degree, Yemen and Saudi Arabia are fighting full-blown or proto-insurgencies. These conflicts have led to thousands of deaths and imprisonments, as well as full-scale suspensions of human rights. Not surprisingly, many Arabs are bitter at their governments, which are thus vulnerable to having jihadist movements focus more on them than on the United States.

Nor are non-Arab Muslim countries off the hook. Indonesia and Bangladesh, the world's largest Muslim countries, both face local terrorist groups linked to al-Qaeda, and Afghanistan faces the remnants of the Taliban. Pakistan, of course, is home to myriad jihadist groups. None of these governments are accepted as legitimate by the jihadist community: some are too democratic, some too close to the West, and none sufficiently Islamic.

Even countries on the periphery of the Muslim world are ripe for diversion. India in Kashmir, Russia in Chechnya and other parts of the Caucasus, China in Xinjiang province, the Philippines, Thailand, Nigeria and Israel are all countries where a non-Muslim government faces internal dissent from a Muslim community. These are logical places for the next jihad if the goal is to remove foreigners from the lands of Islam or Muslims from the dominance of other religious communities.

These potential diversions are political, but where values rather than policies are at issue the United States still has advantages. To be sure, Hollywood, American television and American music offers the world such blasphemous ideas as freedom of speech, women's equality, and the rights of homosexuals as well as a steady diet of teen sexuality and the subversion of the traditional family hierarchy. Many of the issues that have caught Muslim extremists' ire in recent years, however, have been European: Dutch filmmaker Theo Van Gogh's graphic film criticising the treatment of women under Islam; France's ban on headscarves for Muslim girls in school; the publication of cartoons mocking the Prophet Mohammed in Denmark. Unlike Europe, the United States does not face significant tension from a large Muslim population, so similar reactions are less likely, though not impossible.[48]

Diversion is likely to work particularly well against potential al-Qaeda affiliates and the loose network of bin Laden admirers, as opposed to the al-Qaeda core. The affiliates are usually engaged in bitter wars against local regimes, which already take most of their attention. These individuals are not yet fully committed to attacking the United States. Diversion would make the United States even less attractive as a target. Similarly, the imaginations of individual jihadists in Europe or in the Muslim world would be seized by the supposed outrages of other countries, not America.

The advantages of diversion can be measured in saved American lives and dollars. To be blunt, others will die so Americans will live. Al-Qaeda and local movements would attack in Britain, Russia, Indonesia, Egypt, Saudi Arabia and so on, but not, or less frequently, in the United States. Nor would the United States have to undertake as many costly defensive measures. Other policy concerns—trade, nuclear proliferation, and so on—could receive the attention they deserve. Over time, diversion might exacerbate fault lines within the jihadist movement. Without a single enemy on which to focus their anger, jihadists might start to fight one another over priorities and resources.

Needless to say, a diversion strategy has several severe problems. Diversion, of course, requires policy changes—in short, concessions—to be meaningful. Parts of the jihadist movement may decide the United States is no longer public enemy number one, but only if US policies and values give less offence or another state commits a grievance that rises to the level of perceived US crimes. Most importantly today, the United States would have to withdraw from Iraq—ideally, from the jihadists' point of view, with its tail between its legs. The United States would also have to cut off Israel. Being more sympathetic to the Palestinians and pushing hard for a two-state solution is not enough: the United States would have to be seen as a critic of Israel, not a friend. Washington would also have to be more like Japan in its foreign policy toward the Muslim world: trade is okay, but political and military influence is not.

Even if these policy transformations occurred, parts of the jihad would resist being diverted. It would take many years to convince sceptical and conspiratorial jihadists that the United States was showing new colours. Moreover, the list of grievances against the United States is exceptionally long. Even some who would be diverted might only be distracted temporarily. The efforts of Arab regimes to divert their home-grown jihadists to Afghanistan to fight and die in the struggle against the Soviets worked in the short term, but when that struggle ended they found themselves confronting a far more dangerous foe. As former CIA officer Milton Beardon noted, these fighters' didn't die in great numbers. They died in tiny numbers, and they did come back.'[49]

Diversion would also relieve pressure on the al-Qaeda core, perhaps enabling it to reconstitute itself. Because the jihad is global, keeping it down requires a global response, which the United States now orchestrates. Equally importantly, US pressure greatly reduces other countries' incentives to look the other way at jihadists on their territory. Although the jihadists may intend no harm to their hosts, many states avoid tolerating them for fear of infuriating the United States, a risky move for any state.

Conversely, if the United States tried to divert the jihadists, it would infuriate US allies and other countries. In essence, the United States would be inviting terrorists to focus on killing other people, just not Americans. Even if this were not a declared policy, its contours would become known to a degree, and gaining diplomatic support from the affected countries would be far more difficult.

Even more importantly, while diversion would reduce the threat to US citizens, it would not diminish—in fact it is intended to increase—the threat to other countries, thus implicating many US interests around the globe. The stability of Pakistan is a vital US interest. Moreover, a greater al-Qaeda threat to Saudi Arabia risks instability in the world's largest oil producer. If the already strong Pakistani jihadist movement grew, it would further threaten stability in an already tottering state suffering from rampant corruption, severe economic problems, ethnic strife and a border war with India. Add to this lethal mix Pakistan's nuclear programme and you have the stuff of nightmares.

It would be disastrous should the jihadists ever capture a state, or even gain significant influence over one as they did in Afghanistan under the Taliban, or before that in Sudan. Al-Qaeda was able to use these countries, remote and poor as they were, as bases to construct a global army. The organisation was able to make its network far stronger and to bolster like-minded groups around the world. Recruitment, training, propaganda, indoctrination and other vital organisational efforts became far more effective when the groups had the security of a state to fall back on, rely on and exploit. Within these countries, the humanitarian costs were high. Afghanistan continued to be wracked by civil war, and the Taliban turned away international aid organisations trying to help its desperate citizens. Citizens who did not share the Taliban's extreme credo suffered brutal repression.

These problems would grow exponentially should jihadists come to power in a rich state like Saudi Arabia or a powerful one like Pakistan. Al-Qaeda's yearly budget at its peak was around $30m; the Saudi state, in contrast, took in revenues of almost $150bn in 2005. Spending a fraction of that money on advancing the jihadist cause would transform the movement's capabilities and size. Pakistan's situation is even more troubling. The government budget, at about $15bn, is only a tenth that of Saudi Arabia, but Islamabad controls a large army and several nuclear weapons. If this were controlled by jihadists, a nuclear exchange with India that would kill tens of millions would be one possibility, as would a launch against Israel or a Pakistan-backed terrorist strike on the United States.

Diverting jihadists away from the US homeland to Iraq is particularly dangerous. This strategy assumes a finite number of jihadists who, logically, can only be in one place at a time. However, the Iraq War has proven a generator of terrorism, inspiring thousands of young Muslims against the United States. There are more than enough jihadists to go around. Moreover, in Iraq they are picking up new skills and joining a network that makes them exponentially more dangerous.

It is difficult to pursue diversion without running these risks. US efforts to weaken the jihadists, even if surreptitious, would still surface through leaks at home and the occasional statements of allies. Over time, it would be impossible to carry out such a policy covertly. In addition, the United States cannot simply pick and choose and hope to appease the jihadists. Though leaving Iraq would address one grievance, al-Qaeda's list was drawn well before the US invasion and would remain after the last US soldier left Iraq.

However, one aspect of diversion should be kept in mind even if the strategy as a whole is rejected: the United States need not fight every battle and should try to avoid creating new enemies when possible. Many local groups are for now focused on local governments. Unless there is good reason to think these groups will soon join al-Qaeda, the United States should be leery of confronting them directly or otherwise making new enemies.

Strategy Six: delegitimation

A longer-term strategy involves trying to undermine support for terrorists by delegitimising their tactics and ideas. Governments may also use moderate and respected voices in a particular community—Muslim preachers for the jihadists, labour unions for leftists, cultural heroes for ethno-nationalist groups, and so on—to condemn terrorists. Governments can also spotlight defectors from the group. Explaining government positions, highlighting the extreme views and brutality of the terrorist group, and otherwise employing standard political tactics of making yourself look good and your opponent bad can, in theory, reduce terrorists' ability to recruit and raise money and, by winning over the populace to the government's side, increase intelligence collection.

Terrorism requires the deliberate killing of non-combatants. This is rarely popular. Few publics, no matter how bloodthirsty, want women and children to die. Thus, terrorists start out as at a disadvantage in convincing the public to see them as just. Even the terrorists' ideas, while less controversial than their use of violence, can be attacked with relative ease. Some jihadists consider the vast majority of Muslims to be apostates, hardly a viewpoint that will make them popular. Most roundly condemn the concept of democracy, even though it is supported widely in the Arab world.[50] In addition, jihadists have declared many popular activities such as sports and music to be deviations from true Islam. Such positions greatly affect the level of public support the jihadists receive.

Theologically, the terrorists are on thin ice. The vast majority of Muslim scholars have different interpretations concerning the declaration of jihad, the role of popular input into decision-making, the legitimacy of various regimes in the Muslim world and the permissibility of deviance from the strict codes the terrorists proclaim. Many of these clerics have views on these issues that would not comfort Western audiences, but are far removed from those of the terrorists.

Saudi Arabia has pursued this strategy successfully in its anti-terrorism campaign that began in earnest after the May 2003 attacks in the kingdom. At the behest of the regime, Saudi Arabia's usually bland media explicitly portrayed the gruesome impact of attacks by al-Qaeda in the Arabian Peninsula on Muslim civilians. The result was a wave of popular revulsion against the jihadists. This forced them to shift tactics away from Muslim civilians, a shift that made operations much harder and shows that their credibility has been damaged. Saudi Arabia was also able to convert several prominent clerics from adversaries and critics into regime supporters. This campaign helped convince many Saudis to reject the radicals, hurting their efforts to recruit and fundraise and giving the Saudi regime the ability to better solicit information from the populace.[51]

One common criticism of efforts to delegitimise terrorists is that no amount of propaganda could convince someone like Osama bin Laden and his diehard followers to lay down their arms. This is true, but it misses the point. Delegitimising terrorists has little impact on those already in the organisation. They have already drunk the Kool-Aid. Rather, efforts to delegitimise terrorists affect both would-be recruits and potential financiers. In addition to shaping the attitudes of these more active parts of the jihadist movement, delegitimising the terrorists also shapes the public mood, which has profound effects on the ability to gather intelligence and on the long-term desirability of reform.

One of the biggest advantages of delegitimation is that it has relatively few costs. The investments are in people and changing tactics. The United States would not have to deploy troops, change its alliance structure, or otherwise shake up its security to engage in delegitimation.

Delegitimation, however, will be less effective if it is not tied to policy changes. Perceived atrocities in Iraq or more images like those from Abu Ghraib will drown out outrage over an atrocity like Beslan or disagreement with the jihadists' condemnation of democracy. Even if other governments are the messengers, the anger US policies generate will make it difficult to reduce support for anti-US groups.

Delegitimation also requires restraint on the part of the United States and its allies. The essence of this strategy is to highlight the horrific violence and extreme goals of the foe. If US actions take centre stage instead, as high-profile measures such as invading other countries or other dramatic uses of military force inevitably will, the jihadists will draw support simply by portraying themselves as defending the Muslim community—their means and ultimate goals will be lost in the din.

Strategy seven: transforming terrorist breeding grounds

The most ambitious approach, and the most difficult, is to transform countries that breed terrorists. Bush argued for this approach eloquently in a speech before the National Endowment for Democracy in 2005, describing one aspect of US counter-terrorism strategy:

> If the peoples of that region are permitted to choose their own destiny, and advance by their own energy and by their participation as free men and women, then the extremists will be marginalized, and the flow of violent radicalism to the rest of the world will slow, and eventually end. By standing for the hope and freedom of others, we make our own freedom more secure.[52]

According to this strategy, the sclerotic rule of the Al Saud, the brutality of the Mubarak government and other grievances can all be redressed through ballots, not bullets. The president's views have some support from scholars of terrorism. Ted Robert Gurr, for example, notes that in democracies reforms can greatly reduce support for terrorism and win over potential terrorist recruits.[53]

The greatest attraction of this ambitious approach is that it promises a longterm solution to the terrorism problem. Killing and capturing al-Qaeda leaders, building defences or encouraging jihadist groups to attack elsewhere all push back the problem, at best. But if some of the grievances that lead to terrorism can be addressed, the supply of money and recruits might dry up. Northern Ireland offers perhaps the best example. Credible British offers of political power to Irish nationalists made the use of violence seem increasingly unnecessary. Over time, and it took decades, the IRA leadership recognised that they had more to gain by working with a democratic system.[54]

The disadvantages largely lie in the areas of feasibility and costs. There is no recipe for making a democracy. In addition to honest elections and the protection of minority rights, common building blocks of democracy include the rule of law, a free press, independent civic organisations like unions and professional groups, and a sense of trust among citizens. In a country like Algeria, all of these are lacking. As the United States discovered in Iraq and Afghanistan, it can influence the process, but much of the real work must be done by locals, many of whom are at best half-hearted democrats. And at times aggressive US diplomacy discredits would-be democrats in the eyes of anti-US nationalists. But only promoting more modest change opens Washington to criticism for allowing regimes like Mubarak's to stay in power. An additional problem with this strategy is that for truly transformative change, the United States must often ask allies like the Al Saud to risk surrendering power, something most regimes are loathe to do.

Democracy may also produce Islamist regimes that, while not jihadist in orientation, would oppose US foreign policy and social goals. In Palestine and Iraq, candidates linked to the terrorist group Hamas and pro-Iran militants have won elections. Islamists have done well in elections in Morocco, Egypt, Yemen, Bahrain and Saudi Arabia and probably would have won outright were it not for tight regime control over the results. As Middle East specialist F. Gregory Gause III contends, 'the problem with promoting democracy in the Arab world is not that Arabs do not like democracy; it is that Washington probably would not like the governments Arab democracy would produce'.[55] An Islamist victory in Egypt, for example, might lead to a decrease in women's rights, a harsher stand against Israel, or more criticism of the US position in Iraq. At the very least, such a government would be less inclined to cooperate with the CIA in hunting suspected terrorists. At most, it might expel the US military from the bases it uses in Egypt and actively support groups like Hamas that use terrorism against Israel.

Making the right choice

Making the best strategic choice depends on the ultimate definition of victory. US goals should be realistic even if they are ambitious. Politicians of both parties regularly talk about 'eliminating' terrorism, failing to recognise that the tactic has been around for literally thousands of years and is almost impossible to eradicate. Counter-terrorism specialist Paul Pillar points out that 'terrorism can be reduced and controlled, not defeated'.[56] And even Pillar's more cautious objective must be qualified yet further with the obvious caveat that the price—in human, financial and policy terms—must be acceptable.

With this realistic goal in mind, the more dramatic approaches—crushing the terrorists unilaterally through overwhelming force and transforming terrorist breeding grounds via democratisation—become far less appealing. They are both likely to fail and are tremendously costly, a prohibitive combination. Diversion, too, is highly risky, as well as immoral, and is difficult to implement. Despite their theoretical potential, in reality these approaches are costly and probably not feasible.

A more effective approach is to encourage allies to fight terrorists more effectively, recognising that allies are usually the key to successful counter-terrorism efforts. With allied help, terrorists can be contained and, in the long term, their many divisions will rise to the fore. Delegitimation can, to a degree, further this process. Defences have value, but the most important defensive measures involve improving domestic intelligence and ensuring the support of the Muslim community rather than trying to harden every potential terrorist target.

It is vital that there be a real debate on the proper course. Too many options are presented as cost free or as coexisting harmoniously with other forms of counter-terrorism, when in fact they are risky and loaded with trade-offs. Many political promises are grandiose, leading the public to expect a decisive victory at little cost. A more informed debate will help lay the foundation for a stronger counter-terrorism policy that can better be sustained in the decades to come.

Daniel Byman is the Director of the Center for Peace and Security Studies at Georgetown University's School of Foreign Service and a Senior Fellow at the Saban Center for Middle East Policy at the Brookings Institution.

Notes

1. For a cogent review of these problems, see Stephen D. Biddle, *American Grand Strategy after 9/11: An Assessment* (Carlisle, PA: US Army War College, April 2005), p. 22.
2. Leading recent works on terrorism include Bruce Hoffman, *Inside Terrorism* (New York: Columbia University Press, 2006); Max Abrams, 'Why Terrorism Does Not Work', *International Security,* vol. 31, no. 2, Fall 2006, pp. 42–78; Robert Trager and Dessislava Zagorcheva, 'Deterring Terrorism: It Can Be Done', *International Security,* vol. 30, no. 3, Winter 2005–06, pp. 87–123; and Robert Reich (ed.), *Origins of Terrorism* (Washington DC: Woodrow Wilson Press, 1998). Robert Pape, *Dying to Win* (New York: Random House, 2005), addresses the tactic of suicide bombing. For works on al-Qaeda, see Michael Scheuer, *Through Our Enemies' Eyes* (Washington DC: Brassey's, 2006); Marc Sageman, *Understanding Terror Networks* (Philadelphia, PA: University of Pennsylvania Press, 2004); National Academy of Public Administration, *Transforming the FBI* (September 2005), Peter Bergen, *The Osama bin Laden I Know* (New York: The Free Press, 2006). Two superb journalistic accounts of US counter-terrorism are Steve Coll, *Ghost Wars* (Harmondsworth: Penguin Press, 2004) and Lawrence Wright, *The Looming Tower* (New York: Knopf, 2006).
3. Works on counter-terrorism include Paul Pillar, *Terrorism and U.S. Foreign Policy* (Washington DC: Brookings, 2001); and Barry R. Posen, 'The Struggle against Terrorism: Grand Strategy, Strategy, and Tactics', *International Security,* vol 26, no. 3, Winter 2001, pp. 39–55.
4. The 2006 *National Strategy for Combating Terror* emphasised killing and arresting terrorists abroad, denying them the support of states, preventing them from gaining access to weapons of mass destruction, and spreading democracy. The strategy is ostensibly directed against all terrorists, but in practice the US effort is concentrated against al-Qaeda and the broader jihadist movement it supports. The Bush administration has at times been criticised for being too broad in its approach.
5. For a review, see Geneive Abdo, *No God but God: Egypt and the Triumph of Islam* (New York: Oxford University Press, 2000) and International Crisis Group, *Islamism in North Africa II: Egypt's Opportunity* (Brussels: ICG, 2004).
6. Michael Scheuer, *Imperial Hubris* (Washington DC: Brassey's, 2004), p. 241.
7. Henri Barkey, 'Turkey and the PKK: A Pyrrhic Victory?', in Robert Art and Louise Richardson (eds) *Democracy and Counterterrorism Lessons from the Past* (Washington DC: USIP Press, 2007), pp. 343–82.
8. Several reports indicate that the PKK is reviving in Iraq now. Michael Hastings, 'Blacksnake's Lair: From Deep in the Hills, Kurdish Rebels are Stirring up Turkey and Iran, and Threatening the One Calm Part of Iraq', *Newsweek,* 9 October 2006.
9. Bob Woodward, '50 Countries Detain 360 Suspects at CIA's Behest', *Washington Post,* 22 November 2001. Paul Pillar is critical of the use of law-enforcement techniques in isolation but notes they can be a valuable component of a broader counter-terrorism strategy. See Pillar, *Terrorism and U.S. Foreign Policy,* pp. 80–89; Paul R. Pillar, 'Counterterrorism after Al-Qaeda', *The Washington Quarterly,* vol. 27, no. 3, 2004, pp. 101–13, and Paul R. Pillar, 'Intelligence', in Audrey Kurth Cronin and James M. Ludes (eds), *Attacking Terrorism: Elements of a Grand Strategy* (Washington DC: Georgetown University Press, 2004), p. 115.
10. National Academy of Public Administration, *Transforming the FBI, p. 16.*
11. Saxby Chambliss, Subcommittee on Terrorism and Homeland Security House Permanent Select Committee on Intelligence, 'Counterterrorism Intelligence Capabilities and Performance Prior to 9–11', July 2002.
12. John Diamond, 'It's No Secret: CIA Scouting for Recruits', *USA Today,* 22 November 2005.
13. Abdo, *No God But God,* p. 78; Gilles kepel, *Jihad: The Trail of Political Islam* (Cambridge, MA: Harvard University Press, 2003), pp. 275–89.
14. Andrew Higgins and Christopher Cooper, 'CIA-backed Team used Brutal Means to Break Up Terrorist Cell in Albania', *Wall Street Journal,* 20 November 2001.
15. Daniel L. Byman, 'Friends Like These: Counterinsurgency and the War on Terrorism', *International Security,* vol. 31, no. 2, Fall 2006, pp. 79–115.

16. Fu'ad Husayn, 'Al-Zarqawi, the Second Generation of Al-Qa'ida', serialised in *Al Quds Al-'Arabi,* May and June 2005.
17. Daniel Byman, 'Remaking Alliances for the War on Terrorism', *Journal of Strategic Studies,* vol. 29, no. 5, October 2006, pp. 767–811.
18. To be clear, in contrast to the Cold War policy of containment, this is not based on the territorial containment of an enemy. Rather, the goal is to try to prevent the danger from growing and, as this is happening, wait for internal contradictions to weaken the adversary further.
19. Philip B. Heymann, *Terrorism and America: A Commonsense Strategy for a Democratic Society* (Cambridge, MA: MIT Press, 2000), p. 158.
20. John Mueller, 'Six Rather Unusual Propositions about Terrorism', *Terrorism and Political Violence,* vol. 17, no. 4, 2005, pp. 487–8.
21. Clark Chapman and Allan Harris, 'A Skeptical Look at September 11: How We Can Defeat Terrorism by Reacting To It More Rationally', *Skeptical Inquirer,* September-October 2002, pp. 29–34.
22. For useful reviews, see Hala Jaber, *Hezbollah: Born With A Vengeance* (New York: Columbia University Press, 1997) and Judith Palmer Harik, *Hezbollah: The Changing Face of Terrorism* (New York: I.B. Tauris, 2004).
23. Daniel Levitas, *The Terrorist Next Door* (New York: St Martin's Griffin, 2004), p. 324.
24. Kepel, *Jihad,* p. 304.
25. International Crisis Group, *Hizbollah: Rebel Group without a Cause?* (Brussels: ICG, 2003); James Kitfield, 'The Iranian Connection', *National Journal,* May 2002, p. 1469.
26. See John Mueller, 'The Banality of "Ethnic War"', *International Security,* vol. 25, no. 1, Summer 2000, pp. 42–70.
27. Terrorism expert Marc Sageman articulates this view when he notes, 'The old Al Qaeda is hiding away in caves someplace'. Marlena Telvick, 'Al Qaeda Today: The New Face of the Global Jihad', Frontline, available at http://www.pbs.org/wgbh/pages/frontline/shows/front/etc/today.html. Sageman's claim overstates al-Qaeda's decline, but his basic point that the core is less capable is true. Often, though their sole link is through web sites that spread the jihad, the ranks of sympathisers swell even more.
28. Pillar, 'Intelligence', p. 115.
29. The primary criticism of the barrier is on the grounds that it both effectively annexes Palestinian territory and that it inhibits the flow of goods into Israel from Palestinian areas, further hurting the Palestinian economy. The former criticism in particular would not apply to the United States.
30. Avi Dicter and Daniel Byman, *Israel's Lessons for Fighting Terrorists and Their Implications for the United States,* Saban Analysis Paper, no 8 (Washington DC: Brookings, 2006), p. 7.
31. Pillar, 'Intelligence', p. 125.
32. *Report of the Accountability Review Boards on the Embassy Bombings in Nairobi and Dar es Salaam* (Washington DC: 1999).
33. Statement of Cathleen A. Berrick, Director, Homeland Security and Justice, Testimony Before the Committee on Government Reform, House of Representatives, 2003. Aviation Security: Efforts to Measure Effectiveness and Strengthen Security Programs, 20 November 2003. GAO-040285T: 22.
34. According to James Fallows, more than 80% of the entire TSA's budget ($5.3bn) in 2005 went to cover the cost of airport screening. This left less than $1bn for all other forms of transportation, including roads, bridges, subways, ports and so on, which are more frequented by Americans than airlines. A total of $4.7bn was requested to support TSA's aviation security efforts in the FY2007 budget. Fallows 2005; United States Department of Homeland Security 2006. James Fallows, 'Success Without Victory', *Atlantic Monthly,* January-February 2005; United States Department of Homeland Security, Budget-in-brief (FY2007), http://www.dhs.gov/interweb/assetlibrary/Budget_BIB-FY2007.pdf.
35. Steve Orr, 'No Change in Airport Screening', *Rochester Democrat & Chronicle,* 27 November 2004.

36. Scott Higham and Robert O'Harrow, Jr. 'Contracting Rush for Security Led to Waste, Abuse', *Washington Post,* 22 May 2005, P. A1.

37. Eric Lipton, 'US to Spend Billions More to Alter Security Systems', *New York Times,* 7 May 2005.

38. For a review of terrorist innovation, see Brian A. Jackson, John C. Baker, Peter Chalk, Kim Cragin, John V. Parachini and Horacio R. Trujillo, *Aptitude for Destruction: Organizational Learning in Terrorist Groups and Its Implications for Combating Terrorism* (Santa Monica, CA: RAND, 2005).

39. Dicter and Byman, Israel's Lessons, pp. 5–8.

40. Michael Isikoff and Mark Hosenball, 'Wrong Priorities?', *Newsweek,* 7 September 2005, http://www.msnbc.msn.com/id/9246373/site/newsweek/fromRL.1/.

41. James Risen and Eric Lichtbau, 'Bush Lets US Spy on Callers without Courts', *New York Times,* 16 December 2005, p. A1.

42. Muslim Public Affairs Council, *MPAC Special Report: Religion & Identity of Muslim American Youth Post-London Attacks* (Washington DC: Muslim Public Affairs Council, 2005).

43. Institute of International Education, 'International Student Enrollment Growth Slows in 2002/2003', press release, 3 Novemeber 2003, http://opendoors.iienetwork.org/?=36523.

44. Jeremy Shapiro and Benedicte Suzan, 'The French Experience of Counterterrorism', *Survival,* vol. 45, no. 1, Spring 2003, p. 68.

45. See, for example, Michael Scott Doran, 'Somebody Else's Civil War', *Foreign Affairs,* vol. 81, no. 1, January-February 2002, pp. 22–42.

46. Richard Falkenrath, Remarks at the Brookings Institution Panel on 'How to Win the War on Terrorism', 22 September 2005, available at http://www.brookings.edu/fp/saba/events/20050922_panel1.pdf.

47. 'President Addresses Nation, Discusses Iraq, War on Terror', speech at Fort Bragg, 28 June 2005, http://www.whitehouse.gov/news/releases/2005/06/20050628-7.html; see also 'President Discusses War on Terror', talk at the National Defense University, 8 March 2005.

48. Many American Muslims are educated professionals who are well integrated into American society. Often, they have higher average incomes than do non-Muslims. The various plots uncovered since 11 September have all involved small, disconnected groups and individuals rather than a larger, country-wide network. Polls conducted in 2006 show that Americans associate far fewer negative images of Muslims than do Europeans who were also polled. Pew Global Attitudes Project, 'The Great Divide', 22 March 2006, p. 6, http://pewglobal.org/reports/display.php?ReportID=253; Daniel Benjamin and Steven Simon, *The Next Attack* (New York: Times Books, 2005), p. 119; Nicole J. Henderson, Christopher W. Ortiz, Naomi F. Sugie and Joel Miller, *Law Enforcement & Arab American Community Relations After September 11, 2001: Engagement in a Time of Uncertainly* (New York: Vera Institute of Justice, 2006), pp. 17–18.

49. Scheuer, *Through our Enemies' Eyes,* p. 111.

50. United Nations Development Programme, *Arab Human Development Report* (New York: United Nations Publications, 2003), p. 19.

51. The Saudi regime has effectively engaged in the 'war of ideas'. By converting several prominent clerics from adversaries and critics to regime supporters, the regime was able to use highly credible voices to undercut support for the radicals. The jihadists' own missteps in targeting, such as killing Muslims and Arabs in early attacks, made it easier for the regime to gain the backing of their former critics and to paint the jihadists as murderous thugs in the eyes of the Saudi people. The Saudi government also lined up clergy more openly sympathetic to the regime to condemn the jihadists. It pressed hard to ensure that state-backed clerics offered a united front against the jihadists. Saudi Arabia also pushed groups like Hamas and other radical organisations it backs to condemn the violence. Finally, the Saudis also published confessions of captured terrorists to show their ignorance and brutality.

52. 'President Discusses War on Terror at National Endowment for Democracy', speech before the National Endowment for Democracy, 5 October 2005.

53. Ted Robert Gurr, 'Terrorism in Democracies: Its Social and Political Bases', in Walter Reich (ed.), *Origins of Terrorism: Psychologies, Ideologies, Theologies, and States of Mind* (New York: Cambridge University Press, 1990), pp. 87–98.

54. Ed Maloney, *A Secret History of the IRA* (New York: W.W. Norton, 2002), pp. 375–479.

55. F. Gregory Gause III, 'Can Democracy Stop Terrorism?', *Foreign Affairs,* vol. 84, no. 5, September-October 2005, pp. 62–76.

56. Pillar, *Terrorism and U.S. Foreign Policy,* p. 218.

Russell D. Howard*

Preemptive Military Doctrine

No Other Choice

Emphasis on the preemptive uses of force is a response to the terrorist attacks of September 11, 2001, which brought home the necessity of addressing potentially catastrophic threats before the United States is attacked.[1] The first manifestation of this more forceful security doctrine was President George W. Bush's seminal September 20, 2001 address to a joint session of Congress in which he vowed to hold responsible both those who perpetuate attacks against the United States and those who harbor them.[2] The preemption concept was more clearly articulated in a speech delivered on June 1, 2002 to graduating cadets at the U.S. Military Academy at West Point, in which President Bush asserted his administration's intention to carry out preemptive military attacks if necessary to protect American lives.[3]

The West Point speech signaled a historic shift from long-accepted Cold War applications of the use of force. "For much of the last century," the President Bush said, "America's defense relied on the Cold War doctrines of deterrence and containment. In some cases, those strategies still apply." However, he contended, "new threats also require new thinking."

> Deterrence—the promise of massive retaliation against nations—means nothing against shadowy terrorist networks with no nation or citizens to defend. Containment is not possible when unbalanced dictators with weapons of mass destruction can deliver those weapons on missiles or secretly provide them to terrorist allies.[4]

This paper endorses what has come to be known as the "Doctrine of Preemption," the principle that a preemptive strategy is necessary in a post–Cold War security environment, when America's most dangerous adversaries are transnational, non-state actors with access to weapons of mass destruction and an intent to use them. In support of this position, a number of policy and legal rationales will be explored.

During the Cold War, international terrorism was essentially a small but dangerous sideshow to the greater, bipolar, Cold War drama. Terrorism in this era was almost always the province of groups of militants that had the backing of political forces and states hostile to the United States. What is new today is the emergence of terrorism that is not ideological in a traditional political sense. Instead, it is inspired largely by religious extremists and ethnic separatists. These may be individuals, like the Unabomber, or similarly minded people

---

*The author is indebted to Christian Westra for his invaluable assistance in updating this article.

working in cells, small groups, or larger coalitions.[5] They do not answer completely to any government, they operate across national borders, and they have access to sophisticated funding sources and advanced technology.[6]

The new terrorist groups are not bound by the same constraints or motivated by the same goals as nation-states. They are not amenable to traditional diplomacy or military deterrence because there is no state to negotiate with or to retaliate against. Nor are they concerned about limiting casualties. Under the old rules, "terrorists wanted a lot of people watching, not a lot of people dead."[7] They did not want large body counts; they wanted converts and a seat at the table. Today's terrorists are less concerned about converts; rather than wanting a seat at the table, "they want to destroy the table and everyone sitting at it."[8] Religious terrorists, al Qaeda in particular, want casualties—lots of them.[9]

Today's terrorism is not ideological like Communism or capitalism, with values that can be debated in the classroom or voted on at the polls. Instead, it is an adaptation of an ancient tactic. The major difference between modern terrorism and its historical antecedents is that the "new terrorism" is better financed and has a worldwide reach, thanks to globalization and the information revolution. The new terrorism can harness the power of the Internet, using advanced communications systems to move vast sums from Karachi to London or to connect disenfranchised young people in Queens or Frankfurt with radical clerics living thousands of miles away. For only $28.50, any Internet surfer can purchase *Bacteriological Warfare: A Major Threat to North America,* which explains how to grow deadly bacteria that could be used in a terrorist attack.

Terrorists and WMD

The prospect of terrorists using WMD (weapons of mass destruction, i.e., nuclear, radiological, biological, or chemical weapons) to attack the United States is the single strongest justification for the Doctrine of Preemption. As President Bush explained in 2002:

> When the spread of chemical and biological and nuclear weapons, along with ballistic missile technology occurs, even weak states and small groups could attain a catastrophic power to strike great nations. Our enemies have declared this very intention, and have been caught seeking these terrible weapons. They want the capability to blackmail us, or to harm us, or to harm our friends and we will oppose them with all our power.[10]

Indeed, al Qaeda has threatened the United States with WMD. Discoveries in Afghanistan have confirmed that al Qaeda and other terrorist groups are actively seeking the ability to use biological agents against United States and its allies.[11] According to former UN weapons inspector David Kay, this should not come as a surprise:

> Only a blind, deaf and dumb terrorist group could have survived the last five years and not been exposed at least to the possibility of the use of WMD, while the more discerning terrorists would have found some tactically brilliant possibilities already laid out on the public record.[12]

Steven Miller, director of the International Security Program at Harvard's Kennedy School, agrees that policymakers should be concerned about terrorists' access to nuclear weapons. According to Miller, "opportunities for well-organized and well-financed terrorists to infiltrate a Russian nuclear storage facility are greater than ever."[13] Miller believes there have been more than two-dozen thefts of weapons-usable materials in the former Soviet Union in recent years. Though several suspects have been arrested in undercover sting operations, others may have gotten away.[14] In 1994, Miller points out, "350 grams of plutonium were smuggled on board a Lufthansa flight from Moscow to Munich. Fortunately, SWAT teams confiscated the material as soon as it arrived."[15]

Given the known goals of terrorists, the United States can no longer rely solely on a reactive, crisis-response military posture, as it has in the past. Our inability to deter a potential attacker, the immediacy of today's threats, and the catastrophic consequences of a WMD attack do not permit that option. The United States simply cannot allow its enemies to strike first with nuclear, radiological, biological, or chemical weapons.[16]

Arms Control Protocols and Westphalian Rules No Longer Apply

The United States' inability to negotiate with non-state actors limits the usefulness of diplomacy in reducing the likelihood of chemical, biological, radiological, and nuclear attacks. For example, it is stated U.S. policy not to negotiate with terrorists.[17] The rationale behind this policy is clear: Giving in to terrorist demands will prompt more terrorist activity. This is especially true in hostage situations because negotiations with terrorists could potentially force the United States to risk having to meet certain demands for ransom or safe passage.

However, it would be very beneficial to have a mechanism—presumably secret—that could enable an opportunity to dialogue with terrorists. This would be especially important in regard to transnational, non-state actors who have no formal diplomatic voice. The manner in which this dialogue might take place would depend on the situation. Discussions could be held in secret or through surrogates. Preferably, a dialogue—not necessarily negotiations—with terrorists could be established before an attack that might prevent it from happening, thus avoiding the necessity of preemption. In any case, opening a dialogue is important if for no other reason than that understanding what is really on a terrorist's mind has intelligence value. Even more important, having a terrorist understand what is on our mind may well have at least some deterrent value.

Nuclear arms control and reduction treaties promulgated during the Cold War were, and still are, valuable assets for preventing conflict. They provided baseline agreements that fostered cooperation between nuclear powers and led to greater transparency and confidence-building measures that still exist today. Unfortunately, treaties meant to control and reduce the number of chemical and biological weapons have not been as effective.

The Chemical Weapons Convention (CWC) entered into force on April 29, 1997. It has been signed by 120 states and bans chemical weapons production and storage as well as use. The strength of the convention is that it calls for unprecedented and highly intrusive inspections, including routine and challenge inspection mechanisms. The weakness of the convention is that several countries that pose concerns about chemical proliferation have not joined the CWC regime. These include Libya, North Korea, and Syria.[18]

Biological weapons are also prohibited by a treaty, the Biological and Toxin Weapons Convention (BWC), which entered into force in 1975 and now comprises some 140 members. The strength of the BWC is that it bans an entire class of weapons, prohibiting the development, production, stockpiling, or acquisition of biological agents or toxins of any type or quantity that do not have protective, medical, or other peaceful purposes. "However, the major shortfall of the BWC is its lack of any on-site verification mechanism."[19]

Significantly, arms control conventions only affect state behavior. They have no impact on the behavior of transnational and other non-state actors that might possess and use chemical, biological, or nuclear weapons, or on those rogue states that are not signatories to the conventions.

The major problems the United States has in addressing international WMD threats are outdated military doctrine and the traditional way it employs military force. The traditional uses of military force are defense, deterrence, compellence, and presence. Defense against terrorist use of WMD is extremely difficult, especially in a democracy. Without compromising civil liberties in draconian ways—a goal of terrorists—no defense regime could come close to guaranteeing security against a terrorist intent on attacking the United States with WMD. As former Secretary of Defense Donald Rumsfeld reflected in a speech at the National Defense University in January 2002: "It is not possible to defend against every conceivable kind of attack in every conceivable location at every minute of the day or night. The best, and in some cases, the only defense is a good offense."

Deterrence against nongovernmental actors is also extremely difficult. Where exactly do you retaliate against Osama bin Laden if he launches a biological attack? As James Wirtz and James A. Russell note in a recent article:

> Deterrence generally does not work against terrorists. Stateless and usually spread over wide regions or even among continents, terrorists do not present a viable target for retaliation. The death and destruction that can be visited upon a terrorist organization in a retaliatory attack is greatly exceeded by the damage even a small terrorist cell can inflict on civilian society.[20]

Historically, the United States has employed its military to compel enemies to change their behavior after a crisis has occurred. The National Security Act of 1947 and its subsequent amendments have structured the U.S. security apparatus to react to crises, not prevent them. However, given the nature of the post—Cold War WMD threats, a new strategy must be pursued to compel adversaries to change their behavior before they attack. This is preemption.

Preemption—Not Fighting Fair?

Preemption has long been an important and widely accepted U.S. security policy option.[21] Even so, the preemptive use of military force is a difficult concept for many Americans to accept. For one thing, as Brad Roberts points out, preemption defies certain traditional notions of fair-play:

> Moral philosophy establishes that wars of self-defense are just, whereas wars of aggression are not. But there has long been a healthy debate about precisely what constitutes a war of self-defense. A mid-sixteenth-century scholar of just war wrote, "There is a single and only just cause for commencing a war . . . namely, wrong received." In our day Michael Walzer has argued, "Nothing but aggression can justify war. . . . There must actually have been a wrong, and it must actually have been received (or its receipt must be, as it were, only minutes away)."[22]

This view, however, has not been held by all. Hugo Grotius wrote in 1625: "The first just cause of war . . . is an injury, which even though not actually committed, threatens our persons or our property."[23] Grotius emphasized that to safeguard against wars of aggression, it was essential to be certain about the enemy's intent to attack. Later, in 1914, Elihu Root argued that international law did not require the aggrieved state to wait before using force in self-defense "until it is too late to protect itself."[24]

Roberts contends, rightly I think, that there can be "no blanket reply" to the question, "Is there a moral case for preemption?" As Roberts writes, "some acts of preemption will be deemed just, others unjust." In the case of preemption against WMD threats, Roberts argues that the strongest moral case for U.S. preemption exists under the following conditions:

> (1) an aggressor has actually threatened to use his WMD weapons, has taken steps to ready the means to do so, and has specifically threatened the United States (including its territory, citizens, or military forces); (2) those WMD weapons have been built in violation of international law; (3) the aggressor's threatened actions invoke larger questions about the credibility of security guarantees or the balance of power within a region; (4) the president has secured the approval of the U.S. Congress; and (5) the United States has secured the backing of the U.N. Security Council and any relevant regional organization. The prudential tests of last resort, proportionality, and reasonable chance of success must also be met.[25]

I agree with the first four of Robert's conditions but not with the last. The backing of the UN and regional organizations would certainly strengthen the moral argument for preemption but may be impossible to obtain, given China's reluctance to violate sovereignty under any circumstances and Russia's recurring post-Kosovo habit of siding with rogue states like Iran. Moreover, the United States must never forgo the option to act unilaterally.

Domestic Political Support

The commonly held view that the U.S. public disapproves of preemption is simply mistaken. A good example is the 1998 bombing of a Sudanese chemical plant that was suspected of having ties to Osama bin Laden. Even when it was revealed that the plant was probably making nothing sinister, public opinion in the United States was still strongly in favor of the attacks.[26] In fact, two-thirds of Americans approved the military strike, while only 19 percent were opposed.[27]

More recent data show that Congress is in favor of preemption under certain conditions, particularly when conducted against non-state actors intent on harming the U.S. Dr. Scott Silverstone, a professor and researcher at the United States Military Academy, has categorized data from congressional hearings, memos, media articles, and personal statements showing that members of the Senate and House are nearly unanimous in their support for preemption as a strategy. In fact, Silverstone's data show that 90 percent of the Senate favored a preemption strategy against non-state actors. The figure in the House was 81 percent. Remarkably, not one elected official in the House or Senate explicitly rejected the notion of preemptive warfare directed against non-state actors.[28]

Preemption and International Law

A strong case can be made for the legality of preemptive warfare, or what many legal scholars have termed, "anticipatory self-defense," even if it is not permitted under the United Nations Charter.

There is little doubt that the United Nations Charter prohibits anticipatory self-defense. When the architects of the United Nations gathered at San Francisco in 1945, their overriding concern was to ensure that the nations of the world never went to war with each other again. Article 2(4) of the Charter states that member states of the United Nations "shall refrain in their international relations from the threat or use of force against the territorial integrity or political independence of any state."[29] There are only two exceptions to this broad prohibition against the threat or use of force. In instances when the United Nations Security Council determines the "existence of any threat to the peace, breach of the peace, or act of aggression," it may authorize the use of force under Article 39 of the UN Charter.[30] In addition, under Article 51 of the UN Charter, member states of the United Nations are permitted to use force in "individual or collective self-defense" if an "armed attack" against them has occurred.[31]

Might anticipatory self-defense be justified under either Article 39 or Article 51 of the United Nations Charter? Most legal scholars believe the answer is no.[32] Article 39, the so-called "Official Police Action" power, has been invoked by the Security Council on only two occasions—once during the Korean War, and once during the Gulf War. In both instances, hostilities had already commenced. On its face, Article 51 might appear to open the door to the preemptive use of force. After all, the terms "self-defense" and "armed attack" could conceivably have a different meaning in the 21st century than they did in 1945, given the new threats posed by terrorists with access to WMD. Nevertheless, the International Court of Justice has been explicit in emphasizing that self-defense is permitted under Article 51 only after an actual armed attack has occurred.[33] Following this reasoning, the invasion of Afghanistan by the United States after September 11 could conceivably be justified under Article 51, but only because an actual armed attack—perpetrated by individuals sheltered by the Afghan government—had occurred on New York and Washington.

Needless to say, this kind of brittle legalism has been roundly criticized for not reflecting contemporary realities. However noble the intentions of the UN framers may have been, Article 2(4) has failed entirely to prevent the threat or use of force in the international arena.[34] Just as importantly, Articles 2(4), 39, and 51 do not address the threat posed by non-state actors, most notably terrorist groups operating from within states. Some legal scholars believe these observations are legally irrelevant and that the signatory states of the UN Charter are still legally bound to observe all of the Charter's provisions.[35] Others, however, argue that the use of force provisions in the United Nations Charter have fallen into "desuetude," meaning that their legal force has been eroded over time by inconsistent practice.[36] If this were the case, the permissibility of anticipatory self-defense under international law would be determined not with narrow reference to the United Nations Charter, but rather by examining broader preexisting legal norms, or what is often referred to collectively as "customary international law."

Customary international law is said to result from a practice followed by states out of a sense of legal obligation.[37] Although anticipatory self-defense has particular relevance to the post–September 11 world, it is hardly a concept unique to our time. The most notable example of preemption in early U.S. history is the so-called *Caroline* incident.[38] In 1837, an insurrection against Great Britain raged in Canada. America and Britain were at peace but an American ship, the *Caroline,* was suspected by the British of providing assistance to the Canadian rebels. Late one night, a group of British sailors and Canadian loyalists boarded the *Caroline* and killed an American crewmember, setting the ship ablaze before sending it over Niagara Falls. Incensed, the United States public demanded retribution. Secretary of State Daniel Webster protested the incident, and the British government eventually apologized.

From the diplomatic correspondences between Webster and his British counterparts, a new standard for anticipatory self-defense emerged. Under this standard, preemption was deemed acceptable so long as it was "necessary" and "proportionate." Self-defense, Webster wrote, is justified if the "necessity of that self-defense is instant, overwhelming, and leaving no choice of means, and no moment of deliberation."[39] Moreover, Webster added, "the necessity of self-defense, must be limited by that necessity, and kept clearly within it."[40] In other words, under the *Caroline* standard, anticipatory self-defense is legal insofar as it occurs in response to an imminent attack and reflects the actual nature of the threat encountered. As Professor Thomas M. Franck has demonstrated, there is ample evidence of modern state practice to suggest that the *Caroline* standard has the force of customary international law today.[41]

Of course, administering the *Caroline* standard raises considerable challenges, especially in the modern security environment. When is an attack actually imminent? Is a terrorist attack imminent once training camps have been formed, or must policymakers wait until an operation is set to commence? Should the standard for imminence be relaxed when the potential harm from an attack is catastrophic, such as in the case of a nuclear or biological attack? Finally, even if preemption is legal under international law, is it prudent from a geo-strategic perspective? Each of these questions will have to be answered by policymakers on a case-by-case basis, balancing the costs and benefits of action and inaction in each instance. My view is that the *Caroline* standard should be interpreted broadly when there is clear evidence to show that America's security is at risk.

Conclusion

I was on the dais at West Point when President Bush gave his "preemption speech" and was taken with one of his statements, which I paraphrase here. He told the audience: "The gravest danger to freedom lies at the perilous crossroads of radicalism and technology. When the spread of chemical and biological and nuclear weapons, along with ballistic missile technology occurs, even weak states and small groups could attain a catastrophic power to strike great nations." He went on: "Our enemies have declared this very intention, and have been caught seeking these terrible weapons. They want the capability to blackmail us, or to harm us, or to harm our friends—and we will oppose them with all our power."

In my view, "opposing them with all our power" must include the "preemptive use of force" to defeat terrorists before they can inflict pain on the United States. Traditional applications of American power—economic, political, diplomatic, and military used to leverage and influence states in the past—are not effective against non-state actors. Whom do you sanction or embargo? With whom do you negotiate? How do you defend against or deter Osama bin Laden? You don't. The only effective way to influence the bin Ladens of the world is to preempt them before they can act.

Brigadier General Russell D. Howard (Retired) was a career Special Forces officer and is now the Director of the Jebsen Center for Counter-terrorism Studies at the Fletcher School at Tufts University. His recent publications include *Defeating Terrorism,* (McGraw-Hill, 2004), *Homeland Security and Terrorism* (McGraw-Hill, 2005), and *Weapons of Mass Destruction and Terrorism* (McGraw-Hill, 2006).

Notes

1. Michael E. O'Hanlon, Susan Rice, and James B. Steinberg (December 2002), "The New National Security Strategy and Preemption," *Brookings Policy Brief #113,* p. 1.
2. Ibid.
3. President George W. Bush (June 1, 2002), West Point, New York.
4. Ibid.
5. Stephen A. Cambone (1996), *A New Structure for National Security Policy Planning* (Washington, DC: Government Printing Office), p. 43.
6. Gideon Rose (March–April 1999), "It Could Happen Here—Facing the New Terrorism," *Foreign Affairs,* p. 1.
7. Frequently quoted remark made by Brian Jenkins in 1974.
8. Quote attributed to James Woolsey, 1994.
9. Bruce Hoffman (1998), *Inside Terrorism* (New York: Columbia University Press), p. 205.
10. George W. Bush, June 1, 2002.
11. Judith Miller (September 14, 2002), "Lab Suggests Qaeda Planned to Build Arms, Officials Say," *New York Times,* p. 1.
12. David Kay (2001), "WMD Terrorism: Hype or Reality." In James M. Smith and William C. Thomas, eds., *The Terrorism Threat and US Government Response: Operational and Organizational Factors* (US Air Force Academy: INSS Book Series), p. 12.
13. Doug Gavel (Autumn 2002), "Can Nuclear Weapons Be Put Beyond the Reach of Terrorists?" *Kennedy School of Government Bulletin,* p. 43.
14. Ibid., p. 45. Interestingly, in *Just Wars,* Michael Walzer seems to contradict his earlier statements by arguing that "states can rightfully defend themselves against violence that is imminent but not actual."
15. Ibid., p. 48.
16. See the National Security Strategy of the United States.
17. Stansfield Turner (1991), *Terrorism and Democracy* (Boston: Houghton Mifflin Company), p. xii. Actually, Admiral Turner makes the argument that the United States will negotiate with terrorists. See chapter 26, *We Will Make Deals.*
18. "Weapons of Mass Destruction" (1999), *Great Decisions,* p. 51.
19. Ibid., p. 52.
20. James Wirtz and James A. Russell (Spring 2003), "U.S. Policy on Preventive War and Preemption," *The Nonproliferation Review, 10,* no. 1, p. 116.
21. O'Hanlon, et al., p. 4.
22. Brad Roberts (March 1998), "NBC-Armed Rogues: Is there a Moral Case for Preemption?" In Elliott Abrams, ed., *Close Calls: Intervention, Terrorism, Missile Defense, and 'Just War' Today* (EPPC), p. 11.
23. Hugo Grotius, *The Law of War and Peace,* book 2, chapter 1, section 2.
24. Elihu Root (1914), "The Real Monroe Doctrine," *American Journal of International Law, 35,* p. 427.
25. Roberts, p. 13.

Preemptive Military Doctrine **491**

26. "Excerpts: US Editorials Assess Impact of Anti-Terrorist Strikes" (June 14, 2000), *USIS Washington File,* pp. 1–6, http://www.fas.org/man/dod-101/ops/docs/98082307_tpo.html.

27. John Diamond (August 21, 1998), "US Strikes Tougher Stance Against Terrorism," *Cnews,* http://www.canoe.ca/CNEWSStrikeAtTerrorism/aug20_us.html.

28. Multiple conversations with Dr. Scott Silverstone.

29. Charter of the United Nations (1945), Article 2(4).

30. Charter of the United Nations (1945), Article 39.

31. Charter of the United Nations (1945), Article 51. Significantly, states are permitted to use force in self-defense under Article 51 only "until the Security Council has taken measures necessary to maintain international peace and security."

32. See e.g., Mary Ellen O'Connell (2002), "The Myth of Preemptive Self-Defense," *American Society of International Law,* pp. 1–22.

33. *The Republic Nicaragua v. The United States of America,* International Court of Justice (1986).

34. As Professor Thomas M. Franck wrote in a widely read 1970 article, "the high-minded resolve of Article 2(4) mocks us from its grave . . ." such that "the United Nations Charter today bears little more resemblance to the modern world than does a Magellan map." Thomas M. Franck, "Who Killed Article 2(4)?" *American Journal of International Law, 64,* Issue 4 (Oct. 1970), p. 809.

35. See e.g., Louis Henkin (1979), *How Nations Behave: Law and Foreign Policy,* 2nd ed. (Columbia University), pp. 141.

36. See e.g., Michael J. Glennon (2005), "Idealism at the U.N.," *Policy Review,* pp. 3–14; Michael J. Glennon (2001–2002), "The Fog of Law: Self-Defense, Inherence, and Incoherence in Article 51 of the United Nations Charter," *Harvard Journal of Law & Public Policy, 25,* p. 539–558.

37. Statute of the International Court of Justice, Article 38.

38. See Anthony Clark Arend (Spring 2003), "International Law and Preemptive Use of Military Force," *Washington Quarterly,* pp. 90–91 (providing historical context on the *Caroline* incident and analyzing its implications for contemporary anticipatory self-defense).

39. Ibid., p. 91.

40. Ibid.

41. See Thomas M. Franck, *Recourse to Force,* "Anticipatory Self-defense," pp. 97–108.

Paul R. Pillar

Beyond Al Qaeda

Countering a Decentralized Terrorist Threat

The fortunes of Osama bin Laden's al Qaeda, generally viewed as the principal terrorist menace to U.S. interests for the past decade, have fluctuated significantly. The disciplined, centrally directed organization that executed the terrorist spectacular on September 11, 2001 fell on harder times following the subsequent U.S.-led intervention in Afghanistan. The group was rousted from its Taliban-controlled safe haven, most of its senior and mid-level leaders were killed or incarcerated, and most of those still at large became focused at least as much on their own survival as on organizing new terrorist operations. Bin Laden's organization later appeared to rebound, with other operatives stepping up to replace the lost cadres and a parallel resuscitation of its Taliban allies helping to buy it some breathing space in its South Asian redoubt.[1] Even with the rebound, however, al Qaeda is no longer the dominating organization it was at the time of 9/11. Its role in international terrorism has become less a matter of instigation and control than of inspiration and more tenuous connections to specific terrorist operations.

Al Qaeda still is able to inflict substantial damage, but most challenges for counter-terrorist efforts now and for the next several years will come from the larger global network of mostly Sunni Islamic extremists, of which al Qaeda has been the best known part. The name "al Qaeda" often is loosely and misleadingly applied to the entire network, but the network extends far beyond Bin Laden's group. Counterterrorism has become a task of confronting not just al Qaeda but the children and cousins of al Qaeda.

In contrast to al Qaeda's ups and downs, the trajectory of the larger movement over the past few years has been mostly up. Sunni extremism has become a larger, more popu-lous, and more geographically dispersed phenomenon than it was only a few years ago. The roots of this brand of extremism remain very much alive and in some cases are grow-ing deeper. They include closed economic and political systems in much of the Muslim world that deny many young adults the opportunity to build better lives for themselves and also deny them the political representation to voice their grievances peacefully over the lack of such opportunity. Other factors underlying the rise of Islamist terrorism include the paucity of credible alternatives to militant Islam as vehicles of opposition to the established order as well as widespread opposition toward U.S. policies within and toward the Muslim world, especially the U.S. posture toward the Arab–Israeli conflict and the invasion and occupation of Iraq.

The radical Islamist threat comes from an eclectic array of groups, cells, and individ-uals. Offshoots of al Qaeda that carry on bin Laden's malevolent cause and operate under local leaders will remain part of the mix. Another part includes like-minded groups that arise locally but, in the manner of franchisees, adopt the al Qaeda name because it is such a widely recognized brand. These groups include the one in Iraq organized by the late Abu Musab al-Zarqawi, and the Algerian-based organization originally known as the Salafist Group for Call and Combat. Yet another part includes well-established regionally based groups such as Jemaah Islamiya in Southeast Asia. Many of these groups have local objectives but share the transnational anti-Americanism of the larger network. Finally, individuals best labeled simply as jihadists, who carry no group membership card but move through and draw support from the global network of like-minded radical Islamists, also are part of the picture. From their ranks, some individuals likely will emerge with the leadership skills needed to organize operational cells and conduct terrorist attacks.

In a word, the transformation of the terrorist threat from the al Qaeda of September 2001 to the mixture just described is one of *decentralization*. The initiative, direction, and support for anti-U.S. terrorism is coming from more, and more widely scattered, locations than it ever has before. Although any weakening of al Qaeda lessens (but does not eliminate) the risk of particularly large, well-organized, and well-financed terrorist operations, the decentralization of the threat poses offsetting problems for collecting and analyzing counterterrorist intelligence, enlisting foreign support to counter the threat, and sustaining the United States' own commitment to combat it while avoiding further damage to U.S. relations with the Muslim world. For these reasons, the counterterrorist challenges after the defeat of al Qaeda may very well be even more complex than they were before.

Uncertain Intelligence Targets

The small, secretive nature of terrorist plots and the indeterminate number of them—likely to become an even greater problem as the Islamic terrorist threat further decentralizes—always have made terrorism a particularly difficult target. The mission of intelligence in counterterrorism is not only to monitor known terrorist and terrorist groups but also to uncover any groups who *might* attack the United States and its interests. The greater the number of independent actors and centers of terrorist planning and operations, the more difficult that mission becomes. Exhortations to the intelligence community to penetrate terrorist groups are useless if the groups that need to be penetrated have not even been identified.

The U.S. intelligence community's experience in the 1990s may help it adjust to the transformation currently underway. Prior to the bombing in 1993 of the World Trade Center (WTC), the terrorist threat against the United States was thought of chiefly in terms of known, named, discrete groups such as the Lebanese Hizballah. The principal challenges for analysts involved identifying the structure and strength of each group as well as making sense of the pseudonymous "claim names" commonly used in declaring responsibility for attacks. The WTC bombing and the subsequent foiled plot to bomb several other landmarks in New York City introduced the concept of ad hoc terrorists: nameless cells of radicals who come together for the sole purpose of carrying out a specific attack.

The term *ad hoc* subsequently was discarded as suggesting too casual an arrangement and as not reflecting the links to the wider jihadist network that intelligence work through the mid-1990s gradually uncovered. Even with those links, however, the New York plots were examples of a decentralized threat in that they evidently were initiated locally. As demonstrated by the shoestring budget on which the WTC bombers operated, the plots were not directed and financed by bin Laden from a lair in Sudan or South Asia. The threats that U.S. intelligence must monitor today have in a sense returned to what existed in the early 1990s. Now, however, the threat has more moving parts, more geographically dispersed operations, and more ideological momentum.

Much, though not all, of the intelligence community's counterterrorist efforts over the past several years can be applied to the increasingly decentralized threat the world now faces. Even the intelligence work narrowly focused on al Qaeda has unearthed many leads and links, involving anything from telephone calls to shared apartments, that are useful in uncovering other possible centers of terrorist planning and operations. These links are central to intelligence counterterrorist efforts because linkages with known terrorists can uncover other individuals who may be terrorists themselves. Most successful U.S. efforts to disrupt terrorist organizations, including the capture of most of the al Qaeda leadership since September 2001, have resulted from such link analysis.

The looser the operational connections become, however, and the less that Islamist terrorism is instigated by a single figure, the harder it will be to uncover exploitable links and the more likely that the instigators of future terrorist attacks will escape the notice of U.S. intelligence. With a more decentralized network, these individuals will go unnoticed not because data on analysts' screens are misinterpreted but because they will never appear on those screens in the first place.

The 9/11 plot helps to illustrate the point. Retrospective inquiries have given much attention to the tardiness in placing two of the hijackers, Khalid al-Mihdhar and Nawaf al-Hazmi, on U.S. government watch lists. Much less attention has been paid to what made al-Mihdhar and al-Hazmi candidates for a watch list in the first place: their participation in a meeting with an al Qaeda operative in Kuala Lumpur. U.S. intelligence acquired information about the meeting by piecing together al Qaeda's activities in the Far East and developing rosters of al Qaeda intermediaries whose activities could be tracked to gain information that would provide new leads. Although this was skillful and creative intelligence work, it relied on linkages to a known terrorist group, al Qaeda—linkages that existed because bin Laden and senior al Qaeda leadership in South Asia ultimately directed and financed the terrorist operation in question. A decentralized version of the threat will not necessarily leave such a trail.

Muhammad Atta and some of the other September 11 hijackers were never even considered candidates for the watch lists because intelligence reporting had not previously associated them with known terrorists. In fact, one of al Qaeda's criteria for selecting the hijackers almost certainly was that they did not have such traceable associations. In a more decentralized network, such connections are even less likely.

Yet, even a decentralized terrorist threat has some linkages that can be exploited, and this will be important in future counterterrorist efforts by the intelligence community. Within the networks of Sunni Islamic extremists, almost everyone can be linked at least indirectly, such as through their past common experiences in camps in Afghanistan, to almost everyone else. The overwhelming majority of these linkages, however, consists of only casual contacts and do not involve preparations for terrorist operations directed against the United States, as the meeting in Kuala Lumpur evidently did. No intelligence service has the resources to monitor all of these contacts, to compile the life history of every extremist who potentially may become a terrorist, or to construct comprehensive sociograms of the radical Islamist scene. Detecting the perpetrators of the next terrorist attack against the United States therefore will have to go beyond link analysis and increasingly rely on other techniques for picking terrorists out of a crowd.

Mining of financial, travel, and other data on personal actions and circumstances other than mere association with questionable individuals and groups is one such technique.[2] The technique has been increasingly used in recent years, with potential for using it even further. Yet, data mining for counterterrorist purposes always will require a major investment in obtaining and manipulating the data in return for only a modest narrowing of the search for terrorists. Numerous practical difficulties in gaining access to personal information and the lack of a reliable algorithm for processing the data inhibit the effectiveness of this technique. Significant issues regarding personal privacy, which have been raised more frequently amid reports of expanded data mining by the Department of Homeland Security, are an additional complication.[3] The 9/11 attacks, however, significantly lowered the threshold for all investments in counterterrorist operations, including data mining, making this technique worth employing more extensively even if it appears no more cost effective than it did before September 2001.

It is the U.S. population and U.S. policymakers, not the intelligence community, who will have to make the most important adjustment concerning intelligence operations. They will have to lower their expectations regarding how much of the burden of stopping terrorists intelligence can carry. An increasingly decentralized terrorist threat and indeterminate intelligence target will mean that more terrorists and terrorist plots may escape the notice of intelligence services altogether. The transformation of the threat itself, coupled with the inherent limits of intelligence operations implies that more of the counterterrorist burden will have to be borne by other policy instruments, from initiatives to address the reasons individuals gravitate toward terrorism in the first place to physical security measures to defeat attempted attacks.

Fragile International Cooperation

The willingness of governments worldwide to join the campaign against terrorism has increased significantly over the last 25 years—a welcome change from earlier days when many regimes were more apt to condone terrorism than to condemn it because of their support for "national liberation movements." September 11 seemed to strengthen further a global consensus in confronting terrorism. This apparent collective commitment, however, should not be taken for granted. Despite many governments' declarations that they stand with the United States in combating terrorism, each decision by a foreign government on whether to cooperate reflects calculations about the threat that nation faces from particular terrorist groups, its relations with the United States, any incentives Washington offers for its cooperation, domestic opinion, and the potential effect of enhanced counterterrorist measures on its domestic interests. Such calculations can change, and the perceived net advantage of cooperating may be slim. In short, global cooperation against terrorism already is fragile.

Much of foreign governments' willingness to help has depended on al Qaeda's record and menacing capabilities. The enormity of the 9/11 attacks and the unprecedented impact they had on the U.S. government's priorities and policies have accounted for much of the increased willingness among foreign governments to assist in efforts to combat terrorism. The threat al Qaeda has posed to some of the governments themselves, particularly the Saudi regime, also has helped the United States gain cooperation. The bombings in Riyadh in May and November of 2003 were wake-up calls that partly overcame numerous reasons for the Saudis' sluggishness in cracking down on Islamic extremists in their midst. Most of the victims of the November bombing were Arabs of modest means; this sloppy targeting undoubtedly cost al Qaeda some of its support in the kingdom. Since then, the Saudi government has exerted, with significant success, markedly more effort than it did previously in combating jihadist groups on its own territory.

Foreign cooperation will become more problematic as the issue moves beyond al Qaeda. How will governments respond to a U.S. appeal to move against groups that never have inflicted comparable horrors on the United States or on any other nation, or against groups that do not conspicuously pose the kind of threat that al Qaeda has posed to Saudi Arabia? How can regimes be motivated to tackle Islamic groups that may represent an emerging terrorist threat but have not yet resorted to terrorism? A possible example is the Central Asian-based Hizb al-Tahrir, which operates legally in many other places, including the United Kingdom. Without the special focus that comes from a fight against the group that accomplished 9/11, many of the past reasons for foot-dragging in counterterrorism are likely to reassert themselves. These reasons include the sympathy that governments or their populations feel for many of the anti-Western or anti-imperialist themes in whose name terrorists claim to act, an aversion to doing Washington's bidding against interests closer to home, and a general reluctance to rock local boats.

Problems that the United States already has encountered in dealing with Lebanese Hizballah illustrate some of the difficulties in enlisting foreign help against terrorist groups—even highly capable groups—other than al Qaeda.[4] Hizballah's bombing of the U.S. Marine barracks in Beirut in 1983 is second only to 9/11 in the number of American deaths attributable to a terrorist attack. Hizballah's terrorist apparatus, led by its longtime chief Imad Mughniyah, remains formidable. The dominant view of Hizballah in Lebanon and elsewhere in the Middle East, however, is that the group is a legitimate participant in Lebanese politics. The group holds seats in parliament and provides social services in much of the country. Hizballah's miscalculations that led to its war with Israel in the summer of 2006, and its military setbacks in that war, may have done little to diminish its political standing.[5] Despite the events two decades ago in Lebanon, including other bombings and a series of kidnappings of Westerners, Hizballah's political status has prevented U.S. officials from effectively appealing for cooperation against Hizballah in the way that the 9/11 attacks allowed them to appeal for cooperation against al Qaeda. Notwithstanding the major potential terrorist threat it poses, Hizballah has not been clearly implicated in any terrorist attack on Americans since the bombing of Khobar Towers more than a decade ago.

A limitation to foreign willingness to cooperate with the United States on counterterrorism is skepticism among foreign publics and even elites that the most powerful nation on earth needs to be preoccupied with small bands of radicals. Even the depth of the trauma that 9/11 caused the American public does not seem to be fully appreciated in many areas overseas, particularly in the Middle East. Such skepticism is likely to be all the greater when the U.S. preoccupation is no longer with the group that carried out 9/11.

Any reduced foreign support for counterterrorism will not be clear or sudden. No foreign government will declare that it supports terrorists. Instead, foreign governments may be a little slower to act, a little less forthcoming with information, or slightly more apt to cite domestic impediments to cooperation. Whether counterterrorist cooperation weakens will rest largely on whether and how Washington responds to the concerns and needs of its foreign partners.

Muslim Distrust

Skepticism and distrust among Muslims across the world about U.S. counterterrorist efforts have impeded international cooperation and may become an even bigger problem in a post–al Qaeda era. With Muslims—especially Muslims claiming to act in the name of their religion—still dominating international terrorism, Muslims will still dominate Washington's counterterrorist target list. This fact will continue to encourage questions about whether the so-called war on terrorism is really a war on Islam. Many Muslims ask whether a sustained counterterrorist campaign has less to do with fighting terrorism than with maintaining the political status quo in countries with pro-U.S. regimes. Many Muslims also see the campaign as part of a religiously based war between the Muslim world and a Judeo-Christian West.

The "war on terrorism" terminology exacerbates this problem, partly because a war is most clearly understood as a war against somebody rather than a metaphorical war against a tactic. The problem has been minimized insofar as counterterrorist operations have been aimed primarily at a particular group, al Qaeda. The less the fight is conducted against a single named foe, the greater the problem of misinterpreting the term *war*. The extension of the *war on terrorism* label to the invasion and occupation of Iraq has exacerbated the problem. Even though a portion of the violence that has plagued Iraq is appropriately labeled as terrorism, the Bush administration undertook the military operation in Iraq primarily for reasons other than counterterrorism, feeding Muslim misperceptions and fears that the United States also has ulterior motives every other time it talks about fighting terrorism.

Such perceptions among Muslims will strengthen the roots of the very Islamist terrorism that already poses the principal threat to U.S. interests. They will encourage a sense that the Muslim world as a whole is in a struggle with the Judeo-Christian West and foster a view of the United States as the chief adversary of Muslims worldwide. Given the fact that Islamist extremism is likely to continue to be the driving force behind significant terrorist threats to U.S. interests, fighting terrorism without the effort being perceived simply as a war against Muslims may be a challenge that can only be lessened and not avoided altogether. Senior U.S. officials have been careful to disavow any antipathy toward Muslims, which has helped to some extent. Deeds rather than words will shape most Muslims' attitudes, however, which means that U.S. policies toward Iraq and the Arab-Israeli conflict in particular will be especially influential.

Maintaining a Commitment

Perhaps the greatest future challenge that a more decentralized terrorist threat poses to U.S. counterterrorist efforts concerns the perseverance and determination of the United States itself. The American public has shown that its commitment to counterterrorism can be as fickle as that of foreign publics. Over the past quarter century, Americans and their government have given variable attention, priority, and resources to U.S. counterterrorist programs, with interest and efforts spiking in the aftermath of a major terrorist incident and declining as time passes without an attack.

It took a disaster of the dimensions of 9/11 to generate the strong U.S. attention to counterterrorism during the past several years. Although intended to topple the twin towers and kill thousands, the 1993 WTC bombing did not spark anything close to a similar amount of attention. Bin Laden and the prowess his group demonstrated with overseas attacks had come to be fully appreciated among counterterrorist specialists within the U.S. government by at least the late 1990s, but not among the American public. U.S. citizens and their elected leaders and representatives respond far more readily to dramatic events in their midst than to warnings and analysis about threatening events yet to occur. The further the events of September 2001 fade into the past, the more difficult it will be to keep Americans focused on the danger posed by terrorism, especially that posed by terrorists other than the perpetrators of 9/11.

The U.S. response to the bombing of commuter trains in Madrid in March 2004 suggests how difficult it is to energize or reenergize Americans about counterterrorism. Commentary in the United States about the attack focused less on the continued potency of a global terrorist threat than on inter-allied differences over the Iraq war, with charges of "appeasement" leveled against Spanish voters for ousting the governing party in an election held three days after the attack. For most Americans, the difference between terrorism inside the United States and terrorism against even a close ally is huge, with only the former capable of boosting their commitment to counterterrorism.

Here again, the "war on terrorism" metaphor is unhelpful. Americans tend to think in non-Clausewitzian terms, with war and peace seen as markedly different and clearly separated states of being. War entails special sacrifices and rules that Americans do not want to endure in peacetime. Peace means to them demobilization, relaxation of the nation's guard, and a return to nonmartial pursuits. In U.S. history, peace usually has meant either victory, as with World War II, or withdrawal and a rejection of the reasons for having gone to war in the first place, such as with the Vietnam War. Americans are not accustomed to the concept of a war that is necessary and waged with good reason but offers no prospect of ending with a clear peace and especially a clear victory.[6]

U.S. leaders have conveyed some of the right cautions to the public. Former Secretary of Defense Donald Rumsfeld correctly observed that the "war on terrorism" will not end with a surrender on the deck of the *USS Missouri.*[7] Attitudes in the United States, however, will be shaped less by such words of caution than by the historically based American conception of war and peace. Moreover, not having a clear end is not the same as having no end—and the latter is, for practical purposes, what the United States faces in countering terrorism during the years ahead.

An end, whether clear or not, will be even more elusive in the fight against terrorism than was true of the Cold War. Although the Cold War did not conclude with the signing of any surrender agreement on a battleship, its end nonetheless was fairly distinct, highlighted by the crumbling of the Berlin Wall in November 1989 and of the Soviet Union in December 1991. It also entailed an indisputable victory for the West, achieved with the collapse of a single arch foe. Success in counterterrorism offers no such prospect.

The sense of being at war has been sustained thus far not only by rhetoric about a "war on terrorism" but also by certain practices that resemble those used in real shooting wars of the past, such as indefinite detention of prisoners without recourse to civilian courts. Although useful in mustering support for the invasion, the application of the *war on terrorism* label to the campaign in Iraq will compound the difficulty of sustaining domestic public support for counterterrorism in a post–al Qaeda era. With the Bush administration having placed so much attention on state sponsorship of terrorism, and on one (now eliminated) state sponsor in particular, further appeals to make still more sacrifices to defeat disparate and often nameless groups are apt to confuse many U.S. citizens.

Moreover, the costs and agony of the Iraq war mean that not only the Bush administration but also its successors will face increased skepticism about the credibility of warnings concerning threats to U.S. security, including terrorist threats. The existence of a specific, recognizable, hated terrorist enemy has helped the U.S. population retain its focus. As long as al Qaeda exists, even in a weakened form, it will serve that function. Yet, when will al Qaeda be perceived as having ceased to exist? The group's demise will be nowhere near as clear as, say, the fall of a government.

For much of the American public, the signal that terrorism has been vanquished is likely to be the death or capture of bin Laden. Americans tend to personalize their conflicts by concentrating their animosity on a single despised leader, a role that Adolf Hitler and Saddam Hussein played at different times. This personalized perspective often leads to an overestimation of the effect of taking out the hated leader, as if the conflict were a game of chess in which checkmate of the king ends the contest. The euphoria following Saddam's capture in December 2003 is an example. Bin Laden since 2001 probably has played a role in al Qaeda's operations almost as limited and indirect as Saddam's influence was on the Iraqi insurgency during his eight months in hiding. Yet, this is where any similarities with Iraq end. The elimination of bin Laden, if followed by a year or more without another major al Qaeda operation against the United States, would lead many Americans to believe that the time had come to declare victory in the "war on terrorism" and move on to other concerns. Meanwhile, bin Laden's death would not end or even cripple the radical Islamist movement. Fragments of his organization will spread, subdivide, and inject themselves into other parts of the worldwide Islamist network, like a metastasizing cancer that lives on with sometimes lethal effects even after the original tumor has been excised.

Context and Consequences

Any erosion in the U.S. commitment to counterterrorism that may occur in the years ahead will depend not only on popular perceptions (or misperceptions) of the terrorist threat but also on the broader policy environment in which national security decisions are made. Available resources constitute part of that environment. The resources devoted to counterterrorist operations may decline not because of a specific decision to reduce them but because reductions in spending for national security overall would reduce funds available for counterterrorism. Surges in both defense spending and budget deficits under the Bush administration make some such reductions likely during the next several years. Departmental comptrollers seeking to spread the pain of budget cuts will inflict some of that pain on counterterrorist programs.

Controversies over privacy and civil liberties constitute another part of the policy environment. The United States already has experienced a backlash against some provisions of the principal post–9/11 counterterrorist legislation, the USA PATRIOT Act, as well as the domestic use of other counterterrorist tools. In the wake of the attacks, the U.S. government's investigative powers expanded in some ways that would have been unthinkable earlier. If the clear danger represented by al Qaeda appears to recede, pressures to roll back those powers will increase.

Any diminution, for whatever combination of reasons, of the priority the United States gives to counterterrorist operations will have consequences that go well beyond specific counterterrorist programs. At home, the impact would be seen in everything from reduced vigilance by baggage screeners to less tolerance by citizens for the daily inconveniences associated with stricter security measures. Abroad, a weaker commitment to counterterrorism on the part of the U.S. public would make it more difficult for U.S. diplomats to insist on cooperation from foreign governments.

How long any reduction of the U.S. commitment to counterterrorism lasts depends on how much time passes before the next major terrorist attack against U.S. interests, especially the next such attack on U.S. soil. Time, as always, is more on the side of the terrorist, whose patience and historical sense is greater than that of the average American. Americans' perception of the threat almost certainly will decline more rapidly than the threat itself.

The United States thus faces during the coming years an unfortunate combination of a possibly premature celebration along with a continuing and complicating terrorist threat. The counterterrorist successes against al Qaeda thus far have been impressive and important, and the capture or death of bin Laden will unleash a popular reaction that probably will be nothing short of ecstatic. That joy could be a harmful diversion, however, from attention that will be needed more than ever in the face of remaining problems: difficulty in cementing the counterterrorist cooperation of foreign partners, antagonism and alienation within the Muslim world that breeds more terrorists, and added complexity for intelligence services charged with tracking the threat.

The chief counterterrorist problem confronting U.S. leaders in the years ahead will be a variation of an old challenge: sustaining a national commitment to fighting terrorism even in the absence of a well-defined and clearly perceived danger. A demise of al Qaeda will make the need for that commitment less apparent to most U.S. citizens, even though the danger will persist in a different form. Political leaders will bear the heavy burden of instilling that commitment, and they will have to do so with analysis, education, and their powers of persuasion, not just with slogans and war cries. That will be a difficult task.

Paul R. Pillar is a Visiting Professor and member of the faculty of the Security Studies Program at Georgetown University. He is also a National Intelligence Officer for the Middle East and South Asia at the CIA. Dr. Pillar has spent more than twenty years in the intelligence community and is author of *Terrorism and U.S. Foreign Policy.*

Notes

1. Bruce Hoffman, "Challenges for the U.S. Special Operations Command Posed by the Global Terrorist Threat: Al Qaeda On the Run or On the March?" Testimony to the House Armed Services Subcommittee on Terrorism, Unconventional Threats, and Capabilities, February

14, 2007. Available at http://armedservices.house.gov/pdfs/TUTC021407/Hoffman_Testimony021407.pdf.

2. Paul R. Pillar, "Statement to Joint Inquiry of the Senate Select Committee on Intelligence and the House Permanent Select Committee on Intelligence," October 8, 2002. Available at www.dni.gov/nic/testimony_8oct2002.html.

3. Ellen Nakashima, "Collecting of Details on Travelers Documented," *Washington Post,* September 22, 2007, A1.

4. See Daniel Byman, "Should Hizballah Be Next?" *Foreign Affairs, 82,* no. 6 (November/December 2003): 54–66.

5. Paul Salem, "The Future of Lebanon," *Foreign Affairs, 85,* no. 6 (November/December 2006): 13–22.

6. One of the more thoughtful statements that looks to a "victory" against terrorism is found in Gabriel Schoenfeld, "Could September 11 Have Been Averted?" *Commentary, 112,* no. 5 (December 2001): 21–29. See also subsequent correspondence about Schonfeld's article in *Commentary, 113,* no. 2 (February 2002): 12–16.

7. Donald Rumsfeld, interview, *Face the Nation,* CBS, September 23, 2001.

Steven Simon and Jeff Martini

Terrorism: Denying Al Qaeda Its Popular Support

A consensus among states is emerging, undoubtedly hastened by the September 11 attacks, that terrorism is of universal concern and in direct violation of the principles of the international community. This agreement contrasts markedly with the deep division on the issue immediately following the process of decolonization in the mid-twentieth century. At that time, many newly independent states were reticent to cede the authority over coercive means wholly to state actors, thereby denying legitimacy to future freedom fighters. Today, however, the number of states that have rejected the legitimacy of terrorism has reached critical mass, with holdouts increasingly forced to capitulate (Libya) or to be dealt with as rogue nations (Sudan).[1]

A convergence in strategic interests has certainly helped to bridge this divide between the West and the developing world. Significantly, many of the newly independent states of the 1950s and 1960s now face terrorism problems of their own. The governments of still other states seem to manipulate the global war on terrorism to provide the necessary pretext for cracking down on long-standing domestic opposition movements. The decreasing likelihood of states debating the merits of terrorism, however, is also at least partly attributable to efforts to propagate international norms.

Studies of terrorism frequently address the concept of target audiences, groups generally defined as those whom terrorists seek to intimidate or influence through violence. However, it is also important to understand terrorists' other target audience—the aggrieved populations that they purport to represent. This latter group, not to be confused with terrorists' actual cadres, extends to a broader, less radicalized population that has the power to confer a degree of legitimacy on the terrorists simply by responding positively to their tactics. In the case of Al Qaeda, this group consists of diffuse or very loosely aligned supporters who welcome the news of a new terrorist attack or do not make an effort to distance themselves from Al Qaeda's claim to represent their cause. Denying terrorists the support of these constituents is a crucial component in the war on terrorism and requires approaches that go beyond the standard strategies employed in the current campaign. Marshaling international norms to stigmatize terrorism further stands as one such initiative that would deny terrorists the approval of these populations, pushing the terrorists' tactics farther toward the margins.

What's in a Norm?

Norms are generally defined as "a standard of appropriate behavior for actors with a given identity."[2] A "standard" is thus meant to imply a behavioral regularity.[3] "Appropriate,"

502

on the other hand, alludes to a subjective understanding of what is "proper," or how one "ought" to behave.[4] Simply put, from the perspective of norm proponents, there are no such things as bad norms.[5] Moreover, in the context of the war on terrorism, norms are not simply abstract moral guidelines, but powerful ordering principles with very practical implications.

In the life cycle of norms, norm entrepreneurs[6] play a crucial role as catalysts in the earliest stages of development. They are the community leaders who through persuasion, mobilization, and activism begin to create the initial momentum that, if sustained, can lead to general acceptance and eventually institutionalization of these ideas.[7] Operationalizing the norm, however, requires the constructive engagement of holdouts that continue to reject its relevance. Appeals can be tailored either to the universality of the concept or to its compatibility with the violators' own value system if it too obligates the prescribed behavior. In effect, norm entrepreneurs provide the information and publicity that can be leveraged to convince or shame norm violators into compliance.

The Helsinki Process is a good example of an initiative designed to provoke this type of cognitive dissonance. These negotiations between the West and the Soviet bloc, which were eventually codified in a series of principles that committed the signatories to mutual respect of territorial sovereignty and basic human rights, drew attention to the incompatibility between the former Soviet Union's self-professed commitment to the rights of individuals and individuals' obligations to the party as well as the state under Communist rule.[8] Although the Helsinki Final Act of August 1975 did not establish any real enforcement body, the agreement provided a foundation for future negotiation and, importantly, a convenient platform for the West to promote its own view of the respective obligations of individuals and society, an area in which the West had a clear stake in resolving in favor of personal liberties.[9]

Defining Standards of Behavior

The establishment of legal codes defining states' rights and restraints regarding the use of force is a crucial first step in creating the conditions for accountability. Subsequently, rewarding compliant behavior and sanctioning noncompliant behavior creates the necessary incentives to spread the norm through a process of socialization.

The Geneva conventions are probably the most notable instance of an effort to codify limits on states' use of force. Although their precise application is sometimes disputed, the conventions provide a powerful reference for the treatment of noncombatants in wartime. In addition, the international community has endorsed a number of terrorism-specific initiatives such as the Hague Convention for the Unlawful Seizure of Aircraft (1970); the Convention Against the Taking of Hostages (1979); and, more recently, UN Security Council Resolution 1373 (2001), which criminalizes a host of activities that have been used to support or provide a haven for terrorist organizations. The acceptance and eventual internalization of an emerging norm demands passage of a series of litmus tests, most critically the norm's durability in the face of challenges.[10] The first step, however, must be the clear communication of a standard or expectation of behavior. The aforementioned agreements help to provide this framework.

In effect, terrorists disregard two fundamental prohibitions. First, violence is not a legitimate means of solving political disputes, particularly when the aggressors are nonstate actors. This transcends Max Weber's well-known formulation that states have a monopoly over the legitimate use of force. A critical legitimizing condition when considering the use of force is that the agent in question is a sovereign power. Even in the language of those who assert Muslims' fundamental right to physical jihad, historical precedents suggest that resort to force requires authorization from some higher authority, particularly when the battle is for the expansion of Islam rather than the collective defense of the *ummah*.

The second norm essential to delegitimizing the strategy of terrorism is the belief that noncombatants are entitled to immunity and should not be subject to attack. Although terrorists often attempt to circumscribe this restraint by stressing their adversaries' own record of civilian casualties, the fact that this argument is made at all is a tacit recognition of the relevance of proportionality.

Importantly, these two norms are more than just theoretical constructs; their practical implications have long been debated both in Western and Islamic traditions. The Western discourses of *jus in bello* (what type of force is justified) and *jus ad bellum* (when force is justified) have led to the development of formal and informal codes regulating belligerents' responsibilities and obligations in wartime. Although the specific manifestations of these traditions have, of course, varied according to the particular historical context, general trends can be identified. Whether one speaks of the Hebraic, Roman, early Christian, or Germanic conceptions of war, each included provisions outlining justifications for war as well as treatments of the distinction between combatant and noncombatant.[11] Gradually, these notions have coalesced, developing into a Western consensus prohibiting tactics that are indiscriminate or disproportionate in scope and limiting the use of force to instances of self-defense.[12] Thus, although these rules are still contravened, their *de jure* acceptance does provide states with important normative referents that help order expectations and behavior.

Similarly, Arab culture and Islamic thought have a parallel tradition of theorizing on the definition of just war. Islamic interpretations also vary widely depending on the particular temporal, social, and political context. The Koran may be ubiquitous in the Muslim world, but its precise application and the interpretation of it and other essential texts differ considerably.[13] Nevertheless, overriding themes emerge regulating force based on obligations both to God and to fellow man, Muslim or otherwise. Fred Donner, a scholar of the Islamic tradition, notes "examples of injunctions against killing women, children, and other noncombatants; similarly, [juristic literature] bars attacks on the enemy without first inviting them to embrace Islam, discusses the problem of 'double effect' (e.g., unintended deaths of noncombatants during a nighttime assault), and so on."[14] Stepping back from the polarizing and largely misunderstood concept of jihad, a great deal of common ground actually exists on the restrictions applied to the use of force. What remains is the search for a mechanism to institutionalize these restrictions at the state and community level that would significantly help to undermine popular support for terrorist organizations.

Enforcing Compliance

Once they are defined and recognized, the second step is to enforce adherence to a norm. The U.S. decision to publish its list of active state sponsors of terrorism—and in the process shame nations such as Cuba, Libya, Iran, Sudan, and Syria, all of which have been suspected of aiding terrorist organizations or being slow to recognize the emerging norm against terrorism—is one example of how Washington seeks to enforce the international norm against terrorism. The Financial Aid Task Force (FATF), which publishes a list of "Non-Cooperative Countries and Territories," uses a similar strategy in the fight against money laundering and terrorist financiers. Punishing states with military action or economic sanctions, such as the sanctions regime against Libya imposed in the wake of the bombing of Pan Am Flight 103, the cruise missile strikes against Sudan and Afghanistan in 1998 in the aftermath of Al Qaeda's attacks on the U.S. embassies in Nairobi and Dar es Salaam, and the present Syria Accountability Act predicated in part on Damascus' continued support of terrorist organizations, stands as an even more coercive approach. In short, the United States has long appealed to norms to build coalitions against terrorism.

Norm adherence should not be confused with or even imply voluntary agreement absent coercion. For example, compellance, or "acquiescence through fear,"[15] is one of several means to secure adherence to a norm. What matters most is the expectation that actors comply with a code of behavior. At least initially, their rationale for compliance may be and often is self-interest or fear, but their adherence reinforces the pressure on others to follow suit. Over time, habitual compliance lends the norm a "taken-for-granted quality,"[16] relieving norm proponents from the need to police its enforcement. A good example is the norm that developed against the slave trade, a case in which Britain, throughout the nineteenth century, employed its naval resources and credible threats of force to ensure the success of its antislavery campaign.[17] Other norms even compel states to use force, such as the emerging norm for states to intervene in the case of genocide or other humanitarian disasters.[18] In short, the propagation of a norm is not an abstract exercise in consensus building; it often involves a good bit of arm-twisting, and depending on the nature of the enforcement regime, the emerging norms may come with sharp teeth.

Deepening the Norm against Terrorism

To enforce the norm against state-supported terrorism, a top-down approach has largely been successful, with fewer states (with some notable exceptions, including Syria and Iran) now willing openly to flaunt the prohibitions against supporting terrorist organizations. To what extent these norms have diffused to the general population, however, is an open question. It is also a critical one, in that today's most dangerous terrorist threat, Al Qaeda and its affiliate groups, has attained a surprisingly wide base of support throughout the Muslim world. Indeed, a study by the Pew Research Institute in June 2003 found that "solid majorities in the Palestinian Authority, Indonesia, and Jordan—and nearly half of those in Morocco and Pakistan—say they have some confidence in Osama bin Laden 'to do the right thing regarding world affairs.'"[19]

The creation of norms goes to the heart of this issue and stands as one means of addressing the gulf between the values to which states and their respective populations subscribe. Can the emerging consensus from the top-down effort spread to Muslim populations more generally, or must a second initiative be undertaken to coalesce support for restraints on violence at a grassroots level? In what ways would such a bottom-up approach differ from the experience of state-driven initiatives?

The Top-Down Agenda

The international community undoubtedly should continue its efforts to delegitimize state-supported terrorism. Both UN Security Council Resolution 1373 and the FATF Eight Special Recommendations, which criminalizes the financial support of terrorist organizations, stand as important recent initiatives. Additionally, the international community should push to elicit unequivocal denunciations of terrorism from regional bodies such as the Arab League and the Organization of Islamic Conference. Both of these organizations have ratified antiterrorism conventions, but in an attempt to satisfy the international community without delegitimizing the Palestinian struggle in the process, they define terrorism in such a way as to render their commitment less forceful. One caveat in the Arab Convention for the Suppression of Terrorism, for example, states, "All cases of struggle by whatever means, including armed struggle, against foreign occupation and aggression for liberation and self-determination, in accordance with the principles of international law, shall not be regarded as a [terrorist] offence. This provision shall not apply to any act prejudicing the territorial integrity of any Arab State."[20] Thus according to this provision, liberation movements, unless they threaten a member state of the Arab League, may be exempt from the terrorist label.

Work also must be done to reinforce and broaden prohibitions against the funding of terrorist organizations, particularly those with multiple personalities such as the military, political, and social welfare wings of Hamas. Increasingly, terrorist groups are compartmentalizing their operations in order to bypass existing regulations. This not only serves to reopen avenues to outside funding but also provides a convenient veneer of legitimacy for the terrorists. Whether or not these groups do good social work is in many ways beside the point.[21] Their ties to terrorism and the benefit this relationship bestows on the parent organization is the critical question. For example, that Hamas provides much needed social services in Gaza is not disputed. The possible diversion of financing meant for these humanitarian projects to terrorist operations, however, is problematic. Indeed, the social welfare arm of Hamas has legitimized the less noble tactics of the organization, allowing Hamas to promote itself as something other than a strictly terrorist organization. Not until September of last year did the European Union finally accede to U.S. pressure to cut off funding to affiliate groups of Hamas. The difficulty in reaching consensus on this issue points to the need to define support for terrorism more broadly.

Additionally, the definition of state culpability must be expanded to include other indirect support to terrorists, such as willful neglect in securing borders or a failure to crack down on activities such as the narcotics trade that may facilitate terrorist activities by providing access to hard currency, transnational networks, etc. Thus far, the propagation of norms has appropriately focused on direct support for terrorists, but holding states accountable to some minimum level of effort in deterring terrorists from using their territory as a base of operations or policing criminal networks that have natural linkages with terrorist organizations is a logical next step. In sum, to sustain momentum, the international community should raise the bar to reflect an expectation that states not just passively accept their obligations to refrain from supporting terrorist organizations, but also proactively take steps to eliminate them.

Finally, the depoliticization of efforts to strengthen international norms is necessary to create objective metrics for judging state commitments to the war on terrorism as well as an effective enforcement regime. Rather than the current sliding scale that defines state support of terrorism differently based on political considerations, standards should be harmonized. Whether the case in question is Pakistan's support for Kashmiri groups or Iran's arming of Hizballah, inconsistently applying standards does not aid efforts to eliminate terrorism. Similarly, although defining terrorism is notoriously difficult, terrorist organizations should be classified based on the tactics they use rather than a quid pro quo whereby, for example, states make their co-operation in the global war on terrorism contingent upon defining bother-some opposition movements in their own country as terrorist organizations.

Developing Norms from the Bottom Up

Although state-driven initiatives have made and continue to make significant progress, such initiatives must be complimented by a parallel bottom-up approach to deny terrorist groups access to their bases of popular support. Top-down initiatives are limited because state diplomacy is often at odds with the value systems of a state's citizenry. This is particularly true in the Middle East, where few regimes can be described as being truly representative. Moreover, a number of states have charted a decidedly pro-Western course (Egypt, Jordan, Morocco, Turkey) while significant segments of their populations hold very different political and cultural sensibilities.

Secondly, although states have crucial roles to play in regulating the use of force, terrorism is fundamentally a subnational phenomenon. As such, its elimination will require changing perceptions at the community level. To expect state-driven initiatives alone to be commensurate with the task is to assume complete state sovereignty as well as states' unhindered ability to project their authority. This is not always the case, and thus states alone are inadequate to the task; self-policing at the community level is required to deny terrorists the room to operate. Moreover, only refusal by the aggrieved populations that terrorists purport to defend to implicitly justify the violence committed on their behalf—by remaining silent or, worse, acting as the terrorists' cheering section—can weaken terrorists' populist cover.

What makes these bottom-up efforts so difficult is the fundamental difference in their implementation from the state-driven initiatives that have dominated previous efforts. Namely, although a process of coercion, whereby the strong can compel weak states to submit to their will, can expedite the propagation of norms in the international system, norm creation at the subnational level will require either appealing to the community's self-interest or to the inherent legitimacy of the norms themselves.[22] Diffuse ideological support for terrorists is simply not subject to the logic of conventional power politics. Therefore, U.S. efforts must rely primarily on persuasion to stigmatize the use of terrorist tactics.

Practical Steps Forward at the Grassroots Level

What then can the United States do to expedite the emergence of norms against violence at the community level? Acknowledging that change is difficult to institute from the top down, the United States should find creative means to support the efforts of local norm entrepreneurs. That said, providing this support is much more complicated than simply identifying members of a society that are sympathetic to the notion that violence is not the preferred means of settling disputes. The (negative) net effect of U.S. backing for Mahmoud Abbas during his brief tenure as the Palestinian prime minister in the summer of 2003 illustrates the potential pitfalls of overtly supporting a norm entrepreneur. The Bush administration's vocal support of Abbas simply undermined his domestic support. In the future, the United States should support norm entrepreneurs in a way that enables their work without also leading to their labeling as a U.S. proxy.

Fortunately, more subtle ways do exist to support norm entrepreneurs without engendering this backlash. However, such efforts will require time and patience. Contributing to the development of local institutions that promote norm convergence with Western values is one method that allows local norm entrepreneurs to receive support while remaining an arms length from its source. U.S./EU support for Birzeit University in Palestine, an institution that is both independent and (relatively) liberal, is an example of this approach. Bringing scholars and students to the West is another potential means to generate the conditions under which norm entrepreneurs may grow as intellectuals and activists. The resulting epistemic communities, or associations based on shared academic training, represent one type of norm entrepreneurship that has had significant success in advancing value-based agendas. Notable examples include loose organizations of natural scientists—coalitions whose members have very different cultural backgrounds but similar professional training—that have succeeded in mobilizing the international community to rethink state obligations toward the environment.[23]

The United States also needs to improve its public diplomacy, specifically by communicating the compatibility of U.S. policy and values with the aspirations of those living in the Muslim world. This does not imply a foreign policy driven by global opinion, but the United States should clearly explain the rationale behind its decisions, which in turn should be carried out in a manner that demonstrates respect for the sensibilities and cultural sensitivities of others. Absent this effort, Muslim audiences have no compelling alternative to the tortured logic of Al Qaeda.[24] Better communication will require significant investment in the U.S. capacity to reach audiences in the Middle East, either via mass media or through a buttressed and better-trained Foreign Service.[25] The goal of such a process would not be to indoctrinate but rather to engage dissenters and provoke introspection among those prone to supporting terrorism framed as resistance.

Change often does come from the bottom up, and overwhelming military force is not always the most effective means of communication. Important historical precedents exist of introspection catalyzing dramatic shifts in thinking as well as policy. The Soviet Union's liberalization and South Africa's rejection of apartheid are two notable examples. Neither took place within a strategic vacuum, but both changes in posture reflected internal unease with the unifying logic of the regime.[26] Another example is the U.S. drive in the 1970s to rein in the CIA and to prohibit assassination as a foreign policy tool. At that time, spreading awareness that the CIA had plotted the murder of a number of foreign leaders under the administrations of Dwight D. Eisenhower, John F. Kennedy, Lyndon B. Johnson, and Richard M. Nixon provoked concerns that the United States was forfeiting any claims to moral leadership.[27] The investigating Church Committee's public admonishment was intended in part to recapture some credibility in the international community and to foster a norm against assassination internationally.

Today, Executive Order (EO) 12333, a successor to earlier efforts undertaken during the Ford administration, embodies the code against assassination, with every administration since confirming its expression of self-restraint. Although the order is consistent with the stipulations of the Hague Convention IV (1907), of which the United States is a party, EO 12333 goes a step further in specifying the restrictions as well as including a prohibition against indirect participation in an assassination plot.[28] This unilateral expression of U.S. willingness to sanction its own breaches and excesses is the same process of self-reflection that the United States should be promoting elsewhere. Today, the prisoner abuse scandal in Abu Ghraib calls for an even more robust effort at self-policing to salvage some of the credibility that the United States has lost from this episode. The blatant disregard for human rights not only invites backlash, but also cripples U.S. ability to exert moral influence and promote a broader norm against the use of unregulated violence.

Finally, a corresponding effort must be made to address the material conditions under which terrorists prey on the frustrations of the disenfranchised. Any attempt to win hearts and minds that simply skirts around root causes dooms itself to failure. Poverty, lack of social mobility, a poor educational infrastructure, and the denial of basic human rights all contribute to the hopelessness that terrorists exploit. Unfortunately, these conditions are widespread in the developing world and, even with enhanced commitment to development initiatives, these issues will persist far into the future. Progress in addressing root causes will help pave the way for broader acceptance of norms against terrorism at the subnational level. The slow and incremental nature of that progress should not deter the West from dramatically increasing its investment and commitment to addressing root causes.

The Feedback Loop: Norms Are Working

In general, the compulsion of norm-breakers to offer ex post facto justifications of their actions provides evidence that a threshold has been crossed and, moreover, that the boundary is becoming more well defined.[29] A useful example of this is the U.S. need to rationalize its continued use of antipersonnel landmines in the Korean Demilitarized Zone. In this case, the norm has not yet reached a point where the United States has been forced to cease employing these devices, but it does carry enough weight to compel the United States to explain its position and to adhere to certain limitations, thus signaling a shift in thinking on this issue.[30]

In the case of terrorism specifically, recent messages attributed to Al Qaeda suggest a consensus growing within the Muslim world against the targeting of noncombatants. Following the bombings in Casablanca, Riyadh, and Istanbul in 2003, operations that amounted essentially to Muslim-on-Muslim violence, Al Qaeda made repeated attempts to justify the indiscriminate nature of their attacks explicitly. For example, on November 17, 2003, members of Al Qaeda sent the following message to the Arabic daily *Al Quds Al Arabi*:

> Some claim that we consider most Muslims as non-believers and sanction killing them. How do we go everywhere to protect them and then sanction shedding their blood? This cannot be accepted by sound reason, let alone a Muslim who knows the rulings of God. We have repeatedly warned Muslims against approaching the places of infidels, and

we now renew the warning. Moreover, it is impermissible, according to Shari'a . . . to mix with those infidels, neither in their homes nor in work places, until they stop their crusading war against Islam and Muslims.[31]

Similarly, attackers described the Muhaya residential compound bombed in Riyadh as "teeming with Arab translators for the U.S. intelligence services."[32] These determined efforts to revise the nature of targets are not insignificant; the attackers' evident compulsion to redefine the identity of those killed indicates fear over the implication of killing civilians. In short, Al Qaeda's statements suggest that disregard for the sanctity of noncombatants is no longer without political cost among their constituencies. The norm is spreading.

The Place for Norms in U.S. Strategy

Promoting respect for the rule of law, both domestically and at the international level, is in the U.S. national interest. Because the United States carries enormous normative weight in the international system, its values exert disproportionate influence in the development of international norms.[33] Free trade is one example of this dynamic whereby the United States and other leading economies have used their leverage to lobby for a more uniform international trade regime and, on the strength of this effort, have created an expectation reducing barriers to trade and reinforcing their own self interest. Thus, norms are not so much about imposing restraints on dominant states as subjecting the entire state system to the rules by which dominant states would prefer to play.[34] Moreover, in the specific case of restricting the use of violence, creating some semblance of order benefits the entire international community in that it allows states to pursue other national interests beyond narrow security concerns.

In effect, norms mitigate the need for states to operate assuming the worst of others. Whether or not other states behave as the United States would like, the predictability of their behavior is quite helpful. Subscription to or rejection of a norm stands as an important means for state actors to signal their intentions, reducing the considerable transaction costs of this uncertainty. In this sense, order has intrinsic benefits for all states. Although other methods, including the projection of overwhelming force, can also foster this type of environment, international norms offer a more efficient, cost-effective approach.

Finally, the propagation of norms as a method of combating terrorism need not come at the exclusion of other complimentary approaches. Ideational change is necessarily a long, slow process, and the propagation of norms is unlikely to make the world dramatically safer in the near term. On the other hand, the current mix of preemptive force, counterterrorism, and homeland security strategies are a quick fix. They will not serve as sustainable, long-term solutions without a parallel commitment to strengthening and broadening coalitions against terrorism. Norms have the potential to hold these coalitions together, absent the U.S. ability to affect conformity through coercion.

History is replete with examples of norms developing to limit the use of force. Whether we are speaking of outlawing the assassination of world leaders, prohibiting the use of chemical weapons, or exempting medical personnel from being targeted in wartime, ideas and values have played a key role in limiting the circumstances when violence may be employed legitimately. In all these examples, however, the critical actors were states and the benchmark for compliance was state behavior. With respect to terrorism, the case must be made to publics directly. In short, delegitimizing terrorism requires establishing consensus both at the community and national levels.

The United States and the international community can help to build these norms not with patronizing platitudes, but by patiently articulating a compelling alternative to the logic of terrorism. Notable examples exist of aggrieved populations that chose to reject violence, be it the antiapartheid struggle or the majority of black Americans during the civil rights movement. In each instance, indigenous norm entrepreneurs overcame significant resistance to their causes to effect ideational and structural change. Corollaries exist in the Arab World; the West must find a way to support their efforts.

Steven Simon is Hasib J. Sabbagh Senior Fellow for Middle Eastern Studies at the Council on Foreign Relations in Washington D.C. Previously, Dr. Simon was a senior analyst on the Middle East and terrorism at RAND Corporation. Jeff Martini is a research assistant at RAND.

Notes

1. Ilias Bantekas, "The International Law of Terrorist Financing," *American Journal of International Law* 97, no. 2 (April 2003): 318.
2. Martha Finnemore, *National Interests in International Society* (Ithaca: Cornell University Press, 1996), p. 22; Peter Katzenstein, ed., *The Culture of National Security* (New York: Columbia University Press, 1996), p. 5.
3. Christopher Gelpi, "Crime and Punishment: The Role of Norms in Crisis Bargaining," *American Political Science Review* 91, no. 2 (June 1997): 340.
4. Ibid.
5. Martha Finnemore and Kathryn Sikkink, "International Norm Dynamics and Political Change," *International Organization* 52, no. 4 (Autumn 1998): 892.
6. Finnemore and Sikkink employ the term "norm entrepreneur" while others prefer "transnational moral entrepreneur." For the latter usage, see Ethan Nadelmann, "Global Prohibition Regimes: The Evolution of Norms in International Society," *International Organization* 44, no. 4 (Autumn 1990): 485.
7. Finnemore and Sikkink, "International Norm Dynamics and Political Change," p. 904.
8. Geoffrey Edwards, "Human Rights and Basket III Issues: Areas of Change and Continuity," *International Affairs* 61, no. 4 (Autumn 1985): 632.
9. Ibid.
10. Jeffrey Legro identifies durability, specificity, and concordance as the three benchmarks of a norm's robustness. Jeffrey Legro, "Which Norms Matter? Revisiting the 'Failure' of Internationalism," *International Organization* 51, no. 1 (Winter 1997): 34.
11. James Turner Johnson, "Historical Roots and Sources of the Just War Tradition in Western Culture," in *Just War and Jihad,* eds. John Kelsay and James Turner Johnson (Westport, Conn.: Greenwood Publishing Group, 1991), pp. 7–12; Michael Walzer, *Just and Unjust Wars: A Moral Argument With Historical Illustrations* (New York: Basic Books, 1977).
12. Johnson, "Historical Roots and Sources of the Just War Tradition in Western Culture," p. 15.
13. These would of course include the Sunna and the Hadith.
14. Fred Donner, "Sources of Islamic Conceptions of War," in *Just War and Jihad,* eds. John Kelsay and James Turner Johnson (Westport, Conn.: Greenwood Publishing Group, 1991), pp. 31–33.
15. Ian Hurd describes "compellance" in this fashion: "Coercion refers to a relation of asymmetrical physical power among agents, where this asymmetry is applied to changing the behavior of the weaker agent. The operative mechanism is fear or simple 'compellance'; fear produces acquiescence." Ian Hurd, "Legitimacy and Authority in International Politics," *International*

Organization 53, no. 2 (Spring 1999): 383. See Thomas Schelling, *Arms and Influence* (New Haven, Conn.: Yale University Press, 1966).

16. Finnemore and Sikkink, "International Norm Dynamics and Political Change," p. 895.

17. Nadelmann, "Global Prohibition Regimes," p. 492.

18. See Martha Finnemore, *The Purpose of Intervention* (Cornell: Cornell University Press, 2003).

19. Pew Global Attitudes Project, "Views of a Changing World," June 2003, p. 3.

20. "The Arab Convention for the Suppression of Terrorism," April 1998, http://www.albab.com/arab/docs/league/terrorism98.htm (accessed September 17, 2004).

21. For a more in-depth discussion, see International Crisis Group, "Islamic Social Welfare Activism in the Occupied Palestinian Territories: A Legitimate Target?" *Middle East Report,* no. 13 (April 2, 2003), pp. 18–20.

22. Hurd, "Legitimacy and Authority in International Politics," p. 383.

23. Peter Haas, "Introduction: Epistemic Communities and International Policy Coordination," *International Organization* 52, no. 1 (Winter 1992): 5.

24. Edward P. Djerejian et al., "Changing Minds Winning Peace," *Report of the Advisory Group on Public Diplomacy for the Arab and Muslim World,* October 1, 2003, p. 8.

25. Ibid.

26. For the role of ideas in the Soviet transformation, see Janice Gross Stein, "Political Learning by Doing: Gorbachev as Uncommitted Thinker and Motivated Learner," *International Organization* 48, no. 2 (Spring 1994): 155–163.

27. Daniel Schorr, "Stop Winking at the Ban," *Christian Science Monitor,* September 21, 2001; Thomas Ward, "Norms and International Security: The Case of International Assassination," *International Security* 25, no. 1 (Summer 2000).

28. Elizabeth B. Bazen, "Assassination Ban and E.O. 12333: A Brief Summary," *CRS Report for Congress,* RS21037, January 4, 2002, http://www.fas.org/irp/crs/RS21037.pdf (accessed October 9, 2004).

29. Finnemore and Sikkink, "International Norm Dynamics and Political Change," p. 892.

30. Ibid.

31. Abu Hafs Al Masri Brigades, "A Statement From the Jihad Rule About the Islamic Iron Hammer Operation," November 15, 2003, http://www.homelandsecurityus.com/Turkey.htm (accessed October 9, 2004).

32. Ibid.

33. Nadelmann, "Global Prohibition Regimes," pp. 484–485.

34. A more detailed discussion on this phenomenon can be found in Hedley Bull, *The Anarchical Society* (New York: Columbia University Press, 1977).

Matthew Levitt, 2004

Untangling the Terror Web: Identifying and Counteracting the Phenomenon of Crossover Between Terrorist Groups

Counterterrorism should be seen not as an effort to rid the world of terrorism, but as an ongoing struggle to constrict the operating environment in which terrorists raise funds, procure documents, engage in support activities, and conduct attacks. One of the most effective ways to constrict the operating environment and crack down on terrorist financing is to target the network of interlocking logistical support groups. Many of these groups are not particular to a single terrorist organization. In fact, militant Islamist organizations from the al Qaeda to Hamas interact and support one another in the international matrix of logistical, financial, and sometimes operational terrorist activity. This matrix of relationships is what makes the threat of international terrorism so dangerous. Prosecuting the war on terror, whether on the battlefield or in the courtroom, demands greater attention to the web of interaction among these various groups and state sponsors. Indeed, as this paper suggests, concerted action against terrorist financing is one of the best ways to advance not only the war on terror, but other national security priorities such as pursuing the Roadmap to Israeli-Palestinian peace, and the stabilization of Iraq.

Pundits and politicians alike tend to think of the war on terror against al Qaeda as a completely disparate phenomenon from the battle against other terrorist groups. This is, in part, a logical supposition as groups like Hamas and Hezbollah do not belong to the more tightly knit family of al Qaeda-associated terrorist groups. Hezbollah and Palestinian terrorist groups do not conduct joint operational activity with al Qaeda, and despite some ad hoc cooperation and personal relationships, they have no official or institutional links. Nonetheless, these groups are no less benign for their independence from al Qaeda.

Indeed, the overall strength and effectiveness of the war on terror is undermined by the failure to appreciate these overarching connections. The interconnectivity between radical Islamist terrorist groups, including those that do not plan and implement attacks together, demands a more coordinated and comprehensive counterterrorism strategy than simply trying to target each of these groups individually, one at a time. Though historically this proved effective in the battle against leftist European groups in the 1970s and 1980s, the links between radical Islamist groups are qualitatively different than the informal links that existed between leftist European terrorist organizations.

Networks and relationships best describe the current state of international terrorism. This matrix of relationships between terrorists who belong to one or another group is what makes the threat of international terrorism so dangerous today. For example, while there are no known headquarter-to-headquarter links between al Qaeda and Hezbollah, the two groups are known to have held senior level meetings over the past decade and to maintain ad hoc, person-to-person ties in the areas of training and logistical support activities. As recent attacks in Casablanca and Istanbul reemphasized, these relationships—not particular group affiliations—are the driving force behind al Qaeda's continued ability to conduct devastating terrorist attacks, even after two and a half years of the war on terror.

Too often people insist on pigeonholing terrorists as members of one group or another, as if such operatives carry membership cards in their wallets. In reality, much of the "network of networks" that characterizes today's terrorist threat is informal and unstructured. Not every al Qaeda operative has pledged an oath of allegiance (a *bayat*) to Osama bin Laden, while many terrorists maintain affiliations with members of other terrorist groups and facilitate one another's activities. This analysis applies to Palestinian terrorist groups as well. Groups like Hamas have no concrete connections to the al Qaeda "network of networks." However, in the area of terrorist financing and logistical support there is significant overlap and cooperation between these and other terrorist groups.

Between "Operatives" and "Supporters"

September 11 drove home the central role logistical and financial support networks play in international terrorist operations. Clearly, individuals who provide such support must be recognized as terrorists of the same caliber as those who use that support to execute attacks. To be sure, taken together the plethora of individuals, organizations and other fronts that provided logistical and financial support to the 9-11 plotters combine to form the single most significant enabling factor behind the September 11 attacks. Indeed, prior to September 11, officials frequently made the mistake of distinguishing between terrorist "operatives" and terrorist "supporters." Several of the September 11 plotters were identified as terrorist "supporters" prior to the attacks, but were not apprehended because they were not considered terrorist "operatives."

By now it should be clear to investigators, intelligence officers and decision makers alike that the logistical and financial supporters of terrorism warrant increased attention, not only because they facilitate acts of terror and radicalize and recruit future terrorists, but because distinguishing between "supporters" and "operatives" assures that the plotters of the next terrorist attack—today's "supporters"—will only be identified after they conduct whatever attack they are now planning—and are thus transformed into "operatives." In particular, any serious effort to crack down on terrorist financing, so critical to disrupt terrorist activity, demands paying special attention to these support networks.

Key Nodes in the Matrix of Terror Financing

A close examination of these networks reveals there are key nodes in this matrix that have become the preferred conduits used by terrorists from multiple terrorist groups to fund and facilitate attacks. Shutting down these organizations, front companies and charities will go a long way toward curtailing logistical support and stemming the flow of funds to and among terrorist groups.

Many critics of the economic war on terrorism mistakenly suggest that because the amount of money that has been frozen internationally is in the low millions, very little has actually been accomplished. The dollar amount frozen, however, is a poor litmus test. Terrorist groups will always find other sources of funding. A more telling yardstick that the amount of money frozen and put into an escrow account is whether authorities have shut down the key nodes through which terrorists raise, launder and transfer funds.

Indeed, similarly unrealistic litmus tests are applied to the war on terrorism itself. Too often people talk about winning the war on terrorism, defeating al Qaeda, or ending terrorism. But the fact is, one cannot defeat terrorism. Terrorism in one form or another has been around for centuries and will be around for many more. It has not, however, always presented as critical a national security challenge as it does today—nor will it necessarily continue to do so. Bringing the phenomenon of terrorism back down to tolerable levels is a very attainable goal.[1] Counterterrorism, therefore, is not about defeating terrorism, it is about constricting the operating environment—making it harder for terrorists to operate at every level, such as conducting operations, procuring and transferring false documents, ferrying fugitives from one place to another, and financing, laundering, and transferring funds. Authorities need to make it more difficult for terrorists to conduct their operational, logistical and financial activities, and to deny them the freedom of movement to conduct these activities. In fact, one can so constrict a terrorist group's operating environment that it will eventually suffocate. In its day, the Abu Nidal organization was the al Qaeda of its time, and it no longer exists. A time will come when the primary international terrorist threat will no longer be posed by al Qaeda, but by other nascent groups.

If, therefore, we are serious about constricting terrorists' operating environment and cracking down on terrorist financing, then we need to look at key nodes in the network of terrorists' logistical support groups.

Many of these organizations are not particular to one terrorist group. Militant Islamist groups from al Qaeda to Hamas interact and support one another in an international matrix of logistical, financial, and sometimes operational terrorist activity. As former National Security Council terrorism czar Richard Clarke recently testified, "al Qaeda is a small part of the overall challenge we face from radical terrorist groups which associate themselves with Islam. Autonomous cells, regional affiliate groups, radical Palestinian organizations, and groups sponsored by Iran's Revolutionary Guards are engaged in mutual support arrangements, including funding."[2]

In short, inattention to any one part of the web of militant Islamist terror undermines the effectiveness of measures taken against other parts of that web.

Links between Terror Groups:
The Network of Relationships

September 11 produced a political will, markedly absent after previous attacks, to take concrete action to counter and disrupt the terrorist threat to America and its allies. These efforts, however, tend to focus on al Qaeda to the exclusion of other groups. Al Qaeda and these other groups, however, maintain logistical and financial links that reveal a matrix of illicit activity on an international scale. Indeed, if authorities are serious about cracking down on terrorist financing, they must not only prevent the purportedly political or social-welfare wings of terrorist groups from flourishing; they must take concrete steps to disrupt their activities. Accomplishing this requires an appreciation of the network of relationships that exists between various terrorists groups.

Consider the following examples of the terror web:

- In November 2001, the U.S. government designated the al-Taqwa banking system as a terrorist entity for "provid[ing] cash transfer mechanisms for Al Qaida."[3] But al-Taqwa also financed the activities of several other terrorist organizations, including Hamas. In fact, not only was al-Taqwa originally established in 1988 with seed money from the Egyptian Muslim Brotherhood, but Hamas members and individuals tied to al Qaeda feature prominently among its shareholders.[4] According to the February 2002 testimony of Deputy Assistant Secretary of the Treasury Juan C. Zarate, "$60 million collected annually for Hamas was moved to accounts with Bank al-Taqwa."[5] Six years earlier, a 1996 report by Italian intelligence had already linked al-Taqwa to Hamas and other Palestinian groups, as well as to the Algerian Armed Islamic Group and the Egyptian al-Gama'a al-Islamiyya.[6]

- According to court documents, two men played central roles in radicalizing, training and funding the cell of American Muslims in Portland that tried to enter Afghanistan via China and Hong Kong to fight alongside al Qaeda and the Taliban against U.S. forces. In another sign of the crossover between terrorist elements, one of these men is associated with Palestinian terrorism, the other with al Qaeda. According to court documents, Ali Khaled Steitiye, a Hamas supporter who underwent terrorist training in South Lebanon and an unindicted coconspirator in the Portland case, engaged in weapons training with members of the Portland cell. Steitiye possessed several weapons, "which were used by members of the conspiracy to engage in weapons training to prepare the conspirators to assist the forces in the territory of Afghanistan controlled by the Taliban, including those associated with al-Qaeda, against the United States and its allies."[7]

  Steitiye's collaborator was Sheikh Mohammed Abdirahman Kariye, a co-founder of the designated al Qaeda front organization Global Relief Foundation. According to an FBI affidavit, cell members were secretly recorded describing how Kariye, the Imam of the local mosque, instructed his followers to fight with their fellow Muslims against Americans in Afghanistan. Kariye provided $2,000 to cover the travel costs of the cell members, money he acquired from members of the mosque. According to the affidavit, one cell member, Jeffrey Battle, explained that in the wake of Stietiye's arrest in October 2001, "Kariye directed the group of jihadists to return to the United States if they were unable to enter Afghanistan."[8]

- In May 2003, several individual European countries joined the United States in freezing the assets of the al Aqsa International Foundation, a Hamas front organization funding "Palestinian fighters" while recording its disbursements as "contributions for charitable projects."[9] Significantly, al Aqsa's representative in Yemen, Mohammed Ali Hasan al-Moayad, was arrested not only for funding Hamas, but also for providing money, arms, communication gear and recruits to al Qaeda.[10] According to an Israeli report on Hezbollah's global activity, the head of the al Aqsa International Foundation office in the Netherlands indicated the office raised funds for Hezbollah in coordination with the group's main office in Germany.[11]

Networks of Relationships Case Study: Abu Musab al Zarqawi

The case of Abu Musab al Zarqawi (aka Fadel Nazzal Khalayleh) offers a particular insightful perspective on the scope of the informal links, personal relationships, and organizational crossover between disparate terrorist operatives and groups. As the Zarqawi case makes abundantly clear, such networks of relationships are both geographically and organizationally diverse.

Following Secretary of State Colin Powell's February 6 address to the United Nations Security Council, some questioned his description of the "sinister nexus between Iraq and the al Qaeda terrorist network."[12] In fact, the relationship between Baghdad and terrorism mirrors the way in which today's international terrorist groups function: not as tightly structured hierarchies, but rather as shadowy networks that, when necessary, strike ad hoc tactical alliances, bridging religious and ideological schisms. Osama bin Laden's calls on Muslims to come to Iraq's defense, even as he derided the "infidel" regime in Baghdad, are a case in point.[13]

One of the more active terrorist networks in recent years has been that of Abu Musab al-Zarqawi. At least 116 terrorist operatives from Zarqawi's global network have been arrested, including members in France, Italy, Spain, Britain, Germany, Turkey, Jordan, and Saudi Arabia.[14] For example:

Turkey: On February 15, 2002, Turkish police intercepted two Palestinians and a Jordanian who entered Turkey illegally from Iran on their way to conduct bombing attacks in Israel. Zarqawi had dispatched the three men, reportedly members of Beyyiat al-Imam (a group linked to al Qaeda) who fought for the Taliban and received terrorist training in Afghanistan, while he was in Iran.[15] More recently, Abdelatif Mourafik (alias Malek the Andalusian, or Malek the North African), a Moroccan Zarqawi associate wanted for his role in the May 2003 Casablanca suicide bombings, was arrested in Turkey in the fall of 2003.[16] Indeed, according to early assessments by Turkish officials, Zarqawi was the planner behind the two sets of double suicide bombings in Istanbul in November 2003.[17]

Germany: Although the al-Tawhid terrorist cell apprehended in Germany in April 2002 has been tied to Abu Qatada in Britain, Zarqawi controlled its activities. Eight men were arrested, and raids yielded hundreds of forged passports from Iran, Iraq, Jordan, Denmark, and other countries. According to German prosecutors, the group facilitated the escape of terrorist fugitives from Afghanistan to Europe and planned to attack U.S. or Israeli interests in Germany.[18]

Jordan: While in Syria, Zarqawi planned and facilitated the October 2002 assassination of U.S. Agency for International Development official Lawrence Foley in Amman.[19] Jordanian prime minister Abu Ragheb Ali announced that the Libyan and Jordanian suspects arrested in December in connection with the attack received funding and instructions from Zarqawi and had intended to conduct further attacks against "foreign embassies, Jordanian officials, some diplomatic personnel, especially Americans and Israelis."[20] Moreover, during his UN address, Powell revealed that after the murder, an associate of the assassin "left Jordan to go to Iraq to obtain weapons and explosives for further operations."[21] In addition, a key Zarqawi deputy called Foley's assassins on a satellite phone to congratulate them while he was driving out of Iraq toward Turkey, a mistake that led to his capture and confirmation that an al Qaeda cell was operating out of Iraq.[22]

Poison plots: Powell also disclosed that Abuwatia, a detainee who graduated from Zarqawi's terrorist camp in Afghanistan, admitted to dispatching at least nine North African extremists to Europe to conduct poison and explosive attacks.[23] European officials maintain Zarqawi is the al Qaeda coordinator for attacks there, where chemical attacks were thwarted in Britain, France and Italy.[24] Similarly, Director of Central Intelligence George Tenet has stated that the Zarqawi network was behind poison plots in Europe this year.[25]

Although Zarqawi's active role in organizing terrorist operations suggests that he himself is a major terrorist leader, it is useful to clarify his links to other groups so as to better understand how international terrorism works. There is no precise organizational or command structure to the assemblage of groups that fall under al Qaeda's umbrella or that cooperate with the organization. Hence, whether Zarqawi swore allegiance (*bayat*) to bin Laden makes little difference in whether the two would work together at promoting a common agenda.

The range of actors who have given Zarqawi safe haven and support clearly illustrate the current modus operandi of terrorist networks. Consider his movements since he first surfaced as a terrorist suspect in 1999, when he led Jund al-Shams, an Islamic extremist group and al Qaeda affiliate operating primarily in Syria and Jordan.[26]

Jordan: Zarqawi has been a fugitive since 1999 when Jordanian authorities first tied him to radical Islamic activity leading Jund al-Shams. In 2000, a Jordanian court sentenced him in absentia to fifteen years of hard labor for his role in the al Qaeda millennial terror plot targeting Western interests in Jordan.[27]

Taliban-ruled Afghanistan: In 2000, Zarqawi traveled to Afghanistan, where he oversaw an al Qaeda training camp and worked on chemical and biological weapons.[28] Such camps served as open universities, educating terrorists from a wide array of local and international groups. These students in turn established relationships and networks, like the anti-Soviet mujahedin before them. With every success in the war on terrorism, such networks become increasingly essential to al Qaeda, providing a new cadre of terrorist operatives.

Iran and Iraq: In early 2002, Zarqawi was wounded in the leg while fighting against U.S.-led coalition forces in Afghanistan. He escaped to Iran, then traveled to Iraq in May 2002, where his wounded leg was amputated and replaced with a prosthetic device. According to Secretary Powell, Zarqawi then spent two months recovering in Baghdad, during which time "nearly two dozen extremists converged on Baghdad and established a base of operations there. These al Qaeda affiliates, based in Baghdad, now coordinate the movement of people, money, and supplies into and throughout Iraq for his network, and they've now been operating freely in the capital for more than eight months."[29] Prior to the war in Iraq, Zarqawi had returned to the Ansar al-Islam camp in northern Iraq run by his Jund al-Shams lieutenants. There, he enjoyed safe haven and free passage into and out of Ansar-held areas:[30] Zarqawi is now said to be back in Iran, where he continues to operate with the full knowledge of the regime in Tehran.[31]

Syria and Lebanon: From Baghdad, Zarqawi traveled to Syria and possibly Lebanon.[32] U.S. intelligence officials have definitively linked Zaraqawi to Hezbollah, magnifying their concerns about the ad hoc tactical relationship brewing between Iran's Shi'i proxy and the loosely affiliated al Qaeda network.

In September, when U.S. authorities designated Zarqawi and several of his associates as "Specially Designated Global Terrorist" entities, they revealed that Zarqawi not only has "ties" to Hezbollah, but that plans were in place for his deputies to meet with both Hezbollah and Asbat al Ansar (a Lebanese Sunni terrorist group tied to al Qaeda) "and any other group that would enable them to smuggle mujaheddin into Palestine" in an effort "to smuggle operatives into Israel to conduct operations."[33] Zarqawi received "more than $35,000" in mid-2001 "for work in Palestine," which included "finding a mechanism that would enable more suicide martyrs to enter Israel" as well as "to provide training on explosives, poisons, and remote controlled devices."[34]

At the same time, the Zarqawi network was planning attacks on Jewish or Israeli targets in Europe. According to the Treasury Department, Zarqawi met an associate named Mohamed Abu Dhess in Iran in early September 2001 "and instructed him to commit terrorist attacks against Jewish or Israeli facilities in Germany with 'his [Zarqawi's] people'."[35]

The Matrix of International Terror in Context: the War on Terror, Israeli-Palestinian Conflict, and War in Iraq

Three critical and interrelated national security priorities currently dominate the U.S. foreign policy agenda: the war on terror, the war in Iraq, and the Israeli-Palestinian conflict. Indeed, each is made that much more difficult to navigate by the complicating factor of the dizzying matrix of relationships between various terrorist groups, fronts, and individual members that define international terrorism today.

Again, consider a few examples:

War on Terror: Working Through Organizational Crossover

Hamas funding comes from sources closely tied to other groups, especially al Qaeda. Take for example Muhammad Zouaydi, a senior al Qaeda financier in Madrid whose home and offices were searched. Spanish investigators found a five-page fax dated October 24, 2001, revealing Zouaydi was not only financing the Hamburg cell responsible for the September 11 attacks, but also Hamas. In the fax, which Zouaydi kept for his records, the Hebron Muslim Youth Association solicited funds from the Islamic Association of Spain. According to Spanish prosecutors, "the Hebron Muslim Youth Association is an organization known to belong to the Palestinian terrorist organization Hamas which is financed by activists of said organization living abroad." Spanish police also say Zouaydi gave $6,600 to Sheikh Helal Jamal, a Palestinian religious figure in Madrid tied to Hamas.[36]

U.S. authorities detained Abdurahman Muhammad Alamoudi, head of the American Muslim Foundation, on charges he was engaging in financial transactions with Libya, a state sponsor of terror subject to U.S. sanctions. According to court documents, $340,000 in cash was seized from Alamoudi on August 16, 2003, as he attempted to board a plane in London bound for Damascus. An unidentified Libyan delivered the cash to Alamoudi in his hotel room the previous night. According to the Bureau of Immigration and Customs Enforcement (ICE), the money may have been "intended for delivery in Damascus to one or more of the terrorists or terrorist organizations in Syria." Alamoudi has publicly lauded Hezbollah and Hamas, expressed his preference for attacks that "hit a Zionist target in America or Europe or elsewhere but not like what happened at the Embassy in Kenya," and was an officer of charities in Northern Virginia tied to Hamas and al Qaeda.[37] Alluding to Hamas, Assistant U.S. Attorney Steve Ward added that "in addition to dealing with Libya, [Alamoudi] has a more direct connection with terrorist organizations designated by the United States government."[38]

According to an affidavit prepared for his bail hearing, Alamoudi laundered and transferred hundreds of thousands of dollars through charities he ran to terrorist groups, including al Qaeda and Hamas.[39] In 2000, for example, a group that received $160,000 from a charity run by Alamoudi was subsequently implicated in the millennial plot foiled that December.[40] In 2002, two of Alamoudi's other organizations, the Success Foundation and the Happy Hearts Trust, sent $95,000 to Hamas front organizations in Jordan and Israel, including the Humanitarian Relief Association and Human Appeal International.[41] Beyond this, court documents assert that tens of thousands of dollars more went through other organizations run by Alamoudi to Hamas.[42]

Similar crossover between funding for Hamas and al Qaeda was recently exposed in the case of Soliman Biheiri, another individual at the center of the massive terror financing investigation in Northern Virginia. Biheiri, described by U.S. officials as "the U.S. banker for the Muslim Brotherhood," headed a since defunct investment company called BMI Inc. in New Jersey[43] The original investors in the company, suspected of financing Hamas, al Qaeda and perhaps other designated terrorist groups, include Yassin al Qadi and Hamas leader Mousa Abu Marzook (both listed as Specially Designated Global Terrorists by the U.S. government), as well as Abdullah Awad bin Laden (Osama Bin Laden's nephew and the former head of the U.S. offices of suspected al Qaeda front the World Assembly of Muslim Youth, WAMY).[44]

Such links are not a new phenomenon. The leader of a Pakistani jihadi organization openly admitted to having "person-to-person contacts" with other groups, adding, "sometimes fighters from Hamas and Hezbollah help us." Asked where his group meets groups like Hamas and Hezbollah," the Pakistani answered, "a good place to meet is in Iran." Offering insight into the importance of interpersonal relationships between members of disparate terrorist groups, he added, "We don't involve other organizations. Just individuals."[45]

Another such link was revealed when U.S. immigration officials briefly detained Muhammad Jamal Khalifa, bin Laden's brother-in-law and a senior IIRO official and al Qaeda financier, in San Francisco in December 1994. Among the material found in his belongings "were extensive discussions of assassination, the use of explosives, military training and jihad as well as details of Islamist movements such as Hamas and Palestinian Islamic Jihad." Khalifa maintained relations with Hamas members working for the IIRO in the Philippines even after he left the organization to open a branch of the Muwafaq Foundation there.[46]

Iraq: Foreign Jihadists and Domestic Baathists Teaming Up to Attack Americans

Even as coalition forces try to plant the seeds of a pluralistic society in Iraq, these trends are being uprooted by swarms of radicals from across the Muslim world who enter Iraq— primarily from Syria and Iran but also from Saudi Arabia—to take advantage of Iraq's new-found status as a failing state. Iraq has now become a magnet for Baathists, Sunni terrorists, Shia radicals and others opposed to the development of a peaceful, pluralistic society in Iraq, much like Afghanistan, Somalia, parts of Yemen, Georgia's Pankisi Gorge, Chechnya and other undergoverned territories.

These destabilizing forces include individual radicals and terrorist groups, but also neighboring states, such as Syria and Iran, both of which allow terrorist elements to cross their borders into Iraq. U.S administrator Paul Bremer, also a noted authority on international terrorism, recently told CNN, "We've certainly seen foreign fighters who sort of fit the al Qaeda profile—people traveling on documents from Syria, Yemen, Sudan, in some cases Saudi Arabia, some of the terrorist groups we've attacked in the west of the country."[47]

According to press reports, coalition intelligence agencies intercepted conversations between radical Islamists from Saudi Arabia and Iraqi Baathists. Officials were reportedly surprised by this, noting the conservative fundamentalist ideology of Saudi extremists, while Baathists are more often moderate if not secular Muslims.[48]

But such cooperation borne of opportunism and a narrow mutual interest in targeting coalition forces should be no surprise. Almost as soon as coalition forces crossed into Iraq, reports leaked out of thousands of Arab irregular forces—some volunteers, some members of terrorist groups like Palestinian Islamic Jihad, Hezbollah and Fatah splinter groups—crossing the Syrian border into Iraq to battle coalition forces. Coalition commanders commonly referred to these irregulars as "Syrians" because so many of them were Syrian, and many carried Syrian travel documents, in some cases specifically marked "reason for entry: Jihad. Length of stay: Indefinite."[49] In one case, U.S. military forces captured a large group of Syrians and confiscated seventy suicide jackets—each filled with twenty-two pounds of military grade C4 explosives, and mercury detonators.[50] In another case, soldiers found several hundred thousands dollars on a bus that came from Syria, together with "leaflets suggesting that Iraqis would be rewarded if they killed Americans."[51] Syrian Foreign Minister Farouq al Shara explained his country's facilitating terrorists' travel to Iraq by asserting quite plainly, "Syria's interest is to see the invaders defeated in Iraq."[52] In case some planners were still unclear on the developing trend, Osama Bin Laden issued a tape-recorded message to the "mujahideen brothers in Iraq" in February stressing "the importance of the martyrdom operations against the enemy."[53] Most recently, Sunni clerics meeting in Stockholm in mid-July at a conference of the European Council for Fatwa and Research approved the use of suicide attacks in Iraq (and Palestine and Kashmir).[54]

Israeli-Palestinian Conflict: Likely Cross-group Cooperation in Gaza Bombing

The recent bombing of a U.S. convoy in Gaza on October 15, 2003, which killed three American contract employees of the U.S. embassy in Tel Aviv and injured a fourth, was neither unprecedented nor unexpected. Indeed, U.S. embassy employees narrowly escaped injury in a similar attack last June, when unknown assailants detonated two bombs near their vehicle.[55] No group has claimed responsibility for the October 15 attack. But Palestinian security officials quickly arrested several members of the Popular Resistance Committee (PRC), a conglomeration of former and current members of Fatah, Islamic Jihad, Hamas and the various Palestinian security forces. Whether the PRC is responsible is unclear. But such a strike would certainly be in keeping with its methods: The group's most daring and successful attack was a February 14, 2002 roadside bombing that demolished an Israeli armored tank. Indeed, that attack was executed with the assistance of a Hezbollah agent who infiltrated Palestinian territory to provide the PRC with technical and operational advice.[56]

Although Hezbollah has not killed Americans recently, it does target them, as CIA Director George Tenet testified in February 2002.[57] Indeed, throughout the 1990's Hezbollah operatives were especially active surveiling American and other interests throughout Southeast Asia.[58] Moreover, according to statements by captured operatives and other information made public by Israeli intelligence, Hezbollah and Lebanon-based operatives from Iran's Islamic Revolutionary Guard Corps have recruited a network of rogue Fatah cells to serve as Hezbollah's West Bank cadres.[59] Hezbollah is particularly well known for its skill at manufacturing and placing sophisticated roadside bombs, a skill the group has now transferred to the West Bank and Gaza. Aside from Hezbollah's role in the aforementioned 2002 tank bombing, in mid-2002 Israeli authorities discovered a type of mine in Hebron that had previously been used only by Hezbollah in Lebanon. Israeli authorities conducting a search in Hebron during that same month arrested Fawzi Ayub, a Hezbollah operative who had entered the territories by sea using his own Canadian passport.[60]

Authorities are also concerned al Qaeda operatives could link up with Palestinian militias and terrorist groups to target Israeli and American interests there. Recently released information indicates that the Mombassa attacks were no aberration, and that al Qaeda is intent on entering the Israeli-Palestinian arena. In August, Israel submitted a report to the UN stating that it had thwarted several attempts by al Qaeda operatives carrying foreign passports to enter Israel in order to gather intelligence and conduct attacks.[61] Israel also noted that it had captured Palestinians recruited by al Qaeda abroad to conduct attacks in Israel. Moreover, pamphlets signed by the "Bin Laden Brigades of Palestine" have been found in Palestinian areas encouraging Palestinians to continue "in the footsteps of Osama bin Laden."[62] Last month, such reports found support in the United States: The U.S. Treasury Department highlighted al Qaeda plans and funding for attacks in Israel, including "training on explosives . . . and remote controlled devices" such as the one employed on October 15 in Gaza.[63]

Regardless of who bombed the U.S. convoy in Gaza, the attack highlights the increasingly international nature of the Israeli-Palestinian conflict and the devastating cost of failing to identify and confront the increasingly common crossover between otherwise disparate terrorist groups.

The Terror Matrix as an Impediment to Fighting the War on Terror

To be sure, failure to understand the crossover and cooperation between international terrorist groups has already undermined efforts to prosecute the war on terror, both on the global battlefield and in the courtroom.

For example, this lack of understanding has frustrated efforts to curb the flow of funds to al Qaeda and other terrorists. A senior delegation of U.S. Treasury officials traveled to Europe in November 2002 to solicit European cooperation in a trans-Atlantic effort to block the international assets of about a dozen of the most egregious terror financiers. The effort failed however, because European officials were unsatisfied with the fact that the majority of evidence the Americans presented to support their request focused on these financiers' support of groups like Hamas. Material pointing to their financing of al Qaeda activities was limited out of fear of exposing sensitive sources and methods behind such intelligence, while evidence of their funding of Hamas was more readily available. The Americans were told they would have to produce evidence these financiers were funding more than just Hamas (i.e., al Qaeda) if they expected European cooperation.[64]

Similarly, the EU has yet to designate the al Aqsa International Foundation as a terrorist entity, despite its known ties to Hamas, al Qaeda and possibly Hezbollah.

Myopic perspectives such as this, blind to the crossover between terror networks, have also undermined criminal prosecutions of terrorists, including several cases in the United States.

As the myriad of companies, charities, and other suspected terrorist front organizations now under investigation in Northern Virginia highlight, there is a critical need to break away from the tendency to adhere to a strict compartmentalization of terrorist groups in investigating terrorism cases. Investigating the family of organizations in Northern Virginia—including the Safa Group, SAAR Foundation, Success Foundation and many more—strictly as a Hamas, Palestinian Islamic Jihad (PIJ), or al Qaeda cases—clearly did not work. Indeed, the tentacles of this entrenched network are suspected of providing tremendous logistical and financial support to a variety of international terrorist groups.

Tracing these financial trails, however, proved immensely difficult given the various groups' proactive efforts to layer their transactions and obfuscate the terrorist intentions of their many transactions. More than anything, the links between various personalities tied to these organizations on the one hand and to a laundry list of terrorist groups, fronts and operatives on the other, keyed investigators into the network's terror financing and support activities.

Progress on this complex web of front organizations appears to have developed only with the passage of the USA Patriot Act, which facilitated the sharing of intelligence among prosecutors and permitted cross-referencing of information across previously compartmentalized terrorism investigations.

Conclusion

Money has not been a constraint on the activities of al Qaeda, Palestinian terrorist groups, or the jihadists and Ba'athists fighting coalition forces in Iraq. This will continue to be the case until more serious action is taken toward restricting the financing of terrorism, which is indeed one of the most effective ways to advance the war on terror, the Roadmap to Israeli Palestinian peace, and the stabilization of Iraq.

The principal terrorist threat today stems from the web of shadowy relationships between loosely affiliated groups. The sponsors of such groups further complicate the web, be they states or substate actors. Indeed, there is no precise organizational or command structure to the assemblage of groups that cooperate with al Qaeda or fall under the organization's umbrella. Given the multifarious links between international terrorist groups and their relationships with state sponsors of terrorism such as Iran and Syria, the war on terror will be most effective if it has a strategic focus on the full matrix of international terrorism rather than a tactical focus on al Qaeda. Prosecuting the war on terror, whether on the battlefield or in the courtroom, demands greater attention to the web of interaction among these various groups and state sponsors.

Matthew A. Levitt is a senior fellow and director of the Stein Program on Terrorism, Intelligence, and Policy at The Washington Institute for Near East Policy. From 2005 to early 2007, Dr. Levitt served as deputy assistant secretary for intelligence and analysis at the U.S. Department of the Treasury. He previously served as an FBI analyst specializing in tactical and strategic analysis in support of counterterrorism operations.

Notes

1. Without trying to quantify current and tolerable levels of terrorism, one can safely assert that reducing the threat of radical Islamic terrorism, the source of the vast majority of terrorist threats today, would significantly reduce the threat level from one in which each day brings several new terror threats to one in which such threats, while perhaps no less dangerous, are far less frequent.
2. Richard A. Clarke, "Statement before the United States Senate Banking Committee," 22 October 2003, (www.senate.gov/banking/files/clarke.pdf).
3. John B. Taylor, "Statement from the US Department of the Treasury," 7 November 2001, (www.treas.gov/press/releases/po771.htm).
4. "The United States and Italy Designate Twenty-Five New Financiers of Terror," Department of the Treasury Office of Public Affairs, PO-3380, 29 August 2002, (www.ustreas.gov/press/releases/po3380.htm) and Lucy Komisar, "Shareholders in the Bank of Terror?" Salon.com, 15 March 2002; and Mark Hosenball, "Terror's Cash Flow," *Newsweek,* 25 March 2002, 28, 29.
5. Testimony of Juan C. Zarate, Deputy Assistant Secretary, Terrorism and Violent Crime, U.S. Department of the Treasury, House Financial Subcommittee Oversight and Investigations, 12 February 2002.
6. Ibid.
7. *United States of America v. Jeffrey Leon Battle et al.,* United States District Court for the District of Oregon, No. CR 02-399 HA, 2 October 2003.
8. Les Zaitz, "FBI Affidavit Alleges Imam Bankrolled Plot," *The Oregonian,* 23 August 2003, A01.
9. "Treasury Designates Al-Aqsa International Foundation as Financier of Terror: Charity Linked to Funding of the Hamas Terrorist Organization," Department of the Treasury, Office of Public Affairs, 29 May 2003, (www.treas.gov/pres/releases/js439.htm).
10. *USA v. Mohammed Ali Hasan Al-Moayad,* Affidavit in Support of Arrest Warrant, Eastern District of New York, 5 January 2003.

11. "Hezbollah: Profile of the Lebanese Shiite Terrorist Organization of Global Reach Sponsored by Iran and Supported by Syria," Intelligence and Terrorism Information Center, The Center for Special Studies, Special Information Paper, June 2003, (www.intelligence.org.il/eng/bu/hizbullah/hezbollah.htm).

12. Secretary of State Colin Powell, "Remarks to the United Nations Security Council," 5 February 2003, (www.state.gov/secretary/rm/2003/17300.htm).

13. Audio Message by Osama bin Laden, Al-Jazeera Television, 11February 2003. See BBC transcript, (www.news.bbc.co.uk/2/hi/middle_east/2751019.htm).

14. Secretary of State Colin Powell, "Remarks to the United Nations Security Council" 5 February 2003, (www.state.gov/secretary/rm/2003/17300.htm).

15. Douglas Frantz and James Risen, "A Secret Iran-Arafat Connection is Seen Fueling the Mideast Fire," *The New York Times,* 24 March 2002, A1; and David Kaplan, "Run and Gun: Al Qaeda Arrests and Intelligence Hauls Bring New Energy to the War on Terrorism," *U.S. News and World Report,* 30 September 2002, 36-38, 41.

16. Sebastian Rotella and Richard C. Paddock, "Experts See Major Shift in Al Qaeda's Strategy," *Los Angeles Times,* 19 November 2003, AI.

17. "Istanbul's attacks mastermind identified, consul's window makes appeal," Agence France Presse, 27 November 2003.

18. Philipp Jaklin and Hugh Williamson, "Terror Suspects Detained in Germany," *Financial Times,* 24 April 2002, 6; Edmund L. Andrews, "German Officials Find More Terrorist Groups, and Some Disturbing Parallels," *The New York Times,* 26 April 2002, A12.

19. Secretary of State Colin Powell, "Remarks to the United Nations Security Council," 5 February 2003, <www.state.gov/secretary/rm/2003/17300.htm> and "Treasury Designates Six Al Qaeda Terrorists," U.S. Department of the Treasury press release (JS-757), 24 September 2003, (www.treasury.gov/press/release/js757.htm).

20. "Al Qaeda man behind murder of US diplomat hiding in northern Iraq: Jordan," *Agence France Presse,* 18 December 2002.

21. Secretary of State Colin Powell, "Remarks to the United Nations Security Council," 5 February 2003, (www.state.gov/secretary/rm/2003/17300.htm).

22. Ibid.

23. Ibid.

24. Elaine Sciolino and Desmond Butler, "Europeans Fear That the Threat From Radical Islamists Is Increasing," *The New York Times,* 8 December 2002, A32.

25. George J. Tenet, "Worldwide Threat—Converging Dangers in a Post-9/11 World: Testimony of Director of Central Intelligence George J. Tenet before the Senate Select Committee on Intelligence," 6 February 2002, (http://www.cia.gov/cia/public_affiars/speeches/2002/dci_speech_02062002.html).

26. "Treasury Designates Six Al Qaeda Terrorists," US Department of the Treasury press release (JS-757), 24 September 2003, (http://www.treasury.gov/press/releases/js757.htm).

27. "Al Qaeda man behind murder of US diplomat hiding in northern Iraq: Jordan," *Agency France Press,* 18 December 2002.

28. Secretary of State Colin Powell, "Remarks to the United Security Council," 5 February 2003, (www.state.gov/secretary/rm/2003/17300.htm).

29. Ibid.

30. Ibid.

31. *Al-Sharq al-Awsat,* 1 June 2003; A European intelligence official subsequently confirmed this report in an interview with the author, September 2003.

32. David E. Kaplan, Angie Cannon, Mark Mazzetti, Douglas Pasternak, Kevin Whitelaw, Aamir Latif, "Run and Gun," *U.S. News and World Report,* 30 September 2002, 36.

33. "Treasury Designates Six Al Qaeda Terrorists," US Department of the Treasury press release (JS-757), 24 September 2003, (http://www.treasury.gov/press/releases/js757.htm).

34. Ibid.

35. Ibid.

36. Central Trial Court No. 5, Spanish National High Court (*Audiencia Nacional*), CASE 35/2002 (ordinary procedure), Don Baltasar Garzon Real, Magistrado Juez del Juzgado Central de Instrucción 19 July 2002.

37. Declaration in Support of Detention, *USA v. Abdurahman Muhammad Alamoudi,* case No 03-1009M, Alexandria Division, Eastern District of Virginia, 30 September 2003.

38. Douglas Farah, "US Says Activist Funded Terrosists; Leader of Muslim Groups Denied Bail," *The Washington Post,* 1 October 2003, A6.

39. Douglas Farah, "US Indicts Prominent Muslim, Affidavit: Alamoudi Funded Terrorists," *The Washington Post,* 24 October 2003. A1.

40. Ibid.

41. Ibid, and Glenn R. Simpson, "Unraveling Terror's Finances," *Wall Street Journal,* 24 October 2003, A2.

42. Ibid.

43. Glenn R. Simpson, "The U.S. Provides Details of Terror-Financing Web Defunct Investment Firm In New Jersey Is the Hub; Suspect to Stay in Custody," *The Wall Street Journal,* 15 September 2003.

44. Ibid.; For information on WAMY's ties to terrorism see "Combating Terrorist Financing, Despite the Saudis," Policywatch #673, The Washington Institute for Near East Policy, 1 November 2002, (www.washingtoninstitute.org/watch/Policywatch/policywatch2002/673.htm).

45. Jessica Stern, *Terror in the Name of God: Why Religious Militants Kill* (New York: Harper Collins, 2003), 211.

46. Rohan Gunaratna, *Inside Al Qaeda: Global Network of Terror* (New York: Columbia University Press, 2002), 114, 145.

47. "Bremer says Hundreds of international terrorists in Iraq," *Agence France Presse,* 24 August 2003.

48. Raymond Bonner, "The Struggle for Iraq: Weapons; Iraqi Arms Catches Cited in Attacks," *The New York Times,* 14 October 2003, A1.

49. Luke Hunt, "Evidence of Iraq's 'terrorist ties' mounts, but bin Laden link elusive," *Agence France Presse,* 16 April 2003.

50. Ibid.

51. Bernard Weinraub, "Fighters from Syria Among Iraqi Prisoners in an American Camp." *The New York Times,* 20 April 2003, B4.

52. "Syria Hits Back at U.S. Says It Supports 'Iraqi People' Against Invaders," Agence France Presse, March 31, 2003.

53. Audio Message by Osama bin Laden, Al-Jazeera Television, 11February 2003. See BBC transcript, (news.bbc.co.uk/2/hi/middle_east/2751019,htm).

54. Arnaud de Borchgrave, "Clerics OK suicide-bombers," *United Press International,* 15 August 2003.

55. Margot Dudkevitch, "IDF thwarts two suicide bombings," *Jerusalem Post,* 29 June 2003.

56. James Bennett, "Israeli Killed As His Commandos Demolish West Bank House," *The New York Times,* 16 February 2002, A4.

57. George J. Tenet, "Worldwide Threat—Converging Dangers in a Post-9/11 World: Testimony of Director of Central Intelligence George J. Tenet before the Senate Select Committee on Intelligence," 6 February 2002, (http://www.cia.gov/cia/public_affairs/speeches/2002/dci_speech_02062002.html).

58. Maria Ressa, *Seeds of Terror: An Eyewitness Account of al Qaeda's Newest Center of Operations in Southeast Asia* (New York; Free Press, 2003), Pp.129-132; see also Matthew Levitt, "From the Beqa'a Valley to the Blue Ridge Mountains: Hezbollah's Global Presence and Operations", Lecture presented at The International Policy Institute for Counter-Terrorism (ICT), Third Annual Conference, "Post Modern Terrorism: Trends Scenarios, and Future Threats," 7–10 September 2003, Herzliya, Israel.

59. Matthew Levitt, "Hezbollah's West Bank Foothold," *Peacewatch* #429, The Washington Institute for Near East Policy, 20 August 2003, (www.washingtoninstitute.org/watch/Peacewatch/peacewatch2003/429.htm).

60. "Hezbollah (part 1): Profile of the Lebanese Shiite Terrorist Organization of Global Reach Sponsored by Iran and Supported by Syria," Intelligence and Terrorism Information Center at the Center for Special Studies, Israel, June 2003; and author interview with intelligence sources, July 2003, available at (www.intelligence.org.il/eng/bu/hizbullah/hezbollah.htm).

61. Anna Driver, "Israel Says al Qaeda Active in Palestinian Areas," *Reuters,* 5 August 2003.

62. Ibid.

63. "Treasury Designates Six Al Qaeda Terrorists," US Department of the Treasury press release (JS-757), 24 September 2003, (www.treasury.gov/press/release/js757.htm).

64. Testimony of Jimmy Gurule, Under Secretary for Enforcement, U.S. Department of the Treasury, Before the U.S. Senaté Judiciary Committee, November 20, 2002. (www.ustreas. gov/press/releases/po3635.htm) and Douglas Farah, "U.S. Pinpoints Top Al Qaeda Financiers, Treasury Official Heads to Europe to Seek Help in Freezing Backers' Assets," *The Washington Post,* 18 October 2002. A26.

Chapter 9

Leveraging the Role of the Private Sector

Just weeks after the attacks on September 11, the U.S. government launched an attack against the terrorist financial infrastructure—a critical front in the war on terrorism. After all, terrorists face great difficulty in planning and executing sophisticated attacks without access to extensive financial resources. Without money, terrorists cannot sustain their operations let alone expand to new fronts, recruit new members, or purchase new weapons. Given the global nature of the world economy, however, governments are unable to restrict access to financial institutions without the cooperation of other nations as well as the private sector. The global private sector in particular has become a critical player in stemming the finances of terrorist groups, and thus, leveraging the role of the private sector is essential for counterterrorism efforts.

Despite major international efforts to curb terrorist financing, Mark Basile is doubtful that al Qaeda has yet to be significantly starved of its funding. Basile outlines how al Qaeda has managed to build a network of financiers who have skillfully hidden al Qaeda assets in legitimate and illegitimate businesses, and who have also "learned to effectively leverage the global financial system of capital markets." In his article, Basile explains why al Qaeda's financial system is not only healthy but that it may be likely to withstand international efforts to date—in particular, since "al Qaeda has built a significant base of Islamic charities in Saudi Arabia with international divisions that have not been scrutinized or controlled by the regime."

By attacking the World Trade Center—a symbol of the global economy but also home to hundreds of businesses—al Qaeda terrorists made clear their intent to target the private sector in their attacks. According to Kelly Hicks and Roseann McSorley, the 9/11 attacks "showed how ill-prepared the financial sector was for an event as massive and shocking as bringing down skyscrapers full of thousands of people." The authors argue that "while the U.S. government began to deal with the lessons of 9/11 . . . the finance industry set about strengthening its own security posture."

In their article, Hicks and McSorley detail how changes to the various building blocks that comprise a robust security posture for a typical financial firm—communications, awareness training, crisis management, intelligence, physical security countermeasures, and the development of public private partnerships—have "strengthened the ability of financial institutions to support local law enforcement in ways that enable the latter to commit more of their precious resources toward countering terrorist activities, rather than ensuring the safety of people on a large-scale." In other words, by being better prepared for terrorist attacks, the private sector can play an important role in minimizing the effects of an attack and thereby assist public agencies responsible for crisis management.

Beyond assisting with the curbing of terrorist financing and facilitating effective crisis management, however, "the private sector also has the potential to be involved in a different way: as partners in intelligence gathering and information sharing with U.S. government agencies charged with counterterrorism responsibilities." Stacy Reiter Neal suggests that "by leveraging their existing strengths—international presence, local employees, micro-level knowledge of cities and regions, and strong, well-managed organizational structures—multinational corporations are uniquely positioned to gather street-level, open-source intelligence and to observe security trends that can aid counterterrorism professionals and policymakers." In her article, Neal reviews existing efforts and proposals for collaboration between the private sector and government—public-private partnerships—as well as barriers to deeper collaboration between public and private entities. Neal concludes that "the possibilities presented by successful public-private intelligence partnerships are immeasurable," but that they are limited by the lack of organization and clear policies and procedures for information sharing. According to Neal, "resolving these issues will be essential to creating a successful cross-sector information-sharing system."

Mark Basile, 2004

Going to the Source: Why Al Qaeda's Financial Network Is Likely to Withstand the Current War on Terrorist Financing

On 24 September 2001, President Bush announced the first stage of the War on Terrorism with an attack against the terrorist financial infrastructure. Since then, the impact of this attack on Al Qaeda's ability to operate has been minimal, for three reasons. First, Al Qaeda has built a strong network of financiers and operatives who are both frugally minded and business savvy. As a result, terrorist finances are often hidden in legitimate and illegitimate businesses and disguised as commodities and cash. Second, Al Qaeda has learned to effectively leverage the global financial system of capital markets. Small financial transfers, underregulated Islamic banking networks and informal transfer systems throughout the world make it almost impossible to stop Al Qaeda from moving money. Third, Al Qaeda has built a significant base of Islamic charities in Saudi Arabia with international divisions that have not been scrutinized or controlled by the regime. As a result, Al Qaeda's sophisticated financial network may be able to sustain international efforts to disrupt it. Financial regulations imposed to reduce terrorist financing must be applied more broadly and be supported by significant resources. An improvement in the war on terrorist financing requires better international coordination, more effective use of financial regulations, and regulating the Saudi Arabian charity structure.

The war on terrorist financing is currently ill-equipped to starve Al Qaeda of its funding. Al Qaeda is an effective organization that has taken advantage of the weaknesses in global financial markets to develop a network of financing options that cannot be easily overcome. This article will examine the mechanisms that enable Al Qaeda to continue to raise and disperse funds for future operations, and policy options to improve the ability of regulators to reduce Al Qaeda's financial strength.

Al Qaeda's strengths include its network structure and doctrine, which leverages wealthy donors and charities for funding, as well as training operatives to develop self-funding strategies. Al Qaeda's strength is a global financial system of licit and illicit companies, private investors, government sponsors, and religious "charities" that fund Al Qaeda operations.

Al Qaeda always benefits from numerous financial channels, away from government regulation and control. U.S. domestic regulations will have an impact on Al Qaeda finances in the United States, but applying these regulations to international markets and foreign banking systems is problematic. In addition, Al Qaeda always has a fallback financial system to rely on, including the underregulated Islamic banking system and the international hawala transfer system. The hawala system is Al Qaeda's most effective means of money movement through cash smuggling.[1]

Al Qaeda benefits from weak U.S. foreign policy and coalition building with allies, such as Saudi Arabia, who are unwilling to effectively implement stringent regulations to stem terrorist funding. Al Qaeda benefits from the weak financial regulations of failed states and weak regulation of charities throughout the Middle East to fund its organization. As such, the United States must make a significant foreign policy push for banking oversight and regulation in the Middle East and a local government crackdown on the unregulated charity structure in Saudi Arabia. The United States must use diplomatic and economic tools to push developing countries toward higher standards of regulation in order to cut off Al Qaeda sources of funding.

Al Qaeda's financial structure is well equipped to last in a long war on terrorist financing against the United States and its allies. Most of the evidence underlying this author's arguments is based on academic research, public trials, and Congressional testimony from authorities on Al Qaeda, terrorist financing, and financial regulation. The primary evidence on Al Qaeda that supports many of these findings is based on interviews with Al Qaeda detainees and documents found in Al Qaeda facilities; evidence that may be fabricated because Al Qaeda operatives are taught the tools of denial and deception when conducting operations. Therefore, there is always a possibility, especially before the war on terrorism has come to a conclusion and more evidence is available, that the information provided by detained Al Qaeda operatives and confiscated Al Qaeda paperwork is misleading or incomplete.

The Background of Al Qaeda's Financial Network

> It is neither a single group nor a coalition of groups: it comprises a core base or bases in Afghanistan, satellite terrorist cells worldwide, a conglomerate of Islamist political parties, and other largely independent terrorist groups that it draws on for offensive actions and other responsibilities.[2]

Unlike the leaders of other terrorist organizations, Osama Bin Laden did not rise to power primarily as a religious authority, military hero, or political figure. He was a wealthy financier from a wealthy Saudi family with close ties to the United States. Although his personal fortune is estimated to be between $30 and $200 million, it is quite clear that his organization, Al Qaeda, does not rest on his financial coattails. Rather, Al Qaeda operates a significant financial network, approximated at over $300 million in value, dispersing between $30 and $40 million per year.[3] This network has grown from its origins as the financing arm of the Mujahideen in Afghanistan to a decentralized network of financial capabilities that leverages a limited set of funding channels to fund its organization.

Al Qaeda uses limited funding channels very effectively. In its *Guidance for Financial Institutions in Detecting Terrorist Financing,* the Financial Action Task Force (FATF) on Money Laundering claims that terrorists raise funds from two sources: states and "revenue-generating" activities including fraud, narcotics trafficking, kidnapping, and extortion in addition to running legitimate businesses.[4] Al Qaeda is notable for primarily using fraud and legitimate businesses to support a network, rather than engaging in the full spectrum of "revenue-generating" activities.

The decentralized nature of Al Qaeda makes the overall financial structure very self-sufficient and potentially regenerative. The leadership structure comprises four committees, each reporting to a council of leadership members, the *majlis al-shura,*[5] which, in turn, reports directly to the Emir-General of Al Qaeda. The committee structure includes military, business, religious, and media arms. The business and finance committee, a group of professional bankers, accountants, and financiers,[6] is responsible for setting up and running the financial network that sustains Al Qaeda, from providing logistics for operational cells and bases, to sourcing funds from charities and other sources. It runs a number of illegitimate and legitimate businesses as part of its network. Diamond trading, import-export, manufacturing, transport, and financial services are businesses that Al Qaeda owns and uses. Until recently, the financial arm was run by one of bin Laden's close associates, Mustafa Ahmed al-Hawsawi, who was recently captured. Although the capture of Hawsawi was a good step in the war on terrorist financing, it also showed how Al Qaeda can adapt: Hawsawi was presumably replaced as early as October 2002 by an Egyptian named Abdullah Ahmed Abdullah.[7]

Al Qaeda keeps the funding for its operational cells unconnected from the network of sources from which it raises funds. Al Qaeda requires terrorist cells to be self-managed and often self-sufficient when it comes to finances. Separately, Al Qaeda relies on its businesses and charities to send funding to Al Qaeda's central base of financial operations. In this manner, Al Qaeda runs its sources of funding separately from the funding needs of terrorist cells.[8] This keeps Al Qaeda's financial sources as discreet as possible while allowing operational cells to deploy without ever giving away information on Al Qaeda's underlying financial network.

A Flexible, Extensive, and Deep Financial Network

Al Qaeda's financial capabilities benefit from a network of wealthy supporters, a number of legitimate and illegitimate businesses, and a consistent source of funding from Islamic charities. Moreover, Al Qaeda compounds this financial base of strength with an operational doctrine that teaches deception and denial, frugal financial behavior, and self-sustaining financing tools to its operatives. Al Qaeda's financial network is strong and adaptive, built on a base of networked financiers and operationally strong terrorists. Its means for sourcing funds, managing or hiding funds, and dispersing funds are numerous and complex. To date, each Al Qaeda cell that has conducted a successful operation has received or raised funds from a different channel. The flexibility of Al Qaeda's financial network relies on three strengths of its network: the operational doctrine, the extensive financial network of financiers and businesses, and the consistent source of funding from Islamic charities.

Operational Doctrine

Al Qaeda's operational doctrine breeds frugal financial practices and a self-sustaining attitude in the field. Parts of Al Qaeda's doctrine are exposed in the military training manual of Al Qaeda, *Declaration of Jihad against the Country's Tyrants,* which instructs its operatives in the tools of deception and denial.[9] In the section on financial security precautions, the commander of the cell is instructed to divide finances into funds to be invested for financial return and funds to be saved for operations. In general, these funds must be dispersed, occasionally left with non-members of the cell, and the locations of the funds are not to be divulged to cell soldiers,[10] thus reducing the chances that a captured cell will divulge the source of its financing. The cell commander is given responsibility for the effective allocation, use, and occasionally raising of cell funds.

Al Qaeda operatives are also taught to use credit card fraud, document forgery, and other criminal scams to support their objectives. This self-sufficiency hurt the early cells of Al Qaeda, notably the first World Trade Center bombing cell in 1993. In the early part of the 1990s, Al Qaeda either did not have the necessary resources, or at least chose not to use them for its operational cells. Ramzi Yousef, the mastermind and commander of the first World Trade Center bombing was financed by donations from a Holy Water company in the Middle East.[11] Yet the limited nature of Yousef's funding not only caused him to build a bomb that was too small, but also forced one of his operatives, Mohammed Salameh, to foolishly try to retrieve the deposit on the rental truck used to hold the bomb.[12]

Although Al Qaeda's doctrine is frugal in spirit, it is intelligent in its funding allocations. In the days before 11 September 2001, Al Qaeda operatives returned unused funds from their cell in the form of wire transfers for over $20,000 dollars to Al Qaeda leaders in the Middle East. At the same time, the operational commanders did not spare any expense in buying business-class seats so that the hijackers were in the optimal position to take over the cabin.[13]

Businesses and Financiers

Al Qaeda's financial strength is also based on its ability to raise funds from legitimate and illegitimate business and from its network of financiers. In the time since September 11, many Al Qaeda legitimate businesses and financiers have been exposed. However, Al Qaeda is still able to operate businesses in states that are failing around the world such as diamond trafficking in Africa and honey trading out of Yemen, and many financiers still exist that have not been exposed.

The United States shut down a number of Al Qaeda's businesses in the war in Afghanistan, but Al Qaeda continues to run businesses in developing parts of the world. One such business is the diamond business, which Al Qaeda runs in Liberia and Burkina Faso, two countries involved in the illicit diamond trade. Al Qaeda diamond trafficking, which has gone undisturbed since 1998 when it was established in the $20 million industry in West Africa, represents an illegitimate business that Al Qaeda has significantly profited from by working with a number of local companies.[14] In addition to illicit diamond trading, Al Qaeda engages in legitimate business, such as honey trading. Although some claim that this business is a cover for smuggling of money, weapons, and drugs,[15] the business may also be legitimate because the honey trade in the Middle East is important to the culture, religion, and trade. Regardless of how Al Qaeda uses the business, its ability to successfully run overt businesses in honey and covert businesses in gems illustrates a complexity in Al Qaeda's financial network.

The 19 hijackers on 11 September 2001 used less than $500,000[16] from 20 key financiers to fund the hijacking of 4 American commercial jetliners. This $500,000 was transferred to the hijackers in a large number of small installments over time, through different financial channels, indirectly passed to the terrorists from the Middle East, through Germany, the United Arab Emirates (UAE), and Malaysia.[17] The source of these funds was unclear to U.S. authorities until a recent document, recovered from the Arlington, Texas headquarters of Benevolence International Foundation (BIF), listed 20 top Al Qaeda financiers, known as the Golden Chain.[18] In the United States Court case against the President of BIF, Ennam Arnaout, it was suggested that this list of 20 financiers helped provide the funding for the 9/11 cell. More importantly, if true, these 20 individuals highlight the deep pockets of Al Qaeda financiers.

Islamic Charities

The third contributor to Al Qaeda's financial resilience is income from charities. Since September 11, the U.S. arms of a number of Islamic charities that funded Al Qaeda have been shut down and their assets have been frozen. Many of these charities were run by Al Qaeda operatives, such as Ennam Arnaout, who was sentenced to 11 years in prison for money-laundering rather than terrorism. Of course, while charities on U.S. soil are governed by American regulations, Middle East-based charities are not constrained by U.S. law. These charities not only represent a seemingly uncontrollable source of funding, they are also a stable source of funding.

Zakat, or alms giving, is one of the five pillars of Islam, a religious duty for all Muslims. As such, Islamic charities through the Middle East and the rest of the world have a consistent source of funding from religious Muslims. Although the vast majority of charities are legitimate enterprises, funding community development in Islamic communities, a number also have close ties to terrorist groups. Additionally, a number of terrorist organizations, such as Hamas and Hezbollah, include charity and nongovernmental organizations (NGOs) as an overt part of their organizational structure, which raises questions of whether charitable funds are channeled to charitable purposes or terrorism. In the case of Al Qaeda, charities and NGOs act primarily under cover in their financing of terrorism, rather than funding any charitable purposes Al Qaeda may have. Many of these charities were not specifically created to fully fund Al Qaeda, but have since become supportive of its cause.

Many of the charities that support Al Qaeda financially have done so since the Soviet Afghan war. Three of the charities that have come to the attention of the U.S. Justice Department are the Muslim World League (MWL), Benevolence International Foundation, and Qatar Charitable Society (QCS).[19] Even though there were public suggestions that these charities funded Al Qaeda as early as 1993, it was not until a year after 9/11 that the Treasury Department froze the assets of the first two charities.[20] Each of these charities has existed for many years; in the case of the Muslim World League, since 1962.

The case against Ennam Arnaout and his Islamic charity, BIF, uncovered the illegal and yet virtually undetectable ability of Al Qaeda to pull funds from its charities. Funds would be allocated, and accounted for, by the charity for community development and charitable activities. Once the full amount was pulled out for the charitable project, a small percentage (around 10%) of the cash was skimmed off the top and physically passed to an Al Qaeda operative who deposited this clean money into Al Qaeda accounts in the Middle East or dispersed it to operational cells in other parts where Al Qaeda operates, such as Bosnia.[21]

The problem with MWL, BIF, and any Islamic charity that supports Al Qaeda is two-fold. First, because their objectives are typically noble and many of their activities may be justifiable, shutting them down may create serious problems for local beneficiaries and have negative impacts on humanitarian needs that the charity is funding. Second, there are typically other illegitimate charities that will accept the cash when charities like MWL and BIF are closed down. While religious Muslims are called to give to charities, with the belief that their money is being used toward an ethical cause, the cash flow out of charities is very loosely regulated and easy to move to terrorist organizations, often without the donor's knowledge or consent. This is especially beneficial to Al Qaeda because the money that is received from charities is clean money, and unlike illicit financing sources, does not need to be laundered.

Al Qaeda has a flexible, extensive, and deep financial network. Its flexibility lies in its doctrinal ability to self-fund operations and save money by the frugal behavior of its operatives. Glimpses of the extensive nature of the network are evident by the deep pockets of financiers and the diversity of legitimate and illegitimate businesses on which Al Qaeda has relied. Finally, Al Qaeda has its hands in the pockets of unknowing Muslims, who, in fulfilling their religious duty to give alms to charities are unknowingly funding terrorist operations.

Al Qaeda's Financial Channels

> Al Qaeda has three financial systems organized by bankers who are as "aware of the cracks inside the Western Financial System as they are aware of lines on their own hands."
>
> —Osama bin Laden in an interview in a Pakistani newspaper[22]

Presumably, the three primary financial systems that Osama Bin Laden divulged include the formal international banking system, the Islamic Banking financial system, and the underground hawala system. Al Qaeda uses these three financial systems, each under varying degrees of regulation, to channel its funds around the world. More recently, Al Qaeda has also used a fourth financial channel in physical movement of cash, diamonds, and precious metals in suitcases in order to evade government oversight.[23]

International Banking System

Al Qaeda's financial network reaches around the world. Although U.S. regulations and legislation have allowed the government to freeze terrorist assets in U.S. jurisdictions, it has limited abilities outside of the U.S. financial system. Al Qaeda's only limitation, in the wake of U.S. regulations and legislation, is a greater difficulty of moving money into the United States. There are two primary reasons that regulations in the international environment are not a long-term solution to winning the war on terrorist financing. The first is that the legal and regulatory structures of foreign financial markets are different and financial transfers regulations between these markets are not yet designed to identify terrorist funds. The second is that Al Qaeda has a global financial system of non-U.S. based regulated and unregulated banks, including the Islamic banking system, through which it can still transfer, store, and invest its funds.

The global financial system was not created to stop the war on terrorist financing. After Bretton Woods, central bank control of international finance decreased, as global currencies floated on international capital markets and investors put their money in places with strong economic activity. In the last 30 years, regulation of global capital markets has decreased as many countries have been gaining access to markets in New York, London, Tokyo, and Hong Kong. The goal of investing in these markets is to gain access to cheaper sources of financing and more stable rates of return. Countries that integrate into capital markets accordingly reduce their cost of capital. Tighter integration also requires faster transactions and allocation of funds, a benefit that increased regulation reduces.

In the developing world, central banks often still control foreign financial transactions. In general, economists believe that when central banks allow their currency to be traded and transacted freely, local investors will choose to invest internationally and repatriate gains into local markets. This type of laissez-faire attitude suggests that access to international markets will cause efficiencies that will force developing countries to develop their own internal financial and banking oversight to protect their new sources of funds. Unfortunately, reducing central bank control in developing countries may also allow terrorists to easily access global financial markets and rely on commercial banking systems with limited oversight.

Islamic Banking

In addition to benefiting from weak banking oversight in the developing world and the unlikely direction of reduced capital market integration, Al Qaeda also takes advantage of a financial structure close to home: the Islamic banking network. This global financial network has strong relationships through the third world, notable tax havens, and most importantly most of the developed world, including the United Kingdom and United States. The Islamic banking system is legitimate and operates under *sharia,* Islamic law, which prohibits bankers or customers from earning interest on funds. The profits that banks do earn (not specifically called "interest") are used for internal bank projects or are given to charities. Because of *sharia,* Islamic banks typically have excess cash (the interest) that must be allocated.[24] Reputable Islamic banks typically have Sharia Boards[25] who act as a religious and accounting standards committee, making decisions about what financial instruments their bank is able to use under Islamic law.[26] Unfortunately, even with Sharia Boards (who have had their share of scandals[27]), Islamic banks are known for lacking regulatory oversight, and the unclear guidelines for the use of interest make Islamic banks a possible source of funding for Al Qaeda.

Al Qaeda is no different from other terrorist organizations, arms smugglers, and drug traffickers in its use of Islamic banks. As the leading financial institutions of areas of the world rich with oil and natural resources, Islamic banks are the primary channel for investment and transactions into the Middle East and many other parts of the developing world. Therefore, they are networked into sophisticated capital markets around the world. Al Qaeda uses front companies to funnel its finances through this system. For example, the Advice and Reformation Committee, a presumed front for Al Qaeda, received funds in a Barclay's account from correspondent Islamic banks in Sudan, Dubai, and the UAE. The funds in the Barclay's account were then forwarded to operational cells in Western Europe by the signatory on the account, a presumed Al Qaeda associate.[28] To bin Laden's advantage, the correspondent nature of Islamic banks to Western banks allows for transfers that receive less scrutiny. This advantage is also detrimental to international efforts to curb the transfers as international trade relies on banking ties between the Middle East and the Western banks. Condemning the correspondent nature of this banking relationship may hurt the movement of terrorist funds, but it will also significantly impact the ability of large corporations to invest in the region and therefore is likely infeasible.

Hawalas

The hawala system, in the United States and globally, is used by legitimate persons and terrorists to move money around the world without the detection of the global banking system.[29] Similar to the Islamic Banking system, it is governed by Sharia law, but accounts are not kept, nor are financial instruments provided.[30] The legitimate hawala network has not yet been regulated, which makes it an opportune channel for Al Qaeda to use in transferring funds, not only internationally, but into the United States.

Hawala, the Arabic word for "transfer,"[31] refers to an informal global network of individuals who transact cash for their clients, similar to a wiring service. In a hawala, no money transfers are made between traders. Instead, a phone call or fax is sent from one hawaladar to another hawaladar, instructing the latter to dispense cash to the intended recipient. This cash transaction itself is not accounted for, as the hawaladars only hold balances against each other that will eventually be settled through a single wire transfer, movement of precious stones, or other means.[32] The hawala system is an ancient one that is particularly important in parts of the world with weak banking infrastructure and few bank accounts, such as the developing world.

Although Congress tried to regulate the hawala system in the United States in 1994, proposed legislation did not pass. Although the USA Patriot Act requires hawala registration in the United States, strict enforcement may be a difficult task. Executive Order 13224 closed down the Somalia Al Barakaat hawala office in the United States soon after the attacks of September 11. Unfortunately, such enforcement against one of the financial channels of 9/11 is reactive and provides little improvement in proactively preventing terrorist funds from moving through hawalas. Furthermore, even if the United States could put regulations on U.S.-based hawalas, it would be unable to have any affect on the international network of traders. Nevertheless, one of the Treasury Departments' annual money laundering priorities is to "concentrate on informal value transfer systems, such as hawalas, as a means of moving money."[33] Unfortunately, the hawala network can also be used as a money-laundering apparatus, where dirty funds are given to a trader on the inbound side of a transaction and clean funds are dispersed on the outbound side of the transaction.

Financial Regulations Used Against Terrorist Financing

> We will starve terrorists of funding, turn them against each other, rout them out of their safe hiding places, and bring them to justice.
>
> —President George W. Bush, 24 September 2001[34]

The United States has attempted to curb the funding capabilities of Al Qaeda and other terrorist organizations by passing strict money-laundering laws, ensuring tighter regulation of less structured transactions and by giving closer scrutiny to the financial network that Al Qaeda uses to fund operations. Executive Order 13224, the International Emergency Economic Powers Act (IEEPA), and the USA PATRIOT of 2001 (the Patriot Act) have all addressed the issue of terrorist financing. Although results have been significant on U.S. soil, and to a certain extent, European soil, these American regulations have had limited success in constraining Al Qaeda's international network. If the goal was to prevent Al Qaeda financing from entering the U.S. capital markets, then many of the regulations might be considered successful and appropriate. But, as President Bush said on his passage of Executive Order 13224, the war on terrorist financing must "starve" the terrorists and "route them out of their safe hiding places." In this area of regulation, the war on terrorist financing may only achieve success in blocking funds in the United States.

Although U.S. regulations have frozen terrorist assets in U.S. jurisdiction, these regulations will have limited success outside of the U.S. financial system. Eighteen months after the war on terrorist financing was announced,[35] its success must be judged at two levels: blocking Al Qaeda funds in U.S. jurisdictions and blocking Al Qaeda funds in non-U.S. jurisdictions. By 10 June 2002, $112 million had been seized from all terrorist organizations (including Al Qaeda), $34.3 million blocked domestically, and $77.8 million internationally.[36] Unfortunately, the specific magnitude of this action on Al Qaeda is impossible to judge without knowing how much of the funds specified were Al Qaeda's and how big Al Qaeda's financial network was originally.

Not withstanding Executive Order 13224, the IEEPA, improvements in the Financial Crimes Enforcement Network (FinCEN), and new attention to anti-money laundering laws, the UN member nations and some foreign bodies believe that the overall war on Al Qaeda financing has waned in its second year. In a report of the Monitoring Group on Al Qaeda, the United Nations suggested that only $10 million in funds has been blocked since the original $112 million, and that Al Qaeda still raises over $46 million a year from financiers in North Africa, the Middle East, Europe, and Asia.[37] The report also suggests that these funds are often transferred from accounts in developed markets, but once Al Qaeda receives funds it often converts the assets into untraceable gold, precious metals, and gems.

American regulatory action against Al Qaeda finances is effective within the financial system that the government controls. When President Bush signed Executive Order 12334, and invoked the IEEPA, funds in U.S. banks that were linked with terrorist groups or activities were frozen and people under U.S. jurisdiction were prevented from doing business with terrorist organizations and individuals.

The Patriot Act and the National Money Laundering Strategies have realigned the administrative focus on tighter money-laundering reporting requirements. The 2002 National Money Laundering Strategy in particular made "effectiveness of efforts to combat terrorist financing" and "dismantling terrorist financial networks" its top two goals.[38] These actions are a direct turnaround in policy as of the attacks of 9/11. Before the attacks, Treasury Secretary Paul O'Neill and the Bush Administration opposed any and all new upgrades to money-laundering legislation.[39]

The Financial Crimes Enforcement Network (FinCEN) is one of the most practical groups for fighting terrorist financing, especially when the funds come from "clean" sources and are transacted through "non-traditional" systems.[40] FinCEN and banking agencies have put some regulatory pressure on the business community to report possible terrorist financing activities, in the form of Suspicious Activity Reports (SARs). Unfortunately, SARs have a $5,000 threshold, and Al Qaeda can easily transfer smaller sums of money to avoid suspicion, as they did to discretely fund the 9/11 cell.

Although domestic legislation has improved U.S. ability to fight terrorist financing on U.S. soil, organizational barriers have limited the government's success. Tracking terrorist finances is a joint effort between the CIA, FBI, Treasury Department, Justice

Department, and elements of the Department of Homeland Security. Most of the asset freezing is done by the Justice Department and the Treasury Department, and yet the Foreign Terrorist Asset Tracking Center, intended to be the lead organization on terrorist financing is housed within the CIA, which has limited overt diplomatic powers. Although the CIA's involvement is important in tracking foreign assets and catching terrorists, the war of terrorist financing requires diplomatic and legal actions that domestic law enforcement and international diplomatic efforts must coordinate. Unfortunately, Treasury is prevented from taking the lead on terrorist financing, even though it must enforce such regulations. This could cause timing problems if Treasury were unable to quickly shut down terrorist bank accounts in U.S. banks.

The U.S. government should be hesitant to apply strenuous regulations to global capital markets, such as New York, because the regulations themselves may hurt the liquid nature of its international transactions. However, freezing U.S.-based bank accounts is one action the Treasury can take without adverse effects on capital markets, although freezing Middle East bank accounts may lead to a significant decrease in Middle Eastern investment accounts in U.S.-controlled banks. Controlling foreign import and export financial flows will also significantly hurt global capital markets in developing countries. More generally, free market principles are often not compatible with the regulatory mechanisms that are intended to protect them from terrorist abuse.

Central bank control of foreign transactions is generally not a favorable long-term economic condition for developing countries. However, such countries also have loosely regulated banking systems that are ideal for Al Qaeda. An appropriate solution requires international private industry participation. Large international companies, especially those involved in developing markets, rely on access to global capital markets. These companies, typically of American or European origin, are often important to the developing economic prosperity. A war on terrorist financing and improvements in developing market banking regulation must put these new companies in a leadership role. Given their U.S. or EU origins, large international companies are often subject to their own country's financial jurisdiction. Therefore, stringent accounting regulations may transcend to developing markets through international investment, rather than local government enforcement. This transfer of regulatory ideals may enable developing markets to continue to grow legitimately rather than turning into financial havens for terrorists. However, the onus of such regulatory change is on the international companies, whose ethical standards are often called into question in the international arena.

Global markets and foreign financial systems are simply not built for scrupulous regulations that can catch terrorist financing. Therefore, shutting down links in Al Qaeda's financial web, outside of developed financial markets like the United States, will be very challenging. Even other developed markets like Europe either suffer from limited financial institutional capabilities (supported by the low volume of Suspicious Activity Reports[41]) or legal systems with "stringent evidentiary standards" to block terrorist assets.[42] Regardless of the problem, international markets do not operate in the same way that the American formal financial system operates. As a result, U.S.-based terrorist financing initiatives will not apply effectively when enforced in other countries. Moreover, limiting liquidity between international capital markets will only increase the cost of capital in such markets, causing economic losses and general discontent for upstanding global investors.

Within the current actions on its war on terrorist financing, the United States has limited regulatory power to impact Al Qaeda's financial network outside of the United States.

Even if increasing regulatory constraints from Executive Order 13224, IEEPA, and the Patriot Act create a more vigil environment within U.S. jurisdictions, the United States faces an uphill battle in enforcing regulatory actions in foreign markets. The formal financial system has not benefited in the past from regulatory controls and is unlikely to withstand long periods of slower international transfers. Foreign banking and financial systems are not equipped to build the regulatory environments that are required to fight an effective war on terrorist financing. And, even if regulatory actions were somewhat effective against terrorist transactions domestically and internationally, Al Qaeda has access to a well-established, global, unregulated hawala system. This system is strongly networked with hawaladars in the United States and Europe as well as in the failing states of the developing world, where Al Qaeda recruits, trains, and builds capabilities.

Current U.S. financial regulations used to target terrorist financing are incompatible with the international financial system and foreign banking systems. Unfortunately, even if international systems could follow the U.S. lead and develop self-regulating capabilities that were agreeable across nations, Al Qaeda could still easily transfer funds through the global Islamic banking network and correspondent banks or the unregulated hawala system.

Recommendations for Diplomatic Action in the War on Terrorist Financing

> We will direct every resource at our command to win the war against terrorists, every means of diplomacy, every tool of intelligence, every instrument of law enforcement, every financial influence.
>
> —President George W. Bush, 24 September 2001

The United States has, to date, failed to strike the heart of Al Qaeda's financial structure: its charities and financier network in the Middle East. Not only has the United States failed to use every diplomatic tool, but it has also failed to use every financial and economic tool at its disposal. Although U.S. efforts domestically to track down and freeze Al Qaeda finances have had some success with the use of the Patriot Act, Executive Order 13224, and the IEEPA, the United States is not using all of the tools at its disposal to eliminate Al Qaeda's international financial base. First, it seems that the Bush administration is hesitant to take further diplomatic and regulatory action in the international community. U.S. work with international bodies such as the Financial Action Task Force (FATF) and the United Nations Counter-Terrorism Committee has not gone far enough. Second, the U.S. has not used all of its tools to impose change in unregulated offshore markets and underregulated markets that are known for terrorist financing. Third, and most important, the United States has begun to lose the diplomatic battle to fight financial networks in the Middle East. More specifically, the United States must put significant diplomatic and economic pressure on Saudi Arabia to stem charity flows to Al Qaeda, the single largest source of Al Qaeda funding.[43]

Working with the International Community

The United States must work closely with international bodies that are able to bridge the differences in financial structures between the United States and foreign allies. An independent task force of the Council on Foreign Relations recommended that the United

States create a new international organization dedicated solely to curbing terrorist financing. Their rationale was that such an organization would "drive other countries—whose efforts are woefully inadequate—to greater effectiveness and cooperation."[44] Unfortunately, the United States has begun to lose international allies recently over its policies in Iraq, and gaining credibility and support for a U.S.-led organization could be very difficult. An alternative to this suggestion is the empowerment of the existing FATF, an international body representing 29 governments, established by the G-7 in 1989. The FATF published a report in April 2002 to help financial institutions in detecting terrorist financing.[45] The FATF was also instrumental in "naming and shaming" international money-laundering havens, publishing best practices for regulating charities and suggestions to "bring the hawala system out from the shadows."[46] Given these recent actions and leadership role on key terrorist financing issues, the United States must leverage the international success of the FATF and push them toward an implementation approach of their guidelines. However, the FATF has until now remained a standards body, with limited enforcement power and resources. The organization should change to certify international financial regulators that can be assigned to international banking communities.

Al Qaeda benefits from its ability to wait out political pressures in the international community. In the war on terrorism financing, the gap in European and U.S. relations is widening at the same time as the United States and the United Nations disagree on the effectiveness of the war on terrorist financing. The difference in financial systems is not the only barrier in U.S.-EU relations. As a report by the Watson Institute at Brown University suggests, the EU is significantly ill-equipped to detect and track terrorist transactions. The report states that whereas the U.S. Treasury Office of Foreign Assets Control (OFAC) has more than 100 staff "working full time on implementation of financial sanctions, the Bank of England had a staff of about seven, the French Ministry of Finance has two people working part-time, the German Bundesbank had one, and the European Commission in Brussels had only one person and a half-time assistant."[47] At the same time, a recent report by the United Nations Counter-Terrorism Committee suggested that the war on terrorist financing has had limited results. Rather than collaborate with the United Nations on such measurements, the United States has failed to provide complete information on suspected Al Qaeda members.[48] In summary, the United States must look to the international community and its allies for more support and in return must share intelligence and resources to track Al Qaeda finances and operatives.

Using All of the Financial Tools in the Toolbox

We put the world's financial institutions on notice: if you do business with terrorists, if you support them or sponsor them, you will not do business with the United States of America.[49]

—President George W. Bush

Under the "special measures" section of the Patriot Act, and sections of the IEEPA, the United States has the ability to cut off foreign countries from U.S. capital markets. This tool is currently being used in a threatening way to force a number of countries to improve their regulatory environment. The "special measures" section has also been evoked by the Secretary of the Treasury against Nauru and until recently Ukraine to cut off their access to American capital markets. Unfortunately, neither of these countries is a source of terrorist finances, although certainly their money-laundering credentials are extensive.[50] Of the current list of countries under scrutiny by the Treasury's Foreign Asset Control Office,[51] certain key Middle East countries are missing, including Egypt, the United Arab Emirates, and Saudi Arabia, whereas poorer states such as Iran and Libya are listed.

According to Lee Wolosky, Chairman of the National Commission on Terrorist Attacks Upon the United States, "Al Qaeda has been particularly attracted to operating in under-regulated jurisdictions, places with limited bank supervision, no anti-money laundering laws, ineffective enforcement institutions, and a culture of no-questions-asked bank secrecy."[52] While foreign investors have a number of choices outside of U.S. capital markets, invoking the "special measures" provision against offshore, unregulated markets in the Cayman Islands and other financial havens would send a clear sign to financial markets on the legitimacy of such offshore markets. In order to push the international community to regulate itself, the United States must deny certain countries and territories access to its capital markets. To flush Al Qaeda funds out of these underregulated markets, the United States must use all of the tools at its disposal, specifically listing countries that are not implementing appropriate levels of terrorist financing regulations.

Saudi Arabian Charities

The diplomatic relationship between the Saudi Royal Family and the U.S. administration has been historically strong, although Islamic extremism in Saudi Arabia and popular anti-American sentiment jeopardizes the strength of the Saudi Royal Family's regime. As the wealthiest state in the Middle East, the home of Osama bin Laden, his Golden Chain, and most of his prominent charities, Saudi Arabia is the source of Al Qaeda's funding that must be addressed directly and continuously.

"Charitable and humanitarian organizations have long been a preferred venue for terrorist financing, with or without the knowledge of the organizations or their donors."[53] Al Qaeda is no exception to this rule. Since 9/11, U.S. and allied authorities have discovered a number of charities that were financing Al Qaeda's operations. However, with the exception of U.S.-based charities, the United States has been powerless within its own right to shut down many of these charities in territories outside of U.S. and NATO command and has had to rely on international cooperation. If the United States is going to have a significant impact on the financial network of Al Qaeda, it must direct efforts at the source of Al Qaeda's finances—Islamic charities in Saudi Arabia. This requires consistent and devoted diplomatic efforts with Saudi Arabia to include FATF inspectors and set up internationally monitored Financial Intelligence Units (FIUs) through the Egmont Group.

Al Qaeda's charity structure is critical to its long-term funding needs. In the Middle East, zakat requires all Muslims to give 2.5% of their income to charitable organizations. Without regulation, Muslims can justify giving such alms to any charitable organizations. The Saudi government recently passed new regulations governing private fundraising and is now encouraging that funds be donated only through established groups operating under the direct patronage of the royal family. Unfortunately, some of these approved groups feature prominently on U.S. terrorist lists.[54] And even if the Saudis shut down these approved groups, "encouraging" Saudis to use established groups is not incentive enough for those that oppose the Saudi Royal Family and the United States. While it is unlikely the Muslims will accept the regulating of zakat without significant public resistance, the Saudi regime must regulate the charity structure itself, while ensuring that innocent Saudis are still encouraged to fulfill their religious duty. New legislation in August 2003 increased penalties for terror financing to up to 15 years in jail and significant fines.[55] However, these penalties are unlikely stringent enough for the Saudi Arabian Monetary Agency to enforce.

The Saudi Royal Family must also seek out those Saudis that are intentionally funding Al Qaeda with law enforcement efforts and a FIU. Unfortunately, "one Saudi official stated that a Saudi organization created to crack down on charities that fund terrorism has been ineffective because its personnel do not want to uncover high-ranking Saudis actively financing such charities."[56] In this case, executive leadership and support is required on both sides of the U.S.-Saudi relationship. If high-ranking Saudis are connected to charities that fund Al Qaeda, the United States must push to have these charities closed and the high-ranking Saudis removed from power and prosecuted. Regardless of its relationship with Saudi Arabia, the United States must also freeze the assets of charities and, when possible, expose guilty Saudi leadership. Although uncovering highlevel scandals within the Saudi government may be somewhat destabilizing in the short term, it is a better long-run alternative than continuing to fund a terrorist organization that is against both the United States and Saudi Arabia.

The United States has known for some time about the Saudi charities that fund and support Al Qaeda. In 1998, Mercy International Relief Organization smuggled weapons into Kenya from Somalia for Al Qaeda,[57] and recent discoveries have shown that Benevolence International Foundation raised funds in America for support of Al Qaeda operatives in Bosnia.[58] Regardless of whether a Saudi charity is smuggling weapons or smuggling money, the Saudi government, with the strong support and enforcement of U.S. diplomatic action must shut these charities down. This is not an action that has been successful under current U.S.-Saudi diplomatic relations. Regardless of close historic ties between the United States and Saudi Arabia, the United States must address Saudi charities, with or without Saudi government support. In the absence of rigid Saudi support, the United States may take a number of financial actions. Such actions may include stringent actions such as adding Saudi Arabia to the list of IEEPA culprits or less stringent action such as limiting foreign direct investment into Saudi Arabia. While the later policy may create dissent in the U.S. business community, it will also force U.S. businesses to put pressure on the Saudi regime.

The United States and Saudi Arabia share many interests in the war against terrorism. President Bush must abide by his words on 7 November 2001: "if you do business with terrorists, if you support them or sponsor them, you will not do business with the United States of America." The United States must use all its diplomatic and economic tools to address the largest source of Al Qaeda's fundraising: charities and financiers in Saudi Arabia.

U.S. diplomacy cannot be underrated in the war on terrorist financing. Al Qaeda's financial pockets are deep outside of the United States, and therefore, the United States must take decisive action with allies in Europe and the Middle East to stop funding to Al Qaeda. In addition, the United States must diplomatically provide options to help countries regulate their financial systems and defend them against Al Qaeda abuses. In situations where countries are unwilling to take decisive and immediate action, at the strategic and tactical level, the United States must leverage economic tools to persuade foreign countries to comply.

Conclusion and Suggestions for Further Research

The war on terrorist financing may be purging terrorist funds from U.S. and European bank accounts, but it is not attacking the source of Al Qaeda's financial network. Al Qaeda's flexibility and financial doctrine make cutting of funds very difficult. This difficulty is compounded by the inability of U.S. regulations to have a significant effect outside of U.S. markets. Therefore, the United States must build more aggressive international coalitions and use all of its regulatory tools to stem the flow of financing to Al Qaeda. This starts with two actions: empowering and backing the FATF to impose terrorist financing regulations internationally and taking decisive action on Saudi Arabia's financial network of charities.

Given the complexity of the international financial system and the numerous foreign banking systems that connect to it, the United States must support an international organization in the global war on terrorist financing. This organization must be responsible for oversight of illegal international transactions, enforcing a progressive schedule of banking oversight in developing countries (working with organizations like the IMF and OECD) and exposing illegal terrorist financial havens around the world. Such an organization requires the full support and financial backing of the U.S. coalition on the war on terrorism.

Unfortunately, taking the war on terrorist financing to Saudi Arabia poses a significant change in U.S. foreign policy. Saudi Arabia's inability to control the financial flows to terrorist groups poses a problem to U.S. national security that must be directly addressed. While U.S. regulators in the Saudi banking system will not be well received, the United States must nonetheless require the Saudi government to invite international banking inspectors in to regulate their financial systems. It is not enough for the Saudi government to request that Muslims give zakat through government charities, it must also regulate and oversee the charity structure.

Although charity oversight will certainly cut off many sources of Al Qaeda's financing, there will always be financiers who are willing to fund Al Qaeda in cash. Whereas tighter regulation and banking oversight will fix structural problems, no regulations will prevent the basic smuggling of cash and the existence of financiers sympathetic to Al Qaeda's cause. Therefore, the United States must continue to support the fighting of financial networks as part of the larger war on terrorism with military, political, and social capabilities.

Terrorist financial sources have evolved significantly from the days of state-based terrorist financing. In this relatively new field of research, Al Qaeda represents just one example of how non-state actors fund global operations. As such, there are a number of further research topics on fighting terrorist financing and fighting Al Qaeda's network structure. The United States has only started to uncover the network of financiers behind Al Qaeda and other international terrorist organizations such as Hezbollah, a topic that will grow as more evidence is uncovered. While terrorist financing continues to evolve, so does the international financial system, as regulations change and markets increase their level of integration. Limited research has looked at how the international financial systems are inefficient in their tracking of terrorist financing. In addition, balancing the development of economic prosperity with preventing terrorist abuses of the system is a topic that development and security organizations must continue to study. Looking in particular at Al Qaeda, further research should look at preemptive tools to identify economically strong non-state actors that threaten U.S. national security. While there were many signs of the attacks on 9/11, in hindsight, the financial trail of Al Qaeda was one indication of the nature of their threat on U.S. soil that might have been exposed yet failed to translate into financial regulation against the channels that funded the World Trade Center attack in 1993.

The war on Al Qaeda's financial network is certainly not over. Al Qaeda is able to leverage a number of financial systems to hide funds from U.S. and allied governments as well as leverage an underregulated base of Islamic charities for funding. A decisive victory in the war on terrorist financing requires a more aggressive U.S. foreign policy on issues of finance. While U.S. political and military policy has directly targeted threats to national security, the United States has not adequately addressed the financial networks that support international terrorist groups like Al Qaeda.

Notes

1. Congress, Senate, Committee on Banking, Housing, and Urban Affairs, Subcommitee on International Trade and Finance, *Hawala and Underground Terrorist Financing Mechanisms: Hearing before the Subcommittee on International Trade and Finance.* 107th Congress., 1st sess., 14 November 2001.
2. Rohan Gunartna, *Inside Al Qaeda: Global Network of Terror* (New York: Columbia University Press, 2002), p. 54.
3. R. T. Naylor, *Wages of Crime: Black Markets, Illegal Finance, and the Underworld Economy* (Ithaca: Cornell University Press, 2002), p. 288.
4. Financial Action Task Force on Money Laundering, "Guidance for Financial Institutions in Detecting Terrorist Financing," April 2002; available at (http://www.fatf-gafi.org/TerFinance_en.htm).
5. Gunaratna, *Inside Al Qaeda,* 57.
6. Ibid., p. 61.
7. Susan Schmidt and Douglas Farah, "Al Qaeda's New Leaders; Six Militants Emerge from Ranks to Fill Void," *The Washington Post,* 29 October 2002, p. A01.
8. "Government's Evidentiary Proffer Supporting the Admissibility of Co-Conspirator Statements," *United States of America v. Ennam Arnaout.* United States District Court Northern District of Illinois, Eastern Division. Case # 02 CR 892. 31 January 2003.
9. "Declaration of Jihad Against the Country's Tyrants, Military Series," recovered by Manchester Police from home of Nazihal Wadih Raghie, 10 May 2000, p. 66. www.usdoj.gov/ag/trainingmanuel.htm.
10. Ibid., p. 22
11. Mark Hubard, "Bankrolling bin Laden," *The Financial Times,* 20 November 2001, p. 10.
12. Gunaratna, *Inside Al Qaeda,* 64.
13. Ibid., p. 65.
14. Douglas Farah, "Report Says Africans Harbored Al Qaeda; Terror Assets Hidden in Gem-Buying Spree," *The Washington Post,* 29 December 2002, p. A01.
15. Judith Miller and Jeff Gerth, "Trade in Honey is Said to Provide Money and Cover for Bin Laden," *The New York Times,* 11 October 2001, p. A01.
16. Council on Foreign Relations, "Terrorism Q&A," available at (http://www.terrorismanswers.com/ responses/money.htm).
17. Gunaratna, *Inside Al Qaeda,* 104.
18. "Government's Evidentiary Proffer Supporting the Admissibility of Co-Conspirator Statements," p. 30.

19. U.S. Congress. House. Committee on Financial Services, Subcommittee on Oversight and Investigations, *Progress since 9/11: The Effectiveness of U.S. Anti-Terrorist Financing Efforts,* 108th Cong. 1st sess., 11 March 2003.

20. Office of Public Affairs, United States Treasury Department, "Treasury Department Statement on the Designation of Wa'el Hamza Julidan." 6 September 2002. Document #PO-3397.

21. "Government's Evidentiary Proffer Supporting the Admissibility of Co-Conspirator Statements," pp. 65–74.

22. Congress. Senate. Committee on Banking, Housing, and Urban Affairs, Subcommittee on International Trade and Finance, *Hawala and Underground Terrorist Financing Mechanisms: Hearing before the Subcommittee on International Trade and Finance.* 107th Cong., 1st sess., 14 November 2001.

23. U.S. General Accounting Office, *Terrorist Financing: U.S. Agencies Should Systematically Assess Terrorists' Use of Alternative Financing Mechanisms,* United States General Accounting Office, November 2003, GAO-04-163, p. 19.

24. Ibrahim Warde, *Islamic Finance in the Global Economy* (Edinburgh: Edinburgh University Press, 2000), p. 144.

25. Reputable Islamic banks typically are part of the International Association of Islamic Banks (IAIB)

26. Warde, *Islamic Finance in the Global Economy,* p. 227.

27. Ibid., p. 227.

28. Loretta Napoleoni, *Modern Jihad: Tracing the Dollars behind the Terror Networks* (Sterling, VA: Pluto Press, 2003), p. 126.

29. Warde, *Islamic Finance in the Global Economy,* p. 227.

30. Napoleoni, *Modern Jihad,* p. 125

31. Hawala is also translated as "trust," but according to Ibrahim Warde, an Islamic banking scholar, the word actually means "transfer" in Arabic.

32. U.S. General Accounting Office, *Terrorist Financing,* p. 18.

33. National Money Laundering Strategy, July 2002, p. 21.

34. Fact Sheet on Terrorist Financing Executive Order, 24 September 2001, available at ⟨http://www.whitehouse.gov/news/releases/2001/09/print/20010924-2.htm⟩.

35. President George W. Bush announced the war on terrorist financing with the passage of Executive Order 13224 on 24 September 2001.

36. National Money Laundering Strategy, July 2002, p. 18.

37. Colum Lynch, "War on Al Qaeda Funds Stalled; Network 'Fit and Well,' Ready to Strike, Draft of U.N. Report Says," *The Washington Post,* 29 August 2002, p. A01.

38. National Money Laundering Strategy, July 2002, p. iii.

39. Ibrahim Warde, "The War on Terrorist Financing," Lecture at the Fletcher School of Law and Diplomacy, Tufts University, 7 April 2003.

40. In the National Money Laundering Strategy, The Department of Treasury and Department of Justice define "Non-traditional" systems as a family of monetary remittance systems that provide for the transfer of value outside of the regulated financial industry. National Money Laundering Strategy, July 2002, p. 21.

41. Maurice R. Greenberg (Chair), "Terrorist Financing: Report of an Independent Task Force Sponsored by the Council on Foreign Relations," *Council on Foreign Relations,* New York, October 2002, p. 21.

42. Ibid.

43. U.S. Congress. House. Committee on Financial Services, Subcommittee on Oversight and Investigations, *Progress since 9/11.*

44. Greenberg, "Terrorist Financing," p. 5.

45. Financial Action Task Force on Money Laundering, "Guidance for Financial Institutions in Detecting Terrorist Financing," April 2002; available at ⟨http://www.fatf-gafi.org/TerFinance_en.htm⟩.

46. Lee Wolosky, *Public Hearing on the National Commission on Terrorist Attacks Upon the United States,* 1 April 2003 available at (http://www.9-11commission.gov/hearings/hearing1/witness_wolosky.htm).
47. Greenberg, "Terrorist Financing," p. 22.
48. Lynch, "War on Al Qaeda Funds Stalled," p. A01.
49. Remarks of President George W. Bush, 7 November 2001.
50. Wolosky, *Public Hearing on the National Commission on Terrorist Attacks Upon the United States.*
51. A list of countries currently under scrutiny can be found at (http://www.ustreas.gov/offices/enforcement/ ofac/sanctions/index.htm).
52. Wolosky, *Public Hearing on the National Commission on Terrorist Attacks Upon the United States.*
53. Matthew Levitt, *The Network of Terrorist Financing,* Washington Institute, 15 August 2002, available at (http://www.washingtoninstitute.org/media/levitt/levitt080102.htm).
54. Ibid.
55. Royal Embassy of Saudi Arabia, *Initiatives and Actions Taken by the Kingdom of Saudi Arabia in the War on Terrorism,* Royal Embassy of Saudi Arabia, Washington, DC, September 2003, available at (http://www.saudiembassy.net), p. 9.
56. Levitt, *The Network of Terrorist Financing.*
57. Levitt, *The Network of Terrorist Financing.*
58. "Government's Evidentiary Proffer Supporting the Admissibility of Co-Conspirator Statements," pp. 65–74.

Kelly Hicks and Roseann McSorley

Global Terrorism and the Private Sector

The Impact of 9/11 on Security Awareness and Operations in Financial Institutions

Since the terrorist attacks on September 11, 2001, many changes have occurred in the structure and composition of security departments in the world's largest financial institutions. The 9/11 attacks on the World Trade Center (WTC) showed how ill-prepared the financial sector was for an event as massive and shocking as bringing down skyscrapers full of thousands of people—and attacking the very nerve center of the U.S. military. The fact that it was accomplished by a relatively small group with a modest budget, seemingly right under the noses of the U.S. government's leading intelligence agencies, is significant. While the U.S. government began to deal with the lessons of 9/11 (among them, poor intelligence sharing and lack of interoperability between government agencies), the finance industry set about strengthening its own security posture. The points that were clearest to industry leaders were clear: safeguard your people, refine your ability to communicate efficiently in a catastrophic situation, and be able to continue and resume your operations in the aftermath.

Not only have internal mechanisms been set up for enhanced communications and greater staff awareness, but also professional working groups called "Public Private Partnerships" have been launched in major global cities such as Hong Kong, London, and New York. This combination of internal and external security activities has strengthened the ability of financial institutions to support local law enforcement in ways that enable the latter to commit more of their precious resources toward countering terrorist activities, rather than ensuring the safety of people on a large scale (as was the focus of the authorities in the pre–9/11 days). This paper presents a road map for strengthening the intelligence and security information-sharing relationship between the public and private sectors.[1] It focuses on specific building blocks that comprise a robust security posture for a typical financial firm. In the six years since 9/11, recognizable progress has been made in the following general areas, which the industry considers to be the essential core elements of a program that will strengthen security and mitigate risk:

- communications
- awareness training
- crisis management
- intelligence

- physical security countermeasures
- development of public-private partnerships between local financial institutions and government, province, and local level anti-terrorism authorities

1. Communications

For financial firms, poor communications between company leaders and employees is the most widely acknowledged shortcoming of the crisis management response to the terror attacks of 9/11. Effective and resilient communications are key to strengthening a firm's ability to safeguard their people, processes, information, and physical assets. Being able to rapidly and efficiently convey the firm's intent regarding evacuation, business recovery operations, global liquidity, etc., are the building blocks to preserving a business, as well as assisting law enforcement and public services in focusing their resources and energy toward dealing with a wide area disaster situation. The challenge of effective communications can be divided into two key areas: staff communications (i.e., people safety) and crisis communications (i.e., management command and control for global business continuity).

Staff Communications

The ability to communicate quickly and thoroughly with employees was recognized almost immediately as a crucial capability during the 9/11 attacks. John Thain, formerly of Goldman Sachs and currently chairman of the New York Stock Exchange, recalled the feeling of utter helplessness as the WTC attack unfolded, and he could not get messages out to staff or locate key people. This was a concern that affected more than one CEO or senior manager, and led to a number of considerations on how to deal with this stark vulnerability.

One outcome of the communication challenge following 9/11 was the development of public address systems beyond those already installed in most large office buildings as part of the fire command station. Many financial firms are tenants of multi-tenant office buildings, which are controlled by a property management company who contracts the lobby security and fire command station staff. The property manager and the CEO of a financial firm may have very differing views on the conduct of security and safety during a crisis. Reflecting on the confusing and often incomplete announcements that came over building public announcement (PA) systems during 9/11, firms such as Goldman Sachs and Lehmann Brothers began to consider how companies could create their own means to reach their staff with carefully crafted messages directly from the firm's management (rather than the building management, whose imperatives may conflict with that of the tenant firm). The message itself would ostensibly be crafted based on internal procedures that company had developed for crisis response, which will be discussed later in this section. Having the ability to communicate directly with staff, in single buildings or in a campus arrangement, became an investment decision that some premier financial firms readily made. This alternate system has become an integral part of the crisis response framework in some firms, undergoing regular testing and drilling. According to Thain, the improved communications capability has dramatically increased the comfort level among leadership that they could reach out to employees in an emergency. Among employees, improved communications has enhanced confidence that messages delivered over the PA system would be accurate and designed to enhance their survivability. All of this, of course, is made operational through frequent, focused (i.e. limited scale) drills and exercises that reinforce basic communication, command center and equipment setup, and internal information escalation procedures.

Crisis Communications

All firms that engaged in enhanced communications practices following 9/11 discovered that a structured escalation of information was necessary in all cases, from the most mundane type of incident to the most urgent crisis. This is because, often, a crisis develops as an outgrowth of a seemingly small incident that can worsen if information about the situation is not escalated quickly to decision makers who can deal with it properly. Most firms attempt to address this by forming crisis teams that represent phases or levels of operations. The phases may be called by a different name from firm to firm, due to each one's particular "culture" and experiences, but the general framework is the same across all firms. The phases of an escalation framework generally equate to:

- **First responders**—building security, as well as maintenance workers who monitor building operations functions (power, chilled water, networking) and would likely be the first to see an incident unfolding.

- **Crisis management team**—an interdisciplinary group of mid-level managers that represents the core functions of a firm, such as corporate services, human resources, corporate communications, legal, security, business continuity, technology, and real estate. These functions are aligned similarly but not exactly, depending on each firm's size and needs.

- **Business decision team**—a team formed by the business managers of the firm, who would use the information and advice of the crisis managers to make informed decisions on the handling of the situation as well as potential downstream business recovery operations.

These levels are linked by means of a resilient notification and communications system, which ties the command and control structure together. The escalation of information moves through the levels from first responder to crisis managers to business decision makers, forming the fundamental structure for crisis communications and management followed by most firms. The level of detail and complexity (not to mention expense) in some of these crisis structures is remarkable. Six years after 9/11, the "basic equipment" of the crisis communications systems includes dedicated command centers with satellite phones, laptop ports, television and teleconferencing capabilities, etc. Many firms have networked and drilled this functionality globally and are state of the art. A sample chart that outlines suggested levels of escalation and stakeholders at each level is presented below. This model is an adequate representation of a crisis management hierarchy as well as communications flow.

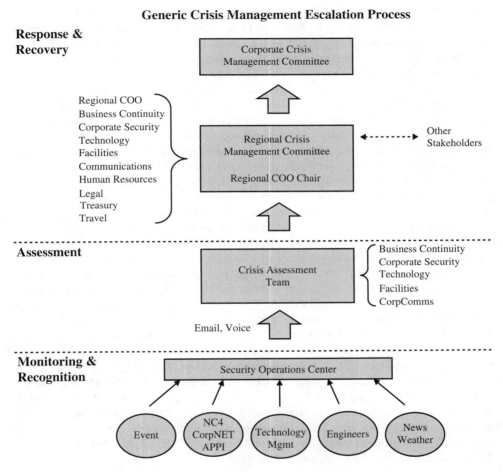

Generic Crisis Management Escalation Process

Figure 1. Example of a corporate crisis escalation mod.

2. Awareness Training

Another important impact of the rise of global terrorism on financial firms is the recognition of the need to train employees to respond quickly and calmly during a crisis situation so that their survival and operational capability is not impinged. Training and awareness is executed in major firms in a number of key areas, including crisis response, life safety, and threat awareness.

When a fire engine shows up in front of a building on Wall Street, without warning and with lights flashing, employees may panic and begin to self-evacuate. This anecdotal observation is a truism in almost any Wall Street firm, even six years after 9/11.[2] People were traumatized from the events they could not control or understand, and the common reaction has been to take matters into their own hands in any potential emergency situation. This frames the main challenge facing security managers—to keep staff safe and focused during an emergency or crisis.

To address this challenge, some firms have targeted mid-level managers from the trade floors and trained them in leadership techniques (specifically, panic reduction and how to be decisive in an uncertain situation). This has generally been successful, at least in instilling confidence and greater awareness among these managers, who form an important link between the leaders of the firm, the security management, and the protective services (police and fire). Without proper leadership, a situation in which thousands of employees are exposed in an instant to a life-threatening situation, could lead to mass casualties. The difference in having some prominent leaders—trained and aware, to step forward and manage information flow, mitigate panic, and maintain order—is a clear advantage to senior financial leaders who are used to managing risk on an order of magnitude.

Another aspect of this challenge that must be addressed is awareness training for the general employee population themselves. This includes any contractors or consultants who occupy a space in the firm, and thereby deserve the same protection as the full-time employees. The most effective way to address their needs is through mass marketing of crisis awareness and response procedures. This typically involves desk drops of information pamphlets with security hotline numbers, "go bag" contents lists, and other important information.[3] Additionally, at least two firms have developed online training modules with interactive test questions and scenarios, designed to imbed and if periodically retested, reinforce the main tenets of the awareness program among all employees.

Firms are also required by law to train their employees monthly in "fire and life safety" procedures. This regulated and routine training augments the awareness training, and if carefully coordinated can include such aspects as "shelter in place" and other innovative procedures that have been developed specifically to address staff safety during chemical or biological, as well as multiple bomb scenarios.[4] All of this must be reinforced and updated to account for technical and legal evolutions.

The effectiveness of this training has been found to be marginal, as most firms do not enforce attendance of training sessions. This is an aspect that involves leadership—if the firm's leaders endorse, attend, and support such programs, employees will naturally do the same. This leadership aspect is one of the pivotal points in staff safety that directly impact survivability, continuity of business operations, and ultimately the robustness of the financial industry. If this link is weakened, all else will fail. Therefore, leadership cannot be stressed enough as the key factor in the success of awareness programs.

3. Crisis Management

Closely tied to communications, crisis management represents the nerve center of effective response to terrorism and natural hazards. In 2003, after the August 14th blackout, one major Wall Street firm, which we will call "Firm X" for confidentiality reasons, committed itself to investing a substantial amount of time, manpower, and resources into a world-class crisis management program. The development of the program is still evolving within several major firms and has had many refinements, but insights into the program's developmental stages will be discussed in the following section.

Firm X has been looked upon by competitors as the market leader in investment banking, if not in financial risk-taking itself. Firm X also has a lesser known but equally important reputation for assuming risk by having less sunk cost invested directly into elaborate contingency measures. This was not to say at all that Wall Street did not recognize the need for effective response to the post 9/11 threats. On the contrary, the presence of strong leadership endorsement and involvement ensured that such a program would be developed. However, Firm X implemented its program with very lean resources, which is a Firm X trait. Firm X is not a large firm as compared to AIG or Chase. Within Firm X, structures such as technology, security, and especially business continuity are small and lack elaborate and redundant processes. The leaders of Firm X felt that streamlined approaches could be taken—teaming up of various interdisciplinary or "cross-divisional" groups were the hallmark of accomplishing almost any complex mission. In the crisis management arena, the approach was to co-lead from the security and business continuity groups, combining the natural planning features of building and staff security and safety with networking resiliency and business recovery planning expertise. To this co-leadership model were joined the other pieces of the structure as mentioned above—HR, communications, legal, etc. This core team became the catalyst for all crisis management policy design, training conceptualization and execution, team formulation, command center management, and management oversight reporting.

The result in eighteen months from mid 2003 to the end of 2004 was remarkable. The effectiveness of the cross-divisional ownership of key pieces of the program was clearly a result of the innovative and resource-conscious approach. At the end of that first period, more than 20 crisis command centers had been established in five global locations, and more than 10,000 staff had been trained in the crisis response and general threat awareness procedures. Additionally, major crisis team exercises had taken place in all major global hubs, and the lessons-learned were being addressed for remediation. A key to the success of the crisis training exercises was keeping them small in scale initially, within one region rather than globally. This would be widened gradually in future exercises, only after the regions were solidly able to set up command centers and establish effective communications without error in two or more exercises. Also important to the program's success was diligent after action review and remediation of the lessons-learned. Tying crisis management teams together in global scale drills—in a "pass the baton" fashion—was the final stage of training and drilling. But it usually took more than six months to execute properly on this scale, once the regional processes were mature enough—and this cannot be rushed; all members of the various crisis teams must be familiarized with the program and their own personal roles before elaborate exercises can be conducted.

Some of the leadership lessons were profound. For example, no one had realized before conducting a few leadership crisis drills how absolutely paramount structured and redundant communications were. Also, few business leaders had realized how fast a certain crisis situation needed to be escalated to the very top of the firm's core leadership in order to conduct survival of the firm-level decisions. There were many other lessons learned that directly contributed to the design of a very efficient program in Firm X. As a common benchmarking and best practices procedure among Wall Street firms, lessons learned by one firm are actively shared and adapted for use by all, to the extent feasible.

4. Intelligence

The terrorist attacks of 9/11 did not directly lead firms to adopt internal intelligence capabilities, as most corporate security entities already had some kind of an intelligence function, a natural feature of their operational capability. However, following 9/11, given the imperative of increased risk in global operating environments where terrorism is a destabilizing factor in local politics, some firms saw the need to establish a separate function within their security department to deal solely with gathering intelligence. This enhanced intelligence capability could be used to support decision making necessary to protect employees, critical facilities, critical data and systems and infrastructure—on a global basis.

Before 9/11 (and in some cases, now), companies largely relied on the background knowledge and experience that their security employees may have brought with them from previous careers. Many of these employees were prior government officials, such as FBI, CIA, or military. In global multinational firms, this background array includes MI-5 and 6 in the UK, Bundesgrenzschutz (BGS) or Bundesnachrichtendienst (BND) in Germany, and Special Duties Unit (SDU) in Hong Kong. None of this represents a change from the norm prior to 9/11 and still is the method of operating in many firms today. However, 9/11 had the effect of compelling firms to be much more broadly focused and proactive in their intelligence gathering efforts. In other words, firms began seeking ways to leverage their employees' past government or military careers in a more meaningful way, to reestablish contacts within their former organizations with the goal of sharing information. This also led to firms actively recruiting individuals based on their intelligence background, to further bolster this concept. The advent of the Overseas Security Advisory Council or OSAC was an important piece in accomplishing the desired end-state of having a greater internal intelligence fusion between private and public sector entities. This type of organization provides a fusion point for the sharing of intelligence information and are highly valued for their role as interface between the myriad government agencies and the private sector.

For financial firms, intelligence shapes security operations and the development of protective countermeasures. Countermeasures range from building protection, anti-fraud and executive protection, to travel advisory and crisis management support. In addition to the OSAC and ISAC [Information Sharing and Analysis Center] type organizations, a firm's intelligence personnel can access many different types of unclassified information that may be available through past professional relationships as well as newly developed ones with standing law enforcement and government agencies. The information shared with financial firms on an informal basis is crucial to a firm's being able to put together a picture of the threats and risks they face in their global operating environments. Many firms still do not carry a very elaborate or even separate intelligence function within their security departments. Rather, they typically outsource their intelligence needs to vendors who can provide a relatively reliable threat management capability for a price. Intelligence vendors normally consist of groups of prior government intelligence officials who provide contract work in information analysis for the private sector and even governments. Their capabilities are normally very good and can include persons with current security clearances on their staff. Vendors provide a necessary analytical function and service to many financial firms, either supplanting the need for a permanent intelligence function, or augmenting an existing one.

The functionality of a separate intelligence department, if given a clear mission and adequate resources to accomplish it, is invaluable. For example, a global intelligence team, comprised of two to three individuals in each major regional hub of a global company, can process a substantial volume of information on a daily basis. Such a setup may include a separate operations function for information collection, an analysis function for processing and creating products, and possibly a distribution or business relations function for the direct provision of intelligence reports to certain business lines that use the security-related reports in their own research. This fusion point is crucial—for example, the degree to which an intelligence function is going to augment the normal research function of equity trading and sales or investment banking must be carefully coordinated so that the intelligence-gathering functions and the end user are clear with each other on the information requirements and the specific deliverables to the business. This is crucial in a relationship between the security department and the business line (just as it is important to be crystal clear within the supported branches within the security department, even though there is not as great a knowledge gap between the intelligence provider and the recipient). Intelligence, properly integrated into a security department's various functions (building protection, executive protection, crisis management), can lead and provide steady, crucial information support in the major areas of a corporate security department.

5. Physical Security Countermeasures

As mentioned in the previous section, intelligence can lead—through detailed threat assessments and timely provision of threat information—the development of security countermeasures and general support to a security department. This is not a reaction or an outgrowth of 9/11 or global terrorism per se. However, the degree to which intelligence is refined as a function and integrated into the security process of a firm reflects the recognition that global operating environments are more dangerous because of the direct impact of terrorism on security and stability in countries. Major areas in which intelligence can support the strengthening of security and countermeasures are as follows:

- **Critical facilities protection**—careful and empirical threat and trends analysis will help security personnel to determine which facilities face the greatest threat, and which measures (stronger access control, additional guards, bollards, etc,) are necessary based on their gap analysis.
- **Crisis management**—intelligence forms the key link in the information flow between the local authorities (with whom firms must have strong relations, even in an environment with a mature public-private partnership) and the leadership of the firm's crisis management team.
- **VIP protection**—a firm's most senior executives require close protection, especially in high or extreme risk operating environments. Intelligence threat assessments, based on the empirical analysis mentioned above, can enhance this protection function's awareness level and the security measures implemented for the VIP during the travel. For example, using a helicopter or an armored vehicle may be a decision resulting from a critical assessment.

- **Support to special corporate events**—intelligence threat assessments are also useful in the establishment of the protective measures for special events held by businesses of the firm in locations that may have an existing threat of "extremist" demonstrations, high crime, or potential terrorist acts. Holding the event in a protected location rather than at a popular Western hotel is an example of mitigating the threat of terrorist targeting or collateral damage.

These are but a few of the ways in which a mature intelligence function may be used to support a large global financial firm. Probably the most important lesson learned in establishing such a function, however, is that it takes time (resources, training) and patience to build a truly effective intelligence team. From the beginning, a nongovernment intelligence team is at a significant disadvantage because it must compete with governments and sophisticated vendors for an informational edge. Furthermore, the intelligence department of a financial firm cannot be seen as gathering classified information, for obvious legal reasons. However, through public-private partnerships, the FBI and Department of Homeland Security can share government intelligence that is deemed appropriate to the strengthening of private security capabilities.

6. Public-Private Partnerships (PPP)

Arguably, information sharing between the private and public sectors is a two-way street. After attending countless seminars, road shows, summits, and symposia on the topic, this author feels that both sides of the partnership are not doing all they can to work together seamlessly and efficiently. Of course there are natural barriers to the relationship that must be overcome, but this will only happen if communications are constant and based on familiarity and trust. Also, each side must have a basic understanding of the information requirements of the other—what are the information needs, and how the information can best be conveyed back and forth is the most important aspect of a PPP. An anecdotal example of a PPP startup meeting bears this out. At a recent security summit conducted in a major city between a financial firm and several government agencies for the purpose of establishing a PPP, both sides seemed to talk past each other on key aspects of information sharing. An FBI representative clearly saw it as a matter of "how the finance industry can help the FBI," and suggested that firms "should feel free to come to us with your information so we can do our jobs better." There was not much else offered by the FBI representative that would stimulate a solid establishment of a PPP relationship based on that level of input. If the situation is that a financial firm does not know what the FBI wants to know, especially a terrorism financing technique or a complex investigation trend, then they will not know what information is important to share.

A New Scotland Yard representative at the summit provided a different viewpoint, which called for more sharing on the part of the authorities. He presented a case example wherein a firm was offered the opportunity to participate in the investigation of the 7/7 bombings in London. Scotland Yard had reached an impasse because they failed to see anything provocative in the financial records of one of the major conspirators, Mohammad Siddique Kahn. The firm participants were given a look at all the evidence gathered on Kahn. They were asked to review the records for abnormalities. The firm immediately saw items of interest to them that the police investigators did not know to focus on. The result was that Kahn was identified and linked to the bombings through very innocuous and low-value banking transactions—very different outcomes than the New Scotland Yard investigators had expected (they were looking for large monetary transactions). Presenting this example helped the New Scotland Yard official to make the important point to the assembled financial representatives, that intelligence sharing under a PPP is a two-way street and a two-way learning experience. This anecdote is illustrative of what a functioning and mutually beneficial relationship between government and private sector should entail.

Back to the point about "actionable intelligence"—firms have finite resources committed to protection of their critical facilities, data, and infrastructure. They need information that is up to date, addresses the nature of the threat, and is not watered-down to the point of being useless. For example, if a suicide bomb threat exists for New York City subway systems, all the private sector needs to know is that they should advise their staff to use alternate means of transportation to and from work during the affected period. The firm's security management can then structure the appropriate communications for their people, and get the job done. A daily report from Homeland Security, called "private-sector threat summary," would be an effective means to convey this information at little or no cost to DHS. This would potentially provide information that can be taken directly from sensitive or classified contexts and provided where the need is greatest. Timeliness is important as well, but not always crucial. For example, an interrogation of a terror suspect that leads to the disclosure of a cell planning an attack using vaporized biological or chemical weapons—if disclosed to them—will prompt financial firms to create internal practices of shutting down a building's HVAC system during an incident. Or, they may install chemical detectors or UV lights on their air intake filters, adding a layer of protection and proactivity to their response capability. In this particular case, it does not matter if the information is timely, just that it can be shared inter-sectorally, without stripping out the most important elements, such as means of delivery of the toxin, and the intended target location.

Taking a look from the other side, many financial firms do not appear committed to security intelligence information gathering, much less sharing with outsiders. Some of this is due to internal policies restricting the release of information a firm considers integral to its competitive edge in a particular region. Or it may simply be that a firm has not committed the time and resources to tie together its internal operational risk (emerging markets-focused) entities with its security intelligence team. These two are often not inherently linked and must be brought together to identify, analyze, and balance collection requirements according to their needs. This is a huge undertaking and until a firm's leadership recognizes and pushes for this process to take place, this important linkage will continue to be a critical gap. Other factors impeding sharing from the finance industry side include restrictions in some countries that preclude the sharing of any personal data, which is a big issue in many firms.

Efficient two-way intelligence sharing between public and private sector will continue to be a challenge. The PPP is an adequate but underdeveloped platform for this sharing. A combination of streamlined sharing from the government side and better organization for information development on the corporate side will help the process to mature and be of value to both sides.

7. Conclusion

Since 9/11, a number of crucial areas have emerged as important to the robustness and resiliency of the financial sector. The extent to which financial firms have implemented functioning countermeasures to their perceived threats is commendable, but much work and refinement still needs to be done. There are areas of unevenness across the industry, mainly due to the size of the firm—especially the nature of its global operations and emerging markets—that limit the degree to which awareness programs and security processes mature within a firm. Variation in leadership decisions regarding the emphasis placed on the mitigation of threats and risks is also a source of the imbalances across the industry, as some firms are less (or more) willing to take risks than others. This aside, there are several key areas that are "must-haves" in terms of a firm's readiness: solid crisis communications and response procedures, efficient intelligence gathering and dissemination processes. Communications and intelligence should be linked to specific requirements based on risk analysis, and provided in a succinct and digestible manner to all clients. Finally, countermeasures that fit the intelligence threat picture, as well as the budget, resources, and risk appetite of the firm are necessary to assure protection of staff, facilities, information, and infrastructure.

The extent to which the efforts of financial institutions to enhance their security awareness and operations has contributed to supporting law enforcement in combating terrorism is still a work in progress. Clearly, the measures taken to strengthen staff awareness and crisis escalation procedures in many major Wall Street firms have helped ensure a much more efficient response to many types of disasters. This shows significant progress from years past, and is recognized by law enforcement and local first responders as more than lip service. But there is still much to be done, especially in the area of intelligence sharing—a push of information—from federal, state, and local entities to the private sector, to identify emerging threats for the private sector, so that the countermeasures implemented by financial firms are aligned to the threat environment and appropriately scaled. Intelligence fusion, frequent threat briefings, tabletop exercises and other means will help provide meaningful ways to bridge the information gaps and join all parties in the information sharing process.

Kelly Hicks specializes in corporate security for a major Wall Street firm. He retired from the US Army in 2000, having served as the Army Attaché to Hong Kong, as well as the China and Northeast Asia military policy advisor to the Army Staff and Army Secretariat. Prior to that, he served as a Special Forces officer in Latin America and Asia, specializing in counterterrorism. Hicks holds a Masters degree in China-US Modern Relations from Harvard University and an undergraduate degree in Anthropology.

Roseann McSorley is the Regional Head of Security, Business Continuity and Crisis Management for a major Wall Street firm. Roseann joined the Central Business Continuity Management (BCM) team in her firm in October 1998 and was responsible for business continuity for the Equities businesses. In September of 1999, she assumed responsibility for the Regional BCM team and helped to lead the efforts to recover her firm's business after the World Trade Center attacks in September, 2001. After 9/11, Roseann has shared her firm's successful recovery experience with many different organizations and regulators, both domestically and globally. She continues to be active in many industry organizations.

Notes

1. The findings and opinions are those of the writer, and do not reflect the position of a particular financial firm.
2. Note: Use of the term *Wall Street* in the context of this paper is meant to keep certain firms unnamed in specific proprietary areas of terrorism response. Also, the term is not all-encompassing of every Wall Street firm, but instead will only apply to most large globally operating firms, whose investments in robust response programs are noted in the community.
3. A go-bag is a kit that a person can use in an emergency when a quick exit is required. A go-bag can include as smoke mask, flashlight, space blanket, and other accessories that can be put together or purchased commercially. Go-bags are distributed to employees to give them some survival items to take with them during an evacuation. They usually include some extra money, keys, and other necessities in case the building is lost.
4. Shelter in place (SIP) is a technique that large office buildings use to help protect employees from the effects of a blast or outside emergency. SIP is managed by announcements from security personnel telling employees to move to the core of the building (near elevator lobby and away from the windows in events where there may be a bomb outside). In a chemical attack situation, employees may be told to remain at their desks and not to attempt to go outside. In all cases, the movement of employees is controlled by announcements from security.

Stacy Reiter Neal*

Cross-Sector Intelligence Partnerships

Is Public-Private Information Sharing a Neglected Counterterrorism Tool?

In the early 21st century, transnational terrorism poses one of the most grave threats to national governments and their international economic interests. As U.S. business has "gone global," so too has terrorism: The multinational corporation has changed the way business transactions are executed across borders, but at the same time, the transnational non-state actor has transformed terrorism—once a phenomenon with a largely local impact—into a global issue. For more than a decade, globalization has been a key driver in the development of both business and terrorism. While multinational corporations have discovered ways to profit from the threat of terrorism—the private security industry generates billions of dollars in annual revenues—they have also increasingly become terrorist targets themselves, accounting for more than 80 percent of attacks against U.S. interests in 2000, and 90 percent in 2001.[1] However, beyond profits and losses, the private sector also has the potential to be involved in a different way: as partners in intelligence gathering and information sharing with U.S. government agencies charged with counterterrorism responsibilities. By leveraging their existing strengths—international presence, local employees, micro-level knowledge of cities and regions, and strong, well-managed organizational structures—multinational corporations are uniquely positioned to gather street-level, open-source intelligence and to observe security trends that can aid counterterrorism professionals and policymakers.

Although some public-private partnerships in intelligence and counterterrorism have been attempted, many existing information-sharing programs deal with the flow of information from the top-down. This chapter will investigate existing efforts and proposals for collaboration between the private sector and government to mutually enhance security and intelligence capabilities. After reviewing these initiatives, the potential issues inhibiting intelligence information sharing between these entities—in both directions—will be discussed. Finally, the chapter will consider prospects for in-depth public-private cooperation and sustained input from businesses to federal counterterrorism intelligence operations.

*The author would like to extend her sincere thanks to Robert Riegle, director of the State & Local Program Office, Office of Intelligence & Analysis, U.S. Department of Homeland Security, for his thoughtful review of this chapter.

Existing Efforts at Public-Private Intelligence Cooperation

Since the terrorist attacks of September 11, 2001, businesses have been forced to confront the realities of transnational terrorism. By targeting the World Trade Center towers in New York—home to powerful U.S. businesses and considered to be a definitive symbol of robust U.S. financial and commercial markets—al Qaeda pointedly took aim at the private sector as an extension of United States economic power. In the context of a climate of increased vigilance triggered by the attacks and the compulsory response, the U.S. private sector began to face the implications of transnational terrorism and respond to overtures for stronger partnerships with federal agencies. However, such relationships had been considered well before the 9/11 attacks.

Pre–9/11 Initiatives

As early as the 1970s and 1980s, American companies operating abroad were concerned about being the targets of terrorist activity, and were aware of "increased cooperation among national and international terrorist organizations in the form of common financial and technical support that [would] encourage additional terrorist attacks against United States MNCs [multinational corporations]."[2] The establishment of the U.S. State Department's Overseas Security Advisory Council (OSAC) in 1985 was an early effort at public-private information sharing. As a Federal Advisory Committee with a U.S. government charter, OSAC "help[s] companies do business abroad and to identify security risks in foreign locales," and membership includes security representatives from the private sector.[3] OSAC is intended to "provide for regular and timely interchange of information between the Private Sector and the State Department concerning developments in the overseas security environment."[4] During the time of OSAC's creation, the often limited and local interests of both companies and terrorist organizations operating during the 1970s and 1980s meant that U.S. government involvement was not broad in scope.[5] However, today, OSAC recognizes the increasing threat of terrorism to U.S. interests abroad, and has broadened its council membership to include "30 private sector and 4 public sector member organizations" drawn from a total constituency base of "more than 3,500 U.S. companies, educational institutions, religious, and non-governmental organizations."[6] The continued strength of the OSAC partnership, its success in various national environments and across diverse sectors, and its efficient dissemination of vital security information from public and private sources have caused some to view the OSAC model as a viable template for future public-private information-sharing initiatives.[7]

The 1993 World Trade Center attack and a subsequent increase in international incidents directed at U.S. companies abroad spurred some "effective intelligence and law enforcement efforts" to prevent international terrorist plots targeting U.S. businesses, most notably the thwarting of the 1995 plan by an al Qaeda affiliate to "destroy a dozen U.S. airline flights on Asia-Pacific routes."[8] Certainly, these incidents and the real possibility of similar events in the future prompted consideration of public-private information sharing to prevent terrorism aimed at both business and other targets. From 1993 to 2000, the growing sense of the terrorist threat to critical infrastructure industries, such as telecommunications, banking, and transportation, prompted a series of government responses, including the 1996 creation of the President's Commission on Critical Infrastructure Protection (PCCIP). This commission identified critical vulnerabilities and appointed lead federal agencies to liaise with certain sectors in developing preparedness plans.[9] The PCCIP and Presidential Decision Directive 63, the product that identified critical infrastructure sectors and partnerships, first raised the issues of willingness by the private sector to cooperate and share proprietary information with the U.S. government—as well as legality and privacy issues that remain unresolved today—and serve as the foundation for present public-private information sharing.[10]

In 1998, the Clinton administration introduced Information Sharing and Analysis Centers (ISACs), which are domestic "private sector organizations (or networks of organizations) . . . [that] disseminate real-time information on threats to critical industries" and which can also serve as coordination clearinghouses in the case of threats to national security.[11] ISACs function as private associations—as in OSAC, the affiliates of ISACs are smaller membership organizations, rather than individual private-sector companies—and lack consistent operating guidelines. The layered ISAC structure, in which individual company input is filtered through associations to the ISAC—essentially an intermediary organization—translates into widely disparate methods of information gathering, sharing, and dissemination, and limits direct federal interaction with private-sector entities. Prior to 9/11, only a few ISACs were created within specialized sectors: financial services, information technology, telecommunications, and electricity.[12] At the time, "the notion of a public-private partnership . . . was fairly new."[13] While ISACs have resulted in some public-private collaboration, early efforts were not as successful as the established OSAC program and did not generate a significant volume of information sharing.[14] In addition, ISAC organization by corporate sector, rather than by region, is problematic. Aside from the difficulty of classifying corporations with diverse interests, sector organization also fosters a narrow approach to potential threats. Since terrorists select targets based on a number of factors, including ease of access, impact, and location, the ISAC model's focus on sectors alone ignores the importance of exchanging relevant information among companies that share common regional interests despite operating in different industries.[15] While ISACs could help to increase threat awareness within sectors, they could arguably be most useful in threat mitigation, which would require coordination across sectors and within geographic areas—much like OSAC.[16]

Thus, while initial efforts were made to develop organizational capacity for public-private collaboration through OSAC, PCCIP, and ISACs, robust and effective public-private sector intelligence or information sharing did not exist prior to 2001. The tragic terrorist attacks of 9/11, however, drastically and irrevocably changed the security context for U.S.-based corporations and the global business community.

Post–9/11 Initiatives

The 9/11 terrorist attacks on U.S. soil illustrated that businesses face terrorist threats not just to individual firms (the focus in the 1970s, 1980s, and early 1990s), but at an industry-wide and regional level and, perhaps most importantly, at a macro-level (the global environment).[17] For some firms, the 9/11 attacks had a direct impact at all three levels, while countless others experienced the secondhand effects of the attacks on the global economy. In particular, the increased presence and assertion of transnational terrorist threats caused the private sector's conception of risk management to change drastically from the pre–9/11 era. The international landscape and the threats contained within it—which had effectively changed overnight—necessitated a "thorough reappraisal of risk assessment methods that must incorporate the disruptive projections of ideological antagonism."[18] Though their direct interests differed, the goals of the private sector and government began to converge around a shared interest in anticipating and thwarting of disruptive and damaging attacks by non-state actors. As government and business developed separate systems for anticipating and addressing these risks, both sectors understood the potential benefits of a more collaborative, even regimented, information-sharing environment. These possibilities led to increased private-sector participation in ISACs and other measures emanating from the new Department of Homeland Security.

Due to the increased push for collaborative security measures following the 9/11 attacks, there was "heightened emphasis by industry to exchange information with government entities" across departments and specialties, especially concerning preparedness efforts.[19] Much of the information-sharing efforts that now exist between the government and private sector, as a result, remain focused on critical infrastructure protection—a natural nexus between business and government concerns. In the post–9/11 environment, new ISACs were created, and by March 2005 the total number had increased to 15, each representing a different "critical sector."

Despite the emergence of additional ISACs, a continuing lack of post–9/11 regulations to "clearly delineate how the ISACs should operate or how the relationship between the ISACs and the federal government should work" resulted in varied ISAC structures—each configuration operating with a different combination of private and public funding.[20] The Energy ISAC required an annual membership of $7,500 in 2002, for which a member "becomes an anonymous part-owner of the site, its data, and its intellectual property,"[21] while the Supply Chain ISAC waives initial sign-up costs and charges only a $500 annual fee and $50 vetting charge upon enrollment, with no ownership benefits for members.[22] Some ISACs offer a tiered fee structure. The Information Technology ISAC has five membership options with decreasing benefits at fee levels of $40,000, $25,000, $10,000, $5,000, and no cost.[23] The Financial Services ISAC offers four membership levels that are associated with varying benefits, ranging from a $10,000 "Premier Membership" that includes credentials, crisis alerts, customized analysis, and access to a "watch desk," down to a free "Basic Participant" level that requires payment per meeting attended.[24] The disparity in funding and structure has resulted in varying "commitment levels" among sector ISACs, which lead to irregular information sharing and a lack of synthesis among sectors to yield information relevant to regional or specific threats. For example, while "nuclear power plant operators have high levels of participation because of regulatory reporting requirements," other sectors participate voluntarily and to a lesser degree due to liability issues.[25] Such uncoordinated efforts across sectors increase the possibility that threat trends or other relevant data will not reach the end users that need it most.

With the creation of the Department of Homeland Security (DHS) in 2002, the federal government attempted to codify its relations with the private sector in the areas of homeland security and counterterrorism. Several specific developments within the DHS have potential to serve as a new basis for collaborative efforts among public and private entities. The now-defunct Information Analysis and Infrastructure Protection (IAIP) Directorate—one of the five original DHS directorates—had a mission "to protect critical infrastructure and to serve as a focal point for synthesizing terrorism-related information."[26] Due to the discrete functions and unique challenges of intelligence and critical infrastructure protection, the intelligence arm of the IAIP Directorate has since been replaced by the Intelligence & Analysis Directorate, with critical infrastructure protection now housed under the National Preparedness Directorate.

The DHS's Homeland Security Information Network makes unclassified but sensitive information available to private-sector executives in critical infrastructure industries.[27] From the other direction, the DHS Private Sector Office was created to provide "a direct line of communication" from the U.S. business community to the federal government, but it "is not intended nor does it act as a conduit for national security sensitive information, either from industry to government or vice versa."[28] Rather, this liaison office "facilitates interaction between DHS and the private sector" and "provides information and education to the private sector regarding the activities of DHS."[29] The transfer of information between the public and private sectors occurs through the DHS State and Local Fusion Centers, which "facilitate sharing information across jurisdictions and function."[30] However, it is important to note that, despite the existence of these information and liaison offices, due to provisions of the Privacy Act of 1974, federal agencies such as the FBI and DHS are greatly limited in "the collection, maintenance, use, and dissemination of personal information" to private entities.[31] Finally, the DHS's Protected Critical Infrastructure Information (PCII) Program encourages "private industry to share its sensitive security-related business information with the Federal government" by making any information submitted through the program protected from public disclosure under the Freedom of Information Act (FOIA) and state and local disclosure laws or use in civil litigation.[32] Companies can upload this sensitive information via an online portal, complete with guidelines and a checklist.[33] However, since the disclosure exemption under PCII has not yet been challenged in court, the program remains little used and essentially untested as a means for private entities to share critical intelligence.[34]

The post–9/11 private ISAC and public DHS entities provide some initial points for intelligence-related interaction between business and government, but much of this interaction is superficial, establishing links while not allowing for the exchange of more in-depth operational intelligence. Therefore, while public-private collaboration has improved since 9/11 due to a recognition of common interests, a willingness to cooperate, and the creation of basic communication channels, the potential for public-private information sharing has not yet been fully tapped.

Potential to Build: The Private Sector's Intelligence Experience and Motivation to Collaborate

Despite the lack of organization and the absence of formal partnerships between the private sector and the government, the private sector already contributes to national security and intelligence efforts in important ways. Businesses provide security products and services, fulfill government contracts, and undertake certain duties that were formerly government domain (such as translation services). These "homeland security products and services" account for "hundreds of billions of dollars."[35] However, the private sector also provides key intelligence data to government in a bottom-up flow of information gathered through interaction with the public on a daily basis. At the most basic level, business are required by the USA PATRIOT Act to allow the government access to records, books, and documents that contain information on employees and customers who might be under suspicion.[36] Further, the U.S. government is able to access "commercial databases for counterterrorism purposes" via several methods, including direct request, monetary purchase, or outright demand.[37] While these information-sharing directives provide useful data, they fail to capitalize on initiative from within the private sector and opportunities to develop enduring partnerships between business and government lasting beyond one-time information exchanges. Also, these single-direction flows of information from the private sector to the public sector, where they are often shared among several agencies, create privacy protection concerns, which will be explored in greater detail in the following section.

Beyond simple proprietary information hand-offs required by new counterterrorism law, "[i]ndustry provides 'intelligence' and information to the public sector about potential terrorist threats."[38] One particularly notable example of this is the initiative a Minnesota-based flight school took in fall 2001 to inform officials about a suspicious student—Zacarias Moussaoui.[39] More recently, an employee in a New Jersey Circuit City store was instrumental in thwarting a plot to attack Fort Dix in January 2006 when he notified authorities that a customer requested suspicious terrorist training footage to be transferred from VHS to DVD.[40] Now, it appears, "[i]n the post–9/11 era, employers more readily notify the government when an employee or customer acts" suspiciously.[41] However, in order for this type of information sharing to succeed, the federal government must facilitate this type of engagement, and the public must find it acceptable for corporations to share customer information with the federal government—a proposition that raises valid concerns for the protection of civil liberties and privacy. The question is whether this increased awareness and potential wealth of ground-level information can be formally translated into a codified information and intelligence-sharing avenue between private firms and counterterrorism officials that benefits the public and private sectors, as well as the public at large.

While collaborative initiatives between government and private sector are in relatively nascent form, the private sector is already well equipped to conduct intelligence gathering and even, to some extent, information analysis. Private businesses have long been involved with independent intelligence gathering since corporations, with operations worth billions of dollars in dozens of countries, must engage in risk management and corporate counterintelligence in order to protect their assets and remain competitive. Companies regularly produce internal risk and vulnerability assessments, and conduct country political risk analysis by analyzing open-source information in order to decide whether to operate in certain foreign emerging markets.[42] In addition, the practice of corporate counterintelligence goes beyond risk assessment, and refers to "all measures taken to discover, assess, and defeat the threats from other corporations, foreign intelligence services, pressure groups, the media, terrorists, extremists, criminals, and others."[43] This type of information gathering is often facilitated by operation in foreign environments, where civil liberties concerns are not as prominent as in a domestic U.S. setting.[44]

Alongside this potential to build collaborative efforts exists a palpable desire on the part of private-sector leaders to provide more information relevant to national security to the federal government. Several studies provide evidence of will and motivation on the part of the private sector but, since no appropriate information-sharing system is in place, this sentiment has yet to be capitalized upon by federal counterterrorism efforts. In a survey of 228 for-profit, privately owned businesses, publicly traded corporations, and nonprofit organizations, a "vast majority—88 percent—have met with a representative from law enforcement, first responders, or homeland security officials,"[45] illustrating a willingness to work collaboratively at some level on national and corporate security issues (if not specifically on intelligence or information sharing). However, with little to no centralized direction from the government regarding the operational intelligence that could easily be gathered by many of these companies, only half of the respondents in the survey indicated that they "regularly ask workers to be alert and report unusual activity that may suggest a terrorist threat," and more than half "do not or probably do not conduct a check of prospective employees and organizations with which they do business for terrorist affiliations."[46] Businesses could easily gather this type of information with the establishment of appropriate internal procedures and if aided by the intelligence community.

Likewise, in a separate study comparing a stratified random sample of 4,000 U.S. companies across nine industry sectors and a sample of 339 security managers at companies belonging to the American Society for Industrial Security (ASIS), information sharing seems even less of a day-to day priority. Only 10 percent of all U.S. companies and 50 percent of ASIS member companies "reported increased contact with law enforcement since 9/11, with almost all the rest indicating no change."[47] Financial, transport, and communication-related companies seemed the most likely to participate in increased contact, while the service industry—a potential source of good day-to-day operational intelligence—were the least likely.[48] In addition, for those companies reporting at least one company contact per year with law enforcement, only 15.5 percent of all companies (66.7 percent of the ASIS member companies) had contact with federal law enforcement.[49] However, of the ASIS member companies that had specific security contacts within law enforcement, 40 percent had terrorism-related contacts and 68 percent had information-sharing contacts.[50] While it is encouraging that ASIS member companies—which are attuned to security and terror issues—state these two areas as major points of collaboration, the lack of prioritization of terrorism and information sharing among the general companies with law enforcement contacts surveyed (under 7 percent and 16 percent, respectively) indicates a lack of awareness of information-sharing initiatives in the private sector as a whole.[51]

The failure to fully capitalize on the private sector's potential to aid government intelligence gathering represents a missed opportunity in national security. The main reason this potential remains untapped is insufficiently organized initiative within the public sector. Organizational direction would make a difference in the participation of private-sector firms—particularly those that prioritize security issues and are engaged in critical infrastructure protection—in intelligence efforts. Basic relationships and a will to cooperate exist in many cases, but could be further fostered with central encouragement. As one study found, corporate CEOs express patriotism and "a sense of duty to the nation," with all "willing to be helpful" and "committed to sharing resources." However, the scope, expectations, and limits of any public-private intelligence collaboration would have to be clearly defined in order for these positive sentiments and important resources to be effectively harnessed for counterterrorism.[52] Thus, despite the existing efforts and the inherent capabilities of the private sector—as well as the obvious will on the part of both the public and private sectors to engage one another in counterterrorism efforts—it appears that "the federal government is not doing nearly enough to harness the capabilities, assets, and goodwill of the private sector to bolster our national state of preparedness."[53] This lack of effective engagement is largely due to difficulties inherent to the information-sharing process, including privacy protection, administrative capacity, control of information flow, and more, which will be discussed in the following section of this chapter.

Difficulties Impeding Public-Private Information Sharing and Intelligence Coordination

Some observers believe that the obstacles blocking effective public-private coordination are insurmountable.[54] The main obstacles to effective intelligence partnerships between the private sector and government include: information security and privacy concerns; the lack of an effective organizational structure to facilitate knowledge exchange; the difficulty in measuring the success of intelligence-sharing in preventing terrorist attacks, and therefore of providing "proof" that investment in intelligence-gathering and information-sharing efforts is needed; and fears about the implications of increased government regulation over the private sector. Each of these areas presents fundamental challenges to the development of a true public-private intelligence partnership that will not be easily overcome, regardless of the potential benefits of cross-sector intelligence cooperation.

Information Security and Privacy: Can Information Safely Flow Both Ways?

The security of shared information is a major concern and a significant obstacle to future public-private intelligence efforts. Since there is no guarantee that information flows will be treated as sensitive, the government and the private sector have found it difficult to establish mutual trust. This suspicion "stems from a lack of history and familiarity in exchanging information between the public and private sectors."[55] The private sector has been reticent to share proprietary information, particularly because information is "the essence of competitive advantage."[56] The misuse of proprietary information in any way may jeopardize future business. Furthermore, existing client confidentiality agreements with customers cannot be easily violated, nor should they from the perspective of the private sector. Revelations of security breaches or other problems at a private firm could ruin the firm's reputation and open it to potential litigation, and the knowledge of additional threats can increase a firm's civil liability exposure.[57] When the private sector is obligated to provide data from commercial databases to the government under the PATRIOT Act, businesses have little control over how that information is used or whether it is adequately protected. This presents an interesting dilemma for the private sector: How should the private sector aid intelligence officials while maintaining data integrity and confidentiality? This question is key to any future collaborative intelligence initiatives between the public and private sectors and is unlikely to be resolved in the near future. In order for the requisite trust to be established between the private sector and the government, privacy and information security systems will have to become better developed.

Legislators have made some efforts to remedy the fears about the misuse or leaking of sensitive information shared by private-sector entities. In September 2001, Senators Robert F. Bennett (R-UT) and Jon Kyl (R-AZ) introduced a bill (S.1456) that was intended to "encourage the secure disclosure and protected exchange of critical infrastructure information."[58] The proposed legislation aimed to create a blanket exemption to the Freedom of Information Act (FOIA) and a "safe harbor provision" for companies that voluntarily disclose critical information "in good faith."[59] The bill was neglected in favor of the passage of a bill introduced in the House of Representatives (H.R.5005), which established the DHS and included provisions for information access and sharing. However, the bill did not include a blanket exemption or protective provisions to the extent of the Bennett-Kyl legislation.[60] While there is now a limited exemption to the FOIA under the previously mentioned PCII program, its protection, having yet to be tested in court, provides inadequate comfort to some executives, who remain "concerned that disclosures will not remain confidential."[61]

Since the "current legal structure does not adequately address" federal use of commercial data, any plausible information-sharing system will have to include "rules that guide government use of information by making decisions more reliable, transparent, and accountable."[62] While government access to data is obviously a vital component of national security strategy, it is also important not to minimize the concerns of the private sector in this dialogue. Unfettered access by government officials may lead to a lack of trust, not only due to insufficient data protection, but also if the information is not reciprocated with intelligence useful for businesses themselves. The private sector will be less willing to cooperate if their contributions to the intelligence not only compromise their business operations, but also go unreciprocated by the government.[63]

Concerns about liability represent a key problem in ensuring information security and privacy. Is the private sector, in agreeing to disclose sensitive information to the government, exempting the government from any future liability concerning leaks of that information? In other words, "who will assure the protection of these data? Who will pay, in the event of a breach in the system?"[64] In addition, knowledge of threat and risk, which corporations may gain through federal cooperation, can also increase private liability to customers and shareholders. These issues affect not only corporate bottom lines, but also the security of businesses against terrorist attacks. Information about the vulnerabilities of the private sector, if accessed by the wrong people, "could be viewed as a road map for terrorists to attack [businesses]."[65] These concerns remain significant barriers to successful public-private information-sharing efforts.[66]

"Unsettled Organizational Landscape"

Is government equipped to handle information inflows from the private sector and to coordinate suitable information outflows? The "unsettled organizational landscape" that currently characterizes federal efforts at private-sector information sharing represents a major obstacle—perhaps the most critical one—to coordinating public-private intelligence partnerships.[67] According to Daniel Prieto, there is no "reliable public partner for the private sector." While ISACs were created to serve as the "primary node for information sharing" between business and federal government, the councils "have struggled to fill that role" for several reasons.[68] Part of the problem is that, as previously mentioned, the privately managed ISACs vary greatly in organization and leadership. Their scope of membership varies from sector to sector, with some ISACs reaching 100 percent of their constituent firms through member associations and others reaching barely 20 percent.[69] The total reach of ISACs extends to "approximately 65 percent of the U.S. private critical infrastructure."[70] The quality and training of staff also varies greatly. Some ISACs are able to access classified data and others only unclassified but sensitive data.[71] Further, in April 2003, an independent ISAC Council was established to coordinate among 11 individual ISACs,[72] creating yet another administrative layer to the public-private coordination puzzle. For these reasons, in devising its own procedures, the DHS has "conspicuously distanced itself from the ISAC model."[73]

Although the DHS "was designated by the Homeland Security Act to play a lead role in facilitating information sharing with the private sector," the department is considered too new to adequately assume this responsibility.[74] In fact, the attendant personnel turnover and transition issues within the newly created DHS have actually "hindered information sharing efforts" over the past four years, both with the private sector and within federal agencies.[75] While the DHS is the sole domestic representative to the Executive Committee of the National Intelligence Council, the department is not the only federal agency to disseminate information to the private sector. As one former executive and security consultant notes of the inter-agency morass, "you might call the FBI and hear one thing, then call the State Department and hear something else. There is, in effect, no quality control."[76] These multiple sources mean there is no central point for information in- and out-flow and a consequent lack of confidence in federal government information systems. In fact, one executive cites "portal fatigue" as a significant damper to sharing efforts.[77] The sheer volume of Web-based information portals, with their attendant passwords, administrative clearances, and often repetitive information, illustrates the lack of centralized information and highlights the frustration of the private sector.[78] As such, in the aforementioned survey of 228 private entities, local law enforcement agencies—rather than the DHS or other federal agencies—were named the "most valuable source of terror threat information," presumably due to their accessibility.[79]

Further, within any organizational structure created to facilitate public-private information-sharing coordination, communication channels need to flow in both directions in order for private-sector intelligence to be provided—something that is not always accomplished within the current federal system. In addition to frustrations caused by the absence of coherent, centralized communication, the occasional submission of government information requests to businesses without a "valid reason for the government to know something" fuels resentment among CEOs. Businesses are generally willing to provide information but want to be able to supply the most focused and helpful information they can[80]—a difficult task when encountering a lack of top-down information, often a by-product of Privacy Act limitations or simply time taken to perform analysis. Regardless of the reasons, the perception among cooperative business leaders that "the federal government is withholding information . . . heightens the reluctance by the private sector to share information with the federal government."[81] There is no value proposition in sharing sensitive information that is not being reciprocated with equally useful and timely information from the government. This may cause private-sector leaders to consider information sharing "another inefficient use of their time."[82]

Many of these organizational issues could be addressed by centralizing private-sector information sharing, perhaps by creating a hub agency that houses sector experts who could gather and analyze information from varied sources and disseminate relevant items to appropriate parties. This hub would serve as a central repository for business-generated intelligence. However, in a system in which "controversy has accompanied the attempts to share information among intelligence agencies," the "next frontier" of sharing between the public and private sectors seems an even more daunting task.[83] Since the DHS remains in a nascent stage of development, and coordination with the private sector does not appear to be at the top of the DHS priority list, it is doubtful that a coherent federal coordination system (both among federal systems and between government and business entities) will emerge anytime soon.

Success Measurement: Will Intelligence Investment by the Private Sector Be "Worth It"?

The success of any counterterrorism initiative is not easily measured. Thwarted attacks may not even register on the radar. Failures in security, evident through tangible consequences, often overshadow the successes of preventive measures. This makes the value proposition of preventive security measures difficult to rationalize in terms of expense, time, or personnel. These issues exist in the public sector, and are no different in the private sector. Consider the following scenario offered by Dean Alexander. A company spends significant amounts of money on counterterrorism measures. No terrorism incident occurs. The question remains whether the "allocation of resources did its job—because there was no terrorist incident—or [whether] it was a waste of money—because no terrorist attack occurred."[84] In the private sector in particular, the potential costs of information sharing or voluntary participation in intelligence gathering for the government will always be questioned. For this reason, success measurement or a "return on investment" in collaborative security will need to be addressed. The tension between providing adequate security for business operations by engaging in a reciprocal information-sharing relationship with the government and allocating non-profit-generating capital to such efforts is a real dilemma in the corporate world. While part of the private sector's motivation to collaborate with federal agencies is altruistic, there is also an implicit expectation that such collaboration will ultimately benefit the corporation and its bottom line.

Regardless of motivations, private-sector investment in intelligence collaborations will be limited by company size and resources, resulting in uneven cooperation across firms or sectors. This uneven participation increases the likelihood that government will engage highly profitable companies or companies within resource-rich industries. In some cases, firms or sectors with few resources but with critical information will inevitably slip through the cracks. On the whole, due to these and other constraints, "overall investment in private sector security initiatives has been modest,"[85] and this trend is likely to extend to information-sharing initiatives. A firmer sense of shared investment and common goals must be fostered within the private sector in order for more intensive intelligence cooperation to take place. Currently, CEOs are "willing to invest time and effort into sharing information with the government," but only "to a point."[86] Possible remedies include increased government funding for intelligence infrastructure development within the private sector or the encouragement of pilot programs within individual companies that could be successfully replicated in other settings with less initial investment of planning time, money, and other valuable resources.

Increased Government Regulation and Oversight: Will the Private Sector Succumb?

Fears about the federalization of private-sector activities—or alternatively, the privatization of federal duties—generate another source of tension for public-private counterterrorism partnerships. This debate has recently focused on the role of private security firms in conducting patrols and details in Iraq. Additionally, increased government regulation of business practices—most heavily felt, perhaps, in the post–9/11 airline industry—creates strain in the private sector (in terms of investment to meet compliance standards or adhere to other regulations). Increased business cooperation with government could, some believe, increase risks for businesses with employees or clients who have broken the law, leading to "future inquiries into business activities."[87]

Insights from the aforementioned National Infrastructure Advisory Council survey of CEOs also clearly illustrate a general reluctance to adhere to increased regulation. While "[a]ll the CEOs interviewed were clearly patriotic and expressed a sense of duty to the nation," they qualified this willingness to help with an indication that "they are reluctant to share information with the government if it means more regulation."[88] However, some argue that increased regulation may "not always [be] in conflict with the best interests of the private sector" and that, in fact, government regulation can "ensure uniformity and enforcement of standards" in terms of security regulations.[89] If additional regulations are to be developed, and the private sector is expected to voluntarily comply, then business and corporate representatives should be involved in the development of these regulations or accountability controls.[90]

Each of these four issues—privacy concerns, lack of organization, incentives for cooperation, and implications of increased regulation—are major issues that must be addressed prior to further public-private intelligence partnership. However, keeping these issues in mind, the following section will attempt to frame recommendations for possible future partnerships.

Prospects for Future Public-Private Intelligence Engagement

Public-private information sharing represents a critical opportunity for gathering useful intelligence that can effectively fight terrorism. For this reason, the federal government should pursue methods to help these partnerships to progress effectively and yield useful results. Given the barriers to collaboration outlined in the previous section, the way forward is not clear. Nevertheless, analysis from various experts, working groups, and private-sector sources indicate that there is significant potential for enhancing collaborative efforts between government and the private sector if the appropriate resources and organizational structures are devoted to them. A concerted effort to "harness" the "patriotism and civic duty" of industry to "improve U.S. security" will entail a new focus on the role of the private sector and a devotion of significant resources to public-private intelligence partnerships.[91]

First, if intelligence partnerships are to become more fully developed, the federal intelligence and homeland security communities need to codify and strengthen the relationship between public and private entities. A reciprocal flow of information is necessary for the private sector to be fully embraced as an intelligence partner. The "tips" must not just flow upward from businesses and corporations, but also from the federal government to identified contacts in the private sector. Increased government sharing of sensitive but unclassified information (and, even classified information when private-sector receptors are cleared to receive it) would assist private businesses in protecting assets, personnel, or other interests and would go a long way in developing a relationship of trust with federal intelligence contacts. However, entrenched institutional attitudes may continue to prevent further cooperation both within the law enforcement and security structure and between public and private entities. Public-private cooperation may face further difficulties when a willingness to partner is "challenged by elements of homeland security that lack experience with such partnerships."[92] As such, if information-sharing relationships between business and government are to be successfully developed, according to Prieto, "[s]haring information must become part of the DNA of the national security, intelligence, and homeland security communities, federal, state and local officials, and the private sector."[93] Thus, the discourse has to move "beyond talking about the need to dramatically improve information sharing with the private sector and hold government officials accountable for actually doing it."[94] Integrating the private sector "into the full government intelligence cycle," from reporting and analysis to dissemination, can also benefit both sides of a true information-sharing partnership.[95] Should the necessary shift in the institutional outlook of government agencies occur, existing studies suggest the private sector would be a willing federal partner.

In addition to shouldering primary responsibility in the coordination and promotion of public-private intelligence partnerships, the national intelligence and homeland security apparatus must also take steps to address the four obstacles outlined in the previous section. Unless properly resolved, the issues of privacy, regulation, organization, and incentives will preclude more in-depth information sharing and intelligence collaboration across sectors. Privacy and information security concerns are not to be minimized, as businesses face legal ramifications for misusing private customer data or a loss in profit when sensitive internal information is made known to industry competitors. Therefore, it will be essential to "clarify laws regarding privacy and insider threats." One possible method of accomplishing this would be the creation of a legal "best practices guide" that would provide CEOs and their government partners with a "clear legal environment in which to operate" and could be issued by a federal agency such as DHS or the FBI.[96] In addition to fostering privacy and security, a sense of shared investment in developing intelligence capabilities could be achieved through the implementation of a matching funding program whereby the federal government matches a percentage of private-sector investment in internal intelligence-gathering or information-sharing apparatuses.

The regulation issue will not likely be settled in the near future, but some degree of federal supervision will undoubtedly be required to monitor and retain control over any information-sharing efforts that span entire industry sectors. To enable increased sharing of threat data from the government to member private-sector firms, the government could require all ISACs to employ or retain personnel with limited security clearances. This would allow for a productive two-way flow of information as well as help to control and monitor flows, keeping sensitive data in the hands of capable people who are cleared and in "need-to-know" positions. Despite concerns among some public-sector officials that private-sector employees cannot be trusted with sensitive threat information, the presence of personnel with security clearances is not new. Under the National Industrial Security Program, established in 1993, thousands of private-sector employees have secured clearances—some at the highest levels—to perform private-sector work related to government business.[97] Since citizens are entrusted with sensitive information on a regular basis, those responsible for information-sharing programs in the private sector should also be granted clearances, allowing some federal regulation of the process.

Organizational capacity for information sharing presents the most critical challenge to any future successes in cross-sector intelligence efforts. The federal government would not be well served by implementing any mandatory information sharing beyond that which is already outlined in the PATRIOT Act. However, developing a voluntary system that engages directly with private-sector entities will take some time. Personal relationships will have to be developed between intelligence community officials and corporate CEOs, a practice that will likely yield the best results if accomplished one-on-one with companies rather than with associations as in the ISAC model.[98] The goal of this more tailored approach to relationships would be to develop government's "[c]apacity to convert information to operational intelligence."[99] This structure presents ample opportunities to address public-private trust issues as well, as it provides a venue through which long-term individual relationships can be built.

Suggestions for future initiatives must also integrate information sharing and intelligence collaboration with other public-private partnerships, which would increase the value of private investment in these measures. There have been numerous successful partnerships in the areas of critical infrastructure security[100] and public health, and these can be used as models for future information-sharing efforts and structures. A repository of these best practices can be found, for example, at the DHS's Lessons Learned Information Sharing (LLIS) Web site, which is a secure, restricted-access, peer-validated Web site that serves as "the national network of Lessons Learned and Best Practices for emergency response providers and homeland security officials" and is "designed to facilitate efforts to prevent, prepare for and respond to acts of terrorism and other incidents across all disciplines and communities throughout the U.S."[101] In addition, the state-level Fusion Center structure—in which a central intelligence amalgamation office is established to coordinate among various state and federal intelligence bodies—can "benefit the [Intelligence Community] as well as the public and private sectors" by providing services, including "Request-For-Information (RFI) vetting and coordination, collaborative analysis, and timely dissemination of information across the full spectrum" of critical infrastructure protection.[102] These models and opportunities within the current system could be synthesized into quite an effective information-sharing apparatus, if only the central organization existed to support it.

The establishment of a central, functional private-sector hub office within DHS is essential if any functional information flow is to be developed. Centrally located analysis will allow the government to appropriately filter information coming in and going out, which will help to reduce the volume of information shared and highlight the most relevant data. Recent developments suggest that such a hub may be on the horizon, though perhaps outside the DHS apparatus. In December 2005, FBI formally established a Domestic Security Alliance Council (DSAC), modeled after the successful OSAC function within the Department of State. DSAC was conceptualized by a team of public- and private-sector officials and brought to the DHS—where it never got off the ground—prior to its establishment at the FBI, with some DHS funding.[103] Described as "a strategic partnership between the FBI and the U.S. private commercial sector," DSAC is intended to "enhance communications and promote the timely and effective exchange of information."[104] The main function of DSAC is an online portal where businesses can upload data relevant to crimes or other activities of a suspicious nature. This data is to be aggregated with other similarly contributed data and examined by FBI analysts, who would then reissue relevant threat information to private-sector partners and the general public. Currently, the DSAC "web portal for information sharing as described in the mission statement . . . is currently under construction,"[105] and the program is not yet staffed with analysts. However, the DSAC portal and its attempt to gather, analyze, and disseminate information from public and private sources in a central hub represents a promising move in the right direction for public-private information-sharing efforts.

While the federal government is ultimately the responsible party in outlining the terms and organizational structure of any potential public-private partnership, the private sector must also bear responsibility for mobilization, innovation, and follow-through on intelligence relationships. Businesses have multiple reasons—some altruistic, some selfish—to consider further intelligence cooperation despite the risks outlined in this chapter. Conversely, while intelligence has traditionally been exclusively government territory, the increasing importance of proprietary private-sector information—as well as of open source data that private entities could readily provide in line with their areas of expertise—makes the private sector a desirable partner for government intelligence. In fact, "[c]ollaboration among companies, in unison with a growing public-private partnership and improved labor-management resolve, is a key element of society's struggle—and ultimate victory—over terror."[106] This opportunity should not be cast aside. Homeland security initiatives "can be improved through private involvement when the government does not have pertinent information and would find it very difficult or prohibitively expensive to acquire it."[107] The minute albeit important details that sector-specific companies are able to gather as part of their everyday operations—fluctuations in market prices, incidence of internal crime, customer patterns, and more—can be valuable to intelligence agencies as they struggle to "connect the dots" in the big picture of terrorist threats. These small pieces of information can translate into operational knowledge if filtered in the right way and directed toward the right people. The possibilities presented by successful public-private intelligence partnerships are immeasurable. Unfortunately, they are now limited primarily by the lack of organization and clear policies and procedures. Resolving these issues will be essential to creating a successful cross-sector information-sharing system.

Stacy Reiter Neal is Associate Director of External Affairs at the Jebsen Center for Counter-Terrorism Studies, a research center housed within The Fletcher School at Tufts University. Ms. Neal holds an M.A. in Law and Diplomacy from The Fletcher School.

Notes

1. Philip E. Auerswald, et al., "Where Private Efficiency Meets Public Vulnerability: The Critical Infrastructure Challenge," from Auerswald, et al., eds., *Seeds of Disaster, Roots of Response: How Private Action Can Reduce Public Vulnerability* (Cambridge, UK: Cambridge University Press, 2006): 7.
2. Michael G. Harvey, "A Survey of Corporate Programs for Managing Terrorist Threats," *Journal of International Business Studies, 24,* no. 3 (Third Quarter, 1993): 466.
3. Todd Datz, "Capital Ideas: As the federal government's influence over security practices grows, CSOs have a few suggestions for improving public-private partnerships," *CSO Magazine,* December 2003. Available at http://www.csoonline.com/read/120103/ideas.html.
4. "About OSAC," Overseas Security Advisory Council Web site. Available at http://www.osac.gov/About/index.cfm.
5. Harvey, 467.
6. "About OSAC."
7. Datz.
8. Dean C. Alexander and Yonah Alexander, *Terrorism and Business: The Impact of September 11, 2001* (Ardsley, NY: Transnational Publishers, 2002), 14.
9. Brian Lopez, "Critical Infrastructure Protection in the United States Since 1993," in Auerswald, et al., eds., *Seeds of Disaster, Roots of Response,* 38–41.
10. Daniel B. Prieto, III, "Information Sharing with the Private Sector: History, Challenges, Innovation, and Prospects," in Auerswald, et al, eds., *Seeds of Disaster, Roots of Response,* 406.
11. Congress of the United States Congressional Budget Office. *Homeland Security and the Private Sector: A CBO Paper,* December 2004, 6. Available at http://www.cbo.gov/ftpdocs/60xx/doc6042/12-20-HomelandSecurity.pdf.
12. Prieto, 406.
13. Molly M. Peterson, "Security: New Centers Foster Information Sharing, Industry; Experts Say," *National Journal's Technology Daily,* October 18, 2002. Available via Lexis-Nexis.
14. Ibid.
15. Conversation with Robert Riegle, Director, State & Local Program Office, Office of Intelligence & Analysis, U.S. Department of Homeland Security, October 23, 2007.
16. Ibid.
17. Michael A. Czinkota, Gary A. Knight, and Peter W. Liesch, "Terrorism and international business: conceptual foundations," in Suder, ed., *Terrorism and the International Business Environment,* 48.
18. Michel Henri Bouchet, "The impact of geopolitical turmoil on country risk and global investment strategy," in Suder, ed., *Terrorism and the International Business Environment,* 91.
19. Alexander and Alexander, 57.
20. Prieto, 406.
21. Willard S. Evans, Jr., "Protecting critical infrastructures by sharing information," *Energy IT, 7,* no. 1 (January/February 2002): 45. Available via Lexis-Nexis.
22. "Join the SC-ISAC," Supply Chain Information Sharing and Analysis Center Web site. Available at http://secure.sc-investigate.net/SC-ISAC/ISACJoin.aspx.
23. "Membership Levels and Associated Benefits," Information Technology-Information Sharing and Analysis Center Web site. Available at www.it-isac.org/showmatrix.php.
24. "Membership Benefits," Financial Services ISAC Web site. Available at www.fsisac.com/membership.

25. Jennifer McAdams, "Bridging the Gap: What makes public/private security alliances succeed? It's not just about the money—except when it is," *Federal Computer Week,* February 26, 2007. Available at www.fcw.com/article97729-02-26-07-Print.

26. Prieto, 407.

27. Ibid, 409.

28. Ibid.

29. Ibid.

30. "State and Local Fusion Centers," U.S. Department of Homeland Security Web site. Available at www.dhs.gov/xinfoshare/programs/gc_1156877184684.shtm.

31. "Overview of the Privacy Act of 1974, 2004 Edition," U.S. Department of Justice Web site. Available at www.usdoj.gov/oip/1974intro.htm.

32. "Protected Critical Infrastructure Information (PCII) Program," U.S. Department of Homeland Security Web site. Available at www.dhs.gov/xinfoshare/programs/editorial_0404.shtm.

33. Ibid.

34. Riegle, October 23, 2007.

35. Dean C. Alexander, *Business Confronts Terrorism: Risks and Responses* (Madison: University of Wisconsin Press, 2004), 13.

36. Stephen J. Schulhofer, *The Enemy Within: Intelligence Gathering, Law Enforcement, and Civil Liberties in the Wake of September 11* (New York: The Century Foundation Press, 2002), 50.

37. Jerry Berman, "Security, Privacy, and Government Access to Commercial Data," in Clayton Northouse, ed., *Protecting What Matters: Technology, Security, and Liberty Since 9/11* (Washington, DC: Computer Ethics Institute and Brookings Institution Press, 2006), 104, 115.

38. D. Alexander, 114.

39. Ibid.

40. Matt Katz, "Store Clerk's Tip Was Key to Foiling Fort Dix Terror Plot," *USA Today,* May 9, 2007. Available at www.usatoday.com/news/nation/2007-05-09-fort-dix-clerk_N.htm.

41. D. Alexander, 114.

42. Ibid., 90–91.

43. Stuart Poole-Robb and Alan Bailey, *Risky Business: Corruption, Fraud, Terrorism, and Other Threats to Global Business* (London: Kogan Page Ltd., revised edition, 2003), 106.

44. Riegle, October 23, 2007.

45. Institute of Management and Administration, "Corporate Anti-Terrorism: Benchmarks and Best Practices: Executive Summary" New York: Institute of Management & Administration Inc., 2006, 14. Available at www.ioma.com/issues/SPCRPT/1608633-1.html.

46. Ibid., 15–16.

47. American Society for Industrial Security, *The ASIS Foundation Security Report: Scope and Emerging Trends,* 2005, 34. Available at www.asisonline.org/foundation/trendsinsecuritystudy.pdf.

48. Ibid., 35.

49. Ibid.

50. Ibid., 37.

51. Ibid.

52. Stephen E. Flynn and Daniel B. Prieto, *Neglected Defense: Mobilizing the Private Sector to Support Homeland Security* (New York: Council on Foreign Relations *Council Special Report (CSR)* No. 13 (March 2006), 29.

53. Ibid., 6.

54. Ibid., 1.

55. Prieto, 412.

56. Lewis M. Branscomb and Erwann O. Michel-Kerjan, "Public-Private Collaboration on a National and International Scale," in Auerswald, et al., eds., *Seeds of Disaster, Roots of Response,* 398.

57. Ibid.

58. U.S. Congress, Senate, *A bill to facilitate the security of the critical infrastructure of the United States (Critical Information Security Act of 2001),* 107th Congress, 1st Session, 2001, S.1456.

59. U.S. Congress, Senate, Committee on Governmental Affairs, *Securing Our Infrastructure: Private/Public Information Sharing.* 107th Congress, 2nd Session, May 8, 2002.

60. U.S. Congress, House of Representatives, *To establish the Department of Homeland Security, and for other purposes (Homeland Security Act of 2002),* 107th Congress, 2nd Session, 2002, H.R. 5005.

61. D. Alexander, 114.

62. Berman, 116.

63. John T. Chambers and Gilbert G. Gallegos, *Public-Private Sector Intelligence Coordination: Final Report and Recommendations by the Council.* National Infrastructure Advisory Council, U.S. Department of Homeland Security, July 11, 2006. Available at www.dhs.gov/xlibrary/ assets/niac/niac_icwgreport_july06.pdf. See pages 29–33 for private-sector CEO survey results about concerns in information sharing.

64. Branscomb and Michel-Kerjan, 398.

65. Datz.

66. ISAC Council, "Vetting and Trust for Communication among ISACs and Government Entitites," *ISAC Council White Paper,* January 31, 2004, 1. Available at www.isaccouncil.org/ pub/Vetting_and_Trust_013104.pdf.

67. Prieto, 410.

68. Ibid., 411.

69. ISAC Council, "Reach of the Major ISACs," *ISAC Council White Paper,* January 31, 2004. Available at www.isaccouncil.org/pub/Reach_of_the_Major_ISACs_013104.pdf.

70. Ibid. See also Chambers and Gallegos, 18.

71. Chambers and Gallegos, 18.

72. ISAC Council, "Government-Private Sector Relations," *ISAC Council White Paper,* January 31, 2004, 1. Available at www.isaccouncil.org/pub/Government_Private_Sector_Relations_ 013104.pdf.

73. Prieto, 411.

74. Flynn and Prieto, 1.

75. Prieto, 410–411.

76. Datz.

77. Lester J. Johnson, Jr., "Private Sector Information Sharing: The DHS Perspective and Lessons Learned," Statement before the United States House of Representatives Committee on Homeland Security on Intelligence Information Sharing and Terrorism Risk Assessment, Thursday, July 26, 2007, 2–3. Available at http://homeland.house.gov/SiteDocuments/20070726123111- 41306.pdf.

78. Ibid.

79. Institute of Management and Administration, 14.

80. Chambers and Gallegos, 29.

81. Prieto, 415.

82. Chambers and Gallegos, 29.

83. Lloyd Dixon and Robert Reville, "National Security and Private-Sector Risk Management for Terrorism," in Auerswald et al., eds., *Seeds of Disaster, Roots of Response,* 300.

84. D. Alexander, 85.

85. Flynn and Prieto, 2.

86. Ibid., 31.

87. D. Alexander, 118.

88. Chambers and Gallegos, 29.

89. Flynn and Prieto, 30.

90. Chambers and Gallegos, 28.

91. Flynn and Prieto, 3.

92. Charles W. Wessner, *Partnering Against Terrorism: Summary of a Workshop* (Washington, DC: The National Academies Press, 2005), 36.

93. Prieto, 425.

94. Flynn and Prieto, 36.

95. Ibid., 37.

96. Chambers and Gallegos, 23.

97. "National Industrial Security Program," Information Security Oversight Office, National Archives Web site. Available at www.archives.gov/isoo/oversight-groups/nisp/.

98. Ibid., 22.

99. Ibid., 25.

100. See case studies in Wessner and Flynn and Prieto.

101. "Lessons Learned Information Sharing," U.S. Department of Homeland Security Web site. Available at www.llis.dhs.gov.

102. Chambers and Gallegos, 24.

103. Riegle, October 23, 2007.

104. "Background," Domestic Security Alliance Council Web site. Available at www.dsac.gov/Pages/background.htm.

105. Ibid.

106. Yonah Alexander, "Corporate alliances against terrorism," *The Washington Times,* August 19, 2003.

107. John D. Donahue and Richard J. Zeckhauser, "Sharing the Watch: Public-Private Collaboration for Infrastructure Security," in Auerswald et al., eds., *Seeds of Disaster, Roots of Response,* 434.

Chapter 10

Winning the War on Terrorism

Since the attacks on September 11, the United States and its allies have been engaged in what has been controversially called the "war on terrorism." As a major component in this war, U.S. military operations in Afghanistan have aimed to dismantle and destroy the al Qaeda organization—and more broadly, the threat of terrorism—before such threats would again reach U.S. borders. The resurgence of al Qaeda following U.S. interventions in Afghanistan and Iraq, however, has raised critical questions about our ability to defeat al Qaeda and more broadly, the threat of terrorism. Can we win the war on terrorism? What does victory look like? How are we doing so far?

According to Bruce Riedel, "al Qaeda is a more dangerous enemy today than it has ever been before . . . thanks largely to Washington's eagerness to go into Iraq rather than concentrate on hunting down al Qaeda's leaders, the organization now has a solid base of operations in the badlands of Pakistan and an effective franchise in western Iraq." Riedel argues that the U.S. occupation of Iraq has helped bin Laden's strategy of dragging the United States into "bleeding wars" throughout the Islamic world and his end goal of forcing a U.S. withdrawal from the Middle East as he claims to have achieved with the Soviet Union in Afghanistan in the 1980s. Riedel suggests that "decisively defeating al Qaeda will be more difficult now than it would have been a few years ago." Despite setbacks, Riedel remains optimistic that it can still be done. However, victory against al Qaeda will require "a comprehensive strategy over several years, one focused on both attack al Qaeda's leaders and ideas and altering the local conditions that allow them to thrive."

Audrey Kurth Cronin contends that "past experience with the decline of terrorist organizations is vital in dealing with the current threat, and that the United States and its allies must tap into that experience to avoid prior mistakes and to effect al Qaeda's demise." Cronin's in-depth examination of the broader historical and political context of terrorism reveals that the phenomenon of al Qaeda and the challenge of devising an effective response over the long-term are not entirely without precedent. Cronin notes that while "the war on terrorism might be perpetual . . . the war on al Qaeda will end." According to Cronin, "there are at least seven broad explanations for, or critical elements in, the decline and ending of terrorist groups in the modern era." Although al Qaeda is unique to its predecessors in its fluid organization, methods of recruitment, funding, and means of communication, Cronin argues that al Qaeda "is an amalgam of old and new." Consequently, some important lessons for counterterrorism strategies can be learned from the decline of earlier terrorist groups.

Despite the loss of their dedicated sanctuary in Afghanistan and critical networks in key locations such as Saudi Arabia, Major Reid Sawyer and Major Jodi Vittori assess the capacity of al Qaeda as "stronger and more powerful than at any other time since 2002." According to the authors, many of al Qaeda's achievements "are a result of shortcomings in counterterrorism strategies and the failure to challenge al Qaeda across the entire spectrum of conflict. Sawyer and Vittori argue that for the war on terrorism "to succeed, al Qaeda must be understood as a multi-faceted organization *and* a global social movement [emphasis added]." The authors suggest that "al Qaeda's dual nature requires that the U.S. and its allies fight this war on three levels: a war of action, a war of networks and, the most difficult and intractable conflict, a war on ideas. Failing to recognize and address these three interrelated levels will ensure that al Qaeda remains a resilient organization with an increasing capacity for violence."

Brigadier General (ret.) Russell Howard [this book's co-editor] begins the final chapter in this volume by challenging the notion of the "war on terrorism." Rather than a system of beliefs, "terrorism is a means and tactic." General Howard reminds us that historically, "terrorism as a tactic has not been defeated." Terrorist groups, on the other hand, have an average life expectancy of twelve years. Characterizing counterterrorism efforts as a war has thus distorted both the threat that we face and the primary challenge at hand: the defeat of Islamic extremists who threaten the West. General Howard outlines five ways to hasten defeat. First, the struggle against al Qaeda should be called a campaign rather than a war. Second, the national security architecture of the United States needs to be overhauled to meet present-day threats. Third, the extremist ideology of al Qaeda needs to be fought with a better (or more correct) ideology of moderate Islam. Fourth, networks such as al Qaeda should be fought with networks rather than hierarchical bureaucracies. Finally, the need to prepare young Muslims for the challenges of modernization and globalizations requires a well-rounded education that includes foundations in math, the sciences and international relations.

Bruce Riedel

Al Qaeda Strikes Back

Summary: By rushing into Iraq instead of finishing off the hunt for Osama bin Laden, Washington has unwittingly helped its enemies: al Qaeda has more bases, more partners, and more followers today than it did on the eve of 9/11. Now the group is working to set up networks in the Middle East and Africa—and may even try to lure the United States into a war with Iran. Washington must focus on attacking al Qaeda's leaders and ideas and altering the local conditions in which they thrive.

A Fiercer Foe

Al Qaeda is a more dangerous enemy today than it has ever been before. It has suffered some setbacks since September 11, 2001: losing its state within a state in Afghanistan, having several of its top operatives killed, failing in its attempts to overthrow the governments of Egypt, Jordan, and Saudi Arabia. But thanks largely to Washington's eagerness to go into Iraq rather than concentrate on hunting down al Qaeda's leaders, the organization now has a solid base of operations in the badlands of Pakistan and an effective franchise in western Iraq. Its reach has spread throughout the Muslim world, where it has developed a large cadre of operatives, and in Europe, where it can claim the support of some disenfranchised Muslim locals and members of the Arab and Asian diasporas. Osama bin Laden has mounted a successful propaganda campaign to make himself and his movement the primary symbols of Islamic resistance worldwide. His ideas now attract more followers than ever.

Bin Laden's goals remain the same, as does his basic strategy. He seeks to, as he puts it, "provoke and bait" the United States into "bleeding wars" throughout the Islamic world; he wants to bankrupt the country much as he helped bankrupt, he claims, the Soviet Union in Afghanistan in the 1980s. The demoralized "far enemy" would then go home, allowing al Qaeda to focus on destroying its "near enemies," Israel and the "corrupt" regimes of Egypt, Jordan, Pakistan, and Saudi Arabia. The U.S. occupation of Iraq helped move his plan along, and bin Laden has worked hard to turn it into a trap for Washington. Now he may be scheming to extend his strategy by exploiting or even triggering a war between the United States and Iran.

Decisively defeating al Qaeda will be more difficult now than it would have been a few years ago. But it can still be done, if Washington and its partners implement a comprehensive strategy over several years, one focused on both attacking al Qaeda's leaders and ideas and altering the local conditions that allow them to thrive. Otherwise, it will only be a matter of time before al Qaeda strikes the U.S. homeland again.

One Lost, Two Gained

The al Qaeda leadership did not anticipate the rapid collapse of the Taliban regime in Afghanistan in the fall of 2001. Up to that point, Afghanistan had been a fertile breeding ground for the organization. According to some estimates, al Qaeda had trained up to 60,000 jihadists there. Al Qaeda leaders welcomed the invasion by U.S. and coalition forces on the assumption that they would quickly get mired in conflict, as the Soviets had two decades earlier. Al Qaeda and the Taliban thought they had decapitated the Afghan opposition and severely hampered its ability to fight by assassinating the Northern Alliance commander Ahmed Shah Masoud two days before 9/11.

But in December 2001, Mullah Muhammad Omar, the Taliban leader and self-proclaimed "commander of the faithful," to whom bin Laden had sworn allegiance, lost Kandahar, the capital of the Taliban's fiefdom. The Taliban had already lost considerable support among Afghans by the time of the invasion because of their draconian implementation of fundamentalist Islamic law and their harsh crackdown on poppy cultivation, the mainstay of the Afghan economy. But the key to their defeat was the defection of Pakistan. According to Ahmed Rashid, the top expert on the Taliban, up to 60,000 Pakistani volunteers had served in the Taliban militia before 9/11, alongside dozens of active-duty Pakistani army advisers and even small Pakistani army commando units. When these experts left, the Taliban lost their conventional military capability and political patronage, and al Qaeda lost a safe haven for its operational planning, training, and propaganda efforts.

The senior members of al Qaeda and the Taliban recovered quickly. In early 2002, they hid in the badlands along the Pakistani-Afghan border. Fighters went underground, and the trail for the top three men (bin Laden, Mullah Omar, and Ayman al-Zawahiri, bin Laden's top deputy) went cold almost immediately. For the next two years, al Qaeda focused on surviving—and, with the Taliban, on building a new base of operations around Quetta, in the Baluchistan region of Pakistan.

Al Qaeda also moved swiftly to develop a capability in Iraq, where it had little or no presence before 9/11. (The 9/11 Commission found no credible evidence of any operational connection between al Qaeda and Iraq before the attacks, and the infamous report connecting the 9/11 mastermind Mohamed Atta with Iraqi intelligence officers in Prague has been discredited.) On February 11, 2003, bin Laden sent a letter to the Iraqi people, broadcast via the satellite network al Jazeera, warning them to prepare for the "Crusaders' war to occupy one of Islam's former capitals, loot Muslim riches, and install a stooge regime to follow its masters in Washington and Tel Aviv to pave the way for the establishment of Greater Israel." He advised Iraqis to prepare for a long struggle against invading forces and engage in "urban and street warfare" and emphasized "the importance of martyrdom operations which have inflicted unprecedented harm on America and Israel." He even encouraged the jihadists in Iraq to work with "the socialist infidels"—the Baathists—in a "convergence of interests."

Thousands of Arab volunteers, many of them inspired by bin Laden's words, went to Iraq in the run-up to the U.S. invasion. Some joined the fledgling network created by the longtime bin Laden associate Abu Musab al-Zarqawi, who had fled Afghanistan and come to Iraq sometime in 2002 to begin preparations against the invasion. (Zarqawi had been a partner in al Qaeda's millennium plot to blow up the Radisson Hotel and other targets in Amman, Jordan, in December 2000. Later, in Herat, Afghanistan, he ran operations complementary to al Qaeda's.) Zarqawi's network killed an officer of the U.S. Agency for International Development, Laurence Foley, in Amman on October 28, 2002—the first anti-American operation connected to the invasion.

Root and Branch

The U.S. invasion of Iraq took the pressure off al Qaeda in the Pakistani badlands and opened new doors for the group in the Middle East. It also played directly into the hands of al Qaeda leaders by seemingly confirming their claim that the United States was an imperialist force, which helped them reinforce various local alliances. In Iraq, Zarqawi adopted a two-pronged strategy to alienate U.S. allies and destabilize the country. He sought to isolate U.S. forces by driving out all other foreign forces with systematic terrorist attacks, most notably the bombings of the United Nations headquarters and the Jordanian embassy in Baghdad in the summer of 2003. More important, he focused on the fault line in Iraqi society—the divide between Sunnis and Shiites—with the goal of precipitating a civil war. He launched a series of attacks on the Shiite leadership, holy Shiite sites, and Shiite men and women on the street. He organized the assassination of the senior leader of the Supreme Council for the Islamic Revolution in Iraq, Ayatollah Muhammad Baqir al-Hakim, in the summer of 2003, and the bombings of Shiite shrines in Najaf and Baghdad in March 2004 and in Najaf and Karbala in December 2004. Even by the ruthless standards of al Qaeda, Zarqawi excelled.

Zarqawi's strategy did prompt criticism from other jihadi groups and some second-guessing within al Qaeda, but it nevertheless succeeded brilliantly. In a letter to Zarqawi dated July 9, 2005, Zawahiri questioned the wisdom of igniting Sunni-Shiite hatred in the Muslim world, and Zarqawi became known within the movement as al Gharib (the Stranger) because of his extreme views. Still, he pressed ahead, and the al Qaeda leadership in Pakistan never challenged him publicly. Although he led only a small percentage of the Sunni militants in Iraq, Zarqawi was at the cutting edge of the insurgency, the engine of the civil war. By late 2004, he had formally proclaimed his allegiance to bin Laden, and bin Laden had anointed him "the prince of al Qaeda in Iraq."

Zarqawi's group, al Qaeda in Iraq, has continued to foment sectarian unrest. In February 2006, it attacked one of the country's most sacred Shiite sites, the Golden Mosque in Samarra. Zarqawi's death last summer changed little. In October 2006, the group proclaimed the independence of a Sunni state—"the Islamic State of Iraq"—in Sunni-majority areas, such as Baghdad, Mosul, and Anbar Province, declaring its opposition not just to the U.S. occupation but also to the Iranian-backed Shiite region in the south and to the Kurdish region in the north (which it says is supported by Israel). Most of all, al Qaeda in Iraq has continued to orchestrate massacres against Shiites in Baghdad.

The visible success of its partners in Iraq has strengthened the hand of al Qaeda and its allies, old and new, in Pakistan. With the help of tactical advice and, probably, funds from al Qaeda, the Taliban had already regrouped by 2004. In 2005, bin Laden appeared in a Taliban video advising its commanders. By 2006, the Taliban had recovered sufficiently to launch a major offensive in Afghanistan and even attempted to retake Kandahar. New tactics imported from Iraq, such as suicide bombings and the use of improvised explosive devices, became commonplace in Afghanistan. Taliban attacks rose from 1,632 in 2005 to 5,388 in 2006, according to the U.S. military, and suicide operations grew from 27 in 2005 to 139 in 2006. NATO troops held on to the major towns and cities but suffered significant losses, including over 90 dead.

Al Qaeda has also developed closer ties to Kashmiri terrorist groups, such as Lashkar-e-Taiba and Jaish-e-Muhammad. Some of those links predated 9/11. In late 1999, for example, bin Laden (as well as Taliban forces and Pakistani intelligence agents) was intimately involved in the hijacking of an Indian airliner by Kashmiri terrorists—an operation that then Indian Foreign Minister Jaswant Singh has since correctly described as the "dress rehearsal" for 9/11. Al Qaeda and Kashmiri groups have continued their deadly cooperation: the spectacular multiple bombings that rocked Mumbai last July had the marks of al Qaeda's modus operandi, and Indian authorities have linked them to al Qaeda's allies in Kashmir.

Spreading the Word

With two new bases secured and local alliances reinforced, al Qaeda has worked to expand its reach beyond Afghanistan, Pakistan, and Iraq. To vividly showcase its strength, al Qaeda records most of its operations and transmits the gruesome coverage to jihadi Web sites all over the world. The U.S. invasion of Iraq and the chaos that followed were a boon to al Qaeda's propaganda efforts, as they offered tangible evidence, al Qaeda's leaders could argue, both that Washington had imperialist plans and that the jihad against U.S. forces was working.

Bin Laden made a landmark video recording in October 2004, in time for the presidential election in the United States, promising to bankrupt Washington in Afghanistan and Iraq. Largely silent in 2005, he made several announcements in 2006. On the fifth anniversary of 9/11, al Qaeda released a major statement entitled "The Manhattan Raid," featuring previously unseen videos of two of the 9/11 pilots and the most extensive discussion yet on the background and purpose of the operation. Zawahiri, al Qaeda's propaganda point man—whose role is to reassure the faithful that the movement is alive and well—has also become more prolific; he issued at least 15 messages in 2006. Overall, al Qaeda quadrupled its output of videos between 2005 and 2006—all propaganda instruments, of course, but also a means for the organization's leaders to rally its followers and send them instructions. According to one expert, there are also some 4,500 overtly jihadi Web sites that disseminate the al Qaeda leadership's messages.

Al Qaeda has expanded its influence in the Middle East and Europe. It has earned much credibility in the global jihadi subculture. Its grand plans to topple the governments of Egypt, Jordan, and Saudi Arabia have failed, but its attacks against them illustrate the growing breadth of its ambitions and its increasing reach throughout the Middle East. And thanks to the international connections that Zarqawi established, the group has been able to provide foreign foot soldiers for the war in Iraq. Dozens of them have gone—and more continue to go—to Iraq to join the jihad. Most of them appear to be Saudis, although exact numbers are impossible to come by. The most striking case is perhaps that of Muriel Degauque, a Belgian woman and a convert to Islam, who blew herself up in a car-bomb attack against a U.S. convoy in Iraq in November 2005. Conversely, one of the 2005 attacks in Amman involved an Iraqi woman sent by Zarqawi. And thanks to Zarqawi's pipeline, a slew of al Qaeda faithful trained in Iraq can now be sent back to their homelands as experienced fighters.

Al Qaeda's relocation to Pakistan has also provided new opportunities for the group to expand its reach in the West, especially the United Kingdom. Thanks to connections to the Pakistani diaspora, visitors from Pakistan have relatively easy access to the Pakistani community in the United Kingdom, and Pakistani-born Britons can readily travel to Pakistan and back—facilitating recruitment, training, and communications for jihadists. (By one estimate, Pakistan received 400,000 visits from British residents in 2004.) The large communities of immigrants from Pakistan and Bangladesh living in the United Kingdom—and some disaffected Muslim British citizens—have become targets for recruitment. With entry into the United States made more difficult because of U.S. homeland security measures, the United Kingdom has become a focal point of al Qaeda's activities in the West.

In November 2006, Eliza Manningham-Buller, the director general of the British Security Service, known as MI5, said that some 200 networks of Muslims of South Asian descent were being monitored in the United Kingdom. At "the extreme end of this spectrum," Manningham-Buller said, "are resilient networks directed from al Qaeda in Pakistan," and terrorist plots in the United Kingdom "often have links back to al Qaeda in Pakistan, and through those links al Qaeda gives guidance and training to its largely British foot soldiers here on an extensive and growing scale." Since 2001, these foot soldiers are suspected of having plotted 30 or so attacks on targets in the United Kingdom or aircraft leaving for the United States. (All but one of them have been disrupted.) These networks' most notable success was the July 7, 2005, attacks on the London public transport system. Videos later released by Zawahiri left no question that al Qaeda had sponsored the attacks.

Although links between Pakistan and other terrorist attacks in Europe are less well established, al Qaeda's influence on them is almost certain. The extent of al Qaeda's involvement in the March 11, 2004, attack on the Madrid subway is unclear, for example; the bombing may have been an independent, copycat operation. But some sources, including Abdel Bari Atwan, the well-connected editor of Al-Quds al-Arabi, claim it was an al Qaeda operation, and last year Zawahiri publicly counted that act as one of al Qaeda's successful "raids." There is no question, meanwhile, that al Qaeda was behind the November 2003 attacks in Istanbul against Jewish and British targets, including the British consulate, that killed or wounded over 800 people.

Al Qaeda's growing connections to Europe have made the United States more vulnerable, too. If it had not been foiled, the plot last August to destroy ten commercial airliners en route from the United Kingdom to the United States—which has been tied back to the Pakistani-British network and was probably timed to coincide with the sixth anniversary of 9/11—would have been devastating. Last January, John Negroponte, then the director of national intelligence, said that the operation was the most ambitious attempt to slaughter innocents since 9/11. He told the Senate that al Qaeda's core elements "continue to plot attacks against our homeland and other targets, with the objective of inflicting mass casualties. And they are cultivating stronger operational connections and relationships that radiate outward from their leaders' secure hideout in Pakistan to affiliates throughout the Middle East, North Africa, and Europe."

Now What?

Al Qaeda today is a global operation—with a well-oiled propaganda machine based in Pakistan, a secondary but independent base in Iraq, and an expanding reach in Europe. Its leadership is intact. Its decentralized command-and-control structure has allowed it to survive the loss of key operatives such as Zarqawi. Its Taliban allies are making a comeback in Afghanistan, and it is certain to get a big boost there if NATO pulls out. It will also claim a victory when U.S. forces start withdrawing from Iraq. "The waves of the fierce crusader campaign against the Islamic world have broken on the rock of the mujahideen and have reached a dead end in Iraq and Afghanistan," a spokesperson for the newly proclaimed Islamic State of Iraq said on November 29, 2006. "For the first time since the fall of the Ottoman caliphate in the past century, the region is witnessing the revival of Islamic caliphates."

Whether or not such claims are true, al Qaeda is well placed to threaten global security in the near future. Because it thrives on failed and failing states, it will have opportunities to set up new operations. One appealing option may be Lebanon, where extremist Sunni groups have long operated, particularly in the country's second-largest city, Tripoli, which was controlled by a Sunni fundamentalist group during much of the 1980s, before Syria cracked down. If the Lebanese state is further weakened or civil war breaks out, al Qaeda may seek a foothold there. The United Nations force stationed in Lebanon is likely to be a target, since the jihadists consider it to be another crusading army in the Muslim world.

Gaza is another prime candidate: it is already divided between Hamas and Fatah, and there is evidence that a small al Qaeda apparatus is forming there. Israeli security sources have expressed growing alarm about this new al Qaeda presence on their doorstep. Yemen, bin Laden's ancestral homeland, may also make an appealing base. Last November, the group al Qaeda of Jihad Organization in the Land of Yemen claimed credit for attacking oil facilities in the Hadramawt region "as directed by our leader and commander Sheik Osama bin Laden . . . [and in order] to target the Western economy and stop the robbery [and] the looting of Muslim resources." Bangladesh is yet another possibility. The Jihad Movement in Bangladesh was one of the original signatories of bin Laden's 1998 declaration of war on the West. Last year, as bitter feuding between the two main political parties was increasingly ripping the country apart, there were growing indications that Bangladeshi fundamentalist groups were becoming radicalized. The political meltdown now under way in the capital, Dhaka, is creating the type of fractious environment in which al Qaeda thrives.

Africa presents some opportunities, too. Somalia has been a failed state for almost two decades and has had a long history of al Qaeda activity: in November 2002, it served as the base for an attack on two Israeli tourist targets in Kenya. The Ethiopian occupation of Somalia at the beginning of the year temporarily routed the Islamists, but al Qaeda is not finished in Mogadishu. In Algeria, meanwhile, al Qaeda is trying to revive the civil war that killed over 100,000 people in the 1990s. The Algerian Islamist movement the Salafist Group for Preaching and Combat, known by its French initials GSPC, swore allegiance to bin Laden last year, and he ordered that the group be renamed al Qaeda in the Islamic Maghreb. It has since attacked oil targets and police stations, hoping that a spectacular series of assaults, especially on Western targets, could reignite the civil war.

Bin Laden might also be nurturing bolder plans, such as exploiting or even triggering an all-out war between the United States and Iran. Indeed, there is evidence that al Qaeda in Iraq—and elements of the Iraqi Sunni community—increasingly consider Iran's influence in Iraq to be an even greater problem than the U.S. occupation. Al Qaeda worries about the Sunni minority's future in a Shiite-dominated Iraq after the Americans leave. Propaganda material of Sunni jihadists in Iraq and elsewhere openly discusses their fear that Iran will dominate a postoccupation Iraq and seek to restore the type of regional control that the Persian Empire had in the sixteenth century. In a remarkable statement last November, Zarqawi's successor, Abu Hamza al-Masri, thanked President George W. Bush for sending the U.S. Army to Iraq and thus giving al Qaeda the "great historic opportunity" to engage Americans in direct fighting on Arab ground. (He also said that Bush was "the most stupid and ominous president" in U.S. history.) But he warned that the invasion had "revived the glory of the old Persian Safavid Empire in a very short period of time." Similarly, the self-proclaimed emir of the Islamic State of Iraq, Abu Omar al-Baghdadi, issued a statement in February 2007 welcoming news that the U.S. government was considering sending more troops to Iraq and saying that he was eagerly looking forward to an American nuclear attack on Iran.

A war between the "crusaders" and the "Safavids" would benefit the jihad against both groups: by pitting two of its worst enemies against each other, the Sunni Arab jihadi community would be killing two birds with one stone. Al Qaeda would especially like a full-scale U.S. invasion and occupation of Iran, which would presumably oust the Shiite regime in Tehran, further antagonize Muslims worldwide, and expand al Qaeda's battlefield against the United States so that it extends from Anbar Province in the west to the Khyber Pass in the east. It understands that the U.S. military is already too overstretched to invade Iran, but it expects Washington to use nuclear weapons. Baghdadi has told Sunnis in Iran to evacuate towns close to nuclear installations.

The biggest danger is that al Qaeda will deliberately provoke a war with a "false-flag" operation, say, a terrorist attack carried out in a way that would make it appear as though it were Iran's doing. The United States should be extremely wary of such deception. In the event of an attack, accurately assigning blame will require very careful intelligence work. It may require months, or even years, of patient investigating to identify the plotters behind well-planned and well-executed operations, as it did for the 1988 bombing of Pan Am flight 103 over Lockerbie, Scotland, and the 1996 attacks on the U.S. barracks at the Khobar Towers in Saudi Arabia. Presidents George H. W. Bush and Bill Clinton were wise to be patient in both those cases; Washington would be well advised to do the same in the event of a similar attack in the future. In the meantime, it should, of course, continue do its utmost to prevent Iran from acquiring nuclear weapons and from fomenting violence and terrorism in the Middle East by using tough diplomacy and targeted sanctions. And it should not consider a military operation against Iran, as doing so would only strengthen al Qaeda's hand—much as the U.S. invasion and occupation of Iraq have.

War Games

The challenge of defeating al Qaeda is more complex today than it was in 2001. The organization is more diffuse, and its components operate more independently. Bin Laden continues to influence its direction and provide general guidance and, on occasion, specific instructions. But overall the movement is more loosely structured, which leaves more room for independent and copycat terrorist operations.

Partly because of this evolution, Washington needs a grand strategy to defeat al Qaeda. The past five years have demonstrated that a primarily military approach will not work. The focus of Washington's new strategy must be to target al Qaeda's leaders, who provide the inspiration and direction for the global jihad. As long as they are alive and active, they will symbolize successful resistance to the United States and continue to attract new recruits. Settling for having them on the run or hiding in caves is not enough; it is a recipe for defeat, if not already an acknowledgment of failure. The death of bin Laden and his senior associates in Pakistan and Iraq would not end the movement, but it would deal al Qaeda a serious blow.

A critical first step toward decapitating al Qaeda is for Washington to enhance its commitment in Afghanistan. President Bush promised to do so last February, but more needs to be done. Defeating the resurgent Taliban will require a significant increase in NATO forces, and that will require U.S. leadership. The United States should urgently divert more troops from Iraq to Afghanistan as a way to encourage U.S. allies in Afghanistan to help supply the additional troops and equipment needed. NATO should also encourage its partners in the Mediterranean Dialogue—especially Algeria, Egypt, Jordan, Morocco, and Tunisia—to contribute to the stabilization of Afghanistan. It should also create a contact group led by a senior NATO diplomat to engage with all of Afghanistan's neighbors to secure the country's borders, especially the 1,500-mile one with Pakistan. This group should include Iran, which has generally been a helpful player in Afghanistan in the last few years. NATO should reach out to India as well: New Delhi has already provided half a billion dollars in aid for Afghanistan, and, having long been a target of Islamist terrorism, India has a national interest in defeating it.

The United States should supplement this military buildup by taking the lead on a major economic reconstruction program in Afghanistan. Since 2001, the international community has delivered far less aid per capita to Afghanistan, one of the world's poorest countries, than it has to recovering states such as Bosnia. The country's infrastructure must be improved in order to develop a mainstream agricultural economy that can compete with illicit poppy cultivation, which breeds crime and corruption and strengthens the jihadi subculture.

The United States and its partners, including NATO, also need to take a firmer position with the Pakistani government to enlist its help in tracking down al Qaeda leaders. President Pervez Musharraf has taken some important steps against al Qaeda, especially after its attempts to assassinate him, and he has promised more than once a full crackdown on extremism. But mostly he has sought to tame jihadists—without much success—and his government has tolerated those who harbor bin Laden and his lieutenants, Taliban fighters and their Afghan fellow travelers, and Kashmiri terrorists. Many senior Pakistani politicians say privately that they believe Pakistan's Inter-Services Intelligence (ISI) still has extensive links to bin Laden; some even claim it harbors him. Apprehending a few al Qaeda officers would not be enough, and so a systematic crackdown on all terrorists—Arab, Afghan, and Kashmiri—is critical. Hence, Pakistan should no longer be rewarded for its selective counterterrorism efforts. (Washington has already given it some $10 billion in aid since 9/11.) The new Congress must take a sharp look at evidence (including evidence gathered by Afghan authorities) of Pakistani cooperation to assess how it can be improved.

Congress should also press the Bush administration to ensure that Pakistan holds free and fair parliamentary elections this year and that Pakistani opposition leaders are allowed to compete in them. If it makes sense to bring democracy to Afghanistan, then surely it makes sense to bring it to Pakistan. The prevailing theory that strongmen such as Musharraf make for better counterterrorism partners is a canard; Musharraf, for one, has not delivered the goods. The Pakistani army and the ISI have tolerated and sponsored terrorism for the last two decades, and the nexus between Pakistan and terrorism will not be broken until Pakistani officers are back in their barracks and civilian rule is restored.

Iraq is, of course, another critical battlefield in the fight against al Qaeda. But it is time to recognize that engagement there is more of a trap than an opportunity for the United States. Al Qaeda and Iran both want Washington to remain bogged down in the quagmire. Al Qaeda has openly welcomed the chance to fight the United States in Iraq. U.S. diplomacy has certainly been clumsy and counterproductive, but there is little point in reviewing the litany of U.S. mistakes that led to this disaster. The objective now should be to let Iraqis settle their conflicts themselves. Rather than reinforce its failures, the United States should disengage from the civil war in Iraq, with a complete, orderly, and phased troop withdrawal that allows the Iraqi government to take the credit for the pullout and so enhance its legitimacy.

No doubt al Qaeda will claim a victory when the United States leaves Iraq. (It already does so at the sheer mention of withdrawal.) But it is unlikely that the Islamic State of Iraq will fare well after the occupation ends. Anbar and adjacent Sunni provinces have little water, few other natural resources, and no access to the outside world except through hostile territory. The Shiites and the Kurdish militias will have no compunction about attacking the Islamic State of Iraq. (Al Qaeda's own propaganda indicates that it fears the Shiites' wrath after the United States' departure more than it fears what would happen if the Americans stayed.)

Another essential aspect of the United States' war against al Qaeda is the war of ideas. Washington must learn to develop more compelling narratives for its actions. Its calls for bringing democracy to Iraq have not resonated, partly because its actions have not matched its rhetoric. Human rights abuses at Abu Ghraib and Guantánamo Bay have even further sullied the United States' reputation and honor. Washington should emphasize the concrete steps the United States is taking to heal differences between Islam and the West and to bring peace to Palestine and Kashmir, among other areas. Creating a new narrative will probably also require bringing to Washington (and London) new leaders who are untarnished by the events of the last few years.

The repackaging effort will also have to involve concrete actions to address the issues that al Qaeda invokes to win recruits, particularly the Arab-Israeli conflict but also the conflict in Kashmir. The president of the United States must get personally involved in brokering peace in both instances. In the case of the Arab-Israeli conflict, this will not be easy, especially with Hamas in power in Gaza. But neglecting the issue is no solution either. Washington should consider various ideas for getting the opposing sides back to the negotiating table, including the Baker-Hamilton proposal calling for a new international conference. President Bush should also use the United States' enhanced relationship with

India—thanks to the nuclear deal the two countries ratified last year—to encourage the nascent dialogue between India and Pakistan and seek an end to those states' rivalry. Such an end would make it easier for the Pakistani government to crack down on terrorist networks in Kashmir, some of which are partners of al Qaeda.

It is now fashionable to call the struggle against al Qaeda the long war. It need not be so, even though helping to rebuild Afghanistan will require a long-term commitment. Decisive actions in key arenas could bring significant results in short order, and a focused strategy could eventually destroy the al Qaeda movement. On the other hand, a failure to adjust U.S. strategy would increase the risk that al Qaeda will launch another "raid" on the United States, this time perhaps with a weapon of mass destruction. For the last several years, al Qaeda's priority has been to bleed the United States in Afghanistan and Iraq. Striking on U.S. soil has been a lesser goal. If al Qaeda survives, however, sooner or later it will attack the U.S. homeland again.

The Few Setbacks

Despite its overall progress, al Qaeda has suffered several significant setbacks since 9/11, mostly in the Middle East, where it has called for toppling what it considers corrupt pro-U.S. governments. In February 2003, bin Laden wrote a now-famous sermon extolling the "band of knights," the jihadists who had attacked New York and the Pentagon on 9/11, and calling for the overthrow of all apostate leaders in the Persian Gulf—the "Karzais [referring to Afghan President Hamid Karzai] of Riyadh, Kuwait, Bahrain and Qatar." In a follow-up message in December 2004, he argued that in the revolution against Saudi Arabia, then Crown Prince Abdullah (now the king), Defense Minister Sultan bin Abdul Aziz, Interior Minister Nayef bin Abdul Aziz, and Bandar bin Sultan (then the Saudi ambassador to the United States) should be killed. He repeatedly urged jihadists to target the oil sector in Saudi Arabia to drive up world oil prices. According to Saudi officials, these public messages came with secret orders from bin Laden instructing cells to attack soft targets in Saudi Arabia.

The al Qaeda apparatus in the kingdom, which had been quiescent, exploded into action between 2003 and 2006—triggering the most serious and sustained domestic violence since the creation of modern Saudi Arabia in the early twentieth century. Targets included individual Westerners, the housing compounds of oil companies and Western firms such as the Vinnell Corporation, the Abqaiq oil processing facility (which produces 60 percent of Saudi Arabia's oil), the Ministry of the Interior, and the U.S. consulate in Jidda. Although the offensive coincided with the withdrawal of significant U.S. forces from the country, the pullout was not, as some analysts believed, bin Laden's main goal; it was merely a step toward the overthrow of the "corrupt" regimes in the Islamic world and the ultimate destruction of Israel.

But the Saudi internal security forces fought back very effectively. According to Saudi authorities, they foiled more than 25 major attacks and by the end of 2006 had killed or captured over 260 terrorists, including all but one of the 26 men on the country's most wanted list. The backbone of the al Qaeda movement in the kingdom was apparently broken. After 9/11, al Qaeda also launched an offensive in Egypt, the home country of Zawahiri, preaching the overthrow of President Hosni Mubarak. Hotels and tourist sites in the Sinai frequented by Israelis and Westerners were struck in October 2004 and July 2005—the July attacks, in Sharm al-Sheikh, killed almost a hundred people, outdoing the worst terrorist strike in Egypt up to that point (the Luxor massacre of 1997, which has also been linked to Zawahiri).

But the violence never spread beyond the Sinai; the Egyptian security apparatus kept the threat away from Cairo and the center of Egyptian political life. Terrorists and al Qaeda sympathizers are almost certainly present in the Sinai today, but they do not threaten the regime. More plots should be expected, however, as Zawahiri has announced a new alliance between al Qaeda and an Egyptian Islamic group led by the brother of Khalid al-Islambuli, the assassin of President Anwar al-Sadat.

Like bin Laden and Zawahiri, Zarqawi tried—and failed—to overthrow the leader of his home country, King Abdullah of Jordan. The Jordanian security forces foiled most of his plots. A plan to strike the headquarters of the General Intelligence Department, in Amman, with a chemical bomb in April 2004—Zarqawi's most ambitious effort in Jordan—ended with the GID seizing trucks with over 20 tons of chemical explosives. (Zarqawi took credit for the plot but claimed that the Jordanian authorities fabricated the presence of chemical weapons; as he put it, if his group possessed such a device, "we would not hesitate one second to use it on Israeli cities.") Al Qaeda was also responsible for the November 2005 bombing of the Radisson and two other hotels in Amman.

In Saudi Arabia, Egypt, and Jordan, the governments have strengthened the secret police and given them carte blanche to strike al Qaeda and its sympathizers. The United States and its allies in Europe have also provided additional counterterrorism assistance to the targeted regimes and stepped up cooperation with their security forces. The lesson is clear: al Qaeda is still too weak to overthrow established governments equipped with effective security services; it needs failed states to thrive.

Bruce Riedel is a Senior Fellow at the Saban Center for Middle East Policy at the Brookings Institution. He retired last year after 29 years with the Central Intelligence Agency. He served as Special Assistant to the President and Senior Director for Near East Affairs on the National Security Council (1997–2002), Deputy Assistant Secretary of Defense for Near East and South Asian Affairs (1995–97), and National Intelligence Officer for Near East and South Asian Affairs at the National Intelligence Council (1993–95).

Audrey Kurth Cronin

How al-Qaida Ends

The Decline and Demise of Terrorist Groups

The war on terrorism might be perpetual, but the war on al-Qaida will end. Although the al-Qaida network is in many ways distinct from its terrorist predecessors, especially in its protean ability to transform itself from a physical to a virtual organization, it is not completely without precedent. And the challenges of devising an effective response over the long term to a well-established international group are by no means unique. Al-Qaida shares elements of continuity and discontinuity with other terrorist groups, and lessons to be learned from the successes and failures of past and present counterterrorist responses may be applicable to this case. Current research focuses on al-Qaida and its associates, with few serious attempts to analyze them within a broader historical and political context. Yet this context sheds light on crucial assumptions and unanswered questions in the campaign against al-Qaida. What do scholars know about how terrorist movements end? What has worked in previous campaigns? Which of those lessons are relevant to understanding how, and under what circumstances, al-Qaida will end?

Radical Islamists will pose a threat to the United States and its interests for a long time to come. But there is a difference between sporadic and local acts of terrorism by religious extremists and the coordinated growth of al-Qaida, with its signature of meticulous planning, mass casualties, and global reach. A central assumption of early U.S. planning was that the elimination of al-Qaida would bring the war on terrorism (or the global struggle against violent extremism) to an end. Yet al-Qaida itself is a moving target, with experts arguing that it has changed structure and form numerous times. As a result, the strategy to counter this group is composed of tactics such as targeting its leader, Osama bin Laden, and his top lieutenants and denying the organization the ability, finances, and territory to regroup. Similar approaches have been employed against other terrorist organizations, with sharply varied outcomes. Careful analysis of comparable situations can shed light on what is required to close out an epoch dominated by al-Qaida terrorism.

Terrorism studies are often event driven, spurred by attacks and the need to analyze and respond more effectively to a specific threat.[1] As a result, the bulk of traditional research on terrorism has been descriptive analysis focused on one group, detailing its organization, structure, tactics, leadership, and so on. True to this pattern, since the terrorist attacks of September 11, 2001, there has been an outpouring of research (bad and good) on al-Qaida, but little attention to analyzing it across functional lines within a wider body of knowledge and research on terrorist groups. To the extent that broader crosscutting research has been done, the weight of it rests on questions of the causes of this threat, as well as the arguably narrow matters of the weapons and methods being used or likely to be used. This agenda reflects the strengths of the established international security and defense community, where there is far more expertise, for example, on nuclear weapons and proliferation than on the Arabic-speaking networks that might use them, on operational methods such as suicide attacks than on the operatives who employ them, and on the causes of wars than on how they end. Yet just as war termination may be more vital in its implications for the international system than how wars begin, the question of how the al-Qaida movement ends may be vital to understanding the strategic implications for the United States, its allies, and the shape of the new era.

The question of how terrorist groups decline is insufficiently studied, and the available research is virtually untapped. Yet it has a raft of implications for the challenges posed by al-Qaida and its associates, as well as for the counter-terrorist policies of the United States and its allies, many of which reflect little awareness or scrutiny of the assumptions upon which they rest. For example, national leaders focus on the capture or death of bin Laden as a central objective in the campaign against al-Qaida.[2] Past experience with the decapitation of terrorist groups, however, is not seriously examined for insights into this case. Some analysts concentrate on the root causes of terrorism and urge policies that will shift local public support away from al-Qaida, suggesting a longterm approach toward the movement's gradual decline. Experience from cases where populations have become unwilling to support other causes is little tapped, and resulting changes in the behavior of terrorist organizations separated from their constituencies are hardly known. In other cases, the use of force or other repressive measures against terrorist groups has been successful. Yet the conditions under which that approach has succeeded or failed have not been examined for parallels with al-Qaida. Most observers assume that negotiations would never lead to the end of al-Qaida because it has nonnegotiable, apocalyptic demands. But experience with other terrorist groups that had open-ended or evolving demands is little scrutinized. In short, the substantial history of how terrorism declines and ceases has not been analyzed for its potential relevance to al-Qaida.

The argument here is that past experience with the decline of terrorist organizations is vital in dealing with the current threat, and that the United States and its allies must tap into that experience to avoid prior mistakes and to effect al-Qaida's demise. The article proceeds in four sections. The first provides a brief review of previous research on how terrorism declines or ends; the second is an examination of the endings of other relevant terrorist organizations, with an eye toward determining what has worked in previous campaigns and why; the third offers an analysis of al-Qaida's unique characteristics to determine where comparisons with other groups are appropriate and where they are not; and the fourth addresses how what came before has implications for U.S. and allied policy toward al-Qaida today.

Previous Research on How Terrorism Ends

The study of terrorism is often narrowly conceived and full of gaps; it is not surprising, therefore, that the question of how the phenomenon ends is understudied. The vast majority of contemporary research on terrorism has been conducted by scholars who are relatively new to the subject and unaware of the body of work that has gone before: in the 1990s, for example, 83 percent of the articles published in the major journals of terrorism research were produced by individuals writing on the subject for the first time.[3] Thus far they have made little effort to build on past conclusions, with only halting and disappointing progress in understanding the phenomenon outside its present political context.[4] Not unrelated, a crippling aspect of much of the research on terrorism is its often applied nature; analysts willing to examine more than one group or broader, noncontemporary, conceptual questions are rare.[5] This is somewhat understandable, given that different groups undertake terrorist acts for different reasons, and it is safer to specialize; efforts to accelerate the demise of al-Qaida, however, require more lateral thinking. The thinness of terrorism studies may be giving way to more sustained substantive research in the post-September 11 world, though it is too early to say whether current attention will persist and mature.

Nonetheless, serious research conducted thus far has produced several overlapping themes and approaches in three areas: the relationship between how a terrorist group begins and ends; the search for predictable cycles or phases of terrorist activity; and the comparison of historical counterterrorism cases.

Links Between Beginnings and Endings

Hypotheses about how terrorist groups end are frequently connected to the broader body of hypotheses about what causes terrorism.[6] The assumption is that the origins of terrorism persist throughout the life of terrorist organizations and shed light on sources of their eventual demise. But this is often an oversimplification. Given the close ties between terrorism analysis and government support, when the perception of imminent attacks subsides, support for solid research declines. Work on a declining or defunct terrorist group is therefore typically sparser than is the tackling of its origins and evolution. With such a glaring imbalance in the available research, great care must be taken in generalizing about beginnings and endings of specific terrorist groups.

Recognition of the interplay of internal and external forces in the evolution of terrorism is also crucial. In any given case, the evolution from political awareness to the formation (usually) of a terrorist group to the carrying out of a terrorist attack is a complex process. Some steps in this process may be accidental or opportunistic.[7] Likewise, the process by which a terrorist group declines may be as much determined by innate factors as by external policies or actors.[8] A group may make a bad decision, engage in a counterproductive strategy, or simply implode. It may also have an innate compulsion to act—for example, it may be driven to engage in terrorist attacks to maintain support, to shore up its organizational integrity, or even to foster its continued existence.[9]

Studies of the causes of terrorism frequently begin with analyses of the role of individual operatives or their leaders. These include examinations of the psychologies of individual terrorists,[10] "profiles" of terrorists (and future terrorists) and their organizations,[11] assessments of the conditions that encourage or enable individuals to resort to terrorism,[12] and studies of the distinctive characteristics of terrorist leaders and their followers.[13] The relationship between the motivations and characteristics of individual operatives, on the one hand, and the means to end their violent attacks, on the other, is implied but not always obvious.

Another approach especially favored among terrorism experts is analyzing the organizational dynamics of the group. Important late-twentieth-century research concluded that terrorism is essentially a group activity: by understanding the dynamics of the group, including its shared ideological commitment and group identity, analysts can isolate the means of ending its terrorist attacks.[14] The focus is thus on the dynamics of relationships between members as a way of gaining insight into the vulnerability of the group's hierarchy, the weaknesses of its organizational structure, the group's ideology and world-view, and so on, which in turn potentially sheds light on how a group might unravel. Such research analyzes the behavior of the terrorist group from the perspective of the needs of the organization itself, an approach that was particularly influential in studying the behavior of leftist and ethnonationalist/separatist groups of the 1970s and 1980s.[15]

Many analysts, however, question the relevance of this well-established approach in an era of decentralized, nonhierarchical cell structures that are able to exploit information technology and the tools of globalization.[16] The internet is emerging as the critical new dimension of twenty-first-century global terrorism, with websites and electronic bulletin boards spreading ideological messages, perpetuating terrorist networks, providing links between operatives in cyberspace, and sharing violent images to demonstrate ruthlessness and incite followers to action.[17] Likewise, a growing emphasis on individual initiative, the presence of mission-driven organizations operating with an understanding of the commander's intent, and a lack of traditional logistical trails all have implications for analyzing how terrorist groups end. Cells that operate independently are much more difficult to eliminate and can even gain a kind of immortality. Mission-driven groups are designed to be self-perpetuating and may not fit traditional organizational models of how terrorism ends.

The nature of the grievance that drives a terrorist organization has some bearing on the speed and likelihood of its decline.[18] On average, modern terrorist groups do not exist for long. According to David Rapoport, 90 percent of terrorist organizations have a life span of less than one year; and of those that make it to a year, more than half disappear within a decade.[19] Whether an organization supports a left-wing, right-wing, or ethnonationlist/separatist cause appears to matter in determining its life span. Of these three, terrorist groups motivated by ethnonationalist/separatist causes have had the longest average life span; their greater average longevity seems to result, at least in part, from support among the local populace of the same ethnicity for the group's political or territorial objectives.[20] It is too soon to compile reliable data on the average life span of contemporary terrorist groups motivated by religion (or at least groups that appeal to religious concepts as a mobilizing force); however, the remarkable staying power of early religious terrorist groups such as the Hindu Thugs, in existence for at least 600 years, would seem to indicate the inherent staying power of sacred or spiritually based motivations.[21]

Finally, because of the degree to which terrorism research has been subsidized by governments and biased by later policy imperatives, the role of counterterrorism is often overemphasized. With easier access to government data, researchers tend naturally to stress state behavior. The degree to which terrorist groups evolve independent of government action can be under-appreciated. The result is a strong bias toward tying the decline of such groups to specific government policies, especially after the fact, even though the relationship between cause and effect may be unclear.[22]

Cycles, Stages, Waves, and Phases

Some researchers argue that terrorist attacks conform to a temporal pattern that provides insight into increases and decreases in numbers of attacks. Thus another approach to understanding the life span of a terrorist movement is to search for identifiable cycles.

Walter Enders and Todd Sandler assert that long-term analysis of terrorism trends during the late twentieth century indicates that transnational terrorist attacks run in cycles, with peaks approximately every two years. Enders and Sandler's cycles are tracked across terrorist groups worldwide, shedding light on the likelihood of an attack coming from someone somewhere; indeed, before September 11 they correctly predicted enhanced danger of a high-casualty terrorist attack. But like strategic intelligence that provided general but not tactical warning of the September 11 attacks, Enders and Sandler's findings were of limited use in predicting where the attack would occur, by which group, and by what means.[23] The apparent existence of global statistical patterns is interesting, but it provides no insight into the decline of specific terrorist groups. In his attempt to use mathematical analysis to determine risk assessment for al-Qaida attacks, Jonathan Farley likewise concluded that while the connections between cells can be quantitatively modeled, assumptions about how individual cells operate may be wrong.[24] The usefulness of statistical models based on a large number of assumptions to determine a specific group's decline is limited.

Other experts have focused on the existence of developmental stages through which all terrorist groups evolve, especially psychological stages of growing alienation or moral disengagement for groups, individuals, or both.[25] Leonard Weinberg and Louise Richardson have explored the applicability of a conflict theory framework—including stages of emergence, escalation, and de-escalation—to the life cycles of terrorist groups. They conclude that the framework is useful in examining terrorist groups originating or operating in Western Europe in the late twentieth century, but urge more research in this area to determine whether it is applicable to other places and periods.[26]

Still other analysts suggest that specific types of groups may possess their own developmental stages. Ehud Sprinzak, for example, argued that right-wing groups exhibit a unique cyclical pattern. Driven by grievances specific to their particular group, members direct their hostility against "enemy" segments of the population defined by who they are—with regard to race, religion, sexual preference, ethnicity, and so on—not by what they do. To the extent that the government then defends the target population, the former also becomes a "legitimate" target. But the cycle of violence reflects underlying factors that may continue to exist, and that can experience periods of flare-up and remission, depending on the degree to which the government is able to bring campaigns of violence under control.[27]

Other researchers study the evolution of terrorist groups as types of social movements and are intellectual descendants of Ted Robert Gurr.[28] The more highly developed literature on social movements posits, for example, that terrorism may appear at the end of a cycle of the rise and fall of movements of mass protest.[29] Social movements may just as easily be drawn toward more positive means, however. Understanding the pattern of mobilization may be important for dissecting the origins of an established group but may not be as revealing of its likely end. On the whole, research on social movements gives more insight into the origins of terrorist groups than it does into their decline.

Finally, Rapoport posits another broad hypothesis on the life cycles of terrorist groups. He argues that over the course of modern history, waves of international terrorist activity last about a generation (approximately forty years). These waves are characterized by expansion and contraction and have an international character, with similar activities in several countries driven by a common ideology. Two factors are critical to Rapoport's waves: (1) a transformation in communication or transportation patterns, and (2) a new doctrine or culture. Yet although a wave is composed of terrorist organizations and their activities, the two need not exist concurrently. Rapoport argues that because most individual organizations have short life spans, they often disappear before the overarching wave loses force. The current wave of jihadist terrorism may be different, however, because unlike earlier waves of the modern era, this one is driven by a religious (not a secular) cause. Rapoport is therefore reluctant to predict its end.[30]

Comparative Counterterrorism Cases

Cyclical hypotheses are notoriously difficult to formulate and difficult to prove; they can require so much generalization and qualification that their relevance to specific groups becomes remote. As with many international security questions, an alternative approach has been to assemble volumes of comparative case studies that draw parallel lessons about terrorist organizations, including how they declined and ended or were defeated.[31] These, too, present a host of challenges. First, terrorism studies often look primarily at the attributes of a particular group or at the counterterrorist policies of a state. Rarely are both equally well considered. Because of the heavy state interest in combating terrorism, the emphasis is understandably on a comparison of counterterrorist techniques used by states over the life span of each group, with policy implications for current challenges. Second, with their focus on a relatively narrow functional question, comparative terrorism cases can fall victim to superficiality: regional experts can be reluctant to cede ground to strategic studies experts whom they consider interlopers in their geographic/linguistic/cultural ambit. For this reason, many comparative studies are published as edited collections of articles by regional experts, but these in turn can fail to control relevant variables and to coalesce on a central theme. Third, access to data is a big problem: conducting primary research on contemporary terrorist groups is difficult because making contact with operatives or their targets can be dangerous for both the researchers and their contacts. In addition, governments may restrict access to relevant written sources.[32] Fourth, because of the political nature of terrorism, researchers operate at the intersections of sensitive ideas; maintaining objectivity in studying behavior that is deliberately designed to shock can prove challenging. Finally, studying this phenomenon over a range of terrorist groups in different cultural, historical, and political contexts requires generalization and risks the introduction of distortions when making comparisons.[33] The best case studies are usually completed years after a group has ceased to exist; as a result, their applicability to current challenges is limited. For any given group, it is vital to identify characteristics that distinguish it from its predecessors and those that do not.

How Other Terrorist Groups have Ended

There are at least seven broad explanations for, or critical elements in, the decline and ending of terrorist groups in the modern era: (1) capture or killing of the leader, (2) failure to transition to the next generation, (3) achievement of the group's aims, (4) transition to a legitimate political process, (5) undermining of popular support, (6) repression, and (7) transition from terrorism to other forms of violence. The relevant factors can be both internal and external: terrorist groups implode for reasons that may or may not be related to measures taken against them. Nor are they necessarily separate and distinct. Indeed individual case studies of terrorist groups often reveal that more than one dynamic was responsible for their decline. The typical focus on government counterterrorist measures slights the capabilities and dynamics of the group itself and is frequently misguided; even among groups that decline in response to counterterrorist campaigns, the picture remains complex.[34] Counterterrorist techniques are often best used in combination, and methods can overlap: frequently more than one technique has been employed to respond to a given group at different times. The goal here is to focus on the historical experience of previous groups and study the commonalities, in both the internal and external variables, so as to determine aspects of the processes of terrorist decline that are relevant to al-Qaida. Although listing these seven key factors separately is admittedly artificial, they are analyzed consecutively for the sake of argument and convenience (see Table 1).

Capture or Killing of the Leader

The effects of capturing or killing a terrorist leader have varied greatly depending on variables such as the structure of the organization, whether the leader created a cult of personality, and the presence of a viable successor. Regardless of whether the removal of a leader results in the demise of the terrorist group, the event normally provides critical insight into the depth and nature of the group's popular support and usually represents a turning point. Recent examples of groups that were either destroyed or deeply wounded by the capture of a charismatic leader include Peru's Shining Path (Sendero Luminoso), the Kurdistan Workers' Party (PKK), the Real Irish Republican Army (RIRA), and Japan's Aum Shinrikyo. The U.S. government designates all four as "foreign terrorist organizations."[35]

Shining Path's former leader, Manuel Rubén Abimael Guzmán Reynoso (aka Guzmán), was a highly charismatic philosophy professor who built a powerful Marxist movement through a brutal campaign of executing peasant leaders in Peru's rural areas during the 1980s and early 1990s. Somewhat ironically, Shining Path, which was founded in the late 1960s, began to engage in violence just after the government undertook extensive land reform and restored democracy to the country; the earliest attacks involved the burning of rural ballot boxes in the 1980 presidential election.[36] Increased popular access to a university education helped Guzmán radicalize a growing cadre of impressionable young followers. He consolidated his power in part by expelling or executing dissenters, resulting in unquestioned obedience but also a highly individualistic leadership. By the early 1990s, Shining Path had pushed Peru into a state of near anarchy. Guzmán's capture on September 12, 1992, however, including images of the former leader behind bars recanting and asking his followers to lay down their arms, dealt the group a crushing blow.[37]

Table 1

How Terrorist Groups Decline and End

Key Factors[a]	Notable Historical Examples[b]
Capture/Kill leader(s)	Shining Path
	Kurdistan Workers' Party
	Real Irish Republican Army
	Aum Shinrikyo
Unsuccessful generational transition	Red Brigades
	Second of June Movement
	Weather Underground
	Baader-Meinhof group (Red Army Faction)
	The Order
	Aryan Resistance Army
Achievement of the cause	Irgun/Stern Gang
	African National Congress
Transition to a legitimate political process/ negotiations	Provisional Irish Republican Army
	Palestinian Liberation Organization
	Liberation Tigers of Tamil Eelam[c]
	Moro Islamic Liberation Front
Loss of popular support	Real Irish Republican Army
	Basque Homeland and Freedom (ETA)
	Shining Path
Repression	People's Will
	Shining Path
	Kurdistan Workers' Party
Transition out of terrorism:	
toward criminality	Abu Sayyaf
	Revolutionary Armed Forces of Colombia
toward full insurgency	Khmer Rouge
	Guatemalan Labor Party/Guatemalan National Revolutionary Unit
	Communist Party of Nepal-Maoists
	Kashmiri separatist groups (e.g., Lashkar-e-Toiba and Hizbul Mujahideen)
	Armed Islamic Group (Algeria)

[a]The factors listed here are not mutually exclusive and can be found in combination.
[b]These are illustrative examples, not a comprehensive list.
[c]This peace process is threatened by renewed violence as this article goes to press.

The Kurdistan Workers' Party, an ethnonationalist/separatist group founded in 1974 and dedicated to the establishment of a Kurdish state, also suffered the capture of its charismatic leader, Abdullah Ocalan.[38] Beginning in 1984, the group launched a violent campaign against the Turkish government that claimed as many as 35,000 lives. Ocalan was apprehended in early 1999 in Kenya (apparently as a result of a tip from U.S. intelligence) and returned to Turkey, where a court sentenced him to death.[39] On the day of sentencing, riots and demonstrations broke out among Kurdish populations throughout Europe. Ocalan, whose sentence was later commuted to life imprisonment, advised his followers to refrain from violence.[40] Renamed the Kurdistan Freedom and Democracy Congress (KADEK) and then Kongra-Gel, the group remains on the U.S. terrorist list; however, it has subsequently engaged mainly in political activities on behalf of the Kurds.[41]

The Real Irish Republican Army is a splinter group of the Provisional Irish Republican Army that split off in 1997 after refusing to participate in the peace process. It conducted a series of attacks in 1998, including the notorious Omagh bombing, which killed 29 people (including 9 children) and injured more than 200. The Northern Irish community reacted with such outrage that the group declared a cease-fire and claimed that its killing of civilians was inadvertent. In 2000 the RIRA resumed attacks in London and Northern Ireland, focusing exclusively on government and military targets. In March 2001 authorities arrested the group's leader, Michael McKevitt. From an Irish prison, he and forty other imprisoned members declared that further armed resistance was futile and that the RIRA was "at an end." The group currently has between 100 and 200 active members and continues to carry out attacks; nevertheless, its activities have significantly declined since McKevitt's arrest.[42]

Aum Shinrikyo (now known as "Aleph") is essentially a religious cult founded in 1987 by Shoko Asahara, a half-blind Japanese mystic. Asahara claimed that the world was approaching the apocalypse and used an eclectic blend of Tibetan Buddhist, Hindu, Taoist, and Christian thought to attract an international following, primarily in Japan but also in Australia, Germany, Russia, Sri Lanka, Taiwan, and the United States. Asahara declared that the United States would soon initiate Armageddon by starting World War III against Japan and called on the group's members to take extraordinary measures in preparation for the attack. The notable aspects of this group are its international reach and its use of so-called weapons of mass destruction, particularly anthrax and sarin gas. In March 1995, members of Aum Shinrikyo released sarin gas in the Tokyo subway, resulting in the deaths of 12 people and injuries to another 5,000. Asahara was arrested in May 1995 and sentenced to death in February 2004. The group has shrunk from approximately 45,000 members worldwide in 1995 to fewer than 1,000, many of whom live in Russia.[43]

These are just a few of the contemporary cases where the capture or killing of the leader of a terrorist organization proved to be an important element in the organization's decline. Other examples include the arrest of leaders in groups as diverse as France's Direct Action (Action Directe); El Salvador's People's Liberation Forces (Fuerzas Populares de Liberación); and the U.S. group known as the Covenant, the Sword, and the Arm of the Lord.[44] From a counterterrorism perspective, the killing of a terrorist leader may backfire by creating increased publicity for the group's cause and perhaps making the leader a martyr who will attract new members to the organization (or even subsequent organizations).

Che Guevera is the most famous example of this phenomenon.[45] There is some reason to believe that arresting a leader is more effective in damaging a group than is killing or assassinating him.[46] But even a humiliating arrest can backfire if the incarcerated leader continues to communicate with his group. Sheikh Omar Abd al-Rahman (the so-called Blind Sheikh), convicted of conspiracy in the 1993 bombing of the World Trade Center, is a notable example.[47] In other cases, imprisoned leaders may prompt further violence by group members trying to free them (e.g., the Baader-Meinhof group and, again, al-Rahman).[48] Thus, if a leader is captured and jailed, undermining his credibility and cutting off inflammatory communications are critical to demoralizing his following.

Inability to Pass the Cause on to the Next Generation

The concept of the failure to transition to the next generation is closely related to theories that posit that terrorist violence is associated with the rise and fall of generations, but here it is applied to individual case studies. As mentioned above, the nature of the group's ideology seems to have relevance to the cross-generational staying power of that group. The left-wing/anarchistic groups of the 1970s, for example, were notorious for their inability to articulate a clear vision of their goals that could be handed down to successors after the first generation of radical leaders departed or were eliminated.[49] The Red Brigades, the Second of June Movement, the Japanese Red Army, the Weather Underground Organization/Weathermen, the Symbionese Liberation Army, and the Baader-Meinhof group are all examples of extremely dangerous, violent groups in which a leftist/anarchist ideology became bankrupt, leaving no possibility to transition to a second generation.[50]

Right-wing groups, which draw their inspiration from fascist or racist concepts, can also have difficulty persisting over generations, though, as Martha Crenshaw observes, this may reflect the challenges of tracking them over time rather than their actual disintegration.[51] Examples include the numerous neo-Nazi groups in the United States and elsewhere.[52] Still, the racist causes of many of these groups can persist long after the disappearance of the group itself; their movement underground,[53] or their reemergence under a different name or structure, is common.[54] Extensive examinations by academic experts and the Federal Bureau of Investigation of right-wing groups in the United States during the 1990s, especially after the 1995 Oklahoma City bombing, revealed their tendency to operate according to a common modus operandi, ideology, or intent; this includes the so-called leaderless resistance, which involves individual operatives or small cells functioning independently in pursuit of an understood purpose.[55] Such organizational decentralization complicates conclusions about beginnings and endings of right-wing groups, but it may also militate against truly effective generational transition. Furthermore, to support their activities, some right-wing groups engage in criminal behavior such as the robbing of banks and armored cars, racketeering, and counterfeiting, which, in the United States, has provided evidence trails for federal authorities and undermined group longevity.

The internal process that occurs during the transition from first- to second-generation terrorist leaders is very sensitive. Failure to pass the legacy to a new generation is a common historical explanation for a terrorist group's decline or end.

Achievement of the Cause

Some terrorist organizations cease to exist once they have fulfilled their original objective. Two examples are the Irgun Zvai Leumi (National Military Organization, also known either by its Hebrew acronym ETZEL or simply as Irgun), founded in 1931 to protect Jews with force and to advance the cause of an independent Jewish state, and the African National Congress (ANC). As head of the Irgun, Menachem Begin, who would later become prime minister of Israel, ordered the 1946 bombing of the King David Hotel, headquarters of British rule in Palestine. The attack killed 92 people and hastened Britain's withdrawal. Irgun disbanded with the creation of the state of Israel, when its members transitioned to participation in the new government. The ANC was created in 1912 and turned to terrorist tactics in the 1960s. Its attacks were met with an extremely violent campaign of right-wing counterstrikes as the apartheid regime began to wane.[56] ANC leader Nelson Mandela, imprisoned for terrorist acts from 1964 to 1990, was elected South Africa's first president following the end of apartheid.[57] The last ANC attack occurred in 1989, and the organization became a legal political actor in 1990, having achieved its objective of ending the apartheid regime.

Walter Laqueur divides terrorist groups that attained their objectives into three categories: (1) those with narrow, clearly defined aims that were realistically attainable; (2) those with powerful outside protectors; and (3) those facing imperial powers that were no longer willing or able to hold on to their colonies or protectorates.[58] In the context of twenty-first-century terrorism, additional categories are possible. Although it happens in a minority of cases, using terrorism to achieve an aim does sometimes succeed; to recognize this reality is not to condone the tactic and may even be a prerequisite to effectively countering it.

Negotiations Toward a Legitimate Political Process

The opening of negotiations can be a catalyst for the decline or end of terrorist groups, potentially engendering a range of effects. Groups have transitioned to political legitimacy and away from terrorist behavior after the formal opening of a political process. Examples include the Provisional Irish Republican Army, whose participation in the multiparty talks with the British and Irish governments was crucial to the 1998 Good Friday agreement; the Palestine Liberation Organization (PLO), which entered a peace process with Israel during the 1990s; and the Liberation Tigers of Tamil Eelam (LTTE, or Tamil Tigers), which began talks with the Sri Lankan government, brokered by the Norwegian government, in 2002.[59] But the typical scenario for a terrorist group's decline is usually much more complicated than simply the pursuit or achievement of a negotiated agreement.

Despite the successful negotiated outcomes that can result between the major parties, a common effect of political processes is the splintering of groups into factions that support the negotiations (or their outcome) and those that do not. For example, the IRA splintered into the Real Irish Republican Army;[60] and the Popular Front for the Liberation of Palestine (PFLP), Democratic Front for the Liberation of Palestine, and PFLP–General Command (GC) split with the PLO over the Israeli-Palestinian peace process. From a counterterrorist perspective, dividing groups can be a purpose of the negotiations process, as it isolates and potentially strangles the most radical factions. But such splintering can also occur on the "status quo" (or, usually, pro-government) side, as happened in South Africa (with the Afrikaner white power group Farmers' Force, or Boermag) and in Northern Ireland (with the Ulster Volunteer Force). Governments confront huge difficulties when negotiating with organizations against which they are still fighting in either a counterterrorism campaign or a traditional war.[61] The most extreme case of counterproductive splintering of status quo factions is Colombia, where the signing of the peace accords between the Colombian government and the Popular Liberation Army (Ejército Popular de Liberación, or EPL) in 1984 resulted in the formation of right-wing paramilitary groups that disagreed with the granting of political status to the EPL. Before long, leftist groups, paramilitary units, and the Colombian army stepped up their attacks, unraveling the peace, increasing the violence, and further fractionating the political actors. Worse, splinter groups are often more violent than the "mother" organization, responding to the imperative to demonstrate their existence and signal their dissent. Splinter groups can be seen as engaging in a new "layer" of terrorism with respect to the original group or their own government. This can also be the case, for example, when groups enter elections and take on a governing role. In such situations, the long-term goal (a viable political outcome) and the short-term goal (the reduction in violence) may be at odds.[62]

A wide range of variables can determine the broader outcome of negotiations to end terrorism, including the nature of the organization of the group (with hierarchical groups having an advantage over groups that cannot control their members' actions), the nature of the leadership of the group (where groups with strong leaders have an advantage over those that are decentralized), and the nature of public support for the cause (where groups with ambivalent constituencies may be more likely to compromise). There must also be negotiable aims, which are more likely to exist with territorially based groups than with those that follow left-wing, right-wing, or religious/spiritualist ideologies. Determining the degree to which opening a political dialogue with a terrorist group is a likely avenue for the decline of the group and a reduction in violence is a highly differentiated calculation.

Negotiations, however, need not be a formalized process and need not occur only with the leadership of a group. Arguably, a form of negotiation with a terrorist organization, or more precisely with its members, is the offer of amnesty to those willing to stop engaging in violence and come forth with information about their fellow operatives. The classic case of a successful amnesty is the Italian government's 1979 and 1982 repentance legislation and the Red Brigades.[63] In another case, the government of Alberto Fujimori in Peru offered amnesty to members of Shining Path, both after Guzmán's capture and during the waning days of the group. As Robert Art and Louise Richardson point out in their comparative study of state counterterrorism policies, an amnesty may be most successful when an organization is facing defeat and its members have an incentive to seek a way out of what they see as a losing cause.[64]

Diminishment of Popular Support

Terrorist groups are strategic actors that usually deliberate about their targets and calculate the effects of attacks on their constituent populations. Miscalculations, however, can undermine a group's cause, resulting in plummeting popular support and even its demise. Terrorist groups generally cannot survive without either active or passive support from a surrounding population. Examples of active support include hiding members, raising money, and, especially, joining the organization. Passive support, as the term implies, is more diffuse and includes actions such as ignoring obvious signs of terrorist group activity, declining to cooperate with police investigations, sending money to organizations that act as fronts for the group, and expressing support for the group's objectives.

Popular support for a terrorist group can dissipate for a number of reasons. First, people who are not especially interested in its political aims may fear government counteraction. Apathy is a powerful force; all else being equal, most people naturally prefer to carry on their daily lives without the threat of being targeted by counterterrorism laws, regulations, sanctions, and raids. Sometimes even highly radicalized populations can pull back active or passive support for a group, especially if the government engages in strong repressive measures and people simply become exhausted. The apparent loss of local popular support for Chechen terrorist groups is a good example.

Second, the government may offer supporters of a terrorist group a better alternative. Reform movements, increased spending, and creation of jobs in underserved areas are all tactics that can undermine the sources of terrorist violence. They can also result, however, in increased instability and a heightened sense of opportunity—situations that in the past have led to more terrorist acts. Evidence suggests that the extent to which societal conditions lead to a sense of "indignation" or frustrated ambition among certain segments of society during a period of transition might be a crucial factor for the decision to turn to terrorist violence. Sometimes terrorist attacks are seen as an effort to nudge the flow of history further in one's direction.[65]

Third, populations can become uninterested in the ideology or objectives of a terrorist group; events can evolve independently such that the group's aims become outdated or irrelevant. A sense of historical ripeness or opportunity may have been lost. Examples include many of the Marxist groups inspired by communist ideology and supported by the Soviet Union. This is arguably a major reason why the nature of international terrorism has evolved beyond primary reliance on state sponsorship toward a broader range of criminal or entrepreneurial behavior.

Fourth, a terrorist group's attacks can cause revulsion among its actual or potential public constituency.[66] This is a historically common strategic error and can cause the group to implode. Independent of the counterterrorist activity of a government, a terrorist group may choose a target that a wide range of its constituents consider illegitimate. This occurred, for example, with the Omagh bombing. Despite hasty subsequent statements by RIRA leaders that they did not intend to kill innocent civilians, the group never recovered in the eyes of the community.[67] Other examples of strategic miscalculation abound. In February 1970 the PFLP-GC sabotaged a Swissair plane en route to Tel Aviv, resulting in the deaths of all 47 passengers, 15 of whom were Israelis. The PFLP-GC at first took responsibility but then tried unsuccessfully to retract its claim when popular revulsion began to surface.[68] Similarly, there has been revulsion among the Basque population in Spain to attacks by the separatist group Basque Fatherland and Liberty (Euzkadi Ta Askatasuna, or ETA), which some observers credit with the declining popularity of the group.[69] Public revulsion was a factor in the undermining of support for Sikh separatism in India, a movement directed at establishing an independent state of Khalistan that killed tens of thousands between 1981 and 1995 and was responsible for the assassination of Indian Prime Minister Indira Gandhi on October 31, 1984.[70]

Popular revulsion against terrorist attacks can have immediate effects. Arguably the most well developed and broadly based conduit for resource collection in the world is the connection between the Tamil Tigers and the dispersed Tamil diaspora. The LTTE's desire to avoid the "terrorist organization" label in the post-September 11 world and shore up its base of popular support was an element in the group's December 2001 decision to pursue a negotiated solution.[71] Likewise, a state-sponsored terrorist group can lose support when the state decides that it is no longer interested in using terrorism, responds to pressure from other states, has more important competing goals, or loses the ability to continue its support.[72] Libya's expulsion of the Palestinian terrorist Abu Nidal and cutting off of support to Palestinian groups such as the Palestine Islamic Jihad and the PFLP-GC are notable examples.

Military Force and the Repression of Terrorist Groups

The use of military force has hastened the decline or ended a number of terrorist groups, including the late-nineteenth-century Russian group Narodnaya Volya, Shining Path, and the Kurdistan Workers' Party. From the state's perspective, military force offers a readily available means that is under its control. Although terrorism is indeed arguably a form of war, terrorists use asymmetrical violence, by definition, because they are unable or unwilling to meet a status quo government on the battlefield. Shifting the violence to a form that is familiar and probably advantageous for the state is an understandable response. In some circumstances, it is also successful. Historically, military force has taken two forms: intervention, when the threat is located mainly beyond the borders of the target state (as with Israel's 1982 involvement in Lebanon); or repression, when the threat is considered mainly a domestic one (as with the PKK). More typically, the state will use some combination of the two (as in Colombia).[73]

The effects of the use of repressive military force in some cases may prove to be temporary or counterproductive; in other cases, it may result in the export of the problem to another country. The classic contemporary case is the Russian counterterrorism campaign in Chechnya.[74] Russian involvement in the second Chechen war appears to have produced a transition in the Chechen resistance, with more terrorist attacks in the rest of Russia, greater reliance on suicide bombers, and the growing influence of militant Islamic fighters. To the extent that the Chechens originally engaged in a classic insurgency rather than in terrorism, they have since 2002 altered their tactics toward increasing attacks on Russian civilians. The strong repressive response by the Russian government has apparently facilitated the spread of the conflict to neighboring areas, including Ingushetia and Dagestan. And there seems to be no end in sight, given the increasing radicalization and identification of some Chechen factions with the al-Qaida movement.[75]

Democracies or liberal governments face particular difficulties in repressing terrorist groups. Because military or police action requires a target, the use of force against operatives works best in situations where members of the organization can be separated from the general population. This essentially forces "profiling" or some method of distinguishing members from nonmembers—always a sensitive issue, particularly when the only available means of discrimination relate to how members are defined (race, age, religion, nationality, etc.) rather than to what they do (or are planning to do). Excellent intelligence is essential for the latter (especially in advance of an attack), but even in the best of situations, it is typically scarce. Repressive measures also carry high resource and opportunity costs. Long-term repressive measures against suspected operatives may challenge civil liberties and human rights, undermine domestic support, polarize political parties, and strain the fabric of the state itself, further undercutting the state's ability to respond effectively to future terrorist attacks.

Transition to Another Modus Operandi

In some cases, groups can move from the use of terrorism toward either criminal behavior or more classic conventional warfare. The transition to criminal behavior implies a shift away from a primary emphasis on collecting resources as a means of pursuing political ends toward acquiring material goods and profit that become ends in themselves. Groups that have undertaken such transitions in recent years include Abu Sayyaf in the Philippines and arguably all of the major so-called narco-terrorist groups in Colombia.[76] Beginning in 2000, Abu Sayyaf shifted its focus from bombings and targeted executions to the taking of foreign hostages and their exchange for millions of dollars in ransom.[77] The Revolutionary Armed Forces of Colombia uses a variety of mechanisms to raise funds—including kidnapping for ransom, extortion, and especially drug trafficking—running operations that yield as much as $1 billion annually.[78]

Terrorist groups can also escalate to insurgency or even conventional war, especially if they enjoy state support. Notable examples include the Kashmiri separatist groups, the Khmer Rouge, and the Communist Party of Nepal–Maoists. Transitions in and out of insurgency are especially common among ethnonationalist/separatist groups, whose connection to a particular territory and grounding in an ethnic population provide a natural base; in these situations, the evolution involves changes in size or type of operations (do they operate as a military unit and attack mainly other military targets?) and whether or not the organization holds territory (even temporarily). Terrorism and insurgency are not the same, but they are related. Very weak, territorially based movements may use terrorist attacks and transition to insurgency when they gain strength, especially when their enemy is a state government (as was the case for most groups in the twentieth century). One example is Algeria's Armed Islamic Group, which massacred tens of thousands of civilians in the civil war that followed the Islamic Salvation Front's victory in the 1991 parliamentary elections. The key in understanding the relationship between the two tactics is to analyze the group's motivation, its attraction to a particular constituency, its strength, and the degree to which its goals are associated with control of a piece of territory. Transitions to full-blown conventional war, on the other hand, can occur when the group is able to control the behavior of a state according to its own interests, or even when an act of terrorism has completely unintended consequences.[79]

Is al-Qaida Unique among Terrorist Organizations?

Four characteristics distinguish al-Qaida from its predecessors in either nature or degree: its fluid organization, recruitment methods, funding, and means of communication.

Fluid Organization

The al-Qaida of September 2001 no longer exists. As a result of the war on terrorism, it has evolved into an increasingly diffuse network of affiliated groups, driven by the worldview that al-Qaida represents. In deciding in 1996 to be, essentially, a "visible" organization, running training camps and occupying territory in Afghanistan, al-Qaida may have made an important tactical error; this, in part, explains the immediate success of the U.S.-led coalition's war in Afghanistan.[80] Since then, it has begun to resemble more closely a "global jihad movement," increasingly consisting of web-directed and cyber-linked groups and ad hoc cells.[81] In its evolution, al-Qaida has demonstrated an unusual resilience and international reach. It has become, in the words of Porter Goss, "only one facet of the threat from a broader Sunni jihadist movement."[82] No previous terrorist organization has exhibited the complexity, agility, and global reach of al-Qaida, with its fluid operational style based increasingly on a common mission statement and objectives, rather than on standard operating procedures and an organizational structure.[83]

Al-Qaida has been the focal point of a hybrid terrorist coalition for some time, with ties to inspired freelancers and other terrorist organizations both old and new.[84] Some observers argue that considering al-Qaida an organization is misleading; rather it is more like a nebula of independent entities (including loosely associated individuals) that share an ideology and cooperate with each other.[85] The original umbrella group, the International Islamic Front for Jihad against Jews and Crusaders, formed in 1998, included not only al-Qaida but also groups from Algeria, Bangladesh, Egypt, and Pakistan. A sampling of groups that are connected in some way includes the Moro Islamic Liberation Front (Philippines), Jemaah Islamiyah (Southeast Asia), Egyptian Islamic Jihad (which merged with al-Qaida in 2001), al-Ansar Mujahidin (Chechnya), al-Gama'a al-Islamiyya (primarily Egypt, but has a worldwide presence), Abu Sayyaf (Philippines), the Islamic Movement of Uzbekistan, the Salafist Group for Call and Combat (Algeria), and Harakat ul-Mujahidin (Pakistan/Kashmir). Some experts see al-Qaida's increased reliance on connections to other groups as a sign of weakness; others see it as a worrisome indicator of growing strength, especially with groups that formerly focused on local issues and now display evidence of convergence on al-Qaida's Salafist, anti-U.S., anti-West agenda.[86]

The nature, size, structure, and reach of the coalition have long been subject to debate. Despite claims of some Western experts, no one knows how many members al-Qaida has currently or had in the past. U.S. intelligence sources place the number of individuals who underwent training in camps in Afghanistan from 1996 through the fall of 2001 at between 10,000 and 20,000;[87] the figure is inexact, in part, because of disagreement over the total number of such camps and because not all attendees became members.[88] The International Institute for Strategic Studies in 2004 estimated that 2,000 al-Qaida operatives had been captured or killed and that a pool of 18,000 potential al-Qaida operatives remained.[89] These numbers can be misleading, however: it would be a mistake to think of al-Qaida as a conventional force, because even a few trained fighters can mobilize many willing foot soldiers as martyrs.

Methods of Recruitment

The staying power of al-Qaida is at least in part related to the way the group has perpetuated itself; in many senses, al-Qaida is closer to a social movement than a terrorist group.[90] Involvement in the movement has come not from pressure by senior al-Qaida members but mainly from local volunteers competing to win a chance to train or participate in some fashion.[91] The process seems to be more a matter of "joining" than being recruited,[92] and thus the traditional organizational approach to analyzing this group is misguided. But the draw of al-Qaida should also not be overstated: in the evolving pattern of associations, attraction to the mission or ideology seems to have been a necessary but not sufficient condition. Exposure to an ideology is not enough, as reflected in the general failure of al-Qaida to recruit members in Afghanistan and Sudan, where its headquarters were once located.[93] As psychiatrist Marc Sageman illustrates, social bonds, not ideology, apparently play a more important role in al-Qaida's patterns of global organization.[94]

Sageman's study of established links among identified al-Qaida operatives indicates that they joined the organization mainly because of ties of kinship and friendship, facilitated by what he calls a "bridging person" or entry point, perpetuated in a series of local clusters in the Maghreb and Southeast Asia, for example. In recent years, operatives have been connected to al-Qaida and its agenda in an even more informal way, having apparently not gone to camps or had much formal training: examples include those engaged in the London bombings of July 7 and 21, 2005, the Istanbul attacks of November 15 and 20, 2003, and the Casablanca attacks of May 16, 2003.[95] This loose connectedness is not an accident: bin Laden describes al-Qaida as "the vanguard of the Muslim nation" and does not claim to exercise command and control over his followers.[96] Although many groups boast of a connection to al-Qaida's ideology, there are often no logistical trails and thus no links for traditional intelligence methods to examine.[97] This explains, for example, the tremendous difficulty in establishing connections between a radical mosque, bombers, bomb makers, supporters, and al-Qaida in advance of an attack (not to mention after an attack).

Another concern has been the parallel development of Salafist networks apparently drawing European Muslims into combat against Western forces in Iraq. The European Union's counterterrorism coordinator, Gijs de Vries, for example, has cautioned that these battle-hardened veterans of the Iraq conflict will return to attack Western targets in Europe. The Ansar al-Islam plot to attack the 2004 NATO summit in Turkey was, according to Turkish sources, developed in part by operatives who had fought in Iraq.[98] A proportion of those recently drawn to the al-Qaida movement joined after receiving a Salafist message disseminated over the internet. Such direct messages normally do not pass through the traditional process of vetting by an imam. European counterterrorism officials thus worry about members of an alienated diaspora—sometimes second- and third-generation immigrants—who may be vulnerable to the message because they are not thoroughly trained in fundamental concepts of Islam, are alienated from their parents, and feel isolated in the communities in which they find themselves. The impulse to join the movement arises from a desire to belong to a group in a context where the operative is excluded from, repulsed by, or incapable of successful integration into a Western community.[99]

Thus, with al-Qaida, the twentieth-century focus on structure and function is neither timely nor sufficient. Tracing the command and control relationships in such a dramatically changing movement is enormously difficult,[100] which makes comparisons with earlier, more traditional terrorist groups harder but by no means impossible; one detects parallels, for example, between al-Qaida and the global terrorist movements that developed in the late nineteenth century, including anarchist and social revolutionary groups.[101]

Means of Support

Financial support of al-Qaida has ranged from money channeled through charitable organizations to grants given to local terrorist groups that present promising plans for attacks that serve al-Qaida's general goals.[102] The majority of its operations have relied at most on a small amount of seed money provided by the organization, supplemented by operatives engaged in petty crime and fraud.[103] Indeed, beginning in 2003, many terrorism experts agreed that all-Qaida could best be described as a franchise organization with a marketable "brand."[104] Relatively little money is required for most al-Qaida-associated attacks. As the International Institute for Strategic Studies points out, the 2002 Bali bombing cost less than $35,000, the 2000 USS *Cole* operation about $50,000, and the September 11 attacks less than $500,000.[105]

Another element of support has been the many autonomous businesses owned or controlled by al-Qaida; at one point, bin Laden was reputed to own or control approximately eighty companies around the world. Many of these legitimately continue to earn a profit, providing a self-sustaining source for the movement. International counterterrorism efforts to control al-Qaida financing have reaped at least $147 million in frozen assets.[106] Still, cutting the financial lifeline of an agile and low-cost movement that has reportedly amassed billions of dollars and needs few resources to carry out attacks remains a formidable undertaking.

Choking off funds destined for al-Qaida through regulatory oversight confronts numerous challenges. Formal banking channels are not necessary for many transfers, which instead can occur through informal channels known as "alternative remittance systems," "informal value transfer systems," "parallel banking," or "underground banking." Examples include the much-discussed *hawala* or *hundi* transfer networks and the Black Market Peso Exchange that operate through family ties or unofficial reciprocal arrangements.[107] Value can be stored in commodities such as diamonds and gold that are moved through areas with partial or problematical state sovereignty. Al-Qaida has also used charities to raise and move funds, with a relatively small proportion of gifts being siphoned off for illegitimate purposes, often without the knowledge of donors.[108] Yet efforts to cut off charitable flows to impoverished areas may harm many genuinely needy recipients and could result in heightened resentment, which in turn may generate additional political support for the movement.[109] Al-Qaida's fiscal autonomy makes the network more autonomous than its late-twentieth-century state-sponsored predecessors.

Means of Communication

The al-Qaida movement has successfully used the tools of globalization to enable it to communicate with multiple audiences, including potential new members, new recruits, active supporters, passive sympathizers, neutral observers, enemy governments, and potential victims. These tools include mobile phones, text messaging, instant messaging, and especially websites, email, blogs, and chat rooms, which can be used for administrative tasks, fund-raising, research, and logistical coordination of attacks.[110] Although al-Qaida is not the only terrorist group to exploit these means, it is especially adept at doing so.

A crucial facilitator for the perpetuation of the movement is the use of websites both to convey messages, *fatwas,* claims of attacks, and warnings to the American public, as well as to educate future participants, embed instructions to operatives, and rally sympathizers to the cause. The internet is an important factor in building and perpetuating the image of al-Qaida and in maintaining the organization's reputation. It provides easy access to the media, which facilitates al-Qaida's psychological warfare against the West. Indoctrinating and teaching new recruits is facilitated by the internet, notably through the dissemination of al-Qaida's widely publicized training manual (nicknamed "The Encyclopedia of Jihad") that explains how to organize and run a cell, as well as carry out attacks.[111] Websites and chat rooms are used to offer practical advice and facilitate the fraternal bonds that are crucial to al-Qaida. In a sense, members of the movement no longer need to join an organization at all, for the individual can participate with the stroke of a few keys. The debate over the size, structure, and membership of al-Qaida may be a quaint relic of the twentieth century, displaced by the leveling effects of twenty-first-century technology.

The new means of communication also offer practical advantages. Members of al-Qaida use the web as a vast source of research and data mining to scope out future attack sites or develop new weapons technology at a low cost and a high level of sophistication. On January 15, 2003, for example, U.S. Secretary of Defense Donald Rumsfeld quoted an al-Qaida training manual retrieved by American troops in Afghanistan that advised trainees that at least 80 percent of the information needed about the enemy could be collected from open, legal sources.[112]

Earlier Terrorist Groups, al-Qaida, and U.S. Policy Implications

Al-Qaida's fluid organization, methods of recruitment, funding, and means of communication distinguish it as an advancement in twenty-first-century terrorist groups. Al-Qaida is a product of the times. Yet it also echoes historical predecessors, expanding on such factors as the international links and ideological drive of nineteenth-century anarchists, the open-ended aims of Aum Shinrikyo, the brilliance in public communications of the early PLO, and the taste for mass casualty attacks of twentieth-century Sikh separatists or Hezbollah. Al-Qaida is an amalgam of old and new, reflecting twenty-first-century advances in means or matters of degree rather than true originality; still, most analysts miss the connections with its predecessors and are blinded by its solipsistic rhetoric. That is a mistake. The pressing challenge is to determine which lessons from the decline of earlier terrorist groups are relevant to al-Qaida and which are not.

First, past experience with terrorism indicates that al-Qaida will not end if Osama bin Laden is killed. There are many other reasons to pursue him, including bringing him to justice, removing his leadership and expertise, and increasing esprit de corps on the Western side (whose credibility is sapped because of bin Laden's enduring elusiveness). The argument that his demise will end al-Qaida is tinged with emotion, not dispassionate analysis.

Organizations that have been crippled by the killing of their leader have been hierarchically structured, reflecting to some degree a cult of personality, and have lacked a viable successor. Al-Qaida meets neither of these criteria: it has a mutable structure with a strong, even increasing, emphasis on individual cells and local initiative. It is not the first organization to operate in this way; and the demise of similar terrorist groups required much more than the death of one person.[113] Unlike the PKK and Shining Path, al-Qaida is not driven by a cult of personality; despite his astonishing popularity, bin Laden has deliberately avoided allowing the movement to revolve around his own persona, preferring instead to keep his personal habits private, to talk of the insignificance of his own fate, and to project the image of a humble man eager to die for his beliefs. As for a viable replacement, bin Laden has often spoken openly of a succession plan, and that plan has to a large degree already taken effect. Furthermore, his capture or killing would produce its own countervailing negative consequences, including (most likely) the creation of a powerful martyr. On balance, the removal of bin Laden would have important potential benefits, but to believe that it would kill al-Qaida is to be ahistorical and naive. That al-Qaida is already dead.

Second, although there was a time when the failure to transition to a new generation might have been a viable finale for al-Qaida, that time is long past. Al-Qaida has transitioned to a second, third, and arguably fourth generation. The reason relates especially to the second distinctive element of al-Qaida: its method of recruitment or, more accurately, its attraction of radicalized followers (both individuals and groups), many of whom in turn are connected to existing local networks. Al-Qaida's spread has been compared to a virus or a bacterium, dispersing its contagion to disparate sites.[114] Although this is a seductive analogy, it is also misleading: the perpetuation of al-Qaida is a sentient process involving well-considered marketing strategies and deliberate tactical decisions, not a mindless "disease" process; thinking of it as a "disease" shores up the unfortunate American tendency to avoid analyzing the mentality of the enemy. Al-Qaida is operating with a long-term strategy and is certainly not following the left-wing groups of the 1970s in their failure to articulate a coherent ideological vision or the peripatetic right-wing groups of the twentieth century. It has transitioned beyond its original structure and now represents a multigenerational threat with staying power comparable to the enthnonationalist groups of the twentieth century. Likewise, arguments about whether al-Qaida is best described primarily as an ideology or by its opposition to foreign occupation of Muslim lands are specious: al-Qaida's adherents use both rationales to spread their links. The movement is opportunistic. The challenge for the United States and its allies is to move beyond rigid mind-sets and paradigms, do more in-depth analysis, and be more nimble and strategic in response to al-Qaida's fluid agenda.

The third and fourth models of a terrorist organization's end—achievement of the group's cause and transition toward a political role, negotiations, or amnesty—also bear little relevance to al-Qaida today. It is hard to conceive of al-Qaida fully achieving its aims, in part because those aims have evolved over time, variably including achievement of a pan-Islamic caliphate, the overthrow of non-Islamic regimes, and the expulsion of all infidels from Muslim countries, not to mention support for the Palestinian cause and the killing of Americans and other so-called infidels. Historically, terrorist groups that have achieved their ends have done so by articulating clear, limited objectives. Al-Qaida's goals, at least as articulated over recent years, could not be achieved without overturning an international political and economic system characterized by globalization and predominant U.S. power. As the historical record indicates, negotiations or a transition to a legitimate political process requires feasible terms and a sense of stalemate in the struggle. Also, members of terrorist groups seeking negotiations often have an incentive to find a way out of what they consider a losing cause. None of this describes bin Laden's al-Qaida.

This points to another issue. As al-Qaida has become a hybrid or "virtual organization," rather than a coherent hierarchical organization, swallowing its propaganda and treating it as a unified whole is a mistake. It is possible that bin Laden and his lieutenants have attempted to cobble together such disparate entities (or those entities have opportunistically attached themselves to al-Qaida) that they have stretched beyond the point at which their interests can be represented in this movement. Some of the local groups that have recently claimed an association with al-Qaida have in the past borne more resemblance to ethnonationalist/separatist groups such as the PLO, the IRA, and the LTTE. Examples include local affiliates in Indonesia, Morocco, Tunisia, and Turkey. This is not to argue that these groups' aims are rightful or that their tactics are legitimate. Rather, because of its obsession with the notion of a monolithic al-Qaida, the United States is glossing over both the extensive local variation within terrorist groups and their different goals; these groups have important points of divergence with al-Qaida's agenda, and the United States does no one any favors by failing to seriously analyze and exploit those local differences (except perhaps al-Qaida).

The U.S. objective must be to enlarge the movement's internal inconsistencies and differences. Al-Qaida's aims have become so sweeping that one might wonder whether they genuinely carry within them the achievement of specific local grievances. There is more hope of ending such groups through traditional methods if they are dealt with using traditional tools, even including, on a case-by-case basis, concessions or negotiations with specific local elements that may have negotiable or justifiable terms (albeit pursued through an illegitimate tactic). The key is to emphasize the differences with al-Qaida's agenda and to drive a wedge between the movement and its recent adherents. The historical record of other terrorist groups indicates that it is a mistake to treat al-Qaida as a monolith, to lionize it as if it is an unprecedented phenomenon with all elements equally committed to its aims, for that eliminates a range of proven counterterrorist tools and techniques for ending it. It is also a mistake to nurture al-Qaida's rallying point, a hatred of Americans and a resentment of U.S. policies (especially in Iraq and between Israel and the Palestinians), thereby conveniently facilitating the glossing over of differences within.

Fifth, reducing popular support, both active and passive, is an effective means of hastening the demise of some terrorist groups. This technique has received much attention among critics of George W. Bush and his administration's policies, many of whom argue that concentrating on the "roots" of terrorism is a necessary alternative to the current policy of emphasizing military force. This is a superficial argument, however, as it can be countered that a "roots" approach is precisely at the heart of current U.S. policy: the promotion of democracy may be seen as an idealistic effort to provide an alternative to populations in the Muslim world, frustrated by corrupt governance, discrimination, unemployment, and stagnation. But the participants in this debate are missing the point.[115] The problem is timing: democratization is a decades-long approach to a short-term and immediate problem whose solution must also be measured in months, not just years. The efforts being undertaken are unlikely to have a rapid enough effect to counter the anger, frustration, and sense of humiliation that characterize passive supporters. As for those who actively sustain the movement through terrorist acts, it is obviously a discouraging development that many recent operatives have lived in, or even been natives of, democratic countries—the March 2004 train attacks in Madrid and 2005 bombings in London being notable examples.[116]

The history of terrorism provides little comfort to those who believe that democratization is a good method to reduce active and passive support for terrorist attacks. There is no evidence that democratization correlates with a reduction in terrorism; in fact, available historical data suggest the opposite. Democratization was arguably the cause of much of the terrorism of the twentieth century. Moreover, democracy in the absence of strong political institutions and civil society could very well bring about radical Islamist governments over which the West would have little influence. There are much worse things than terrorism, and it might continue to be treated as a regrettable but necessary accompaniment to change were it not for two potentially serious developments in the twenty-first century: (1) the use of increasingly destructive weapons that push terrorist attacks well beyond the "nuisance" level, and (2) the growing likelihood that terrorism will lead to future systemic war. In any case, the long-term, idealistic, and otherwise admirable policy of democratization, viewed as "Americanization" in many parts of the world, does not represent a sufficiently targeted response to undercutting popular support for al-Qaida.

There are two vulnerabilities, however, where cutting the links between al-Qaida and its supporters hold promise: its means of funding and its means of communication. Efforts to cut off funding through traditional avenues have had some results. But not nearly enough attention is being paid to twenty-first-century communications, especially al-Qaida's presence on the internet. The time has come to recognize that the stateless, anarchical realm of cyberspace requires better tools for monitoring, countermeasures, and, potentially, even control. Previous leaps in cross-border communication such as the telegraph, radio, and telephone engendered counteracting developments in code breaking, monitoring, interception, and wiretapping. This may seem a heretical suggestion for liberal states, especially for a state founded on the right of free speech; however, the international community will inevitably be driven to take countermeasures in response to future attacks. It is time to devote more resources to addressing this problem now. Western analysts have been misguided in focusing on the potential use of the internet for so-called cyberterrorism (i.e., its use in carrying out attacks); the internet is far more dangerous as a tool to shore up and perpetuate the al-Qaida movement's constituency.[117] Preventing or interdicting al-Qaida's ability to disseminate its message and draw adherents into its orbit is crucial. Countering its messages in serious ways, not through the outdated and stilted vehicles of government websites and official statements but through sophisticated alternative sites and images attractive to a new generation, is an urgent priority.

As for the opponent's marketing strategy, al-Qaida and its associates have made serious mistakes of timing, choice of targets, and technique; yet the United States and its allies have done very little to capitalize on them. In particular, the United States tends to act as if al-Qaida is essentially a static enemy that will react to its actions, but then fails to react effectively and strategically to the movement's missteps. The Bali attacks, the May 2003 attacks in Saudi Arabia, the Madrid attacks, the July 2005 London attacks—all were immediately and deliberately trumpeted by al-Qaida associates. Where was the coordinated counterterrorist multimedia response? There is nothing so effective at engendering public revulsion as images of murdered and maimed victims, many of whom resemble family members of would-be recruits, lying on the ground as the result of a terrorist act. Outrage is appropriate. Currently, however, those images are dominated by would-be family members in Iraq, the Palestinian territories, Abu Ghraib, and Guantanamo Bay. The West is completely outflanked on the airwaves, and its countermeasures are virtually nonexistent on the internet. But as the RIRA, PFLP-GC, and ETA cases demonstrate, the al-Qaida movement can undermine itself, if it is given help. A large part of this "war" is arguably being fought not on a battlefield but in cyberspace. The time-honored technique of undermining active and passive support for a terrorist group through in-depth analysis, agile responses to missteps, carefully targeted messages, and cutting-edge technological solutions is a top priority.

This is a crucial moment of opportunity. Polls indicate that many of al-Qaida's potential constituents have been deeply repulsed by recent attacks. According to the Pew Global Attitudes Project, publics in many predominantly Muslim states increasingly see Islamic extremism as a threat to their own countries, express less support for terrorism, have less confidence in bin Laden, and reflect a declining belief in the usefulness of suicide attacks.[118] In these respects, there is a growing range of commonality in the attitudes of Muslim and non-Muslim publics; yet the United States focuses on itself and does little to nurture cooperation. American public diplomacy is the wrong concept. This is not about the United States and its ideals, values, culture, and image abroad: this is about tapping into a growing international norm against killing innocent civilians—whether, for example, on vacation or on their way to work or school—many of whom are deeply religious and many of whom also happen to be Muslims. If the United States and its allies fail to grasp this concept, to work with local cultures and local people to build on common goals and increase their alienation from this movement, then they will have missed a long-established and promising technique for ending a terrorist group such as al-Qaida.

There is little to say about the sixth factor, the use of military repression, in ending al-Qaida. Even though the U.S. military has made important progress in tracking down and killing senior operatives, the movement's ability to evolve has demonstrated the limits of such action, especially when poorly coordinated with other comparatively underfunded approaches and engaged in by a democracy. Although apparently effective, the Turkish government's repression of the PKK and the Peruvian government's suppression of Shining Path, for example, yield few desirable parallels for the current counterterrorist campaign.

Transitioning out of terrorism and toward either criminality or full insurgency is the final, worrisome historical precedent for al-Qaida. In a sense, the network is already doing both. Efforts to cut off funding through the formal banking system have ironically heightened the incentive and necessity to engage in illicit activities, especially narcotics trafficking. With the increasing amount of poppy seed production in Afghanistan, al-Qaida has a natural pipeline to riches. This process is well under way. As for al-Qaida becoming a full insurgency, some analysts believe this has already occurred.[119] Certainly to the extent that Abu Musab al-Zarqawi and his associates in Iraq truly represent an arm of the movement (i.e., al-Qaida in Iraq), that transition is likewise well along. The alliance negotiated between bin Laden and al-Zarqawi is another example of an effective strategic and public relations move for both parties, giving new life to the al-Qaida movement at a time when its leaders are clearly on the run and providing legitimacy and fresh recruits for the insurgency in Iraq. As many commentators have observed, Iraq is an ideal focal point and training ground for this putative global insurgency. The glimmer of hope in this scenario, however, is that the foreigners associated with al-Qaida are not tied to the territory of Iraq in the same way the local population is, and the tensions that will arise between those who want a future for the nascent Iraqi state and those who want a proving ground for a largely alien ideology and virtual organization are likely to increase—especially as the victims of the civil war now unfolding there continue increasingly to be Iraqi civilians. The counter to al-Zarqawi's al-Qaida in Iraq, as it is for other areas of the world with local al-Qaida affiliates, is to tap into the long-standing and deep association between peoples and their territory and to exploit the inevitable resentment toward foreign terrorist agendas, while scrupulously ensuring that the United States is not perceived to be part of those agendas.

If the United States continues to treat al-Qaida as if it were utterly unprecedented, as if the decades-long experience with fighting modern terrorism were totally irrelevant, then it will continue to make predictable and avoidable mistakes in responding to this threat. It will also miss important strategic opportunities. That experience points particularly toward dividing new local affiliates from al-Qaida by understanding and exploiting their differences with the movement, rather than treating the movement as a monolith. It is also crucial to more effectively break the political and logistical connections between the movement and its supporters, reinvigorating time-honored counterterrorism tactics targeted at al-Qaida's unique characteristics, including the perpetuation of its message, its funding, and its communications. Al-Qaida continues to exploit what is essentially a civil war within the Muslim world, attracting alienated Muslims around the globe to its rage-filled movement. Al-Qaida will end when the West removes itself from the heart of this fight, shores up international norms against terrorism, undermines al-Qaida's ties with its followers, and begins to exploit the movement's abundant missteps.

Conclusion

Major powers regularly relearn a seminal lesson of strategic planning, which is that embarking on a long war or campaign without both a grounding in previous experience and a realistic projection of an end state is folly. This is just as true in response to terrorism as it is with more conventional forms of political violence. Terrorism is an illegitimate tactic that by its very nature is purposefully and ruthlessly employed.[120] At the heart of a terrorist's plan is seizing and maintaining the initiative. Policymakers who have no concept of a feasible outcome are unlikely to formulate clear steps to reach it, especially once they are compelled by the inexorable action/reaction, offense/defense dynamic that all too often drives terrorism and counterterrorism. Although history does not repeat itself, ignoring history is the surest way for a state to be manipulated by the tactic of terrorism.

At the highest levels, U.S. counterterrorism policy has been formulated organically and instinctively, in reaction to external stimuli or on the basis of unexamined assumptions, with a strong bias toward U.S. exceptionalism. Sound counterterrorism policy should be based on the full range of historical lessons learned about which policies have worked, and under which conditions, to hasten terrorism's decline and demise. Treating al-Qaida as if it were sui generis is a mistake. As I have argued here, while there are unique aspects to this threat, there are also connections with earlier threats. Speaking of an unprecedented "jihadist" threat, while arguably resonating in a U.S. domestic context, only perpetuates the image and perverse romanticism of the al-Qaida movement abroad, making its ideology more attractive to potential recruits. Such an approach also further undermines any inclination by the United States to review and understand the relationship between historical instances of terrorism and the contemporary plotting of a strategy for accelerating al-Qaida's demise. In short, formulating U.S. counterterrorism strategy as if no other state has ever faced an analogous threat is a serious blunder.

Comparatively speaking, the United States has not had a great deal of experience with terrorism on its territory. In this respect, its response to the shock of al-Qaida's attacks is understandable. But the time for a learning curve is past. Intellectually, it is always much easier to over- or underreact to terrorist attacks than it is to take the initiative and think through the scenarios for how a terrorist group, and a counterterrorist effort, will wind down. Short-term reactive thinking is misguided for two reasons: the extraordinary and expensive effort to end terrorism will be self-perpetuating, and the inept identification of U.S. aims will ensure that the application of means is unfocused and ill informed by past experience. Failing to think through al-Qaida's termination, and how U.S. policy either advances or precludes it, is an error not only for the Bush administration, criticized by some for allegedly wanting an excuse to hype a permanent threat, but also for any administration of either political party that succeeds or replaces it.

Terrorism, like war, never ends; however, individual terrorist campaigns and the groups that wage them always do. A vague U.S. declaration of a war on terrorism has brought with it a vague concept of the closing stages of al-Qaida rather than a compelling road map for how it will be reduced to the level of a minor threat. The only outcome that is inevitable in the current U.S. policy is that militarily focused efforts will end, because of wasteful or counterproductive effort and eventual exhaustion. The threat is real and undeniable, but continuing an ahistorical approach to effecting al-Qaida's end is a recipe for failure, the further alienation of allies, and the squandering of U.S. power.

Audrey Kurth Cronin is Director of Studies of the Changing Character of War Program at Oxford University. Dr. Cronin came to Oxford University from the U.S. National War College, National Defense University, where she was Professor of Strategy and taught courses on international terrorism, strategy, and policy-making. She also worked at the Congressional Research Service, Library of Congress, where she advised Members of Congress and their staffs on terrorism matters.

Notes

1. On this point, see Frederick Schulze, "Breaking the Cycle: Empirical Research and Postgraduate Studies on Terrorism," in Andrew Silke, ed., *Research on Terrorism: Trends, Achievements, and Failures* (London: Frank Cass, 2004), pp. 161–185.
2. See, for example, "CIA Chief Has 'Excellent Idea' Where bin Laden Is," June 22, 2005, http://www.cnn.com/2005/US/06/20/goss.bin.laden/index.html.
3. Andrew Silke, "The Road Less Travelled: Recent Trends in Terrorism Research," in Silke, *Research on Terrorism,* p. 191.
4. Andrew Silke, "An Introduction to Terrorism Research," in Silke, *Research on Terrorism,* pp. 1–29.

5. Silke, *Research on Terrorism,* pp. 208–209.
6. Martha Crenshaw, "How Terrorism Declines," *Terrorism and Political Violence,* Vol. 3, No. 1 (Spring 1991), p. 73; and Jeffrey Ian Ross and Ted Robert Gurr, "Why Terrorism Subsides: A Comparative Study of Canada and the United States," *Comparative Politics,* Vol. 21, No. 4 (July 1989), pp. 407–408. Examples of articles on the drivers of terrorism include Michael Mousseau, "Market Civilization and Its Clash with Terror," *International Security,* Vol. 27, No. 3 (Winter 2002/03), pp. 5–29; and Audrey Kurth Cronin, "Behind the Curve: Globalization and International Terrorism," *International Security,* Vol. 27, No. 3 (Winter 2002/03), pp. 30–58. See also Charles Knight and Melissa Murphy, and Michael Mousseau, "Correspondence: The Sources of Terrorism," *International Security,* Vol. 28, No. 2 (Fall 2003), pp. 192–198.
7. For more on this argument, especially as it relates to the causes of terrorism, see Audrey Kurth Cronin, "Sources of Contemporary Terrorism," in Cronin and James M. Ludes, eds., *Attacking Terrorism: Elements of a Grand Strategy* (Washington, D.C.: Georgetown University Press, 2004), pp. 19–45, especially p. 22.
8. See United States Institute of Peace, "How Terrorism Ends," Special Report, No. 48 (Washington, D.C.: United States Institute of Peace, May 25, 1999), especially the overview section written by Martha Crenshaw, pp. 2–4.
9. For example, Bruce Hoffman compares al-Qaida to the archetypal shark that must continue swimming to survive. See, for example, Ann Scott Tyson, "Al-Qaeda Broken, but Dangerous," *Christian Science Monitor,* June 24, 2002. See also Martha Crenshaw, "Decisions to Use Terrorism: Psychological Constraints on Instrumental Reasoning," *International Social Movements Research,* Vol. 4 (1992), pp. 29–42.
10. Among numerous sources on these subjects, see Martha Crenshaw, "The Psychology of Terrorism: An Agenda for the Twenty-first Century," *Political Psychology,* Vol. 21, No. 2 (June 2000), pp. 405–420; Martha Crenshaw, "The Logic of Terrorism," in Walter Reich, ed., *Origins of Terrorism: Psychologies, Ideologies, Theologies, States of Mind,* 2d ed. (Washington, D.C.: Woodrow Wilson Center Press, 1998), pp. 7–24; and Jerrold Post, "Terrorist Psycho-Logic," in Reich, *Origins of Terrorism,* pp. 25–40.
11. This approach is well established in criminology and intelligence analysis. See, for example, Irene Jung Fiala, "Anything New? The Racial Profiling of Terrorists," *Criminal Justice Studies,* Vol. 16, No. 1 (March 2003), pp. 53–58; Rex A. Hudson, *Who Becomes a Terrorist and Why? The 1999 Government Report on Profiling Terrorists* (Guilford, Conn.: Lyons, 2002); and Paul R. Pillar, "Counterterrorism after al-Qaeda," *Washington Quarterly,* Vol. 27, No. 3 (Summer 2004), p. 105. As Pillar points out, the Transportation Security Administration already uses profiling to screen airline passengers. Ibid.
12. See, for example, Alan Krueger and Jitka Maleckova, "Education, Poverty, Political Violence, and Terrorism: Is There a Causal Connection?" Working Paper, No. 9074 (Cambridge, Mass.: National Bureau of Economic Research, July 2002), p. 2; Alan Richards, *Socio-economic Roots of Radicalism? Towards Explaining the Appeal of Islamic Radicals* (Carlisle, Pa.: Strategic Studies Institute, Army War College, July 2003); Daniel Pipes, "God and Mammon: Does Poverty Cause Militant Islam?" *National Interest,* No. 66 (Winter 2001/2002), pp. 14–21; and Gary T. Dempsey, "Old Folly in a New Disguise: Nation Building to Combat Terrorism," Policy Analysis Series, No. 429 (Washington, D.C.: Cato Institute, March 21, 2002).
13. See, for example, Leonard Weinberg and William Lee Eubank, "Leaders and Followers in Italian Terrorist Groups," *Terrorism and Political Violence,* Vol. 1, No. 2 (April 1989), pp. 156–176.
14. For an organizational analysis of terrorist groups, see David C. Rapoport, ed., *Inside Terrorist Organizations,* 2d ed. (London: Frank Cass, 2001).
15. Martha Crenshaw, "Theories of Terrorism: Instrumental and Organizational Approaches," in Rapoport, *Inside Terrorist Organizations,* pp. 19–27.
16. See, for example, Ian O. Lesser, Bruce Hoffman, John Arguilla, David Ronfeldt, and Michele Zanini, *Countering the New Terrorism* (Santa Monica, Calif.: RAND, 1999); John Arquilla and David F. Ronfeldt, eds., *Networks and Netwars: The Future of Terror, Crime, and Militancy* (Santa Monica, Calif.: RAND, 2001); and Ray Takeyh and Nikolas Gvosdev, "Do Terrorist

Networks Need a Home?" *Washington Quarterly*, Vol. 25, No. 3 (Summer 2002), pp. 97–108; and Matthew Levitt, "Untangling the Terror Web: Identifying and Counteracting the Phenomenon of Crossover between Terrorist Groups," *SAIS Review*, Vol. 24, No. 1 (Winter–Spring 2004), pp. 33–48.

17. Steve Coll and Susan B. Glasser, "Terrorists Turn to the Web as Base of Operations," *Washington Post*, August 7, 2005; Craig Whitlock, "Briton Used Internet as His Bully Pulpit," *Washington Post*, August 8, 2005; and Susan B. Glasser, and Steve Coll, "The Web as Weapon: Zarqawi Intertwines Acts on Ground in Iraq with Propaganda Campaign on the Internet," *Washington Post*, August 9, 2005.

18. United States Institute of Peace, "How Terrorism Ends," p. 1.

19. David C. Rapoport, "Terrorism," in Mary Hawkesworth and Maurice Kogan, eds., *Routledge Encyclopedia of Government and Politics*, Vol. 2 (London: Routledge, 1992), p. 1067. This claim admittedly needs to be updated. A good study of the life span of terrorist organizations, including those that gained purchase in the 1990s, is still waiting to be written.

20. In discussing the longevity of terrorist groups, Martha Crenshaw notes only three significant groups with ethnonationalist ideologies that ceased to exist within ten years of their formation. One of these, the National Organization of Cypriot Fighters (Ethniki Organosis Kyprion Agoniston, or EOKA), disbanded because its goal—the liberation of Cyprus—was achieved. By contrast, a majority of the terrorist groups that she lists as having existed for ten years or longer have recognizable ethnonationalist ideologies, including the Irish Republican Army (in its many forms), Sikh separatist groups, Basque Homeland and Freedom (Euskadi Ta Askatasuna, or ETA), various Palestinian nationalist groups, and the Corsican National Liberation Front. See Crenshaw, "How Terrorism Declines," pp. 69–87.

21. David C. Rapoport, "Fear and Trembling: Terrorism in Three Religious Traditions," *American Political Science Review*, Vol. 78, No. 3 (September 1984), pp. 658–677. Rapoport asserts that before the nineteenth century, religion was the only acceptable cause for terrorism, providing a transcendent purpose that rose above the treacherous and petty political concerns of man.

22. Crenshaw, "How Terrorism Declines," p. 73.

23. Walter Enders and Todd Sandler, "Transnational Terrorism, 1968–2000: Thresholds, Persistence, and Forecasts," *Southern Economic Journal*, Vol. 71, No. 3 (January 2004), pp. 467–482; Todd Sandler, Walter Enders, and Harvey E. Lapan, "Economic Analysis Can Help Fight International Terrorism," *Challenge*, January/February 1991, pp. 10–17; and Walter Enders and Todd Sandler, "Is Transnational Terrorism Becoming More Threatening? A Time-Series Investigation," *Journal of Conflict Resolution*, Vol. 44, No. 3 (June 2000), pp. 307–332.

24. Jonathan David Farley, "Breaking Al-Qaida Cells: A Mathematical Analysis of Counterterrorism Operations (A Guide for Risk Assessment and Decision Making)," *Studies in Conflict and Terrorism*, Vol. 26, No. 6 (November/December 2003), pp. 399–411. See also Bernard Harris, "Mathematical Methods in Combatting Terrorism," *Risk Analysis*, Vol. 24, No. 4 (August 2004), pp. 985–988.

25. For example, referring to the case study of the Weathermen, Ehud Sprinzak argues that left-wing groups evolve through three stages: crisis of confidence, conflict of legitimacy, and crisis of legitimacy. See Sprinzak, "The Psychopolitical Formation of Extreme Left Terrorism in a Democracy: The Case of the Weatherman," in Reich, *Origins of Terrorism*, pp. 65–85. For another argument about the psychological phases for terrorist groups, see Albert Bandura, "Mechanisms of Moral Disengagement," in Reich, *Origins of Terrorism*, pp. 161–191.

26. Leonard Weinberg and Louise Richardson, "Conflict Theory and the Trajectory of Terrorist Campaigns in Western Europe," in Silke, *Research on Terrorism*, pp. 138–160.

27. Ehud Sprinzak, "Right-Wing Terrorism in Comparative Perspective: The Case of Split Delegitimization," in Tore Bjorgo, ed., *Terrorism from the Extreme Right* (London: Frank Cass, 1995), pp. 17–43.

28. Ted Robert Gurr, *Why Men Rebel* (Princeton, N.J.: Princeton University Press, 1970). There is a rich literature from the 1960s and 1970s on political violence, of which terrorism is arguably a subset. Gurr defines political violence as "all collective attacks within a political community against the political regime, its actor—including competing political groups as well as incumbents—or its policies." Ibid., pp. 3–4.

29. Crenshaw, "How Terrorism Declines," p. 82. See also John O. Voll, "Bin Laden and the New Age of Global Terrorism," *Middle East Policy,* Vol. 8, No. 4 (December 2001), pp. 1–5; and Quintan Wiktorowicz, "Framing Jihad: Intra-movement Framing Contests and al-Qaida's Struggle for Sacred Authority," *International Review of Social History,* Vol. 49, Supp. 12 (December 2004), pp. 159–177.

30. David C. Rapoport, "The Four Waves of Modern Terrorism," in Cronin and Ludes, *Attacking Terrorism,* pp. 46–73; and David C. Rapoport, "The Fourth Wave: September 11 in the History of Terrorism," *Current History,* December 2001, pp. 419–424.

31. The best of these is Martha Crenshaw's edited book *Terrorism in Context* (University Park: Pennsylvania State University Press, 1995), because it examines both the evolution of terrorist organizations and the counterterrorist techniques used against them. It explains terrorism as part of broader processes of political and social change. Reflecting its own historical context, however, there is a strong bias toward left-wing and ethnonationalist/separatist groups. In the wake of September 11, Yonah Alexander produced an edited volume of comparative case studies, *Combating Terrorism: Strategies of Ten Countries* (Ann Arbor: University of Michigan Press, 2002), which emphasizes counterterrorist techniques used mainly against European groups. Another promising study is Robert J. Art and Louise Richardson, *Democracy and Terrorism: Lessons from the Past* (Washington, D.C.: United States Institute of Peace, forthcoming).

32. Crenshaw, "How Terrorism Declines," p. 70.

33. Crenshaw, "Thoughts on Relating Terrorism to Historical Contexts," in Crenshaw, *Terrorism in Context,* pp. 3–24. One interesting comparative study of terrorist groups in two countries, Canada and the United States, concluded that four factors led to terrorism's decline: preemption, deterrence, burnout, and backlash. Its applicability was limited by the small number of cases, however, Jeffrey Ian Ross and Ted Robert Gurr, "Why Terrorism Subsides: A Comparative Study of Canada and the United States," *Comparative Politics,* Vol. 21, No. 4 (July 1989), pp. 405–426.

34. Crenshaw argues that the decline of terrorism results from the interplay of three factors: the government's response, the choices of the terrorist group, and the organization's resources. See Crenshaw, "How Terrorism Declines," p. 80. In another article, she further explores the internal and external factors, pointing to how government strategies such as deterrence, enhanced defense, and negotiations interact with terrorist group success, organizational breakdown, dwindling support, and new alternatives for terrorist organizations. See United States Institute of Peace, "How Terrorism Ends," pp. 2–5.

35. See the annual U.S. Department of State *Country Reports on Terrorism* (which, beginning in 2004, replaced *Patterns of Global Terrorism*) at http://www.state.gov/s/ct/rls/crt. In 2003 the PKK was renamed Kongra-Gel, which continues to be a designated group.

36. Audrey Kurth Cronin, Huda Aden, Adam Frost, and Benjamin Jones, *Foreign Terrorist Organizations,* CRS Report for Congress (Washington, D.C.: Congressional Research Service, February 6, 2004), pp. 103–105, Order Code RL32223.

37. Guzmán was sentenced to life in prison in 1992, but the trial was later ruled unconstitutional; he is scheduled to be retried (for a second time). His successor, Oscar Ramírez Duran, also known as Feliciano, continued to direct the movement after Guzmán's capture; but as mentioned earlier, the group's membership sharply plummeted. The State Department has estimated its strength at between 400 and 500 members, down from as many as 10,000 in the late 1980s and early 1990s. See U.S. Department of State, *Patterns of Global Terrorism, 2003,* April 2004, http://www.state.gov/documents/organization/31912.pdf. Duran was likewise captured in July 1999. Some analysts worry that the group may resurge, with notable attacks in 2002 and 2003. See Cronin et al., *Foreign Terrorist Organizations,* p. 103. Although possible, resurgence on a large scale is unlikely: the capture of Guzmán was clearly a watershed. See also Art and Richardson, *Democracy and Counterterrorism.*

38. For an explanation of the meaning of this term and other main typologies of terrorism, see Cronin, "Behind the Curve," pp. 39–42.

39. "U.S. Welcomes Ocalan Capture," Agence France-Presse, February 16, 1999. Ocalan's sentence was later commuted to life in prison.

40. "Turkey Lifts Ocalan Death Sentence," *BBC News,* October 3, 2002,http://news.bbc.co.uk/2/hi/europe/2296679.stm.

41. Cronin et al., *Foreign Terrorist Organizations,* pp. 53–55.

42. Ibid., pp. 88–89; and U.S. Department of State, *Patterns of Global Terrorism, 2003.*

43. Cronin et al., *Foreign Terrorist Organizations,* pp. 17–19; and U.S. Department of State, *Patterns of Global Terrorism, 2003.* According to the State Department, in July 2001 a small group of Aum members was arrested in Russia before it could follow through with its plan to set off bombs near the Imperial Palace in Tokyo, free Asahara, and smuggle him into Russia.

44. Direct Action's four principal leaders, Joelle Aubron, Georges Cipriani, Nathalie Menigon, and Jean-Marc Rouillan, were arrested in February 1987, followed shortly thereafter by Max Frerot, effectively dismantling the leadership of the group and putting an end to its activities. Members of the People's Liberation Forces killed their own deputy leader when she appeared to be interested in negotiating with the Salvadoran government; the leader of the group, Salvador Cayetano Carpio, committed suicide shortly thereafter, resulting in the disintegration of the group and essentially its absorption into a larger organization, the Farabundo Martí National Liberation Front. After a four-day siege of their compound in April 1985, eight leaders of the Covenant, the Sword, and the Arm of the Lord were arrested and imprisoned, effectively ending the group. The Chilean group Manuel Rodriguez Patriotic Front Dissidents essentially ceased to exist because of the arrest of its key leaders in the 1990s. The latter reached a peace agreement with the Salvadoran government in 1991. See the MIPT Terrorism Knowledge Base, a database of domestic and international terrorist organizations, at http://www.tkb.org.

45. Che Guevara was captured and killed by the Bolivian army in October 1967 and subsequently became a legendary figure who inspired leftist and separatist groups in Latin America and throughout the world. Leila Ali Khaled of the Popular Front for the Liberation of Palestine carried the book *My Friend Che* with her when she hijacked TWA flight 840 in August 1969. In the United States, the Weathermen also organized massive protests on the second anniversary of Che's death. Harvey Kushner, *Encyclopedia of Terrorism* (Thousand Oaks, Calif.: Sage, 2003), pp. 155–156, 372, 406.

46. I am grateful to Mia Bloom for sharing this observation.

47. Sheikh Omar is the leader of the Egyptian al-Gama al-Islamiya, which is closely tied with Egyptian Islamic Jihad. Although imprisoned for life in the United States, he has continued to call on his followers to engage in violence, especially against Jews. He was also convicted for plotting to bomb the Holland and Lincoln Tunnels and the United Nations building and to assassinate Senator Alphonse D'Amato and UN Secretary General Boutros Boutros-Ghali. See, for example, Anonymous, *Through Our Enemies' Eyes: Osama bin Laden, Radical Islam, and the Future of America* (Washington, D.C.: Brassey's 2002), p. 274.

48. Members of the Baader-Meinhof group engaged in violence during numerous attempts to free their imprisoned comrades, for example. The Blind Sheikh has also prompted violence aimed at his release. Ibid.

49. For an explanation of the major types of terrorist organizations, see Cronin, "Behind the Curve," pp. 39–42.

50. The Red Army Faction, a successor of the Baader-Meinhof group, arguably continued for some years and transitioned to what it called its "third generation," with claims of attacks in the name of the RAF during the 1980s and early 1990s. The degree to which it truly was the same group is debatable. In any case, the dissolution of the Soviet Union severely undermined its ideology. See entry in MIPT Terrorism Knowledge Base.

51. Crenshaw, "How Terrorism Declines," p. 78. On right-wing groups, see Cronin, "Behind the Curve," pp. 39–42.

52. These include the Christian Patriots, the Aryan Nations, the Ku Klux Klan, and The Order (a short-lived faction of Aryan Nations) in the United States, as well as the Anti-Zionist Movement in Italy and the National Warriors of South Africa.

53. In the United States, the Ku Klux Klan is a notable example.

54. Some groups, such as The Order (active between 1982 and 1984), have been idolized by their admirers and continue to exercise influence.

55. The concept of "leaderless existence" apparently originated with Col. Ulius Louis Amoss, who wrote an essay with this as the title in 1962. It was later popularized by Louis R. Beam Jr., Aryan Nations leader and former Texas Ku Klux Klan Grand Dragon leader. See Beam, "Leaderless Resistance," *The Seditionist,* No. 12 (February 1992).

56. During much of this period, the African National Congress was labeled a terrorist organization by the U.S. Department of Defense but not by the U.S. State Department.

57. The South-West African People's Organization underwent a similar transition: from orchestrating bombings in banks, stores, schools, and service stations to governing Namibia.

58. For example, among those that had outside protectors, Laqueur includes the Palestinian Arab groups and the Croatian Ustasha. For those facing imperial powers not able to hold on to colonies, he includes the IRA (Britain and Ireland after World War I), the Irgun (Britain and the Palestine Mandate after World War II), and the EOKA (Britain and Cyprus, also after World War II). Walter Laqueur, *Terrorism* (London: Weidenfeld and Nicolson, 1977), p. 118.

59. The talks have stopped and started several times, and at this writing are threatened by renewed violence; however, it looks as if they will result in limited Tamil autonomy.

60. Other splinter groups include the Continuity IRA and the Irish National Liberation Army.

61. For a discussion of this problem, see Fred Charles Ilké, *Every War Must End,* 2d ed. (New York: Columbia University Press, 2005), pp. 84–105.

62. Negotiations, however, complicate a terrorist organization's efforts to perpetuate its own absolutist perspective in justifying the use of terrorist violence. See Adrian Guelke, *The Age of Terrorism and the International Political System* (London: I.B. Tauris, 1998), pp. 162–181.

63. Franco Ferracuti, "Ideology and Repentance: Terrorism in Italy," in Reich, *Origins of Terrorism,* pp. 59–64; and Leonard Weinberg, "Italy and the Red Brigades," in Art and Richardson, *Democracy and Counterterrorism.*

64. Other examples cited by Art and Richardson include amnesties or other incentives given to members of the ETA, the Shining Path, the FALN, the IRA, and the Tamil Tigers, with degrees of success related to whether members of a group perceived it as likely to prevail. See "Conclusion," in Art and Richardson, *Democracy and Counterterrorism.*

65. Peter A. Lupsha," Explanation of Political Violence: Some Psychological Theories versus Indignation," *Politics and Society,* Vol. 2, No. 1 (Fall 1971), pp. 89–104; and Luigi Bonanate, "Some Un-anticipated Consequences of Terrorism," *Journal of Peace Research,* Vol. 16, No. 3 (May 1979), pp. 197–211.

66. Terrorist operations, albeit shocking and tragic, at least as often increase the level of public support for the cause and indeed are designed to do so. Examples include the PLO, the Internal Macedonian Revolutionary Organization, the IRA, and nineteenth-century Russian terrorist groups. See Laqueur, *Terrorism.*

67. See Sean Boyne, "The Real IRA: After Omagh, What Now?" *Jane's Intelligence Review,* October 1998, http://www.janes.com/regional_news/europe/news/jir/jir980824_1_n.shtml.

68. MIPT database incident profile, http://64.233.167.104/search?q?cache:vBXLiW4gwekJ:www.tkb.org/Incident.jsp%3FincID%3D372+popular+revulsion+terrorist+group&hl=en. The PFLP-GC has ties with Syria and Libya and may have had a role in the bombing of Pan Am 103 over Lockerbie, Scotland. See Cronin et al., *Foreign Terrorist Organizations,* pp. 80–82; and Kenneth Katzman, *The PLO and Its Factions,* CRS Report for Congress (Washington, D.C.: Congressional Research Service, June 10, 2002), Order Code RS21235. The state sponsorship of this group from the 1980s may have reduced its dependency on a local constituency.

69. See, for example, Goldie Shabad and Franciso José Llera Ramo, "Political Violence in a Democratic State: Basque Terrorism in Spain," in Crenshaw, *Terrorism in Context,* pp. 410–469, especially pp. 455–462.

70. Mark Juergensmeyer, *Terror in the Mind of God: The Global Rise of Religious Violence* (Berkeley: University of California Press, 2000), pp. 84–101. See also C. Christine Fair, "Diaspora Involvement in Insurgencies: Insights from the Khalistan and Tamil Eelam Movements," *Nationalism and Ethnic Politics,* Vol. 11, No. 1 (Spring 2005), pp. 125–156.

71. Fair, "Diaspora Involvement in Insurgencies."

72. For more on state sponsorship, see Daniel Byman, *Deadly Connections: States That Sponsor Terrorism* (Cambridge: Cambridge University Press, 2005).

73. On intervention, see Adam Roberts, "The 'War on Terror' in Historical Perspective," *Survival,* Vol. 47, No. 2 (Summer 2005), pp. 115–121.

74. For recent work on this subject, see Mark Kramer, "The Perils of Counterinsurgency: Russia's War in Chechnya," *International Security,* Vol. 29, No. 3 (Winter 2004/05), pp. 5–63; and Mark Kramer, "Guerrilla Warfare, Counterinsurgency, and Terrorism in the North Caucasus: The Military Dimension of the Russian-Chechen Conflict," *Europe-Asia Studies,* Vol. 57, No. 2 (March 2005), pp. 209–290.

75. The International Institute for Strategic Studies (IISS) claims that Russian forces suffered 4,749 casualties between August 2002 and August 2003, the highest figure since the second Chechen conflict began in 1999. International Institute for Strategic Studies, *The Military Balance, 2003/2004* (London: IISS, 2003), pp. 86–87. For more on the Chechen case, see Audrey Kurth Cronin, "Russia and Chechnya," in Art and Richardson, *Democracy and Counterterrorism.*

76. These would include the Revolutionary Armed Forces of Colombia, the National Liberation Army, and the United Self-Defense Forces of Colombia.

77. See Larry Niksch, *Abu Sayyaf: Target of Philippine-U.S. Antiterrorism Cooperation,* CRS Report for Congress (Washington, D.C.: Congressional Research Service, updated April 8, 2003), Order Code RL31265; and Cronin et al., *Foreign Terrorist Organizations,* pp. 4–7.

78. Cronin et al., *Foreign Terrorist Organizations,* p. 92.

79. As Adam Roberts notes, the outbreak of World War I is a principal example: the Bosnian-Serb student who killed Archduke Franz Ferdinand in July 1914 had no intention of setting off an international cataclysm. See Ratko Parezanin, *Mlada Bosna I prvi svetski rat* [Young Bosnia and the First World War] (Munich: Iskra, 1974), cited in Roberts, "The 'War on Terror' in Historical Perspective," p. 107 n. 15.

80. Rapoport, "The Four Waves of Modern Terrorism," p. 66.

81. Coll and Glasser, "Terrorists Turn to the Web as Base of Operations."

82. Porter J. Goss, director of central intelligence, testimony before the Senate Select Committee on Intelligence, "Global Intelligence Challenges, 2005: Meeting Long-Term Challenges with a Long-Term Strategy," 109th Cong., 2d sess., February 16, 2005, http://www.cia.gov/cia/public_affairs/speeches/2004/Goss_testimony_02162005.html.

83. Possible exceptions include the international anarchist movement, which was confined to Russia, Europe, and the United States.

84. David Johnston, Don Van Natta Jr., and Judith Miller, "Qaida's New Links Increase Threats from Far-Flung Sites," *New York Times,* June 16, 2002. Many commentators have pointed out that al-Qaida is translated as "the base," "the foundation," or even "the method." It was not intended at its founding to be a single structure.

85. Xavier Raufer, "Al-Qaeda: A Different Diagnosis," *Studies in Conflict and Terrorism,* Vol. 26, No. 6 (November/December 2003), pp. 391–398.

86. For an early analysis of the arguments of both sides, see Audrey Kurth Cronin, *Al-Qaeda after the Iraq Conflict,* CRS Report for Congress (Washington, D.C.: Congressional Research Service, May 23, 2003), Order Code RS21529.

87. Central Intelligence Agency, "Afghanistan: An Incubator for International Terrorism," CTC 01-40004, March 27, 2001; and Central Intelligence Agency, "Al-Qa'ida Still Well Positioned to Recruit Terrorists," July 1, 2002, p. 1, both cited in *Final Report of the National Commission on Terrorist Attacks upon the United States* (New York: W.W. Norton, 2004), p. 67 n. 78.

88. Anonymous, *Through Our Enemies' Eyes,* especially pp. 126, 130–131; Marc Sageman, *Understanding Terror Networks* (Philadelphia: University of Pennsylvania Press, 2004), especially p. 121; and David Johnson and Don Van Natta Jr., "U.S. Officials See Signs of a Revived al-Qaida," *New York Times,* May 17, 2003.

89. International Institute for Strategic Studies, *Strategic Survey, 2003/4* (London: Routledge, 2005), p. 6.

90. See also "The Worldwide Threat, 2004: Challenges in a Changing Global Context," testimony of Director of Central Intelligence George J. Tenet before the Senate Select Committee on Intelligence, 108th Cong., 2d sess., February 24, 2004, http://www.cia.gov/cia/public_affairs/speeches/2004/dci_speech_02142004.html.

91. According to Sageman's analysis, operatives have gathered in regional clusters, which he labels "the central staff of al-Qaida," "the Southeast Asian cluster," "the Maghreb cluster," and "the core Arab cluster." Sageman, *Understanding Terror Networks.*

92. Ibid.; and Jeffrey Cozzens, "Islamist Groups Develop New Recruiting Strategies," *Jane's Intelligence Review,* February 1, 2005.

93. Sageman, *Understanding Terrorist Networks,* p. 119. Sageman's book analyzes the patterns of growth of cells involved in past attacks, including vigorous refutation of the thesis that exposure to ideology alone explains the growth of al-Qaida.

94. Ibid., p. 178.

95. Jack Kalpakian, "Building the Human Bomb: The Case of the 16 May 2003 Attacks in Casablanca," *Studies in Conflict and Terrorism,* Vol. 28, No. 2 (March–April 2005), pp. 113–127.

96. Al Jazeera TV, September 10, 2003, cited in Michael Scheuer, "Coalition Warfare: How al-Qaeda Uses the World Islamic Front against Crusaders and Jews, Part I," *Terrorism Focus,* Vol. 2, No. 7, March 31, 2005, http://www.jamestown.org/terrorism/news/article.php?articleid=2369530.

97. Paul Pillar, "Counterterrorism after al-Qaida," *Washington Quarterly,* Vol. 27, No. 3 (Summer 2004), pp. 101–113.

98. Cozzens, "Islamist Groups Develop New Recruiting Strategies."

99. Sageman, *Understanding Terrorist Networks,* especially p. 92.

100. On this point, see Bruce Hoffman, "The Changing Face of al-Qaida and the Global War on Terrorism," *Studies in Conflict and Terrorism,* Vol. 27, No. 6 (December 2004), p. 556.

101. On this subject, see Laqueur, *Terrorism,* especially pp. 3–20; and James Joll, *The Second International, 1889–1914* (London: Weidenfeld and Nicolson, 1955).

102. Bruce Hoffman, "The Leadership Secrets of Osama bin Laden: The Terrorist as CEO," *Atlantic Monthly,* April 2003, pp. 26–27.

103. Sageman, *Understanding Terrorist Networks,* pp. 50–51.

104. See Douglas Farah and Peter Finn, "Terrorism, Inc.: Al-Qaida Franchises Brand of Violence to Groups across World," *Washington Post,* November 21, 2003; Daniel Benjamin, "Are the Sparks Catching?" *Washington Post,* November 23, 2003; and Sebastian Rotella and Richard C. Paddock, "Experts See Major Shift in al-Qaida's Strategy," *Los Angeles Times,* November 19, 2003.

105. International Institute for Strategic Studies, *Strategic Survey,* 2003/4, p. 8.

106. "U.S.: Terror Funding Stymied," *CBS News,* January 11, 2005, http://www.cbsnews.com/stories/2005/01/11/terror/main666168.shtml.

107. These are methods of transferring value anonymously, without electronic traceability or paper trails. See Rensselaer Lee, *Terrorist Financing: The U.S. and International Response,* CRS Report for Congress (Washington, D.C.: Congressional Research Service, December 6, 2002), pp. 11–13, Order Code RL31658.

108. For information on informal financing mechanisms and U.S. efforts to control them, see testimony of Assistant Secretary Juan Carlos Zarate for Terrorist Financing and Financial Crimes, U.S. Department of the Treasury, before the House Financial Services Committee's Subcommittee on Oversight and Investigations, 109th Cong., 2d sess., February 16, 2005, http://www.ustreas.gov/press/releases/js2256.htm.

109. For more on illegal and legal globalized networks of financing, see *Terrorist Financing,* Report of an Independent Task Force Sponsored by the Council on Foreign Relations (New York: Council on Foreign Relations Press, October 2002); *Update on the Global Campaign against Terrorist Financing,* Second Report of an Independent Task Force on Terrorist Financing Sponsored by the Council on Foreign Relations (New York: Council on Foreign Relations Press, June 15, 2004); Loretta Napoleoni, *Modern Jihad: Tracing the Dollars behind*

the Terror Networks (London: Pluto, 2003); Douglas Farah, *Blood from Stones: The Secret Financial Network of Terror* (New York: Broadway Books, 2004); and Thomas J. Biersteker and Sue E. Eckert, eds., *Countering the Financing of Global Terrorism* (London: Routledge, forthcoming).

110. For more on this phenomenon, see Cronin, "Behind the Curve," pp. 30–58.

111. For an analysis of current terrorist use of the internet, see Gabriel Weimann, "www.terror. net: How Modern Terrorism Uses the Internet," Special Report, No. 116 (Washington, D.C.: United States Institute of Peace, March 2004).

112. Ibid., p. 7.

113. Comparable cell-based "immortal" terrorist networks have included the social revolutionary and anarchist movements of the late nineteenth and early twentieth centuries. I am indebted to Timothy Hoyt for this observation.

114. See, for example, Corine Hegland, "Global Jihad," *National Journal,* May 8, 2004, pp. 1396–1402.

115. As Jonathan Monten demonstrates, democratization is a long-standing goal of U.S. foreign policy; with respect to terrorism, however, both the "vindicationists" and the "exemplarists" are missing the point. Monten, "The Roots of the Bush Doctrine: Power, Nationalism, and Democracy Promotion in U.S. Strategy," *International Security,* Vol. 29, No. 4 (Spring 2005), pp. 112–156.

116. Nor will withdrawal from occupation in Iraq and Palestine, for example, solve this problem: al-Qaida-associated suicide attacks in Egypt, Morocco, Saudi Arabia, and Turkey belie that argument. See Robert A. Pape, *Dying to Win: The Strategic Logic of Suicide Terrorism* (New York: Random House, 2005).

117. On the broader significance of using the internet as a means of mobilization, see Audrey Kurth Cronin, "Cyber-mobilization: The New *Levée en Masse," Parameters,* Vol. 36, No. 2 (Summer 2006), pp. 77–87.

118. See "Islamic Extremism: Common Concern for Muslim and Western Publics, Support for Terror Wanes among Muslim Publics," July 14, 2005, http://pewglobal.org/reports/display. php?ReportID=248.

119. Among them is Michael Scheuer, author of Anonymous, *Imperial Hubris.*

120. I have dealt at length with the question of the definition of terrorism elsewhere and will not rehash those arguments here. See, for example Cronin, "Behind the Curve," pp. 32–33.

The author is indebted to Robert Art, David Auerswald, John Collins, Patrick Cronin, Timothy Hoyt, Joel Peters, Harvey Rishikof, Adam Roberts, Karen Wilhelm, and former colleagues and students at the U.S. National War College. The detailed comments of an anonymous reviewer were invaluable, and the Leverhulme Trust provided much-appreciated financial support.

Reid Sawyer and Jodi M. Vittori[1]

The Uncontested Battles

The Role of Actions, Networks, and Ideas in the Fight Against al Qaeda

Introduction

On October 15, 2007, a controversial article in the *Washington Post* reported that some U.S. military officials considered al Qaeda in Iraq (AQI) defeated.[2] While AQI is only one part of the Sunni extremist insurgency in Iraq, it has been the focal point for the broader al Qaeda movement both in terms of money[3] and personnel.[4] Supporters across the Middle East, and increasingly in Europe, have developed strong networks that facilitate the movement of thousands of foreign fighters, supplies, and money to answer AQI's call to arms. In organizational terms, Iraq has acted as a terrorism Petri dish where AQI developed new tactics and measures to attack the United States—both in Iraq and around the world.

Yet sustained and continual pressure on AQI has degraded the organization and disassembled its support networks. Going forward, the ability for AQI to shape the future jihadist fight outside of Iraq will be limited. AQI will face obstacles obtaining funds, distributing money across its network and maintaining a viable organization to attract recruits, for Iraq and for Islamist causes elsewhere. At a cursory glance, it could appear that the United States and its allies have achieved a strategic victory for the United States, and simultaneously, a substantial loss, not only strategically but also morally for the broader al Qaeda organization and its efforts to defeat the United States.

However, AQI is only one subset of a larger, more complex organization. There is no doubt that the potential defeat of AQI is significant, yet it is not clear how this will impede al Qaeda's future development and growth. For the United States and its allies' counterterrorism efforts to succeed, al Qaeda must be understood both as a multifaceted organization and a global social movement. As this paper will demonstrate, al Qaeda's dual nature requires that the United States and its allies fight this war on three levels: a war of action, a war of networks and, the most difficult and intractable conflict, a war of ideas. Failing to recognize and address these three interrelated levels will ensure al Qaeda remains a resilient organization with an increasing capacity for violence.

To illustrate these concepts, this paper consists of three sections. The first section describes the state of the jihad and al Qaeda today. The second explains how al Qaeda simultaneously exists as both an organization and a global social movement, and how these aspects reinforce each other. Finally, the third section explores the three levels on which the conflict is being waged and discusses the implications of systemic failures to contest key battles on each level.

The State of the Jihad Today

Looking at the state of the jihad today there is both good and bad news. No doubt al Qaeda has suffered significant losses since 9/11: Numerous senior leaders, along with thousands of their foot soldiers, have been captured or killed and al Qaeda has lost the freedom of maneuver it once enjoyed in Afghanistan. In the past year alone, al Qaeda faced a number of serious setbacks, the most significant being the damage to the AQI. At the same time, though, al Qaeda has expanded its base of operations, allied with new organizations and increased its worldwide operational tempo.

The Good News

Perhaps the most significant and successful sustained counterterrorism efforts against al Qaeda to date have taken place in Saudi Arabia. For three years, al Qaeda waged war against a variety of targets in Saudi Arabia ranging from attacks on Western housing compounds to Saudi Arabian targets. The resultant counterterrorism actions were staggering. "By the end of 2006 they had killed or captured over 260 terrorists including all but one of the most wanted top 26 in the country. According to the Saudis they foiled more than 25 major attacks."[5] In 2007, security forces interfered with yet another al Qaeda-linked plot to attack oil facilities in Saudi Arabia, by arresting over 172 individuals operating in seven cells and seizing numerous weapons caches and over 5 million dollars.[6] Saudi Arabia has stepped-up efforts to impede the flow of foreign fighters to Iraq and recently has reduced the ability for Saudi financiers to support al Qaeda.

Al Qaeda has also suffered setbacks in other key locations. The severe missteps made by Fatah al-Islam in Lebanon in May 2007 stopped the coalescence of al Qaeda in Lebanon. The resulting conflict in the Palestinian refugee camps between Fatah al-Islam and Lebanon's security forces prevented the use of Lebanese territory and its Palestinian refugee camps, at least in the near-term, as a training ground and strategic reserve for other Islamist conflicts.[7]

Despite repeated attempts, al Qaeda has also failed to establish any meaningful presence in Egypt. A series of attacks in October 2004 and July 2005 focused on Egypt's tourist industry. However, "The Egyptian security apparatus successfully confined the threat to the Sinai and away from the center of the Egyptian political life. A cadre of terrorists and sympathizers almost certainly still exists in Sinai but it does not threaten the regime."[8] Nevertheless, Egypt will remain an attractive and important target for al Qaeda given al Qaeda's stated aims.

In a final example, the *de facto* government of the Islamic Courts in Somalia and its al Qaeda allies were defeated with U.S. assistance in December 2006. The defeat of these factions prevented al Qaeda from gaining any significant foothold in the Horn of Africa, an area al Qaeda has long desired sanctuary.[9]

The Bad News

Even with the pending defeat of al Qaeda in Iraq and continued setbacks in other locations, the outlook for al Qaeda is far from bleak. The succession of arrests of key al Qaeda figures certainly represents tactical, and in some cases strategic, successes.[10] Yet it also demonstrates the depth of al-Qaeda's "bench" and the commitment of its members to step forward. The mere fact that al Qaeda has survived for the past six years is a testament to its strength and resilience.[11] This alone represents a substantial setback for counterterrorist governments and an immeasurable moral victory for al Qaeda and its followers. But al Qaeda has done more than simply survive. It has undergone a resurgence. Al Qaeda has experienced unprecedented growth, both in its organization and its associated movements, since 9/11. The organization, and increasingly the movement, remains capable of high degrees of violence.

A telling example of this bleak story is the proliferation of foreign fighters participating in both Afghanistan and Iraq. *The New York Times* recently reported that roughly 100 to 300 of the combatants in Afghanistan were non-Afghans.[12] By all accounts, coalition forces are seeing "an unprecedented level of reports of foreign-fighter involvement."[13] The foreign fighters have proven to be even more extreme than local Taliban militias.[14] In Iraq, the United States recently identified over 500 persons who had come to fight on behalf of al Qaeda and its associated movements from Libya, Morocco, Syria, Algeria, Oman, Yemen, Tunisia, Egypt, Jordan, Saudi Arabia, and even Belgium, France, and the United Kingdom.[15] With these additional fighters, al Qaeda has been able wage jihad on a number of fronts, including the United Kingdom, Indonesia, Iraq, Afghanistan, and the Philippines, among others.

The challenges facing counterterrorist governments today in combating al Qaeda are far greater than on September 12, 2001, as al Qaeda has also made three critical adaptations that have contributed to its survival over the past six years. First, al Qaeda has expanded its global presence and influence through mergers with like-minded groups. Second, the organization has incorporated existing technologies into new tactical applications. Third, the relative sanctuary that al Qaeda enjoys in both the developed world and failing states has provided the organization the critical breathing room necessary to recuperate.

Mergers

A number of organizations—with similar ideologies and goals—have combined efforts with al Qaeda, reaping the benefits of merged activities. These benefits include increased synergies through the sharing of strategic intelligence, resources, and tactical expertise; reinforcement of organizational functions (thus enhancing the durability and survivability of the overall organization); and an expanded global reach. In the past three years, "40 organizations have announced their formation and pledged their allegiance to bin laden, al Qaeda and their strategic objectives."[16] Many have mistakenly viewed al Qaeda's mergers as a sign of weakness, when nothing could be farther from the truth. The continued interest of organizations to join with al Qaeda reflects the significant appeal and pervasive nature of al Qaeda's ideology.

For example, in November 2006, al Qaeda completed a formal merger with the Salafist Group for Preaching and Combat (GSPC), an Islamist organization based in Algeria. While the two groups had been cooperating since 2005, in November 2006, GSPC changed its name to al Qaeda in the Islamic Magreb (AQIM) and took up the al Qaeda banner, launching attacks in Mauritania, Morocco, and Tunisia and conducting its first ever attacks against U.S. interests.[17] Given the large North African Muslim diaspora in Europe, AQIM will continue to expand its existing networks there, enabling al Qaeda's leadership its recruitment, logistics, and propaganda infrastructure.[18]

Technical Innovations

Al Qaeda has displayed great deftness in the adoption and integration of existing technologies into its tactics and operations. The use of technology has allowed al Qaeda to communicate with its members, to appeal to potential constituents and to increase its lethality. Through the use and adaptation of common technologies, al Qaeda has survived and evolved in an increasingly hostile security environment. The rapid diffusion and proliferation of new uses of technology has enhanced the ability of affiliated and home-grown terrorist cells to contribute to the global jihad more than before. Moreover, these technologies, to a degree, have offset the significant advantage the United States possesses in this asymmetrical fight.

Perhaps more so than any other single technology, al Qaeda's use of the Internet has proved invaluable.[19] The virtual world, through chat rooms, password protected forums, and jihadist media sites, fosters relatively secure communication and interaction and creates a supportive community for its members. The Internet offers distinct advantages to al Qaeda, which seeks to nurture and grow a powerful global social movement: first, in recruiting new members; second, in offering "distance learning" opportunities for potential jihadists; and third, by providing tools that enhance tactical operations.

First, al Qaeda utilizes the Internet to raise the consciousness of Muslims around the world. While the Internet is an important tool in the recruitment and radicalization of new members, the Internet has not opened the floodgates of new recruits. Instead, only a small number of individuals have been observed who have transitioned from inquisition to action due to either passive or active engagement with a jihadist forum on the Internet.[20] Person-to-person contact remains the predominant method of recruitment and radicalization.[21] This having been said, however, by providing unfettered access to extremist literature, discussions, and propaganda, the Internet provides the building blocks for those interested to become involved in the global jihad.

Second, the Internet provides a forum to educate and communicate with supporters around the world without having to travel to a training camp.[22] The panoply of Web sites include: instructions for producing explosives, dissemination of training manuals, and ideological materials, such as martyr videos, videotaped beheadings and fatwas, are also available to bolster the movement.[23] However, efforts spawned by these "distance learning opportunities" are often less sophisticated and successful than operations centrally planned and executed by al Qaeda.[24] Regardless of their efficacy, the value of increasing the reach of jihadist training and indoctrination to those who do not have access to experienced jihadists or training camps cannot be underestimated.

Third, the Internet provides tools for jihadists to protect themselves and plan future operations. Jihadists have taken advantage of the proliferation of commercially available encryption programs.[25] Captured materials reveal that al Qaeda members have employed encryption since the early 1990s. For example, Ramzi Yousef, the lead planner of the 1993 World Trade Center bombing, encrypted files concerning the Bojinka plot to destroy eleven U.S. commercial aircraft over the Pacific Ocean in 1995.[26] Wadih el Hage, convicted for his role in the 1998 attacks on the U.S. embassies in East Africa, encrypted his e-mail communications prior to the attacks.[27] Additionally, the use of geospatial tools, such as Google Earth, enhances preoperational reconnaissance and targeting efforts. By using these tools, terrorists can improve target selection,[28] focus reconnaissance efforts, and familiarize their operatives with a given target—all of which enhance operational effectiveness.[29] Al Qaeda's technical innovations extend beyond the Internet however. The tactics continually evolve in order to maintain a level of fear in society, as society becomes accustomed to their tactics. For instance, in the early days of the Iraq insurgency, AQI used beheadings to instill fear in the population. The public gradually became immune to this gruesome tactic, so AQI switched its focus to improvised explosive devices that randomly kill large numbers of people. But the widespread use of improvised explosive devices ultimately desensitized the country to those attacks as well. Recognizing this, AQI recently began using chlorine designated for water treatment in improvised explosive devices to make chlorine bombs, with the intent to sicken or wound more individuals than explosives alone could accomplish.[30] This use of chemical weapons once again ratcheted up the level of fear among the population. It is this continued learning and innovation that has kept al Qaeda tactics one step ahead of counterterror forces.

Sanctuary

Al Qaeda enjoys relative sanctuary in the Federally Administered Tribal Areas (FATA) in western Pakistan. From this secure location, al Qaeda leadership "have reestablished significant control over their once-battered worldwide terror network and over the past year has set up a band of training camps [. . .] near the Afghan border."[31] The return of the region to prominence for training terrorists accomplishes two goals for al Qaeda. First and most important, the continued presence of training camps signal to al Qaeda's worldwide supporters that it remains a vibrant organization, and creates a physical place that supporters can point to as an example of resurgence. Second, the camps provide a physical location for jihadists around the world to gather, train, perpetuate their virulent ideology, and plan for new attacks. These camps are particularly significant for European jihadists, who come to be trained and indoctrinated, and then return home with enhanced "street credibility." With this training and newfound credibility, they become "cell-builders," who now have the luxury to build cells and train those who could not attend such camps.[32]

The U.S. intelligence community has concluded that the FATA sanctuary has allowed al Qaeda to regenerate "key elements of its Homeland attack capability."[33] While this safe haven may not remain indefinitely, it presently is an important factor in al Qaeda's continued resiliency and success as well as its ability to reassert itself as an organization and not simply serve as an inspiration for jihadists around the world.

The Two Dynamics of al Qaeda's Success

Despite being the target of the greatest onslaught of military, law enforcement, and intelligence operations ever brought against a terrorist group, al Qaeda remains a vibrant and robust organization. The vitality of al Qaeda today begs for an explanation of its resiliency and adaptability in a tremendously hostile security environment. The fact that al Qaeda has survived and, in many respects, flourished, reflects two sets of dynamics: al Qaeda's organizational dynamics and the movement associated with al Qaeda. First, we will discuss the dual nature of al Qaeda, and how this increases its ability to withstand the Western onslaught. Second, we will assess the shortcomings of current U.S. counterterrorism strategies, and how these failures have undoubtedly contributed to al Qaeda's continued survival, and indeed, success.

Al Qaeda, the Organization, and al Qaeda, the Movement

Lee Hamilton of the Woodrow Wilson International Center for Scholars has stated that "The mere fact that five years after 9/11 we are still struggling to define the enemy and understand why it hates us is indicative of the vast challenge we face, because if you can't define your enemy with precision, it's very hard to develop an effective counterterrorism strategy."[34] As Mr. Hamilton recognized, efforts to define al Qaeda have largely failed, thereby precluding analytical clarity of the issue and a thorough understanding of its consequences.

Al Qaeda has been described as an organization comprised of multiple networks and also as an ideology that has transcended the organization resulting in a distributed social movement. While both of these descriptive labels may be technically true, neither accurately reflects the dual nature of al Qaeda. Instead, al Qaeda needs to be understood as possessing aspects of both an organization and a movement, and that the relationship between these aspects reinforces and bolsters the overall strength of al Qaeda. Overlooking the relationship between these two aspects results in a misunderstanding of the threat and inhibits the formation of effective counterterrorism strategy.

The Organization

Governments traditionally treat al Qaeda as a networked organization with a command-and-control structure, some level of hierarchy (however loose it may be), foreign fighter facilitation networks, operational cells, logistical support elements, and regional "franchised" organizations. These networks present identifiable command-and-control structures that can be observed and targeted by governments through law enforcement or military operations. Such an approach is appealing and makes sense to intelligence and government officials because viewing al Qaeda in this manner facilitates organized attacks on the network. It also provides a mechanism to measure progress by "subtracting" the targeted elements from the sum total of the organization.

However appealing the organizational view of al Qaeda may be, this approach presents an incomplete and somewhat inaccurate picture of al Qaeda. Viewing al Qaeda as an organized network overlooks the very essence of the organization that has provided al Qaeda with its resilience and lifeblood over the past six years: its broad and geographically diverse movement. Furthermore, this approach suggests that the threat can be defeated or managed by attacking organizational elements, but ignores the fact that as long as the al Qaeda's ideology remains attractive and individuals see incentives to answer the call to arms, al Qaeda will continue to survive.

The Movement

The social movement that is al Qaeda is multigenerational, without a geographic center, transnational in nature, virtual in design, and exceptionally difficult to detect and interdict. The movement is neither organized nor directed by the existing al Qaeda leadership, but rather, is inspired and sustained by al Qaeda's ideology, the perceptions of U.S. and Western occupation of Iraq and a pervasive hatred of the United States. The movement is comprised of supporters, sympathizers, and inspired "home-grown" operational terrorist cells representing a spectrum from the most dedicated adherents of al Qaeda's ideology to those who conveniently use portions of al Qaeda's teachings to serve their own interests but that do not necessarily subscribe to the end state of a global caliphate. The movement provides al Qaeda with its recruits and supporters and is, in short, the engine driving regeneration within al Qaeda.

The core of this larger movement emanates from the small Salafist sub-sect of Islam. This sub-sect encompasses many groups who consider the world to be in a state of *jahaliyya* (a world in chaos) like that which existed before the establishment of Islam. All Salafists reify the concept of *tawhid* (the unity of God), that God is supreme and unique and that any traditions or other religious aspects that have occurred after the Prophet Mohammad and his four successors (the *Rashiduun*) are un-Islamic. While most Salafists seek to convert society to their view of Islam through education or politics, the jihadists focus on the need for warfare and revolution to promote the Salafist cause.[35] As such, Salafism in general, and the subset of Salafist-jihadists in particular, form a larger movement of ideologues and potential sympathizers to support al Qaeda.

The genius in al Qaeda's ideology is that it allows disparate groups and individuals to locate their particular grievances in a larger framework that transcends any local or national concerns. The deterritorialized nature of Islam combined with al Qaeda's reinterpretation of religious principles and the reimagination of history has created a poignant and appealing story for many. Al Qaeda's leadership understands the need to remain relevant and continue to fight for increased "market share." For instance, second-in-command Ayman Zawahiri, in an interview with the al-Sahab media network on May 5, 2007, attempted to appeal to African Americans, American Indians, and Hispanics in terms of oppression and not religion, by invoking the image of using Malcom X.[36] By emphasizing factors of oppression instead of framing the conflict in religious terms, he tailored his message to new audience segments.[37]

While government officials and intelligence analysts recognize the existence of a movement surrounding al Qaeda, these same officials prefer to avoid viewing al Qaeda as a diffuse social movement. Insofar as al Qaeda is a movement—an amorphous, undefined, transnational collection of people and ideas that lacks definable structure or borders—it becomes difficult to identify and target key nodes. Furthermore, there is no assurance that targeting these nodes would have any effect on the overall movement. This leaves government officials without clear and discernable metrics to gauge the success or failure of their efforts against al Qaeda.

The Dynamic Between the Organization and the Movement

An appreciation that the two dimensions of al Qaeda exist in a mutually reinforcing manner will help governments avoid the dilemma of choosing between a myopic focus on the organization and a broader and potentially ineffective framework for combating the movement. Figure 1 highlights this interaction between these two dimensions:

This model depicts the principal component parts of the organization and the movement. For the organization to be effective, it requires leadership, networks, and the resources. The leaders of an organization are responsible for selecting subordinate leaders within the organization, setting direction and priorities and managing the organization through crises. It is the leadership that enables groups to plan, coordinate, and execute their attacks.[38] Without good leadership, the personnel, training, and expertise will be useless. Moreover,

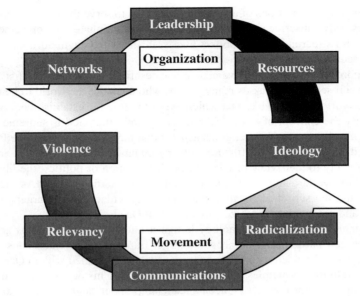

Figure 1. Al Qaeda's Enabling Components

Rohan Gunaratna has described al Qaeda as a "network of networks."[39] The ability to create, maintain, and leverage multiple networks enables the organization to remain viable and evade elimination. Without such diverse networks, al Qaeda would present counterterrorist forces with either a single target, or there would be such an exceptionally disconnected set of disparate groups that there would be no global jihad.

For the movement to be effective, its message must remain relevant, it must possess a dynamic method of communicating its ideology, and it must be able to continue to radicalize potential recruits. Despite al Qaeda's relatively small size, its radical interpretation of history and Islamic theology has had a disproportionate influence on both the fundamentalist and mainstream discourse. Al Qaeda's ability to keep its message relevant is a factor that cannot be overstated. As Mr. Gunaratna [to be consistent with other names] has noted, as long as al Qaeda can appeal to Muslims worldwide to share its ideas, aims, and objectives, then support and operational cells can regenerate.[40] Were al Qaeda to become irrelevant, it would quickly find itself threatened by other organizations and leaders for primacy within the larger jihadist movement. This, in turn, would invariably lead to a decline in recruitment, and eventually, the organization would disappear. Equally as important as the message is the means to communicate that message to a diverse and geographically dispersed audience. As such, it is the ideology, communicative capability, and relevance that facilitate the contribution of resources to the organization, and it is the resources the organization expends through "propaganda by deed" that keeps the movement invigorated.

The groundswell of the supporting movement thus increases the resource base available to the organization. All terrorist organizations require resources to acquire or build weapons; to provide monetary support for compartmented terrorist cells, travel expenses, logistics operations; and to gain access their targets. As with any skill-intensive organization, the most important resource is human capital. The radicalization efforts within the movement directly dictate the regenerative capacity of the organization. Finally, the more resources the organization can generate over time, the less pressure its leaders will face from within the organization for reform, the more the organization can withstand external pressures and the greater ability to prosecute its terror campaigns.

Additionally, two critical and related elements connect the organization and the movement: violence and ideology. For al Qaeda, violence is the currency of the organization. Through violence, al Qaeda communicates with a number of audiences—the direct target of the violent act, the wider community of actors threatened by al Qaeda, its supporters, and even the organization's own members—keeping the organization relevant both in terms of its enemies and its supporters. In this way, violence serves three functions for the organization. First, violence is used for instrumental reasons[41]—to create fear among a population, to provoke an overly severe response by counterterror governments, or to coerce governments to change some policy. Second, violence serves organizational purposes by promoting it as *the* authentic vanguard of the people it purports to represent.[42] Third, violence can be performative or symbolic, communicating a larger message to a variety of audiences.[43] It is al Qaeda's violence that keeps them in the headlines, without which it is just another activist group that would gradually face from the public's priorities.

If violence is the currency of the organization, then ideology is the connective tissue binding the disparate members of the movement together as well as connecting the movement with the terrorist organization. Ideology "frames organizational structure, leadership and membership motivation, recruitment and support, and shapes the strategies and tactics adopted by the group."[44] Additionally, the ideology legitimizes al Qaeda's violence, by presenting the need for violence as a religious duty.

Shortcomings in Counterterrorist Efforts

The success that al Qaeda has realized in the past six years is not wholly attributable to its foresight, strategic planning, or organizational design. In reality, many of al Qaeda's achievements are a result of the shortcomings in counterterrorism strategies and the failure to challenge al Qaeda across the entire spectrum of conflict. Four principal areas of counterterrorism strategy will be discussed in this article. First, as discussed above, current counterterrorism efforts are focused almost exclusively on al Qaeda as an organization, often ignoring the widely distributed social movement. Second, the continued conflict in Iraq has provided jihadists around the globe a renewed focus and commitment to target the United States and coalition partners. Third, counterterrorism efforts have been too narrowly focused on tactical objectives at the expense of the operational and strategic objectives. Fourth, the failure to contest key battles—geographical, ideological, and organizational—has allowed al Qaeda unprecedented access to new and expanding resources including sanctuaries, the power of the dominant Salafi-jihadist narrative, and advantageous mergers with other extremist organizations.

A Myopic Focus

As discussed above in some detail, al Qaeda today is both an organization and geographically and ethnically diverse movement. However, most current counterterrorism strategies do not take into account both aspects of al Qaeda's existence, preferring to focus on only organizational qualities. Effective counterterrorism strategies must account for al Qaeda's dual nature. Failure to include the less-well-defined social movement in the equation will result in an incomplete strategy, skewed to tactical counterterrorism operations while ignoring the broader, more complicated social dimensions of the threat. The ultimate consequence is that such a narrow view will only prolong the life of al Qaeda and increase the danger to the United States and its interests around the world.

The War in Iraq

The war in Iraq creates challenges for counterterrorist strategies. The recently declassified National Intelligence Estimate indicated that "[al Qaeda's] association with AQI helps al Qa'ida [*sic*] to energize the broader Sunni extremist community, raise resources, and to recruit and indoctrinate operatives, including for Homeland attacks."[45] Morally, AQI has been a clarion call for those who are fighting in the name of Islam. The occupation and perceived neocolonial designs of the United States in Iraq have had a decided impact on world opinion, and particularly the Sunni extremist community. "Two new studies, one by the Saudi government and one by an Israeli think tank . . . found that most foreign fighters in Iraq were not terrorists before the Iraq war, but were 'radicalized by the war itself.' "[46]

The failure of AQI to achieve a decisive victory against the United States in Iraq and the likely defeat of the organization may not have resulted in the desired strategic impact. The defeat of AQI is an important achievement, yet it is unclear that the defeat of AQI will significantly hurt the progression of the broader al Qaeda movement. While the fear of "bleed-out" of fighters from Iraq remains, the real danger arises from the tactical lessons learned by al Qaeda in the course of fighting the United States over the past four years in Iraq. Undoubtedly, al Qaeda will disseminate this knowledge with extremists far and wide. Examples have already been witnessed of technology transfer from Iraq to other theaters of operation.[47] Additionally, Sunni extremists will frame AQI's defeat in ways to promote their views. For them, it will serve as U.S. hegemony and of the U.S.'s desire to destroy Sunni Islam. They will also highlight the loss of life and tremendous expense incurred by the United States as an example of what can be accomplished by motivated Islamic fighters.

Unbalanced Approach to the Fight

This perhaps is the single greatest contributing factor aiding al Qaeda's resurgence. It is a conceptual failure to view the struggle against al Qaeda as a singular conflict, rather than three distinct yet related efforts. While it is indeed a war consisting of tactical operations, it is also a war against regional and global jihadist networks and, perhaps most importantly, a conflict of ideas and ideologies. Since al Qaeda's declaration of war against the United States in 1996, al Qaeda has been waging this struggle across all three of these levels. Bin Laden and his lieutenants presciently understood that operations at each level reinforced efforts on the other levels. The initial failure by the United States to recognize these three distinct levels and the subsequent failure to develop a multifaceted counterterrorism strategy to address them has permitted al Qaeda to conduct a global terror campaign unabated and virtually unchecked.

The first level is a *war of action*.[48] It is the war that Americans are most familiar with; it is predominantly pursued using the military and intelligence instruments of national power. Fought by al Qaeda and governments alike, the war of action consists of premeditated, preemptive, and preventative strikes and is measured in minutes, hours, and days. For al Qaeda and its affiliates, this level is comprised of individual bombings and coordinated attacks, in other words, tactical operations. For the United States, this level of war involves intelligence operations to find individuals or cells associated with al Qaeda, and either capture or kill them. As such, success in this arena tends to erode the organizational aspects of al Qaeda: its resources (including recruits) and its leadership. Certainly, enough success on the tactical level will eventually degrade al Qaeda's ability to recruit and remain relevant, but only so long as new recruits are not available.

The mid-term fight, the *war of networks,*[49] is waged in terms of months and years. These battles focus on the extensive network structure of the organization that is al Qaeda, its affiliated organizations such as AQI or AQIM and the al Qaeda movement. This aspect of the conflict focuses not only on the organization, but also on elements of the broader movement. Beyond targeting the command-and-control elements of the operational cells, the war of networks must be also aimed at the multiple and overlapping support networks that facilitate the recruitment, radicalization, and movement of foreign fighters; the acquisition and distribution of chemical precursors for conventional explosives; and communications. These networks can be small and geographically limited to a particular province or transnational. The complexity of network operations explains the fact that it can take months, or even years, to realize success. Still, despite the difficulty, the war of networks is where counterterrorism forces can best constrain the terrorists' strategic operating environment, thus limiting their effectiveness.

Since 2001, counterterrorism forces have achieved some significant success in the war of networks. Al Qaeda has been forced from its sanctuary in Afghanistan while large numbers of al Qaeda's senior leaders and even greater numbers of its fighters have been captured. Yet, as important as these victories have been, the impact of these actions in the larger picture is limited. The resurgent foreign fighter network in Afghanistan is an important reminder of this dilemma. Ultimately, no matter the successes on the tactical level, the failure to succeed across *all* levels of this fight will allow al Qaeda to respond and adapt. It is a biological truth that if an organism is not stressed enough, for long enough, it will grow stronger. The evolutionary process has been kind to al Qaeda.

The *war of ideas*[50] is the most complex and difficult for counterterrorist governments to comprehend, and it will be a long-term fight waged over years and decades. Al Qaeda has masterfully conducted an ideological campaign over the last decade and set the agenda with regards to the role of Islam versus secular ideas throughout the Islamic world. Unfortunately, the United States, and the West overall, have yet to contest this battle space, allowing al Qaeda's narrative to become the dominant, and in many cases the sole, narrative. This is the realm where the movement portion of al Qaeda is at its zenith—where the ideas of al Qaeda's extremist version of Islam collide with those of the majority of Muslims as well as those of the West. The United States has assumed that it is communicating a message of democracy, capitalism, the rule of law and civil liberties, and that this automatically resonates with all of humanity. Unfortunately, centuries of Western foreign policy, and the last 40 years of U.S. foreign policy, have given these terms negative connotations in the region.

It is this realm that is the proverbial "long war"—a war not unlike that of the Cold War. While there was certainly a great deal at stake militarily, economically, and diplomatically, in the end, the Cold War was about a battle of ideas—whether capitalism and democracy would win out over totalitarianism. In the end, sometimes through intentional planning by leaders in the West, and other times, through simple luck and a desire for individual dignity and rights, the Western narrative eventually won. Now a similar battle is raging. Again, it is a battle between those espousing individual civil liberties, democracy, capitalism, and the rule of law versus totalitarianism. However, unlike in the Cold War, the United States and the West is not aggressively pursuing its narrative, which leaves al Qaeda's as one of the few voices being heard.

These three wars are inexorably linked together and cannot be separated. Victories by al Qaeda in the war of action allow the organization to mobilize greater resources and build more comprehensive networks. The stronger the networks become, the more they reify al Qaeda's ideology and allow for new members to participate in the fight.[51] In turn, this reified ideology brings new recruits and resources for future al Qaeda actions. As such, all three levels are mutually reinforcing.

The Conceded Battles

The above sections identified three areas where counterterrorism governments are less than effective, and, which together, lead to the fourth and final area—the conceded battle-grounds. There is an imbalance between the attention paid to terrorism within declared combat zones (Iraq, Afghanistan, and the Horn of Africa) and that directed outside of these zones. While it is easy to argue that this is to be expected, this is an insufficient answer and points to the obvious imbalance between military means and the other instruments of national power. Contesting the wars of actions and networks within the declared combat zones of Iraq and Afghanistan is not enough. Al Qaeda must also be aggressively challenged in other key locations and on other key issues. A quick tour around unchallenged aspects of the jihadist diaspora will illustrate the gravity of the situation:

- Al Qaeda has established relative sanctuary in Pakistan for the senior leadership and reestablished training camps in the surrounding areas.
- It has conducted a merger with an Algerian organization (AQIM), subsequently gaining access to European and North African networks.
- Al Qaeda established a limited relationship and presence inside of Lebanon.
- Al Qaeda may be working with and potentially merging with LIFG.[52]
- Al Qaeda has reestablished a limited presence in Yemen.[53]

In fact, even a cursory investigation of these events reveals, in the majority of cases, there was ample reporting and warning of these events in the media prior to their coming to fruition. There are two principal uncontested areas that we will address: geographical and ideological factors.

Contesting Geography

Typically, counterterrorism fights are defined by nature of the enemy and less defined by geography. The relatively high degree of security al Qaeda enjoys in the FATA reminds us that even terrorists exist in physical space and must reside somewhere. The expansion of jihadist forces in Lebanon is a prime example of our failure to act.

Al Qaeda has long identified states of central concern—Egypt, Jordan, Lebanon, Palestinian Territories, Saudi Arabia, Syria, and Yemen—in their writings and has worked to establish active presence in all of these locations at one time or another. However, the periphery of the jihadist diaspora is equally important, if not more so, to al Qaeda's long-term future. The ability for al Qaeda to gain a foothold in the periphery, either in terms of sanctuary or in terms of alignment with local groups, would serve to provide access to new "markets" in the hope of gaining new constituents.[54] Peripheral states such as Nigeria hold special promise for al Qaeda.

> The openings for terrorist infiltration cannot be overlooked. Osama Bin Laden himself listed Nigeria as a priority target. So far, there is no indication that terrorist networks have taken hold in Nigeria nor that even many radical Islamic figures have contemplated a policy of violence. But Nigerians have already been found within the ranks of the GSPC [now AQIM] and the potential for linkages between terrorist groups and Nigeria's already well developed criminal and drug trafficking groups is a worrisome prospect.[55]

Even states, such as Bangladesh, that may not normally be thought of as al Qaeda strongholds present risks for U.S. interests. In Bangladesh, the formation of an

> umbrella group [that] advocates an extremist jihadist rhetoric that closely resonates with bin Laden's line. The movement seeks the creation of a transnational caliphate that will eventually take in all of Bagladesh, Assam, north Bengal, and Burma's Arakan province, and has been identified as a key propaganda and logistical conduit for al Qaeda in South Asia. Indian and Western intelligence sources fear that many of the al Qaeda and Taliban members who entered the country between 2001 and 2002 are now training the [umbrella group] and may be seeking to establish the group as a concerted operational wing for cross-regional attacks in South Asia.[56]

All of these examples point to the very real challenges faced by the United States or any counterterror government—combating al Qaeda within sovereign states requires the assistance and permission of these states. There are no easy or quick answers to this challenge but the difficulty does not permit us to concede the future.

Contesting Ideology

Defeating a cell or a network does not constitute long-term success. Terrorism "is a vicious by-product of ideological extremism [as such] government and society must develop an ideological response to make it difficult for terrorist groups to replenish their human losses and material wastage."[57] As intimated in the discussion on the war of ideas above, counterterror governments have failed to contest this space. Instead, their actions have often been counterproductive and have only worsened the situation.

Most "studies of terrorism frequently address the concept of target audiences, groups generally defined as those whom terrorists seek to intimidate or influence through violence. However, it is also important to understand terrorists' other target audience—the aggrieved populations that they purport to represent."[58] Counterterrorism is a fight not only *with* the terrorists but also *for* the uncommitted population, which is a far broader group that "has the power to confer a degree of legitimacy on the terrorists simply by responding positively to [al Qaeda's] tactics."[59] Counterterror governments must appreciate what they can and cannot influence within the narrative space. The division of the narrative space in such terms allows for the development of a sophisticated and nuanced approach to countering the narrative. For those areas in which governments can compete, they should focus on separating the terrorists from their message. Governments should challenge the terrorists' assertion that they alone represent and speak for the people. Perhaps more important, governments must recognize where they cannot *directly* affect or shape the narrative and set enabling conditions for other agents to work to counter al Qaeda's narrative.

Fighting this battle will not be easy. "Friendly governments wishing to cooperate with the United States on regional security issues may be constrained by domestic perceptions. It is fundamentally difficult for non-Muslims to influence perceptions about their own religion. Only Muslims themselves have the credibility to challenge the misuse of Islam by radicals."[60] Nonetheless, governments cannot abdicate their role in contesting this vital space.

We must be careful not to leave the reader with the impression that al Qaeda is a hyper-capable organization that is successfully executing a global grand strategy. In fact, we argue that even the resurgent al Qaeda is far from this caricature. While al Qaeda may not be capable of launching and executing a global grand strategy, their actions have been "good enough." In other words, for al Qaeda to "succeed," it does not have to be perfect, invincible, or even dominant. Instead, al Qaeda only has to stay relevant and survive. The future demands that we look *across* the three levels of this conflict and expand our horizons to better anticipate potential events and opportunities where al Qaeda could claim a "victory" and take action to challenge these contests. When the United States and its allies do not even "show up" to play, one should not be surprised when al Qaeda "wins."

Conclusions and Some Recommendations

Al Qaeda's ability to change and adapt both in anticipation of, and in reaction to, the changing security environment provides a great deal of insight about the organization and its associated movement. Organizations that fail to adapt to external changes become obsolete or worse. Yet, despite the loss of their dedicated sanctuary in Afghanistan, the inability to operate training camps "openly," and the loss of critical networks in key locations such as Saudi Arabia, al Qaeda today is stronger and more powerful than at any other time since 2002. The declassified Key Judgments of the 2007 National Intelligence Estimate stated that

> Al-Qa'ida is and will remain the most serious terrorist threat to the Homeland, as its central leadership continues to plan high-impact plots, while pushing others in extremist Sunni communities to mimic its efforts and to supplement its capabilities. We assess the group has protected or regenerated key elements of its Homeland attack capability, including: a safehaven in the Pakistan Federally Administered Tribal Areas (FATA), operational lieutenants, and its top leadership.[61]

Yet, as discussed above, al Qaeda's resurgence is not due solely to the al Qaeda's actions. Its success or failure also hinges on our actions or inactions. Principal among these is the inability to fashion an effective and responsive counterterror strategy that organizes governmental forces effectively across the three wars and integrates their actions into a comprehensive, forward-looking strategy. The unfortunate reality exists that the war against al Qaeda has been primarily fought along the war of action level. This is not to say that the war of networks has been ignored. Yet, outside of the declared combat zones of Afghanistan and Iraq, it is hard to find evidence of a coordinated interagency effort to combat al Qaeda's extensive networks. Given these issues, we advocate the following two policy prescriptions: unity of command and a more comprehensive and nuanced informational campaign.

First, there must be unity of command in the fight against Salafist jihadists that encompasses all the instruments of United States power: military, diplomatic, economic, intelligence, law enforcement, and so forth. With this unity of command must come a "forcing function"—one agency or individual who has the ability to create an overall counter-jihadist national strategy, and then implement those actions across the relevant government agencies. With this would come a greater capability for the United States to fight across the spectrum of conflict, rather than focusing almost solely on the aspects of the war of action. As this forcing function would facilitate the integration of these aspects, it would also create more efficiency and effectiveness.

Second, the United States has failed to galvanize our resources to contest the war of ideas; this is the singular most important battle that we are not fighting. The United States should not be afraid to let the realities of the Salafist jihadists speak for themselves. These groups have produced a myriad of CDs, DVDs, and Internet media for their own propaganda purposes. On such media, they proudly display the beheading of hostages, torture of university students, stoning of women, and the like. Realizing that much of what the United States and West says is immediately suspect in much of the world, why not let the actions of movements associated with al Qaeda speak for themselves? While such acts may not deter hard-core adherents to this ideology, it may take some of the "wind out of the sails" of the more passive supporters of the movement. After all, militias and former insurgents in Iraq have not begun to rally to the American and allied forces because of a sudden love of the United States, but rather, because compared to the violence perpetrated by al Qaeda-associated forces, the U.S. side became the better option. By not restricting al Qaeda's propaganda, al Qaeda would be forced to defend their actions. While a dominant narrative, it is ultimately self-defeating. In areas around the world where al Qaeda has attempted to gain a foothold—Bosnia, Chechnya, western Iraq—they have been rejected by the people in each of these locations. As such, they would be forced to either explain their actions, modify their actions and demands, or face the commensurate loss in public sympathy.

However, not only must the United States advocate its message to foreign audiences, but it must communicate the message here at home. As economist Friedrich Hayek noted at the end of World War II, as the West and USSR were beginning to square off for what would become the Cold War:

> It is a lamentable fact that democracies in their dealings with dictators before the war, not less than in their attempts at propaganda and in the discussion of their war aims, have shown an inner insecurity and uncertainly of aim which can be explained only by confusion about their own ideals and the nature of the differences which separated them from the enemy.[62]

This is not to argue that the American public must be made paranoid, looking for a terrorist behind every tree. Nevertheless, fighting this war requires some sacrifices, including spreading the costs amongst society. For instance, this may require reevaluating of foreign policy initiatives and the alignment of those initiatives with the message being communicated to these populations. It also means reducing the U.S. reliance on oil.

In conclusion, currently, through a combination of strategic planning, trial and error, and luck, al Qaeda is changing at a faster pace than that which the United States is willing to adapt. As such, while it has suffered some devastating losses, including its former sanctuaries in Afghanistan and western Iraq, it has demonstrated the operational durability to adapt and still move forward. Only through coordinated efforts by the United States with regards to its own actions can the United States adapt as needed. Only in doing so can the United States, along with close cooperation with our allies, hope to respond, and better yet, aggressively attack al Qaeda throughout its organization and movement and along all three planes of warfare. Only then will the organization and movement no longer be able to regenerate itself forcing it into decline. Doing so will be the only means for an already long war to be that much shorter.

Major Reid Sawyer, a career military intelligence officer, is the former Executive Director and founding member of the Combating Terrorism Center at the United States Military Academy. He is currently a fellow with the Center and an adjunct assistant professor at the School of International and Public Affairs at Columbia University, where he teaches a graduate seminar on terrorism studies. As an intelligence officer, Major Sawyer previously served in a variety of special operations assignments. Major Sawyer earned his undergraduate degree from the United States Military Academy and holds a masters of public administration from Columbia University where he is completing his doctorate degree. Major Sawyer has lectured widely on the topic of terrorism and counterterrorism. He is also the co-editor of *Defeating Terrorism*.

Major Jodi M. Vittori is a PhD candidate at the University of Denver's Graduate School of International Studies. She previously served as an instructor in the US Air Force Academy's Department of Political Science, as well as thirteen years as an intelligence officer, including assignments in the Middle East, Bosnia-Herzegovina and the Republic of Korea. Recent publications include "The Business of Terror: Al Qaeda as a Multinational Corporation" in *Internationale Politik Transnational Edition* 6 No. 3, Summer 2005, "Gambling With History: The Making of a Democratic Iraq" in *Air and Space Power Journal Chronicles,* June 2004 (with Dr. Brent Talbot), and "The Gang's All Here: The Globalization of Gang Activity" in *The Journal of Gang Research,* Spring 2007.

Notes

1. The views expressed in this paper are those of the authors and not of the U.S. Military Academy, the Department of the Army, the Department of the Air Force, or any other agency of the U.S. Government.
2. Thomas E. Ricks and Karen DeYoung, "Al Qaeda in Iraq Reported Crippled," *Washington Post,* October 15, 2007.

3. "Suspected '100 Million Dollar Al Qaeda Financier' Netted in Iraq," (Agence France-Presse, October 4, 2007). An al Qaeda financier that was "suspected of handing over 50,000 dollars a month to al Qaeda [in Iraq] using his leather merchant business as a front" was captured in central Baghdad. This money was raised from a network of al Qaeda supporters in Europe and the Middle East. However, these amounts are small in comparison to the millions of dollars AQI raises annually through criminal enterprises inside of Iraq. According to the *Los Angeles Times,* this is just one example of the rampant corruption and crime that feeds all the various insurgent groups. Alexander Zavis, "Iraqi Militants Feed on Corruption," *Los Angeles Times,* October 26, 2007.

4. Ricks and DeYoung, "Al Qaeda in Iraq Reported Crippled."

5. Bruce Riedel, "Al Qaeda Five Years after the Fall of Kahndahar" (Brookings Institution, January 18, 2007).

6. Craig Whitlock and Robin Wright, "Saudis Say They Broke up Suicide Plots," *Washington Post* (April 28, 2007), http://www.washingtonpost.com/wp-dyn/content/article/2007/04/27/AR2007042700649.html?hpid=topnews, "Saudi Arrests Suspects Planning Oil Attacks" (Reuters, April 27, 2007).

7. Of note, there has been some disagreement over how closely Fatah al-Islam is relataed to al Qaeda. Rebecca Bloom, "Backgrounder: Fatah Al-Islam" (Council on Foreign Relations, June 8, 2007). However, even if Shakir al Absi, leader of Fatah al-Islam, never actually swore *bayat* to Usama bin Laden, it is clear given the close affiliations of those he trains, as well as his relationship with Abu Musab al Zarqawi, that he has had extremely close ties with the al Qaeda network. For information on European recruits training in Lebanon, see Lorenzo Vidino, "Current Trends in Jihadi Networks in Europe," *Terrorism Monitor,* 5, no. 20 (October 25, 2007), http://jamestown.org/terrorism/news/article.php?articleid=2373743. For information on North African-affiliated terrorists (such as those of al Qaeda in the Islamic Magreb) using Fatah al-Islam training centers, see Andrew Black, "Lebanon Another Waypoint for North Africans Headed to Iraq," *Terrorism Focus, 4,* no. 17 (June 5, 2007), http://jamestown.org/terrorism/news/article.php?articleid=2373446.

8. Riedel, "Al Qaeda Five Years after the Fall of Kahndahar."

9. Jeffrey Haynes, "Islam and Democracy in East Africa," *Democratization, 13,* no. 3 (2006): 498.

10. For instance the capture of Kahlid Sheikh Mohammad or Hadi al-Iraqi, among others, clearly are significant victories for counterterrorism forces.

11. Organizational resiliency, a construct well explored in organizational theory literature, captures the essence of the al Qaeda's survival and regeneration since October 2001. "Resilience refers to a dynamic process encompassing positive adaptation within the context of significant adversity"[11] [emphasis in original]. Organizational adaptation does not represent a static state, but rather a "dynamic" process. Adaptation results from both proactive measures taken by an organization and organizational responses to exogenous shocks. Suniya S. Luthar, Dante Cicchetti, and Bronwyn Becker, "The Construct of Resilience: A Critical Evaluation and Guide for Future Work," *Child Development, 71,* no. 3 (2000).

12. David Rohde, "Foreign Fighters of Harsher Bent Bolster Taliban," *New York Times,* October 30, 2007.

13. Ibid.

14. Ibid.

15. "U.S. Says Finds List of Qaeda Fighters in Iraq" (Agence France-Presse, October 3, 2007).

16. Michael Scheuer, "Al-Qaeda and Algeria's G.S.P.C.: Part of a Much Bigger Picture," *Terrorism Focus, 4,* no. 8 (April 3, 2007), http://www.jamestown.org/terrorism/news/article.php?articleid=2373295.

17. Andrew McGregor, "Leadership Disputes Plaque Al-Qaeda in the Islamic Magreb," *Terrorism Focus,* 4, no. 30 (2007), http://www.jamestown.org/terrorism/news/article.php?issue_id=4240.

18. Alison Pargeter, "North African Immigrants in Europe and Political Violence," *Studies in Conflict and Terrorism, 29,* no. 8 (2006). 733–735.

19. This topic is more fully explored in Jarret Brachman's contribution to this volume, "Hi-Tech Terror: Al-Qaeda's Use of New Technology."

20. Aidan Kirby and Shawn Brimely, "Home-Grown Terrorism," *Boston Globe* (June 8, 2006), http://www.boston.com/news/globe/editorial_opinion/oped/articles/2006/06/08/home_grown_terrorism/. Certain members of the cell of 18 Toronto youth were reported radicalized from contact with jihadist cites on the Internet.

21. "The process of transformation from an alienated individual to a committed activist is commonly seen in religious sects and terrorists groups and requires investment in intense and lengthy personal interactions. This implies that the fear that vulnerable young Muslims may be recruited to the Jihad through internet messages is overblown. Reading and sending messages about the Jihad on the Internet may make these individuals receptive to its appeal, but direct involvement requires interaction." Michael Taarnby, "Recruitment of Islamist Terrorists in Europe: Trends and Perspectives," (January 14, 2005), http://www.justitsministeriet.dk/fileadmin/downloads/Forskning_og_dokumentation/Rekruttering_af_islamistiske_terrorister_i_Europa.pdf.

22. "A World Wide Web of Terror," *Economist* (July 12, 2007), http://www.economist.com/world/displaystory.cfm?story_id=9472498.

23. Gabriel Weinmann, "Virtual Disputes: The Use of the Internet for Terrorist Debates," *Studies in Conflict and Terrorism, 29,* no. 7 (2006), Evan F. Kohlmann, "The Real Online Terrorist Threat," *Foreign Affairs, 85,* no. 5 (2006), Michael Moss, "What to Do About Pixels of Hate," New York Times October 21, 2007.

24. Moreover, the Internet does not provide the same opportunity to establish and strengthen personal relationships as the camps once did.

25. Encryption programs such as PGP, or Pretty Good Protection, and steganography software allow users to protect their information during transmission on the Internet. Steganography programs allow the user to embed images or files within other images that are not visible unless the user knows the hidden files exist and has the appropriate encryption key. More than 100 programs exist on the Internet that can perform these functions to varying degrees.

26. Jamie Gorelick, "Computer Encryption" (US House Judiciary Committee Concerning Computer Encryption, September 25, 1996).

27. *Indictment of Wadih El Hage, United States of America v. Usama Bin Laden, 98-Cr-1023* (1998).

28. Clancy Chassay and Bobbie Johnson, "Google Earth Used to Target Israel," *Guardian* (October 25, 2007), http://www.guardian.co.uk/technology/2007/oct/25/google.israel/print.

29. Al Qaeda in the Islamic Magreb (AQIM) released a video showing preparations to attack U.S. workers in Algeria and shows Google Earth images marking bus route carrying Haliburton workers, the preparation of two bombs and the attack itself.

30. Three attacks occurred in Iraq on March 16, 2007 in the space of three hours: one involved a pickup truck carrying chlorine and explosives exploded wounding one and killing another; two hours later a dump truck carrying chlorine was used, which wounded over 100 residents south of Fallujah, causing them to require medical attention for "skin and lung irritation and vomiting"; the third, less than an hour later, involved a tanker carrying 200 gallons of chlorine, which "sickened about 250 people." "U.S. Says Iraq Chlorine Bomb Factor Was Al Qaeda's" (Reuters, February 24, 2007), Karin Brulliard, "Chlorine Blast Kills 8; 6 Troops Also Die in Iraq," *Washington Post,* March 18, 2007.

31. Mark Mazzetti and David Rohde, "Terror Officials See Al Qaeda Chiefs Regaining Power," *New York Times* (February 19, 2007), http://www.nytimes.com/2007/02/19/world/asia/19intel.html?_r=1&oref=slogin. Dirk Laabs and Sebastian Rotella, "Terrorists in Training Head to Pakistan," *Los Angeles Times,* October 14, 2007. Souad Mekhennet and Michael Moss, "Europeans Get Terror Training inside Pakistan," *New York Times,* September 10, 2007. Hassan Abbas, "Increasing Talibanization in Pakistan's Seven Tribal Agencies," *Terrorism Monitor, 5,* no. 18 (September 27, 2007), http://jamestown.org/terrorism/news/article.php?articleid=2373679.

32. Musab al-Suri authored a 1500 page treatise on waging jihad in the post-9/11 environment entitled "Global Islamic Resistance Call." In it, he used the term "cell builders" to be those

who create and train their own cells after returning from al Qaeda camps. Paul Cruickshank and Mohannad Hage Ali, "Abu Musab Al Suri: Architect of the New Al Qaeda," *Studies in Conflict and Terrorism, 30,* no. 1 (2007).

33. "National Intelligence Estimate: The Terrorist Threat to the U.S. Homeland" (Office of the Director of National Intelligence, July 2007).

34. Lee Hamilton et al., *State of the Struggle* (Washington, DC: Council on Global Terrorism, 2006), 3.

35. A commonly used term in the media to describe this phenomenon is that of "Wahhabism"; however, most adherents to this creed describe themselves as Muwahiddun ("Unitarians") or Salafiyyun, from "salaf" meaning "follow" or "precede." For additional information on this particular subset of Islam, see Quintan Wiktorowicz, "Anatomy of the Salafi Movement," *Studies in Conflict and Terrorism, 29,* no. 3 (2006). Christopher Blanchard, "The Islamic Traditions of Wahhabism and Salafiyya," (Library of Congress Congressional Research Service, 2005).

36. "As-Sahab Video of Third Interview with Dr. Ayman Al-Zawahiri" (SITE Institute, May 5, 2007).

37. Steven R. Corman and Jill S. Schiefelbein, "Communication and Media Strategy in the Jihadi War of Ideas" (Consortium for Strategic Communication, April 20, 2006).

38. Kim Cragin and Sara A. Daly, *The Dynamic Terrorist Threat: An Assessment of Group Motivations and Capabilities in a Changing World* (Santa Monica, CA: RAND, 2004). 40.

39. Rohan Gunaratna, *Inside Al Qaeda: Global Network of Terror* (New York: Columbia University Press, 2002).

40. Ibid., 232.

41. Martha Crenshaw, "Theories of Terrorism: Instrumental and Organizational Approaches," in *Inside Terrorist Organizations,* ed. David C. Rapoport, *Cass Series on Political Violence* (London: Frank Cass, 2001), 13.

42. Ibid., 19.

43. Mark Juergensmeyer, *Terror in the Mind of God: The Global Rise of Religious Violence,* 3rd ed., Comparative Studies in Religion and Society (Berkeley, CA: University of California Press, 2003), 124–125.

44. Rohan Gunaratna, "Ideology in Terrorism and Counter Terrorism: Lessons from Combating Al Qaeda and Al Jemaah Al Islamiyah in Southeast Asia" (CSRC, September 2005), 1.

45. "National Intelligence Estimate: The Terrorist Threat to the U.S. Homeland."

46. Tom Regan, "Studies: War Radicalized Most Foreign Fighters in Iraq," *Christian Science Monitor* (July 18, 2005), http://www.csmonitor.com/2005/0718/dailyUpdate.html. The authors wish to note that this argument should not be taken as either support for or against removing U.S. troops from Iraq in the near term. It is merely acknowledgment that the 2003 U.S. invasion of Iraq has had a radicalizing effect.

47. Al Qaeda insurgents in Afghanistan have adopted the particular methods of improvised explosive device construction and the increased use of suicide bombers. Jihadist leaders have even gone so far as to travel from Afghanistan to Iraq and vice versa to exchange ideas. For further information see Michael Scheuer, "Afghanistan and Iraq: Two Sunni War Theaters Evolving into One?" *Terrorism Focus, 4,* no. 10 (April 17, 2007), http://www.jamestown.org/terrorism/news/article.php?articleid=2373330.

48. An unnamed government official offered the idea that the war against al Qaeda is really three wars: a war of action, one of networks and a war of ideas.

49. Der Derian first used the concept of a war of networks in 2001, writing that "From the start, it was apparent that 9-11 was and would continue to be a war of networks." James Der Derian, "The War of Networks," *Theory & Event, 5,* no. 4 (2001).

50. The term *war of ideas* has become so common that attribution is not possible.

51. The Madrid bombing on March 11, 2004 highlights the interrelated nature of two levels. While the Spanish cell had limited, if any, meaningful contact with any al Qaeda members, the ten bombs that killed 191 people and wounded more than 1800 was hailed as a victory for global jihad. Additionally, several members of the Spanish cell were not strongly religious and one

of the leaders was involved in the drug trade. Yet, within a month bin Laden referenced the Madrid attacks and offered a peace treaty with the West. By linking the Madrid attacks (War of Action) with the larger global jihad (War of Ideas), bin Laden was leveraging an action on one level to reinforce another level in the strategic jihad despite the fact that the attacks were not planned, coordinated, directed, or financed by al Qaeda. Nonetheless, the tragic loss of life and fallout from the elections provided al Qaeda an important moment on the international stage and set the example for other "home-grown" terrorists that share al Qaeda's world view to follow.

52. The Libyan Islamic Fighting Group (LIFG) was formed in the early 1990s by Libyans who had fought the Soviets in Afghanistan. In November 2007, some elements of the organization claimed to have signed a formal merger with the al Qaeda leadership. "Libyan Islamists 'Join Al-Qaeda'," *BBC* (November 3, 2007), http://news.bbc.co.uk/2/hi/africa/7076604.stm.

53. Gregory D. Johnsen, "Is Al-Qaeda in Yemen Regrouping?," *Terrorism Focus, 4,* no. 15 (May 22, 2007), http://jamestown.org/terrorism/news/article.php?articleid=2373414. Francis T. Miko, "Removing Terrorist Sanctuaries: The 9/11 Commission Recommendations and US Policy" (Library of Congress Congressional Research Service, 2005).

54. Key states in this group include Algeria, Bangladesh, Indonesia, Malaysia, Nigeria, the Philippines, and Uzbekistan.

55. Princeton N. Lyman, Testimony before the House Committee on International Relations Subcommittee on Africa, "Fighting Terrorism in Africa," April 1, 2004.

56. Angel Rabasa et al., *Beyond Al-Qaeda: The Global Jihadist Movement* (Santa Monica, CA: RAND, 2006), 102–103.

57. Gunaratna, "Ideology in Terrorism and Counter Terrorism: Lessons from Combating Al Qaeda and Al Jemaah Al Islamiyah in Southeast Asia," 1.

58. Ibid.

59. Steve Simon and Jeff Martini, "Terrorism: Denying Al Qaeda Its Popular Support," *Washington Quarterly, 28,* no. 1 (2004–2005): 131–132.

60. Angel Rabasa et al., "The Muslim World after 9/11" (Santa Monica, CA: RAND Corporation, 2004).

61. "National Intelligence Estimate: The Terrorist Threat to the U.S. Homeland." This declassified estimate also cites Iraq as the key force in mobilizing the larger jihadist community to support al Qaeda's goals.

62. Friedrich A. Hayek, *The Road to Serfdom* (Chicago: University of Chicago Press, 1994), 8.

Bibliography

Abbas, Hassan. "Increasing Talibanization in Pakistan's Seven Tribal Agencies." *Terrorism Monitor,* no. 18 (September 27, 2007), http://jamestown.org/terrorism/news/article.php?articleid=2373679.

"As-Sahab Video of Third Interview with Dr. Ayman Al-Zawahiri." SITE Institute, May 5, 2007.

Black, Andrew. "Lebanon Another Waypoint for North Africans Headed to Iraq." *Terrorism Focus,* no. 17 (June 5, 2007), http://jamestown.org/terrorism/news/article.php?articleid=2373446.

Blanchard, Christopher. "The Islamic Traditions of Wahhabism and Salafiyya." Library of Congress Congressional Research Service, 2005.

Bloom, Rebecca. "Backgrounder: Fatah Al-Islam." Council on Foreign Relations, June 8, 2007.

Brulliard, Karin. "Chlorine Blast Kills 8; 6 Troops Also Die in Iraq." *Washington Post,* March 18, 2007.

Chandler, Michael, and Rohan Gunaratna. *Countering Terrorism: Can We Meet the Threat of Global Violence?:* Reaktion Books, 2007.

Chassay, Clancy, and Bobbie Johnson. "Google Earth Used to Target Israel." *Guardian* (October 25, 2007), http://www.guardian.co.uk/technology/2007/oct/25/google.israel/print.

Corman, Steven R., and Jill S. Schiefelbein. "Communication and Media Strategy in the Jihadi War of Ideas." Consortium for Strategic Communication, April 20, 2006.

Cragin, Kim, and Sara A. Daly. *The Dynamic Terrorist Threat: An Assessment of Group Motivations and Capabilities in a Changing World.* Santa Monica, CA: RAND, 2004.

Crenshaw, Martha. "Theories of Terrorism: Instrumental and Organizational Approaches." In *Inside Terrorist Organizations,* edited by David C. Rapoport, 13–31. London: Frank Cass, 2001.

Cruickshank, Paul, and Mohannad Hage Ali. "Abu Musab Al Suri: Architect of the New Al Qaeda." *Studies in Conflict and Terrorism, 30,* no. 1 (2007): 1–14.

Der Derian, James. "The War of Networks." *Theory & Event, 5,* no. 4 (2001).

Princeton N. Lyman, Testimony before the House Committee on International Relations Subcommittee on Africa. "Fighting Terrorism in Africa," April 1, 2004.

Gorelick, Jamie. "Computer Encryption." U.S. House Judiciary Committee Concerning Computer Encryption, September 25, 1996.

Gunaratna, Rohan. "Ideology in Terrorism and Counter Terrorism: Lessons from Combating Al Qaeda and Al Jemaah Al Islamiyah in Southeast Asia." CSRC, September 2005.

———. *Inside Al Qaeda: Global Network of Terror.* New York : Columbia University Press, 2002.

Hamilton, Lee, Bruce Hoffman, Brian Jenkins, Paul Pillar, Xavier Raufer, Walter Reich, and Fernando Reinares. *State of the Struggle.* Washington, DC: Council on Global Terrorism, 2006.

Hayek, Friedrich A. *The Road to Serfdom.* Chicago: University of Chicago Press, 1994.

Haynes, Jeffrey. "Islam and Democracy in East Africa." *Democratization, 13,* no. 3 (2006): 490–507.

Indictment of Wadih El Hage, United States of America v. Usama Bin Laden, 98-Cr-1023 (1998).

Johnsen, Gregory D. "Is Al-Qaeda in Yemen Regrouping?" *Terrorism Focus,* no. 15 (May 22, 2007), http://jamestown.org/terrorism/news/article.php?articleid=2373414.

Juergensmeyer, Mark. *Terror in the Mind of God: The Global Rise of Religious Violence,* 3rd ed., Comparative Studies in Religion and Society. Berkeley, CA: University of California Press, 2003.

Kirby, Aidan, and Shawn Brimely. "Home-Grown Terrorism." *Boston Globe* (June 8, 2006), http://www.boston.com/news/globe/editorial_opinion/oped/articles/2006/06/08/home_grown_terrorism/.

Kohlmann, Evan F. "The Real Online Terrorist Threat." *Foreign Affairs, 85,* no. 5 (2006): 115–124.

Laabs, Dirk, and Sebastian Rotella. "Terrorists in Training Head to Pakistan." *Los Angeles Times,* October 14, 2007.

"Libyan Islamists 'Join Al-Qaeda'." *BBC* (November 3, 2007), http://news.bbc.co.uk/2/hi/africa/7076604.stm.

Luthar, Suniya S., Dante Cicchetti, and Bronwyn Becker. "The Construct of Resilience: A Critical Evaluation and Guide for Future Work." *Child Development, 71,* no. 3 (2000): 543–562.

Mazzetti, Mark, and David Rohde. "Terror Officials See Al Qaeda Chiefs Regaining Power." *New York Times* (February 19, 2007), http://www.nytimes.com/2007/02/19/world/asia/19intel.html?_r=1&oref=slogin.

McGregor, Andrew. "Leadership Disputes Plaque Al-Qaeda in the Islamic Magreb." *Terrorism Focus,* no. 30 (2007), http://www.jamestown.org/terrorism/news/article.php?issue_id=4240.

Mekhennet, Souad, and Michael Moss. "Europeans Get Terror Training inside Pakistan." *New York Times,* September 10, 2007.

Miko, Francis T. "Removing Terrorist Sanctuaries: The 9/11 Commission Recommendations and Us Policy." Library of Congress Congressional Research Service, 2005.

Moss, Michael. "What to Do About Pixels of Hate." *New York Times,* October 21, 2007.

"National Intelligence Estimate: The Terrorist Threat to the U.S. Homeland." Office of the Director of National Intelligence, July 2007.

Pargeter, Alison. "North African Immigrants in Europe and Political Violence." *Studies in Conflict and Terrorism, 29,* no. 8 (2006): 731–747.

Rabasa, Angel, Cheryl Benard, Peter Chalk, C. Christine Fair, Theodore W. Karasik, Rollie Lal, Ian O. Lesser, and David E. Thaler. "The Muslim World after 9/11." Santa Monica, CA: RAND Corporation, 2004.

Rabasa, Angel, Peter Chalk, Kim Cragin, Sara A. Daly, Heather S. Gregg, Theodore W. Karasik, Kevin A. O'Brien, and William Rosenau. *Beyond Al-Qaeda: The Global Jihadist Movement.* Santa Monica, CA: RAND Corporation, 2006.

Regan, Tom. "Studies: War Radicalized Most Foreign Fighters in Iraq." *Christian Science Monitor* (July 18, 2005), http://www.csmonitor.com/2005/0718/dailyUpdate.html.

Ricks, Thomas E., and Karen DeYoung. "Al-Qaeda in Iraq Reported Crippled." *Washington Post,* October 15, 2007, A01.

Riedel, Bruce. "Al-Qaeda Five Years after the Fall of Kahndahar." Brookings Institution, January 18, 2007.

Rohde, David. "Foreign Fighters of Harsher Bent Bolster Taliban." *New York Times,* October 30, 2007.

"Saudi Arrests Suspects Planning Oil Attacks." Reuters, April 27, 2007.

Scheuer, Michael. "Afghanistan and Iraq: Two Sunni War Theaters Evolving into One?" *Terrorism Focus,* no. 10 (April 17, 2007), http://www.jamestown.org/terrorism/news/article.php?articleid=2373330.

———. "Al-Qaeda and Algeria's G.S.P.C.: Part of a Much Bigger Picture." *Terrorism Focus,* no. 8 (April 3, 2007), http://www.jamestown.org/terrorism/news/article.php?articleid=2373295.

Simon, Steve, and Jeff Martini. "Terrorism: Denying Al Qaeda Its Popular Support." *Washington Quarterly, 28,* no. 1 (2004–2005): 131–145.

"Suspected '100 Million Dollar Al-Qaeda Financier' Netted in Iraq." Agence France-Presse, October 4, 2007.

Taarnby, Michael. "Recruitment of Islamist Terrorists in Europe: Trends and Perspectives." (January 14, 2005), http://www.justitsministeriet.dk/fileadmin/downloads/Forskning_og_dokumentation/Rekruttering_af_islamistiske_terrorister_i_Europa.pdf.

"U.S. Says Finds List of Qaeda Fighters in Iraq." Agence France-Presse, October 3, 2007.

"U.S. Says Iraq Chlorine Bomb Factor Was Al Qaeda's." Reuters, February 24, 2007.

Vidino, Lorenzo. "Current Trends in Jihadi Networks in Europe." *Terrorism Monitor,* no. 20 (October 25, 2007), http://jamestown.org/terrorism/news/article.php?articleid=2373743.

Weinmann, Gabriel. "Virtual Disputes: The Use of the Internet for Terrorist Debates." *Studies in Conflict and Terrorism, 29,* no. 7 (2006): 623–639.

Whitlock, Craig, and Robin Wright. "Saudis Say They Broke up Suicide Plots." *Washington Post* (April 28, 2007), http://www.washingtonpost.com/wp-dyn/content/article/2007/04/27/AR2007042700649.html?hpid=topnews

Wiktorowicz, Quintan. "Anatomy of the Salafi Movement." *Studies in Conflict and Terrorism, 29,* no. 3 (2006): 207–239.

"A World Wide Web of Terror." *Economist* (July 12, 2007), http://www.economist.com/world/displaystory.cfm?story_id=9472498.

Zavis, Alexander. "Iraqi Militants Feed on Corruption." *Los Angeles Times,* October 26, 2007.

Russell D. Howard

Winning the Campaign against Terrorists

Five Considerations

The title of this article may at first seem odd to most readers because the term "campaign against terrorists" is used instead of the more universally recognized "global war on terrorism." Most national security pundits, officials, military leaders, and the president advance the notion that the United States is at war with "terrorism" and that "terrorism" must be defeated. Indeed, there are ample well-researched and well-articulated articles, books, oped pieces, and examples of congressional testimony advancing the premise that "terrorism" can be defeated—as if "terrorism" were a system of belief such as "Nazism" in Germany during the 1930s and 1940s or "Communism" (however discounted or distorted) in North Korea today.

This article is based on different premises. To this author, and increasingly others, terrorism cannot be viewed as an "ism" like communism, fascism, socialism, capitalism, and other ideologies. To the extent the suffix "ism" suggests a body of thought or system of belief that can be defeated with force or a better "ism," terrorism is a misnomer.[1] Instead, terrorism is a means and tactic defined as the intentional use of violence against civilian populations in order to achieve political ends. The U.S. and its allies are not at war with the means or tactic, but with those seeking those political ends—who happen to be terrorists.

Terrorism is a tactic that has been used for centuries and will continue to be used in the future. History tells us—at least to date—that terrorism as a tactic has not been defeated, but specific terrorist groups have. Some terrorist groups—the Thugs in India come to mind—survived for centuries; however, that is not the norm. According to Dr. Rohan Gunaratna, the average life expectancy of a modern terrorist group is twelve years.[2] Like terrorist groups of the past, al Qaeda will also be defeated. Obviously, al Qaeda has surpassed the "twelve-year average," but eventually the organization—along with its surrogate and franchise groups—will also be defeated.

This chapter outlines five ways to hasten al Qaeda's defeat. They are:

1. If you are not going to fight a war, do not call it a war!

2. Rewrite the National Security Act of 1947 to address the present-day threat.

3. Fight an ideology with a better (or more correct) ideology.

4. Fight networks with networks.

5. Educate, educate, and educate susceptible youth.

1. If you are not going to fight a war, do not call it a war!

Somewhat unique to U.S. political rhetoric is the misuse of the word "war." Perhaps because a sense of urgency or required motivation, American politicians give "warfare status" to non-warlike circumstances. Examples include the Johnson administration's "War on Poverty" and the Reagan administration's "War on Drugs." By any definition, neither were wars: they were not waged against states (as outlined in the Webster Dictionary's definition of war), nor were they "fought" using all of elements of power at America's disposal. Similarly, the so-called "War on Terror" is not a war by any definition. The U.S. is not threatened by nor engaged in conflict with any state. Instead, the U.S. and the West are threatened by transnational, non-state actors such as al Qaeda, who attack globally and pursue the acquisition of weapons of mass destruction (WMD).

Certainly, the American public does not think it is at war. Americans have traditionally displayed an extraordinary degree of resourcefulness and self-sacrifice in times of war.[3] The best example of that tradition is World War II, when the war effort became an immediate extension of America's national will and purpose.[4] Today, says Stephen Flynn, "We are breaking with that tradition. Our nation faces grave peril, but we seem unwilling to mobilize at home to confront the threat before us."[5] For example, at the height of World War II, the United States committed roughly thirty-six percent of its gross domestic product (GDP) to the war effort and had more than twelve million men and women in uniform at the end of the war. Presently, less than four percent of U.S. GDP is committed to the campaign against terrorism, and of the 2.6 million men and women presently in uniform, 1.4 million are in the National Guard and Reserve.[6] Unlike the World War II era, when consumer goods were rationed and America's productive capacity was focused on the war effort, today there are no shortages, no rationing, and the production of goods and services for the consumer market is operating uninterrupted.

America's traditional allies do not consider the battle against terrorism to be a war, either. The United Kingdom stopped using the term "global war on terrorism" in April 2007. Hilary Benn, Britain's International Development Secretary, said, "In the UK, we do not use the phrase 'war on terror' because we can't win by military means alone, and because this isn't us against one organized enemy with a clear identity and a coherent set of objectives."[7] To states such as the United Kingdom, Spain, and France, which have had terrorism problems for decades, a "war on terror" suggests the use of a military operation to achieve a solution. Instead, these states prefer—and in many cases have been successful in achieving—police operations that help achieve political solutions. More important, several European countries are home to large Muslim populations which, like their counterparts in their homes of origin, are not enamored with the term "global war on terrorism." Allies such as the UK and France must calibrate their willingness to be "coalition partners" with the hostility such a partnership raises within large Muslim communities in both countries.

Clearly, when first articulated by President Bush and authorized by the U.S. Congress on September 18, 2001, the term "war on terrorism" was meant to galvanize the American people. The phrase, much like other sayings invoked by the administration, such as "you can run but you can't hide" and "you are either with us or against us," were intended to rally the American public to the task at hand—and they worked. Unfortunately, when the American president and legislature speak, the whole world, not just the intended American audience, listens. As a result, these terms were and continue to be interpreted very differently by non-Americans. For example, many Muslims—up to seventy percent in Morocco, Egypt, and Pakistan, according to one poll—interpret "war on terror" to mean war against their religion.[8] Steven Kull, an editor at WorldPublicOpinion.org, a Washington-based group that conducted the poll, said, "While U.S. leaders may frame the conflict as a war on terrorism, people in the Islamic world clearly perceive the U.S. as being at war with Islam."[9]

Because the U.S. and its allies are not really fighting a war, the fight against terrorist groups should not be called a war. It should instead be called what it is: a campaign against Islamic extremists who threaten the West. The threat cannot be underestimated. The use of asymmetric tactics and networked structures make today's enemy very different from—and arguably more dangerous than—traditional, state-centric threats. However, to defeat the Islamic extremist threat, the U.S. will require the support of its friends, allies, and American public, none of which believe or behave as if they are at war.

2. Rewrite the National Security Act of 1947 to address the present-day threat

America's current national security organization and law is based on the National Security Act (NSA) of 1947, which created the Department of Defense, the U.S. Air Force, the Central Intelligence Agency, and the National Security Council. This legislation was intended to correct coordination and operations deficiencies observed during World War II and to address the emerging Soviet threat. For the most part, it worked: the U.S. prevailed in the Cold War and averted nuclear disaster. However, during the past several years (and particularly since 9/11), many observers have questioned whether the NSA and the institutions and treaty regimes it created can adequately address the challenges of post-Cold War global security.

Clearly, the global security environment has changed since the end of the Cold War. No longer do superpowers and their surrogates compete for the world's allegiance and resources. No longer do realist and idealist theories based on sovereign state behavior and state interaction provide satisfactory frameworks for discussing (and solving) American and international security challenges. Today, instead of an adversarial superpower, the West's major security threats include transnational, non-state terrorist groups with access to WMD; failed, failing, and rogue states; and international criminal cartels. These entities are the main sources of international and domestic terrorism, transnational crime, ethnic and religious conflict, the opportunity for WMD proliferation, and other new security threats.

Unfortunately, the 1947 NSA was not designed, and has not been adequately adapted, to address these threats. It was promulgated in and for a bipolar, state-centric, balance-of-power environment. The present security environment is less state-centric, is not bipolar, and has an unbalanced power distribution (very much in America's favor). Threats to U.S. security are more diverse and pervasive than during the Cold War. Too often—think of 9/11 as one of many instances—the American failure to predict, prevent, and protect against terrorist and other threats is a result of outdated security legislation, organizations, and doctrine.

It is beyond the scope of this paper to examine all of the NSA's deficiencies. However, a short example highlighting the Central Intelligence Agency (CIA) is illustrative of the NSA's problems. According to Dr. Amy Zegart, professor of public policy at UCLA, the NSA has limited the CIA's effectiveness in two lasting ways. First, it gave the CIA responsibility for coordinating all U.S. intelligence agencies—six different agencies at the time—but granted the agency little authority to do so.[10] The Department of Defense retained the control of the overwhelming majority of the intelligence budget, while the CIA director was given discretion over less than twenty percent of intelligence funds and "had no real ability to hire, fire, move, or manage personnel working in any of the other multiple intelligence agencies."[11] Second, the NSA protected the existing territory of the various intelligence agencies, "making clear that existing intelligence agencies should 'continue to collect, evaluate, correlate, and disseminate' their own intelligence unfettered."[12] The CIA was actually "legally barred from gathering intelligence about American citizens on American soil, conducting any law enforcement or police activities, or performing other internal security functions."[13] These restrictions "arose partly from fears of creating an American Gestapo," but also from "intense lobbying" by then-FBI Director J. Edgar Hoover.[14] The result was a critical bifurcated structural split between foreign and domestic intelligence; the CIA was responsible for tracking enemies abroad and the FBI responsible for finding them at home. Decades later, the 9/11 Commission deemed the intelligence community's structure—a direct result of the NSA—to be one of the "institutional failings" exploited by al Qaeda.[15]

Today, the Director of National Intelligence (DNI) has taken over many of the functions that formerly fell under the domain of the CIA director. Created by the Intelligence Reform and Terrorism Prevention Act of 2004, the DNI is appointed by the President with Senate consent. However, according to Zegart, the DNI structure "retains nearly all of the same design flaws as the CIA under the NSA." The DNI, "like the CIA director before him, is struggling to make an even greater number of U.S. intelligence agencies"—now sixteen discrete organizations—operate in unison, while working with weak statutory powers and competing for more funding.[16] Today's "more hidden, mobile, and adaptive enemy than the Soviet Union ever was" only further complicates the DNI's mission.[17]

Rewriting the NSA would be a difficult task, but it is achievable. The model for such a rewrite is the Goldwater-Nichols Act of 1986, which reorganized the Department of Defense and corrected the problems of inter-service rivalry, bloated command structures, and incessant turf battles. As chairman of the Investigations Subcommittee of the House Armed Services Committee, Congressman Bill Nichols studied the problem and led the campaign to force new legislation. However, it took the commitment of two strong-willed senators—Republican Barry Goldwater and Democrat Sam Nunn—to pass legislation over the objections of the Department of Defense (Secretary of the Navy John Lehman in particular was a major obstacle) and many in the Reagan administration.[18] Goldwater and Nunn's opposite characteristics complicated the work of their entrenched opponents. Unfortunately, the Goldwater-Nichols Act, which passed in both the House and Senate by wide margins, did not go far enough. Correcting the problems of inter-service rivalries was a good first step, but correcting the problems of inter-agency rivalries is the next and more formidable step.

It will take a courageous team of legislators to push NSA reorganization legislation through what one can predict will be strong resistance from entrenched bureaucracies. Potential candidates for this endeavor are Senators Chuck Hagel, a Republican from Nebraska, and Jack Reed, a Democrat from Rhode Island. Both are military veterans keenly interested in international affairs and national security issues. Both are no-nonsense legislators with impeccable foreign policy credentials. Both are tough, reasonable, and articulate. Most important, like Goldwater and Nunn before them, they are friends. Perhaps they can lead the campaign to formulate the laws that will prepare the U.S. for the security challenges it will face in the future.[19]

3. Fight an ideology with a better (or more correct) ideology

Ideology is the glue that holds al Qaeda and like-minded groups together. Osama bin Laden and other Islamist terrorists draw on a long tradition of intolerance within an extreme view of Islam dating "from Ibn Taimiyyah, through the founders of Wahhabism, through the Muslim Brotherhood, to Sayyid Qutb"—one which "does not distinguish politics from religion, thus distorting both."[20] This radical form of Islam "calls for the establishment of a Caliphate across the Islamic world, beginning with the expulsion of the infidel from Muslim lands."[21] It preaches that "every Muslim has their part to play and every Muslim can achieve Martyrdom" by waging jihad and, if necessary, conducting suicide operations.[22]

Al Qaeda's ideology does not require a hierarchical organization to spread; "indeed, it has spread like wildfire through Madrassas, radical Mosques, and the Internet" based on its ability to allow "any Muslim extremist, acting alone, in a cell, or as part of a network . . . [to] take up this cause, and incite others to take up the cause too."[23] According to the 9/11 Commission, this ideology "is fed by grievances stressed by bin Laden and widely felt throughout the Muslim world—against the U.S. military presence in the Middle East, policies perceived as anti-Arab and anti-Muslim, and support of Israel."[24] Osama bin Laden and like-minded extremists say what they mean: to them America is the font of all evil, the "head of the snake," and it must be converted or destroyed.[25] Further, this stance "is not a position with which Americans can bargain or negotiate. With it there is no common ground—not even respect for life—on which to begin a dialogue."[26]

Who can negotiate with or discount an ideology that many say is corrupt? If it is true that neither the Koran nor Muhammad's example justifies the attacks of 9/11, and that al Qaeda employs narrow, self-serving interpretations to justify their actions, who can refute them?[27] Who can take back what some call a hijacked religion?[28] The answer is Muslims themselves. If, as some speculate, a very small percentage of Muslims are extremists, why is the extremist voice so loud?[29] Why is it that "moderate" Muslims do not rise up and denounce those who they feel have given Islam a bad name? Three reasons come to mind.

First, "liberal" Islam was badly bludgeoned by the militaristic, populist regimes that came to power in the Middle East in the 1950s. These regimes espoused belligerent nationalism, were ferocious in preserving indigenous heritage, and were deeply suspicious of any ideas originating in the Western empires they expelled from their territories. These regimes "stood for unity, uniformity and one-man, one-party rule, and sought to manipulate religion to win the populace to their cause."[30] Not much has changed. Moderate Muslims advocating democratic reform in the Middle East do not fare well with the reigning governments in the region. As a recent RAND Corporation study notes, "the principal obstacle to building moderate Muslim networks in the Middle East is the lack of extant, widespread liberal movements to network; only small groups and scattered individuals exist there today."[31] Lacking moderate political outlets in secular Arab states, public dissatisfaction with the status quo is often channeled through the Muslim Brotherhood and other Islamist factions, not via democratic-minded Muslims, who often lack visibility and influence.[32]

Second, moderate Muslims are not united, nor do they speak with one voice. The community's various viewpoints and factions result in poor organization—an area in which extremists excel.[33] Very few moderate Muslim spokesmen have the communication abilities to propagate their message effectively. According to the RAND study, "This weakness is especially evident in audio-visual narrowcasting. Of the four hundred or so known tape-cassette preachers, none are moderate. The majority are radical, a minority traditionalist."[34]

Third, moderate Muslims are afraid—very afraid. Moderate Muslims run the risk of being labeled apostates (*takfir*) by extremists, an accusation that can result in death. For example, on April 10, 2006 "an Egyptian group calling itself the "al-Jama'ah Consultative Council . . . disseminated a hit list of moderate Muslims" accused of being apostates.[35] The group gave those on the list three days to "disavow" their moderate views or be killed.[36] The threat read:

> We will follow them everywhere they go and at anytime; and they can never be far from the swords of truth, and they are closer to us that our shoelaces. They are monitored day and night. We are fully aware of their hiding places, their houses, their children's schools, and the times when their wives are alone at home. We gave our rules to the soldiers of God to execute the rule of God so that their blood can become close to God [to kill them] and burn their houses. And we thank God that many of those infidels and atheists do not exist in the land of Islam, so that they do not defile the Islamic land with their rotten blood. They are in the land of infidelity, the land of idols, pagans, and Cross worshippers: in America, Canada, Switzerland, and Italy. If they existed on a spot in the Islamic land, let us wash the places of their slaughter and beheading seven times to purify the Islamic land of the impurity of their blood. And let us captivate their women and enslave their children loot them. Let us apply the Islamic rule to them; and whoever kills one of them, will get his loot.[37]

So, how can the U.S. and the West help moderate Muslims regain their voices and take back their religion? Very carefully and indirectly, or the strategy will not work. Any moderate Muslim, be it an individual or group, known for receiving aid from the West are immediately tainted and accused of being collaborators by extremists. Therefore, indirect aid "filtered" through philanthropic organizations (taking a page from the al Qaeda playbook) to moderates willing to fight back would be helpful.[38]

Another way to assist moderate Muslims might be to do nothing at all. For example a recent article in *USA Today* entitled "Pakistani Public Turning against Islamic Militants" noted that seventy-four percent of Pakistanis polled are fed up with Taliban and al Qaeda-led extremism in their country.[39] According to the article, "Pakistanis are appalled by [the Taliban's] brutal brand of Islam," to the extent that "some local militias have taken up arms against the Taliban's al Qaeda-linked foreign allies similar to the way Iraqi insurgents set aside differences with U.S. forces this year to drive out al Qaeda militants.[40] Furthermore, *al Jazeera,* a news network often maligned as being anti-West, might be part of the solution. True, the popular media outlet is critical of the West (particularly the U.S.) and autocratic Arab states allied with the West. However, it is also critical of al Qaeda and Islamic extremism. For example, in October 2007 al Qaeda sympathizers unleashed a torrent of anger against *al Jazeera* television, accusing it of misrepresenting Osama bin Laden's comments on a videotape and criticizing the network on militant online forums.[41] According to observers, "the reaction highlighted militants' surprise at bin Laden's words, and their dismay at the deep divisions among al Qaeda and other Iraqi militants that he appeared to be trying to heal."[42] The Western media's arguments underscoring Islamist extremist shortcomings may fall on deaf ears in the Muslim world, but *al Jazeera*'s don't.

4. Fight networks with networks[43]

As noted in the Arquilla, Ronfeldt, and Zanini chapter and this author's opening chapter in this volume, today's terrorists have moved from centralized, hierarchical, bureaucratic organizations to decentralized, flatter, looser, and less hierarchical organizational structures. Historically, when al Qaeda had sanctuary in Sudan until 1996 and Afghanistan until 2002, it had been a top-down organization with strong central leadership control over almost all aspects of its operations. However, its defeat in Afghanistan and continued Western-led military operations against al Qaeda have served to isolate its leadership and sever or complicate communications links with its operatives, which are scattered around the globe.[44]

Since it lost its sanctuary in Afghanistan, al Qaeda has evolved into a much more decentralized organization relying on allied groups or semi-autonomous networked cells to carry out deadly operations and the Internet to rectify its communications problems.[45] Al Qaeda's covert networks are loosely affiliated and not led by any central authority. What binds the networks together is an ideology—a radical view of Islam that advocates a revolutionary struggle, to be waged by means of violence, political action, and propaganda against the secular Muslim regimes (the near enemy) and Israel and the West (the far enemy).[46] Al Qaeda's networked cells operate independently, with their members rarely knowing the identity of others or of anyone higher up in the organization's hierarchy. Because they do not form ties outside their cells and minimize their ties within the network, al Qaeda operators are difficult to find, kill, or capture. For example, the ties between members of the 9/11 hijacker network and outsiders were non-existent. However, "the hijacker's network"—like most al Qaeda-related networks—"had a hidden strength" in its "massive redundancy through trusted prior contacts."[47] These contacts were based on tribal affiliation or common experiences in madrassas or training camps, making the network very resilient. These historical ties "were solidly in place as the hijackers made their way to America" and are in place today among al Qaeda's networked cells.[48]

The U.S. is fighting al Qaeda's networks with hierarchical, bureaucratic security organizations that were adequate during the Cold War era, when the adversary was similarly organized.[49] However, hierarchies do not fight networks very well. An example from the private sector can perhaps best illustrate this concept. Similar to post-9/11 al Qaeda, the online marketplace craigslist is a decentralized, leaderless, Internet-based network that is beating its hierarchical and bureaucratic competition. Craigslist users generate and monitor content, so that in a "day-to-day kind of way, the people who use the site run it."[50] The site has grown from humble beginnings in San Francisco to a network found in 50 countries and 450 cities around the world.[51] Three million people use craigslist every month, generating over eight billion page views.[52] All listings—which feature everything from garage-sale items to event tickets to used cars to potential dates—are free, with the exception of job listings posted by for-profit companies.[53] One study based in the San Francisco market showed that local newspapers—which charge for classified ads and take up to two days to publish them—were losing as much as $50 million a year in revenue to craigslist.[54] While craigslist and al Qaeda are obviously very different organizations, their success over conventional organizations can be attributed to a common factor: networked structure. While "trust in an ideology" is the glue that holds al Qaeda together, "trust in community" is the glue that holds craigslist together.[55]

Like al Qaeda and craigslist, the U.S. needs nimbleness that cannot be found in a hierarchy, but is inherent in networks. For example, Arquilla and Ronfeldt—who coined the phrase "it takes a network to fight a network"—suggest that the U.S. needs to become more "networked" by breaking down the barriers between structures or sectors, such as civil and military, federal and local, or foreign and domestic. For example, the events of 9/11 proved that, acting on their own, neither the FBI nor the CIA could thwart terrorism. However, for these sectors to cooperate effectively, they require the assistance of a law enforcement network that crosses all agencies and levels of government. They need networked communications systems to capture, analyze, transform, fuse, and act upon information across public and private organizations at a speed, cost, and level of reliability that to date have proven impossible. Similarly, the Centers for Disease Control and Prevention cannot adequately respond to an anthrax or smallpox outbreak or other bioterrorism incidents on its own. An effective response would require the activation of robust public health and emergency responder networks.[56]

Finally, progress in the form of public-private partnerships to fight cyber-terror and protect critical infrastructure may be a model to follow in the future. According to Stephen Goldberg and William Eggers, in a world in which elusive, decentralized, non-state entities such as al Qaeda and Hezbollah represent the biggest threat to Western democracies, "the networked approach has become critical to national security."[57] As these scholars note, "In simpler times the federal government might have employed a command-and-control approach for such a critical initiative. But in the wake of the September 11 terrorist attacks, a centralized approach was neither feasible nor desirable.[58] The government alone cannot thwart attacks on technological networks, telephone systems, power grids, financial systems, dams, municipal water systems, and the rest of our nation's critical infrastructure because of one staggering fact: between 85 and 90 percent of the U.S. infrastructure is privately owned.[59]

To work in tandem with these private-sector infrastructure owners, the U.S. government has formed several multi-sector networks to coordinate security efforts. For example, Information Sharing and Analysis Centers (ISACs)—networks that promote public-private communication, information-sharing, and preparedness for possible critical infrastructure attacks—exist in the financial, telecommunications, chemical, transportation, food, energy, and information technology sectors.[60] In addition, President George W. Bush's federal cyber-security initiative was built around a "cornerstone" of public-private partnership.

The president stated, "Only by acting together can we build a more secure future in cyberspace."[61] Models such as these demonstrate the government's recognition of today's more complicated homeland security problems. While these limited critical infrastructure and cyber-security initiatives do not address all aspects of fighting terrorism and have met with limited success, they represent a shift in federal strategy—an important step toward "fighting networks with networks."

5. Educate, Educate, and Educate Susceptible Youth

Much of the Muslim world, but particularly the Middle East, has regressed economically while many former third world countries—the four "Asian Tigers" (Taiwan, South Korea, Singapore, and Hong Kong) as well as China, India, and Vietnam come to mind—are flourishing in the globalized world. A recent *Newsweek* article highlights some statistics that illustrate the point: "In the early 1960s, Egypt—the Arab world's most populous country—exported manufactured goods at roughly the same per capita level as South Korea and Taiwan. Now . . . [South Korea and Taiwan] export more in three days than Egypt does all year."[62] According to the article, "the Arab world is in a state of long-term deglobalization, more isolated today than it was twenty, thirty, or forty years ago."[63] Despite large oil revenues, the region's share of world trade and investment been halved in the past twenty-five years, and its proportion of global manufacturing exports has dropped to less than one percent.[64] Disturbingly, to "keep pace with an exploding population of young job-seekers," the region will have to create seventy million jobs in the next thirteen years if it hopes to keep unemployment down to the global norm.[65]

There are many social, cultural, and political reasons for the lackluster economic performance, but one looms large: "poor technical skills due to decrepit university systems (no Arab school ranks among the world's best)."[66] Indeed, at a time when education in international relations, math, science, and other technical and social disciplines are prerequisites for competitiveness in a globalized world, religious teaching in madrassas seems to be the emphasis in greater Arabia and other Muslim countries. This has the potential to be a recipe for disaster. While no one discounts the importance of religious education, the existence of millions of madrassa graduates—who may be experts on Islam but lacking in technical skills—will not help the region compete, or perhaps even survive, in an increasingly globalized world. Actually, the notion of a cohort of millions of unskilled and unemployed younger workers with no upward mobility is a recipe for disaster, since this segment of the population is ripe for recruitment by al Qaeda and other extremist groups.

Pakistan offers a good case study for the dangers of an over-emphasis on religious education and a neglect of modern skill attainment. According to the 9/11 Commission Report, "Pakistan's endemic poverty, widespread corruption, and often ineffective government create opportunities for Islamist recruitment. Poor education is a particular concern."[67] Millions of Pakistani families send their children to madrassas because these schools are the only educational opportunity that is available (or affordable). Unfortunately, many madrassas have been used as incubators for violent extremism. According to the police commander of Karachi, Pakistan, "there are 859 madrassas teaching more than 200,000 youngsters in his city alone."[68] Not all madrassas in Karachi or any city actively preach jihadi militancy, but even those without direct links to violence may promote an ideology that provides religious justification for such attacks.[69] Exploiting Karachi's rapid, unplanned, and unregulated urbanization and its masses of young, disaffected youth, these madrassas use the "pulpit to promote sectarian and jihadi violence."[70]

Similar situations exist in many other Muslim countries, including Bangladesh, Yemen, and Saudi Arabia. Other regions are affected, too, as a significant number of young Southeast Asians are studying at madrassas in Pakistan and Yemen. According to the Australian government, these students "have been influenced by some of the more doctrinaire versions of Islam—particularly the closely-related Salafi and Wahhabi streams."[71] Saudi Arabia's financial influence has also helped promote extremism in Southeast Asia through the funding of madrassas.[72]

What can be done to counteract the influence of madrassas? At a minimum, an effort should be made to close down those schools that have proven links with extremist militant groups.[73] Additionally, developing alternative schools and curriculums that do not feature purely religious education may be a partial answer. The schools and curriculum could compete with or supplement madrassas depending on local educational policy and custom. Ideally, oil-rich Arab states such as Saudi Arabia should contribute funds to this type of educational development. Perhaps instead of funding extremist education in madrassas, the world's richest oil producing countries should help fund regional programs that educate future generations of engineers, scientists, and entrepreneurs, who will keep Middle Eastern economies running once the oil runs out.

Also, and alternatively, it might be a mission of the West to help. One of the major recommendations of the 9/11 Commission was for the U.S. to cooperate with other countries to directly support the building and operating of primary and secondary schools in select Muslim states.[74] Additionally, the Commission recommended more support for vocational education in trades and business skills.[75] If, as reported, the war in Iraq is costing $200 million per day, it seems possible and logical to earmark a very small portion of that amount for useful educational alternatives that, in the end, might produce conditions that will make military action unnecessary.[76]

Concluding Remarks: It's Just Common Sense

The United States needs to take a more comprehensive and proactive response to the terrorist threat. It must use all of its elements of power—economic, political, diplomatic, communications, civil defense, education, and the military—in eliminating the threat from Islamist extremism. Make no mistake: al Qaeda and its like-minded surrogate, franchise, and aspirational groups are the number one "clear and present" danger the U.S. faces today. Defeating them is an important national and international objective—and they will be defeated. However, it will take more than military and police activity to do so. As much as anything, a successful strategy to defeat al Qaeda will require a good dose of common sense. The five means of addressing the threat outlined in this chapter are a start.

If the U.S. is not fighting a war against terror—and it is not—then common sense should tell us to stop calling it a war. Neither the American public nor U.S. allies think or act like they are involved in a war. Instead, a more suitable term should be used: campaign, effort, operation, struggle—any will do. It should simply not be called a war, and certainly not a crusade. Common sense also should tell us that U.S. laws should make it easy for the numerous security, intelligence, and defense departments, agencies, and bureaus to defeat Islamist extremists. They currently do not. In fact, the National Security Act of 1947 does not include language appropriate for addressing transnational, non-state actors that act globally and are trying to obtain weapons of mass destruction (and how could it, since al Qaeda and other Islamist extremists were not a problem in 1947?). To solve this problem, the law should be changed to reflect today's security realities.

If al Qaeda were a state—organized hierarchically, engaged in multi-lateral, multi-state discourse, and susceptible to diplomatic, economic, and conventional military means of persuasion—then our hierarchical, state-centric, military approach to defeating the organization might work. However, al Qaeda is not a state: it owns no territory, does not participate in international diplomacy, and it does not respond to international norms. Al Qaeda is a non-state actor with global reach and ambition. It is a network of networks whose basic organizing block is a cell. Al Qaeda is not bureaucratic or hierarchical, has no central authority, and can function without a "commander in chief." Common sense might tell us that to fight a network, it will take a network—and that the U.S. and its allies might have to become more networked themselves.

The 2003 U.S. National Strategy for Combating Terrorism unfortunately informed the American public that "terrorism" was the nation's enemy. Common sense should tell us that, by definition, terrorism is a means or a tactic—not an enemy. Islamist extremists are the enemy, as is their ideology: a radical form of Islam that has been discredited by most Muslims, who argue that al Qaeda's distorted version of Islam is contrary to the essence of the true Islamic spirit.[77] Fortunately, there is some good news: the 2006 version of the Combating Terrorism Strategy correctly identifies extremists and their distorted ideology as the enemy. Common sense then dictates that countering a distorted ideology (Islamic extremism) can best be done by those who understand the alternative ideology: "moderate" Muslims who can refute the distortions promulgated by al Qaeda and likeminded groups. For a variety of reasons identified earlier in this paper, many—not all—moderate Muslims are hesitant to be critical of extremists such as al Qaeda. For their future, as well as those of the U.S. and its allies, moderate Muslims need to stand up and be recognized, and they will likely need some form of Western support to do so.

Finally, this chapter posited that education may be a key component in defeating Islamist extremism and extremists. Young Muslims and their counterparts around the world will need a well-rounded education emphasizing modern disciplines and skill sets in order to survive and prosper in an increasingly globalized world. Religious education is important, not just to Muslims, but to those of all faiths. However, only learning about religion may not prepare one for the challenges of modernization and globalization, which require a foundation in math, the sciences, and international relations. Who should ensure that Muslim youth receive a balanced education experience? Muslim countries, of course—it is to their advantage. However, the U.S. and its allies can help. As Craig Cohen of the Center for Strategic and International Studies urged the U.S. House of Representatives at a hearing on madrassa reform, "Let's become the country that provides opportunity for young Pakistanis, rather than the country that is at war with Islam, which is how we are perceived today."[78] This statement makes a lot of common sense.

Brigadier General Russell D. Howard (Retired) was a career Special Forces officer and is now the Director of the Jebsen Center for Counter-terrorism Studies at the Fletcher School at Tufts University. His recent publications include *Defeating Terrorism,* (McGraw-Hill, 2004), *Homeland Security and Terrorism* (McGraw-Hill, 2005), and *Weapons of Mass Destruction and Terrorism* (McGraw-Hill, 2006).

Notes

1. Jonah Goldberg, "Enough Already! Time to Stop the War on Terrorism," *National Review Online,* April 10, 2002. Available at <http://article.nationalreview.com/?q=MTRiZGRhYT dhNDdmYjRlZTJmMDA0NGIyOTI3MjJhZTY=>.
2. Multiple conversations with Dr. Rohan Gunaratna over a six-year research association.
3. Stephen Flynn, *America the Vulnerable* (New York: Harper Collins, 2004), x.
4. David Halberstam, *War in Time of Peace* (Simon and Schuster: New York, 2001), 496.
5. Flynn, x.
6. "Air Force Association Statement of Policy," September 12, 2004. Available at <www.afa.org/AboutUs/PolicyIssues05.asp>.
7. "Benn criticizes 'war on terror' idea," *The Guardian,* April 16, 2007. Available at <www.guardian.co.uk/terrorism/story/0,,2058226,00.html>.
8. Michael Nichols, "Muslims Believe U.S. Goal to Weaken Islam—Poll," *Reuters,* April 24, 2007. Available at <www.reuters.com/article/politicsNews/idUSN2332112320070424?feed Type=RSS>.
9. Ibid.
10. Amy Zegart, "The CIA's License to Fail," *Los Angeles Times,* September 23, 2007. Available at <www.isop.ucla.edu/article.asp?parentid=78595>.
11. Ibid.
12. Ibid.
13. Ibid.
14. Amy Zegart, *Flawed by Design: the Evolution of the CIA, JCS , and NSC* (Palo Alto, CA: Stanford University Press, 1999), 268.
15. Zegart, "The CIA's License to Fail." See also *The 9/11 Commission Report* (New York: W.W. Norton & Company, 2004), 265.
16. Zegart, "The CIA's License to Fail."
17. Ibid.
18. Russell Howard, "Reorganizing Defense—Book Review," *Joint Force Quarterly* No. 32 (Autumn 2002), 137.
19. This is an original thought, but it is not unique. A study currently being undertaken by group led by James Locher, III has arrived at the same conclusion. For those who want to understand the difficulty of changing the law, see James Locher, *Victory on the Potomac* (College Station, TX: Texas A&M University Press, 2002).
20. *The 9/11 Commission Report.* (New York: W. W. Norton, 2005), 362.
21. Gerald Howarth, "Can the War on Terror be Won?" Speech to the Conservative Way Forward, January 18, 2005. Available at <www.geraldhowarth.org.uk/record.jsp?type= speech&ID=9>.
22. Ibid.
23. Ibid.
24. *The 9/11 Commission Report,* 362.
25. Ibid.
26. Ibid.
27. Karen Armstrong, "Is Islam Violent?" in *Taking Back Islam: American Muslims Reclaim Their Faith,* ed. Michael Wolfe (USA: Rodale, 2002), 25.
28. Jonathan Rauch, "Islam has been Hijacked and Only Muslims Can Save It," *Reason Online,* October 13, 2001. Available at <www.reason.com/news/show/34589.html>.

29. Kurt Campbell and Richard Weitz, "Non-Military Strategies for Countering Islamist Terrorism: Lessons Learned From Past Counterinsurgencies," *The Princeton Project on National Security,* September 27, 2006, p. 7. Available at <www.hudson.org/files/publications/Counterinsurgency-Princeton-Campell-Weitz.pdf>.
30. Emanuel Sivan, "The Clash Within Islam," *Survival,* Vol. 45. No. 1 (Spring 2003), 36.
31. Angel Rabasa, Cheryl Benard, Lowell H. Schwartz, and Peter Sickle, *Building Moderate Muslim Networks* (Santa Monica: RAND Corporation, 2007), 113. Available at <www.rand.org/pubs/monographs/2007/RAND_MG574.pdf>.
32. Ibid, 114.
33. Sivan, 40.
34. Ibid.
35. M. Zuhdi Jasser, "Death Threats Against a List of Moderate Muslims in the West," *Plugged in Arizona,* April 13, 2006. Available at <www.azcentral.com/blogs/index.php?blog=174&title=al_jama_ah_consultative_council_distribu&more=1&c=1&tb=1&pb=1&blogtype=PluggedinAZ>.
36. Ibid.
37. Ibid.
38. This was a common theme articulated at the "Islam in Democratic Societies" conference hosted by the Jebsen Center for Counter-Terrorism Studies and the Hudson Institute on April 26, 2006 in Medford, Massachusetts.
39. Paul Wiseman and Zafar M. Sheikh, "Pakistani Public Turning Against Islamic Militants," *USA Today,* October, 27, 2007, 1A.
40. Ibid.
41. "Extremists Slam al-Jazeera Over bin Laden Tape," *Taipei Times,* October 27, 2007, 7.
42. Ibid.
43. John Arquilla, David Ronfeldt, and Michele Zanini, "Networks, Netwar, and Information-Age Terrorism," in *Terrorism and Counterterrorism: Understanding the New Security Environment,* eds. Russell D. Howard and Reid L. Sawyer (Dubuque, IA: McGraw-Hill, 2006), 108.
44. Cofer Black, testimony at the "Al Qaeda: Threat to the United States and its Allies" hearings before the House Sub-Committee on Terrorism, Non-Proliferation, and Human Rights, April 1, 2004 Available at <http://commdocs.house.gov/committees/intlrel/hfa92869.000/hfa92869_0.HTM>.
45. Ibid.
46. Christopher Henzel, "The Origins of al Qaeda's Ideology: Implications for U.S. Strategy," *Parameters,* Vol. 35, No. 1 (Spring 2005), 76. Available at <www.carlisle.army.mil/usawc/Parameters/05spring/henzel.htm>.
47. Valdis E. Krebs, "Uncloaking Terrorist Networks," *First Monday,* Vol. 7, No. 4 (April 2002), 4. Available at <www.firstmonday.org/issues/issue7_4/krebs/index.html>.
48. Ibid.
49. Peter Buxbaum, "DoD Needs its Networks to be Unconventional to Fight Terrorism," *Government Computer News Online,* November 15, 2006. Available at <www.gcn.com/online/vol1_no1/42583-1.html?topic=defense-technology>.
50. Ori Brafman and Rod A. Beckstrom," *The Starfish and the Spider: The Unstoppable Power of Leaderless Organizations* (New York: Penguin, 2006), 65.
51. "craigslist factsheet," from craigslist.org. Available at <www.craigslist.org/about/factsheet.html>.
52. Ibid.
53. Brafman and Beckstrom, 65.
54. Philip Weiss, "A Guy Named Craig," *New York Magazine,* January 16, 2006. Available at <http://nymag.com/nymetro/news/media/internet/15500/>.
55. Brafman and Beckstrom, 66.
56. Stephen Goldsmith and William D. Eggers, *Governing by Network: The New Shape of the Public Sector.* (Washington, DC: Brookings Institution Press, 2004), 5.
57. Ibid, 3.

58. Ibid.
59. Ibid.
60. Ibid.
61. Ibid.
62. Marcus Noland and Howard Pack, "The Inward East: The Arab world's economies are getting ever less globalized," *Newsweek,* October 29, 2007, 38. Available at <www.newsweek.com/id/57419/output/print>.
63. Ibid.
64. Ibid.
65. Ibid.
66. Ibid, 39.
67. *The 9/11 Commission Report,* 367.
68. Ibid.
69. International Crisis Group, "Pakistan: Karachi's Madrassas and Violent Extremism," *Asia Report,* No. 130 (March 29, 2007). Available at <www.crisisgroup.org/home/index.cfm?l=1&id=4742>.
70. Ibid.
71. "Transnational Terrorism: The Threat to Australia," Government of Australia Department of Foreign Affairs and Trade *White Paper,* March 29, 2004. Available at <www.dfat.gov.au/publications/terrorism/index.html>.
72. Ibid.
73. Hassan Abbas, "Ulema Versus Ijtihad: Understanding the Nature of the Crisis in the Muslim World," *al Nakhla: The Fletcher School Online Journal for Issues Related to Southwest Asia and Islamic Civilization,* Article 1(Fall 2004), 4. Available at <http://fletcher.tufts.edu/al_nakhlah/archives/fall2004/abbas.pdf>.
74. *The 9/11 Commission Report,* 378
75. Ibid.
76. Martin Wolk, "Cost of Iraq War Could Surpass $1 Trillion," *MSNBC.com,* March 17, 2006. Available at <www.msnbc.msn.com/id/11880954>.
77. Abbas, 1.
78. Anwer Iqbal, "Education Termed Key to Defeating Extremists," *Dawn E-Paper,* May 11, 2007. Available at <www.dawn.com/2007/05/11/top19.htm>.

Acknowledgments

Unit I Defining the Threat

Chapter 1

From *Inside Terrorism* by Bruce Hoffman (Columbia University Press, 2006). Copyright © 2006 by Columbia University Press. Reprinted by permission.

From *Terrorism: Theirs & Ours* by Eqbal Amhad and David Barsamian (Seven Stories Press, 2001). Copyright © 2001 by Seven Stories Press. Reprinted by permission.

From *Origins of Terrorism: Psychologies, Idelogies, Theologies, States of Mind,* Walter Reich, eds., (Woodrow Wilson Center Press, 1998). Copyright © 1998 by Johns Hopkins University Press. Reprinted by permission.

Chapter 2

From *International Terrorism,* vol. 27, no.3, Winter 2002/03, pp. 30–58. Copyright © 2003 by MIT Press Journals. Reprinted by permission.

From *Washington Quarterly,* vol. 25, no. 3, Summer 2002, pp. 97–108. Copyright © 2002 by Center for Strategic & International Studies. Reprinted by permission.

From *Washington Quarterly,* vol. 29, no. 2, Spring 2006, pp. 27–53. Copyright © 2006 by Center for Strategic & International Studies. Reprinted by permission.

Chapter 3

Copyright © 2007 by The McGraw-Hill Companies.

From *Countering the New Terrorism* by John Arguilla, David Ronfeldt, and Michele Zanini (RAND Corporation, 1999). Copyright © 1999 by Rand Corporation. Reprinted by permission.

From *Washington Quarterly,* 2004. Copyright © 2007 by Center for Strategic & International Studies. Reprinted by permission.

Copyright © 2007 by The McGraw-Hill Companies.

Chapter 4

Chapter 5

Unit II Countering the Terrorist Threat

Chapter 6

Chapter 10

Index